T0180639

Lecture Notes in Computer Science   **14007**

Founding Editors

Gerhard Goos

Juris Hartmanis

Editorial Board Members

Elisa Bertino, *Purdue University, West Lafayette, IN, USA*

Wen Gao, *Peking University, Beijing, China*

Bernhard Steffen◉, *TU Dortmund University, Dortmund, Germany*

Moti Yung◉, *Columbia University, New York, NY, USA*

The series Lecture Notes in Computer Science (LNCS), including its subseries Lecture Notes in Artificial Intelligence (LNAI) and Lecture Notes in Bioinformatics (LNBI), has established itself as a medium for the publication of new developments in computer science and information technology research, teaching, and education.

LNCS enjoys close cooperation with the computer science R & D community, the series counts many renowned academics among its volume editors and paper authors, and collaborates with prestigious societies. Its mission is to serve this international community by providing an invaluable service, mainly focused on the publication of conference and workshop proceedings and postproceedings. LNCS commenced publication in 1973.

Carmit Hazay · Martijn Stam
Editors

Advances in Cryptology – EUROCRYPT 2023

42nd Annual International Conference on the Theory
and Applications of Cryptographic Techniques
Lyon, France, April 23–27, 2023
Proceedings, Part IV

 Springer

Editors
Carmit Hazay 🆔
Bar-Ilan University
Ramat Gan, Israel

Martijn Stam 🆔
Simula UiB
Bergen, Norway

ISSN 0302-9743 ISSN 1611-3349 (electronic)
Lecture Notes in Computer Science
ISBN 978-3-031-30633-4 ISBN 978-3-031-30634-1 (eBook)
https://doi.org/10.1007/978-3-031-30634-1

This Springer imprint is published by the registered company Springer Nature Switzerland AG
The registered company address is: Gewerbestrasse 11, 6330 Cham, Switzerland

Preface

The 42nd Annual International Conference on the Theory and Applications of Cryptographic Techniques, Eurocrypt 2023, was held in Lyon, France between April 23–27 under the auspices of the International Association for Cryptologic Research. The conference had a record number of 415 submissions, out of which 109 were accepted.

Preparation for the academic aspects of the conference started in earnest well over a year ago, with the selection of a program committee, consisting of 79 regular members and six area chairs. The area chairs played an important part in enabling a high-quality review process; their role was expanded considerably from last year and, for the first time, properly formalized. Each area chair was in charge of moderating the discussions of the papers assigned under their area, guiding PC members and reviewers to consensus where possible, and helping us in making final decisions. We created six areas and assigned the following area chairs: Ran Canetti for Theoretical Foundations; Rosario Gennaro for Public Key Primitives with Advanced Functionalities; Tibor Jager for Classic Public Key Cryptography; Marc Joye for Secure and Efficient Implementation, Cryptographic Engineering, and Real-World Cryptography; Gregor Leander for Symmetric Cryptology; and finally Arpita Patra for Multi-party Computation and Zero-Knowledge.

Prior to the submission deadline, PC members were introduced to the reviewing process; for this purpose we created a slide deck that explained what we expected from everyone involved in the process and how PC members could use the reviewing system (HotCRP) used by us. An important aspect of the reviewing process is the reviewing form, which we modified based on the Crypto'22 form as designed by Yevgeniy Dodis and Tom Shrimpton. As is customary for IACR general conferences, the reviewing process was two-sided anonymous.

Out of the 415 submissions, four were desk rejected due to violations of the Call for Papers (non-anonymous submission or significant deviations from the submission format). For the remaining submissions, the review process proceeded in two stages. In the first stage, every paper was reviewed by at least three reviewers. For 109 papers a clear, negative consensus emerged and an early reject decision was reached and communicated to the authors on the 8th of December 2022. This initial phase of early rejections allowed the program committee to concentrate on the delicate task of selecting a program amongst the more promising submissions, while simultaneously offering the authors of the rejected papers the opportunity to take advantage of the early, full feedback to improve their work for a future occasion.

The remaining 302 papers progressed to an interactive discussion phase, which was open for two weeks (ending slightly before the Christmas break). During this period, the authors had access to their reviews (apart from some PC only fields) and were asked to address questions and requests for clarifications explicitly formulated in the reviews. It gave authors and reviewers the opportunity to communicate directly (yet anonymously) with each other during several rounds of interaction. For some papers, the multiple rounds helped in clarifying both the reviewers' questions and the authors' responses.

For a smaller subset of papers, a second interactive discussion phase took place in the beginning of January allowing authors to respond to new, relevant insights by the PC. Eventually, 109 papers were selected for the program.

The best paper award was granted to the paper "An Efficient Key Recovery Attack on SIDH" by Wouter Castryck and Thomas Decru for presenting the first efficient key recovery attack against the Supersingular Isogeny Diffie-Hellman (SIDH) problem. Two further, related papers were invited to the Journal of Cryptology: "Breaking SIDH in Polynomial Time" by Damien Robert and "A Direct Key Recovery Attack on SIDH" by Luciano Maino, Chloe Martindale, Lorenz Panny, Giacomo Pope and Benjamin Wesolowski.

Accepted papers written exclusively by researchers who were within four years of PhD graduation at the time of submission were eligible for the Early Career Best Paper Award. There were a number of strong candidates and the paper "Worst-Case Subexponential Attacks on PRGs of Constant Degree or Constant Locality" by Akın Ünal was awarded this honor.

The program further included two invited talks: Guy Rothblum opened the program with his talk on "Indistinguishable Predictions and Multi-group Fair Learning" (an extended abstract of his talk appears in these proceedings) and later during the conference Vadim Lyubashevsky gave a talk on "Lattice Cryptography: What Happened and What's Next".

First and foremost, we would like to thank Kevin McCurley and Kay McKelly for their tireless efforts in the background, making the whole process so much smoother for us to run. Thanks also to our previous co-chairs Orr Dunkelman, Stefan Dziembowski, Yevgeniy Dodis, Thomas Shrimpton, Shweta Agrawal and Dongdai Lin for sharing the lessons they learned and allowing us to build on their foundations. We thank Guy and Vadim for accepting to give two excellent invited talks. Of course, no program can be selected without submissions, so we thank both the authors of accepted papers, as well as those whose papers did not make it (we sincerely hope that, notwithstanding the disappointing outcome, you found the reviews and interaction constructive). The reviewing was led by our PC members, who often engaged expert subreviewers to write high-quality, insightful reviews and engage directly in the discussions, and we are grateful to both our PC members and the subreviewers. As the IACR's general conferences grow from year to year, a very special thank you to our area chairs, our job would frankly not have been possible without Ran, Rosario, Tibor, Marc, Gregor, and Arpita's tireless efforts leading the individual papers' discussions. And, last but not least, we would like to thank the general chairs: Damien Stehlé, Alain Passelègue, and Benjamin Wesolowski who worked very hard to make this conference happen.

April 2023   Carmit Hazay
                                                        Martijn Stam

Organization

General Co-chairs

Damien Stehlé   ENS de Lyon and Institut Universitaire de France,
                              France
Alain Passelègue   Inria, France
Benjamin Wesolowski   CNRS and ENS de Lyon, France

Program Co-chairs

Carmit Hazay   Bar-Ilan University, Israel
Martijn Stam   Simula UiB, Norway

Area Chairs

Ran Canetti   Boston University, USA
(for Theoretical Foundations)

Rosario Gennaro   Protocol Labs and CUNY, USA
(for Public Key Primitives with Advanced Functionalities)

Tibor Jager   University of Wuppertal, Germany
(for Classic Public Key Cryptography)

Marc Joye   Zama, France
(for Secure and Efficient Implementation, Cryptographic Engineering, and Real-World Cryptography)

Gregor Leander   Ruhr-Universität Bochum, Germany
(for Symmetric Cryptology)

Arpita Patra   Google and IISc Bangalore, India
(for Multi-party Computation and Zero-Knowledge)

Program Committee

Masayuki Abe	NTT Social Informatics Laboratories and Kyoto University, Japan
Adi Akavia	University of Haifa, Israel
Prabhanjan Ananth	UC Santa Barbara, USA
Gilad Asharov	Bar-Ilan University, Israel
Marshall Ball	New York University, USA
Christof Beierle	Ruhr University Bochum, Germany
Mihir Bellare	UC San Diego, USA
Tim Beyne	KU Leuven, Belgium
Andrej Bogdanov	Chinese University of Hong Kong, China
Xavier Bonnetain	Inria, France
Joppe Bos	NXP Semiconductors, Belgium
Chris Brzuska	Aalto University, Finland
Ignacio Cascudo	IMDEA Software Institute, Spain
Nishanth Chandran	Microsoft Research India, India
Chitchanok Chuengsatiansup	The University of Melbourne, Australia
Michele Ciampi	The University of Edinburgh, UK
Ran Cohen	Reichman University, Israel
Jean-Sébastien Coron	University of Luxembourg, Luxembourg
Bernardo David	IT University of Copenhagen, Denmark
Christoph Dobraunig	Intel Labs, Intel Corporation, Hillsboro, USA
Léo Ducas	CWI Amsterdam and Leiden University, Netherlands
Maria Eichlseder	Graz University of Technology, Austria
Pooya Farshim	IOHK and Durham University, UK
Serge Fehr	CWI Amsterdam and Leiden University, Netherlands
Dario Fiore	IMDEA Software Institute, Spain
Pierre-Alain Fouque	Université Rennes 1 and Institut Universitaire de France, France
Steven Galbraith	University of Auckland, New Zealand
Chaya Ganesh	IISc Bangalore, India
Si Gao	Huawei Technologies Co., Ltd., China
Daniel Genkin	GeorgiaTech, USA
Craig Gentry	TripleBlind, USA
Benedikt Gierlichs	KU Leuven, Belgium
Rishab Goyal	UW-Madison, USA
Vipul Goyal	NTT Research and CMU, USA
Viet Tung Hoang	Florida State University, USA
Andreas Hülsing	Eindhoven University of Technology, Netherlands

Antoine Joux · CISPA, Helmholtz Center for Cybersecurity, Germany

Karen Klein · ETH Zurich, Switzerland

Markulf Kohlweiss · University of Edinburgh and IOHK, UK

Jooyoung Lee · KAIST, Korea

Gaëtan Leurent · Inria, France

Shengli Liu · Shanghai Jiao Tong University, China

Yunwen Liu · Cryptape Technology Co., Ltd., China

Stefan Lucks · Bauhaus-Universität Weimar, Germany

Hemanta Maji · Purdue, USA

Alexander May · Ruhr University Bochum, Germany

Nele Mentens · Leiden University, Netherlands and KU Leuven, Belgium

Tal Moran · Reichman University, Israel

Michael Naehrig · Microsoft Research, USA

Ngoc Khanh Nguyen · EPFL, Switzerland

Emmanuela Orsini · Bocconi University, Italy and KU Leuven, Belgium

Jiaxin Pan · NTNU, Norway

Omkant Pandey · Stony Brook University, USA

Anat Paskin-Cherniavsky · Ariel University, Israel

Chris Peikert · University of Michigan and Algorand, Inc., USA

Léo Perrin · Inria, France

Giuseppe Persiano · Università di Salerno, Italy

Thomas Peters · UCLouvain, Belgium

Christophe Petit · Université libre de Bruxelles, Belgium and University of Birmingham, UK

Krzysztof Pietrzak · ISTA, Austria

Bertram Poettering · IBM Research Europe – Zurich, Switzerland

Bart Preneel · KU Leuven, Belgium

Divya Ravi · Aarhus University, Denmark

Christian Rechberger · TU Graz, Austria

Ron Rothblum · Technion, Israel

Carla Ràfols · Universitat Pompeu Fabra, Spain

Paul Rösler · FAU Erlangen-Nürnberg, Germany

Yu Sasaki · NTT Social Informatics Laboratories, NIST Associate, Japan

Dominique Schröder · FAU Erlangen-Nürnberg, Germany

Omri Shmueli · Tel Aviv University, Israel

Janno Siim · Simula UiB, Norway

Daniel Slamanig · AIT Austrian Institute of Technology, Austria

Yifan Song · Tsinghua University, China

Qiang Tang	The University of Sydney, Australia
Serge Vaudenay	EPFL, Switzerland
Fernando Virdia	Intel Labs, Switzerland
Meiqin Wang	Shandong University, China
Mor Weiss	Bar-Ilan University, Israel
David Wu	UT Austin, USA

Additional Reviewers

Behzad Abdolmaleki	Katharina Boudgoust
Damiano Abram	Christina Boura
Hamza Abusalah	Zvika Brakerski
Leo Ackermann	Lennart Braun
Amit Agarwal	Marek Broll
Ghous Amjad	Ileana Buhan
Benny Applebaum	Matteo Campanelli
Gal Arnon	Federico Canale
Thomas Attema	Anne Canteaut
Benedikt Auerbach	Gaëtan Cassiers
Lukas Aumayr	Wouter Castryck
Gennaro Avitabile	Pyrros Chaidos
Melissa Azouaoui	André Chailloux
Saikrishna Badrinarayanan	T.-H. Hubert Chan
Karim Baghery	Anirudh Chandramouli
Kunpeng Bai	Rohit Chatterjee
Shi Bai	Hao Chen
David Balbás	Long Chen
Manuel Barbosa	Mingjie Chen
Khashayar Barooti	Yanbo Chen
James Bartusek	Yanlin Chen
Andrea Basso	Yilei Chen
Balthazar Bauer	Yu Long Chen
Carsten Baum	Wei Cheng
Michiel van Beirendonck	Céline Chevalier
Josh Benaloh	James Chiang
Fabrice Benhamouda	Wonhee Cho
Ward Beullens	Wonseok Choi
Amit Singh Bhati	Wutichai Chongchitmate
Ritam Bhaumik	Hien Chu
Alexander Bienstock	Valerio Cini
Alexander Block	Christine Cloostermans
Jonathan Bootle	Andrea Coladangelo
Cecilia Boschini	Daniel Collins

Sandro Coretti-Drayton
Craig Costello
Elizabeth Crites
Miguel Cueto Noval
Jan-Pieter D'Anvers
Sourav Das
Alex Davidson
Gabrielle De Micheli
Cyprien Delpech de Saint Guilhem
Patrick Derbez
Lalita Devadas
Siemen Dhooghe
Jesus Diaz
Khue Do
Jelle Don
Rafael Dowsley
Avijit Dutta
Sébastien Duval
Christoph Egger
Tariq Elahi
Lynn Engelberts
Felix Engelmann
Muhammed F. Esgin
Thomas Espitau
Andre Esser
Simona Etinski
Prastudy Fauzi
Patrick Felke
Hanwen Feng
Rex Fernando
Tako Boris Fouotsa
Danilo Francati
Sapir Freizeit
Paul Frixons
Rachit Garg
Sanjam Garg
Aymeric Genêt
Marios Georgiou
Satrajit Ghosh
Niv Gilboa
Valerie Gilchrist
Emanuele Giunta
Aarushi Goel
Eli Goldin
Junqing Gong

Alonso González
Lorenzo Grassi
Jiaxin Guan
Zichen Gui
Aurore Guillevic
Aditya Gulati
Aldo Gunsing
Chun Guo
Divya Gupta
Felix Günther
Hosein Hadipour
Mohammad Hajiabadi
Shai Halevi
Peter Hall
Shuai Han
Patrick Harasser
David Heath
Lena Heimberger
Alexandra Henzinger
Julia Hesse
Minki Hhan
Dennis Hofheinz
Maya-Iggy van Hoof
Sam Hopkins
Akinori Hosoyamada
Kristina Hostáková
Martha Norberg Hovd
Yu-Hsuan Huang
Loïs Huguenin-Dumittan
Kathrin Hövelmanns
Yuval Ishai
Muhammad Ishaq
Tetsu Iwata
Michael John Jacobson, Jr.
Aayush Jain
Samuel Jaques
Jinhyuck Jeong
Corentin Jeudy
Ashwin Jha
Mingming Jiang
Zhengzhong Jin
Thomas Johansson
David Joseph
Daniel Jost
Fatih Kaleoglu

Novak Kaluderovic
Chethan Kamath
Shuichi Katsumata
Marcel Keller
John Kelsey
Erin Kenney
Hamidreza Khorasgani
Hamidreza Khoshakhlagh
Seongkwang Kim
Elena Kirshanova
Fuyuki Kitagawa
Bor de Kock
Konrad Kohbrok
Lisa Kohl
Sebastian Kolby
Dimitris Kolonelos
Ilan Komargodski
Yashvanth Kondi
Venkata Koppula
Alexis Korb
Matthias Krause
Hugo Krawczyk
Toomas Krips
Mike Kudinov
Péter Kutas
Thijs Laarhoven
Yi-Fu Lai
Baptiste Lambin
Nathalie Lang
Abel Laval
Laurens Le Jeune
Byeonghak Lee
Changmin Lee
Eysa Lee
Seunghoon Lee
Sihyun Lee
Dominik Leichtle
Jannis Leuther
Shai Levin
Chaoyun Li
Yanan Li
Yiming Li
Xiao Liang
Jyun-Jie Liao
Benoît Libert

Wei-Kai Lin
Yao-Ting Lin
Helger Lipmaa
Eik List
Fukang Liu
Jiahui Liu
Qipeng Liu
Xiangyu Liu
Chen-Da Liu-Zhang
Satya Lokam
Alex Lombardi
Patrick Longa
George Lu
Jinyu Lu
Xianhui Lu
Yuan Lu
Zhenliang Lu
Ji Luo
You Lyu
Reinhard Lüftenegger
Urmila Mahadev
Mohammad Mahmoody
Mohammad Mahzoun
Christian Majenz
Nikolaos Makriyannis
Varun Maram
Laurane Marco
Ange Martinelli
Daniel Masny
Noam Mazor
Matthias Meijers
Fredrik Meisingseth
Florian Mendel
Bart Mennink
Simon-Philipp Merz
Tony Metger
Pierre Meyer
Brice Minaud
Kazuhiko Minematsu
Victor Mollimard
Tomoyuki Morimae
Nicky Mouha
Tamer Mour
Marcel Nageler
Mridul Nandi

María Naya-Plasencia
Patrick Neumann
Hai Nguyen
Ky Nguyen
Phong Q. Nguyen
Ryo Nishimaki
Olga Nissenbaum
Anca Nitulescu
Ariel Nof
Julian Nowakowski
Adam O'Neill
Sai Lakshmi Bhavana Obbattu
Miyako Ohkubo
Eran Omri
Claudio Orlandi
Michele Orrù
Elisabeth Oswald
Omer Paneth
Guillermo Pascual-Perez
Kenneth G. Paterson
Sikhar Patranabis
Alice Pellet-Mary
Maxime Plancon
Antigoni Polychroniadou
Alexander Poremba
Bernardo Portela
Eamonn Postlethwaite
Emmanuel Prouff
Kirthivaasan Puniamurthy
Octavio Pérez Kempner
Luowen Qian
Tian Qiu
Willy Quach
Håvard Raddum
Srinivasan Raghuraman
Justin Raizes
Sebastian Ramacher
Hugues Randriambololona
Shahram Rasoolzadeh
Simon Rastikian
Joost Renes
Nicolas Resch
Alfredo Rial Duran
Doreen Riepel
Silvia Ritsch

Melissa Rossi
Mike Rosulek
Yann Rotella
Lawrence Roy
Roozbeh Sarenche
Amirreza Sarencheh
Pratik Sarkar
Arish Sateesan
Christian Schaffner
Carl Richard Theodor Schneider
Markus Schofnegger
Peter Scholl
André Schrottenloher
Gregor Seiler
Sruthi Sekar
Nicolas Sendrier
Meghna Sengupta
Jinrui Sha
Akash Shah
Siamak Shahandashti
Moni Shahar
Shahed Sharif
Laura Shea
Abhi Shelat
Yaobin Shen
Sina Shiehian
Jad Silbak
Alice Silverberg
Luisa Siniscalchi
Tomer Solomon
Karl Southern
Nicholas Spooner
Sriram Sridhar
Srivatsan Sridhar
Akshayaram Srinivasan
François-Xavier Standaert
Uri Stemmer
Lukas Stennes
Patrick Steuer
Christoph Striecks
Patrick Struck
Chao Sun
Erkan Tairi
Akira Takahashi
Abdullah Talayhan

Titouan Tanguy
Stefano Tessaro
Emmanuel Thomé
Sri AravindaKrishnan Thyagarajan
Yan Bo Ti
Mehdi Tibouchi
Tyge Tiessen
Bénédikt Tran
Andreas Trügler
Daniel Tschudi
Aleksei Udovenko
Jonathan Ullman
Dominique Unruh
Vinod Vaikuntanathan
Daniele Venturi
Michiel Verbauwhede
Javier Verbel
Gilles Villard
Mikhail Volkhov
Satyanarayana Vusirikala
Benedikt Wagner
Roman Walch
Hendrik Waldner
Alexandre Wallet
Michael Walter
Mingyuan Wang
Yuyu Wang
Florian Weber
Hoeteck Wee
Puwen Wei
Charlotte Weitkaemper

Weiqiang Wen
Benjamin Wesolowski
Daniel Wichs
Wessel van Woerden
Ke Wu
Keita Xagawa
Hanshen Xiao
Jiayu Xu
Yingfei Yan
Xiuyu Ye
Kevin Yeo
Eylon Yogev
Albert Yu
Aaram Yun
Alexandros Zacharakis
Thomas Zacharias
Michal Zajac
Greg Zaverucha
Runzhi Zeng
Cong Zhang
Lei Zhang
Ren Zhang
Xinrui Zhang
Yuqing Zhao
Yu Zhou
Dionysis Zindros
Giorgos Zirdelis
Lukas Zobernig
Arne Tobias Ødegaard
Morten Øygarden

Sponsoring Institutions

- Platinum Sponsor: Université Rennes 1 and PEPR Quantique, Zama
- Gold Sponsor: Apple, Cryptolab, ENS de Lyon, ENS PSL, Huawei, Sandbox AQ, Thales, TII
- Silver Sponsor: Algorand Foundation, ANSSI, AWS, PQShield
- Bronze Sponsor: Cosmian, CryptoExperts, CryptoNext Security, IBM, Idemia, Inria, LIP

Contents – Part IV

Side-Channels and Masking

Blockcipher and Hash Function Cryptanalysis

Truncated Boomerang Attacks
and Application to AES-Based Ciphers

Augustin Bariant$^{(\boxtimes)}$ (iD) and Gaëtan Leurent$^{(\boxtimes)}$ (iD)

Inria, Paris, France
gaetan.leurent@inria.fr

Abstract. The boomerang attack is a cryptanalysis technique that combines two short differentials instead of using a single long differential. It has been applied to many primitives, and results in the best known attacks against several AES-based ciphers (Kiasu-BC, Deoxys-BC). In this paper, we introduce a general framework for boomerang attacks with truncated differentials.

We show that the use of truncated differentials provides a significant improvement over the best boomerang attacks in the literature. In particular, we take into account structures on the plaintext and ciphertext sides, and include an analysis of the key recovery step. On 6-round AES, we obtain a competitive structural distinguisher with complexity 2^{87} and a key recovery attack with complexity 2^{61}.

The truncated boomerang attack is particularly effective against tweakable AES variants. We apply it to 8-round Kiasu-BC, resulting in the best known attack with complexity 2^{83} (rather than 2^{103}). We also show an interesting use of the 6-round distinguisher on the full TNT-AES, a tweakable block cipher using 6-round AES as a building block. Finally, we apply this framework to Deoxys-BC, using a MILP model to find optimal trails automatically. We obtain the best attacks against round-reduced versions of all variants of Deoxys-BC.

Keywords: Truncated differential · Boomerang attack · AES · Kiasu · Deoxys · TNT-AES · MILP

1 Introduction

The AES [15] is the most widely used block cipher today, and we have a good understanding of its security. Its round function is strongly byte-aligned; this simplifies the analysis with the wide-trail strategy, and many cryptanalysis techniques rely on truncated trails to take advantage of this property. After 20 years of analysis, we have a high confidence in the design, and many recent tweakable proposals reuse the AES round function with different tweakey schedules (Kiasu-BC [26], Deoxys-BC [28], and TNT-AES [1]). However, an attacker can introduce a difference in the additional tweak of these constructions, so they must be analysed in the related-tweak model, and by extension in the related-key model. In these models, the boomerang attack is particularly effective because both high-probability

© International Association for Cryptologic Research 2023
C. Hazay and M. Stam (Eds.): EUROCRYPT 2023, LNCS 14007, pp. 3–35, 2023.
https://doi.org/10.1007/978-3-031-30634-1_1

differentials composing the boomerang reach more rounds. In particular, the best known attacks against Kiasu-BC and Deoxys-BC are boomerang attacks (Tables 2 and 3).

In this work, we carefully and systematically analyse the interaction between truncated differentials and boomerang attacks. Our approach is similar to the analysis of impossible differential attacks in [11]: we aim at providing a unified formula taking into account many details of a broad class of attacks. We integrate and improve a set of techniques proposed in different variants of the boomerang attack, leading to the best boomerang attacks against several AES-based ciphers.

Our Results. We present a generic framework to describe boomerang attacks based on truncated differentials (Sect. 3). Instead of first building a boomerang distinguisher and then appending extra key recovery rounds, we consider the truncated boomerang attack as a whole, including the key recovery exploiting the first and last round transitions. The framework integrates and improves on previous analyses, including structures of plaintexts and ciphertexts [9], and truncated differentials as introduced by Wagner [39]. Our improvements come principally from the use of structures of ciphertexts, which were underused in recent works. We also consider boomerang trails with smaller probability than the random case, and mount attacks by gathering enough samples to detect the bias.

We first apply our framework to reduced AES (Sect. 4). On 6-round AES, we obtain a distinguisher with complexity 2^{87}, and a key-recovery with complexity 2^{61}, improving the previous best boomerang attack with complexity 2^{71} [10].

We adapt the key-recovery attack to 8-round Kiasu-BC (Sect. 5) by revisiting a previous boomerang attack with complexity 2^{103} [18]. Using structures of ciphertexts, we obtain the best attack against Kiasu-BC, with complexity 2^{83}.

We also apply a variant of the 6-round attack to the full TNT-AES [1], and obtain a marginal distinguisher with complexity slightly below 2^{128} (Sect. 6). The attack is not competitive with the generic attack against TNT with complexity $\mathcal{O}(\sqrt{n} \cdot 2^{3n/4})$ [25], but it uses a lower memory (2^{32} instead of 2^{96}), and it can distinguish TNT with 6-round AES from TNT with a PRP. Moreover, this is the first property of 6-round AES that can be used to target a generic construction using 6-round AES as a building block (to the best of our knowledge). We also provide an attack on reduced TNT-AES, using a 5-round boomerang trail.

In Sect. 7, we build a MILP model implementing our framework, to find good parameters for the full attack automatically. The model allows both fixed differences and truncated differences, and takes into account the complexity of the key recovery, instead of just optimizing a boomerang distinguisher. It confirms that our basic attack on AES is optimal within our framework.

Finally, we apply the MILP model to Deoxys-BC, and obtain improved attacks against most variants (Sect. 8). Although the boomerang trails on AES and Deoxys-BC are quite different, the underlying analysis is the same.

Due to space constraints, some results are only available in the full version of this paper [6]. Our code is also available as additional data [7].

Distinguishers and Key-Recovery Attacks. In this work, we report distinguishers and key-recovery attacks, with key-recovery typically having a lower complexity on the same number of rounds. Obviously, a key-recovery attack can be used as a distinguisher, but we focus on structural distinguishers that only use statistical properties of the block cipher, without guessing subkey material (denoted as "independent of the secret key" in [24]). Indeed, a series of recent works have proposed complex distinguishers on 5-round [24] and 6-round AES [2,5,33], and we obtain similar results with simpler techniques. This notion of distinguisher is not clearly defined, but our distinguishers can be used with secret S-Boxes, which is not the case for most key-recovery attacks.

2   Preliminaries

2.1   The AES Round Function

AES was designed in 1998 by Daemen and Rijmen (as Rijndael) and won the NIST standardization competition in 2000 [15]. Three instances of the cipher exist, for key sizes of 128, 196 and 256 bits, but we only consider AES-128 in this paper. Since we do not exploit the AES key schedule, we only describe the round function. AES-128 operates on a 128-bit state, represented as a 4×4-byte array, and iterates on 10 rounds a round function composed of the following operations:

- **SubBytes**: The AES S-Box is applied to each byte of the state.
- **ShiftRows**: The second row is shifted by 1 cell to the left, the third row by 2 cells, and the fourth row by 3 cells.
- **MixColumns**: Each column is multiplied by an MDS Matrix.
- **AddRoundKey**: Each byte is XORed with a byte of the round key.

There is one extra AddRoundKey operation before the first round, and the last round omits the MixColumns operation.

Due to the popularity of the AES, and its availability in hardware on several platforms, many constructions reuse its round function. In particular, Kiasu [27] and Deoxys [28] are two tweakable block ciphers that reuse the AES round function, with a modified tweakey schedule (combining the key and tweak) to compute the round (tweak)keys. Deoxys has been selected in the CAESAR portfolio. TNT-AES [1] is another tweakable block cipher using the AES round function, where the tweak is only XORed to the internal state twice.

Kiasu-BC Tweakey Schedule. Kiasu-BC has a 128-bit key and 64-bit tweak, with 10 rounds. The round tweakeys are computed as $k_i + t$ where k_i is the round key following the AES key schedule, and t is the tweak (encoded in the first two rows). In particular, Kiasu-BC with the zero tweak is the same as the AES.

Table 1. AES distinguisher and key recovery attacks with known and secret S-Boxes. CP: chosen plaintexts/ACC: chosen plaintexts and adaptively-chosen ciphertexts

	Rounds	Type	Data		Time	Ref
AES Distinguishers	5	Multiple-of-n	2^{32}	CP	$2^{36.6}$	[24]
	6	Yoyo	$2^{122.8}$	ACC	$2^{121.8}$	[33]
	6	Exchange attack	$2^{88.2}$	CP	$2^{88.2}$	[5]
	6	Exchange attack	2^{84}	ACC	2^{83}	[4]
	6	Truncated differential	$2^{89.4}$	CP	$2^{96.5}$	[2]
	6	Truncated boomerang	2^{87}	ACC	2^{87}	Subsect. 4.1
AES Key-recovery	6	Square	2^{32}	CP	2^{71}	[14]
	6	Partial-sum	2^{32}	CP	2^{48}	[21]
	6	Boomerang	2^{71}	ACC	2^{71}	[10]
	6	Mixture	2^{26}	CP	2^{80}	[3]
	6	Retracing boomerang	2^{55}	ACC	2^{80}	[19]
	6	Boomeyong	$2^{79.7}$	ACC	2^{78}	[32]
	6	Truncated boomerang	2^{59}	ACC	2^{61}	Subsect. 4.2
AES Secret S-Box KR	5	Square	2^{40}	CP	2^{40}	[37]
	5	Multiple-of-n	$2^{53.3}$	CP	$2^{52.6}$	[22]
	5	Retracing boomerang	$2^{25.8}$	ACC	$2^{25.8}$	[19]
	6	Square	2^{64}	CP	2^{90}	[37]
	6	Truncated boomerang	2^{94}	ACC	2^{94}	Subsect. 4.3

Table 2. Boomerang (B) and rectangle (R) attacks against variants of Deoxys-BC. Most attacks succeed with probability 1/2.

Model	Rnd	Previous					New			
			Data	Time	Mem	Ref		Data	Time	Mem	Ref
RTK1	8						B	2^{88}	2^{88}	2^{73}	*Full version* [6]
	9						B	2^{135}	2^{174}	2^{129}	*Full version* [6]
RTK2	8	B	2^{28}	2^{28}	2^{27}	[34][a]	B	2^{27}	2^{27}	2^{27}	*Full version* [6]
	9	B	2^{98}	2^{112}	2^{17}	[34]	B	$2^{55.2}$	$2^{55.2}$	$2^{55.2}$	*Full version* [6]
	10	B	$2^{98.4}$	$2^{109.1}$	2^{88}	[42]	B	$2^{94.2}$	$2^{95.2}$	$2^{94.2}$	Sect. 8
	11	R	$2^{122.1}$	$2^{249.9}$	$2^{128.2}$	[42]	B	2^{129}	$2^{223.9}$	2^{129}	Sect. 8
RTK3	10	B	2^{22}	2^{22}	2^{17}	[34]	B	$2^{19.4}$	$2^{19.4}$	2^{18}	*Full version* [6]
	11	B	2^{100}	2^{100}	2^{17}	[34]	B	$2^{32.7}$	$2^{32.7}$	$2^{32.7}$	*Full version* [6]
	12	B	2^{98}	2^{98}	2^{64}	[42]	B	$2^{67.4}$	$2^{67.4}$	2^{65}	*Full version* [6]
	13	R	$2^{125.2}$	$2^{186.7}$	2^{136}	[43]	B	$2^{126.7}$	$2^{170.2}$	$2^{126.7}$	Sect. 8
	14	R	$2^{125.2}$	$2^{282.7}$	2^{136}	[43]	B	2^{129}	$2^{278.8}$	2^{129}	*Full version* [6]

[a]The probability of Sasaki's trail is 2^{-56} with structures, thus we believe that the complexity of the attack is actually 2^{30} in data and time and 2^{29} in memory.

Table 3. Attacks against Kiasu-BC and TNT-AES

	Rounds	Type	Data		Time	Ref
Kiasu-BC	7	Square (KR)	$2^{43.6}$	CP	$2^{48.5}$	[17]
	8	Meet-in-the-Middle (KR)	2^{116}	CP	2^{116}	[38]
	8	Imposs. Diff (KR)	2^{118}	CP	2^{118}	[18]
	8	Boomerang (KR)	2^{103}	ACC	$2^{103.1}$	[18]
	8	Truncated boomerang (KR)	2^{83}	ACC	2^{83}	Sect. 5
TNT-AES	*-5-*	Boomerang (dist.)	2^{126}	ACC	2^{126}	[1]
	5-*-*	Impossible differential (KR)	$2^{113.6}$	CP	$2^{113.6}$	[25]
	--*	Generic (dist.)	$2^{99.5}$	CP	$2^{99.5}$	[25]
	-5-	Truncated boomerang (dist.)	2^{76}	ACC	2^{76}	*Full version* [6]
	5-5-*	Truncated boomerang (KR)	2^{87}	ACC	2^{87}	*Full version* [6]
	-6-	Truncated boomerang (dist.)	$2^{127.8}$	ACC	$2^{127.8}$	Sect. 6

Deoxys-BC Tweakey Schedule. Deoxys-BC has two variants: Deoxys-BC-256 has a 256-bit tweakey with 14 rounds, and Deoxys-BC-384 has a 384-bit tweakey with 16 rounds. The tweakey material is composed of a variable length key and tweak summing to 256 or 384 bits; for simplicity, we assume that the key length is a multiple of 128. The tweakey material is divided in words of 128 bits (denoted TK^i). Eventually, the round tweakey of round j is defined as:

$$STK_j = \begin{cases} RC_j + TK_j^1 + TK_j^2 & \text{For Deoxys-BC-256} \\ RC_j + TK_j^1 + TK_j^2 + TK_j^3 & \text{For Deoxys-BC-384} \end{cases}$$

TK_j^i is the tweakey state, initialized as $TK_0^i = TK^i$ and updated with

$$TK_{j+1}^1 = h(TK_j^1) \quad TK_{j+1}^2 = h(\mathsf{LFSR}_2(TK_j^2)) \quad TK_{j+1}^3 = h(\mathsf{LFSR}_3(TK_j^3))$$

where h is a byte permutation, and LFSR_2 and LFSR_3 are LFSRs that operate in parallel on each byte of the tweakey. This construction (the STK construction [27]) ensures that differences in subtweakey byte position may only cancel out up to $i - 1$ times every 15 rounds if differences are introduced in i tweakey words.

Notations. We denote E a block cipher operating on a state of n bits. In a 4×4 matrix, the bytes are numbered in the AES order (column-major) When k_i is a sub(twea)key, we denote $k_i^{eq} = \mathsf{MixColumns}^{-1}(k_i)$.

2.2 Differentials and Truncated Differentials

We use $+$ to denote the XOR operation (the addition in $\mathbb{F}_{2^u}^v$). A differential is defined by an input difference $\Delta_{\text{in}} \in \{0,1\}^n$ and an output difference $\Delta_{\text{out}} \in \{0,1\}^n$. We use the notation $\Delta_{\text{in}} \xrightarrow[E]{p} \Delta_{\text{out}}$ when a differential exists with probability p, where the probability is defined over a random plaintext P:

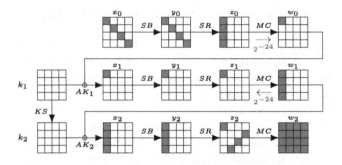

Fig. 1. Example of a truncated differential trail on 3-round AES.

$$p = \Pr[\Delta_{\text{in}} \xrightarrow[E]{} \Delta_{\text{out}}] = \Pr\left[E(P) + E(P + \Delta_{\text{in}}) = \Delta_{\text{out}}\right]$$

Since E is a permutation, we have $\Pr[\Delta_{\text{in}} \xrightarrow[E]{} \Delta_{\text{out}}] = \Pr[\Delta_{\text{out}} \xrightarrow[E^{-1}]{} \Delta_{\text{in}}]$.

A truncated differential is defined by a set of input differences $\mathcal{D}_{\text{in}}$ and a set of output differences $\mathcal{D}_{\text{out}}$. We use the notation $\mathcal{D}_{\text{in}} \xrightarrow[E]{\vec{p}} \mathcal{D}_{\text{out}}$ to denote the existence of a truncated differential with probability $\vec{p}$, defined as (with Avg denoting the average):

$$\vec{p} = \operatorname*{Avg}_{\Delta_{\text{in}} \in \mathcal{D}_{\text{in}}} \Pr\left[E(P) + E(P + \Delta_{\text{in}}) \in \mathcal{D}_{\text{out}}\right]$$

We also define the probability of the reverse truncated differential as

$$\bar{p} = \operatorname*{Avg}_{\Delta_{\text{out}} \in \mathcal{D}_{\text{out}}} \Pr\left[E^{-1}(P) + E^{-1}(P + \Delta_{\text{out}}) \in \mathcal{D}_{\text{in}}\right]$$

In general, the two probabilities are different, and related as follow:

$$\frac{\vec{p}}{|\mathcal{D}_{\text{out}}|} = \frac{\bar{p}}{|\mathcal{D}_{\text{in}}|} = \operatorname*{Avg}_{\Delta_{\text{in}} \in \mathcal{D}_{\text{in}}, \Delta_{\text{out}} \in \mathcal{D}_{\text{out}}} \Pr\left[E(P) + E(P + \Delta_{\text{in}}) = \Delta_{\text{out}}\right]$$

Figure 1 gives an example of a truncated differential on 3 rounds of AES, with respectively 4, 1, and 4 active S-Boxes in each round. The probability of the truncated differential is $\vec{p} = 2^{-24}$ and the reverse probability is $\bar{p} = 2^{-24}$.

2.3 Boomerang Attacks

Boomerang attacks, introduced by Wagner in 1999 [39], use adaptive plaintext and ciphertext queries to generate quartets with specific differences at an intermediate state of the cipher. The attacker decomposes the full cipher E into two subciphers E_0 (the upper part) and E_1 (the lower part), with $E = E_1 \circ E_0$, with high probability differentials on E_0 and E_1 (of probabilities p and q), denoted respectively $\Delta_{\text{in}} \xrightarrow[E_0]{p} \Delta_{\text{out}}$ and $\nabla_{\text{in}} \xrightarrow[E_1]{q} \nabla_{\text{out}}$. The attack proceeds as follows:

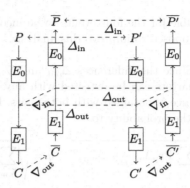

Fig. 2. Construction of a boomerang quartet.

1. Generate pairs of plaintext (P, P') such that $P + P' = \Delta_{in}$, and query the corresponding ciphertexts $(C, C') = (E(P), E(P'))$.
2. Shift the ciphertexts pairs into new pairs $(\overline{C}, \overline{C'}) = (C + \nabla_{out}, C' + \nabla_{out})$ and query their decryptions $(\overline{P}, \overline{P'}) = (E^{-1}(\overline{C}), E^{-1}(\overline{C'}))$.
3. Look for pairs with $\overline{P} + \overline{P'} = \Delta_{in}$.

Analysis. We have $E_0(P) = E_1^{-1}(C)$ because $E = E_1 \circ E_0$. In particular,

$$E_0(\overline{P}) + E_0(\overline{P'}) = E_1^{-1}(\overline{C}) + E_1^{-1}(\overline{C'}) + E_0(P) + E_1^{-1}(C) + E_0(P') + E_1^{-1}(C')$$

Moreover, the differentials in E_0 and E_1 imply that:

$$\Pr[E_0(P) + E_0(P') = \Delta_{out}] = p$$
$$\Pr[E_1^{-1}(C) + E_1^{-1}(\overline{C}) = \nabla_{in}] = q$$
$$\Pr[E_1^{-1}(C') + E_1^{-1}(\overline{C'}) = \nabla_{in}] = q$$

When the three events are satisfied, we obtain $E_0(\overline{P}) + E_0(\overline{P'}) = \Delta_{out}$ and with an additional probability p, $\overline{P} + \overline{P'} = \Delta_{in}$. Finally, assuming that all events are independent, we compute the boomerang trail probability p_b as a lower bound of the probability of the boomerang relation $\overline{P} + \overline{P'} = \Delta_{in}$:

$$\Pr\left[E^{-1}(E(P) + \nabla_{out}) + E^{-1}(E(P + \Delta_{in}) + \nabla_{out}) = \Delta_{in}\right] \geq p_b = p^2 \times q^2$$

Figure 2 shows the construction of a boomerang quartet. When $p^2 \times q^2 \gg 2^{-n}$, this gives a distinguisher for the cipher using $\mathcal{O}(p^{-2} \times q^{-2})$ quartets because the probability of detecting a quartet is 2^{-n} for a random permutation. In most cases, the distinguisher can be converted into a key recovery by exploiting key dependencies in the distinguisher.

2.4 Improvements of the Boomerang Attack

Analysis of the Connection Probability. The analysis above assumes that the four pairs involved in a boomerang quartet follow their corresponding differentials independently. In practice, we usually obtain a probability higher than

p^2q^2, but it is also possible for the four events to be incompatible [30]. Several techniques have been proposed to improve this analysis.

Multiple Differentials. Since the differences Δ_{out} and ∇_{in} are not used by the attacker, boomerang quartets can be detected with any internal difference, as long as the same difference is obtained with both pairs. Following the analysis of [8,39], this increases the probability to

$$p_b = \hat{p}^2\hat{q}^2 \qquad \hat{p} = \sqrt{\sum_{\Delta_{\text{out}}} \Pr[\Delta_{\text{in}} \xrightarrow{E_0} \Delta_{\text{out}}]^2} \qquad \hat{q} = \sqrt{\sum_{\nabla_{\text{in}}} \Pr[\nabla_{\text{in}} \xrightarrow{E_1} \nabla_{\text{out}}]^2}$$

The Sandwich Attack. Instead of splitting the cipher E into two parts $E = E_1 \circ E_0$, Dunkelman, Keller and Shamir [20] proposed to split it in three parts $E = E_1 \circ E_m \circ E_0$ with a small E_m in the middle. For the analysis, they evaluate the probability of the boomerang trail using the connection probability r of E_m:

$$\Pr\left[\overline{P} + \overline{P}' = \Delta_{\text{in}}\right] \geq p_b = p^2q^2r$$
$$r = \Pr\left[E_m^{-1}(E_m(X) + \nabla_{\text{in}}) + E_m^{-1}(E_m(X + \Delta_{\text{out}}) + \nabla_{\text{in}}) = \Delta_{\text{out}}\right]$$

The connection probability r can be evaluated experimentally, and some specific choices of E_m result in $r = 1$ (in particular, when E_m is the identity, we fall back to the standard analysis of boomerangs). The Boomerang Connectivity Table (BCT) was later introduced [13] to analyze the case where E_m is an S-Box layer. The case where E_m is composed of several rounds has been analyzed in further works [16,36,40]. Recent works also show that setting E_m to a single S-Box layer might lead to inaccurate connection probabilities [41].

Structures. Biham, Dunkelman and Shamir have introduced a variant of the boomerang attack using structures for the key recovery [9]. They start from a boomerang distinguisher with fixed differences Δ_{in} and ∇_{out}, and add extra rounds at the beginning and at the end. By propagating the differences Δ_{in} and ∇_{out}, they obtain a set of possible input differences $\mathcal{D}_{\text{in}}$ and output differences $\mathcal{D}_{\text{out}}$. In a typical SPN cipher, these sets are vector spaces.

The attacker builds a structure $P + \mathcal{D}_{\text{in}} = \{P + \delta : \delta \in \mathcal{D}_{\text{in}}\}$, and uses it as starting point for the attack. A structure of $|\mathcal{D}_{\text{in}}|$ elements defines $|\mathcal{D}_{\text{in}}|^2/2$ pairs, and $|\mathcal{D}_{\text{in}}|/2$ of them lead to the fixed difference Δ_{in}. Therefore, the use of structures covers additional rounds without increasing the data complexity.

Structures can also be used on the ciphertext side, by shifting each ciphertext with all differences in $\mathcal{D}_{\text{out}}$. However, many later works do not use structures on the ciphertext side.

Retracing Boomerang. Dunkelman et al. [19] proposed an improvement where the ciphertexts are chosen so that the two returning pairs $(C, \overline{C})$ and $(C', \overline{C'})$ are dependant: if one passes the trail on E_1, the other passes it too. This increases the probability of the trail to $p_b = p^2q$. In the same spirit, Rahman et al. [32] recently proposed a boomerang attack embedding a yoyo distinguisher.

3 Truncated Boomerang Attacks

We consider boomerang attacks with truncated differentials, as introduced by Wagner in the original paper [39]. We obtain a key-recovery attack, improving on the use of structures of Biham *et al.* [9] by considering truncated differentials for the full cipher, instead of starting from a shorter boomerang distinguisher with fixed input/output differences and adding truncated trails for the key-recovery rounds. Some boomerang attacks of this type have been proposed on AES [10] and Kiasu-BC [18], but they only use structures on the plaintext side. Our framework unifies and improves on previous boomerang attacks, using truncated differentials for E_0 and E_1, and structures on both sides.

3.1 Truncated Boomerang Distinguisher

Let us consider two truncated differentials $\mathcal{D}_{in}^0 \xrightarrow[E_0]{p} \mathcal{D}_{out}^0$ and $\mathcal{D}_{in}^1 \xrightarrow[E_1]{q} \mathcal{D}_{out}^1$ with probabilities $\vec{p}, \bar{p}$ and $\vec{q}, \bar{q}$ on E_0 and E_1. We assume that $\mathcal{D}_{in}^0$ is a vector subspace of $\{0,1\}^n$ and $0 \notin \mathcal{D}_{out}^1$. The truncated boomerang attack proceeds as follows:

1. Choose a random plaintext P_0, and query the encryption oracle over the structure $P_0 + \mathcal{D}_{in}^0$; for each $i \in \mathcal{D}_{in}^0$, we define $P_i = P_0 + i$ and $C_i = E(P_i)$.
2. For each ciphertext C_i, query the decryption oracle over the set $C_i + \mathcal{D}_{out}^1$: for each $j \in \mathcal{D}_{out}^1$, we define $\overline{C_i}^j = C_i + j$ and $\overline{P_i}^j = E^{-1}(\overline{C_i}^j)$.
3. Count the number of pairs $(\overline{P_i}^j, \overline{P_{i'}}^{j'})$ with $\overline{P_i}^j + \overline{P_{i'}}^{j'} \in \mathcal{D}_{in}^0$ (and $i \neq i'$). This can be done efficiently by projecting the plaintext values on the orthogonal complement of $\mathcal{D}_{in}^0$ in $\{0,1\}^n$, and looking for collisions.
4. If needed, repeat steps 1 to 3 with different plaintext structures.

Analysis. We consider a potential quartet $(P, P', \overline{P}, \overline{P'})$ corresponding to $(C, C', \overline{C}, \overline{C'})$, with $P + P' \in \mathcal{D}_{in}^0$ and $C + \overline{C}, C' + \overline{C'} \in \mathcal{D}_{out}^1$. We have:

$$\Pr[E_0(P) + E_0(P') \in \mathcal{D}_{out}^0] = \vec{p}$$
$$\Pr[E_1^{-1}(C) + E_1^{-1}(\overline{C}) \in \mathcal{D}_{in}^1] = \bar{q}$$
$$\Pr[E_1^{-1}(C') + E_1^{-1}(\overline{C'}) \in \mathcal{D}_{in}^1] = \bar{q}$$

Following the sandwich attack analysis (with $E_m = \mathrm{id}$), we define the connection probability:

$$r = \Pr\left[E_0(\overline{P}) + E_0(\overline{P'}) \in \mathcal{D}_{out}^0 \;\middle|\; \begin{array}{l} E_0(P) + E_0(P') \in \mathcal{D}_{out}^0 \\ E_1^{-1}(C) + E_1^{-1}(\overline{C}) \in \mathcal{D}_{in}^1 \\ E_1^{-1}(C') + E_1^{-1}(\overline{C'}) \in \mathcal{D}_{in}^1 \end{array} \right]$$

If the four events hold, we have $\overline{P} + \overline{P'} \in \mathcal{D}_{in}^0$ with an additional probability $\bar{p}$. This analysis of the truncated boomerang distinguisher is the same as proposed by Wagner [39], but our attack is more general with structures on both sides.

In general, we have $E_1^{-1}(C) + E_1^{-1}(\overline{C})$ and $E_1^{-1}(C') + E_1^{-1}(\overline{C'})$ in $\mathcal{D}_{in}^1$, therefore they are equal with probability $|\mathcal{D}_{in}^1|^{-1}$, and this implies $E_0(\overline{P}) + E_0(\overline{P'}) \in \mathcal{D}_{out}^0$; hence $r \geq |\mathcal{D}_{in}^1|^{-1}$. Moreover, if $\mathcal{D}_{in}^1$ and $\mathcal{D}_{out}^0$ are vector subspaces, then $\Sigma = E_0(P) + E_0(P') + E_0(\overline{P}) + E_0(\overline{P'}) \in \mathcal{D}_{in}^1$; in particular, $\Sigma \in \mathcal{D}_{out}^0$ with probability $|\mathcal{D}_{out}^0 \cap \mathcal{D}_{in}^1| / |\mathcal{D}_{in}^1|$; this implies $E_0(\overline{P}) + E_0(\overline{P'}) \in \mathcal{D}_{out}^0$ hence $r \geq |\mathcal{D}_{out}^0 \cap \mathcal{D}_{in}^1| / |\mathcal{D}_{in}^1|$.

Assuming that all the events are independent, each quartet $(P_i, P_{i'}, \overline{P}_i^j, \overline{P}_{i'}^{j'})$, defined by a pair $(i, j), (i', j')$, follows the truncated boomerang trail with probability p_b, and randomly satisfies $\overline{P}_i^j + \overline{P}_{i'}^{j'} \in \mathcal{D}_{in}^0$ with probability $p_\$$:

$$p_b = \vec{p} \cdot \bar{\vec{p}} \cdot \vec{q}^2 \cdot r \qquad\qquad r \geq |\mathcal{D}_{in}^1|^{-1} \qquad (1)$$

$$p_\$ = |\mathcal{D}_{in}^0| / 2^n \qquad\qquad (2)$$

We assume that the boomerang probability can be well approximated as $p_b + p_\$$. We distinguish the cipher E from a random permutation when the expected number of remaining quartets (quartets with $\overline{P}_i^j + \overline{P}_{i'}^{j'} \in \mathcal{D}_{in}^0$) is significantly higher for E than for a random permutation. We define the signal-to-noise ratio:

$$\sigma = p_b / p_\$ \qquad\qquad (3)$$

When $\sigma \gg 1$, we obtain a distinguisher using $Q = \mathcal{O}(p_b^{-1})$ quartets. More precisely, with $Q = \mu \cdot p_b^{-1}$ (μ a small constant) we expect μ remaining quartets with the cipher E, versus $\mu \cdot \sigma^{-1} \ll 1$ for a random permutation. A distinguisher that detects the presence of at least one quartet has a success rate of $1 - e^{-\mu}$.

When σ is smaller, we need to collect a large number of quartets, and compare the expected number of remaining quartets q_b for E and $q_\$$ in the random case:

$$q_b = Q \times (p_\$ + p_b) = Q \times p_\$(1 + \sigma) \qquad\qquad q_\$ = Q \times p_\$$$

We detect the bias with $Q = \mathcal{O}(p_\$^{-1}\sigma^{-2}) = \mathcal{O}(p_b^{-1}\sigma^{-1})$ samples, following [29, Theorem 2]. Using $Q = c \times p_b^{-1}\sigma^{-1}$ with a small constant c and setting a threshold at $Q \times p_\$(1 + \sigma/2)$, the distinguisher has a success rate of $\Phi(\sqrt{c}/2)$, with Φ the cumulative distribution function of the standard normal distribution.

If Q is smaller than the number of quartets in a full structure $(|\mathcal{D}_{in}^0|^2|\mathcal{D}_{out}^1|^2/2)$, we use a partial structure with only $\sqrt{2Q}$ elements. Otherwise, we need $N = 2Q \times |\mathcal{D}_{in}^0|^{-2}|\mathcal{D}_{out}^1|^{-2}$ structures of $S = |\mathcal{D}_{in}^0||\mathcal{D}_{out}^1|$ elements. Finally, we obtain a distinguisher with a constant probability of success with the following complexity in number of quartets, time, data, and memory:

$$Q = \mathcal{O}\left(\max(p_b^{-1}, \sigma^{-1} \cdot p_b^{-1})\right) \qquad\qquad (4)$$

$$T = D = \max(\sqrt{2Q}, 2Q \times |\mathcal{D}_{in}^1|^{-1}|\mathcal{D}_{out}^1|^{-1}) \qquad\qquad (5)$$

$$M = \min(D, |\mathcal{D}_{in}^0||\mathcal{D}_{out}^1|) \qquad\qquad (6)$$

Application to 6-Round AES. To explain the truncated boomerang distinguisher in practice, we give a truncated boomerang trail on 6-round AES in

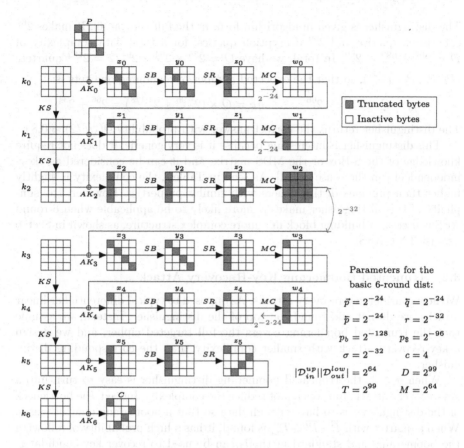

Fig. 3. A truncated boomerang trail on 6-round AES.

Fig. 3, using the 3-round trail of Fig. 1 twice. $\mathcal{D}_{in}^0$ and $\mathcal{D}_{in}^1$ are the sets of all states that have zeros on all diagonals except the main one. $\mathcal{D}_{out}^0$ is the same as the output set of Fig. 1, and $\mathcal{D}_{out}^1$ is active on the main anti-diagonal (it differs because we omit the last MixColumns operation). We have

$$|\mathcal{D}_{in}^0| = |\mathcal{D}_{out}^0| = 2^{32} \qquad \vec{p} = 2^{-24} \qquad \bar{p} = 2^{-24}$$
$$|\mathcal{D}_{in}^1| = |\mathcal{D}_{out}^1| = 2^{32} \qquad \vec{q} = 2^{-24} \qquad \bar{q} = 2^{-24}$$

Since $\mathcal{D}_{out}^0 \cap \mathcal{D}_{in}^1 = \{0\}$, we have $r = |\mathcal{D}_{in}^1|^{-1}$, and the analysis above gives the following parameters:

$$p_b = \vec{p} \cdot \bar{p} \cdot \vec{q}^2 \times |\mathcal{D}_{in}^1|^{-1} = 2^{-128} \qquad \sigma = 2^{-32}$$
$$p_\$ = |\mathcal{D}_{in}^0|/2^n = 2^{-96} \qquad Q = c \cdot 2^{160}$$

Using $c = 4$ and the formulas of Eqs. (4), (5), and (6), we obtain a distinguisher with complexity:

$$T = D = 2^{99} \qquad M = 2^{64}$$

The distinguisher is given in algorithm form in the full version [6]. It makes 2^{67} encryption queries and 2^{99} decryption queries, for a total data complexity of $D = 2^{67} + 2^{99} \approx 2^{99}$. In total, we have $Q = 2^{35} \times 2^{64} \times 2^{64}/2 = 2^{162}$ quartets $(P_i, P_{i'}, \overline{P_i}^j, \overline{P_{i'}}^{j'})$, so that the expected number of remaining quartets is:

$$q_\$ = Q \times 2^{-96} = 2^{66} \qquad q_E = Q \times (2^{-96} + 2^{-128}) = 2^{66} + 2^{34}$$

The distinguisher returns the correct answer with probability $\Phi(\sqrt{c}/2) \approx 0.84$.

This distinguisher is interesting because it is very generic: it does not require knowledge of the S-Box or the MDS matrix, and it can be considered as "key-independent" in the sense of [24]. As seen in Table 1, the complexity is slightly higher than previous distinguishers with similar properties. However, the simplicity of this distinguisher makes it more likely to be applicable when 6-round AES is used as a building block in a more complex structure, as shown in Sect. 6 against TNT-AES.

3.2   Truncated Boomerang Key-Recovery Attack

We now consider key-recovery attacks. As opposed to typical differential or linear attacks, we do not add rounds on top of the distinguisher. Instead, we assume that the truncated boomerang covers the full targeted cipher, and we design a key-recovery attack with smaller complexity than the corresponding distinguisher.

When $\sigma \geq 1$, the truncated boomerang distinguisher is easy to turn into a key-recovery attack, but we cannot reduce the complexity. Indeed, the bottleneck of the distinguisher is to have enough data so that a boomerang quartet exists. When a quartet with $\overline{P} + \overline{P'} \in \mathcal{D}_{in}^0$ is found, it has a high probability of following the boomerang, and standard methods can be used to recover key candidates. Therefore, we focus on the case $\sigma \ll 1$, where the distinguisher requires multiple quartets following the boomerang.

Given a candidate quartet with $\overline{P} + \overline{P'} \in \mathcal{D}_{in}^0$, we can extract some key information assuming that it follows the boomerang. If this is the case, we have two pairs of known plaintexts (P, P') and $(\overline{P}, \overline{P'})$ following the truncated differential $\mathcal{D}_{in}^0 \xrightarrow[E_0]{p} \mathcal{D}_{out}^0$, and two pairs of known ciphertexts $(C, \overline{C})$ and $(C', \overline{C'})$ following the truncated differential $\mathcal{D}_{in}^1 \xrightarrow[E_1]{q} \mathcal{D}_{out}^1$. Using standard techniques from differential cryptanalysis, we can usually extract partial information about the first and last subkeys. We denote by κ the number of key bits that can be extracted, and by ℓ the average number of κ-bit key candidates suggested by a quartet. Note that the key information suggested by a quartet might be incompatible between both pairs of plaintexts following the upper differential (or between both pairs of ciphertexts following the lower differential), in this case the quartet is discarded.

We follow the standard approach to identify the most likely candidates for the κ bits of key: we build a table of 2^κ counters corresponding to key candidates, and we increment the counter of each key suggested by each quartet. With enough data, the right key is expected to be among the top $2^{\kappa-a}$ counters (a denotes the advantage of the attack).

Analysis. Following the previous analysis, we expect $Q \times (p_\$ + p_b)$ quartets with $\overline{P} + \overline{P'} \in \mathcal{D}_{\text{in}}^0$: $Q \times p_b$ quartets following the boomerang trail (right quartets), and $Q \times p_\$$ false positives. For a right quartet, the correct key is among the deduced key candidates, and for a wrong quartet, we expect that ℓ random key candidates are deduced. Assuming that all the quartets behave independently, the wrong counters follow the binomial distribution $\mathcal{B}(Q, (p_\$ + p_b) \times \ell \times 2^{-\kappa})$ and the right counter follows the distribution $\mathcal{B}(Q, p_\$ \times \ell \times 2^{-\kappa} + p_b)$. We denote the probabilities of suggesting a wrong key and the right key as:

$$p_w = (p_\$ + p_b) \times \ell \times 2^{-\kappa} \approx p_\$ \times \ell \times 2^{-\kappa} \tag{7}$$

$$p_0 = p_\$ \times \ell \times 2^{-\kappa} + p_b \approx p_w + p_b \tag{8}$$

We obtain a higher signal-to-noise ratio $\tilde{\sigma}$ than previously:

$$\tilde{\sigma} = p_b/p_w = \sigma \times 2^\kappa/\ell \tag{9}$$

When $\tilde{\sigma} \gg 1$, only a handful of right quartets are necessary to have the right key ranked first, so that $Q = \mathcal{O}(p_b^{-1})$.

When $\tilde{\sigma} \ll 1$, the counters can be approximated by normal distributions, and we use the work of Selçuk [35, Theorem 3] to evaluate the number of samples needed to have the right key among the top $2^{\kappa-a}$ key candidates (depending on the success rate). For a fixed value of a, we need Q proportional to $p_b^{-1}\tilde{\sigma}^{-1}$, and the complexity increases linearly in a. Finally, the increased signal-to-noise ratio $\tilde{\sigma} \gg \sigma$ reduces the data complexity to:

$$Q = \mathcal{O}\left(\max(p_b^{-1}, \tilde{\sigma}^{-1} \times p_b^{-1})\right) \tag{10}$$

$$D = \max(\sqrt{2Q}, 2Q \times |\mathcal{D}_{\text{in}}^0|^{-1}|\mathcal{D}_{\text{out}}^1|^{-1}) \tag{11}$$

The time complexity is harder to evaluate; it can be bounded with T_E the cost of an oracle call (by convention, $T_E = 1$), and T_C the cost of deducing key candidates from a quartet:

$$T = D \times T_E + Q \times p_\$ \times T_C \tag{12}$$

When $T_C \ll 2^n \times |\mathcal{D}_{\text{in}}^0|^{-2}|\mathcal{D}_{\text{out}}^1|^{-1}$, we have $Q \times p_\$ \times T_C \ll D$ and the second term is negligible; the cost of the attack is thus dominated by the oracle queries. Otherwise, it is often possible to reduce the second term with more advanced filtering, but this requires a dedicated analysis for each attack.

After recovering $2^{\kappa-a}$ candidates for the κ-bit partial key, the full key can be recovered by exhaustive search of the remaining bits with complexity 2^{n-a}, or by launching a variant of the attack on a different set of key bits.

Success Probability. When $\tilde{\sigma} \ll 1$, the average values of right and wrong counters are high enough to approximate them with normal distributions. In that case, the success rate can be evaluated using the formula given by [35], under additional assumptions about the independence of key counters, and order statistics:

$$P_S = \Phi\left(\frac{\sqrt{\mu\tilde{\sigma}} - \Phi^{-1}(1 - 2^{-a})}{\sqrt{\tilde{\sigma} + 1}}\right) \tag{13}$$

with $\mu = Q \times p_b$ the expected number of right quartets.

When $\tilde{\sigma}$ is high, the binomial distributions of right and wrong counters have their average values respectively $Q \times p_b \approx 1$ and $Q \times p_w \ll 1$. As discussed in [35, Sect. 3.2.1], the normal approximation is inaccurate in this case; we obtain a more accurate estimate of the success probability using a Poisson approximation.

Extracting Key Candidates. When the truncated differentials are described by truncated trails (with a set of intermediate differences at each step), the parameters ℓ and κ can often be deduced directly from the trail. We assume that E_0 starts with the addition of a subkey K_0, followed by an S-Box layer SB, and we denote the set of differences after the S-Box layer by $\mathcal{D}^0_{\text{mid}}$:

$$E_0 = \tilde{E}_0 \circ \text{SB} \circ \text{AK}_{K_0} \qquad \mathcal{D}^0_{\text{in}} \xrightarrow[\text{SB}]{p_0} \mathcal{D}^0_{\text{mid}} \qquad \mathcal{D}^0_{\text{mid}} \xrightarrow[\tilde{E}_0]{p_1} \mathcal{D}^0_{\text{out}}$$

We also assume that $\mathcal{D}^0_{\text{in}}$ is a vector subspace aligned with the S-Box layer (each S-Box is either inactive, or active with all possible differences). $\mathcal{D}^0_{\text{mid}}$ is a subset of $\mathcal{D}^0_{\text{in}}$; typically it is constructed so that some parts of the state have fixed differences after the linear layer. For instance, in the AES trail of Fig. 1, $\mathcal{D}^0_{\text{mid}}$ corresponds to differences δ such that MixColumns(ShiftRows(δ)) is active only on the first cell, with $|\mathcal{D}^0_{\text{mid}}| = 2^8$ and $\vec{p}_0 = 2^{-24}$. In general, we have:

$$\vec{p}_0 = |\mathcal{D}^0_{\text{mid}}|/|\mathcal{D}^0_{\text{in}}| \qquad\qquad \vec{p} = \vec{p}_0 \times \vec{p}_1 \qquad (14)$$

We consider a pair (P, P'), and assume that it follows the truncated trail, *i.e.* $\text{SB}(P + K_0) + \text{SB}(P' + K_0) \in \mathcal{D}^0_{\text{mid}}$. This constrains the partial subkey $K_{0|\mathcal{D}^0_{\text{in}}}$ corresponding to the active S-Boxes in SB. More precisely, for each difference δ in $\mathcal{D}^0_{\text{mid}}$, we expect on average 0.5 unordered pairs $\{X, X'\}$ such that $X + X' = P + P'$ and $\text{SB}(X) + \text{SB}(X') = \delta$ (restricted to the active bytes $\mathcal{D}^0_{\text{mid}}$). This pair can be recovered efficiently after pre-computing the DDT of the S-Box, and we deduce two possible keys $X + P$ and $X + P'$. Therefore, we have the following parameters when extracting key candidates from a pair (P, P'):

$$\ell^0 = |\mathcal{D}^0_{\text{mid}}| \qquad \kappa^0 = \log_2(|\mathcal{D}^0_{\text{in}}|) \qquad T^0_C = \ell^0 = |\mathcal{D}^0_{\text{mid}}|$$

Starting from a candidate quartet, we have two different pairs (P, P') and $(\overline{P}, \overline{P}')$ assumed to follow the upper differential. Therefore, we expect only $|\mathcal{D}^0_{\text{mid}}|^2/|\mathcal{D}^0_{\text{in}}|$ key candidates compatible with both pairs. We apply the same reasoning to the lower trail (using ciphertext pairs), and deduce the parameters ℓ and κ for a quartet in the general case:

$$\ell = |\mathcal{D}^0_{\text{mid}}|^2 \cdot |\mathcal{D}^1_{\text{mid}}|^2 \cdot |\mathcal{D}^0_{\text{in}}|^{-1} \cdot |\mathcal{D}^1_{\text{out}}|^{-1} \qquad \kappa = \log_2(|\mathcal{D}^0_{\text{in}}| \cdot |\mathcal{D}^1_{\text{out}}|) \qquad (15)$$

Using the probability $\vec{p}_0$ for the first round and $\tilde{q}_0$ for the last round, we have

$$\ell \cdot 2^{-\kappa} = \vec{p}_0^{\,2} \cdot \tilde{q}_0^{\,2} \qquad (16)$$

For the lower trail, we only have to process a fraction $|\mathcal{D}^0_{\text{mid}}|^2/|\mathcal{D}^0_{\text{in}}|$ of the candidate quartets (with a key compatible with both pairs). In particular, when $|\mathcal{D}^0_{\text{mid}}|^2 \ll |\mathcal{D}^0_{\text{in}}|$, the time complexity is dominated by the first extraction step: $T_C = |\mathcal{D}^0_{\text{mid}}|$.

Application to 6-Round AES. This attack can directly be applied to AES, using the same 3-round trails as in the previous section (see Fig. 3):

$$|\mathcal{D}_{\text{in}}^0| = |\mathcal{D}_{\text{out}}^0| = 2^{32} \qquad |\mathcal{D}_{\text{mid}}^0| = 2^8 \qquad \vec{p} = 2^{-24} \qquad \overleftarrow{p} = 2^{-24}$$

$$|\mathcal{D}_{\text{in}}^1| = |\mathcal{D}_{\text{out}}^1| = 2^{32} \qquad |\mathcal{D}_{\text{mid}}^1| = 2^8 \qquad \vec{q} = 2^{-24} \qquad \overleftarrow{q} = 2^{-24}$$

Using the parameters of the key extraction, our analysis results in

$$\ell = |\mathcal{D}_{\text{mid}}^0|^2 \cdot |\mathcal{D}_{\text{mid}}^1|^2 \cdot |\mathcal{D}_{\text{in}}^0|^{-1} \cdot |\mathcal{D}_{\text{out}}^1|^{-1} = 2^{-32} \qquad \kappa = \log_2(|\mathcal{D}_{\text{in}}^0| \cdot |\mathcal{D}_{\text{out}}^1|) = 64$$

$$p_b = \vec{p} \cdot \overleftarrow{p} \cdot \vec{q}^2 \times |\mathcal{D}_{\text{in}}^1|^{-1} = 2^{-128}$$

$$p_w = |\mathcal{D}_{\text{in}}^0| \times 2^{-n} \times \ell \times 2^{-\kappa} = 2^{-192} \qquad \tilde{\sigma} = 2^{64}$$

Since $\tilde{\sigma} \gg 1$, we only need a few right quartets; with $\mu = 4$ we obtain

$$Q = \mu \times p_b^{-1} = 2^{130} \qquad\qquad D = 2^{67}$$

Time Complexity. With these parameters, the attack complexity is dominated by the oracle queries. We use 8 structures of 2^{64} elements; in each structure we detect $2^{64} \times 2^{63} \times p_\$ = 2^{31}$ pairs with $\overline{P} + \overline{P}' \in \mathcal{D}_{\text{in}}^0$, resulting in $8 \times 2^{31} = 2^{34}$ candidate quartets in total. Each quartet suggests on average 2^{-32} candidates for 64 bits of key (for most of the quartets, there is no key compatible with both sides of the quartet). Finally, we expect 2^2 suggestions of wrong keys (each key is suggested 2^{-62} times on average), and $\mu = 4$ suggestions for the correct key. With high probability, the key with the most suggestions is the correct one.

We implemented the attack on a reduced AES with 4-bit S-Boxes, and it behaves as expected [7].

4   Optimized Boomerang Attacks on 6-Round AES

As shown by Biryukov [10], boomerang attacks on AES can be optimized using multiple trails. We now present improved versions of our attacks using this technique, including a 6-round key-recovery attack with complexity 2^{61}. The improvement compared to the attack of Biryukov with complexity 2^{71} is due to the use of structures on the ciphertext side.

4.1   Optimized Distinguisher

Instead of only considering the trail of Fig. 1 with fixed positions for all the active bytes, we consider a collection of four different trails for upper part:

The collection can be considered as a truncated differential $\mathcal{D}_{\text{in}}^0 \xrightarrow[E_0]{p} \mathcal{D}_{\text{out}}^0$ with

$$\vec{p} = 2^{-22} \qquad\qquad \overleftarrow{p} = 2^{-24} \qquad\qquad |\mathcal{D}_{\text{in}}^0| = 2^{32} \qquad\qquad |\mathcal{D}_{\text{out}}^0| = 2^{34}$$

Similarly, we consider four trails for the lower part:

Again, this can be considered as a truncated differential $\mathcal{D}_{in}^1 \xrightarrow[E_1]{q} \mathcal{D}_{out}^1$ with

$$\vec{q} = 2^{-24} \qquad \overleftarrow{q} = 2^{-22} \qquad |\mathcal{D}_{in}^1| = 2^{34} \qquad |\mathcal{D}_{out}^1| = 2^{32}$$

The analysis of the previous sections can be applied as-is with these trails. We obtain a better attack because we increase $\vec{p}$ and $\overleftarrow{q}$ by a factor 4, even though $|\mathcal{D}_{in}^1|$ increases by a factor 4; we obtain $p_b = 2^{-124}$ instead of 2^{-128}. The distinguisher is exactly the same because $\mathcal{D}_{in}^0$ and $\mathcal{D}_{out}^1$ are the same, but this improved analysis shows that the complexity of the distinguisher can be reduced to $T = D = 2^{91}$ (with $c = 4$, $\sigma = 2^{-28}$ and $Q = 2^{154}$).

Larger Set $\mathcal{D}_{out}^1$. We further improve the distinguisher using a collection of 16 trails with the following input and output sets for the lower trail:

This collection can be considered as a truncated differential $\mathcal{D}_{in}^1 \xrightarrow[E_1]{q} \mathcal{D}_{out}^1$ with

$$\vec{q} = 2^{-22} \qquad \overleftarrow{q} = 2^{-22} \qquad |\mathcal{D}_{in}^1| = 2^{34} \qquad |\mathcal{D}_{out}^1| = 2^{34}$$

This does not affect the probability p_b, but generates larger structures; the complexity is reduced to $T = D = 2^{89}$ with $Q = 2^{154}$.

Different Set $\overline{\mathcal{D}}_{in}^0$ for Returning Pairs.
Following Biryukov [10], we use a higher probability differential for the returning pair $(\overline{P}, \overline{P'})$, different from for the initial pair (P, P'), and with a larger set $\overline{\mathcal{D}}_{in}^0$. We consider the same collection of 16 trails as above, corresponding to a truncated differential $\overline{\mathcal{D}}_{in}^0 \xrightarrow[E_0]{\overline{p}} \mathcal{D}_{out}^0$ with

$$\vec{\overline{p}} = 2^{-22} \qquad \overleftarrow{\overline{p}} = 2^{-22} \qquad |\overline{\mathcal{D}}_{in}^0| = 2^{34} \qquad |\mathcal{D}_{out}^0| = 2^{34}$$

This corresponds to keeping quartets with a single active diagonal in $\overline{P} + \overline{P'}$, but not necessarily the main one. We adapt our analysis to account for the two distinct upper differentials and we obtain

$$p_b = \vec{p} \cdot \vec{\overline{p}} \cdot \overleftarrow{q}^2 \times |\mathcal{D}_{in}^1|^{-1} = 2^{-122} \qquad \sigma = 2^{-28}$$
$$p_\$ = |\overline{\mathcal{D}}_{in}^0|/2^n = 2^{-94} \qquad Q = 2^{152}$$

Finally, we obtain a distinguisher with complexity $T = D = 2^{87}$ (with $c = 4$).

4.2   Optimized Key-Recovery Attack

For a key-recovery attack, we can use the trails above to obtain an attack with complexity $T = D = 2^{62.5}$. We keep the set $\mathcal{D}^1_{\text{out}}$ active only in the first column ($|\mathcal{D}^1_{\text{out}}| = 2^{32}$) in order to extract information on the same key for each quartet. More details are given in the full version [6].

In order to further reduce the complexity of this attack, we use truncated boomerang characteristics with lower signal-to-noise ratios, taking advantage of the additional filter provided by the key extraction. Following [10], we modify the truncated trail on the returning side $(\overline{P}, \overline{P}')$ to allow any combination of two active diagonals in input, leading to the following parameters:

$$\overline{\mathcal{D}}^0_{\text{in}} = \left\{ \boxed{}, \boxed{}, \boxed{}, \boxed{}, \boxed{}, \boxed{} \right\}$$

$$\vec{p} = 2^{-22} \quad \overleftarrow{p} = 2^{-24} \qquad\qquad |\mathcal{D}^0_{\text{in}}| = 2^{32} \qquad |\mathcal{D}^0_{\text{out}}| = 2^{34} \quad |\mathcal{D}^0_{\text{mid}}| = 2^{10}$$

$$\overline{\vec{p}} = 2^{-46} \quad \overline{\overleftarrow{p}} = 6 \times 2^{-16} = 2^{-13.4} \quad |\overline{\mathcal{D}}^0_{\text{in}}| = 6 \times 2^{64} \quad |\mathcal{D}^0_{\text{out}}| = 2^{34}$$

$$\vec{q} = 2^{-24} \quad \overleftarrow{q} = 2^{-22} \qquad\qquad |\mathcal{D}^1_{\text{in}}| = 2^{34} \qquad |\mathcal{D}^1_{\text{out}}| = 2^{32} \quad |\mathcal{D}^1_{\text{mid}}| = 2^{10}$$

When extracting the key, we recover information about the main diagonal of k_0 from (P, P'), and information about the first anti-diagonal of k_6 from $(C, \overline{C})$ and $(C', \overline{C}')$ (note that $(\overline{P}, \overline{P}')$ is not necessarily active in the main diagonal). Moreover, the key suggested by $(C, \overline{C})$ and $(C', \overline{C}')$ must lead to the same active byte in z_4, so that

$$\ell^0 = 2^{10} \quad \kappa^0 = 32 \quad \ell^1 = 2^{-14} \quad \kappa^1 = 32 \quad \ell = 2^{-4} \quad \kappa = 64$$

Using the previous analysis, we obtain

$$p_b = \vec{p} \cdot \overline{\overleftarrow{p}} \cdot \vec{q}^{\,2} \times |\mathcal{D}^1_{\text{in}}|^{-1} = 2^{-113.4}$$

$$p_w = |\overline{\mathcal{D}}^0_{\text{in}}| 2^{-n} \times \ell \times 2^{-\kappa} = 2^{-129.4} \qquad\qquad \tilde{\sigma} = 2^{16}$$

Since $\tilde{\sigma} \gg 1$, a few right quartets are sufficient for the success of this attack; we use $\mu = 8$, this corresponds to $Q = 2^{116.4}$ and we use a partial structure of $D = 2^{58.7}$ elements.

Success Probability. We assume that the attacker keeps key candidates with counter values of at least 5. With $\tilde{\sigma} \gg 1$, we approximate the wrong key counters by Poisson distributions with $\lambda = Q \times p_w = 2^{-13}$, each of which equal 5 or more with probability $1 - e^{-\lambda}(1 + \lambda + \lambda^2/2 + \lambda^3/6 + \lambda^4/24) \approx 2^{-71.9}$; we don't expect to keep any wrong keys. On the other hand, the counter for the right key follows a Poisson distribution with $\lambda = \mu = 8$. It reaches a value of 5 or more with probability ≈ 0.9.

Time Complexity. After recovering a candidate for 64 bits of key (32 bits of k_0 and 32 bits of k_6), we repeat the attack with $\mathcal{D}_{in}^0$ in a different diagonal and use the partial knowledge of k_6 to increase the probability $\bar{q}$. This step has a negligible complexity.

The time complexity is balanced between oracle queries and extracting key candidates. Indeed, we filter $2^{58.7} \times 2^{57.7} \times |\overline{\mathcal{D}}_{in}^0| \times 2^{-n} = 2^{55}$ candidates with $\overline{P} + \overline{P}' \in \overline{\mathcal{D}}_{in}^0$ using 6 hash tables indexed by each combination of two active columns. The complexity T_C to generate key candidates for a given quartet is essentially 4×2^{10} accesses to a small table; we approximate it as $T_C \approx 2^{5.4} T_E$ (since one encryption has 6×16 S-Boxes). Finally, the time complexity is

$$T = 2^{58.7} T_E + 2^{55} T_C \approx 2^{60.8} T_E$$

4.3   Key-Recovery with Secret S-Boxes

The techniques described in Subsect. 3.2 assume that the S-Box and MDS matrix are known to the attacker in order to extract key information. However, it is also possible to extract key information with an unknown S-Box under some conditions. Following [23], we assume that all S-Boxes in a column are identical, and that the MDS matrix has two identical coefficients in each row.

As a concrete example, we consider the AES MixColumns matrix

$$\mathsf{MC} = \begin{bmatrix} 2 & 3 & 1 & 1 \\ 1 & 2 & 3 & 1 \\ 1 & 1 & 2 & 3 \\ 3 & 1 & 1 & 2 \end{bmatrix}$$

We consider a pair $(C, \overline{C})$ following the truncated trail of Fig. 3. According to the trail, the difference before the last round (w_4) is in a set of 2^8 differences; in particular, the difference in cell 1 is equal to the difference in cell 2:

$$w_4 + \overline{w}_4 \in \left\{ \begin{bmatrix} 2\delta & 0 & 0 & 0 \\ \delta & 0 & 0 & 0 \\ \delta & 0 & 0 & 0 \\ 3\delta & 0 & 0 & 0 \end{bmatrix} : \delta \in \{0,1\}^8 \right\} = \left\{ \mathsf{MC} \cdot \begin{bmatrix} \delta & 0 & 0 & 0 \\ 0 & 0 & 0 & 0 \\ 0 & 0 & 0 & 0 \\ 0 & 0 & 0 & 0 \end{bmatrix} : \delta \in \{0,1\}^8 \right\}$$

Moreover, we assume that the differences in cells 13 and 10 of the ciphertext are equal (they are moved to cell 1 and 2 by ShiftRows)

$$C + \overline{C} = \begin{bmatrix} \alpha & 0 & 0 & 0 \\ 0 & 0 & 0 & \beta \\ 0 & 0 & \beta & 0 \\ 0 & \gamma & 0 & 0 \end{bmatrix}$$

In this case, S-Boxes 1 and 2 in the last round follow the same transition $\delta \to \beta$. With high probability, this implies that the unordered pairs of input/output are equal; in particular $\{C[13] + k_6[13], \overline{C}[13] + k_6[13]\} = \{C[10] + k_6[10], \overline{C}[10] + k_6[10]\}$. This suggests two key candidates:

$$k_6[13] + k_6[10] \in \{C[13] + C[10], C[13] + \overline{C}[10]\}$$

In order to use this property in a truncated boomerang attack, we use the multiple upper trails of Subsect. 4.1, and a single lower trail with a restricted

$\mathcal{D}_{\text{out}}^1$ of size 2^{24} to ensure that $C + \overline{C}$ and $C' + \overline{C}'$ have the required properties for all quartets considered:

$$\mathcal{D}_{\text{out}}^1 = \left\{ \begin{bmatrix} a & 0 & 0 & 0 \\ 0 & 0 & 0 & b \\ 0 & 0 & b & 0 \\ 0 & c & 0 & 0 \end{bmatrix} : a, b, c \in \{0,1\}^8 \right\}$$

The corresponding parameters are:

$$\vec{p} = 2^{-22} \qquad \overleftarrow{p} = 2^{-24} \qquad |\mathcal{D}_{\text{in}}^0| = 2^{32} \qquad |\mathcal{D}_{\text{out}}^0| = 2^{34}$$

$$\overline{\vec{p}} = 2^{-22} \qquad \overline{\overleftarrow{p}} = 2^{-22} \qquad |\overline{\mathcal{D}}_{\text{in}}^0| = 2^{34} \qquad |\mathcal{D}_{\text{out}}^0| = 2^{34}$$

$$\vec{q} = 2^{-32} \qquad \overleftarrow{q} = 2^{-24} \qquad |\mathcal{D}_{\text{in}}^1| = 2^{32} \qquad |\mathcal{D}_{\text{out}}^1| = 2^{24}$$

For each quartet, the pair $(C, \overline{C})$ suggests two values for $k_6[13] + k_6[10]$, and $C', \overline{C}'$ also suggests two values. Therefore a quartet suggests on average $\ell = 2^{-6}$ values for $\kappa = 8$ bits of key. Using the analysis of Subsect. 3.2, we obtain:

$$p_b = \vec{p} \cdot \overline{\overleftarrow{p}} \cdot \overleftarrow{q}^2 \times |\mathcal{D}_{\text{in}}^1|^{-1} = 2^{-124} \qquad \tilde{\sigma} = 2^{-16}$$

$$p_w = |\overline{\mathcal{D}}_{\text{in}}^0| \times 2^{-n} \times \ell \cdot 2^{-\kappa} = 2^{-108} \qquad Q = \mathcal{O}(2^{140})$$

To obtain a high probability of success we use $Q = 2^{145}$, i.e. $D = 2^{90}$. Since $\tilde{\sigma} \ll 1$, the counter distribution of the right key can be approximated to the normal distribution $\mathcal{N}(2^{37} + 2^{21}, 2^{37})$ while wrong key counters distributions can be approximated to $\mathcal{N}(2^{37}, 2^{37})$. We expect the correct key to be ranked first with very high probability ($P_S > 0.99$ using the formula from [35]).

The time complexity is dominated by the oracle queries: for each structure of 2^{56} plaintexts/ciphertexts, we filter $2^{56} \times 2^{55} \times |\overline{\mathcal{D}}_{\text{in}}^0| \times 2^{-n} = 2^{17}$ candidate quartets with $\overline{P} + \overline{P}' \in \overline{\mathcal{D}}_{\text{in}}^0$, and the time to extract the key candidates is negligible. We can repeat the attack to recover up to 16 key bytes in different positions, with a complexity of $D = T = 2^{94}$ (but only 12 recovered bytes are linearly independent).

5   Application to 8-Round Kiasu-BC

Kiasu-BC [26] is an instance of the TWEAKEY framework [27], reusing the AES round function in a tweakable block cipher. The 6-round boomerang attack on the AES can be extended to 8-round Kiasu-BC by taking advantage of the tweak input to cancel state differences in order to have one inactive round in the upper and lower trails. Indeed, the best known attack on Kiasu-BC is an 8-round attack with complexity 2^{103} in data and time [18] following this idea. Following our framework, we improve this attack with a better use of structures.

Truncated Boomerang. Since we use a tweak difference Δ_{tw}, we slightly generalize our truncated differential framework to allow a set of tweak differences $\mathcal{D}_{\text{tw}}$. We start from a 4-round truncated trail $(\mathcal{D}_{\text{in}}, \mathcal{D}_{\text{tw}}) \xrightarrow{p}_{E} \mathcal{D}_{\text{out}}$ with probability 2^{-32}, similar to the 3-round trail of previous sections:

$\mathcal{D}_{tw}$ is the set of differences active in the first cell of the tweak; following the tweakey schedule of Kiasu-BC, this results in a tweakey difference in $\mathcal{D}_{tw}$ at each round. We obtain an 8-round boomerang with two 4-round differentials:

$$\vec{p} = 2^{-32} \qquad \bar{p} = 2^{-32} \qquad |\mathcal{D}_{in}^0| = 2^{32} \qquad |\mathcal{D}_{out}^0| = 2^{32} \qquad |\mathcal{D}_{tw}^0| = 2^8$$
$$\vec{q} = 2^{-32} \qquad \bar{q} = 2^{-32} \qquad |\mathcal{D}_{in}^1| = 2^{32} \qquad |\mathcal{D}_{out}^1| = 2^{32} \qquad |\mathcal{D}_{tw}^1| = 2^8$$

Following the analysis of the AES attack in Subsect. 3.2, we deduce on average $\ell = 2^{-32}$ candidates of $\kappa = 64$ key bits per quartet. Therefore, we obtain

$$p_b = \vec{p} \cdot \bar{p} \cdot \vec{q}^2 \times |\mathcal{D}_{in}^1|^{-1} = 2^{-160}$$
$$p_w = |\mathcal{D}_{in}^0|/2^n \times \ell \times 2^{-\kappa} = 2^{-192} \qquad\qquad \tilde{\sigma} = 2^{32}$$

Since $\tilde{\sigma} \gg 1$, we only need a few right quartets. Taking $\mu = 4$, we obtain an attack with $Q = 2^{162}$ quartets. We take advantage of the tweak to build larger structures (iterating over the tweak and data inputs), of size $|\mathcal{D}_{in}^0| \cdot |\mathcal{D}_{tw}^0| \cdot |\mathcal{D}_{out}^1| \cdot |\mathcal{D}_{tw}^1| = 2^{80}$. Thus we only need 8 structures, with data complexity $D = 2^{83}$. In each structure of 2^{80} elements, we expect 2^{63} quartets with $\overline{P} + \overline{P}' \in \mathcal{D}_{in}^0$, therefore the time complexity for the key recovery is negligible, and $T = D = 2^{83}$.

Success Probability. There are 2^{66} quartets with $\overline{P} + \overline{P}' \in \mathcal{D}_{in}^0$, suggesting on average 2^{-32} key candidates each; hence a total of 2^{34} candidates for 64 bits of key. We keep key candidates whose counter reaches 2 or more. Modeling counters for wrong keys with a Poisson distribution with $\lambda = 2^{-30}$, the probability for a specific wrong key counter to be at least 2 is $1 - e^{-\lambda}(1 + \lambda) \approx 2^{-61}$; therefore we expect to keep 8 wrong keys. On the other hand, the counter for the right key follows a Poisson distribution with $\lambda = 4$. It reaches a value of 2 or more with probability ≈ 0.9.

As in the AES attacks, we recover the full key by repeating the attack with $\mathcal{D}_{in}^0$ in a different diagonal. Taking advantage of the recovered values of the last round key, this adds a negligible complexity.

6   Application to TNT-AES

TNT-AES is a tweakable block cipher reusing the AES round function published at Eurocrypt 2020 [1]. It is part of the Tweak-aNd-Tweak framework, building a tweakable block cipher $\tilde{E}$ from a block cipher E:

$$\tilde{E}_{K_0,K_1,K_2} : P, T \mapsto C = E_{K_2}\Big(T + E_{K_1}\big(T + E_{K_0}(P)\big)\Big)$$

In order to improve its efficiency, TNT-AES uses a 6-round AES as building block E. The designers of TNT proved its security up to $2^{2n/3}$ queries, and conjectured a higher security bound. Later work [25] proved the bound to be at least $\Omega(2^{3n/4})$ queries, and exhibited a distinguisher with $\mathcal{O}(\sqrt{n} \cdot 2^{3n/4})$ queries.

Truncated Boomerang. Our attack focuses on the middle cipher E_{K_1}, between both tweak additions. In order to skip the initial and final ciphers E_{K_0} and E_{K_2}, we introduce differences in the tweak, instead of introducing them in the plaintext and ciphertext. We fix a plaintext P, and consider four tweaks $T, T', \overline{T}, \overline{T}'$ to create quartets as follows:

1. Query $C = \tilde{E}(P, T)$ and $C' = \tilde{E}(P, T')$
2. Query $\overline{P} = \tilde{E}^{-1}(C, \overline{T})$ and $\overline{P}' = \tilde{E}^{-1}(C', \overline{T}')$
3. Detect when $\overline{P} = \overline{P}'$

We denote the inputs and outputs of E_{K_1} as X and Y, with $Y = E_{K_1}(X)$:

$$X = E_{K_0}(P) + T \quad X' = E_{K_0}(P) + T' \quad \overline{X} = E_{K_0}(\overline{P}) + \overline{T} \quad \overline{X}' = E_{K_0}(\overline{P}') + \overline{T}'$$
$$Y = E_{K_2}^{-1}(C) + T \quad Y' = E_{K_2}^{-1}(C') + T' \quad \overline{Y} = E_{K_2}^{-1}(C) + \overline{T} \quad \overline{Y}' = E_{K_2}^{-1}(C') + \overline{T}'$$

When $\overline{P} = \overline{P}'$, we have a boomerang quartet for E_{K1} with differences

$$X + X' = T + T' = \Delta_{\text{in}} \qquad \overline{X} + \overline{X}' = \overline{T} + \overline{T}' = \Delta'_{\text{in}}$$
$$Y + \overline{Y} = T + \overline{T} = \nabla_{\text{out}} \qquad Y' + \overline{Y}' = T' + \overline{T}' = \nabla'_{\text{out}}$$

When using a truncated boomerang trail (with a fixed P and a set of tweaks), there are two important limitations compared to the previous attacks:

- We only detect when the difference $\overline{X} + \overline{X}'$ matches exactly $\overline{T} + \overline{T}'$, instead of detecting a set of differences $\mathcal{D}_{\text{in}}^0$. The boomerang trail probability decreases.
- We necessarily have $\Delta_{\text{in}} + \Delta'_{\text{in}} = \nabla_{\text{out}} + \nabla'_{\text{out}}$. For the 6-round AES truncated boomerang trail of Fig. 3, this implies $\Delta_{\text{in}} = \Delta'_{\text{in}}$ and $\nabla_{\text{out}} = \nabla'_{\text{out}}$. Therefore, we cannot take advantage of structures on the ciphertext side.

Nonetheless, truncated boomerangs can be used with structures of tweaks on the plaintext side, and the analysis of the middle rounds as truncated differentials significantly reduces the complexity compared to the analysis of [1].

Upper Differential. We use the same collection of 4 upper trails as in our optimized attack on AES:

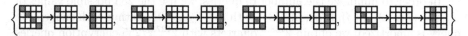

We have the following parameters

$$\vec{p} = 2^{-22} \qquad \bar{p} = 2^{-24} \qquad |\mathcal{D}_{\text{in}}^0| = 2^{32} \qquad |\mathcal{D}_{\text{out}}^0| = 2^{34}$$

For the return trail, we must hit a fixed $\overline{T} + \overline{T}' = \Delta_{\text{in}}^0$:

$$\vec{\bar{p}} = 2^{-22} \qquad \bar{\bar{p}} = 2^{-56} \qquad |\overline{\mathcal{D}}_{\text{in}}^0| = 2^0 \qquad |\mathcal{D}_{\text{out}}^0| = 2^{34}$$

Lower Differential. Since we cannot use structures on the ciphertext side, we use a fixed value Δ_{out}^1 to maximize the probability of the trail. We observe that in an AES column, the transition $\delta \rightarrow (*, 0, 0, 0)$ through a layer of inverse S-Boxes followed by inverse MixColumns happens with probability $2272/2^{32} \approx 2^{-20.85}$ with $\delta = (L(\beta/2), L(\beta), L(\beta), L(\beta/3))$, with L the linear transform inside the AES S-Box (see the full version [6] for more details). We choose $\Delta_{\text{out}}^1 =$ MixColumns(ShiftRows(δ)):

$$\vec{q} = 2^{-52.85} \qquad \overleftarrow{q} = 2^{-20.85} \qquad |\mathcal{D}_{\text{in}}^1| = 2^{32} \qquad |\mathcal{D}_{\text{out}}^1| = 2^0$$

Boomerang Trail Probability. We obtain:

$$p_b = \vec{p} \cdot \overleftarrow{p} \cdot \overleftrightarrow{q}^2 \times |\mathcal{D}_{\text{in}}^1|^{-1} = 2^{-151.7} \qquad p_\$ = |\overline{\mathcal{D}}_{\text{in}}^0|/2^n = 2^{-128}$$

As shown in the full version, we obtain a slightly better probability p_b by carefully analyzing the boomerang, and correlation between the sides:

$$p_b = 2^{-151.4}$$

It is not possible to recover actual key material with this attack because X is unknown. However, we can use $E_{K_0}(P) + K_1$ as an equivalent subkey if all queries are made with the same P. Using the pair (X, X') we extract $\ell = 2^{10}$ candidates for $\kappa = 32$ key bits. Unfortunately, we cannot use the pairs $(Y, \overline{Y})$ for filtering on the ciphertext side since the unknown value Y is different in each quartet. Similarly, the pair $(\overline{X}, \overline{X}')$ is unusable for key extraction. Therefore,

$$p_b = 2^{-151.4} \qquad p_w = p_\$ \times \ell \times 2^{-\kappa} = 2^{-150} \qquad \tilde{\sigma} = 2^{-1.4}$$

With $\tilde{\sigma} < 1$, we need $Q = c \cdot \tilde{\sigma}^{-1} \cdot p_b^{-1}$ with a small constant c; we take $c = 64$, $Q = 2^{158.8}$. Since we have structures of size 2^{32}, this corresponds to $D = 2^{127.8}$.

Distinguisher. With $2^{127.8}$ queries we obtain a distinguisher between TNT-AES (using 6-round AES as the building block) and a PRP (or TNT using a PRP). This obviously does not threaten the security of TNT-AES, but we believe that it is an interesting use case showing that a 6-round boomerang distinguisher can be extended to a larger scheme, even if the attack is marginal.

In order to minimize the number of queries, we use the 255 possible values of $\Delta_{\text{out}}^1 = (L(\beta/2), L(\beta), L(\beta), L(\beta/3))$ with $\beta \in \mathbb{F}_{256} \setminus \{0\}$, so that each encryption query is amortized: we obtain $2^{158.8}$ quartets with $2^{127.8}/255$ encryption queries and $2^{127.8}$ decryption queries. After collecting the quartets, we expect that the counter corresponding to the right key follows the distribution $\mathcal{N}(2^{8.8} + 2^{7.4}, 2^{8.8})$ while counters for the wrong keys follow the distribution $\mathcal{N}(2^{8.8}, 2^{8.8})$ (the distance between the expected values is 8 times the standard deviation).

We obtain a distinguisher by observing whether the maximum counter is higher than a threshold $t = 2^{8.8} + 7 \times 2^{4.4}$. The probability that all counters for wrong keys are lower than t is $\Phi(7)^{2^{32}} \approx 0.995$, therefore the probability of false positive is 0.005. The probability that the counter for the right key is higher than t is $\Phi(1) = 0.84$ so the probability of false negative is 0.16.

Finally, we can increase the success rate by running three attacks in parallel using three input sets $\mathcal{D}_{in}^0$, $\mathcal{D}_{in}'^0$, $\mathcal{D}_{in}''^0$ on three different diagonals. Using superstructures of 2^{96} values, we run all three attacks with the same queries, and generate counters for three sets of 2^{32} equivalent keys. Using a threshold of $t = 2^{8.8} + 7.1 \times 2^{4.4}$, we keep the probability of false positive below 1%, while the probability that at least one of the three counters corresponding to right keys is higher than the threshold increases to 99%.

TNT with 5-Round AES. A reduced version of TNT-AES with 5 AES rounds can be attacked more efficiently, using a probability-one truncated differential for one half of the cipher. In the full version [6] we give a distinguisher with 2^{76} queries, and a key-recovery with complexity 2^{87}.

7 Modeling the Framework Using MILP

MILP modelling encodes a cryptographic problem as a Mixed Integer Linear Programming problem, and uses an available solver to find optimal solutions. This method was applied to the search of boomerang distinguisher on Deoxys by Cid *et al.* [12]. Their MILP model encodes the activity of each state byte with a binary variable that equals 1 if its corresponding byte is active and 0 if not, and that is constrained depending on the activity pattern of Deoxys operations. In order to build a boomerang trail, their model includes two separate differential trails with two overlapping rounds in the middle (in order to account for the ladder switch and the BCT analysis). The objective function to minimize is roughly the number of active S-Boxes, *i.e.* the sum of all variables representing the activity of S-Box input (or output) bytes.

After generating the optimal boomerang template, they instantiate active bytes with concrete differences that maximize S-Box transition probabilities. An important contribution of their work is an analysis of the degrees of freedom of the tweakey differences. Their MILP model counts the number of linear relations between the tweakey differences and ensures that at least one degree of freedom remains in the final trail, otherwise it is unlikely to find concrete differences for the tweakey.

In 2019, Zhao et al. [42,43] improved this MILP model by adding two extra rounds at the end of the lower trail, containing truncated differences.

Our MILP Model. Previous works [12,34,43] showed that the best attack is not always obtained with the best distinguisher. Therefore we follow the same high-level approach as in [31]: our main objective is to cover the full boomerang attack with the MILP model. We give an overview of the model in the full version [6], and for more details the full code is available [7]. Our model is based on [12]; the main improvement is to allow 4 possible states for each byte of the trail, instead of only 2 (active or inactive):

- inactive, with a zero difference, denoted as ▫;
- active with a *fixed* non-zero difference, denoted as ▪;
- active with an *unknown* (truncated) difference, denoted as ▪.
- active with an *equal* (but unknown) difference for both pairs, denoted as ▪.

From these possible states, we can deduce the parameters of the attacks, including the structure size, which allows us to ask the MILP solver to minimize the formula for the data complexity of the attack given in Subsect. 3.2.

Bytes with *equal* differences encode relations between the two different pairs that follow the same trail, rather than properties of a trail by itself. This allows the MILP model to capture trails like the 6-round AES boomerang of Fig. 3. The model does not encode linear relations between active bytes (*e.g.* the set of differences for w_2 of Fig. 3 is active on all bytes but has size 2^{32}), but using this type of constraint is sufficient in many cases because it is propagated through the linear layer.

Our model generates boomerang trails without instanciating the differences. In order to derive concrete attacks from the trail, we instantiate the trail with differences that optimize the different S-Box transitions.

Limitations of the MILP Model. Our model handles only fixed differences in the tweakey. More importantly, although our model takes into account the ladder switch to compute the boomerang connection probability, it does not accurately compute the connection probability. Some boomerang trails given in a previous version of this paper were even found incompatible by Song et al. [41]. More generally, some boomerang trails returned by the MILP are not instantiable. When that happens in practice, we modify the boomerang trail squeleton or we generate a different trail using the MILP solver.

To instantiate boomerang trails generated by the MILP, we use the tables DDT, BCT [13], UBCT, LBCT and EBCT, introduced in [16,36,40]. In order to ensure that the trails are not incompatible, we verified experimentally the probability of the middle rounds [7]. For each trail, we indicate the rounds that have been checked, with the theoretical probability p_{th} for the middle rounds, and the experimental value observed p_{exp}. In some attacks, the experimental probability slightly differs from the theoretical one; we deduce an adjusted trail probability $\tilde{p}_b$ that is used to calculate the complexity of the attack.

7.1   Results on AES-128 and Kiasu-BC

We use the MILP model to search for attacks on AES-128 and Kiasu-BC and compare them with the results of the previous sections.

On AES-128, the model returns a trail corresponding to Fig. 3 with a full *equal* state in w_2. This confirms the optimality of our truncated trail within our framework. However, the model does not handle multiple trails, so that it cannot suggest the improved attack of Sect. 4.

On Kiasu-BC, the model cannot find the attack of Sect. 5, because it does not handle truncated differences in the tweak. With fixed difference in the tweak, the best trail found by the solver is unfortunately not instantiable, because of incompatibilities in the middle rounds. The solver nevertheless ensures that no attack with complexity less than 2^{80} exist in that framework.

8   Application to Deoxys-BC

Deoxys-BC [28] is a tweakable block cipher of the TWEAKEY framework [27] based the AES round function, on which the best known attacks are based on boomerangs [12,34,42,43]. Due to the large choice of tweakey differences, finding the best truncated boomerang trails manually is a tedious work. Instead, we use our MILP model of Sect. 7.

In the single tweakey model, the analysis is exactly that of the AES, and the best known boomerang attack is given in Sect. 4.

In the related tweakey model, the attacker can insert differences in some of the tweakey words TK^i. Depending on the tweak size and differences used, this can be either a single-key attack with chosen tweaks, or a related-key attack. We denote as RTKr a model with differences in r 128-bit states, corresponding to:

- RTK1: single-key attacks on any variant with at least 128 bits of tweak.
- RTK2: single-key attacks on Deoxys-BC-384 with 256 bits of tweak, or related-key attacks on Deoxys-BC-256.
- RTK3: related-key attacks on Deoxys-BC-384.

For 13-round Deoxys-BC in the RTK3 model, we selected a non-optimal trail in terms of data complexity, which was better in time complexity. For 8-round and 9-round Deoxys-BC in the RKT1 model and 10-round Deoxys-BC in the RTK2 model, we modified the squeleton of the trail returned by the MILP because the original one was not instantiable. During other difference instantiations, we sometimes applied slight manual improvements. For instance, for minor gains, we introduced state changing bytes: fixed on the forward trail but truncated on the return trail.

Description of the Attacks. In the related-tweakey model, the attacker queries two sets of $|\mathcal{D}_{in}^0|$ plaintexts (under tweaks T and T'), and each ciphertext is shifted $|\mathcal{D}_{out}^1|$ times with a new tweak ($\overline{T}$ and $\overline{T}'$ respectively). In total a structure of size $S = |\mathcal{D}_{in}^0| \times |\mathcal{D}_{out}^1|$ requires $2S$ decryption queries (or $4S$ if $|\mathcal{D}_{out}^1| = 1$) and generates S^2 quartets.

The values of ℓ and κ mentioned on the figures are the one used in our attacks, corresponding either to a 1-round or to a 2-round key-recovery. Each attack recovers a partial key, aiming for a success rate of $1/2$, comparable to previous analysis; we assume that the rest of the key can be recovered efficiently afterwards. When $\tilde{\sigma} \gg 1$, the number μ of right quartets required varies from 1 to 4. In particular, if $p_b \gg \ell \cdot p_{\$}$, we expect no wrong quartet and $\mu = 1$ suffices, else several right quartets are needed to get the correct key ranked first.

10-Round Deoxys-BC in the RTK2 Model (Fig. 4). Query one partial structure of $2^{93.2}$ ciphertexts, so that on average, $\mu = 2^{93.2+93.2} \cdot \tilde{p}_b = 2$ quartets follow the trail. For each element of the structure, deduce on average 1 candidate for 30 bits of key on the plaintext side: 1 candidate for $tk_0[4, 9, 14]$ and 1 representant of the 4 possible candidates each for $tk_0[3]$[1]. In total, there are on average $2^{93.2+93.2-56-30} = 2^{100.4}$ candidate quartets matching on the ciphertext bytes with a known difference and on the key candidate.

For each quartet, retrieve 2^{-8} candidates for $tk_{10}[9]$ with 2 table accesses. This costs $2^{101.4}$ table accesses, and since an encryption makes $10 \times 16 = 2^{7.3}$ S-Box calls, this step costs $2^{94.1}$ equivalent encryptions. For each of the $2^{100.4-8} = 2^{92.4}$ remaining quartets, retrieve on average 2^{-32} candidates of $tk_{10}[0, 1, 2, 3, 4, 5, 6, 7]$. Finally, recover 2^{-16} candidates for $tk_9^{eq}[1, 6]$. There remains $2^{92.4-32-16} = 2^{44.4}$ quartets with a 118-bit key candidate. The only candidate suggested twice is expected to be the right candidate. The time complexity is $2^{94.2} + 2^{94.1} \approx 2^{95.2}$, thus $(D, T, M) = (2^{94.2}, 2^{95.2}, 2^{94.2})$.

11-Round Deoxys-BC in the RTK2 Model. The MILP solver did not return a pertinent trail for this key setting. Instead, we use the 10-round trail and append a round at the beginning. First, query the full encryption codebook with $\overline{T}, \overline{T}'$ and store it. Then, guess the full tk_0. Perform the 10-round attack, by using the same ciphertext structure for each guess of tk_0 and simulating encryption queries with fetches in the codebook. We chose $\mu = 4$ and for each key guess, the 10-round attack with partial structures of $2^{93.7}$ elements gives $2^{45.4}$ candidates for 118 bits, for a time complexity of $2^{95.1}$. If we suppose that a fetch to the codebook costs an encryption in time complexity, we end up with $T = 2^{128}(2^{94.7} + 2^{95.1}) = 2^{223.9}$. The probability that one of the counters is at least 4 is $2^{-295+116+128} = 2^{-51}$, so in average, the correct key is ranked first. This gives $(D, T, M) = (2^{129}, 2^{223.9}, 2^{129})$.

13-Round Deoxys-BC in the RTK3 Model (Fig. 5). Query a partial structure of $2^{125.65}$ plaintexts. On average, $\mu = 2^{125.65} \cdot 2^{125.65} \cdot \tilde{p}_b = 4$ quartets follow the trail.

1. For each element of the structure, retrieve the representant k of the 2^6 possible key values of $tk_{13}[13, 14, 15]$ that satisfy the transition $y_{12} \rightarrow x_{12}$. k defines 18 key bits.

---

[1] S-Box 3 on the plaintext side has two pairs $(x, x + \delta), (x', x' + \delta)$ following the transition fixed by the trail. Instead of listing four key candidates, we identify one of the 2^6 cosets of $\langle \delta, x + x' \rangle$.

2. Guess the value of the tweakey material $tk_0[2, 7, 8, 13]$. Set $\delta =$ 0x7e42c465 and $\delta_{\text{in}} =$ 0x00007a00, and look for collisions between:

$$v = y_0[2, 7, 8, 13] \quad \| \; \overline{y_0}[2, 7, 8, 13] \quad \| \; \overline{P}[0, 5, 10, 15] \quad \| \; k$$
$$v' = y_0'[2, 7, 8, 13] + \delta \; \| \; \overline{y_0'}[2, 7, 8, 13] + \delta \; \| \; \overline{P'}[0, 5, 10, 15] + \delta_{\text{in}} \; \| \; k'$$

This step costs $2^{32} \cdot 2 \cdot 2^{125.65} = 2^{158.65}$ in time complexity. On average, $2^{125.65} \cdot 2^{125.65} \cdot 2^{-114} = 2^{137.3}$ quartets remain for each $tk_0[2, 7, 8, 13]$ ($2^{169.3}$ in total).

3. For each quartet, retrieve $2^{7+7-32} = 2^{-18}$ values of $tk_0[3, 4, 9, 14]$ such that the difference in $w_0[4]$ is compatible with the S-Box transition in the next round. In order to minimize the complexity, first deduce the $2^{7+7-8} = 2^6$ pairs of column differences compatible with a key candidate for $tk_0[3]$, by only checking the first S-Box. Then, deduce the $2^{6-8} = 2^{-2}$ pairs of columns compatible with a key candidate for $tk_0[4]$ with the second S-Box. Finally deduce $tk_0[9, 14]$.
   This step requires $2^8 + 2^7 = 2^{8.6}$ table accesses per quartet, therefore a total of $2^{8.6+169.3} = 2^{177.9}$ accesses; and $2^{32+137.3-18} = 2^{151.3}$ quartets remain.

4. For each quartet, retrieve $2^{7+7-32} = 2^{-18}$ values of $tk_0[1, 6, 11, 12]$ and $2^{24+24-32} = 2^{16}$ key candidates for $tk_{13}[8, 9, 10, 11]$. Recover $x_{12}[8, 9, 10, 11]$ and the difference in $y_{11}[2, 7, 8]$. Retrieve 2^{-24} candidates for $tk_{12}^{eq}[2, 7, 8]$. $2^{151.3-18+16-24} = 2^{125.3}$ quartets remain.

5. For each quartet, recover the difference in $x_1[4, 14]$ and the value of $w_0[4, 14]$ from the known key bytes of tk_0. Retrieve $2 \cdot 2 \cdot 2^{-8} = 2^{-6}$ values of $tk_1[4]$ and 2^{-6} values for $tk_1[14]$ (2 candidates are deduced per pair because the differences are already compatible). $2^{125.3} \cdot 2^{-12} = 2^{113.3}$ quartets remain.

6. Eventually, each of the $2^{113.3}$ quartets determines in average 1 candidate of $18 + 32 + 32 + 32 + 32 + 24 + 16 = 186$ bits. We model a wrong counter with a poisson distribution with $\lambda = 2^{-72.7}$. The probability that any wrong counter is at least 3 is $(1 - e^{-\lambda}(1 + \lambda + \lambda^2/2)) \cdot 2^{184} \approx 2^{-34.7}$. The correct counter follows the poisson distribution with $\lambda = 4$ and it is at least 3 with probability 0.76. Therefore, the success probability of this attack is 0.76.

Complexity analysis. The time complexity is dominated by the $2^{177.9}$ table accesses of step 3. An encryption of 13-round Deoxys-BC has 16×13 S-Boxes, so the time complexity is equivalent to $2^{177.9}/208 = 2^{170.2}$ encryptions. Thus $(D, T, M) = (2^{126.7}, 2^{170.2}, 2^{126.7})$.

Other Variants. Due to space constraints, the attacks found on other variants of Deoxys-BC are detailed in the full version of this paper [6].

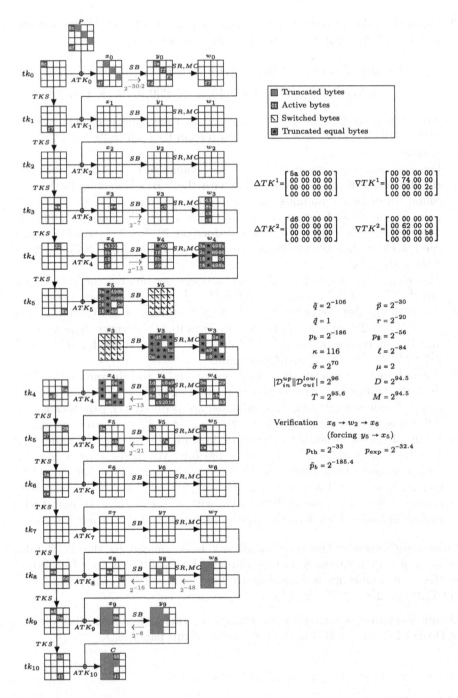

Fig. 4. Truncated boomerang attack on 10-round Deoxys-BC in the RTK2 model, starting from the ciphertext side. This attack succeeds with probability 1/2. Middle rounds are analyzed with UBCT, LBCT and EBCT (probabilities on the trail).

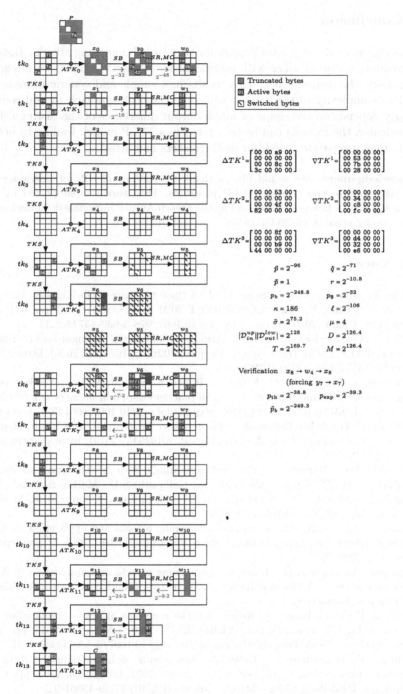

Fig. 5. Truncated boomerang attacks on 13-round Deoxys-BC in the RTK3 model, starting from the plaintext side. This attack succeeds with probability 0.76. Middle rounds are analyzed with the ladder switch and single BCT (probability r).

9   Conclusion

In this paper, we develop a framework for truncated boomerang attacks. Instead of extending a distinguisher with additional key-recovery rounds, we integrate them inside the distinguisher. This results in a simple and generic formula for the data complexity of the attack, while the classical approach to add rounds strongly depends on the shape of input/output differences of the distinguisher. In particular, the formula can be integrated in a MILP model, leading to better results than a separate search for distinguishers and attacks.

Acknowledgement. We would like to thank the authors of [12] for providing the code they used to generate the MILP programs. This work was supported by the French Ministry of Defence (AID), and by the French Agence Nationale de la Recherche (ANR), under grant ANR-20-CE48-0017 (project SELECT).

References

1. Bao, Z., Guo, C., Guo, J., Song, L.: TNT: how to tweak a block cipher. In: Canteaut, A., Ishai, Y. (eds.) EUROCRYPT 2020. LNCS, vol. 12106, pp. 641–673. Springer, Cham (2020). https://doi.org/10.1007/978-3-030-45724-2_22
2. Bao, Z., Guo, J., List, E.: Extended truncated-differential distinguishers on round-reduced AES. IACR Trans. Symm. Cryptol. **2020**(3), 197–261 (2020). https://doi.org/10.13154/tosc.v2020.i3.197-261
3. Bar-On, A., Dunkelman, O., Keller, N., Ronen, E., Shamir, A.: Improved key recovery attacks on reduced-round AES with practical data and memory complexities. J. Cryptol. **33**(3), 1003–1043 (2019). https://doi.org/10.1007/s00145-019-09336-w
4. Bardeh, N.G.: A key-independent distinguisher for 6-round AES in an adaptive setting. Cryptology ePrint Archive, Report 2019/945 (2019). https://eprint.iacr.org/2019/945
5. Bardeh, N.G., Rønjom, S.: The exchange attack: *how to distinguish six rounds of AES with $2^{88.2}$ chosen plaintexts*. In: Galbraith, S.D., Moriai, S. (eds.) ASIACRYPT 2019. LNCS, vol. 11923, pp. 347–370. Springer, Cham (2019). https://doi.org/10.1007/978-3-030-34618-8_12
6. Bariant, A., Leurent, G.: Truncated boomerang attacks and application to AES-based ciphers. Cryptology ePrint Archive, Report 2022/701 (2022). https://eprint.iacr.org/2022/701
7. Bariant, A., Leurent, G.: Truncated boomerang attacks and application to AES-based ciphers – Additional data (2023). https://github.com/AugustinBariant/Truncated_boomerangs
8. Biham, E., Dunkelman, O., Keller, N.: The rectangle attack — rectangling the serpent. In: Pfitzmann, B. (ed.) EUROCRYPT 2001. LNCS, vol. 2045, pp. 340–357. Springer, Heidelberg (2001). https://doi.org/10.1007/3-540-44987-6_21
9. Biham, E., Dunkelman, O., Keller, N.: New results on boomerang and rectangle attacks. In: Daemen, J., Rijmen, V. (eds.) FSE 2002. LNCS, vol. 2365, pp. 1–16. Springer, Heidelberg (2002). https://doi.org/10.1007/3-540-45661-9_1

10. Biryukov, A.: The boomerang attack on 5 and 6-round reduced AES. In: Dobbertin, H., Rijmen, V., Sowa, A. (eds.) AES 2004. LNCS, vol. 3373, pp. 11–15. Springer, Heidelberg (2005). https://doi.org/10.1007/11506447_2

11. Boura, C., Lallemand, V., Naya-Plasencia, M., Suder, V.: Making the impossible possible. J. Cryptol. **31**(1), 101–133 (2017). https://doi.org/10.1007/s00145-016-9251-7

12. Cid, C., Huang, T., Peyrin, T., Sasaki, Y., Song, L.: A security analysis of Deoxys and its internal tweakable block ciphers. IACR Trans. Symm. Cryptol. **2017**(3), 73–107 (2017). https://doi.org/10.13154/tosc.v2017.i3.73-107

13. Cid, C., Huang, T., Peyrin, T., Sasaki, Y., Song, L.: Boomerang connectivity table: a new cryptanalysis tool. In: Nielsen, J.B., Rijmen, V. (eds.) EUROCRYPT 2018. LNCS, vol. 10821, pp. 683–714. Springer, Cham (2018). https://doi.org/10.1007/978-3-319-78375-8_22

14. Daemen, J., Knudsen, L., Rijmen, V.: The block cipher square. In: Biham, E. (ed.) FSE 1997. LNCS, vol. 1267, pp. 149–165. Springer, Heidelberg (1997). https://doi.org/10.1007/BFb0052343

15. Daemen, J., Rijmen, V.: The Design of Rijndael, vol. 2. Springer, Heidelberg (2002). https://doi.org/10.1007/978-3-662-04722-4

16. Delaune, S., Derbez, P., Vavrille, M.: Catching the fastest boomerangs application to SKINNY. IACR Trans. Symm. Cryptol. **2020**(4), 104–129 (2020). https://doi.org/10.46586/tosc.v2020.i4.104-129

17. Dobraunig, C., Eichlseder, M., Mendel, F.: Square attack on 7-round Kiasu-BC. In: Manulis, M., Sadeghi, A.-R., Schneider, S. (eds.) ACNS 2016. LNCS, vol. 9696, pp. 500–517. Springer, Cham (2016). https://doi.org/10.1007/978-3-319-39555-5_27

18. Dobraunig, C., List, E.: Impossible-differential and boomerang cryptanalysis of round-reduced Kiasu-BC. In: Handschuh, H. (ed.) CT-RSA 2017. LNCS, vol. 10159, pp. 207–222. Springer, Cham (2017). https://doi.org/10.1007/978-3-319-52153-4_12

19. Dunkelman, O., Keller, N., Ronen, E., Shamir, A.: The retracing boomerang attack. In: Canteaut, A., Ishai, Y. (eds.) EUROCRYPT 2020. LNCS, vol. 12105, pp. 280–309. Springer, Cham (2020). https://doi.org/10.1007/978-3-030-45721-1_11

20. Dunkelman, O., Keller, N., Shamir, A.: A practical-time related-key attack on the KASUMI cryptosystem used in GSM and 3G telephony. In: Rabin, T. (ed.) CRYPTO 2010. LNCS, vol. 6223, pp. 393–410. Springer, Heidelberg (2010). https://doi.org/10.1007/978-3-642-14623-7_21

21. Ferguson, N., et al.: Improved cryptanalysis of Rijndael. In: Goos, G., Hartmanis, J., van Leeuwen, J., Schneier, B. (eds.) FSE 2000. LNCS, vol. 1978, pp. 213–230. Springer, Heidelberg (2001). https://doi.org/10.1007/3-540-44706-7_15

22. Grassi, L.: MixColumns properties and attacks on (round-reduced) AES with a single secret S-box. In: Smart, N.P. (ed.) CT-RSA 2018. LNCS, vol. 10808, pp. 243–263. Springer, Cham (2018). https://doi.org/10.1007/978-3-319-76953-0_13

23. Grassi, L., Rechberger, C., Rønjom, S.: Subspace trail cryptanalysis and its applications to AES. IACR Trans. Symm. Cryptol. **2016**(2), 192–225 (2016). https://doi.org/10.13154/tosc.v2016.i2.192-225, https://tosc.iacr.org/index.php/ToSC/article/view/571

24. Grassi, L., Rechberger, C., Rønjom, S.: A new structural-differential property of 5-round AES. In: Coron, J.-S., Nielsen, J.B. (eds.) EUROCRYPT 2017. LNCS, vol. 10211, pp. 289–317. Springer, Cham (2017). https://doi.org/10.1007/978-3-319-56614-6_10

25. Guo, C., Guo, J., List, E., Song, L.: Towards closing the security gap of tweak-and-tweak (TNT). In: Moriai, S., Wang, H. (eds.) ASIACRYPT 2020. LNCS, vol. 12491, pp. 567–597. Springer, Cham (2020). https://doi.org/10.1007/978-3-030-64837-4_19

26. Jean, J., Nikolić, I., Peyrin, T.: Kiasu v1. Submitted to the CAESAR competition (2014)

27. Jean, J., Nikolić, I., Peyrin, T.: Tweaks and keys for block ciphers: the TWEAKEY framework. In: Sarkar, P., Iwata, T. (eds.) ASIACRYPT 2014. LNCS, vol. 8874, pp. 274–288. Springer, Heidelberg (2014). https://doi.org/10.1007/978-3-662-45608-8_15

28. Jean, J., Nikolić, I., Peyrin, T., Seurin, Y.: The Deoxys AEAD family. J. Cryptol. **34**(3), 1–51 (2021). https://doi.org/10.1007/s00145-021-09397-w

29. Mantin, I., Shamir, A.: A practical attack on broadcast RC4. In: Matsui, M. (ed.) FSE 2001. LNCS, vol. 2355, pp. 152–164. Springer, Heidelberg (2002). https://doi.org/10.1007/3-540-45473-X_13

30. Murphy, S.: The return of the cryptographic boomerang. IEEE Trans. Inf. Theory **57**(4), 2517–2521 (2011)

31. Qin, L., Dong, X., Wang, X., Jia, K., Liu, Y.: Automated search oriented to key recovery on ciphers with linear key schedule. IACR Trans. Symm. Cryptol. **2021**(2), 249–291 (2021). https://doi.org/10.46586/tosc.v2021.i2.249-291

32. Rahman, M., Saha, D., Paul, G.: Boomeyong: embedding yoyo within boomerang and its applications to key recovery attacks on AES and Pholkos. IACR Trans. Symm. Cryptol. **2021**(3), 137–169 (2021). https://doi.org/10.46586/tosc.v2021.i3.137-169

33. Rønjom, S., Bardeh, N.G., Helleseth, T.: Yoyo tricks with AES. In: Takagi, T., Peyrin, T. (eds.) ASIACRYPT 2017. LNCS, vol. 10624, pp. 217–243. Springer, Cham (2017). https://doi.org/10.1007/978-3-319-70694-8_8

34. Sasaki, Y.: Improved related-tweakey boomerang attacks on Deoxys-BC. In: Joux, A., Nitaj, A., Rachidi, T. (eds.) AFRICACRYPT 2018. LNCS, vol. 10831, pp. 87–106. Springer, Cham (2018). https://doi.org/10.1007/978-3-319-89339-6_6

35. Selçuk, A.A.: On probability of success in linear and differential cryptanalysis. J. Cryptol. **21**(1), 131–147 (2007). https://doi.org/10.1007/s00145-007-9013-7

36. Song, L., Qin, X., Hu, L.: Boomerang connectivity table revisited. IACR Trans. Symm. Cryptol. **2019**(1), 118–141 (2019). https://doi.org/10.13154/tosc.v2019.i1.118-141

37. Tiessen, T., Knudsen, L.R., Kölbl, S., Lauridsen, M.M.: Security of the AES with a secret S-box. In: Leander, G. (ed.) FSE 2015. LNCS, vol. 9054, pp. 175–189. Springer, Heidelberg (2015). https://doi.org/10.1007/978-3-662-48116-5_9

38. Tolba, M., Abdelkhalek, A., Youssef, A.M.: A meet in the middle attack on reduced round Kiasu-BC. IEICE Trans. Fundam. Electron. Commun. Comput. Sci. **99**(10), 1888–1890 (2016)

39. Wagner, D.: The boomerang attack. In: Knudsen, L. (ed.) FSE 1999. LNCS, vol. 1636, pp. 156–170. Springer, Heidelberg (1999). https://doi.org/10.1007/3-540-48519-8_12

40. Wang, H., Peyrin, T.: Boomerang switch in multiple rounds. IACR Trans. Symm. Cryptol. **2019**(1), 142–169 (2019). https://doi.org/10.13154/tosc.v2019.i1.142-169

41. Yang, Q., Song, L., Sun, S., Shi, D., Hu, L.: New properties of the double boomerang connectivity table. IACR Trans. Symmetric Cryptol. **2022**(4), 208–242 (2022). https://doi.org/10.46586/tosc.v2022.i4.208-242, https://tosc.iacr.org/index.php/ToSC/article/view/9977

42. Zhao, B., Dong, X., Jia, K.: New related-tweakey boomerang and rectangle attacks on deoxys-bc including BDT effect. IACR Trans. Symm. Cryptol. **2019**(3), 121–151 (2019). https://doi.org/10.13154/tosc.v2019.i3.121-151

43. Zhao, B., Dong, X., Jia, K., Meier, W.: Improved related-tweakey rectangle attacks on reduced-round Deoxys-BC-384 and Deoxys-I-256-128. In: Hao, F., Ruj, S., Sen Gupta, S. (eds.) INDOCRYPT 2019. LNCS, vol. 11898, pp. 139–159. Springer, Cham (2019). https://doi.org/10.1007/978-3-030-35423-7_7

Better Steady than Speedy: Full Break of SPEEDY-7-192

Christina Boura[1]([✉]), Nicolas David[2], Rachelle Heim Boissier[1],
and María Naya-Plasencia[2]

[1] Université Paris-Saclay, UVSQ, CNRS, Laboratoire de mathématiques de
Versailles, 78000 Versailles, France
{christina.boura,rachelle.heim}@uvsq.fr
[2] Inria, Paris, France
{nicolas.david,maria.naya-plasencia}@inria.fr

Abstract. Differential attacks are among the most important families of cryptanalysis against symmetric primitives. Since their introduction in 1990, several improvements to the basic technique as well as many dedicated attacks against symmetric primitives have been proposed. Most of the proposed improvements concern the key-recovery part. However, when designing a new primitive, the security analysis regarding differential attacks is often limited to finding the best trails over a limited number of rounds with branch and bound techniques, and a poor heuristic is then applied to deduce the total number of rounds a differential attack could reach. In this work we analyze the security of the SPEEDY family of block ciphers against differential cryptanalysis and show how to optimize many of the steps of the key-recovery procedure for this type of attacks. For this, we implemented a search for finding optimal trails for this cipher and their associated multiple probabilities under some constraints and applied non-trivial techniques to obtain optimal data and key-sieving. This permitted us to fully break SPEEDY-7-192, the 7-round variant of SPEEDY supposed to provide 192-bit security. Our work demonstrates among others the need to better understand the subtleties of differential cryptanalysis in order to get meaningful estimates on the security offered by a cipher against these attacks.

Keywords: differential cryptanalysis · block ciphers · SPEEDY · security claim · key recovery

1 Introduction

Differential cryptanalysis is a very powerful technique to analyse block ciphers. It was introduced in 1990 by Biham and Shamir who used this method to break the Data Encryption Standard (DES). The idea of this technique applied to block ciphers is to exploit input differences that propagate through the cipher to output differences with a probability higher than what is expected for a random permutation.

© International Association for Cryptologic Research 2023
C. Hazay and M. Stam (Eds.): EUROCRYPT 2023, LNCS 14007, pp. 36–66, 2023.
https://doi.org/10.1007/978-3-031-30634-1_2

Differential cryptanalysis is arguably the most well-known and studied technique in symmetric cryptography. Indeed, in the last 30 years, differential attacks have been applied to analyze a high number of primitives: [4,6–9,14,20,23], to cite only a few. In parallel, several refinements and generalizations of the basic technique were introduced together with some new dedicated methods. One can for example mention the technique of truncated differentials [18], the use of structures to reduce data complexity (a technique already introduced in [8]), the technique of probabilistic neutral bits [16] or the conditional differential attacks [17]. However, applying differential cryptanalysis on a new cipher is in general a laborious, complex and potentially error-prone procedure. Indeed, combining together the different improvements and techniques for mounting interesting differential attacks is highly non-trivial. This is the reason why the designers of a new primitive provide most of the time only basic arguments on the security of their design against differential attacks. This is done for example by applying the branch-and-bound algorithm to determine the highest number of rounds covered by a single differential trail. Based on this, and without getting into too many details, designers then provide an estimate on the number of rounds that the key recovery steps could reach on top of the differential distinguisher. This estimation is used to state security claims, sometimes conservative, sometimes not, depending on the target application scenario. Examples of such kind of claims exist for almost all modern symmetric designs [1–3,10,13].

In this work we analyze SPEEDY against differential attacks. SPEEDY is a new ultra-low latency family of block ciphers [19], designed by Leander, Moos, Moradi and Rasoolzadeh. The authors provided in [19] a preliminary analysis that suggested that all versions of this cipher should be immune against this type of attack. However, we demonstrate here that SPEEDY-7-192 can be fully broken with differential cryptanalysis. Our attack that uses improved techniques for the key-recovery part, demonstrates in practice that a more in-depth analysis of a primitive against differential cryptanalysis is necessary in order to provide precise estimates of its security margin.

1.1 Our Contribution

We analyzed SPEEDY, a new ultra-low latency family of block ciphers [19] against differential attacks. More precisely, we managed to break the full version of SPEEDY-7-192, one of the three main variants of this family. This variant iterates over 7 rounds and its designers claimed 192-bit time and data security. Our attack has a time of $2^{187.84}$ and data complexity of $2^{187.28}$, and is thus more than 2^4 times faster than exhaustive search, contradicting therefore the security claim. We shared our results with the designers, that have agreed and acknowledged our attack. This attack is based on a 5.5-round distinguisher and is extended to 7 rounds, therefore it contradicts another claim of the designers: "the attacker cannot add more than one round to extend a distinguisher". Our attack is non-trivial and is based on improved techniques for the key-recovery part. We believe that most of these ideas could be generalized to be applied to differential attacks against other ciphers and we hope that this work can be seen as a step towards a general framework that could help in the future designers precisely estimate the security margin of their design against differential cryptanalysis.

Finally, we provide a brief summary of our differential attacks on the $r = 5$ and $r = 6$-round variants of SPEEDY-r-192 even if the attacks on the other variants do not contradict the designers' security claims, but they provide the best known attacks on these variants up to date. A summary of all our attacks together with other third-party cryptanalysis results on SPEEDY is given in Table 1.

Table 1. Summary of SPEEDY cryptanalysis

Algorithm	# rounds attacked	Ref.	Data	Time (in C_E)	Memory	Security claim $(\mathcal{T}, \mathcal{D})$
SPEEDY-5-192	3	[22]	$2^{17.6}$	$2^{52.5}$	$2^{25.5}$	$(2^{128}, 2^{64})$
SPEEDY-5-192	5	this work	$2^{101.65}$	$2^{107.8}$	2^{42}	$(2^{128}, 2^{64})$
SPEEDY-6-192	5.5	this work	$2^{121.65}$	$2^{127.8}$	2^{42}	$(2^{128}, 2^{128})$
SPEEDY-6-192	6	this work	$2^{121.65}$	$2^{151.67}$	2^{42}	$(2^{128}, 2^{128})$
SPEEDY-7-192	7	this work	$2^{187.28}$	$2^{187.84}$	2^{42}	$(2^{192}, 2^{192})$

The rest of the paper is organized as follows. In Sect. 2, we summarize the classical framework for differential attacks and deduce generic complexity formulas. In Sect. 3, we present the SPEEDY family of block ciphers and describe our methodology for finding good differential trails. Our attack on SPEEDY-7-192 is given in Sect. 4. Finally, our results on the other main variants of the SPEEDY family are briefly presented in Sect. 5. This section also discusses open problems and directions.

2   Differential Cryptanalysis

Differential attacks are a very popular chosen-plaintext cryptanalysis technique against symmetric primitives [5]. The invention of this technique in 1990 was devastating for the ciphers of the time, as demonstrated by the breaks of both full FEAL and full DES [6,8] among others. Similarly to the majority of attacks against block ciphers, differential attacks are built around a distinguisher. A differential distinguisher exploits as a distinguishing property the existence of a pair of differences $(a, b) \in \mathbb{F}_2^n$, where n is the block size, such that the input difference a propagates through some rounds of the cipher to the output difference b with a probability significantly higher than 2^{-n}. This distinguisher can then be extended a few rounds in both directions by adding some rounds that will serve as the key recovery part. In this part, an attacker will guess a reduced part of the key, and using this knowledge will be able to compute the first and/or the last state of the distinguisher in order to check if some plaintext or ciphertext pair follows the differential.

The goal of this section is to provide a global overview of a differential key recovery attack that extends a fixed differential in both directions together with generic formulas representing its time, data and memory complexity.

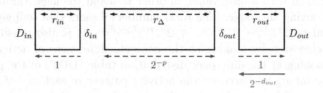

Fig. 1. Differential cryptanalysis context.

We start by considering a differential $\Delta = (\delta_{in}, \delta_{out})$ of probability $P = 2^{-p}$ covering r_Δ rounds. The difference δ_{in} (resp. δ_{out}) then maps to a truncated difference in D_{in}, r_{in} rounds before (resp. D_{out} and r_{out}) with probability 1. We denote by d_{in} (resp. d_{out}) the log_2 of the size of the input (resp. output) difference such that $|D_{in}| = 2^{d_{in}}$ (resp. $|D_{out}| = 2^{d_{out}}$). Note that the attack can be done in both directions (encryption or decryption) and the most interesting direction is determined by the concrete parameters. Without any further improvements, the data and time complexities should be the same in both directions, while the memory complexity is given by the size of one structure ($2^{d_{in}}$ or $2^{d_{out}}$). Similarly to our attack on SPEEDY-7-192, we will present a procedure in which we make calls to the decryption oracle (i.e. by generating ciphertexts). However, the general description of the attack remains unchanged regardless of the direction. To obtain the description of a chosen plaintext attack, it suffices to replace in what follows "ciphertexts", D_{out} and d_{out} by "plaintexts", D_{in} and d_{in}.

Data Complexity. In order to have enough data to expect that one pair satisfies the differential, we will use *structures*, as it is often done in differential attacks. A structure is a set of ciphertexts that have a fixed value in the non-active bits, and that take all possible values in the remaining d_{out} bits. This approach permits us to build ($2^{2d_{out}-1}$) pairs inside a structure. The probability to start from a difference in D_{out} and to fall back to a difference δ_{out} is usually $2^{-d_{out}}$. This means that to have one pair that satisfies the differential trail, we need a total of $2^{p+d_{out}}$ pairs that we will obtain by using 2^s structures where s is such that $2^{s+2d_{out}-1} = 2^{p+d_{out}}$, that is $s = p - d_{out} + 1$. Therefore, we need to generate $2^{d_{out}+s} = 2^{p+1}$ ciphertexts and thus the data complexity is $\mathcal{D} = 2^{p+1}$.

Pair Sieving. Since performing the key recovery phase with all the $2^{p+d_{out}}$ pairs is too costly in general, the attacker will very probably need to perform a sieving step which will permit her to discard pairs that cannot follow the differential trail. This can be done efficiently by just looking at the plaintext corresponding to each ciphertext inside a structure: the attacker will only keep those ciphertext pairs, for which the difference of the corresponding plaintext pairs belongs to D_{in}, i.e. only those pairs that have the same value on the $n - d_{in}$ non-active bits in the plaintext. This can be efficiently done by ordering the list of structures of size $2^{d_{out}}$ with respect to the values of the non-active bits in the plaintext, or even with a hash table, in order to avoid the logarithmic factor of sorting and sieving the table. The total number of pairs that will get through this sieve will be $2^{s+2d_{out}-1-n+d_{in}} = 2^{p-n+d_{in}+d_{out}}$. It is also possible to add an extra sieving step by looking at the concrete differences of active S-boxes. Indeed, by looking at the difference distribution table (DDT) of the primitive's S-box and by taking into account the activity pattern of each one of the active S-boxes, it is possible to further sieve the remaining pairs by removing all those that have an impossible difference on the concerned words. This approach was for example used in [12]. We denote by C_S the average cost of sieving a pair. This cost is in general quite small as it might simply correspond to a table lookup. However this is not always the case, as we will see in the attack of Sect. 4. Indeed, in our case, this cost will be a little higher than what it would have been with a straightforward approach, as we will consider simultaneously several configurations for the sieving filter.

Key Recovery. Although all of the pairs that were kept after the sieving step are candidates for having followed the differential, we now want to keep only those such that there exists an associated key that actually leads to the differential. By considering the first and last rounds, and performing partial key guesses that we will merge thanks to efficient list merging algorithms like the ones presented in [21], we can obtain quite low additional factors. In particular, we will denote by C_{KR}, the average cost to perform the key recovery steps per pair. The optimal way of doing this will depend on the round function structure of the analyzed cipher. However this is a step that can typically be done with a small factor. Its goal is to generate a final number of triplets formed by plaintext (or ciphertext) pairs and candidate associated keys that we expect smaller than the original number of pairs (and of the exhaustive search cost), and the cost of finding the secret key given these triplets is not expected to be the complexity bottleneck. In Sect. 4.4 we show some improved techniques to reduce this cost, and provide an example of such an accelerated key search in the context of SPEEDY.

Total Time and Memory Complexity. We denote by C_E the cost of one encryption. Taking into account the data generation, the data sieve and the key recovery steps described above, the *time complexity* T^1 is given by

$$T = \left(2^{p+1} + 2^{p+1}\frac{C_S}{C_E} + 2^{s+2d_{out}-1-n+d_{in}}\frac{C_{KR}}{C_E}\right)C_E.$$

---

[1] If k is the size of the secret key, for the attack to be valid, the time complexity T should be smaller than $2^k C_E$.

We present in the next two sections an application of the techniques introduced in Sect. 2 against the SPEEDY family of block ciphers. Section 3 is dedicated to the distinguisher part, while Sect. 4 describes the key recovery part for SPEEDY-7-192.

3 Finding Good Differentials on SPEEDY

We start by briefly presenting the specifications of the SPEEDY family of ciphers.

3.1 Specifications of the SPEEDY Family of Block Ciphers

The SPEEDY family of ciphers is a family of lightweight block ciphers introduced by Leander, Moos, Moradi and Rasoolzadeh at CHES 2021 [19]. The main design goal of these primitives was to be fast in CMOS hardware by achieving extremely low latency. This goal was notably reached thanks to the design of a dedicated 6-bit bijective S-box.

There are different SPEEDY variants that differ in block size, key size and number of rounds. More precisely, the block cipher SPEEDY-r-6ℓ has a block and key size of 6ℓ bits and is iterated over r rounds. The internal state is viewed as a $\ell \times 6$ rectangle-array of bits. Following the notation of [19], we will denote by $x_{[i,j]}$, $0 \leq i < \ell$, $0 \leq j < 6$, the bit located at row i and column j of the state x. Note that all indices start from zero and the zero-th bit or word is always considered to be the most significant one. Furthermore, if there is an addition or a subtraction in the indices of the state, this is done modulo ℓ for the first (row) index and in modulo 6 for the second (column) index.

The default block and key size for SPEEDY is 192 bits and this instance is denoted by SPEEDY-r-192. It is suggested to iterate this instance over 5,6 or 7 rounds. Next, we provide the specifications of the round function for SPEEDY-r-192. Note that for this variant, the state is seen as $(\ell \times 6)$-bit rectangle, with $\ell = 32$.

Round Function of SPEEDY-r-192. The internal state is first initialized with the 192-bit plaintext. Then, a round function $\mathcal{R}_r$ is applied to the state r times, where r is typically 5, 6 or 7. The round function is composed of four operations: First, AddRoundKey (A_{k_r}) XORs the round subkey k_r to the state. Then, the SubBox (SB) operation applies a 6-bit S-box to each row of the state. Follows the ShiftColumns (SC) operation that rotates each column of the state by a different offset. These two operations (SB and SC) are repeated twice in an alternating manner. After this, the MixColumns (MC) operation multiplies each column of the state by a binary matrix. Finally, a constant c_r is XORed to the state by the AddRoundConstant (AC) operation. Note that, for the last round, the last ShiftColumns as well as the MixColumns and the AddRoundConstant operations are omitted, while a post-whitening key is XORed to the state. The round function $\mathcal{R}_r$ for the rounds $0 \leq r < \mathbf{r} - 1$ while also for the round $\mathbf{r} - 1$ are depicted in Fig. 2.

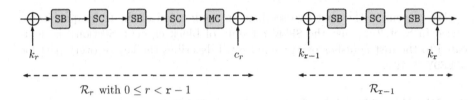

Fig. 2. The round function of SPEEDY-r-192 for the first $r-1$ rounds (left) and the last round (right).

Table 2. Table representation of the 6-bit S-box S

x	0	1	2	3	4	5	6	7	8	9	10	11	12	13	14	15
S(x)	8	0	9	3	56	16	41	19	12	13	4	7	48	1	32	35
x	16	17	18	19	20	21	22	23	24	25	26	27	28	29	30	31
S(x)	26	18	24	50	62	22	44	54	28	29	20	55	52	5	36	39
x	32	33	34	35	36	37	38	39	40	41	42	43	44	45	46	47
S(x)	2	6	11	15	51	23	33	21	10	27	14	31	49	17	37	53
x	48	49	50	51	52	53	54	55	56	57	58	59	60	61	62	63
S(x)	34	38	42	46	58	30	40	60	43	59	47	63	57	25	45	61

In the rest of our paper, we assume that the input (resp. output) to each of the described operations is a vector x (resp. y) $\in \mathbb{F}_2^{32 \times 6}$.

- **AddRoundKey (A_{k_r})**: The 192-bit round key k_r is XORed to the internal state. Hence,
$$y_{[i,j]} = x_{[i,j]} \oplus k_{r[i,j]}.$$

- **SubBox (SB)**: A 6-bit S-box S is applied to each row of the state. More precisely, for each row i, $0 \leq i < 32$, SB operates as follows:
$$(y_{[i,0]}, y_{[i,1]}, y_{[i,2]}, y_{[i,3]}, y_{[i,4]}, y_{[i,5]}) = S(x_{[i,0]}, x_{[i,1]}, x_{[i,2]}, x_{[i,3]}, x_{[i,4]}, x_{[i,5]}).$$

The table representation of the S-box S is given in Table 2.

- **ShiftColumns (SC)**: This operation rotates the j-th column of the state, $0 \leq j < 6$, upside by j bits:
$$y_{[i,j]} = y_{[i+j,j]}.$$

- **MixColumns (MC)**: The MC operation of SPEEDY applies column-wise and is based on a cyclic binary matrix $\alpha = (\alpha_1, \alpha_2, \alpha_3, \alpha_4, \alpha_5, \alpha_6)$ whose values depend on the number of rows ℓ:
$$y_{[i,j]} = x_{[i,j]} \oplus x_{[i+\alpha_1,j]} \oplus x_{[i+\alpha_2,j]} \oplus x_{[i+\alpha_3,j]} \oplus x_{[i+\alpha_4,j]} \oplus x_{[i+\alpha_5,j]} \oplus x_{[i+\alpha_6,j]}.$$

Recall that the additions $i + \alpha_*$ are considered mod ℓ.
For $\ell = 32$, $\alpha = (1, 5, 9, 15, 21, 26)$.

- **AddRoundConstant** (A_{c_r}): The 192-bit round constant c_r is XORed to the internal state. Hence,

$$y_{[i,j]} = x_{[i,j]} \oplus c_{r[i,j]}$$

As this operation is not relevant to our analysis we omit the description of the constant values.

Key Schedule. The 192-bit master key of SPEEDY-r-192 is loaded to the state of the first round key k_0. To obtain the next round key, the key schedule consists in simply applying a bit-permutation PB. Hence,

$$k_{r+1} = \text{PB}(k_r), \text{ with } k_{r+1[i',j']} = k_{r[i,j]},$$

Table 3. The bit-permutation P for SPEEDY-r-192 with $\beta = 7$ and $\gamma = 1$.

i	0	1	2	3	4	5	6	7	8	9	10	11	12	13	14	15
P(i)	1	8	15	22	29	36	43	50	57	64	71	78	85	92	99	106

i	16	17	18	19	20	21	22	23	24	25	26	27	28	29	30	31
P(i)	113	120	127	134	141	148	155	162	169	176	183	190	5	12	19	26

i	32	33	34	35	36	37	38	39	40	41	42	43	44	45	46	47
P(i)	33	40	47	54	61	68	75	82	89	96	103	110	117	124	131	138

i	48	49	50	51	52	53	54	55	56	57	58	59	60	61	62	63
P(i)	145	152	159	166	173	180	187	2	9	16	23	30	37	44	51	58

i	64	65	66	67	68	69	70	71	72	73	74	75	76	77	78	79
P(i)	65	72	79	86	93	100	107	114	121	128	135	142	149	156	163	170

i	80	81	82	83	84	85	86	87	88	89	90	91	92	93	94	95
P(i)	177	184	191	6	13	20	27	34	41	48	55	62	69	76	83	90

i	96	97	98	99	100	101	102	103	104	105	106	107	108	109	110	111
P(i)	97	104	111	118	125	132	139	146	153	160	167	174	181	188	3	10

i	112	113	114	115	116	117	118	119	120	121	122	123	124	125	126	127
P(i)	17	24	31	38	45	52	59	66	73	80	87	94	101	108	115	122

i	128	129	130	131	132	133	134	135	136	137	138	139	140	141	142	143
P(i)	129	136	143	150	157	164	171	178	185	0	7	14	21	28	35	42

i	144	145	146	147	148	149	150	151	152	153	154	155	156	157	158	159
P(i)	49	56	63	70	77	84	91	98	105	112	119	126	133	140	147	154

i	160	161	162	163	164	165	166	167	168	169	170	171	172	173	174	175
P(i)	161	168	175	182	189	4	11	18	25	32	39	46	53	60	67	74

i	176	177	178	179	180	181	182	183	184	185	186	187	188	189	190	191
P(i)	81	88	95	102	109	116	123	130	137	144	151	158	165	172	179	186

such that

$$(i', j') := P(i, j) \text{ with } (6i' + j') \equiv (\beta \cdot (6i + j) + \gamma) \mod 6\ell,$$

where β and γ are parameters depending on the block length of the cipher and that satisfy the condition that $\gcd(\beta, 6\ell) = 1$. For SPEEDY-r-192, the parameters $\beta = 7$ and $\gamma = 1$ are suggested, leading to the permutation P described in Table 3.

Security Claims. The authors made security claims for the three main versions of SPEEDY-r-192. For the 5-round version the authors expect no attack with complexity better than 2^{128} in time when data complexity is limited to 2^{64}. On the other hand, SPEEDY-6-192 should achieve 128-bit security, while SPEEDY-7-192 is expected to provide full 192-bit security.

3.2   Differential Properties of SPEEDY

We describe in this section the differential properties of the non-linear and linear layer of SPEEDY.

Differential Properties of the S-Box. The SPEEDY family of cipher employs a 6-bit S-box S whose differential uniformity is $\delta_S = 8$. This means that the highest probability of a differential transition through S is 2^{-3}. One particularity of this S-box that we exploit in our attacks is that almost all 1-bit to 1-bit differential transitions are possible. Moreover, these minimal weight transitions often have a relatively high probability. Table 4 summarizes all these transitions, together with their corresponding probability. The full DDT is given in [11].

Table 4. Summary of all the 1-bit input differences α to 1-bit output differences β. The corresponding probability can be obtained by multiplying the coefficients of the table by 2^{-5}. The symbol - means that the corresponding transition is impossible.

α/β	1	2	4	8	16	32
1	2	-	4	2	4	2
2	1	2	4	4	2	2
4	-	3	2	-	3	1
8	1	1	3	3	1	1
16	-	-	4	4	3	4
32	1	1	2	3	1	-

Another particularity is that 1-bit to 1-bit differential transitions can be chained within one round through the SB ○ SC ○ SB operation. All of them are possible and three of them achieve the maximum probability of 2^{-6}.

Differential Properties of the MixColumns Operation. The branch number of the MC operation is 8, which is the maximum possible value for the vector α chosen. As the maximum differential probability over 1 round is 2^{-6}, this means that an upper bound on the probability of any differential transition over two rounds is $(2^{-6})^8 = 2^{-48}$. The inverse MixColumns operation is defined with the vector

$$\alpha^{-1} = (4, 5, 6, 7, 10, 12, 14, 15, 16, 18, 19, 20, 21, 22, 23, 24, 25, 28).$$

This means in particular, that a column with a single active bit, will lead after the inverse of the MixColumns operation to 19 active bits, while a column with two active bits will be transformed after the inverse MixColumns to a column with at least 12 active bits.

3.3   Searching for Good Differential Trails

We describe in this section the methodology we followed to find the trails used in our attacks. Our idea was to precompute at first all good one-round trails and then chain them to create longer trails with high probability.

Searching for Good One-Round Trails. Let M be the matrix used in the MixColumns operation. In order to find good one-round trails, we first computed and stored all ordered pairs of columns $(x, M(x)) \in \mathbb{F}_2^{32} \times \mathbb{F}_2^{32}$ such that both columns x and $M(x)$ have at most 7 active bits each. This led to a total of 5248 pairs $(x, M(x)) \in \mathbb{F}_2^{32} \times \mathbb{F}_2^{32}$. However, these 5248 pairs can be divided into 164 equivalence classes, each equivalence class corresponding to the 32 rotations of a different activity pattern inside a column. We then stored in a table T one representative per equivalence class and used these pairs to precompute and store all 1-round trails satisfying some particular criteria. To describe this phase we need to introduce the following notation. Let st[0] be the initial state for our computation. We denote by st[1] the resulting state after applying MC to st[0], st[2] the state after applying SB to st[1], st[3] the state after applying SC to st[2], st[4] the state after applying SB to st[3], st[5] the state after applying SC to st[4] and finally st[6] the state after applying MC to st[5]:

$$st[0] \xrightarrow{MC} st[1] \xrightarrow{SB} st[2] \xrightarrow{SC} st[3] \xrightarrow{SB} st[4] \xrightarrow{SC} st[5] \xrightarrow{MC} st[6].$$

We computed all such propagations ($\mathtt{st[0]}$, $\mathtt{st[6]}$) satisfying the following conditions:

- $\mathtt{st[0]}$ has a single active column c_0 such that $(c_0, M(c_0)) \in \mathsf{T}$,
- $\mathtt{st[5]}$ has a single active column c_5 such that $(c_5, M(c_5)) \in \mathsf{T}$,
- $\mathtt{st[2]}$ has at most two active bits per row,
- the probability of the trail ($\mathtt{st[0]}$, $\mathtt{st[6]}$) is strictly higher than 2^{-49}.

For all trails satisfying the above conditions, we stored in a table the states ($\mathtt{st[0]}$, $\mathtt{st[5]}$) together with the probability of the corresponding trail. We obtained a total number of 48923 one-round trails, which we stored. Note that each trail can be shifted column-wise to form 32 other valid one-round trails. Thus, in total, there are 1565536 one-round trails which satisfy our criteria.

We now justify the criteria used for computing these 1-round trails. Our main constraint was computing time, as considering all 1-round trails is computationally infeasible. Furthermore, as we wanted to store the trails and reuse them, memory needed to be reasonable as well. Limiting the computation to states with a single active column before and after each $\mathtt{MixColumns}$ computation is a reasonable assumption, as states with more active columns would lead by the inverse $\mathtt{ShiftColumns}$ operation to many active rows. Furthermore, by doing initial experiments for computing long trails, we noticed that all good trails found never had more than 7 active bits in a column. This can be explained by the fact that more active rows naturally lead to lower probability transitions through the $\mathtt{SubBox}$ operation. We then limited the transition through the first $\mathtt{SubBox}$ operation to only transitions from rows with Hamming weight one to rows with Hamming weight at most two. While transitions activating in the output more bits per row can still lead to good trails respecting the other criteria, only a small proportion of these transitions does so, while the computational gain for not considering them is huge. Finally, we limited the probability of the trails to 2^{-49} in order not to have to store too many trails for the second phase. This particular bound came from our initial experiments, were we noticed that the probability of all 1-round trails that were part of the longer trails we found, had probability strictly higher than this bound.

We claim by no means that the chosen criteria lead to all the one-round trails that could be part of optimal longer trails, however we believe that our strategy is a reasonable trade-off between optimality and efficiency.

Searching for Longer Trails. In a second step we used the precomputed 1-round trails to create longer ones. To do so, we started by chaining our precomputed one-round trails in order to obtain r-round trails.

To begin, we exhaustively ran through all the precomputed one-round trails and searched for the ones that can be chained. Recall here that the starting state and ending state of each round trail are the states just before the MixColumns application. The chaining condition is very simple and consists in simply verifying that the final state of a one-round trail is the same as a column-wise rotation of the starting state of the following one by an integer $0 \leq \iota < 32$. Note that when $\iota \neq 0$, the full one-round trail concerned is also rotated column-wise. Also note that doing so, we only obtain an element of an equivalence class modulo the column-wise rotation. In order to make our search efficient, we first sorted the states by Hamming weight and active column coordinate of their initial and final state. Following this procedure, we found 1476978 2-round trails, each of them giving by rotation another 32 valid 2-round trails. We followed a similar procedure to obtain 46471749 3-round trails which can also be rotated column-wise to obtain 32 times more valid 3-round trails. To compute the 4-round trails we use in our attack on the 7-round version, we chained the 2-round trails with themselves rather than using the 3-round trails in order for the search to be more efficient. We stored the most interesting 4-round trails we found based on criteria of low probability and adaptability to the key recovery step as described in the next section.

From now on, for each r-round trail, we use the following notations. Let $\mathtt{st^{start}}[k]$ (resp. $\mathtt{st^{end}}[k]$) be the starting state (resp. the ending state) of each one-round trail composing the r-round trail, for $0 \leq k < r$. Denote also by $\mathtt{c_{start}}$ the active column of $\mathtt{st^{start}}[0]$ and by $\mathtt{c_{end}}$ the active column of $\mathtt{st^{end}}[r-1]$. Let w_0 be the Hamming weight of $\mathtt{c_{start}}$ (i.e. the number of active bits in $\mathtt{c_{start}}$) and let w_1 be the Hamming weight of $M(\mathtt{c_{end}})$, where M is the matrix used in MixColumns. Finally denote by P_k, the probability of the round k, for $0 \leq k < r$. The probability of the r-round trail, that we will call from now on *core trail*, is then given by $P_0 \times P_1 \times \cdots \times P_{r-1}$.

Extending the Core Trail. To build our attack, we need to choose an r-round trail that will be extended one round backwards and half a round forwards as shown in Fig. 3. In this section, we describe the criteria that we used to select an r-round trail that is likely to result in a good $(r+1.5)$-round trail. The resulting $(r+1.5)$-round trail must have good probability, but also needs to be adapted to our key recovery step. In particular, as we will argue in detail in Sect. 4, it is important to have differentials that will allow for efficient sieving in the plaintext. In particular, it is desirable that the $(r+1.5)$-round trail we construct has a sufficient number of inactive rows on the plaintext.

First, as described above, we need to make sure that the r-round trail selected leads to a $(r+1.5)$-round trail with good probability. For a r-round trail, the probability of the resulting $(r+1.5)$-round trail can be upper-bounded by $2^{-(w_0+1)\times 3} \times P_0 \times P_1 \times \cdots \times P_{r-1} \times 2^{-w_1 \times 3}$. Indeed, if w_0 is the Hamming weight of c_{start}, then by computing backwards one round there will be at least $w_0 + 1$ active S-boxes. As the highest probability transition through an S-box has probability 2^{-3}, the highest possible probability of this prepended round will be $2^{-(w_0+1)\times3}$. In the same way, if w_1 is the Hamming weight of $M(c_{end})$, then there will be exactly w_1 active S-boxes through the first S-box layer of the next round. Thus, the probability of the appended half round will be at most $2^{-w_1\times3}$. We generated all possible r-round core trails following the procedure described above and kept the ones providing high estimated probabilities.

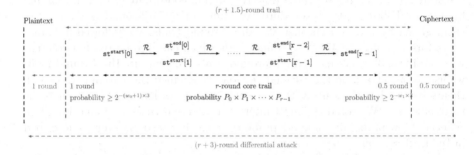

Fig. 3. Generating $(r + 1.5)$-round trails from core r-round trails and extending them to mount $(r + 3)$-round attacks on **SPEEDY**.

Second, we want the r-round trail selected to lead to a $(r + 1.5)$-round trail that has a significant number of inactive rows on the plaintext in order for the sieving step to be efficient. First, consider the initial state of the r-round trail. The rows that are active in this state are exactly the rows that will be active in the state that follows the first SC operation in round 0 of the $(r + 1.5)$-round trail. To achieve better sieving, we want the transition from this state through $SC^{-1} \circ SB^{-1}$ to lead to an initial state of the $(r + 1.5)$-round trail that has low Hamming weight. To achieve this, not only the number of active rows but also the way those are distributed inside this state play a role for the efficiency of the sieving procedure. Let L be the size of a block of consecutive rows, where all rows are non-active except for l out of them. An example of such a state is shown below with $L = 15$ and $l = 3$.

Large values of L combined with small values of l naturally lead to better complexities. Indeed, we can carefully control the l active rows with some probability at a given cost. By doing so, we can generate a number of inactive rows in the plaintext as high as $L - 5 - l$, thus leading to a sieving of $2^{-[(L-5-l)]\times6}$.

Using the above criteria, we selected an r-round trail, which we then extended in two ways, starting first by appending a round backwards. This led to an $(r+1)$-round trail. Then, to further improve the probability of our trail $(r+1)$-round trail, we relied on the technique of multiple differentials.

3.4 Multiple Differentials

The technique of multiple differentials consists in considering multiple $(r+1)$-round differential trails that all have the same input and output difference. To make the description of our technique simpler, we will describe how we built our multiple differentials in the case of our 7-round attack. In this case, $r = 4$. For our 7-round attack, the chosen 4-round core trail is the one displayed in red in Fig. 4. This trail has probability $2^{-161.15}$. As shown in Fig. 4, we extended it by one round backwards and obtained a 5-round trail of probability $p_{main} = 2^{-170.56}$. We call this trail the *main trail*. Note that it is possible to extend the 4-round core trail backwards with probability 2^{-6} for one round. However, this propagation, due to the diffusion properties of the inverse MixColumns transformation would lead to a column with 19 active bits (see Sect. 3.2). Such a scenario would have complicated the key-recovery phase and was not retained.

We limited our search to trails with probability smaller or equal to $p_{max} = p_{main} \times 2^{-25}$. Our new trails must thus verify that

- their input difference is such that the bits of coordinate

$$(i, j) \in \{2, 3, 4, 7, 8, 10, 12, 14, 16, 17, 18, 25, 27, 29\} \times \{1\}$$

  are active, whilst the other bits are inactive in the first state of Fig. 4;
- their output difference is such the bits of coordinate

$$(i, j) \in \{1, 15, 16, 19, 21, 25, 31\} \times \{3\}$$

  are active, whilst the other bits are inactive in the second state surrounded by red in Fig. 4.

To build our new trails, we rely on an algorithm that operates round by round.

Initial Round. We start by building a list of potential initial one-round trails. We denote the initial state by st[0], the state after the application of MC by st[1], and so on so forth as we did when constructing our one-round trails. We construct our initial one-round trails in a similar fashion to the way we constructed the one-round trails used to build our main trail. More precisely, we want our potential initial one-round trails to satisfy the following conditions:

- st[0] verifies the input condition;
- st[5] has a single active column c_5 such that $(c_5, M(c_5)) \in T$;
- st[2] has at most two active bits per row.

In order to make the search more efficient, we added constraints on these initial round trails' probability and Hamming weight, using the fact that $(st[0], st[6])$ must belong to a larger 5-round trail such that the probability of this larger trail is at most p_{max}. We will not describe these constraints in detail as they are very similar to previous techniques we used to build trails of reasonable probability. We obtained 6 potential initial round trails. Because of the second condition above, these new trails can be chained to our previously computed one-round trails. This property will be used to build our multiples.

Chaining the Initial Round. In order to find trails that satisfy our truncated differential constraints, we must now chain the potential initial round trails to the previously computed one-round trails. We do so in two steps in order for the chaining to be computationally feasible.

1. We chain the 2-round trails pre-computed to the potential initial one-round trails to form potential initial three-round trails. We get 8049 such 3-round trails.
2. We chain these potential initial 3-round trails to the previously computed 2-round trails to obtain 5-round trails.

We found 409 5-round trails that matched all our criteria. By adding their corresponding probabilities, we found a final probability of $2^{-169.95}$. As one can notice, using multiple differentials allows to improve the probability of the r-round differential, but this improvement is not as important as one would have expected by the number of found trails. This is due to the fact that all of the additional trails found had unfortunately quite bad probabilities compared to the main one.

5.5-Round Differential Trail. We describe now the 5.5-round differential trail we used to attack SPEEDY-7-192 in the following section. This trail is depicted in Fig. 4.

As stated before, the 5-round trail has probability $2^{-170.56}$, which is improved to $2^{-169.95}$ by using multiple trails. We then extended this differential 0.5 round forwards. For this step we followed a particular approach. To go through the last S-box layer of the distinguisher part (see the before last state of Fig. 4) an attacker has several choices. One extreme would be to fix to some concrete output value the transitions through all active S-boxes. This comes at a cost of a certain probability, but if we choose the transitions carefully we can guarantee very few active rows on the ciphertext. The other extreme is to consider truncated output differences for all the active S-boxes of this state. Thus the transition through the SubBox layer happens with probability 1, but almost all rows will be active in the output leading to very large structures of ciphertexts. What we decided to do is a trade-off between these two scenarios. More precisely, we decided to fix the transition 0x4 → 0x10 for the active S-boxes of rows 5, 11 and 19 and to allow more transitions for the S-boxes of rows 0 and 28. The choice of these two rows comes from the fact that after the SC operation, these two S-boxes activate some common rows. Our goal was to activate at most 7 rows after the SC operation (last state of Fig. 4) and for this we computed the highest probability to have at most 4 rows active between rows 23 and 31 and also row 0 after SC. We exhausted all possible configurations and we found the best one to be the one having the rows $24, 27, 28$ and 31 active after SC. One possibility for this was to force the output difference of the S-box of row 0 to be of the form $(0,*,0,0,*,0)$ and the output difference of the S-box of row 28 to be of the form $(*,*,0,0,*,0)$, where $*$ means that the corresponding bit is potentially active. The probability then to start from any difference of the above form in rows 0 and 28 and to activate at most the rows $24, 27, 28$ and 31 after the SC is $2^{-3.41}$. This fact, together with the probability of $2^{-3.41}$ for the transition $\mathtt{0x4} \rightarrow \mathtt{0x10}$ for the other three active rows, gives a total probability of $2^{-13.64}$.

To summarize, as can be seen from Fig. 4, our 5.5-round trail has then a total probability of

$$2^{-169.95} \times 2^{-13.64} = 2^{-183.59}.$$

4   Attack on SPEEDY-7-192

SPEEDY-7-192 is the variant of the SPEEDY family suggested for applications where a security of 192 bits is needed. We show in this section, by using the techniques and ideas introduced earlier, how to recover the secret key of this version with less than 2^{192} encryptions. In addition, we will propose two ideas that will allow us to optimize the complexity of the attack: one, already used for instance in [12], is to not consider the rounds as blocks regarding their treatment with respect to the differential distinguisher or the truncated part, but include some row transitions in the differential and let the rest go as truncated in the same round which we will apply in the input and output of the attack; the other is to consider the detailed equations over two rounds with merging techniques that will allow us to optimize the complexity of the key guessing part.

Our attack has a data complexity of $2^{187.28}$, a time complexity of $2^{187.84}$ and a memory complexity of 2^{42} and contradicts thus the designers' security claim for this variant, as has been acknowledged by them. More importantly, this crypt-analysis highlights that the security margin for this variant was overestimated. Our attack uses the differential found with the ideas from Sect. 2 and the implemented method described in Sect. 3.3. As described before, the main differential trail depicted in Fig. 4 covers 5.5 rounds and its probability, when taken together with its associated multiple trails described in Sect. 3.4, is $2^{183.59}$. The trail of Fig. 4 can then be extended one round backwards and half a round forwards as shown in Fig. 5, to finally cover 7 rounds. This fact contradicts a particular statement of the designers that wrote that a one-round security margin for the key-recovery part should be sufficient.

4.1   Trade-Off Between Differential Probability and Efficient Sieving

Our attack is performed in the decryption direction. The first step is to generate a number of relevant ciphertexts to implement the attack. If we impose no extra

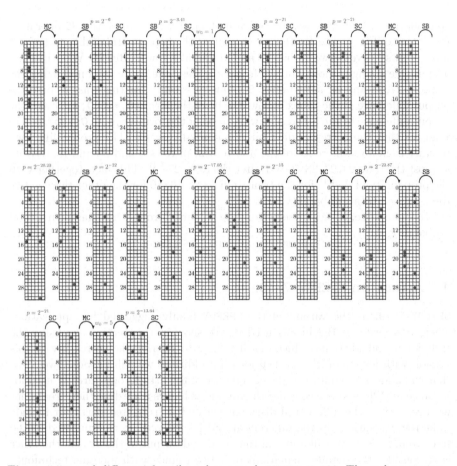

Fig. 4. 5.5-round differential trail used to attack SPEEDY-7-192. The red part corresponds to the 4-round core trail, while the blue part corresponds to the 1.5-round extension. Grey bits are bits with unknown difference. The two states surrounded in red are the starting and final states of the multiple differentials considered. (Color figure online)

condition on the extension of the distinguisher to the plaintexts ($\delta_{in} \rightarrow D_{in}$ as denoted in Fig. 1) then D_{in} will have all but one rows active (see Fig. 4). This would lead to a very limited sieving and would thus leave us with too many potential pairs on which to perform the key recovery. For this reason, we propose a first improvement. This improvement consists in restricting the permitted transitions through the second S-box layer of Round 0. More precisely, the condition is that the three active bits in rows 26, 28 and 30 after the second S-box only generate a maximum of three active rows in the plaintext state (among rows 26 to 31 and among rows 0 to 2). This condition allows to have 7 inactive rows (instead of 1 before) in the plaintext state at the cost of decreasing the overall differential probability. We denote by P_{in} the probability that it is

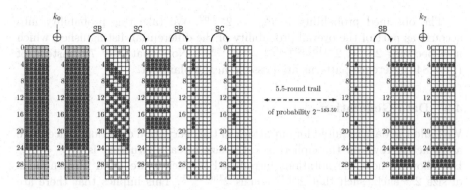

Fig. 5. Key recovery part of the 7-round attack against SPEEDY-7-192

verified. As we show next, since this probability is relatively high, the impact on the overall differential probability is limited Fig. 6.

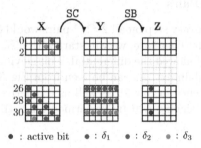

● : active bit   ● : δ_1 ● : δ_2 ● : δ_3

Fig. 6. Transition of rows 26, 28 and 30 through the inverse of the second SB of round 0.

To compute P_{in}, we start with the state **Z**, corresponding to the state after the second S-box application of Round 0, where the rows 26, 28 and 30 all have an active difference of 010000. Therefore, on the state **Y**, we consider differences $\delta_1, \delta_2, \delta_3$ that propagate to 010000 through the S-box layer with probability $\mathbb{P}(\delta_1), \mathbb{P}(\delta_2), \mathbb{P}(\delta_3)$ respectively. Propagating backwards through SC, we obtain $\mathbf{X}_{\delta_1,\delta_2,\delta_3} = \text{SC}^{-1}(\mathbf{Y}_{\delta_1,\delta_2,\delta_3})$. We are interested in states $\mathbf{X}_{\delta_1,\delta_2,\delta_3}$ that have at most three nonzero rows among rows 26 to 31 and among rows 0 to 2. We define the function $\mathbb{1}_3$ as follows:

$$\mathbb{1}_3(\mathbf{X}_{\delta_1,\delta_2,\delta_3}) = \begin{cases} 0 \text{ if } \mathbf{X}_{\delta_1,\delta_2,\delta_3} \text{ has more than 3 nonzero rows} \\ 1 \text{ else.} \end{cases}$$

The overall probability for the transition is given by the formula

$$P_{in} = \int_{\delta_1,\delta_2,\delta_3} \mathbb{1}_3(\mathbf{X}_{\delta_1,\delta_2,\delta_3}) \mathbb{P}(\delta_1)\mathbb{P}(\delta_2)\mathbb{P}(\delta_3).$$

The obtained probability is $P_{in} = 2^{-2.69}$. We take this probability into account as part of the overall probability of the differential distinguisher, which now becomes $2^{p^*} = 2^{-(183.59+2.69)} = 2^{-186.28}$. Note that only 78 (instead of $\binom{9}{3} = 84$) difference patterns are possible in the plaintext.

4.2 Data Generation

We build the data required for our attack in the decryption direction. Since there are 7 active rows on the ciphertexts, the size of each structure is $2^{7 \times 6} = 2^{42}$. By following now the notations introduced in Sect. 2, we build 2^s structures of size 2^{42} each, such that 2^{s+42} equals $2^{186.28+1}$. This implies that there are $2^s = 2^{145.28}$ structures and $2^{145.28+2 \cdot 42-1} = 2^{228.28}$ potential pairs. The cost of the data generation is $2^{187.28}C_E$, where C_E is the cost of one encryption and can be estimated as $6*(1+6+6+6)+1+6+6 = 128$ bit-operations. Indeed, MC, SB are 6 bit-operations, the cost of AK is 1, and all these transformations can be applied in parallel.

4.3 Sieving of the Pairs

Performing the key-recovery step on all $2^{228.28}$ pairs would exceed the complexity of the exhaustive search. Therefore, we will start with a sieving step to eliminate pairs that cannot have followed the differential. This sieving is done by looking at the differences in the plaintext. As can be seen from Fig. 5, the 'good' plaintext pairs have a zero-difference in row 25 as well as 6 inactive rows among rows 26 to 31 and 0 to 2. The sieving will be performed on both the inactive and the active rows.

Inactive Rows. Each inactive row represents a 6-bit filter. We consider each of the 78 possible difference pattern in the plaintext. For each pattern, since there are 7 inactive rows at the input, the sieving obtained from these rows is 2^{-42}.

Active Rows $[3 - 24]$. We can proceed to a sieving on each of these 22 active rows by taking into account the first S-box layer of Round 0. To make this step clear, we start by explaining the sieve on row 6. As can be seen from Fig. 5, to follow the differential, a plaintext pair should generate after the application of the S-box a truncated difference of the form $(0,*,*,*,0,0)$. By looking at the DDT of SPEEDY's S-box, we see that the input differences 0x16, 0x2d and 0x3c never propagate to an output difference of the form $(0,*,*,*,0,0)$. Thus, any pair with one of those three plaintext differences at row 0 can be sieved out. This gives us a filter of $log_2(61/64) = 0.07$, as shown in Table 5. The filters for the other active rows are computed similarly and are reported in Table 5.

Considering the 78 Different Patterns in the Rows $[26-31]$ *and* $[0-2]$. Recall that there are in total 78 possible patterns *pat*, and each one corresponds to a subset of exactly 3 active rows among rows 26 to 31 and 0 to 2 in the plaintext. We start from the difference $(0,1,0,0,0,0)$ on the rows 26, 28 and 30 after the

Table 5. Sieving in the active rows [3 − 24] of the plaintext.

row	filter	row	filter	row	filter	row	filter
3	0.42	9	0.02	15	0.09	21	0.07
4	0.48	10	0.05	16	0.07	22	0.17
5	0.07	11	0.07	17	0.09	23	0.51
6	0.07	12	0.12	18	0	24	1.42
7	0.07	13	0.02	19	0.02		
8	0	14	0.07	20	0		

total filter 3.9

second S-box of Round 0. Then we propagate this difference backwards through the two S-box layers of Round 0 and discard all the differences that do not follow the pattern considered. The number of possible differences on the plaintext allows us to filter $2^{-f_{pat}} = \frac{\#\text{Possible differences}}{2^{3 \cdot 6}}$ (see [11] for the 78 possible values of f_{pat}).

Summarizing the Sieving Step. For a pattern *pat*, the sieving corresponding to the inactive rows is 2^{-42} while the one on the active rows is $2^{-3.9} \cdot 2^{-f_{pat}}$. Thus, the total number of potential pairs for the key recovery step is

$$\sum_{pat} 2^{228.28 - 45.9 - f_{pat}} = 2^{182.38} \sum_{pat} 2^{-f_{pat}} = 2^{186.42}.$$

This sieving step is the reason why we decided to perform the attack in the decryption direction. Indeed, using the 78 patterns in initial structures would have further increased the complexity.

4.4   Recovering the Key

In this section, we describe our improved key recovery step. The key recovery algorithm is performed for each pair on the fly. As explained in the last section, the total number of pairs we will try in this step is $2^{186.42}$. For each pair, we check whether there exists a key that allows the pair to follow the differential. If not, the pair is discarded. Otherwise, as we will show, we obtain a partial key on which all bits are determined but a small number n_l which is equal to 8 on average. For each of the remaining pairs and associated partial key, we then try exhaustively all possible 2^{n_l} keys. For each pair, the key recovery is divided into three stages which can be summarized as follows. First, we determine bits of the last subkey k_7 using the fact that if the pair follows the trail, then it must belong to δ_{out} before the last SB application. Since the key schedule of SPEEDY consists simply in a permutation of the key bits, this in turn constrains the bits of k_0. Second, we determine more bits of k_0 using the fact that the pair must belong to δ_{in}. Lastly, we determine a few extra key bits using the penultimate S-box application (first S-box application of the last round).

Stage 1 - Last Subkey Addition (k_7). For each pair, we start by determining several bits of k_7. As can be seen from Fig. 5, the ciphertext pairs are active on the rows [4,10,18,24,27,28,31]. For the rows [4,10,18,27,31] (respectively row 24), we want the partial key to be such that these rows satisfy the differential $(0,1,0,0,0,0)$ (respectively $(0,0,0,0,1,0)$) before the last SB application. For each pair, this determines $6 \times 6 = 36$ key bits on average. The case of row 28 is only slightly different. If active, there are 2^6 possibilities for the six key bits, but 4 different patterns are possible before SB. A correct pattern is thus reached with probability 2^{-4}. The row 28 can thus determine 6 additional key bits at the cost of 2^2 guesses on average. This stage thus allows us to determine up to 42 key bits at the cost of 2^2 guesses. In Table 6, we detail which key bits of the master key are fixed after determining the value of k_7 on the rows corresponding to one of the 7 active rows in the ciphertext.

Table 6. Guessed master key bits from the subkey k_7. Each row corresponds to one of the 7 active rows of the ciphertexts.

row							row						
4	145	8	63	118	173	36	27	55	110	165	28	83	138
10	13	68	123	178	41	96	28	1	56	111	166	29	84
18	157	20	75	130	185	48	31	31	86	141	4	59	114
24	25	80	135	190	53	108							

About the Potentially Active Ciphertext Rows. For the sake of simplicity, we consider in this analysis that the four ciphertext rows [24,27,28,31] are active, as it simplifies the key guessing procedure. In fact, we could just discard the pairs that do not verify this, leaving us with $2^{24+24-1} - 2^{47-6} \approx 2^{46.91}$ pairs for the partial structure on 4 lines instead of 2^{47}, but with a higher probability of reaching a good difference before the penultimate SB. In practice, there is no need to discard this data. It can also be treated with similar methods to the one presented here. Although these methods are slightly more expensive than the one presented here as a few more key bits might have to be partially guessed, they are used to handle a very small proportion of data. Thus, the difference in the cost will be negligible. We thus limit our explanations to the predominant case, with all the rows active. We allow rows [4,10,18] to be non active. For each of these rows, this gives on average a probability of 2^{-6} of having a difference that can match the required one (including the 0 difference). Thus, on average, only one 6-bit key word leads to the desired difference.

Stage 2 - First Subkey Addition (k_0). We now focus on the addition of the first subkey k_0. This key recovery stage is performed row by row, and the order in which each row is treated is important in order to keep our time complexity as low as possible. For each row, we will use available information from both SubBox layers of Round 0 to determine more triplets of possible pairs and associated key. Table 7 helps us understand how to exploit the first S-box of Round 0 for rows [3,...,24]. Recall that these rows are active rows in the plaintext and that they allowed us to perform a specific sieving given in Sect. 4.3. For each row, Table 7 provides the following information:

- **Key determined** gives the number of key bits already determined during Stage 1 (*i.e.* with subkey k_7).
- **Key left** gives the number of key bits that remain to be determined for this row (note that the sum of **Key determined** and **Key left** is always 6).
- **Differential Filter** gives the value of the filter that was applied during the sieving step to each pair.
- **Fixed bits** gives the amount of inactive bits after the first SubBox layer.
- **First S-box Cost** gives the overall cost in bits for a given row to check the propagation through the first SubBox. Since one can precompute the valid pairs of values and associated partial keys for each row, this cost is equal to (**Key left** + **Differential filter** - **Fixed bits**) rather than **Key left**. For each row and for each key, the probability that they satisfy the differential is $2^{\text{Differential filter}-\text{Fixed bits}}$. In particular, for rows where the value of **First S-box Cost** is negative, then for each pair, there exists a key that satisfies the differential with probability < 1. Such rows allow us to discard more pairs.

Since row 25 is inactive, it does not provide any information about k_0 through the first SB. For the sake of simplicity, we do not analyze how to exploit the rows 0 to 2 and 26 to 31. This could have been done by looking at the case of each specific pattern, but it wouldn't have significantly improved the attack whilst considerably lengthening the description of the key recovery step.

To perform the key recovery, we will also look into the propagation through the second S-box. More precisely, we will use the conditions set on the rows [3,4,5,8,9,11,13,15,17,18,19] after the application of the second S-box to sieve the pairs. At the output of the second S-box, these rows must have the exact difference (0,1,0,0,0,0). This provides us with a 2^{-6} filter, but it is not straightforward how to exploit it. Indeed, because of the SC step, each row at the output of the second S-box layer depends on 6 rows at the output of the first S-box layer. It thus seems that in order to get a 2^{-6} filter, one first has to guess 6 rows of k_7, which is very costly. However, we use several improved techniques in order to get filters without having to guess too many rows before the first S-box step. We describe these techniques through an example which can be found in the paragraph dedicated to the rows [18,19,22,21,23] below. We now describe in detail the first three steps of Stage 2. Table 8 sums up the rest of Stage 2.

Rows [4]. We start by considering row 4. This row allows us to perform a filter of -0.52 at the first S-box level of Round 0.

Table 7. This table represents the information used for efficiently solving the key-recovery part of the attack. Each line in the table is associated to the same row in the state. The column `Key determined` indicates how many bits are already known from Stage 1 (those bits are depicted in red), and `Key left` is the number of bits that remains to be known. `Fixed bits` represents the number of inactive bits after the first SB of Round 0 and that therefore can be used to perform a sieving on the candidate keys. The `cost` is the difference between the previous values, and the `second filter` denotes the active rows in the second SB, as they will provide an additional filtering to produce the fixed output difference.

row							Key determined	Key left	Differential Filter	Fixed bits	First S-box Cost
0	0	1	2	3	4	5	2	4	*	*	*
1	6	7	8	9	10	11	1	5	*	*	*
2	12	13	14	15	16	17	1	5	*	*	*
3	18	19	20	21	22	23	1	5	0.42	4	1.42
4	24	25	26	27	28	29	3	3	0.48	4	-0.52
5	30	31	32	33	34	35	1	5	0.07	3	2.07
6	36	37	38	39	40	41	2	4	0.07	3	1.07
7	42	43	44	45	46	47	0	6	0.07	3	3.07
8	48	49	50	51	52	53	2	4	0	2	2
9	54	55	56	57	58	59	3	3	0.02	2	1.02
10	60	61	62	63	64	65	1	5	0.05	3	2.05
11	66	67	68	69	70	71	1	5	0.07	3	2.07
12	72	73	74	75	76	77	1	5	0.12	3	2.12
13	78	79	80	81	82	83	2	4	0.02	2	2.02
14	84	85	86	87	88	89	2	4	0.07	3	1.07
15	90	91	92	93	94	95	0	6	0.09	3	3.09
16	96	97	98	99	100	101	1	5	0.07	3	2.07
17	102	103	104	105	106	107	0	6	0.09	3	3.09
18	108	109	110	111	112	113	3	3	0	2	1
19	114	115	116	117	118	119	2	4	0.02	2	2.02
20	120	121	122	123	124	125	1	5	0	2	3
21	126	127	128	129	130	131	1	5	0.07	3	2.07
22	132	133	134	135	136	137	1	5	0.17	3	2.17
23	138	139	140	141	142	143	2	4	0.51	4	0.51
24	144	145	146	147	148	149	1	5	1.42	5	1.42
25	150	151	152	153	154	155	0	6	*	*	*
26	156	157	158	159	160	161	1	5	*	*	*
27	162	163	164	165	166	167	2	4	*	*	*
28	168	169	170	171	172	173	1	5	*	*	*
29	174	175	176	177	178	179	1	5	*	*	*
30	180	181	182	183	184	185	1	5	*	*	*
31	186	187	188	189	190	191	1	5	*	*	*

Rows [18,19,20,21,23]. We next consider the rows 18,19,20,21 and 23. To understand why these rows are the next ones we consider, one must take into account the second S-box transition. Indeed, consider the rows [17,18,19] after the second S-box transition. These three rows are active, and must thus have the exact difference (0,1,0,0,0,0). Since these rows are positioned next to each other, one does not need to guess $3 \times 6 = 18$ rows at the input of the first S-box, but only 8, namely the rows [17,18,...,24]. Further, we show that to get a filter, one does not need to guess all of the 8 rows on which the rows [17,18,19] after the second S-box transition depend. We start by precomputing all the pairs of values that are in the codomain of the function

$$a, b, c, d, e, f \mapsto \left(S^{-1}(a, b, c, d, e, f), S^{-1}(a, b, c, d, e \oplus 1, f) \right)$$

and store them in a table of size 2^6. We can thus build precomputed table of size 2^{18} which contains all possible valid values of rows [17,18,19] at the entry the second S-box layer. We guess the rows [18,19,20,21,23] at the entry of the first S-box. In total, 13 bits of the rows [18,19,22,21,23] later impact the rows [17,18,19] at the entry of the second S-box. There are thus 2^{26} possible pairs of values for these bits, whilst in total, the table contains 2^{18} possible pairs that verify the condition at the output of the S-box on the rows [17,18,19]. This thus results in a 2^{-8} filter. More precisely each pair matches a pre-computed valid pair in the table of size 2^{18} with probability 2^{-8}. In particular, whenever a pair is not discarded, the rows [17,18,19] before the second S-box are completely determined. This will allow us to filter more pairs as we guess more rows in the plaintext which impact the value of the rows [17,18,19] before the second S-box. The guess of rows 18,19,21 and 23 can be done with merging techniques developed in [15] resulting in a reduction of the guessing cost from $2^{2.02+2.07+1+0.51+2.17} = 2^{7.77}$ to $2^{4.09} + 2^{3.68} + 2^{7.77-8} = 2^{4.94}$, or else can be more efficiently performed with small precomputations regarding these partial transitions with a cost for each step given by the number of remaining solutions, so $2^{7.77-8} = 2^{-0.23}$ in this example.

Row 24. The next step consists in guessing row 24. As we have described previously, for the pairs that have not been discarded yet, the three rows [17,18,19] before the second S-box are fixed. Two bits of row 24 later impact the value of these rows. Thus, we obtain an extra 2^{-2} filter. Therefore, as can be seen from Table 7 we obtain a partial guessing cost of $2^{1.42}$ and a partial data cost of $2^{-0.58}$.

The next steps of the key recovery are described in Table 8. This table must to be read from top to bottom. Its columns provide the following informations:

- **Row guessed at the input.** This column displays the coordinate of the row guessed. The column considered first is at the top and the last one is at the bottom.
- **Partial guessing cost.** This column displays the cost of guessing each row and checking that the first S-box transition is valid (See Table 7).

- **Partial data filter.** For each row, this column displays the log of the probability that a valid partial key exists for each pair, taking into account the filter provided by the constraints after the second S-box. This column provides information on the evolution of the data after guessing each row (or group of rows). For a (group of) row(s), if the entry on this column is $-x$, then the number of pairs remaining after handling this (these) column(s) is multiplied by 2^{-x}.
- **Row determined at second S-box.** This column displays the second S-box rows that are fully determined after a given guess.

Table 8. Description of Stage 2 of the key recovery.

Row guessed at the input	Partial guessing cost	Partial data filter	Row determined at second S-box
4	-0.52	-0.52	
18,19,22,21,23	4.9	-0.23	17,18,19
24	1.42	-0.58	
20	3	-3	15
17	3.09	-0.91	
16	2.07	0.07	13
15	3.09	-0.91	
14	1.07	-0.93	11
13	2.02	-1.98	
11	2.07	0.07	9
12	2.12	-1.88	8
9	1	-3	
10	2.05	-1.95	
8	2	0	5
6	1.07	-0.93	3
5	2.07	-1.93	
7	3.07	-0.93	
3	1.42	-0.58	

The complexity of the key recovery so far is given by the formula

$$[2^{186.42+2}2^{-0.52}(2^{4.94} + 2^{-0.23}(2^{1.42} + 2^{-0.58}(2^3 + 2^{-3}(\cdots(2^{1.42} + 2^{0.58})))))] \, 2^{-7}C_E$$
$$= 2^{186.15}C_E$$

and there are $2^{168.3}$ remaining pairs.

Stage 3 - Back to k_7 Using the Penultimate S-Box. For the remaining key bits, we will go back to k_7 and study the penultimate S-box. A similar approach to the second S-box is applied here: instead of using the second S-box transition to perform a guess and filter approach, the penultimate S-box is used. For each row of k_7, Table 9 shows which bits of the master key still need to be guessed (the bits in black). For each pair, we wish to find partial keys such that they lead to the difference 000100 before the first S-box of the last round on rows [0,5,11,19,31]. For each of these rows, Table 10 displays which rows of k_7 need to be guessed in order to check the transition to 000100 before the first S-box of the last round. More precisely, it provides the following information.

- Row considered. This column displays the coordinate of the row before the first S-box of the last round which will be used to filter the right key guesses.
- Involved rows of k_7. This column displays which rows of k_7 must be guessed in order to check the condition on the row considered before the first S-box of the last round.
- Number of missing bits. This columns displays the number of bits in the involved rows of k_7 that have not yet been determined.

For each remaining pair and for each of these five transitions, we recover the key bits that allow this transition and put them in tabs. By merging them, we then recover the pairs and associated partial keys that allow the whole state transition. After this step, only the key bits [15,16,152,153,159,180,187,188] are left to determine. This is done by guessing them. The complexity associated to this step is

$$2^{168.3}(2^8 + 2^8 + 2^9 + 2^{10} + 2^{10} + 2^{11}(1 + 2^8)) = 2^{180.31}C_E.$$

Table 9. In red, the master key bits that have already been determined. In black, the bits that still need to be determined.

row							Key left	row							Key left
0	169	32	87	142	5	60	2	16	73	128	183	46	101	156	2
1	115	170	33	88	143	6	2	17	19	74	129	184	47	102	1
2	61	116	171	34	89	144	1	18	157	20	75	130	185	48	0
3	7	62	117	172	35	90	2	19	103	158	21	76	131	186	2
4	145	8	63	118	173	36	0	20	49	104	159	22	77	132	1
5	91	146	9	64	119	174	2	21	187	50	105	160	23	78	1
6	37	92	147	10	65	120	1	22	133	188	51	106	161	24	1
7	175	38	93	148	11	66	2	23	79	134	189	52	107	162	2
8	121	176	39	94	149	12	2	24	25	80	135	190	53	108	0
9	67	122	177	40	95	150	2	25	163	26	81	136	191	54	2
10	13	68	123	178	41	96	0	26	109	164	27	82	137	0	2
11	151	14	69	124	179	42	3	27	55	110	165	28	83	138	0
12	97	152	15	70	125	180	3	28	1	56	111	166	29	84	2
13	43	98	153	16	71	126	2	29	139	2	57	112	167	30	2
14	181	44	99	154	17	72	3	30	85	140	3	58	113	168	2
15	127	182	45	100	155	18	2	31	31	86	141	4	59	114	0

Table 10. Description of Stage 3 of the key recovery.

Row	Involved rows of k_7	# missing bits	Row	Involved rows of k_7	# missing bits
0	27,28,29,30,31,0	8	19	14,15,16,17,18,19	10
5	0,1,2,3,4,5	9	31	23,24,25,26,27,28	8
11	6,7,8,9,10,11	10			

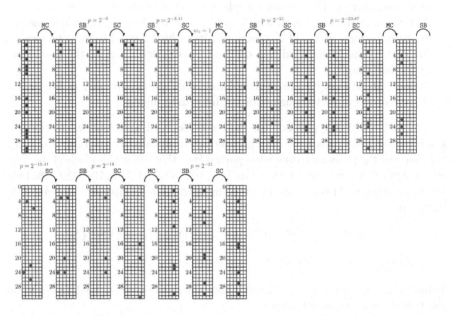

Fig. 7. 3.5-round differential trail used to attack SPEEDY-5-192. The red part corresponds to the 2-round core trail, while the blue part corresponds to the 1.5-round extension (Color figure online).

Complexity Summary. The final time complexity of our attack is

$$T = 2^{187.28}C_E + 2^{179.42}C_E + 2^{186.15}C_E + 2^{180.31}C_E = 2^{187.84}C_E$$

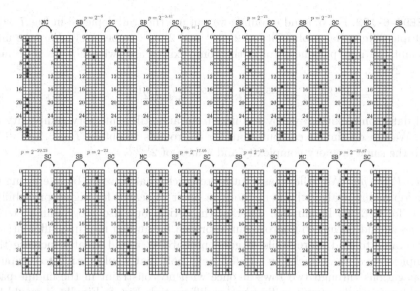

Fig. 8. 4.5-round differential trail used to attack SPEEDY-6-192. The red part corresponds to the 3-round core trail, while the blue part to the 1.5-round extension (Color figure online).

5   Discussion and Conclusion

We presented in this work an attack on SPEEDY-7-192 that fully breaks this variant of the SPEEDY family of ciphers. In parallel, we could also build attacks on other variants, even if our attacks on these smaller-round versions do not contradict the corresponding security claims. For completeness we provide a summary of these attacks, that are at the best of our knowledge the best known attacks on these versions.

SPEEDY-5-192. Following the trail depicted in Fig. 7 and its associated multiple differential probability of $2^{104.02}$, computed as explained in Sect. 3.4, we can build a differential attack on 5 rounds, very similar to the 7-round one. We just need to take into account the new parameters. Note that the complexity for the key recovery is extrapolated from the 7 round version, since the first round is the same and we have the same amount of key bits, we expect similar complexity for the first part of the key recovery. Regarding 5 rounds the new complexity is given by (with $C_E = 2^{6.47}$ here):

$$\mathcal{T} = 2^{107.71}C_E + 2^{100.38}C_E + 2^{105.38}C_E + 2^{86.85}C_E \approx 2^{107.98}C_E,$$

a data complexity of $2^{107.71}$ and a memory complexity of 2^{42}. The authors stated that this version should achieve 128-bit security when data complexity is limited to 2^{64}. Therefore, due to the data limitation, our attack does not contradict the security claim of the designers but still represents the best known attack against SPEEDY-5-192.

SPEEDY-6-192. For 5.5 and 6 rounds we can use the trail depicted in Fig. 7 with multiple differential probability of $2^{125.41}$ and $2^{149.28}$ respectively. We take into account the new parameters and the complexities are (with $C_E^{5.5} = 2^{6.67}$ and $C_E^6 = 2^{6.75}$):

$$\mathcal{T}_6 = 2^{152.97} C_E + 2^{145.36} C_E + 2^{150.36} C_E + 2^{132.36} \approx 2^{153.19} C_E,$$

and data complexity given by the first term and still a memory complexity of 2^{42}. We can do similar computations for 5.5 rounds to obtain $\mathcal{T}_{5.5} = 2^{129.34} C_E$ with the same memory complexity and a data of $2^{129.1}$.

Open Problems. We believe, as a future research, that it would be interesting to develop different algorithmic methods in order to search for higher-probability trails for SPEEDY. In parallel, different theoretical but also programming techniques should permit to improve our approach for finding multiple differentials. Being able to find more trails of good probability would greatly increase the complexities of the attacks. In parallel, new tools that would permit to compute propagations through two rows at once with no constraint in the middle part would potentially permit to find better differentials Fig. 8. Finally, it would be interesting to develop an automatic tool for differential cryptanalysis that could give an approximate of the best attack complexity for certain types of ciphers.

Acknowledgements. This project has received funding from the European Research Council (ERC) under the European Union's Horizon 2020 research and innovation program (grant agreement no. 714294 - acronym QUASYModo). It was also partially supported by the French Agence Nationale de la Recherche through the SWAP project under Contract ANR-21-CE39-0012. We would also like to thank Shahram Rasoolzadeh and Zahra Ahmadian for fruitful discussions and for pointing out an error in our initial analysis.

References

1. Banik, S., et al.: WARP: revisiting GFN for lightweight 128-bit block cipher. In: Dunkelman, O., Jacobson, Jr., M.J., O'Flynn, C. (eds.) SAC 2020. LNCS, vol. 12804, pp. 535–564. Springer, Cham (2021). https://doi.org/10.1007/978-3-030-81652-0_21
2. Banik, S., Pandey, S.K., Peyrin, T., Sasaki, Yu., Sim, S.M., Todo, Y.: GIFT: a small present. In: Fischer, W., Homma, N. (eds.) CHES 2017. LNCS, vol. 10529, pp. 321–345. Springer, Cham (2017). https://doi.org/10.1007/978-3-319-66787-4_16
3. Beierle, C., et al.: The SKINNY family of block ciphers and its low-latency variant MANTIS. In: Robshaw, M., Katz, J. (eds.) CRYPTO 2016. LNCS, vol. 9815, pp. 123–153. Springer, Heidelberg (2016). https://doi.org/10.1007/978-3-662-53008-5_5
4. Biham, E., Furman, V., Misztal, M., Rijmen, V.: Differential cryptanalysis of Q. In: Matsui, M. (ed.) FSE 2001. LNCS, vol. 2355, pp. 174–186. Springer, Heidelberg (2002). https://doi.org/10.1007/3-540-45473-X_15
5. Biham, E., Shamir, A.: Differential cryptanalysis of DES-like cryptosystems. In: Menezes, A.J., Vanstone, S.A. (eds.) CRYPTO 1990. LNCS, vol. 537, pp. 2–21. Springer, Heidelberg (1991). https://doi.org/10.1007/3-540-38424-3_1

6. Biham, E., Shamir, A.: Differential cryptanalysis of feal and n-hash. In: Davies, D.W. (ed.) EUROCRYPT 1991. LNCS, vol. 547, pp. 1–16. Springer, Heidelberg (1991). https://doi.org/10.1007/3-540-46416-6_1

7. Biham, E., Shamir, A.: Differential cryptanalysis of Snefru, Khafre, REDOC-II, LOKI and Lucifer. In: Feigenbaum, J. (ed.) CRYPTO 1991. LNCS, vol. 576, pp. 156–171. Springer, Heidelberg (1992). https://doi.org/10.1007/3-540-46766-1_11

8. Biham, E., Shamir, A.: Differential cryptanalysis of the full 16-round DES. In: Brickell, E.F. (ed.) CRYPTO 1992. LNCS, vol. 740, pp. 487–496. Springer, Heidelberg (1993). https://doi.org/10.1007/3-540-48071-4_34

9. Blondeau, C., Gérard, B.: Multiple differential cryptanalysis: theory and practice. In: Joux, A. (ed.) FSE 2011. LNCS, vol. 6733, pp. 35–54. Springer, Heidelberg (2011). https://doi.org/10.1007/978-3-642-21702-9_3

10. Bogdanov, A., et al.: PRESENT: an ultra-lightweight block cipher. In: Paillier, P., Verbauwhede, I. (eds.) CHES 2007. LNCS, vol. 4727, pp. 450–466. Springer, Heidelberg (2007). https://doi.org/10.1007/978-3-540-74735-2_31

11. Boura, C., David, N., Heim Boissier, R., Naya-Plasencia, M.: Better steady than speedy: full break of SPEEDY-7-192. Cryptology ePrint Archive, Paper 2022/1351 (2022). https://eprint.iacr.org/2022/1351

12. Broll, M., et al.: New attacks from old distinguishers improved attacks on serpent. In: Galbraith, S.D. (ed.) CT-RSA 2022. LNCS, vol. 13161, pp. 484–510. Springer, Cham (2022). https://doi.org/10.1007/978-3-030-95312-6_20

13. Canteaut, A., et al.: Saturnin: a suite of lightweight symmetric algorithms for post-quantum security. IACR Trans. Symmetric Cryptol. **2020**(S1), 160–207 (2020). https://doi.org/10.13154/tosc.v2020.iS1.160-207

14. Canteaut, A., Fuhr, T., Gilbert, H., Naya-Plasencia, M., Reinhard, J.-R.: Multiple differential cryptanalysis of round-reduced PRINCE. In: Cid, C., Rechberger, C. (eds.) FSE 2014. LNCS, vol. 8540, pp. 591–610. Springer, Heidelberg (2015). https://doi.org/10.1007/978-3-662-46706-0_30

15. Canteaut, A., Naya-Plasencia, M., Vayssière, B.: Sieve-in-the-middle: improved MITM attacks. In: Canetti, R., Garay, J.A. (eds.) CRYPTO 2013. LNCS, vol. 8042, pp. 222–240. Springer, Heidelberg (2013). https://doi.org/10.1007/978-3-642-40041-4_13

16. Choudhuri, A.R., Maitra, S.: Differential cryptanalysis of Salsa and ChaCha - an evaluation with a hybrid model. Cryptology ePrint Archive, Paper 2016/377 (2016). https://eprint.iacr.org/2016/377

17. Knellwolf, S., Meier, W., Naya-Plasencia, M.: Conditional differential cryptanalysis of NLFSR-based cryptosystems. In: Abe, M. (ed.) ASIACRYPT 2010. LNCS, vol. 6477, pp. 130–145. Springer, Heidelberg (2010). https://doi.org/10.1007/978-3-642-17373-8_8

18. Knudsen, L.R.: Truncated and higher order differentials. In: Preneel, B. (ed.) FSE 1994. LNCS, vol. 1008, pp. 196–211. Springer, Heidelberg (1995). https://doi.org/10.1007/3-540-60590-8_16

19. Leander, G., Moos, T., Moradi, A., Rasoolzadeh, S.: The SPEEDY family of block ciphers engineering an ultra low-latency cipher from gate level for secure processor architectures. IACR Trans. Cryptogr. Hardw. Embed. Syst. **2021**(4), 510–545 (2021). https://doi.org/10.46586/tches.v2021.i4.510-545

20. Leurent, G.: Improved differential-linear cryptanalysis of 7-round chaskey with partitioning. In: Fischlin, M., Coron, J.-S. (eds.) EUROCRYPT 2016. LNCS, vol. 9665, pp. 344–371. Springer, Heidelberg (2016). https://doi.org/10.1007/978-3-662-49890-3_14

21. Naya-Plasencia, M.: How to improve rebound attacks. In: Rogaway, P. (ed.) CRYPTO 2011. LNCS, vol. 6841, pp. 188–205. Springer, Heidelberg (2011). https://doi.org/10.1007/978-3-642-22792-9_11
22. Rohit, R., Sarkar, S.: Cryptanalysis of reduced round SPEEDY. In: AFRICACRYPT 2022, pp. 133–149. LNCS, Springer, Heidelberg (2022). https://doi.org/10.1007/978-3-031-17433-9_6
23. Wang, M.: Differential cryptanalysis of reduced-round PRESENT. In: Vaudenay, S. (ed.) AFRICACRYPT 2008. LNCS, vol. 5023, pp. 40–49. Springer, Heidelberg (2008). https://doi.org/10.1007/978-3-540-68164-9_4

Exploiting Non-full Key Additions: Full-Fledged Automatic Demirci-Selçuk Meet-in-the-Middle Cryptanalysis of SKINNY

Danping Shi[1,2], Siwei Sun[3(✉)], Ling Song[4], Lei Hu[1,2], and Qianqian Yang[1,2]

[1] State Key Laboratory of Information Security, Institute of Information Engineering, Chinese Academy of Sciences, Beijing, China
{shidanping,hulei,yangqianqian}@iie.ac.cn
[2] School of Cyber Security, University of Chinese Academy of Sciences, Beijing, China
[3] School of Cryptology, University of Chinese Academy of Sciences, Beijing, China
sunsiwei@ucas.ac.cn
[4] Jinan University, Guangzhou, China

Abstract. The Demirci-Selçuk meet-in-the-middle (DS-MITM) attack is a sophisticated variant of differential attacks. Due to its sophistication, it is hard to efficiently find the best DS-MITM attacks on most ciphers *except* for AES. Moreover, the current automatic tools only capture the most basic version of DS-MITM attacks, and the critical techniques developed for enhancing the attacks (e.g., differential enumeration and key-dependent-sieve) still rely on manual work. In this paper, we develop a full-fledged automatic framework integrating all known techniques (differential enumeration, key-dependent-sieve, and key bridging, etc.) for the DS-MITM attack that can produce key-recovery attacks directly rather than only search for distinguishers. Moreover, we develop a new technique that is able to exploit partial key additions to generate more linear relations beneficial to the attacks. We apply the framework to the SKINNY family of block ciphers and significantly improved results are obtained. In particular, all known DS-MITM attacks on the respective versions of SKINNY are improved by at least 2 rounds, and the data, memory, or time complexities of some attacks are reduced even compared to previous best attacks penetrating less rounds.

Keywords: Demirci-Selçuk MITM Attacks · Differential Enumeration · Key-dependent Sieve · SKINNY

1 Introduction

DS-MITM attack was introduced by Demirci and Selçuk [6] to attack AES in FSE 2008. Let $\{P^0, P^1, \ldots, P^{255}\}$ be a set of 2^8 plaintexts for 4-round AES

© International Association for Cryptologic Research 2023
C. Hazay and M. Stam (Eds.): EUROCRYPT 2023, LNCS 14007, pp. 67–97, 2023.
https://doi.org/10.1007/978-3-031-30634-1_3

such that the i-th $(0 \leq i < 16)$ byte of these plaintexts traversing $\mathbb{F}_2^8$ and all other bytes of them are fixed to some constant. Basically, Demirci and Selçuk in [6] showed that the value of the sequence $C^0[j]||C^1[j]|| \ldots ||C^{255}[j]$ formed by concatenating the jth byte of the corresponding ciphertexts $\{C^0, C^1, \ldots, C^{255}\}$ of $\{P^0, P^1, \ldots, P^{255}\}$ can be fully determined by 25 8-bit parameters. Moreover, it is observed in [7] that the value of the sequence $C^0[j] \oplus C^1[j]||C^0 \oplus C^2[j]|| \ldots, C^0 \oplus C^{255}[j]$ can be fully determined by 24 8-bit parameters. Therefore, $C^0[j] \oplus C^1[j]||C^0 \oplus C^2[j]|| \ldots, C^0 \oplus C^{255}[j]$ can take at most $(2^8)^{24}$ different values, while for a random 255-byte sequence, it has $(2^8)^{255}$ possibilities. Obviously, this behavior forms a distinguisher. In this work, we say that the degree of freedom of the output sequence is 24 bytes.

Since then, many improvement techniques have been proposed to enhance the attack [8–10,13,16], and DS-MITM produces the best cryptanalytic results on AES in the single-key model [10,16,17]. In 2010, Dunkelman et al. introduced the so-called *differential enumeration* technique to reduce the degree of freedom of the output sequence, where the input plaintext set is constructed such that it contains one message conforming to a given truncated differential [13]. The *differential enumeration* technique was further improved in [8]. Also, Dunkelman et al. exploited the algebraic relations (named as *key bridges*) to reduce the space of the candidate keys [13]. Another improvement is to consider a multiset, i.e. an unordered set with multiplicity, other than an ordered sequence, which reduces the possibilities by a factor 4 [13]. The key-dependent-sieve technique was introduced in [16] to further reduce the degree of freedom of the output sequence by considering the relations induced by the key-schedule algorithm on the parameters that fully determine the value of the output sequence.

In order to find DS-MITM attack efficiently, some tools have been proposed in the literature. In [8,9], a dedicated search algorithm for DS-MITM attacks implemented in C/C++ was presented by Derbez and Fouque. Shi et al. proposed a constraint programming (CP) based approach for automatizing the search of DS-MITM distinguishers, whose most important advantage is the decoupling of the modeling and resolution processes of the cryptanalytic technique [20]. However, the CP-based model presented in [20] only capture the most basic version of the DS-MITM attack, and those critical techniques developed for enhancing the attacks (e.g., differential enumeration and key-dependent-sieve) still rely on manual work.

Our Contributions. We develop a full-fledged automatic framework for DS-MITM attacks on *tweakable* block ciphers that integrates all known techniques, including but not limited to differential enumeration, key-dependent-sieve, and key bridging techniques. This tool makes full use of the ability of choosing tweaks when the target cipher is a tweakable block cipher, and our tool is able to output a configuration of a DS-MITM key-recovery attack directly, and thus avoid trapping into the situation where an optimal distinguisher may lead to a sub-optimal key-recovery attack. Note that the automation of the differential enumeration technique is highly nontrivial, and it is enabled by a thorough analysis on how to synthesize the objective function from the variables involved in the model.

Moreover, we propose a method for describing the dependencies between the variables linked by a linear transformation and a *non-full* key addition based on the rank of a matrix derived from the linear transformation. With this method, the dependencies within the rounds of an iterative block cipher due to non-full key additions can be fully exploited to reduce the degree of freedom of the output sequence. Note that this technique alone can improve the previous best DS-MITM attack on SKINNY-128-384 by 1 round in the single-key and single-tweak setting as shown in Section G.

We apply the framework to the SKINNY family of block ciphers and the results are summarized in Table 1, from which we can see that all known DS-MITM attacks on the respective versions of SKINNY are improved by at least 2 rounds, and the data, memory, or time complexities of some attacks are reduced even compared to previous best attacks penetrating less rounds. We note that most of the key-recovery attacks listed in Table 1 are not extended from the best distinguishers we can find by changing the objective of the model to identify the optimal distinguishers instead of the best key-recovery attacks.

Organization. In Sect. 2, we give a brief description of DS-MITM attack and SKINNY block cipher. Then in Sect. 3, we present the generalized new non-full key-addition technique. In Sect. 4, we present a unified full-fledged automatic framework integrating all known techniques (e.g. differential enumeration, key-dependent-sieve, tweak-difference cancellation, non-full key-addition) for the DS-MITM attack and apply it to SKINNY. Section 5 presents the results of SKINNY. Finally, we propose some discussions in Sect. 6. Please refer to the full version [21] for more details. Relevant source codes can be found via https:// github.com/shidanping/DS-MITM.

2   Primarily

2.1   Notations

The following notations will be used in this paper.

- The input state of rth round is denoted by $\mathbf{S}_r$ and jth cell of n-cell state $\mathbf{S}_r$ is represented by $\mathbf{S}_r[j]$. Let P^k represent kth plaintext and C^k represent associated ciphertext. The parameter of P^k in the internal cell $\mathbf{S}_r[j]$ is denoted by $P^k[\mathbf{S}_r[j]]$. Let $P \oplus P'[\mathbf{S}_r[j]]$ represent $P[\mathbf{S}_r[j]] \oplus P'[\mathbf{S}_r[j]]$.
- Assume $\mathcal{B} = [\mathbf{S}_r[j_0], \mathbf{S}_r[j_1], \ldots, \mathbf{S}_r[j_t]]$ is a sequence of positions. Then the concatenation $P[\mathbf{S}_r[j_0]]\|P[\mathbf{S}_r[j_1]] \ldots \|P[\mathbf{S}_r[j_t]]$ of P ($P \oplus P'$ respectively) in positions specified by $\mathcal{B}$ is denoted by $P[\mathcal{B}]$ ($P \oplus P'[\mathcal{B}]$ respectively). The set of $\{P[\mathbf{S}_r[j_0]], P[\mathbf{S}_r[j_1]], \ldots, P[\mathbf{S}_r[j_t]]\}$ is also represented by $\{P[j] : j \in \mathcal{B}\}$.
- Let $\mathcal{E}_1$ and $\mathcal{E}_r$ be 1-round and r-round function of an iterative block cipher respectively. $\mathcal{E}_1$ maps input state $\mathbf{S}_r$ to output state $\mathbf{S}_{r+1} = \mathcal{E}_1(\mathbf{S}_r)$.
- $|*|$ represents the size of a set or table $*$.

A δ-set was first proposed by Daemen and Rijmen [5], which is a structure of 256 plaintexts by traversing one byte while sharing same value in other bytes. Lin et al. extended the definition of δ-set to multiple active bytes [19].

Table 1. Summary results of SKINNY in the single-key setting, where ID, ZC, Int and MITM denote the impossible differential, zero correlation, integral and classic meet-in-the-middle attack respectively

Version	Approach	R_{attack}	Time	Data	Memory	CT	Ref.
SKINNY-128-128	ID	17	$2^{120.8}$	$2^{118.5}$	$2^{97.5}$		[23]
	ID	17	$2^{116.51}$	$2^{116.37}$	2^{80}	✗	[15]
	DS-MITM	17	$2^{122.06}$	2^{96}	$2^{118.91}$		Sect. L, Fig. 35
SKINNY-128-256	ID	19	$2^{119.8}$	2^{62}	2^{110}		[23]
	ID	19	$2^{219.23}$	$2^{117.86}$	2^{208}		[15]
	DS-MITM	19	$2^{238.26}$	2^{96}	$2^{210.99}$	✗	[14]
	DS-MITM	19	$2^{235.05}$	2^{96}	$2^{207.7}$		Sect. I, Fig. 29
	DS-MITM	20	$2^{254.28}$	2^{96}	$2^{250.99}$		Sect. H, Fig. 27
	DS-MITM	21	$2^{234.84}$	2^{96}	$2^{183.52}$		Sect. A, Fig. 13(8-bit tweak)
	DS-MITM	21	$2^{234.99}$	2^{64}	$2^{231.86}$	✓	Sect. C, Fig. 17(8-bit tweak)
	Int	22	2^{216}	$2^{113.58}$	2^{216}		[15]
SKINNY-128-384	ID	22	$2^{373.48}$	$2^{92.22}$	$2^{147.22}$		[22]
	ID	21	$2^{347.35}$	$2^{122.89}$	2^{336}		[15]
	MITM	23	2^{368}	2^{120}	2^{16}	✗	[2]
	DS-MITM	22	$2^{366.28}$	2^{96}	$2^{370.99}$		[4]
	DS-MITM	23	2^{372}	2^{96}	$2^{352.46}$		Sect. G, Fig. 25
	DS-MITM	25	$2^{363.83}$	2^{96}	$2^{336.39}$	✓	Sect. 5.2, Fig. 11(8-bit tweak)
	Int	26	2^{344}	2^{121}	2^{340}		[15]
SKINNY-64-128	ID	18	2^{116}	2^{60}	2^{112}		[12]
	ID	19	$2^{119.8}$	2^{60}	2^{112}		[23]
	ID	19	$2^{110.34}$	$2^{60.86}$	2^{104}	✗	[15]
	DS-MITM	18	$2^{126.32}$	2^{32}	$2^{61.91}$		[14]
	DS-MITM	19	$2^{123.43}$	2^{52}	$2^{126.95}$		Sect. N, Fig. 39
	DS-MITM	21	$2^{119.32}$	2^{60}	$2^{114.81}$		Sect. D, Fig. 19(8-bit tweak)
	ZC/Integral	20	$2^{97.5}$	$2^{68.4}$	2^{82}	✓	[1]
	Int	22	2^{110}	$2^{57.58}$	2^{108}		[15]
SKINNY-64-192	ID	22	$2^{183.97}$	$2^{47.84}$	$2^{74.84}$		[22]
	ID	21	$2^{174.42}$	$2^{62.43}$	2^{168}		[15]
	MITM	23	2^{188}	2^{52}	2^{4}		[11]
	MITM	23	2^{188}	2^{28}	2^{4}		[2]
	MITM	23	2^{184}	2^{60}	2^{8}	✗	[2]
	DS-MITM	21	$2^{186.63}$	2^{60}	$2^{133.99}$		[14]
	DS-MITM	21	$2^{180.01}$	2^{44}	$2^{191.55}$		Sect. K, Fig. 33
	DS-MITM	23	$2^{179.9}$	2^{32}	$2^{183.49}$		Sect. F, Fig. 23(8-bit tweak)
	DS-MITM	23	$2^{174.9}$	2^{56}	$2^{179.46}$	✓	Sect. E, Fig. 21(16-bit tweak)
	ZC/Integral	23	$2^{155.6}$	$2^{73.2}$	2^{138}		[1]
	Int	26	2^{172}	2^{61}	2^{172}		[15]
SKINNY-64-64	ID	17	$2^{61.8}$	$2^{59.5}$	$2^{49.6}$		[23]
	ID	17	2^{59}	$2^{58.79}$	2^{40}	✗	[15]
	DS-MITM	17	$2^{62.06}$	2^{48}	$2^{61.91}$		Sect. O, Fig. 41

[1] ✓ represents chosen-tweak model (CT).

Definition 1 ($\delta(\mathcal{A})$-set). *A set of messages* $\{P^0, P^1, \ldots, P^N\}$ *that are all different in positions specified by* $\mathcal{A}$ *($P^0 \oplus P^k[\mathcal{A}] = k$) and all equal in other positions, where* $\mathcal{A} = [\mathbf{S}_r[j_0], \mathbf{S}_r[j_1], \ldots, \mathbf{S}_r[j_s]]$ *is a sequence of positions.*

An ordered difference sequence of the associated $\delta(\mathcal{A})$-set expressed in Definition 2 will be utilized in DS-MITM attack.

Definition 2 ($\Delta \mathcal{E}_r(\delta(\mathcal{A}))[\mathcal{B}]$-sequence). *An ordered sequence* $P^0[\mathcal{B}] \oplus P^1[\mathcal{B}] \|$ $P^0[\mathcal{B}] \oplus P^2[\mathcal{B}]\| \ldots \|P^0[\mathcal{B}] \oplus P^N[\mathcal{B}]$ *in positions specified by* $\mathcal{B}$ *of the associated* $\delta(\mathcal{A})$-set by encrypting the $\delta(\mathcal{A})$-set $\{P^0, P^1, \ldots, P^N\}$ by function $\mathcal{E}_r$, where $\mathcal{A} = [\mathbf{S}_{r_0}[j_0], \mathbf{S}_{r_0}[j_1], \ldots, \mathbf{S}_{r_0}[j_s]]$ and $\mathcal{B} = [\mathbf{S}_{r_1}[i_0], \ldots, \mathbf{S}_{r_1}[i_t]]$ represent two sequences of positions.*

2.2 Basic DS-MITM Attack

In this section, we present a brief overview of the previous DS-MITM attack. A cipher is usually split into three consecutive parts of r_0, r_1, and r_2 rounds, respectively. The DS-MITM attack consists of a precomputation phase and an online phase.

Precomputation Phase. The precomputation phase is to construct a distinguisher on the second part of r_1 rounds. Constructing a distinguisher is to find a pair of $(\mathcal{A}, \mathcal{B})$ to construct a $\delta(\mathcal{A})$-set satisfying that the size of the space of the values that the output sequence $\Delta \mathcal{E}_{r_1}(\delta(\mathcal{A}))[\mathcal{B}]$ may take is less than that for a random sequence. For a reduced block cipher $\mathcal{E}_{r_1}$, $\Delta \mathcal{E}_{r_1}(\delta(\mathcal{A}))[\mathcal{B}]$ sequence is usually uniquely determined by several internal parameters. Then the size of the space of the values that $\Delta \mathcal{E}_{r_1}(\delta(\mathcal{A}))[\mathcal{B}]$ may take is portrayed by the size of all possible values space of these internal parameters. A lookup table will be built to save all possible values that $\Delta \mathcal{E}_{r_1}(\delta(\mathcal{A}))[\mathcal{B}]$ may take for all possible values of these internal parameters, which will be represented by $Tab_{\Delta \mathcal{E}_{r_1}(\delta(\mathcal{A}))[\mathcal{B}]}$ below.

A basic distinguisher on toy cipher is described by Proposition 1. We will give concrete examples of the following concepts on a 3-round toy SPN block cipher with a 4-byte block size (Fig. 1). The round function of the toy block cipher consists of a Substitution layer $\mathbb{SB}$ (substitute each cell by a Sbox), a linear layer $\mathbb{L}$ (update state by left-multiplying a binary matrix $[[0,1,1,1], [1,0,1,1], [1,1,0,1], [1,1,1,0]]$) and a key addition layer $\mathbb{AK}$ (update the state by XORing the round keys). To make the description clearer for the SPN block cipher, let $\mathbf{S}_i$ represent the input state of ith round and $\mathbf{S}_i^{\mathbb{SB}}$ be the output state of the Substitution layer below.

Proposition 1. *Let* $\mathcal{A} = [\mathbf{S}_0[3]], \mathcal{B} = [\mathbf{S}_3[1]]$. *Construct a* $\delta(\mathcal{A})$-set $\{P^0, P^1, \ldots, P^{255}\}$ *satisfying that* $P^0 \oplus P^i[\mathcal{A}] = i, i \in \{1, \ldots, 255\}$, *the output difference sequence* $\Delta \mathcal{E}_3(\delta(\mathcal{A}))[\mathcal{B}] = P^0 \oplus P^1[\mathbf{S}_3[1]]\| \ldots \|P^0 \oplus P^{255}[\mathbf{S}_3[1]]$ *can be uniquely determined by 7 internal parameters:*

$$P^0[\mathbf{S}_0[3]], \{P^0[\mathbf{S}_1[j]] : j \in [0, 1, 2]\}, \{P^0[\mathbf{S}_2[j]] : j \in [0, 2, 3]\}.$$

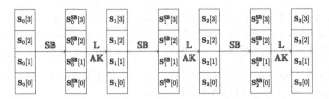

Fig. 1. A 3-round toy SPN block cipher

Proof. For each plaintext $P^i, i \in \{1, \ldots, 255\}$, $P^0 \oplus P^i[\mathbf{S}_0[j]] = 0, \forall j \in [0, 1, 2]$ and $P^0 \oplus P^i[\mathbf{S}_0[3]] = i$ from $\delta(\mathcal{A})$-set definition. So only the difference in $\mathbf{S}_0[3]$ is non-zero. Thus with the knowledge of $P^0[\mathbf{S}_0[3]]$, $P^0 \oplus P^i[\mathbf{S}_0^{\mathbb{SB}}[3]]$ can be deduced, while $\forall j \in [0, 1, 2], P^0 \oplus P^i[\mathbf{S}_0^{\mathbb{SB}}[j]] = 0$. $\{P \oplus P^i[\mathbf{S}_1[j]] : \forall j \in [0, \ldots, 3]\}$ can be deduced and $P^0 \oplus P^i[\mathbf{S}_1[3]] = 0$. Iterate this process, $\Delta\mathcal{E}_3(\delta(\mathcal{A}))[\mathcal{B}]$ can be uniquely determined by the above 7 internal parameters. Thus $\Delta\mathcal{E}_3(\delta(\mathcal{A}))[\mathcal{B}]$ can take at most $(2^8)^7$ possible values, while it has $(2^8)^{255}$ possibilities for a random 255-byte sequence. A distinguisher is constructed and a lookup table $Tab_{\Delta\mathcal{E}_{r_1}(\delta(\mathcal{A}))[\mathcal{B}]}$ is built to save all possible values of $\Delta\mathcal{E}_3(\delta(\mathcal{A}))[\mathcal{B}]$.

Online Phase. The online phase is to guess round-keys involved in r_0 rounds to identify a $\delta(A)$-set for the distinguisher. Then guess round-keys involved in r_2 rounds to compute the value of $\Delta\mathcal{E}_{r_1}(\delta(\mathcal{A}))[\mathcal{B}]$ by partially decrypting the associated $\delta(A)$-set through r_2 rounds. Check whether the sequence in the lookup table $Tab_{\Delta\mathcal{E}_{r_1}(\delta(\mathcal{A}))[\mathcal{B}]}$, obtain the candidate of guessed round-keys involved in r_0, r_2 rounds that pass the test.

2.3   Techniques for Enhancing the DS-MITM Attack

Several improvement techniques are introduced to further reduce the time or memory complexity in the precomputation phase and online phase.

Differential Enumeration Technique. The main bottleneck technique is the differential enumeration technique introduced by Dunkelman et al. in Asiacrypt 2010 [13]. Try many pairs of messages to find one pair of (P, P') conforming to a truncated differential characteristic and construct a $\delta(\mathcal{A})$-set from P ($P \in \delta(\mathcal{A})$), which leads to a reduction of the possible values space of the internal parameters. In [8], Derbez et al. introduced the improved differential enumeration technique by finding that many values of the internal parameters are not reached if the $\delta(\mathcal{A})$-set constructed from a message conforming to a specified truncated differential characteristic.

Property 1 (Differential property of S-box). Given an input and output difference pair of $(\Delta_{in}, \Delta_{out})$ of an Sbox, the equation $\mathrm{Sbox}(x) \oplus \mathrm{Sbox}(x \oplus \Delta_{in}) = \Delta_{out}$ has one solution on average.

For example in Proposition 1, assume (P^0, P') conforms to the truncated differential trail shown in Fig. 2 and $P^0 \in \delta(\mathcal{A})$-set. Then 6 parameters of

$\{P^0[\mathbf{S}_0[3]]\} \cup \{P^0[\mathbf{S}_1[j]], j \in [0, 1, 2]\} \cup \{P^0 \oplus P'[\mathbf{S}_0^{\mathrm{SB}}[3]]\} \cup \{P^0 \oplus P'[\mathbf{S}_3[1]]\}$
can determine the output sequence in Proposition 1. Because three parameters
of $P^0[\mathbf{S}_2[j]] (j \in [0, 2, 3])$ can be deduced from $P^0 \oplus P'[\mathbf{S}_2[j]]$ and $P^0 \oplus P'[\mathbf{S}_2^{\mathrm{SB}}[j]])$
according to Property 1, while it is obvious that $P^0 \oplus P'[\mathbf{S}_2[j]]$ and $P^0 \oplus P'[\mathbf{S}_2^{\mathrm{SB}}[j]]$
can be deduced from the above 6 internal parameters. Then $\Delta\mathcal{E}_3(\delta(\mathcal{A}))[\mathcal{B}]$ can
take at most $(2^8)^6$ possible values, and the size of the precomputation table
$Tab_{\Delta\mathcal{E}_3(\delta(\mathcal{A}))[\mathcal{B}]}$ is reduced by 1 byte.

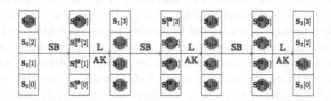

Fig. 2. A truncated differential trail on toy cipher

Key-Dependent-Sieve Technique. In [16], Li et al. introduced this technique to
reduce the possibilities of the values that the internal parameters may reach,
which is achieved by utilizing the relations on round keys deduced from these
internal parameters.

Tweak-Difference Cancellation Technique. In [18], the difference in tweak is utilized to cancel a difference in the state, called tweak-difference cancellation in
this paper. Then differences of a $\delta(\mathcal{A})$-set at more cells will be zero, which leads
to fewer internal parameters that determine the output sequence.

Key-Bridging Technique. The technique utilizes the dependent relations on keys
involved in the key-recovery phase to reduce the guessed keys space [13], which
is a general method used in most key-recovery attacks.

2.4 Brief Description of SKINNY Block Cipher

SKINNY is a family of tweakable block cipher [3]. SKINNY-64 and SKINNY-128
have 64-bit and 128-bit block size respectively. In both versions, the states are
arranged as 4×4-array, where the size of each cell is 4-bit in SKINNY-64 case
and 8-bit in SKINNY-128 case. The input state of rth round is denoted by

$$\mathbf{S}_r = \begin{pmatrix} \mathbf{S}_r[0] & \mathbf{S}_r[1] & \mathbf{S}_r[2] & \mathbf{S}_r[3] \\ \mathbf{S}_r[4] & \mathbf{S}_r[5] & \mathbf{S}_r[6] & \mathbf{S}_r[7] \\ \mathbf{S}_r[8] & \mathbf{S}_r[9] & \mathbf{S}_r[10] & \mathbf{S}_r[11] \\ \mathbf{S}_r[12] & \mathbf{S}_r[13] & \mathbf{S}_r[14] & \mathbf{S}_r[15] \end{pmatrix}.$$

For each block size n, SKINNY-n can take three tweakey size $t = n, t = 2n$, and, $t = 3n$. SKINNY-n-t denotes the version with block size n and tweakey
size t. t-bit tweakey can be arranged as t/n 4×4-array $TKz, z \in \{1, \ldots, t/n\}$.

Each tweakey is first updated by a permutation PT $(TKz[j] \leftarrow TKz[PT[j]], z \in \{1, 2, 3\})$ for each round. Then every cell of the first and second rows of TK2 and TK3 is individually updated with an LFSR (The details of LFSR can be found in [3]).

$$PT = (9, 15, 8, 13, 10, 14, 12, 11, 0, 1, 2, 3, 4, 5, 6, 7).$$

The round function is composed of 5 operations: SubCells (SB), AddConstants (AC), AddRoundTweakey (AK), ShiftRows (SR) and MixColumns (MC). In the following, let $\mathbf{S}_r^{\mathrm{SB}}$, $\mathbf{S}_r^{\mathrm{AK}}$ and $\mathbf{S}_r^{\mathrm{SR}}$ denote the output state of SubCells, AddRoundTweakey and ShiftRows respectively (Fig. 10). The sum of updated t/n tweakey arrays is denoted by RK_r, which is the round-key of rth round.

SubCells is to substitute each cell by a 4-bit $(n = 64)$ or 8-bit $(n = 128)$ Sbox. AddConstants is to update the state by XORing constants, which is omitted because constants have no effect on this attack. AddRoundTweakey is to update the state by XORing the first two rows of state with t/n tweakey arrays, i.e. $\mathbf{S}_r^{\mathrm{AK}}[j] = \mathbf{S}_r^{\mathrm{SB}}[j] \oplus RK_r[j], 0 \leq j \leq 7$. ShiftRows is to rotate i-th row to the right by i cells. MixColumns is to multiply each column by the binary matrix MC:

$$MC = \begin{pmatrix} 1 & 0 & 1 & 1 \\ 1 & 0 & 0 & 0 \\ 0 & 1 & 1 & 0 \\ 1 & 0 & 1 & 0 \end{pmatrix}.$$

3   The Non-full Key-Addition Technique

A new general improvement technique, referred to as *non-full key-addition technique*, is introduced for block ciphers where partial states are updated by the round keys. The previous best DS-MITM attack on SKINNY-128–384 can directly be improved by one round by utilizing the technique alone (in Sect. G). When partial states are updated by round keys, states between two consecutive rounds are not totally independent. Many dependencies within internal parameters are ignored in previous attacks, which are effective for further reducing the space of the values that internal parameters may take.

Assume only the first two bytes are updated by XORing the round-keys RK_r in the key addition layer of the toy cipher. Then $\mathbf{S}_{r+1} = \mathbb{L}(\mathbf{S}_r^{\mathrm{SB}}) \oplus (RK_r[0], RK_r[1], \quad 0, 0)$. Then variables in $\{\mathbf{S}_r[0], \mathbf{S}_r[1], \mathbf{S}_r[2], \mathbf{S}_r[3], \mathbf{S}_{r+1}[2], \mathbf{S}_{r+1}[3]\}$ are not independent and linked by Sbox and linear layer without round-key knowledge. For example, the degree of freedom of $\{\mathbf{S}_1[0], \mathbf{S}_1[1], \mathbf{S}_1[2], \mathbf{S}_2[2], \mathbf{S}_2[3]\}$ is 4. This dependency will lead to that 5 parameters of $\{P^0[\mathbf{S}_1[j]] : j \in [0, 1, 2]\} \cup \{P^0[\mathbf{S}_2[j]] : j \in [2, 3]\}$ in Proposition 1 can take at most $(2^8)^4$ possible values. So the space of values that the output sequence may take is further reduced by 1 byte. This example can be seen as taking $g_1 = (1, 1, 1, 0, 1, 1)$ defined in the below Property 2.

This article will describe the non-full key-addition technique in Property 2 from a more general and comprehensive perspective. For simplicity, we will introduce this technique on a regular round function. Note that the technique for other round functions can be considered in a similar way. The constant addition is omitted in this description as it has no effect on the property.

Property 2. Assume $\mathbf{S}_{r+1} = \mathbb{L}(\mathbf{S}_r^{\mathbb{SB}}) \oplus (RK_r[0], \ldots, RK_r[s-1], 0, \ldots), \mathbf{S}_r^{\mathbb{SB}} = (\text{Sbox}(\mathbf{S}_r[0]), \ldots, \text{Sbox}(\mathbf{S}_r[n-1]))$, where s partial cells are updated by the round-key RK_r and $\mathbb{L}$ is the linear transformation matrix. Introduce a vector $g_r = (g_r[0], g_r[1], \ldots, g_r[2n-s-1]) \in \mathbb{F}_2^{2n-s}$ corresponding to $(\mathbf{S}_r[0], \ldots, \mathbf{S}_r[n-1], \mathbf{S}_{r+1}[s], \ldots, \mathbf{S}_{r+1}[n-1])$. For each possible value of g_r, compute the rank β_{g_r} of the matrix consisting of $\{\overrightarrow{\mathbf{e}_j} : g_r[j] = 1, j \in [0, \ldots, n-1]\}$ and $\{\mathbb{L}_j : g_r[n+j-s] = 1, j \in [s, \ldots, n-1]\}$, where $\overrightarrow{\mathbf{e}_j}$ is the n-dimensional unit vector with jth bit 1 and $\mathbb{L}_j$ is the jth row of the linear transformation matrix. For any plaintext P, parameters of $\{P[\mathbf{S}_r[j]] : g_r[j] = 1, j \in [0, \ldots, n-1]\} \cup \{P[\mathbf{S}_{r+1}[j]] : g_r[n+(j-s)] = 1, j \in [s, \ldots, n-1]\}$ can take at most $(2^c)^{\beta_{g_r}}$ possible values, where c is the size of each cell. We also say that the possible values space of these internal parameters is reduced by $\sum_{j=0}^{2n-1-s} g_r[j] - \beta_{g_r}$ cells.

As each $\mathbf{S}_r^{\mathbb{SB}}[j]$ can be expressed by $\text{Sbox}(\mathbf{S}_r[j])$. Thus the relations on $\mathbf{S}_r^{\mathbb{SB}}[j]$ can be converted to that on $\mathbf{S}_r[j]$ directly. Note that all possible values of $(g_r[0], \ldots, g_r[2n-1-s], \sum_{j=0}^{2n-1-s} g_r[j] - \beta_{g_r})$ can be built directly from $\mathbb{L}$. This way of description makes the technique easy to be modeled in the full-fledged search framework in Sect. 4.5.

4   Full-Fledged Framework with New Improvement Techniques

4.1   A High Level Overview

Before stating our new framework of modelling DS-MITM attack with four additional new techniques that have not been included in the basic model in Asiacrypt 2018 [20], we would like to give a high-level description of the unified framework which supports a full package of techniques. In particular, we highlight the variables that will be introduced for realizing these functions.

Basic DS-MITM distinguisher. Impose constraints over three types (typeX, typeY, typeZ) of 0–1 variables to describe the basic distinguisher [20].

Differential enumeration. Note that the automation of the differential enumeration technique is highly nontrivial and the key point is to synthesize internal parameters that will uniquely determine the output sequence from the combination of the basic model and truncated differential trail. It is enabled by introducing an important proposition (Proposition 3). To modelling the differential enumeration technique, a new type, i.e., typeT, of 0–1 variables for each cell are first introduced to describe the traditional truncated differential trail. Two new types (typeGT, typeGZ) of 0–1 variables for each cell are introduced to synthesize the internal parameters that determine the output sequence, where typeGT variables describe the internal parameters whose values will be bounded by truncated differential trail and typeGZ variables describe the remaining internal parameters.

Key-dependent sieve. To modelling the key-dependent-sieve technique, the internal parameters that determine the output sequence described by typeGT and typeGZ variables are unified by a new type, i.e., typeV, of 0–1 variables, and a new type typeK of 0–1 variables are introduced to describe the round-keys deduced from these internal parameters.

Non-full key-addition. To modelling the non-full key-addition technique, introduce integer variables for each round to describe the reduced cells with typeV variables introduced for the key-dependent-sieve technique.

Tweak-difference cancellation. Note that the tweak values input to each round are known to the attackers, which can be treated as constants in the computation of the output difference. But we need to consider the injected tweak-difference by tweak addition operation when imposing constraints over typeX variables following the forward differential propagation rule. We will introduce typeX variables for each tweak cell and describe forward differential trail propagation for both tweak addition and tweak schedule.

Key-recovery phase. The methods for modelling the phase of deducing the guessed round-keys to construct $\delta(\mathcal{A})$-set and obtain $\Delta\mathcal{E}_{r_1}(\delta(\mathcal{A}))[\mathcal{B}]$ sequence by partially decrypting the associated $\delta(\mathcal{A})$-set can refer to Shi et al.'s work [20], which are achieved by introducing typeM variables involved in first r_0 rounds and typeW type variables involved in last r_2 rounds and impose constraints over typeM variables to form *a backward differential trail* and constraints over typeW variables to form *a forward determination trail*. To consider the differential enumeration in this paper, we also need to model the phase of obtaining a pair conforming to the truncated differential trail of the distinguisher. We will introduce new type, i.e., typeE, of 0–1 variables for each cell involved in r_0 and r_2 rounds, and impose constraints over typeE to form *a backward differential trail* through the first r_0 rounds and *a forward differential trail* through the last r_2 rounds. And typeE-$\mathbf{S}_{r_0}$ should be equal to typeT-$\mathbf{S}_{r_0}$, while typeE-$\mathbf{S}_{r_0+r_1}$ should be equal to typeT-$\mathbf{S}_{r_0+r_1}$.

4.2   Modelling the Basic DS-MITM Distinguisher

In [20], Shi et al. proposed a modelling method for the basic DS-MITM attack based on constraints programming (CP). In this section, we review and describe Shi et al.'s modelling method for finding DS-MITM distinguisher in a more unified way. We encourage the readers to go through this section since new terminologies are introduced and will be used to enhance the expressiveness of our framework.

As defined in [20], three types (typeX, typeY, typeZ) of 0–1 variables for each cell are introduced. Let typeX-*, typeY-* and typeZ-* denote the type variables in a cell or a state * respectively below. Constraints over typeX variables follows the so-called *forward differential propagation rule*. Constraints over typeY variables follows so-called *backward determination propagation rule.* Assume the distinguisher is constructed on the second part of r_1 rounds $(r_0, r_0 + 1, \ldots, r_0 + r_1 - 1)$.

typeX Variables

– Generalized propagation rule for typeX variables is presented in Definition 3, and typeX variables form a so-called *forward differential trail.*

Definition 3 (forward differential trail). *Let* $\mathbf{S}_{i+1} = f(\mathbf{S}_i)$ *for* $0 \leq i \leq r - 1$, *where* f *is the round function of an iterative block cipher and* $\mathbf{S}_i = (\mathbf{S}_i[0], \mathbf{S}_i[1], \ldots, \mathbf{S}_i[n-1])$ *is the n-cell input state of the ith round. Introduce typeX variables for each cell: typeX-$\mathbf{S}_i$ = (typeX-$\mathbf{S}_i[0]$, typeX-$\mathbf{S}_i[1]$, \ldots, typeX-$\mathbf{S}_i[n-1]$)* $\in \{0,1\}^n, 0 \leq i \leq r$. *Define* $\overline{\mathcal{A}_i} = [\mathbf{S}_i[j] : typeX\text{-}\mathbf{S}_i[j] = 0, j \in [0, \ldots, n-1]]$. *We call (typeX-$\mathbf{S}_0$ $\xrightarrow{f}$ typeX-$\mathbf{S}_1$ $\xrightarrow{f}$ $\cdots$ $\xrightarrow{f}$ typeX-$\mathbf{S}_r$) a valid forward differential trail if for each pair of* (P, P') *satisfying* $P \oplus P'[j] = 0, \forall j \in \overline{\mathcal{A}_i}$, *obtain*

$$P \oplus P'[j] = 0, \forall j \in \overline{\mathcal{A}_{i+1}}.$$

– typeX variables are defined with the following implications.

$$\text{typeX-}* = \begin{cases} 0(\square) \\ 1(\boxtimes) \end{cases}$$

– Informally, constraints over typeX variables follow the differential propagation rule with probability 1. And typeX-$\mathbf{S}_{i+1}[j] = 0$ indicates that $\mathbf{S}_{i+1}[j]$ is always a in-active cell (internal difference at $\mathbf{S}_{i+1}[j]$ is always 0) for any pair of (P, P') satisfying $P \oplus P'[\mathbf{S}_0[j]] = 0, \forall j \in \overline{\mathcal{A}_0}$. A valid forward differential trail on the toy cipher is shown in Fig. 3. In the figure, $\overline{\mathcal{A}_0} = [\mathbf{S}_0[j] : j \in [0, 1, 2]], \overline{\mathcal{A}_1} = [\mathbf{S}_1[3]]$, and typeX-$\mathbf{S}_0 = (0, 0, 0, 1) \longrightarrow$ typeX-$\mathbf{S}_1 = (1, 1, 1, 0)$ is valid. Because output difference $P \oplus P'[\mathbf{S}_1[3]]$, for any pair of (P, P') in-active at positions specified by $[\mathbf{S}_0[j] : j \in [0, 1, 2]]$, is always 0. Imposed constraints over typeX variables following this propagation rule through all specific operations (S-box, $MC, \ldots$) please refer to [20].

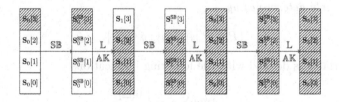

Fig. 3. A valid forward differential trail on toy cipher

An opposite direction *backward differential trail* is also presented in Definition 4 and a backward differential trail on toy cipher is shown in Fig. 4.

Definition 4 (backward differential trail). *Let* $\mathbf{S}_{i+1} = f(\mathbf{S}_i)$ *for* $0 \leq i \leq r - 1$, *where* f *is the round function of an iterative block cipher and* $\mathbf{S}_i = (\mathbf{S}_i[0], \mathbf{S}_i[1], \ldots, \mathbf{S}_i[n-1])$ *is the n-cell input state of ith round. Introduce typeX variables for each cell:* $typeX\text{-}\mathbf{S}_i = (typeX\text{-}\mathbf{S}_i[0], typeX\text{-}\mathbf{S}_i[1], \ldots, typeX\text{-}\mathbf{S}_i[n-1]) \in \{0,1\}^n, 0 \leq i \leq r.$ *Define* $\overline{\mathcal{A}_i} = \{\mathbf{S}_i[j] : typeX\text{-}\mathbf{S}_i[j] = 0, j \in [0, \ldots, n-1]\}.$ *We call* $(typeX\text{-}\mathbf{S}_0 \xleftarrow{f^{-1}} typeX\text{-}\mathbf{S}_1 \xleftarrow{f^{-1}} \cdots \xleftarrow{f^{-1}} typeX\text{-}\mathbf{S}_r)$ *a valid backward differential trail if for any pair of* (P, P') *satisfying* $P \oplus P'[j] = 0, \forall j \in \overline{\mathcal{A}_{i+1}}$, *obtain*

$$P \oplus P'[j] = 0, \forall j \in \overline{\mathcal{A}_i}.$$

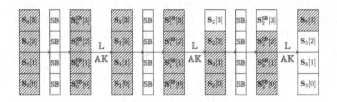

Fig. 4. A valid backward differential trail on toy cipher

typeY Variables

– Generalized propagation rule for typeY variables is proposed in Definition 5, and typeY variables form the so-called *backward determination trail*.

Definition 5 (backward determination trail). *Let* $\mathbf{S}_{i+1} = f(\mathbf{S}_i)$ *for* $0 \leq i \leq r - 1$, *where* f *is the round function of an iterative block cipher and* $\mathbf{S}_i = (\mathbf{S}_i[0], \mathbf{S}_i[1], \ldots, \mathbf{S}_i[n-1])$ *is the n-cell input state of ith round. Introduce typeY variables for each cell:* $typeY\text{-}\mathbf{S}_i = (typeY\text{-}\mathbf{S}_i[0], \ldots, typeY\text{-}\mathbf{S}_i[n-1]) \in \{0,1\}^n, 0 \leq i \leq r.$ *Define* $\mathcal{B}_i = \{\mathbf{S}_i[j] : typeY\text{-}\mathbf{S}_i[j] = 1, j \in [0, \ldots, n-1]\}.$ *We call* $(typeY\text{-}\mathbf{S}_0 \xrightarrow{f} typeY\text{-}\mathbf{S}_1 \xrightarrow{f} \cdots \xrightarrow{f} typeY\text{-}\mathbf{S}_r)$ *a valid backward determination trail if for any pair of* (P, P'), *each difference among*

$$\{P \oplus P'[j] : j \in \mathcal{B}_{i+1}\}$$

can be uniquely determined by

$$\{P \oplus P'[j], P[j] : j \in \mathcal{B}_i\}.$$

– This variable is defined with the following implications.

$$typeY\text{-}* = \begin{cases} 0(\square) \\ 1(\blacksquare) \end{cases}$$

– Informally, $typeY\text{-}\mathbf{S}_i[j] = 0$ indicates that difference in each cell in $\mathcal{B}_{i+1}$ is independent of the knowledge of $\mathbf{S}_i[j]$. A valid backward determination trail on the toy cipher is shown in Fig. 5. In the figure, $\mathcal{B}_2 = [\mathbf{S}_2[j] :$

$j \in [0, 2, 3]]$, $\mathcal{B}_3 = [\mathbf{S}_3[1]]$, and typeY-$\mathbf{S}_2 = (1, 0, 1, 1) \longrightarrow$ typeY-$\mathbf{S}_3 = (0, 1, 0, 0)$ is valid, because $P \oplus P'[\mathbf{S}_3[1]]$ can be uniquely determined by $\{P \oplus P'[\mathbf{S}_2[j]], P[\mathbf{S}_2[j]] : j \in [0, 2, 3]\}$. Imposed constraints over typeY variables following the propagation rule through all specific operations please refer to [20].

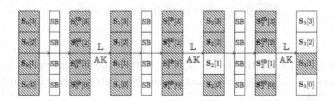

Fig. 5. A valid backward determination on toy cipher

An opposite direction *forward determination trail* is also defined in [20].

Remark 1. In the backward determination trail definition, the $\{P[\mathbf{S}_i[j]], j \in \mathcal{B}_i\}$ can be omitted in case of f is a linear operation.

typeZ Variables

– This variable is imposed for each cell satisfying the rule that typeZ-* (▨) equals 1 if and only if typeX-* = 1 (▨) and typeY-* = 1 (▧).

Objective Function

Proposition 2 ([20]). *Assume* (typeX-$\mathbf{S}_{r_0} \xrightarrow{f}$ typeX-$\mathbf{S}_{r_0+1} \xrightarrow{f} \cdots \xrightarrow{f}$ typeX-$\mathbf{S}_{r_0+r_1}$) *is a forward differential trail and* (typeY-$\mathbf{S}_{r_0} \xrightarrow{f}$ typeY-$\mathbf{S}_{r_0+1} \xrightarrow{f} \cdots \xrightarrow{f}$ typeY-$\mathbf{S}_{r_0+r_1}$) *is a backward determination trail. Impose constraints over* (typeX-$\mathbf{S}_i[j]$, typeY-$\mathbf{S}_i[j]$, typeZ-$\mathbf{S}_i[j]$) *for each cell following the rule that* typeZ-$\mathbf{S}_i[j] = 1$ *if and only if* typeX-$\mathbf{S}_i[j] = 1$ *and* typeY-$\mathbf{S}_i[j] = 1$. *Let* $\mathcal{A} = \mathcal{A}_{r_0} = [\mathbf{S}_{r_0}[j] : typeX\text{-}\mathbf{S}_{r_0}[j] = 1, j \in [0, \ldots, n]]$, $\mathcal{B} = \mathcal{B}_{r_0+r_1} = [\mathbf{S}_{r_0+r_1}[j] : typeY\text{-}\mathbf{S}_{r_0+r_1}[j] = 1, j \in [0, \ldots, n]]$. *For any constructed* $\delta(\mathcal{A})$-*set* $\{P^0, P^1, \ldots, P^{N-1}\}$, *the output difference sequence* $\Delta\mathcal{E}_{r_1}(\delta(\mathcal{A}))[\mathcal{B}]$ *can be uniquely determined by the following internal parameters:*

$$\{P^0[\mathbf{S}_i[j]] : typeZ\text{-}\mathbf{S}_i[j] = 1, r_0 \leq i \leq r_0 + r_1 - 1, j \in [0, \ldots, n]\}.$$

In the basic model, the objective function can be obtained from Proposition 2. The example in Proposition 1 can be obtained directly from this Proposition 2, which is also illustrated in Fig. 6. The lookup table $Tab_{\Delta\mathcal{E}_r(\delta(\mathcal{A}))[\mathcal{B}]}$ will be built to save all values of $\Delta\mathcal{E}_{r_1}(\delta(\mathcal{A}))[\mathcal{B}]$ for all possible values of

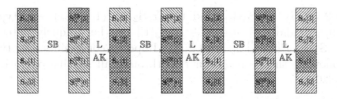

Fig. 6. A valid typeZ trail on toy cipher

$\{P^0[\mathbf{S}_i[j]] : \text{typeZ-}\mathbf{S}_i[j] = 1, r_0 \leq i \leq r_0 + r_1 - 1, j \in [0, \ldots, n]\}$. And the smaller the size of the table is, the better the distinguisher is. Thus in the basic model, the objective function of the distinguisher is constrained to Minimize $(\sum_{i=r_0}^{r_0+r_1-1} \sum_{j=0}^{n-1} \text{typeZ-}\mathbf{S}_i[j])$.

Remark 2. Sometimes multiset is considered instead of the output difference sequence, i.e. an unordered set with multiplicity. The model for searching the ordered sequence and unordered multiset are almost the same. For simplicity, the objective function is defined for the ordered sequence below, while the experiments for SKINNY are both done by considering the ordered sequence and unordered multiset.

4.3   Modelling the Differential Enumeration Technique

The basic idea of the differential enumeration technique is to try many pairs of messages to find one pair of (P, P') conforming to a specified truncated differential characteristic and construct a $\delta(\mathcal{A})$-set from P. The space of the values that the output sequence may take is reduced because of fewer internal parameters that determine the sequence.

It is highly nontrivial to synthesize objective function, which is enabled by an important Proposition 3. Three types (typeT, typeGT, typeGZ) of 0–1 variables for each cell are introduced. Constraints over typeT variables will follow a valid truncated differential propagation rule. In order to automatically synthesize the internal parameters from the combination of the basic distinguisher and truncated differential trail. Two new types (typeGT, typeGZ) of 0–1 variables for each cell are introduced to describe the internal parameters that determine the output sequence. And the parameters whose values are bounded by the truncated differential trail are represented by typeGT variables while the remaining internal parameters are described by typeGZ variables.

typeT Variables

– Constraints over typeT variables follow the traditional valid truncated differential propagation rule in the encryption direction. typeT variable is defined with the following implications.

$$\text{typeT-}* = \begin{cases} 0(\square) : \text{if the cell is in-active in the truncated differential trail,} \\ 1(\blacksquare) : \text{if the cell is active in the truncated differential trail.} \end{cases}$$

- (typeT-$\mathbf{S}_0 \xrightarrow{f}$ typeT-$\mathbf{S}_1 \xrightarrow{f} \cdots \xrightarrow{f}$ typeT-$\mathbf{S}_r$) represents a valid truncated differential trail through the encryption round function f. A valid truncated differential trail on the toy cipher is shown in Fig. 7.

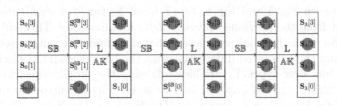

Fig. 7. A truncated differential trail on the toy cipher

typeGT Variables

- Generalized propagation rule for typeGT variables is proposed in Definition 6 and typeGT variables form a so-called *typeT-based backward determination trail*.

Definition 6 (typeT-based backward determination trail). *Let* $\mathbf{S}_{i+1} = f(\mathbf{S}_i)$ *for* $0 \leq i \leq r - 1$, *where* f *is the round function of an iterative block cipher,* $\mathbf{S}_i = (\mathbf{S}_i[0], \mathbf{S}_i[1], \ldots, \mathbf{S}_i[n-1])$ *is the* n-*cell input state of* ith *round, and* (typeT-$\mathbf{S}_0 \xrightarrow{f}$ typeT-$\mathbf{S}_1 \xrightarrow{f} \cdots \xrightarrow{f}$ typeT-$\mathbf{S}_r$) *is a valid truncated differential trail. Introduce typeGT variables for each cell:* typeGT-$\mathbf{S}_i = ($typeGT-$\mathbf{S}_i[0], \ldots,$ typeGT-$\mathbf{S}_i[n-1]) \in \{0,1\}^n, 0 \leq i \leq r$. *Define* $\mathcal{G}_i = [\mathbf{S}_i[j] :$ typeGT-$\mathbf{S}_i[j] = 1, j \in [0, \ldots, n-1]]$. *We call* (typeGT-$\mathbf{S}_0 \xrightarrow{f}$ typeGT-$\mathbf{S}_1 \xrightarrow{f} \cdots \xrightarrow{f}$ typeGT-$\mathbf{S}_r$) *a typeT-based backward determination trail if for each pair of* (P, P') *conforming to the truncated differential trail defined by typeT variables, obtain each difference in*

$$\{P \oplus P'[j] : j \in \mathcal{G}_{i+1}\}$$

can be uniquely determined by

$$\{P \oplus P'[j], P[j] : j \in \mathcal{G}_i\}.$$

- typeGT variable for each cell is defined with the following implications.

$$\text{typeGT-}* = \begin{cases} 0(\square) \\ 1(\blacksquare) \end{cases} \tag{1}$$

- Informally, typeGT-$\mathbf{S}_i[j] = 0$ indicates whether the difference in each cell in $\mathcal{G}_{i+1}$ is independent of knowledge of $\mathbf{S}_i[j]$ or $\mathbf{S}_i[j]$ is in-active in the truncated differential trail (typeT-$\mathbf{S}_i[j] = 0$), which is different from *backward*

dewtermination definition 5. A valid typeT-based backward determination trail on the toy cipher is shown in Fig. 8. In the figure, $\mathcal{G}_0 = [\mathbf{S}_0[0]], \mathcal{G}_1 = [\mathbf{S}_1[j] : j \in [1,2,3]]$, and typeGT-$\mathbf{S}_0 = (1,0,0,0) \rightarrow$ typeGT-$\mathbf{S}_1 = (0,1,1,1)$ is valid. $\{P \oplus P'[\mathbf{S}_1[j]] : j \in [1,2,3]\}$ can be uniquely determined by $\{P \oplus P'[\mathbf{S}_0[0]], P[\mathbf{S}_0[0]]\}$ because $\forall j \in [1,2,3], P \oplus P'[\mathbf{S}_0[j]] = 0$ if (P, P') conforms to the truncated differential trail defined by ◙. From the comparison between Fig. 5 and Fig. 8, *typeT-based backward determination trail* is different from the previous *backward determination trail*. This will lead to a reduction of the internal parameters that determine the output sequence by combining the truncated differential with the basic DS-MITM distinguisher.
- Constraints over typeGT variables following the propagation rule through all operations can be imposed in two steps. Firstly, introduce dummy 0–1 variables for each cell: Dm-$\mathbf{S}_i = (\text{Dm-}\mathbf{S}_i[0], \dots, \text{Dm-}\mathbf{S}_i[n-1]) \in \{0,1\}^n$, and impose constraints over (Dm-$\mathbf{S}_i$, typeGT-$\mathbf{S}_{i+1}$) following backward determination propagation rule (Definition 5). Secondly, impose constraints over (Dm-$\mathbf{S}_i[j]$, typeT-$\mathbf{S}_i[j]$, typeGT-$\mathbf{S}_i[j]$) following the rule that typeGT-$\mathbf{S}_i[j] = 1$ if and only if Dm-$\mathbf{S}_i[j] = $ typeT-$\mathbf{S}_i[j] = 1$, which can be easily generated by using convex hull computation method.

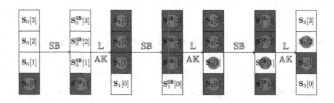

Fig. 8. A typeT-based backward determination trail on toy cipher

A *typeT-based forward determination trail* is also presented in Definition 7.

Definition 7 (typeT-based forward determination trail). *Let* $\mathbf{S}_{i+1} = f(\mathbf{S}_i)$ *for* $0 \leq i \leq r-1$, *where* f *is the round function of an iterative block cipher,* $\mathbf{S}_i = (\mathbf{S}_i[0], \mathbf{S}_i[1], \dots, \mathbf{S}_i[n-1])$ *is the n-cell input state of ith round, and* (typeT-$\mathbf{S}_0 \rightarrow$ typeT-$\mathbf{S}_1 \rightarrow \cdots \rightarrow$ typeT-$\mathbf{S}_r$) *is a valid truncated differential trail. Introduce typeGT variables for each cell:* typeGT-$\mathbf{S}_i = $ (typeGT-$\mathbf{S}_i[0], \dots,$ typeGT- $\mathbf{S}_i[n-1]) \in \{0,1\}^n, 0 \leq i \leq r$. *Define* $\mathcal{G}_i = \{\mathbf{S}_i[j] :$ typeGT-$\mathbf{S}_i[j] = 1, j \in [0, \dots, n-1]\}$. *We call* (typeGT-$\mathbf{S}_0 \xleftarrow{f^{-1}}$ typeGT-$\mathbf{S}_1 \xleftarrow{f^{-1}}$ $\cdots \xleftarrow{f^{-1}}$ typeY-$\mathbf{S}_r$) *a typeT-based forward determination differential trail if for each pair of* (P, P') *conforming to the truncated differential propagation trail defined by typeT variables, obtain each difference in*

$$\{P \oplus P'[j] : j \in \mathcal{G}_i\}$$

can be uniquely determined by

$$\{P \oplus P'[j] : j \in \mathcal{G}_{i+1}\}, \{P[j] : j \in \mathcal{G}_i\}.$$

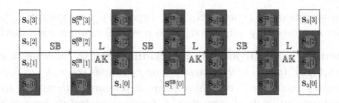

Fig. 9. A typeT-based forward determination trail on toy cipher

typeGZ Variables

– This variable is imposed following the rule of Eq. (2).

$$\text{typeGZ-*} = \begin{cases} 1(\blacksquare) : \text{if typeZ-*} = 1 \text{ and typeGT-*} = 0, \\ 0(\square) : \text{otherwise}. \end{cases} \tag{2}$$

– These variables are utilized to consider the remaining internal parameters that determine the output difference except those covered by typeGT variables (typeGT-* = 1). Constraints over these variables following the rule can be easily generated by the convex hull computation method.

Objective Function Based on Differential Enumeration Technique. An important Proposition 3 is proposed based on the six types variables (typeX, typeY, typeZ, typeT, typeGT, typeGZ). Then this proposition is applied to automatically synthesize the objective function for the distinguisher based on the differential enumeration technique.

The following description is based on the assumption that Sbox has differential Property 1, which is usually true. And the differential Property 1 will be utilized where *typeT-backward determination trail* and *typeT-based forward determination trail* meet. Denote R_M be the round where two trails meet. Let $\mathbf{S}_{R_M}$ and $\mathbf{S}^{\text{SB}}_{R_M}$ represent the input and output state of the $\mathbb{SB}$-layer of round R_M, respectively. To combine the basic DS-MITM distinguisher and the differential enumeration technique, typeGT variables in R_M should be initialized by typeZ and typeT variables as shown in Eq. (3) and Eq. (4) for two reasons. Firstly, the differential Property 1 can be utilized in the active Sbox of the truncated differential trail. Secondly, we only care about internal parameters that determine the output difference (typeZ-* = 1). For a complete search of r_1 rounds distinguisher, all possible R_M should be tried. The following description of the proposition is for an individual model with a fixed (r_1, R_M).

$$\text{typeGT-}\mathbf{S}_{R_M}[j] = \begin{cases} 1, & \text{if typeT-}\mathbf{S}_{R_M}[j] = 1 \text{ and typeZ-}\mathbf{S}_{R_M}[j] = 1, \\ 0, & \text{otherwise}. \end{cases} \tag{3}$$

$$\text{typeGT-}\mathbf{S}^{\text{SB}}_{R_M}[j] = \begin{cases} 1, & \text{if typeT-}\mathbf{S}^{\text{SB}}_{R_M}[j] = 1 \text{ and typeZ-}\mathbf{S}^{\text{SB}}_{R_M}[j] = 1, \\ 0, & \text{otherwise}. \end{cases} \tag{4}$$

The constraints over (typeGT-$\mathbf{S}_{R_M}[j]$, typeT-$\mathbf{S}_{R_M}[j]$, typeZ-$\mathbf{S}_{R_M}[j]$) following the rules can be easily generated by convex hull computation method.

Proposition 3 (New Objective Function). *Impose constraints over three types (typeX,typeY,typeZ) of 0–1 variables on r_1 rounds $(r_0, r_0+1, \ldots, r_0+r_1-1)$. typeX variables and typeY variables form a forward differential trail and a backward determination trail respectively. Impose constraints over (typeX-$\mathbf{S}_i[j]$, typeY-$\mathbf{S}_i[j]$,typeZ-$\mathbf{S}_i[j]$) for each cell following the rule that typeZ-$\mathbf{S}_i[j] = 1$ if and only if typeX-$\mathbf{S}_i[j] = 1$ and typeY-$\mathbf{S}_i[j] = 1$. (typeGT-$\mathbf{S}_{r_0} \xrightarrow{\mathcal{E}_1}$ typeGT-$\mathbf{S}_{r_0+1} \xrightarrow{\mathcal{E}_1}$ $\cdots \xrightarrow{\mathcal{E}_1}$ typeGT-$\mathbf{S}_{R_M}$) and (typeGT-$\mathbf{S}_{R_M}^{\mathbb{SB}} \xleftarrow{\mathcal{E}_1^{-1}}$ typeGT-$\mathbf{S}_{R_M+1} \xleftarrow{\mathcal{E}_1^{-1}} \cdots \xleftarrow{\mathcal{E}_1^{-1}}$ typeGT-$\mathbf{S}_{r_0+r_1}$) form a typeT-based backward determination trail (Definition 6) and a typeT-based forward determination trail (Definition 7) respectively. typeGT- $\mathbf{S}_{R_M}$ and typeGT- $\mathbf{S}_{R_M}^{\mathbb{SB}}$ are initialized by Eq. (3) and Eq. (4). Define $\mathcal{A} = [\mathbf{S}_{r_0}[j] : \text{typeX-}\mathbf{S}_{r_0}[j] = 1, j \in [0, \ldots, n-1]], \mathcal{B} = [\mathbf{S}_{r_0+r_1}[j] : \text{typeY-}\mathbf{S}_{r_0+r_1}[j] = 1, j \in [0, \ldots, n-1]]$. Assume (P^0, P') conforms to the truncated differential trail defined by typeT variables. For any $\delta(\mathcal{A})$-set $\{P^0, P^1, \ldots, P^{N-1}\}$ constructed from the message P^0 $(P^0 \in \delta(\mathcal{A}))$, the output difference sequence $\Delta\mathcal{E}_{r_1}(\delta(\mathcal{A}))[\mathcal{B}]$ can be uniquely determined by the following internal parameters:*

$$\{P^0 \oplus P'[\mathbf{S}_{r_0}[j]] : \text{typeGT-}\mathbf{S}_{r_0}[j] = 1, j \in [0, \ldots, n-1]\},$$
$$\{P^0 \oplus P'[\mathbf{S}_{r_0+r_1}[j]] : \text{typeGT-}\mathbf{S}_{r_0+r_1}[j] = 1, j \in [0, \ldots, n-1]\},$$
$$\{P^0[\mathbf{S}_i[j]] : \text{typeGT-}\mathbf{S}_i[j] = 1, r_0 \le i \le r_0+r_1-1, i \ne R_M, j \in [0, \ldots, n-1]\},$$
$$\{P^0[\mathbf{S}_i[j]] : \text{typeGZ-}\mathbf{S}_i[j] = 1, r_0 \le i \le r_0+r_1-1, j \in [0, \ldots, n-1]\}.$$

$$(5)$$

Proof. According to Proposition 2, the output sequence can be uniquely determined by $\{P^0[\mathbf{S}_r[j]] : \text{typeZ-}\mathbf{S}_r[j] = 1, r_0 \le r \le r_0+r_1-1, j \in [0, \ldots, n-1]\}$, in which all except $\{P^0[\mathbf{S}_{R_M}[j]] : \text{typeZ-}\mathbf{S}_{R_M}[j] = 1, j \in [0, \ldots, n-1]\}$ have been included by $\{P^0[\mathbf{S}_r[j]] : \text{typeGT-}\mathbf{S}_r[j] = 1 \text{ or typeGZ-}\mathbf{S}_r[j] = 1, r \ne R_M, j \in [0, \ldots, n-1]\}$ from the definition of typeGZ variables shown in Eq. (2). If we can prove that $\{P^0[\mathbf{S}_{R_M}[j]] : \text{typeZ-}\mathbf{S}_{R_M}[j] = 1, j \in [0, \ldots, n-1]\}$ can be uniquely determined by above internal parameters, the proof is complete.

Firstly, if (P^0, P') conforms to the truncated differential described by typeT variables and (typeGT-$\mathbf{S}_{r-1} \xrightarrow{\mathcal{E}_1}$ typeGT-$\mathbf{S}_r$) forms a typeT-based backward determination trail, then $\{P^0 \oplus P'[\mathbf{S}_r[j]] : \text{typeGT-}\mathbf{S}_r[j] = 1, j \in [0, \ldots, n-1]\}$ can be uniquely determined by $\{P^0 \oplus P'[\mathbf{S}_{r-1}[j]] : \text{typeGT-}\mathbf{S}_{r-1}[j] = 1, j \in [0, \ldots, n-1]\}$ and $\{P^0[\mathbf{S}_{r-1}[j]] : \text{typeGT-}\mathbf{S}_{r-1}[j] = 1, j \in [0, \ldots, n-1]\}$ (Definition 6). Thus iterate the process on r to obtain that $\{P^0 \oplus P'[\mathbf{S}_{R_M}[j]] : \text{typeGT-}\mathbf{S}_{R_M}[j] = 1, j \in [0, \ldots, n-1]\}$ can be uniquely determined by $\{P^0[\mathbf{S}_r[j]] : \text{typeGT-}\mathbf{S}_r[j] = 1, r_0 \le r \le R_M - 1, j \in [0, \ldots, n-1]\} \cup \{P^0 \oplus P'[\mathbf{S}_{r_0}[j]] : \text{typeGT-}\mathbf{S}_{r_0}[j] = 1, j \in [0, \ldots, n-1]\}$.

Secondly, if (P^0, P') conforms to the truncated differential trail described by typeT variables and (typeGT-$\mathbf{S}_r \xleftarrow{\mathcal{E}_1^{-1}}$ typeGT-$\mathbf{S}_{r+1}$) forms a typeT-based forward determination trail (Definition 7). Then $\{P^0 \oplus P'[\mathbf{S}_r] : \text{typeGT-}\mathbf{S}_r[j] = 1, j \in [0, \ldots, n-1]\}$ can be uniquely determined by $\{P^0 \oplus P'[\mathbf{S}_{r+1}[j]] : \text{typeGT-}\mathbf{S}_{r+1}[j] = 1, j \in [0, \ldots, n-1]\}$ and $\{P^0[\mathbf{S}_r[j]] : \text{typeGT-}\mathbf{S}_r[j] = 1, j \in [0, \ldots, n-1]\}$. Iterate this process on r to obtain that $\{P^0 \oplus P'[\mathbf{S}_{R_M}^{\text{SB}}[j]] : \text{typeGT-}\mathbf{S}_{R_M}^{\text{SB}}[j] = 1, j \in [0, \ldots, n-1]\}$ can be uniquely determined by $\{P^0[\mathbf{S}_r[j]] : \text{typeGT-}\mathbf{S}_r[j] = 1, R_M + 1 \leq r \leq r_0 + r_1 - 1, j \in [0, \ldots, n-1]\} \cup \{P^0 \oplus P'[\mathbf{S}_{r_0+r_1}[j]] : \text{typeGT-}\mathbf{S}_{r_0+r_1}[j] = 1, j \in [0, \ldots, n-1]\}$.

Apply differential Property 1 on $(P^0 \oplus P'[\mathbf{S}_{R_M}[j]], P^0 \oplus P'[\mathbf{S}_{R_M}^{\text{SB}}[j]])$ to deduce $\{P^0[\mathbf{S}_{R_M}[j]] : \text{typeGT-}\mathbf{S}_{R_M}[j] = 1, j \in [0, \ldots, n-1]\}$. Thus $\{P^0[\mathbf{S}_{R_M}[j]] : \text{typeZ-}\mathbf{S}_{R_M}[j] = 1, j \in [0, \ldots, n-1]\}$ are uniquely determined with the remaining parameters of $\{P^0[\mathbf{S}_{R_M}[j]] : \text{typeGZ-}\mathbf{S}_{R_M}[j] = 1, j \in [0, \ldots, n-1]\}$.

The objective function is constrained to Minimize OBJ, where

$$OBJ = \sum_{i=r_0}^{i=r_0+r_1-1} \sum_{j=0}^{j=n-1} \text{typeGZ-}S_i[j] + \sum_{i=r_0, i\neq R_M}^{i=r_0+r_1-1} \sum_{j=0}^{j=n-1} \text{typeGT-}S_i[j]$$
$$+ \sum_{i\in\{r_0, r_0+r_1\}} \sum_{j=0}^{j=n-1} \text{typeGT-}S_i[j]. \tag{6}$$

Remark 3. The above objective function is a unified expression for the generalized model with the differential enumeration technique. The actual objective function OBJ_{Dis} of the distinguisher is OBJ minus the reduced space by the key-dependent-sieve or non-full key-addition techniques et al. Details of the attack phase on SKINNY will be given in Proposition 4 as an example of the proof, which can be automatically deduced by Proposition 3.

4.4 Modelling Key-Dependent-Sieve Technique

Some round keys can be deduced from the internal parameters that determine the output difference sequence. The key-dependent-sieve technique is to utilize the dependent relations on these round keys to reduce the possible values space of the internal parameters, which is an important technique and has not been included in the previous automatic search model in [20].

One type typeV of 0–1 variable for each state cell and one type typeK of 0–1 variable for each round-key cell will be introduced to describe whether the round-key cell can be deduced from the internal parameters listed in Eq. (5) that determine the output difference sequence. We will give a description of modelling the technique on a regular round function. Assume $\mathbf{S}_{r+1} = \mathbb{L}(\mathbf{S}_r^{\text{SB}}) \oplus RK_r$, where $\mathbb{L}$ is a linear transformation matrix and RK_r is the round-key.

typeV Variables

– This variable is imposed following the rule listed in Eq. (7).

$$\text{typeV-}* = \begin{cases} 1 : \text{if typeGZ-}* = 1 \text{ or typeGT-}* = 1, \\ 0 : \text{otherwise.} \end{cases} \tag{7}$$

According to Proposition 3, the internal parameter satisfying typeGZ-$*$ = 1 or typeGT-$*$ = 1 is needed to determine the output sequence, which is unified by typeV-$*$ = 1.

typeK Variables

- Describe $RK_r[j]$ as $\mathbf{S}_{r+1}[j] \oplus \mathbb{L}(\mathbf{S}_r^{\text{SB}}[j_0], \mathbf{S}_r^{\text{SB}}[j_1], \ldots, \mathbf{S}_r^{\text{SB}}[j_s]])$. A new type typeK of 0–1 variables are introduced for each round-key cell following the rule listed in Eq. (8).

$$\text{typeK-}RK_r[j] = \begin{cases} 1(\blacksquare) : \text{if typeV-}\mathbf{S}_{r+1}[j] = 1, \text{typeV-}\mathbf{S}_r^{\text{SB}}[j_i] = 1, \forall i, \\ 0(\square) : \text{otherwise}. \end{cases} \qquad (8)$$

The possible values space of the internal parameters can be reduced by the number of relations on these deduced round-key cells satisfying typeK-$RK_r[j]$ = 1. And the various relations for specified cipher can be included in the model dynamically.

Model of Key-Dependent-Sieve for SKINNY. For SKINNY described in Sect. 2.4, each round-key cell $RK_r[j]$ is related to only one position of each master tweakey array TKz. $RK_r[j]$ can be uniquely determined by $\{TKz[PT^r[j]] : z \in \{1, \ldots, t/n\}\}$. PT^r (PT^{-r} respectively) represents the composite permutation of $PT \circ \cdots \circ PT$ ($PT^{-1} \circ \cdots \circ PT^{-1}$ respectively). For each $j \in \{0, 1, \ldots, 15\}$, $\{RK_r[PT^{-r}[j]] : r \in \{r_0, \ldots, r_0 + r_1 - 1\}\}$ are uniquely determined by $\{TKz[j] : z \in \{1, \ldots, t/n\}\}$. In attack figures, j will be listed in each round-cell $RK_r[PT^{-r}[j]]$. Assume N_j cells in $\{RK_r[PT^{-r}[j]] : r \in \{r_0, \ldots, r_0 + r_1 - 1\}\}$ will be deduced from the internal parameters that determine the output sequence. Then $N_j = \sum\limits_{r=r_0}^{r_0+r_1-1} \text{typeK-}RK_r[PT^{-r}[j]]$. Each relation on these N_j round-key cells can be converted to a relation on those internal parameters. As $\{RK_r[PT^{-r}[j]] : r \in \{r_0, \ldots, r_0 + r_1 - 1\}\}$ are uniquely determined by $\{TKz[j] : z \in \{1, \ldots, t/n\}\}$, the possible values space of internal parameters can be reduced by $N_j - t/n$ cells from $N_j - t/n$ independent relations on these N_j round-keys if $N_j > t/n$.

Introduce an integer variable $Cut_{keysieve_j}$ for each position j to represent the reduced cells. Constraints over $\{Cut_{keysieve_j}, \sum\limits_{r=r_0}^{r_0+r_1-1} \text{typeK-}RK_r[PT^{-r}[j]]\}$ are imposed satisfying $Cut_{keysieve_j} = \text{Max}(0, \sum\limits_{r=r_0}^{r_0+r_1-1} \text{typeK-}RK_r[PT^{-r}[j]] - t/n)$. Then the overall reduced cells by key-dependent-sieve technique are $\sum\limits_{j=0}^{15} Cut_{keysieve_j}$ and denoted by $Cut_{keysieve}$ listed in attack figures.

4.5 Modelling the Non-full Key-Addition Technique

The non-full key-addition exploits the relations on the parameters that determine the output difference sequence and Proposition 3 shows that these internal parameters satisfy typeGT-* = 1 or typeGZ-* =1. And typeGT-* = 1 or typeGZ-* =1 has been unified by typeV-* = 1 in Sect. 4.4. Property 2 shows how to exploit all possible dependencies within parameters. Introduce an integer variable Cut_r for each round to represent the reduced cells, restrict $(\text{typeV-}\mathbf{S}_r[0], \ldots, \text{typeV-}\mathbf{S}_r[n-1], \text{typeV-}\mathbf{S}_{r+1}[s] \ldots, \text{typeV-}\mathbf{S}_{r+1}[n-1], Cut_r)$ to take values in the subset of all possible values of $(g_r[0], \ldots, g_r[2n-1-s], \sum_{j=0}^{2n-1-s} g_r[j] - \beta_{g_r})$ shown in Property 2. Constraints over these variables can be imposed by a system of linear inequalities by using the convex hull computation method.

Model of Non-full Key-Addition for SKINNY. The round function of SKINNY is a little different from that defined in Property 2. The technique can be also considered in a similar way. For SKINNY, the first two rows of state before the ShiftRows will be updated by XORing the round-keys. We will model the technique for each column of SKINNY, and the property for all columns are the same. Thus each column of SKINNY can be simply described by $(y_0, y_1, y_2, y_3) = \mathbb{L}(x_0 \oplus rk_0, x_1 \oplus rk_1, x_2, x_3)$, where $\mathbb{L} = MC \circ SR$ is the composite linear transformation matrix. For example, $y_i = \mathbf{S}_{r+1}[4 \cdot i]$ and $x_i = \mathbf{S}_r^{\text{SB}}[4 \cdot i + (-i)\%4]$ for 0th column. In SKINNY case, introduce vector $g = (g[0], \ldots, g[5]) \in \mathbb{F}_2^6$ corresponding to $(x_2, x_3, y_0, y_1, y_2, y_3)$. For each possible value of g, obtain the rank β_g of matrix consisting of $\{\mathbb{L}_j^{-1} : g[j-2] = 1, j \in [2,3]\}$ and $\{\overrightarrow{\mathbf{e}_j} : g[j+2] = 1, j \in [0, \ldots, 3]\}$. Introduce an integer Cut_1 for each column to describe the reduced cells. According to Property 2, restrict $(\text{typeV-}x_2, \text{typeV-}x_3, \text{typeV-}y_0, \ldots, \text{typeV-}y_3, Cut_1)$ to take values in the subset of all possible values of $(g[0], \ldots, g[5], \sum_{j=0}^{5} g[j] - \beta_g)$. The reduced cells in each column of SKINNY by this technique are listed below of MC in attack figures of SKINNY. The overall reduction number by utilizing the technique is denoted by $Cut_{nonfull}$ in attack figures.

4.6 Modelling the Tweak-Difference Cancellation Technique

For tweakable block cipher, the attack considers the output sequence of the associated $\delta(\mathcal{A})$-set by encrypting a plaintext-tweak combination $\{(P^0, TW^0), \ldots, (P^N, TW^N)\}$, where TW^N represents the selected tweak for P^i. The tweak differences can be controlled to cancel the state difference in one round, then differences of the $\delta(\mathcal{A})$-set at more internal cells will be zero, which leads to fewer internal parameters that determine the output sequence. The tweak-difference is proved to be an effective technique for attacks of SKINNY and has not been included in the previous automatic search model in [20].

Assume the tweak difference will be injected to the state by tweak addition. The tweak addition operation and tweak schedule should be considered when imposing constraints over typeX variables following *the forward differential propagation rule* (informally differential propagation with probability 1). We need to introduce typeX variables for each tweak cell, and impose the constraints over typeX variables through each tweak addition following forward differential propagation rule in Definition 3 except for the round with tweak-difference cancellation. For the round with tweak-difference cancellation, the tweak materials are controlled to cancel state difference. Assume the tweak addition operation is expressed by $y = x \oplus rT$, where rT represents the tweak material input to the internal state cell.

The propagation rules for the round with tweak-difference cancellation is

$$\text{typeX-}y = \begin{cases} 0 : \text{typeX-}x = \text{typeX-}rT = 0, \\ 1 : \text{typeX-}x \oplus \text{typeX-}rT = 1, \\ 0 \text{ or } 1 : \text{typeX-}x = \text{typeX-}rT = 1, \end{cases} \tag{9}$$

while the propagation rule for other rounds is the forward differential propagation rule presented in Definition 3:

$$\text{typeX-}y = \begin{cases} 0 : \text{typeX-}x = \text{typeX-}rT = 0, \\ 1 : \text{others}. \end{cases} \tag{10}$$

The constraints over $(\text{typeX-}x, \text{typeX-}rT, \text{typeX-}y)$ following the rules of Eq. (9) or Eq. (10) can be imposed by using the convex hull computation method. Note that tweak differences are known to attackers and can be treated as constants except in the description of *forward differential trail*. In order to inject fewer differences from the tweak, the tweak differences are usually controlled to cancel the state difference in the first round of the distinguisher.

Model of Tweak-Difference Cancellation for SKINNY. We will introduce typeX variables for each round-key cell $RK_r[j]$. If one of $\{TKz[j] : z \in \{1, \ldots, t/n\}\}$ is loaded with tweak material, the tweak difference will propagate to round-key $RK_r[PT^{-r}[j]]$. If typeX-$RK_r[j] = 1$ (⊠), at least one of $\{TKz[PT^r[j]] : z \in \{1, \ldots, t/n\}\}$ is loaded with tweak material. Tweak difference introduced in one position is more controllable and sufficient to cancel state difference in the first round of distinguisher. For simplicity, we will give the description of attacks by loading tweak material on the positions of $TK1$. For example in Fig. 10 and Fig. 11, tweak materials will be loaded in $TK1[1]$ and are controlled to cancel state difference in 4th round.

4.7   Modelling the Key-Recovery Phase

Firstly, the key-recovery phase is to find a pair of plaintext (P, P') conforming to the truncated differential trail. Secondly, guess round-keys involved in r_0 rounds to construct a $\delta(\mathcal{A})$-set from P for the distinguisher. Finally, guess round-keys involved in last r_2 rounds $(r_0 + r_1, r_0 + r_1 + 1, \ldots, r_0 + r_1 + r_2 - 1)$ to obtain the value of $\Delta Enc_{r_1}(\delta(\mathcal{A}))[\mathcal{B}]$ sequence by partially decrypting the associated $\delta(\mathcal{A})$-set. The methods for modelling the last two phases please refer to Shi et al.'s work [20], which are achieved by introducing two new type variables following a backward differential propagation rule through the first r_0 rounds and a forward determination propagation rule through the last r_2 rounds. And a key-bridging technique is performed for SKINNY [4].

Here we also need to model the phase of constructing a plaintext structure to find a pair of (P, P') conforming to the truncated differential trail of the distinguisher. In order to construct plaintext structure and observe ciphertext difference for each pair of plaintexts in the structure, we should propagate the input difference of the distinguisher with probability 1 from round r_0 to plaintext and propagate the output difference of the distinguisher with probability 1 from round $r_0 + r_1$ to ciphertext. Introduce typeE type variables for each state involved in first r_0 rounds and last r_2 rounds. Impose constrains over typeE variables satisfying that (typeE-$\mathbf{S}_0 \xleftarrow{\mathcal{E}_1^{-1}} \cdots \xleftarrow{\mathcal{E}_1^{-1}}$ typeE-$\mathbf{S}_{r_0}$) form a *backward differential trail* and ($typeE-\mathbf{S}_{r_0+r_1} \xrightarrow{\mathcal{E}_1} \cdots \xrightarrow{\mathcal{E}_1}$ typeE-$\mathbf{S}_{r_{r_0+r_1+r_2}}$) form a *forward differential trail*. Besides, typeE-$\mathbf{S}_{r_0}[j] = $ typeT-$\mathbf{S}_{r_0}[j]$ and typeE-$\mathbf{S}_{r_0+r_1}[j] = $ typeT-$\mathbf{S}_{r_0+r_1}[j], \forall j \in \{0, \dots, n-1\}$ will be imposed. According to the definition of forward and backward differential trails, we have the following observation. The plaintext structure to find a pair conforming to the truncated differential can be constructed by a $\delta(\mathcal{A}^T)$-set of $\{P^0, P^i, \dots, P^N\}$ satisfying that $P^0 \oplus P^i[j] = 0, \forall j \notin \mathcal{A}^T$, where $\mathcal{A}^T = [\mathbf{S}_0[j] : \text{typeE-}\mathbf{S}_0[j] = 1, j \in [0, \dots, n-1]]$. It is fairly straightforward to see the online phase of attacks on SKINNY in Sect. 2.4 and Fig. 11.

5 Results of SKINNY Block Cipher

All of the known improvement techniques (differential enumeration, key-dependent-sieve, non-full key-addition, tweak-difference cancellation, key-bridging) are integrated into the automatic search for the best DS-MITM attack on SKINNY. This full-fledged automatic model for SKINNY makes full use of the ability to choose tweaks and output the DS-MITM key-recovery attack directly.

The results are summarized in Table 1. All known DS-MITM attacks on the respective versions of SKINNY are improved, and the data, memory, or time complexities of some attacks are reduced even compared to previous best attacks penetrating less rounds. The previous best 10.5-round distinguisher for SKINNY-128-384 is also improved by 2.5 rounds by changing the objective of the model to identify the best distinguishers, which is presented in Sections P.

5.1 Brief Illustration of Figures and Complexity Computation

The attack phase can be easily verified from all figures, and so does the attack complexities. We would give a brief illustration of attack figures on the SKINNY family and the unified attack complexities computation methods. We will only give one detailed attack phase on SKINNY-128-384 (Fig. 10 and Fig. 11) to help readers understand and check the model.

Figure illustration in distinguisher figures

- ▨ and ⊠ form a forward differential trail (Definition 3) and a backward determination trail (Definition 5) respectively.
- □ cells represent the internal parameters that determine the output difference according to Proposition 2.
- The reduced cells by applying the non-full key-addition technique on □ cells of each column are listed below of the operation MC. The total reduced number is represented by $Cut_{NonFull}$.
- ■ cells denote the round-keys deduced from these □ cells. The $Cut_{Keysieve}$ represents the reduced number by utilizing the key-dependent-sieve technique on these deduced ■ round-keys.
- The number j listed in the round-key cell represents that this round-key cell can be uniquely determined by $\{TKz[j] : z \in \{1 \ldots, t/n\}\}$. If ▨ is drawn in this round-key cell, then $TK1[j]$ is loaded by tweak material.

Complexity in precomputation phase. The time complexity for constructing a lookup table to save all possibilities is $N \cdot 2^{c \cdot OBJ_{Dis}} \cdot \rho$, where N is the size of the $\delta(\mathcal{A})$-set ($N = |\delta(\mathcal{A})|$), c is the length of each cell, ρ is typically computed by the number of active S-box (⊠) divided by total number of S-box in attacked rounds of SKINNY, and OBJ_{Dis} is the objective function of the distinguisher defined in remark 3. And the memory complexity is $(N-1) \cdot (|\mathcal{B}| \cdot c) \cdot 2^{OBJ_{Dis} \cdot c}$, where $|\mathcal{B} \cdot c|$ is the length of each output sequence $\Delta\mathcal{E}_r(\delta(\mathcal{A}))[\mathcal{B}]$.

Figure illustration in the online key-recovery phase

- ▨ cells form a backward differential trail (Definition 4).
- ■ cells denote the round-keys involved to construct a plaintext structure to identify a $\delta(\mathcal{A})$-set and obtain the output sequence by partially decrypting the associated $\delta(\mathcal{A})$-set. The key-bridging technique can be utilized in these round-keys, which is also presented in the following attack on SKINNY-128-384.

Complexity in the online phase. The time complexity in the online phase is $N \cdot 2^{OBJ_{KC} \cdot c} \cdot \rho_1$, where N is the size of the $\delta(\mathcal{A})$-set, c is the length of the cell, ρ_1 is typically computed by number of active Sbox (▨) divided by total number of S-box, and OBJ_{KC} represents objective function of the key-recovery attack defined by the number of guessed round-keys. The data complexity is $2^{N_{data} \cdot c}$, where N_{data} is the number of ▨ at Round 0.

5.2   25 Rounds Attack on SKINNY-128-384 (376-Bit Key, 8-Bit Tweak)

Load the 8-bit tweak material in $TK1[1]$, which will propagate to round-keys $RK_r[PT^{-r}[j]]$: $\{RK_0[1], RK_1[9], RK_2[0] \ldots\}$.

Precomputation phase

Proposition 4 (11-round distinguisher on SKINNY-128-384 (Fig. 10)).
Define $\mathcal{A} = [\mathbf{S}_4[2]], \mathcal{B} = [\mathbf{S}_{15}[10]]$. *Construct a* $\delta(\mathcal{A})$-*set of* $\{P^0, P^1, \ldots, P^{N-1}\}$ *and a tweak material set of* $\{TW^0, TW^1, \ldots, TW^N\}$ *satisfying that* $P^i[\mathbf{S}_4[2]] \oplus P^0[\mathbf{S}_4[2]] = i$ *and* $TW^i[RK_4[2]] = P^i[\mathbf{S}_4^{\mathrm{SB}}[2]] \oplus P^0[\mathbf{S}_4^{\mathrm{SB}}[2]], \forall i \in \{0, 1, \ldots, N-1\}$. *Then* $\Delta\mathcal{E}_{11}(\delta(\mathcal{A}))[\mathcal{B}]$ *sequence can only take at most* $(2^8)^{41}$ *values.*

Proof. After the tweak-difference cancellation, $P^i \oplus P^0[\mathbf{S}_6[j]] = 0, j \in [0, \ldots, 15]$, $\forall i \in \{1, \ldots, N-1\}$. Then $P^i \oplus P^0[\mathbf{S}_7[9]] = TW^i \oplus TW^0[RK_6[4]]$, so $\{P^0, P^1, \ldots, P^N\}$ also identify a $\delta(\mathcal{A}')$-set for $\mathcal{A}' = [\mathbf{S}_7[9]]$. It is trivial from Proposition 2 that the output difference sequence $\Delta\mathcal{E}_{11}(\delta(\mathcal{A}))[\mathcal{B}]$ can be uniquely determined by following 46-cell internal parameters ($\square$):

$$P^0[\mathbf{S}_7[9]], \{P^0[\mathbf{S}_8[j]] : j \in [3, 11, 15]\}, \{P^0[\mathbf{S}_9[j]] : j \in [1, 2, 3, 7, 9, 11, 13, 15]\}$$

$$\{P^0[\mathbf{S}_{10}[j]] : j \notin [4, 10, 12, 13]\}, \{P^0[\mathbf{S}_{11}[j]] : j \notin [0, 4, 5, 13, 15]\}$$

$$\{P^0[\mathbf{S}_{12}[j]] : j \in [1, 3, 5, 8, 11, 14]\}, \{P^0[\mathbf{S}_{13}[j]] : j \in [1, 7, 10]\}, \{P^0[\mathbf{S}_{14}] : j \in [5, 8]\}.$$

Non-full key-addition technique. According to Property 2, the possible values space of the internal parameters can be reduced by 5 bytes from following relations on internal parameters in the 9th round, 10th round, 11th round:

- 1 in $\{P^0[\mathbf{S}_9[15]], P^0[\mathbf{S}_{10}[2]], P^0[\mathbf{S}_{10}[14]]\}$ as $P^0[\mathbf{S}_9[15]] = P^0[\mathbf{S}_{10}[2]] \oplus P^0[\mathbf{S}_{10}[14]]$,
- 1 in $\{P^0[\mathbf{S}_9[9]], P^0[\mathbf{S}_{10}[7]], P^0[\mathbf{S}_{10}[15]]\}$ as $P^0[\mathbf{S}_9[9]] = P^0[\mathbf{S}_{10}[7]] \oplus P^0[\mathbf{S}_{10}[15]]$,
- 2 in $\{P^0[\mathbf{S}_{10}[8]], P^0[\mathbf{S}_{10}[15]], P^0[\mathbf{S}_{11}[2]], P^0[\mathbf{S}_{11}[6]], P^0[\mathbf{S}_{11}[14]]\}$ as $P^0[\mathbf{S}_{10}[8]] = P^0[\mathbf{S}_{11}[6]] \oplus P^0[\mathbf{S}_{11}[14]], P^0[\mathbf{S}_{10}[15]] = P^0[\mathbf{S}_{11}[2]] \oplus P^0[\mathbf{S}_{11}[14]]$,
- 1 in $\{P^0[\mathbf{S}_{11}[11]], P^0[\mathbf{S}_{11}[14]], P^0[\mathbf{S}_{12}[1]], P^0[\mathbf{S}_{12}[5]]\}$ as $P^0[\mathbf{S}_{11}[11]] \oplus P^0[\mathbf{S}_{11}[14]] = P^0[\mathbf{S}_{12}[1]] \oplus P^0[\mathbf{S}_{12}[5]]$.

Thus $\Delta\mathcal{E}_{11}(\delta(\mathcal{A}))[\mathcal{B}]$ sequence can be uniquely determined by 41-cell internal bytes. $N = |\delta(\mathcal{A})| = 43$ is enough to construct the distinguish for SKINNY, because there are $2^{8 \cdot 42}$ possibilities for a random 42-byte sequence. Build a lookup table $Tab_{\Delta\mathcal{E}_{11}(\delta(\mathcal{A}))[\mathcal{B}]}$ to save all of the $2^{8 \cdot 41}$ possibilities.

Complexity. The time complexity to construct a hash table in the precomputation phase to save all possibilities is $43 \cdot 2^{41 \cdot 8} \cdot \frac{47}{16 \cdot 25} \approx 2^{330.31}$. And the memory complexity is $42 \cdot 8 \cdot 2^{41 \cdot 8} \approx 2^{336.39}$.

Online Phase.

The 25-round attack on SKINNY-128-384 can be extended by adding 4 rounds at the start and 10 rounds at the end (Fig. 11). $\blacksquare$ cells represent involved guessed round-keys in the online phase.

- Query an arbitrate plaintext-tweak combination of P^0 and TW^0 such that $TW^0[RK_4[2]] = 0$ to obtain the corresponding ciphertext C^0.
- For each possible value of these active round-keys ($\blacksquare$):
    step 1 Deduce internal parameters of P^0 in active cells ($\boxtimes$): $P^0[\mathbf{S}_4[2]]$, $P^0[\mathbf{S}_3[15]], \{P^0[\mathbf{S}_2[j]] : j \in [0, 6, 9, 12]\}, \{P^0[\mathbf{S}_1[j]] : j \in [2, 4, 5, 7, 8, 10, 13]\}$.

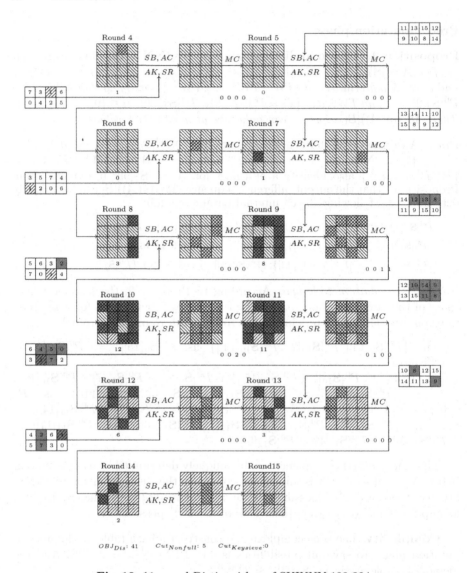

Fig. 10. 11-round Distinguisher of SKINNY-128-384

$\mathcal{A} = [S_4[2]], \mathcal{B} = [S_{15}[10]]$. Load tweak material in $TK1[1]$. The output difference can be uniquely determined by 46-cells internal parameters (□). 5 bytes are reduced by the non-full key-addition technique, which are listed below of each MC. $|\delta(\mathcal{A})| = 43$ is enough to construct distinguish. As the output sequence of SKINNY-128-384 can take at most $2^{8\cdot41}$ possible values, while there are $2^{8\cdot42}$ possibilities for a random 42-byte sequence. Each number j listed in round-key cell represents that these round-key cells can be uniquely determined by $\{TKz[j] : z \in \{1,\dots,t/n\}\}$. ☒ on the round-key cell represents that the tweak

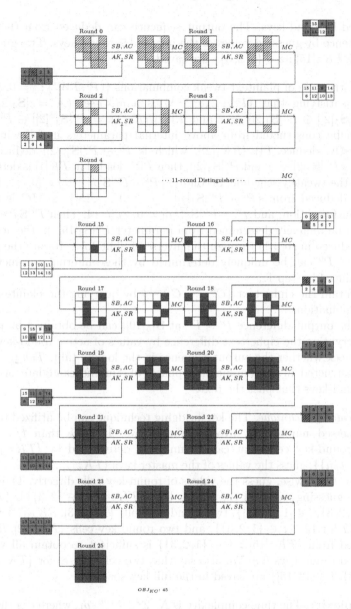

Fig. 11. 25-round attack on SKINNY-128-384

material loaded in $TK1[j]$ will propagate to this cell, where tweak-difference may be injected.

☒ describe a backward differential trail to determine the plaintext structure that will identify a $\delta(\mathcal{A})$-set for the distinguisher. All internal parameters of P in ☒ cells of $\mathbf{S}_i, 1 \leq i \leq 4$ can be deduced from plaintext by guessing values of involved ■ round-keys. The output sequence can deduced from the cipher-text difference by guessing values of the involved ■ round-keys. Two guesses for $\{TKz[12], TKz[15] : z \in \{1, 2, 3\}\}$ are saved.

step 2 A structure of plaintext-tweak combinations $\{(P^i, TW^i) : i = 0, \ldots, N - 1\}$ satisfying that $\{P^0, \ldots, P^{N-1}\}$ is a $\delta(\mathcal{A})$-set $(\mathcal{A} = [\mathbf{S}_4[2]])$ with $P^i[\mathbf{S}_4[2]] \oplus P^0[\mathbf{S}_4[2]] = i$ and $TW^i[RK_4[2]] = P^i[\mathbf{S}_4^{\text{SB}}[2]] \oplus P^0[\mathbf{S}_4^{\text{SB}}[2]]$ can be constructed from above internal parameters in following ways. Firstly, deduce $TW^i[RK_4[2]]$, which is $P^i \oplus P^0[\mathbf{S}_4^{\text{SB}}[2]]$ deduced from $P^i \oplus P^0[\mathbf{S}_4[2]] = i$ and $P^0[\mathbf{S}_4[2]]$, then TW^i loaded in $TK[1]$ is determined by the tweakey schedule. Secondly, $\{P^i \oplus P^0[\mathbf{S}_3^{\text{SR}}[j]] : j \in [0, \ldots, 15]\}$ can be deduced from $\{P^i \oplus P^0[\mathbf{S}_4[j]] : j \in [0, \ldots, 15]\}$ as MC is a linear transformation, and $P^i \oplus P^0[\mathbf{S}_3^{\text{SR}}[j]] = 0, \forall j \neq 14$. Then $P^i[\mathbf{S}_3] \oplus P^0[\mathbf{S}_3]$ can be uniquely determined from parameter $P^0[\mathbf{S}_3[15]]$ in the active cell (deduced in step 1) through the inverse of ShiftRows. Iterate the process, $P^i \oplus P^0$ can be uniquely determined by these internal parameters (▨) deduced in step 1.
step 3 Obtain the ciphertext $\{C^0, \ldots, C^{N-1}\}$ by querying the plaintext-tweak combinations.
step 4 The output difference $P^i \oplus P^0$ at $\mathbf{S}_{15}[10]]$ can be obtained by partially decrypting the ciphertext difference by values of active round-keys (■).
step 5 Check whether the output sequence in the lookup table $Tab_{\Delta \mathcal{E}_{11}(\delta(\mathcal{A}))[\mathcal{B}]}$ constructed in precomputation phase, obtain the candidate of guessed round-keys that past the text.

- *Key-bridging technique.* The key-bridging technique can be utilized to reduce the guessed number of involved round-keys. If more than t/n cells in these round-key cells that can be uniquely determined by $\{TKz[j] : z \in \{1, \ldots, t/n\}\}$, guess the values of the master keys $\{TKz[j] : z \in \{1, \ldots, t/n\}\}$ directly. Otherwise, guess the values of round-key cells directly. Thus in this attack, guessing values of the master keys $\{TKz[1] : z \in \{2, 3\}\} \cup \{TKz[j] : z \in \{1, 2, 3\}, j \notin [1, 12, 15]\}$, two round-key cells $\{RK_{21}[3], RK_{23}[7]\}$ updated from $\{TKz[12] : z \in \{1, 2, 3\}\}$, and two round-key cells $\{RK_{21}[2], RK_{23}[4]\}$ updated from $\{TKz[15] : z \in \{1, 2, 3\}\}$ is sufficient to obtain all values of involved round keys (■). We also say that two cell guesses for $\{TKz[j] : z \in \{1, 2, 3\}, j \in [12, 15]\}$ are saved in the full key space.

Complexity. The time complexity is $N \cdot 2^{OBJ_{KC} \cdot c} \cdot \rho_1$, where c is the length of the cell, ρ_1 is typically computed by number of active S-box (▨) divided by total number of S-box, which is $43 \cdot 2^{45 \cdot 8} \cdot \frac{132}{16 \cdot 25} \approx 2^{363.83}$. The data complexity is $2^{8 \cdot 12} = 2^{96}$.

6 Discussions

- We also apply our method to AES. Our tool can recover the previous best DS-MITM attacks. However no better result is obtained.

- Different results in the single-key chosen-tweak setting and single-tweak are listed in Table 2 and Table 3 respectively, which illustrate that most of key-recovery attacks are not extended from the best distinguishers.
- What is more, the best key-recovery attacks on SKINNY are produced without utilizing the differential enumeration technique that has been included in the model, while the best distinguishers are produced by utilizing this technique. The best 13-round distinguisher of SKINNY-128-384 (Fig. 42) in the single-key single-tweak setting is presented in Sect. P, which improves the previous best 10.5-round distinguisher by 2.5 rounds, and can not be extended to the best attack. We guess the reason is the design of the linear layer. The backward differential and backward determination trails through the linear layer of SKINNY from the same input are different, while they are the same through the linear layer of AES. Then the involved round-keys for finding a pair of plaintexts conforming to a truncated differential trail and for constructing a $\delta(\mathcal{A})$-set are different.
- Interestingly, the time of searching for the best attack is less than that of searching for the best distinguisher sometimes. For example, the best 25-round key-recovery attack on SKINNY-128-384 in the single-key chosen-tweak setting is produced in 331 s, while the best 13-round distinguisher in the single-key single-tweak setting is produced in 1012 s.

Acknowledgments. We thank anonymous reviewers for their valuable comments. This research is supported by the National Key R&D Program of China (Grants No. 2022YFB2701900, 2018YFA0704704), the National Natural Science Foundation of China (Grants No. 62172410, 62022036, 62132008, 62032014, 62202460), the Youth Innovation Promotion Association of Chinese Academy of Sciences, and the Fundamental Research Funds for the Central Universities.

References

1. Ankele, R., Dobraunig, C., Guo, J., Lambooij, E., Leander, G., Todo, Y.: Zero-correlation attacks on tweakable block ciphers with linear tweakey expansion. IACR Trans. Symmetric Cryptol. **2019**(1), 192–235 (2019). https://doi.org/10.13154/tosc.v2019.i1.192-235

2. Bao, Z., Guo, J., Shi, D., Tu, Y.: Superposition meet-in-the-middle attacks: updates on fundamental security of AES-like hashing. In: Dodis, Y., Shrimpton, T. (eds.) Advances in Cryptology - CRYPTO 2022–42nd Annual International Cryptology Conference, CRYPTO 2022, Santa Barbara, CA, USA, 15–18 August 2022, Proceedings, Part I. LNCS, vol. 13507, pp. 64–93. Springer, Cham (2022). https://doi.org/10.1007/978-3-031-15802-5_3

3. Beierle, C., et al.: The SKINNY family of block ciphers and its low-latency variant MANTIS. In: Robshaw, M., Katz, J. (eds.) CRYPTO 2016. LNCS, vol. 9815, pp. 123–153. Springer, Heidelberg (2016). https://doi.org/10.1007/978-3-662-53008-5_5

4. Chen, Q., Shi, D., Sun, S., Hu, L.: Automatic Demirci-Selçuk meet-in-the-middle attack on SKINNY with key-bridging. In: Zhou, J., Luo, X., Shen, Q., Xu, Z. (eds.) ICICS 2019. LNCS, vol. 11999, pp. 233–247. Springer, Cham (2020). https://doi.org/10.1007/978-3-030-41579-2_14

5. Daemen, J., Rijmen, V.: The Design of Rijndael - The Advanced Encryption Standard (AES), Second Edition. Information Security and Cryptography. Springer, Heidelberg (2020). https://doi.org/10.1007/978-3-662-60769-5
6. Demirci, H., Selçuk, A.A.: A meet-in-the-middle attack on 8-round AES. In: Nyberg, K. (ed.) FSE 2008. LNCS, vol. 5086, pp. 116–126. Springer, Heidelberg (2008). https://doi.org/10.1007/978-3-540-71039-4_7
7. Demirci, H., Taşkın, İ, Çoban, M., Baysal, A.: Improved meet-in-the-middle attacks on AES. In: Roy, B., Sendrier, N. (eds.) INDOCRYPT 2009. LNCS, vol. 5922, pp. 144–156. Springer, Heidelberg (2009). https://doi.org/10.1007/978-3-642-10628-6_10
8. Derbez, P., Fouque, P.-A.: Exhausting Demirci-Selçuk meet-in-the-middle attacks against reduced-round AES. In: Moriai, S. (ed.) FSE 2013. LNCS, vol. 8424, pp. 541–560. Springer, Heidelberg (2014). https://doi.org/10.1007/978-3-662-43933-3_28
9. Derbez, P., Fouque, P.-A.: Automatic search of meet-in-the-middle and impossible differential attacks. In: Robshaw, M., Katz, J. (eds.) CRYPTO 2016. LNCS, vol. 9815, pp. 157–184. Springer, Heidelberg (2016). https://doi.org/10.1007/978-3-662-53008-5_6
10. Derbez, P., Fouque, P.-A., Jean, J.: Improved key recovery attacks on reduced-round , in the single-key setting. In: Johansson, T., Nguyen, P.Q. (eds.) EUROCRYPT 2013. LNCS, vol. 7881, pp. 371–387. Springer, Heidelberg (2013). https://doi.org/10.1007/978-3-642-38348-9_23
11. Dong, X., Hua, J., Sun, S., Li, Z., Wang, X., Hu, L.: Meet-in-the-middle attacks revisited: key-recovery, collision, and preimage attacks. In: Malkin, T., Peikert, C. (eds.) CRYPTO 2021. LNCS, vol. 12827, pp. 278–308. Springer, Cham (2021). https://doi.org/10.1007/978-3-030-84252-9_10
12. Dunkelman, O., Huang, S., Lambooij, E., Perle, S.: Biased differential distinguisher - cryptanalysis of reduced-round SKINNY. Inf. Comput. **281**, 104796 (2021). https://doi.org/10.1016/j.ic.2021.104796
13. Dunkelman, O., Keller, N., Shamir, A.: Improved single-key attacks on 8-round AES-192 and AES-256. In: Abe, M. (ed.) ASIACRYPT 2010. LNCS, vol. 6477, pp. 158–176. Springer, Heidelberg (2010). https://doi.org/10.1007/978-3-642-17373-8_10
14. Hadipour, H., Eichlseder, M.: Autoguess: a tool for finding guess-and-determine attacks and key bridges. In: Ateniese, G., Venturi, D. (eds.) Applied Cryptography and Network Security - 20th International Conference, ACNS 2022, Rome, Italy, 20–23 June 2022, Proceedings. LNCS, vol. 13269, pp. 230–250. Springer (2022). https://doi.org/10.1007/978-3-031-09234-3_12
15. Hadipour, H., Sadeghi, S., Eichlseder, M.: Finding the impossible: automated search for full impossible differential, zero-correlation, and integral attacks. IACR Cryptology ePrint Archive, p. 1147 (2022). https://eprint.iacr.org/2022/1147
16. Li, L., Jia, K., Wang, X.: Improved single-key attacks on 9-round AES-192/256. In: Cid, C., Rechberger, C. (eds.) FSE 2014. LNCS, vol. 8540, pp. 127–146. Springer, Heidelberg (2015). https://doi.org/10.1007/978-3-662-46706-0_7
17. Li, R., Jin, C.: Meet-in-the-middle attacks on 10-round AES-256. Des. Codes Crypt. **80**(3), 459–471 (2015). https://doi.org/10.1007/s10623-015-0113-3
18. Li, R., Jin, C.: Meet-in-the-middle attacks on round-reduced tweakable block cipher Deoxys-BC. IET Inf. Secur. **13**(1), 70–75 (2019). https://doi.org/10.1049/iet-ifs.2018.5091

19. Lin, L., Wu, W., Wang, Y., Zhang, L.: General model of the single-key meet-in-the-middle distinguisher on the word-oriented block cipher. In: Lee, H.-S., Han, D.-G. (eds.) ICISC 2013. LNCS, vol. 8565, pp. 203–223. Springer, Cham (2014). https://doi.org/10.1007/978-3-319-12160-4_13

20. Shi, D., Sun, S., Derbez, P., Todo, Y., Sun, B., Hu, L.: Programming the Demirci-Selçuk meet-in-the-middle attack with constraints. In: Peyrin, T., Galbraith, S. (eds.) ASIACRYPT 2018. LNCS, vol. 11273, pp. 3–34. Springer, Cham (2018). https://doi.org/10.1007/978-3-030-03329-3_1

21. Shi, D., Sun, S., Song, L., Hu, L., Yang, Q.: Exploiting non-full key additions: full-fledged automatic Demirci-Selcuk meet-in-the-middle cryptanalysis of skinny. IACR Cryptology ePrint Archive, p. 255 (2023). https://eprint.iacr.org/2023/255

22. Tolba, M., Abdelkhalek, A., Youssef, A.M.: Impossible differential cryptanalysis of reduced-round SKINNY. In: Joye, M., Nitaj, A. (eds.) AFRICACRYPT 2017. LNCS, vol. 10239, pp. 117–134. Springer, Cham (2017). https://doi.org/10.1007/978-3-319-57339-7_7

23. Yang, D., Qi, W., Chen, H.: Impossible differential attacks on the SKINNY family of block ciphers. IET Inf. Secur. 11(6), 377–385 (2017). https://doi.org/10.1049/iet-ifs.2016.0488

Efficient Detection of High Probability Statistical Properties of Cryptosystems via Surrogate Differentiation

Itai Dinur[1], Orr Dunkelman[2], Nathan Keller[3], Eyal Ronen[4(✉)], and Adi Shamir[5]

[1] Computer Science Department, Ben Gurion University, Be'er Sheva, Israel
dinuri@cs.bgu.ac.il
[2] Computer Science Department, University of Haifa, Haifa, Israel
orrd@cs.haifa.ac.il
[3] Department of Mathematics, Bar-Ilan University, Ramat Gan, Israel
Nathan.Keller@biu.ac.il
[4] Computer Science Department, Tel Aviv University, Tel Aviv-Yafo, Israel
eyal.ronen@cs.tau.ac.il
[5] Computer Science Department, Weizmann Institute of Science, Rehovot, Israel
adi.shamir@weizmann.ac.il

Abstract. A central problem in cryptanalysis is to find all the significant deviations from randomness in a given n-bit cryptographic primitive. When n is small (e.g., an 8-bit S-box), this is easy to do, but for large n, the only practical way to find such statistical properties was to exploit the internal structure of the primitive and to speed up the search with a variety of heuristic rules of thumb. However, such bottom-up techniques can miss many properties, especially in cryptosystems which are designed to have hidden trapdoors.

In this paper we consider the top-down version of the problem in which the cryptographic primitive is given as a structureless black box, and reduce the complexity of the best known techniques for finding all its significant differential and linear properties by a large factor of $2^{n/2}$. Our main new tool is the idea of using *surrogate differentiation*. In the context of finding differential properties, it enables us to simultaneously find information about all the differentials of the form $f(x) \oplus f(x \oplus \alpha)$ in all possible directions α by differentiating f in a single randomly chosen direction γ (which is unrelated to the α's). In the context of finding linear properties, surrogate differentiation can be combined in a highly effective way with the Fast Fourier Transform. For 64-bit cryptographic primitives, this technique makes it possible to automatically find in about 2^{64} time all their differentials with probability $p \geq 2^{-32}$ and all their linear approximations with bias $|p| \geq 2^{-16}$ (using 2^{64} memory); previous algorithms for these problems required at least 2^{96} time. Similar techniques can be used to significantly improve the best known time complexities of finding related key differentials, second-order differentials, and boomerangs. In addition, we show how to run variants of these algorithms which require no memory, and how to detect such

C. Hazay and M. Stam (Eds.): EUROCRYPT 2023, LNCS 14007, pp. 98–127, 2023.
https://doi.org/10.1007/978-3-031-30634-1_4

statistical properties even in trapdoored cryptosystems whose designers specifically try to evade our techniques.

1 Introduction

Most cryptanalytic techniques against block ciphers exploit the existence of some statistical property which happens with a higher than expected probability. It is thus essential to find all such anomalies (or to demonstrate that none exists) whenever we are designing a new cryptosystem or attacking an existing cryptosystem developed by others. Note that such a search has to be carried out only once for each cryptosystem, and if it is successful, its results can be used to find an unlimited number of actual keys. Consequently, even a lengthy computational effort to find such properties can be justified.

Due to the centrality of this topic, many papers had been published about it over the last 30 years. Almost all of them had taken a bottom-up approach, in which the attacker first finds the statistical properties of small local elements (such as S-boxes), and then tries to 'glue' them together into a high probability global property. The analysis of a small n-bit S-box (e.g., with $n = 8$) is easy: For example, all its differential properties (which can be grouped together in the form of a difference distribution table, denoted by DDT) and all its linear properties (which can be grouped together in the form of a linear approximation table, denoted by LAT) can be found exhaustively in time 2^{2n}. However, the process of constructing the global properties is usually guided by various heuristics (such as testing only low Hamming weight differences, or using only the highest probability local properties), and thus it can miss many properties. In fact, knowledge of these heuristic restrictions can be exploited by the designers of trapdoored ciphers to evade attacks. For example, it is easy to attach a keyed decorrelation module [37] at the beginning and the end of a cipher in order to force any high probability differential characteristic to have high Hamming weight input and output differences. Other constructions of trapdoored cryptosystems can be found in [35] (with a planted high probability differential characteristic) and [36] (with a planted high probability linear approximation).

Even in standard (non-trapdoored) cryptosystems, such bottom-up techniques can be error-prone: There are many known cases in which the global probability differs significantly from the product of the local probabilities due to subtle correlations (as demonstrated in [12,18,33]), and where a high probability property results from the accumulation of many low probability properties along many differential characteristics or within the linear hull (which was a crucial element in the attacks described in [25,27]). Finally, it is difficult to apply such bottom-up techniques to designs in which the basic operations are block-wide (see, for example, [9]), are defined in terms of large primitives (e.g., 32-bit S-boxes), are available only in the form of a hardware token (with no description of its internal structure), or are provided in an obfuscated form (as done in many whitebox cryptosystems such as [14]).

Developing efficient top-down techniques for finding all the usable statistical properties of functions $f : \{0,1\}^n \to \{0,1\}^n$ with a large n seems to be a hard problem, which had been solved so far only in some special cases. For example, the differential properties of a moderately large cryptographic primitive which uses only additions, rotations, and XOR's (an ARX design) were studied in [8–10], and were used to mount differential attacks on Simon, Speck, Ascon, LEA, and other ciphers. The related problem of finding linear biases in the same special case of ARX ciphers was studied in [30,31,39], whose results were used to mount linear attacks on Speck and SM4. Another special case discussed in [1,11,13], is when the adversary uses heuristics to guess the most likely input differences, and wants to simultaneously find all the corresponding output differences in high probability differentials. The related problem of finding all high probability linear biases when the most likely input or output mask is guessed using heuristics was studied in [20]. Notice that without such heuristics, any algorithm of this type has a high complexity of $\Omega(2^n)$. A different type of top-down algorithm is described in [15], which deals with general black box functions f, but can find only iterative differential characteristics (in which the input difference is equal to the output difference). Finally, in the quantum setting (which is not the computation model we use in this paper) there are several papers (e.g., [29,38]) which show how to find in polynomial time differential properties in a general f, but only when their probabilities p are extremely close to 1.

When we try to apply a top-down analysis to a large black box function f (e.g., a full cryptosystem with $n = 64$), finding all the 2^{2n} entries in its DDT and LAT becomes both infeasible and unnecessary, since almost all the known attacks use only their highest entries. If we are only interested in differentials $\alpha \to \beta$ which happen with probability that exceeds p, the best previously available technique (described in Sect. 2) is to try all the possible input differences α, and to compute for each α the output differences $f(x) \oplus f(x \oplus \alpha)$ for $\mathcal{O}(p^{-1})$ randomly chosen values of x. This reduces the time complexity of finding all the significant entries in the DDT from 2^{2n} to $2^n p^{-1}$. The corresponding algorithm for finding all the significant entries in the LAT requires $2^n p^{-2}$ time (see [20]).

In this paper we introduce a new type of top-down technique which can reduce these two complexities by a major factor of $2^{n/2}$. The main new technique we use is *surrogate differentiation*, in which we obtain information on f by examining its derivative in an arbitrary direction which is not directly related to the statistical properties we want to find. For example, when we search for a differential property in which some input difference α is mapped to some output difference β with high probability p, we want to differentiate the function f in a particular direction α by considering pairs of inputs of the form $(x, x \oplus \alpha)$ and following the evolution of $f(x) \oplus f(x \oplus \alpha)$. This differentiation of f simultaneously achieves two very different purposes: It eliminates certain constants from the expression (for example, an unknown key which was XOR'ed to the input), and it makes it possible to exploit a sequence of high-probability differential events in order to successfully predict the output difference. However, when we try to find all the high probability properties in a new cryptosystem, we do not know a-priori the actual directions α with respect to which we want to differentiate f. Our novel idea is that if we replace the real but unknown α by an unrelated but known *surrogate value*[1] γ, we can still benefit from the elimination of unknown constants, and we can save a lot of time by using the same arbitrarily chosen surrogate value $\gamma \neq 0$ to simultaneously analyze all the possible values of α via a single unified computation.

The new idea of surrogate differentiation yields a plethora of algorithms with significantly improved complexities for detecting a large variety of statistical properties in general black box functions. In the case of differentials with probability p, our new algorithm (described in Sect. 2) requires $\mathcal{O}(2^{n/2}p^{-1})$ time, compared to the best previous time complexity of $\mathcal{O}(2^n p^{-1})$. This new complexity is almost optimal, as an information-theoretic argument shows that any algorithm for this problem requires $\Omega(2^{n/2}p^{-1/2})$ evaluations of the black-box function f.

A worst-case variant of this algorithm can deal with backdoored functions: This variant requires $\mathcal{O}(2^{n/2}p^{-3/2})$ time, and detects a hidden differential with probability p even in trapdoor cryptosystems in which the locations of the right pairs with respect to the characteristic were chosen adversarially. In addition, we present a memoryless variant of this algorithm whose time complexity is $\mathcal{O}(\max(2^{n/2}p^{-2}, p^{-3}))$. At the end of the section, we describe an experimental verification of our worst-case algorithm which finds all the high-probability 5-round and 6-round differentials of the NSA-designed cryptosystem Speck, and compares our top-down results to the bottom-up analysis presented in [10].

Our next algorithm (described in Sect. 3) can detect all linear biases of at least p in time $\mathcal{O}(2^{n/2}p^{-2})$. Note that in terms of complexity, the results on differential and linear properties are comparable, since to sense a bias of p we need $\mathcal{O}(p^{-2})$ data, whereas to sense a differential with probability p we need only $\mathcal{O}(p^{-1})$ data.

These improvements make it possible to apply a top-down analysis to full size cryptosystems with $n = 64$, and to find in about 2^{64} time all their differentials with probabilities $p \geq 2^{-32}$ and all their linear biases $|p| \geq 2^{-16}$. Previously, these tasks had required at least 2^{96} time.

In Sect. 4 and we report improved algorithms for boomerangs, related-key differentials, and second-order differentials. The full attacks are given in the full version of the paper at [16]. Here, one cannot hope to obtain an algorithm as good as for differential and linear properties, as information-theoretic arguments yield lower bounds of $\Omega(2^{3n/4}p^{-1/4})$ for second-order differentials and boomerangs and $\Omega(2^n p^{-1/2})$ for related-key differentials. Our new algorithms have complexities of at most $\mathcal{O}(2^n p^{-2})$ for all three types of properties, thus making it possible to detect such properties for 32-bit and sometimes 48-bit constructions in a practical amount of time.

A summary of our main results can be found in Table 1.

---

[1] According to Wikipedia, a surrogate marker in clinical trials is a known measure which may correlate with the unknown clinical markers we would like to follow, but does not necessarily have a guaranteed relationship.

Table 1. Our main results for probabilities $p \geq 2^{-n/2}$ and biases $|p| \geq 2^{-n/4}$

Property	Time	Data	Memory	Section
Differentials (fundamental alg)	$\mathcal{O}(2^{n/2}p^{-1})$	$\mathcal{O}(2^{n/2}p^{-1})$	$\mathcal{O}(2^{n/2}p^{-1})$	Sect. 2.2
Differentials (memory-efficient)	$\tilde{\mathcal{O}}(2^{n/2}p^{-1})$	$\tilde{\mathcal{O}}(2^{n/2}p^{-1})$	$\tilde{\mathcal{O}}(p^{-2})$	App. 2.4
Differentials (memoryless)	$\mathcal{O}(2^{n/2}p^{-2})$	$\mathcal{O}(2^{n/2}p^{-2})$	$\mathcal{O}(1)$	Sect. 2.3
Differentials (worst-case)	$\mathcal{O}(2^{n/2}p^{-3/2})$	$\mathcal{O}(2^{n/2}p^{-3/2})$	$\mathcal{O}(2^{n/2}p^{-1/2})$	Sect. 2.5
Linear approximations	$\mathcal{O}(2^{n/2}p^{-2})$	$\mathcal{O}(2^{n/2}p^{-2})$	$\mathcal{O}(2^{n/2}p^{-2})$	Sect. 3
Boomerangs	$\mathcal{O}(2^{n}p^{-1})$	$\mathcal{O}(2^{n})$	$\mathcal{O}(2^{n}p^{-1})$	Full version [16]
Second-order differentials	$\mathcal{O}(2^{n}p^{-2})$	$\mathcal{O}(2^{n})$	$\mathcal{O}(2^{n}p^{-2})$	Full version [16]
Related-Key differentials	$\mathcal{O}(2^{n}p^{-2})$	$\mathcal{O}(2^{n}p^{-1})$	$\mathcal{O}(2^{n}p^{-1})$	Full Version [16]

n — block size and key size.

Our research leads to many interesting open problems, some of which are listed in the concluding Sect. 5. In particular, in spite of the significant improvements over previous results, our upper bounds still do not match the best known lower bounds, and there are additional statistical properties to which we do not know how to apply our new techniques.

2   Efficient Algorithms for Detecting High-Probability Differentials

Differential cryptanalysis [6] is a central cryptanalytic technique, based on tracing the development of differences during the encryption process of a pair of plaintexts. The central notion in differential cryptanalysis is a *differential*. We say that the differential $\alpha \rightarrow \beta$ for the function $f : \{0,1\}^n \rightarrow \{0,1\}^n$ holds with probability p, if $\Pr[f(x) \oplus f(x \oplus \alpha) = \beta] = p$, where $x \in \{0,1\}^n$ is chosen uniformly at random. The pairs $(x, x \oplus \alpha)$ that satisfy $f(x) \oplus f(x \oplus \alpha) = \beta$ are called *right pairs* with respect to the differential. As differential attacks exploit high-probability differentials, a central goal in differential cryptanalysis is to detect high-probability differentials efficiently.

In this section we present an algorithm that allows detecting all differentials of $f : \{0,1\}^n \rightarrow \{0,1\}^n$ that hold with probability $\geq p$, with complexity of $\mathcal{O}(2^{n/2}p^{-1})$. This algorithm is almost optimal, as by an information-theoretic lower bound presented below, any generic algorithm for this task has complexity of $\Omega(2^{n/2}p^{-1/2})$. We also present three variants of the algorithm: a worst-case algorithm that allows detecting with a high probability also high-probability differentials that are adversarially hidden, a memoryless algorithm with only a slightly higher time complexity, and a memory-efficient algorithm that allows reducing the memory complexity to $\mathcal{O}(p^{-2})$ without increasing the data and time complexities. We then experimentally verify our algorithm, by using it to detect all high-probability differentials of 5-round and 6-round variants of SPECK [2].

Throughout this paper (and especially when we estimate running times and the probability of false alarms) we assume that the black-box function behaves in a sufficiently random way. Any gross deviation (such as the discovery of a huge multicollision in a supposedly random function, which can slow our algorithms) is likely to cast serious doubts about the soundness of the cryptosystem's design, even if no high probability differential or linear properties are actually found. In addition, for the sake of clarity we ignore poly-logarithmic factors (i.e., factors that are polynomial in n) in all our probability and complexity estimates.

We also note that all our algorithms are probabilistic in nature and rely on some randomness assumptions which are addressed later on. Furthermore, we present those algorithms for a specific (random) key, i.e., we directly analyze a given permutation. First, in most practical applications, the effect of the key on probabilities of statistical properties is minor, and thus, computing the probabilities for a random fixed key gives a good approximation for the actual probabilities. Second, our main algorithms can incorporate multiple keys in order to reduce the dependency on a single fixed key, either by running it multiple times for different keys, or in some of the algorithms, incorporating the different keys into the algorithm.

For the sake of simplicity, we first analyze the algorithms in the scenario where f has only one differential $\alpha \to \beta$ that holds with probability p, while all other differentials have significantly lower probabilities. We then show that the algorithms can be easily generalized to finding all $\geq p$-probability differentials, with no increase in the complexity. In addition, we first present the algorithms under the natural assumption that $p \geq 2^{-n/2}$, and afterwards explain the adjustments required for smaller values of p.

2.1 Previous Algorithms and a Lower Bound

Previous Algorithms. Algorithms for detecting high-probability differentials are abundant in the literature. However, almost all of them operate in a bottom-up fashion, that is, construct a 'long' differential characteristic[2] by concatenating 'short' differential characteristics, and use the probability of the differential characteristic as a lower bound on the probability of the differential. In such algorithms, the short differential characteristics can be found easily and the challenge is to find characteristics that can be 'glued together'.

Top-down algorithms for finding high-probability differentials were considered in several special cases: In [9], Biryukov and Velichkov initiated the study of algorithms detecting all high-probability differentials of the addition operation in ARX ciphers – a problem they coined 'constructing the partial DDT (pDDT)' of the operation. Several follow-up papers (e.g., [8,10]) further studied the pDDT and used it in attacks on the ciphers SIMON, SPECK, Ascon, and LEA. In [1], Albrecht and Leander initiated the study of the case where the adversary had guessed the input difference of a differential using some heuristic, and is interested in finding all output differences to which it leads with a high probability.

---

[2] We remind the reader that a differential characteristic predicts all the intermediate differences, whereas a differential is concerned only with the input difference and the output difference.

Essentially the same problem was studied in several other works (e.g., [11,13]), under the name of *multiple differential cryptanalysis*, and its algorithms for solving it were used in attacks on SPECK (see [3,21]). In [15], Dinur et al. studied the problem of finding all high-probability *iterative* differentials of general functions, and used their results in attacks on the cipher Simon and on the iterated Even-Mansour construction. In [29], Li and Yang showed that in the quantum setting, differentials with probability very close to 1 can be detected in polynomial time (in n), using the Bernstein-Vazirani algorithm [4]. The follow-up paper [38] further enhanced the technique and used it to attack several block cipher constructions. While these works obtained significant advancements in special cases, neither of them applies in general.

A natural top-down algorithm for detecting all differentials of a function $f : \{0,1\}^n \to \{0,1\}^n$ that hold with probability $\geq p$ is the following adaptation of the classical algorithm for constructing the Difference Distribution Table (DDT):

1. For all $\alpha \in \{0,1\}^n$, do:
   (a) Choose $4/p$ random values $x_1, x_2, \ldots, x_{4/p} \in \{0,1\}^n$.
   (b) For each $1 \leq i \leq 4/p$, compute $f(x_i) \oplus f(x_i \oplus \alpha)$ and insert it into a hash table.
   (c) Output all values β that appear in the table at least 2 times.

The data and time complexity of the algorithm is $\mathcal{O}(2^n p^{-1})$ and its memory complexity is $\mathcal{O}(p^{-1})$. The probability of a differential with probability $\geq p$ to be detected is more than 90% (according to standard approximation by a Poisson distribution), and the probability of a differential with probability $\ll p$ to be detected by mistake is small.

Lower Bound. A simple information-theoretic argument yields a lower bound of $\Omega(2^{n/2} p^{-1/2})$ for the task of generically detecting a differential $\alpha \to \beta$ that holds with probability p. Indeed, in order to detect such a differential, the adversary must observe at least one pair with input difference α and output difference β. Assuming that those pairs are distributed randomly, this means that the adversary must observe $\Omega(1/p)$ pairs with input difference α for all α values, i.e., a total of $\mathcal{O}(2^n \cdot p^{-1})$ pairs is needed. This number of pairs cannot be generated (even to cover most values of α) unless the plaintext set is of size $\Omega(2^{n/2} p^{-1/2})$. Thus, the complexity of any algorithm for our problem is $\Omega(2^{n/2} p^{-1/2})$.

2.2   The Fundamental Algorithm

In this subsection we present a probabilistic algorithm which almost matches the lower bound, and under some randomness assumptions finds any probability-p differential (with overwhelming probability) $\alpha \to \beta$ with data, memory, and time complexity of $\tilde{\mathcal{O}}(\max(2^{n/2} p^{-1}, p^{-2}))$. We also note that the memory complexity of the algorithm can be improved to $\mathcal{O}(p^{-2})$ without affecting the data and time complexities, as will be shown in the memory-efficient algorithm of Appendix 2.4.

Main Idea. The main observation behind the algorithm is that the output difference β can be cancelled by differentiating with a completely unrelated surrogate difference γ, and searching for right pairs $(x, x \oplus \alpha)$ for which $(x \oplus \gamma, x \oplus \gamma \oplus \alpha)$ is also a right pair. The search for two "companion" right pairs instead of a single pair has some price, and is the reason of the complexity being higher than the lower bound by a factor of $p^{-1/2}$.

Detailed Description. We choose an arbitrary nonzero value $\gamma \in \{0,1\}^n$, and consider the function $g_\gamma : \{0,1\}^n \to \{0,1\}^n$ defined by $g_\gamma(x) = f(x) \oplus f(x \oplus \gamma)$. We examine the *collisions* in the function $g_\gamma(x)$. Observe that if both $(x, x \oplus \alpha)$ and $(x \oplus \gamma, x \oplus \gamma \oplus \alpha)$ are *right pairs* with respect to the differential $\alpha \to \beta$, then

$$g_\gamma(x) \oplus g_\gamma(x \oplus \alpha) = \Big(f(x) \oplus f(x \oplus \gamma) \Big) \oplus \Big(f(x \oplus \alpha) \oplus f(x \oplus \alpha \oplus \gamma) \Big)$$
$$= \Big(f(x) \oplus f(x \oplus \alpha) \Big) \oplus \Big(f(x \oplus \gamma) \oplus f(x \oplus \alpha \oplus \gamma) \Big) = \beta \oplus \beta = 0$$

and thus, the pair $(x, x \oplus \alpha)$ yields a collision in g_γ, as depicted in Fig. 1. We call quartets $(x, x \oplus \alpha, x \oplus \gamma, x \oplus \alpha \oplus \gamma)$ for which this is satisfied *right quartets* for g_γ.

The fundamental algorithm is detailed in Algorithm 1. In the detection phase, we find collisions in g_γ for random inputs. From each collision, we calculate the corresponding (input difference, output difference) pair, denoted by (α, β), and increase its counter by one. Than, in the verification phase, we go over all such (α, β) pairs that were suggested sufficiently many times (i.e., with high counters). For each such (α, β) pair, we verify that indeed the probability of the differential $\alpha \to \beta$ is larger than p. We do that by taking $\mathcal{O}(p^{-1})$ random pairs with input difference α, and test that sufficiently many of them have an output difference β.

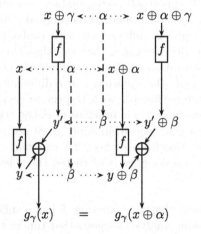

Fig. 1. A Right Quartet for the Fundamental Algorithm

Algorithm 1: The Fundamental Algorithm

Initialize an empty list L of counter tuples (α, β, cnt) and an empty hash table H.

Choose $M = \sqrt{n} \cdot 2^{n/2} p^{-1}$ distinct random values $x_1, x_2, \ldots, x_M \in \{0,1\}^n$.

Pick at random an n-bit non-zero value γ.

for *all* $1 \le i \le M$ **do**

    Compute $g_\gamma(x_i)$ and insert it into a hash table H.

//Detection phase

for *all collisions $g_\gamma(x_i) = g_\gamma(x_j)$ in the hash table* **do**

    Compute the suggested (input difference, output difference) pair
    $(\alpha = x_i \oplus x_j,\ \beta = f(x_i) \oplus f(x_j))$.

    if *$(\alpha, \beta, *) \notin L$* **then**

        add $(\alpha, \beta, 1)$ to L.

    else

        Increment the counter of the tuple (α, β, cnt) to $(\alpha, \beta, cnt + 1)$.

//Verification phase

for *each $(\alpha, \beta, cnt) \in L$ s.t. $cnt \ge n/4$* **do**

    Pick n/p distinct random values $\chi_1, \chi_2, \ldots, \chi_{n/p} \in \{0,1\}^n$.

    Count how many times $f(\chi_i) \oplus f(\chi_i \oplus \alpha) = \beta$.

    If the counter is greater than $n/2$, output (α, β).

Randomness Assumptions. The correctness of the fundamental algorithm relies on the following randomness assumptions. We assume that for any γ the event that the pair $(x \oplus \gamma, x \oplus \gamma \oplus \alpha)$ is a right pair is independent of the event that the pair $(x, x \oplus \alpha)$ is a right pair (which is similar to some of the randomness assumptions of the boomerang attack). Under this assumption, the probability of the quartet to be a right quartet for a random $x \in \{0,1\}^n$ is p^2, and thus, the expected number of collisions (each corresponding to a quartet) of this form is $p^2 2^{n-1}$ (the division by 2 is since each pair is counted twice).

In the presence of multiple differentials with probability p (or close to p) we also need to assume (for the claim that the algorithm finds almost all differentials), that the distribution of right quartets for a given differential is not affected by the existence of other quartets (for a different differential).

Both assumptions are reasonable with respect to cryptographic primitives, and were used, in different contexts in previous works on cryptanalysis [7,24]. We show in Sect. 2.5 a worst-case algorithm which does not rely on these assumptions. Furthermore, the algorithm of Sect. 2.5 can find such high probability differentials even when the designer constructed the scheme to withstand the fundamental algorithm.

Success Analysis. Assume that the function f has a differential $\alpha \to \beta$ with probability p. Our following analysis suggests that (under the above randomness assumptions) this differential is going to be detected with probability higher than 99%. Furthermore, we show that the probability of a differential with probability much lower than p, e.g., $p/10$, to be proposed by our algorithm is negligible.

The data contains $M = \sqrt{n} \cdot 2^{n/2}/p$ inputs, that can be combined into $n/2 \cdot 2^n/p^2$ pairs (of $g_\gamma()$ outputs). Each such pair (of $g_\gamma()$ outputs) determines an α value, and thus, for each α value we expect about $n/2 \cdot 1/p^2$ pairs $(x, x \oplus \alpha)$ and $(x \oplus \gamma, x \oplus \gamma \oplus \alpha)$. As per our randomness assumption, each of these two pairs is right w.r.t. the differential $\alpha \to \beta$ with probability p. Hence, out of the $n/(2 \cdot p^2)$ pairs (of pairs), we expect $n/2$ cases where both pairs $(x, x \oplus \alpha)$ and $(x \oplus \gamma, x \oplus \gamma \oplus \alpha)$ are right ones. When these pairs are right pairs, they suggest a collision in the output of $g_\gamma()$. Hence, we expect $n/2$ collisions in H for the (input difference, output difference) pair (α, β).

Assuming that the number of actual collisions follows the Poisson distribution with a mean value $n/2$ (which is the approximation of the binomial distribution in this case) with a very high probability, the counter of (α, β) is advanced at least $n/4$ times. We list this probability for common values of n in Table 2 and will offer the full analysis in the full version of the paper. Thus, the differential $\alpha \to \beta$ is detected with probability of over 99%. This holds for all differentials with probability at least p.

We note that the verification step at the end of the algorithm verifies that the candidate (α, β) offers a differential. The probability of an (α, β) with probability p (or higher) to fail the verification step is negligible (again under the assumption that the number of right pairs follows the Poisson distribution with a mean value of $n/2$).

Table 2. Probability that a high (low) probability differential is detected by the fundamental algorithm leading to a true (false) positive result

Detection Probability\Block Size	$n = 32$	$n = 64$	$n = 128$	$n = 256$	$n = 512$
High prob. differential (true positive)	0.99	0.999	0.999996	$1 - 2^{-32.7}$	$1 - 2^{-61.4}$
Low prob. differential (false positive)	$2^{-36.6}$	$2^{-71.0}$	$2^{-139.1}$	$2^{-275.0}$	$2^{-546.2}$

We now turn our attention to the probability that a "wrong" differential is detected (i.e., a differential with probability less than $p/10$). We start the discussion with the detection phase (what is the chance that such a differential is suggested). Table 2 contains the probability of a low probability differential (i.e., with probability at most $p/10$) to be offered more than $n/4$ times in $n/(2 \cdot p^2)$ quartets. While the full analysis will be given in the full version of the paper, it is easy to see that the probability of such a differential to be detected is lower than 2^{-n}. Hence, as there are at most $10 \cdot 2^n/p$ differentials with probability $p/10$, we expect at most $\mathcal{O}(1/p)$ such differentials to be analyzed in the verification step.

We note that the probability of a differential to pass the verification step is equal to the probability of the detection phase. This follows the fact that we picked the number of pairs and the threshold to be the same as in the detection phase. As the number of right pairs following a differential is distributed according to the Poisson distribution is the same, we conclude that these are the same passing probabilities. We note that if one can reduce the complexity of the verification step in exchange for possibly higher number of "wrong" differentials which pass the verification step.

Of course, the probability of those differentials to pass the verification step is negligible.

Complexity Analysis. We first note that if there are no differentials with probability even close to p (e.g., all other differentials happen with probability close to 2^{-n}), the probability of a collision in $g_\gamma()$ is 2^{-n}. Hence, the data is expected to contain $M^2/2 \cdot 2^{-n} = (\sqrt{n}2^{n/2}/p)^2/2 \cdot 2^{-n} = n \cdot p^{-2}$ "random" collisions, for which the proposed (input difference, output difference) values are distributed randomly over the 2^{2n} possible values. Hence, the probability that some random (input difference, output difference) phase is suggested $n/4$ times is negligible.

As discussed above, the probability that a differential $\alpha' \to \beta'$ with probability at most $p/10$ is suggested in the detection phase is less than 2^{-n} (see Table 2). Hence, at most $10/p$ such differentials are expected to pass the detection phase.

The time complexity of the data collection phase is $2 \cdot M = \sqrt{n}2^{-n/2+1}/p$ calls to $f(\cdot)$ (in addition to M XORs and M memory accesses).

If there is a single high probability differential, and not too many "wrong" differentials, we expect besides the collisions related to it to have another $\mathcal{O}(n/p^2)$ random collisions. Each such collision is expected to be suggesting a single value[3] for (α', β'). As stated above, we expect to have about $\mathcal{O}(n/p^2)$ collisions, and they are expected to be distributed uniformly (even for the high probability differential). Hence, we expect only a few increments to take place.

If there are many "wrong" differentials (i.e., with probability lower than $p/10$, but not negligible), we expect many collisions — we expect about $n/200$ collisions for each such differential. While the chances of any such differential to pass into the verification step is negligible (and there are at most $\mathcal{O}(n/p)$ of those), they can still incur a very high computational load — there are at most $10 \cdot 2^n/p$ such differentials, and if each of them leads to $n/200$ collisions, we expect about $\mathcal{O}(n \cdot 2^n/p)$ collisions. However, when there are many of those, we can identify that the function which is studied is far from being a "random" function, which would suggest it is not suitable for cryptographic uses.[4]

The verification step takes $\mathcal{O}(n/p)$ for each differential that passed the detection phase. When there is a single right differential and only very low probability differentials, then this step costs $2n/p$ calls to $f(\cdot)$. When there are multiple "wrong" differentials, as noted before, we expect to have $2n/p$ calls to $f(\cdot)$ for each of them, i.e., about $20n/p^2$ calls for $f(\cdot)$ in total.

Hence, the time complexity of the verification step is expected to be $\mathcal{O}(n/p)$ when there are not many "wrong" differentials. When there are many of those (an event which is detected in the detection step), the complexity is $\mathcal{O}(n/p^2)$.

---

[3] If there are more than two values colliding, then each pair of collisions suggests a value for α' and β'.

[4] In other words, one can easily define a statistical test based on the fundamental algorithm, and reject that function as a random function (or a random permutation) if the number of collisions exceeds $\mathcal{O}(n/p^2)$.

The memory complexity of the algorithm is determined by the hash table size and the size of the list L. The size of the hash table is $\mathcal{O}(M) = \mathcal{O}(\sqrt{n}2^{n/2}/p)$ words of memory. The size of the list L depends on the number of collisions. As mentioned above, when there are only differentials with negligible probability (besides the right differential), this list is going to contain $\mathcal{O}(n/p^2)$ values (each corresponding to a random collision) and about n ones for the real differential. When there are many "wrong" differentials, the size of this list is going to grow (and this would be a good indication that the function $f(\cdot)$ is not a "good" pseudo-random function).

To conclude, the time complexity of the algorithm is $\mathcal{O}(n \cdot 2^{n/2}/p)$ calls to $f(\cdot)$ and similar memory complexity. This holds as long as there are not too many "wrong" differentials which exist in the scheme (i.e., there are not too many differentials with probability below $p/10$ that are detected). The existence of many of those may suggest that the function is not suitable for cryptographic uses, and while the fundamental algorithm succeeds in finding the high probability differential (and discarding all "wrong" differentials), its complexity may be higher.

The case $p \leq 2^{-n/2}$. The algorithm can be applied in this case as well, however the number of plaintexts pairs of g_γ it examines – $\mathcal{O}(2^n p^{-2})$ – is larger than 2^{2n-1}, which is the total number of plaintext pairs of g_γ. In order to obtain more than 2^{2n-1} plaintext pairs, we can consider functions g_{γ_i} for different values of the 'surrogate' difference γ_i. (This trick is similar to the use of 'flavors' in Hellman's classical time/memory tradeoff attack [23]). Note however that collisions are meaningful only within the same function g_γ and not between two functions g_{γ_i} and g_{γ_j}. Thus, in order to obtain $\mathcal{O}(2^n p^{-2})$ pairs, we have to consider the entire codebook of 2^n inputs for $\mathcal{O}(2^{-n} p^{-2})$ functions g_{γ_i}.

Thus, the data complexity of the algorithm in this case is 2^n (the entire codebook), and the time and memory complexity is $\mathcal{O}(p^{-2})$, which is the expected total number of collisions in the functions g_{γ_i}. Recall that the simple algorithm described above allows detecting a probability-p differential in time $\mathcal{O}(2^n p^{-1})$. Our algorithm outperforms this algorithm for all values of p.

Unifying the two ranges of p values, the data complexity of the algorithm is $\mathcal{O}(\min(2^{n/2} p^{-1}, 2^n))$ and its time and memory complexity is $\mathcal{O}(\max(2^{n/2} p^{-1}, p^{-2}))$.

Detecting All High-Probability Differentials. If there are k differentials with probability p, the algorithm will simply detect all of them, with no additional cost. (The only case in which some additional cost is incurred is when there are *lots* of high-probability differentials: If $k > \max(2^{n/2} p^{-1}, p^{-2})$, then the complexity is $\mathcal{O}(k)$, as the function g_γ is expected to have $\mathcal{O}(k)$ collisions.)

We note that for the above complexity analysis we assume that there are not too many differentials which are suggested in the detection phase. When this happens, the time complexity of the algorithm may not be correct. Specifically, if there are more than $2^{n/2}$ differentials with probability higher than p, we expect the verification step to be more expensive than the detection phase. We note that the existence of many high probability differentials (which can be detected by observing there are many candidates for the verification step), may suggest that the studied primitive is far from being a secure one.

2.3   A Memoryless Variant of the Algorithm

We now present a memoryless variant of the algorithm, with query complexity[5] of $\mathcal{O}(2^{n/2}p^{-2})$ and time complexity of $\mathcal{O}(\max(2^{n/2}p^{-2}, p^{-3}))$. In other words, the cost for using only a constant-sized memory is increasing the data and time complexity by a factor of $1/p$, compared to the fundamental algorithm presented above. This variant outperforms all previously known algorithms for this task for all $p \geq 2^{-n/2}$. Moreover, it is trivially parallelizable.

The Algorithm. A memoryless variant of the fundamental algorithm presented above is given in Algorithm 2. Note that the collision finding steps for each value of i are completely independent. This allows for a simple parallelization of the algorithm.

Algorithm 2: The Memoryless Algorithm

---

while (α, β) *were not identified* **do**
    Pick at random an n-bit non-zero value γ.
    //Collision finding phase
    Find a collision $g_\gamma(x) = g_\gamma(y)$ in the function g_γ using Pollard Rho's algorithm.
    Denote $\alpha = x \oplus y$, $\beta = f(x) \oplus f(y)$.
    Choose c/p random values $y_1, y_2, \ldots, y_{c/p} \in \{0,1\}^n$. (*c* depends on the success rate)
    //Verification phase
    for $j = 1, 2, \ldots, c/p$ **do**
        Check whether $f(y_i) \oplus f(y_i \oplus \alpha) = \beta$.
        If equality is obtained at least $c/2$ times, output (α, β) and break.

Analysis. By the analysis presented above, assuming that there are not too many "wrong" differentials, collisions suggested by right pairs form a fraction of about p^2 of the collisions of g_γ. This follows the fact that out of the $\mathcal{O}(1/p^2)$ collisions found by the fundemental algorithm and thus, after $1/p^2$ collisions found by the Pollard Rho algorithm, we expect such a special collision. In such a case, the values of (α, β) it suggests will be verified in the last steps with a high probability. On the other hand, input differences suggested by 'random' collisions will not be approved in these steps. We note that the value of c depends on the success

---

[5] We alert the reader that as we discuss a memoryless algorithm, the algorithm cannot store previous values. Instead, we discuss "query" complexity to refer to the number of evaluations of the function $f(\cdot)$, which may be higher than 2^n.

rate. If we wish to make sure that there are no false positive left, we need to pick c such that the probability that the $\mathcal{O}(1/p^2)$ proposed differentials (each collision suggests a differential) are filtered. Hence, c can be picked accordingly (see for example Table 2).

The data complexity of the algorithm is $\mathcal{O}(2^{n/2}p^{-2})$ queries (as each application of Pollard's Rho requires $\mathcal{O}(2^{n/2})$ adaptively chosen inputs). Note that in order to avoid obtaining the same collisions many times, we use different functions g_{γ_i}, which comes at no additional cost as each collision is searched separately. As for the time complexity – if $p \geq 2^{-n/2}$, then the time complexity of the verification phase (which is p^{-3}) is smaller than the time complexity of the Pollard Rho phase, and thus, the overall time complexity is $\mathcal{O}(2^{n/2}p^{-2})$. If $p < 2^{-n/2}$ then the verification phase is dominant, and thus, the overall time complexity is $\mathcal{O}(p^{-3})$. Therefore, the overall time complexity of the algorithm (for any p, unifying the two regions) is $\mathcal{O}(\max(2^{n/2}p^{-2}, p^{-3}))$.

Detecting All High-Probability Differentials. If there are k differential characteristics with probability p, the algorithm will simply detect all of them, by being called $k \cdot \ln(k)$ more times (due to the Coupon collector's nature of the problem — each collision suggests a different (α, β) pair, but those may repeat). Again, as before, if there is a huge number of such high probability differentials, the complexity of the algorithm may "explode".

Comparison with Previous Algorithms. The complexity of our algorithm should not be compared against the adaptation of the DDT computation (with complexity $\mathcal{O}(2^n p^{-1})$) presented above, as this adaptation does not apply in the memoryless setting. In fact, the natural adaptation of the DDT computation to memoryless detection of probability-p differentials has complexity of $\mathcal{O}(2^{2n}p^{-1})$, as one has to check each candidate differential $\alpha \rightarrow \beta$ separately, and each such check requires $\mathcal{O}(1/p)$ time. Therefore, our algorithm is significantly faster.

However, for values of $p < 2^{-n/2}$ our algorithm is outperformed by an adaptation of the NestedRho algorithm [17]. The NestedRho algorithm considers a function $h : \{0,1\}^n \rightarrow \{0,1\}^n$ and detects – in a memoryless manner – all values $y \in \{0,1\}^n$ such that $\Pr[h(x) = y] \geq p$, when $x \in \{0,1\}^n$ is chosen uniformly at random. In our case (i.e., search for differentials), for each fixed input α, one can consider the function $h_\alpha(x) = f(x) \oplus f(x \oplus \alpha)$, and apply to it the NestedRho algorithm to detect all values β such $\Pr[h(x) = \beta] \geq p$, which are exactly all values of β such that the differential $\alpha \rightarrow \beta$ holds with probability $\geq p$. This yields an algorithm with time complexity $2^n \cdot T$, where T is the the complexity of the NestedRho algorithm for the corresponding value of p. Substituting the results from [17], one obtains complexity of $2^n p^{-1}$ for $p > 2^{-n/2}$, $2^{n/2}p^{-2}$ for $2^{-3n/4} < p < 2^{-n/2}$, $2^{-n}p^{-4}$ for $2^{-7n/8} < p < 2^{-3n/4}$, etc.

Our algorithm is faster than this variant of NestedRho for $p \geq 2^{-n/2}$, as $2^{n/2}p^{-2} < 2^n p^{-1}$ in this range. For $p < 2^{-n/2}$, the adaptation of NestedRho is faster.

Algorithm 3: Algorithm for Detecting High-Probability Boomerangs

---

Initialize an empty array of $2n$-bit counters and an empty hash table H.
Choose $S = 32/p$ random values $\gamma_1, \gamma_2, \ldots, \gamma_S$.
Pick at random an n-bit non-zero value γ.
for *all* $1 \leq i \leq S$ **do**

> **for** *all* $x \in \{0,1\}^n$ **do**
> > Compute $g_{\gamma_i}(x)$ and insert it into a hash table H.
>
> **for** *all collisions* $g_{\gamma_i}(x_i) = g_{\gamma_i}(x_j)$ *in the hash table* **do**
> > Increment the counter that corresponds to the (input,output) pair
> > $(x_i \oplus x_j, f(x_i) \oplus f(x_i \oplus \gamma_i))$.

Output each (input, output) pair (α, β) whose counter was advanced at least 8 times.

2.4 A Fixed Amount of Available Memory Variant of the High-Probability Differentials Detection Algorithm

Recall that the fundamental algorithm has time and memory complexities of $\mathcal{O}(\max(2^{n/2}p^{-1}, p^{-2}))$, while the memoryless variant has time complexity of $\mathcal{O}(\max(2^{n/2}p^{-2}, p^{-3}))$ (but is suboptimal for $p < 2^{-n/2}$).

We show how to exploit a fixed amount of available memory to obtain trade-offs between these two algorithms. In fact (assuming $p \geq 2^{-n/2}$), we describe an algorithm with time complexity of $\tilde{\mathcal{O}}(2^{n/2}p^{-1})$, similarly to the fundamental algorithm. Yet, this algorithm has reduced memory complexity of $\tilde{\mathcal{O}}(p^{-2})$, and can therefore be considered as a strict improvement over the fundamental algorithm.

In particular, we describe two different tradeoff algorithms, where the first is an extension of the memoryless algorithm and is preferable for small values S of memory (compared to $1/p$). The second algorithm is an extension of the fundamental algorithm and performs better for larger values of S.

Both of the tradeoff algorithms use the classical Parallel Collision Search (PCS) algorithm [34], which finds C collision pairs in a random function $f : \{0,1\}^n \rightarrow \{0,1\}^n$ with memory of $S = \tilde{\mathcal{O}}(C)$ bits in time complexity T such that $T = \tilde{\mathcal{O}}(C \cdot 2^{n/2}S^{-1/2})$.

Tradeoff Algorithm 1. Recall that we need to find $C = \mathcal{O}(p^{-2})$ collisions in the function g_γ (which we assume to behave as a random function for the sake of the analysis). Given memory $S = \tilde{\mathcal{O}}(C) = \tilde{\mathcal{O}}(p^{-2})$, this is done in time complexity of $T = \tilde{\mathcal{O}}(p^{-2}2^{n/2}S^{-1/2})$ using the PCS algorithm.

The first tradeoff algorithm tests all these $\tilde{\mathcal{O}}(p^{-2})$ collisions (as in the memoryless algorithm), requiring additional time complexity of $\tilde{\mathcal{O}}(p^{-3})$. Consequently, the overall time complexity becomes

$$\tilde{\mathcal{O}}(\max(2^{n/2}p^{-2}S^{-1/2}, p^{-3}))$$

(assuming $S = \tilde{\mathcal{O}}(p^{-2})$). Thus, the complexity of the testing phase is negligible in case $p \geq S^{1/2} \cdot 2^{-n/2}$.

Tradeoff Algorithm 2. For larger values of S (and assuming $S = \tilde{O}(2^n)$), the second tradeoff algorithm eliminates the testing phase by finding more collisions (similarly to the fundamental algorithm). Specifically, an internal loop of the PCS algorithm finds a batch of (about) S collisions in g_γ in time $2^{n/2}S^{1/2}$. We repeat this loop (using different flavors) until we find two collisions that suggest the same input-output difference. The probability of this event is about $(S \cdot p^2)^2 = S^2 p^4$, and hence the total time complexity is

$$\tilde{O}(2^{n/2}S^{1/2}S^{-2}p^{-4}) = \tilde{O}(2^{n/2}p^{-4}S^{-3/2}).$$

This complexity is better than that of the first tradeoff algorithm in the case $2^{n/2}p^{-4}S^{-3/2} < p^{-3}$, or $p > 2^{n/2}S^{-3/2}$ (i.e., $S > 2^{n/3}p^{-2/3}$).

In particular, for $S = \tilde{O}(p^{-2})$ (assuming $p \geq 2^{-n/2}$), the time complexity of the algorithm is $\tilde{O}(2^{n/2}p^{-1})$, which is an improvement over the fundamental algorithm as claimed above.

We note that as for the memoryless algorithm, variants of the NestedRho algorithm become faster than the algorithms described above for small values of p and S.

2.5   A Worst-Case Variant of the Algorithm

While the fundamental algorithm presented above succeeds with a high probability when the right pairs with respect to the differentials are distributed randomly, it can be easily fooled by a trapdoor designer capable of planting the right pairs adversarially. For example, if the $t = p2^{n-1}$ right pairs with respect to the differential characteristic $\alpha \to \beta$ form a linear subspace, then only for $2t$ values of γ (which reside in this subspace) there exists some x such that both $(x, x \oplus \alpha)$ and $(x \oplus \gamma, x \oplus \gamma \oplus \alpha)$ are right pairs. As for all other values of γ, the fundamental algorithm fails almost surely, its success probability is at most $2t/2^n = p$, which might be very small.

In this section we present a worst-case algorithm which receives a function $f : \{0,1\}^n \to \{0,1\}^n$ that may be designed adversarially, and allows detecting a hidden differential characteristic that holds with probability p or distinguishing f from a random function. The memory complexity of the algorithm is $\tilde{O}(2^{n/2}p^{-1/2})$ and its data and time complexity are $\tilde{O}(2^{n/2}p^{-3/2})$. Note that the time complexity is higher than that of the fundamental algorithm by only a factor of $\tilde{O}(p^{-1/2})$.

The Algorithm. The worst-case algorithm is given in Algorithm 4. We note that for $p > 2^{-n/3}$ one can simplify the algorithm (as explained later).

Analysis. We first analyze the success probability of the algorithm in finding the differentials with probability at least p.

Lemma 1. *For $1 \leq i \leq S$, consider iteration i of the algorithm. Then,*

1. *For $0 < \epsilon < 1$, the counter for every differential whose probability is at most $p \cdot \epsilon$ is incremented with probability at most $16 \cdot p \cdot \epsilon^2$.*

Algorithm 4: Worst-Case Algorithm

Initialize an empty list L of counter tuples (α, β, cnt).
Choose $S = 200n/p$ random non-zero values $\gamma_1, \gamma_2, \ldots, \gamma_S$.
for *all* $1 \leq i \leq S$ **do**

    Choose $M = 4 \cdot 2^{n/2} p^{-1/2}$ random values $x_1, x_2, \ldots, x_M \in \{0,1\}^n$.
    Initialize an empty list L_{tmp} of differential tuples (α, β) and an empty hash
    table H.
    for *all* $1 \leq j \leq M$ **do**
        Compute $g_{\gamma_i}(x_j)$ and insert it into a hash table H.

    for *all collisions* $g_{\gamma_i}(x_j) = g_{\gamma_i}(x_{j'})$ *in the hash table* **do**
        Compute the suggested (input difference, output difference) pair
        $(\alpha = x_i \oplus x_j, \ \beta = f(x_i) \oplus f(x_j))$.
        if $(\alpha, \beta) \notin L_{tmp}$ **then**
            add (α, β) to L_{tmp}.

    for *each tuple* $(\alpha, \beta) \in L_{tmp}$ **do**
        if $(\alpha, \beta, *) \notin L$ **then**
            add $(\alpha, \beta, 1)$ to L.
        else
            Increment the counter of the tuple (α, β, cnt) to $(\alpha, \beta, cnt + 1)$

For each $(\alpha, \beta, cnt) \in L$ such that $cnt \geq 0.28S \cdot p = 56n$ output the (input difference, output difference) pair (α, β).

---

2. *Assume that $n > 1$ and $p \cdot 2^n \geq 4$. Then, the counter for every differential whose probability is at least p is incremented with probability at least $\frac{2p}{5}$.*

Proof. Let $0 \leq q \leq 1$ and fix a differential (α, β) whose probability is q.

Consider $x_1, x_2, \ldots, x_M \in \{0,1\}^n$ picked at iteration i. For a value of γ_i, we call a pair $(x_j, x_{j'})$ γ_i-surrogate-right if both $(x_j, x_{j'})$ and $(x_j \oplus \gamma_i, x_{j'} \oplus \gamma_i)$ are right pairs.

Assume that $(x_j, x_{j'})$ is a right pair. Note that $(x_j \oplus \gamma_i) \oplus (x_{j'} \oplus \gamma_i) = x_j \oplus x_{j'} = \alpha$, and since γ_i is uniform, $(x_j \oplus \gamma_i, x_{j'} \oplus \gamma_i)$ is uniformly distributed among all pairs with difference α. Consequently,

$$\Pr_{\gamma_i}[(x_j \oplus \gamma_i, x_{j'} \oplus \gamma_i) \text{ is right} \mid (x_j, x_{j'}) \text{ is right}] = \frac{q \cdot 2^n - 2}{2^n - 2}. \tag{1}$$

Let $\mathcal{E}_{j,j'}$ be an indicator for the event that $(x_j, x_{j'})$ is a right pair. Note that for any $j \neq j'$,

$$\Pr[\mathcal{E}_{j,j'}] = 2^{-n}q,$$

and denote $q' = 2^{-n}q$.

Let $\mathcal{G}$ count the number of unordered γ_i-surrogate-right pairs. Note that the counter for (α, β) is incremented in iteration i if and only if $\mathcal{G} > 0$. Therefore, we analyze $\Pr[\mathcal{G} > 0]$ under the assumptions of each part of the lemma.

Part 1. We prove part 1 of the lemma (assuming $q \leq p\epsilon$)

For any γ_i and $j \neq j'$, let $\mathcal{G}_{j,j'}$ be an indicator for the event that $(x_j, x_{j'})$ is a γ_i-surrogate-right pair. We have

$$\mathrm{E}[\mathcal{G}_{j,j'}] = \Pr[\mathcal{G}_{j,j'} = 1] = \Pr[(x_j, x_{j'}) \text{ is } \gamma_i\text{-surrogate-right}] =$$
$$\Pr[(x_j, x_{j'}) \text{ is right}] \cdot \Pr_{\gamma_i}[(x_j \oplus \gamma_i, x_{j'} \oplus \gamma_i) \text{ is right} \mid (x_j, x_{j'}) \text{ is right}] =$$
$$q' \cdot \tfrac{q \cdot 2^n - 2}{2^n - 2} \leq q' \cdot q.$$

Therefore,

$$\mathrm{E}[\mathcal{G}] = \sum_{j < j'} \mathrm{E}[\mathcal{G}_{j,j'}] = 1/2 \cdot M(M-1) \cdot q' \cdot q \leq \tag{2}$$
$$M^2 \cdot 2^{-n} q \cdot q = 16 \cdot 2^n p^{-1} 2^{-n} q^2 \leq 16 \cdot p \cdot \epsilon^2.$$

By Markov's inequality, $\Pr[\mathcal{G} > 0] = \Pr[\mathcal{G} \geq 1] \leq 16 \cdot p \cdot \epsilon^2$, concluding the first part of the lemma.

Part 2. We prove part 2 of the lemma (assuming $q \geq p$).

Let $\mathcal{E}$ count the number of unordered right pairs in $x_1, x_2, \ldots, x_M$. We begin by lower bounding $\Pr[\mathcal{E} > 0]$. We have

$$\mathrm{E}[\mathcal{E}] = \sum_{j < j'} \mathcal{E}_{j,j'} = 1/2 \cdot M(M-1)q',$$

and

$$\mathrm{E}[\mathcal{E}^2] = \mathrm{E}[(\textstyle\sum_{j_1 < j_2} \mathcal{E}_{j_1,j_2})^2] \leq$$
$$1/2 \cdot M(M-1) \mathrm{E}[\mathcal{E}_{j_1,j_2}^2] +$$
$$M^2(M-1) \cdot \textstyle\sum_{\{j_1,j_2,j_3\} \text{ distinct}} \mathrm{E}[\mathcal{E}_{j_1,j_2} \mathcal{E}_{j_1,j_3}] +$$
$$1/4 \cdot M^2(M-1)^2 \textstyle\sum_{\{j_1,j_2,j_3,j_4\} \text{ distinct}} \mathrm{E}[\mathcal{E}_{j_1,j_2} \mathcal{E}_{j_3,j_4}] \leq$$
$$1/2 \cdot M(M-1)q' + 0 + 1/4 \cdot M^2(M-1)^2(q')^2 =$$
$$1/4 \cdot M(M-1)q' \cdot (2 + M(M-1)q'),$$

where the last inequality uses the fact that $\Pr[\mathcal{E}_{j_1,j_2} \mathcal{E}_{j_1,j_3} = 1] = 0$, while the random variables $\mathcal{E}_{j_1,j_2}$ and $\mathcal{E}_{j_3,j_4}$ are negatively correlated.

Hence, by the second moment method,

$$\Pr[\mathcal{E} > 0] \geq \frac{(\mathrm{E}[\mathcal{E}])^2}{\mathrm{E}[\mathcal{E}^2]} \geq$$
$$\frac{1/4 \cdot M^2(M-1)^2(q')^2}{1/4 \cdot M(M-1)q' \cdot (2 + M(M-1)q')} = \frac{M(M-1)q'}{2 + M(M-1)q'}.$$

Recall that $M = 4 \cdot 2^{n/2} p^{-1/2}$, and since $n > 1$, then $M - 1 \geq M/2$. Therefore, $M(M-1)q' \geq 1/2 \cdot M^2 2^{-n} q \geq M^2 2^{-n} p = 8$, and

$$\Pr[\mathcal{E} > 0] \geq \frac{8}{10} = \frac{4}{5}.$$

Combining this with (1) we obtain

$$\Pr[\mathcal{G} > 0] \geq$$
$$\Pr[\mathcal{E} > 0] \cdot \Pr_{\gamma_i}[(x_j \oplus \gamma_i, x_{j'} \oplus \gamma_i) \text{ is right} \mid (x_j, x_{j'}) \text{ is right}] \geq \tfrac{4}{5} \cdot \tfrac{q \cdot 2^n - 2}{2^n - 2} \geq \tfrac{2p}{5},$$

where the last inequality uses the assumption that $q \cdot 2^n \geq p \cdot 2^n \geq 4$ (and therefore $\frac{p \cdot 2^n - 2}{2^n - 2} \geq \frac{p}{2}$). This concludes the proof of the second part of the lemma. ∎

Lemma 2 (Correctness of Algorithm 4). *Assume that $n > 1$ and $p \cdot 2^n \geq 4$. Then, with probability at least $1 - 2^{-0.4n}$:*

1. *No differential with probability at most $p/10$ is output by the algorithm, and*
2. *All differentials with probability at least p are output by the algorithm.*

Note that the lemma does not guarantee anything about differentials with probability in the range $(p/10, p)$. This has to be taken into account when setting the value of p.

Proof. Fix a differential (α, β) and assume that it is output in an iteration with probability q. Let $\mathcal{C}$ be the value of the counter for this differential at the end of the algorithm. We have

$$E[\mathcal{C}] = S \cdot q.$$

Since the iterations are independent we will use a standard Chernoff bound, which states that for any $0 < c < 1$,

$$\Pr[|\mathcal{C} - E[\mathcal{C}]| \geq c \cdot E[\mathcal{C}]] \leq e^{-\frac{c^2 \cdot E[\mathcal{C}]}{3}}.$$

Recall that the differential is output if its counter value is at least $0.28 S \cdot p$.

Case 1. If the probability of the differential is at most $p/10$, by the first part of Lemma 1 (invoked with $\epsilon = 1/10$), $E[\mathcal{C}] \leq 1/6 \cdot S \cdot p$. By the Chernoff bound,

$$\Pr[\mathcal{C} \geq 0.28\, S \cdot p] \leq \Pr[|\mathcal{C} - E[\mathcal{C}]| \geq 0.1 \cdot S \cdot p] =$$
$$\Pr[|\mathcal{C} - E[\mathcal{C}]| \geq \frac{0.1 \cdot S \cdot p}{E[\mathcal{C}]} \cdot E[\mathcal{C}]] \leq$$
$$e^{-\frac{(0.1 \cdot S \cdot p)^2}{3 \cdot E[\mathcal{C}]}} \leq e^{-\frac{S \cdot p}{50}} \leq e^{-4n} < 2^{-2.4n},$$

as $S = 200n/p$. Taking a union bound over 2^{2n} values of (α, β) values gives the first part of the lemma.

Case 2. By the second part of Lemma 1, if the probability of the differential is at least p, then $E[\mathcal{C}] \geq 2/5 \cdot S \cdot p$. By the Chernoff bound,

$$\Pr[\mathcal{C} \leq 0.28\, S \cdot p] \leq \Pr[|\mathcal{C} - E[\mathcal{C}]| \geq E[\mathcal{C}] - 0.28 \cdot S \cdot p] \leq$$
$$\Pr[|\mathcal{C} - E[\mathcal{C}]| \geq 0.3\, E[\mathcal{C}]] \leq$$
$$e^{-\frac{0.09 \cdot E[\mathcal{C}]}{3}} \leq e^{-\frac{S \cdot p}{100}} \leq e^{-2n} < 2^{-2.4n},$$

as $S = 200n/p$. Taking a union bound over 2^{2n} (α, β) values gives the second part of the lemma. ∎

Lemma 3 (Time Complexity of Algorithm 4). *Let $q_{\alpha,\beta}$ denote the probability of the differential (α, β) in f. Then, the expected time complexity of Algorithm 4 is*

$$\tilde{O}\left(2^{n/2} p^{-3/2} + p^{-2} \cdot \sum_{(\alpha,\beta)|\alpha \neq 0} q_{\alpha,\beta}^2\right).$$

We note that for a random function, we have $q_{\alpha,\beta} = \tilde{\mathcal{O}}(2^{-n})$ for all (α,β) with very high probability, implying that $\sum_{(\alpha,\beta)|\alpha\neq 0} q_{\alpha,\beta}^2 = \tilde{\mathcal{O}}(1)$. In this case, the second term in the complexity formula is $\tilde{\mathcal{O}}(p^{-2}) \ll \tilde{\mathcal{O}}(2^{n/2}p^{-3/2})$ (assuming $p \gg 2^{-n}$), and therefore can be neglected. For an arbitrary function, the term $\sum_{(\alpha,\beta)|\alpha\neq 0} q_{\alpha,\beta}^2$ may become dominant. This happens when the DDT of f has many unusually large entries. The analysis below implies that we can still detect this property in time complexity $\tilde{\mathcal{O}}(2^{n/2}p^{-3/2})$, as it results in an unusually high number of collisions in the hash table H (even though we may not be able to find the largest entry whose probability is p).

Proof. Ignoring collisions in the hash table, the expected time complexity is $\tilde{\mathcal{O}}(S \cdot M) = \tilde{\mathcal{O}}(2^{n/2}p^{-3/2})$. We show that the expected number of collisions in each one of the S iterations is $\tilde{\mathcal{O}}(p^{-1}\sum_{(\alpha,\beta)|\alpha\neq 0} q_{\alpha,\beta}^2)$, which completes the proof.

Fix some iteration i and a differential (α,β) with probability $q_{\alpha,\beta}$. Recall from the proof of Lemma 1 that the number of collisions in the hash table resulting from (α,β) is equal to the number γ_i-surrogate-right pairs. By (2), $E[\mathcal{G}] \leq 16 \cdot p^{-1}q_{\alpha,\beta}^2$. Summing this expression over all (α,β) concludes the proof. ∎

The case of $p > 2^{-n/3}$. We note that the analysis suggests that for a given γ_i value we expect $\mathcal{O}(1/p)$ collisions, and we can test each of those using the verification procedure of the fundamental algorithm in time $\mathcal{O}(1/p)$. Hence, instead of storing L_{tmp} and collecting those, we can just take any (α,β) difference suggested, and test them. Hence, when $1/p^2 < 2^{n/2}p^{-1/2}$ (i.e., which implies $p > 2^{-n/3}$), we do not need the counters (as we essentially wait for the first time (α,β) is suggested). The analysis above is of course still valid (up to the fact that the memory complexity can be reduced).

2.6 Experimental Verification

We implemented and experimentally verified the worst-case variant of the algorithm described in Sect. 2.5 (which was designed to find even planted differential properties whose right pairs were adversarially chosen in order to evade the fundamental algorithm). We used our algorithm to search for all the high-probability 5-round and 6-round differentials of the NSA-designed SPECK [2]. Our top-down algorithm automatically found all the state-of-the-art differential properties which were constructed by the bottom-up analysis presented in [10]. In particular, the best 5-round differential we found was

$$(0x0211, 0x0a04) \rightarrow (0x8000, 0x840a) \quad with \quad p \approx 2^{-9}$$

and the best 6-round differential we found was

$$(0x0211, 0x0a04) \rightarrow (0x850a, 0x9520) \quad with \quad p \approx 2^{-13}.$$

3   Efficient Algorithms for Detecting High-Probability Linear Approximations

Linear cryptanalysis [32] is a central cryptanalytic technique, based on exploiting probabilistic relations between the parities of a subset of the plaintext bits and a subset of the ciphertext bits. The central notion in linear cryptanalysis is a *linear approximation*. We say that the linear approximation $\alpha \to \beta$ for the function $f : \{0,1\}^n \to \{0,1\}^n$ holds with bias p, if $\Pr[\beta \cdot f(x) = \alpha \cdot x] = \frac{1}{2} + p$, where $x \in \{0,1\}^n$ is chosen uniformly at random and '$\cdot$' denotes a scalar product over $GF(2^n)$. The values x that satisfy $\beta \cdot f(x) = \alpha \cdot x$ are called *right values* with respect to the approximation. As linear attacks exploit approximations with a high bias (in absolute value), a central goal in linear cryptanalysis is to detect high-bias approximations efficiently.

In this section we present an algorithm that allows detecting all linear approximations of $f : \{0,1\}^n \to \{0,1\}^n$ with bias $\geq p$ in absolute value with complexity of $\mathcal{O}(2^{n/2}p^{-2})$, provided $p \geq 2^{-n/4}$.

For the sake of simplicity, we omit the words 'in absolute value' in the sequel, but throughout this section, all 'high-bias' approximations detected by the algorithms include those with a strong negative bias.

3.1   Previous Algorithms and a Lower Bound

Previous Algorithms. Algorithms for detecting high-bias linear approximations are abundant in the literature. However, as was described in the introduction, almost all of them operate in a bottom-up fashion, that is, construct a 'long' linear approximation by concatenating 'short' linear approximations. In such algorithms, the short approximations can be found easily and the challenge is to find approximations that can be 'glued together'. Top-down algorithms for finding high-bias linear approximations were considered in several papers, under the name *partial linear approximation table* (pLAT), and were applied to attack the ciphers Speck and SM4 [30,31,39]. However, all these papers considered the special case of the addition operation in ARX ciphers, and not the general case.

A linear approximation with bias of $\pm 1/2$ can be found in polynomial time in n, by solving a system of $2n$ linear bit equations in the variables α, β. For somewhat smaller biases, algorithms for the Learning Parity with Noise (LPN) problem (see, e.g., [19] and the references therein) can be used to detect (α, β) in time faster than 2^n. However, the amount of noise increases rapidly as the bias is reduced, so that these algorithms are not effective even for moderately small biases like $1/4$.

A natural top-down algorithm for detecting all linear approximations of a function $f : \{0,1\}^n \to \{0,1\}^n$ that hold with bias $\geq p$ is the following adaptation of the classical algorithm for constructing the Linear Approximation Table (LAT), which also uses the classical Goldreich-Levin algorithm [22]:

1. For all $\beta \in \{0,1\}^n$, do:

(a) Define an auxiliary Boolean function $f_\beta : \{0,1\}^n \rightarrow \{0,1\}$ by $f_\beta(x) = \beta \cdot f(x)$.

(b) Use the Goldreich-Levin algorithm to find all Fourier coefficients $\hat{f}_\beta(\alpha)$ that are larger than p in absolute value.

(c) For each such α, output the pair (α, β) as the (input,output) mask of a high-bias linear approximation.

The time complexity of the algorithm is $\tilde{\mathcal{O}}(2^n p^{-6})$, as the Goldreich-Levin algorithm (whose complexity is $\tilde{\mathcal{O}}(p^{-6})$) is applied 2^n times. Refined variants of the algorithm (see [20] and the references therein) allow reducing the complexity to $\tilde{\mathcal{O}}(2^n p^{-2})$. By the analysis of the Goldreich-Levin algorithm, with a high probability all linear approximations with bias $\geq p$ are detected, and no linear approximation with bias $\ll p$ is detected by mistake.

Lower Bound. Unlike the case of differentials, the information-theoretic lower bound for finding high-bias linear approximations is rather low. Indeed, $\mathcal{O}(p^{-2})$ samples are sufficient for detecting any linear approximation that holds with bias $\geq p$ with a high probability. Given this amount of samples, all linear approximations can be detected by an exhaustive search over all possible values of (α, β), reusing the same data set.

3.2 A New Efficient Algorithm

In this subsection we present an algorithm which detects a 'hidden' linear approximation $\alpha \rightarrow \beta$ that holds with a bias of p, with data, memory, and time complexity of $\mathcal{O}(2^{n/2} p^{-2})$. In fact, it detects all linear approximations that hold with a bias of $\geq p$ with the same complexity (unless the number of such approximations is extremely large, in which case the complexity is approximately equal to the number of approximations). The algorithm uses surrogate differentiation, as well as a shrinking step and application of the Fast Fourier Transform (or more precisely, the Walsh-Hadamard transform).

Main Idea. The basic observation behind the algorithm is that the input mask α of the linear approximation can be 'cancelled' by using surrogate differentiation – that is, by considering the function $g_\gamma(x) = f(x) \oplus f(x \oplus \gamma)$ for an arbitrary nonzero value γ and examining its linear approximations of the form $0 \rightarrow \beta$. Indeed, note that for any fixed γ, we have

$$\beta \cdot g_\gamma(x) = \beta \cdot (f(x) \oplus f(x \oplus \gamma)) = (\beta \cdot f(x) \oplus \alpha \cdot x) \oplus (\beta \cdot f(x \oplus \gamma) \oplus \alpha \cdot (x \oplus \gamma)) \oplus \alpha \cdot \gamma.$$

As $\alpha \cdot \gamma$ is a constant that does not depend on x, it affects only the *sign* of the bias of the approximation $0 \rightarrow \beta$ via g_γ but not its absolute value. Hence, we can assume that $\alpha \cdot \gamma = 0$ and neglect it, remembering that the sign of the bias may be reversed. After neglecting this term, we see that $\beta \cdot g_\gamma(x) = 0$ if and only if either both $x, x \oplus \gamma$ are 'right values' with respect to the approximation $\alpha \rightarrow \beta$ for f, or neither of them is. Therefore, the linear approximation $0 \rightarrow \beta$

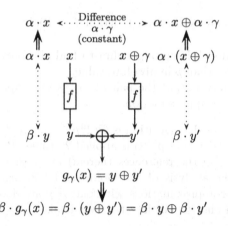

Fig. 2. The relation between the linear approximation $\alpha \to \beta$ for f and the linear approximation $0 \to \beta$ for g_γ.

for g_γ holds with bias of $\pm 2p^2$ (as a concatenation of two linear approximations with bias β). The relation between the approximation $\alpha \to \beta$ for f and the approximation $0 \to \beta$ for g_γ is demonstrated in Fig. 2.

While the bias of approximations of this form (i.e., $2p^2$) is significantly lower than the bias of the original approximation of f, they do not contain the parameter α, which will allow us to detect them more efficiently. We note that in this technique we create a linear relation between two outputs of f, using two linear approximations that connect these outputs of f to the corresponding inputs and an unknown but fixed relation between the inputs. Similar ideas were used in differential-linear cryptanalysis [26], e.g., in the differential-linear attack on the cipher COCONUT98 [5], where a decorrelation module applied in the middle of the cipher makes the output difference of the differential (which is the difference between the inputs to the linear approximation) unknown, but leaves it fixed.

Detailed Description. As written above, we choose an arbitrary nonzero value $\gamma \in \{0,1\}^n$, and consider the function $g_\gamma : \{0,1\}^n \to \{0,1\}^n$ defined by $g_\gamma(x) = f(x) \oplus f(x \oplus \gamma)$. We want to find all linear approximations of g_γ of the form $0 \to \beta$ that hold with bias $\geq 2p^2$. In other words, we want to find all high values in the *row* of the LAT of g_γ that corresponds to input mask 0. Note that this task is different from the usual way of computing the LAT, which works column-wise (i.e., by fixing the output mask β, as was described above). Usually, these tasks are equivalent, as the rows in the LAT of a permutation correspond to columns in the LAT of the inverse permutation. However, in our case, we do not have access to the inverse of g_γ (which is not even well defined since g_γ is not a permutation), and so a somewhat more complex procedure is needed.

A standard way to achieve this goal is to define an auxiliary function $h_\gamma : \{0,1\}^n \to \mathbb{Z}_{\geq 0}$ by $h_\gamma(y) = |\{x \in \{0,1\}^n : g_\gamma(x) = y\}|$. Note that for each mask

β, the bias of the linear approximation $0 \to \beta$ for g_γ is

$$\frac{1}{2} \left(|\{x : g_\gamma(x) \cdot \beta = 0\}| - |\{x : g_\gamma(x) \cdot \beta = 1\}| \right) = \frac{1}{2} \hat{h}_\gamma(\beta).$$

Hence, the values of β we search for consist of the set $\{\beta \in \{0,1\}^n : |\hat{h}_\gamma(\beta)| \geq 4p^2\}$. Using the aforementioned enhanced variants of the Goldreich-Levin algorithm, all these values can be found in time $\tilde{O}(p^{-2})$, once all inputs of h_γ are known. However, computing all these inputs requires 2^n time, and we aim at a significantly faster algorithm.

Instead, we first apply a *shrinking transformation*, in a way that resembles the LF1 algorithm [28] for the LPN problem. Specifically, we shrink the output size of g_γ to $n/2 + \lfloor \log(p^{-2}) \rfloor$ bits by looking only at values x such that the last $\lceil n/2 - \log(p^{-2}) \rceil$ bits of $g_\gamma(x)$ are zeros.[6] (The choice of the range's size is explained below). Note that for any β, the contribution of each of these values of x to the linear approximation $0 \to \beta$ of g_γ is equal to its contribution to the linear approximation $0 \to \bar{\beta}$ of the restriction of g_γ to the first $n/2 + \lfloor \log(p^{-2}) \rfloor$ output bits, where $\bar{\beta}$ is the restriction of β to the same bits. Hence, we can find $\bar{\beta}$ by examining the restricted function $\bar{g}_\gamma$ whose range is $\{0,1\}^{n/2+\lfloor \log(p^{-2}) \rfloor}$, and find the rest of β by repeating the procedure with restriction to the last bits.

Once the shrinking is applied, we find all linear approximations of the form $0 \to \bar{\beta}$ of the function $\bar{g}_\gamma$ by defining the corresponding auxiliary function $\bar{h}_\gamma : \{0,1\}^{n/2+\lfloor \log(p^{-2}) \rfloor} \to \mathbb{Z}_{\geq 0}$ and computing its Walsh-Hadamard transform. The values $\bar{\beta}$ such that $|\hat{\bar{h}}_\gamma(\bar{\beta})| \geq 4p^2$ are those which correspond to the high-bias approximations we search for, as was explained above. The fundamental algorithm is detailed in Algorithm 5. In the first part of the algorithm, for a vector $y \in \{0,1\}^m$, we denote by y_{upper} (resp., y_{lower}) the truncation of y to the $n/2 + \lfloor \log(p^{-2}) \rfloor$ upper (resp., lower) bits. In the second part of the algorithm, we denote by $y_{upper'}$ (resp., $y_{lower'}$) the truncation of y to the $n/2 + \lfloor \log(p^{-1}) \rfloor$ upper (resp., lower) bits.

Randomness Assumptions. The correctness of the fundamental algorithm relies on the following randomness assumptions. We assume that for any γ, the event that x satisfies the linear approximation is independent of the event that $x + \gamma$ satisfies the approximation (which is similar to some of the randomness assumptions of differential-linear attacks). Under this assumption, the probability that either both $x, x + \gamma$ or neither of them satisfy the approximation is $1/2 \pm 2p^2$.

In the presence of multiple linear approximations with bias p (or close to p) we also need to assume that the distribution of values which satisfy one linear approximation is not affected by the distribution of values that satisfy the other high-bias approximations.

Success Analysis. Assume that the function f has a linear approximation $\alpha \to \beta$ with bias p. Our following analysis suggests that (under the above randomness

---

[6] We note that one can choose any constant as the "target", as long as it is consistent with the constant used in the second part of algorithm mentioned later.

Algorithm 5: Efficient Algorithm for Detecting Linear Approximations

---

Initialize the following empty lists: L_1, L_2 of counter tuples (y', cnt), where y' is $n/2 + \lfloor \log(p^{-2}) \rfloor$ bits long; $\bar{L}_1, \bar{L}_2$ of $n/2 + \lfloor \log(p^{-1}) \rfloor$-bit values; $L_3, L_4, \bar{L}_3, \bar{L}_4$ of $n/2 + \lfloor \log(p^{-1}) \rfloor$-bit values; and L_5 of n-bit values.

Choose $M = n \cdot 2^{n/2} p^{-2}$ random distinct values $x_1, x_2, \ldots, x_M \in \{0,1\}^n$.

Pick at random an n-bit non-zero value γ.

for *all* $1 \leq i \leq M$ **do**

> Compute $g_\gamma(x_i)$.
>
> **if** *the last $n/2 - \lceil \log(p^{-2}) \rceil$ bits of $g_\gamma(x)$ are zeros* **then**
>
>> **if** $(g_\gamma(x)_{upper}, *) \notin L_1$ **then**
>>> add $(g_\gamma(x)_{upper}, 1)$ to L_1.
>>
>> **else**
>>> Increment the counter of $(g_\gamma(x)_{upper}, cnt)$ to $(g_\gamma(x)_{upper}, cnt + 1)$
>
> **if** *the first $n/2 - \lceil \log(p^{-2}) \rceil$ bits of $g_\gamma(x)$ are zeros* **then**
>
>> **if** $(g_\gamma(x)_{lower}, *) \notin L_2$ **then**
>>> add $(g_\gamma(x)_{lower}, 1)$ to L_2.
>>
>> **else**
>>> Increment the counter of $(g_\gamma(x)_{lower}, cnt)$ to $(g_\gamma(x)_{lower}, cnt + 1)$

//First Walsh-Hadamard Transform (WHT) phase – Finding β

for $i=1,2$ **do**

> Define $\bar{h}_{\gamma,i} : \{0,1\}^{n/2 + \lfloor \log(p^{-2}) \rfloor} \to \mathbb{Z}_{\geq 0} = cnt$ (for $(y', cnt) \in L_i$).
>
> Apply the fast WHT to $\bar{h}_{\gamma,i}$ to find all values $\bar{\beta}$ such that $|\hat{\bar{h}}_{\gamma,i}(\bar{\beta})| \geq 2p^2$.
> Store these values in the list $\bar{L}_i$.

Add to L_5 all values $\beta \in \{0,1\}^n$ such that $\beta_{upper} \in \bar{L}_1$ and $\beta_{lower} \in \bar{L}_2$.

for *all* $1 \leq i \leq n \cdot 2^{n/2} p^{-1}$ **do**

> **if** *the last $n/2 - \lceil \log(p^{-1}) \rceil$ bits of x_i are zeros* **then**
>> Insert $(x_i)_{upper'}$ to L_3.
>
> **if** *the first $n/2 - \lceil \log(p^{-1}) \rceil$ bits of x_i are zeros* **then**
>> Insert $(x_i)_{lower'}$ to L_4.

for *all* $\beta \in L_5$ **do**

> Define the function $f_\beta(x) : \{0,1\}^n \to \{0,1\}$ by $f_\beta(x) = (-1)^{\beta \cdot f(x)}$.
>
> //Second Walsh-Hadamard Transform phase – Finding α
>
> Define the function $\bar{h}_{\beta,3} : \{0,1\}^{n/2 + \lfloor \log(p^{-1}) \rfloor} \to \{-1,0,1\}$ by $\bar{h}_{\beta,3}(x) = f_\beta(x)$ if $x_{upper'} \in L_3$ and $\bar{h}_{\beta,3}(x) = 0$ otherwise.
>
> Define the function $\bar{h}_{\beta,4} : \{0,1\}^{n/2 + \lfloor \log(p^{-1}) \rfloor} \to \{-1,0,1\}$ by $\bar{h}_{\beta,4}(x) = f_\beta(x)$ if $x_{lower'} \in L_4$ and $\bar{h}_{\beta,4}(x) = 0$ otherwise.
>
> **for** $i=3,4$ **do**
>> Apply the fast WHT to $\bar{h}_{\beta,i}$ to find all values $\bar{\alpha}$ such that $|\hat{\bar{h}}_{\beta,i}(\bar{\alpha})| \geq p$.
>> Store these values in the list $\bar{L}_i$.
>
> Output (α, β) for all $\alpha \in \{0,1\}^n$ such that $\alpha_{upper'} \in \bar{L}_3$ and $\alpha_{lower'} \in \bar{L}_4$.

---

assumptions) this approximation is going to be detected with an overwhelming probability. Furthermore, we show that the probability of a linear approximation with bias much lower than p, e.g., $p/10$, to be proposed by our algorithm is negligible.

The data contains $M = n \cdot 2^{n/2}/p^2$ inputs. After the first shrinking phase, the sum of the counters in each of the lists L_1, L_2 is expected to be between $n/2p^4$ and n/p^4 (depending on p, due to the rounding), and with an overwhelming probability is at least $n/4p^4$. (The high probability comes from the multiplication of the amount of data by a factor of n.) This size of the lists guarantees that for any β s.t. there exists a linear approximation $\alpha \to \beta$ with bias $\geq p$, we have $|\hat{\bar{h}}_{\gamma,1}(\beta_{upper})| \geq 2p^2$ and $|\hat{\bar{h}}_{\gamma,2}(\beta_{lower})| \geq 2p^2$ with an overwhelming probability, and hence, β is going to be suggested at the first stage of the algorithm. On the other hand, for any β s.t. for any α, the bias of the linear approximation $\alpha \to \beta$ is less than $p/10$, we have $|\hat{\bar{h}}_{\gamma,1}(\beta_{upper})| < 2p^2$ and $|\hat{\bar{h}}_{\gamma,2}(\beta_{lower})| < 2p^2$ with an overwhelming probability, and hence, β is not going to be suggested at the first stage of the algorithm.

At the second stage of the algorithm (which is performed for any value of β that was suggested at the first stage), the expected size of the lists L_3, L_4 is between $n/2p^2$ and n/p^2 (depending on p, due to the rounding), and with an overwhelming probability is at least $n/4p^2$. (The high probability comes from the multiplication of the amount of data by a factor of n.) This size of the lists guarantees that for any α s.t. $\alpha \to \beta$ with bias $\geq p$, we have $|\hat{\bar{h}}_{\beta,3}(\alpha_{upper'})| \geq p$ and $|\hat{\bar{h}}_{\beta,2}(\alpha_{lower'})| \geq p$ with an overwhelming probability, and hence, α is going to be suggested at the second stage of the algorithm. On the other hand, for any α s.t. the bias of the linear approximation $\alpha \to \beta$ is less than $p/10$, we have $|\hat{\bar{h}}_{\beta,3}(\alpha_{upper'})| < p$ and $|\hat{\bar{h}}_{\beta,4}(\alpha_{lower'})| < p$ with an overwhelming probability, and hence, α is not going to be suggested at the second stage of the algorithm.

We note that unlike the case of differential characteristics, an additional verification step is not needed, since the Walsh-Hadamard steps filter out all linear approximations with bias of $< p/10$ with an overwhelming probability. A full analysis will be presented in the full version of the paper.

Complexity Analysis. The first shrinking step of the algorithm has complexity of $\mathcal{O}(n2^{n/2}p^{-2})$. As the filtering step checks the equality of $n/2 - \lceil \log(p^{-2}) \rceil$ output bits to zeros, the sum of the counters in each of the lists L_1, L_2 is expected to be $\mathcal{O}(np^{-4})$. The functions $\bar{h}_{\gamma,i}$ are on $n/2 + \lfloor \log(p^{-2}) \rfloor$ bits, and hence, applying the Walsh-Hadamard transform to each of them requires about $\mathcal{O}(n^2 2^{n/2}p^{-2})$. As explained above, after this step for each value β s.t. there exists a linear approximation $\alpha \to \beta$ with bias $\geq p$, the values β_{upper} and β_{lower} will be suggested with an overwhelming probability. The suggestions for β can be reconstructed from the suggested values of β_{upper} and β_{lower} efficiently, by going over the possible values of the $2\lfloor \log(p^{-2}) \rfloor$ common bits of β_{upper} and β_{lower}, finding collisions and completing the value of β for the colliding values. Thus, the complexity of this stage is negligible w.r.t. the complexity of the previous stages.

The second phase of the algorithm is performed for all values of β suggested in the first part. For each such value of β, the complexity of the shrinking phase is $\mathcal{O}(n2^{n/2}p^{-1})$ and the sizes of the lists L_3, L_4 constructed in it is expected to be $\mathcal{O}(np^{-2})$. The functions $\bar{h}_{\beta,i}$ are on $n/2 + \lfloor \log(p^{-1}) \rfloor$ bits, and hence, applying the Walsh-Hadamard transform to each of them requires about $\mathcal{O}(n^2 2^{n/2}p^{-1})$ steps. As was explained above, after this step for each value α s.t. the bias of the linear approximation $\alpha \to \beta$ is $\geq p$, the values $\alpha_{upper'}$ and $\alpha_{lower'}$ will be suggested with an overwhelming probability. The suggestions for α can be reconstructed from the suggested values of $\alpha_{upper'}$ and $\alpha_{lower'}$ efficiently, like in the first phase of the algorithm.

Hence, the time complexity of the algorithm is $\mathcal{O}(n^2 2^{n/2}p^{-2} + tn^2 2^{n/2}p^{-1})$, where t is the number of values of β suggested in the first phase of the algorithm. Therefore, if the number of values of β s.t. there exists α for which the linear approximation $\alpha \to \beta$ holds with a bias of $\geq p$ is $\mathcal{O}(p^{-1})$ then the time complexity of the algorithm is $\mathcal{O}(n^2 2^{n/2}p^{-2} = \tilde{\mathcal{O}}(2^{n/2}p^{-2})$ and the algorithm outputs all linear approximations with a bias of $\geq p$. If the number of such values of β is $\gg p^{-1}$, then the algorithm still outputs all of the high-bias approximations, but its time complexity is increased, proportionally to the number of β values.

The data complexity of the algorithm is $\mathcal{O}(n2^{n/2}p^{-2})$ and the memory complexity is $\mathcal{O}(n2^{n/2}p^{-2})$ (which is dominated by storing the data and applying the fast Walsh-Hadamard transform in the first phase of the algorithm. We note that the output size of the shrinking was chosen in order to balance the complexities of the first shrinking and the first Walsh-Hadamard transform steps (while the complexity of the following steps is significantly lower, unless the algorithm suggests many values of β, as was explained above).

4 Detecting Other High-Probability Statistical Properties

Finally, we use surrogate differentiation to devise algorithms for detecting three other types of statistical properties commonly used in cryptanalysis: boomerangs, second-order differentials, and related-key differentials. As mentioned in the introduction, here we cannot hope for complexity as low as $O(2^{n/2})$, as in all three cases, the information-theoretic lower bound is at least $\Omega(2^{3n/4}p^{-1/4})$. We present algorithms for all three cases with complexity of at most $O(2^n p^{-2})$, which improves over the previously known results by a factor of at least $2^{n/2}$. Our algorithms allow, for the first time, to detect all high-probability boomerangs, second-order differentials and related-key differentials in 48-bit ciphers. The algorithms for Boomerangs, second-order differentials, and related-key differentials can be found in the full version of the paper [16].

5 Summary and Open Problems

In this paper we presented major complexity improvements in the best known techniques for detecting a wide variety of statistical properties of cryptographic primitives which deviate from random behavior in a significant way. The new algorithms can be applied to any black-box function, and in particular they are fast enough to be directly used to analyze 64-bit cryptosystems.

Besides the obvious question of whether our techniques can be further improved, here are some of the problems left open by our research:

1. Can we use similar techniques to speed up the search for other cryptanalytic properties?
2. Can we close the small gap of $\sqrt{p^{-1}}$ between the upper and lower bounds on the time needed to find the significant differentials of a function f?
3. Can surrogate differentiation could be used to solve other problems in cryptography and complexity theory?

Acknowledgements. We would like to thank the reviewers of this paper for their detailed and constructive comments. The first author was supported in part by the Israeli Science Foundation through grant No. 1903/20. The second author was supported in part by the Center for Cyber, Law, and Policy in conjunction with the Israel National Cyber Bureau in the Prime Minister's Office and by the Israeli Science Foundation through grants No. 880/18 and 3380/19. The third author was supported by the European Research Council under the ERC starting grant agreement n. 757731 (LightCrypt) and by the BIU Center for Research in Applied Cryptography and Cyber Security in conjunction with the Israel National Cyber Bureau in the Prime Minister's Office. The fourth author is partially supported by Len Blavatnik and the Blavatnik Family foundation, the Blavatnik ICRC, and Robert Bosch Technologies Israel Ltd. He is a member of CPIIS.

References

1. Albrecht, M.R., Leander, G.: An all-in-one approach to differential cryptanalysis for small block ciphers. In: Knudsen, L.R., Wu, H. (eds.) SAC 2012. LNCS, vol. 7707, pp. 1–15. Springer, Heidelberg (2013). https://doi.org/10.1007/978-3-642-35999-6_1
2. Beaulieu, R., Shors, D., Smith, J., Treatman-Clark, S., Weeks, B., Wingers, L.: The SIMON and SPECK Families of Lightweight Block Ciphers. IACR Cryptol. ePrint Arch. report 404/2013 (2013)
3. Benamira, A., Gerault, D., Peyrin, T., Tan, Q.Q.: A deeper look at machine learning-based cryptanalysis. In: Canteaut, A., Standaert, F.-X. (eds.) EURO-CRYPT 2021. LNCS, vol. 12696, pp. 805–835. Springer, Cham (2021). https://doi.org/10.1007/978-3-030-77870-5_28
4. Bernstein, E., Vazirani, U.V.: Quantum complexity theory. SIAM J. Comput. **26**(5), 1411–1473 (1997). https://doi.org/10.1137/S0097539796300921
5. Biham, E., Dunkelman, O., Keller, N.: Enhancing differential-linear cryptanalysis. In: Zheng, Y. (ed.) ASIACRYPT 2002. LNCS, vol. 2501, pp. 254–266. Springer, Heidelberg (2002). https://doi.org/10.1007/3-540-36178-2_16
6. Biham, E., Shamir, A.: Differential Cryptanalysis of the Data Encryption Standard. Springer, Heidelberg (1993). https://doi.org/10.1007/978-1-4613-9314-6
7. Biryukov, Alex: The Boomerang Attack on 5 and 6-Round Reduced AES. In: Dobbertin, Hans, Rijmen, Vincent, Sowa, Aleksandra (eds.) AES 2004. LNCS, vol. 3373, pp. 11–15. Springer, Heidelberg (2005). https://doi.org/10.1007/11506447_2

8. Biryukov, A., Roy, A., Velichkov, V.: Differential analysis of block ciphers SIMON and SPECK. In: Cid, C., Rechberger, C. (eds.) FSE 2014. LNCS, vol. 8540, pp. 546–570. Springer, Heidelberg (2015). https://doi.org/10.1007/978-3-662-46706-0_28

9. Biryukov, A., Velichkov, V.: Automatic search for differential trails in ARX ciphers. In: Benaloh, J. (ed.) CT-RSA 2014. LNCS, vol. 8366, pp. 227–250. Springer, Cham (2014). https://doi.org/10.1007/978-3-319-04852-9_12

10. Biryukov, A., Velichkov, V., Le Corre, Y.: Automatic search for the best trails in ARX: Application to block cipher SPECK. In: Peyrin, T. (ed.) FSE 2016. LNCS, vol. 9783, pp. 289–310. Springer, Heidelberg (2016). https://doi.org/10.1007/978-3-662-52993-5_15

11. Blondeau, C., Gérard, B., Nyberg, K.: [Multiple differential cryptanalysis using , and X2 statistics]. In: Visconti, I., De Prisco, R. (eds.) SCN 2012. LNCS, vol. 7485, pp. 343–360. Springer, Heidelberg (2012). https://doi.org/10.1007/978-3-642-32928-9_19

12. Blondeau, C., Leander, G., Nyberg, K.: Differential-linear cryptanalysis revisited. J. Cryptol. 30(3), 859–888 (2017). https://doi.org/10.1007/s00145-016-9237-5

13. Blondeau, C., Nyberg, K.: New links between differential and linear cryptanalysis. In: Advances in Cryptology - Proceedings of EUROCRYPT 2013. LNCS, vol. 7881, pp. 388–404. Springer, Heidelberg (2013). https://doi.org/10.1007/978-3-642-38348-9_24

14. Chow, S., Eisen, P.A., Johnson, H., van Oorschot, P.C.: A White-Box DES implementation for DRM applications. In: Proceedings of DRM 2002. LNCS, vol. 2696, pp. 1–15. Springer, Heidelberg (2002). https://doi.org/10.1007/978-3-540-44993-5_1

15. Dinur, I., Dunkelman, O., Gutman, M., Shamir, A.: Improved top-down techniques in differential cryptanalysis. In: Proceedings of LATINCRYPT 2015. LNCS, vol. 9230, pp. 139–156. Springer, Cham (2015). https://doi.org/10.1007/978-3-319-22174-8_8

16. Dinur, I., Dunkelman, O., Keller, N., Ronen, E., Shamir, A.: Efficient detection of high probability statistical properties of cryptosystems via surrogate differentiation. IACR Cryptol. ePrint Arch. report 2023/288 (2023)

17. Dinur, I., Dunkelman, O., Keller, N., Shamir, A.: Memory-efficient algorithms for finding needles in haystacks. In: Advances in Cryptology - Proceedings of CRYPTO 2016, Part II. LNCS, vol. 9815, pp. 185–206. Springer, Heidelberg (2016). https://doi.org/10.1007/978-3-662-53008-5_7

18. Dunkelman, O., Keller, N., Shamir, A.: A practical-time related-key attack on the KASUMI cryptosystem used in GSM and 3G telephony. J. Cryptol. 27(4), 824–849 (2013). https://doi.org/10.1007/s00145-013-9154-9

19. Esser, A., Kübler, R., May, A.: LPN decoded. In: Advances in Cryptology - Proceedings of CRYPTO 2017, Part II. LNCS, vol. 10402, pp. 486–514. Springer, Cham (2017). https://doi.org/10.1007/978-3-319-63715-0_17

20. Fourquet, R., Loidreau, P., Tavernier, C.: Finding good linear approximations of block ciphers and its application to cryptanalysis of reduced round DES (2009). https://perso.univ-rennes1.fr/pierre.loidreau/articles/wcc_2009/wcc_2009.pdf

21. Gohr, A.: Improving attacks on round-reduced speck32/64 using deep learning. In: Advances in Cryptology - Proceedings of CRYPTO 2019, Part II. LNCS, vol. 11693, pp. 150–179. Springer, Cham (2019). https://doi.org/10.1007/978-3-030-26951-7_6

22. Goldreich, O., Levin, L.A.: A hard-core predicate for all one-way functions. In: Proceedings of STOC 1989, pp. 25–32. ACM (1989). https://doi.org/10.1145/73007.73010
23. Hellman, M.E.: A cryptanalytic time-memory trade-off. IEEE Trans. Inf. Theory **26**(4), 401–406 (1980). https://doi.org/10.1109/TIT.1980.1056220
24. Kim, J., Hong, S., Preneel, B., Biham, E., Dunkelman, O., Keller, N.: Related-key boomerang and rectangle attacks: Theory and experimental analysis. IEEE Trans. Inf. Theory **58**(7), 4948–4966 (2012). https://doi.org/10.1109/TIT.2012.2191655
25. Kölbl, S., Leander, G., Tiessen, T.: Observations on the SIMON block cipher family. In: Gennaro, R., Robshaw, M. (eds.) Advances in Cryptology – CRYPTO 2015: 35th Annual Cryptology Conference, Santa Barbara, CA, USA, August 16-20, 2015, Proceedings, Part I, pp. 161–185. Springer, Heidelberg (2015). https://doi.org/10.1007/978-3-662-47989-6_8
26. Langford, S.K., Hellman, M.E.: Differential-linear cryptanalysis. In: Desmedt, Y.G. (ed.) CRYPTO 1994. LNCS, vol. 839, pp. 17–25. Springer, Heidelberg (1994). https://doi.org/10.1007/3-540-48658-5_3
27. Leurent, G., Pernot, C., Schrottenloher, A.: Clustering effect in Simon and Simeck. In: Tibouchi, M., Wang, H. (eds.) ASIACRYPT 2021. LNCS, vol. 13090, pp. 272–302. Springer, Cham (2021). https://doi.org/10.1007/978-3-030-92062-3_10
28. Levieil, É., Fouque, P.-A.: An improved LPN algorithm. In: De Prisco, R., Yung, M. (eds.) SCN 2006. LNCS, vol. 4116, pp. 348–359. Springer, Heidelberg (2006). https://doi.org/10.1007/11832072_24
29. Li, H., Yang, L.: Quantum differential cryptanalysis to the block ciphers. arxiv:1511.08800 (2015)
30. Liu, Y., Fu, K., Wang, W., Sun, L., Wang, M.: Linear cryptanalysis of reduced-round SPECK. Inf. Process. Lett. **116**(3), 259–266 (2016)
31. Liu, Y., Liang, H., Wang, W., Wang, M.: New linear cryptanalysis of Chinese commercial block cipher standard SM4. Secur. Commun. Netw. **2017**, 1461520:1–1461520:10 (2017). https://doi.org/10.1155/2017/1461520
32. Matsui, M.: Linear cryptanalysis method for DES cipher. In: Helleseth, T. (ed.) EUROCRYPT 1993. LNCS, vol. 765, pp. 386–397. Springer, Heidelberg (1994). https://doi.org/10.1007/3-540-48285-7_33
33. Murphy, S.: The return of the cryptographic boomerang. IEEE Trans. Inf. Theory **57**(4), 2517–2521 (2011). https://doi.org/10.1109/TIT.2011.2111091
34. van Oorschot, P.C., Wiener, M.J.: Parallel collision search with cryptanalytic applications. J. Cryptol. **12**(1), 1–28 (1999). https://doi.org/10.1007/PL00003816
35. Peyrin, T., Wang, H.: The MALICIOUS framework: Embedding backdoors into tweakable block ciphers. In: Micciancio, D., Ristenpart, T. (eds.) CRYPTO 2020. LNCS, vol. 12172, pp. 249–278. Springer, Cham (2020). https://doi.org/10.1007/978-3-030-56877-1_9
36. Rijmen, V., Preneel, B.: A family of trapdoor ciphers. In: Biham, E. (ed.) FSE 1997. LNCS, vol. 1267, pp. 139–148. Springer, Heidelberg (1997). https://doi.org/10.1007/BFb0052342
37. Vaudenay, S.: Decorrelation: a theory for block cipher security. J. Cryptol. **16**(4), 249–286 (2003). https://doi.org/10.1007/s00145-003-0220-6
38. Xie, H., Yang, L.: Using Bernstein–Vazirani algorithm to attack block ciphers. Design Codes Cryptogr. **87**(5), 1161–1182 (2018). https://doi.org/10.1007/s10623-018-0510-5
39. Yao, Y., Zhang, B., Wu, W.: Automatic search for linear trails of the SPECK family. In: Lopez, J., Mitchell, C.J. (eds.) ISC 2015. LNCS, vol. 9290, pp. 158–176. Springer, Cham (2015). https://doi.org/10.1007/978-3-319-23318-5_9

Finding the Impossible: Automated Search for Full Impossible-Differential, Zero-Correlation, and Integral Attacks

Hosein Hadipour[1]([✉]), Sadegh Sadeghi[2], and Maria Eichlseder[1]

[1] Graz University of Technology, Graz, Austria
{hossein.hadipour,maria.eichlseder}@iaik.tugraz.at
[2] Department of Mathematics, Institute for Advanced Studies in Basic Sciences (IASBS), Zanjan, Iran

Abstract. Impossible differential (ID), zero-correlation (ZC), and integral attacks are a family of important attacks on block ciphers. For example, the impossible differential attack was the first cryptanalytic attack on 7 rounds of AES. Evaluating the security of block ciphers against these attacks is very important but also challenging: Finding these attacks usually implies a combinatorial optimization problem involving many parameters and constraints that is very hard to solve using manual approaches. Automated solvers, such as Constraint Programming (CP) solvers, can help the cryptanalyst to find suitable attacks. However, previous CP-based methods focus on finding only the ID, ZC, and integral distinguishers, often only in a limited search space. Notably, none can be extended to a unified optimization problem for finding full attacks, including efficient key-recovery steps.

In this paper, we present a new CP-based method to search for ID, ZC, and integral distinguishers and extend it to a unified constraint optimization problem for finding full ID, ZC, and integral attacks. To show the effectiveness and usefulness of our method, we applied it to several block ciphers, including SKINNY, CRAFT, SKINNYe-v2, and SKINNYee. For the ISO standard block cipher SKINNY, we significantly improve all existing ID, ZC, and integral attacks. In particular, we improve the integral attacks on SKINNY-n-$3n$ and SKINNY-n-$2n$ by 3 and 2 rounds, respectively, obtaining the best cryptanalytic results on these variants in the single-key setting. We improve the ZC attack on SKINNY-n-n (SKINNY-n-$2n$) by 2 (resp. 1) rounds. We also improve the ID attacks on all variants of SKINNY. Particularly, we improve the time complexity of the best previous single-tweakey (related-tweakey) ID attack on SKINNY-128-256 (resp. SKINNY-128-384) by a factor of $2^{22.57}$ (resp. $2^{15.39}$). On CRAFT, we propose a 21-round (20-round) ID (resp. ZC) attack, which improves the best previous single-tweakey attack by 2 (resp. 1) rounds. Using our new model, we also provide several practical integral distinguishers for reduced-round SKINNY, CRAFT, and Deoxys-BC. Our method is generic and applicable to other strongly aligned block ciphers.

Keywords: Impossible differential attacks · Zero-correlation attacks · Integral attacks · SKINNY · SKINNYe · CRAFT · SKINNYee · Deoxys-BC

© International Association for Cryptologic Research 2023
C. Hazay and M. Stam (Eds.): EUROCRYPT 2023, LNCS 14007, pp. 128–157, 2023.
https://doi.org/10.1007/978-3-031-30634-1_5

1 Introduction

The impossible differential (ID) attack, independently introduced by Biham et al. [5] and Knudsen [25], is one of the most important attacks on block ciphers. For example, the ID attack is the first attack breaking 7 rounds of AES-128 [28]. The ID attack exploits an impossible differential in a block cipher, which usually originates from slow diffusion, to retrieve the master key. The zero-correlation (ZC) attack, first introduced by Bogdanov and Rijmen [8], is the dual method of the ID attack in the context of linear analysis, which exploits an unbiased linear approximation to retrieve the master key.

The integral attack is another important attack on block ciphers which was first introduced as a theoretical generalization of differential analysis by Lai [26] and as a practical attack by Daemen et al. [13]. The core idea of integral attacks is finding a set of inputs such that the sum of the resulting outputs is key-independent in some positions. At ASIACRYPT 2012, Bogdanov et al. established a link between the (multidimensional) ZC approximation and integral distinguishers [7]. Sun et al. at CRYPTO 2015 [41] developed further the links among the ID, ZC, and integral attacks. Thanks to this link, we can use search techniques for ZC distinguishers to find integral distinguishers. Ankele et al. studied the influence of the tweakey schedule in ZC analysis of tweakable block ciphers at ToSC 2019 [1] and showed that taking the tweakey schedule into account can result in a longer ZC distinguisher.

The search for ID, ZC, and integral attacks on a block cipher contains two main phases: finding a distinguisher and mounting a key recovery based on the discovered distinguisher. One of the main techniques to find ID and ZC distinguishers is the miss-in-the-middle technique [5,7]. The idea is to find two differences (linear masks) that propagate halfway through the cipher forward and backward with certainty but contradict each other in the middle. However, applying this technique requires tracing the propagation of differences (resp. linear masks) at the word- or bit-level of block ciphers, which is a time-consuming and potentially error-prone process using a manual approach. When it comes to the key recovery, we should extend the distinguisher at both sides and trace the propagation of more cryptographic properties taking many critical parameters into account. In general, finding an optimum complete ID, ZC, or integral attack usually implies a combinatorial optimization problem which is very hard to solve using a manual approach, especially when the block size is large and there are many possible solutions. Therefore, developing automatic tools is important to evaluate the security of block ciphers against these attacks, mainly, in designing and analyzing lightweight cryptographic primitives, where a higher precision in security analysis lets us minimize security margins.

One approach to solving the optimization problems stemming from cryptanalytic attacks is developing dedicated algorithms. For instance, in CRYPTO 2016, Derbez and Fouque proposed a dedicated algorithm [14] to find $\mathcal{DS}$-MITM and ID attacks. However, developing and implementing efficient algorithms is difficult and implies a hard programming task. In addition, other researchers may want to adapt these algorithms to other problems with some common features and some differences. This may, again, be very difficult and time-consuming.

Another approach is converting the cryptanalytic problem into a constraint satisfaction problem (CSP) or a constraint optimization problem (COP) and then solving it with off-the-shelf constraint programming (CP) solvers. Recently, many CP-based approaches have been introduced to solve challenging symmetric cryptanalysis problems, which outperform the previous manual or dedicated methods in terms of accuracy and efficiency [20,30,37,39,46]. For example, at EUROCRYPT 2017, Sasaki and Todo proposed a new automatic tool based on mixed integer linear programming (MILP) solvers to find ID distinguishers [37]. Cui et al. proposed a similar approach to find ID and ZC distinguishers [12]. Sun et al. recently proposed a new CP-based method to search for ID and ZC distinguishers at ToSC 2020 [42].

Although the automatic methods to search for ID, ZC, and integral attacks had significant advances over the past years, they still have some basic limitations:

- The CP models for finding ID/ZC distinguishers proposed in [12,37,43] rely on the unsatisfiability of the models where the input/output difference/mask is fixed. This is also the case in all existing CP models to search for integral distinguishers based on division property [15,44] or monomial prediction [19,23]. However, finding an optimal key recovery attack is an optimization problem, which is based on satisfiability. Hence, the previous CP models for finding the ID, ZC, and integral distinguishers can not be extended to a unified optimization model for finding a complete attack. The previous CP models for finding ID, ZC, and integral distinguishers also require checking each input/output property individually. As a result, it is computationally hard to find all possible distinguishers when the block size is large enough.
- The CP model proposed in [42] employs the miss-in-the-middle technique to find ID/ZC distinguishers. This approach does not fix the input/output differences/masks. However, the compatibility between the two parts of the distinguisher is checked outside of the CP model by iterating over a loop where the activeness pattern of a state cell at the meeting point should be fixed in each iteration.
- All previous CP models regarding ID, ZC, and integral attacks only focus on finding the longest distinguishers. However, many other important factors affect the final complexity of these attacks, which we can not take into account by only modeling the distinguisher part. For example, the position and the number of active cells in the input/output of the distinguisher, the number of filters in verifying the desired properties at the input/output of distinguishers, and the number of involved key bits in the key recovery are only a few critical parameters that affect the final complexity of the attack but can be considered only by modeling the key recovery part. We show that the best attack does not necessarily require the longest distinguisher. Hence, it is important to unify the key recovery and distinguishing phases for finding better ID, ZC, and integral attacks.

- The tool introduced by Derbez and Fouque [14] is the only tool to find full ID attacks. However, this tool is based on a dedicated algorithm implemented in C/C++ and is not as generic as the CP-based methods. In addition, this tool can not take all critical parameters of ID attacks into account to minimize the final complexity. As other limitations, this tool can not find related-(twea)key ID attacks and is not applicable for ZC and integral attacks.
- None of the previous automatic tools takes the relationship between ZC and integral attacks into account to find ZC distinguishers suitable for integral key recovery. Particularly, there is no automatic tool to take the meet-in-the-middle technique into account for ZC-based integral attacks.

Our Contributions. We propose a new generic, CP-based, and easy-to-use automatic method to find full ID, ZC, and integral attacks, addressing the above limitations. Unlike all previous CP models for these distinguishers, which are based on unsatisfiability, our CP model relies on satisfiability for finding distinguishers. This way, each solution of our CP models corresponds to an ID, ZC, or integral distinguisher. This key feature enables us to extend our distinguisher models to a unified model for finding an optimal key-recovery attack. Furthermore, our unified CP model takes advantage of key-bridging and meet-in-the-middle techniques. To show the usefulness of our method, we apply it to SKINNY[3], CRAFT [4], SKINNYe-v2 [31], and SKINNYee [32] and significantly improve the ZC, ID, and integral attacks on these ciphers. Table 1 summarizes our results.

- We improve the integral attacks on SKINNY-n-$2n$ and SKINNY-n-$3n$ by 2 and 3 rounds, respectively. To the best of our knowledge, our integral attacks are the best single-key attacks on these variants of SKINNY.
- We improve the ZC attacks on SKINNY-n-n (SKINNY-n-$2n$) by 2 (resp. 1) rounds. We also propose the first 21-round ZC attack on SKINNY-n-$3n$. Our ZC attacks are the best attacks on SKINNY in a known-plaintext setting.
- On CRAFT, we provide a 21-round (20-round) single-tweakey ID (resp. ZC) attack that is 2 (resp. 1) rounds longer than the best previous single-tweakey attack proposed on this cipher at ASIACRYPT 2022 [40].
- We improve all previous single-tweakey ID attacks on all variants of SKINNY. We reduce the time complexity of the ID attack on SKINNY-128-256 by a factor of $2^{22.57}$. Our ID attacks are the best single-tweakey attacks on SKINNY-128-128, and all variants of SKINNY-64. We also improved the related-tweakey ID attack on SKINNY-n-$3n$.
- We provide the first third-party analysis of SKINNYee by proposing 26-round integral and 27-round ID attacks.
- We propose several practical integral distinguishers for reduced round of Deoxys-BC, SKINNY, CRAFT, and SKINNYe-v2/ee (see Table 3).
- Our tool identified several flaws in previous cryptanalytic results on SKINNY (see Table 2). Our tool is efficient and can find all reported results in a few seconds when running on a regular laptop. Its source code is publicly available at the following link: https://github.com/hadipourh/zero

Table 1. Summary of our cryptanalytic results. ID/ZC/Int = impossible differential, zero-correlation, integral. STK/RTK = single/related-tweakey. SK = single-key with given keysize, CP/KP = chosen/known plaintext, CT = chosen tweak. †: attack has minor issues.

Cipher	#R	Time	Data	Mem.	Attack	Setting/Model	Ref.
SKINNY-64-192	**21**	$2^{185.83}$	$2^{62.63}$	2^{49}	ZC	STK/KP	[21, G.3]
	21	$2^{180.50}$	2^{62}	2^{170}	ID	STK/CP	[47]
	21	$\mathbf{2^{174.42}}$	$2^{62.43}$	2^{168}	ID	STK/CP	[21, F.3]
	23†	$2^{155.60}$	$2^{73.20}$	2^{138}	Int †	180,SK/CP,CT	[1]
	26	2^{172}	2^{61}	2^{172}	Int	180,SK/CP,CT	[21, H.2]
	27	2^{189}	$2^{63.53}$	2^{184}	ID	RTK/CP	[27]
	27	$\mathbf{2^{183.26}}$	$2^{63.64}$	2^{172}	ID	RTK/CP	[21, F.4]
SKINNY-128-384	**21**	$2^{372.82}$	$2^{122.81}$	2^{98}	ZC	STK/KP	[21, G.3]
	21	$2^{353.60}$	2^{123}	2^{341}	ID	STK/CP	[47]
	21	$\mathbf{2^{347.35}}$	$2^{122.89}$	2^{336}	ID	STK/CP	[21, F.3]
	26	2^{344}	2^{121}	2^{340}	Int	360,SK/CP,CT	[21, H.2]
	27	2^{378}	$2^{126.03}$	2^{368}	ID	RTK/CP	[27]
	27	$\mathbf{2^{362.61}}$	$2^{124.99}$	2^{344}	ID	RTK/CP	[21, F.4]
SKINNY-64-128	18	2^{126}	$2^{62.68}$	2^{64}	ZC	STK /KP	[36]
	19	$2^{119.12}$	$2^{62.89}$	2^{49}	ZC	STK/KP	[21, G.2]
	19	$2^{119.80}$	2^{62}	2^{110}	ID	STK/CP	[47]
	19	$\mathbf{2^{110.34}}$	$2^{60.86}$	2^{104}	ID	STK/CP	[21, F.2]
	20†	$2^{97.50}$	$2^{68.40}$	2^{82}	Int †	120,SK/CP,CT	[1]
	22	2^{110}	$2^{57.58}$	2^{108}	Int	120,SK/CP,CT	[21, H.1]
SKINNY-128-256	**19**	$2^{240.07}$	$2^{122.90}$	2^{98}	ZC	STK/KP	[21, G.2]
	19	$2^{241.80}$	2^{123}	2^{221}	ID	STK/CP	[47]
	19	$\mathbf{2^{219.23}}$	$2^{117.86}$	2^{208}	ID	STK/CP	[21, F.2]
	22	2^{216}	$2^{113.58}$	2^{216}	Int	240,SK/CP,CT	[21, H.1]
SKINNY-64-64	14	2^{62}	$2^{62.58}$	2^{64}	ZC	STK/KP	[36]
	16	$2^{62.71}$	$2^{61.35}$	$2^{37.80}$	ZC	STK/KP	[21, G.1]
	17	$2^{61.80}$	$2^{59.50}$	$2^{49.60}$	ID	STK/CP	[47]
	17	$\mathbf{2^{59}}$	$2^{58.79}$	2^{40}	ID	STK/CP	[21, F.1]
SKINNY-128-128	**16**	$2^{122.79}$	$2^{122.30}$	$2^{74.80}$	ZC	STK/KP	[21, G.1]
	17	$2^{120.80}$	$2^{118.50}$	$2^{97.50}$	ID	STK/CP	[47]
	17	$\mathbf{2^{116.51}}$	$2^{116.37}$	2^{80}	ID	STK/CP	[21, F.1]
CRAFT	**20**	$2^{120.43}$	$2^{62.89}$	2^{49}	ZC	STK/KP	[21, K.2]
	21	$2^{106.53}$	$2^{60.99}$	2^{100}	ID	STK/CP	[21, K.3]
SKINNYee	**26**	2^{113}	2^{66}	2^{108}	Int	SK/CP,CT	[21, I.3]
	27	$2^{123.04}$	$2^{62.79}$	2^{108}	ID	RTK/CP	[21, I.2]
SKINNYe-v2	**30**	2^{232}	2^{65}	2^{228}	Int	240,SK/CP,CT	[21, H.3]

Outline. We recall the background on ID and ZC attacks and review the link between ZC and integral attacks in Sect. 2. In Sect. 3, we show how to convert the problem of searching for ID and ZC distinguishers to a CSP problem. In Sect. 4, we show how to extend our distinguisher models to create a unified model for finding optimum ID attacks. We discuss the extension of our models for ZC and integral attacks in Sect. 5, and finally conclude in Sect. 6. For detailed attack procedures of all analyzed ciphers, we refer to the full version of our paper [21].

Table 2. Attacks with a serious flaw (invalid attacks).

Cipher	Attack	#R	Setting/Model	Ref.	Flaw
SKINNY-n-n	ID	18	STK/CP	[45]	Sect. 4.2
SKINNY-n-$2n$	ID	20	STK/CP	[45]	Sect. 4.2
	ZC/Int †	22	SK/CP, CT	[48]	Sect. 3
SKINNY-n-$3n$	ID	22	STK/CP	[45]	Sect. 4.2
	ZC/Int †	26	SK/CP, CT	[48]	Sect. 3

† [48] was published after publishing the first version of our paper.

2 Background

Here, we recall the basics of ID and ZC attacks and briefly review the link between the ZC and integral attacks. We also introduce the notations we use in the rest of this paper. We refer to the full version of our paper for the specification of SKINNY and SKINNYe [21, C], CRAFT [21, K.1], and SKINNYee [21, I.1].

2.1 Impossible Differential Attack

The impossible differential attack was independently introduced by Biham et al. [5] and Knudsen [25]. The core idea of an impossible differential attack is exploiting an impossible differential in a cipher to retrieve the key by discarding all key candidates leading to such an impossible differential. The first requirement of the ID attack is an ID distinguisher, i.e., an input difference that can never propagate to a particular output difference. Then, we extend the ID distinguisher by some rounds backward and forward. A candidate for the key that partially encrypts/decrypts a given pair to the impossible differential is certainly not valid. The goal is to discard as many wrong keys as possible. Lastly, we uniquely retrieve the key by exhaustively searching the remaining candidates.

We recall the complexity analysis of the ID attack based on [10,11]. Let E be a block cipher with n-bit block size and k-bit key. As illustrated in Fig. 1, assume that there is an impossible differential $\Delta_U \nrightarrow \Delta_L$ for r_D rounds of E denoted by E_D. Suppose that Δ_U (Δ_L) propagates backward (resp. forward) with probability 1 through E_B^{-1} (resp. E_F) to Δ_B (Δ_F), and $|\Delta_B|$ ($|\Delta_F|$) denotes

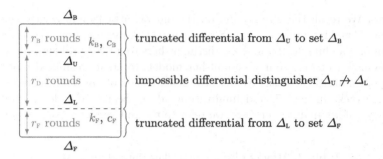

Fig. 1. Main parameters of the ID attack using an r_D-round impossible differential distinguisher $\Delta_\mathrm{U} \not\to \Delta_\mathrm{L}$. The distinguisher is extended with truncated differential propagation to sets $\Delta_\mathrm{U} \to \Delta_\mathrm{B}$ over r_B rounds backwards and $\Delta_\mathrm{L} \to \Delta_\mathrm{F}$ over r_F rounds forward. The inverse differentials $\Delta_\mathrm{B} \to \Delta_\mathrm{U}$ and $\Delta_\mathrm{F} \to \Delta_\mathrm{L}$ involve $k_\mathrm{B}, k_\mathrm{F}$ key bits and have weight $c_\mathrm{B}, c_\mathrm{F}$, respectively.

the dimension of vector space Δ_B (resp. Δ_F). Let c_B (c_F) be the number of bit-conditions that should be satisfied for $\Delta_\mathrm{B} \to \Delta_\mathrm{U}$ (resp. $\Delta_\mathrm{L} \leftarrow \Delta_\mathrm{F}$), i.e., $\Pr(\Delta_\mathrm{B} \to \Delta_\mathrm{U}) = 2^{-c_\mathrm{B}}$ (resp. $\Pr(\Delta_\mathrm{L} \leftarrow \Delta_\mathrm{F}) = 2^{-c_\mathrm{F}}$). Moreover, assume that k_B (k_F) denotes the key information, typically subkey bits, involved in E_B (resp. E_F). With these assumptions we can divide the ID attacks into three steps:

- *Step 1: Pair Generation.* Given access to the encryption oracle (and possibly the decryption oracle), we generate N pairs $(x, y) \in \{0, 1\}^{2n}$ such that $x \oplus y \in \Delta_\mathrm{B}$ and $E(x) \oplus E(y) \in \Delta_\mathrm{F}$ and store them. This is a limited birthday problem, and according to [11] the complexity of this step is:

$$T_0 = \max\left\{\min_{\Delta \in \{\Delta_\mathrm{B}, \Delta_\mathrm{F}\}}\left\{\sqrt{N2^{n+1-|\Delta|}}\right\}, N2^{n+1-|\Delta_\mathrm{B}|-|\Delta_\mathrm{F}|}\right\} \qquad (1)$$

- *Step 2: Guess-and-Filter.* The goal of this step is to discard all subkeys in $k_\mathrm{B} \cup k_\mathrm{F}$ which are invalidated by at least one of the generated pairs. Rather than guessing all subkeys $k_\mathrm{B} \cup k_\mathrm{F}$ at once and testing them with all pairs, we can optimize this step by using the *early abort* technique [29]: We divide $k_\mathrm{B} \cup k_\mathrm{F}$ into smaller subsets, typically the round keys, and guess them step by step. At each step, we reduce the remaining pairs by checking if they satisfy the conditions of the truncated differential trail through E_B and E_F. The minimum number of partial encryptions/decryptions in this step is [10]:

$$T_1 + T_2 = N + 2^{|k_\mathrm{B} \cup k_\mathrm{F}|}\frac{N}{2^{c_\mathrm{B}+c_\mathrm{F}}} \qquad (2)$$

- *Step 3: Exhaustive Search.* The probability that a wrong key survives through the guess-and-filter step is $P = \left(1 - 2^{-(c_\mathrm{B}+c_\mathrm{F})}\right)^N$. Therefore, the number of candidates after performing the guess-and-filter is $P \cdot 2^{|k_\mathrm{B} \cup k_\mathrm{F}|}$ on average. On the other hand, the guess-and-filter step does not involve $k - |k_\mathrm{B} \cup k_\mathrm{F}|$ bits of key information. As a result, to uniquely determine the key, we should exhaustively search a space of size $T_3 = 2^{k-|k_\mathrm{B} \cup k_\mathrm{F}|} \cdot P \cdot 2^{|k_\mathrm{B} \cup k_\mathrm{F}|} = 2^k \cdot P$.

Then, the total time complexity of the ID attack is:

$$T_{tot} = (T_0 + (T_1 + T_2) C_{E'} + T_3) C_E, \qquad (3)$$

where C_E denotes the cost of one full encryption, and $C_{E'}$ represents the ratio of the cost for one partial encryption to the full encryption.

To keep the data complexity less than the full codebook, we require $T_0 < 2^n$. In addition, to retrieve at least one bit of key information in the guess-and-filter step, $P < \frac{1}{2}$ should hold. Note that Eq. 2 is the average time complexity of the guess-and-filter step; for each ID attack, we must evaluate its complexity accurately to ensure we meet this bound in practice. To see the complexity analysis of the ID attack in the related-(twea)key setting, refer to [21, A].

2.2 Multidimensional Zero-Correlation Attack

Zero-correlation attacks, firstly introduced by Bogdanov and Rijmen [8], are the dual of the ID attack in the context of linear analysis and exploit a linear approximation with zero correlation. The major limitation of the basic ZC attack is its enormous data complexity, equal to the full codebook. To reduce the data complexity of the ZC attack, Bogdanov and Wang proposed the multiple ZC attack at FSE 2012 [9], which utilizes multiple ZC linear approximations. However, the multiple ZC attack relies on the assumption that all involved ZC approximations are independent, which limits its applications. To overcome this assumption of, Bogdanov et al. introduced the multidimensional ZC attack at ASIACRYPT 2012 [7]. We briefly recall the basics of multidimensional ZC attack.

Let E_D represent the reduced-round block cipher E with a block size of n bits. Assume that the correlation of m independent linear approximations $\langle u_i, x \rangle + \langle w_i, E_D(x) \rangle$ and all their nonzero linear combinations are zero, where $u_i, w_i, x \in \mathbb{F}_2^n$, for $i = 0, \ldots, m - 1$. We denote by $l = 2^m$ the number of ZC linear approximations. In addition, assume we are given N input/output pairs $(x, y = E_D(x))$. Then, we can construct a function from $\mathbb{F}_2^n$ to $\mathbb{F}_2^m$ which maps x to $z(x) = (z_0, \ldots, z_{m-1})$, where $z_i := \langle u_i, x \rangle + \langle w_i, E_D(x) \rangle$ for all i. The idea of the multidimensional ZC distinguisher is that the output of this function follows the *multivariate hypergeometric distribution*, whereas the m-tuples of bits drawn at random from a uniform distribution on $\mathbb{F}_2^m$ follow a *multinomial distribution* [7]. For sufficiently large N, we distinguish E_D from a random permutation as follows.

We initialize 2^m counters $V[z]$ to zero, $z \in \mathbb{F}_2^m$. Then, for each of the N pairs (x, y), we compute $z_i = \langle u_i, x \rangle + \langle w_i, y \rangle$ for all $i = 0, \ldots, 2^m - 1$, and increment $V[z]$ where $z = (z_0, \ldots, z_{m-1})$. Finally, we compute the following statistic:

$$T = \frac{N \cdot 2^m}{1 - 2^{-m}} \sum_{z=0}^{2^m - 1} \left(\frac{V[z]}{N} - \frac{1}{2^m} \right)^2. \qquad (4)$$

For the pairs (x, y) derived from E_D, i.e., $y = E_D(x)$, the statistic T follows a χ^2-distribution with mean $\mu_0 = (l-1)\frac{2^n - N}{2^n - 1}$ and variance $\sigma_0^2 = 2(l-1)(\frac{2^n - N}{2^n - 1})^2$.

However, it follows a χ^2-distribution with mean $\mu_1 = (l - 1)$ and variance $\sigma_1^2 = 2(l - 1)$ for a random permutation [7]. By defining a decision threshold $\tau = \mu_0 + \sigma_0 Z_{1-\alpha} = \mu_1 - \sigma_1 Z_{1-\beta}$, the output of test is 'cipher', i.e., the pairs are derived from E_D, if $T \leq \tau$. Otherwise, the output of the test is 'random'.

This test may wrongfully classify E_D as a random permutation (type-I error) or may wrongfully accept a random permutation as E_D (type-II error). Let the probability of the type-I and type-II errors be α and β. Then, the number of required pairs N to successfully distinguish E_D from a random permutation is [7]:

$$N = \frac{2^n(Z_{1-\alpha} + Z_{1-\beta})}{\sqrt{l/2} - Z_{1-\beta}}, \tag{5}$$

where $Z_{1-\alpha}$, and $Z_{1-\beta}$ are respective quantiles of the standard normal distribution. Thus, the data complexity of the multidimensional ZC attack depends on the number of ZC approximations, $l = 2^m$, and the error probabilities α and β.

To mount a key recovery based on a multidimensional ZC distinguisher for E_D, we extend E_D by a few rounds at both ends, $E = E_F \circ E_D \circ E_B$. Given N plaintext/ciphertext pairs $(p, c = E(p))$, we can recover the key in two steps:

- *Step 1: Guess-and-filter.* We guess the value of involved key bits in E_B (E_F) and partially encrypt (decrypt) the plaintexts (ciphertexts) to derive N pairs (x, y) for the input $x = E_B(p)$ and output $y = E_F^{-1}(c)$ of E_D. Assuming that wrong keys yield pairs (x, y) randomly chosen from $\mathbb{F}_2^{2n}$, we use the statistic T to discard all keys for which $T \leq \tau$.
- *Step 2: Exhaustive Search.* Finally, we exhaustively search the remaining key candidates to find the correct key.

The time complexity of the guess-and-filter step depends on the number of pairs N and the size of involved key bits in E_B and E_F. Given that typically a subset of internal variables is involved in the partial encryptions/decryptions, we can take advantage of the partial sum technique [16] to reduce the time complexity of the guess-and-filter step. Moreover, by adjusting the value of α and β, we can make a trade-off between the time and data complexities as α and β affect the data, and β influences the time complexity of the exhaustive search.

2.3   Relation Between the Zero-Correlation and Integral Attacks

Bogdanov et al. [7] showed that an integral distinguisher[1] always implies a ZC distinguisher, but its converse is true only if the input and output linear masks of the ZC distinguisher are independent. Later, Sun et al. [41] proposed the following theorem that the conditions for deriving an integral distinguisher from a ZC linear hull in [7] can be removed.

Theorem 1 (Sun et al. [41]). *Let $F : \mathbb{F}_2^n \to \mathbb{F}_2^n$ be a vectorial Boolean function. Assume A is a subspace of $\mathbb{F}_2^n$ and $\beta \in \mathbb{F}_2^n \setminus \{0\}$ such that (α, β) is a ZC*

---

[1] Under the definition that integral property is a balanced vectorial Boolean function.

approximation for any $\alpha \in A$. *Then, for any* $\lambda \in \mathbb{F}_2^n$, $\langle \beta, F(x + \lambda) \rangle$ *is balanced over the set*

$$A^\perp = \{x \in \mathbb{F}_2^n \mid \forall\, \alpha \in A : \langle \alpha, x \rangle = 0\}.$$

According to Theorem 1, the data complexity of the resulting integral distinguisher is 2^{n-m}, where n is the block size and m is the dimension of the linear space spanned by the input linear masks in the corresponding ZC linear hull.

At ToSC 2019, Ankele et al. [1] considered the effect of the tweakey on ZC distinguishers of tweakable block ciphers (TBCs). They showed that taking the tweakey schedule into account can lead to a longer ZC distinguisher and thus a longer integral distinguisher. They proposed Theorem 2, which provides an algorithm to find ZC linear hulls for TBCs following the super-position tweakey (STK) construction of the TWEAKEY framework [24] (see Fig. 2).

Theorem 2 (Ankele et al. [1]). *Let* $E_K(T, P) : \mathbb{F}_2^{t \times n} \to \mathbb{F}_2^n$ *be a TBC following the STK construction. Assume that the tweakey schedule of* E_K *has* z *parallel paths and applies a permutation* h *on the tweakey cells in each path. Let* (Γ_0, Γ_r) *be a pair of linear masks for* r *rounds of* E_K, *and* $\Gamma_1, \ldots, \Gamma_{r-1}$ *represents a possible sequence for the intermediate linear masks. If there is a cell position* i *such that any possible sequence* $\Gamma_0[i], \Gamma_1[h^{-1}(i)], \Gamma_2[h^{-2}(i)], \ldots \Gamma_r[h^{-r}(i)]$ *has at most* z *linearly active cells, then* (Γ_0, Γ_r) *yields a ZC linear hull for* r *rounds of* E.

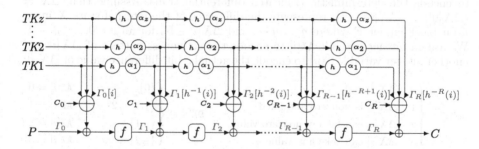

Fig. 2. The STK construction of the TWEAKEY framework.

Ankele et al. used Theorem 2 to manually find ZC linear hulls for several twekable block ciphers including SKINNY, QARMA [2], and MANTIS[3]. Later, Hadipour et al. [22] proposed a bitwise automatic method based on SAT to search for ZC linear hulls of tweakable block ciphers. This automatic method was then reused by Niu et al. [34] to revisit the ZC linear hulls of SKINNY-64-{128,192}.

2.4 Constraint Satisfaction and Constraint Optimization Problems

A constraint satisfaction problem (CSP) is a mathematical problem including a set of constraints over a set of variables that should be satisfied. More formally, a CSP is a triple $(\mathcal{X}, \mathcal{D}, \mathcal{C})$, where $\mathcal{X} = \{X_0, X_1, \ldots, X_{n-1}\}$ is a set of variables;

$\mathcal{D} = \{\mathcal{D}_0, \mathcal{D}_1, \ldots, \mathcal{D}_{n-1}\}$ is the set of domains such that $X_i \in \mathcal{D}_i$, $0 \le i \le n-1$; and $\mathcal{C} = \{\mathcal{C}_0, \mathcal{C}_1, \ldots, \mathcal{C}_{n-1}\}$ is a set of constraints. Each constraint $\mathcal{C}_j \in \mathcal{C}$ is a tuple $(\mathcal{S}_j, \mathcal{R}_j)$, where $\mathcal{S}_j = \{X_{i_0}, \ldots, X_{i_{k-1}}\} \subseteq \mathcal{X}$ and $\mathcal{R}_j$ is a relation on the corresponding domains, i.e., $\mathcal{R}_j \subseteq \mathcal{D}_{i_0} \times \cdots \times \mathcal{D}_{i_{k-1}}$.

Any value assignment of the variables satisfying all constraints of a CSP problem is a feasible solution. The constraint optimization problem extends the CSP problem by including an objective function to be minimized (or maximized). Searching for the solution of a CSP or COP problem is referred to as constraint programming (CP), and the solvers performing the search are called CP solvers.

In this paper, we use MiniZinc [33] to model and solve the CSP and COP problems over integer and real numbers. MiniZinc allows modeling the CSP and COP problems in a high-level and solver-independent way. It compiles the model into FlatZinc, a standard language supported by a wide range of CP solvers. For CSP/COP problems over integer numbers, we use Or-Tools [35], and for CSP/COP problems over real numbers, we employ Gurobi [17] as the solver.

2.5 Encoding Deterministic Truncated Trails

Here, we recall the method proposed in [42] to encode deterministic truncated differential trails. Thanks to the duality relation between differential and linear analysis, one can adjust this method for deterministic truncated linear trails; thus, we omit the details for the linear trails. We define two types of variables to encode the deterministic truncated differential trails. Assume that $\Delta X = (\Delta X[0], \ldots, \Delta X[m-1])$ represents the difference of the internal state X in an n-bit block cipher E, where $n = m \cdot c$, and $\Delta X[i] \in \mathbb{F}_2^c$ for all $i = 0, \ldots, m-1$. We use an integer variable $\mathtt{AX}[i]$ to encode the activeness pattern of $\Delta X[i]$ and another integer variable $\mathtt{DX}[i]$ to encode the actual c-bit difference value of $\Delta X[i]$:

$$\mathtt{AX}[i] = \begin{cases} 0 & \Delta X[i] = 0 \\ 1 & \Delta X[i] \text{ is nonzero and fixed} \\ 2 & \Delta X[i] \text{ can be any nonzero value} \\ 3 & \Delta X[i] \text{ can take any value} \end{cases} \qquad \mathtt{DX}[i] \in \begin{cases} \{0\} & \mathtt{AX}[i] = 0 \\ \{1, \ldots, 2^c - 1\} & \mathtt{AX}[i] = 1 \\ \{-1\} & \mathtt{AX}[i] = 2 \\ \{-2\} & \mathtt{AX}[i] = 3 \end{cases}$$

Then, we link $\mathtt{AX}[i]$ and $\mathtt{DX}[i]$ for all $i = 0, \ldots, m-1$ as follows:

$$Link(\mathtt{AX}[i], \mathtt{DX}[i]) := \begin{cases} \textit{if } \mathtt{AX}[i] = 0 \textit{ then } \mathtt{DX}[i] = 0 \\ \textit{elseif } \mathtt{AX}[i] = 1 \textit{ then } \mathtt{DX}[i] > 0 \\ \textit{elseif } \mathtt{AX}[i] = 2 \textit{ then } \mathtt{DX}[i] = -1 \\ \textit{else } \mathtt{DX}[i] = -2 \textit{ endif} \end{cases}$$

MiniZinc supports conditional expression '$\textit{if-then-else-endif}$', so we do not need to convert to integer inequalities. Next, we briefly explain the propagation rules of deterministic truncated differential trails.

Proposition 1 (Branching). *For $F : \mathbb{F}_2^c \to \mathbb{F}_2^{2c}$, $F(X) = (Y, Z)$ where $Z = Y = X$, the valid transitions for deterministic truncated differential trails satisfy*

$$Branch(AX, DX, AY, DY, AZ, DZ) := (AZ = AX \wedge DZ = DX \wedge AY = AX \wedge DY = DX)$$

Proposition 2 (XOR). *For $F : \mathbb{F}_2^{2c} \to \mathbb{F}_2^c$, $F(X,Y) = Z$ where $Z = X \oplus Y$, the valid transitions for deterministic truncated differential trails satisfy*

$$
XOR(AX, DX, AY, DY, AZ, DZ) := \begin{cases} \textit{if } AX + AY > 2 \textit{ then } AZ = 3 \wedge DZ = -2 \\ \textit{elseif } AX + AY = 1 \textit{ then } AZ = 1 \wedge DZ = DX + DY \\ \textit{elseif } AX = AY = 0 \textit{ then } AZ = 0 \wedge DZ = 0 \\ \textit{elseif } DX + DY < 0 \textit{ then } AZ = 2 \wedge DZ = -1 \\ \textit{elseif } DX = DY \textit{ then } AZ = 0 \wedge DZ = 0 \\ \textit{else } AZ = 1 \wedge DZ = DX \oplus DY \textit{ endif} \end{cases}
$$

Proposition 3 (S-box). *Assume that $S : \mathbb{F}_2^c \to \mathbb{F}_2^c$ is a c-bit S-box and $Y = S(X)$. The valid transitions for deterministic truncated differential trails satisfy*

$$
S\text{-}box(AX, AY) := (AY \neq 1 \ \wedge \ AX + AY \in \{0, 3, 4, 6\} \ \wedge \ AY \geq AX \ \wedge \ AY - AX \leq 1)
$$

For encoding the MDS matrices, see [21, B]. To encode non-MDS matrices, such as the matrix employed in **SKINNY**, as described in [21, D], we can use the rules of XOR and branching to encode the propagation.

3   Modeling the Distinguishers

Although the key recovery of ZC and ID attacks are different, the construction of ZC and ID distinguishers relies on the same approach, which is the miss-in-the-middle technique [5,6]. The idea is to find two differences (linear masks) that propagate halfway through the cipher forward and backward with certainty but contradict each other in the middle. The incompatibility between these propagations results in an impossible differential (resp. unbiased linear hull).

Suppose we are looking for an ID or ZC distinguisher for E_D, which represents r_D rounds of a block cipher E. Moreover, we assume that the block size of E is n bits, where $n = m \cdot c$ with c being the cell size and m being the number of cells. We convert the miss-in-the-middle technique to a CSP problem to automatically find ID and ZC distinguishers. We first divide E_D into two parts, as illustrated in Fig. 3: An upper part E_U covering r_U rounds and a lower part E_L of r_L rounds. Hereafter, we refer to the trails discovered for E_U (E_L) as the upper (lower) trail. We denote the internal state of E_U (E_L) after r rounds by XU_r (XL_r). The state XU_{r_U} (or XL_0) at the intersection of E_U and E_L is called the meeting point.

Let $\texttt{AXU}_r$ and $\texttt{AXL}_r$ denote the activeness pattern of the state variables XU_r and XL_r, as shown in Fig. 3. Let $\texttt{DXU}_r$ and $\texttt{DXL}_r$ denote the actual difference values in round r of E_U and E_L. We encode the deterministic truncated differential trail propagation through E_U and E_L in opposite directions as two independent CSP problems using the rules described in Sect. 2.5. We exclude trivial solutions by adding the constraints $\sum_{i=0}^{m-1} \texttt{AXU}_0[i] \neq 0$ and $\sum_{i=0}^{m-1} \texttt{AXL}_{r_L} \neq 0$. Let $CSP_U(\texttt{AXU}_0, \texttt{DXU}_0, \dots, \texttt{AXU}_{r_U}, \texttt{DXU}_{r_U})$ be the model for propagation of deterministic truncated trails over E_U and $CSP_L(\texttt{AXL}_0, \texttt{DXL}_0, \dots, \texttt{AXL}_{r_L}, \texttt{DXL}_{r_L})$ for E_L^{-1}.

The last internal state in E_U and the first internal state of E_L overlap at the meeting point as they correspond to the same internals state. We define some additional constraints to ensure the incompatibility between the deterministic differential trails of E_U and E_L at the position of the meeting point:

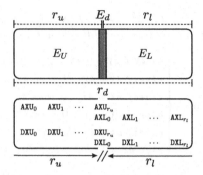

Fig. 3. Modeling the miss-in-the-middle technique as a CSP problem

$CSP_M(\text{AXU}_{r_L}, \text{DXU}_{r_L}, \text{AXL}_0, \text{DXL}_0) :=$

$$\bigvee_{i=0}^{m-1} \left(\begin{array}{l} (\text{AXU}_{r_U}[i] + \text{AXL}_0[i] > 0) \wedge \\ (\text{AXU}_{r_U}[i] + \text{AXL}_0[i] < 3) \wedge \\ \text{AXU}_{r_U}[i] \neq \text{AXL}_0[i] \end{array} \right) \vee \bigvee_{i=0}^{m-1} \left(\begin{array}{l} \text{AXU}_{r_U}[i] = 1 \wedge \\ \text{AXL}_0[i] = 1 \wedge \\ \text{DXU}_{r_U}[i] \neq \text{DXL}_0[i] \end{array} \right) = \textit{True} \qquad (6)$$

The constraints included in CSP_M guarantee the incompatibility between the upper and lower deterministic trails in at least one cell at the meeting point. Lastly, we define $CSP_D := CSP_U \wedge CSP_L \wedge CSP_M$, which is the union of all three CSPs. As a result, any feasible solution of CSP_D corresponds to an impossible differential. We can follow the same approach to find ZC distinguishers.

Although we encode the deterministic truncated trails in the same way as [42], our method to search for distinguishers has some important differences. Sun et al. [42] solves CSP_U and CSP_L separately through a loop where the activeness pattern of a cell at the meeting point is fixed in each iteration. The main advantage of our model is that any solutions of CSP_D corresponds to an ID (or ZC) distinguisher. In addition, we do not constrain the value of our model at the input/output or at meeting point. These key feature enables us to extend our model for the key recovery and build a unified COP for finding the nearly optimum ID and ZC attacks in the next sections.

We showed how to encode and detect the contradiction in the meeting point. However, the contradiction may occur in other positions, such as in the tweakey schedule (see Theorem 2), leading to longer distinguishers. Next, we show how to generalize this approach to detect the contradiction in the tweakey schedule while searching for ZC-integral distinguishers according to Theorem 2.

Consider a block cipher E that follows the STK construction with z parallel independent paths in the tweakey schedule. Assume that E applies the permutation h to shuffle the position of cells in each path of tweakey schedule. Let $STK_r[i]$ be the ith cell of subtweakey after r rounds. For all $i = 0, \ldots, m-1$, we define the integer variable $\text{ASTK}_r[i] \in \{0, 1, 2, 3\}$, to indicate the activeness pattern of $STK_r[i]$. Then we define the following constraints to ensure that there is a contradiction in the tweakey schedule and the condition of Theorem 2 holds:

$$CSP_{TK}(\text{ASTK}_0, \ldots, \text{ASTK}_{r_D-1}) :=$$

$$\bigvee_{i=0}^{m-1} \left(\left(\left(\sum_{r=0}^{r_D-1} \textit{bool2int}\left(\text{ASTK}_r[h^{-r}(i)] \neq 0\right) \leq z \right) \wedge \bigvee_{r=0}^{r_D-1} \left(\text{ASTK}_r[h^{-r}(i)] = 1\right) \right) \vee \left(\bigwedge_{r=0}^{r_D-1} \text{ASTK}_r[h^{-r}(i)] = 0 \right) \right) \tag{7}$$

Equation 7 guarantees that at least one path of the tweakey schedule has at most z active cells, or it is totally inactive. Finally, we create the CSP problem $CSP_D :=$ $CSP_U \wedge CSP_L \wedge CSP_{TK}$ to find ZC distinguishers of tweakable block ciphers taking the tweakey schedule into account. According to Eq. 7, if the sequence of linear masks in the involved tweakey lane has z non-zero values, i.e., $\{1, 2\}$, then at least one of the taken non-zero values should be 1. We also practically verified on reduced-round examples that this condition is indeed necessary to obtain valid ZC-integral distinguishers. This essential condition is ignored in [48]; unfortunately, their claimed distinguishers (and hence their attacks) are invalid. We contacted the authors of [48], and they confirmed our claim.

In our model for distinguisher, we assume that the round keys are independent. Thus, our method regards even those differential or linear propagations over multiple rounds that cannot occur due to the global dependency between the round keys as possible propagations. We also consider the S-box as a black box and do not exploit its internal structure. As a result, regardless of the (twea)key schedule and the choice of S-box, the ID/ZC/Integral distinguishers discovered by our method are always valid.

Before extending our models for key recovery, we first show some of the interesting features of our new model for distinguishers. We can optimize the desired property by adding an objective function to our CSP models for finding distinguishers. According to Theorem 1, maximizing the number of active cells at the input of the ZC linear hull is equivalent to minimizing the data complexity of the corresponding integral distinguisher. Therefore, we maximize the integer addition of the activeness pattern at the input of the ZC-Integral distinguisher. Thanks to this feature, we discovered many practical integral distinguishers for reduced-round Deoxys-BC, SKINNY, SKINNYe-v2, SKINNYee, and CRAFT. Table 3 briefly describes the specification of our integral distinguishers for five ciphers. We note that finding integral distinguishers with minimum data complexity is a challenging task using division property [15,44] or monomial prediction [19,23], especially when the block cipher employs large S-boxes. However, our tool can find integral distinguishers with low data complexity by only one iteration that takes a few seconds on a regular laptop. For a more detailed comparison between our method and monomial prediction or division property, see [21, M].

4   Modeling the Key Recovery for Impossible Differentials

In this section, we present a generic framework which receives four integer numbers (r_B, r_U, r_L, r_F) specifying the lengths of each part in Fig. 1, and outputs an optimized full ID attack for $r = r_B + r_U + r_L + r_F$ rounds of the targeted block cipher. To this end, we extend the CSP model for ID distinguishers in Sect. 3 to make a unified COP model for finding an optimized full ID attack taking all critical parameters affecting the final complexity into account.

Table 3. Summary of integral distinguishers for some ciphers, cell size $c \in \{4,8\}$.

Cipher	#Rounds	Data complexity	Ref
SKINNY-n-n	10/11/12	$\mathbf{2^{5\cdot c}/2^{8\cdot c}/2^{13\cdot c}}$	[21, J]
SKINNY-n-$2n$	12/13/14	$\mathbf{2^{6\cdot c}/2^{9\cdot c}/2^{14\cdot c}}$	[21, J]
SKINNY-n-$3n$	14/15/16	$\mathbf{2^{7\cdot c}/2^{10\cdot c}/2^{15\cdot c}}$	[21, J]
SKINNYe-v2/SKINNYee	16/17/18	$\mathbf{2^{32}/2^{44}/2^{64}}$	[21, J]
CRAFT	12/13/14/15	$\mathbf{2^{28}/2^{44}/2^{56}/2^{64}}$	[21, K.4]
Deoxys-BC-256	5/6	$\mathbf{2^{24}/2^{56}}$	[21, L]
Deoxys-BC-384	6/7	$\mathbf{2^{32}/2^{64}}$	[21, L]

Before discussing our framework, we first reformulate the complexity analysis of the ID attack to make it compatible with our COP model. Suppose that the block size is n bits and the key size is k bits. Let N be the number of pairs generated in the pair generation phase, and P represents the probability that a wrong key survives the guess-and-filter step. According to Sect. 2.1, $P = (1-2^{-(c_B+c_F)})^N$. Let g be the number of key bits we can retrieve through the guess-and-filter step, i.e., $P = 2^{-g}$. Since $P < \frac{1}{2}$, we have $1 < g \leq |k_B \cup k_F|$. Assuming that $(1 - 2^{-(c_B+c_F)})^N \approx e^{-N\cdot 2^{-(c_B+c_F)}}$, we have $N = 2^{c_B+c_F+\log_2(g)-0.53}$. Moreover, suppose that $LG(g) = \log_2(g) - 0.53$. Therefore, we can reformulate the complexity analysis of the ID attack as follows:

$$T_0 = \max \left\{ \begin{array}{c} \min_{\Delta \in \{\Delta_B, \Delta_F\}} \{2^{\frac{c_B+c_F+n+1-|\Delta|+LG(g)}{2}}\}, \\ 2^{c_B+c_F+n+1-|\Delta_B|-|\Delta_F|+LG(g)} \end{array} \right\}, \ T_0 < 2^n,$$

$$T_1 = 2^{c_B+c_F+LG(g)}, \ T_2 = 2^{|k_B \cup k_F|+LG(g)}, \ T_3 = 2^{k-g}, \qquad (8)$$

$$T_{\text{tot}} = (T_0 + (T_1 + T_2)\,C_{E'} + T_3)\,C_E, \ T_{\text{tot}} < 2^k,$$

$$M_{\text{tot}} = \min\{2^{c_B+c_F+LG(g)}, 2^{|k_B \cup k_F|}\}, \ M_{\text{tot}} < 2^k.$$

When searching for an optimal full ID attack, we aim to minimize the total time complexity while keeping the memory and data complexities under the threshold values. As can be seen in Eq. 8, $c_B, c_F, |\Delta_B|, |\Delta_F|$, and $|k_B \cup k_F|$, are the critical parameters which directly affect the final complexity of the ID attack. To determine $(c_B, |\Delta_B|)$, we need to model the propagation of truncated differential trails through E_B, taking the probability of all differential cancellations into account. To determine k_B, we need to detect the state cells whose difference or data values are needed through the partial encryption over E_B. The same applies for partial decryption over E_F^{-1} to determine $c_F, |\Delta_F|, k_F$. Moreover, to determine the actual size of $k_B \cup k_F$, we should take the (twea)key schedule and key-bridging technique into account.

4.1   Overview of the COP Model

Our model includes several components:

- **Model the distinguisher** as in Sect. 3. Unlike the previous methods, our model imposes no constraints on the input/output of the distinguisher.

- **Model the difference propagation in outer parts** for truncated trails $\Delta_{\mathrm{B}} \xleftarrow{E_{\mathrm{B}}^{-1}}$ Δ_{U} and $\Delta_{\mathrm{L}} \xrightarrow{E_{\mathrm{F}}} \Delta_{\mathrm{F}}$ with probability one. Unlike our model for the distinguisher part, where we use integer variables with domain $\{0,\ldots,3\}$, here, we only use binary variables to encode active/inactive cells. We also model the number of filters c_{B} and c_{F} using new binary variables and constraints to encode the probability of $\Delta_{\mathrm{B}} \xrightarrow{E_{\mathrm{B}}} \Delta_{\mathrm{U}}$ and $\Delta_{\mathrm{L}} \xleftarrow{E_{\mathrm{F}}^{-1}} \Delta_{\mathrm{F}}$.

- **Model the guess-and-determine in outer parts.** In this component, we model the determination relationships over E_{B} and E_{F} to detect the state cells whose difference or data values must be known for verifying the differences Δ_{U}, and Δ_{L}. Moreover, we model the relation between round (twea)keys and the internal state to detect the (twea)key cells whose values should be guessed during the determination of data values over E_{B}, and E_{F}.

- **Model the key bridging.** In this component, we model the (twea)key schedule to determine the number of involved sub-(twea)keys in the key recovery. For this, we can use the general CP-based model for key-bridging proposed by Hadipour and Eichlseder in [18], or cipher-dedicated models.

- **Model the complexity formulas.** In this component, we model the complexity formulas in Eq. 8 with the following constraints:

$$
\begin{aligned}
&D[0] := min_{\Delta \in \{\Delta_{\mathrm{B}}, \Delta_{\mathrm{F}}\}} \{ \tfrac{1}{2}(c_{\mathrm{B}} + c_{\mathrm{F}} + n + 1 - |\Delta| + LG(g)) \}, \\
&D[1] := c_{\mathrm{B}} + c_{\mathrm{F}} + n + 1 - |\Delta_{\mathrm{B}}| - |\Delta_{\mathrm{F}}| + LG(g), \\
&T[0] := max\{D[0], D[1]\}, \quad T[0] < n, \\
&T[1] := c_{\mathrm{B}} + c_{\mathrm{F}} + LG(g), \quad T[2] := |k_{\mathrm{B}} \cup k_{\mathrm{F}}| + LG(g), \quad T[3] := k - g, \\
&T := max\{T[0], T[1], T[2], T[3]\}, \quad T < k.
\end{aligned} \tag{9}
$$

Lastly, we set the objective function to `Minimize T`.

All variables in our model are binary or integer variables with a limited domain except for D and $T[i]$ for $i \in \{0,1,2,3\}$ in Eq. 9, which are real numbers. MiniZinc and many MILP solvers such as Gurobi support `max`, and `min` operators. We also precompute the values of $LG(g)$ with 3 floating point precision for all $g \in \{2,\ldots,k\}$, and use the `table` feature of MiniZinc to model $LG(g)$. As a result, our COP model considers all the critical parameters of the ID attacks. We recall that the only inputs of our tool are four integer numbers to specify the lengths of $E_{\mathrm{B}}, E_{\mathrm{U}}, E_{\mathrm{L}}$, and E_{F}. So, one can try different lengths for these four parts to find a nearly optimal attack. We can also modify the objective function of our model to minimize the data or memory complexities where time or any other parameter is constrained. One can extend this single-tweakey model for the related-tweakey setting, as we will show next.

4.2   Detailed Model for **SKINNY**

Next, we show in more detail how to perform each step. To this end, we build the COP model for finding full related-tweakey ID attacks on **SKINNY** as an example. We choose the largest variant of **SKINNY**, i.e., **SKINNY**-n-$3n$ with cell size $c \in \{4,8\}$ to explain our model (see [21, C] for the cipher specification). In what follows, given four integer numbers $r_{\mathrm{B}}, r_{\mathrm{U}}, r_{\mathrm{L}}, r_{\mathrm{F}}$, we model the full ID attack on $r = r_{\mathrm{B}} + r_{\mathrm{U}} + r_{\mathrm{L}} + r_{\mathrm{F}}$ rounds of **SKINNY**, where $r_{\mathrm{D}} = r_{\mathrm{U}} + r_{\mathrm{L}}$ is the length of the distinguisher and r_{B}, and r_{F} are the lengths of extended parts in backward and forward directions, respectively.

Model the Distinguisher. We first model the difference propagation through the tweakey schedule of SKINNY. For the tweakey schedule of SKINNY, we can either use the word-wise model proposed in [3] or a bit-wise model (see Algorithm 1). Here, we explain the bit-wise model. The tweakey path of $TK1$ only shuffles the position of tweakey cells in each round. Thus, for tweakey path $TK1$, we only define the integer variable DTK1$[i]$ to encode the c-bit difference in the ith cell of $TK1$. For tweakey path TKm, where $m \in \{2, 3\}$, we define the integer variables DTK$m_r[i]$ to encode the c-bit difference value in the ith cell of TKm_r, where $0 \leq i \leq 15$. We also define the integer variables ASTK$_r[i]$ and DSTK$_r[i]$ to encode the activeness pattern as well as the c-bit difference value in the ith cell of STK_r. Our CSP model for the tweakey schedule of SKINNY is a bit-wise model. We use the `table` feature of MiniZinc to encode the LFSRs. To this end, we first precompute the LFSR as a lookup table and then constrain the variables at the input/output of LFSR to satisfy the precomputed lookup table. This approach is applicable for encoding any function that can be represented as an integer lookup table, such as DDT/LAT of S-boxes. We tested word-wise and bit-wise models and found the word-wise model more efficient.

Algorithm 1: CSP model for the tweakey schedule of SKINNY

Input: Four integer numbers $(r_\text{B}, r_\text{U}, r_\text{L}, r_\text{F})$
Output: CSP_{DTK}

1 $R \leftarrow r_\text{B} + r_\text{U} + r_\text{L} + r_\text{F} - 1$;
2 Declare an empty CSP model $\mathcal{M}$;
3 $\mathcal{M}.\text{var} \leftarrow \{\text{DTK1}[i] \in \{0, \ldots, 2^c - 1\} : 0 \leq i \leq 15\}$;
4 $\mathcal{M}.\text{var} \leftarrow \{\text{DTK2}_r[i] \in \{0, \ldots, 2^c - 1\} : 0 \leq r \leq R, \, 0 \leq i \leq 15\}$;
5 $\mathcal{M}.\text{var} \leftarrow \{\text{DTK3}_r[i] \in \{0, \ldots, 2^c - 1\} : 0 \leq r \leq R, \, 0 \leq i \leq 15\}$;
6 $\mathcal{M}.\text{var} \leftarrow \{\text{ASTK}_r[i] \in \{0, 1\} : 0 \leq r \leq R, \, 0 \leq i \leq 7\}$;
7 $\mathcal{M}.\text{var} \leftarrow \{\text{DSTK}_r[i] \in \{0, \ldots, 2^c - 1\} : 0 \leq r \leq R, \, 0 \leq i \leq 7\}$;
8 **for** $r = 0, \ldots, R; \; i = 0, \ldots, 7$ **do**
9 $\quad \lfloor \; \mathcal{M}.\text{con} \leftarrow Link(\text{ASTK}_r[i], \text{DSTK}_r[i])$;

10 **for** $r = 1, \ldots, R; \; i = 0, \ldots 15$ **do**
11 $\quad$ **if** $i \leq 7$ **then**
12 $\quad\quad \lfloor \; \mathcal{M}.\text{con} \leftarrow table([\text{DTK2}_{r-1}[h(i)], \text{DTK2}_r[i]], lfsr2)$;
13 $\quad\quad \lfloor \; \mathcal{M}.\text{con} \leftarrow table([\text{DTK3}_{r-1}[h(i)], \text{DTK3}_r[i]], lfsr3)$;
14 $\quad$ **else**
15 $\quad\quad \lfloor \; \mathcal{M}.\text{con} \leftarrow \text{DTK2}_r[i] = \text{DTK2}_{r-1}[h(i)]$;
16 $\quad\quad \lfloor \; \mathcal{M}.\text{con} \leftarrow \text{DTK3}_r[i] = \text{DTK3}_{r-1}[h(i)]$;

17 **for** $r = 0, \ldots, R; \; i = 0, \ldots 7$ **do**
18 $\quad \lfloor \; \mathcal{M}.\text{con} \leftarrow \text{DSTK}_r[i] = \text{DTK1}[h^r(i)] \oplus \text{DTK2}_r[i] \oplus \text{DTK3}_r[i]$;

19 **return** $\mathcal{M}$;

In the data path of SKINNY, SubCells, AddRoundTweakey, and MixColumns can change the activeness pattern of the state while propagating the deterministic differences. Thus, for the internal state before and after these basic operations, we define two types of variables to encode the activeness pattern and difference value in each state cell. Next, as described in Algorithm 2 and [21, algorithm 6], we build CSP_U

and CSP_L. We also build the CSP_M according to Eq. 6. The combined CSP model is $CSP_D := CSP_U \land CSP_L \land CSP_M \land CSP_{DTK}$. Hence, any feasible solution of CSP_D corresponds to a related-tweakey ID distinguisher for SKINNY-n-$3n$. By setting DTK3$_0$ in Algorithm 1 to zero, we can find related-tweakey ID distinguishers for SKINNY-n-$2n$. We can also set DTK1, DTK2$_0$, DTK3$_0$ in Algorithm 1 to zero to find single-tweakey ID distinguishers of SKINNY.

Algorithm 2: CSP_U for upper trail in distinguisher of SKINNY

Input: CSP_{DTK}.var and the integer numbers r_B, r_U
Output: CSP_U

1 $r_{off} \leftarrow r_B$;
2 Declare an empty CSP model $\mathcal{M}$;
3 $\mathcal{M}$.var $\leftarrow CSP_{DTK}$.var;
4 $\mathcal{M}$.var $\leftarrow \{\text{AXU}_r[i] \in \{0,1,2,3\} : 0 \le r \le r_U, 0 \le i \le 15\}$;
5 $\mathcal{M}$.var $\leftarrow \{\text{DXU}_r[i] \in \{-2, \ldots, 2^c - 1\} : 0 \le r \le r_U, 0 \le i \le 15\}$;
6 $\mathcal{M}$.var $\leftarrow \{\text{AYU}_r[i] \in \{0,1,2,3\} : 0 \le r \le r_U, 0 \le i \le 15\}$;
7 $\mathcal{M}$.var $\leftarrow \{\text{DYU}_r[i] \in \{-2, \ldots, 2^c - 1\} : 0 \le r \le r_U, 0 \le i \le 15\}$;
8 $\mathcal{M}$.var $\leftarrow \{\text{AZU}_r[i] \in \{0,1,2,3\} : 0 \le r \le r_U, 0 \le i \le 15\}$;
9 $\mathcal{M}$.var $\leftarrow \{\text{DZU}_r[i] \in \{-2, \ldots, 2^c - 1\} : 0 \le r \le r_U, 0 \le i \le 15\}$;
10 $\mathcal{M}$.con $\leftarrow \sum_{i=0}^{15} \text{AXU}_0[i] + \sum_{i=0}^{15} \text{DTK1}[i] + \sum_{i=0}^{15} \text{DTK2}_0 + \sum_{i=0}^{15} \text{DTK3}_0[i] \ge 1$;
11 **for** $r = 0, \ldots, r_U - 1$, $i = 0, \ldots, 15$ **do**
12 $\mathcal{M}$.con $\leftarrow Link(\text{AXU}_r[i],\text{DXU}_r[i]) \land Link(\text{AYU}_r[i],\text{DYU}_r[i]) \land Link(\text{AZU}_r[i],\text{DZU}_r[i])$;

13 **for** $r = 0, \ldots, r_U - 1$, $i = 0, \ldots, 15$ **do**
14 $\mathcal{M}$.con $\leftarrow S\text{-}box(\text{AXU}_r[i], \text{AYU}_r[i])$;

15 **for** $r = 0, \ldots, r_U - 1$, $i = 0, \ldots, 7$ **do**
16 $\mathcal{M}$.con $\leftarrow XOR(\text{AXU}_r[i], \text{DXU}_r[i], \text{ASTK}_{r_{off}+r}[i], \text{DSTK}_{r_{off}+r}[i], \text{AZU}_r[i], \text{DZU}_r[i])$;
17 $\mathcal{M}$.con $\leftarrow (\text{AZU}_r[i+8] = \text{AYU}_r[i+8]) \land (\text{DZU}_r[i+8] = \text{DYU}_r[i+8])$;

18 **for** $r = 0, \ldots, r_U - 1$, $i = 0, \ldots, 3$ **do**
19 $I_1 \leftarrow [\text{AZU}_r[P[i]], \text{AZU}_r[P[i+4]], \text{AZU}_r[P[i+8]], \text{AZU}_r[P[i+12]]]$;
20 $I_2 \leftarrow [\text{DZU}_r[P[i]], \text{DZU}_r[P[i+4]], \text{DZU}_r[P[i+8]], \text{DZU}_r[P[i+12]]]$;
21 $O_1 \leftarrow [\text{AXU}_{r+1}[i], \text{AXU}_{r+1}[i+4], \text{AXU}_{r+1}[i+8], \text{AXU}_{r+1}[i+12]]$;
22 $O_2 \leftarrow [\text{DXU}_{r+1}[i], \text{DXU}_{r+1}[i+4], \text{DXU}_{r+1}[i+8], \text{DXU}_{r+1}[i+12]]$;
23 $\mathcal{M}$.con $\leftarrow Mdiff(I_1, I_2, O_1, O_2)$;

24 **return** $\mathcal{M}$;

The first operation in the round function of SKINNY is SubCells. However, we can consider the first SubCells layer as a part of E_B and start the distinguisher after it. This way, our model takes advantage of the differential cancellation over the AddRoundTweakey and MixColumns layers to derive longer distinguishers. It happens if the input differences in the internal state (or tweakey paths) are fixed and can cancel out each other through AddRoundTweakey or MixColumns. In this case, we skip the constraints in line 14 of Algorithm 2 for the first round, $r = 0$.

Model the Difference Propagation in Outer Parts. To model the deterministic difference propagations $\Delta_B \xleftarrow{E_B^{-1}} \Delta_U$, and $\Delta_L \xrightarrow{E_F} \Delta_F$, we define a binary variable for each state cell to indicate whether its difference value is zero. Since the SubCells layer does not change the status of state cells in terms of having zero/nonzero differences, we ignore it in this model.

To model the probability of difference propagations $\Delta_{\mathrm{B}} \xrightarrow{E_{\mathrm{B}}} \Delta_{\mathrm{U}}$, and $\Delta_{\mathrm{L}} \xleftarrow{E_{\mathrm{F}}^{-1}} \Delta_{\mathrm{F}}$, note that there are two types of probabilistic transitions. The first type is differential cancellation through an XOR operation. The second type is any differential transition (truncated $\xrightarrow{S}$ fixed) for S-boxes; this is only considered at the distinguisher's boundary, at the first S-box layer of E_{F} or the last of E_{B}.

Let $Z = X \oplus Y$, where $X, Y, Z \in \mathbb{F}_2^c$. Let $\mathtt{AX}, \mathtt{AY}, \mathtt{AZ} \in \{0,1\}$ indicate whether the difference of X, Y, Z are zero. We define the new constraint XOR_1 to model the difference propagation with probability one through XOR:

$$XOR_1(\mathtt{AX}, \mathtt{AY}, \mathtt{AZ}) := (\mathtt{AZ} \geq \mathtt{AX}) \wedge (\mathtt{AZ} \geq \mathtt{AY}) \wedge (\mathtt{AZ} \leq \mathtt{AX} + \mathtt{AY}) \qquad (10)$$

We define a binary variable $\mathtt{CB}_r[i]$ ($\mathtt{CF}_r[i]$) for each XOR operation in the rth round of E_{B} (resp. E_{F}) to indicate whether there is a difference cancellation over the corresponding XOR, where $0 \leq i \leq 19$. We also define the following constraint to encode the differential cancellation for each XOR operation:

$$XOR_p(\mathtt{AX}, \mathtt{AY}, \mathtt{AZ}, \mathtt{CB}) := if\ (\mathtt{AX} + \mathtt{AY} = 2 \wedge \mathtt{AZ} = 0)\ then\ \mathtt{CB} = 1\ else\ \mathtt{CB} = 0 \qquad (11)$$

Algorithm 3 and [21, algorithm 7] describe our model for difference propagation over E_{B} and E_{F}. We combine CSP_{B}^{dp} and CSP_{F}^{dp} into $CSP_{\mathrm{DP}} := CSP_{\mathrm{B}}^{dp} \wedge CSP_{\mathrm{F}}^{dp}$ to model the difference propagation through the outer parts.

Model the Guess-and-Determine in Outer Parts. We now detect the state cells whose difference or value is needed for the filters in $\Delta_{\mathrm{B}} \to \Delta_{\mathrm{U}}$ and $\Delta_{\mathrm{L}} \leftarrow \Delta_{\mathrm{F}}$.

We first discuss detecting the state cells whose difference values are needed. The difference value in a state cell is needed if the corresponding state cell contributes to a filter, i.e., a differential cancellation. We know that AddRoundTweakey and MixColumns are the only places where a differential cancellation may occur. We thus define the binary variables $\mathtt{KDXB}_r[i]$ and $\mathtt{KDZB}_r[i]$ to indicate whether the difference value of $X_r[i]$ and $Z_r[i]$ over E_b should be known. We recall that the difference cancellation through each XOR over E_b is already encoded by $\mathtt{CB}_r[i]$. If $\mathtt{CB}_r[i] = 1$, then the difference value in the state cells contributing to this differential cancellation is needed. For instance, if $\mathtt{CB}_r[i] = 1$, then $\mathtt{KDZB}_r[P[i+4]] = 1$ and $\mathtt{KDZB}_r[P[i+4]] = 1$, where $0 \leq i \leq 3$ and $0 \leq r \leq r_u - 1$. Besides detecting the new state cells whose difference values are needed in each round, we encode the propagation of this property from the previous rounds, as in lines 14–17 of Algorithm 4. We also define new constraint (line 11) to link the beginning of E_{U} to the end of E_{B}. For E_{F}, we also define new binary variables $\mathtt{KDXF}_r[i]$ and $\mathtt{KDZF}_r[i]$ to indicate whether the difference values of $X_r[i]$ and $Z_r[i]$ are needed. Then, we follow a similar approach to model the determination of difference values.

When modeling the determination of data values, SubCells comes into effect. We explain modeling the determination of data values over S-boxes in E_{B}; a similar model can be used for E_{F}. Suppose that $Y_r[i] = S(X_r[i])$, and the value of ΔX_r is known. If we want to determine the value of $\Delta Y_r[i]$, e.g., to check a filter, we need to know the value of $X_r[i]$. Accordingly, we need the value of $X_r[i]$ if either we want to determine $Y_r[i]$, or we want to determine $\Delta Y_r[i]$. On the other hand, if neither data nor difference values after the S-box is needed, we do not need to know the data value before the S-box. Therefore, we define binary variables $\mathtt{KXB}_r[i]$ and $\mathtt{KYB}_r[i]$ to indicate whether the

---

Algorithm 3: CSP_B^{dp} difference propagation through E_B for SKINNY

Input: $CSP_{DTK}.\text{var}$, $CSP_U.\text{var}$ and the integer number r_B
Output: CSP_B^{dp}

1 Declare an empty CSP model $\mathcal{M}$;
2 $\mathcal{M}.\text{var} \leftarrow CSP_{DTK}.\text{var}$;
3 $\mathcal{M}.\text{var} \leftarrow \{\text{AXB}_r[i] \in \{0,1\} : 0 \leq r \leq r_B,\ 0 \leq i \leq 15\}$;
4 $\mathcal{M}.\text{var} \leftarrow \{\text{AZB}_r[i] \in \{0,1\} : 0 \leq r \leq r_B - 1,\ 0 \leq i \leq 15\}$;
5 $\mathcal{M}.\text{var} \leftarrow \{\text{CB}_r[i] \in \{0,1\} : 0 \leq r \leq r_B - 1,\ 0 \leq i \leq 19\}$;
6 **for** $i = 0,\dots,15$ **do**
7 $\quad\lfloor\ \mathcal{M}.\text{con} \leftarrow if\ \text{AXU}_0[i] \geq 1\ then\ \text{AXB}_{r_B}[i] = 1\ else\ \text{AXB}_{r_B}[i] = 0$;

8 **for** $r = 0,\dots,r_B - 1,\ i = 0,\dots,3$ **do**

9 $\quad\ \mathcal{M}.\text{con} \leftarrow Minvdiff_1\left(\begin{pmatrix} \text{AXB}_{r+1}[i] \\ \text{AXB}_{r+1}[i+4] \\ \text{AXB}_{r+1}[i+8] \\ \text{AXB}_{r+1}[i+12] \end{pmatrix}, \begin{pmatrix} \text{AZB}_r[P[i]] \\ \text{AZB}_r[P[i+4]] \\ \text{AZB}_r[P[i+8]] \\ \text{AZB}_r[P[i+12]] \end{pmatrix}\right)$;

10 $\quad\ \mathcal{M}.\text{con} \leftarrow XOR_p(\text{AZB}_r[P[i+4]], \text{AZB}_r[P[i+8]], \text{AXB}_{r+1}[i+8], \text{CB}_r[i])$;
11 $\quad\ \mathcal{M}.\text{con} \leftarrow XOR_p(\text{AZB}_r[P[i]], \text{AZB}_r[P[i+8]], \text{AXB}_{r+1}[i+12], \text{CB}_r[i+4])$;
12 $\quad\lfloor\ \mathcal{M}.\text{con} \leftarrow XOR_p(\text{AXB}_{r+1}[i+12], \text{AZB}_r[P[i+12]], \text{AXB}_{r+1}[i], \text{CB}_r[i+8])$;

13 **for** $r = 0,\dots,r_B - 1,\ i = 0,\dots,7$ **do**
14 $\quad\ \mathcal{M}.\text{con} \leftarrow XOR_1(\text{AZB}_r[i], \text{ASTK}_r[i], \text{AXB}_r[i])$;
15 $\quad\ \mathcal{M}.\text{con} \leftarrow XOR_p(\text{AXB}_r[i], \text{ASTK}_r[i], \text{AZB}_r[i], \text{CB}_r[i+12])$;
16 $\quad\lfloor\ \mathcal{M}.\text{con} \leftarrow (\text{AXB}_r[i+8] = \text{AZB}_r[i+8])$;

17 **return** $\mathcal{M}$;

---

values of $X_r[i]$ and $Y_r[i]$ are needed. Then, we model the determination flow over the S-boxes as follows:

$$S\text{-}box_{gd}(\text{KXB}_r[i], \text{KYB}_r[i], \text{KDXB}_r[i]) := \begin{cases} (\text{KYB}_r[i] \geq \text{KXB}_r[i]) \wedge (\text{KYB}_r[i] \geq \text{KDXB}_r[i]) \wedge \\ (\text{KYB}_r[i] \leq \text{KXB}_r[i] + \text{KDXB}_r[i]) \end{cases}$$

We also model MixColumns according to [21, Equation 16] when encoding the determination of data values over E_B and E_F.

We now explain how to detect the subtweakey cells that are involved in the determination of data values. Let $\text{IKB}_r[i]$ be a binary variable that indicates whether the ith cell of subtweakey in the rth round of E_B is involved, where $0 \leq r \leq r_B - 1$ and $0 \leq i \leq 15$. One can see that $\text{IKB}_r[i] = 1$ if and only if $i \leq 7$ and $\text{KYB}_r[i] = 1$. Otherwise $\text{IKB}_r[i] = 0$. We define binary variables $\text{IKF}_r[i]$ to encode the involved subtweakey in E_F similarly. Algorithm 4 and [21, algorithm 8] describe our CSP models for the guess-and-determine through E_B and E_F. We refer to $CSP_{GD} := CSP_B^{gd} \wedge CSP_F^{gd}$ as our CSP model for the guess-and-determine through the outer parts.

Model the Key Bridging. Although the subtweakeys involved in E_B and E_F are separated by r_D rounds, they may have some relations due to the tweakey schedule. Guessing the values of some involved key cells may determine the value of others. Key-bridging uses the relations between subwteakeys to reduce the number of actual guessed key variables. We can integrate the generic CSP model for key-bridging over

---

Algorithm 4: CSP_B^{gd} guess-and-determine through E_B for SKINNY

Input: $CSP_U.\text{var}$, CSP_B^{dp} and the integer number r_B
Output: CSP_B^{gd}

1 Declare an empty CSP model $\mathcal{M}$;

2 $\mathcal{M}.\text{var} \leftarrow CSP_U.\text{var} \cup CSP_B^{dp}.\text{var}$;

3 $\mathcal{M}.\text{var} \leftarrow \{\text{KDXB}_r[i] \in \{0,1\} : 0 \leq r \leq r_B, \ 0 \leq i \leq 15\}$;

4 $\mathcal{M}.\text{con} \leftarrow \{\text{KDXB}_r[i] \leq \text{AXB}_r[i] : 0 \leq r \leq r_B, \ 0 \leq i \leq 15\}$;

5 $\mathcal{M}.\text{var} \leftarrow \{\text{KDZB}_r[i] \in \{0,1\} : 0 \leq r \leq r_B - 1, \ 0 \leq i \leq 15\}$;

6 $\mathcal{M}.\text{con} \leftarrow \{\text{KDZB}_r[i] \leq \text{AZB}_r[i] : 0 \leq r \leq r_B - 1, \ 0 \leq i \leq 15\}$;

7 $\mathcal{M}.\text{var} \leftarrow \{\text{KXB}_r[i] \in \{0,1\} : 0 \leq r \leq r_B, \ 0 \leq i \leq 15\}$;

8 $\mathcal{M}.\text{var} \leftarrow \{\text{KYB}_r[i] \in \{0,1\} : 0 \leq r \leq r_B - 1, \ 0 \leq i \leq 15\}$;

9 $\mathcal{M}.\text{var} \leftarrow \{\text{IKB}_r[i] \in \{0,1\} : 0 \leq r \leq r_B - 1, \ 0 \leq i \leq 15\}$;

10 **for** $i = 0, \ldots, 15$ **do**

11 $\quad$ $\mathcal{M}.\text{con} \leftarrow if \ \text{AXU}_0[i] = 1 \ then \ \text{KDXB}_{r_B}[i] = 1 \ else \ \text{KDXB}_{r_B}[i] = 0$;

12 $\quad$ $\mathcal{M}.\text{con} \leftarrow if \ \text{AYU}_0[i] = 1 \ then \ \text{KXB}_{r_B}[i] = 1 \ else \ \text{KXB}_{r_B}[i] = 0$;

13 **for** $r = 0, \ldots, r_B - 1, \ i = 0, \ldots, 3$ **do**

14 $\quad$ $\mathcal{M}.\text{con} \leftarrow if \ \text{KDXB}_{r+1}[i] = 1 \ then \ \begin{pmatrix} \text{KDZB}_r[P[i]] = \text{AZB}_r[P[i]] \wedge \\ \text{KDZB}_r[P[i+8]] = \text{AZB}_r[P[i+8]] \wedge \\ \text{KDZB}_r[P[i+12]] = \text{AZB}_r[P[i+12]] \end{pmatrix}$;

15 $\quad$ $\mathcal{M}.\text{con} \leftarrow if \ \text{KDXB}_{r+1}[i+4] = 1 \ then \ \text{KDZB}_r[P[i]] = \text{AZB}_r[P[i]]$;

16 $\quad$ $\mathcal{M}.\text{con} \leftarrow if \ \text{KDXB}_{r+1}[i+8] = 1 \ then \ \begin{pmatrix} \text{KDZB}_r[P[i+4]] = \text{AZB}_r[P[i+4]] \wedge \\ \text{KDZB}_r[P[i+8]] = \text{AZB}_r[P[i+8]] \end{pmatrix}$;

17 $\quad$ $\mathcal{M}.\text{con} \leftarrow if \ \text{KDXB}_{r+1}[i+12] = 1 \ then \ \begin{pmatrix} \text{KDZB}_r[P[i]] = \text{AZB}_r[P[i]] \wedge \\ \text{KDZB}_r[P[i+8]] = \text{AZB}_r[P[i+8]] \end{pmatrix}$;

18 $\quad$ $\mathcal{M}.\text{con} \leftarrow if \ \text{CB}_r[i] = 1 \ then \ (\text{KDZB}_r[P[i+4]] = 1 \wedge \text{KDZB}_r[P[i+8]] = 1)$;

19 $\quad$ $\mathcal{M}.\text{con} \leftarrow if \ \text{CB}_r[i+4] = 1 \ then \ (\text{KDZB}_r[P[i]] = 1 \wedge \text{KDZB}_r[P[i+8]] = 1)$;

20 $\quad$ $\mathcal{M}.\text{con} \leftarrow if \ \text{CB}_r[i+8] = 1 \ then \ \begin{pmatrix} \text{KDZB}_r[P[i]] = \text{AZB}_r[P[i]] \wedge \\ \text{KDZB}_r[P[i+8]] = \text{AZB}_r[P[i+8]] \wedge \\ \text{KDZB}_r[P[i+12]] = 1 \end{pmatrix}$;

21 $\quad$ $\mathcal{M}.\text{con} \leftarrow Minvdata \left(\begin{pmatrix} \text{KXB}_{r+1}[i] \\ \text{KXB}_{r+1}[i+4] \\ \text{KXB}_{r+1}[i+8] \\ \text{KXB}_{r+1}[i+12] \end{pmatrix}, \begin{pmatrix} \text{KYB}_r[P[i]] \\ \text{KYB}_r[P[i+4]] \\ \text{KYB}_r[P[i+8]] \\ \text{KYB}_r[P[i+12]] \end{pmatrix} \right)$;

22 **for** $r = 0, \ldots, r_B - 1, \ i = 0, \ldots, 7$ **do**

23 $\quad$ $\mathcal{M}.\text{con} \leftarrow \text{KDXB}_r[i] \geq \text{KDZB}_r[i]$;

24 $\quad$ $\mathcal{M}.\text{con} \leftarrow \text{KDXB}_r[i+8] = \text{KDZB}_r[i+8]$;

25 $\quad$ $\mathcal{M}.\text{con} \leftarrow if \ \text{CB}_r[i+12] = 1 \ then \ \text{KDXB}_r[i] = 1$;

26 $\quad$ $\mathcal{M}.\text{con} \leftarrow (\text{IKB}_r[i] = \text{KYB}_r[i] \wedge \text{IKB}_r[i+8] = 0)$;

27 **for** $r = 0, \ldots, r_B - 1, \ i = 0, \ldots, 15$ **do**

28 $\quad$ $\mathcal{M}.\text{con} \leftarrow S\text{-}box_{gd}(\text{KYB}_r[i], \text{KXB}_r[i], \text{KDXB}_r[i])$;

29 **return** $\mathcal{M}$;

arbitrary tweakey schedules introduced in [18] into our model. However, the tweakey schedule of SKINNY is linear, and we provide a more straightforward method to model the key-bridging of SKINNY. We explain our model for SKINNY-n-$3n$; it can easily be adapted for the smaller variants.

For the ith cell of subtweakey after r rounds, we have $STK_r[i] = TK1[h^r(i)] \oplus LFSR_2^r(TK1[h^r(i)]) \oplus LFSR_3^r(TK3[h^r(i)])$. Accordingly, knowing $STK_r[h^{-r}(i)]$ in 3 rounds yields 3 independent equations in variables $TK1[i]$, $TK2[i]$, $TK3[i]$, which uniquely determine the master tweakey cells $TK1[i]$, $TK2[i]$, and $TK3[i]$. Hence, we do not need to guess $STK_r[h^{-r}(i)]$ for more than 3 different rs. To take this fact into account, we first define new integer variables $\text{IK} \in \{0, \dots, r_B + r_F - 1\}$, $\text{KE} \in \{0, 1, 2, 3\}$, and $\text{KS} \in \{0, \dots, 48\}$. Then, assuming that $r_{\text{off}} = r_B + r_U + r_L$ and $z = 3$, we use the following constraints to model the key-bridging:

$$CSP_{\text{KB}} := \begin{cases} \text{IK}[i] = \displaystyle\sum_{r=0}^{r_B-1} \text{IKB}_r[h^{-r}(i)] + \sum_{r=0}^{r_F-1} \text{IKF}_r[h^{-(r_{\text{off}}+r)}(i)] \text{ for } 0 \le i \le 15, \\ if \text{ IK}[i] \ge z \text{ then } \text{KE}[i] = z \text{ else } \text{KE}[i] = \text{IK}[i] \text{ for } 0 \le i \le 15, \\ \text{KS} = \displaystyle\sum_{i=0}^{15} \text{KE}[i] \end{cases} \quad (12)$$

Model the Complexity Formulas. We now show how to combine all CSP models and model the complexity formulas. The variable KS in Eq. 12 determines the number of involved key cells, corresponding to $|k_B \cup k_F| = \text{c} \cdot \text{KS}$ involved key bits for cell size c. We can model the other critical parameters of the ID attack as shown in Algorithm 5. We combine all CSP problems into a unified model and define an objective function to minimize the time complexity of the ID attack.

Results. We applied our method to find full ID attacks on all variants of SKINNY in both single and related-tweakey settings. Our model includes integer and real variables, so we used Gurobi to solve the resulting COP problems. Table 1 shows our results. Our ID attacks' time, date, and memory complexity are much smaller than the best previous ID attacks. Notably, the time complexity of our 19-round single-tweakey ID attack on SKINNY-128-256 ([21, Figure 8], details in [21, F.2]) is smaller by a factor of $2^{22.57}$ compared to the best previous one [47]. As another example, we improved the time complexity of the related-tweakey ID attack on SKINNY-128-384 by a factor of $2^{15.39}$ [21, Figure 10], with smaller data and memory complexity than the best previous one [27]. Our tool can discover the longest ID distinguishers for SKINNY so far in both single and related-tweakey settings. However, we noticed that the best ID attacks do not necessarily rely on the longest distinguishers. For instance, our single-tweakey ID attacks on SKINNY use 11-round distinguishers, whereas our tool also finds 12-round distinguishers.

We also applied our tool to CRAFT and SKINNYee. On CRAFT, we found a 21-round ID attack which is 2 rounds longer than the best previous single-tweakey attack presented at ASIACRYPT 2022 [40]. For SKINNYee, we found a 27-round related-tweakey ID attack. Our tool can produce all the reported results on a laptop in a few seconds. Besides improving the security evaluation against ID attacks, our tool can significantly reduce human effort and error.

We also used our tool to check the validity of the previous results. To do so, we fix the activeness pattern in our model to that at the input/output of the claimed distinguisher. Moreover, we constrain the time, memory, and data complexities to the claimed bounds. An infeasible model indicates potential issues with the claimed attack. We manually check the attack to find the possible issue in this case. If the model is feasible, we match the claimed critical parameters with the output of our tool. In case of any mismatch, we manually check the corresponding parameter in the claimed attack to ensure it is calculated correctly.

We followed this approach to check the validity of the ID attacks on SKINNY proposed in [45]. For example, our tool returns 'unsatisfiable' when we limit it to find a 22-round ID attack on SKINNY-n-$3n$ with the claimed parameters in [45]. To figure out the issue, we relax the time/memory/data complexity bounds and only fix the activeness pattern according to the claimed distinguisher. This way, our tool returns different attack parameters compared to the claimed ones. According to [45, Sec. 6], $c_B + c_F$ is supposed to be $18c$ for 22-round ID attack on SKINNY-n-$3n$ with cell size c. However, our tool returns $c_B = 6c$ and $c_F = 15c$, and thus $c_B + c_F = 21c$. Accordingly,

---

Algorithm 5: COP model for the full ID attack on SKINNY

Input: Four integer numbers r_B, r_U, r_L, r_F

Output: COP

1   Declare an empty COP model $\mathcal{M}$;

2   $\mathcal{M} \leftarrow CSP_D \wedge CSP_{DP} \wedge CSP_{GD} \wedge CSP_{KB}$;

3   $\mathcal{M}.var \leftarrow g \in \{1, \ldots, z \cdot 16 \cdot c\}$;   /* Corresponding to parameter g */

4   $\mathcal{M}.var \leftarrow C_B \in \{0, \ldots, 20 \cdot r_B + 16\}$;   /* Corresponding to c_B */

5   $\mathcal{M}.var \leftarrow C_F \in \{0, \ldots, 20 \cdot r_F + 16\}$;   /* Corresponding to c_F */

6   $\mathcal{M}.var \leftarrow W_B \in \{0, \ldots, 16\}$;   /* Corresponding to $|\Delta_B|$ */

7   $\mathcal{M}.var \leftarrow W_F \in \{0, \ldots, 16\}$;   /* Corresponding to $|\Delta_F|$ */

8   $\mathcal{M}.var \leftarrow \{D[i] \in [0, z \cdot 16 \cdot c] : i \in \{0, 1, 2, 3\}\}$;   /* For data complexity */

9   $\mathcal{M}.var \leftarrow \{T[i] \in [0, z \cdot 16 \cdot c] : i \in \{0, 1, 2, 3\}\}$;   /* For time complexity */

10   $\mathcal{M}.var \leftarrow T_{max} \in [0, z \cdot 16 \cdot c]$;

11   $\mathcal{M}.var \leftarrow C_B = \sum_{r=1}^{r_B-1} \sum_{i=0}^{19} CB_r[i] + \sum_{i=0}^{15} KXB_{r_B}[i]$;

12   $\mathcal{M}.var \leftarrow C_F = \sum_{r=0}^{r_F-2} \sum_{i=0}^{19} CF_r[i] + \sum_{i=0}^{7} CF_{r_F-1}[i] + \sum_{i=0}^{15} KXF_0[i]$;

13   $\mathcal{M}.var \leftarrow W_B = \sum_{i=0}^{15} AXB_1[i]$;

14   $\mathcal{M}.var \leftarrow W_F = \sum_{i=0}^{15} AXF_{r_F-1}[i]$;

15   $\mathcal{M}.con \leftarrow D[0] = 0.5 \cdot (c(C_B + C_F) + n - c \cdot W_B + LG(g) + 2)$;

16   $\mathcal{M}.con \leftarrow D[1] = 0.5 \cdot (c(C_B + C_F) + n - c \cdot W_F + LG(g) + 2)$;

17   $\mathcal{M}.con \leftarrow D[2] = min(D[0], D[1])$;

18   $\mathcal{M}.con \leftarrow D[3] = c \cdot (C_B + C_F) + n + 1 - c \cdot (W_B + W_F) + LG(g)$;

19   $\mathcal{M}.con \leftarrow T[0] = max(D[2], D[3])$;

20   $\mathcal{M}.con \leftarrow T[1] = c \cdot (C_B + C_F) + LG(g)$;

21   $\mathcal{M}.con \leftarrow T[2] = c \cdot KS$;   /* Corresponding to $|k_B \cup k_F|$ */

22   $\mathcal{M}.con \leftarrow T[3] = k - g$;

23   $\mathcal{M}.con \leftarrow g \leq T[2]$;

24   $\mathcal{M}.con \leftarrow T_{max} = max(T[0], T[1], T[2], T[3])$;

25   $\mathcal{M}.con \leftarrow (T[0] < n \wedge T_{max} < k)$;

26   $\mathcal{M}.obj \leftarrow$ Minimize T_{max};

27   **return** $\mathcal{M}$;

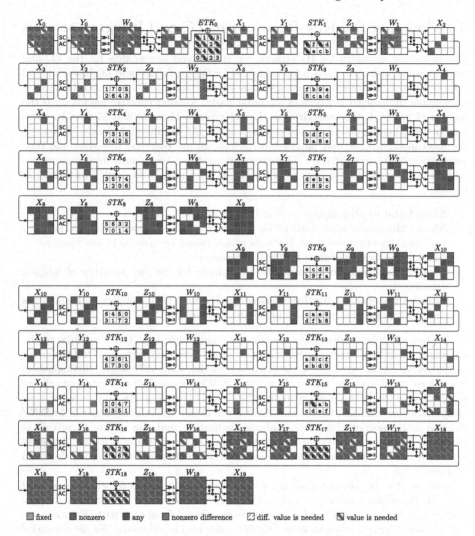

Fig. 4. ID attack on 19 rounds of SKINNY $[n\text{-}2n]$, $|k_B \cup k_F| = 26 \cdot c$, $c_B = 6 \cdot c$, $c_F = 15 \cdot c$, $\Delta_B = 7 \cdot c$, $\Delta_F = 16 \cdot c$

the actual probability that a wrong tweakey is discarded with one pair is about 2^{-21c}. So, the 22-round ID attack on SKINNY-n-3n in [45] requires more data and thus time by a factor of 2^{3c}. The time complexity of the 22-round ID attack on SKINNY-64-192 (SKINNY-128-384) in [45] is $2^{183.97}$ (resp. $2^{373.48}$). As a result, the corrected attack requires more time than the exhaustive search. We also checked the 20-round ID attacks on SKINNY-n-2n in [45]. We noticed that a similar issue makes the corrected attack require more data than the full codebook or more time than the exhaustive search. We contacted the authors of [45], and they confirmed our claim.

5 Modeling the Key Recovery of ZC and Integral Attacks

Similar to our approach for ID attacks, we can extend our models for the ZC and integral distinguishers to make a unified model for finding full ZC and ZC-based integral attacks. One of the critical parameters in the key recovery of ZC and integral attacks is the number of involved key cells in the outer parts. Another effective parameter is the number of involved state cells through the outer parts. Thus, we should consider these parameters when modeling the key recovery of the ZC and integral attacks. Moreover, the meet-in-the-middle and partial-sum techniques are essential to reduce the time complexity of integral attacks. Therefore, taking these techniques into account, we provide a generic CP model for key recovery of ZC and ZC-based integral attacks as follows:

- **Model the distinguisher** as described in Sect. 3.
- **Model the guess-and-determine part** by modeling the value paths in the outer part and detecting the state/key cells whose values are needed in key recovery.
- **Model the key bridging** for the key recovery.
- **Model the meet-in-the-middle technique** for the key recovery of integral attacks.
- **Set the objective function** to minimize the final time complexity, keeping the data and memory complexities under the thresholds.

We only describe modeling the meet-in-the-middle technique. Other modules can be constructed similarly to our models for ID attacks. Given that there is no restriction for the output of ZC-integral distinguishers in our model, some ZC-integral distinguishers might have more than one balanced output cell. With more than one balanced cell, we might be able to use the meet-in-the-middle (MitM) technique [38] to reduce the time complexity. For example, we can use MitM if the ZC-integral distinguisher of SKINNY has two active output cells in one column, indicating that the sum of these cells is balanced. Then, we can recover the integral sums of these two cells for any keyguess separately and merge compatible key guesses that yield the same sum, i.e., that sum to zero overall.

To consider the MitM technique, we model the path values for each output cell of the distinguisher separately in an independent CP submodel. We also define a new integer variable to capture the number of involved key cells in each path. For example, our CP model for integral attacks on SKINNY splits into 16 submodels for the appended rounds after the distinguisher. Each submodel aims at encoding the involved cells in retrieving a certain output cell of the distinguisher. We note that these submodels, together with our CP model for distinguisher, are all combined into one large unified CP model. This way, we can encode and then minimize the complexity of the most critical path, which requires the maximum number of guessed keys in the guess-and-filter step. Similarly to our CP model for ID attacks, our model for ZC and integral attack receives only four integer numbers as input and returns the full ZC or ZC-based integral attack.

We solve our CP models for integral attacks in two steps with two different objective functions:

- We first solve a CP model to minimize the number of involved key cells.
- Next, we limit the number of involved key cells to the output of the previous step and solve the CP model with the objective of maximizing the number of active cells at the input of ZC-integral distinguisher.

As a result, besides reducing the time complexity, we can reduce the data complexity of the resulting integral attacks. To compute the exact final complexity, we introduce an additional helper tool, AutoPSy, which automates the partial-sum technique [16], and apply it as a post-processing step to the CP output. AutoPSy optimizes the column order in each round of partial-sum key recovery.

We applied our unified framework for finding full ZC and integral attacks to CRAFT, SKINNYe-v2, SKINNYee, and all variants of SKINNY and obtained a series of substantially improved results. Table 1 briefly describes our results. More details on our ZC and integral attacks can be found in [21, G, H, I.3]. As can be seen in [21, Figures 14, 15, 19], the inputs of the corresponding ZC distinguishers have 4 active cells, and the outputs have 2 active cells. The previous tools which fix the input/output linear masks to vectors with at most one active cell can not find such a distinguisher.

Our CP models for ZC and integral attacks include only integer variables. Thus, we can take advantage of all integer programming (IP) solvers. We used Or-Tools in this application, and running on a regular laptop, our tool can find all the reported results in a few seconds.

When reproducing the best previous results on SKINNY with our automatic tool, we again noticed some issues in previous works. The previous ZC-integral attacks on SKINNY proposed by Ankele et al. at ToSC 2019 [1] have some minor issues where the propagation in the key recovery part is incorrect. For example, in the 20-round TK2 attack in [1, Figure 20] between X_{18}, Y_{18}, the last row is not shifted; in the 23-round TK3 attack in [1, Figure 22], the mixing between Y_{20}, Z_{20} is not correct. In both cases, this impacts the correctness of all following rounds. However, the attacks can be fixed to obtain similar complexities as claimed.

The comparison with those attacks highlights three advantages of our automated approach: (1) Our approach is much less prone to such small hard-to-spot errors; (2) Our approach can find distinguishers with many active input cells (rather than just one as classical approaches), which is particularly helpful in ZC-integral attacks where a higher input weight implies a lower data complexity; (3) Our approach optimizes the key recovery together with the distinguisher, which together with (2) allows us to attach more key-recovery rounds (7 vs. 5 for TK2 in [1], 9 vs. 7 for TK3 in [1]).

6   Conclusion and Future Works

In this paper, we presented a unified CP model to find full ID, ZC, and ZC-based integral attacks for the first time. Our frameworks are generic and can be applied to word-oriented block ciphers. To show the effectiveness and usefulness of our approach, we applied it to CRAFT, SKINNYe-v2, SKINNYee, and all members of the SKINNY family of block ciphers. In all cases, we obtained a series of substantially improved results compared to the best previous ID, ZC, and integral attacks on these ciphers. Our tool can help the cryptanalysts and the designers of block ciphers to evaluate the security of block ciphers against three important attacks, i.e., ID, ZC, and ZC-based integral attacks, more accurately and efficiently. While we focused on the application to SPN block ciphers, it is also applicable to Feistel ciphers. Applying our approach to other block ciphers such as AES or Feistel ciphers is an interesting direction for future work.

Our improved results show the advantage of our method. However, it also has some limitations. Our CP model for the distinguisher part detects the contradictions in the level of words and does not exploit the internal structure of S-boxes (i.e., DDT/LAT) to consider bit-level contradictions. Thus, one interesting future work is to provide a unified model considering bit-level contradictions. We note that our CP framework for ID, ZC, and integral attacks is modular. The key-recovery part of our CP model can be combined with other CP-based methods for finding distinguishers. For example, regardless of the distinguisher part, one can feed our CP model for the key-recovery part by a set of input/output activeness patterns for the distinguisher part to find the activeness pattern yielding the best key-recovery attack. Next, one can use a more fine-grained CP model that detects bit-level contradictions to check if the selected activeness pattern yields an ID or ZC distinguisher. We recall that in CP models, we can specify a set of input/output activeness patterns by a set of constraints, and we do not have to enumerate all possible input/output activeness patterns. Currently, our tool automatically applies the partial-sum technique as a post-processing step in integral attacks for a refined complexity analysis. Thus, another interesting future work is integrating the partial-sum technique into our CP model for integral attacks. This way, one may be able to improve the integral attacks further.

Acknowledgments. This work has been supported in part by the Austrian Science Fund (FWF SFB project SPyCoDe). The authors would like to thank the anonymous reviewers for their valuable comments and suggestions.

References

1. Ankele, R., Dobraunig, C., Guo, J., Lambooij, E., Leander, G., Todo, Y.: Zero-correlation attacks on tweakable block ciphers with linear tweakey expansion. IACR Trans. Symmetric Cryptol. **2019**(1), 192–235 (2019). https://doi.org/10.13154/tosc.v2019.i1.192-235

2. Avanzi, R.: The QARMA block cipher family. almost MDS matrices over rings with zero divisors, nearly symmetric even-mansour constructions with non-involutory central rounds, and search heuristics for low-latency s-boxes. IACR Trans. Symmetric Cryptol. **2017**(1), 4–44 (2017). https://doi.org/10.13154/tosc.v2017.i1.4-44

3. Beierle, C., Jean, J., Kölbl, S., Leander, G., Moradi, A., Peyrin, T., Sasaki, Yu., Sasdrich, P., Sim, S.M.: The SKINNY family of block ciphers and its low-latency variant MANTIS. In: Robshaw, M., Katz, J. (eds.) CRYPTO 2016. LNCS, vol. 9815, pp. 123–153. Springer, Heidelberg (2016). https://doi.org/10.1007/978-3-662-53008-5_5

4. Beierle, C., Leander, G., Moradi, A., Rasoolzadeh, S.: CRAFT: lightweight tweakable block cipher with efficient protection against DFA attacks. IACR Trans. Symmetric Cryptol. **2019**(1), 5–45 (2019). https://doi.org/10.13154/tosc.v2019.i1.5-45

5. Biham, E., Biryukov, A., Shamir, A.: Cryptanalysis of skipjack reduced to 31 rounds using impossible differentials. In: Stern, J. (ed.) EUROCRYPT 1999. LNCS, vol. 1592, pp. 12–23. Springer, Heidelberg (1999). https://doi.org/10.1007/3-540-48910-X_2

6. Biham, E., Biryukov, A., Shamir, A.: Miss in the middle attacks on IDEA and Khufu. In: Knudsen, L. (ed.) FSE 1999. LNCS, vol. 1636, pp. 124–138. Springer, Heidelberg (1999). https://doi.org/10.1007/3-540-48519-8_10

7. Bogdanov, A., Leander, G., Nyberg, K., Wang, M.: Integral and multidimensional linear distinguishers with correlation zero. In: Wang, X., Sako, K. (eds.)

ASIACRYPT 2012. LNCS, vol. 7658, pp. 244–261. Springer, Heidelberg (2012). https://doi.org/10.1007/978-3-642-34961-4_16

8. Bogdanov, A., Rijmen, V.: Linear hulls with correlation zero and linear cryptanalysis of block ciphers. Des. Codes Crypt. **70**(3), 369–383 (2012). https://doi.org/10.1007/s10623-012-9697-z

9. Bogdanov, A., Wang, M.: Zero correlation linear cryptanalysis with reduced data complexity. In: Canteaut, A. (ed.) FSE 2012. LNCS, vol. 7549, pp. 29–48. Springer, Heidelberg (2012). https://doi.org/10.1007/978-3-642-34047-5_3

10. Boura, C., Lallemand, V., Naya-Plasencia, M., Suder, V.: Making the impossible possible. J. Cryptol. **31**(1), 101–133 (2017). https://doi.org/10.1007/s00145-016-9251-7

11. Boura, C., Naya-Plasencia, M., Suder, V.: Scrutinizing and improving impossible differential attacks: applications to CLEFIA, Camellia, LBlock and SIMON. In: Sarkar, P., Iwata, T. (eds.) ASIACRYPT 2014. LNCS, vol. 8873, pp. 179–199. Springer, Heidelberg (2014). https://doi.org/10.1007/978-3-662-45611-8_10

12. Cui, T., Chen, S., Jia, K., Fu, K., Wang, M.: New automatic search tool for impossible differentials and zero-correlation linear approximations. IACR Cryptol, ePrint Archive, Report 2016/689 (2016), https://eprint.iacr.org/2016/689

13. Daemen, J., Knudsen, L., Rijmen, V.: The block cipher Square. In: Biham, E. (ed.) FSE 1997. LNCS, vol. 1267, pp. 149–165. Springer, Heidelberg (1997). https://doi.org/10.1007/BFb0052343

14. Derbez, P., Fouque, P.-A.: Automatic Search of Meet-in-the-Middle and Impossible Differential Attacks. In: Robshaw, M., Katz, J. (eds.) CRYPTO 2016. LNCS, vol. 9815, pp. 157–184. Springer, Heidelberg (2016). https://doi.org/10.1007/978-3-662-53008-5_6

15. Eskandari, Z., Kidmose, A.B., Kölbl, S., Tiessen, T.: Finding integral distinguishers with ease. In: SAC. LNCS, vol. 11349, pp. 115–138. Springer, Cham (2018). https://doi.org/10.1007/978-3-030-10970-7_6

16. Ferguson, N., et al.: Improved cryptanalysis of Rijndael. In: Goos, G., Hartmanis, J., van Leeuwen, J., Schneier, B. (eds.) FSE 2000. LNCS, vol. 1978, pp. 213–230. Springer, Heidelberg (2001). https://doi.org/10.1007/3-540-44706-7_15

17. Gurobi Optimization LLC: Gurobi Optimizer Reference Manual (2022). https://www.gurobi.com

18. Hadipour, H., Eichlseder, M.: Autoguess: A tool for finding guess-and-determine attacks and key bridges. In: ACNS 2022. LNCS, vol. 13269, pp. 230–250. Springer, Cham (2022). https://doi.org/10.1007/978-3-031-09234-3_12

19. Hadipour, H., Eichlseder, M.: Integral cryptanalysis of WARP based on monomial prediction. IACR Trans. Symmetric Cryptol. **2022**(2), 92–112 (2022). https://doi.org/10.46586/tosc.v2022.i2.92-112

20. Hadipour, H., Nageler, M., Eichlseder, M.: Throwing boomerangs into feistel structures: Application to CLEFIA, WARP, LBlock, LBlock-s and TWINE. IACR Trans. Symmetric Cryptol. **2022**(3), 271–302 (2022). https://doi.org/10.46586/tosc.v2022.i3.271-302

21. Hadipour, H., Sadeghi, S., Eichlseder, M.: Finding the impossible: Automated search for full impossible differential, zero-correlation, and integral attacks. IACR Cryptology ePrint Archive, Report 2022/1147, p. 92 (2022). https://eprint.iacr.org/2022/1147

22. Hadipour, H., Sadeghi, S., Niknam, M.M., Song, L., Bagheri, N.: Comprehensive security analysis of CRAFT. IACR Trans. Symmetric Cryptol. **2019**(4), 290–317 (2019). https://doi.org/10.13154/tosc.v2019.i4.290-317

23. Hu, K., Sun, S., Wang, M., Wang, Q.: An algebraic formulation of the division property: revisiting degree evaluations, cube attacks, and key-independent sums. In: Moriai, S., Wang, H. (eds.) ASIACRYPT 2020. LNCS, vol. 12491, pp. 446–476. Springer, Cham (2020). https://doi.org/10.1007/978-3-030-64837-4_15

24. Jean, J., Nikolić, I., Peyrin, T.: Tweaks and keys for block ciphers: The TWEAKEY framework. In: Sarkar, P., Iwata, T. (eds.) ASIACRYPT 2014. LNCS, vol. 8874, pp. 274–288. Springer, Heidelberg (2014). https://doi.org/10.1007/978-3-662-45608-8_15

25. Knudsen, L.: Deal-a 128-bit block cipher. Complexity **258**(2), 216 (1998)

26. Lai, X.: Higher order derivatives and differential cryptanalysis, pp. 227–233 (1994). https://doi.org/10.1007/978-1-4615-2694-0_23

27. Liu, G., Ghosh, M., Song, L.: Security analysis of SKINNY under related-tweakey settings. IACR Trans. Symmetric Cryptol. **2017**(3), 37–72 (2017). https://doi.org/10.13154/tosc.v2017.i3.37-72

28. Lu, J., Dunkelman, O., Keller, N., Kim, J.: New impossible differential attacks on AES. In: Chowdhury, D.R., Rijmen, V., Das, A. (eds.) INDOCRYPT 2008. LNCS, vol. 5365, pp. 279–293. Springer, Heidelberg (2008). https://doi.org/10.1007/978-3-540-89754-5_22

29. Lu, J., Kim, J., Keller, N., Dunkelman, O.: Improving the efficiency of impossible differential cryptanalysis of reduced camellia and MISTY1. In: Malkin, T. (ed.) CT-RSA 2008. LNCS, vol. 4964, pp. 370–386. Springer, Heidelberg (2008). https://doi.org/10.1007/978-3-540-79263-5_24

30. Mouha, N., Wang, Q., Gu, D., Preneel, B.: Differential and linear cryptanalysis using mixed-integer linear programming. In: Wu, C.-K., Yung, M., Lin, D. (eds.) Inscrypt 2011. LNCS, vol. 7537, pp. 57–76. Springer, Heidelberg (2012). https://doi.org/10.1007/978-3-642-34704-7_5

31. Naito, Y., Sasaki, Yu., Sugawara, T.: Lightweight authenticated encryption mode suitable for threshold implementation. In: Canteaut, A., Ishai, Y. (eds.) EUROCRYPT 2020. LNCS, vol. 12106, pp. 705–735. Springer, Cham (2020). https://doi.org/10.1007/978-3-030-45724-2_24

32. Naito, Y., Sasaki, Y., Sugawara, T.: Secret can be public: Low-memory AEAD mode for high-order masking. In: CRYPTO 2022. LNCS, vol. 13509, pp. 315–345. Springer, Cham (2022). https://doi.org/10.1007/978-3-031-15982-4_11

33. Nethercote, N., Stuckey, P.J., Becket, R., Brand, S., Duck, G.J., Tack, G.: MiniZinc: towards a standard CP modelling language. In: Bessière, C. (ed.) CP 2007. LNCS, vol. 4741, pp. 529–543. Springer, Heidelberg (2007). https://doi.org/10.1007/978-3-540-74970-7_38

34. Niu, C., Li, M., Sun, S., Wang, M.: Zero-correlation linear cryptanalysis with equal treatment for plaintexts and tweakeys. In: Paterson, K.G. (ed.) CT-RSA 2021. LNCS, vol. 12704, pp. 126–147. Springer, Cham (2021). https://doi.org/10.1007/978-3-030-75539-3_6

35. Perron, L., Furnon, V.: OR-Tools. https://developers.google.com/optimization/

36. Sadeghi, S., Mohammadi, T., Bagheri, N.: Cryptanalysis of reduced round SKINNY block cipher. IACR Trans. Symmetric Cryptol. **2018**(3), 124–162 (2018). https://doi.org/10.13154/tosc.v2018.i3.124-162

37. Sasaki, Yu., Todo, Y.: New impossible differential search tool from design and cryptanalysis aspects. In: Coron, J.-S., Nielsen, J.B. (eds.) EUROCRYPT 2017. LNCS, vol. 10212, pp. 185–215. Springer, Cham (2017). https://doi.org/10.1007/978-3-319-56617-7_7

38. Sasaki, Yu., Wang, L.: Meet-in-the-middle technique for integral attacks against feistel ciphers. In: Knudsen, L.R., Wu, H. (eds.) SAC 2012. LNCS, vol. 7707, pp. 234–251. Springer, Heidelberg (2013). https://doi.org/10.1007/978-3-642-35999-6_16

39. Shi, D., Sun, S., Derbez, P., Todo, Y., Sun, B., Hu, L.: Programming the Demirci-Selçuk meet-in-the-middle attack with constraints. In: Peyrin, T., Galbraith, S. (eds.) ASIACRYPT 2018. LNCS, vol. 11273, pp. 3–34. Springer, Cham (2018). https://doi.org/10.1007/978-3-030-03329-3_1

40. Song, L., et al.: Optimizing rectangle attacks: A unified and generic framework for key recovery. In: ASIACRYPT 2022. LNCS, vol. 13791, pp. 410–440. Springer, Cham (2022). https://doi.org/10.1007/978-3-031-22963-3_14

41. Sun, B., et al.: Links among impossible differential, integral and zero correlation linear cryptanalysis. In: Gennaro, R., Robshaw, M. (eds.) CRYPTO 2015. LNCS, vol. 9215, pp. 95–115. Springer, Heidelberg (2015). https://doi.org/10.1007/978-3-662-47989-6_5

42. Sun, L., Gerault, D., Wang, W., Wang, M.: On the usage of deterministic (related-key) truncated differentials and multidimensional linear approximations for spn ciphers. IACR Trans. Symmetric Cryptol. **2020**(3), 262–287 (2020). https://doi.org/10.13154/tosc.v2020.i3.262-287

43. Sun, S., et al.: Analysis of aes, skinny, and others with constraint programming. IACR Trans. Symmetric Cryptol. **2017**(1), 281–306 (2017). https://doi.org/10.13154/tosc.v2017.i1.281-306

44. Todo, Y.: Structural evaluation by generalized integral property. In: EUROCRYPT 2015. LNCS, vol. 9056, pp. 287–314. Springer, Cham (2015). https://doi.org/10.1007/978-3-662-46800-5_12

45. Tolba, M., Abdelkhalek, A., Youssef, A.M.: Impossible differential cryptanalysis of reduced-round SKINNY. In: Joye, M., Nitaj, A. (eds.) AFRICACRYPT 2017. LNCS, vol. 10239, pp. 117–134. Springer, Cham (2017). https://doi.org/10.1007/978-3-319-57339-7_7

46. Xiang, Z., Zhang, W., Bao, Z., Lin, D.: Applying MILP Method to Searching Integral Distinguishers Based on Division Property for 6 Lightweight Block Ciphers. In: Cheon, J.H., Takagi, T. (eds.) ASIACRYPT 2016. LNCS, vol. 10031, pp. 648–678. Springer, Heidelberg (2016). https://doi.org/10.1007/978-3-662-53887-6_24

47. Yang, D., Qi, W., Chen, H.: Impossible differential attacks on the SKINNY family of block ciphers. IET Inf. Secur. **11**(6), 377–385 (2017). https://doi.org/10.1049/iet-ifs.2016.0488

48. Zhang, Y., Cui, T., Wang, C.: Zero-correlation linear attack on reduced-round SKINNY. Frontiers of Comput. Sci. **17**(174808 (2023)), 377–385 (2022). https://doi.org/10.1007/s11704-022-2206-2

Meet-in-the-Middle Preimage Attacks on Sponge-Based Hashing

Lingyue Qin[1,2,4,7], Jialiang Hua[3], Xiaoyang Dong[3,4,7(✉)], Hailun Yan[5], and Xiaoyun Wang[3,4,6,7]

[1] BNRist, Tsinghua University, Beijing, China
qinly@tsinghua.edu.cn
[2] State Key Laboratory of Cryptology, P. O. Box 5159, Beijing 100878, China
[3] Institute for Advanced Study, BNRist, Tsinghua University, Beijing, China
{huajl18,xiaoyangdong,xiaoyunwang}@tsinghua.edu.cn
[4] Zhongguancun Laboratory, Beijing, China
[5] School of Cryptology, University of Chinese Academy of Sciences, Beijing, China
hailun.yan@ucas.ac.cn
[6] Key Laboratory of Cryptologic Technology and Information Security
(Ministry of Education), School of Cyber Science and Technology,
Shandong University, Qingdao, China
[7] National Financial Cryptography Research Center, Beijing, China

Abstract. The Meet-in-the-Middle (MitM) attack has been widely applied to preimage attacks on Merkle-Damgård (MD) hashing. In this paper, we introduce a generic framework of the MitM attack on sponge-based hashing. We find certain bit conditions can significantly reduce the diffusion of the unknown bits and lead to longer MitM characteristics. To find good or optimal configurations of MitM attacks, e.g., the bit conditions, the neutral sets, and the matching points, we introduce the bit-level MILP-based automatic tools on Keccak, Ascon and Xoodyak. To reduce the scale of bit-level models and make them solvable in reasonable time, a series of properties of the targeted hashing are considered in the modelling, such as the linear structure and CP-kernel for Keccak, the Boolean expression of Sbox for Ascon. Finally, we give an improved 4-round preimage attack on Keccak-512/SHA3, and break a nearly 10 years' cryptanalysis record. We also give the first preimage attacks on 3-/4-round Ascon-XOF and 3-round Xoodyak-XOF.

Keywords: MitM · Automatic Tool · Keccak/SHA3 · Ascon · Xoodyak

1 Introduction

The Meet-in-the-Middle (MitM) attack proposed by Diffie and Hellman in 1977 [22] is a generic technique for cryptanalysis of symmetric-key primitives. The essence of the MitM attack is actually an efficient way to exhaustively search a space for the right candidate based on the birthday attack, i.e., dividing the whole space into two independent subsets (also known as neutral sets) and

The full version of the paper is available at https://eprint.iacr.org/2022/1714.

C. Hazay and M. Stam (Eds.): EUROCRYPT 2023, LNCS 14007, pp. 158–188, 2023.
https://doi.org/10.1007/978-3-031-30634-1_6

then finding matches from the two subsets. Suppose $E_K(\cdot)$ to be a block cipher whose size is n-bit such that $C = E_K(P) = F_{K_2}(F_{K_1}(P))$, where $K = K_1\|K_2$ has n bits, and K_1 and K_2 are independent key materials of $n/2$ bits. For a given plaintext-ciphertext pair (P, C), a naive exhaust search attack needs a time complexity 2^n to find the key. However, the birthday-paradox based MitM attack computes independently $F_{K_1}(P)$ and $F_{K_2}^{-1}(C)$ with independent guesses of K_1 and K_2, and searches collision between $F_{K_1}(P)$ and $F_{K_2}^{-1}(C)$ to find the K with a time complexity about $2^{n/2}$. In the past decades, the MitM attack has been widely applied to the cryptanalysis on block ciphers [12,30,40,50] and hash functions [2,34,59]. In the meantime, various techniques have been introduced to improve the framework of MitM attack, such as internal state guessing [30], splice-and-cut [2], initial structure [59], bicliques [11], 3-subset MitM [12], indirect-partial matching [2,59], sieve-in-the-middle [15], match-box [32], dissection [24], differential-aided MitM [14,31,41], nonlinear constrained neutral words [28], etc. Till now, the MitM attack and its variants have broken MD4 [34,44], MD5 [59], KeeLoq [39], HAVAL [4,60], GOST [40], GEA-1/2 [1,7], etc.

At CRYPTO 2011 and 2016, several ad-hoc automatic tools [13,19] were proposed for MitM attacks. At IWSEC 2018, Sasaki [57] introduced MILP-based MitM attacks on GIFT block cipher. At EUROCRYPT 2021, Bao et al. [5] introduced the MILP-based automatic search framework for MitM preimage attacks on AES-like hashing, whose compression function is built from AES-like block cipher or permutations. At CRYPTO 2021, Dong et al. [28] further extended Bao et al.'s model into key-recovery and collision attacks. At CRYPTO 2022, Schrottenloher and Stevens [61] simplified the language of the automatic model and applied it in both classic and quantum settings. Bao et al. [6] considered the MitM attack in a view of the superposition states.

When applying to hash functions, most of the MitM attacks targeted on Merkle-Damgård [17,51] domain extender, whose compression function is usually built from a block cipher and PGV hashing modes [54], such as Davies-Meyer (DM), Matyas-Meyer-Oseas (MMO) and Miyaguchi-Preneel (MP). The goal of the MitM attack is to find a sequence of internal states which satisfy a closed computational path: there is a relation between the value before the first round and the value after the last round in previous applications of MitM attacks. For example, when attacking block-cipher based hashing modes (DM, MMO, MP, etc.), the closed computation path is computed across the first and last rounds via the feed-forward mechanism of the hashing modes. While when attacking block ciphers, the closed computation path is linked via an encryption/decryption oracle. As shown in Fig. 1, one starts by separating the path in two chunks (splice-and-cut): the backward chunk and the forward chunk depending on different neutral sets. Both chunks form independent computation paths. One then finds a partial match between them at certain round.

When considering the new hashing mode, i.e., sponge-based hashing, there is no feed-forward mechanism anymore, e.g. Keccak. We have to try novel ways to build the so-called closed computational path for MitM attack. Most preimage attacks on sponge-based hashing focus on the analysis on Keccak/SHA-3

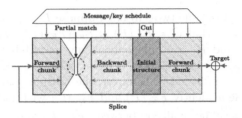

Fig. 1. The closed computation path of the MitM attack

with linearization technique. At ASIACRYPT 2016, Guo et al. [35] introduced the *linear structure* technique to linearise several rounds of `Keccak` and derived upto 4-round preimage attacks. Later, Guo et al.'s attacks were improved by the cross-linear structure [46] at ToSC 2017 and *allocating approach* [45] at EURO-CRYPT 2019. Further improvements in this line were proposed in [37,47,48,56]. At EUROCRYPT 2021, Dinur [23] gave the preimage attacks on `Keccak` by solving multivariate equation systems. Additionally, theoretical preimage attacks marginally better than exhaustive attacks were studied in [8,52].

At INDOCRYPT 2011, an MitM attack on 2-round `Keccak` is given by Naya-Plasencia et al. [53]. However, their MitM attack is different from what we are considering. In [53], after computing the inverse of one round `Keccak` from the target, partial internal states are known. Then, Naya-Plasencia et al. divide the message block into many independent parts and compute forward independently for each part until the known internal states, and filter the messages. Naya-Plasencia et al.'s attack is more like a divide-and-conquer and the birthday attack is not used.

Our Contributions
We apply the birthday-paradox based MitM attack[1], which has been widely used to attack Merkle-Damgård [17,51] hashing with PGV modes as well as block ciphers, to the sponge-based hash functions. Additionally, by applying bit conditions, the diffusion of the two neutral sets can be controlled and reduced, and therefore lead to longer MitM characteristics. Finally, we propose a generic MitM framework with conditions for sponge-based hash functions.

To apply our framework to `Keccak`, `Ascon-XOF` and `Xoodyak-XOF`, we have to search sound configurations for MitM attack, including the choice of the two neutral sets, the bit conditions, the matching points etc. As `Keccak`, `Ascon` are bit-level hashing, we introduce the bit-level MILP-based automatic tools to detect those configurations. Different from the previous byte-level MitM MILP models [5,28,61], the bit-level modelling usually leads to huge scale MILP models and makes it hard to solve in reasonable time. Therefore, we explore detailed properties of dedicated ciphers to reduce the models. For `Keccak`, we apply the linear structures in starting states and CP-kernel properties in matching phase. For `Ascon`, the Boolean expressions of the Sbox are explored in the starting states

---

[1] The Demirci-Selçuk MitM attacks [10,18,20,21,29] are not considered in this paper, which is a quite different technique.

and matching points. In previous modellings [5,28], cells depending on both two neutral sets are always regarded as useless and unknown in the MitM attack. The unknown cells can significantly reduce the number of known cells when propagating (somewhat like polluting), since any known cells will become unknown by operating with the unknown cells. Inspired by the *indirect-partial matching* technique [2,59], the cells depending on the additions of the two neutral sets are also useful and should not be regarded as unknown in the automatic searching models. Therefore, we introduce new constraints for those kinds of cells and reduce the polluting speed of the unknown cells.

At last, we derive a better 4-round preimage attack on Keccak/SHA3-512 than Morawiecki et al.'s rotational cryptanalysis [52] at FSE 2013, that breaks their nearly 10 years' record. While previous preimage attack on Keccak-512 with linear structure techniques [35] (including improvements with various techniques [36,48,56]) only reaches 3 rounds. For Ascon-XOF, the first 3-round and 4-round preimage attacks are given. For Xoodyak-XOF, the first 3-round preimage attack is given. A summary of the related results are given in Table 1.

Table 1. A Summary of the Attacks. Lin. Stru.: Linear Structure. MitM: MitM Attack. Diff.: Differential. †: this attack ignores the padding bits.

Target	Attacks	Methods	Rounds	Time	Memory	Ref.
Keccak-512	Preimage	Lin.Stru.	2	2^{384}	-	[35]
		Lin.Stru.	2	2^{321}	-	[56]
		Lin.Stru.	2	2^{270}	-	[48]
		Lin.Stru.	2	2^{252}	-	[36]
		Lin.Stru.	3	2^{482}	-	[35]
		Lin.Stru.	3	2^{475}	-	[56]
		Lin.Stru.	3	2^{452}	-	[48]
		Lin.Stru.	3	2^{426}	-	[36]
		Rotational	4	2^{506}	-	[52]
		MitM	4	$2^{504.58}$	2^{108}	Sect. 4.3
	Collision	Diff.	2	Practical	-	[53]
		Diff.	3	Practical	-	[25]
Xoodyak-XOF	Preimage	Neural	1	-	-	[49]
		MitM	3	$2^{125.06}$	2^{97}	Sect. 5.2
Ascon-XOF	Preimage	Cube-like	2	2^{103}	-	[27]
		MitM	3	$2^{120.58}$	2^{39}	Full Ver. [55]
		MitM	4	$2^{124.67}$	2^{54}	Sect. 6.2
		Algebraic†	6	$2^{127.3}$	-	[27]
	Collision	Diff.	2	2^{103}	-	[33]

Comparison to Schrottenloher and Stevens's MitM attack. At CRYPTO 2022, Schrottenloher and Stevens [61] introduced preimage attacks on SPHINCS+-Haraka [3], which is sponge-based hashing with permutation Haraka [43]. Their MitM attack computes from the two ends, i.e., the known inner part and the target, to the middle matching part. Combining with the guess-and-determine technique, they derived a 3.5-round (out of 5 rounds) quantum preimage attack on SPHINCS+-Haraka. As stated in [61, Section 3.1], their frameworks do not lead to interesting results on Ascon [27]. The reason may be that for Keccak or Ascon the inverse of one round is not as easy as Haraka. Our framework mainly uses the forward computation, and leads to novel results on both Keccak and Ascon.

2 Preliminaries

In the section, we give some brief descriptions of the Meet-in-the-Middle attack, the sponge-based hash function, the Keccak-f permutation, Ascon-Hash and Ascon-XOF, Xoodyak and Xoodoo permutation.

2.1 The Meet-in-the-Middle Attack

Since the pioneering works on preimage attacks on Merkle-Damgård hashing, e.g. MD4, MD5, and HAVAL [2,34,44,59], techniques such as *splice-and-cut* [2], *initial structure* [59] and *indirect-partial matching* have been invented to significantly improve the MitM approach. As shown in Fig. 1, in the MitM attack, the compression function is divided at certain intermediate rounds (initial structure) into two chunks. One chunk is computed forward (named as forward chunk), and the other is computed backward (named as backward chunk). One of them is computed across the first and last rounds via the feed-forward mechanism of the hashing mode, and they end at a common intermediate round (partial matching point) and form a closed computation path of the MitM attack. In each of the chunks, the computation involves at least one distinct message word (or a few bits of it), such that they can be computed over all possible values of the involved message word(s) independently from the message word(s) involved in the other chunk (the distinct words are called neutral words). In the initial structure, the two chunks overlapped and the neutral words for both chunks appear simultaneously, but still, the computations of the two chunks on the neutral words are independent. The highlevel framework is in Fig. 1, which can be divided into three configurations:

1. The chunk separation – the positions of initial structure and matching points.
2. The neutral sets – the selection on the two neutral sets (denoted as ■ or ■ sets), which determines the degree of freedom (DoF) for each chunk.
3. The matching – the deterministic relation used for matching, which determines the filtering ability (degree of matching, DoM).

After setting up the configurations, the basic attack procedure goes as follows.

1. Choose constants for the initial structure.
2. For all 2^{d_1} values of ■ neutral set, compute backward from the initial structure to the matching points to generate a table L_1, whose indices are the values for matching, and the elements are the values of ■ neutral set.
3. Similarly, build L_2 for 2^{d_2} values of ■ neutral set with forward computation.
4. Check whether there is an m-bit match on indices between L_1 and L_2.
5. For the pairs surviving the partial match, check for a full-state match. Steps 1–5 will be repeated until we find a full match.

The attack complexity. Denote the size of the target by h, and the number of bits for the match by m. An MitM episode is performed with time $2^{\max(d_1,d_2)} + 2^{d_1+d_2-m}$ and the total time complexity of the attack is:

$$2^{h-(d_1+d_2)} \cdot \left(2^{\max(d_1,d_2)} + 2^{d_1+d_2-m}\right) \simeq 2^{h-\min(d_1,d_2,m)}. \tag{1}$$

To illustrate how the MitM attack works, we detail the 7-round attack on AES-hashing of Sasaki [58] in the Supplementary Material A in our full version paper [55] as an example.

2.2 The Sponge-Based Hash Function

The sponge construction [9] shown in Fig. 2 takes a variable-length message as input and produces a digest of any desired length. The b-bit internal state is composed of an outer part of r bits and an inner part of c bits, where r is the rate and c is the capacity. To evaluate the sponge function, one proceeds in three phases with an inner permutation f:

1. **Initialization:** Initialize the b-bit state with the given value (all 0's for Keccak) before proceeding the message blocks.
2. **Absorbing:** The message is padded and split into blocks of r bits. Absorb each r-bit block M_i by XORing into the internal state.
3. **Squeezing:** Produce the digest.

We named the hash functions with sponge construction as the sponge-based hash functions, e.g. Keccak [9], Ascon [27], Xoodyak [16], to name a few.

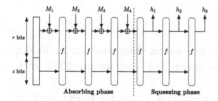

Fig. 2. The sponge construction

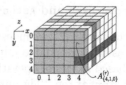

Fig. 3. The Keccak state

2.3   The Keccak-f Permutations

The Keccak hash function family [9] specifies 7 Keccak permutations, denoted Keccak-$f[b]$, where $b \in \{25, 50, 100, 200, 400, 800, 1600\}$ is the width of the permutation. In this paper, we focus on Keccak-$f[1600]$, where the state A is arranged as 5×5 64-bit lanes as depicted in Fig. 3. Let $A_{\{x,y,z\}}^{(r)}$ denote the bit located at the x-th column, y-th row and z-th lane in the round r ($r \geq 0$), where $0 \leq x \leq 4$, $0 \leq y \leq 4$, $0 \leq z \leq 63$. For Keccak in the rest of this paper, all the coordinates are considered modulo 5 for x and y and modulo 64 for z. The function Keccak-$f[1600]$ consists of 24 rounds which consists of five operations $\iota \circ \chi \circ \pi \circ \rho \circ \theta$. Denote the internal states of round r as

$$A^{(r)} \xrightarrow{\theta} \theta^{(r)} \xrightarrow{\rho} \rho^{(r)} \xrightarrow{\pi} \pi^{(r)} \xrightarrow{\chi} \chi^{(r)} \xrightarrow{\iota} A^{(r+1)}.$$

Operations in each round are:

$$
\begin{aligned}
\theta: \quad & \theta_{\{x,y,z\}}^{(r)} = A_{\{x,y,z\}}^{(r)} \oplus \sum\nolimits_{y'=0}^{4} (A_{\{x-1,y',z\}}^{(r)} \oplus A_{\{x+1,y',z-1\}}^{(r)}), \\
\rho: \quad & \rho_{\{x,y,z\}}^{(r)} = \theta_{\{x,y,z-\gamma[x,y]\}}^{(r)}, \\
\pi: \quad & \pi_{\{y,2x+3y,z\}}^{(r)} = \rho_{\{x,y,z\}}^{(r)}, \\
\chi: \quad & \chi_{\{x,y,z\}}^{(r)} = \pi_{\{x,y,z\}}^{(r)} \oplus (\pi_{\{x+1,y,z\}}^{(r)} \oplus 1) \cdot \pi_{\{x+2,y,z\}}^{(r)}, \\
\iota: \quad & A^{(r+1)} = \chi^{(r)} \oplus RC_r,
\end{aligned}
\tag{2}
$$

where $\gamma[x,y]$'s are constants given in the Supplementary Material B in our full version paper [55], RC_r is round-dependent constant.

The Keccak and SHA3 Hash Function. The Keccak hash function follows the sponge construction. For Keccak$[r, c, d]$, the capacity is c, the bitrate is r and the diversifier is d. NIST standardized four SHA3-l versions ($l \in 224, 256, 384, 512$), where $c = 2l$ and $r = 1600 - 2l$. The only difference of Keccak and SHA3 is the padding rule. The padding rule for Keccak is padding the message with '10*1', which is a single bit 1 followed by the minimum number of 0 bits followed by a single bit 1, to make the whole length to a multiple of $(1600 - 2l)$. For SHA3, the message is padded with '0110*1'. However, the padding rule does not affect the final time complexity of our attack.

2.4   Ascon-Hash and Ascon-XOF

The Ascon family [27] includes the hash functions Ascon-Hash and Ascon-Hasha as well as the extendable output functions Ascon-XOF and Ascon-XOFa with sponge-based modes of operations.

Ascon Permutation. The inner permutation applies 12 round functions to a 320-bit state. The state A is split into five 64-bit words, and denote $A_{\{x,y\}}^{(r)}$ to be the x-th (column) bit of the y-th (row) 64-bit word, where $0 \leq y \leq 4$, $0 \leq x \leq 63$. The round function consists of three operations p_C, p_S and p_L. Denote the internal states of round r as $A^{(r)} \xrightarrow{p_S \circ p_C} S^{(r)} \xrightarrow{p_L} A^{(r+1)}$.

- **Addition of Constants** p_C: $A^{(r)}_{\{*,2\}} = A^{(r)}_{\{*,2\}} \oplus RC_r$.
- **Substitution Layer** p_S: For each x, this step updates the columns $A^{(r)}_{\{x,*\}}$ using the 5-bit Sbox. Assume the S-box maps $(a_0, a_1, a_2, a_3, a_4) \in \mathbb{F}_2^5$ to $(b_0, b_1, b_2, b_3, b_4) \in \mathbb{F}_2^5$, where a_0 is the most significant bit. The algebraic normal form (ANF) of the Sbox is as follows:

$$
\begin{aligned}
b_0 &= a_4 a_1 + a_3 + a_2 a_1 + a_2 + a_1 a_0 + a_1 + a_0, \\
b_1 &= a_4 + a_3 a_2 + a_3 a_1 + a_3 + a_2 a_1 + a_2 + a_1 + a_0, \\
b_2 &= a_4 a_3 + a_4 + a_2 + a_1 + 1, \\
b_3 &= a_4 a_0 + a_4 + a_3 a_0 + a_3 + a_2 + a_1 + a_0, \\
b_4 &= a_4 a_1 + a_4 + a_3 + a_1 a_0 + a_1.
\end{aligned}
\tag{3}
$$

- **Linear Diffusion Layer** p_L:

$$
\begin{aligned}
A^{(r+1)}_{\{*,0\}} &\leftarrow S^{(r)}_{\{*,0\}} \oplus (S^{(r)}_{\{*,0\}} \ggg 19) \oplus (S^{(r)}_{\{*,0\}} \ggg 28), \\
A^{(r+1)}_{\{*,1\}} &\leftarrow S^{(r)}_{\{*,1\}} \oplus (S^{(r)}_{\{*,1\}} \ggg 61) \oplus (S^{(r)}_{\{*,1\}} \ggg 39), \\
A^{(r+1)}_{\{*,2\}} &\leftarrow S^{(r)}_{\{*,2\}} \oplus (S^{(r)}_{\{*,2\}} \ggg 1) \oplus (S^{(r)}_{\{*,2\}} \ggg 6), \\
A^{(r+1)}_{\{*,3\}} &\leftarrow S^{(r)}_{\{*,3\}} \oplus (S^{(r)}_{\{*,3\}} \ggg 10) \oplus (S^{(r)}_{\{*,3\}} \ggg 17), \\
A^{(r+1)}_{\{*,4\}} &\leftarrow S^{(r)}_{\{*,4\}} \oplus (S^{(r)}_{\{*,4\}} \ggg 7) \oplus (S^{(r)}_{\{*,4\}} \ggg 41).
\end{aligned}
$$

Ascon -Hash and Ascon-XOF. The state A is composed of the outer part with 64 bits $A_{\{*,0\}}$ and the inner part 256 bits $A_{\{*,i\}}$ ($i = 1, 2, 3, 4$). For Ascon-Hash, the output size is 256 bits, and the security claim is 2^{128}. For Ascon-XOF, the output can have arbitrary length and the security claim against preimage attack is $\min(2^{128}, 2^l)$, where l is the output length. In this paper, we target on Ascon-XOF with a 128-bit hash value and a 128-bit security claim against preimage attack.

2.5 Xoodyak and Xoodoo Permutation

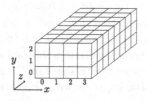

Fig. 4. Toy version of the Xoodoo state. The order in y is opposite to Keccak

Internally, Xoodyak makes use of the Xoodoo permutation [16], whose state (shown in Fig. 4) bit denoted by $A^{(r)}_{\{x,y,z\}}$ is located at the x-th column, y-th row and z-th lane in the round r, where $0 \le x \le 3$, $0 \le y \le 2$, $0 \le z \le 31$. For

Xoodoo, all the coordinates are considered modulo 4 for x, modulo 3 for y and modulo 32 for z. The permutation consists of the iteration of a round function $R = \rho_{east} \circ \chi \circ \iota \circ \rho_{west} \circ \theta$. The number of rounds is a parameter, which is 12 in Xoodyak. Denote the internal states of the round r as

$$A^{(r)} \xrightarrow{\theta} \theta^{(r)} \xrightarrow{\rho_{west}} \rho^{(r)} \xrightarrow{\iota} \iota^{(r)} \xrightarrow{\chi} \chi^{(r)} \xrightarrow{\rho_{east}} A^{(r+1)}.$$

$$
\begin{aligned}
\theta &: \quad \theta^{(r)}_{\{x,y,z\}} = A^{(r)}_{\{x,y,z\}} \oplus \sum_{y'=0}^{2}(A^{(r)}_{\{x-1,y',z-5\}} \oplus A^{(r)}_{\{x-1,y',z-14\}}), \\
\rho_{west} &: \quad \rho^{(r)}_{\{x,0,z\}} = \theta^{(r)}_{\{x,0,z\}}, \ \rho^{(r)}_{\{x,1,z\}} = \theta^{(r)}_{\{x-1,1,z\}}, \ \rho^{(r)}_{\{x,2,z\}} = \theta^{(r)}_{\{x,2,z-11\}}, \\
\iota &: \quad \iota^{(r)}_{\{0,0,z\}} = \rho^{(r)}_{\{0,0,z\}} \oplus RC_r, \text{ where } RC_r \text{ is round-dependent constant,} \quad (4) \\
\chi &: \quad \chi^{(r)}_{\{x,y,z\}} = \iota^{(r)}_{\{x,y,z\}} \oplus (\iota^{(r)}_{\{x,y+1,z\}} \oplus 1) \cdot \iota^{(r)}_{\{x,y+2,z\}}, \\
\rho_{east} &: \quad A^{(r+1)}_{\{x,0,z\}} = \chi^{(r)}_{\{x,0,z\}}, \ A^{(r+1)}_{\{x,1,z\}} = \chi^{(r)}_{\{x,1,z-1\}}, \ A^{(r+1)}_{\{x,2,z\}} = \chi^{(r)}_{\{x-2,2,z-8\}}.
\end{aligned}
$$

Xoodyak can serve as a XOF, i.e. Xoodyak-XOF, which offers arbitrary output length l. The preimage resistance is $\min(2^{128}, 2^l)$. We target on Xoodyak-XOF with output of 128-bit hash value and 128-bit absorbed message block.

3   Meet-in-the-Middle Attack on Sponge-Based Hashing

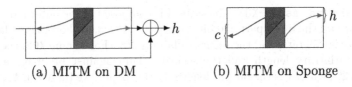

(a) MITM on DM   (b) MITM on Sponge

Fig. 5. Differences in MitM attack on PGV and sponge hash functions (Color figure online)

The essence of the Meet-in-the-Middle attack is actually an efficient way to exhaustively search a space for the right one based on the birthday attack. Taken the MitM attack on DM construction (Fig. 5(a)) as an example, suppose the size of the internal state is n, the size of the output is h ($n \geq h$). In the perspective of exhaust search attack, one chooses a random internal state to verify if it leads to the given h-bit target. After searching a space of 2^h internal states, one will find the preimage. In the MitM attacks, as shown in Fig. 5(a), the attacker starts from the internal state in the middle, which is divided into two independent forward and backward chunks (marked in red and blue, respectively). One computes the two chunks independently until the matching point to filter the wrong internal states. The details are given in Sect. 2.1.

When considering the sponge-based hashing, if we start from some similar internal states in the middle (as shown in Fig. 5(b)) to search preimage with the given target, the internal state has to satisfy not only the target in forward computation, but also the c-bit inner part in backward computation. In other words, we have to search a space with $2^{(h+c)}$ internal states to meet the target and the inner part. Taking the complexity of exhaustive search (i.e., 2^h) into consideration, it may be not a good idea to search a $(h + c)$-bit space even with MitM. For sponge-based hashing, we do not follow the conventional start-from-the-middle way to drive the MitM attack. We try to search a more compact space to find the preimage. In fact, we choose to search the r-bit outer part. With the known c-bit inner part, a search of h-bit subspace of the outer part (if $r > h$) with MitM method is enough to find the preimage. The highlevel framework of the MitM approach is shown in Fig. 6 and highlighted in the green box. Since we start from the outer part and try to satisfy the h-bit target, only forward computations are involved. Like the MitM attack in Sect. 2.1, we need to specify the configurations: the two neutral sets of the outer part, the two independent forward computation chunks, the matching points. We may partially solve the inverse of the permutation from the h-bit target to get some internal bits. Thereafter, by forward computing the two independent chunks until those internal bits, the deterministic relations on the two neutral sets were established, which act as the matching point.

3.1   The Conditions in the MitM Attack

The key point of the MitM is to extend the number of rounds of the independent computation path for blue or red neutral words. For Keccak, we have $\chi : b_i = a_i \oplus (a_{i+1} \oplus 1) \cdot a_{i+2}$. Supposing a_{i+1} is blue neutral word and a_i is red neutral word, then b_i depends on both blue and red neutral words if $a_{i+2} = 1$, otherwise b_i only depends on the red neutral words a_i. That is what we called "conditions".

Setting conditions to control the characteristic can trace back to Wang et al.'s collision attacks with message modification techniques [62,63]. Then, conditions are applied to enhance the probability of the differentials, i.e., the conditional differential cryptanalysis [42]. Later, conditions are used to reduce the diffusion of the cube variables in dynamic cube attack [26] and conditional cube attacks [38]. In MitM attack, the conditions were used to build MitM attacks [2,59] on MD/SHA hashing with ARX structure. For modular addition $X + Y = Z$ $(X, Y, Z \in \mathbb{F}_2^{32})$, particularly the computation of i-th and $(i + 1)$-th bits, assume that the carry from $(i - 1)$-th bit to i-th bit is 0. Then, the $(i + 1)$-th bit of Z is computed as $Z_{\{i+1\}} = X_{\{i+1\}} \oplus Y_{\{i+1\}} \oplus X_{\{i\}} \cdot Y_{\{i\}}$. When $X_{\{i+1\}}$ is blue neutral word and $Y_{\{i\}}$ is red neutral word, the idea of making $X_{\{i\}} = 0$ as a condition so that $Z_{\{i+1\}}$ is only affected by blue neutral word.

In this paper, we try to apply conditions to reduce the diffusion of the red/blue neutral words, and expect to find longer MitM characteristics. In our MitM attack on sponge-based hashing, the conditions usually depend on bits from both inner part (capacity) and outer part (rate). In order to modify certain conditions, we have to modify bits from the inner part. Therefore, as shown in Fig. 6, we place the MitM attack in the processing of the last message block and modify the conditions determined by inner part by randomly changing the first several message blocks (e.g. M_1 in Fig. 6). Suppose there are μ conditions only determined by the inner part[2], the probability to find one right M_1 satisfying all the conditions is about $2^{-\mu}$.

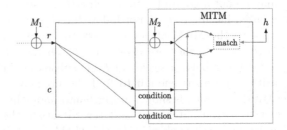

Fig. 6. Framework of the MitM attack on sponge-based hashing

Once we find one right M_1, we assign arbitrary values to all bits except those neutral bits for M_2. Then, an MitM episode is performed:

1. Suppose the two neutral sets of the outer part are of 2^{d_1} and 2^{d_2} values, respectively, which are marked by the ■ and ■ color. For each of 2^{d_1} values, compute forward to the matching points.
2. For each of 2^{d_2} values, compute forward to the matching points.
3. Compute backward with the known h-bit target to the matching points to derive an m-bit matching.
4. Filter states.

The complexity of the MitM episode is $2^{\max(d_1,d_2)} + 2^{d_1+d_2-m}$, which actually checks $2^{d_1+d_2}$ M_2. In order to find a preimage of h, we have to repeat the episode for $2^{h-(d_1+d_2)}$ times. After the conditions in inner part are satisfied, suppose there are 2^{η} non-neutral bits in M_2 that provide 2^{η} MitM episodes. If $\eta+d_1+d_2 < h$, we have to find $2^{h-(\eta+d_1+d_2)}$ M_1, which all satisfy the conditions in the inner part of the last permutation. The total time complexity is

$$2^{h-(\eta+d_1+d_2)} \cdot 2^{\mu} + 2^{h-(d_1+d_2)} \cdot \left(2^{\max(d_1,d_2)} + 2^{d_1+d_2-m}\right). \qquad (5)$$

4   MitM Preimage Attack on Keccak

This section first gives some techniques and properties in previous preimage attacks on Keccak. Then we propose our MILP model for the MitM attack on Keccak. As an application, we mount a 4-round preimage attack on Keccak-512.

---

[2] Note that, if the conditions are determined by both outer part and inner part, then for given inner part, it is possible to change the message block (i.e., M_2 in Fig. 6) to modify the conditions.

4.1   Preliminaries on Keccak

Most previous preimage attacks on Keccak/SHA3 are with the linearization technique. The *linear structure* technique allows to linearize the underlying permutation of Keccak for several rounds. In our attack, we also apply the *linear structure* technique proposed by Guo et al. [35] to linearize one round of Keccak, in order to speed up the search.

Linear Structure. We give an example to explain the *linear structure* technique. As shown in Fig. 7, the variables $v_{0,z}$ and $v_{1,z}$ $(0 \leq z \leq 63)$ are allocated as $A_{\{0,0,z\}}^{(0)} = v_{0,z}$, $A_{\{0,1,z\}}^{(0)} = v_{0,z} \oplus c_{0,z}$, $A_{\{2,0,z\}}^{(0)} = v_{1,z}$, $A_{\{2,1,z\}}^{(0)} = v_{1,z} \oplus c_{1,z}$, where $c_{0,z}$ and $c_{1,z}$ $(0 \leq z \leq 63)$ are constants. After the θ operation, the variables will not diffuse. After the π operation, any two variables are not adjacent in a row, and all outputs of $A^{(1)}$ are linear. To further reduce the diffusion of the variables in χ operation, one can add restricted constraints to the value of constant bits. For example, for the row $\pi_{\{*,0,z\}}^{(0)}$, setting two bit conditions $\pi_{\{1,0,z\}}^{(0)} = 0$ and $\pi_{\{4,0,z\}}^{(0)} = 1$, the other bits except $A_{\{0,0,z\}}^{(1)}$ in $A_{\{*,0,z\}}^{(1)}$ will be constants. Those conditions can be satisfied by modifying the message block and inner part.

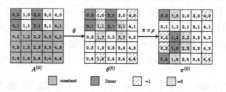

Fig. 7. The linear structure of 1-round Keccak-512

Properties of the Sbox χ. Guo et al. proposed several properties of the Sbox χ, which help to mount preimage attacks on Keccak [35]. Those properties can be also applied in our MitM attack, so we give a brief introduction in the following. Assume $\chi : \mathbb{F}_2^5 \rightarrow \mathbb{F}_2^5$ maps $(a_0, a_1, a_2, a_3, a_4)$ to $(b_0, b_1, b_2, b_3, b_4)$ as

$$b_i = a_i \oplus (a_{i+1} \oplus 1) \cdot a_{i+2}, \tag{6}$$

where all indices are modulo 5. The inverse operation χ^{-1} is

$$a_i = b_i \oplus (b_{i+1} \oplus 1) \cdot (b_{i+2} \oplus (b_{i+3} \oplus 1) \cdot b_{i+4}). \tag{7}$$

Property 1. [35] When there are three known consecutive output bits, two linear equations of the input bits can be constructed. E.g., assuming that (b_0, b_1, b_2) are known, two linear equations on (a_0, a_1, a_2, a_3) are constructed as

$$b_0 = a_0 \oplus (b_1 \oplus 1) \cdot a_2, \quad b_1 = a_1 \oplus (b_2 \oplus 1) \cdot a_3. \tag{8}$$

4.2   MILP Model of the MitM Preimage Attack on Keccak

In previous MILP models [5,28] of the MitM attack, each bit can take one of the four colors (■, ■, ■, and □). Generally, the □ bits depending on both ■ and ■, are unknown and useless in the MitM attack. In our model, bits whose Boolean expression depending on the addition of ■ and ■ (not multiplied) can also be used in our MitM attack, which is known as *the indirect-partial matching technique* [2,59] and ignored by previous automatic models [5,28]. Therefore, we introduce another color, i.e., □. In our MILP models, there are five colors (■, ■, ■, □, and □). We first introduce a new efficient encoding scheme of those colors. Applying the *linear structure* technique, we can skip the first round and construct the model from the second round. Then we model the attribute propagation of the five colors over the five operations in each round of Keccak. We also model the matching phase with the CP-kernel for Keccak. With all above works, we build an automatic MILP model for the MitM preimage attack on Keccak.

Encoding Scheme. Since there are 5 colors to encode in the MILP model, the previous 2-bit encoding method [5,28] is not suitable and we introduce a new 3-bit encoding scheme, i.e., each bit is represented by three 0–1 variables $(\omega_0, \omega_1, \omega_2)$:

- Gray ■: $(1,1,1)$, global constant bits,
- Red ■ : $(0,1,1)$, bits determined by ■ bits and ■ bits of starting state,
- Blue ■ : $(1,1,0)$, bits determined by ■ bits and ■ bits of starting state,
- Green □ : $(0,1,0)$, bits determined by ■ bits, ■ bits and ■ bits, but the expression does not contain the product of ■ and ■ bits,
- White □ : $(0,0,0)$, bits dependent on the product of ■ and ■ bits.

We set ω_1 to 0 for □ and to 1 for any other color (■, ■, ■, □). So □ bit can be quickly detected by the value of ω_1. Then we set ω_0 to 1 for (■, ■) and to 0 for other color (■, □, □). Similarly for ω_2.

Modelling the Starting State with the Linear Structure Technique. In the starting state, each of the 1600 bits takes one color of ■, ■ and ■. We allocate variables $\alpha_{\{x,y,z\}}$ and $\beta_{\{x,y,z\}}$ for the bit with index $\{x,y,z\}$, where $\alpha_{\{x,y,z\}} = 1$ if and only if the bit is ■ and $\beta_{\{x,y,z\}} = 1$ if and only if the bit is ■. Therefore, we can compute the initial DoF by $\lambda_\mathcal{B} = \sum \alpha_{\{x,y,z\}}, \lambda_\mathcal{R} = \sum \beta_{\{x,y,z\}}$. For Keccak, we apply the 1-round restricted linear structure as the example given in Sect. 4.1. Denote the starting state after XORing message block by $A^{(0)}$. The bits in $A^{(0)}_{\{0,0,z\}}$, $A^{(0)}_{\{0,1,z\}}$, $A^{(0)}_{\{2,0,z\}}$ and $A^{(0)}_{\{2,1,z\}}$ can be colored as ■ or ■. And the remaining bits of $A^{(0)}$ need to be ■. In order to control the diffusion of θ operation, $A^{(0)}_{\{0,0,z\}}$ and $A^{(0)}_{\{0,1,z\}}$ should be the same color and the $A^{(0)}_{\{0,0,z\}} \oplus A^{(0)}_{\{0,1,z\}}$ should be constant, which consumes one degree of freedom. Similarly for $A^{(0)}_{\{2,0,z\}}$ and $A^{(0)}_{\{2,1,z\}}$. Thereafter, the coloring pattern keeps the same over the first θ operation. Then with the conditions set in $\pi^{(0)}$ as introduced in Sect. 4.1, we can omit the first χ operation and construct the model from $A^{(1)}$ only considering the linear operation $\pi \circ \rho$ from $A^{(0)}$.

Modelling the Attribute Propagation. The round function of Keccak consists of five operations θ, ρ, π, χ and ι. The linear operations ρ and π only change the position of each bit of the state. The operation ι can be ignored because it will not change the coloring pattern.

Modelling the θ operation. At first, we give the rule of XOR with an arbitrary number of inputs under the new coloring scheme. We name the rule of by XOR-RULE, which involves five rules:

1. XOR-RULE-1: If the inputs have (0,0,0) □ bit, the output is □.
2. XOR-RULE-2: If the inputs are all (1,1,1) ■ bits, the output is ■.
3. XOR-RULE-3: If the inputs have (1,1,0) ■(≥ 1) and ■(≥ 0) bits, the output will be ■ without consuming DoF, or ■ by consuming one DoF of ■.
4. XOR-RULE-4: If the inputs have (0,1,1) ■(≥ 1) and ■(≥ 0) bits, the output will be ■ without consuming DoF, or ■ by consuming one DoF of ■.
5. XOR-RULE-5: If the inputs have (0,1,0) □ bits, or have at least two kinds of ■, ■ and □ bits:
   (a) the output can be □ without consuming DoF.
   (b) the output can be ■ (or ■) by consuming one DoF of ■ (or ■).
   (c) the output can be ■ by consuming one DoF of ■ and one DoF of ■.

Fig. 8. 5-XOR-RULE ("*" represents the bit can be any color)

We give some valid coloring patterns of 5 inputs of XOR, which are named by 5-XOR-RULE, as shown in Fig. 8. Similar to previous MitM attacks [5], we can use some new variables to identify which rule is applied in different cases. We define three 0–1 variables ν_i ($i \in \{0,1,2\}$), where $\nu_0 = 1$ if and only if all the ω_0's of the 5 input bits are 1, similar to the cases $i = 1, 2$. The above five rules can be represented by (ν_0, ν_1, ν_2):

1. (ν_0, ν_1, ν_2) = ($*, 0, *$), XOR-RULE-1 is applied.
2. (ν_0, ν_1, ν_2) = ($1, 1, 1$), XOR-RULE-2 is applied.
3. (ν_0, ν_1, ν_2) = ($1, 1, 0$), XOR-RULE-3 is applied.
4. (ν_0, ν_1, ν_2) = ($0, 1, 1$), XOR-RULE-4 is applied.
5. (ν_0, ν_1, ν_2) = ($0, 1, 0$), XOR-RULE-5 is applied.

Taking (ν_0, ν_1, ν_2) = ($1, 1, 0$) as an example. $\nu_1 = 1$ means that all the ω_1's of the input bits are 1 and there is no □ bit. $\nu_0 = 1$ means that there only may have the ■ or ■. $\nu_2 = 1$ means that there must have ■ or □ or □. Based on the above analysis, we can deduce that when (ν_0, ν_1, ν_2) = ($1, 1, 0$), there only have ■ and ■ and the number of ■ is greater than or equal to one, where XOR-RULE-3 is applied. Denote the output bit as $(\omega_0^O, \omega_1^O, \omega_2^O)$ and the consumed DoF of ■ bits and ■ bits are $(\delta_\mathcal{R}, \delta_\mathcal{B})$, we can derive

$$
\begin{cases}
\omega_0^O - \nu_0 \geq 0, \quad -\omega_0^O + \nu_1 \geq 0, \\
\omega_1^O - \nu_1 = 0, \\
\omega_2^O - \nu_2 \geq 0, \quad -\omega_2^O + \nu_1 \geq 0,
\end{cases}
\qquad
\begin{cases}
\delta_\mathcal{R} - \omega_0^O + \nu_0 = 0, \\
\delta_\mathcal{B} - \omega_2^O + \nu_2 = 0.
\end{cases}
\tag{9}
$$

In the θ operation, the expression of the output bit is XORing 11 input bits. If we directly compute the XORing value of the 11 input bits, we may double counting the consumption of DoF. For example, given (x, z), we compute $\theta_{\{x,0,z\}}^{(r)}$ and $\theta_{\{x,1,z\}}^{(r)}$ by $\theta_{\{x,y,z\}}^{(r)} = A_{\{x,y,z\}}^{(r)} \oplus \sum_{y'=0}^{4} (A_{\{x-1,y',z\}}^{(r)} \oplus A_{\{x+1,y',z-1\}}^{(r)})$. If bits in the common formula $\sum_{y'=0}^{4} (A_{\{x-1,y',z\}}^{(r)} \oplus A_{\{x+1,y',z-1\}}^{(r)})$ are only determined by ■ bits, and $A_{\{x,0,z\}}^{(r)}$, $A_{\{x,1,z\}}^{(r)}$ are ■ bits, we can let the summation bit of $\sum_{y'=0}^{4} (A_{\{x-1,y',z\}}^{(r)} \oplus A_{\{x+1,y',z-1\}}^{(r)})$ be ■ by consuming only one DoF of ■. Thereafter, the two output bits $\theta_{\{x,0,z\}}^{(r)}$, $\theta_{\{x,1,z\}}^{(r)}$ will be ■. However, if we directly set the two output bits $\theta_{\{x,0,z\}}^{(r)}$, $\theta_{\{x,1,z\}}^{(r)}$ to be ■ by the XOR-RULE individually, we have to consume 2 DoF of ■. To solve this problem, we depose the θ operation to three steps in our model, as described in the following expressions:

$$
C_{\{x,z\}}^{(r)} = A_{\{x,0,z\}}^{(r)} \oplus A_{\{x,1,z\}}^{(r)} \oplus A_{\{x,2,z\}}^{(r)} \oplus A_{\{x,3,z\}}^{(r)} \oplus A_{\{x,4,z\}}^{(r)},
$$
$$
D_{\{x,z\}}^{(r)} = C_{\{x-1,z\}}^{(r)} \oplus C_{\{x+1,z-1\}}^{(r)},
$$
$$
\theta_{\{x,y,z\}}^{(r)} = A_{\{x,y,z\}}^{(r)} \oplus D_{\{x,z\}}^{(r)}.
$$

At first, we compute the coloring pattern of $C_{\{x,z\}}^{(r)}$. Then, we compute the coloring pattern of $D_{\{x,z\}}^{(r)}$ and compute $\theta_{\{x,y,z\}}^{(r)}$ at last.

Modelling the χ operation. For the χ operation in the round 0, we add conditions to control the diffusion of the ■ or ■ and the first χ is omitted. For the χ operation from round 1, we build the SBOX-RULE. The χ operation maps $(a_0, a_1, a_2, a_3, a_4)$ to $(b_0, b_1, b_2, b_3, b_4)$. According to Eq. (6), $b_i = a_i \oplus (a_{i+1} \oplus 1) \cdot a_{i+2}$. Hence, for each output bit b_i, we determine its color by (a_i, a_{i+1}, a_{i+2}):

1. If there are □ bits in (a_i, a_{i+1}, a_{i+2}), the output is □.
2. If there are all ■ bits, the output is ■.
3. If there are only ■(≥ 1) and ■(≥ 0) bits, the output will be ■.
4. If there are only ■(≥ 1) and ■(≥ 0) bits, the output will be ■.
5. If there are □, or more than two kinds of ■, ■ and □ bits in (a_i, a_{i+1}, a_{i+2}):
   (a) if a_{i+1} and a_{i+2} are all ■ (or ■), the output is □.
   (b) if a_{i+1} or a_{i+2} is ■, the output is □.
   (c) if a_{i+1} and a_{i+2} are of arbitrarily two kinds of ■, ■, □, the output is □.

The rules SBOX-RULE restrict the coloring pattern of $(a_i, a_{i+1}, a_{i+2}, b_i)$ to the subset of $\mathbb{F}_2^{12}$, which is described by the linear inequalities by using the convex hull computation. Some valid coloring patterns are shown in Fig. 9.

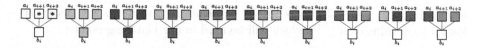

Fig. 9. SBOX-RULE for Keccak ("*" represents the bit can be any color)

Modelling the Matching Phase. Suppose the first 512 bits of $A^{(r+1)}$ are the hash value. In order to attack more rounds, we try to compute certain bits or relations in $A^{(r)}$ by the hash value in $A^{(r+1)}$, to act as the matching points.

Leaked linear relations of $A^{(r)}$. From the 512-bit hash, we know $A^{(r+1)}_{\{*,0,*\}}$ and the first 3 lanes of $A^{(r+1)}_{\{*,1,*\}}$. From $A^{(r+1)}_{\{*,0,*\}}$, we deduce $\pi^{(r)}_{\{*,0,*\}}$ from Eq. (7). Applying the inverse of the operations ρ and π to $\pi^{(r)}_{\{*,0,*\}}$, we can deduce

$$\theta^{(r)}_{\{x,x,z\}} = \pi^{(r)}_{\{x,0,z+\gamma[x,x]\}}, \forall\, 0 \le x \le 4, 0 \le z \le 63. \tag{10}$$

In addition, according to Eq. (8), two linear equations can be deduced from the first three bits of each row of $A^{(r+1)}_{\{*,1,*\}}$, which are given as

$$A^{(r+1)}_{\{0,1,z\}} = \pi^{(r)}_{\{0,1,z\}} \oplus (A^{(r+1)}_{\{1,1,z\}} \oplus 1) \cdot \pi^{(r)}_{\{2,1,z\}},$$
$$A^{(r+1)}_{\{1,1,z\}} = \pi^{(r)}_{\{1,1,z\}} \oplus (A^{(r+1)}_{\{2,1,z\}} \oplus 1) \cdot \pi^{(r)}_{\{3,1,z\}}.$$

Then applying the inverse of ρ and π, the linear equations are transformed to

$$A^{(r+1)}_{\{0,1,z\}} = \theta^{(r)}_{\{3,0,z-\gamma[3,0]\}} \oplus (A^{(r+1)}_{\{1,1,z\}} \oplus 1) \cdot \theta^{(r)}_{\{0,2,z-\gamma[0,2]\}},$$
$$A^{(r+1)}_{\{1,1,z\}} = \theta^{(r)}_{\{4,1,z-\gamma[4,1]\}} \oplus (A^{(r+1)}_{\{2,1,z\}} \oplus 1) \cdot \theta^{(r)}_{\{1,3,z-\gamma[1,3]\}}. \tag{11}$$

With the known value $\theta^{(r)}_{\{x,x,z\}}$ ($0 \le x \le 4, 0 \le z \le 63$) by (10), we add the same known values (underlined) to both sides of (11), which are

$$A^{(r+1)}_{\{0,1,z\}} \oplus \underline{\theta^{(r)}_{\{3,3,z-\gamma[3,0]\}}} \oplus (A^{(r+1)}_{\{1,1,z\}} \oplus 1) \cdot \underline{\theta^{(r)}_{\{0,0,z-\gamma[0,2]\}}}$$
$$= \theta^{(r)}_{\{3,0,z-\gamma[3,0]\}} \oplus \underline{\theta^{(r)}_{\{3,3,z-\gamma[3,0]\}}} \oplus (A^{(r+1)}_{\{1,1,z\}} \oplus 1) \cdot (\theta^{(r)}_{\{0,2,z-\gamma[0,2]\}} \oplus \underline{\theta^{(r)}_{\{0,0,z-\gamma[0,2]\}}})$$
$$A^{(r+1)}_{\{1,1,z\}} \oplus \underline{\theta^{(r)}_{\{4,4,z-\gamma[4,1]\}}} \oplus (A^{(r+1)}_{\{2,1,z\}} \oplus 1) \cdot \underline{\theta^{(r)}_{\{1,1,z-\gamma[1,3]\}}}$$
$$= \theta^{(r)}_{\{4,1,z-\gamma[4,1]\}} \oplus \underline{\theta^{(r)}_{\{4,4,z-\gamma[4,1]\}}} \oplus (A^{(r+1)}_{\{2,1,z\}} \oplus 1) \cdot (\theta^{(r)}_{\{1,3,z-\gamma[1,3]\}} \oplus \underline{\theta^{(r)}_{\{1,1,z-\gamma[1,3]\}}}). \tag{12}$$

According to the CP-kernel property [9] of operation θ, we deduce

$$\theta^{(r)}_{\{3,0,z-\gamma[3,0]\}} \oplus \theta^{(r)}_{\{3,3,z-\gamma[3,0]\}} = A^{(r)}_{\{3,0,z-\gamma[3,0]\}} \oplus A^{(r)}_{\{3,3,z-\gamma[3,0]\}},$$
$$\theta^{(r)}_{\{0,2,z-\gamma[0,2]\}} \oplus \theta^{(r)}_{\{0,0,z-\gamma[0,2]\}} = A^{(r)}_{\{0,2,z-\gamma[0,2]\}} \oplus A^{(r)}_{\{0,0,z-\gamma[0,2]\}},$$
$$\theta^{(r)}_{\{4,1,z-\gamma[4,1]\}} \oplus \theta^{(r)}_{\{4,4,z-\gamma[4,1]\}} = A^{(r)}_{\{4,1,z-\gamma[4,1]\}} \oplus A^{(r)}_{\{4,4,z-\gamma[4,1]\}},$$
$$\theta^{(r)}_{\{1,3,z-\gamma[1,3]\}} \oplus \theta^{(r)}_{\{1,1,z-\gamma[1,3]\}} = A^{(r)}_{\{1,3,z-\gamma[1,3]\}} \oplus A^{(r)}_{\{1,1,z-\gamma[1,3]\}}. \tag{13}$$

Combining (12) and (13), there are linear relations on bits in $A^{(r)}$ with the known hash value of $A^{(r+1)}$, which will be used in our matching points:

$$
\begin{aligned}
A^{(r)}_{\{3,0,z-\gamma[3,0]\}} &\oplus A^{(r)}_{\{3,3,z-\gamma[3,0]\}} \oplus (A^{(r+1)}_{\{1,1,z\}} \oplus 1) \cdot (A^{(r)}_{\{0,2,z-\gamma[0,2]\}} \oplus A^{(r)}_{\{0,0,z-\gamma[0,2]\}}) \\
&= A^{(r+1)}_{\{0,1,z\}} \oplus \theta^{(r)}_{\{3,3,z-\gamma[3,0]\}} \oplus (A^{(r+1)}_{\{1,1,z\}} \oplus 1) \cdot \theta^{(r)}_{\{0,0,z-\gamma[0,2]\}},
\end{aligned}
\tag{14}
$$

$$
\begin{aligned}
A^{(r)}_{\{4,1,z-\gamma[4,1]\}} &\oplus A^{(r)}_{\{4,4,z-\gamma[4,1]\}} \oplus (A^{(r+1)}_{\{2,1,z\}} \oplus 1) \cdot (A^{(r)}_{\{1,3,z-\gamma[1,3]\}} \oplus A^{(r)}_{\{1,1,z-\gamma[1,3]\}}) \\
&= A^{(r+1)}_{\{1,1,z\}} \oplus \theta^{(r)}_{\{4,4,z-\gamma[4,1]\}} \oplus (A^{(r+1)}_{\{2,1,z\}} \oplus 1) \cdot \theta^{(r)}_{\{1,1,z-\gamma[1,3]\}}.
\end{aligned}
\tag{15}
$$

Observation 1 (Conditions in Matching Points of Keccak). *In* (14)*, if four bits* $(A^{(r)}_{\{3,0,z-\gamma[3,0]\}}, A^{(r)}_{\{3,3,z-\gamma[3,0]\}}, A^{(r)}_{\{0,2,z-\gamma[0,2]\}}, A^{(r)}_{\{0,0,z-\gamma[0,2]\}})$ *in* $A^{(r)}$ *satisfy the following two conditions, there is a 1-bit filter:*

(1) There has no $\square$ in $(A^{(r)}_{\{3,0,z-\gamma[3,0]\}}, A^{(r)}_{\{3,3,z-\gamma[3,0]\}}, A^{(r)}_{\{0,2,z-\gamma[0,2]\}}, A^{(r)}_{\{0,0,z-\gamma[0,2]\}})$.

(2) $(A^{(r)}_{\{3,0,z-\gamma[3,0]\}}, A^{(r)}_{\{3,3,z-\gamma[3,0]\}})$ *is of* $(\blacksquare,\blacksquare)$, $(\blacksquare,\square)$, $(\blacksquare,\square)$, $(\square,\square)$, *or* $(\square,\square)$, *or opposite order* .

We introduce a binary variable $\delta_\mathcal{M}$ to represent whether there is a filtering. Similarly to the XOR-RULE, we add three 0–1 variables ν_i ($i \in \{0,1,2\}$), where $\nu_i = 1$ ($i = 0,2$) if and only if all ω_i's of $(A^{(r)}_{\{3,0,z-\gamma[3,0]\}}, A^{(r)}_{\{3,3,z-\gamma[3,0]\}})$ are 1, and $\nu_1 = 1$ if and only if all ω_1's of $(A^{(r)}_{\{3,0,z-\gamma[3,0]\}}, A^{(r)}_{\{3,3,z-\gamma[3,0]\}}, A^{(r)}_{\{0,2,z-\gamma[0,2]\}}, A^{(r)}_{\{0,0,z-\gamma[0,2]\}})$ are 1. We can derive

$$
\begin{cases}
\nu_1 - \delta_\mathcal{M} \geq 0, \quad -\nu_0 - \delta_\mathcal{M} + 1 \geq 0, \quad -\nu_2 - \delta_\mathcal{M} + 1 \geq 0, \\
\nu_0 - \nu_1 + \nu_2 + \delta_\mathcal{M} \geq 0.
\end{cases}
$$

The Objective Function. Let $l_\mathcal{R}$, and $l_\mathcal{B}$ be the accumulated consumption of DoF of $\blacksquare$ and $\blacksquare$, i.e., $l_\mathcal{R} = \sum \delta_\mathcal{R}$ and $l_\mathcal{B} = \sum \delta_\mathcal{B}$. Therefore, we can get $\mathrm{DoF}_\mathcal{R} = \lambda_\mathcal{R} - l_\mathcal{R}$, $\mathrm{DoF}_\mathcal{B} = \lambda_\mathcal{B} - l_\mathcal{B}$. We also have $\mathrm{DoM} = \sum \delta_\mathcal{M}$. According to the time complexity given by Eq. (1), we need to maximize the value of $\min\{\mathrm{DoF}_\mathcal{R}, \mathrm{DoF}_\mathcal{B}, \mathrm{DoM}\}$ to find the optimal attacks. We introduce an auxiliary variable v_{obj}, impose the following constraints, and maximize v_{obj},

$$
\{v_{obj} \leq \mathrm{DoF}_\mathcal{R}, v_{obj} \leq \mathrm{DoF}_\mathcal{B}, v_{obj} \leq \mathrm{DoM}\}.
\tag{16}
$$

4.3   MitM Preimage Attack on 4-Round Keccak-512

We follow the framework in Fig. 6 to perform the attack with (M_1, M_2) and place the MitM attack at M_2. We construct an MILP model for Keccak-512 following Sect. 4.2. The code is in https://github.com/qly14/MITM-Preimage-Attack.git. By solving with our MILP model, we mount a 4-round MitM preimage attack on Keccak-512, as in Fig. 10 and figures in the Supplementary Material B in our full version paper [55], which contains 3 additional symbols:

- $\blacksquare$, $\blacksquare$: there consumes one degree of freedom of $\blacksquare$ to let the bit be $\square$ or $\blacksquare$.
- $\square$: there consumes one degree of freedom of $\blacksquare$ to let the bit be $\blacksquare$.
- $\boxed{m}$: $\square$ bits used for matching.

Conditions in the Linear Structure. State $A^{(0)}$ contains 16 ■ bits and 216 ■ bits. We take the similar strategy with [48] to get 1-round linear structure of Keccak. We introduce 116 binary variables $v = \{v_0, v_1, \cdots, v_{115}\}$ and 116 binary variables $c = \{c_0, c_1, \cdots, c_{115}\}$. Those variables v_i's and c_i's are placed at the $16 + 216 = 232$ ■ and ■ bits in $A^{(0)}$ as in Fig. 10. For example, we set $A^{(0)}_{\{0,0,0\}} = v_0$ and $A^{(0)}_{\{0,1,0\}} = v_0 \oplus c_0$. When we choose $c \in \mathbb{F}_2^{116}$ to be arbitrary constant, the θ operation will act as identity with regard to the ■ and ■ bits in $A^{(0)}$. To reduce the diffusion of χ in round 0, we need to set some bits conditions in $\pi^{(0)}$ to be constants. According to (6), if a_{i+1} is ■ or ■, we need to set $a_{i+2} = 0$ and $a_i = 1$. So there are totally $232 \times 2 = 464$ conditions on $\pi^{(0)}$. After the inverse of $\rho \circ \pi$, we determine the positions of bit conditions in $\theta^{(0)}$. Taking the state $\theta^{(0)}_{\{*,*,1\}}$ as an example, there are six bit conditions as

$$\theta^{(0)}_{\{1,0,1\}} = 1, \ \theta^{(0)}_{\{1,2,1\}} = 0, \ \theta^{(0)}_{\{1,4,1\}} = 1, \theta^{(0)}_{\{3,1,1\}} = 0, \ \theta^{(0)}_{\{3,2,1\}} = 0, \ \theta^{(0)}_{\{4,4,1\}} = 1. \quad (17)$$

Above conditions can be converted to those on $A^{(0)}$. The bits in $A^{(0)}$ can be divided into two parts: the bits determined by the outer part (i.e., they can be modified by directly changing the absorbed M_2), and the bits determined by inner part. The equations in Eq. (17) can be transformed to

$$A^{(0)}_{\{1,0,1\}} \oplus c_2 \oplus A^{(0)}_{\{0,2,1\}} \oplus A^{(0)}_{\{0,3,1\}} \oplus A^{(0)}_{\{0,4,1\}} \oplus c_1 \oplus A^{(0)}_{\{2,2,0\}} \oplus A^{(0)}_{\{2,3,0\}} \oplus A^{(0)}_{\{2,4,0\}} = 1,$$
$$A^{(0)}_{\{1,2,1\}} \oplus c_2 \oplus A^{(0)}_{\{0,2,1\}} \oplus A^{(0)}_{\{0,3,1\}} \oplus A^{(0)}_{\{0,4,1\}} \oplus c_1 \oplus A^{(0)}_{\{2,2,0\}} \oplus A^{(0)}_{\{2,3,0\}} \oplus A^{(0)}_{\{2,4,0\}} = 0,$$
$$A^{(0)}_{\{1,4,1\}} \oplus c_2 \oplus A^{(0)}_{\{0,2,1\}} \oplus A^{(0)}_{\{0,3,1\}} \oplus A^{(0)}_{\{0,4,1\}} \oplus c_1 \oplus A^{(0)}_{\{2,2,0\}} \oplus A^{(0)}_{\{2,3,0\}} \oplus A^{(0)}_{\{2,4,0\}} = 1,$$
$$A^{(0)}_{\{3,1,1\}} \oplus c_3 \oplus A^{(0)}_{\{2,2,1\}} \oplus A^{(0)}_{\{2,3,1\}} \oplus A^{(0)}_{\{2,4,1\}} \oplus A^{(0)}_{\{4,0,0\}} \oplus A^{(0)}_{\{4,1,0\}} \oplus A^{(0)}_{\{4,2,0\}} \oplus A^{(0)}_{\{4,3,0\}} \oplus A^{(0)}_{\{4,4,0\}} = 0,$$
$$A^{(0)}_{\{3,2,1\}} \oplus c_3 \oplus A^{(0)}_{\{2,2,1\}} \oplus A^{(0)}_{\{2,3,1\}} \oplus A^{(0)}_{\{2,4,1\}} \oplus A^{(0)}_{\{4,0,0\}} \oplus A^{(0)}_{\{4,1,0\}} \oplus A^{(0)}_{\{4,2,0\}} \oplus A^{(0)}_{\{4,3,0\}} \oplus A^{(0)}_{\{4,4,0\}} = 0,$$
$$A^{(0)}_{\{4,4,1\}} \oplus A^{(0)}_{\{3,0,1\}} \oplus A^{(0)}_{\{3,1,1\}} \oplus A^{(0)}_{\{3,2,1\}} \oplus A^{(0)}_{\{3,3,1\}} \oplus A^{(0)}_{\{3,4,1\}} \oplus c_0 \oplus A^{(0)}_{\{0,2,0\}} \oplus A^{(0)}_{\{0,3,0\}} \oplus A^{(0)}_{\{0,4,0\}} = 1,$$
$$(18)$$

where $c_0 = A^{(0)}_{\{0,0,0\}} \oplus A^{(0)}_{\{0,1,0\}}$, $c_1 = A^{(0)}_{\{2,0,0\}} \oplus A^{(0)}_{\{2,1,0\}}$, $c_2 = A^{(0)}_{\{0,0,1\}} \oplus A^{(0)}_{\{0,1,1\}}$, $c_3 = A^{(0)}_{\{2,0,1\}} \oplus A^{(0)}_{\{2,1,1\}}$. Given an inner part, the 464 conditions on state $A^{(0)}$ will be a linear system of the $576 - 116 = 460$ variables of M_2 (marked by bold). We compute the rank of the coefficient matrix of the linear system is 250. In other words, through some linear transformations, there are 214 equations out of the total 464 only determined by the bits of inner part. For example, combining the 2nd and 3rd equations in Eq. (18), we can deduce an equation between two inner part bits $A^{(0)}_{\{1,2,1\}} \oplus A^{(0)}_{\{1,4,1\}} = 1$. We have to randomly test 2^{214} M_1 to compute the inner part satisfying the 214 equations. Then for a right inner part, there are $2^{460-250} = 2^{210}$ solutions of M_2, which make all the 464 equations hold. For each solution of M_2, the ■ and $c \in \mathbb{F}_2^{116}$ in the outer part will be fixed. Then with the fixed inner part, we can conduct the MitM episodes to filter states.

Consumed Degrees of Freedom. As shown in Fig. 10, after adding 464 conditions and consuming 108 ■ and 8 ■ degrees of freedom in round 0, we can derive the coloring pattern in $A^{(1)}$. The remaining degrees of freedom for ■ and ■ are 108 and 8, respectively. We give two examples to explain the consumption of degrees of freedom in the computation from $A^{(1)}$ to $A^{(3)}$.

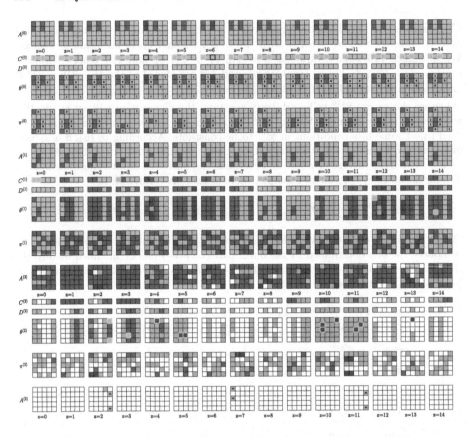

Fig. 10. The MitM preimage attack on 4-round Keccak-512 (part I)

1. For $\theta^{(1)}_{\{0,0,12\}}$ marked by ■ in Fig. 11 (part of Fig. 10), we set an equation of ■ to a constant, which means consuming one DoF of ■ to let $\theta^{(1)}_{\{0,0,12\}}$ be ■, as listed below:

$$A^{(1)}_{\{0,0,12\}} \oplus A^{(1)}_{\{4,0,12\}} \oplus A^{(1)}_{\{4,1,12\}} \oplus A^{(1)}_{\{4,2,12\}} \oplus A^{(1)}_{\{4,3,12\}} \oplus A^{(1)}_{\{4,4,12\}}$$
$$\oplus A^{(1)}_{\{1,0,11\}} \oplus A^{(1)}_{\{1,1,11\}} \oplus A^{(1)}_{\{1,2,11\}} \oplus A^{(1)}_{\{1,3,11\}} \oplus A^{(1)}_{\{1,4,11\}} = const., \quad (19)$$

where the bits marked by red are ■ and others marked by black are ■.

2. For $\theta^{(2)}_{\{1,3,5\}}$ marked by ■ in Fig. 12, we set an equation of ■ to a constant, which means consuming one DoF of ■ to let $\theta^{(2)}_{\{1,3,5\}}$ be ■. Since there have

$$\theta^{(2)}_{\{1,3,5\}} = A^{(2)}_{\{1,3,5\}} \oplus D^{(2)}_{\{1,5\}} = A^{(2)}_{\{1,3,5\}} \oplus C^{(2)}_{\{0,5\}} \oplus C^{(2)}_{\{2,4\}},$$
$$C^{(2)}_{\{0,5\}} = A^{(2)}_{\{0,0,5\}} \oplus A^{(2)}_{\{0,1,5\}} \oplus A^{(2)}_{\{0,2,5\}} \oplus A^{(2)}_{\{0,3,5\}} \oplus A^{(2)}_{\{0,4,5\}},$$
$$C^{(2)}_{\{2,4\}} = A^{(2)}_{\{2,0,4\}} \oplus A^{(2)}_{\{2,1,4\}} \oplus A^{(2)}_{\{2,2,4\}} \oplus A^{(2)}_{\{2,3,4\}} \oplus A^{(2)}_{\{2,4,4\}}.$$

We can set all the ■ involved to be constant:

$$A^{(2)}_{\{1,3,5\}} \oplus A^{(2)}_{\{0,0,5\}} \oplus A^{(2)}_{\{0,1,5\}} \oplus A^{(2)}_{\{0,3,5\}} \oplus A^{(2)}_{\{0,4,5\}}$$
$$A^{(2)}_{\{2,0,4\}} \oplus A^{(2)}_{\{2,1,4\}} \oplus A^{(2)}_{\{2,2,4\}} \oplus A^{(2)}_{\{2,3,4\}} \oplus A^{(2)}_{\{2,4,4\}} = const. \tag{20}$$

Then, we have $\theta^{(2)}_{\{1,3,5\}} = A^{(2)}_{\{0,2,5\}} \oplus const.$

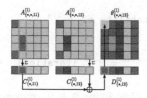

Fig. 11. Example (1) of consumed DoF   **Fig. 12.** Example (2) of consumed DoF

There are totally 100 ■ and ■ in internal states between $A^{(1)}$ and $\theta^{(2)}$, which means that the accumulated consumed degree of freedom of ■ is 100. Denote the 100-bit constants (i.e. constants such as (19) and (20)) as $c_\mathcal{R} \in \mathbb{F}_2^{100}$. At last, the numbers of remaining degrees of freedom for ■ and ■ are both 8 bits.

Matching Strategy with Green Bits. According to Observation 1, we can use $A^{(3)}$ to count the number of matching equations, i.e. $m = 8$. We give an example matching Eq. (21) (marked by ▥ in $A^{(3)}$ with $z = 2$ and $z = 41$ in Fig. 10) according to Eq. (15), which satisfies the matching conditions of Observation 1:

$$A^{(3)}_{\{4,1,2\}} \oplus A^{(3)}_{\{4,4,2\}} \oplus (A^{(4)}_{\{2,1,22\}} \oplus 1) \cdot (A^{(3)}_{\{1,3,41\}} \oplus A^{(3)}_{\{1,1,41\}})$$
$$\oplus A^{(4)}_{\{1,1,22\}} \oplus \theta^{(3)}_{\{4,4,2\}} \oplus (A^{(4)}_{\{2,1,22\}} \oplus 1) \cdot \theta^{(3)}_{\{1,1,41\}} = 0. \tag{21}$$

With known bits in $A^{(4)}$ and $\theta^{(3)}$, the left part of Eq. (21) can be written as Boolean expression (denoted as $f_\mathcal{M}$) on ■, ■ and ■ bits of the starting state. Therefore, denote $f_\mathcal{M} = f_\mathcal{R} \oplus f_\mathcal{B} \oplus f_\mathcal{G}$, where $f_\mathcal{R}$ only contains monomials on ■/□ bits, $f_\mathcal{B}$ contains monomials on ■/□ bits, and $f_\mathcal{G}$ contains monomials on ■ bits and constants. With the given ■ bits, we can compute the value $f_\mathcal{R} \oplus f_\mathcal{G} = f'_\mathcal{M}$ with forward computing Keccak permutation by setting all the ■ bits as 0. Similarly, we get $f_\mathcal{B} \oplus f_\mathcal{G} = f''_\mathcal{M}$ by setting ■ bits as 0. By setting all ■ and ■ bits as 0, we get $f_\mathcal{G} = f'''_\mathcal{M}$. Therefore, we compute $f_\mathcal{R} = f'_\mathcal{M} \oplus f'''_\mathcal{M}$ and $f_\mathcal{B} = f''_\mathcal{M} \oplus f'''_\mathcal{M}$. Then, we can derive the matching equation from Eq. (21) as $f_\mathcal{R} = f_\mathcal{B} \oplus f_\mathcal{G}$.

MitM Attack on 4-Round Keccak-512. In our attack Algorithm 1, we first precompute inversely from $A^{(4)}$ to $A^{(3)}$, and derive 128 Boolean equations similar with Eq. (21). Among them, 8 equations act as the matching points in the MitM phase, and the other 120 equations are used to further filter the partial matched states.

Algorithm 1: Preimage Attack on 4-round Keccak-512

---

1 Precompute inversely from the target to $A^{(3)}$, and derive 128 Boolean equations of similar form with Eq. (21)

2 /* Among them, 8 Boolean equations act as the matching points in the MitM phase. The other 120 Boolean equations are used to further filter the partial matched states.   */

3 **for** 2^x *values of* M_1 **do**

4   Compute the inner part of the 2nd block and solve the system of 464 linear equations

5   **if** *the equations have solutions* /* with probability of 2^{-214} */

6   **then**

7   **for** *each of the* 2^{210} *solutions of* M_2 **do**

8   /* With $x = 400$, there are $2^{400-214+210} = 2^{396}$ iterations */

9   Compute the ■ bits in $A^{(1)}$

10   Traversing the 2^{108} values of ■ in $A^{(1)}$ while fixing ■ as 0, compute forward to determine 100-bit ■/■ bits (denoted as $c_\mathcal{R} \in \mathbb{F}_2^{100}$), and the 8-bit matching point, e.g., in (21), i.e., compute eight $f'_\mathcal{M} = f_\mathcal{R} \oplus f_\mathcal{G}$. Build the table U and store the 108-bit ■ bits of $A^{(1)}$ as well as the 8-bit matching point in $U[c_\mathcal{R}]$.

11   /* This method to solve the nonlinear constrained neutral words is borrowed from Dong et al. [28].   */

12   **for** $c_\mathcal{R} \in \mathbb{F}_2^{100}$ **do**

13   Randomly pick a 108-bit ■ $e \in U[c_\mathcal{R}]$, and set ■ in $A^{(1)}$ as 0, compute to the matching point to get eight $f'''_\mathcal{M} = f_\mathcal{G} + Const(e)$

14   **for** 2^8 *values in* $U[c_\mathcal{R}]$ **do**

15   Restore the values of ■ of $A^{(1)}$ and the corresponding matching point (i.e., eight $f_\mathcal{R} \oplus f_\mathcal{G} = f'_\mathcal{M}$) in a list L_1 (indexed by matching point)

16   **end**

17   **for** 2^8 *values of* ■ **do**

18   Set the 108-bit ■ in $A^{(1)}$ as e. Compute to the matching point to get eight $f''_\mathcal{M} = f_\mathcal{B} + f_\mathcal{G} + Const(e)$. Together with $f'''_\mathcal{M}$, compute $f_\mathcal{B} = f''_\mathcal{M} + f'''_\mathcal{M}$ and store ■ in L_2 indexed by matching point.

19   **end**

20   **for** *values matched between* L_1 *and* L_2 **do**

21   Compute $A^{(3)}$ from the matched ■ and ■ bits

22   **if** $A^{(3)}$ *satisfy the 120 precomputed Boolean equations* /* Probability of 2^{-120} */

23   **then**

24   **if** *it leads to the given hash value* **then**

25   Output the preimage

26   **end**

27   **end**

28   **end**

29   **end**

30   **end**

31   **end**

32 **end**

Following the framework in Fig. 6, we use two message blocks (M_1, M_2) to build the attack as Algorithm 1. In Line 5, once we find solutions of M_2, we can perform 2^{100} MitM episodes in Line 14 to 25 for each of the 2^{210} solutions. For each MitM episode, $2^8 \times 2^8$ internal states are exhausted. Suppose there needs 2^x possible values of M_1. To find a 512-bit target preimage, we need $2^{x-214+210+100+16} = 2^{512}$, i.e., $x = 400$. The steps of Alg. 1 are analyzed below:

- In Line 4, the time complexity is 2^{400} 4-round Keccak and $2^{400} \times 464^3$ bit operations to solve the linear system (the time to solve a system of n linear equations is about $O(n^3)$).
- In Line 9, the time complexity is $2^{400-214+210} \times \frac{1}{4} = 2^{394}$ 4-round Keccak.
- We describe the way to use Eq. (21) as the matching point. In the concrete Keccak attack, we can not set the 108 ■ bits to be 0 when computing $f_\mathcal{B} + f_\mathcal{G} = f''_\mathcal{M}$ and $f_\mathcal{G} = f'''_\mathcal{M}$. This is because, the actual size of the ■ and ■ neutral sets is both 2^8, not 2^{108}. The 100 consumed DoF of ■ bits of $A^{(1)}$ are used to make 100 internal bits (denoted as $c_\mathcal{R} \in \mathbb{F}_2^{100}$) to be ■/■, so the remaining ■ set of size 2^8 can be computed independently to the ■ set.
  We detail the method to derive similar matching equation like "$f_\mathcal{R} = f_\mathcal{B} \oplus f_\mathcal{G}$" or "$f_\mathcal{B} = f_\mathcal{R} \oplus f_\mathcal{G}$" for the two 2^8 ■/■ sets. With fixed ■ bits in $A^{(1)}$ and $c_\mathcal{R} \in \mathbb{F}_2^{100}$, there are 2^8 ■ bits stored in $U[c_\mathcal{R}]$, which is derived in Line 10 of Algorithm 1 following Dong et al.'s method [28]. Setting ■ in $A^{(1)}$ as 0, for each element of $U[c_\mathcal{R}]$, compute forward to the 8 matching equations (e.g. Eq. (21)) to get 8 $f'_\mathcal{M} = f_\mathcal{R} \oplus f_\mathcal{G}$. Randomly pick an element e of $U[c_\mathcal{R}]$ and set ■ in $A^{(1)}$ as 0, to compute the 8 matching equations $f'''_\mathcal{M} = f_\mathcal{G} + Const(e)$, where $Const(e)$ is determined by e. That is, for each of the 2^8 ■, compute $f''_\mathcal{M} = f_\mathcal{B} + f_\mathcal{G} + Const(e)$ by setting the 108 ■ $A^{(1)}$ bits as e. Therefore, we get $f''_\mathcal{M} + f'''_\mathcal{M} = f_\mathcal{B} = f_\mathcal{R} \oplus f_\mathcal{G} = f'_\mathcal{M}$ as filter. To dive into details, we refer the readers to Line 10 to Line 25. In Line 10, the time complexity is $2^{396+108} \times \frac{2}{4} = 2^{503}$ 4-round Keccak, since only two rounds from $A^{(1)}$ to $A^{(3)}$ are needed to compute to derive the ■/■ bits and the matching points.
- In Line 13, the time complexity is $2^{396+100} \times \frac{2}{4} = 2^{495}$ 4-round Keccak.
- In Line 15, this step is just to retrieve $U[c_\mathcal{R}]$ to restore it in L_1 with matching point as index. Suppose one access to the table is equivalent to one Sbox application. The time complexity is $2^{396+100+8} \times \frac{1}{4 \times 320} = 2^{493.36}$ 4-round Keccak, since there are 4×320 Sboxes for 4-round Keccak.
- In Line 18, the time complexity is $2^{396+100+8} \times \frac{2}{4} = 2^{503}$ 4-round Keccak.
- In Line 21, the time is $2^{396+100+8+8-8} \times \frac{2}{4} = 2^{503}$ 4-round Keccak.
- In Line 22, $A^{(3)}$ is checked against the 120 Boolean equations precomputed in Line 1, which acts as a filter of 2^{-120}. After the filter, the time of the final check against the target h is $2^{396+100+8-120} = 2^{384}$ 4-round Keccak.

The total complexity is $2^{400}+2^{400}\times464^3+2^{394}+2^{503}+2^{495}+2^{493.36}+2^{503}+2^{503}+2^{384}\approx$ $2^{504.58}$ 4-round Keccak. The memory to store U is 2^{108}. We also give an experiment of 3-round Keccak-512 in the Supplementary Material C in our full version paper [55].

Remark on padding rule. The last message block has at least 2-bit padding (i.e., '11') for Keccak and 4-bit padding (i.e., '0111') for SHA3. Therefore, we have $x = 402$ for Keccak-512 and $x = 404$ for SHA3-512. However, it only increases the negligible part $2^{400}\times464^3$ in Line 4 to $2^{402}\times464^3$ for Keccak-512 and $2^{404}\times464^3$ for SHA3-512. Therefore the final time complexity is still $2^{504.58}$ 4-round Keccak-512 or SHA3-512 considering the padding. The memory is 2^{108}.

5   MitM Preimage Attack on Xoodyak-XOF

In this section, we list the differences in the MILP model with the model for Keccak in Sect. 4.2, and give an MitM preimage attack on 3-round Xoodyak-XOF.

5.1   MILP Model of the MitM Preimage Attack on Xoodyak-XOF

For Xoodyak, without the help of the *linear structure* technique, the situations of adding conditions to the state before the Sbox χ are more complex. We give the details of the condition rules and the matching rule for Xoodyak in the following.

Modelling the χ operation with conditions in Round 0. The Sbox χ of Xoodyak is different from that of Keccak at the sizes of inputs and outputs, which acts on a column $A^{(r)}_{\{x,*,z\}}$. Assume χ operation maps $(a_0, a_1, a_2) \in \mathbb{F}_2^3$ in to $(b_0, b_1, b_2) \in \mathbb{F}_2^3$ as $b_i = a_i \oplus (a_{i+1} \oplus 1) \cdot a_{i+2}$. In round 0, all the operations between the starting state $A^{(0)}$ and χ are linear, thus the inputs only have ■, ■, □ and ■. We can add conditions on □ bits to control the diffusion. The different rules from the **SBOX-RULE** for Keccak are listed below:

1. If there are two ■ bits and one ■/■/□ bit in (a_0, a_1, a_2), we can add one or two conditions to make one or two outputs to be ■. Without losing generality, suppose a_i is ■ or ■ or □ and both a_{i+1} and a_{i+2} are ■ bits:
   (a) the color of b_i is always same with a_i.
   (b) $a_{i+2}=1$, b_{i+1} will be ■; otherwise, the color of b_{i+1} will be same with a_i.
   (c) $a_{i+1}=0$, b_{i+2} will be ■; otherwise, the color of b_{i+2} will be same with a_i.
2. If there is only one ■ bit and the other two are among (■, ■)/(■, □)/(■, □), we add conditions to reduce the number of □ in the output. If a_i is ■:
   (a) b_i is always be □.
   (b) $a_i=0$, the color of b_{i+1} will be same with a_{i+1} and b_{i+2} will be □.
   (c) $a_i=1$, b_{i+1} will be □ and the color of b_{i+2} will be same with a_{i+2}.
   (d) without conditions on a_i, both b_{i+1} and b_{i+2} will be □.

The rules can be described by a system of linear inequalities by using the convex hull computation. Some valid coloring patterns are shown in Fig. 13.

Fig. 13. Some valid coloring patterns with conditions for χ

Modelling the Matching Phase. Suppose the 128 bits in the top plane $A^{(r+1)}_{\{*,2,*\}}$ of $A^{(r+1)}$ is the hash value. We can easily compute the top plane of state $\chi^{(r)}_{\{*,2,*\}}$ by the inverse of ρ_{east}. Each bit of $\chi^{(r)}_{\{*,2,*\}}$ is computed by $b_2 = a_2 \oplus (a_0 \oplus 1) \cdot a_1$, where (a_0, a_1, a_2) comes from the input column of each Sbox in $\iota^{(r)}$. Hence, we deduce the deterministic relations of $\iota^{(r)}$ to count the DoMs.

Observation 2 (Conditions in Matching Points of Xoodyak). *If (a_0, a_1, a_2) satisfy the following conditions, we say there is a 1-bit matching:*

1. *There is no $\square$ bit in (a_0, a_1, a_2).*
2. *There is no the product of $\blacksquare$ and $\blacksquare$, concretely, (a_0, a_1) should not be $(\blacksquare, \blacksquare)$ or $(\blacksquare, \square)$ or $(\blacksquare, \square)$ or $(\square, \square)$, or opposite order.*
3. *In fact, (a_0, a_1, a_2) should be $(\blacksquare, *, \square)$ or $(*, \blacksquare, \square)$ or $(\blacksquare, \blacksquare, \square)$ or $(\blacksquare, \blacksquare, \square)$ or $(\blacksquare, \blacksquare, \blacksquare)$ or $(\blacksquare, \blacksquare, \blacksquare)$, where '$*$' is $\blacksquare$ or $\blacksquare$ or $\square$ or $\blacksquare$. We exclude several cases such as $(\blacksquare, \square, \blacksquare)$, since it is a filter if $\square = 1$, but not for $\square = 0$.*

5.2   MitM Preimage Attack on 3-Round Xoodyak-XOF

We also follow the framework in Fig. 6 and perform the attack with two message blocks (M_1, M_2), where M_2 has two padding bits '10'. The MitM attack is placed in the 2nd block. Solving with our MILP model for Xoodyak, we get a 3-round MitM preimage attack, shown in the Supplementary Material D in our full version paper [55]. The starting state $A^{(0)}$ contains 4 $\blacksquare$ bits and 97 $\blacksquare$ bits. There are totally 53 conditions on $\blacksquare$ bits of $\iota^{(0)}$ (see Supplementary Material D in our full version paper [55]). In the computation from $A^{(0)}$ to $\iota^{(2)}$, the accumulated consumed degree of freedom of $\blacksquare$ is 93 and there is no DoF of $\blacksquare$ consumed. Therefore, $\text{DoF}_{\mathcal{B}} = 4$, $\text{DoF}_{\mathcal{R}} = 97 - 93 = 4$. The degree of matching is counted by the deterministic relations of $\iota^{(2)}$ according to Observation 2, we get $\text{DoM} = 4$, where

$$\chi^{(2)}_{\{2,2,4\}} = \iota^{(2)}_{\{2,2,4\}} \oplus (\iota^{(2)}_{\{2,0,4\}} \oplus 1) \cdot \iota^{(2)}_{\{2,1,4\}}, \; \chi^{(2)}_{\{1,2,10\}} = \iota^{(2)}_{\{1,2,10\}} \oplus (\iota^{(2)}_{\{1,0,10\}} \oplus 1) \cdot \iota^{(2)}_{\{1,1,10\}},$$

$$\chi^{(2)}_{\{1,2,19\}} = \iota^{(2)}_{\{1,2,19\}} \oplus (\iota^{(2)}_{\{1,0,19\}} \oplus 1) \cdot \iota^{(2)}_{\{1,1,19\}}, \; \chi^{(2)}_{\{2,2,22\}} = \iota^{(2)}_{\{2,2,22\}} \oplus (\iota^{(2)}_{\{2,0,22\}} \oplus 1) \cdot \iota^{(2)}_{\{2,1,22\}}. \tag{22}$$

In the starting state $A^{(0)}$, there are 25 ■ bits which can be modified by changing M_2. The 53 conditions can form a linear system taking the 25 bits of M_2 as variables and the 256 bits inner part as constants. The rank of the coefficient matrix is 13. Therefore, we have to randomly test $2^{(53-13)} = 2^{40}$ M_1 to satisfy the 40 equations only determined by the inner part. Then for a right inner part, there are $2^{25-13} = 2^{12}$ solutions of M_2, which make all the 53 equations hold. The attack algorithm is similar to the attack on Keccak (see Supplementary Material D in our full version paper [55]). The total complexity is $2^{125.06}$ 3-round Xoodyak-XOF, and the memory to store U is 2^{97}.

6   MitM Preimage Attack on Ascon-XOF

In this section, we list the details of the MILP model for Ascon-XOF different from that for Keccak, and give an MitM preimage attack on 4-round Ascon-XOF.

6.1   MILP Model of the MitM Preimage Attack on Ascon-XOF

The Sbox of Ascon is much more complex than Keccak. In round 0, we add the conditions to the starting state to control the diffusion over the p_S operation.

Modelling the Starting State with Conditions. In the starting state $A^{(0)}$, the 64-bit outer part can be ■ or ■ bits, while the last 256-bit inner part is of ■. Assume p_S maps $(a_0, a_1, a_2, a_3, a_4)$ to $(b_0, b_1, b_2, b_3, b_4)$, where the a_0 is in the outer part and (a_1, a_2, a_3, a_4) are in the inner part. When a_0 is ■ and others are ■, all the output bits excluding b_2 should be ■ according to Equ. (3) (case 1 in Fig. 14). However, if we add some conditions on (a_1, a_2, a_3, a_4), for example $a_1 = 1$ and $a_3 + a_4 = 1$, then according to Eq. (3), b_0 and b_3 can also be ■ (case 2 in Fig. 14). We add conditions on the bits in the inner part of $A^{(0)}$ to control the diffusion of ■ and ■ over p_S. We name the rule by CondSBOX-RULE:

1. Condition on a_1: when $a_1 = 1$, b_0 is ■ and the color of b_4 is the same with a_0; when $a_1 = 0$, b_4 is ■ and the color of b_0 is the same with a_0.
2. Condition on $a_3 + a_4$: when $a_3 + a_4 = 1$, b_3 is ■; when $a_3 + a_4 = 0$, the color b_3 is the same with a_0.

Some valid coloring patterns of CondSBOX-RULE are shown in Fig. 14.

Fig. 14. Some valid red coloring patterns of CondSBOX-RULE (Color figure online) (Similar to blue bits)

Modelling the Sbox of Ascon. We also build the Sbox operation without conditions, which is applied from round 1. According to Eq. (3), for each output bit b_i, we determine its color by all the five inputs $(a_0, a_1, a_2, a_3, a_4)$ and build the constraints independently. Taking b_0 as an example, $b_0 = a_4a_1 + a_3 + a_2a_1 + a_2 + a_1a_0 + a_1 + a_0$, we determine its color according to the following rules:

1. If there are □ bits in $(a_0, a_1, a_2, a_3, a_4)$, b_0 is □.
2. If there are all ■ bits, b_0 is ■.
3. If there are only ■(≥ 1) and ■(≥ 0) bits, b_0 will be ■.
4. If there are only ■(≥ 1) and ■(≥ 0) bits, b_0 will be ■.
5. If there are □, or more than two kinds of ■, ■ and □ bits in $(a_0, a_1, a_2, a_3, a_4)$:
   (a) if (a_0, a_1, a_2, a_4) are only ■ and ■ (or ■ and ■), b_0 is □.
   (b) if a_1 is ■ or (a_0, a_2, a_4) are ■, b_0 is □.
   (c) if one of the three pairs (a_1, a_4), (a_1, a_2) and (a_0, a_1) is (■,■) or (■,□) or (■,□) or (□,□), or opposite order, b_0 is □.

Those rules for b_0 can be described by linear inequalities using the convex hull computation. The rules for b_1, b_2, b_3 and b_4 can be constructed by the same way.

Modelling the Matching Phase. We target on Ascon-XOF with a 128-bit hash value, which needs two output blocks. Suppose the 64-bit word $A^{(r+1)}_{\{*,0\}}$ of $A^{(r+1)}$ is the first 64-bit hash value of the first output block. We can easily compute the first 64 bits of state $S^{(r)}$ from the hash value by the inverse of p_L. Each bit of the first 64 bits of $S^{(r)}$ is computed by $b_0 = a_4 a_1 + a_3 + a_2 a_1 + a_2 + a_1 a_0 + a_1 + a_0$ by Eq. (3), where $(a_0, a_1, a_2, a_3, a_4)$ comes from the inputs of each Sbox in $A^{(r)}$. Hence, we deduce the deterministic relations of $A^{(r)}$ to count the degree of freedom of matching.

Observation 3 (Conditions in Matching Points of Ascon). *If $(a_0, a_1, a_2, a_3, a_4)$ satisfy the following conditions, we say there is a 1-bit matching:*

1. *There is no □ bit in $(a_0, a_1, a_2, a_3, a_4)$.*
2. *There have ■ and ■ bits, or □ bit in $(a_0, a_1, a_2, a_3, a_4)$.*
3. *There is no product of ■ and ■, concretely, (a_1, a_4) should not be (■,■) or (■,□) or (■,□) or (□,□), or opposite order, and same to (a_1, a_2) and (a_0, a_1).*

6.2   MitM Preimage Attack on 4-Round Ascon-XOF

Applying the MILP model, we find a 4-round MitM preimage attack (see Supplementary Material E in our full version paper [55]). The starting state $A^{(0)}$ contains 4 ■ bits and 54 ■ bits. There are totally 44 conditions on ■ of $A^{(0)}$ (see Supplementary Material E in our full version paper [55]). In the computation from $A^{(0)}$ to $A^{(3)}$, the accumulated consumed degrees of freedom of ■ is 50 and there is no DoF of ■ consumed. Therefore, $\mathrm{DoF}_\mathcal{B} = 4$, $\mathrm{DoF}_\mathcal{R} = 54 - 50 = 4$. The four matching bit equations (DoM = 4) are derived by $A^{(3)}$ with Observation 3, which are:

$$
\begin{cases}
A^{(3)}_{\{15,4\}} \cdot A^{(3)}_{\{15,1\}} + \cdots + A^{(3)}_{\{15,2\}} \cdot A^{(3)}_{\{15,1\}} + A^{(3)}_{\{15,2\}} + A^{(3)}_{\{15,1\}} \cdot A^{(3)}_{\{15,0\}} + A^{(3)}_{\{15,1\}} + A^{(3)}_{\{15,0\}} = S^{(3)}_{\{15,0\}}, \\
A^{(3)}_{\{25,4\}} \cdot A^{(3)}_{\{25,1\}} + \cdots + A^{(3)}_{\{25,2\}} \cdot A^{(3)}_{\{25,1\}} + A^{(3)}_{\{25,2\}} + A^{(3)}_{\{25,1\}} \cdot A^{(3)}_{\{25,0\}} + A^{(3)}_{\{25,1\}} + A^{(3)}_{\{25,0\}} = S^{(3)}_{\{25,0\}}, \\
A^{(3)}_{\{47,4\}} \cdot A^{(3)}_{\{47,1\}} + \cdots + A^{(3)}_{\{47,2\}} \cdot A^{(3)}_{\{47,1\}} + A^{(3)}_{\{47,2\}} + A^{(3)}_{\{47,1\}} \cdot A^{(3)}_{\{47,0\}} + A^{(3)}_{\{47,1\}} + A^{(3)}_{\{47,0\}} = S^{(3)}_{\{47,0\}}, \\
A^{(3)}_{\{57,4\}} \cdot A^{(3)}_{\{57,1\}} + \cdots + A^{(3)}_{\{57,2\}} \cdot A^{(3)}_{\{57,1\}} + A^{(3)}_{\{57,2\}} + A^{(3)}_{\{57,1\}} \cdot A^{(3)}_{\{57,0\}} + A^{(3)}_{\{57,1\}} + A^{(3)}_{\{57,0\}} = S^{(3)}_{\{57,0\}}.
\end{cases}
\tag{23}
$$

Following the framework in Fig. 6, we choose (M_1, M_2) to make the 44 conditions hold, and perform the MitM attack on M_3. The attack algorithm is given in Supplementary Material E in our full version paper [55]. The time is $2^{124.67}$ 4-round Ascon and the memory is 2^{54}. In addition, we give a 3-round MitM preimage attack on Ascon-XOF with time of $2^{120.58}$ 3-round Ascon and memory of 2^{39} (see Supplementary Material E in [55]). An experiment on the MitM episode is given in Supplementary Material F in our full version paper [55].

7   Conclusion and Discussion

In this paper, we give the framework of the MitM attack on sponge-based hashing. To find good attacks, we build bit-level MILP based automatic tools for MitM attacks on Keccak-512, Ascon-XOF, and Xoodyak-XOF. Although the birthday-paradox MitM attack has been widely applied to block ciphers or MD-based hash functions since 1977, this is the first attempt to apply it to Keccak, etc. Our attacks lead to improved or first preimage attacks on reduced-round Keccak-512, Ascon-XOF, and Xoodyak-XOF.

Similar to previous preimage attacks [35, 45], our attack on Keccak also uses the linearization-based techniques. In previous linearization-based preimage attacks [35, 45], all the variables should not be multiplied with each other. In our MitM attack, the variables can be multiplied with each other within each set. For Keccak, to attack more rounds, we use a one-round linear structure to skip the MILP programming of the first round and accelerate the MILP model. It should be noted that the linear structure used in this paper is just a technique to accelerate the search. Moreover, by using the linear structure, the search only covers a small fraction of the whole space of the solutions, which may be not the optimal MitM attack at all. For other instances of Keccak, it is open problem to apply one or two-round linear structures in the search for MitM attacks.

Acknowledgments. We thank the anonymous reviewers from EUROCRYPT 2023 for the valuable comments. This work is supported by the National Key R&D Program of China (2018YFA0704701, 2022YFB2702804, 2022YFB2701900), the Natural Science Foundation of China (62272257, 62202444), Shandong Key Research and Development Program (2020ZLYS09), the Major Scientific and Technological Innovation Project of Shandong, China (2019JZZY010133), the Major Program of Guangdong Basic and Applied Research (2019B030302008), the Fundamental Research Funds for the Central Universities.

References

1. Amzaleg, D., Dinur, I.: Refined cryptanalysis of the GPRS ciphers GEA-1 and GEA-2. In: Dunkelman, O., Dziembowski, S. (eds.) EUROCRYPT 2022, Proceedings, Part III, vol. 13277, pp. 57–85. Springer, Cham (2022). https://doi.org/10.1007/978-3-031-07082-2_3
2. Aoki, K., Sasaki, Yu.: Preimage attacks on one-block MD4, 63-step MD5 and more. In: Avanzi, R.M., Keliher, L., Sica, F. (eds.) SAC 2008. LNCS, vol. 5381, pp. 103–119. Springer, Heidelberg (2009). https://doi.org/10.1007/978-3-642-04159-4_7
3. Aumasson, J.P., et al.: SPHINCS+: Submission to the NIST post-quantum project (2019)
4. Aumasson, J.-P., Meier, W., Mendel, F.: Preimage attacks on 3-pass HAVAL and step-reduced MD5. In: Avanzi, R.M., Keliher, L., Sica, F. (eds.) SAC 2008. LNCS, vol. 5381, pp. 120–135. Springer, Heidelberg (2009). https://doi.org/10.1007/978-3-642-04159-4_8
5. Bao, Z., Dong, X., Guo, J., Li, Z., Shi, D., Sun, S., Wang, X.: Automatic search of meet-in-the-middle preimage attacks on AES-like hashing. In: Canteaut, A., Standaert, F.-X. (eds.) EUROCRYPT 2021, Part I. LNCS, vol. 12696, pp. 771–804. Springer, Cham (2021). https://doi.org/10.1007/978-3-030-77870-5_27

6. Bao, Z., Guo, J., Shi, D., Tu, Y.: Superposition meet-in-the-middle attacks: updates on fundamental security of AES-like hashing. In: CRYPTO 2022, Proceedings, Part I, vol. 13507, pp. 64–93. Springer, Cham (2022). https://doi.org/10.1007/978-3-031-15802-5_3

7. Beierle, C., et al.: Cryptanalysis of the GPRS encryption algorithms GEA-1 and GEA-2. In: Canteaut, A., Standaert, F.-X. (eds.) EUROCRYPT 2021, Part II. LNCS, vol. 12697, pp. 155–183. Springer, Cham (2021). https://doi.org/10.1007/978-3-030-77886-6_6

8. Bernstein, D.J.: Second preimages for 6 (7?(8??)) rounds of Keccak. NIST mailing list (2010)

9. Bertoni, G., Daemen, J., Peeters, M., Van Assche, G.: Keccak sponge function family main document. Submission to NIST (Round 2) 3(30), 320–337 (2009)

10. Biryukov, A., Derbez, P., Perrin, L.: Differential analysis and meet-in-the-middle attack against round-reduced TWINE. In: Leander, G. (ed.) FSE 2015. LNCS, vol. 9054, pp. 3–27. Springer, Heidelberg (2015). https://doi.org/10.1007/978-3-662-48116-5_1

11. Bogdanov, A., Khovratovich, D., Rechberger, C.: Biclique cryptanalysis of the full AES. In: Lee, D.H., Wang, X. (eds.) ASIACRYPT 2011. LNCS, vol. 7073, pp. 344–371. Springer, Heidelberg (2011). https://doi.org/10.1007/978-3-642-25385-0_19

12. Bogdanov, A., Rechberger, C.: A 3-subset meet-in-the-middle attack: cryptanalysis of the lightweight block cipher KTANTAN. In: Biryukov, A., Gong, G., Stinson, D.R. (eds.) SAC 2010. LNCS, vol. 6544, pp. 229–240. Springer, Heidelberg (2011). https://doi.org/10.1007/978-3-642-19574-7_16

13. Bouillaguet, C., Derbez, P., Fouque, P.-A.: Automatic search of attacks on round-reduced AES and applications. In: Rogaway, P. (ed.) CRYPTO 2011. LNCS, vol. 6841, pp. 169–187. Springer, Heidelberg (2011). https://doi.org/10.1007/978-3-642-22792-9_10

14. Boura, C., David, N., Derbez, P., Leander, G., Naya-Plasencia, M.: Differential meet-in-the-middle cryptanalysis. IACR Cryptology ePrint Archive, p. 1640 (2022). eprint.iacr.org/2022/1640

15. Canteaut, A., Naya-Plasencia, M., Vayssière, B.: Sieve-in-the-middle: improved MITM attacks. In: Canetti, R., Garay, J.A. (eds.) CRYPTO 2013, Part I. LNCS, vol. 8042, pp. 222–240. Springer, Heidelberg (2013). https://doi.org/10.1007/978-3-642-40041-4_13

16. Daemen, J., Hoffert, S., Peeters, M., Assche, G.V., Keer, R.V.: Xoodyak, a lightweight cryptographic scheme. IACR Trans. Symmetric Cryptol. 2020(S1), 60–87 (2020). https://doi.org/10.13154/tosc.v2020.iS1.60-87

17. Damgård, I.B.: A design principle for hash functions. In: Brassard, G. (ed.) CRYPTO 1989. LNCS, vol. 435, pp. 416–427. Springer, New York (1990). https://doi.org/10.1007/0-387-34805-0_39

18. Demirci, H., Selçuk, A.A.: A meet-in-the-middle attack on 8-round AES. In: Nyberg, K. (ed.) FSE 2008. LNCS, vol. 5086, pp. 116–126. Springer, Heidelberg (2008). https://doi.org/10.1007/978-3-540-71039-4_7

19. Derbez, P., Fouque, P.-A.: Automatic search of meet-in-the-middle and impossible differential attacks. In: Robshaw, M., Katz, J. (eds.) CRYPTO 2016, Part II. LNCS, vol. 9815, pp. 157–184. Springer, Heidelberg (2016). https://doi.org/10.1007/978-3-662-53008-5_6

20. Derbez, P., Fouque, P.-A., Jean, J.: Improved key recovery attacks on reduced-round , in the single-key setting. In: Johansson, T., Nguyen, P.Q. (eds.) EURO-CRYPT 2013. LNCS, vol. 7881, pp. 371–387. Springer, Heidelberg (2013). https:// doi.org/10.1007/978-3-642-38348-9_23

21. Derbez, P., Perrin, L.: Meet-in-the-middle attacks and structural analysis of round-reduced PRINCE. In: Leander, G. (ed.) FSE 2015. LNCS, vol. 9054, pp. 190–216. Springer, Heidelberg (2015). https://doi.org/10.1007/978-3-662-48116-5_10

22. Diffie, W., Hellman, M.E.: Special feature exhaustive cryptanalysis of the NBS data encryption standard. Computer **10**(6), 74–84 (1977). https://doi.org/10.1109/C-M.1977.217750

23. Dinur, I.: Cryptanalytic applications of the polynomial method for solving multivariate equation systems over GF(2). In: Canteaut, A., Standaert, F.-X. (eds.) EUROCRYPT 2021, PArt I. LNCS, vol. 12696, pp. 374–403. Springer, Cham (2021). https://doi.org/10.1007/978-3-030-77870-5_14

24. Dinur, I., Dunkelman, O., Keller, N., Shamir, A.: Efficient dissection of composite problems, with applications to cryptanalysis, knapsacks, and combinatorial search problems. In: Safavi-Naini, R., Canetti, R. (eds.) CRYPTO 2012. LNCS, vol. 7417, pp. 719–740. Springer, Heidelberg (2012). https://doi.org/10.1007/978-3-642-32009-5_42

25. Dinur, I., Dunkelman, O., Shamir, A.: Collision attacks on Up to 5 rounds of SHA-3 using generalized internal differentials. In: Moriai, S. (ed.) FSE 2013. LNCS, vol. 8424, pp. 219–240. Springer, Heidelberg (2014). https://doi.org/10.1007/978-3-662-43933-3_12

26. Dinur, I., Shamir, A.: Breaking grain-128 with dynamic cube attacks. In: Joux, A. (ed.) FSE 2011. LNCS, vol. 6733, pp. 167–187. Springer, Heidelberg (2011). https://doi.org/10.1007/978-3-642-21702-9_10

27. Dobraunig, C., Eichlseder, M., Mendel, F., Schläffer, M.: Ascon v1.2: lightweight authenticated encryption and hashing. J. Cryptol. **34**(3), 1–42 (2021). https://doi. org/10.1007/s00145-021-09398-9

28. Dong, X., Hua, J., Sun, S., Li, Z., Wang, X., Hu, L.: Meet-in-the-middle attacks revisited: key-recovery, collision, and preimage attacks. In: Malkin, T., Peikert, C. (eds.) CRYPTO 2021, Part III. LNCS, vol. 12827, pp. 278–308. Springer, Cham (2021). https://doi.org/10.1007/978-3-030-84252-9_10

29. Dunkelman, O., Keller, N., Shamir, A.: Improved single-key attacks on 8-round AES-192 and AES-256. In: Abe, M. (ed.) ASIACRYPT 2010. LNCS, vol. 6477, pp. 158–176. Springer, Heidelberg (2010). https://doi.org/10.1007/978-3-642-17373-8_10

30. Dunkelman, O., Sekar, G., Preneel, B.: Improved meet-in-the-middle attacks on reduced-round DES. In: Srinathan, K., Rangan, C.P., Yung, M. (eds.) INDOCRYPT 2007. LNCS, vol. 4859, pp. 86–100. Springer, Heidelberg (2007). https://doi.org/10.1007/978-3-540-77026-8_8

31. Espitau, T., Fouque, P.-A., Karpman, P.: Higher-order differential meet-in-the-middle preimage attacks on SHA-1 and BLAKE. In: Gennaro, R., Robshaw, M. (eds.) CRYPTO 2015, Part I. LNCS, vol. 9215, pp. 683–701. Springer, Heidelberg (2015). https://doi.org/10.1007/978-3-662-47989-6_33

32. Fuhr, T., Minaud, B.: Match box meet-in-the-middle attack against KATAN. In: Cid, C., Rechberger, C. (eds.) FSE 2014. LNCS, vol. 8540, pp. 61–81. Springer, Heidelberg (2015). https://doi.org/10.1007/978-3-662-46706-0_4

33. Gérault, D., Peyrin, T., Tan, Q.Q.: Exploring differential-based distinguishers and forgeries for ASCON. IACR Trans. Symmetric Cryptol. **2021**(3), 102–136 (2021). https://doi.org/10.46586/tosc.v2021.i3.102-136

34. Guo, J., Ling, S., Rechberger, C., Wang, H.: Advanced meet-in-the-middle preimage attacks: first results on full tiger, and improved results on MD4 and SHA-2. In: Abe, M. (ed.) ASIACRYPT 2010. LNCS, vol. 6477, pp. 56–75. Springer, Heidelberg (2010). https://doi.org/10.1007/978-3-642-17373-8_4

35. Guo, J., Liu, M., Song, L.: Linear structures: applications to cryptanalysis of round-reduced KECCAK. In: Cheon, J.H., Takagi, T. (eds.) ASIACRYPT 2016, Part I. LNCS, vol. 10031, pp. 249–274. Springer, Heidelberg (2016). https://doi.org/10.1007/978-3-662-53887-6_9

36. He, L., Lin, X., Yu, H.: Improved preimage attacks on round-reduced Keccak-384/512 via restricted linear structures. Cryptology ePrint Archive, 2022/788

37. He, L., Lin, X., Yu, H.: Improved preimage attacks on 4-round Keccak-224/256. IACR Trans. Symmetric Cryptol. **2021**(1), 217–238 (2021). https://doi.org/10.46586/tosc.v2021.i1.217-238

38. Huang, S., Wang, X., Xu, G., Wang, M., Zhao, J.: Conditional cube attack on reduced-round Keccak sponge function. In: Coron, J.-S., Nielsen, J.B. (eds.) EUROCRYPT 2017, Part II. LNCS, vol. 10211, pp. 259–288. Springer, Cham (2017). https://doi.org/10.1007/978-3-319-56614-6_9

39. Indesteege, S., Keller, N., Dunkelman, O., Biham, E., Preneel, B.: A practical attack on KeeLoq. In: Smart, N. (ed.) EUROCRYPT 2008. LNCS, vol. 4965, pp. 1–18. Springer, Heidelberg (2008). https://doi.org/10.1007/978-3-540-78967-3_1

40. Isobe, T.: A single-key attack on the full GOST block cipher. J. Cryptol. **26**(1), 172–189 (2012). https://doi.org/10.1007/s00145-012-9118-5

41. Knellwolf, S., Khovratovich, D.: New preimage attacks against reduced SHA-1. In: Safavi-Naini, R., Canetti, R. (eds.) CRYPTO 2012. LNCS, vol. 7417, pp. 367–383. Springer, Heidelberg (2012). https://doi.org/10.1007/978-3-642-32009-5_22

42. Knellwolf, S., Meier, W., Naya-Plasencia, M.: Conditional differential cryptanalysis of NLFSR-based cryptosystems. In: Abe, M. (ed.) ASIACRYPT 2010. LNCS, vol. 6477, pp. 130–145. Springer, Heidelberg (2010). https://doi.org/10.1007/978-3-642-17373-8_8

43. Kölbl, S., Lauridsen, M.M., Mendel, F., Rechberger, C.: Haraka v2 - efficient short-input hashing for post-quantum applications. IACR Trans. Symmetric Cryptol. **2016**(2), 1–29 (2016). https://doi.org/10.13154/tosc.v2016.i2.1-29

44. Leurent, G.: MD4 is not one-way. In: Nyberg, K. (ed.) FSE 2008. LNCS, vol. 5086, pp. 412–428. Springer, Heidelberg (2008). https://doi.org/10.1007/978-3-540-71039-4_26

45. Li, T., Sun, Y.: Preimage attacks on round-reduced KECCAK-224/256 via an allocating approach. In: Ishai, Y., Rijmen, V. (eds.) EUROCRYPT 2019, Part III. LNCS, vol. 11478, pp. 556–584. Springer, Cham (2019). https://doi.org/10.1007/978-3-030-17659-4_19

46. Li, T., Sun, Y., Liao, M., Wang, D.: Preimage attacks on the round-reduced Keccak with cross-linear structures. IACR Trans. Symmetric Cryptol. **2017**(4), 39–57 (2017). https://doi.org/10.13154/tosc.v2017.i4.39-57

47. Lin, X., He, L., Yu, H.: Improved preimage attacks on 3-round Keccak-224/256. IACR Trans. Symmetric Cryptol. **2021**(3), 84–101 (2021). https://doi.org/10.46586/tosc.v2021.i3.84-101

48. Liu, F., Isobe, T., Meier, W., Yang, Z.: Algebraic attacks on round-reduced Keccak. In: Baek, J., Ruj, S. (eds.) ACISP 2021. LNCS, vol. 13083, pp. 91–110. Springer, Cham (2021). https://doi.org/10.1007/978-3-030-90567-5_5

49. Liu, G., Lu, J., Li, H., Tang, P., Qiu, W.: Preimage attacks against lightweight scheme Xoodyak based on deep learning. In: Arai, K. (ed.) FICC 2021. AISC, vol. 1364, pp. 637–648. Springer, Cham (2021). https://doi.org/10.1007/978-3-030-73103-8_45

50. Lucks, S.: Attacking triple encryption. In: Vaudenay, S. (ed.) FSE 1998. LNCS, vol. 1372, pp. 239–253. Springer, Heidelberg (1998). https://doi.org/10.1007/3-540-69710-1_16

51. Merkle, R.C.: A certified digital signature. In: Brassard, G. (ed.) CRYPTO 1989. LNCS, vol. 435, pp. 218–238. Springer, New York (1990). https://doi.org/10.1007/0-387-34805-0_21

52. Morawiecki, P., Pieprzyk, J., Srebrny, M.: Rotational cryptanalysis of round-reduced KECCAK. In: Moriai, S. (ed.) FSE 2013. LNCS, vol. 8424, pp. 241–262. Springer, Heidelberg (2014). https://doi.org/10.1007/978-3-662-43933-3_13

53. Naya-Plasencia, M., Röck, A., Meier, W.: Practical analysis of reduced-round KECCAK. In: Bernstein, D.J., Chatterjee, S. (eds.) INDOCRYPT 2011. LNCS, vol. 7107, pp. 236–254. Springer, Heidelberg (2011). https://doi.org/10.1007/978-3-642-25578-6_18

54. Preneel, B., Govaerts, R., Vandewalle, J.: Hash functions based on block ciphers: a synthetic approach. In: Stinson, D.R. (ed.) CRYPTO 1993. LNCS, vol. 773, pp. 368–378. Springer, Heidelberg (1994). https://doi.org/10.1007/3-540-48329-2_31

55. Qin, L., Hua, J., Dong, X., Yan, H., Wang, X.: Meet-in-the-middle preimage attacks on sponge-based hashing. Cryptology ePrint Archive, Paper 2022/1714 (2022). eprint.iacr.org/2022/1714

56. Rajasree, M.S.: Cryptanalysis of round-reduced KECCAK using non-linear structures. In: Hao, F., Ruj, S., Sen Gupta, S. (eds.) INDOCRYPT 2019. LNCS, vol. 11898, pp. 175–192. Springer, Cham (2019). https://doi.org/10.1007/978-3-030-35423-7_9

57. Sasaki, Yu.: Integer linear programming for three-subset meet-in-the-middle attacks: application to GIFT. In: Inomata, A., Yasuda, K. (eds.) IWSEC 2018. LNCS, vol. 11049, pp. 227–243. Springer, Cham (2018). https://doi.org/10.1007/978-3-319-97916-8_15

58. Sasaki, Yu.: Meet-in-the-middle preimage attacks on AES hashing modes and an application to whirlpool. In: Joux, A. (ed.) FSE 2011. LNCS, vol. 6733, pp. 378–396. Springer, Heidelberg (2011). https://doi.org/10.1007/978-3-642-21702-9_22

59. Sasaki, Yu., Aoki, K.: Finding preimages in full MD5 faster than exhaustive search. In: Joux, A. (ed.) EUROCRYPT 2009. LNCS, vol. 5479, pp. 134–152. Springer, Heidelberg (2009). https://doi.org/10.1007/978-3-642-01001-9_8

60. Sasaki, Yu., Aoki, K.: Preimage attacks on 3, 4, and 5-pass HAVAL. In: Pieprzyk, J. (ed.) ASIACRYPT 2008. LNCS, vol. 5350, pp. 253–271. Springer, Heidelberg (2008). https://doi.org/10.1007/978-3-540-89255-7_16

61. Schrottenloher, A., Stevens, M.: Simplified MITM modeling for permutations: new (quantum) attacks. In: Dodis, Y., Shrimpton, T. (eds.) CRYPTO 2022, Proceedings, Part III, vol. 13509, pp. 717–747. Springer, Cham (2022). https://doi.org/10.1007/978-3-031-15982-4_24

62. Wang, X., Yin, Y.L., Yu, H.: Finding collisions in the full SHA-1. In: Shoup, V. (ed.) CRYPTO 2005. LNCS, vol. 3621, pp. 17–36. Springer, Heidelberg (2005). https://doi.org/10.1007/11535218_2

63. Wang, X., Yu, H.: How to break MD5 and other hash functions. In: Cramer, R. (ed.) EUROCRYPT 2005. LNCS, vol. 3494, pp. 19–35. Springer, Heidelberg (2005). https://doi.org/10.1007/11426639_2

Analysis of RIPEMD-160: New Collision Attacks and Finding Characteristics with MILP

Fukang Liu[1,2(✉)], Gaoli Wang[3,4(✉)], Santanu Sarkar[6], Ravi Anand[2],
Willi Meier[7], Yingxin Li[3], and Takanori Isobe[2,5]

[1] Tokyo Institute of Technology, Tokyo, Japan
liufukangs@gmail.com
[2] University of Hyogo, Hyogo, Japan
takanori.isobe@ai.u-hyogo.ac.jp
[3] Shanghai Key Laboratory of Trustworthy Computing, East China Normal University, Shanghai, China
glwang@sei.ecnu.edu.cn, willi.meier@fhnw.ch
[4] State Key Laboratory of Cryptology, Beijing, China
[5] NICT, Tokyo, Japan
[6] Indian Institute of Technology Madras, Chennai, India
santanu@iitm.ac.in
[7] FHNW, Windisch, Switzerland

Abstract. The hash function RIPEMD-160 is an ISO/IEC standard and is being used to generate the bitcoin address together with SHA-256. Despite the fact that many hash functions in the MD-SHA hash family have been broken, RIPEMD-160 remains secure and the best collision attack could only reach up to 34 out of 80 rounds, which was published at CRYPTO 2019. In this paper, we propose a new collision attack on RIPEMD-160 that can reach up to 36 rounds with time complexity $2^{64.5}$. This new attack is facilitated by a new strategy to choose the message differences and new techniques to simultaneously handle the differential conditions on both branches. Moreover, different from all the previous work on RIPEMD-160, we utilize a MILP-based method to search for differential characteristics, where we construct a model to accurately describe the signed difference transitions through its round function. As far as we know, this is the first model targeting the signed difference transitions for the MD-SHA hash family. Indeed, we are more motivated to design this model by the fact that many automatic tools to search for such differential characteristics are not publicly available and implementing them from scratch is too time-consuming and difficult. Hence, we expect that this can be an alternative easy tool for future research, which only requires to write down some simple linear inequalities.

Keywords: RIPEMD-160 · collision attack · signed difference · modular difference · MILP

1 Introduction

Background. The most powerful technique to mount collision attacks on the MD-SHA hash family is to carefully trace the evolutions of the signed difference

© International Association for Cryptologic Research 2023
C. Hazay and M. Stam (Eds.): EUROCRYPT 2023, LNCS 14007, pp. 189–219, 2023.
https://doi.org/10.1007/978-3-031-30634-1_7

through the round functions [29–32]. The feature of the signed difference is that it can capture how a bit is changed, i.e. from 1 to 0 or from 0 to 1. This makes it interact well with the modular difference because each specified signed difference can uniquely determine the corresponding modular difference and XOR difference. It is thus clear that the signed difference carries the information of both the XOR difference and modular difference.

Based on the above crucial observations, in Wang et al.'s seminal work [29–32], they deduced all the collision-generating differential characteristics by hand for a series of famous hash functions, including MD4, MD5, SHA-0 and SHA-1. However, such hand-crafted work is too technical and time-consuming. Therefore, several automatic tools [2,6,14–18,23–25] to search for these differential characteristics have been developed and they have even been applied to much more complex hash functions like SHA-2 [5,6,15,17] and RIPEMD-160 [14,18]. However, most of these tools [2,6,14–18] are not made publicly available. As far as we know, only the tools [23–25] developed by Stevens are open-source. A similar tool developed by Leurent for the ARX cipher Skein is also open-source [9]. However, the tools developed by Stevens are only for MD5 and SHA-1. Tweaking Stevens's tools for different hash functions is not easy because it requires deep understanding of their implementations and there are a few structured documents for the codes. Especially for RIPEMD-160 and SHA-2, their round functions are more complex than those of MD5 and SHA-1, which further increases the difficulty.

On RIPEMD-160. The hash function RIPEMD-160 [4] was proposed at FSE 1996, whose overall structure can be viewed as two parallel MD5-like instances. Such a double-branch structure makes it well resist against Wang et al.'s powerful techniques for the MD-SHA hash family. The main difficulty is to construct suitable collision-generating differential characteristics and to perform the message modification to fulfill the differential conditions on both branches simultaneously.

Due to the increasing difficulty of analyzing the double-branch structure, the progress in analyzing the security of RIPEMD-160 is slow, as can be seen in Table 1. For example, the first practical collision attacks on 30 and 31 rounds of RIPEMD-160 were demonstrated in 2019 and the best collision attack with the same technique could only reach up to 34 rounds [10]. For the semi-free-start (SFS) collision attack, the best attack could only reach up to 40 rounds [11], which was published also in 2019.

As RIPEMD-160 is an ISO/IEC standard and is being used in bitcoin, we believe further understanding its (second-)preimage and collision resistance is of practical interest. In this work, we target the collision resistance, which is generally more meaningful than the SFS collision resistance.

Our Contributions. The contributions of this work are fourfold. Specifically, we propose:

1. A new strategy to choose the message differences which allows to mount a collision attack on 36-round RIPEMD-160.

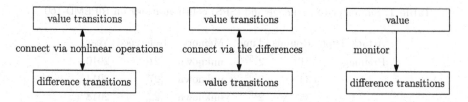

Fig. 1. The comparison between different models (left: [12],middle: [19,24], right: this paper)

2. A state-of-the-art method to efficiently perform the message modification on both branches simultaneously by carefully exploiting the feature of the differential characteristic.
3. A new methodology to search for differential characteristics for RIPEMD-160 that relies on off-the-shelf solvers. This is achieved by constructing a model to describe the signed difference transitions through the round function of RIPEMD-160. As far as we know, it is the first time to use the MILP-based method to search for a *pure signed* differential characteristic
4. A new method to automatically detect the contradictions in the search for signed differential characteristics. Specifically, we propose to use *monitoring variables* representing the values of the internal states to monitor the inconsistency appearing in the signed difference transitions over different rounds. This should be distinguished from Liu et al.'s technique [12] where both the value transitions and difference transitions are involved in a model to avoid the inconsistency, i.e. we do not care about the value transitions because they are costly. This should also be distinguished from the techniques [19,24] where only a model to simply describe two parallel value transitions is used, which is inefficient as no feature of the signed difference propagations is exploited in such a model. The comparison between different methods is shown in Fig. 1.

The source code to search for signed differential characteristics is available at https://github.com/LFKOKAMI/Find_RIPEMD_Trail.git.

Outline of the Paper. In Sect. 2, we introduce the notations and some preliminary works. In Sect. 3, the MILP model to describe the signed difference transitions through RIPEMD-160's round function is detailed. Then, we show the 36-round collision attack in Sect. 4. Finally, we end this paper with some discussions on our techniques in Sect. 5.

2   Preliminaries

2.1   Notation

The following notations are used throughout this paper. $\boxplus$ and $\boxminus$ represent the modular addition and substraction modulo 2^{32}, respectively. $x[i]$ denotes the i-th bit of x and $x[0]$ is the least significant bit. Δx denotes the XOR difference of x' and x, i.e. $\Delta x = x' \oplus x$. δx denotes the modular difference, i.e. $\delta x = x' \boxminus x$.

Table 1. Summary of preimage and (SFS) collision attack on RIPEMD-160

Attack Type	Rounds	Time	Memory	Reference	Year
Preimage	31^a	2^{155}	unknown	[21]	2010
	34	$2^{158.91}$	unknown	[27]	2014
	35^a	$2^{159.38}$	unknown	[22]	2018
SFS collision	36^a	practical		[14]	2012
	42^a	$2^{75.5}$	2^{64}	[18]	2013
	48^a	$2^{76.4}$	2^{64}	[28]	2017
	36	$2^{70.4}$	2^{64}	[18]	2013
	36	$2^{55.1}$	2^{32}	[13]	2017
	36/37	practical		[11]	2019
	40	$2^{74.6}$	negligible	[11]	2019
collision	30/31	practical		[10]	2019
	34	$2^{74.3}$	2^{32}	[10]	2019
	36	$2^{64.5}$	2^{24}	this work	2022

^{a} An attack starting at an intermediate round.

∇x denotes the signed difference between x' and x, i.e. $\nabla x[i] = [\texttt{=}]$ if $x'[i] = x[i]$, $\nabla x[i] = [\texttt{0}]$ if $x'[i] = x[i] = 0$, $\nabla x[i] = [\texttt{1}]$ if $x'[i] = x[i] = 1$, $\nabla x[i] = [\texttt{n}]$ if $(x'[i] = 1, x[i] = 0)$, $\nabla x[i] = [\texttt{u}]$ if $(x'[i] = 0, x[i] = 1)$. $[a, b]$ denotes the set $\{i | a \le i \le b\}$. $\bar{x}$ denotes the bitwise NOT operation on x. Moreover, x^T denotes a column vector and we simply use $x^T[i]$ to represent the i-th element of x^T. Especially, $x^T \ge y^T$ iff $x^T[i] \ge y^T[i]$ for all i, e.g. $(1, 2, 3)^T \ge (0, 2, 1)^T$ as $(1 \ge 0, 2 \ge 2, 3 \ge 1)$.

Definition 1. *The signed difference ∇x is said to be an expansion of the modular difference δx only when ∇x corresponds to the modular difference δx.*

Definition 2. *The hamming weight of the signed difference ∇x is denoted by $\mathbb{H}(\nabla x)$ and $\mathbb{H}(\nabla x)$ is the number of indices i such that $\nabla x[i] \in \{\texttt{n}, \texttt{u}\}$.*

For example, let

$$\nabla x_0 = [\texttt{=n== ==== ==== ==== ==== ==== ==== ====}],$$
$$\nabla x_1 = [\texttt{nu== ==== ==== ==== ==== ==== ==== ====}].$$

Then, both ∇x_0 and ∇x_1 are the expansions of $\delta x = 2^{30}$. Moreover, we have $\mathbb{H}(\nabla x_0) = 1$ and $\mathbb{H}(\nabla x_1) = 2$.

As each signed difference corresponds to a unique modular difference, for convenience, when computing $\delta x \boxplus \delta y$ for a given $(\nabla x, \nabla y)$, we also simply denote $\delta x \boxplus \delta y$ by $\nabla x \boxplus \nabla y$. For the above example, we have $\nabla x_0 \boxplus \nabla x_1 = 2^{31}$.

2.2   Description of RIPEMD-160

RIPEMD-160 [4] was proposed at FSE 1996 by Dobbertin et al. and it is built on the Merkle-Damgård structure. To compress an arbitrary-length message with

RIPEMD-160, the message will be first padded and then divided into several message blocks and each block is of size 512 bits. Supposing there are $\gamma + 1$ message blocks and they are denoted by $M^0, M^1, \ldots, M^\gamma$, the 80-bit hash value $h = (h_0, h_1, h_2, h_3, h_4)$ is computed as follows:

$$IV^{j+1} = H(IV^j, M^j) \text{ for } j \in [0, \gamma],$$
$$h = IV^{\gamma+1},$$

where $H(IV^j, M^j)$ is the compression function of RIPEMD-160, IV^j is a 160-bit chaining variable and IV^0 is a predetermined constant value.

In our collision attack, we aim to find (M^0, M^1) and $(M^0, M^{1'})$ such that

$$H(H(IV_0, M^0), M^1) = H(H(IV_0, M^0), M^{1'})$$

where the number of rounds of H is reduced. In this way, a colliding message pair for the round-reduced RIPEMD-160 can be easily derived.

Let $M = (m_0, m_1, \ldots, m_{15})$ be the 16 message words of size 32 bits each and $IV^0 = (IV_0^0, IV_1^0, \ldots, IV_4^0)$. The specification of the compression function $H(IV^0, M)$ is described below:

$$X_{-5} = Y_{-5} = IV_0^0 \ggg 10, X_{-4} = Y_{-4} = IV_4^0 \ggg 10, X_{-3} = Y_{-3} = IV_3^0 \ggg 10,$$
$$X_{-2} = Y_{-2} = IV_2^0, X_{-1} = Y_{-1} = IV_1^0,$$
$$Q_i^l = X_{i-5} \lll 10 \boxplus \phi_j^l(X_{i-1}, X_{i-2}, X_{i-3} \lll 10) \boxplus m_{\pi_l(i)} \boxplus K_j^l,$$
$$X_i = X_{i-4} \lll 10 \boxplus Q_i^l \lll s_i^l,$$
$$Q_i^r = Y_{i-5} \lll 10 \boxplus \phi_j^r(Y_{i-1}, Y_{i-2}, Y_{i-3} \lll 10) \boxplus m_{\pi_r(i)} \boxplus K_j^r,$$
$$Y_i = Y_{i-4} \lll 10 \boxplus Q_i^r \lll s_i^r,$$

where $i \in [0, 79]$ and $j = \lfloor \frac{i}{16} \rfloor$. Due to the page limit, the specification of $\phi_j^l, \phi_j^r, K_j^l, K_j^r$ can be found in Table 2. $\pi_l(i), \pi_r(i), s_i^l, s_i^r$ can be referred to [4].

Table 2. Boolean functions and round constants in RIPEMD-160

j	ϕ_j^l	ϕ_j^r	K_j^l	K_j^r	Function	Expression
0	XOR	ONX	0x00000000	0x50a28be6	$XOR(x, y, z)$	$x \oplus y \oplus z$
1	IFX	IFZ	0x5a827999	0x5c4dd124	$IFX(x, y, z)$	$(x \wedge y) \oplus (\overline{x} \wedge z)$
2	ONZ	ONZ	0x6ed9eba1	0x6d703ef3	$IFZ(x, y, z)$	$(x \wedge z) \oplus (y \wedge \overline{z})$
3	IFZ	IFX	0x8f1bbcdc	0x7a6d76e9	$ONX(x, y, z)$	$x \oplus (y \vee \overline{z})$
4	ONX	XOR	0xa953fd4e	0x00000000	$ONZ(x, y, z)$	$(x \vee \overline{y}) \oplus z$

After 80 rounds of update, the output of $H(IV^0, M)$ denoted by $IV^1 = (IV_0^1, IV_1^1, \ldots, IV_4^1) \in \mathbb{F}_{2^{32}}^5$ is computed as follows:

$$IV_0^1 = IV_1^0 \boxplus X_{78} \boxplus Y_{77} \lll 10, \quad IV_1^1 = IV_2^0 \boxplus X_{77} \lll 10 \boxplus Y_{76} \lll 10,$$
$$IV_2^1 = IV_3^0 \boxplus X_{76} \lll 10 \boxplus Y_{75} \lll 10, \quad IV_3^1 = IV_4^0 \boxplus X_{75} \lll 10 \boxplus Y_{79},$$
$$IV_4^1 = IV_0^0 \boxplus X_{79} \boxplus Y_{78}.$$

2.3   The Differential Conditions for **RIPEMD-160**

Given a specified signed differential characteristic of RIPEMD-160, it has been shown in [13] that there should also be additional conditions on the modular difference. Specifically, apart from the bit conditions imposed by the differential characteristic, there will also be implicit conditions on each Q_i^l and Q_k^r, which are intermediate values during the round update of RIPEMD-160 as stated above. These implicit conditions are of the following forms:

$$(Q_i^l \boxplus \alpha_i^l) \lll s_i^l = Q_i^l \lll s_i^l \boxplus \beta_i^l,$$
$$(Q_k^r \boxplus \alpha_k^r) \lll s_k^l = Q_k^l \lll s_k^l \boxplus \beta_k^r,$$

where $(\alpha_i^l, \alpha_k^r, \beta_i^l, \beta_k^r)$ are constants and they can be easily derived from the specified differential characteristic. For convenience, we call these implicit conditions and the bit conditions **the differential conditions for a differential characteristic**.

It is possible that the conditions on these (Q_i^l, Q_k^r) contradict with the bit conditions, especially for the dense parts where many bits of the internal states (X_i, X_{i-4}) or (Y_k, Y_{k-4}) are fixed by the differential characteristic due to $Q_i^l = (X_i \boxminus X_{i-4} \lll 10) \ggg s_i^l$ and $Q_k^r = (Y_k \boxminus Y_{k-4} \lll 10) \ggg s_k^r$. Therefore, we should take this into account when searching for a valid differential characteristic. We note that many valid differential characteristics used for the (SFS) collision attacks on round-reduced RIPEMD-160 have been found with Mendel et al.'s tool [10,11,13,14,18]. However, it is unclear how this problem is handled in their tool as the implementation is not publicly available and only a few details of the tool are given in the corresponding papers.

2.4   Previous Methods to Search for Differential Characteristics

In the automatic tools [2,6,14–18,23,25] and Wang et al.'s hand-crafted work, it is common to first linearly propagate the message differences through the internal states backward and forward for several rounds, which can be easily finished either by hand or in a simple automatic way. Then, the signed differences for many internal states are fixed, while there are still some internal states whose signed differences are unknown.

For example, $(\nabla X_{i_0}, \nabla X_{i_0+1}, \ldots, \nabla X_{i_0+i_1})$ and $(\nabla X_{k_0}, \nabla X_{k_0+1}, \ldots, \nabla X_{k_0+k_1})$ are determined at the linear propagation phase where $k_0 > i_0 + i_1$. Then, the aim is to find a valid solution of $(\nabla X_{i_0+i_1+1}, \nabla X_{i_0+i_1+2}, \ldots, \nabla X_{k_0-1})$ to connect $(\nabla X_{i_0}, \nabla X_{i_0+1}, \ldots, \nabla X_{i_0+i_1})$ and $(\nabla X_{k_0}, \nabla X_{k_0+1}, \ldots, \nabla X_{k_0+k_1})$. Achieving the connection is the most technical component in these automatic tools. Its efficiency directly affects the overall performance. The main difficulty to achieve the connection is that many differential conditions are suddenly forced, which makes invalid solutions easily occur.

The most commonly used method for this connection problem is the guess-and-determine technique combined with some heuristic early-stop strategies [2, 6,9,14–18,23,25]. However, the implementation for RIPEMD-160 is not publicly available. There are also some tools [19,24] relying on off-the-shelf solvers for this problem. However, in these tools, the idea is to construct a model to describe two parallel instances of the value transitions. Specifically, does there exist a solution of $(X_{i_0+i_1+1}, X_{i_0+i_1+2}, \ldots, X_{k_0-1})$ and $(X'_{i_0+i_1+1}, X'_{i_0+i_1+2}, \ldots, X'_{k_0-1})$ such that the predetermined signed differences $(\nabla X_{i_0}, \nabla X_{i_0+1}, \ldots, \nabla X_{i_0+i_1})$ and $(\nabla X_{k_0}, \nabla X_{k_0+1}, \ldots, \nabla X_{k_0+k_1})$ can be connected? This can be easily converted into a SAT problem by modelling the value transitions. We tried this method but we could not find desired differential characteristics in practical time. We believe this is mainly because the information of the signed difference propagations cannot be efficiently encoded in such a model.

2.5   On MILP/SAT-Based Automatic Methods

It has become popular to utilize some off-the-shelf solvers to reduce the workload of cryptanalysis in the symmetric-key community. Depending on the used solvers, different languages are required to describe a target problem. Among these automatic methods, the SAT-based and MILP-based methods are mostly used [7,20,26]. For SAT-based methods, it is required to describe the target problem in the Conjunctive Normal Form (CNF) such that the solvers can handle them. For MILP-based methods, it is then required to describe the problem with linear inequalities.

With the software LogicFriday[1], by importing a truth table for some variables, one can easily obtain the minimized CNF in terms of these variables and then convert it into linear inequalities [1]. For example, suppose (x_0, x_1, x_2, x_3) can only take 3 values $\{(0,0,1,1), (1,0,1,0), (1,1,1,1)\}$. With LogicFriday, we can obtain the following equivalent minimized CNF to describe this constraint:

$$x_2 \wedge (x_0 \vee \overline{x_1}) \wedge (\overline{x_1} \vee x_3) \wedge (x_0 \vee x_3) \wedge (\overline{x_0} \vee x_1 \vee \overline{x_3}),$$

i.e. only the above 3 possible values of (x_0, x_1, x_2, x_3) can make the above boolean expression output 1 (true), while the remaining 13 values will make it output 0 (false). The above CNF can be converted into the following linear inequality system:

$$x_2 \geq 1, \ x_0 + (1 - x_1) \geq 1, \ (1 - x_1) + x_3 \geq 1,$$
$$x_0 + x_3 \geq 1, \ (1 - x_0) + x_1 + (1 - x_3) \geq 1.$$

For convenience, we also describe this system with the help of a matrix, as shown below:

$$\mathcal{H} \cdot (x_0, x_1, x_2, x_3)^T \geq (1, 0, 0, 1, -1)^T,$$

where

$$\mathcal{H} = \begin{bmatrix} 0 & 0 & 1 & 0 \\ 1 & -1 & 0 & 0 \\ 0 & -1 & 0 & 1 \\ 1 & 0 & 0 & 1 \\ -1 & 1 & 0 & -1 \end{bmatrix}.$$

---

[1] You can easily download it from https://download.cnet.com/.

3 Finding Signed Differential Characteristics with MILP

In this work, we consider the MILP-based methods to search for signed differential characteristics for RIPEMD-160. To achieve this, the first step is to formulate the problem and the second step is to model the problem with linear inequalities. We emphasize that we tried several different modelling methods before we eventually identified the method described in the paper. Due to the page limit, we only describe the most successful and efficient modelling method.

Formulating the problem is easy. Take the left branch of RIPEMD-160 as an example and it also can be applied to the right branch due to the similarity. Specifically, given $(\nabla X_i, \nabla X_{i+1}, \ldots, \nabla X_{i+4}, \nabla m_{\pi_l(i)})$, how to describe the possible values of ∇X_{i+5} with linear inequalities? In other words, how do the signed differences propagate through the round function and how to describe it with linear inequalities? Once this problem is solved, searching for collision-generating differential characteristics with some chosen message differences is easy as the signed difference transitions through the round function are known and one only needs to add some extra simple constraints to obtain a desired differential characteristic.

3.1 Modelling Signed Difference Transitions

The round function of RIPEMD-160 is of the following form:

$$d_{i+5} = (d_{i+1} \lll 10) \boxplus (F(d_{i+4}, d_{i+3}, d_{i+2} \lll 10) \boxplus (d_i \lll 10) \boxplus m \boxplus c) \lll s.$$

When considering the signed differences, the operation $\lll 10$ only affects the order of variables. From this perspective, to study the signed difference propagation $(\nabla d_i, \nabla d_{i+1}, \nabla d_{i+2}, \nabla d_{i+3}, \nabla d_{i+4}, \nabla m) \rightarrow \nabla d_{i+5}$, we indeed only need to study the signed difference propagation $(\nabla a_0, \nabla a_1, \nabla a_2, \nabla a_3, \nabla a_4, \nabla m) \rightarrow \nabla a_5$, where

$$a_5 = a_1 \boxplus (F(a_4, a_3, a_2) \boxplus a_0 \boxplus m \boxplus c) \lll s. \tag{1}$$

With some intermediate variables $(b_0, b_1, b_2, b_3, b_4, b_5)$, Eq. 1 can be decomposed as

$$b_0 = m \boxplus c, b_1 = F(a_4, a_3, a_2), b_2 = b_0 \boxplus b_1,$$
$$b_3 = b_2 \boxplus a_0, b_4 = b_3 \lll s, b_5 = a_1 \boxplus b_4, a_5 = b_5.$$

As (b_0, b_1, b_2, b_3) are all intermediate state values and m is a free variable that can be controlled by attackers, we only care about their modular differences. In other words, we can arbitrarily choose only one expansion of δb_i $(0 \le i \le 3)$ when constructing the model because one expansion is sufficient to describe the corresponding modular difference. For example, to describe $\delta b_i = \text{0x1}$, we can constrain that ∇b_i only takes [==== ==== ==== ==== ==== ==== ==== ===n] even though ∇b_i indeed can take many possible values. This is because one possible ∇b_i is sufficient to describe the modular difference 0x1. This is critical to improve the whole efficiency as invalid modular differences can be filtered in a much faster way. Our basic idea to construct the model is as follows:

1. Deterministically compute the signed difference transitions for $b_0 = m \boxplus c$, $b_2 = b_0 \boxplus b_1$ and $b_3 = b_2 \boxplus a_0$. Specifically, for each given $(\nabla x, \nabla y)$, uniquely compute one ∇z such that $\delta z = \delta x \boxplus \delta y$, even though there are many such possible ∇z.
2. Compute the signed difference transitions for $b_1 = F(a_4, a_3, a_2)$, where F is a boolean function.
3. Handle the signed difference transitions for $b_4 = b_3 \lll s$, $b_5 = a_1 \boxplus b_4$ and $a_5 = b_5$ according to different situations.

3.2 Describing Signed Differences

To construct the model, we first need to properly describe the signed difference. Different from the XOR difference which can be trivially described with a binary variable, there are 3 important statuses for the signed difference, namely $\{=, \mathtt{n}, \mathtt{u}\}$ and we cannot simply describe them with a binary variable. One may think that it can be described with a variable taking the value from $\{-1, 0, 1\}$, which is also supported by Gurobi. However, such a method is unfriendly to model the signed difference transitions through the boolean functions and the whole performance is bad even if we try some other strategies to make it work.

Finally, we choose to use two binary variables (v, d) to describe a 1-bit signed difference. Moreover, we restrict that (v, d) can only take 3 possible values[2], i.e. $(v, d) \in \{(0, 1), (1, 1), (0, 0)\}$. Specifically, $(v, d) = (0, 1)$ corresponds to $\mathtt{n}$, $(v, d) = (1, 1)$ corresponds to $\mathtt{u}$, and $(v, d) = (0, 0)$ corresponds to $=$. Note that we do not allow $(v, d) = (1, 0)$ because this is redundant and will affect the overall performance. This trick is important to improve the performance.

For convenience, when describing the signed difference of a binary variable κ, we simply use $(\kappa_v, \kappa_d) \in \{(0, 1), (1, 1), (0, 0)\}$ to represent the signed difference $\nabla \kappa$. In many of the following algorithms, we also say such a variable $\nabla \kappa$ is a signed difference variable and it should be viewed as a structure $\nabla \kappa = (\kappa_v, \kappa_d)$.

3.3 Modelling the Modular Addition

We consider the signed difference transition through $z = x \boxplus y$ bit by bit. Moreover, as stated above, we are interested in only one ∇z for a given $(\nabla x, \nabla y)$. To achieve this purpose, we introduce an additional variable ∇c of size 33 to represent the signed differences of the carry bits when computing $\nabla x \boxplus \nabla y$. Then, we use deterministic propagation rules for $(\nabla x[i], \nabla y[i], \nabla c[i]) \rightarrow (\nabla z[i], \nabla c[i+1])$, i.e. each $(\nabla x[i], \nabla y[i], \nabla c[i])$ corresponds to a unique $(\nabla z[i], \nabla c[i+1])$, as shown in Table 3. In this way, ∇z is uniquely determined for each given $(\nabla x, \nabla y)$ and it corresponds to the modular difference $\delta z = \delta x \boxplus \delta y$, which can be easily observed from the propagation rules.

---

[2] Here, it can be found that $d = 1$ means there is a difference and v is the initial value to be changed. Hence, $(v, d) = (0, 1)$ means 0 is changed to 1 and $(v, d) = (1, 1)$ means 1 is changed to 0. We exclude $(v, d) = (1, 0)$ because $(v, d) = (0, 0)$ can carry the same information as $(v, d) = (1, 0)$, i.e. both mean there is no difference.

Let us take [nnu → n=] and [u=u → =u] as examples. For [nnu → n=], it means $2^i \boxplus 2^i \boxminus 2^i = 2^i$. For [u=u → =u], it means $\boxminus 2^i \boxminus 2^i = \boxminus 2^{i+1}$. It is then clear that the modular difference $\delta x \boxplus \delta y$ is correctly recorded by the computed ∇z.

Table 3. The propagation rules for $(\nabla x[i], \nabla y[i], \nabla c[i]) \rightarrow (\nabla z[i], \nabla c[i+1])$

[=== → ==], [==n → n=], [==u → u=], [=n= → n=],
[=u= → u=], [=nn → =n], [=un → ==], [=nu → ==],
[=uu → =u], [n== → n=], [u== → u=], [n=n → =n],
[u=n → ==], [n=u → ==], [u=u → =u], [nn= → =n],
[nu= → ==], [un= → ==], [uu= → =u], [nnn → nn],
[nun → n=], [unn → n=], [nnu → n=], [uun → u=],
[unu → u=], [nuu → u=], [uuu → uu]

According to our way to describe $\{n, u, =\}$, we can convert the above 27 propagation rules in Table 3 into 27 possible values of

$$V_{\text{ADD}} = (x_v[i], x_d[i], y_v[i], y_d[i], c_v[i], c_d[i], z_v[i], z_d[i], c_v[i+1], c_d[i+1]).$$

For example, [n=u → ==] corresponds to the possible value $(0, 1, 0, 0, 1, 1, 0, 0, 0, 0)$. With LogicFriday, we can obtain the corresponding linear inequality system:

$$\mathcal{H}_{\text{ADD}} \cdot V_{\text{ADD}}^T \geq \mathcal{C}_{\text{ADD}}.$$

Algorithm 1 describes how to model the deterministic modular addition. Note that we do not make $\nabla c[0] = [=]$ in Algorithm 1 to increase its flexibility and hence before calling it, the value of $\nabla c[0]$ should be clearly specified.

Algorithm 1. Model $\delta z = \delta x \boxplus \delta y$

1: **procedure** MODADD_MODEL($\nabla x, \nabla y, \nabla c, \nabla z$)
2:     **for** $i = 0$ to 32 **do**
3:         $V_{\text{ADD}} = (x_v[i], x_d[i], y_v[i], y_d[i], c_v[i], c_d[i], z_v[i], z_d[i], c_v[i+1], c_d[i+1])$
4:         add constraints $\mathcal{H}_{\text{ADD}} \cdot V_{\text{ADD}}^T \geq \mathcal{C}_{\text{ADD}}$.

3.4 Modelling the Expansions of the Modular Difference

Given an arbitrary δz, there are many expansions of δz. For example, there are 3 possible expansions of $\delta z = 2^{30}$ as shown below:

$$=n== \quad ==== \quad ==== \quad ==== \quad ==== \quad ==== \quad ==== \quad ====,$$

$$nu== \quad ==== \quad ==== \quad ==== \quad ==== \quad ==== \quad ==== \quad ====,$$

$$uu== \quad ==== \quad ==== \quad ==== \quad ==== \quad ==== \quad ==== \quad ====.$$

Due to our deterministic way to compute the signed difference transitions through the modular addition $z = x \boxplus y$, we lose many possible ∇z. When it is necessary to compute all possible forms of ∇z, we need to tackle the problem of how to model all the possible $\nabla \xi$ from a given ∇z such that $\delta \xi = \delta z$.

To achieve this, we again introduce an additional variable ∇c with $\nabla c[0] = [\texttt{=}]$. Based on the basic fact that $2^i = 2^{i+1} \boxminus 2^i$, $\boxminus 2^i = \boxminus 2^{i+1} + 2^i$, $0 = 0$, $2^{i+1} = 2^{i+1}$ and $\boxminus 2^{i+1} = \boxminus 2^{i+1}$, we can use the following propagation rules in Table 4 to compute all possible $\nabla \xi$ from ∇z.

Table 4. The propagation rules for $(\nabla z[i], \nabla c[i]) \rightarrow (\nabla \xi[i], \nabla c[i+1])$

$[\texttt{nn} \rightarrow \texttt{=n}]$, $[\texttt{uu} \rightarrow \texttt{=u}]$, $[\texttt{nu} \rightarrow \texttt{==}]$, $[\texttt{un} \rightarrow \texttt{==}]$,
$[\texttt{n=} \rightarrow (\texttt{n=}, \texttt{un})]$, $[\texttt{u=} \rightarrow (\texttt{u=}, \texttt{nu})]$,
$[\texttt{=n} \rightarrow (\texttt{n=}, \texttt{un})]$, $[\texttt{=u} \rightarrow (\texttt{u=}, \texttt{nu})]$,
$[\texttt{==} \rightarrow \texttt{==}]$

Similarly, the propagation rules in Table 4 can be converted into 13 possible values of

$$V_{\text{EXP}} = (z_v[i], z_d[i], c_v[i], c_d[i], \xi_v[i], \xi_d[i], c_v[i+1], c_d[i+1]),$$

Note that $[\texttt{n=} \rightarrow (\texttt{n=}, \texttt{un})]$ corresponds to two possible transitions $[\texttt{n=} \rightarrow \texttt{n=}]$ and $[\texttt{n=} \rightarrow \texttt{un}]$. Similar representations will be used throughout this paper. Then, we can obtain the linear inequality system $\mathcal{H}_{\text{EXP}} \cdot V_{\text{EXP}}^T \geq \mathcal{C}_{\text{EXP}}$ to describe Table 4 with LogicFriday.

A Slightly Different Problem. In the procedure to search for signed differential characteristics for the MD-SHA family, it is common to first fix the signed differences of some internal states in advance. In other words, we now consider how to efficiently determine whether a computed ∇z satisfies $\delta \xi \boxminus \delta z = 0$ when $\nabla \xi$ is known and fixed. This is indeed the same with the problem to model the expansions of the modular difference, but we prefer a different method because it does not rely only on a tree structure, i.e. there is no branch.

The following propagation rules for $(\nabla \xi[i], \nabla z[i], \nabla c[i]) \rightarrow (\nabla c[i+1])$ are sufficient to constrain $\delta \xi \boxminus \delta z = 0$, where ∇c is the signed difference of the carry bits when computing $\nabla \xi \boxminus \nabla z$ and $\nabla c[0] = [\texttt{=}]$.

$$[\texttt{===} \rightarrow \texttt{=}],$$
$$[\texttt{=un} \rightarrow \texttt{n}], [\texttt{=nn} \rightarrow \texttt{=}], [\texttt{=uu} \rightarrow \texttt{=}], [\texttt{=nu} \rightarrow \texttt{u}],$$
$$[\texttt{u=n} \rightarrow \texttt{=}], [\texttt{n=n} \rightarrow \texttt{n}], [\texttt{u=u} \rightarrow \texttt{u}], [\texttt{n=u} \rightarrow \texttt{=}],$$
$$[\texttt{nu=} \rightarrow \texttt{n}], [\texttt{nn=} \rightarrow \texttt{=}], [\texttt{uu=} \rightarrow \texttt{=}], [\texttt{un=} \rightarrow \texttt{u}].$$

These 13 propagations rules can be converted into 13 possible values of

$$V_{\text{ZERO}} = (\xi_v[i], \xi_d[i], z_v[i], z_d[i], c_v[i], c_d[i], c_v[i+1], c_d[i+1]).$$

With LogicFriday, we can obtain the corresponding $\mathcal{H}_{\text{ZERO}} \cdot V_{\text{ZERO}}^T \geq \mathcal{C}_{\text{ZERO}}$.

Algorithm 2 describes how to model the expansion of the modular difference. The input isK is a binary variable and is used to provide an option to choose different models.

Algorithm 2. Expansion: derive $\nabla\xi$ from ∇z

1: **procedure** EXPAND_MODEL($\nabla z, \nabla\xi$, isK)
2:     Claim a signed difference vector ∇c of size 33
3:     $\nabla c[0] = [=]$
4:     **for** $i = 0$ to 32 **do**
5:         **if** isK $= 1$ **then**
6:             $V_{\text{ZERO}} = (\xi_v[i], \xi_d[i], z_v[i], z_d[i], c_v[i], c_d[i], c_v[i+1], c_d[i+1])$
7:             $\mathcal{H}_{\text{ZERO}} \cdot V_{\text{ZERO}}^T \geq \mathcal{C}_{\text{ZERO}}$
8:         **else**
9:             $V_{\text{EXP}} = (z_v[i], z_d[i], c_v[i], c_d[i], \xi_v[i], \xi_d[i], c_v[i+1], c_d[i+1])$
10:             add constraints $\mathcal{H}_{\text{EXP}} \cdot V_{\text{EXP}}^T \geq \mathcal{C}_{\text{EXP}}$

3.5   Modelling Boolean Functions

Using some simple boolean functions in the round function is a basic operation in the MD-SHA hash family. For RIPEMD-160, the used boolean functions are shown in Table 2: XOR, ONX, IFZ, IFX and ONZ. Especially, we have

$$w = IFX(x, y, z) = IFZ(y, z, x), \quad w = ONZ(x, y, z) = ONX(z, x, y).$$

The strategies to handle these boolean functions are the same. Due to the space limit, we only explain the difference transitions through $w = ONX(x, y, z)$.

Table 5. The valid values of $(\nabla x[i], \nabla y[i], \nabla z[i], \nabla w[i])$

[====],

[==u=], [==uu], [==un], [==n=], [==nn], [==nu],

[=n==], [=n=n], [=n=u], [=u==], [=u=u], [=u=n],

[n==u], [n==n], [u==n], [u==u],

[=nn=], [=uu=], [=nun], [=nuu], [=unn], [=unu],

[nn=u], [nn==], [nu=u], [nu==], [uu=n], [uu==], [un=n], [un==],

[n=nu], [n=n=], [n=uu], [n=u=], [u=nn], [u=n=], [u=un], [u=u=],

[nnnu], [nnu=], [nun=], [unnn], [uun=], [unu=], [nuuu], [uuun].

The Fast Filtering Model. First, we list all possible $(\nabla x[i], \nabla y[i], \nabla z[i], \nabla w[i])$, as shown in Table 5. Similarly, we can obtain the corresponding inequality system

$$\mathcal{H}_{\text{ONX}} \cdot V_{\text{DF}}^T \geq \mathcal{C}_{\text{ONX}}, \tag{2}$$

$$V_{\text{DF}} = (x_v[i], x_d[i], y_v[i], y_d[i], z_v[i], z_d[i], w_v[i], w_d[i]).$$

The Full Model. In the fast filtering model, we only consider signed difference transitions and ignore the implicit conditions. For example, for $w = ONX(x, y, z)$, when $(\nabla x[i], \nabla y[i], \nabla z[i], \nabla w[i]) = [\text{=n==}]$, there is an implicit condition $z[i] = 1$. Ignoring such implicit conditions will cause invalid differential characteristics because each internal state is used three times in such boolean functions to update different internal states at 3 consecutive rounds. To capture such implicit conditions, a full list of possible $(\nabla x[i], \nabla y[i], \nabla z[i], \nabla w[i], x[i], y[i], z[i])$ is provided in Table 6. For convenience, we call $(x[i], y[i], z[i])$ **monitoring variables** as they are used to store the implicit conditions and hence to monitor the contradictions.

Table 6. The valid values of $(\nabla x[i], \nabla y[i], \nabla z[i], \nabla w[i], x[i], y[i], z[i])$, where $*$ represents that the bit value can take either 0 or 1.

[====,*,*,*],

[==u=,*,1,*], [==uu,1,0,*], [==un,0,0,*], [==n=,*,1,*], [==nn,1,0,*], [==nu,0,0,*],

[=n==,*,*,0], [=n=n,0,*,1], [=n=u,1,*,1], [=u==,*,*,0], [=u=u,0,*,1], [=u=n,1,*,1],

[n==u,*,1,*], [n==uu,*,0,0], [n==n,*,0,1], [u==n,*,1,*], [u==n,*,0,0], [u==u,*,0,1],

[=nn=,*,*,*], [=uu=,*,*,*], [=nun,0,*,*], [=nuu,1,*,*], [=unn,1,*,*], [=unu,0,*,*],

[nn=u,*,*,0], [nn==,*,*,1], [nu=u,*,*,0], [nu==,*,*,1], [uu=n,*,*,0], [uu==,*,*,1],

[un=n,*,*,0], [un==,*,*,1],

[n=nu,*,1,*], [n=n=,*,0,*], [n=uu,*,1,*], [n=u=,*,0,*], [u=nn,*,1,*], [u=n=,*,0,*],

[u=un,*,1,*], [u=u=,*,0,*],

[nnnu,*,*,*], [nnu=,*,*,*], [nun=,*,*,*], [unnn,*,*,*], [uun=,*,*,*], [unu=,*,*,*],

[nuuu,*,*,*], [uuun,*,*,*].

Similarly, based on Table 6, we can obtain the corresponding

$$\mathcal{H}_{\text{ONXFull}} \cdot V_{\text{DFC}}^T \geq C_{\text{ONXFull}}, \tag{3}$$

$$V_{\text{DFC}} = (x_v[i], x_d[i], y_v[i], y_d[i], z_v[i], z_d[i], w_v[i], w_d[i], x[i], y[i], z[i]).$$

Note that in Table 6, $*$ means it can take either 0 or 1, e.g. [==u=,*,1,*] corresponds to 4 possible values: $(0,0,0,0,1,1,0,0,0,1,0)$, $(0,0,0,0,1,1,0,0,0,1,1)$, $(0,0,0,0,1,1,0,0,1,1,0)$ and $(0,0,0,0,1,1,0,0,1,1,1)$.

It is found that some inequalities appear in both Eq. 2 and Eq. 3. This is indeed as expected since the information of Table 5 is fully encoded in Table 6. Therefore, to filter invalid signed difference transitions in a faster way, we will actually use the following linear inequality system

$$\begin{cases} \mathcal{H}_{\text{ONX}} \cdot V_{\text{DF}}^T \geq & C_{\text{ONX}} \\ \mathcal{H}_{\text{ONXCut}} \cdot V_{\text{DFC}}^T \geq & C_{\text{ONXCut}} \end{cases} \tag{4}$$

to describe Table 6. Specifically, $(\mathcal{H}_{\text{ONXCut}}, C_{\text{ONXCut}})$ is obtained by removing the inequalities appearing in Eq. 2 from Eq. 3. Specifically, we check the inequalities specified by $(\mathcal{H}_{\text{ONXFull}}, C_{\text{ONXFull}})$ one by one. If it does not appear in $(\mathcal{H}_{\text{ONX}}, C_{\text{ONX}})$, add it to $(\mathcal{H}_{\text{ONXCut}}, C_{\text{ONXCut}})$.

In this way, we can equivalently say that $(\mathcal{H}_{\mathrm{ONXCut}}, \mathcal{C}_{\mathrm{ONXCut}})$ is purely utilized to describe the implicit conditions as $(\mathcal{H}_{\mathrm{ONX}}, \mathcal{C}_{\mathrm{ONX}})$ can fully describe valid signed difference transitions. This is very important to increase the flexibility of the model as we can add $\mathcal{H}_{\mathrm{ONXCut}} \cdot V_{\mathrm{DFC}}^T \geq \mathcal{C}_{\mathrm{ONXCut}}$ to the model depending on different situations while $\mathcal{H}_{\mathrm{ONX}} \cdot V_{\mathrm{DF}}^T \geq \mathcal{C}_{\mathrm{ONX}}$ is always added. Moreover, the lazy constraint[3] can be applied to $\mathcal{H}_{\mathrm{ONXCut}} \cdot V_{\mathrm{ONXCut}}^T \geq \mathcal{C}_{\mathrm{ONXCut}}$ to improve the performance for some problems. For simplicity, Eq. 2 is called the fast filtering model, while Eq. 4 is called the full model.

Modelling Other Boolean Functions. The above procedure is rather general and we can apply it to other boolean functions.

For $w = XOR(x,y,z)$, the full model can be described with $\mathcal{H}_{\mathrm{XOR}} \cdot V_{\mathrm{DF}}^T \geq \mathcal{C}_{\mathrm{XOR}}$ and $\mathcal{H}_{\mathrm{XORCut}} \cdot V_{\mathrm{DFC}}^T \geq \mathcal{C}_{\mathrm{XORCut}}$, where the fast filtering model is $\mathcal{H}_{\mathrm{XOR}} \cdot V_{\mathrm{DF}}^T \geq \mathcal{C}_{\mathrm{XOR}}$.

For $w = IFZ(x,y,z)$, the full model can be described with: $\mathcal{H}_{\mathrm{IFZ}} \cdot V_{\mathrm{DF}}^T \geq \mathcal{C}_{\mathrm{IFZ}}$ and $\mathcal{H}_{\mathrm{IFZCut}} \cdot V_{\mathrm{DFC}}^T \geq \mathcal{C}_{\mathrm{IFZCut}}$, where the fast filtering model is $\mathcal{H}_{\mathrm{IFZ}} \cdot V_{\mathrm{DF}}^T \geq \mathcal{C}_{\mathrm{IFZ}}$.

Algorithm 3 describes how to model the signed difference signed difference transitions through Boolean functions.

Algorithm 3. Model the signed difference transitions through Boolean functions

1: **procedure** BOOLFAST_MODEL(fNa,$\nabla x, \nabla y, \nabla z, \nabla w$)
2:    **for** $i = 0$ to 32 **do**
3:        $V_{\mathrm{DF}} = (x_v[i], x_d[i], y_v[i], y_d[i], z_v[i], z_d[i], w_v[i], w_d[i])$
4:        **if** fNa $= "ONX"$ **then**
5:            add constraints $\mathcal{H}_{\mathrm{ONX}} \cdot V_{\mathrm{DF}}^T \geq \mathcal{C}_{\mathrm{ONX}}$
6:        **else if** fNa $= "XOR"$ **then**
7:            add constraints $\mathcal{H}_{\mathrm{XOR}} \cdot V_{\mathrm{DF}}^T \geq \mathcal{C}_{\mathrm{XOR}}$
8:        **else if** fNa $= "IFZ"$ **then**
9:            add constraints $\mathcal{H}_{\mathrm{IFZ}} \cdot V_{\mathrm{DF}}^T \geq \mathcal{C}_{\mathrm{IFZ}}$
10: **procedure** BOOLFULL_MODEL(funName,$\nabla x, \nabla y, \nabla z, \nabla w, x, y, z$)
11:    **for** $i = 0$ to 32 **do**
12:        $V_{\mathrm{DFC}} = (x_v[i], x_d[i], y_v[i], y_d[i], z_v[i], z_d[i], w_v[i], w_d[i], x[i], y[i], z[i])$
13:        **if** funName$="ONX"$ **then**
14:            add constraints $\mathcal{H}_{\mathrm{ONXCut}} \cdot V_{\mathrm{DFC}}^T \geq \mathcal{C}_{\mathrm{ONXCut}}$
15:        **else if** funName$="XOR"$ **then**
16:            add constraints $\mathcal{H}_{\mathrm{XORCut}} \cdot V_{\mathrm{DFC}}^T \geq \mathcal{C}_{\mathrm{XORCut}}$
17:        **else if** funName$="IFZ"$ **then**
18:            add constraints $\mathcal{H}_{\mathrm{IFZCut}} \cdot V_{\mathrm{DFC}}^T \geq \mathcal{C}_{\mathrm{IFZCut}}$

3.6   Modelling $a_5 = a_1 \boxplus b_3 \lll s$

This is the special operation in RIPEMD-160 and is another place where contradictions easily occur especially when there are many bit conditions on (a_1, a_5).

---

[3] In Gurobi, the lazy constraint means the constraints that are checked only after a solution is found.

We also note that we will sometimes decompose this computation as

$$b_4 = b_3 \lll s, b_5 = a_1 \boxplus b_4, a_5 = b_5.$$

Due to our deterministic way to compute ∇b_3, many possible ∇b_3 are lost. One idea is to first compute all possible expansions of δb_3 from ∇b_3. Then, the bitwise rotation only affects the order of variables and we immediately obtain all possible ∇b_4. However, what we need is all possible ∇a_5 where $a_5 = a_1 \boxplus b_4$. If we compute $\nabla b_5 = \nabla a_1 \boxplus \nabla b_4$ for each ∇b_4 with the deterministic model for the modular addition and then compute all possible ∇a_5 from ∇b_5 with the model for the expansion, the expansion is used twice and it is too costly because there are too many combinations. However, in some extreme cases, we will use this idea to avoid the contradictions, i.e. the second strategy stated below.

Indeed, it has been studied in [3,13] that $\delta b_4 = ((b_3 \boxplus \delta b_3) \lll s) \boxminus (b_3 \lll s)$ has at most four possible values for a given δb_3. Therefore, ∇b_4 can be divided into four classes and each class corresponds to different δb_4.

The First Strategy. We always choose some δb_4 that hold with a high probability. Then, for each of them, randomly pick one of its expansions ∇b_4. Next, according to $(\nabla a_1, \nabla b_4)$, uniquely determine ∇b_5 with the model for the modular addition. Finally, compute all possible ∇a_5 from ∇b_5 with the model for the expansion. Describing the strategy in words is easy, but how to encode it with linear inequalities?

The most important step is to use linear inequalities to describe how to pick some ∇b_4 holding with a high probability. According to [13], the branch is mainly caused by the carries from the 31st bit and the $(31 - s)$-th bit when computing $b_3 \boxplus \delta b_3$. Therefore, we introduce two variables $(\nabla c_h, \nabla c_m)$ to denote the signed difference of these two carry bits, respectively. Although the two carry bits depend on many bits, we restrict ourselves to only $(\nabla b_3[31], \nabla b_3[30])$ and $(\nabla b_3[31 - s], \nabla b_3[30 - s])$. Then, we fix the propagation rules for

$$(\nabla b_3[31], \nabla b_3[30]) \rightarrow (\nabla b_4[31 + s], \nabla b_4[30 + s], \nabla c_h),$$
$$(\nabla b_3[31 - s], \nabla b_3[30 - s]) \rightarrow (\nabla b_4[31], \nabla b_4[30], \nabla c_m),$$

where the indices are within modulo 32. As the propagation rules are the same for both cases and they are of the same form $(\nabla u, \nabla t) \rightarrow (\nabla \mu, \nabla \tau, \nabla \iota)$, for simplicity, these rules are specified in Table 7. With LogicFriday, Table 7 can be

Table 7. The propagation rules for $(\nabla u, \nabla t) \rightarrow (\nabla \mu, \nabla \tau, \nabla \iota)$

[== → ===],
[n= → (n==, u=n)], [u= → (u==, n=u)],
[un → =u=], [nu → =n=],[=u → =u=], [=n → =n=],
[nn → =un], [uu → =nu].

equivalently described with:

$$\mathcal{H}_{\text{ROT}} \cdot V_{\text{ROT}}^T \geq \mathcal{C}_{\text{ROT}},$$

$$V_{\text{ROT}} = (u_v, u_d, t_v, t_d, \mu_v, \mu_d, \tau_v, \tau_d, \iota_v, \iota_d).$$

For the remaining $\nabla b_4[i]$, they are uniquely determined with

$$\nabla b_4[i] = \nabla b_3[i - s] \text{ for } i \notin \{31, 30, 31 + s, 30 + s\}.$$

An algorithmic description of the first strategy can be referred to Algorithm 4. Later, we need to use $\nabla q[0 : s]$ where $\delta q = \delta a_5 \boxminus \delta a_1 = \delta b_4$ to help detect contradictions (ref. Sect. 3.7). Therefore, we also take ∇q as an input to ROTATE_DIFF_FIRST and whether we compute it depends on the variable isV.

The Second Strategy. For the second strategy, we will allow some low-probability propagations $\delta b_3 \rightarrow \delta b_4$. This is because when there are many bit conditions on (a_1, a_5), it is possible that such a propagation $\delta b_3 \rightarrow \delta b_4$ indeed holds with probability close to 1 under these conditions.

Still we consider $\nabla z = \nabla x \boxplus \nabla y$ and use the variable ∇c to denote the signed differences of the carry bits where $\nabla c[0] = [=]$. The new propagation rules for $(\nabla x[i], \nabla y[i], \nabla c[i]) \rightarrow (\nabla z[i], \nabla c[i + 1])$ are listed in Table 8. In these new rules, the previous rules for the modular addition and the rules for the expansion are combined in a way, i.e. we will consider branches for the modular addition this time because a_5 is no more an intermediate variable but the final output of the round function. As a result, the new model for the modular addition will become much heavier.

Table 8. The new propagation rules for $(\nabla x[i], \nabla y[i], \nabla c[i]) \rightarrow (\nabla z[i], \nabla c[i + 1])$

[=== → ==], [(==n, =n=, n==) → (n=, un)], [(==u, =u=, u==) → (u=, nu)],
[(=un, un=, u=n, =nu, nu=, n=u) → ==], [(=uu, uu=, u=u) → =u],
[(=nn, nn=, n=n) → =n], [nnn → nn], [uuu → uu],
[(nnu, unn, nun) → un], [(uun, nuu, unu) → nu].

With LogicFriday, Table 8 can be equivalently described with

$$\mathcal{H}_{\text{EXPAdd}} \cdot V_{\text{EXPAdd}}^T \geq \mathcal{C}_{\text{EXPAdd}}$$

$$V_{\text{EXPAdd}} = (x_v[i], x_d[i], y_v[i], y_d[i], c_v[i], c_d[i], z_v[i], z_d[i], c_v[i + 1], c_d[i + 1]).$$

The model for the signed difference transitions through $a_5 = a_1 \boxplus (b_3 \lll s)$ with the second strategy is also described in Algorithm 4.

3.7   Detecting More Contradictions

It has been stated in Sect. 2.3 that there are additional implicit conditions. Specifically, for

$$b_4 = b_3 \lll s, b_5 = a_1 \boxplus b_4, a_5 = b_5,$$

Algorithm 4. Model $a_5 = a_1 \boxplus (b_3 \lll s)$

1: **procedure** ROTATE_DIFF_FIRST($s, \nabla b_3, \nabla a_1, \nabla a_5, \nabla q$, isV, isK)
2:     Claim two signed difference vectors $\nabla b_4, \nabla b_5$ of size 32
3:     **for** $i = 0$ to $30 - s$ **do**
4:         $\nabla b_4[i + s \mod 32] = \nabla b_3[i]$
5:     **for** $i = 32 - s$ to 30 **do**
6:         $\nabla b_4[i + s \mod 32] = \nabla b_3[i]$
7:     Claim a signed difference vector ∇c_0 of size 33
8:     Claim a signed difference vector ∇c_h
9:     ROTATE_MODEL($\nabla b_3[31 - s], \nabla b_3[30 - s], \nabla b_4[31], \nabla b_4[30], \nabla c_0[0]$)
10:     ROTATE_MODEL($\nabla b_3[31], \nabla b_3[30], \nabla b_4[31 + s], \nabla b_4[30 + s], \nabla c_h$)
11:     MODADD_MODEL($\nabla a_1, \nabla b_4, \nabla c_0, \nabla b_5$)// $\nabla c_0[0]$ is no longer always [=]
12:     EXPAND_MODEL($\nabla b_5, \nabla a_5$, isK)
13:     **if** isV $= 1$ **then**
14:         Claim a signed difference vector ∇c_1 of size $s + 2$
15:         $\nabla c_1[0] = [\text{=}]$
16:         SIGNED_Q_MODEL($\nabla b_4, \nabla c_0[0], \nabla c_1, \nabla q, s$)// $\nabla q[0 : s] = (\nabla b_4 \boxplus \nabla c_0[0])[0 : s]$
17: **procedure** ROTATE_MODEL($\nabla u, \nabla t, \nabla \mu, \nabla \tau, \nabla \iota$)
18:     $V_{\text{ROT}} = (u_v, u_d, t_v, t_d, \mu_v, \mu_d, \tau_v, \tau_d, \iota_v, \iota_d)$
19:     add constraints $\mathcal{H}_{\text{ROT}} \cdot V_{\text{ROT}}^T \geq C_{\text{ROT}}$
20: **procedure** SIGNED_Q_MODEL($\nabla x, \nabla y, \nabla c, \nabla z, s$)
21:     $V_{\text{ADD}} = (x_v[0], x_d[0], y_v, y_d, c_v[0], c_d[0], z_v[0], z_d[0], c_v[1], c_d[1])$
22:     add constraint $\mathcal{H}_{\text{ADD}} \cdot V_{\text{ADD}}^T \geq C_{\text{ADD}}$
23:     **for** $i = 1$ to $s + 1$ **do**
24:         $V_{\text{ADD}} = (x_v[i], x_d[i], 0, 0, c_v[i], c_d[i], z_v[i], z_d[i], c_v[i + 1], c_d[i + 1])$
25:         add constraint $\mathcal{H}_{\text{ADD}} \cdot V_{\text{ADD}}^T \geq C_{\text{ADD}}$
26:
27: **procedure** ROTATE_DIFF_SECOND($s, \nabla b_3, \nabla a_1, \nabla a_5, \nabla q$, isV)
28:     Claim a signed difference vector ∇b_4 of size 32
29:     EXPAND_MODEL($\nabla b_4, \nabla b_3, 0$)
30:     ADDEXP_MODEL($\nabla a_1, \nabla b_4 \lll s, \nabla a_5$) // $\nabla b_4 \lll s$ only changes the order of ∇b_4
31:     **if** isV $= 1$ **then**
32:         **for** $i = 0$ to $s + 1$ **do**
33:             $\nabla q[i] = \nabla b_4[i - s]$
34: **procedure** ADDEXP_MODEL($\nabla x, \nabla y, \nabla z$)
35:     Claim a signed difference vector ∇c of size 33
36:     $\nabla c[0] = [\text{=}]$
37:     **for** $i = 0$ to 32 **do**
38:         $V_{\text{EXPAdd}} = (x_v[i], x_d[i], y_v[i], y_d[i], c_v[i], c_d[i], z_v[i], z_d[i], c_v[i + 1], c_d[i + 1])$
39:         add constraints $\mathcal{H}_{\text{EXPAdd}} \cdot V_{\text{EXPAdd}}^T \geq C_{\text{EXPAdd}}$.

---

due to the probabilistic propagation $\delta b_3 \rightarrow \delta b_4$, there will be conditions on $q = a_5 \boxminus a_1 = b_3 \lll s$, i.e. there should exist a solution of q to the following equations

$$q = a_5 \boxminus a_1, \delta q = \delta a_5 \boxminus \delta a_1, \delta b_3 \boxplus q \ggg s = (\delta q \boxplus q) \ggg s,$$

where $(\delta b_3, \delta a_5, \delta a_1)$ are fixed according to their specified signed differences $(\nabla b_3, \nabla a_5, \nabla a_1)$.

Algorithm 5. Detect more contradictions in $a_5 = a_1 \boxplus (b_3 \lll s)$

1: **procedure** ROTATE_DIFF_FILTER$(s, \nabla a_5, \nabla a_1, \nabla b_3, \nabla q, a_5, a_1)$
2:     Claim a binary vector q of size 32
3:     COMPUTE_Q$(\nabla a_5, \nabla a_1, a_5, a_1, q)$ //compute q
4:     Claim a binary vector v_0 of size $s + 1$
5:     VAL_DIFF_ADD_MODEL$(\nabla q, q, v_0, s + 1)$//compute $v_0 = (\delta q \boxplus q)[0 : s]$
6:     Claim a binary vector v_1 of size $33 - s$
7:     VAL_DIFF_ADD_MODEL$(\nabla b_3, q \ggg s, v_1, 33 - s)$//compute v_1
8:     add constraint $v_0[0] = v_1[32 - s]$
9:     add constraint $v_0[s] = v_1[0]$
10: **procedure** COMPUTE_Q$(\nabla z, \nabla x, z, x, q)$
11:     **for** $i = 0$ to 32 **do**
12:         DERIVE_COND$(x[i], \nabla x[i])$//derive conditions on x from ∇x
13:         DERIVE_COND$(z[i], \nabla z[i])$//derive conditions on z from ∇z
14:     VAL_ADD_MODEL$(x, q, z, 32)$//$x \boxplus q = z$
15: **procedure** DERIVE_COND$(x, \nabla x)$
16:     //$x = 0$ if $(\nabla x = \text{n})$; $x = 1$ if $(\nabla x = \text{u})$; x is free if $(\nabla x = \text{=})$
17:     add constraint $-x_v + x \geq 0$
18:     add constraint $x_v - x_d - x \geq -1$
19: **procedure** VAL_DIFF_ADD_MODEL$(\nabla a, b, v, l)$//compute $v = (\delta a \boxplus b)[0 : l - 1]$
20:     Claim a signed difference vector ∇c of size l
21:     $\nabla c[0] = [\text{=}]$
22:     **for** $i = 0$ to l **do**
23:         add constraint $2(c_d[i + 1] - 2c_v[i + 1]) + v[i] = (a_d[i] - 2a_v[i]) + b[i] + (c_d[i] - 2c_v[i])$
24:         add constraint $c_d[i + 1] \geq c_v[i + 1]$
25: **procedure** VAL_ADD_MODEL(a, b, v, l)//compute $v = (a \boxplus b)[0 : l - 1]$
26:     Claim a binary vector c of size l
27:     $c[0] = 0$
28:     **for** $i = 0$ to l **do**
29:         add constraint $2c[i + 1] + v[i] = a[i] + b[i] + c[i]$

In our model, the constraints have ensured that δb_4 is one of the 4 possible values computed from δb_3. Since $\delta b_4 = \delta a_5 \boxminus \delta a_1$, there are always solutions to

$$\delta b_3 \boxplus q \ggg s = (\delta q \boxplus q) \ggg s. \tag{5}$$

The problem exists in the additional constraint $q = a_5 \boxminus a_1$. When there are many bit conditions on (a_5, a_1), the number of possible values of q is significantly reduced and it is possible that none of them can make Eq. 5 hold.

As $\delta b_3 \to \delta b_4$ is a possible propagation, taking the careful analysis in [13] into account, we only need to add the following constraints to make the model automatically detect such contradictions:

$$q = a_5 \boxminus a_1,$$
$$(\delta q \boxplus q)[0] = (\delta b_3 \boxplus q \ggg s)[32 - s],$$
$$(\delta q \boxplus q)[s] = (\delta b_3 \boxplus q \ggg s)[0].$$

In ROTATE_DIFF_FIRST and ROTATE_DIFF_SECOND, we have provided an option to compute $\nabla q[0:s]$ according to the binary variable isV and therefore it can be viewed as known. Modelling $\delta q \boxplus q$ and $q = a_5 \boxminus a_1$ is trivial, the details of which can be found from the algorithmic description to detect more contradictions, as shown in Algorithm 5.

Algorithm 6. Model the signed difference transitions for $a_5 = a_1 \boxplus (F(a_4, a_3, a_2) \boxplus a_0 \boxplus m \boxplus c) \lll s$.

1: **procedure** R(fNa,isC,isF,isV,isK, $s, \nabla m, \nabla a_0, \nabla a_1, \nabla a_2, \nabla a_3, \nabla a_4,) \nabla a_5, a_4, a_3,$
$\qquad a_2, a_5, a_1$
2:      Claim signed difference vectors $\nabla b_0, \nabla b_1, \nabla b_2, \nabla b_3$ of size 32
3:      Claim signed difference vectors $\nabla c_2, \nabla c_3$ of size 33.
4:      Claim a signed difference vector ∇q of size $s + 1$.
5:      $\nabla b_0 = \nabla m$
6:      BOOLFAST_MODEL(fNa,$\nabla a_4, \nabla a_3, \nabla a_2, \nabla b_1$)
7:      **if** isC = 1 **then** //involve conditions into the model
8:          BOOLCOND_MODEL(fNa,$\nabla a_4, \nabla a_3, \nabla a_2, \nabla b_1, a_4, a_3, a_2$)
9:      $\nabla c_2[0] = [\texttt{=}], \nabla c_3[0] = [\texttt{=}]$//no carry for the least significant bit
10:      MODADD_MODEL($\nabla b_0, \nabla b_1, \nabla c_2, \nabla b_2$)//$\delta b_2 = \delta b_0 \boxplus \delta b_1$
11:      MODADD_MODEL($\nabla b_2, \nabla a_0, \nabla c_3, \nabla b_3$)//$\delta b_3 = \delta a_0 \boxplus \delta b_2$
12:      **if** isF = 1 **then**//use the first strategy
13:          ROTATE_DIFF_FIRST($s, \nabla b_3, \nabla a_1, \nabla a_5, \nabla q$, isV,isK)
14:      **else**//the second strategy
15:          ROTATE_DIFF_SECOND($s, \nabla b_3, \nabla a_1, \nabla a_5, \nabla q$, isV)
16:      **if** isV = 1 **then**//further detect contradictions
17:          ROTATE_DIFF_FILTER($s, \nabla a_5, \nabla a_1, \nabla b_3, \nabla q, a_5, a_1$)

3.8   The Full Model for RIPEMD-160

With the model for all operations known, it is straightforward to combine them to describe the propagation

$$(\nabla a_0, \nabla a_1, \nabla a_2, \nabla a_3, \nabla a_4, \nabla m) \to \nabla a_5,$$

as shown in Algorithm 6. In the input parameters, fNa is the name of the boolean function, isC is the option to involve the implicit conditions for the boolean functions, isF is the option to use the first or the second strategy to compute ∇b_4, isV is the option to perform the further detection of contradictions, and isK is the option to use different models for the expansions of the modular difference. In other words, depending on the target parts of the differential characteristics, one can flexibly choose different values for these options.

4   Collision Attacks on 36-Round **RIPEMD-160**

In our new collision attacks on round-reduced RIPEMD-160, we choose to inject differences in (m_0, m_6, m_9) because this choice can allow a 36-round collision attack. The pattern of the differential characteristic under such message differences is shown in Fig. 2.

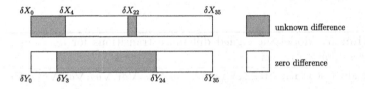

Fig. 2. The pattern of the 36-round differential characteristic

Although we found (m_0, m_6, m_9) according to our experience to analyze the MD-SHA hash family and it is not related to our MILP model, this model is particularly useful when determining their actual modular differences. Specifically, we first considered the message differences of the following form:

$$\delta m_0 = 2^i, \delta m_6 = 0 \boxminus 2^{i+25}, \delta m_9 = 2^{i+12},$$

where the addition in the exponents is modulo 32. However, the obtained differential characteristics are quite unfriendly to the message modification and the probability of the uncontrolled parts is too low. In many cases, the model even outputs that there is no solution for the left branch.

Then, we choose to inject differences in 2 bits of m_0, m_6 and m_9, respectively. For each possible choice, we use the model to minimize $\sum_{i=16}^{24} \mathbb{H}(\nabla Y_i)$. It is found that among all possible choices, the minimal value of $\sum_{i=16}^{24} \mathbb{H}(\nabla Y_i)$ is 12 and we eventually identified the following message differences

$$\delta m_0 = 2^3 \boxplus 2^{22}, \delta m_6 = 0 \boxminus 2^{15} \boxminus 2^{28}, \delta m_9 = 2^2 \boxplus 2^{15}.$$

In addition, with the above message differences, we can also find a suitable solution for the left branch.

In general, with the above message differences, we search for the corresponding collision-generating differential characteristic as follows:

Step 1: Find a valid solution of ∇X_i $(0 \leq i \leq 4)$ and check the differential conditions. If the number of conditions is not that large, just use this solution of ∇X_i $(0 \leq i \leq 4)$ for left branch.

Step 2: Find a valid solution of ∇Y_i $(16 \leq i \leq 24)$ with the MILP model such that $\Delta Y_i = 0$ for $25 \leq i \leq 35$ and we minimize $\sum_{i=16}^{24} \mathbb{H}(\nabla Y_i)$.

Step 3: Find a valid solution of ∇Y_i $(11 \leq i \leq 15)$ with the MILP model such that it can propagate to ∇Y_i $(16 \leq i \leq 24)$ and we minimize $\sum_{i=11}^{15} \mathbb{H}(\nabla Y_i)$.

Step 4: Choose a sparse differential characteristic manually for ∇Y_i $(3 \leq i \leq 5)$ and fix it.

Step 5: Find a solution of ∇Y_i $(6 \leq i \leq 10)$ with the MILP model such that $(\nabla Y_1, \nabla Y_2, \nabla Y_3, \nabla Y_4, \nabla Y_5)$ and $(\nabla Y_{11}, \nabla Y_{12}, \nabla Y_{13}, Y_{14}, \nabla Y_{15})$ can be connected, i.e. the differential characteristic for the right branch is valid.

The found 36-round differential characteristic is displayed in Table 9.

4.1 Fulfilling Differential Conditions

Fulfilling the differential conditions for the 36-round differential characteristic in Table 9 requires nontrivial efforts. Different from the collision attacks on round-reduced RIPEMD-160 [10, 11] where the attackers only need to perform the message modification for one branch, we now need to handle the conditions in both branches simultaneously [8] and the differential characteristic is very dense at the first few rounds for both branches.

The general procedure to fulfill the differential conditions is summarized as follows. As in most collision attacks on MD-SHA hash functions, some minor details for the message modification are omitted here because they are trivial.

Step 1: Exhaust all possible solutions of $(Y_4, Y_5, Y_6, Y_7, Y_8, Y_9)$ and compute the corresponding m_6. Store these m_6s in a table denoted by TAB_M6 and store the tuples $(Y_4, Y_5, Y_6, Y_7, Y_8, Y_9, m_6)$ in a sorted table denoted by TAB_Y_M6, which is sorted according to m_6.

Step 2: Exhaust all possible solutions of $(X_1, X_2, X_3, X_4, X_5, X_6)$ and compute the corresponding m_6. If the obtained m_6 is in TAB_M6_F, store X_1 in a table denote by TAB_X1.

Step 3: Exhaust all possible solutions of $(ONX(Y_{11}, Y_{10}, Y_9 \lll 10), Y_7, Y_8, Y_{12})$ and compute the corresponding m_1. Store these m_1s in a table denoted by TAB_M1.

Step 4: Find a valid M^0 such that the conditions on the newly-obtained chaining variable $(X_{-5}, X_{-4}, X_{-3}, X_{-2}, X_{-1}) = H(CV_0, M^0)$ can hold.

Step 5: For the obtained $(X_{-5}, X_{-4}, \dots, X_{-1})$, exhaust all possible solutions of (X_0, X_1) and compute the corresponding (m_0, m_1). If m_1 is in TAB_M1 and X_1 is in TAB_X1, move to Step 6. Otherwise, try another (X_0, X_1). If all possible values of (X_0, X_1) are traversed, return to Step 4.

Step 6: Exhaust all possible solutions of $(X_2, X_3, X_4, X_5, X_6)$ and compute the corresponding $(m_2, m_3, m_4, m_5, m_6)$. For each obtained m_6, if it is in

Table 9. The 36-round differential characteristic, where $\delta m_0 = 2^3 \boxplus 2^{22}$, $\delta m_6 = 0 \boxminus 2^{15} \boxminus 2^{28}$ and $\delta m_9 = 2^2 \boxplus 2^{15}$.

i	∇X_i	$\pi_l(i)$	i	∇Y_i	$\pi_r(i)$
-5	================================		-5	================================	
-4	================================		-4	================================	
-3	================================		-3	================================	
-2	================================		-2	================================	
-1	================================		-1	================================	
0	nuuuuuuuuuuuuuuuuu=nuuuuuuuuuuu=	0	0	================================	5
1	n===u=u==n=un====uuu=u=nn===u=uu	1	1	================================	14
2	=nun=u=n==n==nn==u==uun==nnu=un=	2	2	=======0=====1============1====	7
3	====nu==========nu=============	3	3	====0=========1==n========0==n1	0
4	nnnnnnnn===unnnnnnnnnnnnnnnnunnn	4	4	=10=n==0========1=n1=101===1=0010	9
5	================================	5	5	=10=10=0010001=101000n0001110010	2
6	================================	6	6	10001nuunnnnnnnnnnnnnn=un1101110	11
7	================================	7	7	0u0n1uun00n10nu01nnun=nuuuuuuuuu	4
8	================================	8	8	n1un0nuuuu1=0u0un0unnnn1nn0nunuu	13
9	================================	9	9	=1=010u1000n00u01uu010n101=n100n	6
10	================================	10	10	u1=0u0110uu=u011=0=1=0=u1=1=0111	15
11	================================	11	11	111n==0=1=1=0n===11==10100n00==0	8
12	================================	12	12	==00==0=0===10==1=01=n0=1100===1	1
13	================================	13	13	==00=0==u==11===0n=1===1u===u01=	10
14	================================	14	14	==u==0===n===n==1=======n===01=	3
15	================================	15	15	=====u========1=0=uu====1=n==10	12
16	================================	7	16	===============n=1============1	6
17	================================	4	17	==0====u=========1==1==========	11
18	================================	13	18	==1=========00=====1==========	3
19	================================	1	19	=========n==11========n======	7
20	================================	10	20	===nu=====================0=	0
21	======u================u=====	6	21	========0=========01=0====1=	13
22	======0===============0====	15	22	====1====1======0==u=11=1=====	5
23	=============1===========1==	3	23	n===1======nu==1=============	10
24	================================	12	24	======u===============0===u=====	14
25	================================	0	25	==================1=====0==	15
26	================================	9	26	==========================1==	8
27	================================	5	27	================================	12
28	================================	2	28	================================	4
29	================================	14	29	================================	9
30	================================	11	30	================================	1
31	================================	8	31	================================	2
32	================================	3	32	================================	15
33	================================	10	33	================================	5
34	================================	14	34	================================	1
35	================================	4	35	================================	3

TAB_M6, move to Step 7. Otherwise, try another $(X_2, X_3, X_4, X_5, X_6)$. If all possible $(X_2, X_3, X_4, X_5, X_6)$ are traversed, return to Step 5.

Step 7: Compute Y_0 using $(Y_{-5}, Y_{-4}, Y_{-3}, Y_{-2}, Y_{-1}) = (X_{-5}, X_{-4}, X_{-3}, X_{-2}, X_{-1})$ and m_5.

Step 8: Retrieve from TAB_Y_M6 the corresponding $(Y_4, Y_5, Y_6, Y_7, Y_8, Y_9)$ according to m_6. For each possible value, move to Step 9. If all possible values are traversed, return to Step 6.

Step 9: Determine (Y_1, Y_2, Y_3) to connect Y_i $(-5 \le i \le 0)$ and Y_j $(4 \le j \le 8)$ by using the degrees of freedom provided by $(m_{14}, m_7, m_9, m_{11}, m_{13})$, the details of which will be explained later. If there exists no solution of (Y_1, Y_2, Y_3), return to Step 8.

Step 10: Traverse all possible values of (Y_{10}, Y_{11}) and compute Y_{12} using

$$(Y_7, Y_8, Y_9, Y_{10}, Y_{11}, m_1).$$

Check the conditions[4] on (Y_{12}, Q_8^l) and if they hold, move to Step 11.

Step 11: Traverse all possible values of Y_{13} and compute Y_{14} using

$$(Y_9, Y_{10}, Y_{11}, Y_{12}, Y_{13}, m_3).$$

Check the conditions on Y_{14} and if they hold, move to Step 12.

Step 12: Traverse all possible values of Y_{15} and compute the corresponding m_{12}. Then, Y_i $(-5 \le i \le 15)$ are all fixed and therefore all m_j $(0 \le i \le 15)$ are fixed. Hence, the remaining internal states X_i $(i \ge 7)$ and Y_j $(j \ge 16)$ can be computed and we check whether the differential conditions on them hold. If they hold, a collision for 36-round RIPEMD-160 is found.

More Details About the Connection (Step 9). Given Y_i $(-5 \le i \le 0)$, Y_j $(4 \le j \le 8)$ and (m_0, m_2, m_4), we aim to find a solution of (Y_1, Y_2, Y_3) such that the computed value of (m_0, m_2, m_4) based on Y_i $(-5 \le i \le 8)$ is consistent with its given value. This is achieved by using the degrees of freedom provided by $(m_{14}, m_7, m_9, m_{11}, m_{13})$. The procedure is described as follows.

Step 9.1. Exhaust all possible valid Y_3. For each valid Y_3, compute Y_2 using $(Y_3, Y_4, Y_5, Y_6, Y_7, m_4)$. If the conditions on (Q_7^r, Y_2, Q_6^r) hold, move to Step 9.2. Otherwise, try another Y_3 until all possible Y_3 are traversed.

Step 9.2. Note that

$$Q_3^r = ONX(Y_2, Y_1, Y_0 \lll 10) \boxplus Y_{-2} \lll 10 \boxplus K_0^r \boxplus m_0,$$
$$Y_3 = Y_{-1} \lll 10 \boxplus Q_3^r \lll s_3^r. \tag{6}$$

In the above equation, only Y_1 is not yet determined. As

$$ONX(x, y, z) = x \oplus (y \wedge \bar{z}),$$

---

[4] After computing Y_{11}, m_8 can be computed using Y_i $(6 \le i \le 11)$. Then, X_8 and Q_8^l can be computed using X_i $(3 \le i \le 7)$ and m_8.

we can uniquely determine $Y_1 \wedge \overline{Y_0} \lll 10$ according to

$$Q_3^r = (Y_3 \boxminus Y_{-1} \lll 10) \ggg s_3^r,$$
$$ONX(Y_2, Y_1, Y_0 \lll 10) = Q_3^r \boxminus (Y_{-2} \lll 10 \boxplus K_0^r \boxplus m_0),$$
$$Y_1 \wedge \overline{Y_0} \lll 10 = ONX(Y_2, Y_1, Y_0 \lll 10) \oplus Y_2.$$

However, as Y_0 has already been determined, the computed $Y_1 \wedge \overline{Y_0} \lll 10$ may contradict with Y_0. Specifically, if $Y_0[i] = 0$ and $(Y_1 \wedge \overline{Y_0} \lll 10)[(i + 10) \mod 32] = 1$, the current Y_3 is invalid and we need to try another Y_3. Otherwise, the current Y_3 is correct and we can simply move to Step 9.3 to enumerate valid Y_1 to ensure Eq. 6 holds. Specifically, if there are n_0 different indices $\{i_1, i_2, \ldots, i_{n_0}\}$ such that

$$Y_0[i_j] = 0, (Y_1 \wedge \overline{Y_0} \lll 10)[(i_j + 10) \mod 32] = 0 \text{ for } 1 \le j \le n_0,$$

there will be 2^{n_0} possible Y_1 and they can be simply enumerated.

Step 9.3. Enumerate all valid Y_1 as explained above. For each Y_1, check the condition on it, i.e. the condition on $Q_5^r = (Y_5 \boxminus Y_1 \lll 10) \ggg s_5^r$. If it holds, compute a new value of m_2 using $(Y_0, Y_1, Y_2, Y_3, Y_4, Y_5)$ and check whether this computed m_2 is consistent with the predetermined m_2. If it is, compute$(m_{14}, m_7, m_9, m_{11}, m_{13})$ using

$$(Y_{-4}, Y_{-3}, Y_{-2}, Y_{-1}, Y_0, Y_1), (Y_{-3}, Y_{-2}, Y_{-1}, Y_0, Y_1, Y_2),$$
$$(Y_{-1}, Y_0, Y_1, Y_2, Y_3, Y_4), (Y_1, Y_2, Y_3, Y_4, Y_5, Y_6), (Y_3, Y_4, Y_5, Y_6, Y_7, Y_8),$$

respectively. Then, compute X_7 and check the conditions on Q_7^l. If the conditions on Q_7^l holds, the connection succeeds and move to Step 10. Otherwise, try another Y_1 until all Y_1 are traversed.

4.2 Complexity Evaluations and Simulations

Let us highlight what we can benefit from our message modification technique. First, we aim to find a valid solution for

$$(X_{-5}, X_{-4}, \ldots, X_6), (Y_{-5}, Y_{-4}, \ldots, Y_9),$$

which corresponds to Step 1 to Step 9. For convenience, we call its solution a **starting point** in our collision attacks. Then, the remaining work is to make the exhaustive search over (Y_{10}, Y_{11}), Y_{13} and Y_{15} in a sequential manner, which is to utilize the degrees of freedom provided by these internal states to fulfill the remaining differential conditions.

On the Exhaustive Search over $(Y_{10}, Y_{11}, Y_{13}, Y_{15})$. Based on the number of bit conditions, there are in total 2^{20}, 2^{18} and 2^{20} possible values of (Y_{10}, Y_{11}), Y_{13} and Y_{15}, respectively. Suppose there are on average 2^{n_1} possible (Y_{10}, Y_{11}) that can pass Step 10. Moreover, for each valid solution (Y_{10}, Y_{11}, Y_{12}), suppose there are on average 2^{n_2} possible Y_{13} that can pass Step 11. Then, the time complexity to exhaust all possible $(Y_{10}, Y_{11}, \ldots, Y_{15})$ is $2^{20} + 2^{18+n_1} + 2^{20+n_1+n_2} \approx 2^{20+n_1+n_2}$.

Experimental results suggest that $n_1 + n_2 \approx 16.5$ where we performed the exhaustive search over (Y_{10}, Y_{11}, Y_{13}) as stated above for 110 valid starting points. We should note that for some starting points, there is no valid solution of (Y_{10}, Y_{11}, Y_{13}) and the probability that there are valid solutions of them is about 0.36.

From the above analysis, we can equivalently say that for each starting point where $(m_0, m_1, m_2, m_3, m_4, m_5, m_6, m_7, m_9, m_{11}, m_{13}, m_{14})$ are fixed, there are about $2^{20+16.5} = 2^{36.5}$ valid values for $(m_{15}, m_8, m_{10}, m_{12})$. More importantly, these $2^{36.5}$ values can be efficiently enumerated by performing the exhaustive search over $(Y_{10}, Y_{11}, Y_{13}, Y_{15})$ as stated above with time complexity $2^{36.5}$, i.e. our exhaustive search strategy is optimal.

On the Required Number of Starting Points. If the differential conditions on the uncontrolled internal states Y_i ($i \geq 16$) and X_j ($j \geq 9$) hold with probability 2^{-p}, we will need to generate $2^{p-36.5}$ starting points to find a collision. According to the calculation, $p = 8 + 55 + 1.5 = 64.5$ where there are 8 bit conditions on $(X_{19}, X_{20}, \ldots, X_{23})$, 55 bit conditions on $(Y_{16}, Y_{17}, \ldots, Y_{26})$ and about 1.5 bit conditions on (Q_{21}^l, Q_{25}^l) and $(Q_{16}^r, Q_{17}^r, \ldots, Q_{28}^l)$. Hence, **it is required to generate about $2^{64.5-36.5} = 2^{28}$ starting points**.

On the Complexity of the Connection. At Step 9, we will need to exhaust 2^{26} possible values of Y_3 as there are 6 bit conditions on it. Then, we need to check the conditions on $(Q_7^r, Y_2, Q_6^r, Q_5^r)$ which hold with probability of about 2^{-4}. Finally, we need to check the consistency in m_2 which holds with probability 2^{-32} and check the condition on Q_7^l holding with probability close to 1.

Moreover, even if the conditions on (Q_7^r, Y_2, Q_6^r) hold, Y_3 is still likely to be invalid due to the contradiction between Y_0 and $Y_0 \wedge \overline{Y_1} \lll 10$. However, this happens only when there exists i such that $Y_0[i] = 0$ and $(Y_0 \wedge \overline{Y_1} \lll 10)[i] = 1$. On the other hand, if $Y_0[i] = 0$ and $(Y_0 \wedge \overline{Y_1} \lll 10)[i] = 0$, we then obtain one free bit in Y_1 and the free bit will be exhausted. Therefore, it is equivalent to stating that there are on average 2^{26} possible (Y_1, Y_3) and they can be exhausted in time 2^{26}.

For each trial of (Y_3, Y_1), the success probability is $2^{-4-32} = 2^{-36}$. Therefore, to generate 2^{28} starting points, we need to try $2^{28+36} = 2^{64}$ times. Hence, **the total time complexity of Step 9 is $2^{28+36} = 2^{64}$** .

On the Complexity of Step 8. As there are on average 2^{26} possible valid values for (Y_1, Y_3), the time complexity of Step 8 is $2^{64-26} = 2^{38}$.

On the Complexity to Exhaust $(X_2, X_3, \ldots, X_6)$. We now evaluate the cost of **Step 6–7** where we need to exhaust all possible values of $(X_2, X_3, \ldots, X_6)$ for a valid $(X_{-5}, X_{-4}, \ldots, X_1)$ obtained at Step 5. By counting the bit conditions, we find that there are in total 28 free bits in $(X_2, X_3, \ldots, X_6)$ for a fixed $(X_{-5}, X_{-4}, \ldots, X_1)$. Hence, the time complexity of this phase is 2^{28}. For each possible value of $(X_2, X_3, \ldots, X_6)$, m_6 will be computed and checked against TAB_M6. Since the size of TAB_M6 is 0x23a000 $\approx 2^{21.15}$, without considering the conditions on Q_i^l ($2 \leq i \leq 6$), the matching probability is about

$2^{-32+21.15} \approx 2^{-10.9}$. Therefore, we can expect to obtain $2^{28-10.9} = 2^{17.1}$ valid solutions of $(X_{-5}, X_{-4}, \ldots, X_6)$ after the exhaustive search. Experiments suggest that there are about 2^{16} such valid solutions. For each such valid value, we need to move to Step 8.

At Step 8, since each m_6 in TAB_M6 corresponds to on average 7 different values of $(Y_4, Y_5, \ldots, Y_9)$ in TAB_Y_M6, Step 8 can also provide about 2.8 free bits. Hence, **the total time complexity of Step 6– 7 is** $2^{38-2.8-16+28} = 2^{47.2}$.

On the Complexity to Find $(X_{-5}, X_{-4}, \ldots, X_1)$. We now evaluate the cost of **Step 4–5**. First, according to the bit conditions on $(X_{-2}, X_{-1}, X_0, X_1)$, for each $(X_{-5}, X_{-4}, \ldots, X_{-1})$ computed from M^0, all state bits of (X_1, X_0) will be directly fixed to fulfill their bit conditions. Hence, we are left to verify whether the computed (X_0, X_1) is valid. First, we need to check whether X_1 is in TAB_X1 and check whether the corresponding m_1 is in TAB_M1. As the size of TAB_X1 is $7800 \approx 2^{14.9}$ and the size of TAB_M1 is 0x1676000 $\approx 2^{24.5}$, the probability it can pass this test is $2^{-17+14.9} \times 2^{-32+24.5} = 2^{-9.6}$. Second, we need to check the conditions on (Q_0^l, Q_1^l) which hold with probability of about $2^{-1.5}$. Therefore, for each computed (X_0, X_1), it is valid with probability $2^{-11.1}$.

Finally, we need to verify the conditions on (X_{-2}, X_{-1}) computed from each M^0 which hold with probability 2^{-30}. Hence, finding a valid $(X_{-5}, X_{-4}, \ldots, X_1)$ requires to try about $2^{30+11.1} = 2^{41.1}$ random M^0. As we need $2^{38-2.8-16} = 2^{19.2}$ such valid solutions, it is required to try $2^{19.2+41.1} = 2^{60.3}$ different M^0. Consequently, **the total time complexity of Step 4–5 is** $2^{60.3}$.

On the Complexity of Step 1–3. We only need to perform Step 1–3 once and we have finished Step 1–3 in practical time. Hence, **the total cost of Step 1–3 is negligible.**

The Total Complexity. According to the above analysis, the time complexity and memory complexity of about collision attacks on 36 rounds of RIPEMD-160 are $2^{64.5}$ and $2^{21.15+2.8} \approx 2^{24}$, respectively.

Simulations. To verify our theoretical analysis and the correctness of our message modification technique, we perform the experiments in the following way. First, we randomly generate $(X_{-5}, X_{-4}, \ldots, X_{-1})$ by always making the conditions on (X_{-2}, X_{-1}) hold because finding their valid values from random M^0 is costly. Then, we compute (X_0, X_1) and check the conditions until we obtain a valid (X_0, X_1). Experimental results match our theoretical analysis for Step 4–5. Next, for each valid $(X_{-5}, X_{-4}, \ldots, X_1)$, we move to Step 6 and try to find valid solutions for $(X_2, X_3, \ldots, X_6)$ and experiments also confirmed our analysis of the time complexity. Then, we move to Step 7–9 to achieve the connection. We find that the success probability of connection is about 2^{-36} and it matches well with our analysis. In this way, we succeed in generating many valid starting points. At last, for each of the obtained starting points, we perform the exhaustive search over $(Y_{10}, Y_{11}, Y_{13}, Y_{15})$ in our way and aim to find a solution for $(Y_{10}, Y_{11}, \ldots, Y_{22})$. The expected time complexity to find a valid $(Y_{10}, Y_{11}, \ldots, Y_{22})$ is about 2^{40} as the conditions on $(Y_{16}, Y_{17}, \ldots, Y_{22})$ hold with probability of about 2^{-40}. Experiments have confirmed this value and we provide

Table 10. A partial solution for the 36-round differential characteristic

i	∇X_i	$\pi_l(i)$	i	∇Y_i	$\pi_r(i)$
-5	1010010101001010110101111001000		-5	1010010101001010110101111001000	
-4	1110111000100000001111011000011		-4	1110111000100000001111011000011	
-3	1111101010110001010011110110010		-3	1111101010110001010011110110010	
-2	0001110001001000010011100010010		-2	0001110001001000010011100010010	
-1	0011101111010110101001000011111		-1	0011101111010110101001000011111	
0	nuuuuuuuuuuuuuuuuuu1nuuuuuuuuuuu1	0	0	10111000110000010010000010111011	5
1	n010u0u11n1un0100uuu1u1nn000u1uu	1	1	11111101010011101100101101100001	14
2	1nun1u0n10n00nn10u10uun01nnu1un1	2	2	01101001000000101010110011010110	7
3	1011nu11111110010nu1110011100011	3	3	00100111110111101n001101000010n1	0
4	nnnnnnnn000unnnnnnnnnnnnnnnnunnnn	4	4	0101n00010010011n10101010110010	9
5	1111111010000010000101011100010	5	5	01001010010001110100n0001110010	2
6	0011000111101110111011010111010	6	6	10001nuunnnnnnnnnnnnnnOun1101110	11
7	0110100000011110101100111100001	7	7	0u0n1uun00n10nu01nnun0nuuuuuuuu	4
8	1001100001011100001001011111011	8	8	n1un0nuuuu110u0un0unnnn1nn0nunuu	13
9	0111110001111000110101010010100	9	9	110010u1000n00u01uu010n1010n100n	6
10	1000010010000000111100110011011	10	10	u100u0110uu0u0111001101u10100111	15
11	0000011010001000101110011101111	11	11	111n110011110n000110110100n00010	8
12	1010011110010011010101011100111110	12	12	00000101001010111010n0111001111	1
13	1001100000000001000100001001011	13	13	10001011u11111010n010001u011u010	10
14	0001101010101101011101001011110110	14	14	01u000011n010n01111001101n010010	3
15	0010000100011111001111001011100	15	15	101110u110100001101uu110010n0010	12
16	=================================	7	16	11010010110011n0101101000001011	6
17	=================================	4	17	0001101u1101110111101111101011110	11
18	=================================	13	18	101000011100000111001101111111110	3
19	=================================	1	19	0111011100n1111001010011n0111111	7
20	=================================	10	20	010nu01001100001010011001010010	0
21	=======u================u=====	6	21	0000111001000101110011011001010	13
22	=======0================0=====	15	22	0001101111010011010u11101001000	5
23	==============1==========1==	3	23	n===1=======nu===1============	10
24	=================================	12	24	=======u============0===u=====	14
25	=================================	0	25	====================1======0==	15
26	=================================	9	26	========================1==	8
27	=================================	5	27	=================================	12
28	=================================	2	28	=================================	4
29	=================================	14	29	=================================	9
30	=================================	11	30	=================================	1
31	=================================	8	31	=================================	2
32	=================================	3	32	=================================	15
33	=================================	10	33	=================================	5
34	=================================	14	34	=================================	1
35	=================================	4	35	=================================	3

m_0	1111101nuu11110101011011100n000		m_8	1000100010011011101011100000111 00
m_1	1110001010001010100011010001010		m_9	011010010011101nu11000111000n01
m_2	0111010000111011001101100000001		m_{10}	10011100001110000100101111001101
m_3	0110010101111100100111010101101		m_{11}	00100100001110000011000100111110
m_4	0101101011110001100101100101001		m_{12}	1000011001101010010101011001001110
m_5	1000001000011001010000110001110		m_{13}	0010001110110111001111110000101001
m_6	00un101111111110u011100000100101		m_{14}	1010001011101100110101010111011101
m_7	110111000010001001100010001000		m_{15}	11010001001001110100011001001011

a solution of $(m_0, m_1, \ldots, m_{15})$ and $(X_{-5}, X_{-4}, \ldots, X_{-1}) = (Y_{-5}, Y_{-4}, \ldots, Y_{-1})$ which can make the conditions on X_i $(0 \leq i \leq 8)$ and Y_j $(0 \leq j \leq 22)$ hold, as shown in Table 10.

5 Further Works and Discussions

As the round functions of the MD-SHA hash family are very similar, we expect that some of our techniques to model the signed difference transitions can be applied to other hash functions that have not yet been broken. The most important target should be SHA-2. However, there are several obstacles to directly apply our techniques to SHA-2. Specifically, in our model, we implicitly rely on the fact that each 32-bit message word is used to update one 32-bit internal state. When it comes to SHA-2, each message word of 32 (resp. 64) bits will be used to update two different internal states of 32 (resp. 64) bits at the same round. In this case, contradictions will much more easily occur and our techniques to detect the inconsistency are insufficient. How to adapt our techniques to SHA-2 is an interesting and meaningful work.

We also notice that in the paper [6] to improve the automatic tool for SHA-2, it is mentioned that relying on off-the-shelf solvers to search for such differential characteristics is inefficient because the information of the signed difference propagations cannot be well exploited. We believe they referred to the models where two parallel instances of value transitions are considered. Obviously, in our model, we have efficiently encoded the information of the signed difference propagations and we believe this is the first important step towards this problem, i.e. how to efficiently rely on off-the-shelf solvers to find such signed differential characteristics.

For RIPEMD-160, we further made some progress by improving the best collision attack by 2 rounds and we believe this work advances the understanding of RIPEMD-160 further.

Acknowledgement. We thank the reviewers of EUROCRYPT 2023 for improving the quality of this paper. Gaoli Wang is supported by the National Key Research and Development Program of China (No. 2022YFB2701900), National Natural Science Foundation of China (No. 62072181), NSFC-ISF Joint Scientific Research Program (No. 61961146004), Shanghai Trusted Industry Internet Software Collaborative Innovation Center. Fukang Liu is supported by Grant-in-Aid for Research Activity Start-up (Grant No. 22K21282). Takanori Isobe is supported by JST, PRESTO Grant Number JPMJPR2031. This research was in part conducted under a contract of "Research and development on new generation cryptography for secure wireless communication services" among "Research and Development for Expansion of Radio Wave Resources (JPJ000254)", which was supported by the Ministry of Internal Affairs and Communications, Japan.

References

1. Abdelkhalek, A., Sasaki, Y., Todo, Y., Tolba, M., Youssef, A.M.: MILP modeling for (large) s-boxes to optimize probability of differential characteristics. IACR Trans. Symmetric Cryptol. 2017(4), 99–129 (2017). https://doi.org/10.13154/tosc.v2017.i4.99-129

2. De Cannière, C., Rechberger, C.: Finding SHA-1 characteristics: general results and applications. In: Lai, X., Chen, K. (eds.) ASIACRYPT 2006. LNCS, vol. 4284, pp. 1–20. Springer, Heidelberg (2006). https://doi.org/10.1007/11935230_1

3. Daum, M.: Cryptanalysis of Hash functions of the MD4-family. Ph.D. thesis, Ruhr University Bochum (2005)

4. Dobbertin, H., Bosselaers, A., Preneel, B.: RIPEMD-160: a strengthened version of ripemd. In: Gollmann, D. (ed.) FSE 1996. LNCS, vol. 1039, pp. 71–82. Springer, Heidelberg (1996). https://doi.org/10.1007/3-540-60865-6_44

5. Dobraunig, C., Eichlseder, M., Mendel, F.: Analysis of SHA-512/224 and SHA-512/256. In: Iwata, T., Cheon, J.H. (eds.) ASIACRYPT 2015. LNCS, vol. 9453, pp. 612–630. Springer, Heidelberg (2015). https://doi.org/10.1007/978-3-662-48800-3_25

6. Eichlseder, M., Mendel, F., Schläffer, M.: Branching heuristics in differential collision search with applications to SHA-512. In: Cid, C., Rechberger, C. (eds.) FSE 2014. LNCS, vol. 8540, pp. 473–488. Springer, Heidelberg (2015). https://doi.org/10.1007/978-3-662-46706-0_24

7. Kölbl, S., Leander, G., Tiessen, T.: Observations on the SIMON block cipher family. In: Gennaro, R., Robshaw, M. (eds.) CRYPTO 2015. LNCS, vol. 9215, pp. 161–185. Springer, Heidelberg (2015). https://doi.org/10.1007/978-3-662-47989-6_8

8. Landelle, F., Peyrin, T.: Cryptanalysis of full RIPEMD-128. In: Johansson, T., Nguyen, P.Q. (eds.) EUROCRYPT 2013. LNCS, vol. 7881, pp. 228–244. Springer, Heidelberg (2013). https://doi.org/10.1007/978-3-642-38348-9_14

9. Leurent, G.: Construction of differential characteristics in ARX designs application to skein. In: Canetti, R., Garay, J.A. (eds.) CRYPTO 2013. LNCS, vol. 8042, pp. 241–258. Springer, Heidelberg (2013). https://doi.org/10.1007/978-3-642-40041-4_14

10. Liu, F., Dobraunig, C., Mendel, F., Isobe, T., Wang, G., Cao, Z.: Efficient collision attack frameworks for RIPEMD-160. In: Boldyreva, A., Micciancio, D. (eds.) CRYPTO 2019. LNCS, vol. 11693, pp. 117–149. Springer, Cham (2019). https://doi.org/10.1007/978-3-030-26951-7_5

11. Liu, F., Dobraunig, C., Mendel, F., Isobe, T., Wang, G., Cao, Z.: New semi-free-start collision attack framework for reduced RIPEMD-160. IACR Trans. Symmetric Cryptol. 2019(3), 169–192 (2019). https://doi.org/10.13154/tosc.v2019.i3.169-192

12. Liu, F., Isobe, T., Meier, W.: Automatic verification of differential characteristics: application to reduced gimli. In: Micciancio, D., Ristenpart, T. (eds.) CRYPTO 2020. LNCS, vol. 12172, pp. 219–248. Springer, Cham (2020). https://doi.org/10.1007/978-3-030-56877-1_8

13. Liu, F., Mendel, F., Wang, G.: Collisions and semi-free-start collisions for round-reduced RIPEMD-160. In: Takagi, T., Peyrin, T. (eds.) ASIACRYPT 2017. LNCS, vol. 10624, pp. 158–186. Springer, Cham (2017). https://doi.org/10.1007/978-3-319-70694-8_6

14. Mendel, F., Nad, T., Scherz, S., Schläffer, M.: Differential attacks on reduced RIPEMD-160. In: Gollmann, D., Freiling, F.C. (eds.) ISC 2012. LNCS, vol. 7483, pp. 23–38. Springer, Heidelberg (2012). https://doi.org/10.1007/978-3-642-33383-5_2

15. Mendel, F., Nad, T., Schläffer, M.: Finding SHA-2 characteristics: searching through a minefield of contradictions. In: Lee, D.H., Wang, X. (eds.) ASIACRYPT 2011. LNCS, vol. 7073, pp. 288–307. Springer, Heidelberg (2011). https://doi.org/10.1007/978-3-642-25385-0_16

16. Mendel, F., Nad, T., Schläffer, M.: Collision attacks on the reduced dual-stream hash function RIPEMD-128. In: Canteaut, A. (ed.) FSE 2012. LNCS, vol. 7549, pp. 226–243. Springer, Heidelberg (2012). https://doi.org/10.1007/978-3-642-34047-5_14

17. Mendel, F., Nad, T., Schläffer, M.: Improving local collisions: new attacks on reduced SHA-256. In: Johansson, T., Nguyen, P.Q. (eds.) EUROCRYPT 2013. LNCS, vol. 7881, pp. 262–278. Springer, Heidelberg (2013). https://doi.org/10.1007/978-3-642-38348-9_16

18. Mendel, F., Peyrin, T., Schläffer, M., Wang, L., Wu, S.: Improved cryptanalysis of reduced RIPEMD-160. In: Sako, K., Sarkar, P. (eds.) ASIACRYPT 2013. LNCS, vol. 8270, pp. 484–503. Springer, Heidelberg (2013). https://doi.org/10.1007/978-3-642-42045-0_25

19. Mironov, I., Zhang, L.: Applications of SAT solvers to cryptanalysis of hash functions. In: Biere, A., Gomes, C.P. (eds.) SAT 2006. LNCS, vol. 4121, pp. 102–115. Springer, Heidelberg (2006). https://doi.org/10.1007/11814948_13

20. Mouha, N., Wang, Q., Gu, D., Preneel, B.: Differential and linear cryptanalysis using mixed-integer linear programming. In: Wu, C.-K., Yung, M., Lin, D. (eds.) Inscrypt 2011. LNCS, vol. 7537, pp. 57–76. Springer, Heidelberg (2012). https://doi.org/10.1007/978-3-642-34704-7_5

21. Ohtahara, C., Sasaki, Yu., Shimoyama, T.: Preimage attacks on step-reduced RIPEMD-128 and RIPEMD-160. In: Lai, X., Yung, M., Lin, D. (eds.) Inscrypt 2010. LNCS, vol. 6584, pp. 169–186. Springer, Heidelberg (2011). https://doi.org/10.1007/978-3-642-21518-6_13

22. Shen, Y., Wang, G.: Improved preimage attacks on RIPEMD-160 and HAS-160. KSII Trans. Internet Inf. Syst. 12(2), 727–746 (2018). https://doi.org/10.3837/tiis.2018.02.011

23. Stevens, M.: New collision attacks on SHA-1 based on optimal joint local-collision analysis. In: Johansson, T., Nguyen, P.Q. (eds.) EUROCRYPT 2013. LNCS, vol. 7881, pp. 245–261. Springer, Heidelberg (2013). https://doi.org/10.1007/978-3-642-38348-9_15

24. Stevens, M., Bursztein, E., Karpman, P., Albertini, A., Markov, Y.: The first collision for full SHA-1. In: Katz, J., Shacham, H. (eds.) CRYPTO 2017. LNCS, vol. 10401, pp. 570–596. Springer, Cham (2017). https://doi.org/10.1007/978-3-319-63688-7_19

25. Stevens, M., et al.: Short chosen-prefix collisions for MD5 and the creation of a rogue CA certificate. In: Halevi, S. (ed.) CRYPTO 2009. LNCS, vol. 5677, pp. 55–69. Springer, Heidelberg (2009). https://doi.org/10.1007/978-3-642-03356-8_4

26. Sun, S., Hu, L., Wang, P., Qiao, K., Ma, X., Song, L.: Automatic security evaluation and (related-key) differential characteristic search: application to SIMON, PRESENT, LBlock, DES(L) and other bit-oriented block ciphers. In: Sarkar, P., Iwata, T. (eds.) ASIACRYPT 2014. LNCS, vol. 8873, pp. 158–178. Springer, Heidelberg (2014). https://doi.org/10.1007/978-3-662-45611-8_9

27. Wang, G., Shen, Y.: (Pseudo-) preimage attacks on step-reduced HAS-160 and RIPEMD-160. In: Chow, S.S.M., Camenisch, J., Hui, L.C.K., Yiu, S.M. (eds.) ISC 2014. LNCS, vol. 8783, pp. 90–103. Springer, Cham (2014). https://doi.org/10.1007/978-3-319-13257-0_6

28. Wang, G., Shen, Y., Liu, F.: Cryptanalysis of 48-step RIPEMD-160. IACR Trans. Symmetric Cryptol. **2017**(2), 177–202 (2017). https://doi.org/10.13154/tosc.v2017.i2.177-202

29. Wang, X., Lai, X., Feng, D., Chen, H., Yu, X.: Cryptanalysis of the hash functions MD4 and RIPEMD. In: Cramer, R. (ed.) EUROCRYPT 2005. LNCS, vol. 3494, pp. 1–18. Springer, Heidelberg (2005). https://doi.org/10.1007/11426639_1

30. Wang, X., Yin, Y.L., Yu, H.: Finding collisions in the full SHA-1. In: Shoup, V. (ed.) CRYPTO 2005. LNCS, vol. 3621, pp. 17–36. Springer, Heidelberg (2005). https://doi.org/10.1007/11535218_2

31. Wang, X., Yu, H.: How to break MD5 and other hash functions. In: Cramer, R. (ed.) EUROCRYPT 2005. LNCS, vol. 3494, pp. 19–35. Springer, Heidelberg (2005). https://doi.org/10.1007/11426639_2

32. Wang, X., Yu, H., Yin, Y.L.: Efficient collision search attacks on SHA-0. In: Shoup, V. (ed.) CRYPTO 2005. LNCS, vol. 3621, pp. 1–16. Springer, Heidelberg (2005). https://doi.org/10.1007/11535218_1

Collision Attacks on Round-Reduced SHA-3 Using Conditional Internal Differentials

Zhongyi Zhang[1,2], Chengan Hou[1,2], and Meicheng Liu[1,2](✉)

[1] State Key Laboratory of Information Security, Institute of Information Engineering, Chinese Academy of Sciences, Beijing, People's Republic of China
{zhangzhongyi0714,houchengan,liumeicheng}@iie.ac.cn
[2] School of Cyber Security, University of Chinese Academy of Sciences, Beijing, People's Republic of China

Abstract. The KECCAK hash function was selected by NIST as the winner of the SHA-3 competition in 2012 and became the SHA-3 hash standard of NIST in 2015. On account of SHA-3's importance in theory and applications, the analysis of its security has attracted increasing attention. In the SHA-3 family, SHA3-512 shows the strongest resistance against collision attacks: the theoretical attacks of SHA3-512 only extend to four rounds by solving polynomial systems with 64 times faster than the birthday attack. Yet for the SHA-3 instance SHAKE256 there are no results on collision attacks that we are aware of in the literatures.

In this paper, we study the collision attacks against round-reduced SHA-3. Inspired by the work of Dinur, Dunkelman and Shamir in 2013, we propose a variant of birthday attack and improve the internal differential cryptanalysis by abstracting new concepts such as *differential transition conditions* and *difference conditions table*. With the help of these techniques, we develop new collision attacks on round-reduced SHA-3 using conditional internal differentials. More exactly, the initial messages constrained by linear conditions pass through the first two rounds of internal differential, and their corresponding inputs entering the last two rounds are divided into different subsets for collision search according to the values of linear conditions. Together with an improved target internal difference algorithm (TIDA), collision attacks on up to 5 rounds of all the six SHA-3 functions are obtained. In particular, collision attacks on 4-round SHA3-512 and 5-round SHAKE256 are achieved with complexity of 2^{237} and 2^{185} respectively. As far as we know, this is the best collision attack on reduced SHA3-512, and it is the first collision attack on reduced SHAKE256.

Keywords: SHA-3 · Hash function · Keccak · Internal differentials · Collision attack · TIDA

Supported by the National Natural Science Foundation of China (Grant No. 62122085 and 12231015) and the Youth Innovation Promotion Association of Chinese Academy of Sciences.

C. Hazay and M. Stam (Eds.): EUROCRYPT 2023, LNCS 14007, pp. 220–251, 2023.
https://doi.org/10.1007/978-3-031-30634-1_8

1   Introduction

The KECCAK hash function [4], designed by Guido Bertoni, Joan Daemen, Michaël Peeters, and Gilles Van Assche [5], was selected as the winner of the SHA-3 competition by the National Institute of Standards and Technology of the USA. In 2015, it was published as the new SHA-3 standard by NIST [11]. The SHA-3 family has four instances with fixed digest sizes, namely SHA3-224, SHA3-256, SHA3-384 and SHA3-512, which correspond to KECCAK$[c] \triangleq$ KECCAK$[r = 1600 - c, c]$, where $c \in \{448, 512, 768, 1024\}$. There are two eXtendable-Output Functions (XOFs) named SHAKE128 and SHAKE256 of the SHA-3 family, which can generate digests with any expected length. In Post-Quantum Cryptography competition (PQC), the two XOFs are applied to all candidate algorithms (CRYSTALS-KYBER, CRYSTALS-Dilithium, FALCON, SPHINCS$^+$) identified by NIST for standardization and all the fourth round candidate KEM algorithms (BIKE, Classic McEliece, HQC, SIKE) [1]. Among them, SPHINCS$^+$ [3] is a stateless hash-based signature scheme including three different versions. One of them is obtained by instantiating the SPHINCS$^+$ construction with SHAKE256.

KECCAK uses a sponge construction, which ensures that messages of any length can be taken as inputs of the hash function. The message is padded and divided into some message blocks with the same length. The size of message block depends on the expected number of output bits. The 1600-bit initial state of KECCAK is XORed the first message block. Then, the state is updated by applying 24-round permutation KECCAK-f to it and XORing another message block, until all blocks are absorbed. In the end, the state is updated again by using 24-round KECCAK-f, and some bits of the state are output as the digest.

Since its publication in 2008, KECCAK has become one of the most important hash functions and received extensive security analysis [2,6,9,10,12–14,16,20]. There are two important security criteria for cryptographic hash functions namely, preimage resistance and collision resistance.

The main focus of this paper is on the security of SHA-3 family against collision attacks. The purpose of a collision attack is to find a pair of different messages such that their digests are the same. In the matter of collision attacks on round-reduced SHA-3 (KECCAK), Dinur, Dunkelman and Shamir [8] presented practical attacks on 4-round KECCAK[448]/KECCAK[512] in 2012, where the authors developed the target difference algorithm to link a 1-round connector to a 3-round high probability difference characteristic. Following the basic framework of [8], Qiao *et al.* completed the connection of 2-round connectors and 3-round difference characteristics using the linearizaion technique and obtained actual collisions for 5-round SHAKE128 [19]. In [12,20], the connectors were improved to 3-round connectors by non-full linearization technique. As a result, the practical collision attacks on 5-round SHA3-224/SHA3-256 were implemented respectively. Almost at the same time as this paper, Huang *et al.* [15] developed new techniques to try to solve the problem of insufficient degrees of freedom, and proposed a collision attack on SHA3-384 with time complexity of $2^{59.64}$. In [13], with the SAT-based automatic search tool and improved connector construction algorithms, Guo *et al.* presented the first quantum collision attacks on SHA-3 instances. More specifically, they extended the classical attacks on SHAKE128 to 6-round and proposed 6-round quantum attacks on SHA3-224 and SHA3-256. For internal differentials, Dinur, Dunkelman and Shamir [9] completed practical collision attacks on 3-round KECCAK[768]/KECCAK[1024] and proposed theoretical attacks on 4-round KECCAK[768] and 5-round KECCAK[512] by using generalized internal differentials. In addition to differential and internal differential, Dinur [7] devised a polynomial method-based algorithm for solving multivariate equation systems and formulated the problem of finding a collision as a non-linear equation system. With the help of this technique, the author obtain a theoretical collision attack on 4-round SHA3-512, where the complexity (2^{263}) is 64 times faster than the birthday attack (2^{269}) considering the bit operations.

Our Contribution. Following the framework of Dinur, Dunkelman and Shamir [9], we improve the generalized internal differentials and present theoretical attacks on all the six SHA-3 variants up to 5 rounds. In detail, the attacks on 4-round SHA3-512 and 5-round SHAKE256 are the best attack results at present as far as we know. Our results and comparison with the related previous work are listed in Table 1. The main contributions with respect to techniques are summarized as follows.

   1. A variant of birthday attack Since an internal difference produces distinct output internal differences after non-linear operation, collision search is actually carried out in several disjoint subsets. We abstract it as a variant of birthday attack. On one hand, it is more convenient for parallel computation. On the other hand, the size of each subset is much smaller than the number of messages, which greatly saves the space of the hash table using in the attack.

   2. Improved generalized internal differentials We introduce the transition condition number to estimate the transition probability of internal differential more accurately. We can construct conditional internal differential characteristics for collision attacks on up to 5 rounds of SHA-3 by adding differential transition conditions to the initial message spaces and their corresponding internal states. This further reduces the time complexity of internal differential cryptanalysis.

   3. Improved target internal difference algorithm We link an internal differential characteristic starting from the second round to the initial state of SHA-3 by solving a linear equation system. With the use of 2-block messages, we change the value of the first block instead of changing an affine subspaces of input internal differences to make the system consistent. And since any affine subspace of the input difference can be selected, in the improved TIDA, we can select a specific set of affine subspaces to obtain internal difference characteristics with high probability.

Conditional Internal Differential Attacks. The technique of *internal differential cryptanalysis* was developed by Peyrin [18] in the cryptanalysis of the Grøstl hash function and generalized by Dinur *et al.* [9] in collision attacks on

Table 1. Comparison of the best collision attacks against the SHA-3 family

Target	Rounds	Complexity	Attack method	Reference
SHA3-224	5	2^{105}	**Internal differential**	**Sect. 6.3**
	5	Practical	Differential	[20]
SHA3-256	5	2^{115}	Internal differential	[9]
	5	2^{105}	**Internal differential**	**Sect. 6.3**
	5	Practical	Differential	[12]
SHA3-384	3	Practical	Internal differential	[9]
	4	2^{147}	Internal differential	[9]
	4	2^{76}	**Internal differential**	**Sect. 6.1**
	4	$2^{59.64}$	Differential	[15]
SHA3-512	3	Practical	Internal differential	[9]
	4	2^{237}	**Internal differential**	**Sect. 6.2**
	4	2^{263}a	Solving polynomial systems	[7]
SHAKE128	5	2^{105}	**Internal differential**	**Sect. 6.3**
	5	Practical	Differential	[19]
	6	$2^{123.5}$	Differential	[13]
SHAKE256	4	2^{76}	**Internal differential**	**Sect. 6.1**
	5	2^{185}	**Internal differential**	**Sect. 6.3**

a The complexity is calculated by bit operations.

SHA-3. This technique resembles standard differential attacks but it uses internal differentials, which consider differences between different parts of a state and follow their statistical evolution, rather than a difference between two states. In [9], Dinur et al. proposed the definitions of the weight of internal differences, which can be used to estimate the transition probability of the internal differences with low weight, and obtained internal differential characteristic with probability 1 for the first round by using algebraic methods.

In this paper, we develop an improved variant of internal differential cryptanalysis to launch collision attacks on SHA-3. We introduce several new techniques such as differential transition conditions of the KECCAK Sbox, which allow us to estimate the transition probability of internal differences more accurately and use conditional internal differentials to reduce more complexity. And since the non-zero internal difference input to χ produces several output internal differences, we can launch a variant of birthday attack. Namely, one or multiple output internal differences will result in a collision subset, so that we can search for collision in each subset.

Improved Target Internal Difference Algorithm. The target internal difference algorithm [9] is a generalization of the target difference algorithm [8], which enables internal differentials to be used to launch collision attacks on 5-round SHA-3. In [9], the output of TIDA is a subspace of the initial messages whose dimension is not enough to produce a collision. Therefore, in the attack on SHA3-256, the TIDA is run multiple times to output enough messages.

The TIDA has two phases, where in the first phase (called the difference phase) it solves a system E composed of linear equations about capacity and all Sboxes to fix the initial internal difference, and in the second phase (called the value phase) it outputs the affine subspace of the initial message by solving a linear system. If 1-block messages are used as the initial messages, in the difference phase, the algorithm will change affine subspaces of the input differences until E is consistent. In our attacks on 5-round SHAKE256, we input 2-block messages into the sponge function as the initial messages. Thus, we just need to change the value of the first block to make E consistent. Since the affine subspaces corresponding to the input differences of Sboxes will lead to distinct transition probabilities of internal differences, after introducing 2-block messages, we select a specific set of affine subspaces which maximize the expected transition probability so that the number of characteristics to launch collision attacks could be reduced. We combine the two phases in the improved TIDA, and reduce the number of iterations for the second phase by using the partial solutions of E. By using the internal differentials with our techniques, we can launch collision attacks on all variants of SHA-3. Our attacks on each variant can reach the most number of rounds at present, except for SHAKE128, though in some cases other attacks reaching the same number of rounds are faster. Specially, the complexity of our attack on 4-round SHA3-512 is 2^{237}, and it is the best result at present. For 4-round SHA3-384, the complexity of our attack is 2^{76}, which is much lower than the result of 2^{147} using the same type of cryptanalysis in [9]. The collision attack on SHAKE256 reaches to 5 rounds for the first time.

Organization. The rest of the paper is organized as follows. In Sect. 2, we describe the SHA-3 hash function. In Sect. 3, some notations used in this paper are given, followed by the overview of our collision attacks and a variant of birthday attack. In Sect. 4, we give the basic concepts of internal differentials and some new concepts. Section 5 presents the framework of attacks and detailed explanations over our techniques. In Sect. 6, the details and results of our attack are given. We conclude the paper in Sect. 7. The internal difference characteristics are postponed to Appendix.

2   Description of SHA-3

In this section, we give a brief description of the sponge construction and the SHA-3 hash function, *i.e.*, the KECCAK hash function. The sponge construction proceeds in two phases: absorbing phase and squeezing phase, as shown in Fig. 1. The message is firstly padded by appending a bit string of 10*1, where 0* represents a shortest string of 0's so that the length of padded message is multiple of r, and cut into r-bit blocks. The b-bit internal state is initialized to be all zeros. In absorbing phase, each message block is XORed into the first r bits of the current state, and then it is applied a fixed permutation to the entire b-bit state. The sponge construction switches to the squeezing phase after all message blocks are processed. In this phase, the first r bits of the state are returned as output and the permutation is applied in each iteration. This process is repeated until all d digest bits are produced. The four instances of SHA-3 family named SHA3-d are defined from KECCAK[c] by appending a two-bit suffix '01' to the message,

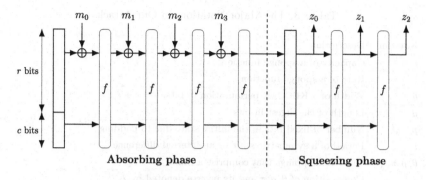

Fig. 1. The sponge construction

where $b = 1600$, $c = 2d$ and $d \in \{224, 256, 384, 512\}$. After that, the padding of KECCAK is applied. SHAKE128 and SHAKE256 are two instances with the capacity $c = 256$ or 512 and any output length d, and the original message M is appended with an additional 4-bit suffix '1111' before applying the padding rule, for any output length. The suffixes "128" and "256" indicate the security strengths that these two functions can generally support. We summarize security strengths of the SHA-3 functions in Table 2.

Table 2. Security strengths of SHA-3 functions

Function	Output Size	Security Strengths in Bits		
		Collision	Preimage	2nd Preimage
SHA3-224	224	112	224	224
SHA3-256	256	128	256	256
SHA3-384	384	192	384	384
SHA3-512	512	256	512	512
SHAKE128	d	$\min(d/2, 128)$	$\geq \min(d, 128)$	$\min(d, 128)$
SHAKE256	d	$\min(d/2, 256)$	$\geq \min(d, 256)$	$\min(d, 256)$

The KECCAK permutation has 24 rounds, which operates on the 1600-bit state s that can be viewed as a 3-dimensional array of bits. One bit of the state at position (x, y, z) is noted as $A[x][y][z]$, where $0 \leq x, y < 5$ and $0 \leq z < 64$. The mapping between the bits of s and those of A is $s[64(5y+x)+z] = A[x][y][z]$. Defined by the designers, $A[\cdot][y][z]$ is a row, $A[x][\cdot][z]$ is a column, and $A[x][y][\cdot]$ is a lane; $A[x][\cdot][\cdot]$ is a sheet, $A[\cdot][y][\cdot]$ is a plane, and $A[\cdot][\cdot][z]$ is a slice.

There are five mappings in each round of the permutation:

$$\theta : A[x][y][z] \leftarrow A[x][y][z] + \sum_{y'=0}^{4} A[x-1][y'][z] + \sum_{y'=0}^{4} A[x+1][y'][z-1].$$

$$\rho : A[x][y][z] \leftarrow A[x][y][z + T(x, y)], \text{where } T(x, y) \text{ is a predefined constant.}$$

$$\pi : A[x][y][z] \leftarrow A[x'][y'][z], \text{where } \begin{pmatrix} x \\ y \end{pmatrix} = \begin{pmatrix} 0 & 1 \\ 2 & 3 \end{pmatrix} \cdot \begin{pmatrix} x' \\ y' \end{pmatrix}.$$

$$\chi : A[x][y][z] \leftarrow A[x][y][z] + (\neg(A[x+1][y][z])) \wedge A[x+2][y][z].$$

$$\iota : A \leftarrow A + RC[n_r], \text{where } RC[n_r] \text{ is the round constants.}$$

Table 3. The Major Notations in Our Attack

Notation	Description
c	Capacity of a sponge function
r	Rate of a sponge function
b	Width of a KECCAK permutation in bits, $b = r + c$
d	Length of the digest in bits
p	Number of fixed bits in the initial state due to padding
i	Period of a symmetric state or an internal difference
$\theta, \rho, \pi, \chi, \iota$	The five mappings that comprise a round
L	Composition of θ, ρ, π and its inverse denoted by L^{-1}
$\mathrm{R}^j(\cdot)$	KECCAK permutation reduced to the first j rounds
$\mathrm{S}(\cdot)$	5-bit Sbox operating on each row of KECCAK state
$\delta_{in}, \delta_{out}$	5-bit input and output differences of an Sbox
$\overline{M}$	Padded message of M. Note that $\overline{M}$ is the last block in our attack
$M_0 \| M_1$	Concatenation of strings M_0 and M_1
$\alpha_i^{(j-1)}$	Input internal difference of the j-th round function with period i
$\beta_i^{(j-1)}$	Input internal difference of χ in the j-th round with period i
$\mathcal{A}_i^{(j-1)}$	Bit value vector before θ in the j-th round with period i
$\mathcal{B}_i^{(j-1)}$	Bit value vector before χ in the j-th round with period i
$\Delta(\cdot)$	Internal difference of one state
$v^{(j-1)}$	Canonical representative state of the internal difference in the j-th round

The addition and multiplication are in $GF(2)$. Since we analyse round-reduced variant with at most 5 rounds, we only give the first five round constants: 0000000000000001, 0000000000008082, 800000000000808a, 8000000080008000, 000000000000808b (given in hexadecimal using the little-endian format).

3   Overview of the Attack

3.1   Notations

We summarize the major notations to be used in this paper in Table 3. In this paper, the addition operation of KECCAK's state is performed on $GF(2)$ or the linear space over $GF(2)$.

3.2   Overview of the Attack

In this section, we give an overview of our collision attacks. Based on the framework of Dinur et al. [9] and a variant of birthday attack, our collision attack consists of two parts, i.e., a high probability internal differential characteristic and several collision subsets generated by the characteristic for finding collisions.

Given an $(n_r - 1.5)$-round internal differential characteristic, there are three stages in our n_r-round collision attacks:

- *Stage 1—Selecting messages stage:* Obtain linear conditions from the 2-round internal differential characteristic and get several subspaces of messages passing the first 2 rounds.
- *Stage 2—Collecting messages stage:* Compute the outputs after $(n_r - 1.5)$ rounds functions from the subspaces found in Stage 1, and store these outputs into different sets.
- *Stage 3—Brust-force searching stage:* By brust force, find a collision from the outputs after target round of each set in Stage 2.

The collecting messages stage and the brute-force searching stage are simple, although they take up the main time complexity. Therefore, the core step of our attack is selecting messages to reduce the complexity of the collision searching stage. In [9], Dinur *et al.* use an algebraic method to reduce the workload of finding messages conforming to the first χ transition. In Sect. 5, we show a new method to select messages passing the first two rounds functions, which saves even more time complexity.

3.3 A Variant of Birthday Attack

When searching for collisions among the outputs of a hash function H, the birthday attack is the simple technique of selecting distinct inputs x_j for $j = 1, 2, \ldots$ randomly and checking for a collision among the $H(x_j)$ values. The probability that no collision is found after 2^t inputs is

$$(1 - 1/2^n)(1 - 2/2^n)\cdots(1 - (2^t - 1)/2^n) \approx e^{-2^t(2^t-1)/2^{n+1}} \tag{1}$$

where 2^n is the cardinality of the range of H [17]. A collision can be found with high probability for $t = n/2$. If t is much smaller than $n/2$, the probability of a collision being found is close to zero. But by repeating the process of selecting 2^t inputs randomly many times, we can also find a collision with high probability. This is a variant of birthday attack, which is reformulated as follows. Assume that the hash function H maps 2^k input subsets $S_1, \ldots, S_{2^k}$ into output subsets $D_1, \ldots, D_{2^k}$ (called collision subsets) and is a random function when it is confined to any set S_j, where S_j $(j = 1, \ldots, 2^k)$ and D_j $(j = 1, \ldots, 2^k)$ are both pairwise disjoint respectively, $|S_j| = 2^l, |D_j| = 2^m$ $(m > 2l)$. If a collision is found with a probability P for $t = n/2$ in Eq. (1), the expected number of the collision subsets to be searched is 2^w $(w \le k)$ with the same success probability P. The relationship between l, m and w is shown as follows:

$$1 - P \approx \left(e^{-2^l(2^l-1)/2^{m+1}}\right)^{2^w} \tag{2}$$

$$= e^{-2^{l+w}(2^l-1)/2^{m+1}} \tag{3}$$

then

$$2l + w = m. \tag{4}$$

For the randomly selected input x in the union of all S_j (denoted as S'), assume that we can determine which output subset $H(x)$ belongs to, but cannot determine the input subset corresponding to x. So the probability of $H(x)$ in subset

D_j is 2^{-k} for any $j \in \{1, \ldots, 2^k\}$. In order to ensure that each collision subset has at least two values on average, the number of randomly selected inputs is at least 2^{k+1}. Therefore, the total number N of inputs we need can be expressed as

$$N = \begin{cases} 2^{(m+w)/2} & k < m, \\ 2^{k+1} & k \geq m. \end{cases} \tag{5}$$

In the attack on 3-round SHA3-512, we use the internal differential characteristic ($k = 20, m = 40$) given in [4] for finding collisions. With 2^{33} random input messages, we can calculate $l = 33 - 20 = 13, w = 40 - 2 \cdot 13 = 14$. This means that we need to search 2^{14} collision subsets to find a collision with probability $(1 - P) \approx 0.4$. When $w = 15$, we can find a collision with a probability close to 1 according to Eq. (2). In this experiment, about 2^5 collision subsets produced collisions, which means that we will get one collision for every 2^{15} collision subsets searched. It can be seen that the experimental value of the collision subset number (w) is very close to the theoretical value.

Assume that H maps a set S of possible inputs into a set D of possible outputs and $S' = \bigcup_{j=1}^{2^k} S_j$, $D' = \bigcup_{j=1}^{2^k} D_j$. In our attack, take 4-round SHA3-512 as an example (Fig. 2). $|S| = 2^{1600}, |D| = 2^{512}, |S'| = 2^{252}, |D_j| = 2^{320}$. There are 2^{156} output subsets D_j, and the size of their union D' is $2^{156+320} = 2^{476}$. By using conditional internal differentials, the probability of transition from S' to D' is 1. We construct the hash table based on the size of D_j instead of D for collision search, and the search can be performed simultaneously in multiple collision subsets. The expected number of inputs to find a collision is 2^{238}.

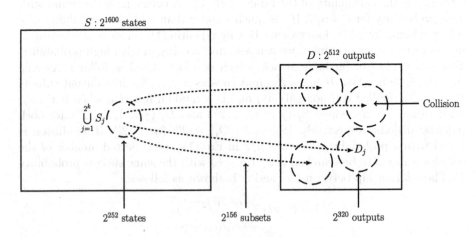

Fig. 2. A variant of birthday attack

4 Description of Internal Difference

In this section we first review the concepts proposed by Dinur *et al.* [9] in their generalization of internal differential, and then define a new metric that can be used to calculate the transition probability of the internal differential more accurately.

4.1 Internal Difference Sets and Representatives

An important property of KECCAK is that if one state has period i in the z-axis (*i.e.*, satisfies $A[x][y][z] = A[x][y][(z+i) \bmod 64]$, for all (x, y, z)), then applying to it any of the θ, ρ, π, χ operations, still maintains the period. This state is called a *symmetric state*. Since the fundamental period corresponding to i is gcd $(i, 64)$, we can redefine $i \in \{1, 2, 4, 8, 16, 32\}$. For $i = 16$, a symmetric state $A[x][y][z]$ is composed of four repetitions of slices 0–15. Each such sequence of slices (0–15, 16–31, 32–47, 48–63) is called a *consecutive slice set* or *CSS* in short. This definition can extend naturally to any $i \in \{1, 2, 4, 8, 16, 32\}$.

Note that the ι operation disturbs the symmetry because all round constants are not periodic. Namely, the round constants are not the same among the CSS.

In an internal differential characteristic, unlike standard differential analysis, the round constant affects the characteristic by introducing a difference between all CSS's. This difference then propagates through the other operations, and its development has to be further studied and controlled. To characterize the difference between general states and symmetric states, the internal difference is defined as follows. Given a period i, the set $\{v + u | u$ is symmetric$\}$ obtained by adding all symmetric states with period i to a single state v is called the *internal difference*, recorded as $[i, v]$. The *zero internal difference* $[i, \mathbf{0}]$ is exactly the set of all symmetric states, and other internal differences $[i, v]$ are cosets of $[i, \mathbf{0}]$ (satisfies $[i, v] = [i, \mathbf{0}] + v$). The state v is called the *representative state*, and all of $[i, v]$ can be regarded as the representative state. In this paper, we choose v satisfying $v[x][y][z] = 0$ $(z \in \{64 - i, \ldots, 63\})$ as the *canonical representative state* (exists uniquely in each internal difference). Since the internal difference is an affine space on $GF(2)$, the action of linear mappings on $[i, v]$ is determined by their action on the representative state. Namely, $\theta([i, v]) = [i, \theta(v)], \rho([i, v]) = [i, \rho(v)], \pi([i, v]) = [i, \pi(v)], \iota([i, v]) = [i, \iota(v)]$.

4.2 Transition Probability of Internal Difference

As in standard differential cryptanalysis, the output difference of the internal difference applying χ depends on the actual input, only if the input difference is zero internal difference, the output difference is unique and also a zero internal difference. In other words, we randomly select several states from the same internal difference as the inputs of χ, and the outputs may belong to different internal differences. As in standard differential analysis, when an internal difference is identified as an input to χ, we need to calculate its all possible output internal differences and the transition probability to a possible output internal difference. For this purpose, we propose the concept of differential transition conditions in combination with the properties of the KECCAK Sbox.

Property 1. Given the input difference $\delta_{in} = (\delta_0, \ldots, \delta_4)^T$ of the 5-bit KECCAK Sbox, the output difference δ_{out} is determined by q $(2 \leq q \leq 4)$ linear conditions with respect to the actual input $x = (x_0, \ldots, x_4)^T$. The q linear conditions $\{l_t(x)\}_{t=0}^{q-1}$ (without constant terms) are called *differential transition conditions*. Equivalently, $\delta_{out} = S(x) \oplus S(x \oplus \delta_{in}) = C \cdot x \oplus \eta$, where $C \in \mathbb{F}_2^{5 \times 5}$ is a matrix $(rank(C) \in \{2, 3, 4\})$ and $\eta \in \mathbb{F}_2^5$ is a constant vector. It can be easily verified that C and η can be represented by δ_{in} as

$$
C = \begin{pmatrix} & \delta_2\,\delta_1 & & \\ & & \delta_3\,\delta_2 & \\ & & & \delta_4\,\delta_3 \\ \delta_4 & & & \delta_0 \\ \delta_1\,\delta_0 & & & \end{pmatrix}, \eta = S(\delta_{in}) = \begin{pmatrix} \delta_0 \oplus (\delta_1 \oplus 1)\delta_2 \\ \delta_1 \oplus (\delta_2 \oplus 1)\delta_3 \\ \delta_2 \oplus (\delta_3 \oplus 1)\delta_4 \\ \delta_3 \oplus (\delta_4 \oplus 1)\delta_0 \\ \delta_4 \oplus (\delta_0 \oplus 1)\delta_1 \end{pmatrix}.
$$

Remark 1. Property 1 holds for the KECCAK Sbox due to its algebraic degree of 2, and a similar property applies to any Sbox with algebraic degree of 2.

Take $\delta_{in} = 0x3$ as an example, the output difference is

$$
\delta_{out} = \begin{pmatrix} 0\,0\,1\,0\,0 \\ 0\,0\,0\,0\,0 \\ 0\,0\,0\,0\,0 \\ 0\,0\,0\,0\,1 \\ 1\,1\,0\,0\,0 \end{pmatrix} \begin{pmatrix} x_0 \\ x_1 \\ x_2 \\ x_3 \\ x_4 \end{pmatrix} \oplus \begin{pmatrix} 1 \\ 1 \\ 0 \\ 1 \\ 0 \end{pmatrix}.
$$

The differential transition conditions are $\{l_0 = x_4, l_1 = x_2, l_2 = x_0 + x_1\}$, and their corresponding output differences are recorded in Table 4. We call the table containing differential transition conditions *difference conditions table* (DCT) of the Sbox. The new table constructed by assigning the differential transition conditions in DCT and recording their resulting output differentials is called *values of difference conditions table* (VDCT).

Table 4. The differential transition conditions of $\delta_{in} = 0x03$

δ_{out}	0x0b	0x1b	0x0a	0x1a	0x03	0x13	0x02	0x12
(l_0, l_1, l_2)	$(0,0,0)$	$(0,0,1)$	$(0,1,0)$	$(0,1,1)$	$(1,0,0)$	$(1,0,1)$	$(1,1,0)$	$(1,1,1)$

In internal differential cryptanalysis, we call the set E composed of all differential transition conditions obtained from the canonical representative state of a internal difference as the differential transition conditions of the internal difference. The rank of E is called the *transition condition number*, and the transition condition number of the i-th round is denoted as k_i. If the transition condition number of $[i, v]$ is k, there are 2^k possible output internal differences and the upper bound of transition probability is 2^{-k}. In Procedure IDTC , we show the details of calculating transition condition number.

Procedure IDTC($A, A', i, DCT, VDCT, E$)

Input: The input internal difference A before χ, the output internal difference A' of A, period i, DCT, VDCT, a linear equation system E.

Output: The updated linear equation system E.

1 **for** *each integer* $j \in [0, 320)$ **do**
2   Obtain the input difference δ_{in} of the j-th Sbox from A.
3   Obtain the output difference δ_{out} of the j-th Sbox from A'.
4   **if** $\delta_{in} \neq 0$ **then**
5   Obtain differential transition conditions $E_0 = \{l_j(W)\}_{j=0}^{q-1}$ from DCT$[\delta_{in}]$, where W is a $25i$-bit variable vector.
6   Obtain value of conditions $(\varepsilon_0, \ldots, \varepsilon_{q-1})$ from VDCT$[\delta_{in}][\delta_{out}]$.
7   Update $E_0 = \{l_j(W) = \varepsilon_j\}_{j=0}^{q-1}$.
8          $E = E \cup E_0$.
9   **end**
10 **end**
11 **return** E

---

5   The Framework and Basic Techniques

In this section, we first present the basic framework of collision attacks on the SHA-3 hash functions with reduced rounds. Then we show the details of techniques and some optimizations for improving our attack.

5.1   The Framework of the Attack

Following the variant of birthday attack, we adopt the strategy of first collecting messages and storing them in different sets, and then performing collision search in each set in turn. Figures 3 and 4 show the basic framework of our attack.

In Stage 1, the probability of the first two rounds in Fig. 3 can be increased to 1 by algebraic methods (as described in next section), while losing exactly $(k_1 + k_2)$ degrees of freedom. In the collecting messages stage, the messages after two round functions and linear operations of the third round (*i.e.*, the first 2.5 rounds) are stored in different sets according to certain rules for the third stage. In Stage 3, the internal difference after 2.5 rounds results in 2^{k_3} different internal differences after the χ operation, and the set generated by the j-th internal difference after another round function is denoted as $D^{(j)}$. Since the probability of collision in the same $D^{(j)}$ is much higher than between different sets, we search for collisions in each $D^{(j)}$ in sequence. But in most cases, we conduct collision search on subsets one by one before χ operation of the last round. In this case, the subsets can be regarded as collision subsets and are pairwise disjoint. Note that all the messages selected in Stage 1 enter a certain collision subset in Stage 3, so we establish an internal differential with probability 1.

In the framework of collision attack on 5-round SHA-3, we select 2-block messages as inputs and use improved target internal difference algorithm (TIDA).

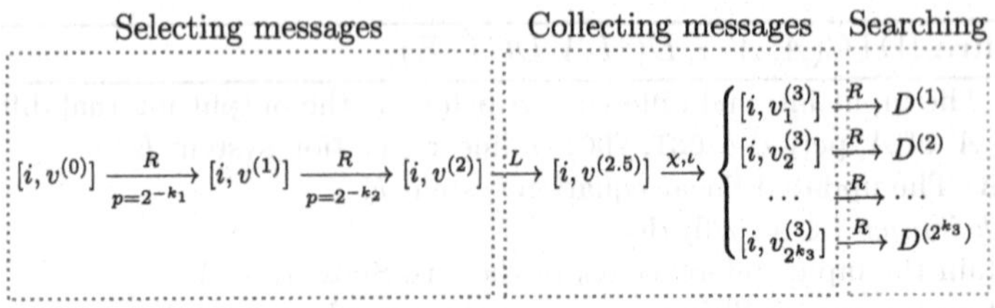

Selecting messages   Collecting messages   Searching

$$[i, v^{(0)}] \xrightarrow[p=2^{-k_1}]{R} [i, v^{(1)}] \xrightarrow[p=2^{-k_2}]{R} [i, v^{(2)}] \xrightarrow{L} [i, v^{(2.5)}] \xrightarrow{\chi, \iota} \begin{cases} [i, v_1^{(3)}] \xrightarrow{R} D^{(1)} \\ [i, v_2^{(3)}] \xrightarrow{R} D^{(2)} \\ \cdots \xrightarrow{R} \cdots \\ [i, v_{2^{k_3}}^{(3)}] \xrightarrow{R} D^{(2^{k_3})} \end{cases}$$

Fig. 3. The framework of 4-round collision attack

TIDA   Selecting messages   Collecting messages   Searching

$$M_0 \xrightarrow{R^5} \oplus \rightarrow [i, v^{(0)}] \xrightarrow[p=2^{-k_1}]{R} [i, v^{(1)}] \xrightarrow[p=2^{-k_2}]{R} [i, v^{(2)}] \xrightarrow[p=2^{-k_3}]{LoR} [i, v^{(3.5)}] \xrightarrow{\chi, \iota} \begin{cases} [i, v_1^{(4)}] \xrightarrow{R} D^{(1)} \\ [i, v_2^{(4)}] \xrightarrow{R} D^{(2)} \\ \cdots \xrightarrow{R} \cdots \\ [i, v_{2^{k_4}}^{(4)}] \xrightarrow{R} D^{(2^{k_4})} \end{cases}$$

with $[i, M_1]$ above $[i, v^{(0)}]$.

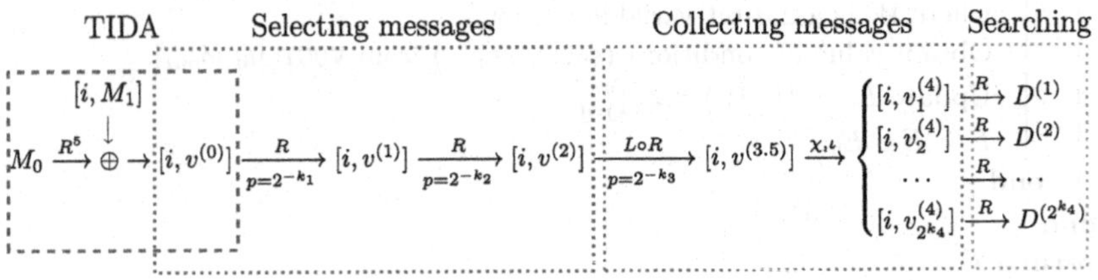

Fig. 4. The framework of 5-round collision attack

The internal differential characteristic used in the attack is given in Characteristic 3 in Appendix A, which covers 2.5 rounds starting from the second round. TIDA is used to find the initial internal difference and the first messages to construct a complete internal differential characteristic with high probability. The full details and analysis of the attack are given in Sect. 5.5.

5.2 Finding Messages Conforming 2-Round Internal Differential Characteristic

In this section, we present an algorithm for finding messages conforming to the first two χ transitions as depicted in Algorithm 1. For a known internal differential characteristic, as shown in Fig. 3, let the states with period i in the internal difference be expressed as follows:

$$u^{(0)} = v^{(0)} + \mathcal{A}_i^{(0)}, u^{(0.5)} = v^{(0.5)} + \mathcal{B}_i^{(0)}, u^{(1)} = v^{(1)} + \mathcal{A}_i^{(1)}, u^{(1.5)} = v^{(1.5)} + \mathcal{B}_i^{(1)},$$

where $u^{(j+0.5)}$ and $v^{(j+0.5)}$ are the state and the internal difference before the $(j+1)$-th χ transition respectively, $\mathcal{A}_i^{(0)}, \mathcal{B}_i^{(0)}, \mathcal{A}_i^{(1)}, \mathcal{B}_i^{(1)}$ are all symmetric state with period i and they have the following vector form (determined by their CSS):

$$\mathcal{A}_i^{(t)} = (a_0^{(t)}, \ldots, a_{25 \cdot i - 1}^{(t)}), \mathcal{B}_i^{(t)} = (b_0^{(t)}, \ldots, b_{25 \cdot i - 1}^{(t)}),$$

where $(a_{j \cdot i}^{(t)}, \ldots, a_{j \cdot i + i - 1}^{(t)})$ are the first i bits of the j-th lane of $\mathcal{A}^{(t)}$, and $\mathcal{A}_i^{(0)}$ satisfies the padding rule and equals to 0 in the capacity part. In order to pass the χ operations of the first two rounds with probability 1, we should find $\mathcal{A}_i^{(0)}$ such that $\mathcal{B}_i^{(0)}$ and $\mathcal{B}_i^{(1)}$ satisfy the respective differential transition conditions

---

Algorithm 1: Finding Messages Passing 2-round Internal Differential

---

Input: An internal differential characteristic, and a period i.
Output: Initial messages conforming 2-round internal differential

1 $E_j = \emptyset, j \in \{0, 1, 2, 3, 4, 5\}$

2 Set $\mathcal{A}_i^{(0)}, \mathcal{B}_i^{(0)}, \mathcal{A}_i^{(1)}, \mathcal{B}_i^{(1)}$ to being $25i$-variable vectors.

3 Add constraints on $\mathcal{A}_i^{(0)}$ such that the symmetric state generated by $\mathcal{A}_i^{(0)}$ satisfies the padding rule and equal to 0 in the capacity part.

4 Obtain the input internal difference $v^{(1.5)}$ and the output internal difference $v^{(2)} + \Delta(RC[2])$ of the second χ from the given characteristic.

5 IDTC($v^{(1.5)}, v^{(2)} + \Delta(RC[2]), i, \text{DCT}, \text{VDCT}, E_1$).

6 Transform $E_1(b_0^{(1)}, \ldots, b_{25 \cdot i-1}^{(1)})$ to $E_1(a_0^{(1)}, \ldots, a_{25 \cdot i-1}^{(1)})$.

7 **for** each $a_j^{(1)}$ appearing in $E_1(\mathcal{A}^{(1)})$ **do**

8      $E_2 = E_2 \cup \{b_{\lfloor j/5i \rfloor \cdot 5i + [(j+i) \bmod 5i]}^{(0)} = x_t\}$.

9      $t = t + 1$.

10 **end**

11 Obtain the input internal difference $v^{(0.5)}$ and the output internal difference $v^{(1)} + \Delta(RC[1])$ of the first χ from the given characteristic.

12 IDTC($v^{(0.5)}, v^{(1)} + \Delta(RC[1]), i, \text{DCT}, \text{VDCT}, E_0$).

13 $E_4 = E_0 \cup E_2$.

14 Transform $E_4(b_0^{(0)}, \ldots, b_{25 \cdot i-1}^{(0)})$ to $E_4(a_0^{(0)}, \ldots, a_{25 \cdot i-1}^{(0)})$.

15 Reduce E_4.

16 **do**

17   Randomly assign values to the free variables in $\{x_j\}_{j=0}^{t-1}$.

18   Obtain E_3 by subsituting E_2 into E_1.

19   Transform $E_3(b_0^{(0)}, \ldots, b_{25 \cdot i-1}^{(0)})$ to $E_3(a_0^{(0)}, \ldots, a_{25 \cdot i-1}^{(0)})$.

20      $E_5 = E_3 \cup E_4$.

21 **while** E_5 is not consistent;

22 Solve E_5 and obtain the initial messages.

23 **return** initial messages

(denoted as $E_0(\mathcal{B}_i^{(0)})$ and $E_1(\mathcal{B}_i^{(1)})$ appearing in Algorithm 1). $E_0(\mathcal{B}_i^{(0)})$ and $E_1(\mathcal{B}_i^{(1)})$ can be transformed into $E_0(\mathcal{A}_i^{(0)})$ and $E_1(\mathcal{A}_i^{(1)})$ by the linear operation $(L(\mathcal{A}_i^{(0)}) = \mathcal{B}_i^{(0)}, L(\mathcal{A}_i^{(1)}) = \mathcal{B}_i^{(1)})$. Since $\mathcal{A}_i^{(1)} = \chi(\mathcal{B}_i^{(0)})$, $a_j^{(1)} = b_j^{(0)} \oplus (b_{j+i}^{(0)} \oplus 1) \cdot b_{j+2i}^{(0)}$, we regard $b_{j+i}^{(0)}$ as a variable x, then

$$
a_j^{(1)} = \begin{cases} b_j^{(0)} \oplus b_{j+2i}^{(0)}, & x = 0, \\ b_j^{(0)}, & x = 1. \end{cases}
$$

In general, all bits $b_{j+i}^{(0)}$ corresponding to the bits $a_j^{(1)}$ appearing in $E_1(\mathcal{A}_i^{(1)})$ are set as intermediate variables $\{x_t\}_{t \in I}$ (I is index set), and the system composed of $b_{j+i}^{(0)} = x_t$ is E_2. Noting that each x_t is the value of a bit $b_j^{(0)}$, it is actually a linear equation about $\mathcal{A}_i^{(0)}$. So $\{x_t\}_{t \in I}$ may be linearly independent. We call the variables in the maximal linearly independent system of $\{x_t\}_{t \in I}$ are the free variables (short for free intermediate variables). After assigning a value to $\{x_t\}_{t \in I}$, E_1 can be expressed as a linear system of $\mathcal{B}_i^{(0)}$, which is also a linear system of $\mathcal{A}_i^{(0)}$, denoted as E_3. For the convenience of calculation, we combine the transition conditions of the first round and assignment conditions $(E_0 \cup E_2)$. Then, by solving the linear system $E_0 \cup E_2 \cup E_3$ and XORing each solution with $v^{(0)}$, the message M conforming 2-round internal differential characteristic is obtained. In fact, all messages M satisfying the first two χ transitions can be found in this way, because we can traverse all possible values of $\{x\}_{t \in I}$. Therefore, we lose $(k_1 + k_2)$ degrees of freedom in total. We need to remove linear related conditions in the linear system and $\{x_t\}_{t \in I}$, the details of algorithm are shown in Algorithm 1. As a simple example, in Fig. 5, we set $k_1 = 3, k_2 = 2$, and the number of free variables is $t = 3$. If the total number of initial messages is 2^n, the differential transition conditions of the first round divides the message spaces into eight subspaces, one of which (named S_1) conforms the first χ transition. Each assignment of the free variables divides the space S into $2^{k_3} = 8$ subspaces, and also divides S_1 into $2^t = 8$ parts (named S_2). The second round differential transition conditions divide each S_2 into $2^{k_2} = 4$ subspaces, one of which (named S_3, as shown by the shadow) conforming the second χ transition. The expected size of S_3 is 2^{n-8}. After all possible values of the free variables are retrieved, about 2^{n-5} messages will conform the first two χ transitions.

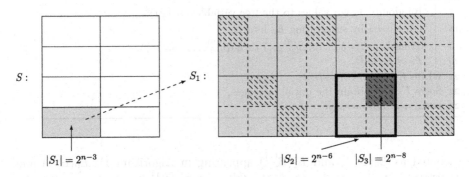

$S:$ $S_1:$

$|S_1| = 2^{n-3}$ $|S_2| = 2^{n-6}$ $|S_3| = 2^{n-8}$

Fig. 5. Message subspaces S and S_1

5.3   Collecting Messages Belonging to Different Internal Difference

We give the details of Stage 2, which collect and store messages into different sets to determine which internal difference the state belongs to after the last linear operation.

For 4-round collision attacks, the values of differential transition conditions of the third round are denoted as $E(\mathcal{B}_i^{(2)}) = \{l_t(\mathcal{B}_i^{(2)})\}_{t=0}^{k_3-1}$, where $\mathcal{B}_i^{(2)} = R^{(2.5)}(M) \oplus v^{(2.5)}$ (M is the message output by Algorithm 1). Then M is stored in $D^{(index)}$ with $index = \sum_{t=0}^{k_3-1} l_t \cdot 2^t$, where $D^{(j)}$ corresponds to the j-th output internal difference. In 5-round collision attacks, we calculate the corresponding data for the 4-th round instead. The details of this step for 4-round collision attacks are shown in Algorithm 2. In order to apply the variant of birthday attack and reduce complexity, in most cases, we will search collisions before the last χ operation, where $D^{(j)}$ is the internal difference of $(n_r - 0.5)$ rounds for n_r-round collision attacks.

Algorithm 2: Store Messages into Set $D^{(i)}$

Input: Message M output from Algorithm 1, subset family
   $\mathcal{D} = \{D^{(0)}, \ldots, D^{(2^{k_3}-1)}\}$, 2.5-round internal differential characteristic.
Output: Subset family $\mathcal{D} = \{D^{(0)}, \ldots, D^{(2^{k_3}-1)}\}$.

1 Compute $\mathcal{B}_i^{(2)} = \texttt{R}^{(2.5)}(M) \oplus \Delta(\texttt{R}^{(2.5)}(M))$ and set $E = \emptyset$.
2 **for** *each integer $j \in [0, 320)$* **do**
3   Get the input difference δ_{in} of the j-th Sbox from $\Delta(\texttt{R}^{(3.5)}(M))$.
4   **if** $\delta_{in} \neq 0$ **then**
5   Get differential ransition conditions E_1 from $\texttt{DCT}[\delta_{in}]$.
6        $E = E \cup E_1$.
7   **end**
8 **end**
9 Reduce $E = \{l_0, \ldots, l_{k_3-1}\}$.
10 Compute $(\eta_0, \ldots, \eta_{k_3-1}) = (l_0(\mathcal{B}_i^{(2)}), \ldots, l_{k_3-1}(\mathcal{B}_i^{(2)}))$.
11 $index = \sum_{j=0}^{k_3-1} \eta_j \cdot 2^j$.
12 $D^{(index)} = D^{(index)} \cup \{M\}$.
13 **return** $\mathcal{D}$

5.4 Bounding the Size of Collision Subset

In the variant of birthday attack, the size of the collision subset determines the time complexity. We use the method in [9] to bound the size of the collision subset.

The collision subset is essentially the output of $\iota \circ \chi$, and the subset of internal difference is the input of χ. Obviously, operation ι can be ignored since it does not affect the size of the collision subset. A property of χ is that it is applied independently on each plane of the state and in particular, maps each plane to itself. When the output is the first d bits of the final state, we bound the number of its possible values by computing the size of which the internal difference is projected onto its first $320\lceil n/320 \rceil$ bits. For $d = 384$ and $d = 448$, the size of collision subset can be bounded more accurately: each output bit $A[x][y][z]$ of χ depends on the 3 input bits $A[x][y][z], A[x+1][y][z]$ and $A[x+2][y][z]$. Therefore, each output lane $A[x][y][\cdot]$ of χ only depends on the 3 input lanes

$A[x][y][\cdot], A[x+1][y][\cdot]$ and $A[x+2][y][\cdot]$. In the case of $d = 384$, the first 5 lanes are mapped to themselves by χ, and the remaining lane depends on only 3 consecutive lanes. For $d = 448$, the 7 output lanes depend on 9 input lanes.

For d-bit collision subset, given that it depends only on the first d' bits before the χ mapping. As the period is i, each lane can assume at most 2^i values. Thus, for $256 \leq d \leq 320$ ($d' = 320$) we obtain a basic bound of 2^{5i} and for $512 \leq d \leq 640$ ($d' = 640$) we obtain a basic bound of 2^{10i}. For $d = 384$ ($d' = 512$) and $d = 448$ ($d' = 576$), the computation can be divided into two parts: the first 5 lanes of the output can assume at most 2^{5i} values, and the remaining bits can assume at most $\min(2^{64}, 2^{3i})$ and $\min(2^{128}, 2^{4i})$ values. From the previous analysis, we obtain a bound of $2^{5i} \cdot \min(2^{64}, 2^{3i})$ for $d = 384$ and a bound of 2^{9i} for $d = 448$. Clearly, the bound only depends on i and d' (which determined by d).

5.5   The Target Internal Difference Algorithm

Dinur et al. [8] explored the *target difference algorithm* (TDA) to link a differential characteristic to the initial state of the KECCAK permutation. In [9], they generalized this method as a variant for internal differential cryptanalysis, which is called *target internal difference algorithm* (TIDA). Analogously, the TIDA is used to link an internal differential characteristic to the initial state, using one permutation round. The initial internal difference of the internal differential characteristic is called the *target internal difference*, denoted by Δ_{T^*}. The outputs of the algorithm are single-block messages whose internal difference after one permutation round is Δ_{T^*}.

In this section, we focus on $\Delta_T = \Delta_{T^*} \oplus \Delta(RC[1])$ and set it as the target internal difference. We modify the output of the algorithm to 2-block messages and apply it to our 5-round collision attack. Namely, given a target internal difference Δ_T, we use TIDA (Algorithm 3) to find 2-block messages $(M_0 \| M_1)$ such that

$$\Delta[\chi \circ L(\mathsf{R}^5(M_0 \| 0^c) \oplus (\overline{M_1} \| 0^c))] = \Delta_T. \tag{6}$$

The first step in constructing the algorithm is to choose period $i = 32$ (and all operations of internal difference are performed on the state that the length of each lane is 32) so that the equations in the algorithm will have enough degrees of freedom. Then, according to a property of χ provided in [8] (as shown in Property 2), the input internal differences corresponding to Δ_T span several affine subspaces.

Property 2 ([8]). For a non-zero 5-bit output difference δ_{out} to a KECCAK Sbox, the set of possible input differences, $\{\delta_{in} | DDT(\delta_{in}, \delta_{out}) > 0\}$, contains at least 5 (and up to 17) 2-dimensional affine subspaces.

We select an 800-dimension subspace (named W) and map it to the initial internal difference $\Delta_I^* = L^{-1}(W)$. The first block M_0 is randomly selected until it satisfies that there is a internal difference Δ_I in $L^{-1}(W)$ equal to the internal difference of $\mathsf{R}^5(M_0 \| 0^c)$ on the padding and capacity bits. Note that the internal

---

Algorithm 3: Target Internal Difference Algorithm (TIDA)

Input: Target internal difference Δ_T, target transition condition number k_T, and target number of rounds n_r.

Output: 2-block message (M_0, M_1), initial internal difference Δ_I, k_1 of $L(\Delta_I)$

1 Set $E_\Delta = \emptyset$ and $\Delta_I^* = L^{-1}(W)$ with a variable vector $W = (w_0, \ldots, w_{799})$.

2 **for** *each non-active Sbox of Δ_T* **do**

3 $\quad\mid\quad E_\Delta = E_\Delta \cup \{w_{5j} = 0, \ldots, w_{5j+4} = 0\}$, for the j-th Sbox.

4 **end**

5 **for** *each active Sbox of Δ_T* **do**

6 $\quad\mid\quad$ Select one 2-dim affine subspace from δ_{in} according to Δ_T.

7 $\quad\mid\quad$ Add 3 affine equations to E_Δ according to the 2-dim affine subspace.

8 **end**

9 **do**

10 $\quad\mid\quad$ Randomly select M_0 and compute $\Delta(\text{R}^{n_r}(M_0))$.

11 $\quad\mid\quad E_c = \{\Delta_I^*[j] = \Delta(\text{R}^{n_r}(M_0))[j]\}_{j=800-p-c/2}^{799}$
    $\quad\mid\quad$ // $\Delta_T^*[j]$ is the j-th bit of Δ_T^*, the same in $\Delta(\text{R}^{n_r}(M_0))$

12 **while** *$E_\Delta \cup E_c$ is not consistent*;

13 Randomly select a solution Δ_I of $E_\Delta \cup E_c$.

14 Calculate k_1 corresponding to Δ_I.

15 **if** $k_1 < k_T$ **then**

16 $\quad\mid\quad$ Set $E_0 = \emptyset$.

17 $\quad\mid\quad$ IDTC($L(\Delta_I), \Delta_T, 32, \text{DCT}, \text{VDCT}, E_0$).

18 $\quad\mid\quad$ **if** *E_0 is consistent* **then**

19 $\quad\mid\quad\quad\mid\quad$ Break.

20 $\quad\mid\quad$ **end**

21 **end**

22 $M_1 = \text{R}^{n_r}(M_0) \oplus \Delta_I \oplus sym$, where sym is a random symmetric state satisfying padding rule and equals to 0 in the capacity part.

23 **return** $(M_0, M_1), \Delta_I, k_1$

---

difference Δ_I is obtained after the first block M_0 is determined, we can calculate the transition condition number k_1 of $L(\Delta_I)$. In order to obtain smaller k_1, we select more M_1 to get several Δ_I and choose the best input internal difference. The remaining bits of Δ_I can be satisfied by modifying the value of the second block M_1. However, due to the insufficient degrees of freedom of the second block, Eq. (1) may not have a solution. In other words, if the transition condition number of $L(\Delta_I)$ is k_1, it results in 2^{k_1} different output internal differences. But the degree of freedom of M_1 is less than 800, not all Sboxes have enough inputs to generate all possible outputs. The number of actual output internal differences may be less than 2^{k_1}, and Δ_T may not be among them. When this occurs, we need to redefine the first block M_0. The details are given in Algorithm 3, and the above process is equivalent to solving equation systems.

6   Results and Complexity Analysis

In this section, we present the details and experimental results of our collision attack on different versions of SHA-3. Given an internal differential characteristic spanning $(n_r - 1.5)$ rounds of the KECCAK permutation, a collision attack on n_r-round SHA-3 consists of the following steps:

1. Construct linear equation systems according to the differential transition conditions of the first two rounds and solve them to get enough initial messages.
2. Pick an arbitrary message obtained in Step 1 and calculate its internal difference after $(n_r - 1.5)$ rounds. If the internal differential characteristic is satisfied, store the message into the corresponding subset. Otherwise, discard the message and go back to Step 2 until collect enough states.
3. Choose an unselected subset.
   (a) Pick a state and store its output after the n_r-th round in a hash table (along with its initial message) and check for a collision.
   (b) If a collision is found, stop and output it. Else if all states are chosen and there is no collision, go back to Step 3. Otherwise, go back to (a).

6.1   Collision Attacks on 4-Round SHA3-384 and SHAKE256

For 4-round SHA3-384 and SHAKE256, we use the same 2.5-round characteristic (Characteristic 1 in Appendix A). We choose $i = 8$ and use the techniques of Sects. 5.1, 5.2 and 5.3. The transition condition numbers of the characteristic are $(k_1, k_2, k_3) = (11, 8, 78)$. The size of $\{x_t\}_{t \in I}$ is 80. There are 59 free variables in SHA3-384 and 72 free variables in SHAKE256. Therefore, in Stage 1, the number of assignments to $\{x_t\}_{t \in I}$ will not exceed 2^{72}.

For SHA3-384 and SHAKE256 ($d \leq 448$), the size of each collision subset is less than k_3. In order to launch collision attack, we need to ensure that there are at least two messages in each collision subset on average. So in the first stage we select 2^{79} messages conforming to the first two χ transitions. For $d = 448$, we can find a collision with good probability by searching 2^{71} collision subsets, and we need fewer collision subsets for smaller d. So the complexity is mainly caused by the first two stages, and it can be reduced by placing eight messages in each state. More specifically, if the initial state can be expressed as $u^{(0)} = \mathcal{A}^{(0)} + v^{(0)}$, where $\mathcal{A}^{(0)}$ is a fully symmetric state with period $i = 8$ and $v^{(0)}$ is the initial internal difference in Characteristic 1. Rewrite $\mathcal{A}^{(0)}$ as follows:

$$\mathcal{A}^{(0)} = (A_8^{(0)}, A_8^{(0)}, A_8^{(0)}, A_8^{(0)}, A_8^{(0)}, A_8^{(0)}, A_8^{(0)}, A_8^{(0)}),$$

where $A_8^{(0)}$ is a CSS of $\mathcal{A}^{(0)}$, and $\mathcal{A} = (\mathcal{A}_1, \ldots, \mathcal{A}_j)$ means each lane of the state $\mathcal{A}$ is the concatenation of the lane corresponding to $\mathcal{A}_k$ ($k = 1, \ldots, j$). The linear operation L acting on the $(5 \times 5 \times 8)$-bit state is denoted by $L_{[8]}$. Due to the property of KECCAK mentioned in Sect. 4.1, $L(\mathcal{A}^{(0)})$ has the following expression:

$$L(\mathcal{A}^{(0)}) = (L_{[8]}(A_8^{(0)}), \ldots, L_{[8]}(A_8^{(0)})).$$

In Characteristic 1, the canonical representative states of the first two rounds are fixed-points of θ. Namely, the states are in the CP-kernel. As a result, The first 2.5 rounds of operation of the messages $u^{(0)}$ selected in Stage 1 can be simplified:

$$
\begin{aligned}
L(u^{(0)}) = \quad & L(\mathcal{A}^{(0)}) + L(v^{(0)}) && = (L_{[8]}(\mathcal{A}_8^{(0)}), \ldots, L_{[8]}(\mathcal{A}_8^{(0)})) + L(v^{(0)}) \\
u^{(0.5)} = \quad & \mathcal{B}^{(0)} + v^{(0.5)} && = (\mathcal{B}_8^{(0)}, \ldots, \mathcal{B}_8^{(0)}) + v^{(0.5)} \\
\iota \circ \chi(u^{(0.5)}) = \quad & \chi(\mathcal{B}^{(0)} + v^{(0.5)}) + RC'[1] && = (\mathcal{A}_8^{(1)}, \ldots, \mathcal{A}_8^{(1)}) + v^{(1)}.
\end{aligned}
$$

Since the last 8 bits in each lane of the canonical representative states are zero, the last CSS of $\mathcal{B}^{(0)} + v^{(0.5)}$ is $\mathcal{B}_8^{(0)}$ which means $\mathcal{A}_8^{(1)} = \chi(\mathcal{B}_8^{(0)})$. In the second round:

$$
\begin{aligned}
L(u^{(1)}) = \quad & L(\mathcal{A}^{(1)}) + L(v^{(1)}) && = (L_{[8]}(\mathcal{A}_8^{(1)}), \ldots, L_{[8]}(\mathcal{A}_8^{(1)})) + L(v^{(1)}) \\
u^{(1.5)} = \quad & \mathcal{B}^{(1)} + v^{(1.5)} && = (\mathcal{B}_8^{(1)}, \ldots, \mathcal{B}_8^{(1)}) + v^{(1.5)} \\
\iota \circ \chi(u^{(1.5)}) = \quad & \chi(\mathcal{B}^{(1)} + v^{(1.5)}) + RC'[2] && = (\mathcal{A}_8^{(2)}, \ldots, \mathcal{A}_8^{(2)}) + v^{(2)},
\end{aligned}
$$

where $\mathcal{A}_8^{(2)} = \chi(\mathcal{B}_8^{(1)})$, $RC'[j] = \Delta(RC[j])$, $j \in \{1,2\}$. And in the third round, $\mathcal{B}_8^{(2)} = L_{[8]}(\mathcal{A}_8^{(2)})$. Therefore, in the collecting messages stage, we can simultaneously calculate eight messages $u_0^{(0)}, \ldots, u_7^{(0)}$ and calculate their transition conditions of the third round in the following way:

$$
L \circ \chi \circ L \circ \chi \circ L(\mathcal{A}_{8,0}^{(0)}, \ldots, \mathcal{A}_{8,7}^{(0)})
$$
$$
= (L_{[8]} \circ \chi \circ L_{[8]} \circ \chi \circ L_{[8]}(\mathcal{A}_{8,0}^{(0)}), \ldots, L_{[8]} \circ \chi \circ L_{[8]} \circ \chi \circ L_{[8]}(\mathcal{A}_{8,7}^{(0)}))
$$
$$
= \quad (\mathcal{B}_{8,0}^{(2)}, \mathcal{B}_{8,1}^{(2)}, \mathcal{B}_{8,2}^{(2)}, \mathcal{B}_{8,3}^{(2)}, \mathcal{B}_{8,4}^{(2)}, \mathcal{B}_{8,5}^{(2)}, \mathcal{B}_{8,6}^{(2)}, \mathcal{B}_{8,7}^{(2)}),
$$

where $\mathcal{A}_{8,j}^{(0)}$ is a CSS of the symmetric state of $u_j^{(0)}$. From each $\mathcal{B}_{8,j}^{(2)}$ we can obtain the transition conditions and calculate the index w_j of its internal difference, then store it into the set $D^{(w_j)}$ (the w_j-th output internal difference after the third χ).

After collecting messages stage, we compute the outputs of each set after $L \circ \chi$ (the state also can be divided into eight parts to simultaneously calculate eight symmetric states) and find a collision. According to the analysis in Sect. 5.4, in order to produce the final collision, the location of the collision needs to be determined. For $256 \leq d \leq 320$, we have to find collisions on the first 5 lanes before the last χ. For $d = 384$, the collision location is the first 8 lanes. And for $d = 448$ and $512 \leq d \leq 640$, the number is 9 and 10. Taking $d = 320$ as an example, if there is a collision $(\mathcal{B}_{8,p}^{(3)}, \mathcal{B}_{8,q}^{(3)})$ on the first 5 lanes, then for any internal difference $\Delta = (\Delta_0, \ldots, \Delta_7)$, $\iota \circ \chi(\mathcal{B}_{8,p}^{(3)} + \Delta_0, \ldots, \mathcal{B}_{8,p}^{(3)} + \Delta_7)$ and $\iota \circ \chi(\mathcal{B}_{8,q}^{(3)} + \Delta_0, \ldots, \mathcal{B}_{8,q}^{(3)} + \Delta_7)$ will be equivalent on the first 320 bits. Therefore, we can calculate their initial symmetric states $\mathcal{A}_{8,p}^{(1)}$ and $\mathcal{A}_{8,q}^{(1)}$, and get the initial messages M_p and M_q by XORing with the initial internal difference. After the previous analysis, we can find a collision $R^4(M_p)$ and $R^4(M_q)$ on the first 320 bits. Note that this technique can be extended naturally to any $i \in \{1, 2, 4, 8, 16, 32\}$. And for $d > 448$, we also need 2^{79} messages to launch attack from the Eq. (1). In all cases, the expected complexity is $2^{79-3} = 2^{76}$. This is 2^{71} times faster than the internal differential attack by Dinur $et\ al.$ [9] for 4-round SHA3-384.

6.2   A Collision Attack on 4-Round SHA3-512

For 4-round SHA3-512, we choose $i = 32$ and used the 2.5-round internal difference characteristic given in Characteristic 2 in Appendix A. The transition condition numbers of the characteristic are $(k_1, k_2, k_3) = (16, 16, 170)$. For $k_3 = 170$, there are 2^{170} different internal differences after the χ mapping of the third round. These internal differences actually compose a 170-dimensional affine space (denoted as U) over $GF(2)$. The projection of the affine space $L \circ \iota(U)$ on the first 10 lanes consists of internal differences which are projected to the first 10 lanes, and its dimension is 156. For $d = 512$, we collect the messages with the same internal difference in the first 10 lanes into a set. Then we need fewer messages for generating collisions.

In selecting messages stage, the size of the variable set $\{x_t\}_{t \in I}$ is 172, and there are 138 free variables. Therefore, we obtain $2^{284-(138+16+16)} = 2^{114}$ expected messages after the variables of $\{x_t\}_{t \in I}$ are assigned each time. Since the size of collision subset is $2^{10 \cdot 32} = 2^{320}$, we need to choose $2^{(320+156)/2} = 2^{238}$ messages, which conforming the first two rounds internal differential characteristic, in order to find a collision with high probability. In order to obtain enough messages, we make $2^{238-114} = 2^{124}$ different assignments to $\{x_t\}_{t \in I}$.

In the next stage, we compute the outputs after 3.5 rounds functions from the subspaces found in Stage 1. Then collect the outputs with the same internal difference in the first 10 lanes into a set.

In searching stage, the sets obtained from the previous step are considered as collision subsets, and we search for collisions on the first 10 lanes in each collision subset in turn. If there is a collision $(\mathcal{B}_{32,0}^{(3)}, \mathcal{B}_{32,1}^{(3)})$ in a collision subset with Δ (projection of the canonical representative state on the first 10 lanes), it will result in a collision $\chi(\widetilde{\mathcal{B}}_{32,0}^{(3)}, \widetilde{\mathcal{B}}_{32,0}^{(3)} \oplus \Delta) = \chi(\widetilde{\mathcal{B}}_{32,1}^{(3)}, \widetilde{\mathcal{B}}_{32,1}^{(3)} \oplus \Delta)$ after 4-round, where $\widetilde{\mathcal{B}}_{32,j}^{(3)}$ is the projection of $\mathcal{B}_{32,j}^{(3)}$ on the first 10 lanes for $j = 0, 1$. In fact, the value of this internal difference does not need to be calculated. We can use the inverse operation to obtain the initial messages corresponding to $\mathcal{B}_{32,0}^{(3)}$ and $\mathcal{B}_{32,1}^{(3)}$, and then calculate the outputs after 4-round function, following Sect. 6.1.

Since period $i = 32$ is half the lane size, we can put the first CSS of two completely symmetric states in each state to represent the corresponding message for calculation (as in Sect. 6.1). The expected time complexity of calculating the output of all messages after 4-round permutation is bounded by $2^{238-1} = 2^{237}$, and the complexity caused by assignment to $\{x_t\}_{t \in I}$ can be ignored. This is 2^{19} times faster than the general birthday attack.

6.3   A Collision Attack on 5-Round SHAKE256

In this section, we present a collision attack on 5-round SHAKE256. Our attack uses internal differential characteristic given in Characteristic 3 in Appendix A, which covers 2.5 rounds satrting from the second round. The transition condition numbers of the characteristic are $(k_2, k_3, k_4) = (21, 18, 16)$. For $[32, \iota^{-1}(v^{(1)})]$, there 129 active Sboxes and 31 non-active Sboxes. Each active Sbox provides 3 linear equations, each non-active Sbox provides 5 linear equations, and the first message block provides 262 linear equations. The size of the linear system used to solve the input internal difference $L(\Delta_I)$ is 804, and the rank is 779. Therefore, we can obtain a consistent linear system $E_\Delta \cup E_c$ by randomly select 2^{25} the first blocks on average. Since the number of variables in the linear system is 800 and the rank is 779, each consistent linear system $E_\Delta \cup E_c$ has 2^{21} solutions (Δ_I). For $i = 32$, the internal differential transition conditions number is the sum of the transition condition numbers of all Sboxes of the canonical representative state. Let $k(S_j)$ be the transition condition number of the j-th Sbox for Δ_T, then we can calculate the expectation of k_1:

$$E(k_1) = \sum_{j=0}^{159} E(k(S_j)). \tag{7}$$

Assume that $\delta_{out}^{(j)}$ is the output difference of S_j and the 2-dimension affine subspace of its possible input differences we choose is $\{\delta_0, \delta_1, \delta_2, \delta_3\}$. For input difference $\delta_{in}^{(j)}$, its transition condition number is the rank of the subspace formed by all possible output differences. So the expectation of $k(S_j)$ is expressed as:

$$E(k(S_j)) = \frac{1}{4} \sum_{j=0}^{3} (5 - \log_2 \mathrm{DDT}(\delta_{in}^{(j)}, \delta_{out}^{(j)})). \tag{8}$$

The expected transition condition number of Δ_I is 410.5, so we can easily obtain massive characteristics with $k_1 < 400$ to get enough messages. The smallest k_1 we have found is 375. We also use the technique in Sect. 6.1 to put two messages in the same state when performing the attack, which reduces the complexity on average by half. In selecting messages stage, the size of $\{x_t\}_{t \in I}$ is 224 and there are 93 free variables for the characteristic. In collecting messages stage, we store the states after 3.5 rounds in different subsets, which are the output internal differences of states after the fourth χ operation. In searching stage, for $d = 384$, the collision subsets are the outputs after 5-th round of subsets in Stage 2. In this case, the size of each collision subset is bounded by $2^{32 \cdot 5 + 64} = 2^{224}$ and the collision subsets are pairwise disjoint. Actually, due to χ acting on the first 5 lanes is bijection, the projection of any collision subset and its internal difference before the last χ is one to one on the first 320 bits. It can be seen from Characteristic 3 that there are $2^{k_3} = 2^{16}$ different internal differences, and their projections on the first 5 lanes can be verified to be different from each other. When conducting collision search, we need to calculate the complete state.

So the time complexity in total is $2^{18+(224+16)/2} = 2^{138}$. If we take the internal difference of 4.5-round as the collision subset, in order to produce a collision after 5-round, we need to find a collision of the first 8 lanes before the last χ. The size of each collision subset is $2^{8\cdot32} = 2^{256}$, which will lead to more time complexity $2^{18+(256+16)/2} = 2^{154}$. For other d, we still search collisions before the last χ and use the techniques in Sect. 6.1 to reduce time complexity. In addition, since $p = 6$ and $c = 512$ in SHAKE256, we can obtain full-bit (1600-bit) collisions by searching for the last $(p + c)$-bit collisions. Assume that the outputs N and N' of 2-block messages $(M_0 || M_1)$ and $(M_0' || M_1')$ are equal in the last 518 bits. We can introduce the third block messages M_2 and M_2' satisfying $N \oplus (\overline{M_2} || 0^c) = N' \oplus (\overline{M_2'} || 0^c)$ to obtain the full-bit collision $\mathrm{R}^5(N \oplus (\overline{M_2} || 0^c)) = \mathrm{R}^5(N' \oplus (\overline{M_2'} || 0^c))$. And the complexity of searching for full-bit collisions is the same as the case of $d \leq 640$.

The number of messages for collision attack and attack complexity are listed in Table 5 for different d. Note that the same internal differential characteristic is also applicable to the collision attacks on SHA3-224, SHA3-256 and SHAKE128, where attack complexities are both the complexity corresponding to $d = 256$.

Table 5. The parameters of characteristics and complexity

d	Number of characteristics	Complexity ($\log_2$)
$256 \sim 320$	1	$106 - 1 = 105$
384	1	138
448	2^{63}	$170 - 1 = 169$
≥ 512	2^{79}	$186 - 1 = 185$

6.4 Summary of Collision Attacks

We summarize different versions of collision attacks in Table 6. For 4-round SHA-3, the first two canonical representative states of Characteristics we used is in CP-kernel. Since ι brings about extra internal differences, we do not find the characteristics where the canonical representative states of the first three rounds are all in CP-kernel. For 5-round SHA-3, we first determine the internal difference of the third round and then search for the appropriate target internal difference. Too few active Sboxes of the target internal difference will make it difficult to find the first block message M_0, and too many will make the differential transition probability of the first round too small, which will consume many degrees of freedom. Therefore, the number of active Sboxes for target internal difference is preferably between 128 and 135.

Table 6. The parameters of characteristics and complexities

Target	n_r	i	DF[a]	k_1	k_2	k_3	k_4	Complexity ($\log_2$)
SHA3-384	4	8	$104 - 4 = 100$	11	8	78	-	$79 - 3 = 76$
SHA3-512	4	32	$288 - 4 = 284$	16	16	170	-	$238 - 1 = 237$
SHAKE256	4	8	$136 - 6 = 130$	16	8	78	-	$79 - 3 = 76$
SHA3-224/SHA3-256/SHAKE128	5	32	≥ 540	-	21	18	16	$106 - 1 = 105$
SHAKE256	5	32	$544 - 6 = 538$	-	21	18	16	≤ 185

[a] Degree of freedom of the initial message space.

7 Conclusions

In this paper, we presented collision attacks on up to 5 rounds of all the six SHA-3 functions by developing conditional internal differential cryptanalysis. We introduced the differential transition conditions to describe the evolution of internal differences and estimate the transition probability more accurately. By solving the linear systems constructed with the difference transition conditions of two rounds, we obtained the messages that conform 2-round internal differential characteristic. According to the linear conditions on their middle states, these messages were divided into different subsets. We described a variant of birthday attack and applied it to these subsets for getting the collisions.

Compared with differential cryptanalysis, searching for internal differential characteristics in CP-kernel might be more difficult because ι cannot be ignored in internal differential cryptanalysis, while the length of internal differential characteristic used in the collision attack is shorter. It seems that standard differential cryptanalysis is more effective for reduced versions of SHA-3 with a low security strength and a large rate, while internal differential has advantages for higher security strengths since the collision is easier produced for a longer digest. In spite of this, our collision attack on each variant of SHA-3 expect SHAKE128 can reach the most rounds at present. For 4-round SHA3-512, our collision attack outperforms the best known attacks, and the collision attack on 5-round SHAKE256 is presented for the first time.

We stress that our attack does not threaten the security of the full SHA-3.

A Internal Differential Characteristics for the Attacks

The internal difference $[i, v]$ is represented by its canonical representative state defined in Sect. 4.1. Each state is given as a matrix of 5×5 lanes of 64 bits, order from left to right, where each lane is given in hexadecimal using the little-endian format. The symbol '-' is used in order to denote a zero 4-bit value.

```
|---------------1|----------------|----------------|------8---------|----------------|
|----------------|----------------|---------1------|------8---------|----------------|
|---------------1|----------------|---------1------|----------------|----------------| R0
|----------------|----------------|----------------|----------------|----------------|
|----------------|----------------|----------------|----------------|----------------|
                                  ↓L
|---------------1|----------------|---------------8|----------------|----------------|
|---------------8|----------------|---------------8|----------------|----------------|
|----------------|-------4------|----------------|----------------|----------------|
|----------------|----------------|----------------|----------------|----------------|
|----------------|-------4------|----------------|----------------|----------------|
                                  ↓χ (p = 2⁻¹¹)
|---------------1|----------------|---------------8|----------------|----------------|
|----------------|----------------|---------------8|----------------|----------------|
|----------------|-------4------|----------------|----------------|----------------|
|----------------|----------------|----------------|----------------|----------------|
|----------------|-------4------|----------------|----------------|----------------|
                                  ↓ι
|----------------|----------------|---------------8|----------------|----------------|
|----------------|----------------|---------------8|----------------|----------------|
|----------------|-------4------|--              |----------------|----------------| R1
|----------------|----------------|----------------|----------------|----------------|
|----------------|-------4------|----------------|----------------|----------------|
                                  ↓L
|----------------|----------------|----------------|----------------|----------------|
|----------------|----------------|----------------|----------------|----------------|
|----------------|----------2--|----------------|----------------|----------------|
|----------------|-------1------|----------------|----------------|----------------|
|---------------2|----------------|----------------|----------------|-------1--------|
                                  ↓χ (p = 2⁻⁸)
|----------------|----------------|----------------|----------------|----------------|
|----------------|----------------|----------------|----------------|----------------|
|----------------|----------2--|----------------|----------------|----------------|
|----------------|-------1------|----------------|----------------|----------------|
|---------------2|----------------|----------------|----------------|-------1--------|
                                  ↓ι
|---------8-82|----------------|----------------|----------------|----------------|
|----------------|----------------|----------------|----------------|----------------|
|----------------|----------2--|----------------|----------------|----------------| R2
|----------------|-------1------|----------------|----------------|----------------|
|---------------2|----------------|----------------|----------------|-------1--------|
                                  ↓L
|-------1----8482|-----8-8-828-8-8|--1-------------|--6-2-2-2-2-2-2-|----4---4-4-----|
|--2-2-2-2-2-2-3-|------1-1-------|-------8----2---|----1-1-1-5-1-1-|---------------4-|
|-----4-----1-1--|----------8---|--4-4-4-4-4-4-6|---------1-1----|---4----1--8----| R2.5
|-----8-8--------|----4---------|---1--|---8-----2-a----|--8------1------|-------1-2------|
|----------------8-|--------81-----|--8-8-----------|---8---------2--|----8----2-2--|
```

The characteristic has a period of $i = 8$ for the 4-round attack on SHA3-384 and SHAKE256, as described in Section 6.1.

Characteristic 1: The 2.5-round internal differential characteristic with probability 2^{-19} and $(k_1, k_2, k_3) = (11, 8, 78)$.

```
|----------------|----------------1--1-|----------------|---------2--2--|----------------|
|----------------|----------------1--1-|----------------|---------2--2--|----------------|
|----------------|----------------|----------------|----------------|----------------| R0
|----------------|----------------|----------------|----------------|----------------|
|----------------|----------------|----------------|----------------|----------------|
                                    ↓L
|----------------|----------------1---1|----------------|----------------|----------------|
|----------2--2-|----------------|----------------|----------------|----------------|
|----------2--2-|----------------|----------------|----------------|----------------|
|----------------|----------------|----------------|----------------|----------------|
|----------------|----------------1--1|----------------|----------------|----------------|
                                    ↓χ  (p = 2^{-16})
|----------------1|----------------1---1|----------------|----------------|----------------|
|----------2--2-|----------------|----------------|----------------|----------------|
|----------2--2-|----------------|----------------|----------------|----------------|
|----------------|----------------|----------------|----------------|----------------|
|----------------|----------------1--1|----------------|----------------|----------------|
                                    ↓ι
|----------------|----------------1--1|----------------|----------------|----------------|
|----------2--2-|----------------|----------------|----------------|----------------|
|----------2--2-|----------------|----------------|----------------|----------------| R1
|----------------|----------------|----------------|----------------|----------------|
|----------------|----------------1--1|----------------|----------------|----------------|
                                    ↓L
|----------------|----------------|----------------|----------------|----------------|
|----------------|----------------|---------1--1--|----------------|----------------|
|----------2---2|----------------|----------------|----------------|----------------|
|----------------|----------2--2--|----------------|----------------|----------------|
|----------------|----------------|----------------|----------------|---------4---4|
                                    ↓χ  (p = 2^{-16})
|----------------|----------------|----------------|----------------|----------------|
|----------------|----------------|---------1--1--|----------------|----------------|
|----------2---2|----------------|----------------|----------------|----------------|
|----------------|----------2--2--|----------------|----------------|----------------|
|----------------|----------------|----------------|----------------|---------4---4|
                                    ↓ι
|----------8-82|----------------|----------------|----------------|----------------|
|----------------|----------------|---------1--1--|----------------|----------------|
|----------2---2|----------------|----------------|----------------|----------------| R2
|----------------|----------2--2--|----------------|----------------|----------------|
|----------------|----------------|----------------|----------------|---------4---4|
                                    ↓L
|---------4-48486|--------2828--2-|----------------1---1-|--------21--21--|--------4-41----|
|--------8-1-8-1-|--------1-----5-|--------2-3-2-3-|--------5-1----|---------4---4-| R2.5
|--------4-5-5--|--------c---c---|--------1--21--2|---------5-1----|-------1-1-1-1-|
|----------28-8|--------4-4-4-4-|--------a-a---8|---------1---1--|---------8-1-8-1|
|--------8---8-|--------84--84--|---------28-8---|---------8-8-8-8|---------8-a-a--|
```

The characteristic has a period of $i = 32$ for the 4-round attack on SHA3-512, as described in Section 6.2.

Characteristic 2: The 2.5-round internal differential characteristic with probability 2^{-32} and $(k_1, k_2, k_3) = (16, 16, 170)$.

```
|--------746a-114|--------b8e2-1a-|--------624---5a|--------6d58-4fd|--------858c-255|
|--------f46a-116|--------b8f2-1e-|--------6642--5a|--------6d58-4f5|--------858c-255|
|--------f46a-116|--------b8e2-1e-|--------6242--5a|--------6d58-4f5|--------858c-255| R1
|--------f46a-156|--------b8e2-1e-|--------6242--5a|--------6d58--f5|--------858c-255|
|--------f46a-116|--------b8e2-1e-|--------6246--5a|--------6d58-4f5|--------858e-257|
```
$$\downarrow L$$
```
|--------8------2|---------------1|----------------|-------8--------|-------8---8---|
|--------8-------|----------------|----------------|----------------|----------8---|
|------------8---|---------------1|----------------|----------------|----------------|
|----------------|----------------|----------------|----------------|----------------|
|--------8----|----------------|----------------|-------8---|----------------|
```
$$\downarrow \chi \ (p = 2^{-21})$$
```
|--------8------2|---------------1|----------------|----------------|----------8---|
|--------8-------|----------------|----------------|----------------|----------8---|
|------------8---|---------------1|----------------|----------------|----------------|
|----------------|----------------|----------------|----------------|----------------|
|--------8----|----------------|----------------|----------------|----------------|
```
$$\downarrow \iota$$
```
|--------8---8-8-|---------------1|----------------|----------------|----------8---|
|--------8-------|----------------|----------------|----------------|----------8---|
|----------8----|---------------1|----------------|----------------|----------------| R2
|----------------|----------------|----------------|----------------|----------------|
|--------8----|----------------|----------------|----------------|----------------|
```
$$\downarrow L$$
```
|--------8---8-8-|----------------|----------------|----------------|----------------|
|----------------|--------------8|----------4--|----------------|----------------|
|--------------2|----------------|----------------|----------------|--------------2|
|--------------4--|--------------8|----------4--|----------------|----------------|
|----------------|----------------|----------------|----------------|----------------|
```
$$\downarrow \chi \ (p = 2^{-18})$$
```
|--------8---8-8-|----------------|----------------|----------------|----------------|
|--------------8|--------------8|----------4--|----------------|----------------|
|--------------2|----------------|----------------|----------------|----------------|
|----------------|--------------8|----------4--|----------------|----------------|
|----------------|----------------|----------------|----------------|----------------|
```
$$\downarrow \iota$$
```
|--------------a|----------------|----------------|----------------|----------------|
|--------------8|--------------8|----------4--|----------------|----------------|
|--------------2|----------------|----------------|----------------|----------------| R3
|----------------|--------------8|----------4--|----------------|----------------|
|----------------|----------------|----------------|----------------|----------------|
```
$$\downarrow L$$
```
|--------------a|--------8---|----------------|----------------|----------------|
|----------------|----------------|----------1-|----------1---|----------------|
|----------------|----------1---|----------------|----------------|----------------| R3.5
|----------------|--------8-|----------------|--------2-----|----------------|
|----------------|----------------|----------------|----------------|----------------|
```

The characteristic has a period of $i = 32$ for the 5-round attack on SHA3-224, SHA3-256, SHAKE128 and SHAKE256, as described in Section 6.3.

Characteristic 3: The 1-3.5 round internal differential characteristic with probability 2^{-39} and $(k_2, k_3, k_4) = (21, 18, 16)$.

B   Appendix: Difference Conditions Table of KECCAK Sbox

Here we list the differential transition conditions of non-zero input differences (Table 7).

Table 7. Difference Conditions Table of KECCAK Sbox

δ_{out}	Differential transition conditions
01	$l_0 = x_4, l_1 = x_1$
02	$l_0 = x_0, l_1 = x_2$
03	$l_0 = x_4, l_1 = x_2, l_2 = x_0 + x_1$
04	$l_0 = x_1, l_1 = x_3$
05	$l_0 = x_4, l_1 = x_3, l_2 = x_1$
06	$l_0 = x_0, l_1 = x_3, l_2 = x_1 + x_2$
07	$l_0 = x_4, l_1 = x_3, l_2 = x_1 + x_2, l_3 = x_0 + x_1$
08	$l_0 = x_2, l_1 = x_4$
09	$l_0 = x_2, l_1 = x_1, l_2 = x_4$
0a	$l_0 = x_0, l_1 = x_4, l_2 = x_2$
0b	$l_0 = x_4, l_1 = x_2, l_2 = x_0 + x_1$
0c	$l_0 = x_1, l_1 = x_4, l_2 = x_2 + x_3$
0d	$l_0 = x_1, l_1 = x_4, l_2 = x_2 + x_3$
0e	$l_0 = x_0, l_1 = x_4, l_2 = x_2 + x_3, l_3 = x_1 + x_2$
0f	$l_0 = x_4, l_1 = x_2 + x_3, l_2 = x_1 + x_2, l_3 = x_0 + x_1$
10	$l_0 = x_3, l_1 = x_0$
11	$l_0 = x_3, l_1 = x_1, l_2 = x_4 + x_0$
12	$l_0 = x_3, l_1 = x_2, l_2 = x_0$
13	$l_0 = x_3, l_1 = x_2, l_2 = x_0 + x_1, l_3 = x_4 + x_0$
14	$l_0 = x_1, l_1 = x_0, l_2 = x_3$
15	$l_0 = x_3, l_1 = x_1, l_2 = x_4 + x_0$
16	$l_0 = x_0, l_1 = x_3, l_2 = x_1 + x_2$
17	$l_0 = x_3, l_1 = x_1 + x_2, l_2 = x_0 + x_1, l_3 = x_4 + x_0$
18	$l_0 = x_2, l_1 = x_0, l_2 = x_3 + x_4$
19	$l_0 = x_2, l_1 = x_1, l_2 = x_4 + x_0, l_3 = x_3 + x_4$
1a	$l_0 = x_2, l_1 = x_0, l_2 = x_3 + x_4$
1b	$l_0 = x_2, l_1 = x_0 + x_1, l_2 = x_4 + x_0, l_3 = x_3 + x_4$
1c	$l_0 = x_1, l_1 = x_0, l_2 = x_3 + x_4, l_3 = x_2 + x_3$
1d	$l_0 = x_1, l_1 = x_4 + x_0, l_2 = x_3 + x_4, l_3 = x_2 + x_3$
1e	$l_0 = x_0, l_1 = x_3 + x_4, l_2 = x_2 + x_3, l_3 = x_1 + x_2$
1f	$l_0 = x_3 + x_4, l_1 = x_2 + x_3, l_2 = x_1 + x_2, l_3 = x_0 + x_1$

C   Appendix: Values of Difference Conditions Table of Keccak Sbox

Here we list the values of differential transition conditions of some input differences, and the other input differences and their differential transition conditions' values can be obtained through cyclic shifting of existing input differences and conditions (Table 8).

Table 8. Values of Difference Conditions Table of Keccak Sbox

$01(<<< j)$	09			19			01			11		
l_0	0			0			1			1		
l_1	0			1			0			1		

$03(<<< j)$	0b	1b	0a	1a	03	13	02	12
l_0	0	0	0	0	1	1	1	1
l_1	0	0	1	1	0	0	1	1
l_2	0	1	0	1	0	1	0	1

$05(<<< j)$	0c	1d	0e	1f	04	15	06	17
l_0	0	0	0	0	1	1	1	1
l_1	0	0	1	1	0	0	1	1
l_2	0	1	0	1	0	1	0	1

$0b(<<< j)$	01	11	02	12	0d	1d	0e	1e
l_0	0	0	0	0	1	1	1	1
l_1	0	0	1	1	0	0	1	1
l_2	0	1	0	1	0	1	0	1

$07(<<< j)$	0f	1f	0e	1e	0d	1d	0c	1c	07	17	06	16	05	15	04	14
l_0	0	0	0	0	0	0	0	0	1	1	1	1	1	1	1	1
l_1	0	0	0	0	1	1	1	1	0	0	0	0	1	1	1	1
l_2	0	0	1	1	0	0	1	1	0	0	1	1	0	0	1	1
l_3	0	1	0	1	0	1	0	1	0	1	0	1	0	1	0	1

$0f(<<< j)$	07	17	06	16	05	15	04	14	0b	1b	0a	1a	09	19	08	18
l_0	0	0	0	0	0	0	0	0	1	1	1	1	1	1	1	1
l_1	0	0	0	0	1	1	1	1	0	0	0	0	1	1	1	1
l_2	0	0	1	1	0	0	1	1	0	0	1	1	0	0	1	1
l_3	0	1	0	1	0	1	0	1	0	1	0	1	0	1	0	1

1f	1f	07	16	0e	15	0d	1c	04	13	0b	1a	02	19	01	10	08
l_0	0	0	0	0	0	0	0	0	1	1	1	1	1	1	1	1
l_1	0	0	0	0	1	1	1	1	0	0	0	0	1	1	1	1
l_2	0	0	1	1	0	0	1	1	0	0	1	1	0	0	1	1
l_3	0	1	0	1	0	1	0	1	0	1	0	1	0	1	0	1

D   Appendix: 2D Affine Subspaces of KECCAK Sbox

Here we give the 2-dimensional affine subspaces and affine equations to the output differences of Sbox using in TIDA (Table 9).

Table 9. 2D Affine Subspaces of KECCAK Sbox

δ_{out}	2D affine subspaces	Corresponding linear equations
01	{01,11,09,19}	$x_0 = 1, x_2 = 0, x_3 = 0$
02	{02,12,03,13}	$x_1 = 1, x_2 = 0, x_3 = 0$
03	{02,12,09,19}	$x_2 = 0, x_0 + x_3 = 0, x_1 + x_3 = 1$
04	{04,06,05,07}	$x_2 = 1, x_3 = 0, x_4 = 0$
05	{04,06,19,1b}	$x_0 + x_2 = 1, x_0 + x_3 = 0, x_0 + x_4 = 0$
06	{04,12,05,13}	$x_3 = 0, x_1 + x_2 = 1, x_1 + x_4 = 0$
07	{04,12,19,0f}	$x_0 + x_3 = 0, x_2 + x_4 = 1, x_0 + x_1 + x_2 = 1$
08	{08,0c,0a,0e}	$x_0 = 0, x_3 = 1, x_4 = 0$
09	{01,11,0e,1e}	$x_0 + x_1 = 1, x_0 + x_2 = 1, x_0 + x_3 = 1$
0a	{08,0c,13,17}	$x_0 + x_1 = 0, x_0 + x_3 = 1, x_0 + x_4 = 0$
0b	{0c,0a,19,1f}	$x_3 = 1, x_0 + x_4 = 0, x_0 + x_1 + x_2 = 1$
0c	{08,0c,0a,0e}	$x_0 = 0, x_3 = 1, x_4 = 0$
0d	{0c,09,0b,0e}	$x_3 = 1, x_4 = 0, x_0 + x_2 = 1$
0e	{08,0c,1b,1f}	$x_3 = 1, x_0 + x_1 = 0, x_0 + x_4 = 0$
0f	{0c,0a,15,13}	$x_0 + x_3 = 1, x_0 + x_4 = 0, x_1 + x_2 = 1$
10	{10,18,14,1c}	$x_0 = 0, x_1 = 0, x_4 = 1$
11	{01,14,09,1c}	$x_1 = 0, x_0 + x_2 = 1, x_0 + x_4 = 1$
12	{02,03,1c,1d}	$x_1 + x_2 = 1, x_1 + x_3 = 1, x_1 + x_4 = 1$
13	{02,09,1c,17}	$x_1 + x_3 = 1, x_2 + x_4 = 0, x_0 + x_1 + x_2 = 1$
14	{10,18,07,0f}	$x_0 + x_1 = 0, x_0 + x_2 = 0, x_0 + x_4 = 1$
15	{06,05,1c,1f}	$x_2 = 1, x_3 + x_4 = 0, x_0 + x_1 + x_3 = 1$
16	{18,14,13,1f}	$x_4 = 1, x_0 + x_1 = 0, x_0 + x_2 + x_3 = 1$
17	{14,05,0d,1c}	$x_1 = 0, x_2 = 1, x_0 + x_4 = 1$
18	{10,0a,15,0f}	$x_0 + x_2 = 0, x_1 + x_3 = 0, x_1 + x_4 = 1$
19	{01,14,0e,1b}	$x_0 + x_2 = 1, x_1 + x_3 = 0, x_0 + x_1 + x_4 = 1$
1a	{18,12,16,1c}	$x_0 = 0, x_4 = 1, x_1 + x_3 = 1$
1b	{12,0a,16,0e}	$x_0 = 0, x_1 = 1, x_3 + x_4 = 1$
1c	{10,18,17,1f}	$x_4 = 1, x_0 + x_1 = 0, x_0 + x_2 = 0$
1d	{16,11,1b,1c}	$x_4 = 1, x_0 + x_2 = 1, x_0 + x_1 + x_3 = 1$
1e	{18,0b,0e,1d}	$x_3 = 1, x_1 + x_4 = 1, x_0 + x_1 + x_2 = 0$
1f	{14,05,0e,1f}	$x_2 = 1, x_1 + x_3 = 0, x_0 + x_1 + x_4 = 1$

References

1. Alagic, G., et al.: Status report on the third round of the NIST post-quantum cryptography standardization process. National Institute of Standards and Technology, Gaithersburg (2022)
2. Bernstein, D.J.: Second preimages for 6 (7? (8??)) rounds of Keccak. NIST mailing list (2010)
3. Bernstein, D.J., et al.: SPHINCS (2017)
4. Bertoni, G., Daemen, J., Peeters, M., Van Assche, G.: Keccak. In: Johansson, T., Nguyen, P.Q. (eds.) EUROCRYPT 2013. LNCS, vol. 7881, pp. 313–314. Springer, Heidelberg (2013). https://doi.org/10.1007/978-3-642-38348-9_19
5. Bertoni, G., Daemen, J., Peeters, M., Van Assche, G.: Keccak sponge function family main document. Submission to NIST (Round 2) **3**(30), 320–337 (2009)
6. Chang, D., Kumar, A., Morawiecki, P., Sanadhya, S.K.: 1st and 2nd preimage attacks on 7, 8 and 9 rounds of Keccak-224,256,384,512. In: SHA-3 Workshop (2014)
7. Dinur, I.: Improved algorithms for solving polynomial systems over GF(2) by multiple parity-counting. In: Marx, D. (ed.) Proceedings of the 2021 ACM-SIAM Symposium on Discrete Algorithms, SODA 2021, Virtual Conference, 10–13 January 2021, pp. 2550–2564. SIAM (2021). https://doi.org/10.1137/1.9781611976465.151
8. Dinur, I., Dunkelman, O., Shamir, A.: New attacks on Keccak-224 and Keccak-256. In: Canteaut, A. (ed.) FSE 2012. LNCS, vol. 7549, pp. 442–461. Springer, Heidelberg (2012). https://doi.org/10.1007/978-3-642-34047-5_25
9. Dinur, I., Dunkelman, O., Shamir, A.: Collision attacks on up to 5 rounds of SHA-3 using generalized internal differentials. In: Moriai, S. (ed.) FSE 2013. LNCS, vol. 8424, pp. 219–240. Springer, Heidelberg (2014). https://doi.org/10.1007/978-3-662-43933-3_12
10. Dinur, I., Dunkelman, O., Shamir, A.: Improved practical attacks on round-reduced Keccak. J. Cryptol. **27**(2), 183–209 (2014)
11. Dworkin, M.J.: SHA-3 Standard: Permutation-Based Hash and Extendable-Output Functions (2015). https://doi.org/10.6028/nist.fips.202
12. Guo, J., Liao, G., Liu, G., Liu, M., Qiao, K., Song, L.: Practical collision attacks against round-reduced SHA-3. J. Cryptol. **33**(1), 228–270 (2019). https://doi.org/10.1007/s00145-019-09313-3
13. Guo, J., Liu, G., Song, L., Tu, Y.: Exploring SAT for cryptanalysis: (Quantum) collision attacks against 6-Round SHA-3. In: Agrawal, S., Lin, D. (eds.) Advances in Cryptology-ASIACRYPT 2022: 28th International Conference on the Theory and Application of Cryptology and Information Security, Taipei, Taiwan, 5–9 December 2022, Proceedings, Part III, pp. 645–674. Springer, Cham (2023). https://doi.org/10.1007/978-3-031-22969-5_22
14. Guo, J., Liu, M., Song, L.: Linear structures: applications to cryptanalysis of round-reduced KECCAK. In: Cheon, J.H., Takagi, T. (eds.) ASIACRYPT 2016. LNCS, vol. 10031, pp. 249–274. Springer, Heidelberg (2016). https://doi.org/10.1007/978-3-662-53887-6_9
15. Huang, S., Ben-Yehuda, O.A., Dunkelman, O., Maximov, A.: Finding collisions against 4-round SHA3-384 in practical time. IACR Trans. Symmetric Cryptol. **2022**, 239–270 (2022)
16. Li, T., Sun, Y.: Preimage attacks on round-reduced KECCAK-224/256 via an allocating approach. In: Ishai, Y., Rijmen, V. (eds.) EUROCRYPT 2019. LNCS, vol. 11478, pp. 556–584. Springer, Cham (2019). https://doi.org/10.1007/978-3-030-17659-4_19

17. Nishimura, K., Sibuya, M.: Probability to meet in the middle. J. Cryptol. **2**(1), 13–22 (1990)
18. Peyrin, T.: Improved differential attacks for ECHO and Grostl. IACR Cryptol. ePrint Arch 2010, 223 (2010). eprint.iacr.org/2010/223
19. Qiao, K., Song, L., Liu, M., Guo, J.: New collision attacks on round-reduced Keccak. In: Coron, J.-S., Nielsen, J.B. (eds.) EUROCRYPT 2017. LNCS, vol. 10212, pp. 216–243. Springer, Cham (2017). https://doi.org/10.1007/978-3-319-56617-7_8
20. Song, L., Liao, G., Guo, J.: Non-full Sbox linearization: applications to collision attacks on round-reduced Keccak. In: Katz, J., Shacham, H. (eds.) Advances in Cryptology - CRYPTO 2017–37th Annual International Cryptology Conference, Santa Barbara, CA, USA, August 20–24, 2017, Proceedings, Part II. LNCS, vol. 10402, pp. 428–451. Springer, Cham (2017). https://doi.org/10.1007/978-3-319-63715-0_15

Symmetric Designs

From Farfalle to MEGAFONO via Ciminion: The PRF HYDRA for MPC Applications

Lorenzo Grassi[1], Morten Øygarden[2], Markus Schofnegger[3], and Roman Walch[4,5,6(✉)]

[1] Radboud University Nijmegen, Nijmegen, The Netherlands
lgrassi@science.ru.nl
[2] Simula UiB, Bergen, Norway
morten.oygarden@simula.no
[3] Horizen Labs, Austin, USA
mschofnegger@horizenlabs.io
[4] Graz University of Technology, Graz, Austria
roman.walch@iaik.tugraz.at
[5] Know-Center GmbH, Graz, Austria
[6] TACEO GmbH, Graz, Austria

Abstract. The area of multi-party computation (MPC) has recently increased in popularity and number of use cases. At the current state of the art, Ciminion, a Farfalle-like cryptographic function, achieves the best performance in MPC applications involving symmetric primitives. However, it has a critical weakness. Its security highly relies on the independence of its subkeys, which is achieved by using an expensive key schedule. Many MPC use cases involving symmetric pseudo-random functions (PRFs) rely on secretly shared symmetric keys, and hence the expensive key schedule must also be computed in MPC. As a result, Ciminion's performance is significantly reduced in these use cases.

In this paper we solve this problem. Following the approach introduced by Ciminion's designers, we present a novel primitive in symmetric cryptography called MEGAFONO. MEGAFONO is a keyed extendable PRF, expanding a fixed-length input to an arbitrary-length output. Similar to Farfalle, an initial keyed permutation is applied to the input, followed by an expansion layer, involving the parallel application of keyed ciphers. The main novelty regards the expansion of the intermediate/internal state for "free", by appending the sum of the internal states of the first permutation to its output. The combination of this and other modifications, together with the impossibility for the attacker to have access to the input state of the expansion layer, make MEGAFONO very efficient in the target application.

As a concrete example, we present the PRF HYDRA, an instance of MEGAFONO based on the HADES strategy and on generalized versions of the Lai–Massey scheme. Based on an extensive security analysis, we implement HYDRA in an MPC framework. The results show that it outperforms all MPC-friendly schemes currently published in the literature.

Keywords: MEGAFONO · HYDRA · Farfalle · Ciminion · MPC Applications

© International Association for Cryptologic Research 2023
C. Hazay and M. Stam (Eds.): EUROCRYPT 2023, LNCS 14007, pp. 255–286, 2023.
https://doi.org/10.1007/978-3-031-30634-1_9

1 Introduction

Secure multi-party computation (MPC) allows several parties to jointly and securely compute a function on their combined private inputs. The correct output is computed and given to all parties (or a subset) while hiding the private inputs from other parties. In this work we focus on secret-sharing based MPC schemes, such as the popular SPDZ protocol [23,24] or protocols based on Shamir's secret sharing [47]. In these protocols private data is shared among all parties, such that each party receives a share which by itself does not contain any information about the initial data. When combined, however, the parties are able to reproduce the shared value. Further, the parties can use these shares to compute complex functions on the data which in turn produce shares of the output.

MPC has been applied to many use cases, including privacy-preserving machine learning [46], private set intersection [40], truthful auctions [13], and revocation in credential systems [38]. In the literature describing these use cases, data is often directly entered from and delivered to the respective parties. However, in practice this data often has to be transferred securely from/to third parties before it can be used in the MPC protocol. Moreover, in some applications, intermediate results of an MPC computation may need to be stored securely in a database. As described in [35], one can use MPC-friendly pseudo-random functions (PRFs), i.e., PRFs designed to be efficient in MPC, to efficiently realize this secure data storage and data transfer by directly encrypting the data using a secret-shared symmetric key.

Besides being used to securely transmit data in given MPC computations, these MPC-friendly PRFs can also be used as a building block to speed up many MPC applications, such as secure database join via an MPC evaluation of a PRF [44], distributed data storage [35], virtual hardware security modules[1], MPC-in-the-head based zero-knowledge proofs [39] and signatures [16], oblivious TLS [1], and many more. *In all these use cases, the symmetric encryption key is shared among all participating parties. Consequently, if one has to apply a key schedule for a given PRF, one has to compute this key schedule at least once in MPC for every fresh symmetric key.*

To be MPC-friendly, a PRF should minimize the number of multiplications in the native field of the MPC protocol. At the current state of the art, Ciminion [26] is one of the most competitive schemes for PRF applications. Proposed at Eurocrypt'21, it is based on the Farfalle mode of operation [10]. However, as we are going to discuss in detail, Ciminion has a serious drawback: *Its security heavily relies on the assumption that the subkeys are independent.* For this requirement, the subkeys are generated via a sponge hash function [11] instantiated via an expensive permutation. As a result, in all (common) cases where the key is shared among the parties, the key schedule cannot be computed locally and needs to be evaluated in MPC. This leads to a significant increase in the multiplicative complexity of Ciminion. In this paper, we approach this problem in two steps. First, we propose MEGAFONO, a new mode of operation inspired by

---

[1] https://www.fintechfutures.com/files/2020/09/vHSM-Whitepaper-v3.pdf.

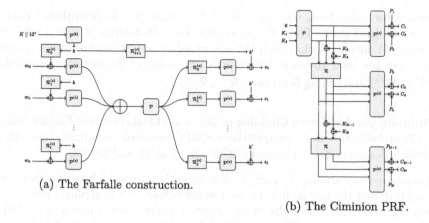

(a) The Farfalle construction.

(b) The Ciminion PRF.

Fig. 1. Farfalle and Ciminion (notation adapted to the one used in this paper).

Farfalle and Ciminion.[2] It is designed to be competitive in all MPC applications. Secondly, we show how to instantiate it in an efficient way. The obtained PRF HYDRA is currently the most competitive MPC-friendly PRF in the literature.

1.1   Related Works: Ciminion and the MPC Protocols

Traditional PRFs (e.g., AES, KECCAK) are not efficient in MPC settings. First, MPC applications usually work over a prime field $\mathbb{F}_p$ for a large p (e.g., $p \approx 2^{128}$), while traditional cryptographic schemes are usually bit-/byte-oriented. Hence, a conversion between $\mathbb{F}_{2^n}$ and $\mathbb{F}_p$ must take place, which can impact the performance. Secondly, traditional schemes are designed to minimize their plain implementation cost, and therefore no particular focus is laid on minimizing specifically the number of nonlinear operations (e.g., AND gates).

For these reasons, several MPC-friendly schemes over $\mathbb{F}_q^t$ for $q = p^s$ and $t \geq 1$ have been proposed in the literature, including LowMC [4], MiMC [3], GMiMC [2], HADESMiMC [32], and *Rescue* [5]. All those schemes are block ciphers – hence, invertible – and they are often used in counter (CTR) mode. However, invertibility is not required in MPC applications, and a lower multiplicative complexity may be achieved by working with non-invertible functions, as recently shown by in [26]. In the following, we briefly discuss the Farfalle construction and the MPC-friendly primitive Ciminion based on it.

Farfalle. Farfalle [10] is an efficiently parallelizable permutation-based construction of arbitrary input and output length, taking as input a key. As shown in Fig. 1a and recalled in Sect. 3, the Farfalle construction consists of a *compression layer* followed by an *expansion layer*. The compression layer produces a single

---

[2] "Megafono" is the Italian word for "megaphone", a cone-shaped horn used to amplify a sound and direct it towards a given direction. Our strategy resembles this goal.

accumulator value from the input data. A permutation is potentially applied to the obtained state. Then, the expansion layer transforms it into a tuple of (truncated) output blocks. Both the compression and expansion layers involve the secret key, and they are instantiated via a set of permutations (namely, $\mathcal{P}^{(c)}, \mathcal{P}, \mathcal{P}^{(e)}$) and rolling functions ($\mathcal{R}_i^{(c)}, \mathcal{R}_i^{(e)}$).

Ciminion. As shown with Ciminion in [26], a modified version of Farfalle based on a Feistel scheme can be competitive for MPC protocols, an application which Farfalle's designers did not consider. Following Fig. 1b and Sect. 3,

(1) compared to Farfalle, the compression phase is missing, a final truncation is applied, and the key addition is performed before $\mathcal{P}^{(e)}$ is applied, and
(2) in contrast to MPC-friendly block ciphers, Ciminion is a *non-invertible* PRF. For encryption it is used as a stream cipher, where the input is defined as the concatenation of the secret key and a nonce.

The main reason why Ciminion is currently the most competitive scheme in MPC protocols is related to one crucial feature of Farfalle, namely the possibility to instantiate its internal permutations with a smaller number of rounds compared to other design strategies. This is possible since the attacker does not have access to the internal states of the Farfalle construction. Hence, while the permutation $\mathcal{P}^{(c)}$ is designed in order to behave like a pseudo-random permutation (PRP), the number of rounds of the permutation $\mathcal{P}^{(e)}$ can be minimized and kept significantly lower for both security and good performance.

Besides minimizing the number of nonlinear operations, Ciminion's designers paid particular attention to the number of linear operations. Indeed, even though the main cost in MPC applications depends on the number of multiplications, other factors (e.g., the number of linear operations) affect efficiency as well.

1.2   The MEGAFONO Design Strategy

The main drawback of Ciminion is the expensive key schedule to generate subkeys that can be considered independent. This implies that Ciminion only excels in MPC applications where the key schedule can be precomputed for a given shared key, or in the (non-common) scenarios where the key is not shared among the parties. However, in the latter case, the party knowing the key can also compute Ciminion's keystream directly in plain (i.e., without MPC) if the nonce and IV are public in a given use case (which is also true for any stream cipher).

Clearly, the easiest solution is the removal of the nonlinear key schedule. However, by e.g. defining the subkey as an affine function of the master key, the security analysis of Ciminion does not hold anymore. As we discuss in detail in Sect. 4, this is a direct consequence of the Farfalle construction itself. Even if the attacker does not have any information about the internal states of Farfalle, they can exploit the fact that its outputs are generated from the **same** unknown input (namely, the output of $\mathcal{P}^{(c)}$ and/or $\mathcal{P}$). Given these outputs and by exploiting the relations of the corresponding unknown inputs (which are related to the definition of the rolling function), the attacker can potentially find the key and break the scheme. For example, this strategy is exploited in the attacks on the Farfalle schemes KRAVATTE and Xoofff [15,19]. In Ciminion, this problem is solved by including additions with independent secret subkeys in the application of the rolling function. In this way, the mentioned relation is unknown due to the presence of the key, and $\mathcal{P}^{(e)}$ can be instantiated via an efficient permutation.

We make the following three crucial changes in the Farfalle design strategy.

1. First, we replace the permutation $\mathcal{P}^{(e)}$ with a keyed permutation $\mathcal{C}_k$.
2. Secondly, we expand the input of this keyed permutation. The second change aims to frustrate algebraic attacks, whose cost is related to both the degree and the number of variables of the nonlinear equation system representing the attacked scheme. In order to create new independent variables for "free" (i.e., without increasing the overall multiplicative complexity), we reuse the computations needed to evaluate $\mathcal{P}$. That is, we define the new variable as the sum of all the internal state of $\mathcal{P}$, and we conjecture that it is sufficiently independent of its output (details are provided in the following).
3. Finally, we replace the truncation in Ciminion with a feed-forward operation, for avoiding to discard any randomness without any impact on the security.

Our result is a new design strategy which we call MEGAFONO.

1.3   The PRF HYDRA

Given the mode of operation, we instantiate it with two distinct permutations, one for the initial phase and one for the expansion phase. As in Ciminion, assuming the first keyed permutation behaves like a PRP and since the attacker does not know the internal states of MEGAFONO, we choose a second permutation that is cheaper to evaluate in the MPC setting. In particular, while the first permutation is evaluated only once, the number of calls to the second permutation (and so the overall cost) is proportional to the output size.

For minimizing the multiplicative complexity, we instantiate the round functions of the keyed permutations $\mathcal{C}_k$ in the expansion part with quadratic functions. However, since no quadratic function is invertible over $\mathbb{F}_p$, we use them in a mode of operation that guarantees invertibility. We opted for the generalized Lai–Massey constructions similar to the ones recently proposed in [33]. Moreover, we show that the approach of using of high-degree power maps with low-degree inverses proposed in *Rescue* does not have any benefits in this scenario.

We instantiate the first permutation $\mathcal{P}$ via the HADES strategy [32], which mixes rounds with full S-box layers and rounds with partial S-box layers. Similar to NEPTUNE [33], we use two different round functions, one for the internal part and one for the external one. We decided to instantiate the internal rounds with a Lai–Massey scheme, and the external ones with invertible power maps.

The obtained PRF scheme called HYDRA is presented in Sect. 5 and Sect. 6, and its security analysis is proposed in Sect. 7.

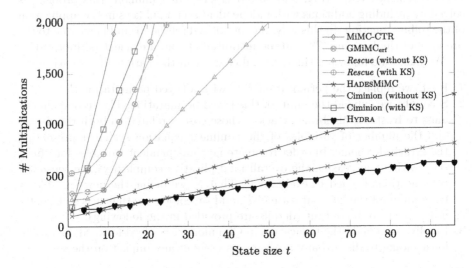

Fig. 2. Number of MPC multiplications of several designs over $\mathbb{F}_p^t$, with $p \approx 2^{128}$ and $t \geq 2$ (security level of 128 bits).

1.4 MPC Performance and Comparison

The performance of any MPC calculation scales with the number of nonlinear operations. In Fig. 2 we compare the number of multiplications required to evaluate different PRFs for various plaintext sizes t using secret shared keys. One can observe that HYDRA requires the smallest number of multiplications, with the difference growing further for larger sizes. The only PRF that is competitive to HYDRA is Ciminion, but only *if the key schedule does not have to be computed*, which happens if shared round keys can be reused from a previous computation. However, this implies that the key schedule was already computed once in MPC, requiring a significant amount of multiplications. HYDRA, on the other hand, does not require the computation of an expensive key schedule and also requires fewer multiplications than Ciminion without a key schedule for larger state sizes.

In Sect. 8, we implement and compare the different PRFs in the MP-SPDZ [41] library and confirm the results expected from Fig. 2. Indeed,

(1) taking key schedules into account, HYDRA is five times faster than Ciminion for $t = 8$, which grows to a factor of 21 for $t = 128$,

(2) without key schedules, Ciminion is only slightly faster than HYDRA for smaller t, until it gets surpassed by HYDRA for $t > 16$, showing that HYDRA is also competitive, even if the round keys are already present.

Compared to all other benchmarked PRFs, HYDRA is significantly faster for any state size t. Furthermore, HYDRA requires the least amount of communication between the parties due to its small number of multiplications, giving it an advantage in low-bandwidth networks. As a result, we suggest to replace each of the benchmarked PRFs with HYDRA in all their use cases, especially if a large number of words need to be encrypted.

1.5   Notation

Throughout the paper, we work over a finite field $\mathbb{F}_q$, where $q = p^s$ for an odd prime number p and an integer $s \geq 1$ (when needed, we will also assume a fixed vector space isomorphism $\mathbb{F}_{p^s} \cong \mathbb{F}_p^s$). We use $\mathbb{F}_q^n$, for $n \geq 1$, to denote the n-dimensional vector space over $\mathbb{F}_q$, and we use the notation $\mathbb{F}_q^\star$ to denote $\mathbb{F}_q$ strings of arbitrary length. The $\cdot \parallel \cdot$ operator denotes the concatenation of two elements. An element $x \in \mathbb{F}_q^t$ is represented as $x = (x_0, x_1, \ldots, x_{t-1})$, where x_i denotes its i-th entry. Given a matrix $M \in \mathbb{F}_q^{t \times s}$, we denote its entry in row r and column c either as $M_{r,c}$ or $M[r, c]$. We use the Fraktur font notation to denote a subspace of $\mathbb{F}_q^r$, while we sometimes use the calligraphic notation to emphasize functions. Given integers $a \geq b \geq 1$, we define the truncation function $\mathcal{T}_{a,b} : \mathbb{F}_q^a \to \mathbb{F}_q^b$ as $\mathcal{T}_{a,b}(x_0, \ldots, x_{a-1}) = (x_0, \ldots, x_{b-1})$. Finally, for MPC, we describe that the value $x \in \mathbb{F}_p$ is secret shared among all parties by $[x]$.

2   Symmetric Primitives for MPC Applications

Here we elaborate on why expensive key schedules are not desirable in many MPC use cases, and we discuss the cost metric in MPC protocols in more details.

2.1   MPC Use Cases and Key Schedules

To highlight that expensive key schedules are not suitable for many scenarios, we describe the use cases discussed in [26] and [35] in greater detail. Concretely, we discuss the data transfer into and out of the MPC protocol, as well as using symmetric PRFs to securely store intermediate results during an MPC evaluation. In the latter case, the setting is the following: The parties want to suspend the MPC evaluation and continue at a later point. As discussed in [35], the trivial solution for this problem is that each party encrypts its share of the data with a symmetric key and stores the encrypted share, e.g., at a cloud provider. The total storage overhead of this approach is a factor n for n MPC parties, since each party stores its encrypted shares of the data. Additionally, each party needs to memorize its symmetric key. The solution to reduce the storage overhead is to use a secret shared symmetric key (i.e., each party knows only a share of the key and the real symmetric key remains hidden), which can directly be sampled as part of the MPC protocol, and encrypt the data using MPC. The resulting ciphertexts cannot be decrypted by any party since no one knows the symmetric key, but can be used inside the MPC protocols at a later point to again create the shares of the data. This approach avoids the storage overhead of the data, and each party only has to memorize its share of the symmetric key which has the same size as the symmetric key itself. However, if the used PRF involves a key schedule, one also has to compute it in MPC for this use case. Other solutions either involve precomputing the round keys, or directly sampling random round keys in MPC instead of sampling a random symmetric key. These approaches require no storage overhead for the encrypted data, but each party needs to memorize its shares of the round keys. In Ciminion, the size of the round keys is equivalent to the size of the encrypted data (when using the same nonce for encrypting the full dataset), hence the whole protocol would be more efficient if each party would just memorize its shares of the dataset instead. Providing fewer round keys and using multiple nonces instead requires the recomputation of Ciminion's initial permutation in MPC, decreasing its performance.

Similar considerations also apply if the MPC parties are different from the actual data providers or if the output of the computation needs to be securely transferred to an external party. The solutions to both problems involve storing the dataset encrypted at some public place (e.g., in a cloud) alongside a public-key encryption of the shares of the symmetric key, such that only the intended recipient can get the shares. If the parties want to avoid expensive key schedules in MPC, they either have to provide shares of the round keys (which have the same size as the encrypted data in Ciminion), or provide fewer round keys alongside multiple nonces, decreasing the performance in MPC.

Remark 1. In this paper, we focus on comparing MPC-friendly PRFs which are optimized for similar use cases as the ones discussed in this section, i.e., use cases which require fast MPC en-/decryption of large amounts of data. Hence, we do not focus on PRFs not defined over $\mathbb{F}_p$ which are optimized for, e.g., Picnic-style signatures, such as LowMC [4], Rain [27], or weakPRF [25].

2.2   Cost Metric for MPC Applications

Modern MPC protocols such as SPDZ [23,24] are usually split into a data-independent *offline phase* and a data-dependent *online phase*. In the offline phase, a bundle of shared correlated randomness is generated, most notably Beaver triples [9] of the form $([a], [b], [a \cdot b])$. This bundle is then used in the online phase to perform the actual computation on the private data.

Roughly speaking, the performance scales with the number of nonlinear operations necessary to evaluate the symmetric primitives in the MPC protocol (sometimes we use the term "multiplication" to refer to the nonlinear operation). This is motivated by the fact that each multiplication requires one Beaver triple, which is computed in the offline phase, as well as one round of communication during the online phase (see [34, Appendix D]. In contrast, linear operations do not require any offline computations and can directly be applied to the shares without communication. Consequently, the number of multiplications is a decent first estimation of the cost metric in MPC, and MPC-friendly PRFs usually try to minimize this number. Whereas each multiplication requires communication between the parties, the depth directly defines the required number of communication rounds, since parallel multiplications can be processed in the same round. Thus, the depth should be low in high-latency networks. To summarize,

- the cost of the offline phase of the MPC protocols directly scales with the number of required Beaver triples (i.e., multiplications), and
- the cost of the online phase scales with both the number of multiplications and the multiplicative depth.

As a concrete example, in many MPC-friendly PRFs, such as HADESMiMC, MiMC, GMiMC, and *Rescue*, the nonlinear layer is instantiated with a power map $R(x) = x^d$ for $d \geq 2$ over $\mathbb{F}_q$. Then, the cost per evaluation is

$$\#\texttt{triples} = \texttt{cost}_d := \text{hw}(d) + \lfloor \log_2(d) \rfloor - 1 , \qquad \texttt{depth}_{\text{online}} = \texttt{cost}_d . \quad (1)$$

Several algorithms to reduce the number of multiplications and communication rounds were developed in the literature. Here we discuss those relevant for our goals. They require random pairs $[r], [r^2]$, and $[r], [r^{-1}]$, which can be generated from Beaver triples in the offline phase (see [34, Appendix D]).

Decreasing the Number of Online Communication Rounds. In the preferred case of $d = 3$, the cost is two Beaver triples and a depth of two. However, in [35] the authors propose a method to reduce the multiplicative depth by delegating the cubing operation to a random value in the offline phase. Hence, all cubings can be performed in parallel reducing the depth. This algorithm (see [34, Appendix D]) requires two triples, but only one online communication round.
Special Case: $R(x) = x^{1/d}$. Optimizations can also be applied for the case $R(x) = x^d$ with very large d. In [5], the authors propose two different algorithms to evaluate R (see [34, Appendix D]), in which the cost of evaluating $R(x) = x^d$ can be reduced to the cost of evaluating $R(x) = x^{1/d}$ (plus an additional multiplication in the online phase) which requires significantly fewer multiplications if $1/d$ is smaller than d. This is, for example, relevant when evaluating *Rescue* with its high-degree power maps in MPC. The algorithm works by delegating the $1/d$ power map evaluation to the offline phase, and evaluating the costly d power map on a random value in plain. Furthermore, since the main MPC work (i.e., $1/d$) is evaluated in the input-independent offline phase, all communication rounds can be parallelized, significantly reducing the multiplicative depth. Using these algorithms and $\texttt{cost}_d$ from Eq. 1, the cost of evaluating x^d in MPC is modified to the following, with a significantly smaller multiplicative depth and a smaller number of multiplications for large d:

$$\#\texttt{triples} = 2 + \min\left\{\texttt{cost}_d, \texttt{cost}_{1/d}\right\} , \qquad \texttt{depth}_{\text{online}} = 2.$$

3   Starting Points of MEGAFONO: Farfalle and Ciminion

Here we recall Farfalle and Ciminion, which are starting points for MEGAFONO.

Farfalle and $^{1/2\times}$Farfalle. Farfalle is a keyed PRF proposed in [10] with inputs and outputs of arbitrary length. As shown in Fig. 1a, it has a compression layer and an expansion layer, each involving the parallel application of a permutation. For our goal, we focus only on the expansion phase, and introduce the term $^{1/2\times}$Farfalle for a modified version of Farfalle that lacks the initial compression phase and only accepts input messages of a fixed size n.

Let $\mathsf{K} \in \mathbb{F}_q^\kappa$ be the secret key for $\kappa \geq 1$. $^{1/2\times}$Farfalle uses a key schedule $\mathcal{K} : \mathbb{F}_q^\kappa \rightarrow (\mathbb{F}_q^n)^\star$ for the subkeys used in the expansion phase, two unkeyed permutations $\mathcal{P}, \mathcal{P}^{(e)} : \mathbb{F}_q^n \rightarrow \mathbb{F}_q^n$, and a rolling function $\mathcal{R} : \mathbb{F}_q^n \rightarrow \mathbb{F}_q^n$.[3] We define $\mathcal{R}_i$ as $\mathcal{R}_i(y) = \rho_i + \mathcal{R} \circ \mathcal{R}_{i-1}(y)$ for each $i \geq 1$ and $\rho_i \in \mathbb{F}_q^n$, where we assume $\mathcal{R}_0$ to be the identity function, i.e., $\mathcal{R}_0(y) = y$. Given an input $x \in \mathbb{F}_q$, $^{1/2\times}$Farfalle $: \mathbb{F}_q^n \rightarrow (\mathbb{F}_q^n)^\star$ operates as $^{1/2\times}$Farfalle$(x) = y_0 \parallel y_1 \parallel y_2 \parallel \cdots \parallel y_j \parallel \cdots$, where $\forall i \geq 0 : y_i := k_{i+1} + \mathcal{P}^{(e)}\left(\mathcal{R}_i\left(\mathcal{P}(x + k_0)\right)\right)$.

From $^{1/2\times}$Farfalle to Ciminion. Ciminion [26] is based on a modified version of $^{1/2\times}$Farfalle over $\mathbb{F}_q^n$ for a certain $n \geq 2$. As shown in Fig. 1b, the main difference with respect to $^{1/2\times}$Farfalle is the definition of the function $k + \mathcal{P}^{(e)}$. In Farfalle/$^{1/2\times}$Farfalle, the key addition is the last operation. In Ciminion, $k + \mathcal{P}^{(e)}(x)$ is replaced by $\mathcal{F}^{(e)}(x+k)$ for a *non-invertible* function $\mathcal{F}^{(e)}$ instantiated via a truncated permutation, i.e., $\mathcal{F}^{(e)}(x+k) := \mathcal{T}_{n,n'} \circ \mathcal{P}^{(e)}(x+k)$ for a certain $1 \leq n' < n$. Moving the key inside the scheme prevents its cancellation when using the difference of two outputs.

In Ciminion, the key schedule $\mathcal{K} : \mathbb{F}_q^\kappa \rightarrow (\mathbb{F}_q^n)^\star$ uses a sponge function [11] instantiated via the permutation $\mathcal{P}$. We refer to [26, Section 2] for more details.

4   The MEGAFONO Strategy for HYDRA

Generating the subkeys of Ciminion via a sponge function and a strong permutation is expensive in terms of multiplications. This makes it inefficient in cases where the secret keys are shared among the parties, as discussed in Sect. 2.1. Another weakness of Ciminion is the final truncation. While it prevents an attacker from computing the inverse of the final permutations $\mathcal{P}^{(e)}$, it is wasteful as it lowers the output of each iteration. To fix these issues, here we propose the MEGAFONO strategy, based on the design strategy of Ciminion (and $^{1/2\times}$Farfalle), but with some crucial modifications.

Definition of Megafono. Let $n \geq 1$ be an integer and let $\mathbb{F}_q$ be a field, where $q = p^s$ for a prime integer $p \geq 2$ and a positive integer $s \geq 1$. Let $\mathsf{K} \in \mathbb{F}_q^\kappa$ be the secret key for $n \geq \kappa \geq 1$. The ingredients of MEGAFONO are

(1) a key schedule $\mathcal{K} : \mathbb{F}_q^\kappa \rightarrow (\mathbb{F}_q^n)^\star$ for generating the subkeys, that is, $\mathcal{K}(\mathsf{K}) = (k_0, k_1, \ldots, k_i, \ldots)$ where $k_i \in \mathbb{F}_q^n$ for each $i \geq 0$,

---

[3] We mention that in [10], authors use the terms "masks" and "(compressing) rolling function" instead of "subkeys" and "key schedule". In Farfalle, the same subkey is used in the expansion phase, that is, $k_1 = k_2 = \cdots = k_i$. Here, we consider the most generic case in which the subkeys are not assumed to be equal.

(2) an iterated unkeyed permutation $\mathcal{P} : \mathbb{F}_q^n \to \mathbb{F}_q^n$ defined as

$$\mathcal{P}(x) = \mathcal{P}_{r-1} \circ \ldots \circ \mathcal{P}_1 \circ \mathcal{P}_0(x) \tag{2}$$

for round permutations $\mathcal{P}_0, \mathcal{P}_1, \ldots, \mathcal{P}_{r-1}$ over $\mathbb{F}_q^n$,
(3) a (sum) function $\mathcal{S} : \mathbb{F}_q^n \to \mathbb{F}_q^n$ defined as

$$\mathcal{S}(x) := \sum_{i=0}^{r-1} \mathcal{P}_i \circ \ldots \circ \mathcal{P}_1 \circ \mathcal{P}_0(x), \tag{3}$$

(4) a function $\mathcal{F}_k : \mathbb{F}_q^{2n} \to \mathbb{F}_q^{2n}$ defined as

$$\mathcal{F}_k(x) := \mathcal{C}_k(x) + x,$$

where $\mathcal{C}_k : \mathbb{F}_q^{2n} \to \mathbb{F}_q^{2n}$ is a block cipher for a secret key $k \in \mathbb{F}_q^{2n}$, and
(5) a rolling function $\mathcal{R} : \mathbb{F}_q^{2n} \to \mathbb{F}_q^{2n}$. For $y, z \in \mathbb{F}^n$, we further define

$$\mathcal{R}_i(y, z) := \varphi_i + \mathcal{R} \circ \mathcal{R}_{i-1}(y, z)$$

for $i \geq 1$, where $\varphi_i \in \mathbb{F}_q^{2n}$ and $\mathcal{R}_0(y, z) = (y, z)$.

MEGAFONO$_\mathsf{K} : \mathbb{F}_q^n \to (\mathbb{F}_q^n)^*$ is a PRF that takes as input an element of $\mathbb{F}_q^n$ and returns an output of a desired length, defined as

$$\text{MEGAFONO}_\mathsf{K}(x) := \mathcal{F}_{k_2}(y, z) \,\|\, \mathcal{F}_{k_3}(\mathcal{R}_1(y, z)) \,\|\, \cdots \,\|\, \mathcal{F}_{k_{i+2}}(\mathcal{R}_i(y, z)) \,\|\, \cdots$$

for $i \in \mathbb{N}$, where $y, z \in \mathbb{F}_q^n$ are defined as

$$y := k_1 + \mathcal{P}(x + k_0) \qquad \text{and} \qquad z := \mathcal{S}(x + k_0).$$

Remark 2. The main goal of MEGAFONO is a secure variant of Ciminion without a heavy key schedule and without relying on independent subkeys $(k_0, k_1, \ldots)$. For this reason, we only consider the case $k = n$ and $\mathcal{K}(\mathsf{K}) = (\mathsf{K}, \ldots, \mathsf{K}, \ldots)$ in the following. Nevertheless, there may be applications in which a key schedule is acceptable, and hence we propose MEGAFONO in its more general form.

Remark 3. The function $\mathcal{F}_k$ is meant to play the role of $\mathcal{P}^{(e)}$ (in the notation we have used to describe Farfalle and Ciminion). We use this notation to emphasize that the function is keyed and that we no longer require it to be a permutation.

4.1   Rationale of MEGAFONO

Following its structure, MEGAFONO shares several characteristics with Ciminion and $^{1/2\times}$Farfalle. Indeed, many attacks on Farfalle (and Ciminion, $^{1/2\times}$Farfalle) discussed in [10, Sect. 5] also apply to MEGAFONO. Here we focus on the differences, by explaining and motivating the criteria for designing MEGAFONO.

Expansion Phase. We emphasize the following point which is crucial for understanding the design rationale of MEGAFONO. As in $^{1/2\times}$Farfalle and Ciminion, the attacker has access to outputs $w_i = \mathcal{F}_k(\mathcal{R}_i(y,z))$ for $i \geq 0$ that depend on a *single common* unknown input (y,z) (in addition to the key). By exploiting the relation among several inputs of $\mathcal{F}_k$ and the knowledge of the corresponding outputs, the attacker can break the entire scheme. Examples of such attacks can be found in [15,19]. In this scenario, one attack consists of solving the system of equations $\{w_i - \mathcal{F}_k(\mathcal{R}_i(y,z)) = 0\}_{i \geq 0}$ with Gröbner bases. We provide details in Sect. 7.4 and point out that the cost depends on several factors, including (i) the number of variables, (ii) the number of equations, (iii) the degree of the equations, and (iv) the considered representative of the system of equations.

Even–Mansour Construction. In Ciminion, the keyed permutation $\mathcal{P}$ is chosen in order to resemble a PRP. Indeed, since $\mathcal{P}$ is computed only once, it has little impact on the overall cost. Further, if $\mathcal{P}$ resembles a PRP, it is unlikely that an attacker can create texts with a special structure at the input of $\mathcal{P}^{(e)}$. This allows for a simplified security analysis of the expansion phase, as it rules out attacks that require control of the inputs of $\mathcal{P}^{(e)}$.

By performing a key addition before the expansion phase, the first part of the scheme becomes an Even–Mansour construction [29] of the form $x \mapsto \mathsf{K} + \mathcal{P}(x + \mathsf{K})$. As proven in [20,28], an Even–Mansour scheme is indistinguishable from a random permutation up to $q^{n/2}$ queries for $\mathsf{K} \in \mathbb{F}_q^n$, assuming both the facts that (i) the unkeyed permutation $\mathcal{P}$ behaves as a pseudo-random public permutation, and that (ii) the attacker knows both the inputs and outputs of the construction. Since $n/2 \cdot \log_2(q)$ is higher than our security level, this allows us to make a security claim on a subcomponent of the entire scheme, and so to further simplify the overall security analysis.

Keyed Permutation in the Expansion Phase. In Farfalle, the final key addition is crucial against attacks inverting the final permutation $\mathcal{P}^{(e)}$. However, an attacker can cancel the influence of the key by using the differences of two outputs if the key schedule is linear. For example, assume that the key schedule for the expansion phase is the identity map (as in Farfalle), and let x be the input of the expansion phase. Let $y_j = \mathsf{K} + \mathcal{P}^{(e)}(\mathcal{R}_j(x))$ and $y_h = \mathsf{K} + \mathcal{P}^{(e)}(\mathcal{R}_h(x))$ be two outputs of the expansion phase. Any difference of the form

$$y_j - y_h = \mathcal{P}^{(e)}(\mathcal{R}_j(x)) - \mathcal{P}^{(e)}(\mathcal{R}_h(x)) \tag{4}$$

results in a system of equations that is *independent of the key* or, equivalently, that depends only on the intermediate unknown state. This is an advantage when trying to solve the associated polynomial system with Gröbner bases.

The key in Ciminion has been moved from the end of $\mathcal{P}^{(e)}$ to the beginning, with the goal of preventing its cancellation by considering differences of the outputs. Inverting $\mathcal{P}^{(e)}$ is instead prevented by introducing a final truncation, which has the side effect of reducing the output size and thus the throughput.

Recently, in [8] the authors showed that moving the key inside of $\mathcal{P}^{(e)}$ is actually *not* sufficient by itself for preventing the construction of a system of equations – similar to (Eq. 4) – which is independent of the secret key. For this reason, instead of working with a permutation-based non-invertible function, we propose to instantiate the last permutation with a block cipher $\mathcal{C}_k$, defined as an iterated permutation with a key addition in each round. In this way, we achieve the advantages of both $^{1/2\times}$ Farfalle and Ciminion. First, the output size of $\mathcal{C}_k$ is equal to the input size and it is not possible to invert $\mathcal{C}_k$ without guessing the key (as in $^{1/2\times}$ Farfalle). Secondly, a carefully chosen $\mathcal{C}_k$ will prevent the possibility to set up a system of equations for the expansion part that is independent of the key by considering differences of outputs (as in Ciminion).

Feed-Forward in Expansion Phase and Nonlinear Rolling Function. The proposed changes in MEGAFONO may allow new potential problems. Let $v_j = \mathcal{C}_k\left(\mathcal{R}_j(y,z)\right)$ and $v_l = \mathcal{C}_k\left(\mathcal{R}_l(y,z)\right)$ be two outputs of the expansion phase for a shared input (y,z) and let $\mathcal{R}'_{j-l}$ denote the function satisfying $\mathcal{R}'_{j-l}\circ\mathcal{R}_l(\cdot) = \mathcal{R}_j(\cdot)$ for $j > l$. Since $\mathcal{C}_k(\cdot)$ is invertible for each fixed k, we have that

$$\forall j > l: \qquad \mathcal{C}_k \circ \mathcal{R}'_{j-l} \circ \mathcal{C}_k^{-1}(v_l) = v_j \implies \mathcal{R}'_{j-l} \circ \mathcal{C}_k^{-1}(v_l) = \mathcal{C}_k^{-1}(v_j).$$

That is, it is possible to set up a system of equations that depend on the keys only (equivalently, that do not depend on the internal unknown state (y,z)). We therefore apply the feed-forward technique on the expansion phase, i.e., we work with $(y,z) \mapsto \mathcal{F}_k(y,z) := \mathcal{C}_k(y,z) + (y,z)$, which prevents this problem.

Assume moreover that the functions $\mathcal{R}_i$, $i \geq 1$ are linear. Given two outputs $w_j = \mathcal{F}_k\left(\mathcal{R}_j(y,z)\right)$ and $w_l = \mathcal{F}_k\left(\mathcal{R}_l(y,z)\right)$,

$$\begin{aligned}
\mathcal{R}'_{j-l}(w_l) - w_j &= \mathcal{R}'_{j-l}\left(\mathcal{F}_k\left(\mathcal{R}_l(y,z)\right)\right) - \mathcal{F}_k\left(\mathcal{R}_j(y,z)\right) \\
&= \mathcal{R}'_{j-l}\left(\mathcal{R}_l(y,z) + \mathcal{C}_k\left(\mathcal{R}_l(y,z)\right)\right) - \mathcal{R}_j(y,z) - \mathcal{C}_k\left(\mathcal{R}_j(y,z)\right) \\
&= \mathcal{R}'_{j-l}\left(\mathcal{R}_l(y,z)\right) + \mathcal{R}'_{j-l}\left(\mathcal{C}_k\left(\mathcal{R}_l(y,z)\right)\right) - \mathcal{R}_j(y,z) - \mathcal{C}_k\left(\mathcal{R}_j(y,z)\right) \\
&= \mathcal{R}'_{j-l}\left(\mathcal{C}_k\left(\mathcal{R}_l(y,z)\right)\right) - \mathcal{C}_k\left(\mathcal{R}_j(y,z)\right)
\end{aligned}$$

for each j,l with $j > l$. Similar equations can be derived for affine $\mathcal{R}_i$. Even if we are not aware of any attack that exploits such an equality, we suggest to work with a nonlinear rolling function. We point out that using a nonlinear function is also suggested by Farfalle's designers in order to frustrate meet-in-the-middle attacks in the expansion phase (see [10, Sect. 5] for more details).

Creating New Variables to Replace a Heavy Key Schedule. Due to the structure of $^{1/2\times}$ Farfalle and Ciminion, and under the assumption that $\mathcal{P}$ behaves like a PRP, an attacker cannot control the inputs and outputs of the expansion phase. However, (meet-in-the-middle) attacks that require only the knowledge of the outputs of such an expansion phase are possible, because multiple outputs are created via a single *common* (unknown) input. The cost of such an attack depends on the number of involved variables and on the degree of the equations. We start by examining how Farfalle and Ciminion prevent such an attack.

Farfalle has been proposed for achieving the best performances in software and/or hardware implementations. For this reason, the field considered in applications is typically $\mathbb{F}_2^n$, where n is large (at least equal to the security level k). This implies that a large number of variables is needed to model the scheme as a polynomial system, which prevents the attack previously described, even when working with a low-degree permutation $\mathcal{P}^{(e)}$. Depending on the details of the permutation, the number of variables could be minimized by working over an equivalent field $\mathbb{F}_{2^l}^m$ where $n = m \cdot l$, without crucially affecting the overall degree of the equations that describe the scheme. For instance, 16 variables, as opposed to 128, are sufficient for describing AES, since all its internal operations (namely, the S-box, ShiftRows, and MixColumns) are naturally defined over $\mathbb{F}_{2^8}^{16}$. This is not the case for SHA-3/Keccak, for which only the nonlinear layer (defined as the concatenation of χ functions) admits a natural description over $\mathbb{F}_{2^5}^{5 \cdot l}$. In general, this scenario can easily be prevented when working with weak-arranged SPN schemes [17] and/or unaligned SPN schemes [14], for which this equivalent representation that minimizes the number of variables comes at the price of huge/prohibitive degrees of the corresponding functions.

Ciminion has, on the other hand, been proposed for minimizing the multiplicative complexity in the natural representation of the scheme over $\mathbb{F}_q^n$ for *large/huge* q and *small* n, namely, the opposite of Farfalle. Hence, in order to work with low-degree permutations $\mathcal{P}^{(e)}$, it is necessary to "artificially" increase the number of variables to prevent attacks. By using a heavy key schedule, one can guarantee that the algebraic relation between the keys $k_0, k_1, k_2, \ldots$ is nontrivial, i.e., described by dense algebraic functions of high degree. Such a complex relation could not be exploited in an algebraic attack, and the attacker is then forced to treat the subkeys as independent variables. To summarize,

- in Farfalle, the (MitM) attack on the expansion phase is prevented by working over a field $\mathbb{F}_p^n$ for a small prime p and a large integer n, and
- in Ciminon, it is prevented by "artificially" increasing the number of variables, working with a heavy key schedule.

None of the two approaches is suitable for our goal, since we mainly target applications over a field $\mathbb{F}_p^n$ for a huge prime p in which a heavy key schedule cannot be computed efficiently. For this reason, we propose to increase the number of variables "for free" by reusing the computation needed to evaluate $\mathcal{P}$. Since $\mathcal{P}$ is instantiated as an iterated permutation in practical use cases, we can fabricate a new $\mathbb{F}_q^n$ element by considering the sum of all internal states of $\mathcal{P}$. This corresponds to the definition of the function $\mathcal{S}$ in Eq. 3. In this way, we can double the size of the internal state (and so, the number of variables) for free.

In more detail, for a given input $x \in \mathbb{F}_q^n$, let $y \in \mathbb{F}_q^n$ be the output $\mathsf{K} + \mathcal{P}(x + \mathsf{K})$, and let $z \in \mathbb{F}_q^n$ be the output $\mathcal{S}(x + \mathsf{K})$. Then y and z are not independent, since $z = \mathcal{S}(\mathcal{P}^{-1}(y - \mathsf{K}))$.[4] However, for proper choices of $\mathcal{P}$ and $\mathcal{S}$, the relation between the two variables is too complex to be exploited in practice, exactly as in the

---

[4] Note that it is not possible to define y as a function of z, since there is no way to uniquely recover x given z.

case of the keys $k_0, k_1, k_2, \ldots$ in Ciminion. As a result, the attacker is forced to consider both y and z as two independent variables, which is exactly our goal.

Similar Techniques in the Literature. For completeness, we mention that the idea of reusing internal states of an iterated function is not new in the literature. E.g., let $E_k^{(r)}$ be an iterated cipher of $r \geq 1$ rounds. In [45], the authors set up a PRF F as the sum of the output of the iterated cipher after r rounds and the output after s rounds for $s \neq r$, that is, $F(x) = E_k^{(r)}(x) + E_k^{(s)}(x)$. Later on, a similar approach has been exploited in the Fork design strategy [6], which is an expanding invertible function defined as $x \mapsto E_{\hat{k}}^{(r_0)}(E_k^{(s)}(x)) \| E_{\tilde{k}}^{(r_1)}(E_k^{(s)}(x))$.

4.2 Modes of Use of MEGAFONO

As in the case of Farfalle and Ciminion, MEGAFONO can be used for key derivation and key-stream generation. It allows amortizing the computation of the key among different computations with the same initial master key K. Besides that, other possible use cases of MEGAFONO are a wide block cipher, in which MEGAFONO is used to instantiate the round function of a contracting Feistel scheme, and a (session-supporting) authenticated encryption scheme. Since these applications were also proposed for Farfalle, we do not describe them here, but refer to [10, Sect. 4] for further details.

We conclude by pointing out the following. MEGAFONO is designed to be competitive for applications that require a natural description over $\mathbb{F}_q^n$, where q is a large prime of order at least 2^{64}. However, this does not mean that MEGAFONO cannot be efficiently used in other applications, e.g., for designing schemes that aim to be competitive in software or hardware. From this point of view, the main difference with respect to Farfalle and Ciminion is the fact that MEGAFONO requires two permutations with different domains, namely, $\mathbb{F}_q^n$ and $\mathbb{F}_q^{2n}$. However, this is not a problem when e.g. considering the family of the SHA-3/Keccak permutations [12], defined over $\mathbb{F}_2^n$ for $n = 25 \cdot 2^l$ for $l \in \{0, 1, \ldots, 6\}$. In this case it is possible to instantiate $\mathcal{P}$ and $\mathcal{C}_k$ with two unkeyed/keyed permutations defined over domains whose size differs by a factor of two. The resulting PRF based on MEGAFONO would be similar to the PRF KRAVATTE based on Farfalle proposed in [10, Sect. 7]. (Proposing concrete round numbers for this version is beyond the scope of this paper. Rather, we leave the open problem to evaluate and compare the performances of the two PRFs for future work.)

5 Specification of HYDRA

5.1 The PRF HYDRA

Let $p > 2^{63}$ (i.e., $\lceil \log_2(p) \rceil \geq 64$) and let $t \geq 4$ be the size of the output. The security level is denoted by κ, where $2^{80} \leq 2^\kappa \leq \min\{p^2, 2^{256}\}$, and $\mathrm{K} \in \mathbb{F}_p^4$ is

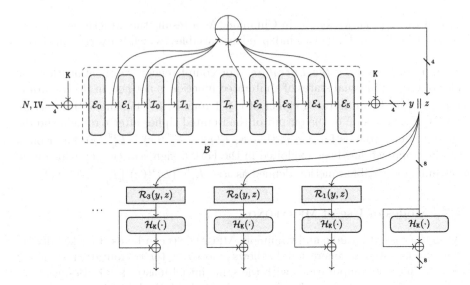

Fig. 3. The HYDRA PRF (where $r := R_{\mathcal{I}} - 1$ for aesthetic reasons).

the master key. We assume that the data available to an attacker is limited to $2^{40} \leq 2^{\kappa/2} \leq \min\{p, 2^{128}\}$. For a plaintext $P \in \mathbb{F}_p^t$, the ciphertext is defined by

$$C = \text{HYDRA}([N \parallel IV]) + P,$$

where $\text{HYDRA} : \mathbb{F}_p^4 \to \mathbb{F}_p^t$ is the HYDRA PRF, $IV \in \mathbb{F}_p^3$ is a fixed initial value and $N \in \mathbb{F}_p$ is a nonce (e.g., a counter).

HYDRA. An overview of HYDRA[5] is given in Fig. 3, where

(1) $y := K + \mathcal{B}([N \parallel IV] + K) \in \mathbb{F}_p^4$ for a certain permutation $\mathcal{B} : \mathbb{F}_p^4 \to \mathbb{F}_p^4$ defined in the following,

(2) $z \in \mathbb{F}_p^4$ defined as $z =: \mathcal{S}_K([N \parallel IV])$ for the non-invertible function $\mathcal{S}_K : \mathbb{F}_p^4 \to \mathbb{F}_p^4$ which corresponds to the sum of the internal states of $K + \mathcal{B}([N \parallel IV] + K)$,

(3) $\mathcal{H}_K : \mathbb{F}_p^8 \to \mathbb{F}_p^8$ is a keyed permutation defined in Sect. 5.4, and

(4) the functions $\mathcal{R}_i : \left(\mathbb{F}_p^4\right)^2 \to \mathbb{F}_p^8$ are defined as

$$\forall i \geq 1 : \qquad \mathcal{R}_i(y, z) := \varphi_i + \mathcal{R} \circ \mathcal{R}_{i-1}(y, z), \tag{5}$$

where $\mathcal{R}_0(y, z) = (y, z)$, and where $\mathcal{R} : \left(\mathbb{F}_p^4\right)^2 \to \mathbb{F}_p^8$ is the rolling function defined in Sect. 5.3, and $\varphi_i \in \mathbb{F}_p^8$ are random constants.

We give an algorithmic description of HYDRA in [34, Appendix E].

---

[5] The (Lernaean) Hydra is a mythological serpentine water monster with many heads. In our case, we can see $\mathcal{B}$ as the body of the Hydra, and the multiple parallel permutations $\mathcal{H}_K$ as its multiple heads.

5.2   The Body of the HYDRA: The Permutation $\mathcal{B}$

The permutation $\mathcal{B} : \mathbb{F}_p^4 \to \mathbb{F}_p^4$ is defined as

$$\mathcal{B}(x) = \underbrace{\mathcal{E}_5 \circ \cdots \circ \mathcal{E}_2}_{4 \text{ times}} \circ \underbrace{\mathcal{I}_{R_\mathcal{I}-1} \circ \cdots \circ \mathcal{I}_0}_{R_\mathcal{I} \text{ times}} \circ \underbrace{\mathcal{E}_1 \circ \mathcal{E}_0}_{2 \text{ times}} (M_\mathcal{E} \times x), \tag{6}$$

where the external and internal rounds $\mathcal{E}_i, \mathcal{I}_j : \mathbb{F}_p^4 \to \mathbb{F}_p^4$ are defined as

$$\mathcal{E}_i(\cdot) = \varphi^{(\mathcal{E},i)} + M_\mathcal{E} \times S_\mathcal{E}(\cdot), \qquad \mathcal{I}_j(\cdot) = \varphi^{(\mathcal{I},j)} + M_\mathcal{I} \times S_\mathcal{I}(\cdot)$$

for $i \in \{0, 1, \ldots, 5\}$ and each $j \in \{0, 1, \ldots, R_\mathcal{I} - 1\}$, where $\varphi^{(\mathcal{E},i)}, \varphi^{(\mathcal{I},j)} \in \mathbb{F}_p^4$ are randomly chosen round constants (we refer to [34, Appendix E] for details on how we generate the pseudo-random constants).

The Round Function $\mathcal{E}$. Let $d \geq 3$ be the *smallest* odd integer such that $\gcd(d, p-1) = 1$. The nonlinear layer $S_\mathcal{E} : \mathbb{F}_p^4 \to \mathbb{F}_p^4$ is defined as

$$S_\mathcal{E}(x_0, x_1, x_2, x_3) = (x_0^d, x_1^d, x_2^d, x_3^d).$$

We require $M_\mathcal{E} \in \mathbb{F}_p^{4 \times 4}$ to be an MDS matrix and recommend an AES-like matrix such as $\mathrm{circ}(2, 3, 1, 1)$ or $\mathrm{circ}(3, 2, 1, 1)$.

The Round Function $\mathcal{I}$. The nonlinear layer $S_\mathcal{I} : \mathbb{F}_p^4 \to \mathbb{F}_p^4$ is defined as $S_\mathcal{I}(x_0, x_1, x_2, x_3) = (y_0, y_1, y_2, y_3)$ where

$$y_l = x_l + \left(\left(\sum_{j=0}^3 (-1)^j \cdot x_j \right)^2 + \left(\sum_{j=0}^3 (-1)^{\lfloor j/2 \rfloor} \cdot x_j \right) \right)^2 \text{ for } 0 \leq l \leq 3. \tag{7}$$

Note that the two vectors $\lambda^{(0)} := (1, -1, 1, -1), \lambda^{(1)} := (1, 1, -1, -1) \in \mathbb{F}_p^4$, that define the coefficients in the sums of (7), are linearly independent and their entries sum to zero. This latter condition is needed to guarantee invertibility by Proposition 1. $M_\mathcal{I} \in \mathbb{F}_p^{4 \times 4}$ is an invertible matrix that satisfies the following conditions (which are justified in [34, Appendix G.2]):

(a) for each $i \in \{0, 1\}$: $\sum_{j=0}^3 \lambda_j^{(i)} \cdot \left(\sum_{l=0}^3 M_\mathcal{I}[j, l] \right) \neq 0$,

(b) for each $i \in \{0, 1\}$ and each $j \in \{0, 1, \ldots, 3\}$: $\quad \sum_{l=0}^3 \lambda_l^{(i)} \cdot M_\mathcal{I}[l, j] \neq 0$, and

(c) its *minimal polynomial* is of maximum degree and irreducible (for preventing infinitely long subspace trails – see [34, Appendix H] for details).

In particular, we suggest using an invertible matrix of the form

$$M_\mathcal{I} = \begin{pmatrix} \mu_{0,0}^{(\mathcal{I})} & 1 & 1 & 1 \\ \mu_{1,0}^{(\mathcal{I})} & \mu_{1,1}^{(\mathcal{I})} & 1 & 1 \\ \mu_{2,0}^{(\mathcal{I})} & 1 & \mu_{2,2}^{(\mathcal{I})} & 1 \\ \mu_{3,0}^{(\mathcal{I})} & 1 & 1 & \mu_{3,3}^{(\mathcal{I})} \end{pmatrix}, \tag{8}$$

for which the conditions *(a)*, *(b)*, and *(c)* are satisfied (we suggest to use the tool given in [34, Appendix H.1] in order to check that the condition *(c)* is satisfied).

5.3   The Rolling Function

The rolling function $\mathcal{R} : \left(\mathbb{F}_p^4\right)^2 \to \mathbb{F}_p^8$ is defined as $\mathcal{R}(y, z) = M_{\mathcal{R}} \times S_{\mathcal{R}}(y, z)$, where a round constant is included in the definition of $\mathcal{R}_i$ (Eq. (5)) and the nonlinear layer $S_{\mathcal{R}}$ is defined as

$$S_{\mathcal{R}}(y_0, y_1, y_2, y_3, z_0, z_1, z_2, z_3) = (y_0 + v, \ldots, y_3 + v, z_0 + w, \ldots, z_3 + w),$$

with $v, w \in \mathbb{F}_p$ defined as

$$v = \left(\sum_{i=0}^{3}(-1)^i \cdot y_i\right) \cdot \left(\sum_{i=0}^{3}(-1)^{\lfloor \frac{i}{2} \rfloor} \cdot z_i\right), \quad w = \left(\sum_{i=0}^{3}(-1)^i \cdot z_i\right) \cdot \left(\sum_{i=0}^{3}(-1)^{\lfloor \frac{i}{2} \rfloor} \cdot y_i\right),$$
$$\tag{9}$$

and the linear layer $M_{\mathcal{R}} \in \mathbb{F}_p^{8 \times 8}$ is defined as

$$M_{\mathcal{R}} = \mathrm{diag}(M_{\mathcal{I}}, M_{\mathcal{I}}) = \begin{pmatrix} M_{\mathcal{I}} & 0^{4 \times 4} \\ 0^{4 \times 4} & M_{\mathcal{I}} \end{pmatrix},$$

where $M_{\mathcal{I}} \in \mathbb{F}_p^{4 \times 4}$ is the matrix just defined for the body's internal rounds.

5.4   The Heads of the HYDRA: The Permutation $\mathcal{H}_K$

The keyed permutation $\mathcal{H}_K : \mathbb{F}_p^8 \to \mathbb{F}_p^8$ is defined as

$$\mathcal{H}_K(y, z) = \underbrace{K' + \mathcal{J}_{R_{\mathcal{H}}-1} \circ (K' + \mathcal{J}_{R_{\mathcal{H}}-2}) \circ \ldots \circ (K' + \mathcal{J}_1) \circ (K' + \mathcal{J}_0)}_{R_{\mathcal{H}} \text{ times}}(y, z),$$

where $K' = K \| (M_{\mathcal{E}} \times K) \in \mathbb{F}_p^8$, and $\mathcal{J}_j : \mathbb{F}_p^8 \to \mathbb{F}_p^8$ is defined as

$$\mathcal{J}_i(\cdot) = \varphi_i + M_{\mathcal{J}} \times S_{\mathcal{J}}(\cdot),$$

where $\varphi_i \in \mathbb{F}_p^8$ are random round constants for each $i \in \{0, 1, \ldots, R_{\mathcal{H}} - 1\}$. The nonlinear layer $S_{\mathcal{J}}(x_0, x_1, \ldots, x_7) = (y_0, \ldots, y_7)$ is defined by

$$y_l = x_l + \left(\sum_{h=0}^{7}(-1)^{\lfloor \frac{h}{4} \rfloor} \cdot x_h\right)^2 \quad \text{for } 0 \le l \le 7.$$

As in (7), we note that the coefficients in the sum, $(1, 1, 1, 1, -1, -1, -1, -1)$, sums to zero. $M_{\mathcal{J}} \in \mathbb{F}_p^{8 \times 8}$ is an invertible matrix that fulfills similar conditions to (a), (b), and (c) described in Sect. 5.2, i.e., (a) $\sum_{h=0}^{7}(-1)^h \cdot \left(\sum_{l=0}^{7} M_{\mathcal{J}}[h, l]\right) \ne 0$, (b) $\sum_{l=0}^{7}(-1)^l \cdot M_{\mathcal{J}}[l, h] \ne 0$, for $h \in \{0, \ldots, 7\}$, and (c) the minimal polynomial of $M_{\mathcal{J}}$ is of maximum degree and irreducible (as detailed in [34, Appendix H]). We recommend that $M_{\mathcal{J}}$ has a similar form to the matrix in Eq. 8 for eight rows and columns.

5.5   Number of Rounds

In order to provide κ bits of security and assuming a data limit of $2^{\kappa/2}$, the number of rounds for the functions $\mathcal{B}$ and $\mathcal{H}_K$ must be at least

$$R_{\mathcal{I}} = \left\lceil 1.125 \cdot \left\lceil \max\left\{ \frac{\kappa}{4} - \log_2(d) + 6, \widehat{R_{\mathcal{I}}} \right\} \right\rceil \right\rceil, \quad R_{\mathcal{H}} = \left\lceil 1.25 \cdot \max\left\{24, 2 + R_{\mathcal{H}}^* \right\} \right\rceil,$$

where $\widehat{R_{\mathcal{I}}}$ and $R_{\mathcal{H}}^*$ are the minimum positive integers that satisfy [34, Appendix G.2] and Eq. 12, respectively. Note that we have added a security margin of 12.5% for $\mathcal{B}$ and 25% for $\mathcal{H}_K$. In [34, Appendix A], we provide a script that returns the number of rounds $R_{\mathcal{I}}$ and $R_{\mathcal{H}}$ for given p and κ. For instance, with $\kappa = 128$, we get $R_{\mathcal{I}} = 42$ and $R_{\mathcal{H}} = 39$. A concrete instantiation of HYDRA's matrices for $p = 2^{127} + 45$ is given in in [34, Appendix C].

About Related-Key Attacks. We do *not* claim security against related-key attacks, since the keys are randomly sampled in each computation, without any input or influence of a potential attacker. Thus, an attacker cannot know or choose any occurring relations between different keys. Indeed, since we focus on MPC protocols in a malicious setting with either honest or dishonest majority (e.g., SPDZ [23,24]), any difference added to one shared key would be immediately detected by the other parties in the protocol. We also emphasize that the same assumption has been made in previous related works [26,32].

6   Design Rationale of $\mathcal{B}$, $\mathcal{R}_i$ and $\mathcal{H}_K$

6.1   The Body $\mathcal{B}$

The HADES Design Strategy. For $\mathcal{B}$, we aim to retain the advantages of HADES [32], in particular the security arguments against statistical attacks and the efficiency of the partial middle rounds. The HADES strategy is a way to design SPN schemes over $\mathbb{F}_q^t$ in which rounds with *full S-box layers* are mixed with rounds with *partial S-box layers*. The external rounds with full S-box layers (t S-boxes in each nonlinear layer) at the beginning and at the end of the construction provide security against statistical attacks. The rounds with partial S-box layers ($t' < t$ S-boxes and $t - t'$ identity functions) in the middle of the construction are more efficient in settings such as MPC and help to prevent algebraic attacks. In all rounds, the linear layer is defined via the multiplication of an MDS matrix.

This strategy has recently been pushed to its limit in NEPTUNE [33], a modified version of the sponge hash function POSEIDON [31]. In such a case, instead of using the same matrix and the same S-box both for the external and the internal rounds, NEPTUNE's designers propose to use two different S-boxes and two different matrices for the external and internal rounds.

The External Rounds of $\mathcal{B}$. As in HADES, POSEIDON, and NEPTUNE, we use the external rounds to provide security against statistical attacks. In the case of HADES and POSEIDON, this is achieved by instantiating the external full rounds with power maps $x \mapsto x^d$ for each of the t words. We recall that this nonlinear layer requires $t \cdot (\mathrm{hw}(d) + \lfloor \log_2(d) \rfloor - 1)$ multiplications (see e.g. [33] for details).

We adopt this approach for $\mathcal{B}$, using 2 external rounds at the beginning and $2 + 2 = 4$ external rounds at the end, where 2 rounds are included as a security margin against statistical attacks (see [34, Appendix G.1] for more details). With respect to HADES and POSEIDON, we do not impose that the number of external rounds at the beginning is equal to the number of external rounds at the end (even if we try to have a balance between them). Instead, we choose the number of external rounds to be even at each side in order to maximize the minimum number of active S-boxes from the wide-trail design strategy [22] (the minimum number of active S-boxes over two consecutive rounds is related to the branch number of the matrix that defines the linear layer).

The Internal Rounds of $\mathcal{B}$. To minimize our primary cost metric (the number of multiplications over $\mathbb{F}_p$), we opt for using maps with degree $2^l \geq 2$ which cost $l \geq 1$ multiplications in the internal rounds. Indeed, let us compare the cost in terms of $\mathbb{F}_p$ multiplications in order to reach a certain degree Δ when using a round instantiated with the quadratic map $x \mapsto x^2$, with one instantiated via an invertible power map $x \mapsto x^d$ with $d \geq 3$, for odd d. Comparing the overall number of $\mathbb{F}_p$ multiplications, the first option is the most competitive, since

$$\underbrace{\lceil \log_2(\Delta) \rceil = \lceil \log_d(\Delta) \cdot \log_2(d) \rceil}_{\text{using } x \mapsto x^2} \leq \underbrace{\lceil \log_d(\Delta) \rceil \cdot (\lfloor \log_2(d) \rfloor + \mathrm{hw}(d) - 1)}_{\text{using } x \mapsto x^d},$$

where $\lceil \log_d(\Delta) \cdot \log_2(d) \rceil \leq \lceil \log_d(\Delta) \rceil \cdot \lceil \log_2(d) \rceil$ and $\lfloor \log_2(d) \rfloor + \mathrm{hw}(d) - 1 \geq \lfloor \log_2(d) \rfloor + 1 = \lceil \log_2(d) \rceil$. For example, consider $d = 3, \Delta = 2^{128}$. With quadratic maps we need 128 $\mathbb{F}_p$ multiplications to reach degree Δ. In the second case, 162 $\mathbb{F}_p$ multiplications are needed, requiring 27% more multiplications in total.

Nonlinear Layer. However, $x \mapsto x^2$ is not invertible, which may affect the security. Therefore, we use the quadratic map in a mode that preserves the invertibility, as in a Feistel or Lai–Massey construction [43]. The latter over $\mathbb{F}_q^2$ is defined as $(x, y) \mapsto (x + F(x - y), y + F(x - y))$, where $F : \mathbb{F}_q \to \mathbb{F}_q$. Generalizations over $\mathbb{F}_p^n$ have recently been proposed [33], including one defined as $(x_0, x_1, \ldots, x_{n-1}) \mapsto (y_0, y_1, \ldots, y_{n-1})$, where $y_i = x_i + F\left(\sum_{j=0}^{n-1}(-1)^j \cdot x_j\right)$ for $i \in \{0, 1, \ldots, n-1\}$ and even $n \geq 3$. This can be further generalized as follows.

Proposition 1. *Let $q = p^s$, where $p \geq 3$ is a prime and s is a positive integer, and let $n \geq 2$. Given $1 \leq l \leq n - 1$, let $\lambda_0^{(i)}, \lambda_1^{(i)}, \ldots, \lambda_{n-1}^{(i)} \in \mathbb{F}_q$ be such that $\sum_{j=0}^{n-1} \lambda_j^{(i)} = 0$ for $i \in \{0, 1, \ldots, l-1\}$. Let $F : \mathbb{F}_q^l \to \mathbb{F}_q$. The Lai-Massey function $\mathcal{F} : \mathbb{F}_q^n \to \mathbb{F}_q^n$ defined as $\mathcal{F}(x_0, \ldots, x_{n-1}) = (y_0, \ldots, y_{n-1})$ is invertible when*

$$y_h = x_h + F\left(\sum_{j=0}^{n-1} \lambda_j^{(0)} \cdot x_j, \sum_{j=0}^{n-1} \lambda_j^{(1)} \cdot x_j, \ldots, \sum_{j=0}^{n-1} \lambda_j^{(l-1)} \cdot x_j\right), \quad \text{for } 0 \leq h \leq n-1.$$

We provide the proof in [34, Appendix F.1]. No conditions are imposed on F. Even if not strictly necessary, we choose $\{\lambda_j^{(0)}\}_{j=0}^{n-1}, \ldots, \{\lambda_j^{(l-1)}\}_{j=0}^{n-1}$ such that they are linearly independent. Since we require $\sum_{j=0}^{n-1} \lambda_j^{(i)} = 0$ for $i \in \{0, \ldots, l - 1\}$, there can be at most $l = n - 1$ linearly independent $\{\lambda_j^{(i)}\}$-vectors.

To reduce the number of rounds and matrix multiplications, we chose a generalized Lai–Massey construction instantiated with a nonlinear function of degree 4 that can be computed with 2 multiplications only.

Linear Layer. The Lai–Massey construction allows for invariant subspaces [48]. Hence, it is crucial to choose the matrix $M_\mathcal{I}$ in order to break them. For this goal, in [34, Appendix H], we show how to adapt the analysis/tool proposed in [36, 37] for breaking arbitrarily long subspace trails for P-SPN schemes to the case of the generalized Lai–Massey constructions. In particular, based on [36, Proposition 13], we show that this result can be always achieved by choosing a matrix for which the minimal polynomial is of maximum degree and irreducible.

Moreover, the interpolation polynomial must be dense. Therefore, we require

(a) for $i \in \{0, 1, \ldots, l - 1\}$: $\sum_{j=0}^{n-1} \lambda_j^{(i)} \cdot \left(\sum_{k=0}^{n-1} M_\mathcal{I}[j, k] \right) \neq 0$,

(b) for $i \in \{0, 1, \ldots, l - 1\}$ and $j \in \{0, 1, \ldots, n - 1\}$: $\sum_{k=0}^{n-1} \lambda_k^{(i)} \cdot M_\mathcal{I}[k, j] \neq 0$.

We give further details on these two conditions in [34, Appendix G.2].

6.2   The Heads $\mathcal{H}_K$

As in Farfalle and Ciminion, the attacker knows the outputs of the expansion phase of MEGAFONO, but cannot choose them (to e.g. set up a chosen-ciphertext attack). By designing $\mathcal{B}$ in order to resemble a PRP, the attacker cannot know or choose the inputs of $\mathcal{H}_K$ (i.e., the output of $\mathcal{B}$). Further, it is not possible to choose inputs of $\mathcal{B}$ which result in specific statistical/algebraic properties at the inputs of $\mathcal{H}_K$. This severely limits the range of attacks that may work at the expansion phase of MEGAFONO, and so of HYDRA.

As a result, we find that the possible attacks are largely algebraic in nature, such as using Gröbner bases. The idea of this attack is to construct a system of equations that links the inputs and the outputs of $\mathcal{H}_K$ in order to find the intermediate variables and the key. In our case, this corresponds to 12 variables: eight to represent the input and four variables related to the key. With this number of variables over such a large field (relative to the security level), we will see in Sect. 7.4 that it will not be necessary for $\mathcal{H}_K$ to reach its maximal degree. Since $\mathcal{H}_K$ is an iterated permutation, it is also possible to introduce new variables at the outputs of each round $\mathcal{J}_i$ in order to reduce the overall cost of the Gröbner basis attack. In such a case, the cost of the attack depends on $\min\{\deg(\mathcal{J}^{-1}), \deg(\mathcal{J})\}$. Indeed, since we can work at round level, each round function $y = \mathcal{J}(x)$ can be rewritten as $\mathcal{J}^{-1}(y) = x$, and the cost of the attack depends on the minimum degree among these equivalent representations.

Therefore, we instantiate the round function of $\mathcal{H}_K$ with a low-degree function, in particular a generalized Lai–Massey construction of degree 2 (where the matrix that defines the linear layer satisfies analogous condition to the ones given for $M_{\mathcal{I}}$). An alternative approach (used e.g. in Rescue) applies both high-degree and low-degree nonlinear power maps (recalled in Sect. 2.2). It is efficient in the MPC setting, and would prompt $\mathcal{H}_K$ to quickly reach its maximal degree. However, since reaching the maximal degree will not be a primary concern of ours (due to the high number of variables), we opt for the former choice of round functions, which allows HYDRA to be fast in the plain setting as well.

6.3   The Rolling Functions $\mathcal{R}_i$

Finally, we consider a nonlinear rolling function, as already done in Xoofff [21] and Ciminion. This has multiple advantages, such as frustrating the meet-in-the-middle attacks on the expansion phase described in [15,19] and previously recalled in Sect. 4.1, and destroying possible relation between consecutive outputs due to the feed-forward operation (see Sect. 4.1 for details).

We work with a rolling function that is different from what is used in the heads, in order to break symmetry. The following (generalized) result ensures the invertibility of the chosen rolling function.

Proposition 2. *Let* $n = 2 \cdot n' \geq 4$, *with* $n' \geq 2$, *and* $\{\lambda_i, \lambda_i', \varphi_i, \varphi_i'\}_{0 \leq i \leq n'-1}$ *be a set of constants in* $\mathbb{F}_p \setminus \{0\}$ *satisfying* $\sum_{i=0}^{n'-1} \lambda_i = \sum_{i=0}^{n'-1} \lambda_i' = \sum_{i=0}^{n'-1} \varphi_i' = 0$. *Let furthermore* $G, H : \mathbb{F}_p \to \mathbb{F}_p$ *be any* $\mathbb{F}_p$ *functions. Then the function* $\mathcal{F}$ *over* $\mathbb{F}_p^n$ *defined as* $\mathcal{F}(x_0, \ldots, x_{n-1}) = (y_0, \ldots, y_{n-1})$ *is invertible for*

$$y_i := \begin{cases} x_i + \left(\sum_{j=n'}^{n-1} \varphi_{j-n'} \cdot x_j \right) \cdot G \left(\sum_{j=0}^{n'-1} \lambda_j \cdot x_j \right) & \text{if } i \in \{0, \ldots, n'-1\}, \\ x_i + \left(\sum_{j=0}^{n'-1} \varphi_j' \cdot x_j \right) \cdot H \left(\sum_{j=n'}^{n-1} \lambda_{j-n'}' \cdot x_j \right) & \text{if } i \in \{n', \ldots, n-1\}. \end{cases}$$

The proof is given in [34, Appendix F.2]. We impose that $(\lambda_0, \ldots, \lambda_{n'-1})$, $(\varphi_0', \ldots, \varphi_{n'-1}') \in \mathbb{F}_p^{n'}$ and $(\varphi_0, \ldots, \varphi_{n'-1})$, $(\lambda_0', \ldots, \lambda_{n'-1}') \in \mathbb{F}_p^{n'}$ are pairwise linearly independent, in order to guarantee that the variables v and w in Eq. 9 are independent (i.e., there is no $\omega \in \mathbb{F}_p$ such that $v = \omega \cdot w$) with high probability.

As before, the matrix $M_{\mathcal{R}}$ is chosen in order to break infinitely long invariant subspace trails. Since the constants that defined the (generalized) Lai-Massey functions (namely, $(1, -1, 1, -1)$ and $(1, 1, -1, -1) \in \mathbb{F}_p^4$) are the same for the rolling function and for the body's internal rounds, we defined $M_{\mathcal{R}}$ via $M_{\mathcal{I}}$.

7   Security Analysis

Inspired by Ciminion, we choose the number of rounds such that $x \mapsto \mathsf{K} + \mathcal{B}(x + \mathsf{K})$ behaves like a PRP (where an attacker is free to choose its inputs and outputs) and no attack works on the expansion phase of HYDRA. In the following, we motivate this choice and justify the number of rounds given in Sect. 5.5.

7.1 Overview

Attacks on the Body. Attacks taking into account the relations between the inputs and the outputs of HYDRA are in general harder than the attacks taking into account the relations between the inputs and the outputs of $\mathcal{B}$. Hence, if an attacker is not able to break $x \mapsto K + \mathcal{B}(x + K)$ if they have full control over the inputs and outputs, they cannot break HYDRA by exploiting the relation of its inputs and outputs. Based on this fact, the chosen number of rounds guarantees that $x \mapsto K + \mathcal{B}(x + K)$ resembles a PRP against attacks with a computational complexity of at most 2^κ and with a data complexity of at most $2^{\kappa/2}$.

We point out that this approach results in a very conservative choice for the number of rounds of $\mathcal{B}$. Indeed, in a realistic attack scenario the outputs of $x \mapsto K + \mathcal{B}(x + K)$ are hidden by $\mathcal{H}_K$, and the overall design will still be secure if $\mathcal{B}$ is instantiated with a smaller number of rounds. However, $\mathcal{B}$ is computed only once, and the overall cost grows linearly with the number of computed heads $\mathcal{H}_K$. Hence, we find that the benefits of allowing us to simplify the security analysis of the heads outweighs this modest increase in computational cost.

Attacks on the Heads. In order to be competitive in MPC, we design $\mathcal{H}_K$ such that HYDRA is secure under the assumption that $K + \mathcal{B}(x+K)$ behaves like a PRP. In particular, the attacker only knows the outputs of the $\mathcal{H}_K$ calls, and cannot choose any inputs with particular statistical or algebraic properties. Hence, the only possibility is to exploit the relations among the outputs of consecutive $\mathcal{H}_K$ calls, which originate from the same (unknown) input $y, z \in \mathbb{F}_p^4$. This can be used when constructing systems of polynomial equations from $\mathcal{H}_K$. Indeed, we will later see that the most competitive attacks are Gröbner basis ones.

7.2 Security Analysis of $\mathcal{B}$

Since $\mathcal{B}$ is heavily based on the HADES construction, its security analysis is also similar. In particular, the external rounds of a HADES design provide security against statistical attacks. Since this part of $\mathcal{B}$ is the same as in HADESMiMC, the security analysis proposed in [32, Sect. 4.1 – 5.1] also applies here. The internal rounds of $\mathcal{B}$ are instantiated with a Lai–Massey scheme, while the internal rounds of HADESMiMC are instantiated with a partial SPN scheme. However, the security argument proposed for HADESMiMC in [32, Sect. 4.2 – 5.2] regarding algebraic attacks can be easily adapted to the case of $\mathcal{B}$.

We refer to [34, Appendix G] for more details. We point out that $x \mapsto K + \mathcal{B}(x + K)$ is an Even–Mansour construction in which $\mathcal{B}$ is independent of the key, while a key addition takes place among every round in HADESMiMC. This fact is taken care of in the analysis proposed in [34, Appendix G], keeping in mind that the Even–Mansour construction cannot guarantee more than $2 \cdot \log_2(p) \geq \kappa$ bits of security [20,28] (this value is reached when $\mathcal{B}$ resembles a PRP).

Finally, in [34, Appendix H] we show how to choose the matrix that defines the linear layer of the internal rounds of $\mathcal{B}$ in order to break the invariant subspace trails of the Lai–Massey scheme, by modifying the strategy proposed in [36] for the case of partial SPN schemes.

7.3   Statistical and Invariant Subspace Attacks on $\mathcal{H}_K$

It is infeasible for the attacker to choose inputs $\{x_j\}_j$ for $\mathcal{B}$ such that the corresponding outputs $\{y_j\}_j$ satisfy certain statistical/algebraic properties, which makes it hard to mount statistical attacks on the heads $\mathcal{H}_K$. However, it is still desirable that $\mathcal{H}_K$ has good statistical properties.

To this end, the matrix $M_{\mathcal{J}} \in \mathbb{F}_p^{8 \times 8}$ is chosen such that no (invariant) subspace trail and probability-1 truncated differential can cover more than 7 rounds (see [34, Appendix H]). Hence, the probability of each differential characteristic over $R_{\mathcal{H}}$ rounds is at most $p^{-\lfloor R_{\mathcal{H}}/8 \rfloor}$, since the maximum differential probability of $S_{\mathcal{J}}$ is p^{-1} (see [34, Appendix I.1]) and at least one $S_{\mathcal{J}}$ function is active every 8 rounds. By choosing $R_{\mathcal{H}} \geq 24$, the probability of each differential characteristic is at most $p^{-3} \leq 2^{-1.5\kappa}$, which we conjecture to be sufficient for preventing differential and, more generally, other statistical attacks in the considered scenario.

7.4   Algebraic and Gröbner Basis Attacks on $\mathcal{H}_K$

It is not possible to mount an interpolation attack, since the input y, z is unknown and the polynomials associated with the various heads differ for each i. Thus, the remainder of this section will be devoted to Gröbner basis attacks.

Note that the variables y and z are clearly not independent, as they both depend on x. Moreover, z can be written as a function of y (the converse does not hold, since the function that outputs z is, in general, not invertible). However, these functions would be dense and reach maximum degree, which implies that the cost of an attack making use of them would be prohibitively expensive. Hence, we will treat y and z as independent variables in the following.

Preliminaries: Gröbner Basis Attacks. The most efficient methods for solving multivariate systems over large finite fields involve computing a Gröbner basis associated with the system. We refer to [18] for details on the underlying theory.

Computing a Gröbner basis (in the grevlex order) is, in general, only one of the steps involved in solving a system of polynomials. In our setting, an attacker is able to set up an overdetermined polynomial system where a unique solution can be expected. In this case it is often possible to read the solution directly from the grevlex Gröbner basis, which is why we will solely focus on the step of computing said basis. There are no general complexity estimates for the running time of state-of-the-art Gröbner basis algorithms such as F_4 [30]. There is, however, an important class of polynomial systems, known as semi-regular (see [7] for a definition), that is well understood. For a semi-regular system the degree of the polynomials encountered in F_4 is expected to reach the degree of regularity D_{reg}, which in this case can be defined as the index of the first non-positive coefficient in the series

$$H(z) = \frac{\prod_{i=1}^{n_e}(1 - z^{d_i})}{(1 - z)^{n_v}},\tag{10}$$

for n_e polynomials in n_v variables, where d_i is the degree of the i-th equation. The estimated complexity of computing a grevlex Gröbner basis is then

$$\mathcal{O}\left(\binom{D_{\mathrm{reg}} + n_v}{n_v}^{\omega}\right),\tag{11}$$

where $2 \le \omega \le 3$ is the linear algebra constant representing the cost of matrix multiplication and D_{reg} the associated degree of regularity [7].

Gröbner Basis Attacks on $\mathcal{H}_K$. There are many possible ways to represent a cryptographic construction as a system of multivariate polynomials, and this choice impacts the performance of the Gröbner basis algorithm. Note that the degree of $\mathcal{H}_K(\mathcal{R}_i(y, z))$ increases with i, and it is therefore not possible to collect enough polynomials for solving by direct linearization at a relatively small degree, as discussed in [34, Appendix G.2]. Instead, we find that the most efficient attack includes only $\mathcal{H}_K(y, z)$ and $\mathcal{H}_K(\mathcal{R}_1(y, z))$ in a representation that introduces new variables and equations for each round. While this increases the number of variables, it keeps the degree low, and allows exploitation of the small number of multiplications in each round. We outline our findings in the following, and we refer to [34, Appendix I.2] for more details on the underlying arguments.

The most promising intermediate modeling can be reduced to a system of $2R_\mathcal{H} + 2$ quadratic equations in $2R_\mathcal{H} - 2$ variables, where $R_\mathcal{H}$ is the number of rounds in $\mathcal{H}_K$. Further analysis shows that the tested systems are semi-regular, and in particular that the degrees encountered in the F_4 algorithm are well-estimated by the series $H(z)$ in Eq. 10. Solving times are also comparable to that of solving randomly generated semi-regular systems with the same parameters. Still, the systems from $\mathcal{H}_K$ are sparser than what can be expected from randomly generated systems. To ensure that this cannot be exploited, we add 2 extra rounds on top of this baseline. Hence, for a security level κ we follow Eq. 11 and define $R_\mathcal{H}^* = R_\mathcal{H}^*(\kappa)$ to be the minimum positive integer such that

$$\binom{2R_\mathcal{H}^* - 2 + D_{\mathrm{reg}}}{2R_\mathcal{H}^* - 2}^2 \ge 2^\kappa,\tag{12}$$

where D_{reg} is computed from Eq. 10 using $n_e = 2R_\mathcal{H}^* + 2$ and $n_v = 2R_\mathcal{H}^* - 2$. We claim that $R_\mathcal{H}^*(\kappa) + 2$ is sufficient to provide κ-bit security against this attack.

Concrete Example for $\kappa = 128$. In this case we get $R_\mathcal{H}^*(128) = 29$, which in turn yields $n_e = 60$ quadratic equations in $n_v = 56$ variables. By expanding the resulting series in Eq. 10, we get $D_{\mathrm{reg}} = 23$ for this system, and the security estimate $\binom{56+23}{56}^2 \approx 2^{130.8}$ follows. Thus, we claim that $R_\mathcal{H}^*(128) + 2 = 31$ is sufficient to provide 128-bit security against Gröbner basis attacks.

Table 1. Online and offline phase performance in MPC for several constructions with state sizes t using a secret shared key. *Prec* is the number of precomputed elements (multiplication triples, squares, inverses). *Depth* describes the number of online communication rounds. The runtime is averaged over 200 runs.

t	Cipher	Rounds	Offline			Online			Combined	
			Prec.	Time ms	Data MB	Depth	Time ms	Data kB	Time ms	Data MB
8	HYDRA	6, 42, 39	**171**	**39.99**	**3.86**	131	6.81	5.37	**46.80**	**3.87**
	Ciminion	90, 14	867	227.47	19.55	735	21.81	28.02	249.29	19.58
	HADESMiMC	6, 71	238	52.66	5.37	79	17.58	5.99	70.24	5.38
	Rescue	10	960	254.80	21.65	**33**	12.65	23.32	267.45	21.68
32	HYDRA	6, 42, 39	**294**	**72.67**	**6.63**	134	**13.36**	**9.69**	**86.03**	**6.64**
	Ciminion	90, 14	3207	910.11	72.30	2895	84.37	103.29	994.47	72.41
	HADESMiMC	6, 71	526	137.49	11.87	79	225.86	13.29	363.35	11.88
	Rescue	10	3840	1253.76	86.60	**33**	109.80	92.82	1363.56	86.70
64	HYDRA	6, 42, 39	**458**	**119.07**	**10.33**	138	**20.57**	**15.45**	**139.64**	**10.35**
	Ciminion	90, 14	6327	2262.55	142.64	5775	178.66	203.64	2441.21	142.84
	HADESMiMC	6, 71	910	251.44	20.53	79	899.55	23.02	1150.99	20.55
	Rescue	10	7680	2851.56	173.20	**33**	402.34	185.50	3253.90	173.39
128	HYDRA	6, 42, 39	**786**	**206.08**	**17.72**	146	**37.49**	**26.97**	**243.58**	**17.75**
	Ciminion	90, 14	12567	4854.43	283.32	11535	328.79	404.34	5183.22	283.72
	HADESMiMC	6, 71	1678	463.59	37.85	79	4371.02	42.47	4834.61	37.89
	Rescue	10	15360	5934.39	346.40	**33**	1549.16	370.84	7483.55	346.77

8   HYDRA in MPC Applications

In this section, we evaluate the performance of HYDRA compared to other PRFs in MPC use cases which assume a secret shared key. We implemented HYDRA and its competitors using the MP-SPDZ library [41][6] (version 0.2.8, files can be found in [34, Appendix A]) and benchmark it using SPDZ [23,24] with the MASCOT [42] offline phase protocol. Concretely, we benchmark a two-party setting in a simulated LAN network (1 Gbit/s and $\ll 1$ ms average round-trip time) using a Xeon E5-2669v4 CPU (2.6 GHz), where each party is assigned only 1 core. SPDZ, and therefore all the PRFs, is instantiated using a 128-bit prime p, with $\gcd(3, p-1) = 1$, thus ensuring that $x \mapsto x^3$ is a permutation, as required by HADESMiMC, *Rescue*, MiMC, GMiMC, and HYDRA. All PRFs are instantiated with $\kappa = 128$. HYDRA requires $4 \cdot R_{\mathcal{E}} \cdot (\text{hw}(d) + \lfloor \log_2(d) \rfloor - 1) + 2 \cdot R_{\mathcal{I}} + (R_{\mathcal{H}} + 2) \cdot \lceil \frac{t}{8} \rceil - 2$ multiplications, hence $130 + 41 \cdot \lceil \frac{t}{8} \rceil$ in this setting.

We implemented all x^3 evaluations using the technique from [35], which requires one precomputed Beaver triple, one precomputed shared random square, and one online communication round. Furthermore, we implemented $x^{1/3}$ (as used in *Rescue*) using the technique described in [5]. MP-SPDZ allows to precompute squares and inverses from Beaver triples in an additional communication round in the offline phase (see Sect. 2).

---

[6] https://github.com/data61/MP-SPDZ/.

In Table 1, we compare the performance of HYDRA to some competitors when encrypting t plaintext words,[7] for a comparison with more PRFs we refer to [34, Appendix J]. We give concrete runtimes, as well as the amount of data transmitted by each party during the evaluation of the offline and online phases. Further, we give the combined number of triples, squares, and inverses which need to be created during the offline phase, as well as the total number of communication rounds (i.e., the depth of the PRF) in the online phase. In the offline phase only the required number of triples, squares, and inverses is precomputed.

Table 1 shows that the offline phase dominates both the overall runtime and the total communication between the parties. HYDRA always requires less precomputation than Ciminion, HADESMiMC, and *Rescue*, hence, it has a significantly more efficient offline phase with the advantage growing with t. Looking at the online phase, HYDRA is faster and requires less communication than its competitors, which is due to the smaller number of multiplications and the better plain performance. While Ciminion is slow due to the expensive key schedule, HADESMiMC requires many expensive MDS matrix multiplications (see [34, Appendix K]) and *Rescue* requires expensive $x^{1/d}$ evaluations.

Table 2. Online and offline phase performance in MPC for several constructions with state sizes t using a secret shared key. *Prec* is the number of precomputed elements (multiplication triples, squares, inverses). *Depth* describes the number of online communication rounds. The runtime is averaged over 200 runs.

t	Cipher	Rounds	Offline			Online			Combined	
			Prec.	Time ms	Data MB	Depth	Time ms	Data kB	Time ms	Data MB
8	HYDRA	6, 42, 39	171	39.99	3.86	131	6.81	5.37	46.80	3.87
	Ciminion (No KS)[a]	90, 14	**148**	**35.64**	**3.34**	107	**3.98**	**5.02**	**39.62**	**3.35**
	Rescue (No KS)[a]	10	480	129.47	10.83	**33**	6.95	11.80	136.42	10.84
32	HYDRA	6, 42, 39	**294**	**72.67**	**6.63**	134	13.36	**9.69**	**86.03**	**6.64**
	Ciminion (No KS)[a]	90, 14	328	80.79	7.40	119	**5.42**	11.16	86.21	7.41
	Rescue (No KS)[a]	10	1920	538.19	43.30	**33**	47.35	46.74	585.54	43.35
64	HYDRA	6, 42, 39	**458**	**119.07**	10.33	138	20.57	**15.45**	**139.64**	10.35
	Ciminion (No KS)[a]	90, 14	568	154.38	12.81	135	**8.05**	19.35	162.42	12.83
	Rescue (No KS)[a]	10	3840	1226.39	86.60	**33**	144.14	93.34	1370.53	86.70
128	HYDRA	6, 42, 39	**786**	**206.08**	**17.72**	146	37.49	**26.97**	**243.58**	**17.75**
	Ciminion (No KS)[a]	90, 14	1048	274.90	23.63	167	**10.70**	35.74	285.60	23.67
	Rescue (No KS)[a]	10	7680	2943.21	173.20	33	737.84	186.52	3681.05	173.39

[a] Assumes round keys are present, i.e., no key schedule computation in MPC.

For the sake of completeness, in Table 2 we also compare the performance of HYDRA to Ciminion and *Rescue* in the case in which the round keys are already present. Comparing HYDRA to Ciminion without a key schedule, one

---

[7] The use cases discussed in this paper basically boil down to encrypting many plaintext words using a secret-shared key. Hence, this benchmark is also representative for the use cases from Sect. 2.1.

can observe that Ciminion's online phase is always faster. However, HYDRA's number of multiplications scales significantly better than Ciminion's, hence, for larger state sizes ($t \geq 32$) HYDRA has a faster offline phase performance, as well as less communication in the online phase.

To summarize, our experiments show that HYDRA is the most efficient PRF in both phases of the MPC protocols. Only if we discard the key schedules, Ciminion is competitive for small state sizes $t < 32$. Thus, using HYDRA leads to a significant performance improvement in MPC use cases, especially in high-throughput conditions. In applications, where the offline phase plays a minor role, e.g., when triples are continuously precomputed and rarely consumed, HYDRA still leads to an performance advantage due to requiring less communication between the parties, however, the advantage will be smaller.

The Effect of the Network. The performance of MPC applications depends on the network speed. A lower bandwidth leads to a larger effect of the communication between the parties on the overall performance. Moreover, a longer round-trip time leads to larger contributions of the number of communication rounds. In the offline phase only shared correlated randomness is created, thus the network performance affects all PRFs in the same way. Consequently, if a PRF has a faster offline phase in the LAN setting, it is also faster in a slower network environment. The situation is different in the online phase: In fast networks, the online phase performance is mostly determined by the plain runtime. In a slower network, more time is spent waiting for the network to deliver packages. HYDRA has a small number of multiplications, hence a preferable offline phase in all networks. Further, it requires little communication in the online phase, making it suitable for low-bandwidth networks. However, it has a larger depth compared to HADESMiMC and *Rescue*, leading to worse runtimes in high-delay networks where runtime is dominated by `round_trip_time` × `depth`. Ciminion's key schedule has a large depth and requires lots of communication between the parties (compare *Data* column in Table 1 and Table 2). Thus, Ciminion is only competitive in slow networks if the key schedule does not need to be computed. Overall, HYDRA has a good balance between a small number of multiplications, little communication, decent plain performance, and a reasonable depth, making it the preferred PRF for MPC applications in most network environments.

Acknowledgments. Lorenzo Grassi is supported by the European Research Council under the ERC advanced grant agreement under grant ERC-2017-ADG Nr. 788980 ESCADA. Morten Øygarden has been funded by The Research Council of Norway through the project "qsIoT: Quantum safe cryptography for the Internet of Things". Roman Walch is supported by the "DDAI" COMET Module within the COMET – Competence Centers for Excellent Technologies Programme, funded by the Austrian Federal Ministry for Transport, Innovation and Technology (bmvit), the Austrian Federal Ministry for Digital and Economic Affairs (bmdw), the Austrian Research Promotion Agency (FFG), the province of Styria (SFG) and partners from industry and academia. The COMET Programme is managed by FFG.

References

1. Abram, D., Damgård, I., Scholl, P., Trieflinger, S.: Oblivious TLS via multi-party computation. In: Paterson, K.G. (ed.) CT-RSA 2021. LNCS, vol. 12704, pp. 51–74. Springer, Cham (2021). https://doi.org/10.1007/978-3-030-75539-3_3
2. Albrecht, M.R., et al.: Feistel structures for MPC, and more. In: Sako, K., Schneider, S., Ryan, P.Y.A. (eds.) ESORICS 2019. LNCS, vol. 11736, pp. 151–171. Springer, Cham (2019). https://doi.org/10.1007/978-3-030-29962-0_8
3. Albrecht, M., Grassi, L., Rechberger, C., Roy, A., Tiessen, T.: MiMC: efficient encryption and cryptographic hashing with minimal multiplicative complexity. In: Cheon, J.H., Takagi, T. (eds.) ASIACRYPT 2016. LNCS, vol. 10031, pp. 191–219. Springer, Heidelberg (2016). https://doi.org/10.1007/978-3-662-53887-6_7
4. Albrecht, M.R., Rechberger, C., Schneider, T., Tiessen, T., Zohner, M.: Ciphers for MPC and FHE. In: Oswald, E., Fischlin, M. (eds.) EUROCRYPT 2015. LNCS, vol. 9056, pp. 430–454. Springer, Heidelberg (2015). https://doi.org/10.1007/978-3-662-46800-5_17
5. Aly, A., Ashur, T., Ben-Sasson, E., Dhooghe, S., Szepieniec, A.: Design of symmetric-key primitives for advanced cryptographic protocols. IACR Trans. Symm. Cryptol. 2020(3), 1–45 (2020). https://doi.org/10.13154/tosc.v2020.i3.1-45
6. Andreeva, E., Lallemand, V., Purnal, A., Reyhanitabar, R., Roy, A., Vizár, D.: Forkcipher: a new primitive for authenticated encryption of very short messages. In: Galbraith, S.D., Moriai, S. (eds.) ASIACRYPT 2019. LNCS, vol. 11922, pp. 153–182. Springer, Cham (2019). https://doi.org/10.1007/978-3-030-34621-8_6
7. Bardet, M., Faugére, J.C., Salvy, B., Yang, B.Y.: Asymptotic behaviour of the degree of regularity of semi-regular polynomial systems. In: Proceedings of MEGA, vol. 5 (2005)
8. Bariant, A., Bouvier, C., Leurent, G., Perrin, L.: Algebraic attacks against some arithmetization-oriented primitives. IACR Trans. Symmetric Cryptol. 2022(3), 73–101 (2022). https://doi.org/10.46586/tosc.v2022.i3.73-101
9. Beaver, D.: Efficient multiparty protocols using circuit randomization. In: Feigenbaum, J. (ed.) CRYPTO 1991. LNCS, vol. 576, pp. 420–432. Springer, Heidelberg (1992). https://doi.org/10.1007/3-540-46766-1_34
10. Bertoni, G., Daemen, J., Hoffert, S., Peeters, M., Assche, G.V., Keer, R.V.: Farfalle: parallel permutation-based cryptography. IACR Trans. Symm. Cryptol. 2017(4), 1–38 (2017). https://doi.org/10.13154/tosc.v2017.i4.1-38
11. Bertoni, G., Daemen, J., Peeters, M., Van Assche, G.: On the indifferentiability of the sponge construction. In: Smart, N. (ed.) EUROCRYPT 2008. LNCS, vol. 4965, pp. 181–197. Springer, Heidelberg (2008). https://doi.org/10.1007/978-3-540-78967-3_11
12. Bertoni, G., Daemen, J., Peeters, M., Van Assche, G.: The KECCAK reference (2011). https://keccak.team/files/Keccak-reference-3.0.pdf
13. Bogetoft, P., Damgård, I., Jakobsen, T., Nielsen, K., Pagter, J., Toft, T.: A practical implementation of secure auctions based on multiparty integer computation. In: Di Crescenzo, G., Rubin, A. (eds.) FC 2006. LNCS, vol. 4107, pp. 142–147. Springer, Heidelberg (2006). https://doi.org/10.1007/11889663_10
14. Bordes, N., Daemen, J., Kuijsters, D., Van Assche, G.: Thinking outside the superbox. In: Malkin, T., Peikert, C. (eds.) CRYPTO 2021. LNCS, vol. 12827, pp. 337–367. Springer, Cham (2021). https://doi.org/10.1007/978-3-030-84252-9_12

15. Chaigneau, C., et al.: Key-recovery attacks on full Kravatte. IACR Trans. Symm. Cryptol. **2018**(1), 5–28 (2018). https://doi.org/10.13154/tosc.v2018.i1.5-28

16. Chase, M., et al.: Post-quantum zero-knowledge and signatures from symmetric-key primitives. In: Thuraisingham, B.M., Evans, D., Malkin, T., Xu, D. (eds.) ACM CCS 2017, pp. 1825–1842. ACM Press (Oct/Nov 2017). https://doi.org/10.1145/3133956.3133997

17. Cid, C., Grassi, L., Gunsing, A., Lüftenegger, R., Rechberger, C., Schofnegger, M.: Influence of the linear layer on the algebraic degree in sp-networks. IACR Trans. Symmetric Cryptol. **2022**(1), 110–137 (2022). https://doi.org/10.46586/tosc.v2022.i1.110-137

18. Cox, D., Little, J., O'Shea, D.: Ideals, varieties, and algorithms: an introduction to computational algebraic geometry and commutative algebra. Springer Science & Business Media (2013)

19. Cui, T., Grassi, L.: Algebraic key-recovery attacks on reduced-round Xoofff. In: Dunkelman, O., Jacobson, Jr., M.J., O'Flynn, C. (eds.) SAC 2020. LNCS, vol. 12804, pp. 171–197. Springer, Cham (2021). https://doi.org/10.1007/978-3-030-81652-0_7

20. Daemen, J.: Limitations of the even-mansour construction. In: Imai, H., Rivest, R.L., Matsumoto, T. (eds.) ASIACRYPT 1991. LNCS, vol. 739, pp. 495–498. Springer, Heidelberg (1993). https://doi.org/10.1007/3-540-57332-1_46

21. Daemen, J., Hoffert, S., Assche, G.V., Keer, R.V.: The design of Xoodoo and Xoofff. IACR Trans. Symm. Cryptol. **2018**(4), 1–38 (2018). https://doi.org/10.13154/tosc.v2018.i4.1-38

22. Daemen, J., Rijmen, V.: The wide trail design strategy. In: Honary, B. (ed.) Cryptography and Coding 2001. LNCS, vol. 2260, pp. 222–238. Springer, Heidelberg (2001). https://doi.org/10.1007/3-540-45325-3_20

23. Damgård, I., Keller, M., Larraia, E., Pastro, V., Scholl, P., Smart, N.P.: Practical covertly secure MPC for dishonest majority – or: breaking the SPDZ limits. In: Crampton, J., Jajodia, S., Mayes, K. (eds.) ESORICS 2013. LNCS, vol. 8134, pp. 1–18. Springer, Heidelberg (2013). https://doi.org/10.1007/978-3-642-40203-6_1

24. Damgård, I., Pastro, V., Smart, N., Zakarias, S.: Multiparty computation from somewhat homomorphic encryption. In: Safavi-Naini, R., Canetti, R. (eds.) CRYPTO 2012. LNCS, vol. 7417, pp. 643–662. Springer, Heidelberg (2012). https://doi.org/10.1007/978-3-642-32009-5_38

25. Dinur, I., et al.: MPC-friendly symmetric cryptography from alternating moduli: candidates, protocols, and applications. In: Malkin, T., Peikert, C. (eds.) CRYPTO 2021. LNCS, vol. 12828, pp. 517–547. Springer, Cham (2021). https://doi.org/10.1007/978-3-030-84259-8_18

26. Dobraunig, C., Grassi, L., Guinet, A., Kuijsters, D.: CIMINION: symmetric encryption based on toffoli-gates over large finite fields. In: Canteaut, A., Standaert, F.-X. (eds.) EUROCRYPT 2021. LNCS, vol. 12697, pp. 3–34. Springer, Cham (2021). https://doi.org/10.1007/978-3-030-77886-6_1

27. Dobraunig, C., Kales, D., Rechberger, C., Schofnegger, M., Zaverucha, G.: Shorter signatures based on tailor-made minimalist symmetric-key cryptom pp. 843–857 (Nov 2022). https://doi.org/10.1145/3548606.3559353

28. Dunkelman, O., Keller, N., Shamir, A.: Minimalism in cryptography: the even-mansour scheme revisited. In: Pointcheval, D., Johansson, T. (eds.) EUROCRYPT 2012. LNCS, vol. 7237, pp. 336–354. Springer, Heidelberg (2012). https://doi.org/10.1007/978-3-642-29011-4_21

29. Even, S., Mansour, Y.: A construction of a cipher from a single pseudorandom permutation. In: Imai, H., Rivest, R.L., Matsumoto, T. (eds.) ASIACRYPT 1991. LNCS, vol. 739, pp. 210–224. Springer, Heidelberg (1993). https://doi.org/10.1007/3-540-57332-1_17

30. Faugére, J.C.: A new efficient algorithm for computing Gröbner bases (F_4). J. Pure Appl. Algebra **139**(1–3), 61–88 (1999)

31. Grassi, L., Khovratovich, D., Rechberger, C., Roy, A., Schofnegger, M.: Poseidon: A new hash function for zero-knowledge proof systems. In: Bailey, M., Greenstadt, R. (eds.) USENIX Security 2021, pp. 519–535. USENIX Association (Aug 2021)

32. Grassi, L., Lüftenegger, R., Rechberger, C., Rotaru, D., Schofnegger, M.: On a generalization of substitution-permutation networks: the HADES design strategy. In: Canteaut, A., Ishai, Y. (eds.) EUROCRYPT 2020. LNCS, vol. 12106, pp. 674–704. Springer, Cham (2020). https://doi.org/10.1007/978-3-030-45724-2_23

33. Grassi, L., Onofri, S., Pedicini, M., Sozzi, L.: Invertible quadratic non-linear layers for mpc-/fhe-/zk-friendly schemes over fnp application to poseidon. IACR Trans. Symmetric Cryptol. **2022**(3), 20–72 (2022). https://doi.org/10.46586/tosc.v2022.i3.20-72

34. Grassi, L., Øygarden, M., Schofnegger, M., Walch, R.: From farfalle to megafono via ciminion: The PRF hydra for MPC applications (2022). https://eprint.iacr.org/2022/342

35. Grassi, L., Rechberger, C., Rotaru, D., Scholl, P., Smart, N.P.: MPC-friendly symmetric key primitives. In: Weippl, E.R., Katzenbeisser, S., Kruegel, C., Myers, A.C., Halevi, S. (eds.) ACM CCS 2016, pp. 430–443. ACM Press (Oct 2016). https://doi.org/10.1145/2976749.2978332

36. Grassi, L., Rechberger, C., Schofnegger, M.: Proving resistance against infinitely long subspace trails: How too choose the linear layer. IACR Trans. Symm. Cryptol. **2021**(2), 314–352 (2021). https://doi.org/10.46586/tosc.v2021.i2.314-352

37. Guo, C., Standaert, F.X., Wang, W., Wang, X., Yu, Y.: Provable security sp networks with partial non-linear layers. IACR Trans. Symm. Cryptol. **2021**(2), 353–388 (2021). https://doi.org/10.46586/tosc.v2021.i2.353-388

38. Helminger, L., Kales, D., Ramacher, S., Walch, R.: Multi-party revocation in Sovrin: performance through distributed trust. In: Paterson, K.G. (ed.) CT-RSA 2021. LNCS, vol. 12704, pp. 527–551. Springer, Cham (2021). https://doi.org/10.1007/978-3-030-75539-3_22

39. Ishai, Y., Kushilevitz, E., Ostrovsky, R., Sahai, A.: Zero-knowledge from secure multiparty computation. In: Johnson, D.S., Feige, U. (eds.) 39th ACM STOC, pp. 21–30. ACM Press (Jun 2007). https://doi.org/10.1145/1250790.1250794

40. Kales, D., Rechberger, C., Schneider, T., Senker, M., Weinert, C.: Mobile private contact discovery at scale. In: Heninger, N., Traynor, P. (eds.) USENIX Security 2019, pp. 1447–1464. USENIX Association (Aug 2019)

41. Keller, M.: MP-SPDZ: A versatile framework for multi-party computation. In: Ligatti, J., Ou, X., Katz, J., Vigna, G. (eds.) ACM CCS 2020, pp. 1575–1590. ACM Press (Nov 2020). https://doi.org/10.1145/3372297.3417872

42. Keller, M., Orsini, E., Scholl, P.: MASCOT: Faster malicious arithmetic secure computation with oblivious transfer. In: Weippl, E.R., Katzenbeisser, S., Kruegel, C., Myers, A.C., Halevi, S. (eds.) ACM CCS 2016, pp. 830–842. ACM Press (Oct 2016). https://doi.org/10.1145/2976749.2978357

43. Lai, X., Massey, J.L.: A proposal for a new block encryption standard. In: Damgård, I.B. (ed.) EUROCRYPT 1990. LNCS, vol. 473, pp. 389–404. Springer, Heidelberg (1991). https://doi.org/10.1007/3-540-46877-3_35

44. Laur, S., Talviste, R., Willemson, J.: From oblivious AES to efficient and secure database join in the multiparty setting. In: Jacobson, M., Locasto, M., Mohassel, P., Safavi-Naini, R. (eds.) ACNS 2013. LNCS, vol. 7954, pp. 84–101. Springer, Heidelberg (2013). https://doi.org/10.1007/978-3-642-38980-1_6
45. Mennink, B., Neves, S.: Optimal PRFs from blockcipher designs. IACR Trans. Symm. Cryptol. **2017**(3), 228–252 (2017). https://doi.org/10.13154/tosc.v2017.i3.228-252
46. Mohassel, P., Zhang, Y.: SecureML: A system for scalable privacy-preserving machine learning. In: 2017 IEEE Symposium on Security and Privacy, pp. 19–38. IEEE Computer Society Press (May 2017). https://doi.org/10.1109/SP.2017.12
47. Shamir, A.: How to share a secret. Commun. ACM **22**(11), 612–613 (1979). https://doi.org/10.1145/359168.359176
48. Vaudenay, S.: On the lai-massey scheme. In: Lam, K.-Y., Okamoto, E., Xing, C. (eds.) ASIACRYPT 1999. LNCS, vol. 1716, pp. 8–19. Springer, Heidelberg (1999). https://doi.org/10.1007/978-3-540-48000-6_2

Coefficient Grouping: Breaking Chaghri and More

Fukang Liu[1,2(✉)], Ravi Anand[2], Libo Wang[2,4(✉)], Willi Meier[5], and Takanori Isobe[2,3]

[1] Tokyo Institute of Technology, Tokyo, Japan
liufukangs@gmail.com
[2] University of Hyogo, Hyogo, Japan
takanori.isobe@ai.u-hyogo.ac.jp
[3] NICT, Tokyo, Japan
[4] Jinan University, Guangzhou, China
[5] FHNW, Windisch, Switzerland
willi.meier@fhnw.ch

Abstract. We propose an efficient technique called coefficient grouping to evaluate the algebraic degree of the FHE-friendly cipher Chaghri, which has been accepted for ACM CCS 2022. It is found that the algebraic degree increases linearly rather than exponentially. As a consequence, we can construct a 13-round distinguisher with time and data complexity of 2^{63} and mount a 13.5-round key-recovery attack. In particular, a higher-order differential attack on 8 rounds of Chaghri can be achieved with time and data complexity of 2^{38}. Hence, it indicates that the full 8 rounds are far from being secure. Furthermore, we also demonstrate the application of our coefficient grouping technique to the design of secure cryptographic components. As a result, a countermeasure is found for Chaghri and it has little overhead compared with the original design. Since more and more symmetric primitives defined over a large finite field are emerging, we believe our new technique can have more applications in the future research.

Keywords: Chaghri · degree evaluation · coefficient grouping · optimization problem · finite field

1 Introduction

In recent years, there is a new trend to design symmetric-key primitives for advanced protocols like secure multi-party computation (MPC), fully homomorphic encryption (FHE) and zero-knowledge proof systems (ZK) [2–5,10,12,15–17,20,21,23,29]. This is mainly motivated by the fact that traditional symmetric-key primitives like AES and SHA-2/SHA-3 are not efficient in these protocols. Therefore, when designing new symmetric-key primitives for them, designers need to be aware of the features of the target MPC/FHE/ZK schemes, e.g. which operations are cost-free and which are costly. For example, for many FHE schemes, a symmetric-key primitive with low multiplicative depth in decryption is desired.

© International Association for Cryptologic Research 2023
C. Hazay and M. Stam (Eds.): EUROCRYPT 2023, LNCS 14007, pp. 287–317, 2023.
https://doi.org/10.1007/978-3-031-30634-1_10

It has been noticed by Canteaut et al. [10] that stream ciphers are a practical solution for efficient homomorphic ciphertext compression and many such stream ciphers have been proposed since then, like Kreyvrium [10], FLIP [29], Rasta [15], Dasta [23], Fasta [12], Masta [21] and Pasta [17]. Among them, Kreyvrium, FLIP, Rasta, Dasta, Fasta are designed over $\mathbb{F}_2$ while Masta and Pasta are designed over $\mathbb{F}_p$ where p is a large prime number. At ACM CCS 2022, an FHE-friendly block cipher called Chaghri [6] defined over $\mathbb{F}_{2^{63}}$ was proposed and it can outperform AES by about 65%.

Along with the new proposals, new cryptanalytic techniques have also been developed. There are some practical examples that several such primitives are broken with new cryptanalytic techniques. Specifically, the variant of MiMC designed over $\mathbb{F}_{2^n}$ is vulnerable against the higher-order differential attack [19]. Jarvis and Friday designed over a large finite field can be broken by Gröbner basis attacks [1]. The first version of FLIP can be practically broken by guess-and-determine attacks [18]. Some important parameters of LowMC and Agrasta are also shown to be insecure against algebraic attacks [14,25–27,30].

Due to the above design-and-break game, cryptographers have started to realize the importance to enrich the pool of cryptanalytic techniques for these new designs. Especially, as many such primitives are defined over a large finite field, it has become urgent to fill the shortcomings of the corresponding crypt-analytic techniques. At CRYPTO 2020, a major breakthrough was made where the higher-order differential attack was extended to finite fields of any character-istics [7]. At the same time, a more refined higher-order differential attack over $\mathbb{F}_{2^n}$ was discovered at ASIACRYPT 2020 [19]. These higher-order differential attacks rely on the degree evaluation. However, in both [7] and [19], the degree is computed in a rather straightforward way and they mainly exploit the low degree of the S-box, i.e. the S-box $x \mapsto x^3$. Although there are some follow-up works [9,11], the corresponding general results still have some limitations and the degree evaluation still seems somewhat straightforward.

Some Related Works. Let us consider a MiMC-like construction defined over $\mathbb{F}_{2^n}$ with an S-box $x \mapsto x^d$ where $d = 2^j + 1$. Then, the general results in [9,11] show that the algebraic degree after r rounds is upper bounded by $\lfloor r\log_2 d \rfloor - j + 1 \approx (r-1)j + 1$. This is obviously ineffective when j is large and n is small as $n < \lfloor r\log_2 d \rfloor - j + 1$ needs to hold to construct a meaningful higher-order differential distinguisher. However, as $(n, d) = (129, 3)$ is one parameter of MiMC, this is indeed quite effective and it implies that the algebraic degree increases linearly. Note that this was first observed in [19] and later generalized in [11].

In [11], the authors considered the SPN ciphers over $\mathbb{F}_{2^n}$. Although Chaghri is also based on the SPN structure, we emphasize that our method is still quite different from [11] and this will be very clear later. This is because we use a much more refined method to evaluate the algebraic degree for any such (n, d) while [9,11] still rely on a very similar bound as in [19] which cannot be effective for large d and small n. Since in Chaghri $(n, d) = (63, 2^{32} + 1)$, we cannot obtain efficient attacks by simply using the bound given in [9,11].

Another related work seems to be the bit-based division property [31], which is a powerful method for the degree evaluation. Recently, the field-based division property [13] has been proposed and used to analyze MiMC. Here, we emphasize that our method is in nature very different from the concept of division property, which should be clear after understanding our method. Moreover, we will give some discussions on the differences on page 13.

Our Contributions. We mainly focus on the higher-order differential attacks on Chaghri. As mentioned above, due to the usage of $(n, d) = (63, 2^{32} + 1)$ in Chaghri, existing methods to bound the algebraic degree become ineffective and we almost cannot violate the designers' claim that the algebraic degree of Chaghri increases exponentially with them. Hence, new techniques are required to break Chaghri. The contributions of this paper are summarized below.

1. A novel and efficient technique called coefficient grouping is proposed for the degree evaluation of Chaghri. The efficiency comes from an efficient representation of the polynomial of any rounds of Chaghri in terms of the input. Specifically, this representation can be determined by a single vector of integers that can be computed in linear time. Furthermore, with this vector of integers, upper bounding the degree is reduced to some well-structured optimization problems that can be efficiently solved, e.g. some can be solved in linear time.

2. For SPN-based ciphers over $\mathbb{F}_{2^n}$, i.e. Chaghri, we demonstrate that it is necessary to first study the increase of the algebraic degree in the univariate case and then study it in the multivariate case. With this strategy and our method to evaluate the algebraic degree, we can break the full 8 rounds of Chaghri with a low data and time complexity of 2^{38}. Moreover, the attack can reach up to 13.5 rounds and this reveals that the original design of Chaghri is flawed. Our results are summarized in Table 1.

3. It is found that the vulnerability of Chaghri exists in the usage of a sparse affine transform (an $\mathbb{F}_2$-linearized affine polynomial), i.e. $B(x) = c_1 x^{2^3} + c_2$, where $c_1, c_2 \in \mathbb{F}_{2^{63}}$ are constants. This can be well explained by our coefficient grouping technique and further shows the advantage of our technique. Hence, we are motivated to design a slightly denser affine transform and further motivated to generalize our coefficient grouping technique to a more complex design. Based on it, we succeed in finding a new affine transform to achieve an almost exponential increase of the algebraic degree. The new affine transform is $B'(x) = c'_1 x + c'_2 x^{2^2} + c'_3 x^{2^8} + c'_4$. By replacing $B(x)$ with $B'(x)$, we can keep the number of rounds of Chaghri unchanged and this has little overhead compared with the original design[1].

Based on the above results, we believe our coefficient technique is useful for both cryptanalysis and design and worth further investigation.

---

[1] The designers of Chaghri have revised their design based on our countermeasures.

Organization. In Sect. 2, we describe the used notations, the block cipher Chaghri and some basic knowledge related to this work. In Sect. 3, the coefficient grouping technique for Chaghri is described. Then, in Sect. 4, we give more details of our attacks on Chaghri in both the univariate and multivariate settings. In Sect. 5, the coefficient grouping technique is further generalized to a more complex design and we describe how to search for a secure affine transform with it. Finally, we conclude the paper in Sect. 6.

Table 1. Summary of our attacks on Chaghri

Attack Type	Rounds	Time	Data	Reference
Distinguisher	8 (full)	2^{38}	2^{38}	Sect. 4
	13	2^{63}	2^{63}	Sect. 4
	13.5	2^{123}	2^{123}	Sect. 4.3
Key recovery	13.5	$2^{96.6}$	2^{63}	Sect. 4.1

2   Preliminaries

2.1   Notation

The following notations will be used throughout this paper.

1. $|\mathcal{S}|$ denotes the size of the set $\mathcal{S}$.
2. $a\%b$ represents $a \bmod b$.
3. $a|b$ denotes that a divides b.
4. $[a, b]$ is a set of integers i satisfying $a \le i \le b$.
5. $H(a)$ is the hamming weight of a.
6. The function $\mathcal{M}_n(x)$ $(x \in \mathbb{N})$ is defined as follows:

$$\mathcal{M}_n(x) = \begin{cases} 2^n - 1 \text{ if } 2^n - 1|x, x \ge 2^n - 1, \\ \%(2^n - 1) \text{ otherwise.} \end{cases}$$

By the definition of $\mathcal{M}_n(x)$, we have $\mathcal{M}_n(x_1 + x_2) = \mathcal{M}_n(\mathcal{M}_n(x_1) + \mathcal{M}_n(x_2))$, $\mathcal{M}_n(2^i) = 2^{i\%n}$ and $\mathcal{M}_n(2^i x) = \mathcal{M}_n(2^{i\%n}\mathcal{M}_n(x))$ for $i \ge 0$.

2.2   On the Finite Field $\mathbb{F}_{p^n}$

For a prime number p and a positive integer n, the finite field $\mathbb{F}_{p^n}$ can be represented as a set of numbers of size p^n. Let α be a primitive element of $\mathbb{F}_{p^n}$. Then each element x in the finite field $\mathbb{F}_{p^n}$ can be written as

$$x = \sum_{i=0}^{n-1} \beta_i \alpha^i,$$

where $\beta_i \in [0, p-1]$. Moreover, the set $\{1, \alpha, \ldots, \alpha^{n-1}\}$ is said to be a polynomial basis of $\mathbb{F}_{p^n}$.

For the element $x \in \mathbb{F}_{p^n}$, it is well-known that

$$\begin{cases} x^{p^n} = x \; \forall x \in \mathbb{F}_{p^n}, \\ x^{p^n - 1} = 1 \; \forall x \in \mathbb{F}_{p^n} \text{ and } x \neq 0. \end{cases}$$

Hence, for two monomials X^a and X^b in the polynomial ring $\mathbb{F}_{2^n}[X]$, there is $X^a \cdot X^b = X^{\mathcal{M}_n(a+b)}$, which is the main reason to define the function $\mathcal{M}_n(x)$.

Moreover, it is also well-known that

$$(x + y)^{p^i} = x^{p^i} + y^{p^i}$$

for $\forall x, y \in \mathbb{F}_{p^n}$ and $i \geq 0$.

The Higher-Order Differential Attack Over $\mathbb{F}_{2^n}$. Throughout this paper, we mainly utilize the idea described in [19] to analyze Chaghri. Specifically, for a given function $\mathcal{F} : \mathbb{F}_{2^n} \to \mathbb{F}_{2^n}$, there always exists a vectorial Boolean function $\mathcal{G} : \mathbb{F}_2^n \to \mathbb{F}_2^n$ such that

$$\sigma : \sum_{i=0}^{n-1} \beta_i \alpha^i \mapsto (\beta_0, \beta_1, \ldots, \beta_{n-1}) \in \mathbb{F}_2^n,$$

$$\sigma(\mathcal{F}(x)) = \mathcal{G}(\sigma(x)) \; \forall x \in \mathbb{F}_{2^n},$$

where $\{1, \alpha, \ldots, \alpha^{n-1}\}$ is a polynomial basis of $\mathbb{F}_{2^n}$.

Let $\deg(\mathcal{G})$ be the algebraic degree of $\mathcal{G}$. For the higher-order differential attack, given any affine vector subspace V of dimension $\deg(\mathcal{G}) + 1$ from $\mathbb{F}_2^n$, there is $\sum_{v \in V} \mathcal{G}(v) = 0$, which implies

$$\sum_{(\beta_0, \beta_1, \ldots, \beta_{n-1}) \in V} \mathcal{F}(\sum_{i=0}^{n-1} \beta_i \alpha^i) = 0.$$

It is well-known that $\deg(\mathcal{G})$ is related to the univariate representation of $\mathcal{F}$, as stated below:

Definition 1 (Univariate degree and algebraic degree). *Let $\mathcal{F}$ and $\mathcal{G}$ be as above. The univariate representation of $\mathcal{F}$ is*

$$\mathcal{F} = \sum_{i=0}^{2^n - 1} u_i X^i,$$

where $u_i \in \mathbb{F}_{2^n}$ for $i \in [0, 2^n - 1]$. The univariate degree of $\mathcal{F}$ denoted by $D_{\mathcal{F}}^u$ is defined as:

$$D_{\mathcal{F}}^u = \max\{i : i \in [0, 2^n - 1], u_i \neq 0\}.$$

Then, $\deg(\mathcal{G})$ can be computed as follows:

$$\deg(\mathcal{G}) = \max\{H(i) : i \in [0, 2^n - 1], u_i \neq 0\}.$$

$\max\{H(i) : i \in [0, 2^n - 1], u_i \neq 0\}$ is also called the algebraic degree of $\mathcal{F}$ denoted by $D_{\mathcal{F}}^a$.

The Multivariate Case. The above higher-order differential attack can also be extended to the multivariate case. Specifically, let $\mathcal{F}(X_1, X_2, \ldots, X_t) : \mathbb{F}_{2^n}^t \to \mathbb{F}_{2^n}$ be a multivariate function in variables $(X_1, X_2, \ldots, X_t)$. Then, its multivariate representation is

$$\mathcal{F} = \sum_{i_1=0}^{2^n-1} \sum_{i_2=0}^{2^n-1} \cdots \sum_{i_t=0}^{2^n-1} u_{i_1,i_2,\ldots,i_t} X_1^{i_1} X_2^{i_2} \cdots X_t^{i_t}.$$

The algebraic degree is then defined as

$$D_{\mathcal{F}}^a = \max\{\sum_{j=1}^{t} H(i_j) : i_j \in [0, 2^n - 1], u_{i_1,i_2,\ldots,i_t} \neq 0\}.$$

Let

$$X_i = \sum_{j=0}^{n-1} \beta_{i,j} \alpha^j, \quad \beta^i = (\beta_{i,0}, \beta_{i,1}, \ldots, \beta_{i,n-1}) \in \mathbb{F}_2^n \text{ where } i \in [1, t].$$

By choosing an affine subspace V of dimension $\dim(V) = D_{\mathcal{F}}^a + 1$ from $\mathbb{F}_2^{n \times t}$, there will be

$$\sum_{(\beta^1, \beta^2, \ldots, \beta^t) \in V} \mathcal{F}(X_1, \ldots, X_t) = 0,$$

which is trivial extension of the univariate case. Specifically, for any monomial $X_1^{\rho_1} X_2^{\rho_2} \cdots X_t^{\rho_t}$, there is $\sum_{i=1}^{t} H(\rho_i) \leq D_{\mathcal{F}}^a$ by definition. For any such affine subspace V, we can denote the corresponding affine subspace of β^i by V_i ($1 \leq i \leq t$) and denote the dimension of V_i by $\dim(V_i)$. Then, there is $\sum_{i=1}^{t} \dim(V_i) = D_{\mathcal{F}}^a + 1 \geq 1 + \sum_{i=1}^{t} H(\rho_i)$. Therefore, there must exist an index i such that $\dim(V_i) \geq H(\rho_i) + 1$, which implies

$$\sum_{\beta^1 \in V_1} \sum_{\beta^2 \in V_2} \cdots \sum_{\beta^i \in V_i} \cdots \sum_{\beta^t \in V_t} X_1^{\rho_1} X_2^{\rho_2} \cdots X_i^{\rho_i} \cdots X_t^{\rho_t} = 0.$$

2.3 Description of Chaghri

The FHE-friendly block cipher Chaghri [6] is defined over a large finite field. There are in total 8 rounds and each round is composed of two steps. Denote the state of Chaghri by $a = (a_1, a_2, a_3) \in \mathbb{F}_{2^{63}}^3$. The round function $R(a)$ of its decryption is described in Algorithm 1. Note that throughout this paper, we are considering the decryption of Chaghri because the designers choose the secure

Algorithm 1. The round function of Chaghri at the $(j+1)^{th}$ round where $0 \leq j \leq 7$

1: **procedure** R(a)
2:     $a_i = G(a_i)$ for $i \in \{1, 2, 3\}$
3:     $a_i = B(a_i)$ for $i \in \{1, 2, 3\}$
4:     $a = M \cdot (a_1, a_2, a_3)^T$
5:     $a_i = a_i + RK[2j+1]_i$ for $i \in \{1, 2, 3\}$
6:     $a_i = G(a_i)$ for $i \in \{1, 2, 3\}$
7:     $a_i = B(a_i)$ for $i \in \{1, 2, 3\}$
8:     $a = M \cdot (a_1, a_2, a_3)^T$
9:     $a_i = a_i + RK[2j+2]_i$ for $i \in \{1, 2, 3\}$

---

number of rounds for Chaghri by mainly analyzing the security of decryption and low multiplicative depth in decryption is desired in FHE schemes. For encryption, the algebraic degree of the S-box is very high and the affine layer is very dense. Hence, our attacks cannot be applied to the encryption of Chaghri.

In Algorithm 1, the round key $RK[j] = (RK[j]_1, RK[j]_2, RK[j]_3) \in \mathbb{F}_{2^{63}}^3$ is generated from a master key $K = (K_1, K_2, K_3) \in \mathbb{F}_{2^{63}}^3$. The whitening key is $RK[0] = (RK[0]_1, RK[0]_2, RK[0]_3)$. We omit the key schedule function as it is not relevant to our attacks. In the following, we explain each component used in the round function, namely G, B and M.

The Nonlinear Function $G(x) : \mathbb{F}_{2^{63}} \to \mathbb{F}_{2^{63}}$. $G(x)$ is defined as $G(x) = x^{2^{32}+1}$.

The Affine Transform $B(x) : \mathbb{F}_{2^{63}} \to \mathbb{F}_{2^{63}}$. $B(x)$ is defined as $B(x) = c_1 x^{2^3} + c_2$ where $c_1, c_2 \in \mathbb{F}_{2^{63}}$ are constants.

The Linear Transform $M : \mathbb{F}_{2^{63}}^3 \to \mathbb{F}_{2^{63}}^3$. M is a 3×3 MDS matrix. The designers do not specify a concrete choice for M and they claim any MDS matrix is suitable. We note here that our attacks apply to any choice of M.

Definition of One Step. According to the round function described in Algorithm 1, the round function is $\text{R}(a) = AK \circ M \circ B \circ G \circ AK \circ M \circ B \circ G(a)$. Similar to [6], one step of Chaghri is defined as $AK \circ M \circ B \circ G(a)$ and we call it the step function of Chaghri.

Notation for the Internal State. We denote the internal state after i steps by $(z_{i,1}, z_{i,2}, z_{i,3})$. For example, the input state is $(z_{0,1}, z_{0,2}, z_{0,3})$, the internal state after 1 step is $(z_{1,1}, z_{1,2}, z_{1,3})$, and the internal state after 1 round is $(z_{2,1}, z_{2,2}, z_{2,3})$. In this paper, we consider R steps of Chaghri.

3   The Coefficient Grouping Technique

We give the intuitive explanation of our new technique with its application to Chaghri. For better understanding, we first only focus on its application to the univariate polynomial and then we discuss how it can be extended to the multivariate case.

Without loss of generality, we consider a general form of $G(x)$ and $B(x)$, as shown below:

$$G(x) = x^{2^{k_0}+2^{k_1}}, B(x) = c_1 x^{2^{k_2}} + c_2.$$

Moreover, we consider the finite field $\mathbb{F}_{2^n}$, i.e. the internal state $a = (a_1, a_2, a_3)$ of Chaghri satisfies $a_i \in \mathbb{F}_{2^n}$ for $i \in [1, 3]$. It should be emphasized that there are constraints on (k_0, k_1, n) to ensure that $G(x)$ is a permutation. Here we only care about its general form of algebraic degree 2. For Chaghri, $(k_0, k_1, k_2) = (32, 0, 3)$ and $n = 63$.

The Main Idea of Our Attacks. We consider an input state which can be represented as univariate polynomials in the variable $X \in \mathbb{F}_{2^n}$, as shown below:

$$z_{0,1} = A_{0,1}X + B_{0,1}, \ z_{0,2} = A_{0,2}X + B_{0,2}, \ z_{0,3} = A_{0,3}X + B_{0,3}, \tag{1}$$

where $A_{0,i}, B_{0,i} \in \mathbb{F}_{2^n}$ $(1 \le i \le 3)$ are randomly chosen constants. In this way, after an arbitrary number of steps, each state word can always be represented as a univariate polynomial in X. Our aim is to compute the upper bound $D_{r,i}$ for the algebraic degree of the univariate polynomial $P_{r,i}(X)$ where $z_{r,i} = P_{r,i}(X)$ $(1 \le i \le 3)$. We say the upper bound for the algebraic degree[2] of r-step Chaghri is D_r where $D_r = \max\{D_{r,1}, D_{r,2}, D_{r,3}\}$. Hence, if $D_r < n$, there exists a higher-order differential attack on r steps of Chaghri with time and data complexity 2^{D_r+1}.

Remark 1. In particular, this attack can be trivially extended for 1 more step by using 2^n data. Specifically, we can consider an input state of the following form:

$$z_{0,1} = X_1, \ z_{0,2} = A_2, \ z_{0,3} = A_3,$$

where $A_2, A_3 \in \mathbb{F}_{2^n}$ are randomly chosen constants and X is the variable. Then, by making $X = B \circ G(X_1 + RK[0]_1)$, the state $(z_{1,1}, z_{1,2}, z_{1,3})$ will be of the same form as in Eq. 1. For such a state $(z_{1,1}, z_{1,2}, z_{1,3})$, after r more steps, the algebraic degree of the univariate polynomials in X is upper bounded by D_r. Since $D_r < n$ and X will traverse all the 2^n possible values when X_1 takes all the 2^n possible values, the higher-order differential attack indeed can reach $r+1$ steps with time and data complexity of 2^n.

---

[2] From the perspective of attackers, D_r can be defined as $\min\{D_{r,1}, D_{r,2}, D_{r,3}\}$ to reduce the time complexity of the attacks. However, due to the strong diffusion of the MDS matrix, using $D_r = \max\{D_{r,1}, D_{r,2}, D_{r,3}\}$ is reasonable and can greatly simplify the attack. This can also be observed from our later analysis of the evolution of the polynomials through the step function of Chaghri, i.e. using $D_r = \max\{D_{r,1}, D_{r,2}, D_{r,3}\}$ is indeed tight according to the experiments.

3.1   Tracing the Form of the Univariate Polynomial

With the input form shown in Eq. 1, the state words $(z_{r,1}, z_{r,2}, z_{r,3})$ can always be represented as univariate polynomials of the following form:

$$z_{r,1} = \sum_{i=1}^{|w_r|} A_{r,i} X^{w_{r,i}}, \ z_{r,2} = \sum_{i=1}^{|w_r|} B_{r,i} X^{w_{r,i}}, \ z_{r,3} = \sum_{i=1}^{|w_r|} C_{r,i} X^{w_{r,i}}$$

where $A_{r,i}, B_{r,i}, C_{r,i} \in \mathbb{F}_{2^n}$ are key-dependent coefficients and we call the set

$$w_r = \{w_{r,1}, w_{r,2}, \ldots, w_{r,|w_r|}\} \subseteq \mathbb{N}$$

the set of all possible exponents for the univariate polynomials after r steps. Note that $0 \in w_r$ since it represents the constant term. It should be mentioned that for $r = 0$, we have

$$w_0 = \{0, 1\}, \tag{2}$$

which corresponds to the input form specified in Eq. 1.

According to the definition of the algebraic degree of a univariate polynomial, we have

$$D_r \leq \max\{H(w_{r,i}) : 1 \leq i \leq |w_r|\}. \tag{3}$$

Analyzing the Evolution of the Polynomial Representations. We are interested in the univariate polynomials to represent $(z_{r+1,1}, z_{r+1,2}, z_{r+1,3})$, i.e. how the polynomials evolve through the step function of Chaghri. The detailed analysis is shown below.

$$G(z_{r,1}) = \Big(\sum_{i=1}^{|w_r|} A_{r,i} X^{w_{r,i}}\Big)^{2^{k_0}+2^{k_1}}$$

$$= \Big(\sum_{i=1}^{|w_r|} A_{r,i} X^{w_{r,i}}\Big)^{2^{k_0}} \Big(\sum_{j=1}^{|w_r|} A_{r,j} X^{w_{r,j}}\Big)^{2^{k_1}} = \sum_{i=1}^{|w_r|} \sum_{j=1}^{|w_r|} A_{r,i,j} X^{\mathcal{M}_n(2^{k_0} w_{r,i} + 2^{k_1} w_{r,j})},$$

where $A_{r,i,j} \in \mathbb{F}_{2^n}$ are key-dependent coefficients.

$$B \circ G(z_{r,1}) = c_1 \Big(\sum_{i=1}^{|w_r|} \sum_{j=1}^{|w_r|} A_{r,i,j} X^{\mathcal{M}_n(2^{k_0} w_{r,i} + 2^{k_1} w_{r,j})}\Big)^{2^{k_2}} + c_2$$

$$= \sum_{i=1}^{|w_r|} \sum_{j=1}^{|w_r|} A'_{r,i,j} X^{\mathcal{M}_n(2^{k_0+k_2} w_{r,i} + 2^{k_1+k_2} w_{r,j})},$$

where $A'_{r,i,j} \in \mathbb{F}_{2^{63}}$ are key-dependent coefficients. c_2 is removed due to $0 \in w_r$.

Similarly, it can be found that

$$B \circ G(z_{r,2}) = \sum_{i=1}^{|w_r|} \sum_{j=1}^{|w_r|} B'_{r,i,j} X^{\mathcal{M}_n(2^{k_0+k_2}w_{r,i}+2^{k_1+k_2}w_{r,j})},$$

$$B \circ G(z_{r,3}) = \sum_{i=1}^{|w_r|} \sum_{j=1}^{|w_r|} C'_{r,i,j} X^{\mathcal{M}_n(2^{k_0+k_2}w_{r,i}+2^{k_1+k_2}w_{r,j})},$$

where $B'_{r,i,j}, C'_{r,i,j} \in \mathbb{F}_{2^n}$ are key-dependent coefficients.

Therefore, we can obtain

$$z_{r+1,1} = \sum_{i=1}^{|w_r|} \sum_{j=1}^{|w_r|} A_{r+1,i,j} X^{\mathcal{M}_n(2^{k_0+k_2}w_{r,i}+2^{k_1+k_2}w_{r,j})},$$

$$z_{r+1,2} = \sum_{i=1}^{|w_r|} \sum_{j=1}^{|w_r|} B_{r+1,i,j} X^{\mathcal{M}_n(2^{k_0+k_2}w_{r,i}+2^{k_1+k_2}w_{r,j})},$$

$$z_{r+1,3} = \sum_{i=1}^{|w_r|} \sum_{j=1}^{|w_r|} C_{r+1,i,j} X^{\mathcal{M}_n(2^{k_0+k_2}w_{r,i}+2^{k_1+k_2}w_{r,j})},$$

where $A_{r+1,i,j}, B_{r+1,i,j}, C_{r+1,i,j} \in \mathbb{F}_{2^{63}}$ are key-dependent coefficients.

Hence, we obtain a relation between the sets w_r and w_{r+1}, as shown below:

$$w_{r+1} = \{e | e = \mathcal{M}_n(2^{k_0+k_2}w_{r,i} + 2^{k_1+k_2}w_{r,j}), 1 \le i,j \le |w_r|\},$$

In this way, for each element $e \in w_{r+2}$, there must exist (i,j,s,t) where $1 \le i,j,s,t \le |w_r|$ such that

$$e = \mathcal{M}_n\left(2^{k_0+k_2}(2^{k_0+k_2}w_{r,i} + 2^{k_1+k_2}w_{r,j}) + 2^{k_1+k_2}(2^{k_0+k_2}w_{r,s} + 2^{k_1+k_2}w_{r,t})\right).$$

In other words,

$$w_{r+2} = \{e | e = \mathcal{M}_n(2^{2k_0+2k_2}w_{r,i} + 2^{k_0+k_1+2k_2}(w_{r,j} + w_{r,s}) + 2^{2k_1+2k_2}w_{r,t}),$$
$$1 \le i,j,s,t \le |w_r|\}.$$

For the concrete parameters of Chaghri, we have

$$w_{r+1} = \{e | e = \mathcal{M}_{63}(2^{35}w_{r,i} + 2^3 w_{r,j}), 1 \le i,j \le |w_r|\},$$

$$w_{r+2} = \{e | e = \mathcal{M}_{63}\left(2^7 w_{r,i} + 2^{38}(w_{r,j} + w_{r,s}) + 2^6 w_{r,t}\right), 1 \le i,j,s,t \le |w_r|\}.$$

Another Representation of the Set $w_{r+\ell}$. Based on the above discussions, it is now clear that there exists another general representation of the set $w_{r+\ell}$. Specifically, it must be of the following form:

$$w_{r+\ell} = \{e | e = \mathcal{M}_n(\sum_{i=1}^{N_{n-1}} 2^{n-1} w_{r,d_{i,n-1}} + \sum_{i=1}^{N_{n-2}} 2^{n-2} w_{r,d_{i,n-2}} + \ldots + \sum_{i=1}^{N_0} 2^0 w_{r,d_{i,0}}),$$
$$\text{where } 1 \le d_{i,j} \le |w_r| \text{ for } 0 \le j \le n-1\}$$

Proof. Proving this form is simple. Specifically, by induction, we only need to prove $w_{r+\ell+1}$ is also of this form when $w_{r+\ell}$ is as above. This is because w_0 is of this form, i.e. for $w_0 = \{w_{0,1}, w_{0,2}\} = \{0,1\} = \{e | e = 2^0 w_{0,i}, 1 \leq i \leq 2\}$, there is

$$N_0 = 1, N_i = 0 \ (1 \leq i \leq n-1). \tag{4}$$

Considering the relation between $w_{r+\ell}$ and $w_{r+\ell+1}$, we have

$$w_{r+\ell+1} = \{e | e = \mathcal{M}_n(2^{k_0+k_2} w_{r+\ell,i} + 2^{k_1+k_2} w_{r+\ell,j}), 1 \leq i,j \leq |w_{r+\ell}|\}.$$

Hence, we have

$$w_{r+\ell+1} = \{e | e = \mathcal{M}_n(\overset{N'_{n-1}}{\underset{i=1}{\sum}} 2^{n-1} w_{r,d'_{i,n-1}} + \overset{N'_{n-2}}{\underset{i=1}{\sum}} 2^{n-2} w_{r,d'_{i,n-2}} + \ldots + \overset{N'_0}{\underset{i=1}{\sum}} 2^0 w_{r,d'_{i,0}}),$$
$$\text{where } 1 \leq d'_{i,j} \leq |w_r| \text{ for } 0 \leq j \leq n-1\},$$

where

$$N'_i = N_{(i-k_1-k_2)\%n} + N_{(i-k_0-k_2)\%n} \text{ for } 0 \leq i \leq n-1. \tag{5}$$

$\square$

In other words, each set w_r can be fully described with a vector of integers $(N^r_{n-1}, N^r_{n-2}, \ldots, N^r_0)$. For w_0, this vector is

$$N^0_0 = 1, N^0_i = 0 \ (1 \leq i \leq n-1).$$

Then, based on the recursive relation specified in Eq. 5, i.e.

$$N^{r+1}_i = N^r_{(i-k_1-k_2)\%n} + N^r_{(i-k_0-k_2)\%n} \text{ for } 0 \leq i \leq n-1, r \geq 0, \tag{6}$$

for any w_r, the corresponding vector of integers $(N^r_{n-1}, N^r_{n-2}, \ldots, N^r_0)$ can be computed in linear time, i.e. with rn times of simple integer additions. Then, the set w_r can be described as follows:

$$w_r = \{e | e = \mathcal{M}_n(\overset{N^r_{n-1}}{\underset{i=1}{\sum}} 2^{n-1} w_{0,d_{i,n-1}} + \overset{N^r_{n-2}}{\underset{i=1}{\sum}} 2^{n-2} w_{0,d_{i,n-2}} + \ldots + \overset{N^r_0}{\underset{i=1}{\sum}} 2^0 w_{0,d_{i,0}}),$$
$$\text{where } 1 \leq d_{i,j} \leq |w_0| \text{ for } 0 \leq j \leq n-1\}. \tag{7}$$

Application to the Chaghri Parameters. For the concrete parameters of Chaghri, the corresponding $(N^1_{62}, N^1_{61}, \ldots, N^1_0)$ for w_1 is

$$N^1_3 = 1, N^1_{35} = 1, N^1_i = 0 \ (i \notin \{3, 35\}, 0 \leq i \leq 62).$$

While for w_2, the corresponding $(N^2_{62}, N^2_{61}, \ldots, N^2_0)$ is

$$N^2_6 = 1, N^2_7 = 1, N^2_{38} = 2, N^2_i = 0 \ (i \notin \{6, 7, 38\}, 0 \leq i \leq 62).$$

For any w_r, we can compute the corresponding $(N^r_{62}, N^r_{61}, \ldots, N^r_0)$ in linear time.

3.2   A Natural Optimization Problem

The last problem we need to deal with is how to compute D_r after giving the vector of integers $(N_{n-1}^r, N_{n-2}^r, \ldots, N_0^r)$. For our representation of w_r, it can be equivalently interpreted in the way that there are in total $N_{n-1}^r + N_{n-2}^r + \ldots + N_0^r$ possible variables that can independently take values from $w_0 = \{0, 1\}$. Hence, the problem to bound D_r becomes a natural optimization problem, as shown below:

$$\text{maximize } H\left(\mathcal{M}_n\left(\sum_{i=0}^{n-1} 2^i \gamma_i\right)\right),$$

$$\text{subject to } 0 \le \gamma_i \le N_i^r \text{ for } i \in [0, n-1].$$

More specifically, due to $w_0 = \{0, 1\}$, w_r specified in Eq. 7 is equivalent to

$$w_r = \left\{\mathcal{M}_n\left(\sum_{i=0}^{n-1} 2^i \gamma_i\right) | 0 \le \gamma_i \le N_i^r \text{ for } i \in [0, n-1]\right\}.$$

After computing N_i^r for $i \in [0, n-1]$, which can be finished in linear time, this problem[3] can be easily encoded as an MILP problem. Specifically, for each integer $m \in [0, 2^n - 1]$, we can assign a bit vector $(m_{n-1}, m_{n-2}, \ldots, m_0)$ for m, i.e. $m = \sum_{i=0}^{n-1} 2^i m_i$. Then, $\mathcal{M}_n(2^j \cdot m)$ just makes m become

$$\left(m_{(n-1-j)\%n}, m_{(n-2-j)\%n}, \ldots, m_{(0-j)\%n}\right),$$

i.e. a change of the order of variables.

The addition is trivial. Specifically, for the addition $\mathcal{M}_n(x+y) = q$ where $x = (x_{n-1}, x_{n-2}, \ldots, x_0)$, $y = (y_{n-1}, y_{n-2}, \ldots, y_0)$ and $q = (q_{n-1}, q_{n-2}, \ldots, q_0)$, by introducing two $(n+1)$-bit vectors $g = (g_n, g_{n-1}, \ldots, g_0)$ and $g' = (g_n', g_{n-1}', \ldots, g_0')$ as well as an n-bit vector $q' = (q_{n-1}', q_{n-2}', \ldots, q_0')$ to represent the intermediate value, we have

$$\begin{cases} g_0 = 0, \ 2g_{i+1} + q_i' = x_i + y_i + g_i \text{ for } i \in [0, n-1], \\ g_0' = g_n, \ 2g_{i+1}' + q_i = q_i' + g_i' \text{ for } i \in [0, n-1]. \end{cases}$$

For the comparison $m \le b$ where $b = (b_{n-1}, b_{n-2}, \ldots, b_0) \in \mathbb{F}_2^n$ is a known integer, it can also be simply described with linear inequalities. Specifically, supposing $b_i = 1$ for any $i \in \{i_1, i_2, \ldots, i_{l-1}, i_l\}$ and $0 \le i_1 < i_2 < \ldots < i_l \le n-1$.

---

[3] Motivated by this work, an ad-hoc algorithm [28] has been developed to solve the above optimization problem in time $\mathcal{O}(n)$. However, in this following, there still remain some other optimization problems which cannot be handled by that $\mathcal{O}(n)$ algorithm [28]. Hence, we only consider the general-purpose solvers for the optimization problems in this paper.

Then $m \leq b$ can be described with the following $n - l$ linear (in)equalities:

$$
\begin{cases}
m_j = 0 \text{ for } i_l < j \leq n - 1, \\
(1 - m_{i_l}) - m_j \geq 0 \text{ for } i_{l-1} < j < i_l, \\
\displaystyle\sum_{s=l-1}^{l} (1 - m_{i_s}) - m_j \geq 0 \text{ for } i_{l-2} < j < i_{l-1}, \\
\qquad\qquad\qquad \cdots \\
\displaystyle\sum_{s=1}^{l} (1 - m_{i_s}) - m_j \geq 0 \text{ for } 0 \leq j < i_1.
\end{cases}
$$

To maximize $H(m)$, we simply write

$$\text{maximize } m_0 + m_1 + \ldots + m_{n-1}.$$

In this way, a simple MILP model can be constructed and the solution of the model is exactly D_r according to Eq. 3.

A Useful Theorem. In the following, we present a useful theorem for the case when the maximal degree is reached.

Theorem 1. *For a given vector of integers* $(N_{n-1}, N_{n-2}, \ldots, N_0)$, *if the solution to the following optimization problem called* **Problem 1** *is* $h \times n$:

$$\text{maximize } \sum_{j=1}^{h} H\left(\mathcal{M}_n(\sum_{i=0}^{n-1} 2^i \gamma_{j,i}) \right),$$

$$\text{subject to } \mathcal{C}_1(\gamma_{1,0}, \gamma_{1,1}, \ldots, \gamma_{h,n-1}, N_0, N_1, \ldots, N_{n-1}),$$

the solution to the following optimization problem called **Problem 2** *must also be* $h \times n$:

$$\text{maximize } \sum_{j=1}^{h} H\left(\mathcal{M}_n(\sum_{i=0}^{n-1} 2^i \nu_j \gamma_{j,i}) \right),$$

$$\text{subject to } \mathcal{C}_1(\gamma_{1,0}, \gamma_{1,1}, \ldots, \gamma_{h,n-1}, N_0, N_1, \ldots, N_{n-1}),$$

where $\nu_j \in \mathbb{N}^+$ *for* $j \in [1, h]$ *and* $\mathcal{C}_1(\gamma_{1,0}, \gamma_{1,1}, \ldots, \gamma_{h,n-1}, N_0, N_1, \ldots, N_{n-1})$ *denotes the set of constraints.*

Proof. Since the solution to **Problem 1** is $h \times n$, for each $j \in [1, h]$, there exists an assignment to $(\gamma_{j,n-1}, \gamma_{j,n-2}, \ldots, \gamma_{j,0})$ denoted by $(\hat{\gamma_{j,n-1}}, \hat{\gamma_{j,n-2}}, \ldots, \hat{\gamma_{j,0}})$ such that

$$\mathcal{M}_n(\sum_{i=0}^{n-1} 2^i \hat{\gamma_{j,i}}) = 2^n - 1.$$

Hence, for each $j \in [1, h]$, we have

$$\mathcal{M}_n(\sum_{i=0}^{n-1} 2^i \nu_j \widehat{\gamma}_{j,i}) = \mathcal{M}_n\left(\nu_j \times \mathcal{M}_n(\sum_{i=0}^{n-1} 2^i \widehat{\gamma}_{j,i})\right) = 2^n - 1.$$

As the upper bound for the solution to **Problem 2** is $h \times n$ and we find an assignment to make its solution be $h \times n$, the solution to **Problem 2** is $h \times n$.

$\square$

Generalization to an Arbitrary Power Function. In the above, we mainly analyze a power function $x \mapsto x^{2^{k_0}+2^{k_1}}$ with algebraic degree 2. It is easy to observe that a similar procedure can be applied to any power function $x \mapsto x^{\sum_{i=1}^{\rho} 2^{\phi_i}}$ over $\mathbb{F}_{2^n}$ with algebraic degree ρ. This is due to the following simple relation:

$$(\sum_{j=1}^{|w_r|} A_j X^{w_{r,j}})^{\sum_{i=1}^{\rho} 2^{\phi_i}} = \sum_{j_1=1}^{|w_r|} \sum_{j_2=1}^{|w_r|} \cdots \sum_{j_\rho=1}^{|w_r|} A_{j_1,j_2,\ldots,j_\rho} X^{2^{\phi_1} w_{r,j_1} + 2^{\phi_2} w_{r,j_2} + \cdots + 2^{\phi_\rho} w_{r,j_\rho}}.$$

By using the same $B(x) = c_1 x^{2^{k_2}} + c_2$, we still can simply use a vector of integers to represent the set of possible exponents. In addition, the recursive relation between the vectors $(N_{n-1}^{r+1}, N_{n-2}^{r+1}, \ldots, N_0^{r+1})$ and $(N_{n-1}^r, N_{n-2}^r, \ldots, N_0^r)$ can be described as below:

$$N_j^{r+1} = \sum_{i=1}^{\rho} N_{(j-\phi_i-k_2)\%n}^r \text{ for } j \in [0, n-1],$$

which implies that these vectors can be computed in linear time. With these vectors, bounding the algebraic degree is then reduced to the same optimization problem. This obviously shows the effectiveness of our coefficient grouping technique.

Comparison with the Literature. First, compared with the well-known degree evaluation technique developed for Keccak [8], our technique does not require to compute the upper bound of the degree at round i before computing the upper bound at round $i+1$. This is mainly because we find an efficient representation of the polynomial of any rounds of Chaghri in terms of the input, which can be determined by a vector of integers and this vector can be computed in linear time. Second, different from the division property that has been well studied in recent years [13,22,24,32], there is no need to use a heavy model to describe the monomial transitions through the round function for each round because they can be simply captured by an efficient recursive relation in our technique. At last, compared with more related works in [9,11,19], when the affine layer is simply $B(x) = c_1 x^{2^{k_2}} + c_2$ and $G(x)$ is any power map over $\mathbb{F}_{2^n}$, tighter bounds can be derived with our technique because our way to describe the polynomial representation after any rounds is more accurate, i.e. we can exclude many redundant monomials that will never appear with our technique while they are treated as possible to appear in these techniques [9,11,19].

4   Cryptanalysis of Full-Round Chaghri

With the above model, the upper bounds for D_r are obtained in seconds, as listed in Table 2.

Table 2. The upper bounds for D_r

r	0	2	4	6	8	10	12	14	16	18	20	22	24	25	26
D_r	1	3	7	12	17	22	27	32	37	42	47	52	58	60	63

Consequently, we can mount a higher-order differential attack on full 8 rounds of Chaghri with data and time complexity of 2^{38}. It also suggests that there is a higher-order differential distinguisher for 12.5 rounds of Chaghri with time and data complexity of 2^{61}. Furthermore, according to Remark 1, we can extend one more step (0.5 round) and construct a higher-order differential distinguisher for 13 rounds of Chaghri with time and data complexity of 2^{63}.

4.1   The Key-Recovery Attack on 13.5 Rounds of Chaghri

We have constructed a 13-round distinguisher with data and time complexity of 2^{63}. Then, we can append 0.5 round for the key recovery. To recover the round key $RK[27]$, an equivalent round key $RK[27]' = (RK[27]'_1, RK[27]'_2, RK[27]'_3)$ is considered, where

$$(RK[27]'_1, RK[27]'_2, RK[27]'_3)^T = M^{-1} \times (RK[27]_1, RK[27]_2, RK[27]_3)^T.$$

Since the operations B^{-1} and G^{-1} work on the internal state in a parallel way, the naive method is to independently guess $RK[27]'_i$ $(1 \leq i \leq 3)$ and compute the corresponding $z_{26,i}$ and check the sum of $z_{26,i}$. If the sum is zero, the guess is correct. Hence, the time complexity of this key-recovery attack is about $3 \times 2^{63} \times 2^{63} < 2^{128}$. Note that after recovering $RK[27]'$, we can compute $RK[27]$ and deduce the master key according to the key schedule function.

Indeed, the key-recovery attack can be more efficient by treating $B^{-1}(RK[27]'_i)$ $(1 \leq i \leq 3)$ as a variable Y_i. Note that $B(x)$ is an affine transform over $\mathbb{F}_{2^{63}}$ and hence $B^{-1}(x)$ is also an affine transform. Then, we can construct a univariate polynomial $P_i(Y_i)$ in terms of Y_i using the condition that the sum of $z_{26,i}$ is 0. The degree of P_i denoted by $\mathcal{D}$ is the degree of the inverse of G and we have $\mathcal{D} = 2^{32} - 1$. Hence, we can estimate the time to construct $P_i(Y_i)$ as about $2^{H(\mathcal{D})} \times 2^{63} = 2^{32+63} = 2^{95}$ field operations. Then, similar to the idea in [19], recovering Y_i is reduced to finding the roots of the univariate polynomial P_i, the time complexity of which can be estimated as $O(\mathcal{D} \times \log(\mathcal{D}) \times \log\log(\mathcal{D}) \times \log(\mathcal{D}) \times \log(2^{63}\mathcal{D}))$ field operations. Hence, we estimate the time complexity to find the roots as 2^{51}. Hence, the time complexity and data complexity of our key-recovery attack on 13.5 rounds of Chaghri are $3 \times (2^{51} + 2^{95}) = 2^{96.6}$ and 2^{63}, respectively.

4.2 Further Refining the Upper Bounds

In this section, we show that before reaching the maximal algebraic degree n, it is possible to refine D_r with more careful analysis. Consider the input state of the following form

$$z_{0,1} = X_1, \ z_{0,2} = A_2, \ z_{0,3} = A_3, \tag{8}$$

where $A_2, A_3 \in \mathbb{F}_{2^n}$ are randomly chosen constants and X_1 is the variable. Let $X = X_1 + RK[0]_1$. In this way, for any number of steps, each state word of Chaghri can be represented as a univariate polynomial in X. For $(z_{1,1}, z_{1,2}, z_{1,3})$, we have

$$z_{1,1} = A_{1,1} X^{\mathcal{M}_n(2^{k_0+k_2}+2^{k_1+k_2})} + B_{1,1},$$
$$z_{1,2} = A_{1,2} X^{\mathcal{M}_n(2^{k_0+k_2}+2^{k_1+k_2})} + B_{1,2},$$
$$z_{1,3} = A_{1,3} X^{\mathcal{M}_n(2^{k_0+k_2}+2^{k_1+k_2})} + B_{1,3},$$

where $A_{1,i}, B_{1,i}$ $(i \in [1,3])$ are constants depending on the key.

Hence, for w_1, we have

$$w_1 = \{\mathcal{M}_n(2^{k_0+k_2} + 2^{k_1+k_2}), 0\}.$$

Then, we have

$$w_r = \{e | e = \mathcal{M}_n\Big(\sum_{i=1}^{N^r_{n-1}} 2^{n-1} w_{1,d_{i,n-1}} + \sum_{i=1}^{N^r_{n-2}} 2^{n-2} w_{1,d_{i,n-2}} + \ldots + \sum_{i=1}^{N^r_0} 2^0 w_{1,d_{i,0}}\Big),$$
$$\text{where } 1 \le d_{i,j} \le 2 \text{ for } 0 \le j \le n-1\}.$$

By making $N^1_0 = 1$ and $N^1_i = 0$ for $i \in [1, n-1]$, we can compute the corresponding $(N^r_{n-1}, N^r_{n-2}, \ldots, N^r_0)$ for $r \ge 1$ with the recursive relation specified in Eq. 6. Computing D_r is then equivalent to the following optimization problem:

$$\text{maximize } H\Big(\mathcal{M}_n \Big(\sum_{i=0}^{n-1} 2^i (2^{k_0+k_2} \gamma_i + 2^{k_1+k_2} \gamma_i) \Big) \Big),$$

$$\text{subject to } 0 \le \gamma_i \le N^r_i \text{ for } i \in [0, n-1].$$

Table 3. The refined upper bounds for D_r in the univariate case

r	0	2	4	6	8	10	12	14	16	18	20	22	24	26	27
D_r	1	3	7	11	16	21	26	32	37	42	47	52	57	62	63

Refined or Unrefined? This refined model is only slightly slower and all the results can still be obtained in seconds as well. The refined upper bounds are shown in Table 3. We have practically verified our attacks on Chaghri for up to 7 rounds. It is found that our refined bounds are correct and tight. It can be found that although the upper bound is slightly better for $r \leq 12$, the complexity to break 8 rounds of Chaghri remains the same. Moreover, the longest higher-order differential distinguisher still only covers 26 steps, which is indeed a direct result of Theorem 1, i.e. the constraints at step r in the unrefined model are the same with those at step $r + 1$ in the refined model and we reach the maximal degree at step 26 in the unrefined model. Due to the high efficiency of the unrefined model, to detect how long a higher-order differential distinguisher can reach, we prefer the unrefined model.

4.3   On the Multivariate Case

After understanding our attack in the univariate case, it is natural to ask whether the distinguisher can be further extended for more steps with a larger set of inputs, e.g. a set of 2^{2n} different inputs. Specifically, with the following input form

$$z_{0,1} = X_1, Z_{0,2} = X_2, Z_{0,3} = A_3,$$

where $A_3 \in \mathbb{F}_{2^n}$ is a randomly chosen constant and X_1, X_2 are variables, whether the attack can be extended for more steps?

Let $X = B \circ G(X_1 + RK[0]_0)$ and $Y = B \circ G(X_2 + RK[0]_1)$. The state $(z_{1,1}, z_{1,2}, z_{1,3})$ can be represented as multivariate polynomials in (X, Y) as below:

$$z_{1,1} = A_{1,1}X + B_{1,1}Y + C_{1,1}, \;\; z_{1,2} = A_{1,2}X + B_{1,2}Y + C_{1,2},$$
$$z_{1,3} = A_{1,3}X + B_{1,3}Y + C_{1,3}.$$

Note that in the following, we will not repeat emphasizing which are constants in the polynomial representation. Instead, we only say which are variables.

To construct the longest higher-order differential distinguisher with at most 2^{2n} data, it suffices to compute the maximal number of steps r where the maximal algebraic degree $2n$ is first reached for the following input state

$$z_{0,1} = A_{0,1}X + B_{0,1}Y + C_{0,1}, \;\; z_{0,2} = A_{0,2}X + B_{0,2}Y + C_{0,2},$$
$$z_{0,3} = A_{0,3}X + B_{0,3}Y + C_{0,3}, \tag{9}$$

where X, Y are variables. As in the univariate case, 1 more step can always be appended before this distinguisher by using 2^{2n} data. This will result in an r-step distinguisher with data and time complexity of 2^{2n}.

For the input form in Eq. 9, the general form of $(z_{r,1}, z_{r,2}, z_{r,3})$ can be written down, as shown below:

$$z_{r,1} = \sum_{i=1}^{|W_r|} A_{r,i} X^{w_{r,i}} Y^{u_{r,i}}, \; z_{r,2} = \sum_{i=1}^{|W_r|} B_{r,i} X^{w_{r,i}} Y^{u_{r,i}}, z_{r,3} = \sum_{i=1}^{|W_r|} C_{r,i} X^{w_{r,i}} Y^{u_{r,i}},$$

where

$$W_r = \{(w_{r,1}, u_{r,1}), (w_{r,2}, u_{r,2}), \ldots, (w_{r,|W_r|}, u_{r,|W_r|})\}.$$

For W_0, we have

$$W_0 = \{(1,0), (0,1), (0,0)\},$$

which corresponds to the input state specified in Eq. 9.

With similar analysis to trace the evolution of the polynomials through G and B, we have

$$W_{r+1} = \{(e_0, e_1)|$$
$$e_0 = \mathcal{M}_n(2^{k_0+k_2} w_{r,i} + 2^{k_1+k_2} w_{r,j}), e_1 = \mathcal{M}_n(2^{k_0+k_2} u_{r,i} + 2^{k_1+k_2} u_{r,j}),$$
$$1 \le i, j \le |W_r|\}.$$

Specifically, we have

$$B \circ G(z_{r,1}) = c_1 \left(\sum_{i=1}^{|W_r|} A_{r,i} X^{w_{r,i}} Y^{u_{r,i}} \right)^{\mathcal{M}_n(2^{k_0+k_2}+2^{k_1+k_2})} + c_2$$

$$= \sum_{i=1}^{|W_r|} \sum_{j=1}^{|W_r|} A_{r+1,i,j} X^{\mathcal{M}_n(2^{k_0+k_2} w_{r,i} + 2^{k_0+k_2} w_{r,j})} Y^{\mathcal{M}_n(2^{k_0+k_2} u_{r,i} + 2^{k_0+k_2} u_{r,j})}.$$

With the similar deduction as in the univariate case, the set W_r can also be represented using a vector of integers $(N_{n-1}^r, N_{n-1}^r, \ldots, N_0^r)$, as shown below:

$$W_r = \{(e_0, e_1)|$$

$$e_0 = \mathcal{M}_n \left(\overset{N_{n-1}^r}{\underset{i=1}{\sum}} 2^{n-1} w_{0,d_{i,n-1}} + \overset{N_{n-2}^r}{\underset{i=1}{\sum}} 2^{n-2} w_{0,d_{i,n-2}} + \ldots + \overset{N_0^r}{\underset{i=1}{\sum}} 2^0 w_{0,d_{i,0}} ,$$

$$e_1 = \mathcal{M}_n \left(\overset{N_{n-1}^r}{\underset{i=1}{\sum}} 2^{n-1} u_{0,d_{i,n-1}} + \overset{N_{n-2}^r}{\underset{i=1}{\sum}} 2^{n-2} u_{0,d_{i,n-2}} + \ldots + \overset{N_0^r}{\underset{i=1}{\sum}} 2^0 u_{0,d_{i,0}} ,$$

where $1 \le d_{i,j} \le |W_0| = 3$ for $0 \le j \le n-1\}$,

where

$$\begin{cases} N_0^0 = 1, N_i^0 = 0 \text{ for } i \in [1, n-1], \\ N_i^r = N_{(i-k_1-k_2)\%n}^{r-1} + N_{(i-k_0-k_2)\%n}^{r-1} \text{ for } 0 \le i \le n-1, r \ge 1. \end{cases}$$

Since

$$W_0 = \{(1,0), (0,1), (0,0)\},$$

i.e. $(w_i^0, u_i^0) \ne (1,1)$ for $i \in [1,3]$, computing the upper bound of the algebraic degree for the multivariate case is also a natural optimization problem[4], as shown

---

[4] Indeed, this problem can also be solved in $\mathcal{O}(n)$ time with the algorithm in [28].

below:

$$\text{maximize } H\left(\mathcal{M}_n(\sum_{i=0}^{n-1} 2^i \gamma_i)\right) + H\left(\mathcal{M}_n(\sum_{i=0}^{n-1} 2^i \lambda_i)\right),$$
$$\text{subject to } 0 \leq \gamma_i + \lambda_i \leq N_i^r \text{ for } i \in [0, n-1].$$

Why $0 \leq \gamma_i + \lambda_i \leq N_i^r$ should hold is due to $(w_{d_{i,j}}^0, u_{d_{i,j}}^0) \neq (1, 1)$ for any index $d_{i,j} \in [1, 3]$.

It is easy to observe that this model is almost the same as that for the univariate case. Applying it to the Chaghri parameters $(k_0, k_1, k_2, n) = (32, 0, 3, 63)$, we obtain the following upper bound for the algebraic degree D_r after r steps, as shown in Table 4. Note that we still use D_r to denote the upper bound for the algebraic degree for r-step Chaghri in the multivariate case. This indicates that the higher-order differential distinguisher can reach at most $26 + 1 = 27$ steps (i.e. 13.5 rounds) using 2^{126} data.

Table 4. The upper bounds for D_r in the multivariate case

r	0	2	4	6	8	10	12	14	16	18	20	22	24	26	27
D_r	1	4	10	20	30	40	50	60	70	80	90	100	111	121	126

The Refined Upper Bounds. Similar to the refined upper bounds for the univariate case, we are interested whether the data complexity of the 13.5-round higher-order differential attack can be further optimized. Specifically, we re-evaluate the upper bound for the algebraic degree by considering the following input form:

$$z_{0,1} = X_1, z_{0,2} = X_2, z_{0,3} = A_3. \tag{10}$$

where only X_1, X_2 are variables. Moreover, we consider the case when X_1 traverses all the 2^n possible values because only in this case will we need to consider the multivariate polynomials to attack more steps. In this case, let $X = B \circ G(X_1 + RK[0]_1)$ and $Y = X_2 + RK[0]_2$. Hence, X will traverse all the 2^n possible values. In this way, we have

$$z_{1,1} = A_{1,1}X + B_{1,1}Y^{\mathcal{M}_n(2^{k_0+k_2}+2^{k_1+k_2})} + C_{1,1},$$
$$z_{1,2} = A_{1,2}X + B_{1,2}Y^{\mathcal{M}_n(2^{k_0+k_2}+2^{k_1+k_2})} + C_{1,2},$$
$$z_{1,3} = A_{1,3}X + B_{1,3}Y^{\mathcal{M}_n(2^{k_0+k_2}+2^{k_1+k_2})} + C_{1,3},$$

where only X, Y are variables. Hence, we have

$$W_1 = \{(0,0), (1,0), (0, \mathcal{M}_n(2^{k_0+k_2} + 2^{k_1+k_2}))\}.$$

Moreover, we have

$$W_r = \{(e_0, e_1)|$$

$$e_0 = \mathcal{M}_n\Big(\sum_{i=1}^{N_{n-1}^r} 2^{n-1} w_{1,d_{i,n-1}} + \sum_{i=1}^{N_{n-2}^r} 2^{n-2} w_{1,d_{i,n-2}} + \ldots + \sum_{i=1}^{N_0^r} 2^0 w_{1,d_{i,0}} \Big),$$

$$e_1 = \mathcal{M}_n\Big(\sum_{i=1}^{N_{n-1}^r} 2^{n-1} u_{1,d_{i,n-1}} + \sum_{i=1}^{N_{n-2}^r} 2^{n-2} u_{1,d_{i,n-2}} + \ldots + \sum_{i=1}^{N_0^r} 2^0 u_{1,d_{i,0}} \Big),$$

where $1 \le d_{i,j} \le |W_1| = 3$ for $0 \le j \le n-1\}$,

where

$$\begin{cases} N_0^1 = 1, N_i^1 = 0 \text{ for } i \in [1, n-1], \\ N_i^r = N_{(i-k_1-k_2)\%n}^{r-1} + N_{(i-k_0-k_2)\%n}^{r-1} \text{ for } 0 \le i \le n-1,\ r \ge 2. \end{cases}$$

In this way, computing D_r is equivalent to solving the following optimization problem:

$$\text{maximize } H\Big(\mathcal{M}_n(\sum_{i=0}^{n-1} 2^i \gamma_i) \Big) + H\Big(\mathcal{M}_n \big(\sum_{i=0}^{n-1} 2^i (2^{k_0+k_2} \lambda_i + 2^{k_1+k_2} \lambda_i) \big) \Big),$$

$$\text{subject to } H\Big(\mathcal{M}_n(\sum_{i=0}^{n-1} 2^i \gamma_i) \Big) = n,\ 0 \le \gamma_i + \lambda_i \le N_i^r \text{ for } i \in [0, n-1].$$

Note that γ_i represents that we assign nonzero values to γ_i variables $w_{1,d_{j,i}}$ and λ_i represents that we assign nonzero values to λ_i variables $u_{1,d_{j,i}}$. Since $(w_{1,d_{j,i}}, u_{1,d_{j,i}})$ cannot be assigned to nonzero values at the same time due to $W_1 = \{(0,0), (1,0), (0, \mathcal{M}_n(2^{k_0+k_2} + 2^{k_1+k_2}))\}$, we have the constraint $0 \le \gamma_i + \lambda_i \le N_i^r$. Moreover, since X will take all the 2^n possible values, we only are interested in the monomials of the form $X^{\rho_1} Y^{\rho_2}$ where $H(\rho_1) \ge n$, i.e. $H(\rho_1) = n$. This is because for the monomial $X^{\rho_1} Y^{\rho_2}$ where $H(\rho_1) < n$, when X takes all the 2^n possible values, the corresponding sum of $X^{\rho_1} Y^{\rho_2}$ is always 0. Hence, we add the constraint $H(\mathcal{M}_n(\sum_{i=0}^{n-1} 2^i \gamma_i)) = n$.

With this model for Chaghri, we obtain in seconds that

$$D_{27} = 122, \quad D_{28} = 126,$$

which are indeed consistent with Theorem 1, i.e. we cannot increase the length of the distinguisher with the refined model. However, $D_{27} = 122$ indicates that the data and time complexity of the 13.5-round distinguisher are both 2^{123}, which improves the results obtained from the unrefined model by a factor of 2^3.

5   Achieving an Almost Exponential Degree Increase

Based on our degree evaluation, it can be observed that the algebraic degree of Chaghri increases linearly in both the univariate case and multivariate case, which contradicts the designers' expectation that it increases exponentially. Therefore, it is natural to ask what countermeasures can be used to achieve an exponential increase of the algebraic degree. In this section, we focus on this problem.

For FHE-friendly ciphers, reducing the multiplicative depth is of great importance. Hence, we still keep the S-box of the form $G(x) = x^{2^{k_0}+2^{k_1}}$, which has algebraic degree 2. For the affine transform $B(x)$, as it is linear over $\mathbb{F}_{2^n}$ and it is almost cost-free for FHE protocols, we are interested whether choosing a different $B(x)$ can achieve an exponential increase of the algebraic degree.

5.1 Searching for Secure Affine Transforms $B(x)$

We consider a general form of $B(x)$ where we omit the constant part, i.e.

$$B(x) = \sum_{i=1}^{|\mathcal{L}|} c'_i x^{2^{\varphi_i}},$$

where $(c'_1, c'_2, \ldots, c'_{|\mathcal{L}|})$ are constants in $\mathbb{F}_{2^{63}}$ such that $B(x)$ is a permutation and $\mathcal{L} = \{\varphi_1, \varphi_2, \ldots, \varphi_{|\mathcal{L}|}\}$. For the S-box, we keep using $G(x) = x^{2^{32}+1}$.

To utilize our coefficient grouping technique for the above general $B(x)$, we need to adjust the general polynomial representation of $(z_{r,1}, z_{r,2}, z_{r,3})$. First, consider the univariate case and the form of $(z_{r,1}, z_{r,2}, z_{r,3})$ can be written as follows where only X is the variable:

$$z_{r,1} = \sum_{i=1}^{|E_{r,1}|} A_{1,i} X^{\omega_{r,1,i}} + \sum_{i=1}^{|E_{r,2}|} A_{2,i} X^{\omega_{r,2,i}} + \ldots \sum_{i=1}^{|E_{r,l_r}|} A_{3,i} X^{\omega_{r,l_r,i}},$$

$$z_{r,2} = \sum_{i=1}^{|E_{r,1}|} B_{1,i} X^{\omega_{r,1,i}} + \sum_{i=1}^{|E_{r,2}|} B_{2,i} X^{\omega_{r,2,i}} + \ldots \sum_{i=1}^{|E_{r,l_r}|} B_{3,i} X^{\omega_{r,l_r,i}},$$

$$z_{r,3} = \sum_{i=1}^{|E_{r,1}|} C_{1,i} X^{\omega_{r,1,i}} + \sum_{i=1}^{|E_{r,2}|} C_{2,i} X^{\omega_{r,2,i}} + \ldots \sum_{i=1}^{|E_{r,l_r}|} C_{3,i} X^{\omega_{r,l_r,i}},$$

where

$$E_{r,j} = \{\omega_{r,j,1}, \omega_{r,j,2}, \ldots, \omega_{r,j,|E_{r,j}|}\} \text{ for } 1 \leq j \leq l_r.$$

In this way, the set of all possible exponents for $(z_{r,1}, z_{r,2}, z_{r,3})$ denoted by E_r can be written as

$$E_r = \bigcup_{i=1}^{l_r} E_{r,i}.$$

For the initial input $(z_{0,1}, z_{0,2}, z_{0,3})$, we use the same form as specified in Eq. 1. In this way, we have

$$E_0 = w_0 = \{0, 1\} = \{w_{0,1}, w_{0,2}\}.$$

Next, we study how the new general polynomial representation evolves through 1 step of Chaghri. First,

$$G(z_{r,i}) = (\sum_{i=1}^{l_r} \sum_{j=1}^{|E_{r,i}|} A_{i,j} X^{\omega_{r,i,j}})^{2^{32}+1}$$

$$= \sum_{i=1}^{l_r} \sum_{j=1}^{|E_{r,i}|} \sum_{s=1}^{l_r} \sum_{t=1}^{|E_{r,s}|} A_{i,j,s,t} X^{\mathcal{M}_{63}(2^{32}\omega_{r,i,j}+\omega_{r,s,t})},$$

$$B \circ G(z_{r,1}) = \sum_{i=1}^{l_r} \sum_{j=1}^{|E_{r,i}|} \sum_{s=1}^{l_r} \sum_{t=1}^{|E_{r,s}|} \sum_{u=1}^{|\mathcal{L}|} A_{i,j,s,t,u} X^{\mathcal{M}_{63}(2^{32+\varphi_u}\omega_{r,i,j}+2^{\varphi_u}\omega_{r,s,t})}.$$

Hence,

$$E_{r+1} = \{e|e = \mathcal{M}_{63}(2^{32+\varphi_u}\omega_{r,i,j} + 2^{\varphi_u}\omega_{r,s,t}),$$
$$1 \leq i, s \leq l_r, \ 1 \leq j \leq |E_{r,i}|, \ 1 \leq t \leq |E_{r,s}|, 1 \leq u \leq |\mathcal{L}|\}.$$

Based on the above recursive relation between E_r and E_{r+1}, with the coefficient grouping technique, E_r can be represented as follows:

$$E_r = \bigcup_{j=1}^{l_r} E_{r,j},$$

$$E_{r,j} = \{e|e = \mathcal{M}_{63}(\sum_{i=1}^{N_{62}^{r,j}} 2^{62} w_{0,d_{i,62}} + \sum_{i=1}^{N_{61}^{r,j}} 2^{61} w_{0,d_{i,61}} + \ldots + \sum_{i=1}^{N_0^{r,j}} 2^0 w_{0,d_{i,0}}),$$

where $1 \leq d_{i,i_0} \leq |w_0|$ for $0 \leq i_0 \leq 62\}.$

Proof. For E_0, there are

$$E_0 = E_{0,1} = w_0 = \{0,1\} = \{w_{0,1}, w_{0,2}\},$$
$$E_{0,1} = \{e|e = \mathcal{M}_{63}(2^0 w_{0,i}), \ 1 \leq i \leq |w_0|\}.$$

Hence, it holds for $r = 0$. Supposing the above new representation of E_r holds, we now prove by induction that it also holds for E_{r+1}. In particular, a similar useful recursive relation can be derived.

Since

$$E_{r+1} = \{e|e = \mathcal{M}_{63}(2^{32+\varphi_u}\omega_{r,i,j} + 2^{\varphi_u}\omega_{r,s,t}),$$
$$1 \leq i, s \leq l_r, \ 1 \leq j \leq |E_{r,i}|, \ 1 \leq t \leq |E_{r,s}|, 1 \leq u \leq |\mathcal{L}|\},$$

we have

$$E_{r+1} = \bigcup_{i=1}^{l_r} \bigcup_{s=1}^{l_r} \bigcup_{u=1}^{|\mathcal{L}|} E_{r+1,i,s,u},$$

$$E_{r+1,i,s,u} = \{e|e = \mathcal{M}_{63}(2^{32+\varphi_u}\omega_{r,i,j} + 2^{\varphi_u}\omega_{r,s,t}), \ 1 \leq j \leq |E_{r,i}|, \ 1 \leq t \leq |E_{r,s}|\}.$$

Since

$$E_{r,j} = \{e | e = \mathcal{M}_{63}(\sum_{i=1}^{N_{62}^{r,j}} 2^{62} w_{0,d_{i,62}} + \sum_{i=1}^{N_{61}^{r,j}} 2^{61} w_{0,d_{i,61}} + \ldots + \sum_{i=1}^{N_0^{r,j}} 2^0 w_{0,d_{i,0}}),$$

$$\text{where } 1 \leq d_{i,i_0} \leq |w_0| \text{ for } 0 \leq i_0 \leq 62\},$$

we have

$$E_{r+1,i,s,u} = \{e | e = \mathcal{M}_{63}(\sum_{j=1}^{N_{62}^{r+1,i,s,u}} 2^{62} w_{0,d_{j,62}} + \ldots + \sum_{j=1}^{N_0^{r+1,i,s,u}} 2^0 w_{0,d_{j,0}}),$$

$$\text{where } 1 \leq d_{j,j_0} \leq |w_0| \text{ for } 0 \leq j_0 \leq 62\},$$

where

$$N_t^{r+1,i,s,u} = N_{(t-32-\varphi_u)\%63}^{r,i} + N_{(t-\varphi_u)\%63}^{r,s} \text{ for } t \in [0,62]. \qquad (11)$$

□

With the above critical observation, we can always decompose E_r as a union of sets, each of which can be solely described with a vector of integers $(N_{62}, N_{61}, \ldots, N_0)$. Moreover, since $E_0 = w_0$, a single vector of integers $(N_{62}^{0,1}, N_{61}^{0,1}, \ldots, N_{61}^{0,1})$ is sufficient to describe E_0 where

$$N_0^{0,1} = 1, N_i^{0,1} = 0 \text{ for } i \in [1,62].$$

Then, based on the recursive relation specified in Eq. 11, for each E_r ($r \geq 1$), we can compute the corresponding sets of vectors of integers to represent E_r. The algorithm is shown in Algorithm 2, where $\mathbf{N}^r$ and $\mathbf{N}^{r+1}$ are the sets of possible vectors of integers describing E_r and E_{r+1}, respectively.

In Algorithm 2, there is a function named REDUCE. This is used to remove the redundant vectors based on the fact that when there are two vectors $(N_{62}, N_{61}, \ldots, N_0)$ and $(N_{62}', N_{61}', \ldots, N_0')$ such that $N_i \geq N_i'$ for each $i \in [0,62]$, the set described with $(N_{62}', N_{61}', \ldots, N_0')$ is just a subset of the set described with $(N_{62}, N_{61}, \ldots, N_0)$.

The Main Idea to Search for a Good Affine Transform. With Algorithm 2, it is now possible to describe how to search for a better affine transform. Specifically, for each E_r, there exist l_r vectors of integers $(N_{62}^{r,i}, N_{61}^{r,i}, \ldots, N_0^{r,i})$ to describe $E_{r,i}$ for $i \in [1, l_r]$. Moreover, if there exists a vector $(N_{62}^{r,i}, N_{61}^{r,i}, \ldots, N_0^{r,i})$ where there are $\mathbb{D}$ nonzero elements, it implies the upper bound for the algebraic degree after r steps is larger than $\mathbb{D}$. This is because it implies that there exists an element $e \in E_r$ such that $H(e) = \mathbb{D}$. Hence, to achieve an exponential increase for the first r ($1 \leq r \leq 5$) steps, we need to ensure that there exists at least one vector $(N_{62}^{r,i}, N_{61}^{r,i}, \ldots, N_0^{r,i})$ where there are 2^r nonzero elements. For $r = 6$, we can slightly relax the constraint and expect that after 7 steps, the maximal degree 63 is reached, i.e. there exists a vector $(N_{62}^{7,i}, N_{61}^{7,i}, \ldots, N_0^{7,i})$

Algorithm 2. Enumerating vectors to represent E_{r+1}

1: **procedure** ENU($\mathbf{N}^r, \mathbf{N}^{r+1}, \mathcal{L}$)
2:     clear $\mathbf{N}^{r+1}$
3:     **for** i in range ($\mathbf{N}^r$.size()) **do**
4:         $(N_{62}^0, N_{61}^0, \ldots, N_0^0) \leftarrow \mathbf{N}^r[i]$
5:         **for** s in range ($\mathbf{N}^r$.size()) **do**
6:             $(N_{62}^1, N_{61}^1, \ldots, N_0^1) \leftarrow \mathbf{N}^r[s]$
7:             **for** $u \in [1, |\mathcal{L}|]$ **do**
8:                 **for** $t \in [0, 62]$ **do**
9:                     $N_t = N_{(t-32-\varphi_u)\%63}^0 + N_{(t-\varphi_u)\%63}^1$
10:                     **if** REDUCE($N_{62}, N_{61}, \ldots, N_0, \mathbf{N}^{r+1}$)$=1$ **then**
11:                         add $(N_{62}, N_{61}, \ldots, N_0)$ to $\mathbf{N}^{r+1}$
12: **procedure** REDUCE($N_{62}, N_{61}, \ldots, N_0, \mathbf{N}$)
13:     **for** i in range ($\mathbf{N}$.size()) **do**
14:         $(N_{62}', N_{61}', \ldots, N_0') \leftarrow \mathbf{N}[i]$
15:         **if** $N_j \geq N_j'$ for all $j \in [0, 62]$ **then**
16:             $\mathbf{N}[i] = (N_{62}, N_{61}, \ldots, N_0)$
17:             return 0
18:         **else if** $N_j' \geq N_j$ for all $j \in [0, 62]$ **then**
19:             return 0
20:     return 1

---

where all the elements are nonzero or there exists a vector $(N_{62}^{7,i}, N_{61}^{7,i}, \ldots, N_0^{7,i})$ such that the solution to the following optimization problem is 63:

$$\text{maximize } H\left(\mathcal{M}_{63}(\sum_{j=0}^{62} 2^j \gamma_j)\right),$$

$$\text{subject to } 0 \leq \gamma_j \leq N_j^{7,i} \text{ for } j \in [0, 62].$$

Searching with Heuristic Strategies. For $r = 0$, there are

$$l_0 = 1, \quad \mathbf{N}^0 = \{(0, 0, \ldots, 0, 1)\}.$$

Then, based on Algorithm 2, for any $r \geq 1$, we can always compute $\mathbf{N}^r$ for any given $\mathcal{L}$. However, the time complexity to compute $\mathbf{N}^r$ becomes exponential in r when $|\mathcal{L}| > 1$ due to the fast diffusion of the monomials. Even for small r, e.g. $r = 5$, if we aim to compute the full set of vectors, it cannot be finished in practical time. However, since we are only interested in vectors where there are a desired number of nonzero elements, we can use some heuristic strategies when computing $\mathbf{N}^r$.

Specifically, for the first r steps ($1 \leq r \leq 5$), we only add the vectors where there are 2^r nonzero elements to $\mathbf{N}^r$ when running Algorithm 2. The underlying reason is that to generate a monomial whose exponent is of hamming weight 2^r at step r, it is required to have two monomials (X^{e_0}, X^{e_1}) where $H(e_0) = H(e_1) = 2^{r-1}$ at step $r-1$. When there exists an empty set $\mathbf{N}^r$ for $1 \leq r \leq 5$, we abandon the current $\mathcal{L}$ and try another $\mathcal{L}$ since it implies we cannot reach the algebraic degree 2^r with the current $\mathcal{L}$. Based on this strategy, we find no candidates for $\mathcal{L}$ when $|\mathcal{L}| = 2$.

Hence, $|\mathcal{L}| = 3$ is taken into account. For $1 \leq r \leq 5$, we still use the above strategies. However, the size of $\mathbf{N}^r$ will increase exponentially. Hence, we further restrict that when the size of $\mathbf{N}^r$ is larger than 2^{13}, exit Algorithm 2 and compute $\mathbf{N}^{r+1}$. For $r = 6$, we only add the vectors where there are at least 55 nonzero elements to $\mathbf{N}^6$. For $r = 7$, when computing $\mathbf{N}^7$ with Algorithm 2, we test whether there is one $(N_{62}^{7,i}, N_{61}^{7,i}, \ldots, N_0^{7,i})$ which can lead to the maximal degree 63. If there is, exit and treat the current $\mathcal{L}$ as a good affine transform. It is found that $\mathcal{L} = \{0, 2, 8\}$ is such a candidate.

With $\mathcal{L} = \{0, 2, 8\}$, for the input of the form specified in Eq. 1, the algebraic degree can reach 63 after 7 steps. Therefore, for the input of the form specified in Eq. 8, the algebraic degree can reach 63 after 8 steps, which is a direct application of Theorem 1. In this way, an almost exponential increase of the algebraic degree is achieved in the univariate setting.

5.2 Evaluating the Algebraic Degree for the Multivariate Case

After obtaining a good affine transform $B(x)$ which can ensure an almost exponential increase of the algebraic degree in the univariate setting, we study how the algebraic degree increases in the multivariate setting. In general, after we reach the maximal algebraic degree in the univariate case, due to the strong diffusion of the MDS matrix and the affine transform, the maximal algebraic degree in the multivariate case can be reached in a few more steps. For Chaghri, we only care about the distinguisher with data complexity and time complexity below 2^{128} since Chaghri only provides 128-bit security. Hence, we only care about when the algebraic degree 128 is reached.

On Two Variables. We first consider the input of the form specified in Eq. 9. Then, similar to the above analysis, the general polynomial representation of $(z_{r,1}, z_{r,2}, z_{r,3})$ can be written as follows:

$$z_{r,1} = \sum_{i=1}^{l_r} \sum_{j=1}^{|U_{r,i}|} A_{i,j} X^{\omega_{r,i,j}} Y^{\mu_{r,i,j}}, \quad z_{r,2} = \sum_{i=1}^{l_r} \sum_{j=1}^{|U_{r,i}|} B_{i,j} X^{\omega_{r,i,j}} Y^{\mu_{r,i,j}},$$

$$z_{r,3} = \sum_{i=1}^{l_r} \sum_{j=1}^{|U_{r,i}|} C_{i,j} X^{\omega_{r,i,j}} Y^{\mu_{r,i,j}},$$

where

$$U_{r,i} = \{(\omega_{r,i,1}, \mu_{r,i,1}), (\omega_{r,i,2}, \mu_{r,i,2}), \ldots, (\omega_{r,i,|U_{r,i}|}, \mu_{r,i,|U_{r,i}|})\} \text{ for } i \in [1, l_r]$$

and $U_r = \bigcup_{i=1}^{l_r} U_{r,i}$ is the set of all possible exponents for $(z_{r,1}, z_{r,2}, z_{r,3})$.

For the input form specified in Eq. 9, we have

$$l_0 = 1, \ U_0 = U_{0,1} = W_0,$$
$$W_0 = \{(0,1), (1,0), (0,0)\} = \{(w_{0,1}, u_{0,1}), (w_{0,2}, u_{0,2}), (w_{0,3}, u_{0,3})\}.$$

Then, by tracing the evolution of the polynomials through 1 step of Chaghri, we can similarly derive

$$U_{r+1} = \{(e_0, e_1)|$$
$$e_0 = \mathcal{M}_{63}(2^{32+\varphi_u} w_{r,i,j} + 2^{\varphi_u} w_{r,s,t}), \ e_1 = \mathcal{M}_{63}(2^{32+\varphi_u} \mu_{r,i,j} + 2^{\varphi_u} \mu_{r,s,t}),$$
$$1 \leq i, s \leq l_r, \ 1 \leq j \leq |U_{r,i}|, \ 1 \leq t \leq |U_{r,s}|, 1 \leq u \leq |\mathcal{L}|\}.$$

With the coefficient grouping technique, similarly, $U_{r,j}$ $(1 \leq j \leq l_r)$ can be represented as

$$U_{r,j} = \{(e_0, e_1)|$$
$$e_0 = \mathcal{M}_{63}(\sum_{i=1}^{N_{62}^{r,j}} 2^{62} w_{0,d_{i,62}} + \sum_{i=1}^{N_{61}^{r,j}} 2^{61} w_{0,d_{i,61}} + \ldots + \sum_{i=1}^{N_0^{r,j}} 2^0 w_{0,d_{i,0}}),$$
$$e_1 = \mathcal{M}_{63}(\sum_{i=1}^{N_{62}^{r,j}} 2^{62} u_{0,d_{i,62}} + \sum_{i=1}^{N_{61}^{r,j}} 2^{61} u_{0,d_{i,61}} + \ldots + \sum_{i=1}^{N_0^{r,j}} 2^0 u_{0,d_{i,0}}),$$
$$1 \leq d_{i,i_0} \leq |W_0|, 0 \leq i_0 \leq 62\},$$

where $W_0 = \{(w_{0,1}, u_{0,1}), (w_{0,2}, u_{0,2}), (w_{0,3}, u_{0,3})\} = \{(0,1), (1,0), (0,0)\}$. Moreover, the recursive relation remains the same as in the univariate case, i.e. Eq. 11. In other words, it is sufficient to describe U_r with a set of vectors of integers and we still denote the set by $\mathbf{N}^r$ to avoid the abuse of notation. Then,

$$\mathbf{N}^0 = \{(0, 0, \ldots, 0, 1)\}$$

and Algorithm 2 can be directly used to compute $\mathbf{N}^r$ for $r \geq 1$.

Supposing there exists a vector $(N_{62}^{r,i}, N_{61}^{r,i}, \ldots, N_0^{r,i})$ in $\mathbf{N}^r$ such that the solution to the following optimization problem is 126, we reach the maximal degree for the input of the form in Eq. 9 after r steps.

$$\text{maximize } H\left(\mathcal{M}_{63}(\sum_{j=0}^{62} 2^j \gamma_j)\right) + H\left(\mathcal{M}_{63}(\sum_{j=0}^{62} 2^j \lambda_j)\right),$$

$$\text{subject to } 0 \leq \gamma_j + \lambda_j \leq N_j^{r,i} \text{ for } j \in [0, 62].$$

Moreover, for the input of the form specified in Eq. 10, the degree 126 can be reached after $r + 1$ steps by applying Theorem 1.

For $\mathcal{L} = \{0, 2, 8\}$, the maximal degree 126 can be reached at $r = 9$ for the input specified in Eq. 10. This implies that 9 steps are secure against the higher-order differential distinguishing attack with complexity below 2^{126}. Compared with the univariate case, only at most 1 more step can be reached. This is indeed as expected due to the strong diffusion effect of the affine transform and MDS matrix.

On Three Variables. Since the algebraic degree will reach 126 after 9 steps when there are 2 variables, we can argue that the algebraic degree will be much larger than 128 after 9 or 10 steps when considering 3 variables. For completeness, we also consider the case when there are 3 variables.

Consider the following input of the form:

$$z_{0,1} = A_{0,1}X + B_{0,1}Y + C_{0,1}Z,$$
$$z_{0,2} = A_{0,2}X + B_{0,2}Y + C_{0,2}Z,$$
$$z_{0,3} = A_{0,3}X + B_{0,3}Y + C_{0,3}Z,$$

where X, Y, Z are variables.

Then, we will have an initial set U_0 of all possible exponents where

$$U_0 = W_0 = \{(0,0,1),(0,1,0),(1,0,0),(0,0,0)\}.$$

To avoid the abuse of notation, we use the same notation as in the case for 2 variables. Then, it can be similarly derived that U_r can be fully described with a set of vectors of integers denoted by $\mathbf{N}^r$ where $\mathbf{N}^0 = \{(0,0,\dots,0,1)\}$ and $\mathbf{N}^r$ $(r \geq 1)$ can be computed with Algorithm 2. With $\mathbf{N}^r$ $(r \geq 1)$, it is possible to give a lower bound for the algebraic degree after r steps for the above input polynomials in (X, Y, Z). Specifically, if there exists a vector $(N_{62}^{r,i}, N_{61}^{r,i}, \dots, N_0^{r,i})$ in $\mathbf{N}^r$ such that the solution to the following optimization problem is SOL, the lower bound is SOL:

$$\text{maximize } H\left(\mathcal{M}_{63}(\sum_{j=0}^{62} 2^j \gamma_j)\right) + H\left(\mathcal{M}_{63}(\sum_{j=0}^{62} 2^j \lambda_j)\right) + H\left(\mathcal{M}_{63}(\sum_{j=0}^{62} 2^j \chi_j)\right),$$

subject to $0 \leq \gamma_j + \lambda_j + \chi_j \leq N_j^{r,i}$ for $j \in [0, 62]$.

As Chaghri only provides 128-bit security, we only need to ensure SOL ≥ 128. It is found that SOL ≥ 187 when $r = 8$ and SOL $= 189$ when $r = 9$, which imply that 9 steps are secure against our higher-order differential distinguishing attack.

5.3   New Parameters for **Chaghri**

According to [6], the total number of rounds T is chosen with the formula $T = 1.5 \times \max\{5, \eta\}$, where η is the maximal number of rounds that can be attacked with time complexity below 2^{128}. With $\mathcal{L} = \{0, 2, 8\}$, we have $\eta = 4$ and hence the total number of rounds T can be kept unchanged, i.e. $T = 8$. In the following, we give an optional assignment to (c_1', c_2', c_3', c_4') such that $B(x) = c_1'x + c_2'x^4 + c_3'x^{256} + c_4'$ is a permutation.

$$c_1' = \alpha^{60} + \alpha^{57} + \alpha^{54} + \alpha^{53} + \alpha^{49} + \alpha^{48} + \alpha^{45} + \alpha^{42} + \alpha^{40} + \alpha^{38}$$
$$+ \alpha^{35} + \alpha^{33} + \alpha^{27} + \alpha^{26} + \alpha^{25} + \alpha^{24} + \alpha^{23} + \alpha^{21} + \alpha^{19} + \alpha^{18}$$
$$+ \alpha^{16} + \alpha^{14} + \alpha^{13} + \alpha^{12} + \alpha^{9} + \alpha^{8} + \alpha^{6} + \alpha^{4},$$
$$c_2' = \alpha^{61} + \alpha^{60} + \alpha^{59} + \alpha^{58} + \alpha^{57} + \alpha^{55} + \alpha^{51} + \alpha^{50} + \alpha^{49} + \alpha^{48}$$
$$+ \alpha^{46} + \alpha^{45} + \alpha^{44} + \alpha^{41} + \alpha^{38} + \alpha^{35} + \alpha^{30} + \alpha^{29} + \alpha^{27} + \alpha^{26}$$
$$+ \alpha^{14} + \alpha^{12} + \alpha^{10} + \alpha^{9} + \alpha^{8} + \alpha^{7} + \alpha^{5} + \alpha,$$
$$c_3' = \alpha^{62} + \alpha^{61} + \alpha^{57} + \alpha^{53} + \alpha^{52} + \alpha^{50} + \alpha^{48} + \alpha^{47} + \alpha^{46} + \alpha^{45}$$
$$+ \alpha^{44} + \alpha^{43} + \alpha^{38} + \alpha^{36} + \alpha^{35} + \alpha^{34} + \alpha^{32} + \alpha^{30} + \alpha^{27} + \alpha^{26}$$
$$+ \alpha^{24} + \alpha^{19} + \alpha^{18} + \alpha^{16} + \alpha^{14} + \alpha^{12} + \alpha^{11} + \alpha^{8} + \alpha^{7} + \alpha^{5} + \alpha^{2} + \alpha,$$
$$c_4' = \alpha^{62} + \alpha^{55} + \alpha^{54} + \alpha^{52} + \alpha^{50} + \alpha^{49} + \alpha^{43} + \alpha^{40} + \alpha^{39} + \alpha^{38} + \alpha^{37}$$
$$+ \alpha^{36} + \alpha^{35} + \alpha^{34} + \alpha^{32} + \alpha^{31} + \alpha^{29} + \alpha^{26} + \alpha^{25} + \alpha^{24} + \alpha^{23} + \alpha^{22}$$
$$+ \alpha^{21} + \alpha^{18} + \alpha^{15} + \alpha^{12} + \alpha^{11} + \alpha^{10} + \alpha^{5} + \alpha^{2} + \alpha.$$

6   Conclusion

We perform an in-depth study on the increase of the algebraic degree of Chaghri by proposing a novel efficient technique called coefficient grouping. In its core, it is an efficient way to represent the polynomial of any rounds of Chaghri in terms of the input. Especially, such an efficient representation can be determined by a single vector of integers that can be computed in linear time. Benefiting from this representation, upper bounding the algebraic degree is reduced to some well-structured optimization problems that can be efficiently solved by either an $\mathcal{O}(n)$ algorithm [28] or the general-purpose solvers.

One important feature of this technique is to use efficient recursive relations to equivalently describe the heavy monomial transitions through the round function. However, in the well-known technique called division property, this has to be modelled round by round and the corresponding cost is high. Especially, with our technique applied to Chaghri, we can compute relatively tight upper bounds of the algebraic degree in linear time, which obviously distinguish it from other techniques.

With this technique, we can break the full 8 rounds of Chaghri with low complexity and can even break up to 13.5 rounds. This is in a way indicates that the lack of techniques to analyze such primitives defined over a large field is still a major issue. With the coefficient grouping technique, we further make a step towards this important question. Specifically, we not only attack a cipher with it, but also describe how to use it to search for secure cryptographic components.

Finally, we mention a few open questions:

- How to find a relatively sparse affine layer that can help achieve the exponential degree increase in a more efficient way?

- Is there a more refined (or even analytical) method to explain how much dense the affine layer should be to achieve an exponential degree increase?
- How to give tight upper bounds of the algebraic degree when the affine layer is dense?

Acknowledgement. We thank Mohammad Mahzoun and Tomer Ashur for carefully checking our results. We also thank the reviewers of EUROCRYPT 2023 for providing many insightful comments. Fukang Liu is supported by Grant-in-Aid for Research Activity Start-up (Grant No. 22K21282). Takanori Isobe is supported by JST, PRESTO Grant Number JPMJPR2031. These research results were also obtained from the commissioned research (No.05801) by National Institute of Information and Communications Technology (NICT), Japan. Libo Wang is supported by the National Natural Science Foundation of China under Grants 62102167, 62032025, and by the Guangdong Basic and Applied Basic Research Foundation under Grants 2022A1515010299, 2020A1515110364.

References

1. Albrecht, M.R., et al.: Algebraic cryptanalysis of STARK-friendly designs: application to MARVELLOUS and MiMC. In: Galbraith, S.D., Moriai, S. (eds.) ASIACRYPT 2019. LNCS, vol. 11923, pp. 371–397. Springer, Cham (2019). https://doi.org/10.1007/978-3-030-34618-8_13

2. Albrecht, M., Grassi, L., Rechberger, C., Roy, A., Tiessen, T.: MiMC: efficient encryption and cryptographic hashing with minimal multiplicative complexity. In: Cheon, J.H., Takagi, T. (eds.) ASIACRYPT 2016. LNCS, vol. 10031, pp. 191–219. Springer, Heidelberg (2016). https://doi.org/10.1007/978-3-662-53887-6_7

3. Albrecht, M.R., Rechberger, C., Schneider, T., Tiessen, T., Zohner, M.: Ciphers for MPC and FHE. In: Oswald, E., Fischlin, M. (eds.) EUROCRYPT 2015. LNCS, vol. 9056, pp. 430–454. Springer, Heidelberg (2015). https://doi.org/10.1007/978-3-662-46800-5_17

4. Aly, A., Ashur, T., Ben-Sasson, E., Dhooghe, S., Szepieniec, A.: Design of symmetric-key primitives for advanced cryptographic protocols. IACR Trans. Symmetric Cryptol. **2020**(3), 1–45 (2020). https://doi.org/10.13154/tosc.v2020.i3.1-45

5. Ashur, T., Dhooghe, S.: MARVELlous: a STARK-friendly family of cryptographic primitives. IACR Cryptol. ePrint Arch., p. 1098 (2018). https://eprint.iacr.org/2018/1098

6. Ashur, T., Mahzoun, M., Toprakhisar, D.: Chaghri – an FHE-friendly block cipher. Cryptology ePrint Archive, Paper 2022/592 (2022). https://eprint.iacr.org/2022/592

7. Beyne, T., et al.: Out of oddity – new cryptanalytic techniques against symmetric primitives optimized for integrity proof systems. In: Micciancio, D., Ristenpart, T. (eds.) CRYPTO 2020. LNCS, vol. 12172, pp. 299–328. Springer, Cham (2020). https://doi.org/10.1007/978-3-030-56877-1_11

8. Boura, C., Canteaut, A., De Cannière, C.: Higher-order differential properties of KECCAK and *Luffa*. In: Joux, A. (ed.) FSE 2011. LNCS, vol. 6733, pp. 252–269. Springer, Heidelberg (2011). https://doi.org/10.1007/978-3-642-21702-9_15

9. Bouvier, C., Canteaut, A., Perrin, L.: On the algebraic degree of iterated power functions. IACR Cryptol. ePrint Arch., p. 366 (2022). https://eprint.iacr.org/2022/366

10. Canteaut, A., et al.: Stream ciphers: a practical solution for efficient homomorphic-ciphertext compression. In: Peyrin, T. (ed.) FSE 2016. LNCS, vol. 9783, pp. 313–333. Springer, Heidelberg (2016). https://doi.org/10.1007/978-3-662-52993-5_16

11. Cid, C., Grassi, L., Gunsing, A., Lüftenegger, R., Rechberger, C., Schofnegger, M.: Influence of the linear layer on the algebraic degree in SP-networks. IACR Trans. Symmetric Cryptol. **2022**(1), 110–137 (2022). https://doi.org/10.46586/tosc.v2022.i1.110-137

12. Cid, C., Indrøy, J.P., Raddum, H.: FASTA – a stream cipher for fast FHE evaluation. In: Galbraith, S.D. (ed.) CT-RSA 2022. LNCS, vol. 13161, pp. 451–483. Springer, Cham (2022). https://doi.org/10.1007/978-3-030-95312-6_19

13. Cui, J., Hu, K., Wang, M., Wei, P.: On the field-based division property: applications to MiMC, Feistel MiMC and GMiMC. In: ASIACRYPT (3). Lecture Notes in Computer Science, vol. 13793, pp. 241–270. Springer, Heidelberg (2022). https://doi.org/10.1007/978-3-031-22969-5_9

14. Dinur, I.: Cryptanalytic applications of the polynomial method for solving multivariate equation systems over GF(2). In: Canteaut, A., Standaert, F.-X. (eds.) EUROCRYPT 2021. LNCS, vol. 12696, pp. 374–403. Springer, Cham (2021). https://doi.org/10.1007/978-3-030-77870-5_14

15. Dobraunig, C., et al.: Rasta: a cipher with low ANDdepth and few ANDs per bit. In: Shacham, H., Boldyreva, A. (eds.) CRYPTO 2018. LNCS, vol. 10991, pp. 662–692. Springer, Cham (2018). https://doi.org/10.1007/978-3-319-96884-1_22

16. Dobraunig, C., Grassi, L., Guinet, A., Kuijsters, D.: CIMINION: symmetric encryption based on toffoli-gates over large finite fields. In: Canteaut, A., Standaert, F.-X. (eds.) EUROCRYPT 2021. LNCS, vol. 12697, pp. 3–34. Springer, Cham (2021). https://doi.org/10.1007/978-3-030-77886-6_1

17. Dobraunig, C., Grassi, L., Helminger, L., Rechberger, C., Schofnegger, M., Walch, R.: Pasta: a case for hybrid homomorphic encryption. IACR Cryptol. ePrint Arch., p. 731 (2021). https://eprint.iacr.org/2021/731

18. Duval, S., Lallemand, V., Rotella, Y.: Cryptanalysis of the FLIP family of stream ciphers. In: Robshaw, M., Katz, J. (eds.) CRYPTO 2016. LNCS, vol. 9814, pp. 457–475. Springer, Heidelberg (2016). https://doi.org/10.1007/978-3-662-53018-4_17

19. Eichlseder, M., et al.: An algebraic attack on ciphers with low-degree round functions: application to full MiMC. In: Moriai, S., Wang, H. (eds.) ASIACRYPT 2020. LNCS, vol. 12491, pp. 477–506. Springer, Cham (2020). https://doi.org/10.1007/978-3-030-64837-4_16

20. Grassi, L., Lüftenegger, R., Rechberger, C., Rotaru, D., Schofnegger, M.: On a generalization of substitution-permutation networks: the HADES design strategy. In: Canteaut, A., Ishai, Y. (eds.) EUROCRYPT 2020. LNCS, vol. 12106, pp. 674–704. Springer, Cham (2020). https://doi.org/10.1007/978-3-030-45724-2_23

21. Ma, H., et al.: Masta: an HE-friendly cipher using modular arithmetic. IEEE Access **8**, 194741–194751 (2020). https://doi.org/10.1109/ACCESS.2020.3033564

22. Hao, Y., Leander, G., Meier, W., Todo, Y., Wang, Q.: Modeling for three-subset division property without unknown subset. In: Canteaut, A., Ishai, Y. (eds.) EUROCRYPT 2020. LNCS, vol. 12105, pp. 466–495. Springer, Cham (2020). https://doi.org/10.1007/978-3-030-45721-1_17

23. Hebborn, P., Leander, G.: Dasta - alternative linear layer for Rasta. IACR Trans. Symmetric Cryptol. **2020**(3), 46–86 (2020). https://doi.org/10.13154/tosc.v2020.i3.46-86

24. Hu, K., Sun, S., Wang, M., Wang, Q.: An algebraic formulation of the division property: revisiting degree evaluations, cube attacks, and key-independent sums. In: Moriai, S., Wang, H. (eds.) ASIACRYPT 2020. LNCS, vol. 12491, pp. 446–476. Springer, Cham (2020). https://doi.org/10.1007/978-3-030-64837-4_15
25. Liu, F., Isobe, T., Meier, W.: Cryptanalysis of full LowMC and LowMC-M with algebraic techniques. In: Malkin, T., Peikert, C. (eds.) CRYPTO 2021. LNCS, vol. 12827, pp. 368–401. Springer, Cham (2021). https://doi.org/10.1007/978-3-030-84252-9_13
26. Liu, F., Sarkar, S., Meier, W., Isobe, T.: Algebraic attacks on rasta and dasta using low-degree equations. In: Tibouchi, M., Wang, H. (eds.) ASIACRYPT 2021. LNCS, vol. 13090, pp. 214–240. Springer, Cham (2021). https://doi.org/10.1007/978-3-030-92062-3_8
27. Liu, F., Sarkar, S., Wang, G., Meier, W., Isobe, T.: Algebraic meet-in-the-middle attack on LowMC. In: ASIACRYPT (1). Lecture Notes in Computer Science, vol. 13791, pp. 225–255. Springer, Heidelberg (2022). https://doi.org/10.1007/978-3-031-22963-3_8
28. Liu, F., Wang, L.: An $\mathcal{O}(n)$ algorithm for coefficient grouping. Cryptology ePrint Archive, Paper 2022/992 (2022). https://eprint.iacr.org/2022/992
29. Méaux, P., Journault, A., Standaert, F.-X., Carlet, C.: Towards stream ciphers for efficient FHE with low-noise ciphertexts. In: Fischlin, M., Coron, J.-S. (eds.) EUROCRYPT 2016. LNCS, vol. 9665, pp. 311–343. Springer, Heidelberg (2016). https://doi.org/10.1007/978-3-662-49890-3_13
30. Rechberger, C., Soleimany, H., Tiessen, T.: Cryptanalysis of low-data instances of full LowMCv2. IACR Trans. Symmetric Cryptol. 2018(3), 163–181 (2018). https://doi.org/10.13154/tosc.v2018.i3.163-181
31. Todo, Y., Morii, M.: Bit-based division property and application to SIMON family. In: Peyrin, T. (ed.) FSE 2016. LNCS, vol. 9783, pp. 357–377. Springer, Heidelberg (2016). https://doi.org/10.1007/978-3-662-52993-5_18
32. Xiang, Z., Zhang, W., Bao, Z., Lin, D.: Applying MILP method to searching integral distinguishers based on division property for 6 lightweight block ciphers. In: Cheon, J.H., Takagi, T. (eds.) ASIACRYPT 2016. LNCS, vol. 10031, pp. 648–678. Springer, Heidelberg (2016). https://doi.org/10.1007/978-3-662-53887-6_24

Pitfalls and Shortcomings
for Decompositions and Alignment

Baptiste Lambin[1,2], Gregor Leander[1], and Patrick Neumann[1(✉)]

[1] Ruhr University Bochum, Bochum, Germany
{gregor.leander,patrick.neumann}@rub.de
[2] University of Luxembourg, Esch-sur-Alzette, Luxembourg
baptiste.lambin@protonmail.com

Abstract. In this paper we, for the first time, study the question under which circumstances decomposing a round function of a Substitution-Permutation Network is possible *uniquely*. More precisely, we provide necessary and sufficient criteria for the non-linear layer on when a decomposition is unique. Our results in particular imply that, when cryptographically strong S-boxes are used, the decomposition is indeed unique. We then apply our findings to the notion of alignment, pointing out that the previous definition allows for primitives that are both aligned and unaligned simultaneously.

As a second result, we present experimental data that shows that alignment might only have limited impact. For this, we compare aligned and unaligned versions of the cipher PRESENT.

Keywords: Supstitution-Permutation Network · Alignment · PRESENT

1 Introduction

Most of the security analysis of symmetric primitives is actually based on their representation and not on the primitive itself: When arguing about the resistance of ciphers or cryptographic permutations, our arguments are in most cases based on a given decomposition of the cipher, in many cases into a linear layer and a set of mappings that are applied in parallel, i.e. S-boxes. While this is very helpful in many cases, it can lead to wrong results in others, see e.g. [3].

Using those ingredients when designing efficient and secure ciphers or cryptographic permutations has a long standing history. It can be seen as having its roots already in Shannon's seminal ideas on confusion and diffusion [25]. While many alternative design strategies exist, the use of S-boxes and linear layers is arguably dominating today's designs and include AES, SHA-3, and many of the primitives for the final round of the NIST lightweight crypto competition.[1]

In this paper we touch upon a very fundamental aspect of this decomposition: its uniqueness.

---

[1] https://csrc.nist.gov/Projects/lightweight-cryptography/finalists.

© International Association for Cryptologic Research 2023
C. Hazay and M. Stam (Eds.): EUROCRYPT 2023, LNCS 14007, pp. 318–347, 2023.
https://doi.org/10.1007/978-3-031-30634-1_11

Decomposing a Round Function. Let us turn the view away from designing a cipher or being given a description of a Substitution-Permutation Network (SPN) but rather to a given round function (or maybe even the composition of several round functions). We can imagine having oracle access to the round function only. Here two natural questions arise. First, how to detect if a given round function is actually an SPN round function, and in a second step, how to find the corresponding decomposition. Those questions have been intensively studied since the last 30 years, starting with the seminal SASAS and ASASA cryptanalysis papers [6,22]. Indeed, there are algorithms that can efficiently find a decomposition into an S-box and a linear layer. In particular, those algorithms answer the existence of a decomposition. Moreover, a natural extension of the decomposition of a round function is the representation of a given block cipher, and having multiple representations of the same cipher can have not only a theoretical impact (some properties might be easier to study using one representation rather than another), but also a practical one, see for example [1,24] where using a different representation to implement the ciphers PRESENT and GIFT can lead to an increase in performances.

However, and this is very surprising for us, while the existence of a decomposition has been studied extensively since almost 30 years, the uniqueness of such a decomposition was, to the best of our knowledge, never studied but always given for granted.

To be very clear, there are obvious, and well known, limitations to a unique decomposition already discussed in [6]. In particular, the order of the S-boxes and their choice up to affine equivalence, i.e. up to composing with affine bijections is clearly not unique. What we are interested in, and what has not been questioned so far, is uniqueness up to those equivalent representations.

Crucially, some security arguments, like counting the number of active S-boxes to bound the probability/absolute correlation of a differential/linear trail, could give different results depending on the decomposition. As we will discuss below, without additional requirements on the S-boxes, a unique decomposition is not guaranteed in general.[2] While this is interesting as a fundamental property of round functions, it also impacts very recent work on alignment.

Alignment - intuitively. Alignment of symmetric primitives is a property that has been initially coined during the SHA-3 competition by the Keccak-team in [5] but actually is an idea that dates back to the wide-trail strategy and the use of super-boxes (or code-concatenation) in order to argue about resistance of block ciphers against differential and linear attacks. Interestingly, while already mentioned more than 10 years ago and since then been used in numerous papers [9,11,13,20], the term was never precisely defined. In all the papers mentioned above the term is used in connection with SPNs and we restrict to those designs here as well.

---

[2] Thankfully, for the case of counting S-boxes those requirements lead to trivial bounds for the probability/absolute correlation of a differential/linear trail, no matter the decomposition.

Intuitively, and this is common in all those papers, alignment is used when the linear layer of an SPN manipulates the state in words, i.e. is word-oriented, and those words are either identical to S-box inputs or consist of multiple S-box inputs (or outputs). However, there are several flavors of this common intuition. For example, several papers mention strong and weak alignment. In [20] the authors mention that no good bounds on the probabilities of differential trails are known for Keccak as it is weakly aligned. Reciprocally, it is argued e.g. in [13] that strong alignment allows proving strong bounds.

The importance of the property, along with its positive and negative connotations, is reflected in several second-round candidates of the NIST lightweight project. For Subterranean the designers state in [11] as a feature that "In a way, the Subterranean round function is the nec plus ultra of weak alignment", while the authors of Saturnin [9] advertise their design "the strongly-aligned version of the wide-trail strategy".

So while many researches might have one (or several) more (or less) precise ideas what alignment with respect to designing a substitution permutation network might mean, a formal definition was not given.

Alignment – defined. This only changed very recently with the work of Bordes *et al.* [8] at CRYPTO 2021 where a definition of alignment was given and its impact on several cryptographically relevant criteria was studied.

Even so it is not stated exactly this way, a round function, with a given decomposition into an S-box layer and a linear layer, is aligned, according to [8], if and only if the primitive has a super-box structure. A super-box structure means that two rounds of the primitive decompose (up to linear changes of input and output) into a set of two or more parallel applications of mappings. Those parallel mappings are then refereed to as super-boxes.

Unfortunately, this definition has shortcomings as discussed below.

The first problem is based on the fact that alignment is defined for a round function with a given description as a fixed S-box and linear layer. Ideally, one would hope that alignment, i.e. the existence of super-boxes, is a property that is inherent to the round function and not to its description only.

The second shortcoming of alignment is its impact on security. In [8] several aligned and unaligned ciphers were compared with respect to e.g. the number of linear and differential characteristics of high probability. Within this selection, ciphers being aligned suffered more from clustering effects. However, the exact impact of alignment on those properties remained unclear. The main reason for this is that the ciphers that are used in the comparisons are very different and it is far from clear whether the difference in the observed behaviours is (mainly) due to alignment or (mainly) due to other properties that separate the ciphers.

Our Contribution

We first present our main result on the uniqueness of decomposition, Theorem 1, in Sect. 2, which states that a decomposition is not unique if and only if (at least) one S-box has maximal differential uniformity and another one has maximal linearity. For better readability, we first present the results and shift the proofs and several more technical insights to Sect. 5.

With respect to alignment, we show in Sect. 3, based on the non-uniqueness of maximal decomposition in general, that there exist round functions that have both an aligned and an unaligned description. We also give a non-artificial example, namely the cipher DEFAULT [2], which is aligned and unaligned at the same time.

Furthermore, in Sect. 4 we present experimental data showing that the impact of alignment with respect to the security criteria studied in [8] may be almost non-existent if we consider alignment as an isolated property. We show this by comparing variants of the same cipher instead of different ciphers. For this we choose the cipher PRESENT. Here, by changing only the original bit-permutation one can nicely create versions that are aligned or unaligned. As we detail, those variants behave very similarly in all aspects, in contrast to the results of [8], see e.g. Fig. 3.

2 Main Results on the Uniqueness of Decompositions

It is easy to see that every round function that is un-keyed (or in which a simple key addition takes place at the end of the round) can be seen as an SPN by simply choosing the non-linear layer to be the round function itself (without the addition of the key in the keyed case) and the linear layer to be the identity. Obviously, this representation of a round function is not very useful. But it already shows that without further restrictions, a decomposition of a round function into non-linear and linear layer cannot be unique. Hence, it is not clear if the properties one infers from one possible decomposition are the same for a different one.

In other words, if we want to infer properties of a round function based on its linear and non-linear layer, we should make sure that it is actually well defined, i. e. it only depends on the round function and not on the choice of decomposition. To give just one example, the arguments made in [3] for the resistance against invariant attacks are only valid for one given decomposition and can be shown to be invalid for another.[3]

Before presenting our results, let us first fix some notations and definitions.

2.1 Preliminaries

Basic Notation. We will denote by $\mathbb{F}_2$ the Galois field with 2 elements and with $+$ the addition in this field, which can be seen as an exclusive or. With $\mathbb{F}_2^n$ we will denote the n dimensional vector space over this field, with x^T the transpose of a (column) vector $x \in \mathbb{F}_2^n$ and with $x^T \cdot y$ the (canonical) inner product of $x, y \in \mathbb{F}_2^n$. Furthermore, we will denote by $\oplus$ the direct sum of vector spaces, i. e. $U \oplus V = W$ if and only if $W = U + V := \{u + v \mid u \in U, v \in V\}$ and

---

[3] The arguments are mainly based on the rational canonical form of the linear layer and this form might change when using linear equivalent S-boxes and modifying the linear layer accordingly.

$U \cap V = \{0\}$ for vector spaces $U, V \subset W$. Given a direct sum $\bigoplus_i U_i = W$ we will denote by $\pi_i^U : W \to U_i$ the projection onto U_i along $\bigoplus_{l \neq i} U_l$, i. e. π_i^U has kernel $\bigoplus_{l \neq i} U_l$, image U_i and is the identity if restricted to U_i.[4] We will also consider the direct sum $\left(\bigoplus_{i \in I} U_i\right) \oplus \left(\bigoplus_{i \notin I} U_i\right)$ and will write $U_I := \bigoplus_{i \in I} U_i$ as well as $\pi_I^U := \sum_{i \in I} \pi_i^U$ for the projection onto $\bigoplus_{i \in I} U_i$ along $\bigoplus_{i \notin I} U_i$ or simply $U_{i \neq l}$ and $\pi_{i \neq l}^U$ if $I = \{i | i \neq l\}$. Also, we will denote by $F_{|U}$ the restriction of a function F to the subset U of its domain.

General Definitions. Let us give some general definitions that we will use throughout this paper.

Definition 1 (Linear/Affine Equivalence). *We call two functions $F, G :$ $\mathbb{F}_2^n \to \mathbb{F}_2^n$ affine equivalent if there exist $a, b \in \mathbb{F}_2^n$ as well as invertible matrices $A, B \in \mathbb{F}_2^{n \times n}$ such that $F(x) = b + B \cdot G(A \cdot x + a)$ for all $x \in \mathbb{F}_2^n$. If $a = 0 = b$ we also call F, G linear equivalent.*

Definition 2 (Differential Uniformity (cf. [23])). *Let $F : U \to V$ for subspaces $U, V \subset \mathbb{F}_2^n$. Then we call $\max_{\alpha \in U \setminus \{0\}, \beta \in V} |\{x \in U | F(x) + F(x + \alpha) = \beta\}|$ the differential uniformity of F and say that it is maximal if it is equal to $|U|$.*

Definition 3 (Linearity, (see [10] for an in-depth discussion)). *Let $F :$ $U \to V$ for subspaces $U, V \subset \mathbb{F}_2^n$. Then we call $\max_{\alpha \in \mathbb{F}_2^n \setminus V^\perp, \beta \in \mathbb{F}_2^n, c \in \mathbb{F}_2} |\{x \in U | \alpha^T \cdot F(x) = \beta^T \cdot x + c\}|$ the linearity of F, where $V^\perp := \{x \in \mathbb{F}_2^n | x^T \cdot y = 0 \; \forall y \in V\}$, and say that it is maximal if it is equal to $|U|$.*

2.2   Defining a (Maximal) Decomposition

Given a (round) function we would like to be able to find a unique decomposition into non-linear and linear layer(s). Similarly to [8], we require the number of S-boxes in the non-linear layer to be maximal. While in general such a decomposition is not unique, we show conditions under which it is. Hence, under these conditions it is possible to infer properties of the round function (such as alignment [8]) based on the linear and non-linear layer(s) of the corresponding unique decomposition.

A Natural Definition. Let us start with formally defining what we understand by a decomposition. Since a non-linear layer typically consists of independent S-boxes (i. e. functions that don't share input and output bits), one can see the S-box layer as the sum of independent functions. For example, the non-linear layer $N : \mathbb{F}_2^{n_1} \times \mathbb{F}_2^{n_2} \to \mathbb{F}_2^{n_1} \times \mathbb{F}_2^{n_2}$ with

$$N \begin{pmatrix} x_1 \\ x_2 \end{pmatrix} = \begin{pmatrix} S_1(x_1) \\ S_2(x_2) \end{pmatrix}$$

---

[4] In other words, the direct sum enables us to express every element $x \in W$ as $\sum_i x_i$ for unique $x_i \in U_i$. Hence, π_j^U is the mapping defined by $x = \sum_i x_i \mapsto x_j$.

and $S_1 : \mathbb{F}_2^{n_1} \to \mathbb{F}_2^{n_1}$ as well as $S_2 : \mathbb{F}_2^{n_2} \to \mathbb{F}_2^{n_2}$ can be seen as

$$N \begin{pmatrix} x_1 \\ x_2 \end{pmatrix} = \begin{pmatrix} S_1(x_1) \\ 0 \end{pmatrix} + \begin{pmatrix} 0 \\ S_2(x_2) \end{pmatrix}$$

where the input/output spaces of those two functions are $\mathbb{F}_2^{n_1} \times 0^{n_2}$ resp. $0^{n_1} \times \mathbb{F}_2^{n_2}$. Note that $\mathbb{F}_2^{n_1} \times 0^{n_2} \oplus 0^{n_1} \times \mathbb{F}_2^{n_2} = \mathbb{F}_2^{n_1} \times \mathbb{F}_2^{n_2}$. A linear layer now only changes the input/output spaces of those functions. Hence, we will define a decomposition of a (round) function by the sum of functions defined on subspaces of the input and output spaces.

Definition 4 (Decomposition). *Let $F : \mathbb{F}_2^n \to \mathbb{F}_2^n$ be bijective. Furthermore, let $U_1, ..., U_d$ and $V_1, ..., V_d$ be non-trivial[5] subspaces of $\mathbb{F}_2^n$ with $\bigoplus_i U_i = \mathbb{F}_2^n = \bigoplus_i V_i$, as well as $F_i : U_i \to V_i$ with*

$$F(x) = F\left(\sum_i \pi_i^U(x)\right) = \sum_i F_i \circ \pi_i^U(x).$$

We call $\{(U_i, V_i, F_i) \mid 1 \leq i \leq d\}$ a decomposition of F. If $d > 1$ we call the decomposition non-trivial.

Note that the reason we need to restrict the definition to non-trivial subspaces is that it is always possible to extend the decomposition by $\hat{F} : \{0\} \to \{0\}$, which does not give any additional information about the (round) function. Moreover, as the order of the functions does not matter, we only consider a set of tuples.

We would like to point out that we actually allow two linear layers, i. e. we are decomposing into $L_2 \circ N \circ L_1$ where L_1 and L_2 are linear layers and N is a non-linear layer. But note that the r round iteration $(L_2 \circ N \circ L_1)^r$ is linear equivalent to $(L_1 \cdot L_2 \circ N)^r$, meaning that both (round) functions, $L_2 \circ N \circ L_1$ and $L_1 \cdot L_2 \circ N$, lead to the same cryptographic properties. With that, allowing two linear layers seems actually more natural than restricting to one linear layer only.

Refining Decompositions. It is easy to see that given a (non-trivial) decomposition $\{(U_i, V_i, F_i) \mid 1 \leq i \leq d\}$ it is always possible to find another decomposition by combining two (or more) of the F_i, i. e. $\{(\bigoplus_{i \in I_l} U_i, \bigoplus_{i \in I_l} V_i, \sum_{i \in I_l} F_i \circ \pi_i^U) \mid 1 \leq l \leq m\}$ is also a decomposition for every partition of the index space $I_1, ..., I_m \subset \{1, ..., d\}$.

Hence, in order for a decomposition to be unique it is clear that one at least has to maximize the number of S-boxes. To this end, we will now define in which case one decomposition is a refinement of another decomposition, which reminds of [8] while technically being different as [8] focuses on the linear layer only.

Definition 5 (Refinement). *Let $F : \mathbb{F}_2^n \to \mathbb{F}_2^n$ be bijective. Let further $D = \{(U_i, V_i, F_i) \mid 1 \leq i \leq d\}$ and $E = \{(W_i, X_i, G_i) \mid 1 \leq i \leq e\}$ be two decompositions of F. We call E a refinement of D if $e > d$ and for all i there exists a value of j such that $W_i \subset U_j$.*

---

[5] More precisely, we allow the subspaces to be equal to $\mathbb{F}_2^n$ but not to be $\{0\}$.

The intuition behind this is that we further decompose each of the individual S-Boxes. Based on this, we can now define a maximal decomposition.

Definition 6 (Maximal Decomposition). *We call a decomposition D maximal if there exists no refinement of D.*

In other words, a decomposition is maximal if we cannot decompose the individual S-boxes any further. It is an interesting question, which we leave open for now, whether two maximal decompositions have to have the same number of S-boxes, or even more, the same size spectrum (see Definition 10 below).

2.3   A Sufficient and Necessary Condition for Unique Decompositions

Knowing the definition of a maximal decomposition, we can now state our main result in context of decompositions.

Theorem 1. *Let $F : \mathbb{F}_2^n \to \mathbb{F}_2^n$ be bijective and let $D = \{(U_i, V_i, F_i) | 1 \leq i \leq d\}$ be a maximal decomposition of F. Then D is unique if and only if there exists no pair (i, k) with $i \neq k$ such that F_i has maximal differential uniformity and F_k has maximal linearity.*

We will prove this in detail in Sect. 5.

Since one of the S-boxes having maximal differential uniformity (resp. maximal linearity) means that the same has to be true for the whole (round) function, we can relax the condition and receive a sufficient, but not necessary, condition.

Corollary 1. *Let $F : \mathbb{F}_2^n \to \mathbb{F}_2^n$ be bijective. If F does not have maximal differential uniformity or maximal linearity then F has a unique maximal decomposition.*

Since differential uniformity and linearity are properties that should already be known for most (if not all) cryptographic primitives, this makes it easy to argue about the uniqueness of their maximal decomposition.

Some Intuition on the Functions without a Unique Maximal Decomposition. Given Theorem 1 it is actually not hard to show (details are given in the full version [17]) that the functions without a unique maximal decomposition are exactly those that are affine equivalent to ones of the form

$$
R\begin{pmatrix} x_1 \\ x_2 \\ x_3 \\ x_4 \end{pmatrix} = \left.\begin{matrix} \left.\begin{pmatrix} f(x_1) \\ g(x_1) + x_2 \end{pmatrix}\right\} \text{S-box(es)} \\ \left.\begin{pmatrix} x_3 \\ h\begin{pmatrix} x_3 \\ x_4 \end{pmatrix} \end{pmatrix}\right\} \text{S-box(es)} \end{matrix}\right.,
$$

where $x_1 \in \mathbb{F}_2^n, x_4 \in \mathbb{F}_2^m$ for integers n, m and $x_2, x_3 \in \mathbb{F}_2$, as well as $f : \mathbb{F}_2^n \to \mathbb{F}_2^n$, $g : \mathbb{F}_2^n \to \mathbb{F}_2$ and $h : \mathbb{F}_2 \times \mathbb{F}_2^m \to \mathbb{F}_2^m$. The reason is that such functions allow us to "mix" S-boxes without changing it, as we can add x_3 (from the second S-box) to x_2 (from the first S-box) before the non-linear layer, but also revert this linear transformation after the non-linear layer by just changing the original linear layer (more details are given in Example 2 of the full version [17]).

Given that one typically tries to minimize the differential uniformity and linearity, it may seem like functions without a unique maximal decomposition are not of interest to cryptographers, but there exists at least one widely-used type of round function that actually has no unique maximal decomposition, namely the one of a generalized Feistel network.

In total, we are able to show that whenever cryptographically strong S-boxes are used the representation of its round function can indeed be used for arguing about its properties, while the same is not always true in the opposing case, as we will see next.

3 Re-aligning Alignment

To give just one example of why the uniqueness of a maximal decomposition can be important, let us take a look at the concept of alignment by Bordes *et al.* [8]. While the intuition should be that a round function is aligned if the primitive has a superbox structure, i. e. the iteration of two rounds exhibits a non-trivial decomposition, the original definition is a bit more involved. Therefore, let us quickly recall the definition of alignment from [8]. For this, we assume that the round function consists of the parallel application of m equally-sized S-boxes, a bijective linear transformation and the addition of a key (resp. constant), i. e. we can write the round function as $L \circ N + c$, where $L \in \mathbb{F}_2^{n \times n}$ is a bijective linear mapping,

$$N = \begin{pmatrix} S_1 \\ \vdots \\ S_m \end{pmatrix}$$

is the non-linear layer, with $S_i : \mathbb{F}_2^{n/m} \to \mathbb{F}_2^{n/m}$ bijective, and $c \in \mathbb{F}_2^n$ is a constant (resp. key). For simplicity, we will use a slightly different but equivalent version of the definition from [8].

Definition 7 (Alignment [8], sub-optimal). *Let $U_i := 0^{(i-1) \cdot n/m} \times \mathbb{F}_2^{n/m} \times 0^{(m-i) \cdot n/m}$ for $i = 1, \ldots, m$. A round function $L \circ N + c$ (as above) is called aligned if L can be written as $T \circ M$ such that*

- *it exists a permutation $\tau : \{1, \ldots, m\} \to \{1, \ldots, m\}$ with $T(U_i) = U_{\tau(i)}$ and*
- *it exists $J \subset \{1, \ldots, m\}$ (non-trivial) such that $M\left(\bigoplus_{i \in J} U_i\right) = \bigoplus_{i \in J} U_i$ and $M\left(\bigoplus_{i \notin J} U_i\right) = \bigoplus_{i \notin J} U_i$,*

where the split between the linear and nonlinear layer is chosen so as to maximize the number of S-boxes in N.[6]

---

[6] This version is equivalent to the one from [8] since $T(U_i) = U_{\tau(i)}$ means that T is the composition of a Π_N-Shuffle and a Π_N aligned linear function. As the composition of a $\Pi_{N'}$ aligned and a Π_N aligned function is obviously $\Pi_{N'}$ aligned if $\Pi_N \leq \Pi_{N'}$, it is then enough to check that M is $\Pi_{N'}$ aligned, with $\Pi_{N'}$ being non-trivial. Since it is only important that $\Pi_{N'}$ is non-trivial, this can be done by checking if $M\left(\bigoplus_{i \in J} U_i\right) = \bigoplus_{i \in J} U_i$ and $M\left(\bigoplus_{i \notin J} U_i\right) = \bigoplus_{i \notin J} U_i$ for some $J \subset \{1, \ldots, m\}$, i. e. checking for all possible $\Pi_{N'}$ with two boxes.

The problem with this definition is that it is not invariant under affine (or even linear) equivalence (of the round function iterated two times), while the existence of a superbox structure is. One non-artificial example where this is indeed a problem is the cipher DEFAULT [2], which is aligned, but a linear equivalent version would not be aligned.

Before we explain the problem in more detail, let us give an alternative definition that is exactly equivalent to the existence of a superbox structure.

Definition 8 (Alignment). *We call a round function R aligned if there exists a non-trivial decomposition of $R \circ R$. In the keyed case we require a non-trivial decomposition for every key.*

Note that whenever a round function is aligned according to the original definition it is indeed aligned, since it implies a non-trivial decomposition of $R \circ R$ with in- and output spaces of a certain form, while a round function that is not aligned according to the original definition could actually be aligned, but the in- and output spaces may not be of the form required in Definition 7.

On the Need of Decomposability for all Keys. On the first glance, requiring decomposibility for all possible key choices may seem as a downside. But note that the original definition does the same (even in the un-keyed case), as it implies a non-trivial decomposition of $R \circ R$ for all possible key/constant additions. Also, there does not seem to be a way around this as the existence of a superbox structure can be key dependent. For instance, let F be self inverse and let $R = F + k$ be the round function for a round key k. Then $R \circ R$ is affine equivalent to $F(F + k)$, which is the identity for $k = 0$ and therefore clearly decomposable, while the same is not necessarily true for $k \neq 0$.

A real world example of a key dependent decomposition is the block cipher CRAFT [4], for which Leander *et al.* show in [19] that there exist some Tweakkeys for which the round function is now very similar to a Feistel network, while originally being an SPN.

That said, it seems to be more in line with [8] to require the existence of a superbox structure for all possible key choices, while clearly a more refined definition would be possible. But, since we show in Sect. 4 that the impact of alignment may be hugely overestimated, we will settle with a definition most true to the original one for now.

Alignment and Generalized Feistel Networks. While there exist non-artificial examples, like the cipher DEFAULT [2], that are aligned according to the definition from [8], but a linear equivalent cipher is not, showing this for DEFAULT is a bit more involved, but does not give further insights into the problem. Hence, we refer to the full version [17] for this and use a more suitable example at

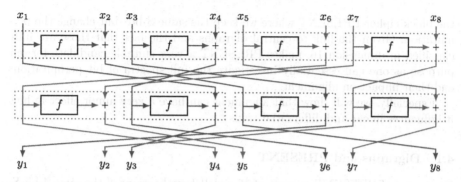

Fig. 1. Example of a round function that is aligned, while a linear equivalent two round composition would not be according to [8]. The colors indicate the alignment resp. superbox structure and the dotted lines the individual S-boxes.

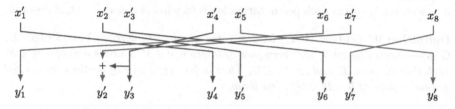

Fig. 2. Linear layer of a (linear) self-equivalent version of the round function from Fig. 1. The colors indicate the initial alignment resp. superbox structure.

this point. Let us have a look at the generalized Feistel network depicted in Fig. 1. Obviously, we can see the permutation of the output as a linear layer and the non-linear transformation of each Feistel branch as an S-box (indicated by the dotted box in the figure). As can be seen, two rounds of this construction result in two independent parts, which shows the existence of a superbox structure. A quick check with the definition from [8] shows that this structure is indeed aligned. But the problem is that the same does not hold true for a linear equivalent version of this two round structure. To see this, note that the linear transformation that adds x_3 to x_2 commutes with the S-box layer. Hence, we can look at a linear equivalent version where we replace the second permutation/linear layer by this linear transformation. Since it commutes with the S-box layer, we end up with the linear layer depicted in Fig. 2 between the two S-box layers. Here we can see that the addition of y_3' to y_2' mixes the two colors, and a quick look at the definition from [8] reveals that this version would not be aligned anymore, while the superbox structure is obviously still present. For more details on this, we refer to the full version [17].

4   Aligned and Unaligned Versions of PRESENT

We are interested in looking at how alignment affects the cryptographic properties of very similar primitives, and to do so we chose to look at variants of the block cipher PRESENT where we keep the same S-box but change the permutation. Given the link to central digraphs and the fact that those are fully classified in dimension 16, makes PRESENT a very suitable candidate for our purpose as one can essentially investigate the full spectra of bit permutations and their impact on alignment.

Especially, we will show that alignment can have a very minor effect in how it influences linear and differential trails.[7]

4.1   Digraphs and PRESENT

One round of PRESENT consists of 16 parallel applications of the same 4-bit S-box followed by a bit permutation of the 64-bit state. The permutation is chosen in such a way that full dependency is reached after two rounds, or more precisely 3 applications of the S-box layer interleaved with two permutation layers. In [16] it was shown how any such permutation leads to what is called a central digraph.

Definition 9. *Let $G = (V, E)$ be a directed graph with vertices V and edges E. G is a central digraph if for every pair of nodes $u, v \in V$ it exists a unique $w \in V$ such that $(u, w) \in E$ and $(w, v) \in E$. That is for every pair of vertices there exist a unique path of length 2 between them.*

A PRESENT-like bit permutation P operating on $\{0, \ldots, 63\}$ gives rise to a central digraph by identifying the 16 S-boxes with 16 vertices and adding an edge from vertex i to vertex j if there exists an output bit of the i-th S-box that is mapped to the j-th S-box in the next round. Note that when restricting to permutations with full dependency after two rounds (thus leading to a central digraph), there are no duplicate edges on this digraph as, for a given S-box, each of its four output bits needs to be sent to a different S-box on the next round.

All Central Digraphs of Order 16 *up to isomorphism.* There are exactly 3492 central digraphs of order 16 up to graph isomorphism, see [16]. Graph isomorphism, translated to the PRESENT-like structure, correspond to permuting the order of S-boxes. Moreover, many PRESENT-like permutations will end up in the same digraph as the order of input and output bits within each S-box is neglected in the graph representation, but relevant for the cipher. As such, not all properties of the cipher can be deduced from the digraph directly. For example, as shown in [18] the number of (linear) trails might well differ for two permutations that correspond to the same digraph. While some properties cannot be deduced from the digraph only, others – in particular alignment – can.

Aligned and Non-aligned Central Digraphs. As mentioned above there are exactly 3492 central digraphs leading to full diffusion after 2 rounds. We can further group them into several sets using the following definition.

---

[7] The code we used to make these experiments is available at: https://doi.org/10.5281/zenodo.7660387.

Definition 10 (Size spectrum of a decomposition). *Let* $F : \mathbb{F}_2^n \to \mathbb{F}_2^n$ *be bijective and let* $D = \{(U_i, V_i, F_i)|1 \leq i \leq d\}$ *be a decomposition of* F. *We call the multiset* $\mathcal{S}_D = \{dim(U_i)|1 \leq i \leq d\}$ *the* size spectrum *of* D.

Moreover, we will say that a digraph G is aligned (resp. unaligned) if the permutations induced from G result in an aligned (resp. unaligned) round function. Recalling the previous sections and in particular Corollary 1, this makes sense as the PRESENT S-box neither has trivial linearity nor differential uniformity and thus its maximal decomposition is unique.

Over all the 3492 central digraphs, their alignment is distributed as follows:

– One single digraph is aligned with a maximal decomposition of size spectrum $\{4, 4, 4, 4\}$. Especially, the original permutation in PRESENT belongs to this class; that is two rounds of PRESENT can be rewritten as consisting of 4 super-boxes of 16 bits each.
– 37 digraphs lead to a maximal decomposition of size spectrum $\{4, 4, 8\}$;
– 1207 digraphs lead to a maximal decomposition of size spectrum $\{4, 12\}$;
– 220 digraphs lead to a maximal decomposition of size spectrum $\{8, 8\}$;
– 2027 digraphs lead to a maximal decomposition of size spectrum $\{16\}$, i.e. all these digraphs are unaligned.

Since our goal is to compare aligned and unaligned versions of PRESENT, we will focus on the two corresponding cases to generate permutations: the (single) case where the maximal decomposition is of size spectrum $\{4, 4, 4, 4\}$, corresponding to the digraph of the original permutation, and the case where the digraph is unaligned. As in [8], we will focus on the linear and differential properties of the resulting variants of PRESENT.

4.2   Linear Cryptanalysis

The idea is to focus only on linear trails with one active S-box per round. This has two advantages. First, it covers the bulk of the correlation used in most of the attacks on PRESENT, cf. [14]. Second, it simplifies the analysis and we can nicely use graph theory and efficient algorithms therein to control the effect of unaligning the original PRESENT permutation.

A linear trail with a single active S-box per round implies for a bit-permutation that has full dependency in two rounds, that only one-to-one bit linear approximations have to be considered through the S-box. There are only 8 possible one-to-one bit transitions with non-zero correlation within the PRESENT S-box, see [7]. For us, the only important point here is that there is no 1-1 transition involving the LSB neither at the input nor at the output of the S-box.

As such, if one were to change the permutation by only modifying the values in the permutation that are affecting the LSB (both at the input and output) of the S-boxes, one would get a new permutation that has the same number of linear trails built from 1-1 transitions. That is, two bit-permutations that only differ in those bits, lead to ciphers with a very similar behaviour with respect to linear attacks. More specifically, this means that an alternative permutation should be built from the following partial permutation, where $\star$ is an undetermined value

$$p^\star = (\star, \star, \star, \star, \star, 17, 33, 49, \star, 18, 34, 50, \star, 19, 35, 51, \star, \star, \star, \star, \star, 21, 37, 53, \star, 22,$$
$$38, 54, \star, 23, 39, 55, \star, \star, \star, \star, \star, 25, 41, 57, \star, 26, 42, 58, \star, 27, 43, 59, \star, \star, \star, \star,$$
$$\star, 29, 45, 61, \star, 30, 46, 62, \star, 31, 47, 63).$$

Extending the Partial Permutation in an Unaligned Way. To build the entire permutation, we want it to both have the above structure (i.e. fits the partial permutation) as well as lead to one of the central digraphs that has the alignment we want to study. Luckily, this can nicely be done with graph theory. The idea is that the partial permutation has to correspond to a sub-graph in one of the central digraphs we aim for.

More explicitly, from the partial permutation $p^\star$, one can deduce a digraph $H^\star$. $H^\star$ contains an edge from vertex i to vertex j if there exists an output bit of index a with $p^\star(a) \neq \star$ in the i-th S-box that is mapped to an input bit of index b with $p^\star(b) \neq \star$ in the j-th S-box in the next round. Then there exists a permutation that both fits the partial permutation *and* leads to one of the 2027 unaligned digraphs G if and only if $H^\star$ is subgraph isomorphic to G.

Such a permutation would then be unaligned while still preserving the linear trails built from 1-1 transitions. We used the subgraph isomorphism solver by McCreesh et al. [21] to find all possible subgraph isomorphisms between $H^\star$ and the unaligned digraphs, and over the 2027 unaligned digraphs, there are 346 that lead to at least one subgraph isomorphism.

Thus, to build alternative permutations, we first choose one of these 346 (unaligned) subgraphs, choose one of the subgraph isomorphism and complete the partial permutation according to this isomorphism to obtain a full permutation. Note that several permutations can be built from a given digraph and subgraph isomorphism, however the exact number is rather hard to evaluate.

By building alternative permutations like this, we can deduce the following proposition that takes care of the most prominent linear trails.

Proposition 1. *For any (aligned or unaligned) permutation generated as described above, the number of linear trails in PRESENT built with only 1-1 transitions is exactly the same as when using the original permutation, and all those trails have an absolute bias of 2^{-3r} over r rounds.*

4.3   Differential Cryptanalysis

Once we obtain a permutation, we can then evaluate different metrics for differential cryptanalysis, and as an echo to [8] we chose to evaluate the number of trails, number of core patterns and number of differentials (i.e. considering the clustering effect of differential trails), which are defined in the following section. We can then repeat the procedure by generating another permutation, possibly also choosing another digraph and/or subgraph isomorphism.

Table 1. Largest deviations observed on the number of differential trails.

	1 permutation per graph			All permutations in the same class		
Rounds	Original	Alternative	Weight	Min. Alt.	Max. Alt.	Weight
2	$2^{48.35}$	$2^{48.21}$	24	$2^{11.11}$	$2^{11.15}$	6
3	$2^{46.29}$	$2^{43.05}$	32	$2^{8.93}$	$2^{9.15}$	8
4	$2^{8.19}$	$2^{6.32}$	12	$2^{7.09}$	$2^{7.52}$	12

Differential Trails. We made experiments to observe how having an unaligned permutation affects the distribution of differential trails (for a formal definition of *differential trails*, we refer to Definition 13 of the full version [17]), more specifically the number of trails of a given weight (i.e. the $-\log_2$ of the probability).

We computed the number of trails up to a given weight over 2, 3 and 4 rounds for both the original permutation as well as for several permutations generated as described in the previous section. The computation was done as an exhaustive search using a standard Branch & Bound algorithm as well as the convolution technique showed in [8] for the first and last round. For 3 rounds, we adapted the algorithm in Appendix A.3 of [8], with some simplifications and optimizations since the linear layer is only a permutation in our case. For 4 rounds, the same algorithm as for 3 rounds is used to generate trails over 3 rounds, which are then manually extended by adding one round at the end.

We give the detailed results in the full version [17], comparing the original permutation to a batch of variant permutations generated in 2 ways: either one random permutation is generated from one random isomorphism for *each* digraph (thus 346 variants considered), or 346 permutations are generated from one isomorphism and one single graph, to showcase that the number of trails remains rather stable within the same class of permutation. We also give a short summary of the largest deviations in Table 1. Each row starts by the number of rounds, followed by 3 entries giving the number of trails for the original (resp. alternative) permutations with the largest gap and for which weight this gap happens, when the alternative permutations are generated as one permutation for one isomorphism for each graph. The remaining 3 entries of the row showcase the largest gap between any of the alternative permutations, which are generated within the same class, showing that in this case the results are rather stable.

Overall, while the (unaligned) alternative permutations tend to lead to lower numbers of trails than the (aligned) original permutation (but not always, e.g. over 4 rounds, there are $\sim 2^{17.31}$ trails of weight 15 for the original permutation while one alternative permutation leads to $\sim 2^{17.40}$ trails of the same weight), the gap between the original and alternative permutations is rather small and the distribution seems to remain very similar.

Core Patterns. In [8], Bordes et al. look at the influence of alignment for truncated differentials (where one only considers whether or not a given S-box has a non-zero difference) over a few block ciphers. However due to PRESENT's linear

Table 2. Largest deviations observed on the number of core patterns. No deviation for 2 rounds when permutations are in the same class.

	1 permutation per graph			All permutations in the same class		
Rounds	Original	Alternative	Active S-boxes	Min. Alt.	Max. Alt.	Active S-boxes
2	$2^{31.48}$	$2^{31.34}$	12	–	–	–
3	$2^{34.18}$	$2^{31.32}$	17	$2^{27.99}$	$2^{28.05}$	15
4	$2^{33.70}$	$2^{31.02}$	18	$2^{31.81}$	$2^{31.92}$	18

layer being a bit-permutation, truncated differentials are not really meaningful to study. Instead, we will consider *core patterns*, which are essentially differential trails without considering the first and last S-box layer. More precisely, core patterns are defined as follows.

Definition 11. *Let* $(\alpha_1, \beta_1, \alpha_2, \ldots, \alpha_r, \beta_r)$ *be a differential trail over* r *rounds with*

$$\alpha_1 \xrightarrow{S} \beta_1 \xrightarrow{P} \alpha_2 \xrightarrow{S} \ldots \xrightarrow{P} \alpha_r \xrightarrow{S} \beta_r$$

Then $(\beta_1, \alpha_2, \ldots, \alpha_r)$ *is called a core pattern.*

While core patterns are still influenced by valid differentials of the S-box for 3 rounds and more, considering them allows us to ignore the effect of the first and last S-box layer that "inflate" the number of trails.

As for differential trails, we computed the number of core patterns for up to a given number of active S-boxes over 2, 3 and 4 rounds, both for the original permutation as well as for a batch of alternative permutations, which are given in details in the full version [17], with a short summary for the largest deviations given in Table 2, structured in the same way as the previous table for differential trails. The algorithm to obtain these results is very similar as for differential trails, except that the bounding step in the Branch & Bound is done over the number of active S-boxes, ignoring the weight of the trails as well as ignoring the first and last S-box layer.

Clustering of Differential Trails. While differential trails are what is usually used to mount differential attacks, it has been shown multiple times (e.g. [12,15,26]) that the actual probability of the underlying differential can deviate quite significantly from the probability of a differential trail because of the *clustering effect*. In short, the probability of a differential (α_1, α_r) is the sum of the probability of all differential trails starting (resp. ending) with α_1 (resp. α_r), see Proposition 2 of the full version [17]. Usually, the *dominant trail hypothesis* is used to argue that the highest probability of any trail fitting a given differential dominates over all other trails, that is, the probability of the differential is about the same as the probability of the trail. However several examples in the literature show that this is not always the case, and as such it is useful to evaluate the actual probability of differentials over a given cipher.

Table 3. Largest deviations observed on the number of differentials.

	1 permutation per graph			All permutations in the same class		
Rounds	Original	Alternative	Weight	Min. Alt.	Max. Alt.	Weight
2	$2^{25.63}$	$2^{25.08}$	12.9556	$2^{15.99}$	$2^{16.02}$	8.97763
3	$2^{30.15}$	$2^{28.69}$	20.8301	$2^{9.07}$	$2^{9.20}$	8

Adapting the algorithm used to compute differential trails, we were able to also compute the probabilities of differentials over 2 and 3 rounds for both the original permutation as well as for several alternative permutations. Again, we give a short summary of the largest observed deviations in Table 3, while the detailed results are given in the full version [17]. As we can see, the distribution for alternative (unaligned) permutations seems quite close to the distribution from the original (aligned) permutation. As an example, in Fig. 3a, we give the *cumulative* histogram of the number of differential of a given weight over 2 rounds, where the red line represents the cumulative histogram for the original permutation, while each alternative permutation is represented by a blue line. Since all the alternative permutations give very close results, their respective lines are all clumped together, which still highlights what we want to show here. Note that while for 2 rounds, the alternative permutations give a very similar curve, for 3 rounds there seems to be a divergence starting around weight 15, while still remaining quite close (we refer to the full version [17] for more details).

To compare this to [8], we give in Fig. 3b the cumulative histogram the authors gave from their analysis of Saturnin, Spongent and Xoodoo, the first two being aligned while the latter being unaligned. Here, the largest gap between Spongent (aligned) and Xoodoo (unaligned) is several orders of magnitude larger than for PRESENT (about 2^{20} near weight 21), and the distributions are very different. Thus, we now have examples of aligned and unaligned ciphers that behave very similar (the PRESENT variants) and very different (Spongent and Xoodoo). Those examples jointly raise doubt about the impact of alignment on its own.

Moreover, the minimal weight for which there is at least one differential is different, while in our experiments when comparing variants of the same cipher, the same minimal weight is achieved both for the (aligned) original permutation as well as for the (unaligned) variants.

While these experiments show that we can find unaligned permutations that are technically better than the original PRESENT permutation, the margin between the two is rather small and the distributions seem to be very close to each other. Overall, the distributions also seem to diverge mostly toward "larger" weights, while low weight trails/differentials are probably the most important ones to focus on, and it's worth recalling that all of these alternative permutations have the exact same linear trails built from 1-1 transitions as the original permutation. At the very least, these experiments clearly show that when comparing aligned vs. unaligned round function of a very similar design, the answer

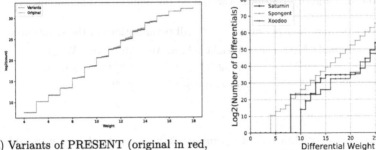

(a) Variants of PRESENT (original in red, variants in blue)

(b) Saturnin, Spongent and Xoodoo [8]

Fig. 3. Cumulative histogram of the number of differentials of a given weight over 2 rounds.

to whether one is clearly better than the other is a lot less clear cut than what was stated in [8].

5   An in Depth Analysis of the Uniqueness of Decompositions

In this section, we will explain the results from Sect. 2 in greater depth. More precisely, we will give more details on decompositions, how one can (possibly) find refinements based on two decompositions, and finally, prove Theorem 1.

Reconstructing a Decomposition Based on the Input Spaces. While the F_i, which can be interpreted as linear transformed S-boxes, are useful for motivating our definition, they are strictly speaking not needed as long as the actual function F is known. To see this, we first note that they can be recovered by projecting onto the corresponding output space.

Corollary 2. *Let $F : \mathbb{F}_2^n \to \mathbb{F}_2^n$ be bijective and let $\{(U_i, V_i, F_i) \mid 1 \leq i \leq d\}$ be a decomposition of F. Then we have that $\pi_i^V \circ F = F_i \circ \pi_i^U$.*

Proof. Since $F = \sum_j F_j \circ \pi_j^U$ and $\pi_i^V \circ F_i$ is the same as F_i in the case that $i = j$ and zero otherwise, the claim follows from

$$\pi_i^V \circ F = \pi_i^V \circ \left(\sum_j F_j \circ \pi_j^U \right) = \sum_j \pi_i^V \circ F_j \circ \pi_j^U = F_i \circ \pi_i^U.$$

$\square$

Now, we show that the F_i provide no additional information, since the restriction of F to U_i is identical to F_i plus some constant that can be recovered by projecting $F(0)$ onto $\bigoplus_{l \neq i} V_l$.

Corollary 3. *Let $F : \mathbb{F}_2^n \to \mathbb{F}_2^n$ be bijective and let $\{(U_i, V_i, F_i) \mid 1 \leq i \leq d\}$ be a decomposition of F. Then we have that $F_i = F_{|U_i} + \pi_{l \neq i}^V \circ F(0)$ and we can write $F = \sum_l F \circ \pi_l^U + (d + 1 \mod 2) \cdot F(0)$.*

Proof. We know that $F = \sum_l F_l \circ \pi_l^U$ by definition. Hence, we have that

$$F \circ \pi_i^U = \sum_l F_l \circ \pi_l^U \circ \pi_i^U = F_i \circ \pi_i^U + \sum_{l \neq i} F_l(0) = F_i \circ \pi_i^U + \sum_{l \neq i} \pi_i^V \circ F(0).$$

Therefore, we get that

$$F = \sum_l F_l \circ \pi_l^U = \sum_l \left(F \circ \pi_l^U + \sum_{i \neq l} \pi_i^V \circ F(0) \right)$$
$$= \sum_l F \circ \pi_l^U + \sum_l (F(0) + \pi_l^V \circ F(0)) = \sum_l F \circ \pi_l^U + (d + 1 \mod 2) \cdot F(0).$$

$\square$

Looking at the S-box layer, we quickly see why this is the case. Assume that

$$N \begin{pmatrix} x_1 \\ x_2 \end{pmatrix} = \begin{pmatrix} S_1(x_1) \\ S_2(x_2) \end{pmatrix}.$$

To isolate S_1, we would fix $x_2 = 0$. But in order to get the second component to be zero for the output space to be a subspace, we have to add $S_2(0)$ to it.

In addition to not having to know the F_i, we also do not need to know the output spaces V_i. But note that it is still important that the output sets are subspaces that are in direct sum.

Corollary 4. *Let $F : \mathbb{F}_2^n \to \mathbb{F}_2^n$ be bijective and let $\{(U_i, V_i, F_i) \mid 1 \leq i \leq d\}$ be a decomposition of F. Then we have that $V_i = F(U_i) + F(0)$.*

Proof. We already know that $V_i = F_i(U_i) = F(U_i) + \pi_{l \neq i}^V \circ F(0)$. The claim now follows from the fact that $\pi_i^V \circ F(0) = F_i(0) \in V_i$. $\square$

Hence, the only thing we need to know for constructing a decomposition are the input spaces. Therefore, if we are able to construct a decomposition of F based on the input spaces U_i by first recovering the output spaces $V_i = F(U_i) + F(0)$, verifying that the V_i are indeed subspaces and in direct sum, and then constructing the F_i as $F_{|U_i} + \pi_{l \neq i}^V \circ F(0)$, validating that $F = \sum_i F_i \circ \pi_i^U$ holds, then we say that the input spaces U_i induce a decomposition of F.

Lemma 1 (Induction of Decomposition). *Let* $F : \mathbb{F}_2^n \rightarrow \mathbb{F}_2^n$ *be bijective. Let further* $U_1, ..., U_d$ *be non-trivial subspaces of* $\mathbb{F}_2^n$ *with* $\bigoplus_i U_i = \mathbb{F}_2^n$ *and let us define* $V_i := F(U_i) + F(0)$. *If the* V_i *are subspaces with* $\bigoplus_i V_i = \mathbb{F}_2^n$ *and if*

$$F = \sum_i F \circ \pi_i^U + (d + 1 \bmod 2) \cdot F(0)$$

then $D = \{(U_i, V_i, F_i) \mid 1 \leq i \leq d\}$ *with* $F_i := F_{|U_i} + \pi_{l \neq i}^V \circ F(0)$ *is a decomposition of* F. *In this case, we say that* $\{U_i \mid 1 \leq i \leq d\}$ *induces the decomposition* D.

Proof. This follows from the observations above and by definition of the F_i, as

$$\sum_i F_i \circ \pi_i^U = \sum_i \left(F_{|U_i} \circ \pi_i^U + \pi_{l \neq i}^V \circ F(0)\right) = \sum_i F \circ \pi_i^U + (d + 1 \bmod 2) \cdot F(0).$$

$\square$

Note that we could have used this as the definition of decomposition. While this does not need the redundant information of the F_i and V_i, it is way less intuitive. Also, when working with decompositions it can be quite useful to have both the F_i and the V_i at hand, too.

Decompositions of Affine Equivalent Functions. We will now show a one-to-one relationship between the decompositions of two affine equivalent functions, which means that the existence of a unique maximal decomposition is actually invariant under affine equivalence.

Lemma 2. *Let* $F, G : \mathbb{F}_2^n \rightarrow \mathbb{F}_2^n$ *be bijective and affine equivalent, i. e.* $F = A \circ G(B + b) + a$ *for invertible matrices* $A, B \in \mathbb{F}_2^{n \times n}$ *and constants* $a, b \in \mathbb{F}_2^n$. *Then* $\{U_i | 1 \leq i \leq d\}$ *induces a decomposition of* F *if and only if* $\{B \cdot U_i | 1 \leq i \leq d\}$ *induces a decomposition of* G.

Proof. Let $\{(U_i, V_i, F_i) \mid 1 \leq i \leq d\}$ be the decomposition of F induced by $\{U_i | 1 \leq i \leq d\}$. It obviously holds that $\bigoplus_i B \cdot U_i = \mathbb{F}_2^n$, as B is invertible. In addition, if we denote by I the identity mapping, we get that

$$A \circ G(B + b) + a = F = \sum_i F \circ \pi_i^U + (d + 1 \bmod 2) \cdot F(0)$$

$$= \sum_i \left(F \circ \pi_i^U + F \circ \pi_{l \neq i}^U \circ B^{-1}(b) + F \circ \pi_i^U \circ B^{-1}(b) + F \circ B^{-1}(b) + F(0)\right)$$

$$+ (d + 1 \bmod 2) \cdot F(0),$$

since we can decompose $F \circ B^{-1}(b)$ into $F \circ \pi_{l \neq i}^U \circ B^{-1}(b) + F \circ \pi_i^U \circ B^{-1}(b) + F(0)$. But, as $\sum_i F \circ \pi_i^U \circ B^{-1}(b) = F \circ B^{-1}(b) + (d+1 \bmod 2) \cdot F(0)$, this is equal to

$$\sum_i \left(F \circ \pi_i^U + F \circ \pi_{l \neq i}^U \circ B^{-1}(b) + F(0) \right) + (d+1 \bmod 2) \cdot F \circ B^{-1}(b)$$

$$= \sum_i F \left(\pi_i^U + \pi_{l \neq i}^U \circ B^{-1}(b) \right) + (d+1 \bmod 2) \cdot F \circ B^{-1}(b)$$

$$= \sum_i F \left(\pi_i^U \left(I + B^{-1}(b) \right) + B^{-1}(b) \right) + (d+1 \bmod 2) \cdot F \circ B^{-1}(b)$$

$$= \sum_i \left(A \circ G \left(B \circ \pi_i^U \left(I + B^{-1}(b) \right) + B \cdot B^{-1}(b) + b \right) + a \right)$$

$$+ (d+1 \bmod 2) \cdot \left(A \circ G \left(B \circ B^{-1}(b) + b \right) + a \right)$$

$$= A \left(\sum_i G \left(B \circ \pi_i^U \left(I + B^{-1}(b) \right) \right) + (d+1 \bmod 2) \cdot G(0) \right) + a.$$

In other words, we have that

$$G = \sum_i G \left(B \circ \pi_i^U \circ B^{-1} \right) + (d+1 \bmod 2) \cdot G(0),$$

where $B \circ \pi_i^U \circ B^{-1}$ are the projections onto $B \cdot U_i$. In addition, we get that

$$A \left(G(B \cdot U_i) + G(0) \right) = F(U_i + B^{-1} \cdot b) + F(B^{-1} \cdot b)$$

$$= \sum_l F \circ \pi_l^U (U_i + B^{-1} \cdot b) + (d+1 \bmod 2) \cdot F(0)$$

$$+ \sum_l F \circ \pi_l^U (B^{-1} \cdot b) + (d+1 \bmod 2) \cdot F(0)$$

$$= F \circ \pi_i^U (U_i) + F \circ \pi_i^U (B^{-1} \cdot b)$$

$$= F_i \circ \pi_i^U (U_i) + \pi_{l \neq i}^V F(0) + F_i \circ \pi_i^U (B^{-1} \cdot b) + \pi_{l \neq i}^V F(0)$$

$$= V_i + F_i \circ \pi_i^U (B^{-1} \cdot b) = V_i.$$

As $\bigoplus_i A^{-1} \cdot V_i = \mathbb{F}_2^n$, it now follows from Lemma 1 that $\{B \cdot U_i | 1 \leq i \leq d\}$ induces a decomposition of G. The reverse direction follows from switching the roles of F and G, as both affine mappings are bijective.   □

This especially shows that a decomposition is invariant (up to changing the F_i) under the addition of constants (e. g. a key), both at the beginning or the end of the round function. Hence, we can ignore such additions.

While the lemma above also enables us to study an affine equivalent version of a function such that one decomposition has a preferable form, e. g. $U_i = 0^{m_i} \times \mathbb{F}_2^{\dim(U_i)} \times 0^{m_i'}$, other decompositions are not necessarily of such a form.

Finding Refinements. In order to judge if a decomposition is maximal we need to know if there exists a refinement. For this, let us try to find a refinement given two decompositions.

Corollary 5. *Let* $F : \mathbb{F}_2^n \to \mathbb{F}_2^n$ *be bijective and let* $\{U_i \mid 1 \le i \le d\}$ *and* $\{W_i \mid 1 \le i \le e\}$ *both induce decompositions of* F. *Then we have that*

$$F + (d \cdot e + 1 \bmod 2) \cdot F(0) = \sum_{i,j} F \circ \pi_i^U \circ \pi_j^W = \sum_{i,j} F \circ \pi_j^W \circ \pi_i^U.$$

Proof. We know that we can write $F = \sum_i F \circ \pi_i^U + (d + 1 \bmod 2) \cdot F(0)$ resp. $F = \sum_j F \circ \pi_j^W + (e + 1 \bmod 2) \cdot F(0)$. This means that

$$F \circ \pi_j^W = \sum_i F \circ \pi_i^U \circ \pi_j^W + (d + 1 \bmod 2) \cdot F(0),$$

which in turn means that

$$F = \sum_j F \circ \pi_j^W + (e + 1 \bmod 2) \cdot F(0)$$

$$= \sum_j \left(\sum_i F \circ \pi_i^U \circ \pi_j^W + (d + 1 \bmod 2) \cdot F(0) \right) + (e + 1 \bmod 2) \cdot F(0)$$

$$= \sum_{i,j} F \circ \pi_i^U \circ \pi_j^W + (d \cdot e + 1 \bmod 2) \cdot F(0).$$

□

As we will see, if $\mathrm{Im}(\pi_i^U \circ \pi_j^W) \cap \mathrm{Im}(\pi_l^U \circ \pi_k^W) = \{0\}$ holds for all $i \ne l$ and $j \ne k$ then we have found a refinement. But as soon as there exists a non-trivial intersection, there exist multiple maximal decompositions. To see that the case of a non-trivial intersection is even possible, let us look at the following example.

Example 1. Let R be as in Sect. 2, i.e.

$$R \begin{pmatrix} x_1 \\ x_2 \\ x_3 \\ x_4 \end{pmatrix} = \begin{pmatrix} f(x_1) \\ g(x_1) + x_2 \\ x_3 \\ h\begin{pmatrix} x_3 \\ x_4 \end{pmatrix} \end{pmatrix} \begin{matrix} \left.\vphantom{\begin{matrix}a\\b\end{matrix}}\right\} \text{S-box} \\[2ex] \left.\vphantom{\begin{matrix}a\\b\end{matrix}}\right\} \text{S-box} \end{matrix},$$

where $x_1 \in \mathbb{F}_2^n, x_4 \in \mathbb{F}_2^m$ for integers n, m and $x_2, x_3 \in \mathbb{F}_2$, as well as $f : \mathbb{F}_2^n \to \mathbb{F}_2^n$, $g : \mathbb{F}_2^n \to \mathbb{F}_2$ and $h : \mathbb{F}_2 \times \mathbb{F}_2^m \to \mathbb{F}_2^m$. Because of Lemma 2 we can ignore a linear layer that would usually mix the output of the two S-boxes.

Let us consider the following subspaces

$$U_1 := \mathbb{F}_2^n \times \mathbb{F}_2 \times 0 \times 0^m, \qquad\qquad U_2 := 0^n \times 0 \times \mathbb{F}_2 \times \mathbb{F}_2^n,$$
$$W_1 := U_1, \qquad\qquad W_2 := \{(0, a, a, b)^T \mid a \in \mathbb{F}_2, b \in \mathbb{F}_2^m\}.$$

It is not too hard to see that both $\{U_1, U_2\}$ and $\{W_1, W_2\}$ induce decompositions (we refer to the full version [17] for more details) while they are obviously not identical, nor is one the refinement of the other. But

$$\mathrm{Im}(\pi_1^U \circ \pi_1^W) \cap \mathrm{Im}(\pi_1^U \circ \pi_2^W) = U_1 \cap 0^n \times \mathbb{F}_2 \times 0 \times 0^m = 0^n \times \mathbb{F}_2 \times 0 \times 0^m \ne \{0\}.$$

5.1 The Case of Trivial Intersections

Based on Corollary 5, one may hope that the set $\{Im(\pi_i^U \circ \pi_j^W)|i,j\} \setminus \{0\}$ induces a decomposition that is a refinement of both initial decompositions. While it is clear that in case of only trivial intersections of those images they form a direct sum, the same is not directly clear for the corresponding output spaces $Im(\pi_i^V \circ \pi_j^X \circ F) = Im(\pi_i^V \circ \pi_j^X)$. Obviously, the intersection can only be non-trivial if $i = l$ as otherwise $Im(\pi_i^U) \cap Im(\pi_l^U) = \{0\}$ already holds, which reduces our analysis to the spaces $Im(\pi_i^U \circ \pi_j^W) \cap Im(\pi_i^U \circ \pi_k^W)$ resp. $Im(\pi_i^V \circ \pi_j^X) \cap Im(\pi_i^V \circ \pi_k^X)$. As the next corollary shows, the input spaces are in direct sum if and only if the output spaces are in direct sum.

Corollary 6. *Let* $F : \mathbb{F}_2^n \to \mathbb{F}_2^n$ *be bijective and let* $\{(U_i, V_i, F_i) \mid 1 \le i \le d\}$ *and* $\{(W_i, X_i, G_i) \mid 1 \le i \le e\}$ *be two decompositions of* F. *Then for all* i, j, k, *it holds that*

$$Im(\pi_i^U \circ \pi_j^W) \cap Im(\pi_i^U \circ \pi_k^W) = \{0\} \Leftrightarrow Im(\pi_i^V \circ \pi_j^X) \cap Im(\pi_i^V \circ \pi_k^X) = \{0\}.$$

Proof. From Corollaries 2 and 3 we know that $F \circ \pi_i^U = F_i \circ \pi_i^U + \pi_{l \ne i}^V \circ F(0) = \pi_i^V \circ F + \pi_{l \ne i}^V F(0)$, which means that

$$
\begin{aligned}
F \circ \pi_i^U \circ \pi_j^W &= \pi_i^V \circ F \circ \pi_j^W + F(0) + \pi_i^V \circ F(0) \\
&= \pi_i^V \left(\pi_j^X \circ F + F(0) + \pi_j^X \circ F(0) \right) + F(0) + \pi_i^V \circ F(0) \\
&= \pi_i^V \circ \pi_j^X \circ F + F(0) + \pi_i^V \circ \pi_j^X \circ F(0) \\
&= \pi_i^V \circ \pi_j^X \left(F + F(0) \right) + F(0).
\end{aligned}
$$

Let $x \in Im(\pi_i^U \circ \pi_j^W) \cap Im(\pi_i^U \circ \pi_k^W)$, i. e. there exist $a, b \in \mathbb{F}_2^n$ such that $\pi_i^U \circ \pi_j^W(a) = x = \pi_i^U \circ \pi_k^W(b)$. This means that

$$F(x) + F(0) = F \circ \pi_i^U \circ \pi_j^W(a) + F(0) = \pi_i^V \circ \pi_j^X \left(F(a) + F(0) \right)$$

and similarly $F(x) + F(0) = \pi_i^V \circ \pi_k^X \left(F(b) + F(0) \right)$, i. e. there exists $c = F(a) + F(0)$ and $d = F(b) + F(0)$ such that $\pi_i^V \circ \pi_j^X(c) = F(x) + F(0) = \pi_i^V \circ \pi_k^X(d)$. As F is a bijection, implying that $F(x) + F(0) = 0$ if and only if $x = 0$ and that the mappings $a \mapsto c$ and $b \mapsto d$ are also bijections, the claim follows. □

Next, we want to show that if $Im(\pi_i^U \circ \pi_j^W) \cap Im(\pi_i^U \circ \pi_k^W) = \{0\}$ holds for all i and $j \ne k$, we either get a refinement or the two decompositions are identical. To do so, we first take a deeper look at compositions of the projections.

Corollary 7. *Let* $U_1, ..., U_d$ *and* $W_1, ..., W_e$ *be subspaces of* $\mathbb{F}_2^n$ *such that* $\bigoplus_i U_i = \mathbb{F}_2^n = \bigoplus_i V_i$. *Then* $Im(\pi_i^U \circ \pi_j^W) \cap Im(\pi_i^U \circ \pi_k^W) = \{0\}$ *hold for all* i *and* $j \ne k$ *if and only if* $\pi_i^U \circ \pi_j^W = \pi_j^W \circ \pi_i^U$ *for all* i, j.

Proof. Let us assume that $Im(\pi_i^U \circ \pi_j^W) \cap Im(\pi_i^U \circ \pi_k^W) = \{0\}$ holds for all i and $j \ne k$. Hence, we know that $\bigoplus_{i,j} Im(\pi_i^U \circ \pi_j^W) = \mathbb{F}_2^n$, and we have to show that $\pi_i^U \circ \pi_j^W = \pi_j^W \circ \pi_i^U$ for all i, j. Since both $\sum_{l,k} \pi_l^U \circ \pi_k^W$ and $\sum_k \pi_k^W$ are the identity, it holds that

$$0 = \pi_i^U + \pi_i^U = \sum_{l,k} \pi_l^U \circ \pi_k^W \circ \pi_i^U + \sum_k \pi_i^U \circ \pi_k^W \circ \pi_i^U = \sum_{l \neq i, k} \pi_l^U \circ \pi_k^W \circ \pi_i^U.$$

As $0 \in \mathrm{Im}(\pi_l^U \circ \pi_k^W)$ for all l, k, and those images are in direct sum, we know that $\pi_l^U \circ \pi_k^W \circ \pi_i^U = 0$ has to hold for all $l \neq i$ and all k. This shows that $\pi_j^W \circ \pi_i^U = \pi_i^U \circ \pi_j^W$, since

$$\pi_j^W \circ \pi_i^U = \sum_l \pi_l^U \circ \pi_j^W \circ \pi_i^U = \pi_i^U \circ \pi_j^W \circ \pi_i^U,$$

but also

$$\pi_i^U \circ \pi_j^W = \sum_l \pi_i^U \circ \pi_j^W \circ \pi_l^U = \pi_i^U \circ \pi_j^W \circ \pi_i^U.$$

Now, let us assume that $\pi_i^U \circ \pi_j^W = \pi_j^W \circ \pi_i^U$ for all i, j, which means that

$$\pi_i^U \circ \pi_j^W \circ \pi_i^U \circ \pi_j^W = \pi_i^U \circ \pi_j^W \circ \pi_j^W \circ \pi_i^U = \pi_i^U \circ \pi_j^W \circ \pi_i^U = \pi_i^U \circ \pi_i^U \circ \pi_j^W = \pi_i^U \circ \pi_j^W,$$

i.e. the $\pi_i^U \circ \pi_j^W$ are projections. If $k \neq j$ then we have that

$$\pi_i^U \circ \pi_j^W \circ \pi_i^U \circ \pi_k^W = \pi_i^U \circ \pi_j^W \circ \pi_k^W \circ \pi_i^U = 0.$$

But also, since $\mathrm{Im}(\pi_i^U \circ \pi_j^W) \cap \mathrm{Im}(\pi_l^U \circ \pi_k^W) \subset \mathrm{Im}(\pi_i^U \circ \pi_j^W)$ and $\pi_i^U \circ \pi_j^W$ is a projection, it has to hold that

$$\{0\} \subset \mathrm{Im}(\pi_i^U \circ \pi_j^W) \cap \mathrm{Im}(\pi_l^U \circ \pi_k^W) = \pi_i^U \circ \pi_j^W \left(\mathrm{Im}(\pi_i^U \circ \pi_j^W) \cap \mathrm{Im}(\pi_l^U \circ \pi_k^W) \right)$$
$$\subset \pi_i^U \circ \pi_j^W \left(\mathrm{Im}(\pi_l^U \circ \pi_k^W) \right) = \{0\}.$$

□

In other words, if all the intersections are trivial, we not only know that we can find a refinement based on the two decompositions, but also that the order in which we do, first decomposing according to the U_i and then refining according to the W_j or the other way around, does not matter since the resulting projections and therefore the subspaces are identical. This leads us to the following lemma.

Lemma 3. *Let $F : \mathbb{F}_2^n \to \mathbb{F}_2^n$ be bijective and let $\{U_i \mid 1 \leq i \leq d\}$ and $\{W_i \mid 1 \leq i \leq e\}$ induce the decompositions D and E of F. If for every i and $j \neq k$ it holds that $\mathrm{Im}(\pi_i^U \circ \pi_j^W) \cap \mathrm{Im}(\pi_i^U \circ \pi_k^W) = \{0\}$ then we can either construct a refinement of D or E induced by the set of input spaces $\{U_i \cap W_j \mid 1 \leq i \leq d, 1 \leq j \leq e\} \setminus \{\{0\}\}$ or $D = E$.*

Proof. By our reasoning above, we already know that if $\mathrm{Im}(\pi_i^U \circ \pi_j^W) \cap \mathrm{Im}(\pi_i^U \circ \pi_k^W) = \{0\}$ holds for every i and $j \neq k$ the images $\mathrm{Im}(\pi_i^U \circ \pi_j^W)$ form a direct sum, as do the images $\mathrm{Im}(\pi_i^V \circ \pi_j^X)$. Note that Corollary 7 shows that $\pi_i^U \circ \pi_j^W = \pi_j^W \circ \pi_i^U$

are the corresponding projections. Therefore, $U_i \supset \text{Im}(\pi_i^U \circ \pi_j^W) = \text{Im}(\pi_j^W \circ \pi_i^U) \subset W_j$, but also $U_i \cap W_j \subset \text{Im}(\pi_j^W)$ and $U_i \cap W_j \subset \text{Im}(\pi_i^U)$, which means that

$$U_i \cap W_j \subset \text{Im}(\pi_i^U \circ \pi_j^W) \subset U_i \cap W_j.$$

Hence, $\text{Im}(\pi_i^U \circ \pi_j^W) = U_i \cap W_j$ and if we remove the trivial subspaces then Corollary 5 shows that the set of input spaces $\{U_i \cap W_j | 1 \leq i \leq d, 1 \leq j \leq e\} \setminus \{\{0\}\}$ induces a decomposition. Also, it obviously holds that $W_j \cap U_i \subset W_j$ and $U_i \cap W_j \subset U_i$, which means that we either got a refinement of D or E, or D is identical to E.   □

5.2   The Case of Non-trivial Intersections

Now, let us look at the case in which at least one intersection of the images is non-trivial. As we will see, this means that (at least) one S-Box has to have maximal differential uniformity and another one has to have maximal linearity. In order to show that, we need the following lemma.

Lemma 4. *Let* $F : \mathbb{F}_2^n \to \mathbb{F}_2^n$ *be bijective and let* $\{(U_i, V_i, F_i) \mid 1 \leq i \leq d\}$ *and* $\{(W_i, X_i, G_i) \mid 1 \leq i \leq e\}$ *be two decompositions of* F. *Then we have that*

$$F\left(\sum_j \pi_i^U \circ \pi_j^W\right) = \sum_j F \circ \pi_i^U \circ \pi_j^W + (e + 1 \bmod 2) \cdot F(0).$$

Proof. The claim follows from

$$F\left(\sum_j \pi_i^U \circ \pi_j^W\right) = F \circ \pi_i^U \left(\sum_j \pi_j^W\right) = F \circ \pi_i^U = \pi_i^V \circ F + \pi_{l \neq i}^V \circ F(0)$$

$$= \pi_i^V \left(\sum_j F \circ \pi_j^W + (e + 1 \bmod 2) \cdot F(0)\right) + \pi_{l \neq i}^V \circ F(0)$$

$$= \sum_j \pi_i^V \circ F \circ \pi_j^W + (e + 1 \bmod 2) \cdot \pi_i^V \circ F(0) + \pi_{l \neq i}^V \circ F(0)$$

$$= \sum_j \left(F \circ \pi_i^U \circ \pi_j^W + \pi_{l \neq i}^V \circ F(0)\right) + (e + 1 \bmod 2) \cdot \pi_i^V \circ F(0) + \pi_{l \neq i}^V \circ F(0)$$

$$= \sum_j F \circ \pi_i^U \circ \pi_j^W + (e + 1 \bmod 2) \cdot F(0).$$

□

Since the inputs to the $F \circ \pi_i^U \circ \pi_j^W$ can be seen as independent as the W_j are in direct sum, this already shows that there has to be some kind of linearity.

Behaviour on the Intersections. Next, we will show that each F_i (resp. the corresponding S-box) has to be affine on each of the subspaces $\text{Im}(\pi_i^U \circ \pi_j^V) \cap \text{Im}(\pi_i^U \circ \pi_k^V)$, which is trivial in the case that those subspaces are $\{0\}$, but gives us more information in the case of a non-trivial intersection. For this, we will first take a deeper look at such intersections.

342   B. Lambin et al.

Corollary 8. *Let* $U_1, ..., U_d, W_1, ..., W_e \subset \mathbb{F}_2^n$ *be subspaces with* $\bigoplus_i U_i = \mathbb{F}_2^n = \bigoplus_i W_i$. *Also, let* P *be a composition of alternating projections* π_i^U, π_j^W. *Then it holds that*

$$Im(P \circ \pi_j^W) \cap Im(P \circ \pi_{k\neq j}^W) = Im(P \circ \pi_j^W \circ \pi_{l\neq i}^U) = Im(P \circ \pi_{k\neq j}^W \circ \pi_{l\neq i}^U).$$

Proof. Note that as $\pi_i^W \circ \pi_{k\neq j}^W = 0$, we can assume that P is either of the form $p \circ ... \circ \pi_i^U \circ \pi_j^W \circ \pi_i^U$ with $p \in \{\pi_i^U \circ \pi_j^W, \pi_j^W \circ \pi_i^U\}$ or $P \circ \pi_{k\neq j}^W$ is zero. As in the second case the claim is obviously true, let us assume that P is of the form $p \circ ... \circ \pi_i^U \circ \pi_j^W \circ \pi_i^U$. It holds that

$$\begin{aligned}
&Im(P \circ \pi_j^W) \cap Im(P \circ \pi_{k\neq j}^W)\\
&= \{P(x)|x \in W_j\} \cap \{P(x')|x' \in W_{k\neq j}\}\\
&= \{y|P(x) = y = P(x'), x \in W_j, x' \in W_{k\neq j}\}\\
&= \{P \circ \pi_j^W(x + x')|P(x) + P(x') = 0, x \in W_j, x' \in W_{k\neq j}\}\\
&= \{P \circ \pi_j^W(\hat{x})|\hat{x} \in \ker(P)\}\\
&\supset Im(P \circ \pi_j^W \circ \pi_{l\neq i}^U)
\end{aligned}$$

as $U_{l\neq i} = \ker(\pi_i^U) \subset \ker(P)$. In addition, we have that

$$\begin{aligned}
\{P \circ \pi_j^W(\hat{x})|\hat{x} \in \ker(P)\} &= \{P \circ \pi_j^W(\hat{x}) + p \circ P(\hat{x})|\hat{x} \in \ker(P)\}\\
&= \{P\left(\pi_j^W(\hat{x}) + \pi_j^W \circ \pi_i^U(\hat{x})\right)|\hat{x} \in \ker(P)\}\\
&= \{P \circ \pi_j^W \circ \pi_{l\neq i}^U(\hat{x})|\hat{x} \in \ker(P)\}\\
&\subset Im(P \circ \pi_j^W \circ \pi_{l\neq i}^U),
\end{aligned}$$

which, together with $\pi_i^U \circ \pi_j^W \circ \pi_{l\neq i}^U = \pi_i^U \circ \left(I + \pi_j^W\right) \circ \pi_{l\neq i}^U = \pi_i^U \circ \pi_{k\neq j}^W \circ \pi_{l\neq i}^U$, where I denotes the identity, completes the proof. $\square$

In other words, if we set $P = \pi_i^U$, the intersections $Im(\pi_i^U \circ \pi_j^V) \cap Im(\pi_i^U \circ \pi_{k\neq j}^V)$ are actually the images of $\pi_i^U \circ \pi_j^W \circ \pi_{l\neq i}^U = \pi_i^U \circ \pi_{k\neq j}^W \circ \pi_{l\neq i}^U$. With this and the lemma above, we can now show that the function has to be affine on those intersection resp. images.

Lemma 5. *Let* $F : \mathbb{F}_2^n \to \mathbb{F}_2^n$ *be bijective and let* $\{(U_i, V_i, F_i) \mid 1 \leq i \leq d\}$ *and* $\{(W_i, X_i, G_i) \mid 1 \leq i \leq e\}$ *be two decompositions of* F. *Then we have that* F *is affine on* $Im(\pi_i^U \circ \pi_j^W \circ \pi_{l\neq i}^U)$ *for every* i, j.

Proof. Let $x, y \in Im(\pi_i^U \circ \pi_j^W \circ \pi_{l\neq i}^U) = Im(\pi_i^U \circ \pi_{k\neq j}^W \circ \pi_{l\neq i}^U)$, i.e. there exist $a, b \in \mathbb{F}_2^n$ such that $x = \pi_i^U \circ \pi_j^W \circ \pi_{l\neq i}^U(a)$ and $y = \pi_i^U \circ \pi_{k\neq j}^W \circ \pi_{l\neq i}^U(b)$. Also, let us define $\hat{W}_1 := W_j$ and $\hat{W}_2 := W_{k\neq j}$. Note that $\{\hat{W}_1, \hat{W}_2\}$ also induces a decomposition, which, combined with the above lemma, leads to

$$F(x+y) = F\left(\pi_i^U \circ \pi_j^W \circ \pi_{l\neq i}^U(a) + \pi_i^U \circ \pi_{k\neq j}^W \circ \pi_{l\neq i}^U(b)\right)$$

$$= F\left(\sum_{r=1,2} \pi_i^U \circ \pi_r^{\hat{W}} \left(\pi_j^W \circ \pi_{l\neq i}^U(a) + \pi_{k\neq j}^W \circ \pi_{l\neq i}^U(b)\right)\right)$$

$$= F \circ \pi_i^U \circ \pi_j^W \circ \pi_{l\neq i}^U(a) + F \circ \pi_i^U \circ \pi_{k\neq j}^W \circ \pi_{l\neq i}^U(b) + F(0)$$

$$= F(x) + F(y) + F(0).$$

□

A direct consequence of this is that $F \circ \pi_i^U \circ \pi_j^W \circ \pi_{l\neq i}^U$ is affine, or equivalent that $F \circ \pi_i^U \circ \pi_j^W \circ \pi_{l\neq i}^U + F(0)$ is linear.[8] But as we can iteratively represent F composed with a projection onto an input space as the projection of F onto the corresponding output space (plus a constant), this gives us the following.

Corollary 9. *Let $F : \mathbb{F}_2^n \to \mathbb{F}_2^n$ be bijective and let $\{(U_i, V_i, F_i) \mid 1 \le i \le d\}$ and $\{(W_i, X_i, G_i) \mid 1 \le i \le e\}$ be two decompositions of F. If $\pi_i^U \circ \pi_j^W \circ \pi_{l\neq i}^U \neq 0$ then there exists an $k \neq i$ such that F_k has maximal linearity.*

Proof. We know that $F \circ \pi_i^U \circ \pi_j^W \circ \pi_{l\neq i}^U + F(0)$ is linear. But this means that

$$F \circ \pi_i^U \circ \pi_j^W \circ \pi_{l\neq i}^U + F(0) = \pi_i^V \left(F \circ \pi_j^W \circ \pi_{l\neq i}^U + F(0)\right)$$

$$= \ldots = \pi_i^V \circ \pi_j^X \circ \pi_{l\neq i}^V (F + F(0))$$

$$= \sum_{l\neq i} \pi_i^V \circ \pi_j^X \circ \pi_l^V \left(F_l \circ \pi_l^U + F_l(0)\right)$$

is also linear. Since the inputs to the F_l are independent, this shows that $\pi_i^V \circ \pi_j^X \circ \pi_l^V \left(F_l \circ \pi_l^U + F_l(0)\right)$ is linear for every $l \neq i$. As $\pi_i^U \circ \pi_j^W \circ \pi_{l\neq i}^U \neq 0$, we also know that $\pi_i^V \circ \pi_j^X \circ \pi_{l\neq i}^V \neq 0$, and therefore there exists a $k \neq i$ such that $\pi_i^V \circ \pi_j^X \circ \pi_k^V \neq 0$, which in turn means that $\pi_i^V \circ \pi_j^X \circ \pi_k^V \left(F_k + F_k(0)\right) \neq 0$. Hence, we can simply select α^T as a non-zero component of $\pi_i^V \circ \pi_j^X \circ \pi_k^V$ and get that $\alpha^T \cdot F_k + \alpha^T \cdot F_k(0)$ is linear and non-trivial, i.e. F_k has maximal linearity. □

In other words, a non-trivial intersection implies a (non-trivial) affine component of one of the S-boxes. But it even implies more.

Non-Trivial Intersections Imply Maximal Differential Uniformity. Knowing that F is affine on these intersections, we are now able to show that this implies maximal differential uniformity of the corresponding F_i.

Lemma 6. *Let $F : \mathbb{F}_2^n \to \mathbb{F}_2^n$ be bijective and let $\{(U_i, V_i, F_i) \mid 1 \le i \le d\}$ and $\{(W_i, X_i, G_i) \mid 1 \le i \le e\}$ be two decompositions of F. If it holds that $Im(\pi_i^U \circ \pi_j^W) \cap Im(\pi_i^U \circ \pi_{k\neq j}^W) \neq \{0\}$ for some i, j then F_i has maximal differential uniformity.*

---

[8] Note that in the case of trivial intersections, we have that $\pi_i^U \circ \pi_j^W \circ \pi_{l\neq i}^U = \pi_j^W \circ \pi_i^U \circ \pi_{l\neq i}^U = 0$, which means that $F \circ \pi_i^U \circ \pi_j^W \circ \pi_{l\neq i}^U + F(0) = 0$.

Proof. Let $\alpha \in \text{Im}(\pi_i^U \circ \pi_j^W) \cap \text{Im}(\pi_i^U \circ \pi_{k \neq j}^W) = \text{Im}(\pi_i^U \circ \pi_j^W \circ \pi_{l \neq i}^U)$ and $x \in U_i = \text{Im}(\pi_i^U \circ \pi_j^W \circ \pi_i^U) + \text{Im}(\pi_i^U \circ \pi_{k \neq j}^W \circ \pi_i^U)$, i.e. we can write $x = x_1 + x_2$ for $x_1 \in \text{Im}(\pi_i^U \circ \pi_j^W \circ \pi_i^U)$ and $x_2 \in \text{Im}(\pi_i^U \circ \pi_{k \neq j}^W \circ \pi_i^U)$. Furthermore, we can find a, b_1, b_2 such that $\alpha = \pi_i^U \circ \pi_j^W \circ \pi_{l \neq i}^U(a)$, $x_1 = \pi_i^U \circ \pi_j^W \circ \pi_i^U(b_1)$ and $x_2 = \pi_i^U \circ \pi_{k \neq j}^W \circ \pi_i^U(b_2)$, which, together with Lemma 4, gives us

$$F(x + \alpha) = F(x_1 + x_2 + \alpha)$$
$$= F\left(\pi_i^U \circ \pi_j^W\left(\pi_{l \neq i}^U(a) + \pi_i^U(b_1)\right) + \pi_i^U \circ \pi_{k \neq j}^W \circ \pi_i^U(b_2)\right)$$
$$= F \circ \pi_i^U \circ \pi_j^W\left(\pi_{l \neq i}^U(a) + \pi_i^U(b_1)\right) + F \circ \pi_i^U \circ \pi_{k \neq j}^W \circ \pi_i^U(b_2) + F(0),$$

where for the last step we use the fact that $\pi_j^W(\hat{a}) = \pi_j^W\left(\pi_j^W(\hat{a}) + \pi_{k \neq j}^W(\hat{b})\right)$ and $\pi_{k \neq j}^W(\hat{b}) = \pi_{k \neq j}^W\left(\pi_j^W(\hat{a}) + \pi_{k \neq j}^W(\hat{b})\right)$. In addition, it is easy to see that that

$$F \circ \pi_i^U \circ \pi_j^W\left(\pi_{l \neq i}^U(a) + \pi_i^U(b_1)\right)$$
$$= \pi_i^V \circ \pi_j^X \circ F\left(\pi_{l \neq i}^U(a) + \pi_i^U(b_1)\right) + F(0) + \pi_i^V \circ \pi_j^X \circ F(0)$$
$$= \pi_i^V \circ \pi_j^X\left(F \circ \pi_{l \neq i}^U(a) + F \circ \pi_i^U(b_1) + F(0)\right) + F(0) + \pi_i^V \circ \pi_j^X \circ F(0)$$
$$= F \circ \pi_i^U \circ \pi_j^W \circ \pi_i^U(b_1) + F \circ \pi_i^U \circ \pi_j^W \circ \pi_{l \neq i}^U(a) + F(0).$$

If we combine those observations and apply Lemma 4 once more, we get that

$$F(x + \alpha)$$
$$= F \circ \pi_i^U \circ \pi_j^W \circ \pi_i^U(b_1) + F \circ \pi_i^U \circ \pi_j^W \circ \pi_{l \neq i}^U(a) + F(0)$$
$$\quad + F \circ \pi_i^U \circ \pi_{k \neq j}^W \circ \pi_i^U(b_2) + F(0)$$
$$= F \circ \pi_i^U\left(\pi_j^W \circ \pi_i^U(b_1) + \pi_{k \neq j}^W \circ \pi_i^U(b_2)\right) + F \circ \pi_i^U \circ \pi_j^W \circ \pi_{l \neq i}^U(a) + F(0)$$
$$= F(x) + F(\alpha) + F(0).$$

In other words, $F(x) + F(x + \alpha) = F(\alpha) + F(0)$ holds for every $x \in U_i$, which means that $F_{|U_i}$ and therefore F_i has maximal differential uniformity. $\square$

Obviously, if one of the F_i has maximal differential uniformity, the same has to be true for the whole (round) function.

Maximal Differential Uniformity Together with Maximal Linearity Implies Non-Unique Maximal Decomposition. Next, we will show that one S-box having maximal differential uniformity and another one having maximal linearity implies that there exists no unique maximal decomposition.

Lemma 7. *Let $F : \mathbb{F}_2^n \to \mathbb{F}_2^n$ be bijective and let $D = \{(U_i, V_i, F_i) | 1 \leq i \leq d\}$ be a maximal decomposition of F. If there exist $i \neq k$ such that F_i has maximal differential uniformity and F_k has maximal linearity then D is not unique.*

Proof. Let us assume that there exists $i \neq k$ such that F_i has maximal differential uniformity, i.e. we can find an $a \in U_i$ such that $F_i(x) + F_i(x + a)$ is constant for all $x \in U_i$, and therefore the same as $F_i(a) + F_i(0)$, and F_k has maximal linearity, i.e. there exists an $\alpha \in \mathbb{F}_2^n \setminus V_k^{\perp}$ and $\beta \in \mathbb{F}_2^n$ such that $\beta^T \cdot x + \alpha^T \cdot F_k(x)$ is constant for all $x \in U_k$, and hence the same as $\alpha^T \cdot F_k(0)$. Let us define $L : \mathbb{F}_2^n \to U_i$ by $L \cdot x := a \cdot \beta^T \cdot \pi_k^U(x)$ for all $x \in \mathbb{F}_2^n$. Then both $\pi_i^U + L$ and $\pi_k^U + L$ are projections, as $\pi_i^U \circ L = L = L \circ \pi_k^U$, $L \circ \pi_i^U = 0 = \pi_k^U \circ L$ and $L^2 = 0$. In addition, their sum is obviously $\pi_i^U + \pi_k^U$, which means that their images together with U_l for $l \notin \{i,k\}$ form a direct sum of $\mathbb{F}_2^n$. Also, as $\text{Im}\left(\pi_i^U + L\right) = U_i + a = U_i$ we have that $F(\text{Im}(\pi_i^U + L)) + F(0) = F(U_i) + F(0) = V_i$ is, by definition, a subspace. To show that $F(\text{Im}(\pi_k^U + L)) + F(0)$ is also a subspace, let us define the projection $P := \pi_k^V + F_i \circ L \circ F_k^{-1} \circ \pi_k^V + F_i(0)$. Note that P is linear, as $F_i(x + a) = F_i(x) + F_i(a) + F_i(0)$ for all $x \in U_i$. Furthermore, P is indeed a projection, since $\pi_k^V \left(\pi_k^V + F_i \circ L \circ F_k^{-1} \circ \pi_k^V + F_i(0)\right) = \pi_k^V$ and therefore $P^2 = P$. We now get that

$$F(\text{Im}(\pi_k^U + L)) + F(0) = \{F\left(\pi_k^U(x) + L \cdot x\right) + F(0) | x \in \mathbb{F}_2^n\}$$

$$= \left\{\sum_l \left(F_l \circ \pi_l^U\left(\pi_k^U(x) + L \cdot x\right) + F_l(0)\right) | x \in U_k\right\}$$

$$= \{F_k \circ \pi_k^U(x) + F_k(0) + F_i \circ L \cdot x + F_i(0) | x \in U_k\}$$

$$= \{y + F_i \circ L \cdot F_k^{-1}\left(y + F_k(0)\right) + F_i(0) | y \in V_k\}$$

$$= \text{Im}(P),$$

which means that $F(\text{Im}(\pi_k^U + L)) + F(0)$ is also a subspace. At last, since

$$F\left(\pi_i^U + L\right) + F\left(\pi_k^U + L\right) = \sum_l F_l \circ \pi_l^U\left(\pi_i^U + L\right) + \sum_l F_l \circ \pi_l^U\left(\pi_k^U + L\right)$$

$$= F_i\left(\pi_i^U + L\right) + F_k(0) + F_i \circ L + F_k \circ \pi_k^U$$

$$= F_i \circ \pi_i^U + F_i \circ L + F_i(0) + F_i \circ L + F_k(0) + F_k \circ \pi_k^U$$

$$= F \circ \pi_i^U + F \circ \pi_k^U,$$

we get that $\sum_{l \notin \{i,k\}} F \circ \pi_l^U + F\left(\pi_i^U + L\right) + F\left(\pi_k^U + L\right) + (d+1 \bmod 2) \cdot F(0) = F$. Therefore, $\{U_l | l \neq k\} \cup \text{Im}\left(\pi_k^U + L\right)$ induces a decomposition of F, different than D but with the same number of S-boxes, which means that D is not unique. $\square$

If we combine all the observations above, we can finally prove Theorem 1.

Proof of Theorem 1. First, let $\{(U_i, V_i, F_i) | 1 \leq i \leq d\}$ be a maximal decomposition of F and assume that there exist $i \neq k$ such that F_i has maximal differential uniformity and F_k has maximal linearity. Then we know from Lemma 7 that this maximal decomposition is not unique.

Now, let $\{(U_i, V_i, F_i) | 1 \leq i \leq d\}$ and $\{(W_i, X_i, G_i) \mid 1 \leq i \leq e\}$ be two different maximal decompositions. We know from Lemma 3 that if all the intersections $\text{Im}(\pi_i^U \circ \pi_j^W) \cap \text{Im}(\pi_i^U \circ \pi_k^W)$ were trivial, we could either refine one of the decompositions or they are identical. But since they are both maximal and not identical, we know that some of those intersection have to be non-trivial. Hence, we can follow from Corollary 9 and Lemma 6 that there exists a pair $i \neq k$ such that F_i has maximal differential uniformity and F_k has maximal linearity. $\square$

6   Conclusion

In this paper we discussed the uniqueness of decompositions, as well as the impact of alignment. With respect to the uniqueness of decomposition, we have seen that this very natural and simple question required quite some technical backup to be finally settled. In our opinion, it is of interest to further explore the possible impact of such non-unique decompositions not only on security and security arguments, but also on implementation aspects.

With respect to the impact of alignment, we show, based on the example of aligned and unaligned versions of PRESENT, that the impact of alignment on its own may only be limited. We therefore encourage further work to either find conditions under which alignment has a meaningful impact, or to show that the impact of plain alignment is insignificant in general. Especially, we would like to advocate for further case studies to try to only change the property under scrutiny, as this produces more convincing results. Another future direction is to develop more fine grained notions that do capture the structural alignment in a non-binary manner.

Finally, and this can be seen as the broader scope, we encourage research that investigates the use of representations of a cipher in arguments for its security.

Acknowledgment. This work was funded by the by the project *Analysis and Protection of Lightweight Cryptographic Algorithms* (432878529) and by DFG (German Research Foudation), under Germany's Excellence Strategy - EXC 2092 CASA - 390781972.

References

1. Aldaya, A.C., García, C.P., Brumley, B.B.: From A to Z: projective coordinates leakage in the wild. IACR Trans. Cryptogr. Hardw. Embed. Syst. **2020**(3), 428–453 (2020)
2. Baksi, A., et al.: DEFAULT: cipher level resistance against differential fault attack. In: Tibouchi, M., Wang, H. (eds.) ASIACRYPT 2021. LNCS, vol. 13091, pp. 124–156. Springer, Cham (2021). https://doi.org/10.1007/978-3-030-92075-3_5
3. Beierle, C., Canteaut, A., Leander, G., Rotella, Y.: Proving resistance against invariant attacks: how to choose the round constants. In: Katz, J., Shacham, H. (eds.) CRYPTO 2017. LNCS, vol. 10402, pp. 647–678. Springer, Cham (2017). https://doi.org/10.1007/978-3-319-63715-0_22
4. Beierle, C., Leander, G., Moradi, A., Rasoolzadeh, S.: CRAFT: lightweight tweakable block cipher with efficient protection against DFA attacks. IACR Trans. Symmetric Cryptol. **2019**(1), 5–45 (2019)
5. Bertoni, G., Daemen, J., Peeters, M., Van Assche, G.: On alignment in Keccak. In: ECRYPT II Hash Workshop, vol. 51, pp. 122 (2011)
6. Biryukov, A., Shamir, A.: Structural cryptanalysis of SASAS. In: Pfitzmann, B. (ed.) EUROCRYPT 2001. LNCS, vol. 2045, pp. 395–405. Springer, Heidelberg (2001). https://doi.org/10.1007/3-540-44987-6_24
7. Bogdanov, A., et al.: PRESENT: an ultra-lightweight block cipher. In: Paillier, P., Verbauwhede, I. (eds.) CHES 2007. LNCS, vol. 4727, pp. 450–466. Springer, Heidelberg (2007). https://doi.org/10.1007/978-3-540-74735-2_31

8. Bordes, N., Daemen, J., Kuijsters, D., Van Assche, G.: Thinking outside the super-box. In: Malkin, T., Peikert, C. (eds.) CRYPTO 2021. LNCS, vol. 12827, pp. 337–367. Springer, Cham (2021). https://doi.org/10.1007/978-3-030-84252-9_12
9. Canteaut, A., et al.: Saturnin: a suite of lightweight symmetric algorithms for post-quantum security. IACR Trans. Symmetric Cryptol. **2020**(S1), 160–207 (2020)
10. Carlet, C.: Boolean Functions for Cryptography and Coding Theory. Cambridge University Press, Cambridge (2021)
11. Daemen, J., Massolino, P.M.C., Mehrdad, A., Rotella, Y.: The subterranean 2.0 cipher suite. IACR Trans. Symmetric Cryptol. **2020**(S1), 262–294 (2020)
12. Daemen, J., Rijmen, V.: Plateau characteristics. IET Inf. Secur. **1**(1), 11–17 (2007)
13. Eichlseder, M., Kales, D.: Clustering related-tweak characteristics: application to MANTIS-6. IACR Trans. Symmetric Cryptol. **2018**(2), 111–132 (2018)
14. Flórez-Gutiérrez, A., Naya-Plasencia, M.: Improving key-recovery in linear attacks: application to 28-round PRESENT. In: Canteaut, A., Ishai, Y. (eds.) EUROCRYPT 2020. LNCS, vol. 12105, pp. 221–249. Springer, Cham (2020). https://doi.org/10.1007/978-3-030-45721-1_9
15. Hall-Andersen, M., Vejre, P.S.: Generating graphs packed with paths estimation of linear approximations and differentials. IACR Trans. Symmetric Cryptol. **2018**(3), 265–289 (2018)
16. Kündgen, A., Leander, G., Thomassen, C.: Switchings, extensions, and reductions in central digraphs. J. Comb. Theory Ser. A **118**(7), 2025–2034 (2011)
17. Lambin, B., Leander, G., Neumann, P.: Pitfalls and shortcomings for decompositions and alignment (full version). Cryptology ePrint Archive, Paper 2023/240 (2023). https://eprint.iacr.org/2023/240
18. Leander, G.: On linear hulls, statistical saturation attacks, PRESENT and a cryptanalysis of PUFFIN. In: Paterson, K.G. (ed.) EUROCRYPT 2011. LNCS, vol. 6632, pp. 303–322. Springer, Heidelberg (2011). https://doi.org/10.1007/978-3-642-20465-4_18
19. Leander, G., Rasoolzadeh, S.: Two sides of the same coin: weak-keys and more efficient variants of CRAFT. IACR Cryptology ePrint Archive, p. 238 (2021)
20. Liu, G., Qiu, W., Yi, T.: New techniques for searching differential trails in Keccak. IACR Trans. Symmetric Cryptol. **2019**(4), 407–437 (2020)
21. McCreesh, C., Prosser, P., Trimble, J.: The Glasgow subgraph solver: using constraint programming to tackle hard subgraph isomorphism problem variants. In: Gadducci, F., Kehrer, T. (eds.) ICGT 2020. LNCS, vol. 12150, pp. 316–324. Springer, Cham (2020). https://doi.org/10.1007/978-3-030-51372-6_19
22. Minaud, B., Derbez, P., Fouque, P.-A., Karpman, P.: Key-recovery attacks on ASASA. In: Iwata, T., Cheon, J.H. (eds.) ASIACRYPT 2015. LNCS, vol. 9453, pp. 3–27. Springer, Heidelberg (2015). https://doi.org/10.1007/978-3-662-48800-3_1
23. Nyberg, K.: Differentially uniform mappings for cryptography. In: Helleseth, T. (ed.) EUROCRYPT 1993. LNCS, vol. 765, pp. 55–64. Springer, Heidelberg (1994). https://doi.org/10.1007/3-540-48285-7_6
24. Reis, T.B.S., Aranha, D.F., López, J.: PRESENT runs fast. In: Fischer, W., Homma, N. (eds.) CHES 2017. LNCS, vol. 10529, pp. 644–664. Springer, Cham (2017). https://doi.org/10.1007/978-3-319-66787-4_31
25. Shannon, C.E.: A mathematical theory of cryptography. Mathematical Theory of Cryptography (1945)
26. Song, L., Huang, Z., Yang, Q.: Automatic differential analysis of ARX block ciphers with application to SPECK and LEA. In: Liu, J.K., Steinfeld, R. (eds.) ACISP 2016, Part II. LNCS, vol. 9723, pp. 379–394. Springer, Cham (2016). https://doi.org/10.1007/978-3-319-40367-0_24

Generic Attack on Duplex-Based AEAD Modes Using Random Function Statistics

Henri Gilbert[1,2], Rachelle Heim Boissier[2(✉)], Louiza Khati[1], and Yann Rotella[2]

[1] ANSSI, Paris, France
[2] Université Paris-Saclay, UVSQ, CNRS,
Laboratoire de Mathématiques de Versailles, Versailles, France
rachelle.heim@uvsq.fr

Abstract. Duplex-based authenticated encryption modes with a sufficiently large key length are proven to be secure up to the birthday bound $2^{\frac{c}{2}}$, where c is the capacity. However this bound is not known to be tight and the complexity of the best known generic attack, which is based on multicollisions, is much larger: it reaches $\frac{2^c}{\alpha}$ where α represents a small security loss factor. There is thus an uncertainty on the true extent of security beyond the bound $2^{\frac{c}{2}}$ provided by such constructions. In this paper, we describe a new generic attack against several duplex-based AEAD modes. Our attack leverages random functions statistics and produces a forgery in time complexity $\mathcal{O}(2^{\frac{3c}{4}})$ using negligible memory and no encryption queries. Furthermore, for some duplex-based modes, our attack recovers the secret key with a negligible amount of additional computations. Most notably, our attack breaks a security claim made by the designers of the NIST lightweight competition candidate XOODYAK. This attack is a step further towards determining the exact security provided by duplex-based constructions.

Keywords: Cryptanalysis · Symmetric cryptography · AEAD ·
Duplex-based constructions · NIST lightweight competition · XOODYAK ·
Random functions

1 Introduction

Authenticated Encryption (AE), which allows to encrypt and authenticate a plaintext message in a combined way, is one of the main workhorses of symmetric cryptography. AE often offers the option to authenticate, in addition to the plaintext message, some extra data which, unlike the plaintext, are transmitted unencrypted. AE is then renamed Authenticated Encryption with Associated Data (AEAD). A considerable research effort was devoted during the last years to the design and analysis of efficient and secure AEAD algorithms. Examples of AEAD mechanisms largely deployed over the Internet are AES-GCM and Chacha20-Poly1305. In 2014–2019, the three-round process of the CAESAR competition for authenticated encryption resulted in the selection of a portfolio of six AEAD mechanisms chosen to address the needs of the three following use cases: lightweight applications, high-performance applications and provision of defense-in-depth features, e.g. nonce misuse resistance. Another symmetric algorithms

© International Association for Cryptologic Research 2023
C. Hazay and M. Stam (Eds.): EUROCRYPT 2023, LNCS 14007, pp. 348–378, 2023.
https://doi.org/10.1007/978-3-031-30634-1_12

selection initiative, the ongoing NIST lightweight cryptography standardization process, aims at selecting (families of) algorithms suitable for use in constrained environment that comprise at least an AEAD mechanism and optionally a cryptographic hashing mechanism. The process was launched in 2018 and has now reached its third round, where ten finalists are still being evaluated.

Most existing AEAD algorithms are either *block cipher-based* or *permutation-based*. In the first case, they result from the application of a suitable mode of operation to a block cipher or a tweakable block cipher. In the second case, they consist in the instantiation of a keyed mode of operation with a public permutation. In this paper, we focus on so-called *duplex-based* keyed modes. Seminal examples of such modes are SpongeWrap and MonkeyDuplex, both introduced by Bertoni, Daemen, Peeters and Van Assche [7,10]. Duplex-based modes can be viewed as an adaptation to the AEAD context of the *Sponge construction* for hash functions introduced by the same authors in [6,8]. After an initialization phase allowing to derive a b-bit state from a key and an IV value, they essentially iterate calls to a key-less public permutation P of the state space $\{0,1\}^b$ in alternance with an injection and/or extraction of data blocks on/from a dedicated r-bit part ($r < b$) of the current state value in order to absorb additional data, encrypt and absorb the plaintext, and produce an authentication tag.[1] The sizes r and $c = b - r$ bits of the state parts affected (resp. unaffected) by data injections or extractions are named the *rate* and the *capacity*. The corresponding state parts are referred to as the *outer* and the *inner* state.

The Security of Duplex-Based Constructions has been extensively studied during the last decade. Let us denote the total time complexity of an attack by $T = \sigma_e + \sigma_d + q_P + t_{extra-op}$, where σ_e and σ_d respectively represent the number of online calls to P caused by the adversary's encryption requests and forgery attempts and q_P represents the number of offline queries to P or its inverse. The last term $t_{extra-op}$ represents the extra computations not taken into account in $\sigma_e + \sigma_d + q_P$, e.g. computations of primitives involved in the initialization and finalization, basic read/write operations in memory, random samplings. It is measured as an equivalent number of P computations.[2] Let us further denote by q_d the number of forgery attempts of the adversary. The initial security arguments for duplex constructions, which leveraged the indifferentiability of the sponge construction for hash functions, only allowed to guarantee the security of the duplex constructions as long as $T \ll min\{2^{\frac{c}{2}}, 2^\kappa\}$ and $q_d \ll 2^\tau$, where κ and τ represent the key length and the tag length. In [27,28], Jovanovic *et al.* showed that in the nonce-respecting setting, the security of a series of duplex constructions can be ensured beyond the birthday bound $2^{\frac{c}{2}}$, namely as long as

---

[1] The name "duplex", that conveys the idea of a bidirectional process, reflects the fact that in such constructions both a data block injection and a data block extraction to/from the current state can potentially take place between two consecutive invocations of P.

[2] Note that in the attack considered in the sequel, $t_{extra-op}$ will in practice be negligible compared to $\sigma_e + \sigma_d + q_P$.

$$T \ll min\{2^{\frac{b}{2}}, \frac{2^c}{\alpha}, 2^\kappa\} \text{ and } q_d \ll 2^\tau, \tag{1}$$

where α represents a small constant upper bounded by r in [27] and a tighter, substantially smaller constant in [28]. The detail of the security proofs sections of [27,28] indicates however that the bounds (1) are only valid under the assumption that σ_d is strongly limited: if one wants to avoid implicit assumptions about σ_d, the bounding conditions (1) must be replaced by the more complete (though still simplified) conditions:

$$T \ll min\{2^{\frac{b}{2}}, \frac{2^c}{\alpha}, \frac{2^c}{\sigma_d}, 2^\kappa\} \text{ and } q_d \ll 2^\tau. \tag{2}$$

Unlike the conditions (1), the complete bounding conditions (2) can hardly be considered as 'beyond-birthday bounds'. For $\sigma_d \geq 2^{\frac{c}{2}}$, the condition $T \ll \frac{2^c}{\sigma_d}$ of (2) indeed implies $T \ll 2^{\frac{c}{2}}$. Thus, the security of the considered duplex-based constructions without assumptions on σ_d can only be guaranteed as long as the birthday condition $T \ll 2^{\frac{c}{2}}$ is met.

The bounding conditions (1) were used for dimensioning the family of duplex AEADs NORX, and led since 2014 to several other AEAD design proposals based on duplex-like constructions with a claimed security level strictly larger than $\frac{c}{2}$. Similar bounds were shown to still hold when instead of limiting the size of injected and extracted data blocks to r bits, one only limits the size of extracted data blocks to r bits but full-state data injections are permitted [30]. This leads to AEAD proposals where the efficiency of the associated data absorption phase is increased. A generalisation of the full-state keyed duplex of [30] with multi-user support, accompanied by a refined security analysis, was published in [20].

Generic Attacks on Duplex-Based Constructions. The best currently known generic attacks on duplex-based constructions are based on multicollisions. These attacks match the security bound $\frac{2^c}{\alpha}$ where α represents a small security loss factor as stated before. They are presented in detail in [28] and can be roughly outlined as follows. First, the adversary submits sufficiently many calls to an encryption oracle in order to find a multicollision among the outer state values of a number ρ of states. Once this has been achieved, an exhaustive search for a c-bit value matching the inner state value of one of these ρ states is likely to succeed after about $\frac{2^c}{\rho}$ trials.

Our Contribution. The end of the former discussion on the security of duplex-based constructions showed that in situations where the possibility of forgery attempts of non-negligible data complexity σ_d is not precluded, the complete bounding conditions (2) only prevent the existence of generic attacks of total complexity $T \ll 2^{\frac{c}{2}}$. It is therefore an open question whether there exists a generic attack of total complexity $\mathcal{T}$ strictly comprised between $2^{\frac{c}{2}}$ and the complexity $\frac{2^c}{\alpha}$ of multicollision-based attacks.[3] In this paper, we provide a positive answer to the former open question by exhibiting a generic attack against a large family of duplex-based constructions of total time complexity $\mathcal{T}$ in $\mathcal{O}(2^{\frac{3c}{4}})$. We rely on the analysis of random function statistics to design a two-phase forgery attack with a precomputation phase of time complexity $\mathcal{O}(2^{\frac{3c}{4}})$ essentially equal to q_P and an actual forgery phase of time complexity $\mathcal{O}(2^{\frac{3c}{4}})$ essentially equal to σ_d. The value σ_d can also be viewed as the data complexity of the attack measured in ciphertext blocks. The attack requires no encryption queries, i.e. $\sigma_e = 0$, and $t_{extra-op}$ is negligible compared to q_P and σ_d. For some of these constructions, our attack recovers the secret key.

Our attack takes advantage of the following property shared by several authenticated encryption modes based on the duplex construction: for a ciphertext built by concatenating a fixed block multiple times, the decryption of a message consists in the iteration of a public function with domain and co-domain $\mathbb{F}_2^c$. This public function is fully determined by the value of the ciphertext block. We are therefore able to precompute some of its parameters offline. Forgery strategies that just assume a "near to average" behaviour of the iterated function, e.g. a cycle length of the path generated by a random point of $\{0,1\}^c$ close to the expected value $\sqrt{\pi 2^c/8}$, do not seem to lead to forgery attack complexities better than $\mathcal{O}(2^c)$. We show that however, the following two-phase attack strategy allows an adversary to produce an existential forgery with a success probability close to 1 and a total (online and offline) computation time $\mathcal{T} = \mathcal{O}(2^{\frac{3c}{4}})$.

1) *In an offline phase*, a significant amount $\mathcal{O}(2^{\frac{3c}{4}})$ of precomputation is dedicated to the detection of a c-bit to c-bit function that possesses exceptional characteristics that exponentially deviate from an average behaviour, thus rendering its use in a forgery attack more efficient.
2) *In an online phase*, the iteration of the function identified in the offline phase is used to produce forgery attempts whose success probability is exceptionally high.

In slightly more detail, the offline phase aims at selecting a ciphertext block that determines a function whose graph possesses a large component in which all paths are terminated by the same exceptionally small cycle, of length at most a small predefined multiple of $2^{\frac{c}{4}}$. This is shown to imply that for long ciphertexts obtained by repeating the selected ciphertext block, the tag is the image of one of the values of the former small cycle by a known function with a probability close to 1. This in turn allows to mount a forgery attack of offline, online and total time complexity $\mathcal{O}(2^{\frac{3c}{4}})$.

The precomputation phase needs to be run only once to break the same construction with as many different keys as desired. Further, we can adjust the trade-off between the precomputation phase and the online phase in order to

---

[3] In other words, the questions whether the "birthday term" $\frac{2^c}{\sigma_d}$ is an artifact of the proofs and whether the capacity value c can be safely dimensioned well below $2s$, where s denotes the targeted security level remain open.

bring the complexity of the latter closer to $\mathcal{O}(2^{\frac{c}{2}})$ at the expense of significantly increasing the complexity of the former.

Previously published generic attacks against hash-based MACs or hash functions also rely on the statistics of random functions [4,29,32,33]. Such attacks also model, as the AEAD attack introduced here, one function that the considered construction allows to iterate as a random function. Yet, while previous attacks generally assume and exploit a "near to average" behaviour of a function selected at random, an essential feature of the attack presented here is that it selects and leverages instances of a function whose behaviour exceptionally deviates from average.

Our attack is applicable to several duplex-based modes such as monkeyWrap, monkeyDuplex or Motorist. Most notably, our attack is applicable to Cyclist, the mode of the Lightweight Cryptography NIST competition finalist XOODYAK [18]. With a key recovery attack of complexity 2^{148} applications of the state update function XOODOO, we break the claim of achieving 184-bit security against plaintext recovery and forgery attacks made by the designers in [18, Corollary 2, p. 72]. Note that this does not threaten the 112-bit security level required by the NIST. Our results are detailed in Sect. 5 and displayed in Table 4.

Organization. The rest of this paper is organized as follows. Section 2 introduces definitions and results related to the statistics of random functions that are relevant for our attack and defines a 'vanilla' duplex-based AEAD mode that only captures those features of duplex-based constructions that are essential to understand our attack. Section 3 presents our attack and analyses its performance using the vanilla mode of Sect. 2 as the target in order to simplify its presentation. Section 4 presents experimental validations of essential features of the attack based on small scale implementations. Section 5 shows that the attack of Sect. 3 is applicable to several real-life duplex modes with minor adaptations. Section 5 also discusses variations encountered in AEADs such as Beetle [16] or Ascon [22] that, on the other hand, prevent the attack.

2   Preliminaries

In this section, we start by introducing key definitions and results related to the statistics of random functions. Next, we describe a simplified duplex-based authenticated encryption mode on which we will rely to describe our attack. This is followed by a short subsection on the security model on which we rely.

2.1   Preliminaries on Random Functions

Let $\mathfrak{F}_n$ be the set of all functions which map a finite set of size $n \in \mathbb{N}^*$ to itself. Without loss of generality, we consider the set $\{1, \ldots, n\}$. Each function f in $\mathfrak{F}_n$ determines a directed graph $G(f)$ in which a vertex goes from node i to node j, $i, j \in \{1, \ldots, n\}$, if and only if $f(i) = j$ [24,31]. In the following, for simplicity reasons, we say that a node belongs to the graph of a function when it belongs to the set of nodes of this graph. We use the term "random function in $\mathfrak{F}_n$" to refer to a function selected uniformly at random in the set $\mathfrak{F}_n$.

For any f in $\mathfrak{F}_n$ and any node x in $G(f)$, we can iterate f and consider the set of *successors* of x

$$\mathcal{S}(x) = \{f^i(x) \mid 0 \le i \le n-1\}.$$

We denote by $s(x)$ the size of this set. Since the graph has a finite number of nodes, the sequence $\{f^i(x)\}_{i \ge 0}$ is eventually periodic. Graphically, it thus corresponds to a path linked to a *cycle* defined as

$$\mathcal{C}(x) = \{f^i(x) \mid \exists j > 0, f^i(x) = f^{i+j}(x)\}.$$

We denote by $\mu(x) = \#\mathcal{C}(x)$ the length of this cycle or *cycle length* and by $\lambda(x) = s(x) - \#\mathcal{C}(x)$ the length of this path or *tail length*. The tail length $\lambda(x)$ is the smallest integer i such that $f^i(x) \in \mathcal{C}(x)$. The set of all nodes $y \in G(f)$ such that $\mathcal{C}(y) = \mathcal{C}(x)$ forms a *connected component*. Since all nodes in the same connected component have the same cycle, the *cycle of a component* is well-defined.

Our cryptanalysis relies on the attacker's ability to find functions which have a large component with a small cycle. We formally characterize what should be understood by "large component with a small cycle" later on. To do so, we will need the two following definitions.

Definition 1 (ν-component). *Let* $0 < \nu < \frac{1}{2}$. *A ν-component is a component that has a cycle of size at most* $n^{\frac{1}{2}-\nu}$.

Definition 2 ((s,ν)-component). *Let* $0 < \nu < \frac{1}{2}$, $0 < s < 1$. *A (s,ν)-component is a ν-component whose size is greater or equal to ns.*

In order to estimate the complexity and success probability of our attack, we rely on the statistical analysis of random functions. Such an analysis has been extensively conducted in combinatorics [21, 23–25, 31]. In this paper, we will need the three following results.

Expectancy of Cycle Length and Tail Length for a Random Point [23]. For a random node x in the graph of a random function $f \in \mathfrak{F}_n$, Flajolet and Odlyzko have computed the asymptotic form of the expectancy of the cycle length $\mu(x)$ and tail length $\lambda(x)$ using generating functions. They obtained an expectancy of $\sqrt{\frac{\pi n}{8}}$ for both.

Probability for a Random Point to Belong to a ν-Component [25]. For a random node x belonging to the graph of a random function $f \in \mathfrak{F}_n$, Harris shows that the probability that $\mu(x)$ is smaller than $n^{\frac{1}{2}-\nu}$ is asymptotically

$$p_\nu = 1 - e^{-\frac{1}{2n^{2\nu}}} + \frac{\sqrt{2\pi}}{n^\nu}\left[1 - \phi(n^{-\nu})\right]$$

$$= \frac{\sqrt{2\pi}}{2n^\nu} + \mathcal{O}\left(\frac{1}{n^{2\nu}}\right)$$

where $\phi(y) = \int_{-\infty}^{y} (2\pi)^{-\frac{1}{2}} e^{-\frac{1}{2}x^2} dx$. This corresponds to the probability for a random node x of the graph of a random function to belong to a ν-component. For example, for $\nu = \frac{1}{4}$ and c a positive integer such that $n = 2^c$, $p_\nu = \frac{\sqrt{2\pi}}{2} \times 2^{-\frac{c}{4}}$.

Probability for a Random Function to Have a (s, ν)-Component [21]. For a random $f \in \mathfrak{F}_n$, the probability $p_{s,\nu}$ that $G(f)$ has a (s, ν)-component has been estimated by DeLaurentis in a paper published at Crypto 1987 [21]. It is shown to be

$$p_{s,\nu} = \sqrt{\frac{2(1-s)}{\pi s}} n^{-\nu} \left[1 + \mathcal{O}\left(r_n(s)\right) \right]$$

where $r_n(s) = s^{-2} n^{-\frac{1}{2} - 3\nu} + s^{\frac{-1}{2}} n^{-\nu} + n^{-\frac{1}{3}}$. Thus, $p_{s,\nu} \approx \sqrt{\frac{2(1-s)}{\pi s}} n^{-\nu}$. For example, if we take $\nu = \frac{1}{4}$, $s = 0.65$ as in Sect. 3.6, and c a positive integer such that $n = 2^c$, $p_{s,\nu} \simeq 0.6 \times 2^{-\frac{c}{4}}$.

Probability for a Random Point to Belong to its Component's Cycle After $l - 1$ Applications of f. Let x be a random point of a random function. Harris [25] gives the asymptotic density function of the number of successors $s(x)$. More precisely, he provides the asymptotic density function f_1 of $\frac{s}{\sqrt{n}}$ for $x > 0$

$$f_1(x) = x e^{-\frac{x^2}{2}} .$$

For l a positive integer, let p_l be the probability that $f^{l-1}(x)$ is in the cycle, that is, the probability that $\lambda(x) \leq l - 1$. Since the number of successors is greater than the tail length, p_l is greater or equal to the probability for x to have strictly less than l successors. Thus, we have

$$p_l \geq 1 - e^{-\frac{l^2}{2n}} .$$

Notational Conventions. For simplicity and readability reasons, when it comes to estimates resulting from statistics on random functions, we will use the sign "$\leq$" where it would be more rigorous to use the smaller or equivalent sign "$\lesssim$" in the rest of the paper.

2.2   Description of a Vanilla Duplex-Based AEAD Mode

The duplex construction was designed by the KECCAK team as a tool to build authenticated encryption modes [7,9]. The first proposal of such a mode is SPONGEWRAP [7], published in 2011. Today, many modes are based on this construction. In this paper, we define the simplified authenticated encryption mode DUPLEXAEAD. DUPLEXAEAD shares its structure with the modes of several duplex-based AEAD schemes. This mode is not meant to be used in practice. It is defined for readability reasons: its sole purpose is to make the description of our attack simpler. We show in Sect. 5 how our attack can be adapted to several real-life duplex-based modes.

DUPLEXAEAD is instantiated with a permutation P which operates on a b-bit state S divided into two parts. The first r bits of the state form the *outer state* $\overline{S}$, whilst the next $c = b - r$ bits form the *inner state* $\widehat{S}$. The state can thus be written as $S = \overline{S}||\widehat{S}$. As stated in Sect. 1, the parameter r is called the *rate* and the parameter c is called the *capacity*. DUPLEXAEAD also involves two other public functions, namely, an initialisation function P_{init} and a finalisation function P_{final}. The encryption algorithm $\mathcal{E}$ takes as input a κ-bit key K, a η-bit nonce N, a plaintext M and associated data A of variable length and returns a ciphertext C and a τ-bit tag T. The decryption algorithm $\mathcal{D}$ takes as input (K, N, A, C, T) and returns the plaintext M if the tag is valid. Otherwise, it returns $\bot$.

We assume for simplicity reasons that the length in bits of the plaintexts processed by DUPLEXAEAD is always divisible by r.[4] Thus, any plaintext M can be split into r-bit blocks, $M = M_0||\cdots||M_{l-1}$, where l is the plaintext length in number of r-bit blocks. The ciphertext's length is equal to the plaintext's length, and can thus also be written $C = C_0||\cdots||C_{l-1}$.

The mode works as follows (see Fig. 1):

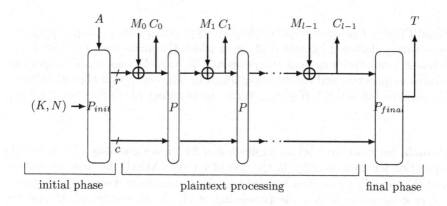

Fig. 1. DUPLEXAEAD in encryption mode.

---

[4] In practice, our cryptanalysis can be easily adapted to attack modes which can process plaintexts of arbitrary length, but this requires a short case-by-case analysis which we provide in Sect. 5. Note that the resulting adjustments have a negligible impact on the complexity of our attack and do not impact its success probability.

Initial Phase. The encryption and decryption algorithms start by an initial phase. The key, the nonce and the associated data are processed by the initialisation function P_{init}. The state is set to the output of P_{init}.

Plaintext Processing. In encryption mode, DUPLEXAEAD then processes the plaintext and generates the ciphertext block by block as follows:

1. The ciphertext block C_i is generated by XORing the outer state to the plaintext block M_i. That is, $C_i \leftarrow \overline{S} \oplus M_i$.
2. The outer state is set to the just computed ciphertext block. That is, $\overline{S} \leftarrow C_i$.
3. The permutation P is applied to the state. That is, $S \leftarrow P(S)$.

Ciphertext Processing. In decryption mode, DUPLEXAEAD then processes the ciphertext. The plaintext M is constructed as the ciphertext is processed but will only be outputted at the end of the final phase if the tag is valid. This phase works as follows:

1. A plaintext block M_i is generated by XORing the outer state to the ciphertext block C_i. That is, $M_i \leftarrow \overline{S} \oplus C_i$.
2. The outer state is set to the value of the ciphertext block. That is, $\overline{S} \leftarrow C_i$.
3. The permutation P is applied to the state. That is, $S \leftarrow P(S)$.

Final Phase. During encryption (resp. decryption), plaintext (resp. ciphertext) processing is followed by a final phase in which the finalisation function P_{final} takes as input the state and computes a τ-bit tag. The encryption algorithm returns a ciphertext and the corresponding tag. The decryption algorithm checks whether the tag is valid. If so, it returns the plaintext M. Otherwise, it returns $\perp$.

Domain Separation. Actual duplex-based AE modes generally rely on domain separation for their security. In the case of DUPLEXAEAD, we assume that the way P_{init} and P_{final} are constructed from P ensures domain separation between the processing of (K, N), the processing of A, the processing of M and the computation of T. This can be done for example by XORing distinct constants to the inner state before P invocations in each phase.

2.3   Security Model

For authenticated encryption, two security notions are involved, namely privacy and integrity. Since our attack aims at breaking integrity, we leave privacy aside. We do not fully formalise the security model but give some *simplified* reminders to the reader.[5] In the integrity setting, we have an adversary $\mathcal{A}$ who has access to the following oracles:

---

[5] For more details see for example [27].

- A primitive oracle $\mathcal{O}_P$ that allows to call the public permutation P or its inverse P^{-1}. It takes as input a value $v \in \mathbb{F}_2^b$ and outputs $P(v) \in \mathbb{F}_2^b$ (resp. $P^{-1}(v) \in \mathbb{F}_2^b$) for a call made to P (resp. P^{-1}).
- An encryption oracle $\mathcal{O}_{enc}$ that takes as inputs a nonce N, associated data A and a plaintext M and returns a ciphertext C and a tag T computed with a secret key K which is randomly sampled once for all (the same key is used by the decryption oracle).[6] It implements the encryption algorithm of the analysed AEAD scheme based on P.
- A decryption oracle $\mathcal{O}_{dec}$ that takes as input a nonce N, associated data A, a ciphertext C and a tag T and, using the key K, returns the corresponding plaintext if the verification is correct, $\perp$ otherwise. Similarly to the previous oracle, it implements the decryption algorithm of the analysed AEAD scheme.

We assume that the adversary $\mathcal{A}$ is **nonce-respecting**. Her goal is to provide a forgery, that is, an input (N, A, C, T) such that $\mathcal{O}_{dec}(N, A, C, T) \neq \perp$ where (C, T) was not outputted by the encryption oracle $\mathcal{O}_{enc}$ on an input $(N, A, \cdot)$ (for any plaintext). The probability to provide a forgery has to be negligible.

As already mentioned in Sect. 1, we denote by q_e, q_d and q_P the number of queries done to respectively the encryption oracle, the decryption oracle and the primitive oracle. We denote by σ_e the total number of plaintext blocks processed by the encryption oracle and by σ_d the total number of ciphertext blocks processed by the decryption oracle.

In this paper, we construct a generic forgery attack against several duplex-based authenticated encryption modes. Our attack is generic in the sense that we do not exploit the properties of the permutation P but only properties of the mode itself [9]. It does not rely on nonce misuse or the release of unverified plaintext. For some modes, our attack also recovers the secret key with a negligible amount of extra computation.

3 Description of the Attack

In this section, we present a generic forgery attack against duplex-based authenticated encryption modes. For the sake of clarity, we first describe how the attack works on the simplified mode DUPLEXAEAD defined in Sect. 2.2. We show how to apply our attack to other authenticated encryption modes in Sect. 5.

3.1 Observation on Duplex-Based AEAD Modes

We describe a simple property of DUPLEXAEAD that is shared with many other duplex-based AE modes: for a ciphertext built by concatenating a fixed block multiple times, the decryption of a plaintext consists in the iteration of a known function with domain and co-domain $\mathbb{F}_2^c$. This property is at the core of our attack. It is depicted in Fig. 2.

---

[6] Each parameter space is well defined according to the analysed AEAD scheme.

Let $\ell \in \mathbb{N}^*$ and $\beta \in \mathbb{F}_2^r$. Let β_ℓ be the ciphertext equal to the concatenation of ℓ r-bit blocks of constant value β, that is

$$\beta_\ell = \underbrace{\beta || \cdots || \beta}_{\ell} \, .$$

During the ciphertext decryption, the value of the outer state at the input of the state update function P is equal to the current ciphertext block. Thus, the decryption of β_ℓ corresponds to the iteration of the function P_β defined as

$$P_\beta : \mathbb{F}_2^c \longrightarrow \mathbb{F}_2^c$$

$$x \longmapsto \widehat{P(\beta || x)} \, .$$

Indeed, let $x_0 \in \mathbb{F}_2^c$ be the value of the inner state obtained at the end of the initial phase from the key, the nonce and the associated data. After processing the first plaintext block, the value of the outer state is equal to the first ciphertext block β. Thus, the input of the state update function is exactly $\beta || x_0$. As a consequence, the value of the inner state going into the second application of P is $\beta || x_1$ where $x_1 = P_\beta(x_0)$. In turn, the third one is $\beta || x_2$ where $x_2 = P_\beta(x_1) = P_\beta^2(x_0)$. When the last plaintext block is constructed, right before the final phase, the state is thus of the form

$$\beta || P_\beta^{\ell-1}(x_0) = \beta || x_{\ell-1} \, .$$

Since the outer part of the state is equal to β, it is known to the attacker. In particular, to recover the value of the state before the final phase, an attacker only needs to determine the value of $x_{\ell-1}$. Since $T = P_{final}(\beta || x_{\ell-1})$, it is sufficient for the attacker to recover the value of $x_{\ell-1}$ to find a forgery (N, A, C, T). As we will show more rigorously later on, our cryptanalysis relies on the fact that without knowing x_0, an attacker is able to select β and ℓ such that she is able to both restrict and predict the space of all possible $x_{\ell-1} = P_\beta^{\ell-1}(x_0)$ with good probability.

3.2 High Level Description of the Attack

Our attack aims at recovering the value of $x_{\ell-1}$. It was devised relying on the random functions statistics introduced in Sect. 2.1. Indeed, let $n = 2^c$. P is a random permutation on $\mathbb{F}_2^b$ and $c = b - r$ is significantly smaller than b. Thus, for any β randomly drawn from $\mathbb{F}_2^r$, we expect P_β to behave as a function randomly drawn from $\mathfrak{F}_n$.

The attack consists of two phases.

Precomputation Phase. First, in a precomputation phase, an offline algorithm finds a value β such that $G(P_\beta)$ has a large component with a small cycle, that is, a (s, ν)-component with great s and ν.

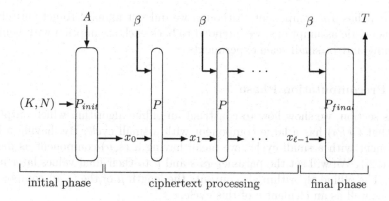

Fig. 2. Decrypting β_ℓ.

Online Phase. Second, in an online phase, (N, A, C, T) queries are submitted to a decryption oracle, where the ciphertext is $C = \beta_\ell$ with ℓ sufficiently large and β is the output of the precomputation algorithm. Recall that β is chosen such that $G(P_\beta)$ has a large component with a small cycle. Since this component is large, it contains the unknown node x_0 with good probability. In that case, for a great enough value of ℓ, $x_{\ell-1}$ belongs to the cycle of this component, which is small. Thus, the number of all possible values for $x_{\ell-1}$ is reduced and can be efficiently exhausted by submitting (N, A, β_ℓ, T) queries to the decryption oracle where

1. tags are produced by applying P_{final} to a state such that $\overline{S} = \beta$ and such that the inner state $\widehat{S}$ belongs to the small cycle of P_β's large component;
2. nonces are either randomly sampled or arbitrary distinct values;[7]
3. the associated data is set to the empty string ε.[8]

Our final attack, which balances the computational cost of the offline and online phases, provides a forgery in time $\mathcal{O}(2^{\frac{3c}{4}})$ with a negligible amount of memory. In the rest of this section, we provide a detailed description together with an analysis of the complexity and success probability of our full attack.

In our complexity and success probability analysis, significant efforts were put towards limiting the use of heuristic assumptions. This is illustrated for example by the use of the probability $p_{s,\nu}$ [21] that a random function has a (s, ν)-component rather than a heuristic estimation of this value from the probability

---

[7] In decryption queries, nonces can be repeated even in a nonce-respecting setting. For the purpose of our attack, x_0 needs to behave as a point randomly sampled in the graph of P_β. Thus, we can either require nonces to be randomly sampled or to be arbitrary distinct values.

[8] For modes other than the full-state duplex, we could set the associated data to any value. In the case of the full-state duplex, the associated data must be chosen carefully (typically, the attack applies when the AD is set to the empty string).

p_ν that it has a ν-component. Although we did not manage to get entirely rid of all heuristic assumptions, we intended to back each assumption with heuristic reasoning and/or small scale experiments.

3.3   Precomputation Phase

In this section, we show how to construct an offline algorithm which outputs β such that $G(P_\beta)$ has a large component with a small cycle. By 'having a large component with a small cycle', we mean having a (s,ν)-component as defined in Sect. 2.1. We will set the parameters s and ν to their final values later in the paper. The offline algorithm also outputs the length μ of the (s,ν)-component's cycle, as well as an element e of this cycle.

Our algorithm samples random values β from $\mathbb{F}_2^r$ and random values x in $\mathbb{F}_2^c$ and investigates whether or not the component on which x is located is a (s,ν)-component of $G(P_\beta)$.

When a random β and a random x are generated, we start by investigating the cycle length of the component on which x is located, that is, whether or not it is a ν-component. Cycle-finding algorithms such as Floyd's or Brent's algorithm provide a straightforward way to determine the component's cycle length. These algorithms are typically used to find collisions on functions with a negligible amount of memory. In fact, the collisions found by these algorithms are located within the functions' cycles. Thus, given a random $\beta \in \mathbb{F}_2^r$, which selects a random $P_\beta \in \mathfrak{F}_n$, and a random $x \in \mathbb{F}_2^c$, cycle-finding algorithms can be used to construct an algorithm which outputs both $\mu(x)$, the cycle length of the connected component on which x is located, and the value of a node in the cycle [26]. We call such an algorithm cycle. The algorithm cycle allows the attacker to determine whether or not the component on which x is located is a ν-component, *i.e.* a component with a cycle of the desired length $\mu(x) \le n^{\frac{1}{2}-\nu}$.

To construct our final precomputation algorithm, two main issues remain to be solved.

Issue 1. If the random β and the random x investigated are such that the component on which x is located is not a (s,ν)-component, it does not necessarily mean that $G(P_\beta)$ does not have a (s,ν)-component. There could be an $x' \ne x$ such that x' belongs to a different component that has the desired cycle length and size. In particular, we must determine whether or not it is worth trying a different $x' \ne x$ when cycle returns a cycle length value that is greater than $n^{\frac{1}{2}-\nu}$ (x's component is not a ν-component). There are two imaginable strategies. The first strategy consists in trying a single random x for each β, and, whenever x has a component with a cycle size smaller than $n^{\frac{1}{2}-\nu}$, investigate whether or not the component has size greater or equal than sn. The second strategy would be to try several x's for each β. We stick to the first strategy. The following argument indeed suggests that the second strategy would be more costly. When conditioned by the failure of the first drawn x, the probability that a second x' succeeds with the same β is at most $\frac{p_{s,\nu}(1-s)}{1-p_{s,\nu}}$ whilst for a new random (β', x'), the probability of success is at least $p_{s,\nu}s$. Thus, the first strategy is better whenever $s > \frac{1}{2-p_{s,\nu}}$ which is always true for our values of s (which are always greater than 0.5) and ν.

Issue 2. Although `cycle` allows to detect ν-components, it does not provide a way to detect (s,ν)-components. Being fully certain that a ν-component has the desired size would be prohibitingly costly. A strategy allowing to estimate that a ν-component is a (s,ν)-component with a sufficiently large probability has to be devised.[9] The algorithm `is_big` implements this strategy. Note that in this algorithm, the notation '$(.,z)$' in Step 4 means that the first output (corresponding to the cycle length) is ignored. Each time the algorithm detects a small cycle, it checks whether or not ω other random nodes belong to the same component. It then computes the proportion s_{obs} of these new randomly chosen points which belong to the desired component. If this number is above a threshold value $s + \delta$ strictly larger than s, it decides that x is likely to belong to a (s,ν)-component and returns β and the values of the cycle. We show that for $\delta = \frac{2.33}{2\sqrt{\omega}}$, a selected component has size greater than s with great probability. Suppose that we have drawn a value β such that β has a ν-component of unknown size $s_\beta n$. In that case, the random variable s_{obs} is the mean of ω Bernoulli variables which are equal to 1 with probability s_β and 0 with probability $1 - s_\beta$. By the Central Limit Theorem (CLT), we have that for all $\epsilon \in \mathbb{R}$,

$$p\left[s_{obs} - s_\beta \le \epsilon\sqrt{\frac{s_\beta(1 - s_\beta)}{\omega}}\right] = p\left(Y \le \epsilon\right)$$

where $Y \rightsquigarrow \mathcal{N}(0,1)$. Thus, since $\delta = 2.33\sqrt{\frac{1}{4\omega}}$ and since for $s_\beta < 1$, $s_\beta(1 - s_\beta) \le \frac{1}{4}$, we have that

$$s_{obs} - s_\beta \le \delta$$

with probability $p_\delta \ge p\left(Y \le 2.33\right) > 0.99$. Suppose that for a random β with a ν-component, we obtain a proportion s_{obs} of random x's in this component such that $s_{obs} \ge s + \delta$ as required in Step 10 of the algorithm `is_big`. We know that with probability $p_\delta \ge 0.99$:

$$s_\beta \ge s_{obs} - \delta \ge s + \delta - \delta = s.$$

As a conclusion, when our final offline algorithm `offline_search` returns a β, then it is such that $G(P_\beta)$ has a ν-component with probability 1, and the component considered has at least the desired size with probability $p_\delta \ge 0.99$.

---

[9] Given a point of the graph x, the introduction of an algorithm which estimates x's component's size is going to significantly complicate our attack's complexity analysis. We believe that we could have designed an attack without this extra algorithm by relying on the fact that a random component is large with great probability. However, unless increasing the complexity of the online phase, we would have then obtained lower success probabilities (roughly around 0.5 rather than close to 1).

Algo. offline_search(ω, s, ν) | Algo. is_big(ω, s, β, μ, e)

Algo. offline_search(ω, s, ν)

1 : **while true do**

2 : $\beta \xleftarrow{\$} \mathbb{F}_2^r$; $x \xleftarrow{\$} \mathbb{F}_2^c$

3 : $(\mu, e) \leftarrow$ cycle(β, x)

4 :   **if** $\mu \leq n^{\frac{1}{2} - \nu}$ **then**

5 :   **if** is_big(ω, s, β, μ, e)

6 :   **return** (β, μ, e)

Algo. is_big(ω, s, β, μ, e)

1 : $\delta \leftarrow \dfrac{2.33}{2\sqrt{\omega}}$; $j \leftarrow 0$

2 : **for** $i = 1..\omega$ **do**

3 : $k \leftarrow 0$; $inside\_big \leftarrow$ **false** ; $y \xleftarrow{\$} \mathbb{F}_2^c$

4 : $(., z) \leftarrow$ cycle(β, y)

5 :   **while** $inside\_big =$ **false and** $k < \mu$ **do**

6 :   **if** $z = e$ **then** $inside\_big \leftarrow$ **true**

7 : $z \leftarrow P_\beta(z)$

8 : $k \leftarrow k + 1$

9 :   **if** $inside\_big$ **then** $j \leftarrow j + 1$

10 : **if** $\dfrac{j}{\omega} \geq s + \delta$ **return true**

11 : **return false**

3.4   Analysis of the Offline Algorithm

In this section, we analyse the success probability and complexity of the offline algorithm. As stated in Sect. 2.3, the complexity is expressed as a number of calls to P. This algorithm is at the core of our attack. It only needs to be executed once. Indeed, once it has succeeded in finding β such that $G(P_\beta)$ has a (s, ν)-component, a duplex-based mode with any key using the permutation P can be attacked.

Complexity of the Cycle-Finding Algorithm. We start by investigating the average complexity of the algorithm cycle. To construct this algorithm, we use Brent's cycle-detection algorithm as a tool [14]. For a random $\beta \in \mathbb{F}_2^r$ and a random $x \in \mathbb{F}_2^c$, Brent's algorithm recovers the cycle length $\mu(x)$ and a node of the cycle $e \in \mathcal{C}(x)$ after at most $2\max(\mu(x), \lambda(x)) + \mu(x)$ applications of P_β. For a random x, the cycle length $\mu(x)$ and the tail length $\lambda(x)$ have the same expectation of $\sqrt{\frac{\pi n}{8}}$ [24] (See Sect. 2.1). Thus, we estimate the average complexity of cycle in number of calls to P to be upper bounded by

$$\mathcal{T}_{\text{cycle}} = 3\sqrt{\frac{\pi n}{8}}.$$

Complexity of the Offline Algorithm. We wish to compute the complexity of the offline algorithm offline_search. First, the memory complexity is negligible. As for the time complexity, we compute the average number of applications of P after which the algorithm returns a block $\beta \in \mathbb{F}_2^r$.

First, we upper bound the average complexity of is_big. This algorithm is executed when a pair (β, x) such that x is located on a ν-component of $G(P_\beta)$ has been selected. It takes as input β, $\mu = \mu(x) \leq n^{\frac{1}{2} - \nu}$, an element e of the cycle of x's component, s and an integer ω. It performs ω times a computation that essentially consists in the generation of a random point of $G(P_\beta)$, one computation of the cycle algorithm, and at most μ point comparisons and $\mu - 1$ P_β invocations. The average complexity of `is_big` is thus upper bounded by

$$\left(\mathcal{T}_{\texttt{cycle}} + n^{\frac{1}{2} - \nu} \right) \omega \,.$$

The following estimation is heuristic, and implicitly relies on the assumption that the average complexity of `cycle` for a random point of a random function does not significantly differ from the average complexity of `cycle` for a random point of a fixed random function that has a ν-component. We provide a reasoning to justify why it seems very unlikely that this assumption would significantly distort the complexity at the end of the section.

We now compute the complexity of `offline_search`. First, we compute the complexity of one single iteration of a Step 1 loop of `offline_search`. Recall that p_ν is the probability for a random node $x \in \mathbb{F}_2^c$ of a random function to belong to a ν-component. Each time a pair (β, x) is generated, the algorithm `cycle` is executed. Then, the algorithm executes `is_big` when a pair is such that x belongs to a ν-component of $G(P_\beta)$, which happens with probability p_ν. Finally, we need to compute after how many Step 1 iterations the algorithm returns a block β on average. At each iteration, the probability to generate a random $\beta \in \mathbb{F}_2^r$ such that $G(P_\beta)$ has a (s, ν)-component is $p_{s,\nu}$. Given such β, the probability that the randomly drawn $x \in \mathbb{F}_2^c$ also belongs to this component is greater than s. Thus, on average, we select a node x in a (s, ν)-component after less than $\frac{1}{p_{s,\nu} s}$ iterations. Heuristically, one can thus expect the overall complexity of our algorithm to be of the following form:

$$\frac{1}{p_{s,\nu} s} \left[\mathcal{T}_{\texttt{cycle}} + p_\nu \left(\mathcal{T}_{\texttt{cycle}} + n^{\frac{1}{2} - \nu} \right) \omega \right] \,.$$

Yet, we need to adjust this expression. Recall that a (s, ν)-component is a ν-component of size *greater or equal* to sn. However, drawing a node in a ν-component of size exactly sn[10] is not enough to make the algorithm stop. Indeed, if a randomly drawn $\beta \in \mathbb{F}_2^r$ is such that $G(P_\beta)$ has a ν-component of size exactly sn, the probability that s_{obs} is greater than $s + \delta$ is smaller than 1% (here, we use the central limit theorem again). We thus need to adjust our computation. To do so, we lower bound the probability that a random pair (β, x) is selected by the probability that it satisfies the two following conditions:

(a) $G(P_\beta)$ has a (s^+, ν)-component with $s^+ \geq s + 2\delta$ (recall that $\delta = \frac{2.33}{2\sqrt{\omega}}$).
(b) x belongs to the (s^+, ν)-component, so that the algorithm `offline_search` randomly draws ω other values in $\mathbb{F}_2^c$ and computes s_{obs}.

Indeed, we show that satisfying these two conditions implies that $s_{obs} \geq s + \delta$ with great probability, which is exactly the condition that needs to be satisfied for the algorithm to return β.

---

[10] or greater than sn, but too close to sn to make the algorithm stop.

Assume that the algorithm randomly draws $\beta \in \mathbb{F}_2^r$ and $x \in \mathbb{F}_2^c$ such that conditions (a) and (b) are satisfied. Then by the central limit theorem, we have that for any $\epsilon \in \mathbb{R}$,

$$p\left[s_{obs} - s^+ \geq \epsilon\sqrt{\frac{s^+(1 - s^+)}{\omega}}\right] = p\left(Y \geq \epsilon\right)$$

where $Y \rightsquigarrow \mathcal{N}(0,1)$. For $\epsilon = -2.33$, we thus have that with probability $p_\delta \geq 0.99$,

$$s_{obs} \geq s^+ - \delta \geq s + \delta.$$

Thus, the probability that a randomly chosen β is selected is lower bounded by $p_{s^+,\nu}s^+p_\delta$. It comes that the average complexity of the offline phase satisfies

$$\mathcal{T}_{\text{offline}} \leq \frac{1}{p_{s^+,\nu}s^+p_\delta}\left[\mathcal{T}_{\text{cycle}} + p_\nu\left(\mathcal{T}_{\text{cycle}} + n^{\frac{1}{2}-\nu}\right)\omega\right]$$

$$= \frac{\mathcal{T}_{\text{cycle}}}{0.99}\left[\sqrt{\frac{\pi}{2(1 - s^+)s^+}}n^\nu\right]\left[1 + p_\nu\omega\left(1 + \frac{n^{\frac{1}{2}-\nu}}{\mathcal{T}_{\text{cycle}}}\right)\right]$$

$$\leq n^{\frac{1}{2}+\nu}\sqrt{\frac{2\pi}{(1 - s^+)s^+}}\left[1 + p_\nu\omega\left(1 + \mathcal{O}(n^{-\nu})\right)\right]$$

$$= n^{\frac{1}{2}+\nu}\sqrt{\frac{2\pi}{(1 - s^+)s^+}}\left[1 + \frac{\sqrt{2\pi}\omega}{2n^\nu} + \mathcal{O}\left(\frac{1}{n^{2\nu}}\right)\right]$$

$$= \left[\frac{1}{\sqrt{(1 - s^+)s^+}}\right]\left[n^{\frac{1}{2}+\nu}\sqrt{2\pi} + n^{\frac{1}{2}}\omega\pi + \mathcal{O}\left(n^{\frac{1}{2}-\nu}\right)\right].$$

For $s^+ = 0.73, \nu = \frac{1}{4}$, the last expression is equivalent to $\sqrt{\frac{2\pi}{(1-s^+)s^+}}n^{\frac{3}{4}} < 6n^{\frac{3}{4}}$.

The previously mentioned heuristic assumption on the similarity of the average tail length of a random point of a random function that has a ν-component and the average tail length of a random point of a random function only underlies the second appearance of $\mathcal{T}_{\text{cycle}}$ in the first bound on $\mathcal{T}_{\text{offline}}$ above. Even if these two statistics differed non-negligibly, this would not significantly distort the complexity. Since is_big is executed only when a ν-component is detected, $\mathcal{T}_{\text{cycle}}$ in its second occurence is multiplied by $p_\nu\omega \ll 1$ whilst it appears otherwise on its own.

Success Probability of the Offline Algorithm. We consider that the algorithm is successful if the value β outputted by the offline algorithm is such that P_β has a (s,ν)-component. We have seen in Sect. 3.3 that when a β is selected (that is, $s_{obs} \geq s + \delta$), the central limit theorem guarantees that the real size of the ν-component investigated is greater than sn with probability p_δ. It comes that the success probability of the offline algorithm p_{offline} is equal to $p_\delta \geq 0.99$.

3.5   Online Phase

In this section, we describe and analyse the online algorithm `online_algo`. The online phase consists in submitting (N, A, C, T) queries to the decryption oracle $\mathcal{O}_{dec}$ with $C = \beta_\ell$ where β has been outputted by the offline algorithm. In the following, we describe how the tags are constructed and how we choose the value of ℓ.

Algo. `online_algo`(β, e, μ, ℓ, m)

---

1 :   **for** $i = 1..m$ **do**

2 : $N \xleftarrow{\$} \mathbb{F}_2^\eta ; y \leftarrow e$

3 :   **for** $j = 1..\mu$ **do**

4 : $T \leftarrow P_{final}(\beta \| y)$

5 :   **if** $\mathcal{O}_{dec}(N, \varepsilon, \beta_\ell, T) \neq \perp$

6 :   **return** $(N, \varepsilon, \beta_\ell, T)$

7 :   **else** $y \leftarrow P_\beta(y)$

8 :   **return false**

Recall that we denote by x_0 the inner state at the end of the decryption's initial phase, and that when the ciphertext C is equal to β_ℓ, the state before the final phase is equal to $\beta \| P_\beta^{\ell-1}(x_0)$. Recall that β, which has been outputted by the offline algorithm, is such that $G(P_\beta)$ has a large component with a small cycle of this large component's cycle. Since this component is large, x_0 belongs to it with great probability. In that case, one can choose ℓ large enough for $P_\beta^\ell(x_0)$ to be likely to reach the small cycle of $G(P_\beta)$'s large component. The number of candidates for the state before the final phase, and thus for the possible tags, is thereby reduced.

More formally, assume that the offline algorithm has been successful, that is, it has outputted β, μ and e such that $G(P_\beta)$ has a (s, ν)-component with a cycle of length μ and such that e is an element of this cycle. If $G(P_\beta)$ has a (s, ν)-component, x_0 belongs to this component with probability greater than or equal to s. If x_0 belongs to the (s, ν)-component, $P_\beta^{\ell-1}(x_0)$ reaches the cycle with the probability p_ℓ introduced in Sect. 2.1. It comes that with probability at least $p_\ell s$, $P_\beta^{\ell-1}(x_0)$ belongs to the cycle. Here, we implicitly rely on the assumption that the random variable tail length of a random point of a random function such that this random point belongs to a (s, ν)-component has the same distribution as the tail length of a random point of a random function. Although we do not believe this assumption to be true in the sense that the distributions are not strictly equal, we believe that they are close enough for it not to impact our attack significantly. Small scale experiments described in Sect. 4 corroborate this assumption.

We now analyse Algorithm `online_algo`. For a nonce $N \in \mathbb{F}_2^\eta$, this online phase consists in submitting the following (N, A, C, T) queries to the decryption oracle:

$$\left(N, \varepsilon, \beta_\ell, P_{final}(\beta || P_\beta^i(e))\right) \quad \text{for } i = 0, \ldots, \mu - 1.$$

Time Complexity. For each nonce, the attacker submits μ decryption queries with a ciphertext of ℓ blocks, and for each decryption query, she must also apply P_{final} to the current state $\beta || y$ where y is the current cycle element and apply P_β to y in order to try exhaustively all the cycle elements. Since $\ell = \mathcal{O}(n^{\frac{1}{2}})$, the time complexity incurred by the above invocations of P_β and P_{final} at each decryption query is negligible compared to the time complexity of a decryption query with $C = \beta_\ell$, that can be approximated by ℓ applications of P. The time complexity for each nonce is thus well approximated by $\mu\ell$ and thus upper bounded by

$$n^{\frac{1}{2}-\nu}\ell.$$

Thus, for m nonces, the average complexity of the online phase in number of calls to P verifies

$$\mathcal{T}_{\texttt{online}} \leq n^{\frac{1}{2}-\nu}m\ell.$$

Probability of success. For each nonce, the probability of success is exactly the probability that $P_\beta^{\ell-1}(x_0)$ belongs to the cycle which we showed to be at least $p_\ell s$. If we repeat this experiment with m nonces, the probability of success is thus at least

$$p_{\texttt{online}} = 1 - (1 - p_\ell s)^m.$$

3.6   Complexity and Success Probability of the Attack

The complexity of the attack is the sum of the complexities of the online algorithm and the offline algorithm. Note that in practice, the attacker only needs to run the precomputation offline algorithm once in order to be able to execute the online phase to attack the same duplex-based mode with any secret key. The average complexity $\mathcal{T}_{\texttt{online}} + \mathcal{T}_{\texttt{offline}}$ of the attack can be upper bounded by

$$n^{\frac{1}{2}-\nu}m\ell + \left[\frac{1}{\sqrt{(1-s^+)s^+}}\right]\left[n^{\frac{1}{2}+\nu}\sqrt{2\pi} + n^{\frac{1}{2}}\omega\pi\right] + \mathcal{O}\left(n^{\frac{1}{2}-\nu}\right).$$

Similarly, the overall success probability of the attack is of the form

$$p_{\texttt{success}} = p_{\texttt{offline}}p_{\texttt{online}} \geq p_\delta\left[1 - (1 - p_\ell s)^m\right]$$

$$\geq 0.99(1 - e^{-mp_\ell s}) \quad (\text{since } \forall x \in \mathbb{R}, e^{-x} > 1 - x).$$

In order to have an overall probability of success $p_{\texttt{success}}$ greater than 0.95, we want $1 - e^{-mp_\ell s}$ to be greater than 0.96. Recall from Sect. 2.1 that $p_\ell \geq 1 - e^{\frac{-\ell^2}{2n}}$. We set $\ell = 3\sqrt{n}$ so that $p_\ell \geq 0.988$. We also set the following values:

- $\omega = 2^{10}$; thus $2\delta = \frac{2.33}{\sqrt{\omega}} < 0.08$;
- $s^+ = 0.73$; thus $s = s^+ - 2\delta = 0.65$.

Since $p_\ell \geq 0.988$ and $s = 0.65$, p_{online} is greater than 0.96 for $m \geq 5$. We thus set $m = 5$. Thus, the complexity has the form

$$15n^{1-\nu} + 6n^{\frac{1}{2}+\nu} + \frac{4\pi 2^{10}}{\sqrt{3}}n^{\frac{1}{2}} + \mathcal{O}\left(n^{\frac{1}{2}-\nu}\right).$$

To balance the above expression, we set $\nu = \frac{1}{4}$, we get an attack of complexity at most $21n^{\frac{3}{4}} + \mathcal{O}(\sqrt{n}) = 21 \times 2^{\frac{3c}{4}} + \mathcal{O}(\sqrt{n})$ in number of calls to P.[11]
    Note that the complexity of the online phase is at most $15n^{1-\nu}$. In particular, given β such that $G(P_\beta)$ has a component of size greater than ns with a cycle length close to 1, the online complexity can be brought close to $2^{\frac{c}{2}+4}$.

3.7   Key-Recovery

For modes such that P_{init} is reversible for known nonce and associated data, our forgery attack also recovers the secret key with $\ell = \mathcal{O}(\sqrt{n})$ extra applications of P, which is negligible compared to the complexity of the forgery. Indeed, if the decryption oracle receives a forgery (N, A, C, T), it returns the corresponding plaintext. This allows the attacker to recover the state at the end of the initial phase with $\ell = \mathcal{O}(\sqrt{n})$ extra applications of P^{-1}.[12] As a consequence, if the function P_{init} is reversible for known nonce and associated data, the attacker recovers the secret key.

4   Small Scale Experiments

Our attack relies on the assumption that the P_β's derived from a public permutation P defined on $\mathbb{F}_2^b$ behave as random functions on $\mathbb{F}_2^c$. To statistically verify this assumption, we implemented some experiments using the permutation XOODOO[12] as P. The main reason behind this choice is its use in the finalist of the NIST lightweight cryptography competition XOODYAK, but another permutation used in practice with a reasonably large value of b would have done just as well. We took toy values compared to XOODYAK for the capacity ($c \leq 40$) in order for computer experiments to remain easy to achieve. Since our attack relies mainly on the random function statistics results introduced in Sect. 2.1, we designed a test for each of these results. We also implemented the algorithm offline_search for small values of c.

---

[11] Note that $\nu = \frac{1}{4}$ is not the fully optimal choice in general. Rather, the optimal choice for ν is $\nu = \frac{1}{2}\left(\frac{1}{2} - \log_n\left(\sqrt{2\pi}/(\sqrt{s^+(1-s^+)}15)\right)\right)$. For example, for $n = 2^{128}$, the optimal choice is approximately 0.256.

[12] The plaintext also allows to verify that the recovered state before the final phase is correct, making the key recovery possible with only a negligible amount of extra computations regardless of the tag length.

Algo. cycle_expectancy(Ω)	Algo. nu_components(Ω, ν)
1: $tot \leftarrow 0$	1: $ctr \leftarrow 0$
2: **for** $i = 1..\Omega$ **do**	2: **for** $i = 1..\Omega$ **do**
3: $\beta \xleftarrow{\$} \mathbb{F}_2^r; x \xleftarrow{\$} \mathbb{F}_2^c$	3: $\beta \xleftarrow{\$} \mathbb{F}_2^r; x \xleftarrow{\$} \mathbb{F}_2^c$
4: $(\mu, e) \leftarrow$ cycle(β, x)	4: $(\mu, e) \leftarrow$ cycle(β, x)
5: $tot \leftarrow tot + \mu$	5: **if** $\mu \leq n^{\frac{1}{2} - \nu}$ **then** $ctr \leftarrow ctr + 1$
6: **return** tot/Ω	6: **return** ctr/Ω

Expectancy of Cycle/Tail Length. We wish to verify that for a random $\beta \in \mathbb{F}_2^r$ and for a random node $x \in G(P_\beta)$, the expectancy of the cycle length $\mu(x)$ and tail length $\lambda(x)$ are both equal to $\sqrt{\frac{\pi n}{8}}$, with $n = 2^c$. Note that the variance of the cycle length and tail length for a random node of a random function is equal to $\sigma_\mu^2 = n\left[\frac{2}{3} - \frac{2\pi}{16}\right]$ [25]. Regarding the cycle length, we use the algorithm cycle_expectancy. After Ω tries, by the Central Limit Theorem, the observed average cycle length mean outputted by the algorithm cycle_expectancy is such that with probability about 0.99:

$$\text{mean} \in \left[\sqrt{\frac{\pi n}{8}} - \frac{2.58\sigma_\mu}{\sqrt{\Omega}}; \sqrt{\frac{\pi n}{8}} + \frac{2.58\sigma_\mu}{\sqrt{\Omega}}\right].$$

Setting $\Omega = 14000$, we verify whether mean is in this interval in our tests (see Table 1). We use a similar algorithm and reasoning for the tail length.[13] As shown in Table 1, all our experimental results match the theory.

Table 1. Expectancy of cycle length and tail length

c	28	32	36	40
Expectancy	10267	41068	164274	657098
Confidence interval	$[10080, 10454]$	$[40321, 41817]$	$[161283, 167266]$	$[645130, 669065]$
tail mean	10323	40971	163732	654775
cycle mean	10255	41620	164445	650156

Probability for a Random Point to Belong to a ν-Component. We wish to verify that for a random $\beta \in \mathbb{F}_2^r$ and for a random node $x \in G(P_\beta)$, the probability that x belongs to a ν-component is p_ν. To do so, we use the algorithm nu_components and focus in practice on experiments where $\nu = \frac{1}{4}$ as it is the value used in our attack. Drawing Ω random (x, β) pairs and computing

---

[13] Here, we make the assumption that the standard deviation for the tail length is the same as the cycle length's. This assumption does not affect our attack, it only affects how to interpret our test results.

the proportion of such pairs such that x belongs to a ν-component of P_β amounts to computing the mean of Ω Bernoulli variables equal to 1 with probability p_ν and 0 with probability $1 - p_\nu$. By the Central Limit Theorem, since the standard variation of the above variables is $\sigma_\nu = \sqrt{p_\nu(1 - p_\nu)}$, we have that

$$\texttt{proportion} \in \left[p_\nu - \frac{2.58\sigma_\nu}{\sqrt{\Omega}} ; p_\nu + \frac{2.58\sigma_\nu}{\sqrt{\Omega}} \right]$$

with probability ≥ 0.99. We verify in our experiments that $\texttt{proportion}$ is indeed in this confidence interval for various values of c and Ω. Our results, which match the theory, are displayed in Table 2.

Table 2. Probability for a random node in the graph of a random function to belong to a ν-component and experimental verification of (the detection of) the occurence of (s, ν)-components.

	c	28	32	36	40
	Ω	71344	142688	285376	570752
ν-component	Expectancy	0.009792	0.004896	0.002448	0.0012
	Conf. interval	$[0.0088, 0.0110]$	$[0.0044, 0.0054]$	$[0.0022, 0.0027]$	$[0.0011, 0.0013]$
	proportion	0.010162	0.004787	0.002400	0.001242
(s, ν)-component	$p_{s+,\nu}s^+p_\delta$	0.002740	0.001370	0.000685	0.000342
	$p_{s,\nu}s$	0.002973	0.001487	0.000743	0.000372
	frequency	0.003714	0.001647	0.000880	0.000517

Probability for a Random Function to Have a (s, ν)-Component. Verifying that for a random $\beta \in \mathbb{F}_2^r$, the probability that $G(P_\beta)$ has a (s, ν)-component is $p_{s,\nu}$ is hard in practice as it is too costly to determine with probability 1 whether or not $G(P_\beta)$ has a (s, ν)-component. Instead, we make an indirect verification. We draw Ω random (x, β) pairs and compute the proportion $\texttt{frequency}$ of such pairs such that:

- P_β has a ν-component (the component to which x belongs);
- the estimated size s_{obs} of this component (given by the proportion, among $\omega = 1000$, of newly chosen random points that belong to this component) is at least $s + \delta$ with $\delta = \frac{2.33}{2\sqrt{\omega}}$, so that the actual size of the component is very likely to be at least sn.[14]

---

[14] To reduce the execution time of the implementation, to detect whether or not two points x, x' are in the same component, we checked whether $\mu(x) = \mu(x')$ instead of doing the exhaustive verification made in $\texttt{is\_big}$.

We compare the found frequency values with two values:

- the lower bound $p_{s,\nu}s$ on the probability that P_β has a (s,ν)-component and x belongs to it;
- the conservative lower bound $p_{s^+,\nu}s^+p_\delta$ on the average value of frequency used in the complexity estimate of the offline algorithm of Sect. 3.4, where $s^+ = s + 2\delta$.

This algorithm is easy to derive from the algorithm offline_search introduced in Sect. 3.3. We make this experiment for various values of Ω and c and with $s = 0.65$, $s^+ = 0.73$, as they are the values used in our attack. Our results match the theory and are displayed in Table 2. The difference (in favour of the adversary) between theoretical bounds and experimental values for frequency in Table 2 can be at least partially explained as follows. The value $p_{s,\nu}$ is the probability that a component is a ν-component of size *greater or equal* to s. The probability that a random point belongs to a (s,ν)-component is thus strictly greater than $p_{s,\nu}s$ as the proportion of the points belonging to a component of size greater than s is greater than s.

Table 3. We provide a few examples of obtained β values such that P_β has a (s,ν)-component with $\mu \ll 2^{\frac{c}{4}}$. Although we only provide one for each c, several values of β are available for each c.

c	β $(b - c$ bits$)$						μ
28	1473b86a	2607d6e5	5234df22	4c111c51	122e188f	37586e28	10
	5b74f306	40ac1d69	2bb9c59f	6e8479b7	3d6ec314	7	
32	67b9632a	032ec1a3	1f3b4f8c	7c641f59	39e3cab6	3aaa4444	4
	73bf377d	7f1f6b35	6412ffb2	523d5180	54465a4f		
36	59189691	3e3769f2	293b1b6f	0cc0af85	7d96b0a4	0e1c201b	122
	137523e8	11f61a60	6c06c85f	762716b7	276c730		
40	7b2fb641	7874c3d6	171abbc2	231ebf22	4e6e1ad3	2d6df079	18
	7e6457aa	7816dd2a	011fe0f3	1de6ee24	56f1ed		

Some Values of β. Lastly, we implemented the algorithm offline_search for small values of c and for $s = 0.65$. A few examples of obtained β values are displayed in Table 3.

**Probability for a Random Point to Belong to its Component's Cycle
After $\ell - 1$ Applications of the Random Function.** In order to verify the
applicability of Harris' result on the number of successors provided in Sect. 2.1
to points randomly drawn in a (s, ν)-component, *a fortiori* when the function is
randomly sampled from the set of all P_β's rather than randomly sampled in $\mathfrak{F}_n$,
we also conducted the following experiment. For all β values displayed in Table 3,
we checked whether the points that were found to be in the (s, ν)-component
had a tail length smaller than $\ell = 3\sqrt{n}$. For all these β, 100% of the points found
to be in the (s, ν)-component have a tail length smaller than ℓ. This gives us
reasonable confidence in the fact that this assumption is realistic and does not
lead to a significant overestimation of the success probability of the attack.

5   Application to Concrete Duplex-Based Modes

In this section, we apply the attack previously described on the simplified
DUPLEXAEAD mode to concrete AEAD duplex-based modes. Whilst our attack
can be easily adapted to many of them as summarized in Table 4, others frustrate our attack. For all the modes presented in Table 4, our attack enables key
recovery.

5.1   Highlights

For the attack to succeed, we identify two requirements:

1. In decryption mode, the ciphertext blocks must overwrite the outer state at
   least in part;
2. The tag must be determined by the state before the final phase, in such a
   way that a correct guess on this state gives us the correct tag.

   As a consequence, we will show that in all modes for which the attack is
applicable, the padding rule applied to the message does not matter, even though
when the padding rule is made block by block the complexity of our attack can
be slightly greater.

   As a main concrete implication, we provide an attack on XOODYAK that
breaks the claim of achieving 184-bit security against plaintext recovery and
forgery attacks made by the designers in [18, Corollary 2, p. 72] but does not
threaten the 112-bit security level required by NIST for the lightweight competition. The attack also breaks the penultimate NORX version NORX v2 [1] but not
the more recent version NORX v3 [2].

   Secondly we highlight two reasons that prevent our attack from applying to
modes such as Beetle [16], Ascon [22] or NORX v3 [2] in Sect. 5.3. We mainly
identify two reasons:

Table 4. Summary of our results. Our attack is the best known generic attack against the modes displayed in blue;[1]r' is the length of the outer state part that is overwritten by ciphertext blocks taking into a account a potential block by block padding such as in monkeyDuplex;[2]Claimed plaintext integrity security level for a key and tag of sufficient, potentially maximal, length;[3]Note that a more efficient (although not generic) attack has been devised in [15].

Mode	monkeyWrap/monkeyDuplex							Cyclist	Motorist	
Scheme	NORX v2[3]		KETJE				KNOT	XOODYAK	KEYAK	
Instance	N-32	N-64	Jr	Sr	Mi	Ma	KNOT-AEAD	XOODYAK	River	Lake
b	512	1024	200	400	800	1600	256 384 384 512	384	800	1600
r	384	768	16	32	128	256	64 192 96 128	192	544	1344
r' [1]	382	766	14	30	126	254	64 192 96 128	192	544	1344
c	128	256	184	368	672	1344	192 192 288 384	192	256	256
Sec. level[2]	128	256	96	128	128	128	125 128 189 253	184	128	128
$\mathcal{T}$	2^{102}	2^{198}	2^{144}	2^{282}	2^{506}	2^{1014}	2^{148} 2^{148} 2^{220} 2^{292}	2^{148}	2^{196}	2^{196}

- the use of a linear application that prevents outer state overwriting such as the *feedback function* proposed in the Beetle mode [16] (requirement 1 is not fulfilled);[15]
- the use of the secret key in the final phase to produce the tag such as in Ascon and NORX v3 [2,22]. Indeed, in that case, a correct guess on the state before the final phase does not determine the tag (requirement 2 is not fulfilled).

5.2   Schemes to Which the Attack Can Be Applied

The attack is applicable to the following duplex-based constructions: the Cyclist, monkeyDuplex and Motorist modes. Therefore, the attack is applicable to XOODYAK, KETJE, KNOT, NORX v2 and KEYAK. This section is made to help the reader check attack details for all AEAD algorithms on which the attack is applicable.

---

[15] Although the first mode that uses a feedback function is COFB [17], this mode is out of scope as it is not duplex-based (in fact, it is not even permutation-based but block-cipher based).

Cyclist Mode. A well known representative of the family of duplex-based ciphers is XOODYAK [18], a finalist of the NIST lightweight cryptography competition.[16] XOODYAK uses the permutation XOODOO as its state update function.

As explained in Sect. 3.5, the specification of the initial phase does not influence the applicability of the attack. Hence, we only focus on the ciphertext processing and the final phase. After the initial phase, a byte is set to '80' and is XORed into the state, but this is only the case for the first block. Thus, we consider that the processing of the first ciphertext block belongs to the initial phase. Moreover, each time a ciphertext block overwrites the outer state, a byte set to '01' is XORed into the state at the bit positions $r + 1, \ldots, r + 8$[17], where $r = 24$ bytes $= 192$ bits [18, p. 68]. Thus, the permutation P on which we need to apply offline_search is

$$P : \mathbb{F}_2^{384} \longrightarrow \mathbb{F}_2^{384}$$
$$s \longmapsto \text{XOODOO}[12](s \oplus 0^{192}||0^7||1||0^{184}).$$

If one considers the padding rule 10^* together with the interface provided by the XOODYAK authors, one can notice that all those transformations are deterministic in the value of the inner state just before processing the last ciphertext block. Hence, we can guess the last state value, and apply the final phase (considering the padding for the last block inside this transformation) to the last block and apply the attack. This means that for any tag length, our attack strategy provides a forgery with a complexity of $2^{148.4}$.

When a valid decryption query is provided to the decryption oracle, the corresponding plaintext is returned. The plaintext allows the attacker to check that her guess on the state before the final phase is correct as she can invert the whole process. Doing so, she can also recover the state just after processing the key. As long as the key is smaller than 44 bytes, it is copied entirely in the state and then A, N and M are processed. Thus, P_{init} is reversible for known N and A. As described in Sect. 3.7 the attack can thus be turned into a key recovery for XOODYAK.

For a t-byte tag and a κ-bit secret key with $\kappa \leq 192$, the authors claim that XOODYAK has a security strength level in bits of $\min(184, \kappa, 8t)$ in computation where the data is limited to $96+\kappa/2$. Our attack breaks this claim for $\kappa \geq 152$ and $t \geq 19$. Our attack not only produces a forgery but also recovers the secret key. Typically, for $\kappa = 192$ and $t = 24$, there should be no attack with a complexity under 2^{184} in time and 2^{192} in data. Yet, our attack has a complexity of $2^{148.4}$.

MonkeyDuplex: KETJE, KNOT and NORX v2. KETJE [12], KNOT-AEAD [34] and NORX v2 [1] use the mode monkeyDuplex defined originally in 2014 for

---

[16] For more details on XOODYAK's specification, we refer to [18] at page 62 for the keyed mode together with pages 67 and 68 for the full description of what is relevant for our analysis. https://csrc.nist.gov/Projects/lightweight-cryptography/.

[17] Note that the rate called r in this paper is denoted by n in XOODYAK's specification.

KETJE [11]. However, those algorithms differ in the padding rule applied to the message.

- In KNOT-AEAD, the padding is made by 'appending a single 1 and the smallest number of 0's to the bit string such that the length of the padded bit string is a multiple of r bits'. Thus, the technique used for XOODYAK can be applied.
- In KETJE and in NORX, the padding is made block by block [12, 1.3, p. 4] and [1, p. 9-10] with the rule pad10*1[r]($|M|$) which is the multi-rate padding as defined in [7]. Both ciphers allow to process bit strings of length smaller or equal[18] to $r' = r - 2$. To deal with this padding rule, we consider that every plaintext block is of length exactly r', meaning that the padding rule is just the concatenation of 11 to each block. By doing the same technique together with the domain separation as for XOODYAK, that is considering that the position corresponding to those two bits are in fact inside the inner state and that the XOR of 11 is part of the KETJE inner permutation P (or part of the NORX inner permutation), we can apply our attack, by considering the effective rate to be $r' = r - 2$ instead of r.

For these three constructions, the final phase is deterministic in the inner state after processing the plaintext or the ciphertext so our attack can be applied. Both ciphers come with 4 different instances and our attack leads to the complexities listed in Table 4. Moreover, when the decryption oracle sends back the plaintext, a key recovery is possible as the state is directly initialized with key and nonce without applying any transformation.

Motorist: KEYAK. KEYAK [13] is a family of authenticated encryption schemes which is a third-round candidate of the CAESAR competition. The features of the Motorist mode that are of interest for our attack are:

- Decryption overwrites the outer state with ciphertext blocks values and in between there are applications of P where P is a KECCAK-p permutation.
- An encoding (in byte) of the size of the processed message blocks is XORed into the state at the $R_a + 1$ byte position, where R_a is the absorbing rate in bytes ($R_a = \frac{r}{8}$).
- For the tag generation, given a (public) tag length, the tag is determined by the state before the final phase.

Thus, the attack can also be applied on KEYAK instances by just changing the function that is iterated and considering the XOR of the bytes that encode the length of ciphertext and associated data to be part of the decryption function.

However, KEYAK comes with instances that can work independently (Pistons), in order to highly parallelize encryption and decryption of large amount of data. To do so, the authors of KEYAK propose to do several initialization in parallel, process independently 4, 8 or more strings and then mix everything together at the end. However, if one would like to guess the tag, one would have

---

[18] This value is called ρ_{max} in [7, p. 335].

to guess independently every inner state in all parallel instances as they are all initialized differently. So, our attack on KEYAK is also applicable on all instances but make sense only for the non-parallelized instances, that is RIVER KEYAK and LAKE KEYAK. For these instances, the key can also be recovered.

5.3   Modes that Frustrate Our Attack

In this section, we will look into authenticated encryption modes to which the attack cannot be applied. Two main features frustrate our cryptanalysis. The first one consists of a final key addition just at the beginning of the final phase and the second one is the use of a *feedback function* as proposed in the mode Beetle [16].

Key-dependent Final Phase. Our attack allows to reduce the space of all possible values of the final state before the final phase. For the modes to which the attack applies, a correct guess on this state can be transformed into a forgery, and, under certain conditions, into a key recovery. However, some proposals such as Ascon [22] or the third version of NORX [2] for the CAESAR competition slightly change the final phase by making it not only dependent on the state after processing the plaintext or ciphertext, but also key dependent. As explained at the beginning of this section, the final tag must be fully determined by the state just before the final phase. When the key is involved in the final phase, even if the correct state value is guessed, an attacker does not know *a priori* the secret key and so the state recovery does not lead to a forgery attack.

Absence of Outer State Overwriting. In another line of research, Chakraborti et al. proposed in 2018 a family of AEAD constructions named Beetle [16]. Beetle is not strictly speaking a duplex-based construction as the use of a *feedback function* between two consecutive invocations of the permutation P avoids, when both a data injection and a data extraction take place, that the r-bit outer state value after the data injection be equal to the extracted data block as in traditional duplexing, and allows to render both values almost independent. Thus, the use of a feedback function prevents the attack by making the outer state overwriting impossible. Unlike duplex-based constructions which do not use a feedback function twist, the Beetle construction is claimed to provide a security level $\min\{\frac{b}{2}, c - \log(r), r\}$ without any restriction on decryption queries [3,16]. The Beetle construction is used in the Beetle and SPARKLE [5] finalists of the NIST lightweight cryptography standardization process.

The same effect also occurs in Subterranean 2.0 [19] which is a second round candidate of the NIST-lightweight competition and a duplex-like proposal. In order to generate the ciphertext blocks, two bits of the state are XORed to serve as a keystream. It prevents the attack in the same way that the feedback function of the Beetle mode does, as the attacker can not predict the value of the outer state before the next application of the update function.

6 Conclusion

In this paper, we provided a generic attack against several duplex-based AEAD modes. Constructed as a forgery attack, our cryptanalysis can be transformed into a key recovery for most modes to which it applies. It has a complexity equivalent to $\mathcal{O}(2^{\frac{3c}{4}})$ applications of the state update function and thus represents an improvement from previous generic attacks against duplex-based modes. It is also memory-less. Further, the complexity of the online phase can be brought close to $2^{\frac{c}{2}}$ at the cost of increasing the time complexity of the pre-computation phase (which needs to be run only once) above $\mathcal{O}(2^{\frac{3c}{4}})$.

References

1. Aumasson, J.P., Jovanovic, P., Neves, S.: NORX v2. Submission to the Caesar competition (2015). https://competitions.cr.yp.to/round2/norxv20.pdf
2. Aumasson, J.P., Jovanovic, P., Neves, S.: NORX v3. Submission to the Caesar competition (2016). https://competitions.cr.yp.to/round3/norxv30.pdf
3. Banik, S., et al.: GIFT-COFB. Cryptology ePrint Archive, Report 2020/738 (2020). https://eprint.iacr.org/2020/738
4. Bao, Z., Guo, J., Wang, L.: Functional graphs and their applications in generic attacks on iterated hash constructions. IACR Trans. Symm. Cryptol. **2018**(1), 201–253 (2018). https://doi.org/10.13154/tosc.v2018.i1.201-253
5. Beierle, C., et al.: Lightweight AEAD and hashing using the Sparkle permutation family. IACR Trans. Symm. Cryptol. **2020**(S1), 208–261 (2020). https://doi.org/10.13154/tosc.v2020.iS1.208-261
6. Bertoni, G., Daemen, J., Peeters, M., Van Assche, G.: On the indifferentiability of the sponge construction. In: Smart, N. (ed.) EUROCRYPT 2008. LNCS, vol. 4965, pp. 181–197. Springer, Heidelberg (2008). https://doi.org/10.1007/978-3-540-78967-3_11
7. Bertoni, G., Daemen, J., Peeters, M., Van Assche, G.: Duplexing the sponge: single-pass authenticated encryption and other applications. In: Miri, A., Vaudenay, S. (eds.) SAC 2011. LNCS, vol. 7118, pp. 320–337. Springer, Heidelberg (2012). https://doi.org/10.1007/978-3-642-28496-0_19
8. Bertoni, G., Daemen, J., Peeters, M., Assche, G.V.: Sponge functions (2007). https://keccak.team/files/SpongeFunctions.pdf
9. Bertoni, G., Daemen, J., Peeters, M., Assche, G.V.: Cryptographic sponge functions (2011). https://keccak.team/files/CSF-0.1.pdf
10. Bertoni, G., Daemen, J., Peeters, M., Assche, G.V.: Permutation-based encryption, authentication and authenticated encryption (2012). http://www.hyperelliptic.org/djb/diac/record.pdf
11. Bertoni, G., Daemen, J., Peeters, M., Assche, G.V., Keer, R.V.: Ketje v1. Submission to Caesar competition (2014). http://competitions.cr.yp.to/round1/ketjev1.pdf
12. Bertoni, G., Daemen, J., Peeters, M., Assche, G.V., Keer, R.V.: Ketje v2. Round 3 candidate for the Caesar competition (2016). http://competitions.cr.yp.to/round3/ketjev2.pdf
13. Bertoni, G., Daemen, J., Peeters, M., Assche, G.V., Keer, R.V.: Keyak v2. Submission to the Caesar competition (2016). https://competitions.cr.yp.to/round3/keyakv22.pdf

14. Brent, R.P.: An improved monte carlo factorization algorithm. In: BIT Numerical Mathematics, Berlin, Heidelberg, p. 176–184 (1980). https://doi.org/10.1007/BF01933190

15. Chaigneau, C., Fuhr, T., Gilbert, H., Jean, J., Reinhard, J.-R.: Cryptanalysis of NORX v2.0. J. Cryptol. **32**(4), 1423–1447 (2018). https://doi.org/10.1007/s00145-018-9297-9

16. Chakraborti, A., Datta, N., Nandi, M., Yasuda, K.: Beetle family of lightweight and secure authenticated encryption ciphers. IACR Trans. Cryptogr. Hardware Embed. Syst. **2018**(2), 218–241 (2018). https://doi.org/10.13154/tches.v2018.i2.218-241, https://tches.iacr.org/index.php/TCHES/article/view/881

17. Chakraborti, A., Iwata, T., Minematsu, K., Nandi, M.: Blockcipher-based authenticated encryption: how small can we go? In: Fischer, W., Homma, N. (eds.) CHES 2017. LNCS, vol. 10529, pp. 277–298. Springer, Cham (2017). https://doi.org/10.1007/978-3-319-66787-4_14

18. Daemen, J., Hoffert, S., Peeters, M., Van Assche, G., Van Keer, R.: Xoodyak, a lightweight cryptographic scheme. IACR Trans. Symm. Cryptol. **2020**(S1), 60–87 (2020). https://doi.org/10.13154/tosc.v2020.iS1.60-87

19. Daemen, J., Massolino, P.M.C., Mehrdad, A., Rotella, Y.: The subterranean 2.0 cipher suite. IACR Trans. Symm. Cryptol. **2020**(S1), 262–294 (2020). https://doi.org/10.13154/tosc.v2020.iS1.262-294

20. Daemen, J., Mennink, B., Van Assche, G.: Full-state keyed duplex with built-in multi-user support. In: Takagi, T., Peyrin, T. (eds.) ASIACRYPT 2017. LNCS, vol. 10625, pp. 606–637. Springer, Cham (2017). https://doi.org/10.1007/978-3-319-70697-9_21

21. DeLaurentis, J.M.: Components and cycles of a random function. In: Pomerance, C. (ed.) CRYPTO 1987. LNCS, vol. 293, pp. 231–242. Springer, Heidelberg (1988). https://doi.org/10.1007/3-540-48184-2_21

22. Dobraunig, C., Eichlseder, M., Mendel, F., Schläffer, M.: ASCON v1.2: lightweight authenticated encryption and hashing. J. Cryptol. **34**(3), 1–42 (2021). https://doi.org/10.1007/s00145-021-09398-9

23. Flajolet, P., Odlyzko, A.M.: Random mapping statistics. In: Quisquater, J.-J., Vandewalle, J. (eds.) EUROCRYPT 1989. LNCS, vol. 434, pp. 329–354. Springer, Heidelberg (1990). https://doi.org/10.1007/3-540-46885-4_34

24. Flajolet, P., Sedgewick, R.: Analytic Combinatorics. Cambridge University Press, Cambridge (2009). http://www.cambridge.org/uk/catalogue/catalogue.asp?isbn=9780521898065

25. Harris, B.: Probability distributions related to random mappings. Ann. Math. Stat. **31**(4), 1045–1062 (1960). https://doi.org/10.1214/aoms/1177705677

26. Joux, A.: Algorithmic Cryptanalysis. Chapman and Hall/CRC, Boca Raton (2009). https://doi.org/10.1201/9781420070033

27. Jovanovic, P., Luykx, A., Mennink, B.: Beyond $2^{c/2}$ security in sponge-based authenticated encryption modes. In: Sarkar, P., Iwata, T. (eds.) ASIACRYPT 2014. LNCS, vol. 8873, pp. 85–104. Springer, Heidelberg (2014). https://doi.org/10.1007/978-3-662-45611-8_5

28. Jovanovic, P., Luykx, A., Mennink, B., Sasaki, Yu., Yasuda, K.: Beyond conventional security in sponge-based authenticated encryption modes. J. Cryptol. **32**(3), 895–940 (2018). https://doi.org/10.1007/s00145-018-9299-7

29. Leurent, G., Peyrin, T., Wang, L.: New generic attacks against hash-based MACs. In: Sako, K., Sarkar, P. (eds.) ASIACRYPT 2013. LNCS, vol. 8270, pp. 1–20. Springer, Heidelberg (2013). https://doi.org/10.1007/978-3-642-42045-0_1

30. Mennink, B., Reyhanitabar, R., Vizár, D.: Security of full-state keyed sponge and duplex: applications to authenticated encryption. In: Iwata, T., Cheon, J.H. (eds.) ASIACRYPT 2015. LNCS, vol. 9453, pp. 465–489. Springer, Heidelberg (2015). https://doi.org/10.1007/978-3-662-48800-3_19
31. Moon, J.W.: Counting Labelled Trees. Canadian Mathematical Congress 1970, William Clowes and Sons (1970)
32. Peyrin, T., Sasaki, Yu., Wang, L.: Generic related-key attacks for HMAC. In: Wang, X., Sako, K. (eds.) ASIACRYPT 2012. LNCS, vol. 7658, pp. 580–597. Springer, Heidelberg (2012). https://doi.org/10.1007/978-3-642-34961-4_35
33. Peyrin, T., Wang, L.: Generic universal forgery attack on iterative hash-based MACs. In: Nguyen, P.Q., Oswald, E. (eds.) EUROCRYPT 2014. LNCS, vol. 8441, pp. 147–164. Springer, Heidelberg (2014). https://doi.org/10.1007/978-3-642-55220-5_9
34. Zhang, W., et al.: KNOT. Round 2 candidate for the NIST Lightweight Cryptography project (2019). https://csrc.nist.gov/CSRC/media/Projects/lightweight-cryptography/documents/round-2/spec-doc-rnd2/knot-spec-round.pdf

Context Discovery and Commitment Attacks
How to Break CCM, EAX, SIV, and More

Sanketh Menda[1]($\boxtimes$), Julia Len[1], Paul Grubbs[2], and Thomas Ristenpart[1]

[1] Cornell Tech, New York, USA
sanketh@cs.cornell.edu
[2] University of Michigan, Ann Arbor, USA

Abstract. A line of recent work has highlighted the importance of context commitment security, which asks that authenticated encryption with associated data (AEAD) schemes will not decrypt the same adversarially-chosen ciphertext under two different, adversarially-chosen contexts (secret key, associated data, and nonce). Despite a spate of recent attacks, many open questions remain around context commitment; most obviously nothing is known about the commitment security of important schemes such as CCM, EAX, and SIV.

We resolve these open questions, and more. Our approach is to, first, introduce a new framework that helps us more granularly define context commitment security in terms of what portions of a context are adversarially controlled. We go on to formulate a new security notion, called context discoverability, which can be viewed as analogous to preimage resistance from the hashing literature. We show that unrestricted context commitment security (the adversary controls all of the two contexts) implies context discoverability security for a class of schemes encompassing most schemes used in practice. Then, we show new context discovery attacks against a wide set of AEAD schemes, including CCM, EAX, SIV, GCM, and OCB3, and, by our general result, this gives new unrestricted context commitment attacks against them.

Finally, we explore the case of restricted context commitment security for the original SIV mode, for which no prior attack techniques work (including our context discovery based ones). We are nevertheless able to give a novel $\mathcal{O}(2^{n/3})$ attack using Wagner's k-tree algorithm for the generalized birthday problem.

Keywords: Secret-key cryptography · AEAD · Committing encryption

1 Introduction

Designers of authenticated encryption with associated data (AEAD) have traditionally targeted security in the sense of confidentiality and ciphertext integrity, first in the context of randomized authenticated encryption [6], and then nonce-based [32] and misuse-resistant AEAD [33].

© International Association for Cryptologic Research 2023
C. Hazay and M. Stam (Eds.): EUROCRYPT 2023, LNCS 14007, pp. 379–407, 2023.
https://doi.org/10.1007/978-3-031-30634-1_13

But in recent years researchers and practitioners have begun realizing that confidentiality and integrity as previously formalized prove insufficient in a variety of contexts. In particular, the community is beginning to appreciate the danger of schemes that are not key committing, meaning that an attacker can compute a ciphertext such that it can successfully decrypt under two (or more) keys. Non-key-committing AEAD was first shown to be a problem in the context of moderation in encrypted messaging [16,24], and later in password-based encryption [29], password-based key exchange [29], key rotation schemes [2], and symmetric hybrid (or envelope) encryption [2].

Even more recently, new definitions have been proposed [5] that target committing to the key, associated data, and nonce. And while there have been proposals for new schemes [2,5] that meet these varying definitions, questions still remain about which current AEAD schemes are committing and in which ways. Moreover, there have been no commitment results shown for a number of important practical AEAD schemes, such as CCM [17], EAX [11], and SIV [33]. Implementing (and standardizing) new AEAD schemes takes time and so understanding which standard AEAD schemes can be securely used in which settings is a pressing issue.

This work makes four main contributions. First, we provide a new, more granular framework for commitment security, which expands on prior ones to better capture practical attack settings. Second, we show the first key commitment attack against the original SIV mode, which was previously an open question. Third, we introduce a new kind of commitment security notion for AEAD—what we call *context discoverability*—which is analogous to preimage resistance for cryptographic hash functions. Fourth, we give context discovery attacks against a range of schemes which, by a general implication, also yield new commitment attacks against those schemes. A summary of our new attacks, including comparison with prior ones, when relevant, is given in Fig. 1.

Granular Commitment Notions. Recall that a nonce-based AEAD encryption algorithm Enc takes as input a key K, nonce N, associated data A, and a message M. It outputs a ciphertext C. Decryption Dec likewise takes in a (K, N, A) triple, which we call the decryption *context*, along with a ciphertext C, and outputs either a message M or special error symbol $\bot$.

While most prior work has focused on key commitment security, which requires commitment to only one part (the key) of the decryption context, Bellare and Hoang (BH) [5] suggest a more expansive sequence of commitment notions for nonce-based AEAD. For the first, CMT-1, an adversary wins if it efficiently computes a ciphertext C and two decryption contexts (K_1, N_1, A_1) and (K_2, N_2, A_2) such that decryption of C under either context works (does not output $\bot$) and $K_1 \neq K_2$. CMT-1 is often called key commitment.[1] CMT-3 relaxes the latter winning condition to allow a win should the decryption contexts differ in any way. We therefore refer to CMT-3 as *context commitment* and schemes that meet CMT-3 as *context committing*. These notions form a strict hierarchy, with CMT-3 being the strongest. Despite this, most prior attacks [2,16,24,29] have focused solely on key commitment (CMT-1).

---

[1] BH refer to this as CMTD-1, but for tidy AEAD schemes, CMT-1 and CMTD-1 are equivalent, so we prefer the compact term.

Our first contribution is to refine further the definitional landscape for nonce-based AEAD schemes in a way that is particularly useful for exploring context commitment attacks. In practice, attackers will often face application-specific restrictions preventing full control over the decryption context. For example, in the Dodis, Grubbs, Ristenpart, and Woodage (DGRW) [16] attacks against Facebook's message franking scheme, the adversary had to build a ciphertext that decrypts under two contexts with equivalent nonces. Their (in BH's terminology) CMT-1 attack takes on a special form, and we would like to be able to formally distinguish between attacks that achieve additional adversarial goals (e.g., different keys but equivalent nonces) and those that may not.

We therefore introduce a new, parameterized security notion that generalizes the BH notions. Our CMT[Σ] notion specifies what we call a setting $\Sigma = (\text{ts}, \text{S}, \text{P})$ that includes a target specifier ts, a context selector S, and a predicate P. The parameters ts and S specify which parts of the context are attacker-controlled versus chosen by the game, and which of the latter are revealed to the attacker. Furthermore, the predicate P takes as input the two decryption contexts and decrypted messages, and outputs whether the pair of tuples satisfy a winning condition. An adversary wins if it outputs a ciphertext and two contexts satisfying the condition that each decrypt the ciphertext without error. The resulting family of commitment notions includes both CMT-1 and CMT-3 but also covers a landscape of further notions.

We highlight two sets of notions. The first set is composed of CMT_k, CMT_n, and CMT_a, which use predicates $(K_1 \neq K_2)$, $(N_1 \neq N_2)$, and $(A_1 \neq A_2)$, respectively. The first notion is equivalent to CMT-1; the latter two are new. All of them are orthogonal to each other and a scheme that meets all three simultaneously achieves CMT-3. We say these notions are *permissive* because the predicates used do not make any demands on other components of the context. In contrast, *restrictive* variants, which we denote via CMT_k^*, CMT_n^*, CMT_a^*, require equality for other context components. For example the first uses predicate $(K_1 \neq K_2) \wedge ((N_1, A_1) = (N_2, A_2))$. These capture the types of restrictions faced in real attacks mentioned above.

Breaking the Original SIV. While prior work has shown (in our terminology) CMT_k^* attacks for GCM [16,24], GCM-SIV [29,35], ChaCha20/Poly1305 [24, 29], XChaCha20/Poly1305 [29], and OCB3 [2], an open question of practical interest [36] is whether there also exists a CMT_k^* attack against Synthetic IV (SIV) mode [33]. We resolve this open question, showing an attack that works in time about 2^{53}. It requires new techniques compared to prior attacks.

SIV combines a PRF F with CTR mode encryption, encrypting by first computing a tag $T = F_K(N, A, M)$ and then applying CTR mode encryption to M, using T as the (synthetic) IV and a second key K'. The tag and CTR mode output are, together, the ciphertext. Decryption recovers the message and then recomputes the tag, rejecting the ciphertext if it does not match. Schmieg [35] and Len, Grubbs, and Ristenpart (LGR) [29] showed that when F is a universal hash-based PRF, in particular GHASH for AES-GCM-SIV, one can achieve a fast CMT_k^* attack.

Scheme	CDY$^*_a$	CDY$^*_n$	CMT$^*_a$	CMT$^*_k$	CMT$_k$	CMT − 3
GCM [19]	★✗ §4	★✗ §4	★✗ §E	☆✗ [16, 24]	☆✗ [16, 24]	☆✗ [16, 24]
SIV [34]	★✗ §4			★✗ §5	★✗ ⟫	★✗ ⟫
CCM [17]	★✗ §4				★✗ ⟫	★✗ ⟫
EAX [11]	★✗ §4	★✗ §4			★✗ ⟫	★✗ ⟫
OCB3 [28]	★✗ §4			☆✗ [2]	☆✗ [2]	☆✗ [2]
PaddingZeros	★✓ ⟫	★✓ ⟫	★✗ §E	☆✓ [2]	☆✓ [5]	★✗ ⟫
KeyHashing	★✓ ⟫	★✓ ⟫	★✗ §E	☆✓ [2]	☆✓ [2]	★✗ ⟫
CAU-C1 [5]	★✓ ⟫	★✓ ⟫		☆✓ [5]	☆✓ [5]	★✗ ⟫

Fig. 1. Summary of context discovery and commitment attacks against a variety of popular AEAD schemes. Symbol ✓ indicates a proof that any attack will take at least 2^{64} time, while symbol ✗ indicates the existence of an attack that takes less than 2^{64} time; symbol ★ indicates results new to this paper and ☆ indicates prior work (citation given). CMT$_k$ and CMT − 3 are from Bellare and Hoang [5], where CMT$_k$ was called CMT-1. The notions CDY$^*_a$, CDY$^*_n$, CMT$^*_a$ and CMT$^*_k$ are introduced in this paper, and are implied by CMT$_k$. Symbol ⟫ indicates that the result is implied from one of the other columns by a reduction shown in this paper. §E indicates Appendix E in the full version.

Their attack does not extend to other versions of SIV, perhaps most notably the original version that uses for F the S2V[CMAC] PRF [33]. This version has been standardized [25] and is available in popular libraries like Tink [3]. For brevity here we describe the simpler case where F is just CMAC; the body will expand on the details. At first it might seem that CMAC's well-known lack of collision resistance (for adversarially-chosen keys), should extend to allow a simple CMT$^*_k$ attack: find K_1, K_2 such that $T = \mathsf{CMAC}_{K_1}(N, A, M) = \mathsf{CMAC}_{K_2}(N, A, M')$ for $M \neq M'$. But the problem is that we need M, M' to also satisfy that

$$M \oplus \mathsf{CTR}_{K'_1}(T) = M' \oplus \mathsf{CTR}_{K'_2}(T) \tag{1}$$

where $\mathsf{CTR}_K(T)$ denotes running counter mode with initialization vector T and block cipher key K. When using a GHASH-based PRF, the second equality condition "plays well" with the algebraic structure of the first condition, making it computationally easy to satisfy both simultaneously. But, here that does not work.

The core enabler for our attack is that we can recast the primary collision finding goal as a generalized birthday bound attack. For block-aligned messages, we show how the two constraints above can be rewritten as a single equation that is the xor-sum of four terms, each taking values over $\{0, 1\}^n$. Were the terms independently and uniformly random, one would immediately have an instance of a 4-sum problem, which can be solved using Wagner's k-tree algorithm [38] in time $\mathcal{O}(2^{n/3})$. But our terms are neither independent nor uniformly random. Nevertheless, our main technical lemma shows that, in the ideal cipher model, the underlying block cipher and the structure of the terms (which are dictated by the details of CMAC-SIV) allows us to analyze the distribution of these terms and show that we can still apply the k-tree algorithm and achieve the same running time. This technique of applying the k-tree algorithm to biased values may be of independent interest.

Putting it all together we achieve a CMT_k^* attack against S2V[CMAC]-SIV that works in time about 2^{53}, making it practical and sufficiently damaging to rule out SIV as suitable for contexts where context commitment matters.

Context Discoverability. Next we introduce a new type of security notion for AEAD. The cryptographic hashing community has long realized the significance of definitions for both collision resistance and preimage resistance [13], the latter of which, roughly speaking, refers to the ability of an attacker to find some input that maps to a target output. In analyzing CMT_k security for schemes, we realized that in many cases we can give very strong attacks that, given any ciphertext, can find a context that decrypts it—a sort of preimage attack against AEAD. To avoid confusion, we refer to this new security goal for AEAD as *context discoverability (CDY)*, as the adversary is tasked with efficiently computing ("discovering") a suitable context for some target ciphertext.

While we have not seen real attacks that exploit context discoverability, since CDY is to CMT what preimage resistance is to collision resistance, we believe that they are inevitable. We therefore view it beneficial to get ahead of the curve and analyze the CDY security before concrete attacks surface.

We formalize a family of CDY definitions similarly to our treatment for CMT. Our $CDY[\Sigma]$ notion is parameterized by a setting $\Sigma = (ts, S)$ that specifies a target specifier ts and a context selector S. Like for $CMT[\Sigma]$, ts and S specify the parts of the context that the attacker can choose and which parts are chosen by the game and either hidden or revealed to the attacker. Unlike CMT, however, the attacker is always given a target ciphertext and needs to only produce one valid decrypting context.

Similar to CMT_k^*, CMT_n^*, CMT_a^*, we define the notions CDY_k^*, CDY_n^*, CDY_a^*. The notion CDY_k^* captures the setting where an adversary is given arbitrary ciphertext C, nonce N, and associated data A, and must produce a key K such that C decrypts under (K, N, A). Similarly, CDY_n^* and CDY_a^* require the adversary to provide a nonce and associated data, respectively, given the other components chosen arbitrarily. These model restricted attack settings where parts of the context are not in the adversary's control.

We also define $CDY^*[ts]$ which generalizes this intuition to any target specifier ts. For example, in $CDY^*[ts = \{n\}]$ the adversary is given arbitrary ciphertext and nonce N, and must produce a key K and associated data A such that the ciphertext decrypts under (K, N, A).

We next analyze the relations between these sets of notions. In particular, we show that if an AEAD scheme is "context compressing"—ciphertexts are decryptable under more than one context—then CMT-3 security implies CDY^*. This is analogous to collision resistance implying preimage resistance, though the details are different. Further, we observe that almost all deployed AEAD schemes are context compressing since they "compress" the nonce and associated data into a shorter tag. This allows us to focus on finding $CDY^*[\Sigma]$ attacks for AEAD

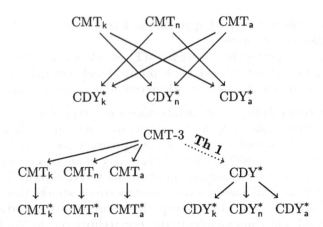

Fig. 2. (Top) Selected relationships between permissive CMT notions and restrictive CDY notions. Solid arrows represent implications. **(Bottom)** Selected relationships between CMT-3 and the notions we introduce in this paper. Solid arrows represent implications. The dotted arrow from CMT-3 to CDY^* holds assuming "context compression" as defined in Theorem 1.

schemes to show that these schemes also do not meet $CMT[\Sigma]$ security. Selected relationships are shown in Fig. 2.

This opens up a new landscape of analysis, which we explore. We characterize a large class of AEAD schemes that use non-preimage resistant MACs and, based on this weakness, we can develop fast CDY_a^* attacks. The set includes CCM, EAX, SIV, GCM, and OCB3. For EAX and CCM, this represents the first attacks of any kind for committing security. For EAX and GCM, we are also able to give CDY_n^* attacks, which is perhaps even more surprising a priori, given that an adversary in this case only controls the nonce.

All this sheds light on the deficiencies of several popular design paradigms for AEAD, when viewed from the perspective of context commitment security. These definitions also allow us to precisely communicate attacks and threat models. For example, CDY might suffice for some applications while others might want the more computationally expensive CMT security.

Revisiting Commitment-Enhancing Mechanisms. Finally, in Appendix E in the full version we use this new framework to analyze proposed mechanisms for commitment security. First, we look at the folklore padding zeros transform which prefixes zeroes to a message before encrypting and verifies the existence of these zeroes at decryption. This transform was recommended in an early OPAQUE draft specification [27, §3.1.1] and was shown by Albertini et al. [2, §5.3] to achieve FROB security and by Bellare and Hoang [5] to achieve CMT-1 security. We show that this transform does not achieve our CMT_a^* notion (and thus CMT-3) for all AEAD schemes, ruling it out as a candidate commitment security transform. We then make similar observations about the CommitKey transform which appends to the ciphertext a hash commitment to the key and the nonce. Finally, we conclude by considering the practical key commitment security of the recent CAU-C1 scheme from BH [5]. While a naive adaptation of DGRW's [16] "invisible salamanders" attack to this scheme takes about 2^{81} time, we show a more optimized attack which takes a little more than 2^{64} time, showing that 64-bit key-committing security does not preclude practical attacks.

Next Steps and Open Problems. Our results resolve a number of open problems about AEAD commitment security, and overall highlight the value of new definitional frameworks that surface different avenues for attack. That said, we leave several open problems, such as whether different flavors of context discovery or commitment attacks can be found against popular schemes—the blank entries in Fig. 1. Our attack techniques do not seem to work against these schemes, but whether positive security results can be shown is unclear.

2 Background

Notation. We refer to elements of $\{0,1\}^*$ as *bitstrings*, denote the length of a bitstring x by $|x|$ and the left-most (i.e., "most-significant") bit by $\mathsf{msb}(x)$. Given two bitstrings x and y, we denote their concatenation by $x \parallel y$, their bitwise xor by $x \oplus y$, and their bitwise and by $x \& y$. Given a number n, we denote its m-bit encoding as $\mathsf{encode}_m(n)$. For a finite set X, we use $x \leftarrow_{\$} X$ to denote sampling a uniform, random element from X and assigning it to x.

Sometimes, we operate in the finite field $\mathrm{GF}(2^n)$ with 2^n elements. This field is defined using an irreducible polynomial $f(\alpha)$ in $\mathrm{GF}(2)[\alpha]$ of degree n. The elements of the field are polynomials $x_0 + x_1\alpha + x_2\alpha^2 + \cdots + x_{n-1}\alpha^{n-1}$ of degree $n-1$ with binary coefficients $x_i \in \mathrm{GF}(2)$. These polynomials can be represented by the n-bit string $x_0 x_1 \cdots x_{n-1}$ of their coefficients. Both addition and subtraction of two n-bit strings, denoted $x+y$ and $x-y$, respectively, is their bitwise xor $x \oplus y$. Multiplication of two n-bit strings, denoted $x \cdot y$, corresponds to the multiplication of the corresponding polynomials x and y followed by modular reduction with the irreducible polynomial $f(\alpha)$.

Probability. An n-*bit random variable* X is one whose value is probabilistically assigned, defined by *probability mass function* $p_X(x) := \Pr[X = x]$. The n-*bit uniform random variable* U is the random variable with the probability mass function $p_U(x) = \frac{1}{2^n}$ for all $x \in \{0,1\}^n$. Given two n-bit random variables X and Y, we define the *total variation distance* between them as

$$\Delta(X, Y) := \max_{i \in \{0,1\}^n} \big| \Pr(X = i) - \Pr(Y = i) \big|.$$

A *random function* F from n-bit strings to m-bit strings is a collection $\{X_i : i \in \{0,1\}^n\}$ of m-bit random variables X_i, one for each n-bit input, such that for all $i \in \{0,1\}^n$, $F(i) := X_i$. A random function F from n-bit strings to m-bit strings is *uniformly random* if, for all $i \in \{0,1\}^n$, $F(i)$ is the m-bit uniform random variable. We say that two random functions F_1 and F_2 from n-bit strings to

m-bit strings are *independent* if, for all $i \in \{0,1\}^n$ and for all $j \in \{0,1\}^n$, $F_1(i)$ and $F_2(j)$ are independent m-bit random variables.

Code-Based Games. To formalize security experiments, we use the *code-based games* framework of Bellare and Rogaway [10]; with refinements from Ristenpart, Shacham, and Shrimpton [31]. A *procedure* P is a sequence of code-like statements that accepts some input and produces some output. We use superscripts like P^Q to denote that procedure P calls procedure Q. We use $(G \Rightarrow x)$ to denote the event that the procedure G outputs x, over the random coins of the procedure. Finally, given a game G and an adversary $\mathcal{A}$, we denote the *advantage* of $\mathcal{A}$ at G by $\mathbf{Adv}_G(\mathcal{A}) := \Pr[G(\mathcal{A}) \Rightarrow \text{true}]$.

Cost of Attacks. We represent cryptanalytic attacks by procedures and compute their cost using a *unit-cost RAM model*. Specifically, following [31], we use the convention that each pseudocode statement of a procedure runs in unit time. This lets us write the running time of a procedure as the maximum number of statements executed, with the maximum taken over all inputs of a given size. Similarly, we define the number of queries as the maximum number of queries executed over inputs of a given size. We recognize that this is a simplification of the real-world (e.g., see Wiener [39]), but for the attacks discussed in this paper, we nevertheless believe that it provides a good estimate.

Pseudorandom Functions. A *pseudorandom function (PRF)* is a function $\mathsf{F} : \mathcal{K} \times \mathcal{M} \to \mathcal{Y}$ defined over a key space $\mathcal{K} \subseteq \{0,1\}^*$, message space $\mathcal{M} \subseteq \{0,1\}^*$, and output space $\mathcal{Y} \subseteq \{0,1\}^*$, that is indistinguishable from a uniform random function. More formally, we define the PRF advantage of an adversary $\mathcal{A}$ as

$$\mathbf{Adv}_{\mathsf{F}}^{\mathrm{prf}}(\mathcal{A}) := \left| \Pr[K \leftarrow_{\$} \mathcal{K} : \mathcal{A}(\mathsf{F}(K, \cdot))] - \Pr[R \leftarrow_{\$} \mathrm{Func} : \mathcal{A}(R)] \right|,$$

and say that F is a PRF if this advantage is small for all adversaries $\mathcal{A}$ that run in a feasible amount of time.

Hash Functions. A *hash function* is a function $\mathsf{H} : \mathcal{K} \times \mathcal{M} \to \mathcal{Y}$, defined over a key space $\mathcal{K} \subseteq \{0,1\}^*$, message space $\mathcal{M} \subseteq \{0,1\}^*$, and hash space $\mathcal{Y} \subseteq \{0,1\}^*$. We define the collision-resistance advantage of adversary $\mathcal{A}$ for H as

$$\mathbf{Adv}_{\mathsf{H}}^{\mathrm{coll}}(\mathcal{A}) := \Pr\big[K \leftarrow_{\$} \mathcal{K}, (M_1, M_2) \leftarrow_{\$} \mathcal{A}(K) :$$
$$(M_1 \neq M_2) \text{ and } (\mathsf{H}(K, M_1) = \mathsf{H}(K, M_2))\big].$$

Block Ciphers and the Ideal Cipher Model. An n-bit *block cipher*, or a block cipher with *block length* n bits, is a function $E : \{0,1\}^n \times \{0,1\}^n \to \{0,1\}^n$, where for each key $k \in \{0,1\}^n$, $E(k, \cdot)$ is a permutation on $\{0,1\}^n$. Since it is a permutation, it has an inverse which we denote by $E^{-1}(k, \cdot)$. To simplify notation, we sometimes use the shorthands $E_k(\cdot) := E(k, \cdot)$ and $E_k^{-1}(\cdot) := E^{-1}(k, \cdot)$.

An n-bit *ideal block cipher* [26] is a random map $E : \{0,1\}^n \times \{0,1\}^n \to \{0,1\}^n$, such that for each key $k \in \{0,1\}^n$, $E_k(\cdot)$ is a permutation on $\{0,1\}^n$. Alternatively, we can think of an ideal block cipher as one where for each key

$k \in \{0,1\}^n$, $E_k(\cdot)$ is uniformly, randomly sampled from the set of permutations on n-bits.

Authenticated Encryption Schemes. An *AEAD scheme* is a triple of algorithms $\mathsf{AEAD} = (\mathsf{Kg}, \mathsf{Enc}, \mathsf{Dec})$, defined over a key space $\mathcal{K} \subseteq \{0,1\}^*$, nonce space $\mathcal{N} \subseteq \{0,1\}^*$, associated data space $\mathcal{A} \subseteq \{0,1\}^*$, message space $\mathcal{M} \subseteq \{0,1\}^*$, and ciphertext space $\mathcal{C} \subseteq \{0,1\}^*$.

1. $\mathsf{Kg} : \varnothing \to \mathcal{K}$ is a randomized algorithm that takes no input and returns a fresh secret key K.
2. $\mathsf{Enc} : (\mathcal{K} \times \mathcal{N} \times \mathcal{A} \times \mathcal{M}) \to (\mathcal{C} \cup \{\bot\})$ is a deterministic algorithm that takes a 4-tuple of a key K, nonce N, associated data A, and message M and returns a ciphertext C or an error (denoted by $\bot$).
3. $\mathsf{Dec} : (\mathcal{K} \times \mathcal{N} \times \mathcal{A} \times \mathcal{C}) \to (\mathcal{M} \cup \{\bot\})$ is a deterministic algorithm that takes a 4-tuple of a key K, nonce N, associated data A, and ciphertext C and returns a plaintext M or an error (denoted by $\bot$).

We call the non-message inputs to Enc—the key, nonce, and associated data—the *encryption context* and the non-ciphertext inputs to Dec—the key, nonce, and associated data—the *decryption context*. And, for a given message, say that an encryption context is *valid* if Enc succeeds (i.e., does not output $\bot$). Similarly, for a given ciphertext, say that a decryption context is *valid* if Dec succeeds (i.e., does not output $\bot$).

For traditional AEAD correctness, we need Enc to be the inverse of Dec. In other words, for any 4-tuple $(K, N, A, M) \in \mathcal{K} \times \mathcal{N} \times \mathcal{A} \times \mathcal{M}$, it holds that

$$\mathsf{Dec}(K, N, A, \mathsf{Enc}(K, N, A, M)) = M .$$

In addition, we impose *tidyness* [30], *ciphertext validity*, and *length uniformity* assumptions. Tidyness requires that for any 4-tuple $(K, N, A, C) \in \mathcal{K} \times \mathcal{N} \times \mathcal{A} \times \mathcal{C}$, it holds that

$$\mathsf{Dec}(K, N, A, C) = M \neq \bot \implies \mathsf{Enc}(K, N, A, M) = C .$$

Ciphertext validity requires that for every ciphertext $C \in \mathcal{C}$ there exists at least one valid decryption context $(K, N, A) \in \mathcal{K} \times \mathcal{N} \times \mathcal{A}$; that is $\mathsf{Dec}(K, N, A, C) \neq \bot$. Length uniformity requires that the length of a ciphertext depends only on the length of the message and length of the associated data.

Finally, for AEAD security, we use the traditional *privacy* and *authenticity* definitions [32, §3].

Committing Authenticated Encryption. A number of prior notions for committing AEAD have been proposed. In Fig. 3 we provide the CMT-1 and CMT-3 games from Bellare and Hoang [5]. The FROB game from Farshim, Orlandi, and Rosie [22] adapted to the AEAD setting by Grubbs, Lu, and Ristenpart [24], is the same except that the final highlighted predicate is changed to "$K_1 = K_2$ or $N_1 \neq N_2$". The FROB game asks the adversary to produce a ciphertext that decrypts under two different keys with the same nonce. The CMT-1 game is more

CMT − 1($\mathcal{A}$):	CMT − 3($\mathcal{A}$):
$((K_1, N_1, A_1), (K_2, N_2, A_2), C) \leftarrow\!\!\$ \mathcal{A}$	$((K_1, N_1, A_1), (K_2, N_2, A_2), C) \leftarrow\!\!\$ \mathcal{A}$
$M_1 \leftarrow \mathsf{AEAD.Dec}(K_1, N_1, A_1, C)$	$M_1 \leftarrow \mathsf{AEAD.Dec}(K_1, N_1, A_1, C)$
$M_2 \leftarrow \mathsf{AEAD.Dec}(K_2, N_2, A_2, C)$	$M_2 \leftarrow \mathsf{AEAD.Dec}(K_2, N_2, A_2, C)$
// decryption success	// decryption success
If $M_1 = \perp$ or $M_2 = \perp$	If $M_1 = \perp$ or $M_2 = \perp$
Return false	Return false
// commitment condition	// commitment condition
If $K_1 = K_2$	If $(K_1, N_1, A_1) = (K_2, N_2, A_2)$
Return false	Return false
Return true	Return true

Fig. 3. (**Left**) The CMT-1 game [5]. (**Right**) The CMT-3 game [5]. The differences are highlighted.

permissive and removes the condition that the nonce be the same. The CMT-3 game is even more permissive and relaxes the different key condition to different keys, nonces, or associated data. Bellare and Hoang [5] show that CMT-3 implies CMT-1, which implies FROB. We will expand on these definitions with a more general framework next.

3   Granular Committing Encryption Definitions

We provide a more general framework for defining commitment security for encryption. As motivation, we observe that while the CMT-1 and the stronger CMT-3 notions provide good security goals for constructions, they do not precisely capture the *way* in which attacks violate security—which parts of the decryption context does the attacker need to control, which parts have been pre-selected by some other party, and which parts are known to the attacker.

These considerations are crucial for determining the exploitability of commitment vulnerabilities in practice. For instance, the vulnerability in Facebook attachment franking [20] exploited by Dodis et al. [16, §3] only works if the nonces are the same; and the key rotation attack described by Albertini et al. [2] only works with keys previously imported to the key management service. And, looking ahead, we propose a variant of the Subscribe with Google attack described by Albertini et al. [2] in which a malicious publisher provides a full decryption context only knowing the honestly published ciphertext.

We provide a more general framework for commitment security notions that more precisely captures attack settings. As we will see in subsequent sections, our definitions provide a clearer explanatory framework for vulnerabilities.

Committing Security Framework. We find it useful to expand the set of security notions to more granularly capture the ways in which the two decryption contexts are selected that generalizes context commitment security. In Fig. 4 we detail the CMT[Σ] game, parameterized by a *setting* $\Sigma = (\mathsf{ts}, \mathsf{S}, \mathsf{P})$ that specifies a *target specifier* ts, a *context selector* S, and a *predicate* P (to be defined next.) The adversary helps compute a ciphertext and two decryption contexts

CMT[ts, S, P]($\mathcal{A}$):

$\mathrm{cat}_c \leftarrow_\$ S$
$\mathrm{cat}_a \leftarrow_\$ \mathcal{A}(\mathsf{Reveal}_{ts}(\mathrm{cat}_c))$
$\mathrm{cat} \leftarrow \mathsf{Merge}_{ts}(\mathrm{cat}_c, \mathrm{cat}_a)$
If $\mathrm{cat} = \bot$:
   Return false
$(C, (K_1, N_1, A_1), (K_2, N_2, A_2)) \leftarrow \mathrm{cat}$
$M_1 \leftarrow \mathsf{AEAD.Dec}(K_1, N_1, A_1, C)$
$M_2 \leftarrow \mathsf{AEAD.Dec}(K_2, N_2, A_2, C)$
If $M_1 = \bot$ or $M_2 = \bot$:
   Return false
Return $\mathsf{P}((K_1, N_1, A_1), (K_2, N_2, A_2))$

Notion	Predicate P
$\mathrm{CMT_k}$	$(K_1 \neq K_2)$
$\mathrm{CMT_n}$	$(N_1 \neq N_2)$
$\mathrm{CMT_a}$	$(A_1 \neq A_2)$
$\mathrm{CMT_k^*}$	$(K_1 \neq K_2) \wedge (N_1, A_1) = (N_2, A_2)$
$\mathrm{CMT_n^*}$	$(N_1 \neq N_2) \wedge (K_1, A_1) = (K_2, A_2)$
$\mathrm{CMT_a^*}$	$(A_1 \neq A_2) \wedge (K_1, N_1) = (K_2, N_2)$

Fig. 4. (Left) The $\mathrm{CMT}[\Sigma]$ commitment security game, parameterized by $\Sigma = (\mathsf{ts}, \mathsf{S}, \mathsf{P})$, a target selector ts, context selector S, and predicate P. **(Right)** Predicates for the permissive notions $\mathrm{CMT_k}$, $\mathrm{CMT_n}$, $\mathrm{CMT_a}$ and restrictive notions $\mathrm{CMT_k^*}$, $\mathrm{CMT_n^*}$, $\mathrm{CMT_a^*}$, where $\mathsf{ts} = \varnothing$.

$(C, (K_1, N_1, A_1), (K_2, N_2, A_2))$, what we call a *commitment attack instance (cat)*. The adversary wins if C decrypts under both decryption contexts, and the two decryption contexts satisfy the predicate P. The parameterization allows attack settings in terms of which portions of the commitment attack instance are attacker controlled versus chosen in some other way, and which of the latter are revealed to the attacker.

We now provide more details. A commitment attack instance is a tuple $(C, (K_1, N_1, A_1), (K_2, N_2, A_2))$ consisting of a ciphertext $C \in \mathcal{C}$; two keys $K_1, K_2 \in \mathcal{K}$; two nonces $N_1, N_2 \in \mathcal{N}$; and two associated data $A_1, A_2 \in \mathcal{A}$. A target specifier ts is a subset of labels $\{\mathsf{C}, \mathsf{k_1}, \mathsf{n_1}, \mathsf{a_1}, \mathsf{k_2}, \mathsf{n_2}, \mathsf{a_2}\} \times \{\cdot, \hat{\cdot}\}$. The left set labels the components of a commitment attack instance, called component labels, and the right set denotes whether the specified component is revealed to the adversary (no hat means revealed and hat means not revealed.) For example, $\mathsf{ts} = \{\mathsf{k_1}, \hat{\mathsf{k_2}}\}$ indicates the K_1 and K_2 in the context, and that K_1 is revealed to the attacker.

A context selector S is a randomized algorithm that takes no input and produces the challenger-defined elements of a commitment attack instance, denoted cat_c, as specified by the target specifier ts. The reveal function Reveal_{ts} parameterized by ts, takes a subset of a commitment attack instance and reveals the components that ts tells it to reveal; i.e., the specified components with no hat. The merge function $\mathsf{Merge}_{ts}(\mathrm{cat}_c, \mathrm{cat}_a)$ parameterized by the target specifier ts, takes two subsets of commitment attack instances cat_c (challenger-defined elements) and cat_a (adversary-defined elements) and works as follows. First, it checks for every component specified by ts that cat_c has a corresponding value. Second, it checks that for every component specified by ts, if cat_a has a value, that it matches the value in cat_c. If either of these checks fail, it outputs $\bot$. Otherwise, it returns their union $\mathrm{cat}_c \cup \mathrm{cat}_a$. Finally, the predicate P takes two decryption contexts output by $\mathsf{Merge}_{ts}(\mathrm{cat}_c, \mathrm{cat}_a)$, and outputs true if they satisfy some criteria (e.g., that $K_1 \neq K_2$), and false otherwise.

We associate to a setting $\Sigma = (\mathsf{ts}, \mathsf{S}, \mathsf{P})$, AEAD Π, and adversary $\mathcal{A}$ the CMT advantage defined as

$$\mathbf{Adv}_{\Pi}^{\mathrm{CMT}[\Sigma]}(\mathcal{A}) := \Pr\left[\, \mathrm{CMT}[\Sigma](\mathcal{A}) \Rightarrow \mathsf{true} \,\right].$$

Taking a concrete security approach, we will track the running time used by $\mathcal{A}$ and provide explicit advantage functions. Adapting our notions to support asymptotic definitions of security is straightforward: in our discussions we will often say a scheme is $\mathrm{CMT}[\Sigma]$ secure as informal shorthand that no adversary can win the $\mathrm{CMT}[\Sigma]$ game with "good" probability using "reasonable" running time.

Capturing CMT-1, CMT-3, and More via Predicates. To understand our definitional framework further, we can start by seeing how to instantiate it to coincide with prior notions. Let $\mathsf{ts} = \varnothing$ indicate the empty target selector, meaning that $\mathcal{A}$ chooses the ciphertext and two decryption contexts fully. Then the set of Σ settings that use the empty target selector defines a family of security goals, indexed solely by predicates, which we denote by $\mathrm{CMT}[\mathsf{P}]$. This family includes CMT-1 by setting $\mathsf{P} := (K_1 \neq K_2)$ and CMT-3 by setting $\mathsf{P} := (K_1, N_1, A_1) \neq (K_2, N_2, A_2)$. Not all instances in this family are interesting: consider, for example, when P always outputs true or false. Nevertheless, the flexibility here allows for more granular specification of adversarial ability. For instance, the predicate that requires $(K_1 \neq K_2) \wedge (N_1 = N_2)$ captures a setting like that of the Dodis et al. [16] attack against Facebook's message franking, which requires that both decryption contexts have the same nonce.

Three games of particular interest are those with predicates that focus on inequality of the three individual context components: $(K_1 \neq K_2)$, $(N_1 \neq N_2)$, and $(A_1 \neq A_2)$. For notational brevity, we let game $\mathrm{CMT}_\mathsf{k} := \mathrm{CMT}[\mathsf{P} = (K_1 \neq K_2)]$ and similarly $\mathrm{CMT}_\mathsf{n} := \mathrm{CMT}[\mathsf{P} = (N_1 \neq N_2)]$ and $\mathrm{CMT}_\mathsf{a} := \mathrm{CMT}[\mathsf{P} = (A_1 \neq A_2)]$. Then CMT_k corresponds to CMT-1, but CMT_n and CMT_a are new. They are also orthogonal to CMT-1, in the sense that we can give schemes that achieve CMT-1 but not CMT_a nor CMT_n security (see Theorem 9 in the full version.) All three are, however, implied by being CMT-3 secure, and a scheme that simultaneously meets CMT_k, CMT_n, and CMT_a also enjoys CMT-3 security (see Lemmas 7 and 8 in the full version.)

Note that CMT_k, CMT_n, and CMT_a are *permissive*: as long as the relevant component is distinct across the two contexts, it does not matter whether the other components are distinct. Also, of interest are *restrictive* versions; for example, we can consider $\mathrm{CMT}_\mathsf{k}^* := \mathrm{CMT}[(K_1 \neq K_2) \wedge (N_1, A_1) = (N_2, A_2)]$ which requires that the nonces and associated data are the same. Similarly, we can define restrictive notions $\mathrm{CMT}_\mathsf{n}^*$ and $\mathrm{CMT}_\mathsf{a}^*$. Restrictive versions are useful as they correspond to attacks that have limited control over the decryption context. Interestingly, these restrictive notions are not equivalent to the corresponding permissive notions, nor does a scheme that simultaneously meets $\mathrm{CMT}_\mathsf{k}^*$, $\mathrm{CMT}_\mathsf{n}^*$, and $\mathrm{CMT}_\mathsf{a}^*$ achieve CMT-3 security (see Theorem 10 in the full version.)

Targeted Attacks. Returning to settings with target specifier ts $\neq \varnothing$, we can further increase the family of notions considered to capture situations where a portion of the context is pre-selected. For instance, in the key rotation example of Albertini et al. [2] mentioned earlier, we would have ts $= \{k_1, k_2\}$ and S $= \{K_1 \leftarrow^\$ \mathcal{K}; K_2 \leftarrow^\$ \mathcal{K}; \text{Return } (K_1, K_2)\}$ to indicate that the malicious sender has to use the two randomly generated keys.

However, not all targeted attack settings are interesting. For some target specifiers ts, we can specify a context selector S such that no adversary can achieve non-zero advantage. In particular, if we have ts $= \{C, k_1, n_1, a_1\}$ and have S pick ciphertext C and context (K_1, N_1, A_1) such that AEAD.Dec(K_1, N_1, A_1, C) returns $\bot$, then no adversary can win the game, making the associated security notion trivial (all schemes achieve it.)

Hiding Target Components. Finally, our game considers target specifiers ts that indicate that some values chosen by S should remain hidden from $\mathcal{A}$. For example, the Subscribe with Google attack described by Albertini et al. [2] can be reframed as a meddler-in-the-middle attack as follows. A publisher creates premium content M_1 and encrypts it using a context (K_1, N_1, A_1) to get a ciphertext C. The ciphertext C is published, but the context (K_1, N_1, A_1) is hidden. A malicious third-party, only looking at the ciphertext C, tries to construct a valid decryption context (K_2, N_2, A_2) and uses that to sell fake paywall bypasses. We can formalize this setting by having the target specifier ts $= \{C, \hat{k}_1, \hat{n}_1, \hat{a}_1\}$, with the context selector S as

$$K_1 \leftarrow^\$ \mathcal{K}; N_1 \leftarrow^\$ \mathcal{N}; A_1 \leftarrow^\$ \mathcal{A}; M_1 \leftarrow^\$ \mathcal{M};$$
$$\text{Return } (\text{AEAD.Enc}(K_1, N_1, A_1, M_1), K_1, N_1, A_1)$$

and with Reveal$_{ts}(C, K_1, N_1, A_1)$ outputting C.

Context Discoverability Security. Dodis et al [16, §5] and Albertini et al. [2, §3.3] have pointed out that traditional CMT games are analogous to collision-resistance for hash functions, in the sense that the goal is to find two different *encryption contexts* (K_1, N_1, A_1, M_1) and (K_2, N_2, A_2, M_2) such that they produce the same ciphertext C. Under this lens, CMT with targeting (and no hiding) is like second preimage resistance, and CMT with targeting and hiding is like preimage resistance. But, the analogy to preimage resistance is not perfect, since we are not asking for *any* preimage but rather one that is not the same as the original. Further, this restriction is unnecessary. Going back to the meddler-in-the-middle example above, it suffices for an on-path attacker to produce any valid context. Thus, we find it useful to define a new preimage resistance-inspired notion of commitment security.

In Fig. 5 we define the game CDY[ts, S], parameterized by a setting $\Sigma = (\text{ts}, \text{S})$ that specifies a target specifier ts and a context selector S. In more detail, a *discoverability attack instance (dat)* is a ciphertext and a decryption context $(C, (K, N, A))$. Here, a target specifier ts is a subset of $\{k, n, a\} \times \{\cdot, \hat{\cdot}\}$ and a context selector S is a randomized algorithm that takes no input and produces a ciphertext and the elements of a decryption context specified by the target specifier ts. The reveal function Reveal$_{ts}$ and the merge function Merge$_{ts}(\text{dat}_c, \text{dat}_a)$

CDY[ts, S]($\mathcal{A}$):	CDY[{k, n}, S]($\mathcal{A}$):	CDY[{k, a}, S]($\mathcal{A}$):
$\mathrm{dat}_c \leftarrow\!\!{\scriptstyle\$}\, \mathsf{S}$	$(C, K, N) \leftarrow\!\!{\scriptstyle\$}\, \mathsf{S}$	$(C, K, A) \leftarrow\!\!{\scriptstyle\$}\, \mathsf{S}$
$\mathrm{dat}_a \leftarrow\!\!{\scriptstyle\$}\, \mathcal{A}(\mathrm{Reveal}_{ts}(t))$	$A \leftarrow\!\!{\scriptstyle\$}\, \mathcal{A}(C, K, N)$	$N \leftarrow\!\!{\scriptstyle\$}\, \mathcal{A}(C, K, A)$
$\mathrm{dat} \leftarrow \mathrm{Merge}_{ts}(\mathrm{dat}_c, \mathrm{dat}_a)$	$M \leftarrow \mathsf{AEAD.Dec}(K, N, A, C)$	$M \leftarrow \mathsf{AEAD.Dec}(K, N, A, C)$
If $\mathrm{dat} = \perp$:	If $M = \perp$:	If $M = \perp$:
$\quad$ Return false	$\quad$ Return false	$\quad$ Return false
$(C, (K, N, A)) \leftarrow \mathrm{dat}$	Return true	Return true
$M \leftarrow \mathsf{AEAD.Dec}(K, N, A, C)$		
If $M = \perp$:		
$\quad$ Return false		
Return true		

Fig. 5. **(Left)** The CDY[ts, S] commitment security game, parameterized by a target specifier ts and a context selector S. **(Middle)** The variant of CDY[Σ] used in the definition of CDY$_\mathsf{a}^*$. **(Right)** The variant of CDY[Σ] used in the definition of CDY$_\mathsf{n}^*$.

work similarly to their CMT counterparts. Finally, the goal of the adversary is to produce *one* valid decryption context for the target ciphertext.

We associate to a setting $\Sigma = (\mathsf{ts}, \mathsf{S})$, AEAD scheme Π, and adversary $\mathcal{A}$ the CDY advantage defined as

$$\mathbf{Adv}_\Pi^{\mathrm{CDY}[\Sigma]}(\mathcal{A}) = \Pr\left[\,\mathrm{CDY}[\Sigma](\mathcal{A}) \Rightarrow \mathsf{true}\,\right].$$

Restricted CDY and Its Variants. To more accurately capture attack settings and to prove relations, we find it useful to define restricted variants of the CDY[Σ] game. A class of games of particular interest are ones that allow targeting under *any* context selector; we call this class *restricted CDY*. For a target specifier ts, let CDY*[ts] be the game where the adversary is given a ciphertext and elements of a decryption context specified by ts, all selected arbitrarily, and needs to produce the remaining elements of a decryption context such that $\mathsf{AEAD.Dec}(K, N, A, C) \neq \perp$. Formally, for an AEAD scheme Π and adversary $\mathcal{A}$, we define the CDY* advantage as

$$\mathbf{Adv}_\Pi^{\mathrm{CDY}^*[\mathsf{ts}]}(\mathcal{A}) = \Pr\left[\,\text{for all S}, \mathrm{CDY}[\mathsf{ts}, \mathsf{S}](\mathcal{A}) \Rightarrow \mathsf{true}\,\right].$$

In addition, we find it useful to define three specific variants of CDY* that allow targeting two-of-three components of a decryption context. Let CDY$_\mathsf{a}^*$ be the game where the adversary is given an arbitrary ciphertext C, key K, and nonce N, and has to produce associated data A such that $\mathsf{AEAD.Dec}(K, N, A, C) \neq \perp$. Formally, for an AEAD scheme Π and adversary $\mathcal{A}$, we define the CDY$_\mathsf{a}^*$ advantage as

$$\mathbf{Adv}_\Pi^{\mathrm{CDY}_\mathsf{a}^*}(\mathcal{A}) = \Pr\left[\,\text{for all S}, \mathrm{CDY}[\{k, n\}, \mathsf{S}](\mathcal{A}) \Rightarrow \mathsf{true}\,\right].$$

The CDY$_\mathsf{k}^*$ and CDY$_\mathsf{n}^*$ games are defined similarly where the adversary has to produce a valid key and nonce respectively such that decryption succeeds when the remaining inputs to decryption are pre-selected. Formally, for an AEAD scheme Π and adversary $\mathcal{A}$, we define the CDY_k^* and CDY_n^* advantage as

$$\mathbf{Adv}_{\Pi}^{\mathrm{CDY}_k^*}(\mathcal{A}) = \Pr\left[\text{ for all } \mathsf{S}, \mathrm{CDY}[\{n, a\}, \mathsf{S}](\mathcal{A}) \Rightarrow \text{true}\right],$$
$$\mathbf{Adv}_{\Pi}^{\mathrm{CDY}_n^*}(\mathcal{A}) = \Pr\left[\text{ for all } \mathsf{S}, \mathrm{CDY}[\{k, a\}, \mathsf{S}](\mathcal{A}) \Rightarrow \text{true}\right].$$

Note that the context selector can only select *valid* ciphertexts, which sidesteps issues with formatting. Without this constraint, a context selector could select a ciphertext that has invalid padding for a scheme that requires valid padding, thereby making the notion trivial (all schemes achieve it.)

Furthermore, specific variants like CDY_a^* may be trivial even with this constraint. For instance, if the ciphertext embeds the nonce, then one can pick some key K, some ciphertext C embedding some nonce N_1, some other nonce N_2, then no CDY_a^* adversary can pick associated data A such that C decrypts correctly under (K, N_2, A). However, in the context of this restricted CDY notion, we think this is desired behavior and delegate capturing nuances like this to the unrestricted CDY notion (which can capture this by restricting to context selectors which ensure that the nonce embedded is the same as the nonce provided.)

With Context Compression, CMT-3 Implies Restricted CDY. A $\mathrm{CDY}[\Sigma]$ attack does not always imply a $\mathrm{CMT}[\Sigma]$ attack. Consider, for example, the "identity" AEAD that has $\mathsf{Enc}(K, N, A, M) \Rightarrow k \parallel n \parallel a \parallel m$ which has an immediate $\mathrm{CDY}[\Sigma]$ attack but is $\mathrm{CMT}[\Sigma]$ secure since a ciphertext can only be decrypted under one context.[2] However, continuing with the hash function analogy, we wonder if a "compression" assumption could make this implication hold. In Theorem 1 we show this statement for $\mathrm{CDY}^*[\mathsf{ts} = \varnothing]$ and $\mathrm{CMT} - 3$. And note that this generalizes to $\mathrm{CDY}^*[\mathsf{ts}]$ for any ts with an appropriate compression assumption. Notably, it holds for CDY_a^* if we assume compression over associated data rather than the full context.

Theorem 1. *Fix some AEAD Π. Then for any adversary $\mathcal{A}$ that wins the $\mathrm{CDY}^*[\mathsf{ts} = \varnothing]$ game, we can give an adversary $\mathcal{B}$ such that*

$$\mathbf{Adv}_{\Pi}^{\mathrm{CDY}^*[\mathsf{ts}=\varnothing]}(\mathcal{A}) \leq 2 \cdot \mathbf{Adv}_{\Pi}^{\mathrm{CMT}-3}(\mathcal{B}) + \mathrm{ProbBadCtx}_{\Pi}, \qquad (2)$$

where $\mathrm{ProbBadCtx}_{\Pi}$ is the probability that a random decryption context, when used for encrypting a random message, is the only valid decryption context for the resulting ciphertext.

Proof. This proof is adapted from Bellare and Rogaway [9, p.147], where they prove a similar theorem for hash functions. We construct an adversary $\mathcal{B}$ that randomly samples a context (K_1, N_1, A_1), encrypts a random message to get a ciphertext C, then asks the CDY adversary $\mathcal{A}$ to produce a decryption context for C to get (K_2, N_2, A_2). This ciphertext generation can be viewed as a valid

---

[2] While the "identity" AEAD is not secure in the sense of privacy [32, §3], one can construct a secure counterexample by using a wide pseudorandom permutation [7].

B:	S:
$K_1 \leftarrow\$ \mathcal{K}$; $N_1 \leftarrow\$ \mathcal{N}$; $A_1 \leftarrow\$ \mathcal{A}$	$K_1 \leftarrow\$ \mathcal{K}$; $N_1 \leftarrow\$ \mathcal{N}$; $A_1 \leftarrow\$ \mathcal{A}$
$M_1 \leftarrow\$ \mathcal{M}$	$M_1 \leftarrow\$ \mathcal{M}$
$\mathrm{ctx}_1 \leftarrow (K_1, N_1, A_1)$	$C \leftarrow \Pi.\mathrm{Enc}(K_1, N_1, A_1, M_1)$
$C \leftarrow \Pi.\mathrm{Enc}(K_1, N_1, A_1, M_1)$	Return C
$\mathrm{ctx}_2 \leftarrow\$ \mathcal{A}(C)$	
If $\mathrm{ctx}_2 = \bot$:	
$\quad$ Return $\bot$	
$(K_1, N_2, A_2) \leftarrow \mathrm{ctx}_2$	
If $(K_1, N_1, A_1) = (K_2, N_2, A_2)$	
$\quad$ Return $\bot$	
Return $(C, (K_1, N_1, A_1), (K_2, N_2, A_2))$	

Fig. 6. Pseudocode for the CMT $-$ 3 adversary $\mathcal{B}$ and CDY* context selector S, used in proof of Theorem 1.

CDY context selector S so $\mathcal{B}$ wins if the returned context is different from the one it sampled; i.e., $(K_1, N_1, A_1) \neq (K_2, N_2, A_2)$. The pseudocode for $\mathcal{B}$ and S is given in Fig. 6 and the success probability is analyzed below.

Per the above discussion the advantage of $\mathcal{B}$ is

$$\mathbf{Adv}_\Pi^{\mathrm{CMT}-3}(\mathcal{B}) = \Pr[(\mathcal{A}(C) \neq \bot) \wedge (\mathrm{ctx}_1 \neq \mathrm{ctx}_2)], \tag{3}$$

where without loss of generality, we are assuming that $\mathcal{A}$ always produces a valid context or fails and produces $\bot$. But, before simplifying this equation, we need to define some terminology. First, let us define the set of valid decryption contexts for a ciphertext as

$$\Gamma(C) := \{(K, N, A) : (\Pi.\mathrm{Dec}(K, N, A, C) \neq \bot)\}.$$

Now, for a given message M, let us also define the set of "bad" decryption contexts which when used for encrypting M, remain the only valid decryption context for the resulting ciphertext

$$\mathrm{BadCtxs}(M) := \{(K, N, A) : |\Gamma(\Pi.\mathrm{Enc}(K, N, A, M))| = 1\}.$$

Finally, let us define the probability that a random decryption context is bad

$$\mathrm{ProbBadCtx}_\Pi := \Pr[(K, N, A) \in \mathrm{BadCtxs}(M)],$$

over the choice $(K, N, A, M) \leftarrow\$ (\mathcal{K} \times \mathcal{N} \times \mathcal{A} \times \mathcal{M})$. Using this notation we can rewrite Eq. 3, where the probabilities are over the choice $(K, N, A, M) \leftarrow\$ (\mathcal{K} \times \mathcal{N} \times \mathcal{A} \times \mathcal{M})$, as

$$\mathbf{Adv}_\Pi^{\mathrm{CMT}-3}(\mathcal{B}) = \Pr[(\mathcal{A}(C) \neq \bot) \wedge (\mathrm{ctx}_1 \neq \mathrm{ctx}_2)]$$
$$\geq \Pr[(\mathcal{A}(C) \neq \bot) \wedge (\mathrm{ctx}_1 \neq \mathrm{ctx}_2) \wedge (\mathrm{ctx}_1 \notin \mathrm{BadCtxs}(M))].$$

Using conditional probability, we can rewrite this term as

$$\Pr[\mathrm{ctx}_1 \neq \mathrm{ctx}_2 \mid (\mathcal{A}(C) \neq \bot) \wedge (\mathrm{ctx}_1 \notin \mathrm{BadCtxs}(m))]$$
$$\cdot \Pr[(\mathcal{A}(C) \neq \bot) \wedge (\mathrm{ctx}_1 \notin \mathrm{BadCtxs}(m))].$$

$\mathcal{B}$:	S:
$K_1 \leftarrow_\$ \mathcal{K};\ N_1 \leftarrow_\$ \mathcal{N};\ A_1 \leftarrow_\$ \mathcal{A}$	$K_1 \leftarrow_\$ \mathcal{K};\ N_1 \leftarrow_\$ \mathcal{N};\ A_1 \leftarrow_\$ \mathcal{A}$
$M_1 \leftarrow_\$ \mathcal{M}$	$M_1 \leftarrow_\$ \mathcal{M}$
$C \leftarrow \Pi.\mathsf{Enc}(K_1, N_1, A_1, M_1)$	$C \leftarrow \Pi.\mathsf{Enc}(K_1, N_1, A_1, M_1)$
$K_2 \leftarrow K_1 + 1;\ N_2 \leftarrow N_1 + 1$	$K_2 \leftarrow K_1 + 1;\ N_2 \leftarrow N_1 + 1$
$A_2 \leftarrow_\$ \mathcal{A}(C, K_2, N_2)$	Return (C, K_2, N_2)
If $A_2 = \perp$	
Return $\perp$	
Return $(C, (K_1, N_1, A_1), (K_2, N_2, A_2))$	

Fig. 7. Pseudocode for the $\mathrm{CMT} - 3$ adversary $\mathcal{B}$ and $\mathrm{CDY}_\mathsf{a}^*$ context selector S, used in proof of Theorem 2.

Recall that if $\mathrm{ctx}_1 \notin \mathsf{BadCtxs}(m)$, then the adversary must choose one of at least two valid contexts, each of which are equally likely to be ctx_1 (even conditioned on C). Thus the probably that it picks ctx_1 is at most $1/2$, and so

$$\mathbf{Adv}_\Pi^{\mathrm{CMT}-3}(\mathcal{B}) \geq \frac{1}{2} \cdot \Pr[(\mathcal{A}(C) \neq \perp) \wedge (\mathrm{ctx}_1 \notin \mathsf{BadCtxs}(m))]$$

$$\geq \frac{1}{2} \cdot (\Pr[\mathcal{A}(C) \neq \perp] - \Pr[\mathrm{ctx}_1 \in \mathsf{BadCtxs}(m)]).$$

Putting it all together, we get that

$$\mathbf{Adv}_\Pi^{\mathrm{CMT}-3}(\mathcal{B}) \geq \frac{1}{2} \cdot \left(\mathbf{Adv}_\Pi^{\mathrm{CDY}^*[\mathsf{ts}=\varnothing]}(\mathcal{A}) - \mathrm{ProbBadCtx}_\Pi \right),$$

and finally rearranging gives the desired result. $\qquad\square$

CMT-3 Implies Restricted Variants of CDY. We now show that if an attack against any of $\mathrm{CDY}_\mathsf{k}^*$, $\mathrm{CDY}_\mathsf{n}^*$, or $\mathrm{CDY}_\mathsf{a}^*$ implies an attack against $\mathrm{CMT} - 3$. The following theorem shows this for $\mathrm{CDY}_\mathsf{a}^*$, but it readily generalizes to $\mathrm{CDY}_\mathsf{k}^*$ and $\mathrm{CDY}_\mathsf{n}^*$.

Theorem 2. *Fix some AEAD Π with key space $|\mathcal{K}| \geq 2$ and nonce space $|\mathcal{N}| \geq 2$. Then for any adversary $\mathcal{A}$ that wins the $\mathrm{CDY}_\mathsf{a}^*$ game, we can give an adversary $\mathcal{B}$ such that*

$$\mathbf{Adv}_\Pi^{\mathrm{CDY}_\mathsf{a}^*}(\mathcal{A}) = \mathbf{Adv}_\Pi^{\mathrm{CMT}-3}(\mathcal{B}),$$

and the runtime of $\mathcal{B}$ is that of $\mathcal{A}$.

Proof. We prove this by constructing $\mathcal{B}$ such that it succeeds whenever $\mathcal{A}$ succeeds. The adversary $\mathcal{B}$ randomly samples a context (K_1, N_1, A_1), encrypts a random message to get a ciphertext C, selects some other key K_2 and nonce N_2 and asks the $\mathrm{CDY}_\mathsf{a}^*$ adversary $\mathcal{A}$ to produce an associated data A_2 such that (K_2, N_2, A_2) can decrypt C. This ciphertext and partial context construction can be viewed as a valid context selector S. The pseudocode for the adversary $\mathcal{B}$ and the context selector S are given in Fig. 7. And, notice that by construction, $\mathcal{B}$ wins whenever $\mathcal{A}$ succeeds. $\qquad\square$

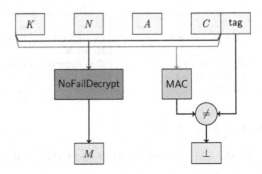

Fig. 8. Decryption structure of AEAD schemes which delegate their authenticity to a MAC. Should the MAC tag comparison fail, the routine outputs an error ($\perp$), otherwise a message is always output by NoFailDecrypt.

This approach of constructing $\mathcal{B}$ readily generalizes to CDY_n^* and CDY_k^*. Further, notice that the $\mathcal{B}$ constructed in Fig. 7 wins CMT_k and CMT_n; and similar relations hold for adversaries $\mathcal{B}$ constructed from CDY_n^* and CDY_k^* adversaries. The following corollary captures these implications.

Corollary 3. *Fix some AEAD Π with key space $|\mathcal{K}| \geq 2$, nonce space $|\mathcal{N}| \geq 2$, and associated data space $|\mathcal{A}| \geq 2$. Then the following three statements hold. First, for any adversary $\mathcal{A}_1$ that wins the CDY_a^* game, we can give an adversary $\mathcal{B}_1$ such that*

$$\mathbf{Adv}_{\Pi}^{\mathrm{CDY}_a^*}(\mathcal{A}_1) = \mathbf{Adv}_{\Pi}^{\mathrm{CMT}_k}(\mathcal{B}_1) = \mathbf{Adv}_{\Pi}^{\mathrm{CMT}_n}(\mathcal{B}_1).$$

Second, for any adversary $\mathcal{A}_2$ that wins the CDY_n^* game, we can give an adversary $\mathcal{B}_2$ such that

$$\mathbf{Adv}_{\Pi}^{\mathrm{CDY}_n^*}(\mathcal{A}_2) = \mathbf{Adv}_{\Pi}^{\mathrm{CMT}_k}(\mathcal{B}_2) = \mathbf{Adv}_{\Pi}^{\mathrm{CMT}_a}(\mathcal{B}_2).$$

Third, for any adversary $\mathcal{A}_3$ that wins the CDY_k^* game, we can give an adversary $\mathcal{B}_3$ such that

$$\mathbf{Adv}_{\Pi}^{\mathrm{CDY}_k^*}(\mathcal{A}_3) = \mathbf{Adv}_{\Pi}^{\mathrm{CMT}_n}(\mathcal{B}_3) = \mathbf{Adv}_{\Pi}^{\mathrm{CMT}_a}(\mathcal{B}_3).$$

And the runtimes of $\mathcal{B}_1$, $\mathcal{B}_2$, and $\mathcal{B}_3$ are that of $\mathcal{A}_1$, $\mathcal{A}_2$, and $\mathcal{A}_3$, respectively.

4   Context Discovery Attacks Against AEAD

We show context discovery attacks on many AEAD schemes which delegate their authenticity to a non-preimage resistant MAC. Specifically, we show CDY_a^* attacks on EAX [11], SIV [34], CCM [17], GCM [19], and OCB3 [28], and CDY_n^* attacks on EAX [11] and GCM [19].

We say that an AEAD delegates its authenticity to a MAC if during decryption, a message is output whenever the MAC comparison succeeds. To formalize

OMAC(K, M):	EAX-Decrypt(K, N, A, C):	$\mathcal{A}(C, K, N)$:
// Compute Constants	// Separate the Tag	$C \parallel \mathsf{tag} \leftarrow C$
$L \leftarrow E_K(0^{128})$	$C \parallel \mathsf{tag} \leftarrow C$	// Compute ξ
$B \leftarrow 2 \cdot L$	// Compute and Check Tag	$\xi \leftarrow \mathsf{tag}$
// split into n-bit blocks	$\mathcal{N} \leftarrow \mathrm{OMAC}(K, 0^{128} \parallel N)$	$\xi \leftarrow \xi \oplus \mathrm{OMAC}_K(0^{128} \parallel N)$
// & xor B to the last block	$\mathcal{H} \leftarrow \mathrm{OMAC}(K, 0^{127}1 \parallel A)$	$\xi \leftarrow \xi \oplus \mathrm{OMAC}_K(0^{126}10 \parallel C)$
Let $M_1, \ldots, M_m \leftarrow M$	$\mathcal{C} \leftarrow \mathrm{OMAC}(K, 0^{126}10 \parallel C)$	// Reconstruct A and Return
$M_m \leftarrow M_m \oplus B$	If $\mathsf{tag} \neq (\mathcal{N} \oplus \mathcal{H} \oplus \mathcal{C})$:	$A \leftarrow E_K^{-1}(\xi)$
// CBC-MAC Evaluation	$\quad$ Return $\perp$	$A \leftarrow A \oplus E_K(0^{127}1) \oplus (2 \cdot E_K(0^{128}))$
$C_0 \leftarrow 0^{128}$	// CTR Decryption	Return (K, N, A)
For $i = 1..m$:	$r \leftarrow \lvert C \rvert / 16 \quad$ // num blocks	
$\quad C_i \leftarrow E_K(C_{i-1} \oplus M_i)$	For $i = 0..(r-1)$:	
Return C_m	$\quad M_i \leftarrow C_i \oplus E_K(\mathcal{N} + i)$	
	Return M	

Fig. 9. (**Left**) Pseudocode for OMAC [11, Fig 1], used in EAX, with block-aligned inputs. (**Middle**) Pseudocode for EAX Mode [11] decryption with 128-bit tag, 128-bit nonce, and block-aligned messages and associated data. (**Right**) Pseudocode for an CDY_a^* attack on EAX.

this, we define NoFailDecrypt as a class of decryption algorithms that never fail. In other words, given a key, nonce, associated data, and ciphertext, they always produce a message. For example, ECB and CTR decryption are NoFailDecrypt algorithms.

With this terminology, we say that an AEAD delegates its authenticity to a MAC if it can be written as a combination of a MAC and a NoFailDecrypt algorithm such that if the MAC check fails, decryption fails; if instead the MAC check passes, then decryption outputs the result of NoFailDecrypt (which never fails). This structure is illustrated in Fig. 8. As a concrete example, for EAX [11] (described in Fig. 9), the MAC corresponds to checking the OMAC tag, and the NoFailDecrypt corresponds to the CTR decryption. In this section, we are particularly interested in schemes that compose this structure with a non-preimage resistant MAC like CMAC [18], GMAC [19, §6.4], or OMAC [11, Fig 1].

The CDY_a^* attacks we show on these schemes have the following outline. Following the definition of the game, the challenger provides the adversary with a ciphertext $C \parallel \mathsf{tag}$, a target key K, and a target nonce N, and asks it to find an associated data A such that $\mathsf{Decrypt}(K, N, A, C \parallel \mathsf{tag}) \neq \perp$. Then, the adversary exploits the lack of preimage resistance to find an associated data A such that $\mathsf{MAC}(K, N, A, C) = \mathsf{tag}$ and returns A. Since, in these schemes, the tag check passing guarantees decryption success, we get that decryption succeeds.

For EAX [11] and GCM [19], we also show CDY_n^* attacks. They proceed in a similar fashion to the CDY_a^* attacks but now the adversary finds a nonce N such that $\mathsf{MAC}(K, N, A, C) = \mathsf{tag}$. But, when the nonce length is shorter than a block (which is always true with GCM, and may be true with EAX), the CDY_n^* attacks are slower than the CDY_a^* attacks.

The remainder of the section details the attacks on EAX. The attacks on SIV, CCM, GCM, and OCB3 are in Appendix B of the full version.

CDY$_a^*$ and CDY$_n^*$ Attacks on EAX. We consider EAX over a 128-bit block cipher as defined in Bellare, Rogaway, and Wagner [11]. For simplicity, we restrict to 128-bit tag, 128-bit nonce,[3] and block-aligned messages and associated data. We note however that this is only to make the exposition simpler and is not necessary for the attack. Pseudocode for the scheme with these parameter choices is given in Fig. 9.

Let's start by contextualizing the CDY$_a^*$ game. The challenger provides us with an m-block ciphertext $C = C_1 \cdots C_m \parallel$ tag, a 128-bit target key K, and a 96-bit target nonce N. And the goal is to find a 1-block associated data A such that EAX-Decrypt$(K, N, A, C) \neq \perp$. Notice from Fig. 9 that decryption passing reduces to the tag check passing. In other words, we can rewrite the goal as finding an associated data A such that

$$\text{tag} = \text{OMAC}_K(0^{128} \parallel N) \oplus \text{OMAC}_K(0^{126}10 \parallel C) \oplus \text{OMAC}_K(0^{127}1 \parallel A). \quad (4)$$

We can rearrange terms to get

$$\text{OMAC}_K(0^{127}1 \parallel A) = \text{tag} \oplus \text{OMAC}_K(0^{128} \parallel N) \oplus \text{OMAC}_K(0^{126}10 \parallel C).$$

Notice that the right-hand side is composed entirely of known terms, thus we can evaluate it to some constant ξ. Using the assumption that A is 1-block, we can expand OMAC_K to get

$$E_K(E_K(0^{127}1) \oplus A \oplus (2 \cdot E_K(0^{128}))) = \xi.$$

Decrypting both sides under K, and solving for A gives

$$A = E_K^{-1}(\xi) \oplus E_K(0^{127}1) \oplus (2 \cdot E_K(0^{128})).$$

The full pseudocode for this attack is given in Fig. 9.

This attack generalizes to other parameter choices. It works as is against an arbitrary-length message, an arbitrary-length tag, and an arbitrary-length nonce. In addition, this attack can also be adapted as a CDY$_n^*$ attack. We start by rewriting Eq. 4 as

$$\text{OMAC}_K(0^{128} \parallel N) = \text{tag} \oplus \text{OMAC}_K(0^{126}10 \parallel C) \oplus \text{OMAC}_K(0^{127}1 \parallel C),$$

and solving for N as we did for A above. Since N is 1 block (128 bits), the reduction is similar, and the success probability remains one. If the nonce length was shorter, then assuming an idealized model like the ideal cipher model, the success probability reduces by a multiplicative factor of $2^{-f \cdot 128}$ where f is the fraction of bytes we do not have control over. For example, if we only had control over 14 of the 16 bytes in an encoded block, then the success probability would reduce by 2^{-16}.

This attack can also be adapted to provide partial control over the output plaintext. Notice that the output plaintext is a CTR decryption under the chosen

---

[3] EAX [11, Figure 4] supports an arbitrary length nonce; 128 bits (16 bytes) is the default in the popular Tink library [3], see [4].

```
SIV-1b-Decrypt(K, C):              CMAC*(K, M):

c ← 1^{n-64}01^{31}01^{31}          S ← CMAC(K, 0^n)
C_1 ∥ tag ← C                       Return CMAC(K, S ⊕ M)
I ← tag
K_1 ∥ K_2 ← K                       CMAC(K, X):
// CTR Decryption
ctr ← I & c                         K_s ← 2 · E_K(0^n)
M ← C_1 ⊕ E_{K_2}(ctr)              Return E_K(K_s ⊕ X)
// IV Check
I' ← CMAC*(K_1, M)
If I ≠ I':
    Return ⊥
Return M
```

Fig. 10. (Left) Pseudocode for SIV Mode [34] decryption with an n-bit message and no associated data. (Right) Pseudocode for CMAC* [34] and CMAC [18] with an n-bit input.

key with the OMAC of the nonce as IV. Assuming an idealized model where the block cipher is an ideal cipher and OMAC is a random function, for every new choice of key and nonce, we get a random output plaintext. So, by trying 2^m key and nonce pairs, we can expect to control m bits of the output plaintext.

5   Restrictive Commitment Attacks via k-Sum Problems

The previous section's CDY_a^* and CDY_n^* attacks against GCM, EAX, OCB3, SIV, and CCM immediately give rise to *permissive* CMT_k attacks against each scheme. This follows from our general result showing that CMT_k security implies CDY_a^* and CDY_n^* (Corollary 3). But this does not imply the ability to build restrictive CMT_k^*, CMT_n^*, or CMT_a^* attacks that require the non-adversarially controlled parts of the two decryption contexts to be identical (see Theorem 10 in the full version.)

Prior work has provided (in our terminology) CMT_k^* attacks for GCM [16, 24], AES-GCM-SIV [29,35], ChaCha20/Poly1305 [24,29], XChaCha20/Poly1305 [29], and OCB3 [2]. An open question of practical interest [36] is whether there is a CMT_k^* attack against SIV. We resolve this open question, showing an attack that works in time about $2^{n/3}$. It requires new techniques related to the fast solution of k-sum problems, as we explain below.

Attack on 1-Block SIV. We consider SIV over an n-bit block cipher (for $n \geq 64$) as defined in the draft NIST specification [34]. For ease of exposition, we restrict to the case of an n-bit message and no associated data, and describe how to generalize this to the multi-block case in Appendix D in the full version. Pseudocode for the scheme with these parameter choices is given in Fig. 10.

Here, the CMT_k^* adversary seeks to produce a ciphertext $C = C_1 \parallel \mathsf{tag}$ and two $2n$-bit keys $K = K_1 \parallel K_2$ and $K' = K_1' \parallel K_2'$ such that SIV-Decrypt$(K, C) \neq \perp$ and SIV-Decrypt$(K', C) \neq \perp$. Notice from Fig. 10 that this reduces to two simultaneous IV checks passing which can be written as

$$\text{tag} = \text{CMAC}^*(K_1, C_1 \oplus E_{K_2}(\text{tag} \mathbin{\&} \text{c})) = \text{CMAC}^*(K_1', C_1 \oplus E_{K_2'}(\text{tag} \mathbin{\&} \text{c}))$$

where $\text{c} = 1^{n-64}01^{31}01^{31}$ is a constant specified by the SIV standard. Our attack strategy will be to choose tag arbitrarily, so we can treat this as a constant value. Towards solving for the remaining variable C_1, we can substitute in the definition of CMAC^* to get

$$\begin{aligned}
\text{tag} &= E_{K_1}((2 \cdot E_{K_1}(0^n)) \oplus E_{K_1}(2 \cdot E_{K_1}(0^n)) \oplus C_1 \oplus E_{K_2}(\text{tag} \mathbin{\&} \text{c})) \\
&= E_{K_1'}((2 \cdot E_{K_1'}(0^n)) \oplus E_{K_1'}(2 \cdot E_{K_1'}(0^n)) \oplus C_1 \oplus E_{K_2'}(\text{tag} \mathbin{\&} \text{c})),
\end{aligned}$$

which we can rearrange the two equalities by solving for the variable C_1, giving us the following:

$$\begin{aligned}
C_1 &= E_{K_1}^{-1}(\text{tag}) \oplus (2 \cdot E_{K_1}(0^n)) \oplus E_{K_1}(2 \cdot E_{K_1}(0^n)) \oplus E_{K_2}(\text{tag} \mathbin{\&} \text{c}) \\
&= E_{K_1'}^{-1}(\text{tag}) \oplus (2 \cdot E_{K_1'}(0^n)) \oplus E_{K_1'}(2 \cdot E_{K_1'}(0^n)) \oplus E_{K_2'}(\text{tag} \mathbin{\&} \text{c}). \quad (5)
\end{aligned}$$

The above implies that it suffices now to find K_1, K_2, K_1', K_2' that satisfy Eq. 5. To ease notation, we define four helper functions, one for each term:

$$\begin{aligned}
F_1(K_1) &:= E_{K_1}^{-1}(\text{tag}) \oplus 2 \cdot E_{K_1}(0^n) \oplus E_{K_1}(2 \cdot E_{K_1}(0^n)), \\
F_2(K_2) &:= E_{K_2}(\text{tag} \mathbin{\&} \text{c}), \\
F_3(K_1) &:= E_{K_1'}^{-1}(\text{tag}) \oplus 2 \cdot E_{K_1'}(0^n) \oplus E_{K_1'}(2 \cdot E_{K_1}(0^n)), \\
F_4(K_2') &:= E_{K_2'}(\text{tag} \mathbin{\&} \text{c}),
\end{aligned}$$

and recast Eq. 5 as a 4-sum problem

$$F_1(K_1) \oplus F_2(K_2) \oplus F_3(K_1') \oplus F_4(K_2') = 0.$$

If these were independent random functions, then we could directly apply Wagner's k-tree algorithm [38] for finding a 4-way collision (also referred to as the generalized birthday problem). But even modeling E as an ideal cipher, the functions are neither random nor independent. For example, $F_1(x) = F_3(x)$ always.

Towards resolving this, we first ensure that the keys K_1, K_2, K_1', and K_2' are domain separated. This can be easily arranged: see Fig. 11 for the pseudocode of our CMT_k^* adversary $\mathcal{A}$ against SIV. We now turn to lower bounding $\mathcal{A}$'s advantage, which consists of two primary steps.

The first is that we argue that, in CMT_k^* when running our adversary against SIV, the helper-function outputs are statistically close to uniform. Then, we show that Wagner's approach works for not-too-biased values.

We observe that F_2 and F_4 trivially behave as independent random functions in the ideal cipher model for E. The analysis for F_1 and F_3 is more involved. We use the following lemma, which bounds the distinguishing advantage between a uniform n-bit string and the output of a single query to either F_1 or F_3.

$\mathcal{A}()$:

$c \leftarrow 1^{n-64}01^{31}01^{31}$

// Arbitrarily pick a tag

$\mathsf{tag} \leftarrow\!\!\$ \{0,1\}^n \setminus \{0^n\}$

// Define helper functions

Def $F_1(K_1) \leftarrow E_{K_1}^{-1}(\mathsf{tag}) \oplus 2 \cdot E_{K_1}(0^n) \oplus E_{K_1}(2 \cdot E_{K_1}(0^n))$

Def $F_2(K_2) \leftarrow E_{K_2}(\mathsf{tag} \;\&\; c)$

Def $F_3(K_1) \leftarrow E_{K_1'}^{-1}(\mathsf{tag}) \oplus 2 \cdot E_{K_1'}(0^n) \oplus E_{K_1'}(2 \cdot E_{K_1}(0^n))$

Def $F_4(K_2') \leftarrow E_{K_2'}(\mathsf{tag} \;\&\; c)$

// Generate lists

For $i = 1, ..., q$:

    $x \leftarrow \mathsf{encode}_{128-2}(i)$

    // Domain separate the keys

    $K_1 \leftarrow 00 \| x$; $K_2 \leftarrow 01 \| x$; $K_1' \leftarrow 10 \| x$; $K_2' \leftarrow 11 \| x$

    // Query a row

    $L_1[i] \leftarrow F_1(K_1)$; $L_2[i] \leftarrow F_2(K_2)$; $L_3[i] \leftarrow F_3(K_1')$; $L_4[i] \leftarrow F_4(K_2')$

// Find an 4-way collision using Wagner's k-tree algorithm [38]

$\mathsf{res} \leftarrow \mathcal{A}.\mathsf{fourWayCollision}(L_1, L_2, L_3, L_4)$

If $\mathsf{res} = \varnothing$:

    Return $\bot$

// Repackage the collision into ciphertext and keys

$(x_1, x_2, x_3, x_4) \leftarrow \mathsf{res}$

$C_1 \leftarrow F_1(x_1) \oplus F_2(x_2)$

$K_1 \leftarrow 00 \| x_1$; $K_2 \leftarrow 01 \| x_2$; $K_1' \leftarrow 10 \| x_3$; $K_2' \leftarrow 11 \| x_4$

Return $C_1 \| \mathsf{tag}, K_1 \| K_2, K_1' \| K_2'$

Fig. 11. Pseudocode for CMT_k^* attack on SIV-1b. The fourWayCollision subroutine is defined in Appendix C in the full version.

Lemma 4. *Let* $\mathsf{tag} \in \{0,1\}^n \setminus \{0^n\}$ *and* σ *be an* n-*bit random permutation with inverse* σ^{-1} *and* U *be the uniform random variable over* n *bit strings. Define* n-*bit random variables (over the choice of* σ)

$$A := \sigma^{-1}(\mathsf{tag}), \qquad B := 2 \cdot \sigma(0^n), \qquad C := \sigma(2 \cdot \sigma(0^n)),$$

where $\cdot$ *denotes multiplication in* $\mathrm{GF}(2^n)$. *Then no adversary that makes one query to a procedure* P *can distinguish between* $P \mapsto (U, U, U)$ *and* $P \mapsto (A, B, C)$ *with probability greater than* $6 \cdot 2^{-n}$.

The proof proceeds by constructing identical-until-bad games and applying the *fundamental lemma of game playing* [10] to discern the distinguishing advantage. The proof appears in Appendix C in the full version.

We combine this with the following technical statement about applying Wagner's k-tree algorithm [38] to almost-random lists.

Theorem 5. *Let* L *be a list of* ℓ *4-tuples* $x = (x_1, x_2, x_3, x_4)$, *where each entry* x *is distinguishable from an 4-tuple of independent uniformly random values with probability at most* ξ. *Let* L_1, L_2, L_3, *and* L_4 *be lists of 1-index* (x_1), *2-index* (x_2), *3-index* (x_3), *and 4-index* (x_4) *elements of* L *respectively. Then Wagner's k-tree algorithm [38] finds a solution* $(y_1, y_2, y_3, y_4) \in L_1 \times L_2 \times L_3 \times L_4$ *such that*

$$y_1 \oplus y_2 \oplus y_3 \oplus y_4 = 0 \,,$$

with probability at least

$$(1 - \ell \cdot \xi)\left(1 - \exp\left(-\frac{\ell^2 \cdot 2^{-n/3}}{8}\right)\right)\left(1 - \exp\left(1 - \frac{\ell^4 \cdot 2^{-4n/3}}{8} - \frac{2}{\ell^4 \cdot 2^{-4n/3}}\right)\right),$$

and time at most

$$20\ell + 4\ell^2 \cdot 2^{-n/3} + 4\mathsf{Sort}(\ell) + 2\mathsf{Sort}((1/2)\ell^2 \cdot 2^{-n/3}) \,,$$

where $\mathsf{Sort}(k)$ denotes the time to sort a list of k items.

The proof proceeds by analyzing the algorithm step-by-step and at each step applying Chernoff bounds [23] to compute a lower bound on the success probability. The proof appears in Appendix C in the full version.

With Lemma 4 and Theorem 5, we can now prove a lower bound on the advantage of the CMT_k^* adversary in Fig. 11.

Theorem 6. Let $\mathcal{A}$ be the CMT_k^* adversary against SIV over an n-bit ideal cipher E, detailed in Fig. 11. It makes $10q$ queries to E and takes at most

$$35q + 4q^2 \cdot 2^{-n/3} + 4\mathsf{Sort}(q) + 2\mathsf{Sort}((1/2)q^2 \cdot 2^{-n/3}) + 11 \,,$$

time, where $\mathsf{Sort}(k)$ is the cost of sorting a list of k items. Then the advantage

$$\mathbf{Adv}_{\mathrm{SIV}}^{\mathrm{CMT}_k^*}(\mathcal{A}) \geq (1 - 8q \cdot 2^{-n})\left(1 - \exp\left(-\frac{q^2 \cdot 2^{-n/3}}{8}\right)\right)$$

$$\left(1 - \exp\left(1 - \frac{q^4 \cdot 2^{-4n/3}}{8} - \frac{2}{q^4 \cdot 2^{-4n/3}}\right)\right). \qquad (6)$$

Proof. By construction, the adversary $\mathcal{A}$ (Fig. 11) wins whenever it finds a collision, so it suffices to lower bound this probability. First, the domain separation over the keys ensures that the two helper functions never query the ideal cipher with the same key. This, by the properties of the ideal cipher, ensures independence of the outputs. Second, F_2 and F_4 call the ideal cipher only once on a fixed output under a new key each invocation, so their outputs are indistinguishable from an n-bit uniform random value. Third, F_1 and F_3 call the ideal cipher three times under the same key each invocation. However, applying Lemma 4 gives us that their outputs are distinguishable from an n-bit uniform random value with probability at most $6 \cdot 2^{-n}$. So, by the union bound, a row of outputs $(F_1(K_1), F_2(K_2), F_3(K_1'), F_4(K_2'))$ is distinguishable from four independent, uniformly random outputs with probability at most $8 \cdot 2^{-n}$. Then, Theorem 5 tells us that the function fourWayCollision called by $\mathcal{A}$ finds a collision with probability at least that of Eq. 6.

It remains to analyze the cost of the adversary $\mathcal{A}$. First, it costs 2 operations to initialize c and tag. Second, since each loop iteration costs 15 operations, the loop costs $15q$ operations. Third, from Theorem 5, finding a 4-way collision on four lists of size q using Wagner's k-tree algorithm [38] costs at most

$$20q + 4q^2 \cdot 2^{-n/3} + 4\mathsf{Sort}(q) + 2\mathsf{Sort}((1/2)q^2 \cdot 2^{-n/3})$$

operations. Fourth, repackaging the collision and returning costs 9 operations. So, the runtime is at most

$$35q + 4q^2 \cdot 2^{-n/3} + 4\mathsf{Sort}(q) + 2\mathsf{Sort}((1/2)q^2 \cdot 2^{-n/3}) + 11 \,.$$

Finally, since each loop iteration makes 10 ideal cipher queries, the algorithm makes $10q$ queries. □

In the following corollary, we show that when the adversary makes approximately $2^{n/3}$ queries, it can win CMT_k^* against SIV with high probability, taking time approximately $2^{n/3}$.

Corollary 7. *Let $\mathcal{A}$ be the CMT_k^* adversary against SIV over an n-bit ideal cipher E, detailed in Fig. 11 with $q = 10 \cdot 2^{n/3}$. It makes $100 \cdot 2^{n/3}$ queries to E and takes at most*

$$750 \cdot 2^{n/3} + 4\mathsf{Sort}(10 \cdot 2^{n/3}) + 2\mathsf{Sort}(50 \cdot 2^{n/3}) + 11 \,,$$

time, where $\mathsf{Sort}(n)$ is the cost of sorting a list of n items. Then

$$\mathbf{Adv}_{\mathrm{SIV}}^{\mathrm{CMT}_k^*}(\mathcal{A}) \geq \left(1 - 80 \cdot 2^{-2n/3}\right)\left(1 - \exp\left(-12.5 \cdot 2^{n/3}\right)\right)(1 - \exp(-1249)) \,.$$

6   Related Work

Key commitment for authenticated encryption was introduced in Farshim, Orlandi, and Rosie [22] through full robustness (FROB), which in turn was inspired by key robustness notions in the public key setting by Abdalla, Bellare, and Neven [1] and refined by Farshim et al. [21]. The FROB game asks that a ciphertext only be able to decrypt under a single key. However, the FROB game was defined for randomized authenticated encryption. Grubbs, Lu, and Ristenpart [24] adapted the FROB game to work with associated data, where they ask that a ciphertext only be able to decrypt under a single key (with no constraints on the associated data.) This notion was further generalized by Bellare and Hoang [5] to the nonce-based setting, with their committing security 1 (CMT-1) definition. The CMT-1 game asks that a ciphertext only be able to decrypt under a single key (with no constraints on the nonce nor the associated data.)

The real-world security implications of key commitment were first highlighted by Dodis et al. [16] where they exploited the lack of key commitment when encrypting attachments in Facebook Messenger's message franking protocol [20] to send abusive images that cannot be reported. Albertini et al. [2] generalized this attack from images to other file formats and called attention to more settings where lack of key commitment can be exploited to defeat integrity. While both these attacks targeted integrity, Len, Grubbs, and Ristenpart [29] introduced partitioning oracle attacks and showed how to use them for password guessing attacks by exploiting lack of key commitment to obtain large speedups over standard dictionary attacks, endangering confidentiality.

Proposals for constructing key committing ciphers also started in the Farshim, Orlandi, and Rosie paper [22] where they showed that single-key Encrypt-then-MAC, Encrypt-and-MAC, and MAC-then-Encrypt constructions produce key committing ciphers, when the MAC is collision-resistant. Grubbs, Lu, and Ristenpart [24] showed that the Encode-then-Encipher construction [8] was key committing. Dodis et al. [16] proposed a faster compression function-based key committing AEAD construction termed *encryptment*, and also discussed the closely related Duplex construction [12], which is also key committing. Albertini et al. [2] formally analyzed the folklore padding zeroes and key hashing transforms and showed that they produce key committing AEAD at a lower performance cost than prior constructions. Bellare and Hoang [5] constructed key committing variants of GCM and GCM-SIV termed CAU-C1 and CAU-SIV-C1, and generic transforms UtC and RtC that can be used to turn unique-nonce secure and nonce-reuse secure AEAD schemes respectively into key committing AEAD schemes.

The potential risk of delegating authenticity of an AEAD entirely to a non-collision-resistant MAC is folklore. Farshim, Orlandi, and Rosie [22] who introduced the notion of committing AEAD also cautioned against using non-collision-resistant MACs and CBC-MAC in particular.

On February 7, 2023, NIST announced the selection of the Ascon family for lightweight cryptography standardization [37]. The finalist version of Ascon [15] specifies two AEAD parameter sets ASCON-128 and ASCON-128A. Both parameter sets specify a 128 bit tag, which by the birthday bound, upper bounds the committing security at 64 bits. But, since the underlying algorithm is a variant of the Duplex construction with a 320-bit permutation, and the same specification specifies parameters a hash function with 128-bit collision resistance, one can specify an AEAD with 128-bit committing security by tweaking parameters.

Concurrent Work. In independent and concurrent work made public very recently, Chan and Rogaway [14] introduced a new definitional framework for committing AE. Their goal is to capture multiple different types of commitment attacks—what they call *misattributions*, or an adversary being able to construct distinct pairs (K, N, A, M) and (K', N', A', M') that both "explain" a single ciphertext C—in a unified way. Their main definition only captures commitment to an entire (K, N, A, M) tuple; but in [14, Appendix A], they briefly describe an extension to only require commitments to a subset of the values.

The extended version of their framework is similar to our CMT[Σ] definition. While both frameworks aim to capture granular win conditions beyond CMT-3, they are orthogonal. Their framework models the multi-key setting with many randomly chosen unknown-to-the-adversary, known-to-the-adversary, and chosen-by-the-adversary keys. While our CMT[Σ] captures the distinction between *permissive* and *restrictive* notions, and settings that impose restrictions on the nonce and associated data. We also introduce the notion of context discoverability and describe its relation to CMT[Σ].

Chan and Rogaway [14] also independently observed that AEAD with non-preimage resistant MACs are vulnerable to commitment attacks and show attacks on GCM and OCB3 similar to the ones we give in Sect. 4.

Acknowledgments. We thank the anonymous reviewers of Eurocrypt 2023 for their feedback. Sanketh thanks Giacomo Pope for helpful discussions. This work was supported in part by NSF grant CNS #2120651, and the NSF Graduate Research Fellowship under Grant No. DGE-2139899.

References

1. Abdalla, M., Bellare, M., Neven, G.: Robust encryption. In: Micciancio, D. (ed.) TCC 2010. LNCS, vol. 5978, pp. 480–497. Springer, Heidelberg (2010). https://doi.org/10.1007/978-3-642-11799-2_28
2. Albertini, A., Duong, T., Gueron, S., Kölbl, S., Luykx, A., Schmieg, S.: How to abuse and fix authenticated encryption without key commitment. In: USENIX Security 2022 (2022). https://ia.cr/2020/1456
3. Ambrosin, M., et al.: Tink (2021). https://github.com/google/tink/releases/tag/v1.6.1
4. Ambrosin, M., et al.: Tink EAX key manager (2021). https://github.com/google/tink/blob/v1.6.1/java_src/src/main/java/com/google/crypto/tink/aead/AesEaxKeyManager.java#L115-L116
5. Bellare, M., Hoang, V.T.: Efficient schemes for committing authenticated encryption. In: Dunkelman, O., Dziembowski, S. (eds.) Advances in Cryptology - EUROCRYPT 2022–41st Annual International Conference on the Theory and Applications of Cryptographic Techniques, Trondheim, Norway, 30 May–3 June 2022, Proceedings, Part II. Lecture Notes in Computer Science, vol. 13276, pp. 845–875. Springer, Heidelberg (2022). https://doi.org/10.1007/978-3-031-07085-3_29
6. Bellare, M., Namprempre, C.: Authenticated encryption: relations among notions and analysis of the generic composition paradigm. J. Cryptol. **21**(4), 469–491 (2008). https://doi.org/10.1007/s00145-008-9026-x
7. Bellare, M., Ristenpart, T., Rogaway, P., Stegers, T.: Format-preserving encryption. In: Jacobson, M.J., Rijmen, V., Safavi-Naini, R. (eds.) SAC 2009. LNCS, vol. 5867, pp. 295–312. Springer, Heidelberg (2009). https://doi.org/10.1007/978-3-642-05445-7_19
8. Bellare, M., Rogaway, P.: Encode-then-encipher encryption: how to exploit nonces or redundancy in plaintexts for efficient cryptography. In: Okamoto, T. (ed.) Advances in Cryptology - ASIACRYPT 2000, 6th International Conference on the Theory and Application of Cryptology and Information Security, Kyoto, Japan, 3–7 December 2000, Proceedings. Lecture Notes in Computer Science, vol. 1976, pp. 317–330. Springer, Heidelberg (2000). https://doi.org/10.1007/3-540-44448-3_24, https://cseweb.ucsd.edu/~mihir/papers/ee.pdf
9. Bellare, M., Rogaway, P.: Introduction to Modern Cryptography (2005). https://web.cs.ucdavis.edu/~rogaway/classes/227/spring05/book/main.pdf

10. Bellare, M., Rogaway, P.: The security of triple encryption and a framework for code-based game-playing proofs. In: Vaudenay, S. (ed.) EUROCRYPT 2006. LNCS, vol. 4004, pp. 409–426. Springer, Heidelberg (2006). https://doi.org/10.1007/11761679_25

11. Bellare, M., Rogaway, P., Wagner, D.A.: The EAX mode of operation. In: Roy, B.K., Meier, W. (eds.) Fast Software Encryption, 11th International Workshop, FSE 2004, Delhi, India, 5–7 February 2004, Revised Papers. Lecture Notes in Computer Science, vol. 3017, pp. 389–407. Springer, Heidelberg (2004). https://doi.org/10.1007/978-3-540-25937-4_25, https://web.cs.ucdavis.edu/~rogaway/papers/eax.pdf

12. Bertoni, G., Daemen, J., Peeters, M., Van Assche, G.: Duplexing the sponge: single-pass authenticated encryption and other applications. In: Miri, A., Vaudenay, S. (eds.) SAC 2011. LNCS, vol. 7118, pp. 320–337. Springer, Heidelberg (2012). https://doi.org/10.1007/978-3-642-28496-0_19

13. Black, J., Rogaway, P., Shrimpton, T.: Black-box analysis of the block-cipher-based hash-function constructions from PGV. In: Yung, M. (ed.) CRYPTO 2002. LNCS, vol. 2442, pp. 320–335. Springer, Heidelberg (2002). https://doi.org/10.1007/3-540-45708-9_21

14. Chan, J., Rogaway, P.: On committing authenticated-encryption. In: Atluri, V., Di Pietro, R., Jensen, C.D., Meng, W. (eds.) Computer Security – ESORICS 2022. ESORICS 2022. Lecture Notes in Computer Science, vol 13555. Springer, Cham (2022). https://doi.org/10.1007/978-3-031-17146-8_14, https://ia.cr/2022/1260

15. Dobraunig, C., Eichlseder, M., Mendel, F., Schläffer, M.: Ascon v1.2: submission to NIST, May 2021. https://csrc.nist.gov/CSRC/media/Projects/lightweight-cryptography/documents/finalist-round/updated-spec-doc/ascon-spec-final.pdf

16. Dodis, Y., Grubbs, P., Ristenpart, T., Woodage, J.: Fast message franking: from invisible salamanders to encryptment. In: Shacham, H., Boldyreva, A. (eds.) CRYPTO 2018. LNCS, vol. 10991, pp. 155–186. Springer, Cham (2018). https://doi.org/10.1007/978-3-319-96884-1_6

17. Dworkin, M.: Recommendation for block cipher modes of operation: the CCM mode for authentication and confidentiality. NIST Special Publication 800-38C (2004). https://doi.org/10.6028/NIST.SP.800-38C

18. Dworkin, M.: Recommendation for block cipher modes of operation: the CMAC mode for authentication. NIST Special Publication 800-38B (2005). https://doi.org/10.6028/NIST.SP.800-38B

19. Dworkin, M.: Recommendation for block cipher modes of operation: galois/counter mode (GCM) and GMAC. NIST Special Publication 800-38D (2017). https://doi.org/10.6028/NIST.SP.800-38D

20. Facebook: Messenger secret conversations: Technical whitepaper (2017). https://about.fb.com/wp-content/uploads/2016/07/messenger-secret-conversations-technical-whitepaper.pdf

21. Farshim, P., Libert, B., Paterson, K.G., Quaglia, E.A.: Robust encryption, revisited. In: Kurosawa, K., Hanaoka, G. (eds.) PKC 2013. LNCS, vol. 7778, pp. 352–368. Springer, Heidelberg (2013). https://doi.org/10.1007/978-3-642-36362-7_22

22. Farshim, P., Orlandi, C., Rosie, R.: Security of symmetric primitives under incorrect usage of keys. IACR Trans. Symmetric Cryptol. **2017**(1), 449–473 (2017). https://doi.org/10.13154/tosc.v2017.i1.449-473

23. Goemans, M.: Chernoff bounds, and some applications (2015). https://math.mit.edu/~goemans/18310S15/chernoff-notes.pdf

24. Grubbs, P., Lu, J., Ristenpart, T.: Message franking via committing authenticated encryption. In: Katz, J., Shacham, H. (eds.) CRYPTO 2017. LNCS, vol. 10403, pp. 66–97. Springer, Cham (2017). https://doi.org/10.1007/978-3-319-63697-9_3

25. Harkins, D.: Synthetic Initialization Vector (SIV) Authenticated Encryption Using the Advanced Encryption Standard (AES). Request for Comments - Informational (2008). https://datatracker.ietf.org/doc/rfc5297/

26. Kilian, J., Rogaway, P.: How to protect DES against exhaustive key search (an analysis of DESX). J. Cryptol. **14**(1), 17–35 (2000). https://doi.org/10.1007/s001450010015

27. Krawczyk, H.: The OPAQUE Asymmetric PAKE Protocol. Technical report, October 2019. https://datatracker.ietf.org/doc/draft-krawczyk-cfrg-opaque/03/

28. Krovetz, T., Rogaway, P.: The OCB Authenticated-Encryption Algorithm. Request for Comments - Informational (2014). https://datatracker.ietf.org/doc/rfc7253/

29. Len, J., Grubbs, P., Ristenpart, T.: Partitioning oracle attacks. In: Bailey, M., Greenstadt, R. (eds.) 30th USENIX Security Symposium, USENIX Security 2021, 11–13 August 2021, pp. 195–212. USENIX Association (2021). https://ia.cr/2020/1491

30. Namprempre, C., Rogaway, P., Shrimpton, T.: Reconsidering generic composition. In: Nguyen, P.Q., Oswald, E. (eds.) EUROCRYPT 2014. LNCS, vol. 8441, pp. 257–274. Springer, Heidelberg (2014). https://doi.org/10.1007/978-3-642-55220-5_15

31. Ristenpart, T., Shacham, H., Shrimpton, T.: Careful with composition: limitations of indifferentiability and universal composability. IACR Cryptol. ePrint Arch., p. 339 (2011). https://ia.cr/2011/339

32. Rogaway, P.: Authenticated-encryption with associated-data. In: Atluri, V. (ed.) Proceedings of the 9th ACM Conference on Computer and Communications Security, CCS 2002, Washington, DC, USA, 18–22 November 2002, pp. 98–107. ACM (2002). https://doi.org/10.1145/586110.586125

33. Rogaway, P., Shrimpton, T.: A provable-security treatment of the key-wrap problem. In: Vaudenay, S. (ed.) EUROCRYPT 2006. LNCS, vol. 4004, pp. 373–390. Springer, Heidelberg (2006). https://doi.org/10.1007/11761679_23

34. Rogaway, P., Shrimpton, T.: The SIV Mode of Operation for Deterministic Authenticated-Encryption (Key Wrap) and Misuse-Resistant Nonce-Based Authenticated-Encryption (2007). https://web.cs.ucdavis.edu/~rogaway/papers/siv.pdf, draft 0.32

35. Schmieg, S.: Invisible Salamanders in AES-GCM-SIV (2020). https://keymaterial.net/2020/09/07/invisible-salamanders-in-aes-gcm-siv/

36. Sophie, indistinguishable from random noise (@SchmiegSophie) (2020). https://web.archive.org/web/20200909134511/twitter.com/SchmiegSophie/status/1303690812933382148, via Twitter

37. N.L.C. Team: NIST announces the selection of the Ascon family for lightweight cryptography standardization, February 2023. https://www.nist.gov/news-events/news/2023/02/lightweight-cryptography-standardization-process-nist-selects-ascon

38. Wagner, D.: A generalized birthday problem. In: Yung, M. (ed.) CRYPTO 2002. LNCS, vol. 2442, pp. 288–304. Springer, Heidelberg (2002). https://doi.org/10.1007/3-540-45708-9_19

39. Wiener, M.J.: The full cost of cryptanalytic attacks. J. Cryptol. **17**(2), 105–124 (2003). https://doi.org/10.1007/s00145-003-0213-5

Impossibility of Indifferentiable Iterated Blockciphers from 3 or Less Primitive Calls

Chun Guo[1,2,3]([✉]), Lei Wang[4]([✉]), and Dongdai Lin[5]([✉])

[1] School of Cyber Science and Technology, Shandong University, Qingdao, China
chun.guo.sc@gmail.com
[2] Key Laboratory of Cryptologic Technology and Information Security of Ministry
of Education, Shandong University, Qingdao 266237, Shandong, China
[3] Shandong Research Institute of Industrial Technology,
Jinan 250102, Shandong, China
[4] Shanghai Jiaotong University, Shanghai, China
wanglei_hb@sjtu.edu.cn
[5] Institute of Information Engineering, Chinese Academy of Sciences, Beijing, China
ddlin@iie.ac.cn

Abstract. Virtually all modern blockciphers are *iterated*. In this paper, we ask: to construct a secure iterated blockcipher "non-trivially", how many calls to random functions and permutations are necessary?

When security means *indistinguishability from a random permutation*, optimality is achieved by the Even-Mansour scheme using 1 call to a public permutation. We seek for the arguably strongest security *indifferentiability from an ideal cipher*, a notion introduced by Maurer et al. (TCC 2004) and popularized by Coron et al. (JoC, 2014).

We provide the first generic negative result/lower bounds: when the key is not too short, no iterated blockcipher making 3 calls is (statistically) indifferentiable. This proves optimality for a 4-call positive result of Guo et al. (Eprint 2016). Furthermore, using 1 or 2 calls, even indifferentiable iterated blockciphers with polynomial keyspace are impossible.

To prove this, we develop an abstraction of idealized iterated blockciphers and establish various basic properties, and apply Extremal Graph Theory results to prove the existence of certain (generalized) non-random properties such as the boomerang and yoyo.

1 Introduction

Iterated Blockciphers. Virtually all modern blockciphers, e.g., DES, AES, PRESENT, Skinny, are designed via iteration [2]. These even include theoretical constructions such as the Luby-Rackoff [40], Iterated Even-Mansour (IEM) ciphers [1,11,23,30] and others [21,29]. In fact, the initialization algorithms of some stream ciphers [50] also follow the iteration paradigm.

The idea of iteration dates back to Shannon [47] or even earlier practice of product ciphers. In general, an iterated structure creates a (usually weak) keyed permutation, typically called its *round*, in a "non-trivial" manner, and then composes such rounds till gaining enough security. By "non-trivial", the round has

Full version available at [28].

to employ smart ideas to resolve non-invertibility of functions [40] or combine keys with keyless permutations [1,11,23]. Such constructs also constitute natural transformations between (pseudo)random functions and (pseudo)random permutations [1,16,21,23,40], which are fundamental in modern cryptography.

While provably secure blockciphers remain out of reach, there is a definite belief that with sufficient iterations, the iterated paradigm does yield enough security. The primary security notion for a blockcipher is *indistinguishability from a random permutation*, i.e., no adversary with bounded oracle queries and black-box access to a permutation can distinguish whether it is interacting with the blockcipher under a random key or a perfectly random permutation. This has probably been the most widely used security assumption for blockciphers. In fact, with certain idealized assumptions and sufficient iterations, the aforementioned Luby-Rackoff [40], IEM [11,23,30] and Swap-Or-Not [29] have been proven indistinguishable (and bounds usually increase with rounds).

The Ideal Cipher Model. Albeit the de-facto standard, indistinguishability is insufficient for a number of important blockcipher-based cryptosystems. For example, some real-world protocols such as f8 and f9 [33] crucially rely on the stronger related-key security of blockciphers [6]. Even worse, in blockcipher-based hash functions [9,10], the adversary can control both the message and the key of the blockcipher and exploit "known-key" or "chosen-key" attacks [8,37] to break collision- or preimage-resistance of the hash. In fact, a mere PRP cannot yield black-box construction of collision resistant hash [48].

Hence, cryptographers have modeled a reliable (κ, n)-blockcipher (i.e., a blockcipher with κ-bit keys and n-bit blocks) as an *ideal cipher* (IC), i.e., a family of 2^κ independent n-bit random permutations that is public to all entities. This is known as the *ideal cipher model* (ICM), and it turned out crucial for proving security for blockcipher-based schemes when the PRP assumption is not enough [9,10,35]. While remaining a heuristic approach [12,41], a proof in the ideal cipher model is typically considered a good indication of security from the point of view of practice. Meanwhile, "being close to ideal" becomes a new standard for blockcipher design and evaluations—much like "being close to a random oracle" for hash functions [7,15]. In fact, distinguishing blockcipher algorithms from "ideal" has been recognized as an important attack vector [8,37].

Indifferentiability. While ICs are unachievable in the standard model [12,41], it remains an interesting problem to build ICs from other public ideal functions. This class of problem shall be addressed with *indifferentiability* introduced by Maurer et al. [41] and popularized by Coron et al. [15]. Indifferentiability is a simulation-based framework that helps assess whether a construction of a target primitive $A^{\mathbf{B}}$ from a lower-level ideal primitive $\mathbf{B}$ is "structurally close" to $\mathbf{C}$, the ideal version of $A^{\mathbf{B}}$ (e.g., the case where A is the IEM cipher, $\mathbf{B}$ is the random permutation $\mathbf{P}$ and $\mathbf{C}$ is an IC was considered in [1]). $A^{\mathbf{B}}$ is *indifferentiable from* $\mathbf{C}$, if for any *differentiator* D there exists an *efficient simulator* $S^{\mathbf{C}}$ querying $\mathbf{B}$ such that the two systems $(A^{\mathbf{B}}, \mathbf{B})$ and $(\mathbf{C}, S^{\mathbf{C}})$ are indistinguishable in the view of D. Indifferentiability comes equipped with a composition theorem [41] which implies that a large class of protocols (see [20,43] for restrictions) are provably secure in the ideal-**B** model if and only if they are provably secure in the ideal-**C** model. Since stronger notions are unachievable in general [20,43], indifferentiability is arguably the strongest security notion for cryptosystems. Due to this and due to the importance of composition, indifferentiability has been applied to various cryptosystems, including iterated hash [7,15], blockciphers [1, 16,21], authenticated encryption [5] and public-key schemes [51].

Therefore, it has been an important direction to evaluate indifferentiability of popular blockcipher constructions [1,16]. The first feasibility was the key-prepended Feistel cipher of Coron et al. [16], which iterates $\Psi^{\mathbf{F}}(K, x_L \| x_R) := x_R \oplus \mathbf{F}(K \| x_L) \| x_L$ with $x_L, x_R \in \{0,1\}^{n/2}$ and $\mathbf{F}$ a public random function. Coron et al. proved indifferentiability with 14 rounds [16] and established equivalence of ideal models. This was later improved to 10 [17] and 8 rounds [19].

Another line of work established indifferentiability for the mentioned IEM ciphers. Concretely, a t-round IEM cipher employs t n-bit random permutations $\mathbf{P}_1, \ldots, \mathbf{P}_t$ and $t + 1$ key derivation functions $\mathsf{kd}_0, \ldots, \mathsf{kd}_t : \{0,1\}^\kappa \to \{0,1\}^n$, and is defined by iterating $\mathrm{EM}_\ell^{\mathbf{P}}(K, x) := \mathsf{kd}_\ell(K) \oplus \mathbf{P}_\ell(\mathsf{kd}_{\ell-1}(K) \oplus x)$. When $\mathsf{kd}_0 = \ldots = \mathsf{kd}_t = \mathbf{F}$ for a random function $\mathbf{F} : \{0,1\}^\kappa \to \{0,1\}^n$, positive results were first proven at 5 rounds [1] and later tightened to 3 rounds [27]. When $\mathsf{kd}_0, \ldots, \mathsf{kd}_t$ are the identity function id, positive results were first proven at 12 rounds [39] and later tightened to 5 rounds [18].

Lower Bounds? We seek for understanding the *complexity* and ask: to have a "non-trivial", provably secure iterated (κ, n)-blockcipher, how many calls to the primitives are *necessary*? Such results may shed lights on *limits on efficiency of widely used paradigms* as well as *boundary of blockcipher designs*.

By "non-trivial", we mean the construction must use some ideas. E.g., if an oracle $\mathcal{O}$ already contains an exponential number of independent n-bit random permutations, then $E^{\mathcal{O}}$ can trivially instantiate an indifferentiable blockcipher. With this in mind, we introduce an oracle $\mathcal{P}$ that "provides all but the goal".

In detail, $\mathcal{P} = (\mathbf{P}_1, \mathbf{P}_2, \ldots, \mathbf{P}_{|\mathcal{I}|})$ is a family of independent random permutations indexed by $i \in \mathcal{I}$, where $\mathbf{P}_i : \{0,1\}^{M(i)} \to \{0,1\}^{m(i)}$ for an integer function $m : \mathcal{I} \to \mathrm{poly}(n)$. The set $\mathcal{I}$ is partitioned into $\mathcal{I}_{\leq n}$ and $\mathcal{I}_{>n}$, such that $i \in \mathcal{I}_{\leq n}$ if and only if $m(i) \leq n$. To avoid trivial results, we require $|\mathcal{I}_{\leq n}| = O(\mathrm{poly}(n))$, so that $\mathcal{P}$ cannot offer exponentially many n-bit permutations. For $i \in \mathcal{I}_{>n}$, it can be $m(i) \gg n$, and an indifferentiable random function/injection can be built by calling such a wide permutation once [5,14]. Thus, such an oracle $\mathcal{P}$ essentially offers the "maximal" power to the constructions. As will be detailed in Sect. 5.1, existing constructions [1,16,39] can be seen as defined upon $\mathcal{P}$.

The status, of course, depends on the security notion. W.r.t. *indistinguishability*, a single permutation-call is already sufficient using the Even-Mansour scheme [23]. We seek for bounds w.r.t. *indifferentiability*. *Specific lower bounds* have been shown: Feistel ciphers [16,19] consume *at least* 6 random function calls, while IEM ciphers need 4 random function/permutation calls [1,18,27]. Despite this and the fruitful positive results mentioned before, no *general lower bounds* are publicly known (except that a polynomial-length random string is insufficient [41]) due to its challenging nature: the adversarial goal is not as clear as [3, 9, 44] (which simply finds collisions or pre-images), and one has to pin-point "non-random" properties that are exploitable within polynomial-queries (unlike [3, 44]) in various cases, and further prove that interactions with ideal ciphers and *all possible simulators* are unlikely to admit such properties.

Our Results. We prove the first general lower bound: *no iterated blockcipher making 3 or less calls to the oracle $\mathcal{P}$ is statistically indifferentiable from ideal ciphers*. This proves *optimality* for the mentioned 4-call positive result [27].

Model and Settings. We consider *iterated blockciphers* that can be written as the composition of *rounds* using keys or derived subkeys. Every *round* is essentially a simpler "1-call" blockcipher *making exactly 1 call to $\mathcal{P}$*, and the total number of $\mathcal{P}$-calls made by the rounds and the key derivation function is a constant.

More concretely, to model rounds/1-call ciphers, we define $E1^{\mathcal{P}}(K, x) := \varphi^{out}(K, \mathcal{P}(\varphi^{in}(K, x)), x)$ with keyspace $\mathcal{K}$ and domain $\{0, 1\}^n$. The *input function* φ^{in} maps $(K, x) \in \mathcal{K} \times \{0, 1\}^n$ into a query (i, δ, z) to $\mathcal{P}$, where $\delta \in \{+, -\}$ indicates the direction, $i \in \mathcal{I}$ indexes the queried permutation and $z \in \{0, 1\}^{M(i)}$ is the concrete query. The *output function* φ^{out} maps the key K, the $\mathcal{P}$ response $z' = \mathcal{P}(\varphi^{in}(K, x))$ and the plaintext x to the ciphertext y.

$E1^{\mathcal{P}}$ must admit efficient inversion within 1 $\mathcal{P}$-call as well. Thus, it is defined $(E1^{-1})^{\mathcal{P}}(K, y) := \gamma^{out}(K, \mathcal{P}(\gamma^{in}(K, y)), y)$ for two other input and output functions γ^{in} and γ^{out}. Arguably, this covers all blockciphers using a single oracle call (which resembles [9]). See Fig. 1 for illustration.

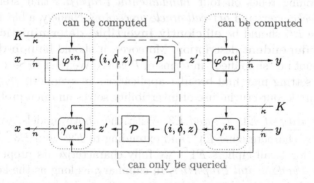

Fig. 1. The general blockcipher $E1^{\mathcal{P}}$ making a single call to its oracle $\mathcal{P}$ for enciphering (up) and deciphering (bottom). $\varphi^{in}, \varphi^{out}, \gamma^{in}$ and γ^{out} are arbitrary (e.g., can be highly non-linear) deterministic and oracle-independent functions, and are computable by the differentiator (as indicated). $\mathcal{P} = (\mathbf{P}_1, \mathbf{P}_2, ...)$ is the mentioned family of random permutations, and it only offers oracle access to the differentiator.

Then, for our model of a t-call iterated blockcipher $Et^{\mathcal{P}} : \mathcal{K} \times \{0, 1\}^n \to \{0, 1\}^n$, the keyspace $\mathcal{K}$ is partitioned into disjoint sets $\mathcal{K}^{(0)}, \mathcal{K}^{(1)}, ... \mathcal{K}^{(t-1)}$, such that for all $K \in \mathcal{K}^{(\ell)}$, it has

$$Et^{\mathcal{P}}(K, x) = \Pi^{\mathcal{P}}_{j_{\ell, t-\ell}}\Big(K\|s, ...\Pi^{\mathcal{P}}_{j_{\ell, 2}}(K\|s, \Pi^{\mathcal{P}}_{j_{\ell, 1}}(K\|s, x))...\Big), \tag{1}$$

where:

(i) $s = \mathsf{kd}^{\mathcal{P}}(K)$ is a subkey and $\mathsf{kd}^{\mathcal{P}}$ makes ℓ calls to $\mathcal{P}$, and
(ii) For each $\ell \in \{0, ..., t-1\}$ and each $\alpha \in \{1, ..., t-\ell\}$, $j_{\ell,\alpha} = \ell(\ell-1)/2 + \alpha$ (so that $Et^{\mathcal{P}}$ is defined upon $\ell(\ell+1)/2$ distinct rounds $\Pi_1, ..., \Pi_{\ell(\ell+1)/2}$), and the round $\Pi_{j_{\ell,\alpha}}^{\mathcal{P}}$ is a 1-call cipher.

See Fig. 2 for illustration of $E2^{\mathcal{P}}$ and Figs. 11 and 12 for pseudocode of $E2^{\mathcal{P}}$ and $E3^{\mathcal{P}}$. This unifies virtually all existing blockcipher constructions. While the same oracle $\mathcal{P}$ is used everywhere in $Et^{\mathcal{P}}$, our subsequent attacks never utilize this oracle reusing, and are applicable even if multiple $\mathcal{P}_1, \mathcal{P}_2, ...$ are used.

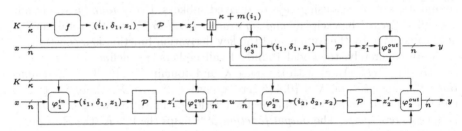

Fig. 2. Encipherment of 2-call iterated blockciphers. (Top) Using one $\mathcal{P}$-call for a key derivation $\mathsf{kd}^{\mathcal{P}}(K) = \mathcal{P}(f(K))$. The function f is deterministic and oracle-independent; (Bottom) Using two $\mathcal{P}$-calls for two rounds, without idealized key derivations.

Our reasoning relies on four *Fundamental Properties* that stem from *the notions of blockciphers* and of *t-call oracle procedures*. Namely, a blockcipher oracle procedure $E^{\mathcal{P}}$ should be **efficiently invertible, deterministic**, and enjoy an **oracle-independent** description. Moreover, it should be **non-degenerate** (i.e., $E^{\mathcal{P}}$ cannot be "simplified" in terms of $\mathcal{P}$ calls). We refer to Sect. 3.1 or 4 for details. Our setting may find broader applications in symmetric cryptography. As a side remark, our crucial use of invertibility solves an open problem of [5].

Differentiability of E1, E2 and E3. With the above models, we prove our main result by characterizing $E1^{\mathcal{P}}$ and extending to $E2^{\mathcal{P}}$ and $E3^{\mathcal{P}}$.

In detail, for 1-call ciphers $E1^{\mathcal{P}}$, we fully characterize its properties, solely based on the *Fundamental Properties*. In summary, as long as the keyspace has $|\mathcal{K}| \geq 2|\mathcal{I}_{\leq n}| + 1 = O(\mathrm{poly}(n))$ (thus, even polynomial keyspace is unachievable!),[1] we can find either $\Omega(\mathrm{poly}(n))$ "inverse-free" encipherments that collide on the $\mathcal{P}$-call and use an entropy-based differentiating approach [41], or find two "non-inverse-free" encipherments $E1^{\mathcal{P}}(K, x)$ and $E1^{\mathcal{P}}(K', x')$ with $\varphi^{in}(K, x) = \varphi^{in}(K', x')$ and use a special regularity property of φ^{in} and γ^{in} to distinguish. We refer to Sect. 3.2 or Theorem 1 for details.

For 2-call iterated cipher $E2^{\mathcal{P}}$, if $\mathcal{K}^{(1)}$ is large enough, i.e., $E2^{\mathcal{P}}$ invokes key derivation for sufficiently many keys, then our differentiators derives $O(\mathrm{poly}(n))$ keys to "collapse" the cipher to a 1-call instance, which has been attacked.

---

[1] Though, trivial constructions with $|\mathcal{K}| \leq |\mathcal{I}_{\leq n}|$ exist since $\mathcal{P}$ may offer $|\mathcal{I}_{\leq n}|$ independent n-bit RPs.

On the other hand, if $\mathcal{K}^{(0)}$ dominates, i.e., $E2^\mathcal{P}$ is a general 2-round blockcipher for most keys, then as long as $\mathcal{K}^{(0)}$ is large enough $|\mathcal{K}^{(0)}| \geq \left(6(3|\mathcal{I}_{\leq n}|)^{\frac{1}{n}} + 5\right)|\mathcal{I}_{\leq n}|+1 = O(\mathrm{poly}(n))$, we can exhibit a general yoyo distinguisher and breaks its *correlation intractability* (a weaker security notion than indifferentiability). We refer to Sect. 3.3 or Theorem 2 for details.

For 3-call iterated ciphers $E3^\mathcal{P}$, if $\mathcal{K}^{(2)}$ or $\mathcal{K}^{(1)}$ is large enough then we again "collapse" it to 1- or 2-call ciphers by deriving $\mathrm{poly}(n)$ keys. If $E3^\mathcal{P}$ is a general 3-round cipher for most keys $\mathcal{K}^{(0)} \subseteq \{0,1\}^\kappa$ with $\kappa \geq 2m_{max} \log_2 |\mathcal{I}_{\leq n}| + 2m_{max}n + 6m_{max} + 4 = \Theta(\mathrm{poly}(n))$, $m_{max} := \max_{i \in \mathcal{I}} m(i)$, we exhibit a universal differentiator that (interestingly) has attack advantage either at least $1/\mathrm{poly}(n) - \mathrm{negl}(n)$ or at least $1 - \mathrm{negl}(n)$, where the concrete polynomial and negligible functions depend on the input functions in the three rounds. We refer to Sect. 3.4 or Theorem 3 for details.

A crucial step is to show the existence of certain non-random properties, which is non-obvious in the general 2- and 3-call ciphers. To this end, we apply Extremal Graph Theory [24,32,38], which bound the maximal number of edges in (bipartite) graphs that do not contain certain structures (a.k.a. *Zarankiewicz numbers* [24]). We refer to Sect. 3 for more detailed overview.

Discussion: Blockcipher Designs. A recent trend is to revisit blockcipher structures and squeeze efficiency for MPC and ZKP settings: see [26] and the references therein. We hope that our work could be a step towards unifying relevant theoretical discussions and shed lights on the "boundary" of designs. We summarize some of our conclusions as follows.

(i) *Expense of overcoming non-invertibility:* if a round/1-call cipher $E1^\mathcal{P}(K, x)$ want to be inverse-free for some (K, x) (e.g., when using non-invertible primitives), then $E1^\mathcal{P}(K, \cdot)$ must admit severe weakness, regardless of its design.

(ii) *Unhelpfulness of wide permutations:* wide permutations with width$> n$ are not "more helpful" in constructing n-bit blockciphers, even if exponentially many are available. This might be another explanation on the difficulty in designing format-preserving encryption schemes (see e.g., [22]).

(iii) *Optimality of popular structures (e.g., the IEM ciphers [18,27]),* in the sense that *no other choice can be better.* This provides the first "excluding-type" theoretical support for practical paradigms.

Besides, since an indifferentiable iterated cipher needs at least 4 calls, our result may be viewed as a theoretical evidence of the advantage (in terms of efficiency) of permutation-based cryptography. Though, we remark that the usual caveats regarding the ideal model apply to this paper: as we consider information-theoretic adversaries, our results do not imply security upper bounds on real-world, computationally bounded adversaries.

Lower Bounds: Functionality Transformations vs. Small-to-Big. Cryptographic constructs consist of two categories: *functionality transformations* and *small-to-big transformations*. The former achieves "non-trivial" new functionality (e.g., our case), while the latter achieve domain or range extension (e.g., PRGs extend range, while hashes extend domain).

A number of existing efficiency lower bounds concerned with *small-to-big transformations*, including hash functions [5,9,25,36,44], PRGs [25,31], signatures [3,25], encryption [25] and injections [5]. A core idea typically employed by these proofs is to apply the pigeonhole principle to force the scheme making the same sequence of primitive calls for exponentially many inputs. This results in either attacks [5,9,44] or unconditional cryptography [3,25,36].

Despite exciting black-box separations [4,34,46], efficiency lower bounds on *functionality transformations* are relatively rare. Our problem *is functionality transforming*: we allow to use wide permutations on $\geq \kappa + n \gg n$ bits, and the domain of our target $E : \{0,1\}^\kappa \times \{0,1\}^n \to \{0,1\}^n$ is thus *not larger*. This difference is crucial, as pigeonhole principle cannot ensure collisions and we have to rely on other properties such as non-degeneracy (see Lemma 3).

Notably, with our oracle $\mathcal{P}$, relevant impossibility results become possible:

(i) A compression function with enough collision or even indifferentiability security can be built using just 1 call to $\mathcal{P}$ via *truncation* [14];
(ii) An indifferentiable injection (or authenticated encryption) can be built using just 1 call to $\mathcal{P}$ via *Encode-then-Encipher* [5].

Still, indifferentiable iterated blockciphers *cannot* be built within 3 calls. These sharp contrasts emphasize the differences between our setting and [5,9].

In a more restricted setting termed *Linicrypt* [13], i.e., cryptosystems are built from random block functions and *linear* diffusion functions, impossibility results regarding encryption [13,42] and circuit garbling [13] exist.

Future Directions. Indeed, blockciphers are *not* necessarily iterated: we serve examples in full version [28]. Intuitively, such designs are weaker than iterated ones with the same number of calls. Though, it is difficult to have a rigorous and clean argument, especially for ciphers with 3 calls. The most intriguing direction is thus to address fully general 2- and 3-call blockciphers, which may shed more lights on iterations. Another intriguing question is whether there are smart ideas to unify the complicated cases in $E3$ analysis. Influences of other aspects such as memory restrictions on adversaries and simulators are also of interest.

On the constructive side, it is intriguing to study the achievability of computational indifferentiability with 3 calls: hardness assumptions on graph problems or key derivation functions might be helpful.

Unlike most practice in symmetric cryptography, our Theorem 3 is asymptotic. The key issue is that our differentiator has to "know" the simulator limitations for its case decision. Classically, simulator (query) complexity is only *polynomially bounded* and seems incompatible with concrete treatments. Fully concrete characterizations may need a new paradigm and are left for future work.

Roadmap. We serve notations and definitions in Sect. 2. Then, as mentioned, we provide a technical overview in Sect. 3.

For the main elaborations, we first formalize the *Fundamental Properties* in Sect. 4. We then give detailed elaborations and characterizations for our 1-call cipher $E1$ as well as its main result in Sect. 5. Our main results on $E2$ and $E3$ are then given in Sect. 6 and 7 respectively. Due to space constraints, detailed proofs are mostly deferred to the full version [28].

2   Preliminaries

Fix n as the security parameter, and write $\mathrm{poly}(n)$ and $\mathrm{negl}(n)$ for arbitrary polynomial and negligible functions respectively. Denote by $\perp$ the empty string. Given $x \in \{0,1\}^n$ and $a \leq n$, denote by $\mathsf{left}_a(x)$ (resp., $\mathsf{right}_a(x)$) the a leftmost (resp., rightmost) bits of x. When two sets A and B are disjoint, we denote $A \sqcup B$ their (disjoint) union. For any domain, denote by id the identity function.

An m-bit random permutation is a permutation that is uniformly selected from $\mathsf{Perm}(m)$, the set of all $(2^m)!$ possible m-bit permutations. Throughout the remaining, we denote by $\mathbf{IC} : \{0,1\}^\kappa \times \{0,1\}^n \to \{0,1\}^n$ an ideal cipher (which is randomly picked from all (κ, n)-blockciphers) with $\kappa = \mathrm{poly}(n)$.

Permutation Family $\mathcal{P}$. As briefed in the Introduction, we consider constructing an n-bit blockcipher from a permutation family oracle $\mathcal{P}$ that "provides all but the goal". In detail, $\mathcal{P} = (\mathbf{P}_1, \mathbf{P}_2, ..., \mathbf{P}_{|\mathcal{I}|})$ provides independent random permutations indexed by $i \in \mathcal{I}$, where $\mathbf{P}_i \in \mathsf{Perm}(m(i))$ for a fixed function $m : \mathcal{I} \to \mathrm{poly}(n)$ (viewed as parameters of $\mathcal{P}$). It can be $m(i) \gg n$ for some $i \in \mathcal{I}$. The index set is thus partitioned as $\mathcal{I} = \mathcal{I}_{\leq n} \sqcup \mathcal{I}_{>n}$, where $i \in \mathcal{I}_{\leq n}$ if and only if $m(i) \leq n$. We require $|\mathcal{I}_{\leq n}| = O(\mathrm{poly}(n))$, while $\mathcal{I}_{>n}$ can be exponentially large. We call permutations with width$> n$ *wide*. Denote by $m_{max} := \max_{i \in \mathcal{I}} m(i)$ and $m_{min} := \min_{I \in \mathcal{I}} m(i)$ the size of largest, resp. smallest permutation in $\mathcal{P}$.

Oracle $\mathcal{P}$ accepts queries of the form (i, δ, z), where $i \in \mathcal{I}$ is the index, $\delta \in \{+, -\}$ indicates if forward $\mathbf{P}_i$ or backward $\mathbf{P}_i^{-1}$ is queried, and $z \in \{0,1\}^{m(i)}$ is the actual $m(i)$-bit input. For $\delta \in \{+, -\}$, we denote $\bar{\delta}$ the opposite of δ.

Indifferentiability. Let $E^{\mathcal{P}}$ be a cryptographic construction that internally queries $\mathcal{P}$, $\mathbf{IC}$ be the ideal crypto object of $E^{\mathcal{P}}$, and $S^{\mathbf{IC}}$ be a simulator that queries $\mathbf{IC}$ and provides the same interfaces as $\mathcal{P}$. Then, for any distinguisher D, the indifferentiability advantage of D against $E^{\mathcal{P}}$ is

$$\mathrm{Adv}^{indif}_{E^{\mathcal{P}}, \mathbf{IC}, S}(D) = \left| \Pr[D^{E^{\mathcal{P}}, \mathcal{P}} = 1] - \Pr[D^{\mathbf{IC}, S^{\mathbf{IC}}} = 1] \right|.$$

$E^{\mathcal{P}}$ is indifferentiable (in the asymptotic sense), as long as for any polynomial-query D: (a) the advantage $\mathrm{Adv}^{indif}_{E^{\mathcal{P}}, \mathbf{IC}, S}(D)$ is $\mathrm{negl}(n)$ w.r.t. the security parameter n for any D, and (b) the number of queries made by S to $\mathbf{IC}$ is $\mathrm{poly}(n)$.

Notations for Differentiators. Consider blockciphers $E1^{\mathcal{P}}, E2^{\mathcal{P}}$ and $E3^{\mathcal{P}}$ built upon the oracle $\mathcal{P}$. By the above, to break indifferentiability, we shall exhibit a differentiator D that "fools" any query-efficient simulator $S^{\mathbf{IC}}$ with non-negligible probability. Notice, D has access to two oracles (E, P) where $\mathrm{E} \in \{E1^{\mathcal{P}}, E2^{\mathcal{P}}, E3^{\mathcal{P}}, \mathbf{IC}\}$ and $\mathrm{P} \in \{\mathcal{P}, S^{\mathbf{IC}}\}$. To describe the interaction between $D^{\mathrm{E},\mathrm{P}}$ and its oracles E, P, we use the expressions $\mathrm{P}(i, \delta, z) \to z'$ to mean that D queries P on (i, δ, z) and P answers with z', and $\mathrm{E}(K, x) \to y$ to mean that E is queried on (K, x) and returns y. Note that in the latter case, the query may be made by S. The notation $E^{-1}(K, y) \to x$ is similar.

As convention, our differentiators always output 1 when it guesses the "real world", and output 0 when it guesses the "ideal" or "simulated world".

Tools from Extremal Graph Theory. Consider a bipartite graph $\mathcal{G} = (\mathcal{V}_L, \mathcal{V}_R, \mathcal{E})$. Intuitively, if $|\mathcal{E}|$ is sufficiently large, then $\mathcal{G}$ must have short cycles (since long cycles will be truncated). This was proven by Hoory [32], and will help establishing the existence of certain structures. To ease applying, we restate Hoory's result [32, Eqs. (1) and (2)] as follows.

Proposition 1. *Let $\mathcal{G} = (\mathcal{V}_L, \mathcal{V}_R, \mathcal{E})$ be a bipartite graph such that:*

(i) $|\mathcal{V}_L|$ and $|\mathcal{V}_R|$ have a common upper bound, i.e., there exists an integer $M > 0$ such that $|\mathcal{V}_L| \leq M$, $|\mathcal{V}_R| \leq M$; and
(ii) $|\mathcal{E}| \geq ((M)^{\frac{1}{t-1}} + 1) \times M$ for some positive integer t.

Then, $\mathcal{G}$ contains a cycle $C_{2\ell}$ with $\ell \leq t$.

If $|\mathcal{E}|$ is large, then $\mathcal{G}$ contains a small complete bipartite graph (a.k.a. biclique). This was proven by Kővári, Sós and Turán [38], and is restated as follows.

Proposition 2. *Let $\mathcal{G} = (\mathcal{V}_L, \mathcal{V}_R, \mathcal{E})$ be a bipartite graph such that:*

(i) There exist two integers $M, N > 0$ such that $|\mathcal{V}_L| \leq M$ and $|\mathcal{V}_R| \leq N$; and
(ii) $|\mathcal{E}| \geq (b-1)^{\frac{1}{a}} \cdot MN^{1-\frac{1}{a}} + (a-1)N$.

Then, $\mathcal{G}$ contains the complete bipartite graph $K_{a,b}$ as a sub-graph.

We refer to the full version [28] for how to concretely derive the two propositions.

3   Technical Overview

As mentioned, we characterize the 1-call model $E1^{\mathcal{P}}$ and then extend the discussion to 2- and 3-call iterated models $E2^{\mathcal{P}}$ and $E3^{\mathcal{P}}$. Below in Sect. 3.1, we first elaborate more on *Fundamental Properties* underlying our reasoning. We then provide intuitions for $E1^{\mathcal{P}}$, $E2^{\mathcal{P}}$ and $E3^{\mathcal{P}}$ in Sect. 3.2, 3.3 and 3.4 in turn.

3.1   Fundamental Properties

As mentioned, our analyses rely on four properties that we believe fundamental to blockcipher oracle procedures. First, the *definition of the notion of blockciphers* yield two properties for a blockcipher oracle procedure $E^{\mathcal{P}}$:

(i) **Efficient invertibility**: blockciphers should be efficiently invertible. Namely, there is a corresponding oracle procedure $(E^{-1})^{\mathcal{P}}$ computing its inverse;
(ii) **Deterministic**: blockciphers should be *deterministic*. For $E^{\mathcal{P}}$, it means for a fixed oracle $\mathcal{P}$, evaluating $E^{\mathcal{P}}(K, x) \to y$ and the corresponding decipherment $(E^{-1})^{\mathcal{P}}(K, y)$ always yield the same transcript of $\mathcal{P}$-queries and responses.

Besides, since an oracle procedure E^P shall have a fixed description that is independent from P, sub-procedures in E^P are **oracle-independent**. We further assume that E^P is **non-degenerate** and cannot be "simplified" in terms of P calls, i.e., no encipherment $E^P(K, x)$ can be approximately computed using less P calls than E^P. Formal definitions will be given in Sect. 4.

3.2   Full Characterization of 1-Call Cipher $E1$

As per mentioned, $E1^P(K, x) := \varphi^{out}(K, P(\varphi^{in}(K, x)))$ and $(E1^{-1})^P(K, y) := \gamma^{out}(K, P(\gamma^{in}(K, y)))$, where φ^{in}, φ^{out}, γ^{in} and γ^{out} can be arbitrary oracle-independent functions. The *Fundamental Properties* already ensure a number of non-trivial properties (on oracle procedures of blockciphers).

Inv-Freeness and Its Oracle-Independence. Our first observation is about inverse-freeness of $E1^P$. An encipherment $E1^P(K, x)$ is *inverse-free* (inv-free for short), if $E1^P(K, x) \to y$ and its corresponding decipherment $(E1^{-1})^P(K, y) \to x$ call $P(i, \delta, \star)$ on the same direction δ; otherwise, $E1^P(K, x)$ is *non-inverse-free* (non-inv-free). In common designs (Feistel, Misty, IEM, etc.), encipherments under a fixed key are either all inv-free or non-inv-free for all plaintext. However, in general, the inv-freeness of $E1^P(K, x)$ may depend on x, admitting *data-dependent* inv-freeness. We serve an example in Fig. 3.

Our observation is that *in $E1^P$, inv-freeness cannot depend on the oracle P*, i.e., one can decide if an encipherment $E1^P(K, x)$ is inv-free without querying P. Intuitively, it is because the query directions of encipherment and decipherment are determined by the input functions φ^{in} and γ^{in}, which are oracle-independent. The formal presentation will be given in Lemma 1. As will be seen, exploitable weakness in an encipherment $E1^P(K, x)$ depends on its inv-freeness, the oracle-independence of which turns out crucial in our attacks.

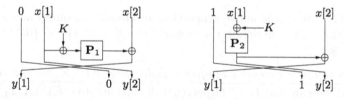

Fig. 3. A 1-call cipher/round that has data-dependent inverse-freeness. (Left) when the leftmost bit of $x = 0\|x[1]\|x[2]$ is 0 (a permutation-based Feistel round); (Right) when the leftmost bit of $x = 1\|x[1]\|x[2]$ is 1 (a Misty-like round).

Properties of Inv-Free $E1^P(K, x)$. For intuitions, consider the key-prepended Feistel round $y = \Psi^F(K, x) := (\text{right}_{n/2}(x) \oplus F(K\|\text{left}_{n/2}(x)))\|\text{left}_{n/2}(x)$. This round is inv-free: an encipherment $\Psi^F(K, x)$ and its corresponding decipherment $(\Psi^{-1})^F(K, y)$ make the same "forward" call to $F(z)$, $z = K\|\text{left}_{n/2}(x) = K\|\text{right}_{n/2}(y)$. This means some information of x is kept in the ciphertext y without "protection". The same property is shared by various Feistel variants

[2, Chapter 1.3.1] (including the Lai-Massey scheme [2, Chapter 1.5]). Casting it into our general model $E1^{\mathcal{P}}$, it means *inv-free $E1^{\mathcal{P}}(K, x) \rightarrow y$ must have* $\varphi^{in}(K, x) = \gamma^{in}(K, y)$.

As a less obvious fact in $\Psi^{\mathbf{F}}$, there necessarily exist many distinct encipherments that make the same **F**-call. I.e., $\Psi^{\mathbf{F}}(K, x)$ calls $\mathbf{F}(z)$ as long as $\text{right}_{n/2}(x) = \text{right}_{n/2}(z)$, and there are $2^{n/2}$ possible x for every z. Similarly for other inv-free designs. It turns out that: *with the non-degeneracy assumption on $E1$, if there is one inv-free $E1^{\mathcal{P}}(K, x)$ then there are $\Omega(\text{poly}(n))$ distinct inv-free $E1^{\mathcal{P}}(K, x_1)$, $E1^{\mathcal{P}}(K, x_2)$, ... that collide on the $\mathcal{P}$-call, i.e.,* $\varphi^{in}(K, x_1) = \varphi^{in}(K, x_2) = ... = \varphi^{in}(K, x)$. This further implies that under each key K, all inv-free $E1^{\mathcal{P}}(K, x)$ give rise to $o(\frac{2^n}{\text{poly}(n)})$ distinct $\mathcal{P}$-calls (even if they can query exponentially many permutations with width$> n$).

We refer to Lemmas 2–4 in Sect. 5.2 for formal elaborations.

Properties of Non-inv-free $E1^{\mathcal{P}}(K, x)$. For intuitions, consider the IEM round $y = \text{EM}^{\mathbf{P}}(K, x) := K \oplus \mathbf{P}(K \oplus x)$, which is non-inv-free since $(\text{EM}^{-1})^{\mathbf{P}}$ always calls $\mathbf{P}^{-1}$. $\text{EM}^{\mathbf{P}}$ is more secure than $\Psi^{\mathbf{F}}$. In fact, attacks against $\text{EM}^{\mathbf{P}}$ have to exploit at least 2 keys K, K' [1, Sect. 3.1, full version] and seek for encipherments $\text{EM}^{\mathbf{P}}(K, x)$ and $\text{EM}^{\mathbf{P}}(K', x')$ that collide on the $\mathbf{P}$-call, i.e., with $K \oplus x = K' \oplus x'$. Such collided encipherments *do exist*, because $\text{EM}^{\mathbf{P}}$ cannot use wide $\mathbf{P}$. Concretely, to invoke a wide $\mathbf{P}$, $\text{EM}^{\mathbf{P}}$ must pad $x \in \{0,1\}^n$ with some "non-trivial" information (e.g., $\mathbf{P}(x\|0)$, or $\mathbf{P}(x\|K)$); but then, by invoking $\mathbf{P}^{-1}$, decipherments are unlikely to "recover" correctly padded $\mathbf{P}$-inputs. In fact, this irrecoverability is the core idea of *Encode-then-Encipher* [5].

It turns out that this irrecoverability stems from oracle-independence. In detail, assuming oracle-independence of φ^{in} and γ^{in}, non-inv-free encipherments $E1^{\mathcal{P}}(K, x)$ can only query permutations with width$\leq n$. Thus, non-inv-free give rise to at most $|\mathcal{I}_{\leq n}|2^{N+1}$ distinct $\mathcal{P}$-calls. We refer to Lemma 5 in Sect. 5.2 for formal elaborations.

Attack $E1^{\mathcal{P}}$. With the above properties, we are able to bump into our differentiator $D1$ on $E1^{\mathcal{P}}$. In detail, the cipher $E1^{\mathcal{P}} : \mathcal{K} \times \{0,1\}^n \rightarrow \{0,1\}^n$ may fall into two cases.

Case 1: there exists at least 1 inv-free encipherment $E1^{\mathcal{P}}(K, x)$. As discussed, this means we can find $t = \Omega(\text{poly}(n))$ distinct inv-free $E1^{\mathcal{P}}(K, x_1), ..., E1^{\mathcal{P}} (K, x_t)$ that make the same $\mathcal{P}$-call $\mathcal{P}(i, \delta, z)$, $(i, \delta, z) = \varphi^{in}(K, x_1) = ... = \varphi^{in}(K, x_t)$. Thus, the restriction of $E1^{\mathcal{P}}(K, \cdot)$ to $\{x_1, ..., x_t\}$ is a bijection defined upon a polynomial-length random string $z' = \mathcal{P}(i, \delta, z)$, and we can apply an entropy-based differentiating approach [41].

Case 2: $E1^{\mathcal{P}}(K, x)$ is non-inv-free for all $(K, x) \in \mathcal{K} \times \{0,1\}^n$. Then, $E1^{\mathcal{P}}(K, x)$ can only invoke the permutations in $\mathcal{P}$ with width$\leq n$ (as discussed). Therefore, the number of possible images of φ^{in} is at most $|\mathcal{I}_{\leq n}|2^{N+1}$. As long as $|\mathcal{K}|2^n \geq |\mathcal{I}_{\leq n}|2^{N+1}$, i.e., the keyspace has $|\mathcal{K}| \geq 2|\mathcal{I}_{\leq n}| + 1$ (which is $O(\text{poly}(n))$, though), the pigeonhole principle guarantees the existence of $(K, x), (K', x') \in \mathcal{K} \times \{0,1\}^n$ with collision $\varphi^{in}(K, x) = \varphi^{in}(K', x')$. $D1$

thus finds such a pair of collided $(K, x), (K', x')$ and attacks by checking if $\gamma^{in}(K, \mathrm{E}(K, x)) = \gamma^{in}(K', \mathrm{E}(K', x'))$.

The formal proof, deferred to the full version [28], is more technical and relies on a sort of "regularity" of the input functions φ^{in} and γ^{in} (Lemma 6).

3.3 Attack 2-Call Iterated Cipher $E2$

Built upon our above results on $E1^{\mathcal{P}}$, we further consider our 2-call model $E2^{\mathcal{P}}$. Recall that the keyspace $\mathcal{K}$ of $E2^{\mathcal{P}}$ can be partitioned $\mathcal{K} = \mathcal{K}^{(0)} \sqcup \mathcal{K}^{(1)}$, such that $E2^{\mathcal{P}}(K, x) = \Pi_3^{\mathcal{P}}(K\|\mathsf{kd}^{\mathcal{P}}(K), x)$ for all $K \in \mathcal{K}^{(1)}$, whereas $E2^{\mathcal{P}}(K, x) = \Pi_2^{\mathcal{P}}(K, \Pi_1^{\mathcal{P}}(K, x))$ for all $K \in \mathcal{K}^{(0)}$. The sub-procedures $\mathsf{kd}^{\mathcal{P}}$ has $\mathsf{kd}^{\mathcal{P}}(K) = \mathcal{P}(f(K))$ for another oracle-independent function f. In addition, for $j = 1, 2, 3$, $\Pi_j^{\mathcal{P}}$ is a 1-call cipher with input and output functions $\varphi_j^{in}, \varphi_j^{out}, \gamma_j^{in}$ and γ_j^{out}. We refer to Fig. 2 for illustration and Fig. 11 for a pseudocode description.

This model $E2^{\mathcal{P}}$ may fall into two cases.

Case 1: $E2^{\mathcal{P}}$ invokes kd for sufficiently many keys. Formally, if the key sets have $|\mathcal{K}^{(1)}| \geq 2|\mathcal{I}_{\leq n}| + 1$, we simply pick $\lambda = 2|\mathcal{I}_{\leq n}| + 1$ keys $K_1, ..., K_\lambda \in \mathcal{K}^{(1)}$ and derive subkeys $s_1 = \mathsf{kd}^{\mathcal{P}}(K_1), ..., s_\lambda = \mathsf{kd}^{\mathcal{P}}(K_\lambda)$. This consumes at most $\lambda = O(\mathrm{poly}(n))$ P-queries. We then view the round $\Pi_3^{\mathcal{P}}$ as a 1-call cipher with keyspace $\{K_1\|s_1, ..., K_\lambda\|s_\lambda\}$ and apply our differentiator $D1$. (It is thus crucial that $D1$ can break $E1$ with polynomial-keyspace.)

Case 2: $E2^{\mathcal{P}}$ is 2-iteration for sufficiently many keys. The concrete condition is $|\mathcal{K}^{(0)}| \geq \left(6\left(3|\mathcal{I}_{\leq n}|\right)^{\frac{1}{n}} + 3\right)|\mathcal{I}_{\leq n}| = O(\mathrm{poly}(n))$. Our idea (non-trivially) generalizes existing specific attacks, which is elaborated as follows.

Outset: Boomerang Property. Our initial intuition lies in a chosen-key boomerang differentiator against the 2-round IEM cipher $y = K \oplus \mathbf{P}_2(K \oplus \mathbf{P}_1(K \oplus x))$, $K \in \{0,1\}^n$ (which is motivated by Andreeva et al.'s [1, Sect. 3.2, full version]). Briefly, for any x, let $u = \mathbf{P}_1(K \oplus x)$. The attack begins by computing four distinct pairs $(K_1, u_1), (K_2, u_2), (K_3, u_3), (K_4, u_4)$ with $u_1 = u_2$, $u_3 = u_4$; $K_1 \oplus u_1 = K_3 \oplus u_3$ and $K_2 \oplus u_2 = K_4 \oplus u_4$. I.e., they induce two collided inputs to $\mathbf{P}_1^{-1}$ and two collide inputs to $\mathbf{P}_2$. Once such four pairs are derived, the differentiator can computes a 4-tuple of cipher inputs/outputs $\left((K_1, x_1, y_1), ..., (K_4, x_4, y_4)\right)$ that has $K_1 \oplus x_1 = K_2 \oplus x_2$, $K_3 \oplus x_3 = K_4 \oplus x_4$; $K_1 \oplus y_1 = K_3 \oplus y_3$, $K_2 \oplus y_2 = K_4 \oplus y_4$; as shown in Fig. 4 (left). Such a 4-tuple satisfies an evasive relation [39] and is hard to found in the ideal world. Actually the involved structure is the basis of the boomerang attack developed in [49].

A similar boomerang can be exhibited in the 2-round Feistel. Motivated by these, our differentiator against the general 2-iteration cipher tries to find pairs $(K_1, u_1), (K_2, u_2), (K_3, u_3), (K_4, u_4) \in \mathcal{K}^{(0)} \times \{0,1\}^n$ that induce similar collided $\mathcal{P}$-calls, i.e., $\gamma_1^{in}(K_1, u_1) = \gamma_1^{in}(K_2, u_2)$, $\gamma_1^{in}(K_3, u_3) = \gamma_1^{in}(K_4, u_4)$; $\varphi_2^{in}(K_1, u_1) = \varphi_2^{in}(K_3, u_3)$ and $\varphi_2^{in}(K_2, u_2) = \varphi_2^{in}(K_4, u_4)$, as shown in Fig. 4 (right). This is a general boomerang property. Unlike Fig. 4 (left), the four encipherments may not be non-inv-free in two rounds: actually, Fig. 4 (right) serves an example where the 1st round of $E2^{\mathcal{P}}(K_3, x_3)$ and $E2^{\mathcal{P}}(K_4, x_4)$ are inv-free.

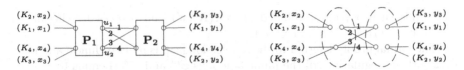

Fig. 4. (Top) Boomerang distinguisher in 2-round IEM. Circles indicate values in domain and range of $\mathbf{P}_1$ and $\mathbf{P}_2$ (in particular, u_1 and u_2 are marked), and lines indicate encipherment flows. To simplify, for lines between $\mathbf{P}_1$ and $\mathbf{P}_2$ the pair (K_j, u_j) is simplified as j. (Bottom) An example of boomerang distinguisher in 2-round general $E2$. Circles indicate values in domain and range of $\mathcal{P}$, and lines indicate encipherment flows. When a line "crosses" a pair of circles, it means the encipherment is non-inv-free in that round, and the two circles (naturally) indicate the $\mathcal{P}$ inputs and outputs; when a line "crosses" a single circle, it means the encipherment is non-inv-free in that round (so that rightward and leftward evaluations reach the same $\mathcal{P}$ input). Thus, the four encipherments are all non-inv-free in the 2nd round; in the 1st round, $E2^{\mathcal{P}}(K_1, x_1)$ and $E2^{\mathcal{P}}(K_2, x_2)$ are non-inv-free, while $E2^{\mathcal{P}}(K_3, x_3)$ and $E2^{\mathcal{P}}(K_4, x_4)$ are inv-free.

From Boomerang to Yoyo. But does such a 4-tuple ever exist? Unlike "concrete" ciphers such as IEM and Feistel, this is unclear in $E2$. To solve this, we apply Hoory's [32] result on girth (i.e., maximal length of cycles in a graph). Briefly, if we view the possible inputs to $\mathcal{P}$ as shores and the pairs $(K, u) \in \mathcal{K}^{(0)} \times \{0, 1\}^n$ as edges, then we can build a bipartite graph $\mathcal{G}$, and the above 4-tuple becomes a 4-cycle C_4 (i.e., cycle of length 4) in $\mathcal{G}$. By Hoory [32] (which is restated in Sect. 2, Proposition 1), as long as the number of edges is large enough, such a 4-cycle or 4-tuple is guaranteed to exist.

However, as will be clear in the analysis (available in [28]), the above requires $\mathcal{K}^{(0)}$ to be of exponential size, which would prohibit its application in our later attack against $E3$. To remedy, we consider longer cycles $C_{2\lambda}, \lambda \leq n+1$. I.e., our differentiator seeks for a 2λ-tuple $\big((K_1, u_1), ..., (K_{2\lambda}, u_{2\lambda})\big)$ that has

$$\varphi_2^{in}(K_1, u_1) = \varphi_2^{in}(K_2, u_2), \qquad \gamma_1^{in}(K_2, u_2) = \gamma_1^{in}(K_3, u_3),$$
$$\varphi_2^{in}(K_3, u_3) = \varphi_2^{in}(K_4, u_4), \qquad \gamma_1^{in}(K_4, u_4) = \gamma_1^{in}(K_5, u_5), \quad ...$$
$$\varphi_2^{in}(K_{2\lambda-1}, u_{2\lambda-1}) = \varphi_2^{in}(K_{2\lambda}, u_{2\lambda}), \qquad \gamma_1^{in}(K_{2\lambda}, u_{2\lambda}) = \gamma_1^{in}(K_1, u_1). \quad (2)$$

Once such a 2λ-tuple is found, our differentiator can computes a 2λ-tuple of $E2$ inputs/outputs $\big((K_1, x_1, y_1), ..., (K_{2\lambda}, x_{2\lambda}, y_{2\lambda})\big)$ that has a "cycle of collisions". I.e., $\gamma_2^{in}(K_1, y_1) = \gamma_2^{in}(K_2, y_2), \varphi_1^{in}(K_2, x_2) = \varphi_1^{in}(K_3, x_3), ..., \gamma_2^{in}(K_{2\lambda-1}, y_{2\lambda-1}) = \gamma_2^{in}(K_{2\lambda}, y_{2\lambda}), \varphi_1^{in}(K_{2\lambda}, x_{2\lambda}) = \varphi_1^{in}(K_1, x_1)$. An example with $\lambda = 4$ is shown in Fig. 5. This is actually a general version of the yoyo distinguisher [45]. By Hoory [32], $|\mathcal{K}^{(0)}| \geq \big(6(3|\mathcal{I}_{\leq n}|)^{\frac{1}{n}} + 3\big)|\mathcal{I}_{\leq n}| = O(\text{poly}(n))$ already suffices for the existence of $\big((K_1, u_1), ..., (K_{2\lambda}, u_{2\lambda})\big)$. Note that Hoory does not apply when $\mathcal{G}$ is a multigraph, but this implies existence of C_2. These solve our first problem.

Non-degenerate Input Functions. Subtleties remain. To argue that no polynomial-query simulator can work out a similar 2λ-tuple of ideal cipher inputs/outputs $\big(\mathbf{IC}(K_1, x_1) = y_1, ..., \mathbf{IC}(K_{2\lambda}, x_{2\lambda}) = y_{2\lambda}\big)$, the input functions φ_1^{in} and γ_2^{in}

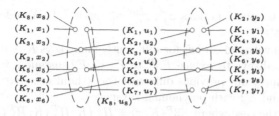

Fig. 5. An example of general yoyo distinguisher with $\lambda = 4$ in $E2$. Meanings of the objects follow Fig. 4.

must be somewhat "non-degenerate". Roughly, $\Pr[x \xleftarrow{\$} \{0,1\}^n : \varphi_1^{in}(K,x) = (i,\delta,z)] = \mathrm{negl}(n)$ and $\Pr[y \xleftarrow{\$} \{0,1\}^n : \gamma_2^{in}(K,y) = (i,\delta,z)] = \mathrm{negl}(n)$ for any K and any (i,δ,z).

Wlog consider φ_1. Indeed, due to the aforementioned "regularity" (Lemma 6), it can be proven $\Pr_x[\varphi_1^{in}(K,x) = (i,\delta,z) \mid \Pi_1^{\mathcal{P}}(K,x)$ non-inv-free$] = \mathrm{negl}(n)$. But $\varphi_1^{in}(K,\cdot)$ may lead $\Omega(2^n/\mathrm{poly}(n))$ distinct inv-free $\Pi_1^{\mathcal{P}}(K,x)$ to the same call $\mathcal{P}(i,\delta,z)$ (i.e., being highly biased), which enables the simulator to cheat.

A complete case-study thus has to consider whether φ_1^{in} and γ_2^{in} are "non-degenerate". However, input functions in virtually all blockciphers are indeed "non-degenerate": otherwise, the round is ridiculously weak. Meanwhile, complete case-study would take us quite far afield. We thereby decide to simplify and introduce *non-degenerate input functions* as an additional assumption for $E2^{\mathcal{P}}$ and $E3^{\mathcal{P}}$, i.e., $\Pr_x[\varphi_1^{in}(K,x) = (i,\delta,z) \mid \Pi_1^{\mathcal{P}}(K,x)$ inv-free$] = \mathrm{negl}(n)$ and $\Pr_y[\gamma_2^{in}(K,y) = (i,\delta,z) \mid (\Pi_2^{-1})^{\mathcal{P}}(K,y)$ inv-free$] = \mathrm{negl}(n)$. We refer to Sect. 6 for more details. With this additional restriction, we prove that no polynomial-query simulator can work out the aforementioned 2λ-tuple. In fact, Eq. (2) defines a novel evasive relation in 2-round general ciphers, which is stronger than differentiability. See Sect. 6 for formal result and [28] for detailed analysis.

It is crucial to restrict our discussion to iterated blockciphers: since the set of valid intermediate values u between the rounds is simply $\{0,1\}^n$, an attacker can pick such a u and compute forward or backward. Indeed, this middle-to-sides approach is common in known- and chosen-key attacks [37].

3.4   Attack 3-Call Iterated Cipher $E3$

We further consider our 3-call model $E3^{\mathcal{P}}$. Recall that $E3^{\mathcal{P}} : \{0,1\}^\kappa \times \{0,1\}^n \to \{0,1\}^n$ has $\kappa = \Theta(\mathrm{poly}(n))$, and its keyspace can be partitioned $\{0,1\}^\kappa = \mathcal{K}^{(0)} \sqcup \mathcal{K}^{(1)} \sqcup \mathcal{K}^{(2)}$, such that:

(i) $E3^{\mathcal{P}}(K,x) = \Pi_6^{\mathcal{P}}(K\|\mathsf{kd}_1^{\mathcal{P}}(K),x)$ for all $K \in \mathcal{K}^{(2)}$;

(ii) $E3^{\mathcal{P}}(K,x) = \Pi_5^{\mathcal{P}}(K\|\mathsf{kd}_2^{\mathcal{P}}(K), \Pi_4^{\mathcal{P}}(K\|\mathsf{kd}_2^{\mathcal{P}}(K),x))$ for all $K \in \mathcal{K}^{(1)}$;

(iii) $E3^{\mathcal{P}}(K,x) = \Pi_3^{\mathcal{P}}(K, \Pi_2^{\mathcal{P}}(K, \Pi_1^{\mathcal{P}}(K,x)))$ for all $K \in \mathcal{K}^{(0)}$.

The sub-procedures $\mathsf{kd}_1^{\mathcal{P}}(K)$ and $\mathsf{kd}_2^{\mathcal{P}}(K)$ derive corresponding subkeys via two and one calls to $\mathcal{P}$ respectively. In addition, for $j = 1, 2, ..., 6$, $\Pi_j^{\mathcal{P}}$ is a 1-call cipher with input and output functions $\varphi_j^{in}, \varphi_j^{out}, \gamma_j^{in}$ and γ_j^{out}. We refer to Fig. 12 for pseudocode of $E3^{\mathcal{P}}$.

When $E3^{\mathcal{P}}$ invokes kd_1 or kd_2 for sufficiently many keys $K \in \{0,1\}^{\kappa}$, we again derive $\mathrm{poly}(n)$ subkeys to reduce $E3^{\mathcal{P}}$ to $E1$ or $E2$ instances with polynomial keyspace, and apply our previous differentiators (thanks to that our differentiators break $E1$ and $E2$ with polynomial keyspace).

The crux is the case where $E3^{\mathcal{P}}(K, x) = \Pi_3^{\mathcal{P}}\big(K, \Pi_2^{\mathcal{P}}\big(K, \Pi_1^{\mathcal{P}}(K, x)\big)\big)$ for virtually all 2^{κ} keys K. Depending on whether the $\Theta(2^{\kappa+n})$ encipherments are "mostly" inv-free or not in the 3 rounds, exploitable non-random properties significantly vary in the $2^3 = 8$ cases and cannot be unified. We thereby have to appeal for a (lengthy) case-study.

Furthermore, note that inv-freeness can be data-dependent, which causes a subtle technical challenge. Namely, without querying P, one cannot fully decide if a certain encipherment is inv-free in the 3 rounds.[2] But querying P would trigger simulator actions in the ideal world, and the simulated P may be defined to change the inv-freeness of the encipherments in question. This turns out a technical challenge, and we call it *decisional inv-free problem*. Our solution is two-fold. First, we identified relevant conditions that are decidable without querying P, so that our differentiator could invoke the right subroutine for case-study without attracting simulator's attention. Meanwhile, to compute (intermediate) values of the encipherments in question, our differentiator (tries the best to) query the enciphering oracle E instead of P to avoid "waking" the simulator. Our case conditions ensure that the ideal cipher responses (in the ideal world) will satisfy our expectations on inv-freeness. We will elaborate more later.

Below we denote by $x \in \{0,1\}^n$ the plaintext, $u = \Pi_1^{\mathcal{P}}(K, x)$ the 1st round output, $w = \Pi_2^{\mathcal{P}}(K, u)$ the 2nd round output and $y = \Pi_3^{\mathcal{P}}(K, w)$ the ciphertext.

Case 1: there are $\Theta(2^{\kappa})$ keys K s.t. only $o(2^n/\mathrm{poly}(n))$ $\Pi_1^{\mathcal{P}}(K, x)$ are non-inv-free, and only $o(2^n/\mathrm{poly}(n))$ $(\Pi_3^{-1})^{\mathcal{P}}(K, y)$ are non-inv-free. Roughly, this means most of the $\Theta(2^{\kappa+n})$ encipherments $E3^{\mathcal{P}}(K, x)$ are inv-free in 1st and 3rd rounds. A famous example is the 3-round Feistel $\mathrm{Feistel3}(K, x) := \Psi^{\mathbf{F}_3}\big(K, \Psi^{\mathbf{F}_2}\big(K, \Psi^{\mathbf{F}_1}(K, x)\big)\big)$. Since the 2nd round could be arbitrary, the "hybrid" cipher $\mathrm{Hyb}(K, x) := \Psi^{\mathbf{F}_3}\big(K, K \oplus \mathbf{P}\big(K \oplus \Psi^{\mathbf{F}_1}(K, x)\big)\big)$ is another example. A fact shared by the two examples is that *there are many encipherments that collide on $\mathbf{F}$- or $\mathbf{P}$-calls in the 2nd round.* Concretely,

- In Feistel3, let $u = \Psi^{\mathbf{F}_1}(K, x)$. Then, for any $z \in \{0,1\}^{n/2}$, all the $2^{n/2}$ encipherments with key K and 1st round output $u = \star\|z$ call $\mathbf{F}_2(K\|z)$;
- In Hyb1, let $u = \Psi^{\mathbf{F}_1}(K, x)$. Then, for any $z \in \{0,1\}^n$, all the 2^n encipherments with (K, u), $K \oplus u = z$, call $\mathbf{P}(z)$.

It turns out that this can be proven in the general 3-round cipher (in this case): there exist $t = \Omega(\mathrm{poly}(n))$ distinct intermediate values

---

[2] E.g., given K and a 1st round output $u \in \{0,1\}^n$, one can decide the inv-freeness of the corresponding encipherment in the 1st and 2nd rounds, since $\Pi_1^{\mathcal{P}}(K, u)$ and $(\Pi_2^{-1})^{\mathcal{P}}(K, u)$ can be decided. But without querying P, one cannot derive $w = \Pi_2^{\mathcal{P}}(K, u)$, and thus cannot decide if the process is inv-free in the 3rd round.

$(K_1, u_1), ..., (K_t, u_t)$ that collide on 2nd round $\mathcal{P}$-call, i.e., $\varphi_2^{in}(K_1, u_1) = ... = \varphi_2^{in}(K_t, u_t) = (i_2, \delta_2, z_2)$, as shown in Fig. 6 (left).

With such a "star" structure, we issue the "central" query $P(i_2, \delta_2, z_2) \rightarrow z_2'$. In the real world, the response z_2' is consistent with $\Omega(\text{poly}(n))$ encipherments. Namely, for all $j \in \{1, ..., t\}$, suppose we evaluate $w_j \leftarrow \varphi_2^{out}(K_j, z_2', u_j)$, $x_j \leftarrow (\Pi_1^{-1})^P(K_j, u_j)$ and $E(K_j, x_j) \rightarrow y_j$. In the real world, if $\Pi_3^P(K_j, w_j)$ is inv-free then it holds $\varphi_3^{in}(K_j, w_j) = \gamma_3^{in}(K_j, y_j)$. In the ideal world, S (roughly) has to find ideal cipher inputs/outputs $\mathbf{IC}(K_j, x_j) = y_j$ that have both inputs and outputs involved in certain collisions, i.e., $\varphi_1^{in}(K_j, x_j) = \gamma_1^{in}(K_j, u_j)$ and $\varphi_3^{in}(K_j, w_j) = \gamma_3^{in}(K_j, y_j)$, the probability of which can be proven negligible. This slightly oversimplifies, and we refer to [28] for details.

The question is: how the *decisional inv-free problem* affects in this case? The point is that: the above strategy only works for encipherments that are inv-free in both 1st and 3rd rounds. When we query $P(i_2, \delta_2, z_2) \rightarrow z_2'$, S may define z_2' such that many of the involved $\Pi_3^P(K_j, w_j)$ become non-inv-free. It seems cumbersome to argue that there remain many (useful) inv-free $\Pi_3^P(K_j, w_j)$.

Such simulator strategies are prohibited by our case condition. In detail, if S want to define z_2' such that $\Pi_3^P(K_j, w_j)$ is non-inv-free for some j, S must find an ideal cipher input/output $\mathbf{IC}(K_j, x_j) = y_j$ such that $(\Pi_3^{-1})^P(K_j, y_j)$ is non-inv-free (otherwise, there appears inconsistency). Though,

– Since it must satisfy $\varphi_1^{in}(K_j, x_j) = \gamma_1^{in}(K_j, u_j)$ ($\Pi_1(K_j, x_j)$ is also inv-free), it cannot be due to a backward query $\mathbf{IC}^{-1}(K_j, y_j) \rightarrow x_j$;
– Since only $o(2^n/\text{poly}(n))$ $(\Pi_3^{-1})^P(K_j, y)$ are non-inv-free for the involved key K_j, it cannot be due to a forward query $\mathbf{IC}(K_j, x_j) \rightarrow y_j$ either.

Thus, our attack strategy will reach $(\Pi_3^{-1})^P(K_j, y_j)$ non-inv-free and succeed.

In our formal elaborations, this case is actually Subcase 3.1. We refer to the full version [28, Sect. 9.1] for details.

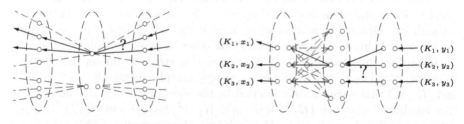

Fig. 6. Query structures used in attacking 3-round general ciphers. (Left) Structures for Case 1. The dashed lines show two examples of "stars": the top "star" centers around an inv-free 2nd round encipherment, while the bottom "star" centers around a non-inv-free 2nd round. (Right) Structures for Case 2. The dashes lines show a simple example of biclique $K_{3,5}$ (we certainly cannot draw "exponential-size"). The bold lines indicate the encipherments sampled by our attack, the arrows indicate the direction of our attack's evaluations, and the ? indicates where our attack checks equalities.

For the remaining, we first focus on the case that there are $\Theta(2^\kappa)$ keys K s.t. $\Omega(2^n/\text{poly}(n))\, \Pi_1^\mathcal{P}(K, x)$ are non-inv-free, and that $\Omega(2^n/\text{poly}(n))\, (\Pi_3^{-1})^\mathcal{P}(K, y)$ are non-inv-free. Depending on whether the $\Omega(2^n/\text{poly}(n))$ 1st round outputs u have $\Pi_2^\mathcal{P}(K, u)$ non-inv-free or not, we further distinguish Case 2 and 3.

Case 2: there are $\Theta(2^\kappa)$ keys K s.t. $\Omega\left(\frac{2^n}{\text{poly}(n)}\right)$ u have $(\Pi_1^{-1})^\mathcal{P}(K, u)$ non-inv-free and $\Pi_2^\mathcal{P}(K, u)$ non-inv-free, and $\Omega\left(\frac{2^n}{\text{poly}(n)}\right)$ $(\Pi_3^{-1})^\mathcal{P}(K, y)$ are non-inv-free. A crucial example is the 3-round IEM cipher $\text{IEM3}(K, x) := K \oplus \mathbf{P}_3\big(K \oplus \mathbf{P}_2\big(K \oplus \mathbf{P}_1(K \oplus x)\big)\big)$. Let $u = \mathbf{P}_1(K \oplus x)$ in IEM3. Let's see an attack for intuition. We begin with three intermediate values $(K_1, u_1), (K_2, u_2), (K_3, u_3)$ that have $K_1 \oplus u_1 = K_2 \oplus u_2 \neq K_3 \oplus u_3$, and then query $\mathbf{P}_1^{-1}$, compute the plaintexts $x_1 \leftarrow K_1 \oplus \mathbf{P}_1^{-1}(u_1)$, $x_2 \leftarrow K_2 \oplus \mathbf{P}_1^{-1}(u_2)$ and $x_3 \leftarrow K_3 \oplus \mathbf{P}_1^{-1}(u_3)$, and acquire the ciphertexts $\mathrm{E}(K_1, x_1) \rightarrow y_1$, $\mathrm{E}(K_2, x_2) \rightarrow y_2$ and $\mathrm{E}(K_3, x_3) \rightarrow y_3$. With these, if we query $\mathbf{P}_3^{-1}(K_1 \oplus y_1) \rightarrow w$ and $\mathbf{P}_3^{-1}(K_2 \oplus y_2) \rightarrow w'$, then the simulator S shall define them such that $w \oplus K_1 = w' \oplus K_2$; if we query $\mathbf{P}_3^{-1}(K_1 \oplus y_1) \rightarrow w$ and $\mathbf{P}_3^{-1}(K_3 \oplus y_3) \rightarrow w'$, then S shall define $w \oplus K_1 \neq w' \oplus K_3$. S cannot know our choice and thus won't be prepared correctly.

To translate this attack to the general 3-round model, we need to grasp its core idea. It turns out to be a structure of exponential size: if we view the range of $\mathbf{P}_1$ and the domain of $\mathbf{P}_2$ as two shores and the pairs (K, u) as edges, then we can build a biclique $K_{3,2^n}$. Due to this, given the $\mathbf{P}_1^{-1}$ and $\mathbf{P}_3^{-1}$ queries, there remain exponential possibilities for the three relevant encipherments $(K_1, x_1), (K_2, x_2)$ and (K_3, x_3), and S cannot pinpoint them. Furthermore, S does not know our choice of $\mathbf{P}_3^{-1}$-queries either. These ideas were also used by Andreeva et al.'s attack on IEM3 [1, Sect. 3.3, full version] (though details slightly deviate).

In the general 3-round cipher, we should view possible inputs to $\mathcal{P}$ as shores and intermediate pairs (K, u) as edges to build a bipartite graph $\mathcal{G}$ (which resembles our previous treatments of 2-iteration), as shown in Fig. 6 (right). Again we need to prove that there indeed exists a biclique $K_{3,2^n}$ as a sub-graph in $\mathcal{G}$, and we resort to *Zarankiewicz numbers* [24]. Concretely, by Kővári, Sós and Turán (KST) [38] (restated in Sect. 2, Proposition 2), as long as κ is large enough (though still $\Theta(n)$), the number of edges is large enough and $K_{3,2^n}$ is guaranteed to exist. This enables finding and exploiting the three encipherments.

Regarding the *decisional inv-free problem*, the setting is simpler than Case 1. In detail, it can be proven that we can sample encipherments $(K_1, x_1), (K_2, x_2)$ and (K_3, x_3) that were unlikely queried by the simulator S. By this and by the case condition, we reach $(\Pi_3^{-1})^\mathcal{P}(K_1, y_1), (\Pi_3^{-1})^\mathcal{P}(K_2, y_2)$ and $(\Pi_3^{-1})^\mathcal{P}(K_3, y_3)$ with non-negligible probability $\Omega(1/\text{poly}(n))$ after querying $\mathrm{E}(K_1, x_1) \rightarrow y_1$, $\mathrm{E}(K_2, x_2) \rightarrow y_2$ and $\mathrm{E}(K_3, x_3) \rightarrow y_3$. This fits into our expectations.

There remain subtleties: similarly to the 2-round case (Sect. 3.3), KST's result [38] only applies to simple graphs. When $\mathcal{G}$ is a multigraph with high multiplicity, we have to resort to a dedicated treatment. Interestingly, using the fact that there can be many edges between a single pair of vertexes, we are able to find three encipherments $(K_1, u_1), (K_2, u_2)$ and (K_3, u_3) that are similar to the above "simple" case. The involved structure is given in Fig. 7 (left). We refer to the full version [28, Sect. 9.2 and 9.3] (Subcase 3.2) for details.

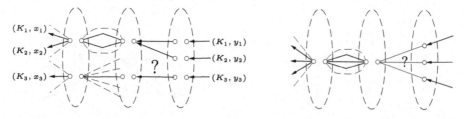

Fig. 7. Query structures used in attacking 3-round general ciphers, when the involved graphs contain heavy multi-edges. (Left) Structures for Case 2. The idea is adapted from Fig. 6 (right). The dashed arcs indicate that there are many (superpolynomial) distinct encipherments "crossing" the same pair of inputs in 1st and 2nd rounds. The dashed lines show that the number of possible encipherments "crossing" the two relevant $\mathcal{P}$-inputs are exponential. (Right) Structures for Case 4. The idea is adapted from Fig. 8 (right): we can find λ useful encipherments within a single pair of $\mathcal{P}$-inputs (in the 1st and 2nd rounds). The use of bold lines, arrows and ? follows Fig. 6.

Case 3: there are $\Theta(2^\kappa)$ keys K s.t. $\Omega\left(\frac{2^n}{\text{poly}(n)}\right)$ u have $(\Pi_1^{-1})^{\mathcal{P}}(K, u)$ non-inv-free and $\Pi_2^{\mathcal{P}}(K, u)$ inv-free, and $\Omega\left(\frac{2^n}{\text{poly}(n)}\right)$ $(\Pi_3^{-1})^{\mathcal{P}}(K, y)$ are non-inv-free. Our attack in this case reuses already discussed ideas. In detail, (roughly) we sample a pair (K, u) from the $\Omega(2^{\kappa+n}/\text{poly}(n))$ pairs that have 1st round non-inv-free while 2nd round inv-free. We then evaluate backward to $x \leftarrow (\Pi_1^{-1})^{\mathrm{P}}(K, u)$, "wrap" by querying $\mathrm{E}(K, x) \rightarrow y$ and further $w \leftarrow (\Pi_3^{-1})^{\mathrm{P}}(K, y)$. Since $\Omega(2^n/\text{poly}(n))$ $(\Pi_3^{-1})^{\mathcal{P}}(K, y)$ are non-inv-free, we reach $(\Pi_3^{-1})^{\mathrm{P}}(K, y)$ non-inv-free with a non-negligible probability and overcome the *decisional inv-free problem*, as shown in Fig. 8 (left). Since $\Pi_2(K, u)$ is inv-free, if we are interacting with the general 3-round cipher then it holds $\varphi_2^{in}(K, u) = \gamma_2^{in}(K, w)$ (as discussed in Sect. 3.2). On the other hand, if we are interacting with the ideal world $(\mathbf{IC}, S^{\mathbf{IC}})$, the simulator S only gains two P-calls $\mathrm{P}(\gamma_1^{in}(K, u))$ and $\mathrm{P}(\gamma_3^{in}(K, y))$. As discussed in Case 2, they won't enable S to pinpoint the encipherment (K, x). Consequently, S is unable to define simulated P and enforce the equality $\varphi_2^{in}(K, u) = \gamma_2^{in}(K, w)$.

In our formal elaborations [28, Sect. 9.4] (which use pigeonhole principle and non-degeneracy of φ_2^{in}), this corresponds to Subcase 3.3.

We then focus on the case that there are $\Theta(2^\kappa)$ keys K s.t. $\Omega(2^n/\text{poly}(n))$ $\Pi_1^{\mathcal{P}}(K, x)$ are non-inv-free, and that $o(2^n/\text{poly}(n))$ $(\Pi_3^{-1})^{\mathcal{P}}(K, y)$ are non-inv-free. Similarly to Case 2 and 3, we further distinguish Case 4 and 5.

Case 4: there are $\Theta(2^\kappa)$ keys K s.t. $\Omega\left(\frac{2^n}{\text{poly}(n)}\right)$ u have $(\Pi_1^{-1})^{\mathcal{P}}(K, u)$ non-inv-free and $\Pi_2^{\mathcal{P}}(K, u)$ non-inv-free, and $o\left(\frac{2^n}{\text{poly}(n)}\right)$ $(\Pi_3^{-1})^{\mathcal{P}}(K, y)$ are non-inv-free. In this case, we reuse the query structures found in Case 2. We also reuse the idea that the inv-free 3rd round allows checking consistency.

In detail, consider the bipartite graph $\mathcal{G}$ built between the 1st and 2nd round (which resembles Case 2). When $\mathcal{G}$ is (roughly) simple, we can find a biclique $K_{\lambda, 2^n}$ with $\lambda = m_{max}$, which resembles Case 2. We then sample one vertex (i_2, δ_2, z_2) from the right shore of $K_{\lambda, 2^n}$, pinpointing λ encipherments

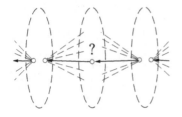 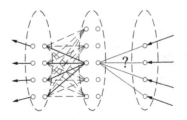

Fig. 8. Query structures used in attacking 3-round general ciphers. (Left) Structures for Case 3. The dashed lines show that the number of possible encipherments "crossing" the two relevant $\mathcal{P}$-inputs are exponential (though, they may not overlap). (Right) Structures for Case 4. The figure shows a simple example with $\lambda = 4$. The use of bold lines, arrows and ? follows Fig. 6.

$(K_1, u_1), ..., (K_\lambda, u_\lambda)$ that invoke $P(i_2, \delta_2, z_2)$ in the 2nd round. See Fig. 8 (left). We then evaluate backward $x_1 \leftarrow (\Pi_1^{-1})^P(K_1, u_1), ..., x_\lambda \leftarrow (\Pi_1^{-1})^P(K_\lambda, u_\lambda)$, "wrap" $E(K_1, x_1) \rightarrow y_1, ..., E(K_\lambda, x_\lambda) \rightarrow y_\lambda$. As only $o\left(\frac{2^n}{poly(n)}\right)$ $(\Pi_3^{-1})^P(K, y)$ are non-inv-free, we likely reach $(\Pi_3^{-1})^P(K_1, y_1), ..., (\Pi_3^{-1})^P(K_\lambda, y_\lambda)$ inv-free and overcome the *decisional inv-free problem*, as shown in Fig. 8 (right).

In the real world, the 2nd round outputs $(K_1, w_1), ..., (K_\lambda, w_\lambda)$ of these encipherments are derivable from $(K_1, w_1), ..., (K_\lambda, w_\lambda)$ using a fixed $z_2' \in \{0, 1\}^{m(i_2)}$. Meanwhile, they have $\varphi_3^{in}(K_1, w_1) = \gamma_3^{in}(K_1, y_1), ..., \varphi_3^{in}(K_\lambda, w_\lambda) = \gamma_3^{in}(K_\lambda, y_\lambda)$. To simulate consistently, the simulator S in the ideal world has to find a corresponding $z_2' \in \{0, 1\}^{m(i_2)}$ satisfying the λ equalities for the ideal cipher responses $y_1, ..., y_\lambda$. Since $\lambda = m_{max}$, this can be proven infeasible.

When $\mathcal{G}$ is a multigraph with high multiplicity, a single pair of vertexes already suffices to pinpoint λ encipherments $(K_1, u_1), ..., (K_\lambda, u_\lambda)$ that invoke the same $P(i_2, \delta_2, z_2)$ in the 2nd round, as shown in Fig. 7 (right). Our above idea thus remains applicable.

In our formal elaborations [28, Sect. 9.5], this corresponds to Subcase 3.4.

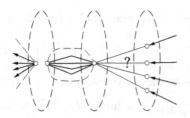 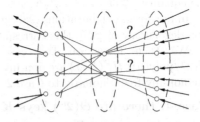

Fig. 9. Query structures used in attacking 3-round general ciphers, Case 5. (Left) When the graph contains heavy multi-edges, we can find λ useful encipherments within a single pair of $\mathcal{P}$-inputs (in the 1st and 2nd rounds). The figure shows a simple example with $\lambda = 4$. (Right) When the graph does not contain too many multi-edges (and the biclique $K_{\lambda,2}$ exists).

Case 5: there are $\Theta(2^\kappa)$ keys K s.t. $\Omega\big(\frac{2^n}{\mathrm{poly}(n)}\big)$ u have $(\Pi_1^{-1})^{\mathcal{P}}(K,u)$ non-inv-free and $\Pi_2^{\mathcal{P}}(K,u)$ inv-free, and $o\big(\frac{2^n}{\mathrm{poly}(n)}\big)$ $(\Pi_3^{-1})^{\mathcal{P}}(K,y)$ are non-inv-free. Again, consider the bipartite graph $\mathcal{G}$ built between the 1st and 2nd round (which resembles Cases 2 and 4). When $\mathcal{G}$ is a multigraph with high multiplicity, we reuse the idea of Case 4 and exploit the structure shown in Fig. 9 (left). The case that $\mathcal{G}$ is (roughly) simple turns out to be the most complicated, and many of our earlier attempts failed. Our eventual idea is built upon a polynomial-size boomerang structure in the 1st and 2nd rounds, which is depicted in Fig. 9 (right).

In detail, we seek for a biclique $K_{\lambda,2}$, $\lambda = O(m_{max})$, in $\mathcal{G}$, as shown in Fig. 9 (right). Again by KST [38], such bicliques exist as long as κ is large enough (though still $\Theta(m_{max}n) = \Theta(\mathrm{poly}(n))$).

The biclique $K_{\lambda,2}$ pinpoints two groups of encipherments, with each group colliding on a 2nd round $\mathcal{P}$-call, as shown in Fig. 9. Therefore, in the real world, there are two $\mathcal{P}$-outputs that are consistent with all the 2λ encipherments. Meanwhile, every encipherment in one group is paired with an encipherment in the other group, such that the two encipherments collide on the 1st round $\mathcal{P}$-call. By these, in the ideal world, the simulator S has to seek for 2λ ideal cipher queries that have both inputs and outputs involved in certain collisions. Namely, the 2λ ideal cipher queries can be arranged in a $2 \times \lambda$ matrix, such that:

- For every pair of ideal cipher queries in every column, the corresponding simulated encipherments collide on the 1st round $\mathcal{P}$-call; and
- For each group of λ ideal cipher queries in each row, there exists a response z_2' that satisfy certain relation with their λ ciphertexts.

When $\lambda = O(m_{max})$, this can be proven infeasible.

In our formal elaborations [28, Sect. 9.6], this corresponds to Subcase 3.5. Some of our earlier failed attempts are also available there.

Other cases: there are $\Theta(2^\kappa)$ keys K s.t. $o\big(\frac{2^n}{\mathrm{poly}(n)}\big)$ $\Pi_1^{\mathcal{P}}(K,x)$ are non-inv-free and $\Omega\big(\frac{2^n}{\mathrm{poly}(n)}\big)$ $(\Pi_3^{-1})^{\mathcal{P}}(K,y)$ are non-inv-free. Then, if most $w = (\Pi_3^{-1})^{\mathcal{P}}(K,y)$ are inv-free w.r.t. Π_2, it follows the above Case 4 by symmetry; if most $w = (\Pi_3^{-1})^{\mathcal{P}}(K,y)$ are non-inv-free w.r.t. Π_2, it follows the above Case 5 by symmetry. We thereby complete the case-study.

Again, we refer to [28, Sect. 9] for the complicated details.

4   Fundamental Properties

By the *notion* of blockciphers, a blockcipher shall be *deterministic* and *efficiently invertible*. The latter has been reflected in Fig. 10 (and Figs. 11 and 12 as well). Below we formalize the former for blockcipher oracle procedures.

Definition 1 (Deterministicness). *An oracle procedure $E^{\mathcal{P}} : \mathcal{K} \times \{0,1\}^n \to \{0,1\}^n$ instantiating a blockcipher must be deterministic, meaning that for* *any* $(K, x) \in \mathcal{K} \times \{0, 1\}^n$, *let* $y = E^{\mathcal{P}}(K, x)$. *Then, the transcripts of* $\mathcal{P}$-*queries and responses obtained during encipherment* $E^{\mathcal{P}}(K, x)$ *and decipherment* $(E^{-1})^{\mathcal{P}}(K, y)$ *are always identical. (E.g., if* $E^{\mathcal{P}}(K, x)$ *queries* $\mathcal{P}(i, \delta, z) \to z'$ *at some stage, then* $(E^{-1})^{\mathcal{P}}(K, y)$ *queries either* $\mathcal{P}(i, \delta, z) \to z'$ *or* $\mathcal{P}(i, \bar{\delta}, z') \to z$ *at some stage.)*

Two more properties/assumptions that we rely on are **oracle-independence of sub-procedures** and **non-degeneracy of** $E^{\mathcal{P}}$.

Oracle-independence means sub-procedures in $E^{\mathcal{P}}$ must be *oracle-independent*. Since the oracle procedure $E^{\mathcal{P}}$ (or black-box cryptographic construction) has a fixed description, this seems obvious (and indeed common in black-box constructions [25] and impossibility proofs [9,44]). Though, we highlight it for clarity. Interestingly, ad hoc blockciphers also strive for such independence (probably to avoid unexpected internal dependency). For example, in AES, the ShiftRows and MixColumns steps are rather independent from SubBytes.

Non-degeneracy means no encipherment $E^{\mathcal{P}}(K, x)$ can be approximately computed using less $\mathcal{P}$ calls than $E^{\mathcal{P}}$, i.e., $E^{\mathcal{P}}$ cannot be "simplified". Formally,

Definition 2 ((Everywhere) Non-degenerate Oracle Procedure). *An oracle procedure* $E^{\mathcal{P}}$ *is (everywhere)* $\varepsilon_{de(E)}$-*non-degenerate, if*

$$\max_{E', K, x} \left\{ \Pr_{\mathcal{P}} \left[(E')^{\mathcal{P}}(K, x) = E^{\mathcal{P}}(K, x) \right] \right\} \leq \varepsilon_{de(E)} = negl(n). \tag{3}$$

where the maximum is taken over all $(K, x) \in \{0, 1\}^{\kappa} \times \{0, 1\}^n$ *and all oracle procedures* $(E')^{\mathcal{P}}$ *such that the number of* $\mathcal{P}$-*calls made during computing* $(E')^{\mathcal{P}}(K, x)$ *is less than* $E^{\mathcal{P}}(K, x)$.

Why non-degenerate? If $E1^{\mathcal{P}}$ is $1/\mathrm{poly}(n)$-non-degenerate, then there is an obvious differentiator with advantage $1/\mathrm{poly}(n) - 2^{-n}$. More importantly, a t-call blockcipher "uses" all of its t $\mathcal{P}$-calls "effectively" only if it is non-degenerate.

5   General 1-Call Blockciphers

We first elaborate on our 1-call cipher model $E1^{\mathcal{P}}$ in Sect. 5.1. Then, we characterize the properties of $E1^{\mathcal{P}}$ in Sect. 5.2. Our formal conclusion on $E1$ insecurity is given in Sect. 5.3.

5.1   General Model of 1-Call Blockciphers/Rounds

We consider any blockcipher oracle procedure $E1^{\mathcal{P}} : \mathcal{K} \times \{0, 1\}^n \to \{0, 1\}^n$ that is built from the permutation family $\mathcal{P}$ in the following way. Let φ^{in} and φ^{out} be two arbitrary deterministic functions that are computable by the computational class of the differentiator(s). Then, $E1^{\mathcal{P}}(K, x) := \varphi^{out}(K, \mathcal{P}(\varphi^{in}(K, x)), x)$.

Since blockciphers are *efficiently invertible* by definitions, $E1^{\mathcal{P}}$ is accomplished by $(E1^{-1})^{\mathcal{P}}(K, y) := \gamma^{out}(K, \mathcal{P}(\gamma^{in}(K, y)), y)$ using two other deterministic functions γ^{in} and γ^{out}. We stress that to ensure $(E1^{-1})^{\mathcal{P}}(K, E1^{\mathcal{P}}(K, x)) \equiv x$, γ^{in} and γ^{out} are strongly correlated with φ^{in} and φ^{out}, and this will be crucial for our attack. A formal description using pseudocode is given in Fig. 10.

```
Algorithm E1^P(K, x) // (K, x) ∈ K × {0,1}^n     Algorithm (E1^{-1})^P(K, x)
(i, δ, z) ← φ^{in}(K, x)                          (i, δ, z) ← γ^{in}(K, y)
z' ← P(i, δ, z)                                   z' ← P(i, δ, z)
y ← φ^{out}(K, z', x)                             x ← γ^{out}(K, z', y)
return y                                          return x
```

Fig. 10. Definition of the 1-call blockcipher $E1^P$. $\varphi^{in}, \varphi^{out}, \gamma^{in}$, and γ^{out} are all deterministic and oracle-independent.

Examples to Facilitate Understanding. First, the key-prepended Feistel round [16] uses $\mathbf{F} : \{0,1\}^{\kappa+n/2} \to \{0,1\}^{n/2}$ and defines $\Psi^{\mathbf{F}}(K, x) := \mathsf{right}_{n/2}(x) \oplus \mathbf{F}(K\|\mathsf{left}_{n/2}(x))\|\mathsf{left}_{n/2}(x)$. It is an $E1$ instance with

$$\varphi^{in}(K, x) := \big(i, +, K\|\mathsf{right}_{n/2}(x)\|[0]_{n/2}\big),$$
$$\varphi^{out}(K, z', x) := \mathsf{right}_{n/2}(x) \oplus \mathsf{right}_{n/2}(z')\|\mathsf{left}_{n/2}(x) \tag{4}$$

using an index i with $m(i) = \kappa + n$ (and truncated permutation [14]).

Second, the IEM round [23] defines $\mathrm{EM}^{\mathbf{P}}(K, x) := K \oplus \mathbf{P}(K \oplus x)$ for $\mathbf{P} \in \mathrm{Perm}(n)$. It is an $E1$ instance with

$$\varphi^{in}(K, x) := (i, +, K \oplus x), \quad \varphi^{out}(K, z', x) := K \oplus z' \tag{5}$$

using an index i with $m(i) = n$.

Finally, a "key-alternating" Misty-R cipher round [2, Chapter 3.18.8] defines $\mathrm{Misty\text{-}R}^{\mathbf{P}}(K, x) := \mathbf{P}\big(K \oplus \mathsf{right}_{n/2}(x)\big)\|\big(\mathsf{left}_{n/2}(x) \oplus \mathbf{P}\big(K \oplus \mathsf{right}_{n/2}(x)\big)\big)$ for $\mathbf{P} \in \mathrm{Perm}(n/2)$. It is an $E1$ instance with

$$\varphi^{in}(K, x) := \big(i, +, K \oplus \mathsf{right}_{n/2}(x)\big), \quad \varphi^{out}(K, z', x) := z'\|\big(\mathsf{left}_{n/2}(x) \oplus z'\big) \tag{6}$$

using an index i with $m(i) = n/2$.

It is easy to see unbalanced Feistel [2, Chapter 1.3.1], Lai-Massey [2, Chapter 1.5] and keyed Feistel rounds are instances of $E1$ as well. Though, $E1$ does not cover multi-line generalized Feistel [2, Chapter 1.3.1] (which makes multiple $\mathcal{P}$ calls per round) and Swap-Or-Not [29] (which uses small-range functions).

5.2 Properties of 1-Call Blockciphers/Rounds

We first introduce several helper sets. We then discuss properties of *data-dependent encipherments*, *inverse-free* and *non-inverse-free encipherments* in turn.

Notations. For any 1-call cipher $E1^{\mathcal{P}} : \mathcal{K} \times \{0,1\}^n \to \{0,1\}^n$ and any K in its keyspace $\mathcal{K}$, define

$$\mathsf{Dom}_{\mathsf{if}}(E1, K) := \Big\{ x \in \{0,1\}^n : \delta = \delta', \text{ where } (i,\delta,z) = \varphi^{in}(K,x),$$
$$(i,\delta',z') = \gamma^{in}(K,y), \ y = E1^{\mathcal{P}}(K,x) \Big\},$$

$$\mathsf{Rng}_{\mathsf{if}}(E1, K) := \Big\{ y \in \{0,1\}^n : \delta = \delta', \text{ where } (i,\delta,z) = \gamma^{in}(K,y),$$
$$(i,\delta',z') = \varphi^{in}(K,x), \ x = (E1^{-1})^{\mathcal{P}}(K,y) \Big\},$$

$$\mathsf{Dom}_{\mathsf{ni}}(E1, K) := \{0,1\}^n \backslash \mathsf{Dom}_{\mathsf{if}}(E1, K), \quad \mathsf{Rng}_{\mathsf{ni}}(E1, K) := \{0,1\}^n \backslash \mathsf{Rng}_{\mathsf{if}}(E1, K). \quad (7)$$

For $x \in \mathsf{Dom}_{\mathsf{if}}(E1, K)$, the encipherment $E1^{\mathcal{P}}(K,x)$ and the corresponding decipherment $(E1^{-1})^{\mathcal{P}}(K,y)$ call $\mathcal{P}$ on the same direction. Therefore, $E1^{\mathcal{P}}(K,x)$ is *inverse-free* (inv-free for short), as reflected by the subscript if. Otherwise, $E1^{\mathcal{P}}(K,x)$ is *non-inverse-free* (non-inv-free), as reflected by ni. We remark that $E1^{\mathcal{P}}(K,x) = E'(\mathcal{P}(f(K)),x)$ is also inv-free, although it may not match classical understandings.

For tag $\in \{\mathsf{ni}, \mathsf{if}\}$, define sets for plaintexts/ciphertexts in $\mathsf{Dom}_{\mathsf{tag}}/\mathsf{Rng}_{\mathsf{tag}}$ that are mapped to a certain $\mathcal{P}$ input (i,δ,z):

$$\mathsf{Dom}_{\mathsf{tag}}(E1, K, i, \delta, z) := \big\{ x \in \mathsf{Dom}_{\mathsf{tag}}(E1, K) : \varphi^{in}(K,x) = (i,\delta,z) \big\},$$
$$\mathsf{Rng}_{\mathsf{tag}}(E1, K, i, \delta, z) := \big\{ y \in \mathsf{Rng}_{\mathsf{tag}}(E1, K) : \gamma^{in}(K,y) = (i,\delta,z) \big\}. \quad (8)$$
$$\mathsf{Dom}_{\mathsf{tag}}(E1, K, i, \delta) := \cup_{z \in \{0,1\}^{m(i)}} \mathsf{Dom}_{\mathsf{tag}}(E1, K, i, \delta, z),$$
$$\mathsf{Rng}_{\mathsf{tag}}(E1, K, i, \delta) := \cup_{z \in \{0,1\}^{m(i)}} \mathsf{Rng}_{\mathsf{tag}}(E1, K, i, \delta, z). \quad (9)$$

We slightly abuse the notation Rng_* to denote the actual ranges of the input functions φ^{in} and γ^{in}. In detail, for tag $\in \{\mathsf{ni}, \mathsf{if}\}$, define

$$\mathsf{Rng}_{\mathsf{tag}}(\varphi^{in}, K) := \big\{ (i,\delta,z) : (i,\delta,z) = \varphi^{in}(K,x) \text{ for some } x \in \mathsf{Dom}_{\mathsf{tag}}(E1, K) \big\},$$
$$\mathsf{Rng}_{\mathsf{tag}}(\gamma^{in}, K) := \big\{ (i,\delta,z) : (i,\delta,z) = \gamma^{in}(K,y) \text{ for some } y \in \mathsf{Rng}_{\mathsf{tag}}(E1, K) \big\}.$$
$$\mathsf{Rng}_{\mathsf{tag}}(\varphi^{in}) := \cup_{K \in \mathcal{K}} \mathsf{Rng}_{\mathsf{tag}}(\varphi^{in}, K), \quad \mathsf{Rng}_{\mathsf{tag}}(\gamma^{in}) := \cup_{K \in \mathcal{K}} \mathsf{Rng}_{\mathsf{tag}}(\gamma^{in}, K). \quad (10)$$

On Data-Dependence. As indicated by the partition $\{0,1\}^n = \mathsf{Dom}_{\mathsf{if}}(E1, K) \sqcup \mathsf{Dom}_{\mathsf{ni}}(E1, K)$, the inv-freeness of $E1^{\mathcal{P}}(K,x)$ can be data-dependent. Though, as mentioned in Sect. 3.1, (surprisingly) *one can decide whether an encipherment $E1^{\mathcal{P}}(K,x)$ is inv-free without querying $\mathcal{P}$*. This turns out crucial in our attacks.

Lemma 1 (Inv-freeness is oracle-independent). *Consider the blockcipher $E1^{\mathcal{P}} : \mathcal{K} \times \{0,1\}^n \to \{0,1\}^n$ in Fig. 10. Then, for any pair $(K,x) \in \mathcal{K} \times \{0,1\}^n$, resp. $(K,y) \in \mathcal{K} \times \{0,1\}^n$, whether $x \in \mathsf{Dom}_{\mathsf{if}}(E1, K)$, resp. $y \in \mathsf{Rng}_{\mathsf{if}}(E1, K)$, can be determined without querying $\mathcal{P}$.*

Proof. Assume otherwise, and let (K, x) be the input such that whether $x \in$ $\mathsf{Dom}_{\mathsf{if}}(E1, K)$ depends on $\mathcal{P}$. Let $(i, \delta, z) = \varphi^{in}(K, x)$ and $y = E1^{\mathcal{P}}(K, x)$. Since $E1^{\mathcal{P}}(K, x)$ only makes one query $\mathcal{P}(i, \delta, z)$ to $\mathcal{P}$, $E1^{\mathcal{P}}(K, x)$ is inv-free if and only if $\mathcal{P}(i, \delta, z)$ is in a certain subset of $\{0, 1\}^{m(i)}$. Namely, there exists a partition $\{0, 1\}^{m(i)} = \mathcal{Z}_\delta \cup \mathcal{Z}_{\bar{\delta}}$ such that $x \in \mathsf{Dom}_{\mathsf{if}}(E1, K)$ if and only if $\mathcal{P}(i, \delta, z) \in \mathcal{Z}_\delta$.

However, let $(i, \delta', z') = \gamma^{in}(K, y)$, then $y \in \mathsf{Rng}_{\mathsf{if}}(E1, K)$ if and only if $\delta' = \delta$. This means it always holds $\mathcal{P}(i, \delta, z) \in \mathcal{Z}_{\delta'}$, where δ' is *fixed* by the definition of the function γ^{in}. This violates our assumption that γ^{in} is oracle-independent.

Therefore, one can decide if $x \in \mathsf{Dom}_{\mathsf{if}}(E1, K)$ solely by computations. The argument for $y \in \mathsf{Rng}_{\mathsf{if}}(E1, K)$ is similar by symmetry. $\quad\square$

Properties of Inv-Free Encipherments. We now formalize the intuitive weaknesses of inv-free encipherments discussed in Sect. 3.1.

Lemma 2 (Inv-freeness preserves partial inputs). *Consider the 1-call blockcipher $E1^{\mathcal{P}}$ in Fig. 10. Then, for any pair (K, x), $x \in \mathsf{Dom}_{\mathsf{if}}(E1, K)$, it holds $\gamma^{in}(K, y) = \varphi^{in}(K, x)$ for $y = E1^{\mathcal{P}}(K, x)$. It further implies $|\mathsf{Dom}_{\mathsf{if}}(E1, i, \delta, z)| = |\mathsf{Rng}_{\mathsf{if}}(E1, i, \delta, z)|$ for any $i \in \mathcal{I}$, $\delta \in \{+, -\}$ and $z \in \{0, 1\}^{m(i)}$.   Proof: this is a straightforward implication of Fig. 10 and Definition 1.*

The second observation follows by non-degeneracy: if there exists one inv-free encipherment $E1^{\mathcal{P}}(K, x)$, then there must exist superpolynomially many.

Lemma 3 (Inv-freeness can't be unique). *Consider the 1-call blockcipher $E1^{\mathcal{P}}$ in Fig. 10. If $E1^{\mathcal{P}}$ is $\varepsilon_{de(E1)}$-non-degenerate in the sense of Definition 2, then for any (K, i, δ, z) such that $\mathsf{Dom}_{\mathsf{if}}(E1, K, i, \delta, z) \neq \emptyset$, it holds*

$$\left|\mathsf{Dom}_{\mathsf{if}}(E1, K, i, \delta, z)\right| > 1/\varepsilon_{de(E1)} = \Omega(poly(n)). \tag{11}$$

Proof. Assume otherwise, i.e., $|\mathsf{Dom}_{\mathsf{if}}(E1, K, i, \delta, z)| \leq \varepsilon_{de(E1)}^{-1}$ for some (K, i, δ, z). By Lemma 2, for any $x \in \mathsf{Dom}_{\mathsf{if}}(E1, K, i, \delta, z)$, the corresponding ciphertext $y = E1^{\mathcal{P}}(K, x)$ must have $y \in \mathsf{Rng}_{\mathsf{if}}(E1, K, i, \delta, z)$. By Lemma 2, $|\mathsf{Rng}_{\mathsf{if}}(E1, K, i, \delta, z)| = |\mathsf{Dom}_{\mathsf{if}}(E1, K, i, \delta, z)| \leq 1/\varepsilon_{de(E1)}$. By these, for any $x \in \mathsf{Dom}_{\mathsf{if}}(E1, K, i, \delta, z)$, one can uniformly pick $y \xleftarrow{\$} \mathsf{Rng}_{\mathsf{if}}(E1, K, i, \delta, z)$ to *encipher (K, x) without querying $\mathcal{P}$ at all*, and the success probability is at least $\varepsilon_{de(E1)}$. This contradicts the assumption that $E1^{\mathcal{P}}$ is $\varepsilon_{de(E1)}$-non-degenerate as Eq. (3). $\quad\square$

An implication of Lemma 3 is that the ranges of φ^{in} and γ^{in} cannot be too large. Due to page limits, the proof is deferred to the full version [28].

Lemma 4 (Functions in inv-free encipherments). *Consider the 1-call blockcipher $E1^{\mathcal{P}}$ in Fig. 10. If $E1^{\mathcal{P}}$ is $\varepsilon_{de(E1)}$-non-degenerate (see Definition 2), then it holds $|\mathsf{Rng}_{\mathsf{if}}(\varphi^{in}, K)| = |\mathsf{Rng}_{\mathsf{if}}(\gamma^{in}, K)| \leq |\mathsf{Dom}_{\mathsf{if}}(E1, K)| \cdot \varepsilon_{de(E1)} \leq 2^n \cdot \varepsilon_{de(E1)}.$*

Properties of Non-inv-free Encipherment. For $E1^{\mathcal{P}}(x)$, $x \in \mathsf{Dom}_{\mathsf{ni}}(E1, K)$, our first observation is that $E1^{\mathcal{P}}(x)$ cannot query *wide random permutations* (as discussed in Sect. 3.2). We now elaborate on the "regularity" of φ^{in} and γ^{in}. For example, in the IEM round (see Eq. (5)), for every $K \in \{0,1\}^n$ we have $|\mathsf{Dom}_{\mathsf{ni}}(E1, K, i, +)| = 2^n = 2^{m(i)}$, and for every $z \in \{0,1\}^n$ we have $|\mathsf{Dom}_{\mathsf{ni}}(E1, K, i, +, z)| = 1 = |\mathsf{Dom}_{\mathsf{ni}}(E1, K, i, +)|/2^{m(i)}$. In the "key-alternating" Misty-R round (see Eq. (5)), we have $|\mathsf{Dom}_{\mathsf{ni}}(E1, K, i, +)| = 2^n$ for $K \in \{0,1\}^{n/2}$ and $|\mathsf{Dom}_{\mathsf{ni}}(E1, K, i, +, z)| = 2^n = |\mathsf{Dom}_{\mathsf{ni}}(E1, K, i, +)|/2^{m(i)}$ with $m(i) = n/2$ for every $z \in \{0,1\}^{n/2}$.

Below we formalize the above first idea and show that the actual ranges of the functions φ^{in} and γ^{in} must be somewhat limited.

Lemma 5 (Non-inv-free encipherments cannot query wide P). *Consider the 1-call blockcipher $E1^{\mathcal{P}}$ in Fig. 10. Then:*

- *For any key $K \in \mathcal{K}$ and any $x \in \mathsf{Dom}_{\mathsf{ni}}(E1, K)$, let $(i, \delta, z) = \varphi^{in}(K, x)$, then it holds $i \in \mathcal{I}_{\leq n}$;*
- *Similarly, for any key $K \in \mathcal{K}$ and any $y \in \mathsf{Rng}_{\mathsf{ni}}(E1, K)$, let $(i, \delta, z) = \gamma^{in}(K, y)$, then it holds $i \in \mathcal{I}_{\leq n}$.*

Consequently, $\left|\mathsf{Rng}_{\mathsf{ni}}(\varphi^{in})\right| \leq |\mathcal{I}_{\leq n}| 2^{N+1}$, $\left|\mathsf{Rng}_{\mathsf{ni}}(\gamma^{in})\right| \leq |\mathcal{I}_{\leq n}| 2^{N+1}$.

Proof. Assume otherwise, then there exists (K, x) such that $x \in \mathsf{Dom}_{\mathsf{ni}}(E1, K)$, and $(i, \delta, z) = \varphi^{in}(K, x)$ has $i \in \mathcal{I}_{>n}$. This means $|z| = m(i) > n$.

Furthermore, the oracle response $\mathcal{P}(\varphi^{in}(K, x)) = z'$ must be that there exists $y \in \mathsf{Rng}_{\mathsf{ni}}(E1, K)$ such that $\gamma^{in}(K, y) = (i, \bar{\delta}, z')$. Since $x \in \mathsf{Dom}_{\mathsf{ni}}(E1, K) \subseteq \{0,1\}^n$ and $y \in \mathsf{Rng}_{\mathsf{ni}}(E1, K) \subseteq \{0,1\}^n$, the number t of z and z' related by such relation is at most 2^n, meaning that $\mathcal{P}(i, \cdot, \cdot)$ must map a set of $t \leq 2^n$ possible z values (that are determined by φ^{in}) to a set of $t \leq 2^n$ possible z' values (that are determined by γ^{in}). This violates the oracle-independence assumption on φ^{in} and γ^{in}. Therefore, for any (K, x), $x \in \mathsf{Dom}_{\mathsf{ni}}(E1, K)$, let $(i, \delta, z) = \varphi^{in}(K, x)$, then it holds $i \in \mathcal{I}_{\leq n}$, i.e., $m(i) \leq n$. It thus follows $\left|\mathsf{Rng}_{\mathsf{ni}}(\varphi^{in})\right| \leq |\{+, -\}| \times |\mathcal{I}_{\leq n}| \times 2^n \leq |\mathcal{I}_{\leq n}| 2^{N+1}$ and $\left|\mathsf{Rng}_{\mathsf{ni}}(\gamma^{in})\right| \leq |\mathcal{I}_{\leq n}| 2^{N+1}$. $\square$

We then formalize the above (somewhat surprising) "regularity" idea (the proof is deferred to [28] due to page limits).

Lemma 6 (Regularity in non-inv-free encipherments). *Consider the 1-call blockcipher $E1^{\mathcal{P}}$ in Fig. 10. Then, for any $K \in \mathcal{K}$ and any $(i, \delta) \in \mathcal{I}_{\leq n} \times \{+, -\}$, the restriction of φ^{in} to $\mathsf{Dom}_{\mathsf{ni}}(E1, K, i, \delta)$ (resp., the restriction of γ^{in} to $\mathsf{Rng}_{\mathsf{ni}}(E1, K, i, \delta)$) is regular. I.e., the following holds for any $z, z' \in \{0,1\}^{m(i)}$*

$$\left|\mathsf{Dom}_{\mathsf{ni}}(E1, K, i, \delta, z)\right| = \left|\mathsf{Rng}_{\mathsf{ni}}(E1, K, i, \bar{\delta}, z')\right| = \frac{\left|\mathsf{Dom}_{\mathsf{ni}}(E1, K, i, \delta)\right|}{2^{m(i)}}.$$

This also means $\left|\mathsf{Dom}_{\mathsf{ni}}(E1, K, i, \delta)\right|$ must be divisible by $2^{m(i)}$.

By Lemma 5, we can derive the collision probability among images of φ^{in} and γ^{in} as follows (the proof is deferred to [28]).

Corollary 1 (Probability of collisions). *For any (i, δ, z) and any set $\mathcal{S} \subseteq \{0,1\}^n$ with $|\mathcal{S}| = poly(n)$, when n is sufficiently large it holds*

$$\Pr\left[y \xleftarrow{\$} \{0,1\}^n \backslash \mathcal{S} : \gamma^{in}(K, y) = (i, \delta, z) \mid y \in \mathsf{Rng}_{\mathsf{ni}}(E1, K)\right] \leq \frac{2}{2^{m_{min}}}, \quad (12)$$

$$\Pr\left[x \xleftarrow{\$} \{0,1\}^n \backslash \mathcal{S} : \varphi^{in}(K, x) = (i, \delta, z) \mid x \in \mathsf{Dom}_{\mathsf{ni}}(E1, K)\right] \leq \frac{2}{2^{m_{min}}}. \quad (13)$$

5.3 Attack 1-Call Blockciphers

After the preparations in Sect. 5.2, we are able to establish insecurity of 1-call ciphers $E1^{\mathcal{P}} : \mathcal{K} \times \{0,1\}^n \to \{0,1\}^n$ of Fig. 10.

Theorem 1 (Differentiability of $E1^{\mathcal{P}}$). *Let $E1^{\mathcal{P}} : \mathcal{K} \times \{0,1\}^n \to \{0,1\}^n$ be a blockcipher defined by Fig. 10. Assume that $E1^{\mathcal{P}}$ is deterministic and $\varepsilon_{de(E1)}$-non-degenerate in the sense of Definition 2, and its keyspace has $|\mathcal{K}| \geq 2|\mathcal{I}_{\leq n}| + 1 = O(poly(n))$. Then, when n is sufficiently large, there exists a differentiator $D1^{E,P}$ making at most $\lceil m_{max}/n \rceil + 2$ queries and has an advantage at least $1 - \frac{m_{max}^2}{2^n} - \frac{2}{2^{m_{min}}} = 1 - negl(n)$.*

It is crucial to restrict $|\mathcal{K}| > |\mathcal{I}_{\leq n}|$: otherwise, $\mathcal{P}$ may already offer $|\mathcal{K}|$ independent n-bit random permutations. There are two purposes to consider $|\mathcal{K}| = poly(n)$. First, it strengthens the negative result (i.e., even indifferentiable cipher of logarithmic key length is impossible). Second, such $D1$ can function as subroutines of $D2$ and $D3$ in Sect. 6 and 7.

The full proof is available in [28].

6 Attack 2-Call Iterated Blockciphers

For 2- and 3-call ciphers, we restrict to *iterated blockciphers* that are built from *key derivation functions* and *rounds*. For a 2-call cipher $E2^{\mathcal{P}}$, this means encipherment $E2^{\mathcal{P}}(K, x)$ must proceed with either of the following flows:

- **Type-I**: $E2^{\mathcal{P}}(K, x) = \Pi_3^{\mathcal{P}}\left(K \| \mathsf{kd}^{\mathcal{P}}(K), x\right)$ for a 1-call function $\mathsf{kd}^{\mathcal{P}} : \{0,1\}^\kappa \to \{0,1\}^{m_{max}}$ and a 1-call cipher $\Pi_3^{\mathcal{P}} : \{0,1\}^{\kappa + m_{max}} \times \{0,1\}^n \to \{0,1\}^n$, or
- **Type-II**: $E2^{\mathcal{P}}(K, x) = \Pi_2^{\mathcal{P}}\left(K, \Pi_1^{\mathcal{P}}(K, x)\right)$ for two 1-call ciphers/rounds $\Pi_1^{\mathcal{P}}, \Pi_2^{\mathcal{P}} : \{0,1\}^\kappa \times \{0,1\}^n \to \{0,1\}^n$.

The keyspace is partitioned $\mathcal{K} = \mathcal{K}^{(0)} \sqcup \mathcal{K}^{(1)}$, such that $E2^{\mathcal{P}}(K, \cdot)$ follows **Type-I** encipherment if and only if $K \in \mathcal{K}^{(1)}$. Formally, we consider the cipher $E2^{\mathcal{P}}$ defined in Fig. 11. As mentioned in the Introduction, there is no need to use multiple $\mathcal{P}_1, \mathcal{P}_2, \ldots$, since $\mathcal{P}$ already provides multiple independent permutations.

As discussed the overview (Sect. 3.3), we make an additional non-degenerate assumption on the input functions φ^{in}. Formally,

Definition 3 (Non-degenerate Keyed Function). *A keyed function $\varphi^{in}(\cdot,\cdot)$ is $\varepsilon_{de(\varphi^{in})}$-non-degenerate, if the following two upper bounds hold (recall from Lemma 1 that the set $\mathsf{Dom}_{if}(E1,K)$ is fully determined by φ^{in}):*

$$\max_{K,(i,\delta,z)} \left\{ \Pr\left[x \xleftarrow{\$} \{0,1\}^n : \varphi^{in}(K,x) = (i,\delta,z) \mid x \in \mathsf{Dom}_{if}(E1,K)\right]\right\} \leq \varepsilon_{de(\varphi^{in})}.$$

$$\max_{x,(i,\delta,z)} \left\{ \Pr\left[K \xleftarrow{\$} \{0,1\}^\kappa : \varphi^{in}(K,x) = (i,\delta,z) \mid x \in \mathsf{Dom}_{if}(E1,K)\right]\right\} \leq \varepsilon_{de(\varphi^{in})}.$$

By default, we assume $\varepsilon_{de(\varphi^{in})} = negl(n)$ is negligible.

Input functions in common inv-free blockciphers are indeed non-degenerate: e.g., key-prepended Feistel round has $\varphi^{in}(K,x) = \left(i,+,K\|\mathsf{right}_{n/2}(x)\|[0]_{n/2}\right)$ (see Eq. (4)) and $\varepsilon_{de(\varphi^{in})} = \max\{1/2^n, 1/2^\kappa\}$.

Theorem 2 (Differentiability of $E2^P$). *Let $E2^P$ be a blockcipher defined by Fig. 10 with keyspace $|\mathcal{K}| \geq \left(6(3|\mathcal{I}_{\leq n}|)^{\frac{1}{n}} + 5\right)|\mathcal{I}_{\leq n}| + 1 = O(poly(n))$. Assume that: (i) for all $j \in \{0,1,2\}$, the round Π_j^P is deterministic and $\varepsilon_{de(\Pi_j)}$-non-degenerate, and (ii) φ_1^{in} and φ_2^{in} are $\varepsilon_{de(\varphi_1^{in})}$- and $\varepsilon_{de(\varphi_2^{in})}$-non-degenerate respectively (see Definition 3). Then, when n is sufficiently large, there exists a differentiator $D2^{E,P}$ making $poly(n)$ queries and has advantage at least $1 - m_{max}{}^2/2^n - 2q^2\varepsilon_{de(\varphi_1^{in})} - 2q^2\varepsilon_{de(\varphi_2^{in})} - 6q^2/2^{m_{min}} = 1 - negl(n)$, where q is the number of **IC**-queries made by $D2$ and S in total.*

We refer to [28] for its proof and Sect. 3.3 for the overview.

Algorithm $E2^P(K,x)$
if $K \in \mathcal{K}^{(1)}$ then
    return $\Pi_3^P(K\|\mathsf{kd}^P(K),x)$
else   // $K \in \mathcal{K}^{(0)}$
    $u \leftarrow \Pi_1^P(K,x)$
    return $\Pi_2^P(K,u)$
end if

Algorithm $(E2^{-1})^P(K,y)$
if $K \in \mathcal{K}^{(1)}$ then
    return $(\Pi_3^{-1})^P(K\|\mathsf{kd}^P(K),y)$
else   // $K \in \mathcal{K}^{(0)}$
    $u \leftarrow (\Pi_2^{-1})^P(K,y)$
    return $(\Pi_1^{-1})^P(K,u)$
end if

Algorithm $\Pi_j^P(K,x)$ // $j \in \{0,1,...,5\}$
$(i_j,\delta_j,z_j) \leftarrow \varphi_j^{in}(K,x)$
$z_j' \leftarrow \mathcal{P}(i_j,\delta_j,z_j)$
$y \leftarrow \varphi_j^{out}(K,z_j',x)$
return y

Algorithm $(\Pi_j^{-1})^P(K,y)$ //
$j \in \{0,1,...,5\}$
$(i_j,\delta_j,z_j) \leftarrow \gamma_j^{in}(K,y)$
$z_j' \leftarrow \mathcal{P}(i_j,\delta_j,z_j)$
$x \leftarrow \varphi_j^{out}(K,z_j',y)$
return x

Algorithm $\mathsf{kd}^P(K)$
$(i,\delta,z) \leftarrow f(K)$
$z' \leftarrow \mathcal{P}(i,\delta,z)$
return z'

Fig. 11. Definition of the 2-call iterated blockcipher $E2^P$.

7 Attack 3-Call Iterated Blockciphers

For 3-call iterated ciphers, $E3^{\mathcal{P}}(K,x)$ can take one of the following three flows:

- **Type-I**: $E3^{\mathcal{P}}(K,x) = \Pi_6^{\mathcal{P}}\big(K\|\mathsf{kd}_1^{\mathcal{P}}(K),x\big)$ for a 2-call KDF $\mathsf{kd}_1^{\mathcal{P}} : \{0,1\}^\kappa \to \{0,1\}^{2m_{max}}$ and a 1-call cipher $\Pi_6^{\mathcal{P}} : \{0,1\}^{\kappa+2m_{max}} \times \{0,1\}^n \to \{0,1\}^n$, or
- **Type-II**: $E3^{\mathcal{P}}(K,x) = \Pi_5^{\mathcal{P}}\big(K\|\mathsf{kd}_2^{\mathcal{P}}(K), \Pi_4^{\mathcal{P}}(K\|\mathsf{kd}_2^{\mathcal{P}}(K),x)\big)$ for a 1-call KDF $\mathsf{kd}_2^{\mathcal{P}} : \{0,1\}^\kappa \to \{0,1\}^{m_{max}}$ and two 1-call ciphers $\Pi_4^{\mathcal{P}}, \Pi_5^{\mathcal{P}} : \{0,1\}^{\kappa+m_{max}} \times \{0,1\}^n \to \{0,1\}^n$, or
- **Type-III**: $E3^{\mathcal{P}}(K,x) = \Pi_3^{\mathcal{P}}\big(K, \Pi_2^{\mathcal{P}}(K, \Pi_1^{\mathcal{P}}(K,x))\big)$ for three 1-call ciphers $\Pi_1^{\mathcal{P}}, \Pi_2^{\mathcal{P}}, \Pi_3^{\mathcal{P}} : \{0,1\}^\kappa \times \{0,1\}^n \to \{0,1\}^n$.

The keyspace is partitioned $\mathcal{K} = \mathcal{K}^{(0)} \sqcup \mathcal{K}^{(1)} \sqcup \mathcal{K}^{(2)}$, such that $E3^{\mathcal{P}}(K,\cdot)$ follows **Type-I**, resp. **Type-II** encipherment if and only if $K \in \mathcal{K}^{(2)}$, resp. $K \in \mathcal{K}^{(1)}$. Formally, $E3^{\mathcal{P}}$ is defined in Fig. 12.

Theorem 3 (Differentiability of $E3^{\mathcal{P}}$). *Let $E3^{\mathcal{P}}$ be a blockcipher defined by Fig. 12 with keyspace $\{0,1\}^\kappa$, $\kappa \geq 2m_{max}\log_2|\mathcal{I}_{\leq n}| + 2m_{max}n + 6m_{max} + 4 = \Theta(poly(n))$. Assume that for $j = 1,2,3,4,5,6$, (i) the round $\Pi_j^{\mathcal{P}}$ is deterministic and $\varepsilon_{de(\Pi_j)}$-non-degenerate, and (ii) φ_j^{in} is $\varepsilon_{de(\varphi_j^{in})}$-non-degenerate (see Definition 3). Then, when n is sufficiently large, there exists a differentiator $D3^{E,P}$ making $poly(n)$ queries to E and P and having advantage either $1/poly(n) - negl(n)$ or $1 - negl(n)$ for some $poly(n)$ and $negl(n)$ determined by φ_j^{in}, $j = 1,2,3,4,5,6$.*

We refer to [28] for its proof and Sect. 3.4 for the overview.

```
Algorithm E3^P(K,x)
if K ∈ K^(2) then
    return Π_6^P(K‖kd_1^P(K),x)
else if K ∈ K^(1) then
    s ← kd_2^P(K)
    return Π_5^P(K‖s, Π_4^P(K‖s,x))
else                        // K ∈ K^(0)
    u ← Π_1^P(K,x)
    return Π_3^P(K, Π_2^P(K,u))
end if

Algorithm kd_1^P(K)
(i_1,δ_1,z_1) ← f_{1,1}(K)
z_1' ← P(i_1,δ_1,z_1)
(i_2,δ_2,z_2) ← f_{1,2}(K,z_1')
z_2' ← P(i_2,δ_2,z_2)
return z_1'‖z_2'
```

```
Algorithm (E3^{-1})^P(K,y)
if K ∈ K^(2) then
    return (Π_6^{-1})^P(K‖kd_1^P(K),y)
else if K ∈ K^(1) then
    s ← kd_2^P(K)
    return (Π_4^{-1})^P(K‖s, (Π_5^{-1})^P(K‖s,y))
else                        // K ∈ K^(0)
    w ← (Π_3^{-1})^P(K,y)
    return (Π_1^{-1})^P(K, (Π_2^{-1})^P(K,w))
end if

Algorithm kd_2^P(K)
(i,δ,z) ← f_{2,1}(K)
z' ← P(i,δ,z)
return z'

// Definitions of Π_j^P(K,x) and
(Π_j^{-1})^P(K,y) are the same as Fig. 11
```

Fig. 12. Definition of the 3-call iterated blockcipher $E3^{\mathcal{P}}$.

Acknowledgment. We thank an anonymous STOC '19 reviewer of [27] for suggesting considering lower bounds. We also thank Mridul Nandi, Wenfeng Qi, Abishanka Saha, Sayantan Paul and Meiqin Wang and EUROCRYPT 2023 reviewers for fruitful comments. This work was partly supported by the National Natural Science Foundation of China (Grant No. 62002202, No. 61872359) and the Taishan Scholars Program (for Young Scientists) of Shandong.

References

1. Andreeva, E., Bogdanov, A., Dodis, Y., Mennink, B., Steinberger, J.P.: On the indifferentiability of key-alternating ciphers. In: Canetti, R., Garay, J.A. (eds.) CRYPTO 2013. LNCS, vol. 8042, pp. 531–550. Springer, Heidelberg (2013). https://doi.org/10.1007/978-3-642-40041-4_29

2. Avanzi, R.: A Salad of Block Ciphers. IACR Cryptology ePrint Archive, p. 1171 (2016). http://eprint.iacr.org/2016/1171

3. Barak, B., Mahmoody-Ghidary, M.: Lower bounds on signatures from symmetric primitives. In: 48th FOCS, pp. 680–688. IEEE (2007). https://doi.org/10.1109/FOCS.2007.38

4. Barak, B., Mahmoody, M.: Merkle's key agreement protocol is optimal: an $O(n^2)$ attack on any key agreement from random oracles. J. Cryptol. **30**(3), 699–734 (2016). https://doi.org/10.1007/s00145-016-9233-9

5. Barbosa, M., Farshim, P.: Indifferentiable authenticated encryption. In: Shacham, H., Boldyreva, A. (eds.) CRYPTO 2018, Part I. LNCS, vol. 10991, pp. 187–220. Springer, Cham (2018). https://doi.org/10.1007/978-3-319-96884-1_7

6. Bellare, M., Kohno, T.: A theoretical treatment of related-key attacks: RKA-PRPs, RKA-PRFs, and applications. In: Biham, E. (ed.) EUROCRYPT 2003. LNCS, vol. 2656, pp. 491–506. Springer, Heidelberg (2003). https://doi.org/10.1007/3-540-39200-9_31

7. Bertoni, G., Daemen, J., Peeters, M., Van Assche, G.: On the indifferentiability of the sponge construction. In: Smart, N. (ed.) EUROCRYPT 2008. LNCS, vol. 4965, pp. 181–197. Springer, Heidelberg (2008). https://doi.org/10.1007/978-3-540-78967-3_11

8. Biryukov, A., Khovratovich, D., Nikolić, I.: Distinguisher and related-key attack on the full AES-256. In: Halevi, S. (ed.) CRYPTO 2009. LNCS, vol. 5677, pp. 231–249. Springer, Heidelberg (2009). https://doi.org/10.1007/978-3-642-03356-8_14

9. Black, J., Cochran, M., Shrimpton, T.: On the impossibility of highly-efficient blockcipher-based hash functions. J. Cryptol. **22**(3), 311–329 (2008). https://doi.org/10.1007/s00145-008-9030-1

10. Black, J., Rogaway, P., Shrimpton, T., Stam, M.: An analysis of the blockcipher-based hash functions from PGV. J. Cryptol. **23**(4), 519–545 (2010). https://doi.org/10.1007/s00145-010-9071-0

11. Bogdanov, A., Knudsen, L.R., Leander, G., Standaert, F.-X., Steinberger, J., Tischhauser, E.: Key-alternating ciphers in a provable setting: encryption using a small number of public permutations. In: Pointcheval, D., Johansson, T. (eds.) EUROCRYPT 2012. LNCS, vol. 7237, pp. 45–62. Springer, Heidelberg (2012). https://doi.org/10.1007/978-3-642-29011-4_5

12. Canetti, R., Goldreich, O., Halevi, S.: The random oracle methodology, revisited. J. ACM **51**(4), 557–594 (2004). https://doi.org/10.1145/1008731.1008734

13. Carmer, B., Rosulek, M.: Linicrypt: a model for practical cryptography. In: Robshaw, M., Katz, J. (eds.) CRYPTO 2016, Part III. LNCS, vol. 9816, pp. 416–445. Springer, Heidelberg (2016). https://doi.org/10.1007/978-3-662-53015-3_15

14. Choi, W., Lee, B., Lee, J.: Indifferentiability of truncated random permutations. In: Galbraith, S.D., Moriai, S. (eds.) ASIACRYPT 2019, Part I. LNCS, vol. 11921, pp. 175–195. Springer, Cham (2019). https://doi.org/10.1007/978-3-030-34578-5_7

15. Coron, J.-S., Dodis, Y., Malinaud, C., Puniya, P.: Merkle-Damgård revisited: how to construct a hash function. In: Shoup, V. (ed.) CRYPTO 2005. LNCS, vol. 3621, pp. 430–448. Springer, Heidelberg (2005). https://doi.org/10.1007/11535218_26

16. Coron, J.-S., Holenstein, T., Künzler, R., Patarin, J., Seurin, Y., Tessaro, S.: How to build an ideal cipher: the indifferentiability of the feistel construction. J. Cryptol. 29(1), 61–114 (2014). https://doi.org/10.1007/s00145-014-9189-6

17. Dachman-Soled, D., Katz, J., Thiruvengadam, A.: 10-round feistel is indifferentiable from an ideal cipher. In: Fischlin, M., Coron, J.-S. (eds.) EUROCRYPT 2016, Part II. LNCS, vol. 9666, pp. 649–678. Springer, Heidelberg (2016). https://doi.org/10.1007/978-3-662-49896-5_23

18. Dai, Y., Seurin, Y., Steinberger, J.P., Thiruvengadam, A.: Indifferentiability of iterated even-mansour ciphers with non-idealized key-schedules: five rounds are necessary and sufficient. In: Katz, J., Shacham, H. (eds.) CRYPTO 2017, Part III. LNCS, vol. 10403, pp. 524–555. Springer, Cham (2017). https://doi.org/10.1007/978-3-319-63697-9_18

19. Dai, Y., Steinberger, J.: Indifferentiability of 8-round feistel networks. In: Robshaw, M., Katz, J. (eds.) CRYPTO 2016, Part I. LNCS, vol. 9814, pp. 95–120. Springer, Heidelberg (2016). https://doi.org/10.1007/978-3-662-53018-4_4

20. Demay, G., Gaži, P., Hirt, M., Maurer, U.: Resource-restricted indifferentiability. In: Johansson, T., Nguyen, P.Q. (eds.) EUROCRYPT 2013. LNCS, vol. 7881, pp. 664–683. Springer, Heidelberg (2013). https://doi.org/10.1007/978-3-642-38348-9_39

21. Dodis, Y., Stam, M., Steinberger, J., Liu, T.: Indifferentiability of confusion-diffusion networks. In: Fischlin, M., Coron, J.-S. (eds.) EUROCRYPT 2016, Part II. LNCS, vol. 9666, pp. 679–704. Springer, Heidelberg (2016). https://doi.org/10.1007/978-3-662-49896-5_24

22. Durak, F.B., Vaudenay, S.: Breaking the FF3 format-preserving encryption standard over small domains. In: Katz, J., Shacham, H. (eds.) CRYPTO 2017, Part II. LNCS, vol. 10402, pp. 679–707. Springer, Cham (2017). https://doi.org/10.1007/978-3-319-63715-0_23

23. Even, S., Mansour, Y.: A construction of a cipher from a single pseudorandom permutation. J. Cryptol. 10(3), 151–161 (1997). https://doi.org/10.1007/s001459900025

24. Füredi, Z., Simonovits, M.: The history of degenerate (bipartite) extremal graph problems. In: Lovász, L., Ruzsa, I.Z., Sós, V.T. (eds.) Erdős Centennial. BSMS, vol. 25, pp. 169–264. Springer, Heidelberg (2013). https://doi.org/10.1007/978-3-642-39286-3_7

25. Gennaro, R., Gertner, Y., Katz, J., Trevisan, L.: Bounds on the efficiency of generic cryptographic constructions. SIAM J. Comput. 35(1), 217–246 (2005). https://doi.org/10.1137/S0097539704443276

26. Grassi, L.: On Generalizations of the Lai-Massey Scheme: the Birth of Amaryllises. Cryptology ePrint Archive, Paper 2022/1245 (2022)

27. Guo, C., Lin, D.: Indifferentiability of 3-Round Even-Mansour with Random Oracle Key Derivation. Cryptology ePrint Archive, Report 2016/894 (2016)

28. Guo, C., Wang, L., Lin, D.: Impossibility of Indifferentiable Iterated Blockciphers from 3 or Less Primitive Calls. Cryptology ePrint Archive, Paper 2023/226 (2023). https://eprint.iacr.org/2023/226

29. Hoang, V.T., Morris, B., Rogaway, P.: An enciphering scheme based on a card shuffle. In: Safavi-Naini, R., Canetti, R. (eds.) CRYPTO 2012. LNCS, vol. 7417, pp. 1–13. Springer, Heidelberg (2012). https://doi.org/10.1007/978-3-642-32009-5_1

30. Hoang, V.T., Tessaro, S.: Key-alternating ciphers and key-length extension: exact bounds and multi-user security. In: Robshaw, M., Katz, J. (eds.) CRYPTO 2016, Part I. LNCS, vol. 9814, pp. 3–32. Springer, Heidelberg (2016). https://doi.org/10.1007/978-3-662-53018-4_1

31. Holenstein, T., Sinha, M.: Constructing a pseudorandom generator requires an almost linear number of calls. In: 53rd Annual IEEE Symposium on Foundations of Computer Science, FOCS 2012, New Brunswick, NJ, USA, 20–23 October 2012, pp. 698–707. IEEE Computer Society (2012). https://doi.org/10.1109/FOCS.2012.51

32. Hoory, S.: The size of bipartite graphs with a given girth. J. Comb. Theory, Ser. B 86(2), 215–220 (2002). https://doi.org/10.1006/jctb.2002.2123

33. Iwata, T., Kohno, T.: New security proofs for the 3GPP confidentiality and integrity algorithms. In: Roy, B., Meier, W. (eds.) FSE 2004. LNCS, vol. 3017, pp. 427–445. Springer, Heidelberg (2004). https://doi.org/10.1007/978-3-540-25937-4_27

34. Kahn, J., Saks, M.E., Smyth, C.D.: A dual version of Reimer's inequality and a proof of Rudich's conjecture. In: Proceedings of the 15th Annual IEEE Conference on Computational Complexity, Florence, Italy, 4–7 July 2000, pp. 98–103. IEEE Computer Society (2000). https://doi.org/10.1109/CCC.2000.856739

35. Kilian, J., Rogaway, P.: How to protect DES against exhaustive key search (an analysis of DESX). J. Cryptol. 14(1), 17–35 (2000). https://doi.org/10.1007/s001450010015

36. Kim, J.H., Simon, D.R., Tetali, P.: Limits on the efficiency of one-way permutation-based hash functions. In: 40th FOCS, pp. 535–542. IEEE (1999). https://doi.org/10.1109/SFFCS.1999.814627

37. Knudsen, L.R., Rijmen, V.: Known-key distinguishers for some block ciphers. In: Kurosawa, K. (ed.) ASIACRYPT 2007. LNCS, vol. 4833, pp. 315–324. Springer, Heidelberg (2007). https://doi.org/10.1007/978-3-540-76900-2_19

38. Kővári, P., T Sós, V., Turán, P.: On a problem of Zarankiewicz. In: Colloquium Mathematicum, vol. 3, pp. 50–57. Polska Akademia Nauk (1954)

39. Lampe, R., Seurin, Y.: How to construct an ideal cipher from a small set of public permutations. In: Sako, K., Sarkar, P. (eds.) ASIACRYPT 2013, Part I. LNCS, vol. 8269, pp. 444–463. Springer, Heidelberg (2013). https://doi.org/10.1007/978-3-642-42033-7_23

40. Luby, M., Rackoff, C.: How to construct pseudorandom permutations from pseudorandom functions. SIAM J. Comput. 17(2), 373–386 (1988). https://doi.org/10.1137/0217022

41. Maurer, U., Renner, R., Holenstein, C.: Indifferentiability, impossibility results on reductions, and applications to the random oracle methodology. In: Naor, M. (ed.) TCC 2004. LNCS, vol. 2951, pp. 21–39. Springer, Heidelberg (2004). https://doi.org/10.1007/978-3-540-24638-1_2

42. Nandi, M.: On the optimality of non-linear computations of length-preserving encryption schemes. In: Iwata, T., Cheon, J.H. (eds.) ASIACRYPT 2015, Part II. LNCS, vol. 9453, pp. 113–133. Springer, Heidelberg (2015). https://doi.org/10.1007/978-3-662-48800-3_5

43. Ristenpart, T., Shacham, H., Shrimpton, T.: Careful with Composition: Limitations of the Indifferentiability Framework. In: Paterson, K.G. (ed.) EUROCRYPT 2011. LNCS, vol. 6632, pp. 487–506. Springer, Cham (2011). https://doi.org/10.1007/978-3-642-20465-4_27

44. Rogaway, P., Steinberger, J.: Security/efficiency tradeoffs for permutation-based hashing. In: Smart, N. (ed.) EUROCRYPT 2008. LNCS, vol. 4965, pp. 220–236. Springer, Heidelberg (2008). https://doi.org/10.1007/978-3-540-78967-3_13

45. Rønjom, S., Bardeh, N.G., Helleseth, T.: Yoyo tricks with AES. In: Takagi, T., Peyrin, T. (eds.) ASIACRYPT 2017, Part I. LNCS, vol. 10624, pp. 217–243. Springer, Cham (2017). https://doi.org/10.1007/978-3-319-70694-8_8

46. Rudich, S.: Limits on the provable consequences of one-way functions. Ph.D. thesis, University of California (1988)

47. Shannon, C.: Communication theory of secrecy system. Bell Syst. Tech. J. **28**, 656–715 (1949)

48. Simon, D.R.: Finding collisions on a one-way street: can secure hash functions be based on general assumptions? In: Nyberg, K. (ed.) EUROCRYPT 1998. LNCS, vol. 1403, pp. 334–345. Springer, Heidelberg (1998). https://doi.org/10.1007/BFb0054137

49. Wagner, D.: The boomerang attack. In: Knudsen, L. (ed.) FSE 1999. LNCS, vol. 1636, pp. 156–170. Springer, Heidelberg (1999). https://doi.org/10.1007/3-540-48519-8_12

50. Wu, H., Preneel, B.: AEGIS: a fast authenticated encryption algorithm. In: Lange, T., Lauter, K., Lisoněk, P. (eds.) SAC 2013. LNCS, vol. 8282, pp. 185–201. Springer, Heidelberg (2014). https://doi.org/10.1007/978-3-662-43414-7_10

51. Zhandry, M., Zhang, C.: Indifferentiability for public key cryptosystems. In: Micciancio, D., Ristenpart, T. (eds.) CRYPTO 2020, Part I. LNCS, vol. 12170, pp. 63–93. Springer, Cham (2020). https://doi.org/10.1007/978-3-030-56784-2_3

Optimal Security for Keyed Hash Functions: Avoiding Time-Space Tradeoffs for Finding Collisions

Cody Freitag[1] , Ashrujit Ghoshal[2(✉)] , and Ilan Komargodski[3]

[1] Cornell Tech, New York, USA
cfreitag@cs.cornell.edu
[2] Paul G. Allen School of Computer Science & Engineering,
University of Washington, Seattle, WA, USA
ashrujit@cs.washington.edu
[3] School of Computer Science and Engineering, Hebrew University of Jerusalem and
NTT Research, 91904 Jerusalem, Israel
ilank@cs.huji.ac.il

Abstract. Cryptographic hash functions map data of arbitrary size to a fixed size digest, and are one of the most commonly used cryptographic objects. As it is infeasible to design an individual hash function for every input size, variable-input length hash functions are built by designing and bootstrapping a single fixed-input length function that looks sufficiently random. To prevent trivial preprocessing attacks, applications often require not just a single hash function but rather a family of keyed hash functions.

The most well-known methods for designing variable-input length hash function families from a fixed idealized function are the Merkle-Damgård and Sponge designs. The former underlies the SHA-1 and SHA-2 constructions and the latter underlies SHA-3. Unfortunately, recent works (Coretti et al. EUROCRYPT 2018, Coretti et al. CRYPTO 2018) show non-trivial time-space tradeoff attacks for finding collisions for both. Thus, this forces a parameter blowup (i.e., efficiency loss) for reaching a certain desired level of security. We ask whether it is possible to build families of keyed hash functions which are *provably* resistant to any non-trivial time-space tradeoff attacks for finding collisions, without incurring significant efficiency costs.

We present several new constructions of keyed hash functions that are provably resistant to any non-trivial time-space tradeoff attacks for finding collisions. Our constructions provide various tradeoffs between their efficiency and the range of parameters where they achieve optimal security for collision resistance. Our main technical contribution is proving optimal security bounds for converting a hash function with a fixed-sized input to a keyed hash function with (potentially larger) fixed-size input. We then use this keyed function as the underlying primitive inside the standard Merkle-Damgård and Merkle tree constructions. We strongly believe that this paradigm of using a keyed inner hash function in these constructions is the right one, for which non-uniform security has not been analyzed prior to this work.

© International Association for Cryptologic Research 2023
C. Hazay and M. Stam (Eds.): EUROCRYPT 2023, LNCS 14007, pp. 440–469, 2023.
https://doi.org/10.1007/978-3-031-30634-1_15

1 Introduction

A cryptographic hash function is a (deterministic) algorithm that takes arbitrary length input data and outputs a fixed length digest. It is one of the most fundamental tools in modern applications of cryptography, underlying numerous widely used applications. For example, it facilitates the hash-and-sign paradigm, proofs-of-work for blockchains, and more. While it is empirically believed that concrete cryptographic hash functions satisfy various useful security properties, formalizing this seems to be currently out of reach. Thus, in the context of provable security, cryptographic hash functions are usually modeled as random oracles, i.e., completely random functions [6]. This allows us to analyze specific properties and argue about the concrete security of systems that use them. In this work, we focus on the property of a hash function being *collision resistant*, i.e., the idea that although collisions exist in abundance in a compressing function, it should be computationally hard to find them.

The task of finding collisions in a given compressing function is only interesting if the adversary is uniform. That is, the adversary is "fixed" before the hash function. Indeed, otherwise, a non-uniform attacker can simply have collisions hardwired. However, the uniform model of security does not capture many real-world adversaries, and therefore it is common to model adversaries as nonuniform in theoretical cryptography. Specifically, non-uniform security captures adversaries that have been designed to attack specific instances, adversaries that have gone through an expensive preprocessing stage, or even protect against (currently unknown) future attacks. Non-uniform security is also necessary for composition within larger systems [18]. For all of these reasons, it is widely believed by the theoretical community that modeling attackers as non-uniform is the right thing to do, despite potentially being overly conservative and including unrealistic attackers.

Dealing with non-uniform attackers in the context of hashing and collision finding makes it necessary to consider a family of keyed hash functions, rather than a single hash function. Collision finding is then defined via the following two-stage game. First, a (keyed) family H of hash functions is fixed, and the attacker can depend arbitrarily on H. Second, a random key key is sampled, and the adversary needs to find a collision in H relative to key. Intuitively, in order to attack the hash function (e.g., find a collision), a non-uniform attacker must either (a) have some hard-coded information about key, or (b) can essentially be treated as uniform.

For applications, we typically want each member of H to operate on unbounded input lengths. That is, $H \colon \{0,1\}^\kappa \times \{0,1\}^* \to \{0,1\}^n$ should be viewed as a two-input function, operating on (key, m), where key $\in \{0,1\}^\kappa$ is the key and $m \in \{0,1\}^*$ is an arbitrary length input. Since it is practically infeasible to design a different hash function for every input length, what happens is that a single basic compressing function $h \colon \{0,1\}^a \to \{0,1\}^n$ for some $a > n$ is designed, and then it is iterated in some way to get a hash function that compresses arbitrarily. For instance, the well-known Merkle-Damgård design [13,24] iterates such a basic compressing function in order to get a variable-input-length hash function that can operate on arbitrary sized data up to some maximum length (e.g., $2^6 4$ bits).

AI-ROM. Since we consider non-uniform security in the random oracle model, we model attackers using the *auxiliary-input random oracle model* (AI-ROM), formally defined by Unruh [27] although implicitly used earlier, for example, by Hellman [20], Yao [28], and Fiat and Naor [15]. In this model, we assume a hash function $h: \{0,1\}^a \to \{0,1\}^n$ with $a > n$ modeled as a completely random one, i.e., a random oracle [6]. The AI-ROM models preprocessing adversaries as two-stage algorithms $(\mathcal{A}_1, \mathcal{A}_2)$ parameterized by S (for "space") and T (for "time"). We refer to such an attacker as an (S,T)-attacker. The first part $\mathcal{A}_1$ (i.e., the offline phase) has unbounded access to h, and its goal is to compute an S-bit "advice" σ for $\mathcal{A}_2$. The second part $\mathcal{A}_2$ (i.e., the online phase) gets the advice σ, can make at most T queries to h, and attempts to accomplish some task involving h. In our case, $\mathcal{A}_2$ gets a random key key $\leftarrow_\$ \{0,1\}^\kappa$ as a challenge and its goal is to come up with a collision in $H(\text{key}, \cdot)$. Aside from the restrictions that $|\sigma| \leq S$ and that $\mathcal{A}_2$ can make at most T queries to h, both $\mathcal{A}_1$ and $\mathcal{A}_2$ are allowed to be computationally unbounded.

Building a Keyed Hash from a Single Hash Function. Observe that for every keyed hash construction, there is an (S,T)-attacker that finds a collision relative to a random key with probability[1] $\Omega(S/2^\kappa + T^2/2^n)$ via the following attack. First, the preprocessing adversary outputs $\Omega(S)$ collisions with respect to arbitrary distinct keys. The online adversary receives a random key. If key is in the remembered list from the preprocessing phase, it outputs the corresponding collision. Otherwise, it performs a T-query birthday-style attack. The adversary wins if either the challenge key appears in one of its preprocessed collisions (giving the $S/2^\kappa$ term) or if the birthday attack succeeds (giving the $T^2/2^n$ term). We refer to this attack as the *naive attack*, and say that a construction is *optimally secure* if there is provably no better attack. This brings us to the main question we consider in this work.

Can we build a keyed hash function (i.e., $H: \{0,1\}^\kappa \times \{0,1\}^* \to \{0,1\}^n$) from non-keyed one (i.e., $h: \{0,1\}^a \to \{0,1\}^n$) with optimal non-uniform security?

If we could design an $h_a: \{0,1\}^a \to \{0,1\}^n$ for every $a \in \mathbb{N}$, then the above task is easy. We can simply parse the input to the appropriate h_a into two parts, one for the key and the other for the input to $H: \{0,1\}^\kappa \times \{0,1\}^* \to \{0,1\}^n$. That is, define $H(\text{key}, m) = h_{\kappa+|m|}(\text{key}\|m)$, where $\|$ stands for string concatenation and $|\cdot|$ stands for bit length. For this construction, Dodis, Guo and Katz [14] showed that the best attack achieves advantage $O(S/2^\kappa + T^2/2^n)$, matching the advantage of the naive attack.

Unfortunately, it is infeasible to design a different hash function for every input length as discussed above. The design of a new h is a delicate and lengthy

---

[1] To simplify notation throughout the introduction, we suppress poly factors in n in the asymptotic $O(\cdot)$ and $\Omega(\cdot)$ notation.

process that could take many years to test and standardize. Having a single hash function is therefore more robust security-wise. Thus, the standard procedure is to design a hash function h with fixed input size and then iterate it in some way to get a hash function that supports arbitrary input lengths.

It may seem that standard domain extension techniques for hash functions (like Merkle-Damgård, Sponge, or Merkle trees) provide a solution for this problem. Indeed, their goal is to take a hash function on a small domain and turn it into a hash function with arbitrary-size domain. But, as we point out next, the standard constructions suffer from a significant security loss. A priori, it is not even clear that this security loss is avoidable.

The Security of Existing Constructions. First, consider (a keyed variant of) the Merkle-Damgård (MD) construction [13,24], perhaps the most widely popular design for getting a hash function on long inputs from one on fixed input sizes. This design is not only extremely fundamental in cryptographic theory, but it also underlies popular hash functions used in practice, most notably MD5, SHA-1, and SHA-2. The MD: $\{0,1\}^\kappa \times \{0,1\}^* \to \{0,1\}^n$ construction iterates the basic hash function $h: \{0,1\}^a \to \{0,1\}^n$ by feeding in input blocks of size $s = a - \max\{\kappa, n\}$ one by one. It first pads the message appropriately such that it is a multiple of s bits. For key $\mathsf{key} \in \{0,1\}^\kappa$ and input $m \in \{0,1\}^s$, define $\mathsf{MD}(\mathsf{key}, m) = h(\mathsf{key} \| m)$. Then, for a longer input $m \in (\{0,1\}^s)^\ell$, viewed as ℓ blocks $m_1, \ldots, m_\ell$ each from $\{0,1\}^s$, recursively define $\mathsf{MD}(\mathsf{key}, (m_1, \ldots, m_\ell)) = h(\mathsf{MD}(\mathsf{key}, (m_1, \ldots, m_{\ell-1})), m_\ell)$. We note that in the standard MD construction (studied, for example, in [1,2,11,17]), key is only explicitly included once when processing the first message block.

Collision resistance of MD in the AI-ROM was first studied by Coretti, Dodis, Guo, and Steinberger [11] and more recently by [1,2,17]. It is known that there is an attack, loosely based on the idea of rainbow tables [20,25], which succeeds in finding a collision with probability $\Omega(S/2^\kappa + ST^2/2^n)$. In typical settings of parameters, the $ST^2/2^n$ term dominates the above expression and in this case it is evident that MD suffers from a significant security loss.

Concretely, in the SHA-1 construction, $a = 678$ and $\kappa = n = 160$. If we model the underlying primitive $h: \{0,1\}^{678} \to \{0,1\}^{160}$ as a perfectly random function, an (S,T)-attacker with $S = 2^{53}$ and $T = 2^{50}$ will find a collision with probability $\approx 2^{-7}$ (essentially completely breaking the scheme).[2] On the other hand, the best one could hope is a construction with maximal advantage $O(S/2^\kappa + T^2/2^n) \approx 2^{-60}$ (obtained by the naive attack).

Another construction we mention is the Sponge [7,8] construction, an alternative to the Merkle-Damgård design that underlies the modern SHA-3 hashing standard. As opposed to MD, the Sponge construction relies on a random *permutation* $\Pi: \{0,1\}^n \to \{0,1\}^n$. Sponge iterates Π by feeding in blocks of size $r < n$ from the input one at a time in a certain way. It results with a keyed hash function $\mathsf{Sp}: \{0,1\}^\kappa \times \{0,1\}^* \to \{0,1\}^r$ with $\kappa + r = n$. Coretti et al. [11]

---

[2] These parameters roughly correspond to an attacker with ≈ 1000 terabytes of memory that uses optimized hardware that can compute 3 billion hashes per second for a long weekend.

(see also [16]) showed that there is a collision finding (S, T)-attack with advantage $\Omega(ST^2/2^\kappa + T^2/2^r)$ against Sp relative to a random key. Again, we see that there is a non-trivial security loss in this construction.

It is important to note that for every choice of S and T the above attacks on Merkle-Damgård and Sponge beat the naive attack. In particular, there is no non-trivial choice of parameters where MD or Sp achieve the optimal security bound.

Lastly, we mention two other popular (variable-input-length) hash function designs: Merkle trees [23] and the BLAKE family [3,4]. The former (Merkle trees) is a popular design that has important features like local opening and can be easily parallelized. Although it is extremely popular both in theory and in practice, we are not aware of a keyed variant that has been studied in the non-uniform setting. The latter (BLAKE) is a runner-up in NIST's competition to create a new hashing standard (where Sponge ended up as the winner). This design is based on the MD design, but they allow the inner hash function h to be keyed at every invocation. We are not aware of a formal study of its security in the non-uniform setting. Looking ahead, two of our main contributions are a proposal and analysis of the non-uniform security of Merkle tree and the MD/ BLAKE design, where the inner hash function h is keyed in every invocation. Concretely, we believe that this is the right notion to consider moving forward, in terms of non-uniform security.

A Different Perspective. Above, we considered the scenario where $h\colon \{0,1\}^a \to \{0,1\}^n$ is given, and we want to build an $H\colon \{0,1\}^\kappa \times \{0,1\}^* \to \{0,1\}^n$ which is as secure as possible for every (S, T)-attacker. A different perspective, slightly more target oriented, is to first fix a desired security level (say 2^{-50}) and the power of adversaries (say $S = T = 2^{60}$) and then understand which h is needed in order to get the desired H. If we use MD (for concreteness) for H, we will need $n \geq 230$, but if we had an optimally secure construction of H, we would need only $n \geq 170$. The latter could potentially be easier to design and argue about.

1.1 Our Results

We provide several constructions of keyed hash functions from non-keyed ones that do not suffer from any security loss (i.e., the naive attack that has advantage $\Theta(S/2^\kappa + T^2/2^n)$ is provably optimal). Our constructions provide various tradeoffs between their efficiency and the range of parameters (S and T) where they achieve optimal security.

Merkle-Damgård and Merkle Trees with a Keyed Inner Hash. All of our constructions can be viewed within a framework that builds on the Merkle-Damgård and Merkle tree constructions.

We start by discussing the MD-based approach. We consider an iterative hashing design where a compression phase is performed in every step using an "inner hash" function. The input for the compression phase is the current state and the next input. At the end, the compression phase outputs the next state.

Of course, the inner hash function in the compression phase can use h as a subroutine. Abstractly, the compression phase for the MD-based construction is

$$y := \mathsf{compress}(\mathsf{key}, y, m),$$

where importantly the compress function takes key as input. See Fig. 1 for an illustration. With this notation, the compression function of the standard MD function (at least as studied in numerous recent works including [1,2,11,17]) is simply $\mathsf{compress}(\mathsf{key}, y, m) = h(y, m)$, and for the first step, y is initialized to key. Notably key is not included in every compression phases.

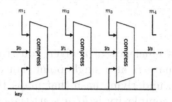

Fig. 1. Our framework for building keyed hash functions based on the Merkle-Damgård construction with a keyed inner compression function.

We next consider a parallelizable hashing design that generalizes the Merkle tree hash function. Here, each input is fed into a "leaf" of the Merkle tree, along with the key value. The compression function is then used to recursively combine outputs in previous levels until a final output is generated. Crucially, we always include key in the compression function. See Fig. 2 for an illustration. This framework provides an alternative to the generalized MD approach described above. It requires at most a factor of two more calls to compress, but it is extremely parallelizable. Further, it provides a local opening property, where someone can prove that an individual message block m_i was included in the hash, without providing the full message.

Our constructions are obtained by different implementations of compress, namely viewing compress as an inner keyed hash function used in the MD and Merkle tree designs. Quantitatively, the MD and Merkle tree approaches give similar results, so we focus our attention on instantiating compress in the case of the MD-based framework. However, all of our main results extend to the setting of the generalized Merkle tree framework, which we provide in the full version.

For simplicity of presentation of our results, we slightly simplify notation and assume that κ (the key length) is equal to n (the output size of the hash function).[3] In our formal theorem statements in the technical sections, κ and n are treated independently when relevant.

---

[3] We note that there are constructions that use $\kappa \neq n$ by design (e.g., BLAKE hash [3, 4] uses $\kappa = n/2$).

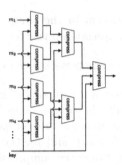

Fig. 2. Our framework for building keyed hash functions based on the Merkle tree construction.

Efficiency: We measure efficiency of a given construction by the number of calls to h needed to evaluate H at a single point. For example, in the standard MD construction with an underlying hash that maps $\{0,1\}^a$ to $\{0,1\}^n$, to hash a b-bit input, the query complexity is $b/(a-n)$ (ignoring rounding[4]). Indeed, every application of h takes as input the previous output (n bits) and so it can process $a - n$ bits from the input each time.

Assuming a Large Inner Hash. Our first result shows that optimal security loss is achievable. That is, we show that there is a way to take a random oracle that operates on a fixed input length and get a keyed hash H that operates on arbitrary-length inputs with the following security guarantee: for any S, T, any (S, T)-attacker has minimal possible advantage in finding a collision in H relative to a random key. In words, the new construction is a variant of MD where we also feed key as input in every block. We refer to this construction as the MD construction with a keyed inner hash, in contrast to the standard MD construction where key is only fed in the first block. At a high level, feeding the key into every invocation of h allows us to reduce the probability of finding a long collision in H to that of finding a collision in h, which achieves optimal security $O(S/2^n + T^2/2^n)$ [14]. Refer to Fig. 3 for an illustration of how the construction works.[5]

---

[4] To be more precise, MD requires $\lceil (b + n + 1)/(a - n) \rceil$ calls to h after padding the input with its length followed by a 1 and a sequence of 0s to fill the remaining current block. However, for ease of presentation, we ignore rounding in the introduction. In the formal theorem statements, we give exact efficiency bounds.

[5] Essentially the same construction appears in Goldwasser-Bellare's lecture notes [19, §8.5] where it is shown that this construction is collision resistant in the uniform setting. Our result shows that this holds in the non-uniform (AI-ROM) setting as well.

Theorem 1 (Informal; see Theorem 8). *Assume $h\colon \{0,1\}^a \to \{0,1\}^n$ is modeled as a random oracle with $a > 2n$. Then, there is an $H_1\colon \{0,1\}^n \times \{0,1\}^* \to \{0,1\}^n$ such that:*

1. *For any $S,T \in \mathbb{N}$ and any (S,T)-attacker, their advantage in finding a collision in $H_1(\mathsf{key},\cdot)$ relative to a random $\mathsf{key} \leftarrow_\$ \{0,1\}^n$ is $O(S/2^n + T^2/2^n)$.*
2. *One evaluation of H_1 on a given key and a b-bit message requires $b/(a-2n)$ queries to h.*

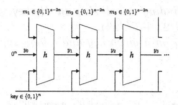

Fig. 3. The construction H_1 underlying Theorem 1 given a hash function $h\colon \{0,1\}^a \to \{0,1\}^n$ for $a > 2n$.

The above result is optimal in terms of security and is almost as efficient as standard MD if $a \geq 2n+\Omega(n)$. For example, if $a = 3n$, processing a b-bit input of H_1 requires querying h as many as $b/(a-2n) = b/n$ times. In the standard MD construction, only $b/(a-n) = b/(2n)$ queries are required, so our construction is less efficient than MD by a small constant factor at most 2 when $a = 3n$.

However, H_1 is significantly less efficient than MD if a is roughly $2n$, i.e. h compresses by a factor of 2. For example, if $a = 2n + 1$, then processing a b-bit input of H_1 requires invoking h as many as b times. However, MD requires only $b/(n+1)$ queries. This is a significant difference. We emphasize that having an efficient construction even when $a \approx 2n$ is not only a technicality but is rather important: concretely, assuming that the basic compressing function shrinks by a factor 2 is extremely common, both in theory and in practice. Thus, our next results are focused on closing this gap.

Instantiating the Keyed Inner Hash with Standard MD. To this end, we start by considering a construction H_2 that works for *any* $a > n$ and only incurs a factor of 2 overhead in terms of efficiency relative to MD. While this may seem too good to be true, we pay in terms of the assumptions we need to make to claim optimal security for collision resistance. Namely, the scheme has "optimal security," meaning any (S,T)-attacker can find a collision with probability at most $O(S/2^n + T^2/2^n)$, only whenever $S \leq T$ and $ST^2 \leq 2^n$.

This main idea behind the construction H_2 is to instantiate the compress function in the MD-based framework of Fig. 1 with a standard MD hash function.

We use key as the key for MD, and we treat $y_{i-1}\|m_i$ as the message. If we use a message block size $|m_i| = n$, this results in only a factor of two overhead relative to MD (essentially, half of the invocations of h incorporate bits of the message m_i, and half of the invocations incorporate bits of the previous output y_{i-1}). This construction is depicted in Fig. 4 and gives the following result.

Theorem 2 (Informal; see Theorem 10**).** *Assume* $h\colon \{0,1\}^a \to \{0,1\}^n$ *is modeled as a random oracle with* $a > n$. *Then, there is an* $H_2\colon \{0,1\}^\kappa \times \{0,1\}^* \to \{0,1\}^n$ *such that:*

1. *For any* $S, T \in \mathbb{N}$ *such that* $S \leq T$, $ST^2 \leq 2^n$, *and any* (S,T)-*attacker, their advantage in finding a collision in* $H_2(\mathsf{key}, \cdot)$ *relative to a random* $\mathsf{key} \leftarrow_\$ \{0,1\}^n$ *is* $O(S/2^n + T^2/2^n)$.
2. *One evaluation of* H_2 *on a given key and a* b-*bit input requires* $2 \cdot b/(a-n)$ *queries to* h.

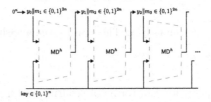

Fig. 4. The construction H_2 underlying Theorem 2 given a hash function $h\colon \{0,1\}^a \to \{0,1\}^n$ for $a > n$. The gray dotted boxes represent the compress function, instantiated with the Merkle-Damgård construction, that uses key $\in \{0,1\}^n$ as the key and $y_{i-1}\|m_i \in \{0,1\}^{2n}$ as the message.

We note that the assumption that $ST^2 \leq 2^n$ in the construction above comes from the fact that best currently known time-space tradeoffs for the collision resistance of standard MD (culminating in [2,17] following the works of [1,9,11]) require this assumption to get optimal bounds when analyzing the ℓ-block MD construction when $\ell \in \omega(1)$. In the special case where we only use a 2-block variant of MD as the underlying compress function, [1] give tight bounds that do not require that $ST^2 \leq 2^n$ (and furthermore, [17] gave tight bounds for all constants ℓ). This motivates our next construction, H_3, which uses the 2-block MD construction for compress, but requires that the input size to h satisfies $a > 3n/2$. See Fig. 5 for an illustration, and the corresponding result is given in the following theorem.

Theorem 3 (Informal; see Corollary 1**).** *Assume* $h\colon \{0,1\}^a \to \{0,1\}^n$ *is modeled as a random oracle with* $a > 3n/2$. *Then, there is an* $H_3\colon \{0,1\}^\kappa \times \{0,1\}^* \to \{0,1\}^n$ *such that:*

1. *For any* $S, T \in \mathbb{N}$ *such that* $S \leq T$ *and any* (S,T)-*attacker, their advantage in finding a collision in* $H_3(\mathsf{key}, \cdot)$ *relative to a random* $\mathsf{key} \leftarrow_\$ \{0,1\}^n$ *is* $O(S/2^n + T^2/2^n)$.

2. *One evaluation of H_3 on a given key and a b-bit input requires $2 \cdot b/(2a - 3n)$ queries to h.*

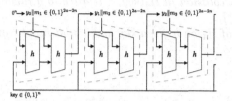

Fig. 5. The construction H_3 underlying Theorem 3 given a hash function $h: \{0,1\}^a \to \{0,1\}^n$ for $a > 3n/2$. The gray dotted boxes represent the compress function, instantiated with a two-block Merkle-Damgård construction, that uses key $\in \{0,1\}^n$ as the key and $y_{i-1}\|m_i \in \{0,1\}^{2a-2n}$ as the message. The $2a - 2n$ bit message is split evenly into the first and second call to h, indicated in the figure by a diamond.

Instantiating the Keyed Inner Hash with a 2-Level Merkle Tree. For our final construction, we seek to build a hash function H_4 that is both efficient and optimally secure whenever $a \approx 2n$ (h is only compressing by a factor of 2), without assuming that $S \leq T$. In particular, $S \gg T$ makes sense in many practical scenarios: the pre-processing attacker may have much more than time T to generate its advice string of size S, the online attacker may have easy random access to a structured advice string, or the online time T may be small for applications that enforce a timeout with fixed-time communication session (see [5] as an example of an attack on a TLS session that requires relatively heavy computation in an offline phase). Lastly, we mention that the bounds we obtain on H_2 and H_3 are tight—there is a non-trivial attack whenever $S > T$ that scales with advantage $\Omega(ST\ell/2^n)$ for standard ℓ-block MD [1,11].

For H_4, we instantiate the compress function from the framework of Fig. 1 using a keyed variant of a Merkle tree construction (this has never been formally defined or analyzed to the best of our knowledge). In our variant, we feed key into all leaves of the Merkle tree. Concretely, in our construction, we use a 2-level Merkle tree and feed key to both of them, corresponding to two distinct invocations of h, and we split the "message" $y_{i-1}\|m_i$ into the remaining input bits for the leaves. The second level of the Merkle tree combines the two outputs from the first level, to produce a n bit output for compress. The full construction of H_4 is illustrated in Fig. 6. We conjecture that this Merkle tree-based construction is optimally secure for collision resistance (see Remark 1 for more details), but analyzing its security turns out to be highly non-trivial. In particular, our current analysis is only optimally secure when $ST^2 \leq 2^n$, as stated in the following theorem.

Theorem 4. *Assume* $h\colon \{0,1\}^a \to \{0,1\}^n$ *is modeled as a random oracle with* $a \geq 2n$. *Then, there is an* $H_4\colon \{0,1\}^\kappa \times \{0,1\}^* \to \{0,1\}^n$ *such that:*

1. *For any* $S, T \in \mathbb{N}$ *such that* $ST^2 \leq 2^n$ *and any* (S,T)*-attacker, their advantage in finding a collision in* $H_4(\mathsf{key}, \cdot)$ *relative to a random* $\mathsf{key} \leftarrow_\$ \{0,1\}^\kappa$ *is* $O(S/2^n + T^2/2^n)$.
2. *One evaluation of* H_4 *on a given key and a* b*-bit input requires* $3 \cdot b/(2a - 3n)$ *queries to* h.

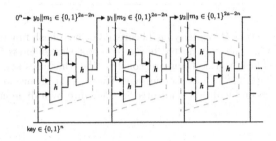

Fig. 6. The construction H_4 underlying Theorem 4 given a hash function $h\colon \{0,1\}^a \to \{0,1\}^n$ for $a \geq 2n$. The gray dotted boxes represent the compress function, instantiated with a two-level Merkle tree, that uses $\mathsf{key} \in \{0,1\}^n$ in each leaf and $y_{i-1}\|m_i \in \{0,1\}^{2a-2n}$ as the message. The $2a - 2n$ bit message is split evenly between the two leaves of the Merkle tree, indicated by a diamond in the figure. We require $a \geq 2n$ so that both outputs from the leaves can be fed into the next layer of the Merkle tree.

We summarize our results in Table 1.

Remark 1 (A conjecture on the security of keyed Merkle trees). The main building block in our construction of Theorem 4 is a Merkle tree where the key value key is included only at the leaves. Concretely, we include a key key in each of the leaves of a Merkle tree and then fill in the rest of the leaves with bits of some message $m \in \{0,1\}^*$, and then run the Merkle tree construction (with an unkeyed hash) as normal to get an n-bit output. In this work, we analyze the simplest case where the Merkle tree has depth 2 with only two leaves. However, this naturally generalizes to any number of ℓ leaves resulting in a tree of depth $O(\log \ell)$.

Table 1. A summary of our results as well as the standard MD construction for reference. The advantage of a construction is given in terms of the probability of (S, T)-attackers to find collisions relative to a random key. The efficiency is measured in terms of the number of calls to h that maps a-bit inputs to n when processing a b-bit input. The assumptions column specifies conditions on various parameters.

	Advantage	Efficiency	Input Size	Assumptions
MD	$\Theta(ST^2/2^n)$	$b/(a-n)$	$a > n$	None
H_1 (Thm. 1)	$\Theta(S/2^n + T^2/2^n)$	$b/(a-2n)$	$a > 2n$	None
H_2 (Thm. 2)	$\Theta(S/2^n + T^2/2^n)$	$2 \cdot b/(a-n)$	$a > n$	$S \leq T, ST^2 \leq 2^n$
H_3 (Thm. 3)	$\Theta(S/2^n + T^2/2^n)$	$2 \cdot b/(2a-3n)$	$a > 1.5n$	$S \leq T$
H_4 (Thm. 4)	$\Theta(S/2^n + T^2/2^n)$	$3 \cdot b/(2a-3n)$	$a \geq 2n$	$ST^2 \leq 2^n$

We conjecture that this approach, where only the leaves are keyed, is as secure as the Merkle tree approach of Fig. 2 where the inner hash function is keyed at every invocation, including interior nodes. This latter approach requires a larger, more complicated, inner hash function, so we would like to avoid this if at all possible.

First, for the simple case of a depth two tree with keyed leaves, we conjecture that the bound we show in this work is not tight (see Theorem 12 for the exact bound we show). Namely, we believe that we should not need to assume $ST^2 \leq 2^n$ (or make any assumptions on S, T) in order to get optimal security. Second, we believe that this intuition should extend to the arbitrary depth Merkle trees that are keyed at the leaves, and we conjecture that it should also achieve optimal (S, T) security without any assumptions on S, T. However, even getting a bound in this case that is optimal in the setting $ST^2 \leq 2^n$ we believe would be very interesting. Additionally, handling deeper Merkle trees could potentially allow for constructions that do not necessarily have even a two-to-one structure, meaning that we could build a keyed hash function based on Merkle trees without assuming the hash function h has input size $a \geq 2n$.

1.2 Related Work

The motivation for this work comes from a recent line of results on the non-uniform security loss of various hashing mechanisms.

For Merkle-Damgård's construction [13,24], this was first studied by Coretti et al. [11] who showed how to find collisions with probability $\Omega(S/2^\kappa + ST^2/2^n)$. The idea is reminiscent of the rainbow tables attack due to Oechslin [25] (in turn building on Hellman [20]). The collisions they get are rather long (of length proportional to T). Akshima et al. [1] generalized the attack to get an ℓ-block collision with probability $\Omega(S/2^\kappa + ST\ell/2^n)$ and showed that this attack is optimal for $\ell = 2$. Ghoshal and Komargodski [17] showed that this attack is optimal for all constant values of ℓ and Akshima, Guo, and Liu [2] almost proved the tightness of the bound for all ℓs by showing that the best possible attack has advantage $O(ST\ell/2^n \cdot (1 + ST^2/2^n) + T^2/2^n)$. For a single-block Merkle-Damgård (i.e., just a compressing random oracle), Dodis, Guo, and Katz [14] showed that including a random key (optimally) defeats preprocessing attacks.

For Sponge [7,8], Coretti, Dodis, and Guo [10] stated a related attack with advantage $\Omega(ST^2/2^\kappa + T^2/2^r)$ (with r being a "rate" parameter of the scheme). Again, this attack resulted in very long collisions. The attack was formalized and extended to ℓ-block collisions with advantage $\Omega(ST\ell/2^\kappa + T^2/2^r)$ by Freitag, Ghoshal and Komargodski [16]. Freitag et al. also proved several upper bounds on the advantage of any attacker, but their bounds are not known to be tight.

Indifferentiability. Our work focuses on collision resistance, but there are other security properties of interest (such as inversion, second preimage resistance, pseudo-randomness, and unpredictability). In the uniform security setting there is a well-known framework called *indifferentiability* (due to Maurer, Renner, and Holenstein [22]) that is used to show that a (wide) class of security goals are simultaneously met. This allows to modularly transition to a (simpler) hybrid world where a complicated hash function construction is replaced with a monolithic random oracle (see, for example, [12]). Such transitions are known to work for all single-stage games but not for multi-stage games [26]. Our non-uniform security model is fundamentally a two-stage model and therefore the indifferentiability framework (as is) does not apply. It is an interesting open problem to find an analogue in the non-uniform setting.

2   Technical Overview

In this section, we give a high level overview of our main techniques. Recall, our goal is to construction a variable-input length, keyed, hash function $H^h\colon \{0,1\}^\kappa \times \{0,1\}^* \to \{0,1\}^n$ from an idealized, fixed-input length hash function $h\colon \{0,1\}^a \to \{0,1\}^n$.

Non-uniform Security in the AI-ROM. We consider non-uniform (S,T)-attackers $\mathcal{A} = (\mathcal{A}_1, \mathcal{A}_2)$ in the auxiliary-input random oracle model (AI-ROM) [27] with the following structure. First, h is randomly sampled from the space of all a-bit to n-bit functions. Then, in the preprocessing phase, $\mathcal{A}_1$ has unbounded access to h and outputs an advice string σ such that $|\sigma| \leq S$. The online phase $\mathcal{A}_2$ receives auxiliary input σ and a random key key $\leftarrow \{0,1\}^\kappa$ as input, and then has to find two distinct messages msg, msg′ such that $H^h(\text{key}, \text{msg}) = H^h(\text{key}, \text{msg}')$ while making at most T queries to h. Our goal is to give constructions H^h such that no (S,T)-attacker as above can find a collision with better than $O(S/2^\kappa + T^2/2^n)$ probability. This is "optimal" in the sense that this matches a naive attack against a purely random H: the preprocessing attacker stores collisions for $\Omega(S)$ keys, and the online attacker either gets "lucky" and receives one of those keys as input or performs a standard birthday-style attack.

Merkle-Damgård Framework with a Keyed Inner Hash. We consider a general framework based on the Merkle-Damgård (MD) transformation where we instantiate the inner hash function with a keyed one. Let $s \in \mathbb{N}$ be the desired message block size. Then, given a function $g \colon \{0,1\}^{\kappa+n+s} \rightarrow \{0,1\}^n$, we can build a function H^g where any attack on the collision resistance of H^g implies an attack on g. The idea behind H^g is as follows. We first break our message up into blocks $m_1, \ldots, m_\ell$ of size $a - \kappa - n$. We initialize the value $y_0 = 0^n$, and for $i = 1, 2, \ldots, \ell$ we compute $y_i = g(\text{key}\|y_{i-1}\|m_i)$. Finally, we output y_ℓ. It is known (e.g. see Sect. 8.5 of [19]) that if you can find a collision in the MD construction H^g for a keyed g in the uniform setting, then this implies you can find a collision in g. Indeed, this reasoning extends to the non-uniform setting with (S, T)-attackers in the AI-ROM. Hence, this shows that H^g is as secure as g. So, our new goal is to construct such a g with "optimal security" given an idealized hash function $h \colon \{0,1\}^a \rightarrow \{0,1\}^n$.

Our first observation is that if $a \geq \kappa + n + s$, then we can simply use $g = h$. Furthermore, h has optimal security $O(S/2^\kappa + T^2/2^n)$ (first formalized by [14] in the AI-ROM), so we are done! So our next goal is to try to use an h from minimal assumptions. Namely, can we get a keyed hash function with arbitrary length input from any $h \colon \{0,1\}^a \rightarrow \{0,1\}^n$ where a is much smaller, i.e. even $a = n + 1$? This will allow us to focus on building as simple a primitive as possible which we can bootstrap to a full variable-input length hash function with optimal security.

Next, we note that for any $a > \max(\kappa, n)$, we can always do the standard Merkle-Damgård transformation using h to construct g, where key is not fed into every invocation of h. For standard MD, it makes sense to set $\kappa = n$ since we use the key key as the initialization vector. Recall, the MD^h construction sets $y_0 = \text{key}$, computes $y_i = h(y_{i-1}\|m_i)$ for $i = 1, \ldots, \ell$, and outputs y_ℓ. This approach has a major downside in that instantiating MD without inserting key into each invocation of h suffers non-trivial time-space tradeoffs. In general, there is an attack on the general MD^h construction with advantage $\Omega(ST^2/2^n)$. This is strictly worse than the optimal bound of $O(S/2^n + T^2/2^n)$ for any setting of parameters with $S, T \gg 1$. However, this attack finds very large—roughly length T—collisions. In our setting, we only care about using MD^h to get a function g with inputs of size $2n + s$. Thus, we leverage a recent line of work (see [1,2,9,11,17]) that shows that if you only use MD^h on ℓ-block messages, then the best known attack has advantage at most $O(ST\ell/2^n + T^2/2^n)$ (and further this is provably tight for constant ℓ [1,17] and, when $ST^2 \leq 2^n$, is provably tight for all ℓ [2]).

So, if we instantiate g in our framework with a fixed-length MD^h construction where we set κ and s to be equal to the output length n, we get a construction for H^h where any (S, T)-attacker has advantage at most $O(ST/2^n + T^2/2^n)$ (up to poly(n) factors). This is only "optimal," however, under the (strong) assumption that $S \leq T$.

Our main technical contribution is instantiating g in the framework above using a new keyed Merkle tree approach, which does not require the assumption that $S \leq T$.

2.1   Keyed Merkle Tree Analysis

For the rest of this technical overview, we focus on our analysis of the keyed Merkle tree construction.

Construction. We start by defining the 2-level construction. We want a keyed function $g: \{0,1\}^{\kappa} \times \{0,1\}^{n+s} \rightarrow \{0,1\}^n$ from a hash function $h: \{0,1\}^a \rightarrow \{0,1\}^n$ where $a \geq 2n$. To do so, we split the $(n+s)$-bit input into two parts, call them m_L, m_R, of size at most $a - \kappa$ (hence we require here that $a - \kappa \geq (n+s)/2$, or $a \geq \kappa + n/2 + s/2$). We concatenate each part with the key key and compute $y_L \leftarrow h(\mathsf{key}\|m_L)$ and $y_R \leftarrow h(\mathsf{key}\|m_R)$. We then concatenate y_L with y_R and feed the resulting string into h to get the output $z \leftarrow h(y_L\|y_R)$ (we require here that $a \geq 2n$). For technical purposes, we "domain separate" each call to h, so $y_L = h_1(\mathsf{key}\|m_L)$, $y_R = h_2(\mathsf{key}\|m_R)$, and $z = h_3(y_L\|y_R)$.

Analysis. We want to bound the probability that any (S,T)-attacker can find a collision in this keyed Merkle tree construction of g. To simplify the analysis here, we consider the case where κ and s are equal to n. Hence, each call to h takes two n-bit inputs and has one n-bit output. We also assume from the start that $ST^2 \leq 2^n$.

We start with the following observation. The probability that any (S,T)-attacker finds a collision at the leaves, corresponding to the calls to h_1, h_2, is at most $O(S/2^n + T^2/2^n)$. Because these calls include the key key, if such an event happened, we could reduce to finding a collision in h directly. So, the challenge is to reason about the advantage of an (S,T)-attacker finding a collision at the second level of the Merkle tree, which is only implicitly related to the key key in the Merkle tree construction. We have to somehow characterize all possible ways that an (S,T)-attack can encode information about h in its advice string from the preprocessing phase.

One of the first tools one often turns to in such analysis is to use the *presampling* technique from [11,27]. We note that if we were to use the presampling technique, we would obtain a term of the form $ST/2^n$ in out bound, which is optimally secure only in the range $S \leq T$. Our main technical contribution is getting an optimally secure protocol for the range $S \gg T$, which therefore requires techniques other than presampling.

The AGL [2] Framework: Reducing to Multi-instance Games. To make our lives significantly easier, we use the multi-instance framework of [2], previously used in somewhat different forms in [1,9,17,21]. At a very high level, this framework gives a way to reason about (S,T)-attackers using an *average-case* advice string rather than a worst-case one. In more detail, they show how to bound the advantage that any (S,T)-attacker $\mathcal{A}$ finds a collision in g^h by the advantage of a (uniform) attacker $\mathcal{B}$ in the following game. First, a random function h is sampled. Then, $\mathcal{B}$ has to win the following game for all $i = 1, \ldots, S$

sequentially, where it is allowed to maintain arbitrary state (that it generates) between each successive game. In each game i, the attacker $\mathcal{B}$ receives a random key key_i, its state from the previous games, and has to come up with a pair of messages $\mathsf{msg}_i, \mathsf{msg}'_i$ such that $g^h(\mathsf{key}_i, \mathsf{msg}_i) = g^h(\mathsf{key}_i, \mathsf{msg}'_i)$ using at most T queries to h. [2,9] show that if the advantage of $\mathcal{B}$ is at most δ^S, then the advantage of the (S,T)-attacker $\mathcal{A}$ is at most 2δ. The magic of this framework is that we can analyze the advantage of $\mathcal{B}$ in each game i only given its state from the previous games, instead of having to reason about arbitrary advice strings as in the case of (S,T)-attackers. Namely, we can lazily sample h on any point that $\mathcal{B}$ has not queried, in a way that is independent of $\mathcal{B}$'s current state.

Note that it suffices to show that the advantage of $\mathcal{B}$ "in game i" is at most δ given it has won all previous games. Let W_i be the event that $\mathcal{B}$ wins game i and $W_{<i}$ be the event that $\mathcal{B}$ wins all games before i. This follows since $\Pr[W_1 \wedge \ldots \wedge W_S] = \prod_{i=1}^{S} \Pr[W_i|W_{<i}] \leq \delta^S$ if $\Pr[W_i|W_{<i}] \leq \delta$ for all $i \in [S]$. Hence, our goal is to show that $\Pr[W_i|W_{<i}] \leq O(S/2^n + T^2/2^n)$, up to $\mathrm{poly}(n)$ factors.

Knowledge Gaining Event: Bounding "Hitting" Queries. Now, to even further simplify the analysis of $\Pr[W_i|W_{<i}]$, we define a key "knowledge gaining event" (based on the techniques of [2]) representing the kind of information that $\mathcal{B}$ may have encoded into its state based on the queries it made to h before game i has started. At a high level, this is an event that we show happens with very small probability (technically at most $2^{-2i \cdot n}$) for an average-case advice string for $\mathcal{B}$ at the start of game i. Then, assuming this event does not occur, we can more easily characterize the strategies of $\mathcal{B}$.

To define this event, we introduce some notation to characterize $\mathcal{B}$'s queries. We refer to all $(i-1) \cdot T$ queries $\mathcal{B}$ makes before the start of game i as "offline" queries, and we refer to the T queries made in game i as "online" queries. An offline query is said to be "hitting" if its output is equal to an output or either of the two inputs to some prior query, i.e. it "hits" a previous query. We are now ready to state our key knowledge gaining event.

- We say that $\mathsf{E}^i_{\mathsf{hit}}$ holds if there are more than $i \cdot \mathrm{poly}(n)$ hitting queries among the $(i-1) \cdot T$ offline queries.

Briefly, we justify why $\mathsf{E}^i_{\mathsf{hit}}$ holds with very small probability. The output for each query is uniformly sampled, and there are at most $3 \cdot (i-1) \cdot T$ values to hit across inputs/outputs in the previous $(i-1) \cdot T$ offline queries. So the probability each offline query is a hitting query is at most $3iT/2^n$, meaning we expect at most $3i^2T^2/2^n$ hitting queries accounting for all $(i-1) \cdot T$ offline queries. Furthermore, we show using a Chernoff bound that there will not be more than $i \cdot \mathrm{poly}(n) \cdot \max(1, iT^2/2^n) = O(i)$ hitting queries (assuming $ST^2 \leq 2^n$) with high probability (recall that we ignore $\mathrm{poly}(n)$ terms).

A Case Analysis Based on Collision Queries. Now, assuming there are at most $i \cdot \mathrm{poly}(n)$ hitting queries, we are ready to show that $\Pr[W_i|W_{<i}] \leq O(S/2^n + T^2/2^n)$. To do so, we look at the following "collision" queries corresponding to the valid collision $\mathsf{msg}_i = (m_L, m_R) \neq \mathsf{msg}'_i = (m'_L, m'_R)$ that $\mathcal{B}$

outputs in game i (we assume that $\mathcal{B}$ makes all of these queries at some point during or before game i).

- Q_1, Q_2, Q_3 are the queries $y_L \leftarrow h_1(\mathsf{key}_i \| m_L)$, $y_R \leftarrow h_2(\mathsf{key}_i \| m_R)$, $z \leftarrow h_3(y_L \| y_R)$, respectively.
- Q'_1, Q'_2, Q'_3 are the queries $y'_L \leftarrow h_1(\mathsf{key}_i \| m'_L)$, $y'_R \leftarrow h_2(\mathsf{key}_i \| m'_R)$, $z \leftarrow h_3(y'_L \| y'_R)$, respectively.

Recall that we assumed the collision occurs among Q_3, Q'_3 (not at the leaves), so it must be the case that $(y_L, y_R) \neq (y'_L, y'_R)$ and queries Q_3, Q'_3 are distinct.

If all of these collision queries are online (were first made during game i), then clearly $\Pr[W_i | W_{<i}] \leq O(T^2/2^n)$. Specifically, as Q_3 and Q'_3 are online (and distinct by assumption) and form a collision, this follows by a birthday bound on at most T online—and hence lazily sampled—queries that $\mathcal{B}$ makes during game i. The challenge comes when analyzing the cases where $\mathcal{B}$ may have made some of these queries before game i, so it could have encoded information about these queries in its state. To do so, we consider the following remaining cases, which cover all possible strategies that $\mathcal{B}$ may employ.

As we already considered when both Q_3, Q'_3 are online queries, it must be the case that one of Q_3, Q'_3 must be an offline query. Assume without loss of generality that Q_3 is offline. Then either (A) both Q_1, Q_2 are online, (B) exactly one of Q_1, Q_2 are online, or Q_1, Q_2 are both offline. The latter case implies that Q_1, Q_2, Q_3 are all offline. Then either is the case that (C) Q'_3 is online, or Q'_3 is also offline. If Q'_3 is also offline, then either we reduce to case (A) or (B) above by symmetry, or it holds that (D) all $Q_1, Q_2, Q_3, Q'_1, Q'_2, Q'_3$ are offline. So, it suffices to show in cases (A-D) that $\Pr[W_i | W_{<i}] \leq \delta \leq O(S/2^n + T^2/2^n)$, at least assuming $ST^2 \leq 2^n$. We proceed to give the main ideas behind each of these cases.

(A) Q_3 is offline but Q_1, Q_2 are online.
There are at most $(i-1) \cdot T$ options for the offline query Q_3. Both online queries Q_1 and Q_2 have to hit such a query, which happens with at most $(i-1) \cdot T \cdot (T/2^n)^2 = O(iT^3/2^{2n}) \leq O(T/2^n)$ when $ST^2 \leq 2^n$ since $i \leq S$.

(B) Q_1, Q_3 are offline but Q_2 is online (symmetrically for Q_1 online and Q_2 offline).
In this case, we claim we can "associate" the key key_i in game i to the query Q_3 since both Q_1 and Q_3 are offline queries. If we can associate key_i to at most k possible Q_3 queries, then this implies the probability the output of some online query hits an input of such an associated query is at most $k \cdot T/2^n$. But how many Q_3 queries can we associate to a key key_i?
In the worst case, key_i may be associated to $(i-1) \cdot T$ many Q_3 queries, but this implies a suboptimal bound of $O(iT^2/2^n)$. But this cannot be true for too many values of key simultaneously. In particular, if a Q_3 query is associated with more than k possible values of key, this means there are k hitting queries, so each Q_3 query can be associated with at most $O(i)$ keys.

This implies there are at most $O(i^2 T)$ pairs of associated key values with potential Q_3 queries, meaning a random key_i value will be associated with at most $O(i^2 T/2^n)$ potential Q_3 values on average. Plugging this average-case bound into k above, this implies a bound of $O(i^2 T^2/2^{2n}) \leq O(S/2^n)$ assuming $ST^2 \leq 2^n$ given $i \leq S$.

(C) Q_1, Q_2, Q_3 are offline but Q_3' is online.

In this case, Q_3' is a distinct query from Q_3 by assumption, but again we can "associate" Q_3 with key_i as above. Then, since Q_3' must share an output with Q_3, the same argument as above gives a bound of $O(S/2^n)$ in this case.

(D) All collision queries $Q_1, Q_2, Q_3, Q_1', Q_2', Q_3'$ are offline.

In this case, we show that every full collision structure with respect to some key among the offline queries leads to a hitting query. Furthermore, two collision structures cannot share the same hitting query. So if there are at most $O(i)$ hitting queries, the probability $Q_1, Q_2, Q_3, Q_1', Q_2', Q_3'$ are all offline for a random key_i is at most $O(i/2^n) \leq O(S/2^n)$.

Thus, we showed that $\Pr[W_i|W_{<i}] \leq O(S/2^n + T^2/2^n)$ no matter when $Q_1, Q_2, Q_3, Q_1', Q_2', Q_3'$ were queried before or during game i. Further, recall the last case where there is a collision at one of the leaves (corresponding to Q_1, Q_1' or Q_2, Q_2'), which can happen with at most $O(S/2^n + T^2/2^n)$ probability since such a collision directly involves key_i. Thus, in all possible cases, we have shown $\Pr[W_i|W_{<i}] \leq \delta \leq O(S/2^n + T^2/2^n)$, at least assuming $ST^2 \leq 2^n$. Finally, by the framework of [2,9], this implies the same bound (up to a multiplicative factor of 2) on the advantage of finding a collision for any (S, T)-attacker.

3 Preliminaries

We let $\mathbb{N} = \{1, 2, 3, \ldots\}$ denote the natural numbers. The set of all functions with domain D and range R is denoted by $\mathsf{Fcs}(D, R)$. We let $*$ denote a wildcard element. For example $(*, z) \in L$ is true if there is an ordered pair in L where z is the second element (the type of the wildcard element shall be clear from the context). For a random variable X we use $\mathsf{E}[X]$ to denote its expected value. We use $x \leftarrow\!\!\ast\, D$ to denote sampling x uniformly sampling from the elements of D. All logarithms in this paper are for base 2 unless otherwise specified.

For a bit-string s, we use $|s|$ to denote the number of bits in s. For two strings s_1, s_2, we use $s_1 \| s_2$ to denote the concatenation of two strings. We use standard regular expression notation where s^* denotes 0 or more copies of s, s^+ denotes one or more copies of s, and s^k denotes k copies of s. Similarly, for a set S, we use S^*, S^+, and S^k to represent 0 or more, 1 or more, of k elements takes from a set S. In particular, we use $\{0,1\}^*$ to represent any arbitrary string of bits. We use the notation $\{0,1\}^{\leq k}$ to represent a string of length at most k.

Chernoff Bound. We state a Chernoff bound which we use in the technical part of the paper.

Proposition 1. *Let* $n \in \mathbb{N}$. *Let* $X_1, X_2, \ldots, X_n$ *be independent* 0-1 *random variables. Let* $X = \sum_{i=1}^{n} X_i$. *Let* μ' *be such that* $\mathsf{E}[X] \leq \mu'$. *Then we have that*

$$\Pr[X \geq (1 + \delta)\mu'] \leq e^{-\frac{\delta\mu'}{3}}.$$

Notice that this version is somewhat non-standard as it even works when we know only an upper bound on the expectation (usually, in standard formulations of Chernoff bound, we need to know the expectation exactly). We have a proof of this Chernoff bound in the full version.

Auxiliary-Input Random Oracle Model (AI-ROM). The auxiliary-input random oracle model, introduced by Unruh [27], captures the power of non-uniform adversaries against random oracles. An attacker $\mathcal{A} = (\mathcal{A}_1, \mathcal{A}_2)$ in this model is formalized as a two stage adversary. In its first stage, which is referred to as the preprocessing phase, $\mathcal{A}_1$ has unbounded access to the random oracle h, and outputs any arbitrary S-bit advice string or auxiliary input σ. In the second stage, referred to as the online phase, gets σ as input, $\mathcal{A}_2$ can make at most T queries to its oracle h. Its aim is to accomplish some task involving h, e.g. find a collision in a construction based on h. We refer to such an adversary $\mathcal{A} = (\mathcal{A}_1, \mathcal{A}_2)$ as an (S, T)-attacker.

Collision Resistance of g^h **in AI-ROM.** We next formalize the keyed-collision resistance of an iterated hash function construction g relative to a hash function $h : \{0,1\}^a \rightarrow \{0,1\}^n$ in the AI-ROM. The construction g has a parameter κ associated with it, where κ is the bit length of key used in g. It first samples a random function $h : \{0,1\}^a \rightarrow \{0,1\}^n$. The adversary $\mathcal{A}_1$ gets unbounded access to h, and it outputs an advice string σ. At this time, $\mathcal{A}_2$ is given the auxiliary input σ, a randomly sampled key from $\{0,1\}^\kappa$, as well as oracle access to h, and it needs to find $\mathsf{msg} \neq \mathsf{msg}'$ such that $g^h(\mathsf{key}, \mathsf{msg}) = g^h(\mathsf{key}, \mathsf{msg}')$. This game, denoted $\mathsf{G}^{\text{ai-cr}}_{g^h}$ is formally defined in Fig. 7.

Definition 1 (AI-CR Advantage). *The advantage of an adversary* $\mathcal{A}$ *against the collision resistance of* g^h *in the AI-ROM is*

$$\mathsf{Adv}^{\text{ai-cr}}_{g^h}(\mathcal{A}) = \Pr\left[\mathsf{G}^{\text{ai-cr}}_{g^h}(\mathcal{A}) = \mathsf{true}\right].$$

For parameters $S, T \in \mathbb{N}$, *we overload notation and denote*

$$\mathsf{Adv}^{\text{ai-cr}}_{g^h}(S, T) = \max_{\mathcal{A}}\left\{\mathsf{Adv}^{\text{ai-cr}}_{g^h}(\mathcal{A})\right\},$$

where the maximum is over all (S, T)-*attackers.*

Throughout the paper, for any (S, T)-attacker $\mathcal{A}$ that outputs messages $\mathsf{msg}, \mathsf{msg}'$ that causes $\mathsf{G}^{\text{ai-cr}}_{g^h}(\mathcal{A})$ to output true on a key key, we assume that $\mathcal{A}$ has fully queried $g^h(\mathsf{key}, \mathsf{msg})$ and $g^h(\mathsf{key}, \mathsf{msg}')$. This is true without loss of generality (up to constant factors in the advantage) as if there exists any (S, T)-attacker $\mathcal{A}$ that does not, you can construct an $(S, T + 2\ell)$-attacker $\mathcal{B}$ that does,

---

Game $G_{g^h}^{\mathsf{ai\text{-}cr}}(\mathcal{A} = (\mathcal{A}_1, \mathcal{A}_2))$

1. $h \leftarrow_\$ \mathsf{Fcs}(\{0,1\}^a, \{0,1\}^n)$
2. $\sigma \leftarrow_\$ \mathcal{A}_1(h)$
3. $\mathsf{key} \leftarrow_\$ \{0,1\}^\kappa$
4. $(\mathsf{msg}, \mathsf{msg}') \leftarrow_\$ \mathcal{A}_2^h(\sigma, \mathsf{key})$
5. Return **true** if:
      (a) $\mathsf{msg} \neq \mathsf{msg}'$, and
      (b) $g^h(\mathsf{key}, \mathsf{msg}) = g^h(\mathsf{key}, \mathsf{msg}')$
6. Else, return **false**

Fig. 7. The collision resistance game $G_{g^h}^{\mathsf{ai\text{-}cr}}$ in AI-ROM for a function g^h based on a random oracle $h : \{0,1\}^a \to \{0,1\}^n$. The construction g^h has a parameter κ associated with it, where κ is the bit length of key used in g.

where g^h requires at most ℓ invocations of h to compute either $g^h(\mathsf{key}, \mathsf{msg})$ or $g^h(\mathsf{key}, \mathsf{msg}')$. As $\ell \leq T$, the resulting attacker will have comparable advantage up to constant factors in T. We note that this is a standard assumption in existing related works in the AI-ROM.

On Padding. The variable-input length hash functions we consider of this work all act on messages which have been parsed into many fixed size blocks of some specified size s. We therefore need a padding function that takes arbitrary length inputs and converts them to a sequence of fixed-size blocks. We need to ensure that this padding function maintains certain properties like injectivity in order to guarantee that if an adversary finds a collision on the padded versions of messages, then it implies a collision with respect to the underlying messages as well. For the purpose of this paper, we define the following padding function, which is a slightly simplified version of the padding function used by the SHA family of hash functions (see [19, Section 8.5] for more discussion on MD-compliant padding functions). The function pad we use takes in a message $\mathsf{msg} \in \{0,1\}^*$, an integer $s \in \mathbb{N}$ representing the size of each block, and an integer n that stipulates that $|\mathsf{msg}| \leq 2^n$. The construction is formally defined as follows.

$\underline{\mathsf{pad}(\mathsf{msg}, s, n):}$

1. Let $k = s - ((|\mathsf{msg}| + n) \bmod s + 1)$.
2. Interpret $|\mathsf{msg}| \in [2^n]$ as an n-bit string.
3. Output $(m_1, \ldots, m_\ell) \in (\{0,1\}^s)^\ell$ where $m_1 \| \ldots \| m_\ell = \mathsf{msg} \| |\mathsf{msg}| \| 1 \| 0^k$.

We formalize the guarantees we use for this padding function in the following theorem.

Theorem 5 (Padding). *Let $s, n \in \mathbb{N}$. The function* $\mathsf{pad}(\mathsf{msg}, s, n)$ *on messages* $\mathsf{msg} \in \{0,1\}^{2^n}$ *satisfies the following properties:*

1. $|\mathsf{pad}(\mathsf{msg}, s, n)| \in (\{0,1\}^s)^\ell$ *for* $\ell = \lceil (|\mathsf{msg}| + n + 1)/s \rceil$.

Construction $\mathsf{KMD}^h(\mathsf{key}, \mathsf{msg})$:

1. $(m_1, m_2, \ldots, m_\ell) \leftarrow \mathsf{pad}(\mathsf{msg}, s, n)$ where $\ell = \lceil (|\mathsf{msg}| + n + 1)/s \rceil$ given by Theorem 5.
2. Initialize $y_0 = 0^n$, and compute $y_i \leftarrow h(\mathsf{key}, y_{i-1} \| m_i)$ for $i = 1, \ldots, \ell$.
3. Output y_ℓ.

Fig. 8. The keyed Merkle-Damgård construction $\mathsf{KMD}^h : \{0,1\}^\kappa \times \{0,1\}^* \to \{0,1\}^n$ given any underlying function $h : \{0,1\}^\kappa \times \{0,1\}^{n+s} \to \{0,1\}^n$, where κ is the key length, n is the output length, and s is the message block size.

2. There is a unique decoding procedure that outputs msg given $\mathsf{pad}(\mathsf{msg}, s, n)$, and outputs $\bot$ on invalid padded messages.
3. If $\mathsf{pad}(\mathsf{msg}, s, n) = \mathsf{pad}(\mathsf{msg}', s, n)$, then $\mathsf{msg} = \mathsf{msg}'$.
4. If $|\mathsf{msg}| < |\mathsf{msg}'|$, then $\mathsf{pad}(\mathsf{msg}, s, n)$ is not a suffix of $\mathsf{pad}(\mathsf{msg}', s, n)$.

We defer the proof of this theorem to the full version.

4   Merkle-Damgård Framework with a Keyed Inner Hash

In this section, we lay out the general framework for our main results, based on the Merkle-Damgård transform using a keyed inner hash. We note that this framework has been explicitly considered in the uniform setting in Sect. 8.5 of the lecture notes of Goldwasser and Bellare [19].[6] We extend this framework to the preprocessing setting, modeled by the AI-ROM of Unruh [27], noting that the high level ideas are similar.

For a key length κ, output length n, and message block size s, we assume an underlying primitive $h : \{0,1\}^\kappa \times \{0,1\}^{n+s} \to \{0,1\}^n$. In other words, viewing the primitive h as a function from $\{0,1\}^a$ to $\{0,1\}^n$, this implies that $a = \kappa + n + s$.

Given such a primitive h, we define the following keyed Merkle-Damgård hash function $\mathsf{KMD}^h : \{0,1\}^\kappa \times \{0,1\}^* \to \{0,1\}^n$. On input key $\mathsf{key} \in \{0,1\}^\kappa$ and message $\mathsf{msg} \in \{0,1\}^*$ of length at most 2^n, the function KMD^h first pads the message to split it into $\ell = \lceil (b + n + 1)/s \rceil$ message blocks of size s as in Theorem 5. It then essentially computes the Merkle-Damgård hash function using the underlying hash function h, except that the key key is inserted into every invocation of h. This is formalized in Fig. 8.

Since the key key is included in every call to the underlying primitive h, it follows that any (S, T)-attacker that finds a collision in KMD^h with respect to a key key also finds a collision in h with respect to key. This is formalized via a reduction, which gives the following theorem. Again, we note that the following

---

[6] The existence of this variant of the Merkle-Damgård transform has gone completely unnoticed in recent works studying non-uniform security of this transformation [1, 2, 11, 17].

theorem very closely follows the reduction given in [19, Section 8.5], but we give the full details in the AI-ROM for completeness.

Theorem 6. *Let* $\kappa, n, s \in \mathbb{N}$. *Let* $h\colon \{0,1\}^{\kappa} \times \{0,1\}^{n+s} \to \{0,1\}^{n}$ *be any function, and let* $\mathsf{KMD}^{h}\colon \{0,1\}^{\kappa} \times \{0,1\}^{*} \to \{0,1\}^{n}$. *Then, for every* $S, T \in \mathbb{N}$, *it holds that*

$$\mathsf{Adv}^{\text{ai-cr}}_{\mathsf{KMD}^{h}}(S,T) \leq \mathsf{Adv}^{\text{ai-cr}}_{h}(S,T).$$

The proof of this theorem is a straightforward reduction, and we defer it to the full version.

Next, we recall that if h is a keyed function modeled as a random oracle (in the AI-ROM of Unruh [27]), Dodis, Guo, and Katz [14] give the following bound on the success probability that any (S,T)-attacker can find a collision in h with respect to a random key.

Theorem 7 ([14]). *Let* $h\colon \{0,1\}^{\kappa} \times \{0,1\}^{b} \to \{0,1\}^{n}$ *be modeled as a random oracle in the AI-ROM. Then, for any* $S, T \in \mathbb{N}$,

$$\mathsf{Adv}^{\text{ai-cr}}_{h}(S,T) \leq \frac{2S + 2\kappa}{2^{\kappa}} + \frac{50\,T^{2}}{2^{n}}.$$

Combining Theorems 6 and 7, we get the following result.

Theorem 8. *Let* $a, \kappa, n \in \mathbb{N}$ *be such that* $a > \kappa + n$. *Let* $h\colon \{0,1\}^{a} \to \{0,1\}^{n}$ *be modeled as a random oracle in the AI-ROM. Then, there is an* $H^{h}\colon \{0,1\}^{\kappa} \times \{0,1\}^{<2^{n}} \to \{0,1\}^{n}$ *such that:*

1. *For any* $S, T \in \mathbb{N}$,

$$\mathsf{Adv}^{\text{ai-cr}}_{H^{h}}(S,T) \leq \frac{2S + 2\kappa}{2^{\kappa}} + \frac{50\,T^{2}}{2^{n}}.$$

2. *One evaluation of* H^{h} *on messages of length* b *requires* $\lceil (b+n+1)/s \rceil$ *queries to* h, *where* $s = a - \kappa - n$.

Proof. As $a > \kappa + n$, we define $s = a - \kappa - n > 0$. Then, we view h as a function from $\{0,1\}^{\kappa} \times \{0,1\}^{n+s}$ to $\{0,1\}^{n}$ and use it in the construction KMD^{h} of Fig. 8 to get the hash function H^{h} required by the theorem.

The bound on the advantage immediately follows as a corollary of Theorems 6 and 7. As for efficiency, we note that padding a message $\mathsf{msg} \in \{0,1\}^{b}$ via Theorem 5 results in a message consisting of ℓ blocks each of length s, where $\ell = \lceil (b+n+1)/s \rceil$. Each block of the message requires a single invocation of h, so evaluating KMD^{h} on msg requires $\ell = \lceil (b+n+1)/s \rceil$ queries to h as required. ∎

Construction $\mathsf{FMD}_b^h(\mathsf{key}, \mathsf{msg})$:

1. Parse msg into ℓ blocks $(m_1, m_2, \ldots, m_\ell)$ each of size s where $\ell = \lceil b/s \rceil$ and m_ℓ is padded with 0s if needed.
2. Initialize $y_0 = \mathsf{key}$, and compute $y_i \leftarrow h(y_{i-1}, m_i)$ for $i = 1, \ldots, \ell$.
3. Output y_ℓ.

Fig. 9. The standard Merkle-Damgård construction with fixed input message length b $\mathsf{FMD}_b^h \colon \{0,1\}^n \times \{0,1\}^b \to \{0,1\}^n$ given any underlying function $h \colon \{0,1\}^n \times \{0,1\}^s \to \{0,1\}^n$, where n is the key and output length, and s is the message block size.

5 Instantiating the Inner Hash: Standard MD

We next consider instantiating the Merkle-Damgård framework of Sect. 4 whenever the underlying hash function $h \colon \{0,1\}^a \to \{0,1\}^n$ has input length a such that $n < a < \kappa + n + s$, where κ is the key length, n is the output length, and s is the desired message block size. Specifically, our goal is to use such a primitive $h \colon \{0,1\}^a \times \{0,1\}^n$ to build a larger (fixed-length) hash function $g^h \colon \{0,1\}^\kappa \times \{0,1\}^{n+s}$ that *can* be plugged into the construction KMD^{g^h}.

The first approach we consider is by simply building g from h using the standard Merkle-Damgård construction where h is not keyed in every invocation. We emphasize that in the standard version of MD, a random initialization vector/ key is still included in the first invocation of h. However, it is not included in the subsequent invocations of h, allowing h to take in smaller inputs overall.

Given an underlying hash function $h \colon \{0,1\}^a \to \{0,1\}^n$ where $a > \max(\kappa, n)$, we define the standard Merkle-Damgård hash function with fixed input message length b $\mathsf{FMD}_b^h \colon \{0,1\}^\kappa \times \{0,1\}^b \to \{0,1\}^n$ as follows. For sake of simplicity and due to the nature of the MD construction, we will assume that the key length κ is equal to the output length n. Let $s = a - n$ be the message block size we will include in each invocation of the underlying h. On input a key $\mathsf{key} \in \{0,1\}^n$ and a message $\mathsf{msg} \in \{0,1\}^b$, the function FMD_b^h splits the message msg into $\ell = \lceil b/s \rceil$ message blocks of size s (adding 0s to the last block if needed). It initializes $y_0 = \mathsf{key}$, and for $i = 1, \ldots, \ell$, computes y_i as the hash of y_{i-1} concatenated with m_i using h. The output of FMD_b^h is then y_ℓ. This is formalized in Fig. 9.

If we instantiate $g^h := \mathsf{FMD}_b^h$ only on input messages of size at most $b = n+s$ as required to instantiate it inside KMD^{g^h}, then we only need to worry about ℓ-block collisions for $\ell = \lceil (n+s)/(a-n) \rceil$. Akshima, Guo, and Liu [2] currently show the best known upper bound on the advantage of finding general ℓ-block collisions in MD^h, given by the following theorem.

Theorem 9 ([2]). *Let* $b, n, s \in \mathbb{N}$ *such that* $b > s$, *and set* $\ell = \lceil b/s \rceil$. *Let* $h \colon \{0,1\}^n \times \{0,1\}^s \to \{0,1\}^n$ *be modeled as a random oracle in the AI-ROM.*

Then, for any $S, T \in \mathbb{N}$,

$$\mathsf{Adv}^{\mathsf{ai\text{-}cr}}_{\mathsf{FMD}^h_b}(S,T) \leq \begin{cases} \frac{200n \cdot (ST + T^2)}{2^n} & \text{if } \ell = 2, \text{and} \\ \frac{34n \cdot ST\ell}{2^n} \cdot \max\left(1, \frac{ST^2}{2^n}\right) + \frac{2 \cdot T^2}{2^n} & \text{if } \ell > 2. \end{cases}$$

We note that Ghoshal and Komargodski [17] give a bound of $O(ST/2^n + T^2/2^n)$ whenever ℓ is a constant, which doesn't require the assumption that $ST^2 \leq 2^n$. However, their bound does not extend to super constant ℓ.

Combined with Theorem 6, we get the following result.

Theorem 10. *Let $a, n, s \in \mathbb{N}$ be such that $a > n$. Let $\ell = \lceil (n+s)/(a-n) \rceil$. Let $h \colon \{0,1\}^a \to \{0,1\}^n$ be modeled as a random oracle in the AI-ROM. Then, there is an $H^h \colon \{0,1\}^\kappa \times \{0,1\}^{<2^n} \to \{0,1\}^n$ such that:*

1. For any $S, T \in \mathbb{N}$,

$$\mathsf{Adv}^{\mathsf{ai\text{-}cr}}_{H^h}(S,T) \leq \begin{cases} \frac{200n \cdot (ST + T^2)}{2^n} & \text{if } \ell = 2, \text{and} \\ \frac{34n \cdot ST\ell}{2^n} \cdot \max\left(1, \frac{ST^2}{2^n}\right) + \frac{2 \cdot T^2}{2^n} & \text{if } \ell > 2. \end{cases}$$

2. One evaluation of H^h on messages of length b requires $\ell \cdot \lceil (b+n+1)/s \rceil$ queries to h.

Proof. As $a > n$, we parse $h \colon \{0,1\}^n \times \{0,1\}^{a-n} \to \{0,1\}^n$ and use it to construct FMD^h_{n+s} as defined in Fig. 9. We then use FMD^h_{n+s} as the primitive underlying our MD-based hash function of Fig. 8. So, we set

$$H^h := \mathsf{KMD}^{\mathsf{FMD}^h_{n+s}}.$$

The bound on the advantage follows as a corollary to Theorems 6 and 9, where the message length required for the FMD^h_{n+s} construction is only $n+s$. Furthermore, this implies that FMD^h_{n+s} requires $\ell = \lceil (n+s)/(a-n) \rceil$ invocations of h per invocation of FMD^h_{n+s}, and $\mathsf{KMD}^{\mathsf{FMD}^h_{n+s}}$ requires $\lceil (b+n+1)/s \rceil$ invocations of FMD^h_{n+s}, giving the resulting efficiency bound. ∎

We emphasize that because our reduction in Theorem 6 is generic, any improvement on the bound of [2,17] for finding an ℓ-block collision in MD will immediately imply an improved bound in Theorem 10.

We next state a corollary of Theorem 10 where we restrict to using $\ell = 2$ invocations of h in the underlying FMD^h_{n+s} construction. For this setting, the bound of [2] above is optimal (up to poly(n) factors), and we observe that the resulting bound matches our desired bound of $O(S/2^n + T^2/2^n)$ whenever $S \leq T$.

Corollary 1. *Let $a, n, s \in \mathbb{N}$ be such that $a \geq 3n/2 + s/2$. Let $h \colon \{0,1\}^a \to \{0,1\}^n$ be modeled as a random oracle in the AI-ROM. Then, there is an $H^h \colon \{0,1\}^\kappa \times \{0,1\}^{<2^n} \to \{0,1\}^n$ such that:*

```
┌─────────────────────────────────────────────────────┐
│  Game $G_{g,S}^{\text{mi-cr}}(\mathcal{B})$           │
│                                                        │
│    1. $h \leftarrow_{\$} \text{Fcs}(\{0,1\}^a,\{0,1\}^n)$ │
│    2. $\text{key}_1, \ldots, \text{key}_S \leftarrow_{\$} \{0,1\}^\kappa$ │
│    3. $\text{st} \leftarrow \bot$                      │
│    4. For $i = 1$ to $S$                               │
│       (a) $(\text{msg}, \text{msg}', \text{st}) \leftarrow_{\$} \mathcal{B}^h(\text{st}, \text{key}_i)$ │
│       (b) Output false if:                             │
│            i. $\text{msg} = \text{msg}'$, or,          │
│           ii. $g^h(\text{key}_i, \text{msg}) \neq g^h(\text{key}_i, \text{msg}')$ │
│    5. Otherwise, output true                           │
└─────────────────────────────────────────────────────┘
```

Fig. 10. The multi-instance game $G_{g^h,S}^{\text{mi-cr}}$, where $\mathcal{B}$ is a uniform adversary with oracle access to the function h.

1. For any $S, T \in \mathbb{N}$,

$$\text{Adv}_{H^h}^{\text{ai-cr}}(S,T) \leq \frac{200n \cdot (ST + T^2)}{2^n}$$

2. One evaluation of H^h on messages of length b requires $2 \cdot \lceil (b + n + 1)/s \rceil$ queries to h.

Proof. Restricting to $\ell = 2$ in Theorem 10, we require that $\ell = \lceil (n + s)/(a - n) \rceil \leq 2$. This holds as long as $a \geq 3n/2 + s/2$, as required. ∎

6   Instantiating the Inner Hash: Two-Level Merkle Tree

In this section, we instantiate the Merkle-Damgård framework of Sect. 4, that uses a keyed inner hash, in the setting where the underlying hash function $h: \{0,1\}^a \to \{0,1\}^n$ satisfies $a \geq \max(2n + 2, \kappa + \lceil n/2 \rceil + 3)$.

The compression function in this instantiation of the MD-based framework, is a Merkle tree with two leaves, where we additionally input the key into each leaf. We describe next the framework introduced in [2] that we use to analyze the collision-resistance of this construction in AI-ROM.

6.1   The AGL [2] Framework

In this section, we briefly introduce the framework given by [2] which is useful in analyzing non-uniform security. An earlier version of this framework was introduced by [1,9] inspired by techniques used in proving constructive Chernoff bounds in [21] and later refined by [1,2,17] to upper bound $\text{Adv}_{g^h}^{\text{ai-cr}}(S,T)$. This framework involves upper bounding the advantage of an (S,T)-attacker using the advantage of a uniform adversary for a multi-instance game that has to find collisions for S randomly chosen values of key.

We define the "multi-instance" game $G_{g^h,S}^{\text{mi-cr}}(\mathcal{B})$ in Fig. 10. We refer an adversary playing $G_{g^h,S}^{\text{mi-cr}}$ and making at most T queries for each key as a (S,T)-MI adversary. For any (S,T)-MI adversary, define

$$\text{Adv}_{g^h}^{\text{mi-cr}}(\mathcal{B}) = \Pr\left[G_{g^h,S}^{\text{mi-cr}}(\mathcal{B}) = \text{true}\right].$$

Further,

$$\text{Adv}_{g^h}^{\text{mi-cr}}(S,T) = \max_{\mathcal{B}} \text{Adv}_{g^h}^{\text{mi-cr}}(\mathcal{B}),$$

where the maximum is taken over all (S,T)-MI adversaries. The following key lemma relates $\text{Adv}_{g^h}^{\text{ai-cr}}(S,T)$ to $\text{Adv}_{g^h}^{\text{mi-cr}}(S,T)$, which is proven in [2].

Lemma 1 ([2]). *Fix $S,T \in \mathbb{N}$ and $0 \leq \delta \leq 1$, if $\text{Adv}_{g^h}^{\text{mi-cr}}(S,T) \leq \delta^S$, then $\text{Adv}_{g^h}^{\text{ai-cr}}(S,T) \leq 2\delta$.*

Offline and Online Queries. Since the adversary in the multi-instance game is stateful, we can assume without loss of generality that it does not repeat queries since they can simply remember the answers. Additionally, [2] formalized the notion of "offline" and "online" queries during a particular instance of the game. When running the adversary on key_i, the queries that were made while the adversary was run on $\text{key}_1, \ldots, \text{key}_{i-1}$ are collectively known as the "offline" queries, and the queries made while running on key_i are "online queries".

6.2   Two-Level Merkle Tree

In this section, we present our construction of a keyed Merkle tree and analyze its collision resistance in the AI-ROM using the framework in the previous section. Specifically, given an underlying hash function $h: \{0,1\}^a \rightarrow \{0,1\}^n$ where $a \geq \max(2n+2, \kappa + \lceil n/2 \rceil + 3)$, we define a keyed, 2-level Merkle tree 2MT_b^h for message length $b \leq 2a - 2\kappa - 4$.

Before we define 2MT_b^h, we introduce notation that allows use to "domain-separate" h into three separate functions. Given a fixed hash function $h: \{0,1\}^a \rightarrow \{0,1\}^n$, we define three domain-separated functions $h_1, h_2, h_3: \{0,1\}^{a-2} \rightarrow \{0,1\}^n$, where $h_i(x)$ outputs $h(\hat{i}\|x)$ where $\hat{i} \in \{0,1\}^2$ is the 2-bit binary representation of i. Moreover, we refer to a query $h(\hat{i}\|*)$ as a query to the function h_i (which is also clearly a query to h).

To construct $2\text{MT}_b^h: \{0,1\}^\kappa \times \{0,1\}^b \rightarrow \{0,1\}^n$, we use h_1 and h_2 above to process the two leaves of the depth-2 Merkle tree, where we include $\text{key} \in \{0,1\}^\kappa$ in each leaf. We then feed those outputs as input to h_3 to get the output of 2MT_b^h. This construction is formalized in Fig. 11.

Our main result of this section is the following theorem, which bounds the probability that any (S,T)-attacker finds a collision in 2MT_b^h.

Theorem 11. *Let $a, \kappa, n \in \mathbb{N}$ be such that $a \geq \max(\kappa + \lceil n/2 \rceil + 3, 2n+2)$. Let $h: \{0,1\}^a \rightarrow \{0,1\}^n$ be modeled as a random oracle in the AI-ROM. Then, for $s = 2a - 2\kappa - n - 4$, the construction $2\text{MT}_{n+s}^h: \{0,1\}^\kappa \times \{0,1\}^{n+s} \rightarrow \{0,1\}^n$ of Fig. 11 satisfies the following.*

$\underline{\textsf{2MT}_b^h(\textsf{key}, \textsf{msg})}$

1. Parse $\textsf{msg} \in \{0,1\}^{2a-2\kappa-4}$ as $\textsf{msg}_L \| \textsf{msg}_R$ where $\textsf{msg}_L, \textsf{msg}_R \in \{0,1\}^{a-\kappa-2}$.
2. Compute $y_L \leftarrow h_1(\textsf{key}\|\textsf{msg}_L)$.
3. Compute $y_R \leftarrow h_2(\textsf{key}\|\textsf{msg}_R)$.
4. Output $z \leftarrow h_3(y_L\|y_R)$.

Fig. 11. The two-level, keyed Merkle tree construction $\textsf{2MT}_b^h \colon \{0,1\}^\kappa \times \{0,1\}^b \to \{0,1\}^n$ with fixed input message length b given any underlying function $h \colon \{0,1\}^a \to \{0,1\}^n$, where $a \geq \max(2n+2, \kappa+3)$ and $b \leq 2a - 2\kappa - 4$. h_1, h_2, h_3 are all domain-separated using the first two bits of h to encode $1, 2, 3$, respectively.

- *For any $S, T \in \mathbb{N}$,*

$$\textsf{Adv}_{g^h}^{\textsf{ai-cr}}(S,T) \leq \left(\frac{S}{2^\kappa} \cdot \left(14n + 42n\gamma + 42n\gamma^2\right) + \frac{T^2}{2^n} \cdot \left(2 + \frac{2\gamma}{T} + \frac{2}{T^2}\right)\right),$$

where $\gamma = ST^2/2^n$.

We prove this theorem using the framework described in Sect. 6.1. So, by Lemma 1, it suffices to prove the following lemma which bounds the advantage of an (S,T)-MI adversary.

Lemma 2. *Let $S, T \in \mathbb{N}$. Then*

$$\textsf{Adv}_{g^h}^{\textsf{mi-cr}}(S,T) \leq \left(\frac{S}{2^\kappa} \cdot \left(7n + 21n \cdot \gamma + 21n \cdot \gamma^2\right) + \frac{T^2}{2^n} \cdot \left(1 + \frac{\gamma}{T} + \frac{1}{T^2}\right)\right)^S,$$

where $\gamma = ST^2/2^n$.

Proof. Following the techniques of [2], we reduce the task of bounding $\textsf{Adv}_{g^h}^{\textsf{mi-cr}}(S,T)$ to that of bounding any T-query adversaries advantage of succeeding in iteration i given that it has succeeded in all previous iterations. Fix any (S,T)-MI attacker $\mathcal{A}$. Let W_i be the indicator random variable that $\mathcal{A}$ wins on $\textsf{key}_i$ in $G_{g^h, S}^{\textsf{mi-cr}}$. Define the random variable $W_{<i} := W_1 \wedge \ldots \wedge W_{i-1}$. We have that

$$\textsf{Adv}_{g^h}^{\textsf{mi-cr}}(\mathcal{A}) = \Pr\left[W_1 \wedge W_2 \wedge \ldots \wedge W_S\right] = \prod_{i=1}^{S} \Pr\left[W_i | W_{<i}\right].$$

We prove in the full version that for every $\mathcal{A}$ and each $i \in [S]$, $\Pr\left[W_{<i+1}\right] \leq (\delta_S)^i$ where

$$\delta_S = \frac{T^2}{2^n} + 7n \cdot \frac{S}{2^\kappa} + 21n \cdot \frac{S^2T^2}{2^{n+\kappa}} + \frac{ST^3}{2^{2n}} + 21n \cdot \frac{S^3T^4}{2^{2n+\kappa}} + \frac{1}{2^n}.$$

It follows that for any (S, T)-MI attacker $\mathcal{A}$,

$$\mathsf{Adv}_{g^h}^{\text{mi-cr}}(\mathcal{A}) = \Pr\left[W_{<S+1}\right] = \prod_{i=1}^{S} \Pr\left[W_i|W_{<i}\right] \leq (\delta_S)^S.$$

As this holds for any such $\mathcal{A}$, it follows that $\mathsf{Adv}_{g^h}^{\text{mi-cr}}(S, T) \leq (\delta_S)^S$, as required by the lemma statement. This completes the proof of Lemma 2.   ∎

6.3   Variable-Input Length Hash from Two-Level Merkle Trees

We combine the construction of Sect. 6.2 with the framework of Sect. 4 to get a variable-input length hash function. This construction is optimally secure as long as $ST^2 \leq 2^n$ and requires an underlying function $h: \{0,1\}^a \to \{0,1\}^n$ where $a \geq \max(\kappa + \lceil n/2 \rceil + 3, 2n + 2)$. This results in the following theorem.

We note if we modify values of κ, n by additive constant factors, we can get the same result as below with only $O(1)$ multiplicative loss in security. In this sense, we can achieve the theorem below assuming a function $h: \{0,1\}^{2n} \to \{0,1\}^n$, i.e. $a = 2n$ so only compressing by a factor exactly two.

Theorem 12. *Let $a, \kappa, n \in \mathbb{N}$ be such that $a \geq \max(\kappa + \lceil n/2 \rceil + 3, 2n + 2)$. Let $h: \{0,1\}^a \to \{0,1\}^n$ be modeled as a random oracle in the AI-ROM. Then, there is an $H^h: \{0,1\}^\kappa \times \{0,1\}^{<2^n} \to \{0,1\}^n$ such that:*

1. For any $S, T \in \mathbb{N}$,

$$\mathsf{Adv}_{H^h}^{\text{ai-cr}}(S, T) \leq \left(\frac{S}{2^\kappa} \cdot \left(14n + 42n\gamma + 42n\gamma^2\right) + \frac{T^2}{2^n} \cdot \left(2 + \frac{2\gamma}{T} + \frac{2}{T^2}\right) \right),$$

where $\gamma = ST^2/2^n$.
2. One evaluation of H^h on a message b bits long requires $3 \cdot \lceil (b + n + 1)/s \rceil$ queries to h where $s = 2a - 2\kappa - n - 4$.

Proof. We define $H := \mathsf{KMD}^{2\mathsf{MT}_{n+s}^h}$ where $2\mathsf{MT}_{n+s}^h$ is defined in Fig. 11. From Theorem 6, we have that $\mathsf{Adv}_{H^h}^{\text{ai-cr}}(S, T)$ is upper bounded by $\mathsf{Adv}_{2\mathsf{MT}_{n+s}^h}^{\text{ai-cr}}(S, T)$. Therefore, the bound on the advantage of any (S, T)-attacker on H^h follows from Theorem 11.

We have that $2\mathsf{MT}_{n+s}^h\{0,1\}^\kappa \times \{0,1\}^{n+s} \to \{0,1\}^n$, for $s = 2a - 2\kappa - n - 4$. A b bit message, after padding, will result in $\lceil (b + n + 1)/s \rceil$ message blocks that are fed into $2\mathsf{MT}_{n+s}^h$. For each call of $2\mathsf{MT}_{n+s}^h$, we need 3 calls to h, which implies the bound on the efficiency of H^h.   ∎

Acknowledgements. Ashrujit Ghoshal's work was partially supported by NSF grants CNS-2026774, CNS-2154174, a JP Morgan Faculty Award, a CISCO Faculty Award, and a gift from Microsoft. Part of Ashrujit Ghoshal's work was done during an internship at NTT Research. Cody Freitag is supported in part by the National Science Foundation Graduate Research Fellowship under Grant No. DGE-2139899 and DARPA Award HR00110C0086. Any opinion, findings, and conclusions or recommendations expressed in this material are those of the authors and do not necessarily reflect the views of the National Science Foundation or the Defense Advanced Research Projects Agency (DARPA). Ilan Komargodski is the incumbent of the Harry & Abe Sherman Senior Lectureship at the School of Computer Science and Engineering at the Hebrew University, supported in part by an Alon Young Faculty Fellowship, by a grant from the Israel Science Foundation (ISF Grant No. 1774/20), and by a grant from the US-Israel Binational Science Foundation and the US National Science Foundation (BSF-NSF Grant No. 2020643).

References

1. Akshima, Cash, D., Drucker, A., Wee, H.: Time-space tradeoffs and short collisions in Merkle-Damgård hash functions. In: Micciancio, D., Ristenpart, T. (eds.) CRYPTO 2020. LNCS, vol. 12170, pp. 157–186. Springer, Cham (2020). https://doi.org/10.1007/978-3-030-56784-2_6
2. Akshima, Guo, S., Liu, Q.: Time-space lower bounds for finding collisions in Merkle-Damgård hash functions. In: Dodis, Y., Shrimpton, T. (eds.) CRYPTO 2022. LNCS, vol. 13509. Springer, Cham (2022). https://doi.org/10.1007/978-3-031-15982-4_7
3. Aumasson, J.P., Henzen, L., Meier, W., Phan, R.C.W.: SHA-3 proposal BLAKE. Submission to NIST, vol. 92 (2008)
4. Aumasson, J., Meier, W., Phan, R.C., Henzen, L.: The Hash Function BLAKE. Information Security and Cryptography, Springer, Heidelberg (2014). https://doi.org/10.1007/978-3-662-44757-4
5. Aviram, N., et al.: DROWN: breaking TLS using SSLv2. In: USENIX, pp. 689–706 (2016). https://doi.org/10.5555/3241094.3241148
6. Bellare, M., Rogaway, P.: Random oracles are practical: a paradigm for designing efficient protocols. In: CCS, pp. 62–73 (1993). https://doi.org/10.1145/168588.168596
7. Bertoni, G., Daemen, J., Peeters, M., Van Assche, G.: On the indifferentiability of the sponge construction. In: Smart, N. (ed.) EUROCRYPT 2008. LNCS, vol. 4965, pp. 181–197. Springer, Heidelberg (2008). https://doi.org/10.1007/978-3-540-78967-3_11
8. Bertoni, G., Daemen, J., Peeters, M., Van Assche, G.: Sponge functions. In: ECRYPT Hash Workshop, vol. 2007. Citeseer (2007)
9. Chung, K., Guo, S., Liu, Q., Qian, L.: Tight quantum time-space tradeoffs for function inversion. In: FOCS, pp. 673–684 (2020). https://doi.org/10.1109/FOCS46700.2020.00068
10. Coretti, S., Dodis, Y., Guo, S.: Non-uniform bounds in the random-permutation, ideal-cipher, and generic-group models. In: Shacham, H., Boldyreva, A. (eds.) CRYPTO 2018. LNCS, vol. 10991, pp. 693–721. Springer, Cham (2018). https://doi.org/10.1007/978-3-319-96884-1_23
11. Coretti, S., Dodis, Y., Guo, S., Steinberger, J.: Random oracles and non-uniformity. In: Nielsen, J.B., Rijmen, V. (eds.) EUROCRYPT 2018. LNCS, vol. 10820, pp. 227–258. Springer, Cham (2018). https://doi.org/10.1007/978-3-319-78381-9_9
12. Coron, J.-S., Dodis, Y., Malinaud, C., Puniya, P.: Merkle-Damgård revisited: how to construct a hash function. In: Shoup, V. (ed.) CRYPTO 2005. LNCS, vol. 3621, pp. 430–448. Springer, Heidelberg (2005). https://doi.org/10.1007/11535218_26

13. Damgård, I.B.: A design principle for hash functions. In: Brassard, G. (ed.) CRYPTO 1989. LNCS, vol. 435, pp. 416–427. Springer, New York (1990). https://doi.org/10.1007/0-387-34805-0_39

14. Dodis, Y., Guo, S., Katz, J.: Fixing cracks in the concrete: random oracles with auxiliary input, revisited. In: Coron, J.-S., Nielsen, J.B. (eds.) EUROCRYPT 2017. LNCS, vol. 10211, pp. 473–495. Springer, Cham (2017). https://doi.org/10.1007/978-3-319-56614-6_16

15. Fiat, A., Naor, M.: Rigorous time/space trade-offs for inverting functions. SIAM J. Comput. 29(3), 790–803 (1999). https://doi.org/10.1137/S0097539795280512

16. Freitag, C., Ghoshal, A., Komargodski, I.: Time-space tradeoffs for sponge hashing: Attacks and limitations for short collisions. In: Dodis, Y., Shrimpton, T. (eds.) CRYPTO 2022. LNCS, vol. 13509. Springer, Cham (2022). https://doi.org/10.1007/978-3-031-15982-4_5

17. Ghoshal, A., Komargodski, I.: On time-space tradeoffs for bounded-length collisions in Merkle-Damgård hashing. In: Dodis, Y., Shrimpton, T. (eds.) CRYPTO 2022. LNCS, vol. 13509. Springer, Cham (2022). https://doi.org/10.1007/978-3-031-15982-4_6

18. Goldreich, O., Krawczyk, H.: On the composition of zero-knowledge proof systems. SIAM J. Comput. 25(1), 169–192 (1996). https://doi.org/10.1137/S0097539791220688

19. Goldwasser, S., Bellare, M.: Lecture notes on cryptography (2008). https://cseweb.ucsd.edu/mihir/papers/gb.pdf

20. Hellman, M.E.: A cryptanalytic time-memory trade-off. IEEE Trans. Inf. Theory 26(4), 401–406 (1980). https://doi.org/10.1109/TIT.1980.1056220

21. Impagliazzo, R., Kabanets, V.: Constructive proofs of concentration bounds. In: Serna, M., Shaltiel, R., Jansen, K., Rolim, J. (eds.) APPROX/RANDOM -2010. LNCS, vol. 6302, pp. 617–631. Springer, Heidelberg (2010). https://doi.org/10.1007/978-3-642-15369-3_46

22. Maurer, U., Renner, R., Holenstein, C.: Indifferentiability, impossibility results on reductions, and applications to the random oracle methodology. In: Naor, M. (ed.) TCC 2004. LNCS, vol. 2951, pp. 21–39. Springer, Heidelberg (2004). https://doi.org/10.1007/978-3-540-24638-1_2

23. Merkle, R.C.: A digital signature based on a conventional encryption function. In: Pomerance, C. (ed.) CRYPTO 1987. LNCS, vol. 293, pp. 369–378. Springer, Heidelberg (1988). https://doi.org/10.1007/3-540-48184-2_32

24. Merkle, R.C.: A certified digital signature. In: Brassard, G. (ed.) CRYPTO 1989. LNCS, vol. 435, pp. 218–238. Springer, New York (1990). https://doi.org/10.1007/0-387-34805-0_21

25. Oechslin, P.: Making a faster cryptanalytic time-memory trade-off. In: Boneh, D. (ed.) CRYPTO 2003. LNCS, vol. 2729, pp. 617–630. Springer, Heidelberg (2003). https://doi.org/10.1007/978-3-540-45146-4_36

26. Ristenpart, T., Shacham, H., Shrimpton, T.: Careful with composition: limitations of the indifferentiability framework. In: Paterson, K.G. (ed.) EUROCRYPT 2011. LNCS, vol. 6632, pp. 487–506. Springer, Heidelberg (2011). https://doi.org/10.1007/978-3-642-20465-4_27

27. Unruh, D.: Random oracles and auxiliary input. In: Menezes, A. (ed.) CRYPTO 2007. LNCS, vol. 4622, pp. 205–223. Springer, Heidelberg (2007). https://doi.org/10.1007/978-3-540-74143-5_12

28. Yao, A.C.: Coherent functions and program checkers (extended abstract). In: STOC, pp. 84–94 (1990). https://doi.org/10.1145/100216.100226

Proof of Mirror Theory for a Wide Range of $\xi_{\max}$

Benoît Cogliati[1], Avijit Dutta[2], Mridul Nandi[2,3], Jacques Patarin[1,4], and Abishanka Saha[3(✉)]

[1] Thales DIS France SAS, Meudon, France
jpatarin@club-internet.fr
[2] Institute for Advancing Intelligence, TCG-CREST, Kolkata, India
[3] Indian Statistical Institute, Kolkata, India
sahaa.1993@gmail.com
[4] Laboratoire de Mathématiques de Versailles, UVSQ, CNRS,
Université Paris-Saclay, Versailles, France

Abstract. In CRYPTO'03, Patarin conjectured a lower bound on the number of distinct solutions $(P_1, \ldots, P_q) \in (\{0,1\}^n)^q$ satisfying a system of equations of the form $X_i \oplus X_j = \lambda_{i,j}$ such that $P_1, P_2, \ldots, P_q$ are pairwise distinct. This result is known as "$P_i \oplus P_j$ Theorem for any $\xi_{\max}$" or alternatively as *Mirror Theory for general $\xi_{\max}$*, which was later proved by Patarin in ICISC'05. Mirror theory for general $\xi_{\max}$ stands as a powerful tool to provide a high-security guarantee for many blockcipher-(or even ideal permutation-) based designs. Unfortunately, the proof of the result contains gaps that are non-trivial to fix. In this work, we present the first complete proof of the $P_i \oplus P_j$ theorem for a wide range of $\xi_{\max}$, typically up to order $O(2^{n/4}/\sqrt{n})$. Furthermore, our proof approach is made simpler by using a new type of equation, dubbed link-deletion equation, that roughly corresponds to half of the so-called orange equations from earlier works. As an illustration of our result, we also revisit the security proofs of two optimally secure blockcipher-based pseudorandom functions, and n-bit security proof for six round Feistel cipher, and provide updated security bounds.

Keywords: Mirror Theory · system of affine equations · PRP · PRF · beyond-birthday-bound security

1 Introduction

Pseudorandom Function (PRF) and Pseudorandom Permutation (PRP) are two fundamental cryptographic objects in symmetric key cryptography. Extensive use of pseudorandom functions in designing cryptographic schemes e.g., authentication protocols, encryption schemes, hash functions, etc. makes it a valuable object from the cryptographic perspective. However, practical candidates for PRF are very scarce. On the other hand, PRP or blockciphers are available in plenty in practice. One can consider a blockcipher to be a pseudorandom function, but due to the PRP-PRF switching lemma, it comes at the cost of birthday-bound security, i.e., if the block size of the blockcipher is n-bits, then one can

© International Association for Cryptologic Research 2023
C. Hazay and M. Stam (Eds.): EUROCRYPT 2023, LNCS 14007, pp. 470–501, 2023.
https://doi.org/10.1007/978-3-031-30634-1_16

consider the blockcipher to be a secure PRF until the number of queries reaches $2^{n/2}$. Such a bound is acceptable when n is moderately large, e.g., 128 bits. However, due to the ongoing trend of lightweight cryptography, several lightweight blockciphers have been designed with smaller block size e.g., 64 bits. In such a situation, a blockcipher is not considered to be a good PRF as birthday-bound security is not adequate with 64 bit block size. Therefore, the natural question arises:

Can we design a pseudorandom function out of lightweight blockciphers that guarantees security beyond the birthday bound?

It turns out that over the past several years researchers have invested a lot of effort in designing such pseudorandom functions [3, 10, 13, 14, 19, 20, 22, 23, 34, 45–47]. Out of several such designs, *xor of two pseudorandom permutations*, $\mathsf{XOR}_2(x) := \mathsf{E}_{k_1}(x) \oplus \mathsf{E}_{k_2}(x)$[1], and its single-keyed variant $\mathsf{XOR}_1(x) := \mathsf{E}_k(0\|x) \oplus \mathsf{E}_k(1\|x)$, are the most popular ones. In a series of papers [39, 40, 42], Patarin claimed that XOR construction (i.e., both XOR_1 and XOR_2) is secure up to $O(2^n)$ queries. Following Patarin's analysis, XOR_2 construction yields the following system of bivariate affine equations:

$$\mathbb{E}_\lambda = \{P_1 \oplus P_2 = \lambda_1, P_3 \oplus P_4 = \lambda_2, \ldots, P_{2q-1} \oplus P_{2q} = \lambda_q\},$$

where $q \geq 1$ and $\lambda := (\lambda_1, \ldots, \lambda_q)$ is a tuple of n-bit binary strings (similarly the XOR_1 construction yields the same system of equations with the additional requirement that $\lambda_1, \ldots, \lambda_q$ are non-zero n-bit binary strings). The entire security analyses for both the constructions rely on finding a good lower bound on the number of solutions $(P_1, \ldots, P_{2q})^2$ to $\mathbb{E}_\lambda$ where (i) for XOR_1 construction, we require that $P_i \neq P_j$ for $i \neq j$, while (ii) for XOR_2 construction, we require that $P_i \neq P_j$ for $i \neq j$, such that i, j are either both odd or both even. During the process of finding the solutions to $\mathbb{E}_\lambda$, assigning values to a variable P_i in $\mathbb{E}_\lambda$ fixes the value of exactly two variables (which are P_i and P_{i+1} if i is odd and P_{i-1}, P_i otherwise) in $\mathbb{E}_\lambda$. However, for a generic bivariate system of affine equations, assigning value to a single variable P_i can fix the values of $k \geq 2$ variables in the set of equations. Patarin [40] named this notion as *block maximality* in a system of bivariate affine equations, denoted as $\xi_{\max}$. It is natural to see that the block maximality of the system of equations $\mathbb{E}_\lambda$ is 2 and thus the security analysis of the XOR construction is reduced to establishing the following result.

"For a given system of bivariate affine equations over a finite group with non-equalities among the variables and $\xi_{\max} = 2$, the number of distinct solutions is always greater than the average number of solutions."

Patarin named this result as **Theorem $P_i \oplus P_j$ for $\xi_{\max} = 2$** [37] (and later in [40], named *Mirror theory* the study of sets of linear equations and linear non-equations in finite groups). This result was stated as a conjecture in [35] and an

---

[1] Here, E_{k_1} and E_{k_2} denote two n-bit independent pseudorandom permutations.

[2] Abusing the notation, we use the same symbol to denote the variables and the solution of a given system of equations.

incomplete and at times unverifiable proof is given in [37]. The result has been acknowledged in the community as a potentially strong approach to establish the optimal security of XOR constructions (i.e., XOR_1 and XOR_2). Beside this result, Patarin [37] also claimed that the number of distinct solutions to a system of q bivariate affine equations with $2 < \xi_{max} \ll 2^{n/2}$ and with non-equality among the variables is always larger than the average number of solutions provided $q \ll 2^n$. Patarin named this result the **Theorem $P_i \oplus P_j$ for any** ξ_{max}. This result was stated as a conjecture [35, Conjecture 8.1] in the context of analysing the security of the Feistel cipher. Only a couple of years later, this result was articulated in many follow-up works for analysing the security of the *xor of two permutations*, and it took a few articles [37,39,40,42] for his result and security argument to evolve. Later, in 2017, this work culminated in a book [32] called *Feistel Ciphers: Security Proofs and Cryptanalysis* by Nachef et al. Unfortunately, some important results were either hard to verify, or stated without proof, which has been reported in multiple works [7,11,15,25,29]. While this has led to some innovations such as the development of the aforementioned χ^2 technique, this state of affairs is unsatisfactory as Mirror Theory is an essential tool for provable security in symmetric cryptography.

1.1   Main Result and Our Contribution

In this paper, our goal is to give a complete and easily verifiable proof of the $P_i \oplus P_j$ Theorem with any ξ_{max}. From a high level, this amounts to lower-bounding the number of solutions of a system of equations of the form $P_i \oplus P_j = \lambda_{ij}$, such that the P_i variables are pairwise distinct.

This result has seen several applications in proving the optimal security bound for several blockcipher and tweakable blockcipher-based schemes such as optimally-secure PRFs, XORP [21,22] and 2k-HtmB-p2 [7] [See Sect. 4]. This result is also applied in the optimal security proof of the Feistel scheme [32,36, 41]. The significance of the last application is due to the wide-ranged use of this scheme. Feistel scheme has been classically used to design many blockciphers (like DES [1], Lucifer [44] etc.), which has the prime advantage over the alternative, substitution permutation networks, of being invertible even if the round functions are not. The Feistel scheme has also been used in format preserving encryption, an important example being the Thorp shuffle [4], which is but an unbalanced Feistel cipher [43]. Along with giving a verifiable proof of the $P_i \oplus P_j$ Theorem with any ξ_{max}, we also provide updated security bounds for these three constructions using our main result, along with proof sketches, to illustrate the impact of the $P_i \oplus P_j$ Theorem with any ξ_{max}.

Notations. For integers $a \leq b$, the set $\{a, a + 1, \cdots, b\}$ is denoted as $[a..b]$ (or simply $[b]$, when $a = 1$). We write $X \leftarrow_\$ S$ to mean that X is sampled uniformly from S and independent of all random variables defined so far. Similarly, we write $X_1, \ldots, X_s \leftarrow_\$ S$ to mean that $X_1, \ldots, X_s$ are uniformly and independently distributed over S. We write X^q to denote a q-tuple $(X_1, \ldots, X_q)$. For $x \in S$, we write $S \setminus x$ to mean $S \setminus \{x\}$. We use $A \sqcup B$ to denote the disjoint union of A and

B (which implicitly means that A and B are disjoint). We consider the vector space $\{0,1\}^n$ over the field $\{0,1\}$, endowed with the two binary operations, $\oplus$ (i.e., addition modulo 2) and multiplication modulo 2. We denote by $N := 2^n$, the number of elements in $\{0,1\}^n$. For a positive integer $e \leq N$, we write $N^{\underline{e}} :=$ $N(N-1)\cdots(N-e+1)$.

A multiset γ is a collection of elements that can repeat. In other words, multiset is an unordered version of a tuple. For $S \in \gamma$, we write γ_{-S} to denote the multiset formed by removing S from γ. We similarly write γ_{+T} to denote the multiset formed by adding an element T to γ. For $S \in \gamma$, we also write γ_{-S+T} to denote the resulting multiset after deleting S and adding T to γ. We say that γ is a **set-system** if it is a multiset of sets. When we want to emphasize an ordering of the elements of γ, we also write the set-system as $\gamma^{[\alpha]} = (\gamma_1, \ldots, \gamma_\alpha)$, which is an enumeration of the sets in γ. In this paper, we consider set-systems γ of non-empty subsets of $\{0,1\}^n$.

System of Difference Equations. Consider a system of difference equations $AX = \Lambda$ over the vector space $\{0,1\}^n$, where $A = (A_{ij})_{i \in [m], j \in [p]}$ is a $m \times p$ matrix with full row rank (and hence consistent), such that each row contains exactly two 1's, and remaining zeros, X is a $p \times 1$ vector of variables and $\Lambda \in (\{0,1\}^n)^m$. As the column sum is zero, we must have $m < p$.[3] Note that each equation in the above system is of the form $X_j \oplus X_k = \lambda_i$ for some i, j, k with $j \neq k$. A solution $X^p \in (\{0,1\}^n)^p$ of the above system is called a *pairwise distinct solution*, or in short a p.d. solution if $X_j \neq X_k$ for $j \neq k \in [p]$. The number of solutions of the system of equations is exactly N^{p-m} which can quite easily be shown by using elementary linear algebra. However, counting the number of p.d. solutions to this system of equations is quite involved. The main aim of this paper is to provide a good lower bound to the number of p.d. solutions.

Graph Theoretic Representation of the System. With every matrix A as described above in the system of difference equations, we can associate a labeled directed graph $G = (V := [p], E, L)$ where the edge set $E = \{(j,k) \in V^2 \mid \exists i \in [m]$ such that $A_{ij} = A_{ik} = 1\}$ and $L(j,k) = \lambda_i$ if $A_{ij} = A_{ik} = 1$. So, whenever there is an edge between j and k, we have directed edges in both directions. Thus, every connected component is strongly connected (there are edges in both directions between two connected vertices). The full row rank of A also implies that the graph G is acyclic and hence is a forest. If the graph G has q components then we must have $|E| = |V| - q$, or $m = p - q$. Given a directed path P from j to k, the equation $X_j \oplus X_k = \bigoplus_{e \in P} L(e)$ is a dependent equation (i.e., it can be obtained by adding a set of equations from the system). So, one can equivalently represent the system of difference equations $AX = \Lambda$ such that the corresponding graph has only star graphs as components. In other words,

---

[3] This is because, the column sum is zero, which implies that the all-1 vector belongs to the kernel of the matrix, implying that it is non-invertible, and since it is already assumed to have full row rank, it cannot possibly have full column rank, hence $m = \text{rank}(A) < p$.

the system of equations corresponding to a component is of the form

$$X_{j_1} \oplus X_{j_\xi} = \lambda_{i_1}, \ldots, X_{j_{\xi-1}} \oplus X_{j_\xi} = \lambda_{i_{\xi-1}}.$$

We call such a system of difference equations *standard system of difference equations*.

Definition 1. *A system of difference equations $AX = \Lambda$ is called* p.d.-consistent *if $\lambda'_i \neq 0$ for all $i \in [m]$ and for all $i \neq i'$ in the same component, $\lambda'_i \neq \lambda'_{i'}$, where $A'X = \Lambda' := \lambda'^m$ is a standard form for the system.*

To have a p.d. solution, p.d.-consistency is a necessary condition. The following theorem provides a lower bound on the number of p.d. solutions for any p.d.-consistent system of difference equations.

Theorem 1 (Main Result). *Let G be the associated graph of a p.d.-consistent system $A_{m \times p} X = \Lambda$, of equations over $\{0,1\}^n$. Suppose the number of vertices in the largest component of G is $\xi_{\max}$. If $p \leq \sqrt{N}$ or $\sqrt{N} \geq \xi^2_{\max} \log_2 N + \xi_{\max}$, and $1 \leq p \leq N/12\xi^2_{\max}$, then the number of p.d. solutions of the system $AX = \Lambda$ is at least $(N)\frac{p}{}/N^m$.*

Remark 1. Note that, in most cryptographic applications (where $N \geq 2^{64}$), $\xi_{\max}$ is either a small constant, or can be shown to be smaller than $\log_2 N$ with overwhelming probability. Typically, this is sufficient to prove that the cryptographic scheme is secure as long as the number q of adversarial queries is upper bounded by $N/12\xi^2_{\max}$, as $(\log_2 N)^3 \leq \sqrt{N}$ for $N \geq 2^{30}$.

1.2 Applications of Theorem $P_i \oplus P_j$ for Any $\xi_{\max}$

Over the years, the Theorem $P_i \oplus P_j$ for any $\xi_{\max}$ has been proven to be a significant result in the context of analysing security bounds of numerous cryptographic designs. Apart from the stand-alone value of XOR_2 or XOR_1 constructions, they are used as a major component in many important blockcipher and tweakable blockcipher-based designs that includes [13,14,18,21,23,24,27,28,33,34,45–47]. However, the security proofs of most of these designs, done by application of the H-Coefficient technique [38], involve fixing the outputs, which in turn determines the inputs, thus getting rid of the adaptive nature of the adversary, and we cannot assume distinctness of these outputs of internal primitives because that would lead to the sub-optimal birthday-bound, rendering the $P_i \oplus P_j$ Theorem for $\xi_{\max} = 2$, useless for these security proofs. Instead, these security proofs require (by application of the H-Coefficient technique [38]) a good lower bound on the number of distinct solutions to a system of bivariate affine equations with a general $\xi_{\max}$ and therein comes the role of the result "Theorem $P_i \oplus P_j$ for any $\xi_{\max}$". It has also been used in proving the beyond-birthday-bound security of many nonce-based MACs including [5,15,16,18,31]. Mennink [30] showed the optimal security bound of EWCDM using this result as the primary underlying tool, and Iwata et al. [22] also used it to show the optimal security bound of

CENC. Despite the debate in the community regarding the correctness of the proof of "Theorem $P_i \oplus P_j$ for any ξ_{max}" [37,40], several authors have used this result to derive an optimal bound for some constructions such as [22,30,48]. This triggers the need for a correct and verifiable proof of these two results, which will eventually help to correctly establish the security proof of the above constructions and improve their security.

1.3 Related Work

Beside the applicability of the Theorem $P_i \oplus P_j$ for general ξ_{max}, the more restricted result of *"Theorem $P_i \oplus P_j$ for $\xi_{max} = 2$"* has already been linked to different cryptographic constructions. In particular, equations of the form $P_{2i-1} \oplus P_{2i} = \lambda_i$, which correspond to a simple variant of the systems we consider in this work, have been considered to prove the security of the XORP[2] construction [9,17,32,37,40]. In [8,42] and [17], systems of the form $\oplus_{j=1}^{k} P_{i,j} = \lambda_i$, where the values $(P_{i,j})_i$ have to be pairwise distinct for $j = 1, \ldots, k$, have been studied to prove the security of the sum of permutations. Recently, a similar problem in the tweakable setting has been examined in [25], with an application to the security of the CLRW2 construction[4]. Mirror Theory has also been considered for nonce-based MACs that rely on an underlying blockcipher or tweakable blockciphers, such as in [15,16,18,26,31]. In that case, constraints also include inequalities of the form $P_i \oplus P_j \neq \lambda_{i,j}$, which also have to be taken into account. Despite the extensive use of the result, its correctness was subject to debate [11]. In [26], Kim et al. have given a verifiable proof of the mirror theory when the number of equations is below the bound $2^{3n/4}$. Datta et al. [12] have extended this result for a system of bivariate affine equations and non-equations. Recently, Dutta et al. [17] and Cogliati and Patarin [9] have independently given a verifiable proof of the "$P_i \oplus P_j$ theorem" for $\xi_{max} = 2$.

Organization. In Sect. 2, we prove an equivalent formulation of our main result through a probability of an event involving disjointness of some random sets, modulo a Proposition, proof of which is postponed to Sect. 3. We give an overview of our proof strategy and a brief comparison with previous proofs in Sect. 3.2. The proof of the Proposition requires a recursive inequality lemma, proof of which is deferred in Sect. A.2. Then, Sect. 4 briefly revisits several proofs that rely on the $P_i \oplus P_j$ Theorem with any ξ_{max}, and provides the corresponding updated security bounds. Finally, we outline possible extensions of our work in Sect. 5.

---

[4] CLRW2 or cascading LRW2 is a tweakable blockcipher, defined as $CLRW2((k_1, k_2, h_1, h_2), t, m) = LRW2((k_2, h_2), t, LRW2((k_1, h_1), t, m))$, with $LRW2((k, h), t, m) = E(k, m \oplus h(t)) \oplus h(t)$, where E is a block cipher, k is the block cipher key, and h is an XOR universal hash function.

2 Probability of Disjointness: An Equivalent Formulation

In order to streamline the proof of Theorem 1, we will operate two distinct changes. First, note that, in order to have solutions, the system has to be p.d. consistent, which corresponds to two distinct conditions: $\lambda_i' \neq 0$ for all $i \in [m]$, and for all $i \neq i'$ in the same component, $\lambda_i' \neq \lambda_{i'}'$. While easy to manipulate, both conditions have to be handled in a different way, which complicates the proof. The simplest fix is to introduce, for every component, an additional λ' value that can be thought to be 0^n. Second, in order to avoid powers of N in our formulas, we prefer switching to a probabilistic formulation where, for every component, we simply sample uniformly at random a value in $\{0,1\}^n$, and consider a disjointness event that is derived from the system of equalities.

More formally, given a set-system $\gamma = \{\gamma_i : i \in [\alpha]\}$, we define the following event:[5]

$$\mathsf{Disj}(\gamma) := \gamma_1 \oplus \mathsf{R}_1, \dots, \gamma_\alpha \oplus \mathsf{R}_\alpha \text{ are disjoint}$$

along with the following probability:

$$\mathsf{P}(\gamma) = \Pr_{\mathsf{R}^\alpha}(\mathsf{Disj}(\gamma)),$$

where $\mathsf{R}_1, \dots, \mathsf{R}_\alpha \leftarrow_\$ \{0,1\}^n$. In words, the event says that a random and independent translation of sets from a collection are disjoint. We write $\|\gamma\| := \sum_{i=1}^\alpha |\gamma_i|$ and $\|\gamma\|_{\max} = \max_i |\gamma_i|$. It is easy to see that the probability of disjointness is invariant under any translation of the sets, i.e., $\mathsf{P}(\gamma) = \mathsf{P}(\gamma')$ where $\gamma_i' = \gamma_i \oplus a_i$ for $a_1, \dots, a_\alpha \in \{0,1\}^n$.

Theorem 1 can be rephrased in the following way.

Theorem 1' (**Equivalent Formulation**). *Let γ be a set-system of elements of $\{0,1\}^n$ such that $\xi_{\max} = \|\gamma\|_{\max}$. If $\|\gamma\| \leq \sqrt{N}$ or $\sqrt{N} \geq \xi_{\max}^2 \log_2 N + \xi_{\max}$, and $1 \leq \|\gamma\| \leq N/12\xi_{\max}^2$, then*

$$\mathsf{P}(\gamma) \geq \frac{(N)^{\|\gamma\|}}{N^{\|\gamma\|}}.$$

The equivalence between both statements is proven in Sect. 2.1. From a high level, the proof of Theorem 1' works in two steps:

1. if γ is small ($\|\gamma\| \leq \sqrt{N}$), then simple calculations show that Theorem 1' holds;
2. otherwise, we prove that, for a well-chosen $a \in T \in \gamma$, one has

$$\mathsf{P}(\gamma) \geq \left(1 - \frac{\|\gamma\| - 1}{N}\right) \mathsf{P}(\gamma'),$$

where γ' is a set system containing exactly the same sets as γ, except that the set T has been replaced with $T \setminus \{a\}$; clearly, applying point 2 repeatedly until $\|\gamma\| \leq \sqrt{N}$ allows us to conclude the proof of Theorem 1'.

---

[5] For a set $A \subseteq \{0,1\}^n$ and a n-bit number $x \in \{0,1\}^n$, $x \oplus A := \{x \oplus a \mid a \in A\}$

Intuitively, the element that we remove from γ is the one that appears, in the associated system of equations, with maximum multiplicity.

More formally, given $z \in \{0,1\}^n \setminus \{0^n\}$, and a set S, we define $\delta_S(z)$ as the number of 2-subsets $\{a, b\}$ of S with $a \oplus b = z$. For a set-system γ, we define

$$\delta_\gamma(z) := \sum_{S \in \gamma} \delta_S(z), \quad \Delta_\gamma := \max_{z \in \{0,1\}^n} \delta_\gamma(z).$$

Clearly, for any set-system γ, $\Delta_\gamma \geq 1$. The underlying statement behind the second point of our proof strategy is the following one.

Proposition 1. *Let λ be a set-system with $\sqrt{N} \leq \|\lambda\| \leq N/12\xi_{\max}^2$ where $\xi_{\max} = \|\lambda\|_{\max}$ satisfies the bound given in Theorem 1', i.e., $\sqrt{N} \geq \xi_{\max}^2 \log_2 N + \xi_{\max}$. Suppose the maximum Δ_λ is attained for $a \oplus b$ with $\{a, b\} \subseteq T \in \lambda$. Then,*

$$P(\lambda) \geq \left(1 - \frac{\|\lambda\| - 1}{N}\right) \cdot P(\lambda_{-a|T})$$

where $\lambda_{-a|T} = \lambda_{-T+T \setminus a}$ (i.e. replacing the element T by $T \setminus a$).

The proof of Proposition 1 is given in Sect. 3, and we explain how to derive Theorem 1' from Proposition 1 in Sect. 2.2.

2.1 Proof of Equivalence

Here we prove why Theorem 1' is an equivalent statement of our main theorem. First, we establish a one-to-one relationship between the number of disjoint favorable solutions r^q with the number of p.d. solutions of systems of equations.

Let $AX = \Lambda$ be a system of difference equations in standard form, and G be its associated graph. For every component C, let L_C be the set of all labels. By definition of p.d.-consistency, all elements of L_C are distinct (and hence it is a set of size $\xi_C - 1$, where ξ_C is the number of vertices in C) nonzero elements. Let i_C denote the center of the star component. Thus, for all other $j \in C$, we have an equation of the form $X_j \oplus X_{i_C} = \lambda_k$ for some k. Now we consider a set-system γ containing all sets of the form $S_C := L_C \cup \{0\}$. Thus, $\|\gamma\| = \sum_C |C| = e$ and $|\gamma| = q$. Let $C_1, \ldots, C_q$, denote the components (written in some order) and let $i_j := i_{C_j}$. Now consider a map f, mapping a p.d. solution x^e of the system to r^q, where $r_j = x_{i_j}$ for all $j \in [q]$. It is easy to see that $S_{C_j} \oplus r_j$ are disjoint sets (as these represent all x values). Moreover, f is clearly injective as a solution is uniquely determined by the tuple $(x_{i_1}, \ldots, x_{i_q})$. So, f is an injective function. Conversely, for any r^q with disjoint $S_{C_j} \oplus r_j$'s, we can define x^e consisting of all values from the set $\sqcup_j(S_{C_j} \oplus r_j)$ in an appropriate order (with $x_{i_j} = r_j$). Clearly, this map is f^{-1} and so f is a bijective function. Hence, the number of p.d. solutions for $AX = \Lambda$ is same as the number of solutions of r^q so that $\text{Disj}(\gamma)$ holds. Second, we note that Theorem 1' can be simply restated as the number of solutions $r^{|\gamma|}$ so that $(\gamma_i \oplus r_i)$'s are disjoint for all $i \in [q]$ is at least

$$\frac{(N)^{\|\gamma\|}}{N^{\|\gamma\| - |\gamma|}} = \frac{(N)^e}{N^{e-q}},$$

where $p - q = m$ corresponds to the number of equations in the system $AX = \Lambda$. This proves the equivalence between our main theorem and the equivalent formulation.

2.2   Proof of Theorem 1'

We first prove the statement when $\|\gamma\| \leq \sqrt{N}$. In this case we remove elements from γ one by one until we end up with a single element. We first note that

$$P(\gamma) = P(\gamma_{-S}) \times \left(1 - \frac{\|\gamma\| - 1}{N}\right) \qquad\qquad if\ |S| = 1 \qquad (1)$$

$$P(\gamma) \geq P(\gamma_{-S}) \times \left(1 - \frac{|S| \times \|\gamma_{-S}\|}{N}\right) \qquad\qquad if\ |S| \geq 2 \qquad (2)$$

where $S \in \gamma$. The above relations are easy to verify (by looking at the restriction imposed on R which translates the set S). Indeed, let us assume $S = \gamma_1$. Then, using the independence of the $(R_i)_{i=1,\dots,|\gamma|}$ random variables, once $R_2, \dots, R_{|\gamma|}$ are chosen such that the equations from $\mathsf{Disj}(\gamma_{-S})$ are satisfied, $\mathsf{Disj}(\gamma)$ adds the following restrictions on R_1:

$$R_1 \oplus x \neq R_i \oplus y \text{ for all } x \in S,\ i \neq 1,\ y \in \gamma_i.$$

Hence, if $|S| = 1$, R_1 has to be different from exactly $\|\gamma\| - 1$ values, while, if $|S| \neq 1$, it has to avoid at most $|S| \times \|\gamma_{-S}\|$ group elements.

Let us write $W_i := (1 - \frac{i}{N})$, so that $\prod_{i=1}^{k-1} W_i = (N)\underline{k}/N^k$. Now we claim that, for $\|\gamma\| \leq \sqrt{N}$,

$$\left(1 - \frac{|S| \times \|\gamma_{-S}\|}{N}\right) \geq \prod_{i=\|\gamma_{-S}\|}^{\|\gamma\|-1} W_i \qquad (3)$$

and hence $P(\gamma) \geq P(\gamma_{-S}) \times \prod_{i=\|\gamma_{-S}\|}^{\|\gamma\|-1} W_i$. After repeatedly removing an element one by one, we have $P(\gamma) \geq \prod_{i=1}^{\|\gamma\|-1} W_i$ which proves the theorem. Now we prove Eq. (3). It is sufficient to show that

$$1 - \frac{ar}{N} \geq \left(1 - \frac{a}{N}\right) \cdots \left(1 - \frac{a+r-1}{N}\right)$$

where $a + r \leq \sqrt{N}$. This can be easily shown by induction on r. For $r = 1$, it is obvious. Now by applying induction hypothesis for r, we obtain

$$\left(1 - \frac{a}{N}\right) \cdots \left(1 - \frac{a+r-1}{N}\right)\left(1 - \frac{a+r}{N}\right) \leq \left(1 - \frac{ar}{N}\right)\left(1 - \frac{a+r}{N}\right)$$

$$\leq 1 - \frac{ar+a}{N} - \frac{r}{N}\left(1 - \frac{a(a+r)}{N}\right) \leq 1 - \frac{ar+a}{N}.$$

For the last inequality we use the fact that $a + r + 1 \leq \sqrt{N}$.

For the next case, we assume that $\sqrt{N} \leq \|\gamma\| \leq N/12\xi_{\max}^2$, i.e. $\|\lambda\|$ is within the required bounds for which Proposition 1 holds. We can create a sequence of nested set-systems $\{\gamma^{(i)}\}_{i=0}^{\sigma}$, with

$$\gamma^{(0)} := \gamma, \quad \|\gamma^{(i+1)}\| = \|\gamma^{(i)}\| - 1, \ \forall i \in [\sigma - 1], \quad \|\gamma^{(\sigma)}\| \leq \sqrt{N},$$

in the following manner: Let $\{x_i, y_i\} \subseteq S_i \in \gamma^{(i)}$ such that $x_i \oplus y_i$ attains the highest multiplicity in $\gamma^{(i)}$, $\Delta_{\gamma^{(i)}}$. We choose one arbitrarily if there exists more than one choice. We define $\gamma^{(i+1)} := \gamma^{(i)}_{-x_i|S_i}$. Now for every $i \in [\sigma - 1]$, if $|S_i| = 1$ we apply Eq. (1), and if $|S_i| \geq 2$, we apply Proposition 1, to obtain

$$\mathsf{P}(\gamma) \geq \mathsf{P}(\gamma^{(\sigma)}) \prod_{i=1}^{\sigma} \left(1 - \frac{\|\gamma\| - i}{N}\right).$$

We already have shown the result for $\gamma^{(\sigma)}$ that $\mathsf{P}(\gamma^{(\sigma)}) \geq (N)_{\|\gamma^{(\sigma)}\|}/N^{\|\gamma^{(\sigma)}\|}$, which completes the proof.

3   Proof of Proposition 1

Notations and Conventions. In the Proposition statement, $\{a, b\} \subseteq T \in \lambda$ and $\Delta_\lambda = \sum_{S \in \lambda} \delta_S(a \oplus b)$. Let $\lambda = \{\lambda_i : i \in [q]\}$ and we write $|\lambda_i| = \xi_i, \xi_{\max} = \max_i \xi_i$ and $\sigma := \sum_i \xi_i$. We also write Δ to denote Δ_λ. Throughout the section we follow this notation. Moreover, we use the notation γ to denote a set-system such that $\gamma \subseteq \lambda$ (as a multiset).

3.1   Initial Condition

Note that, after applying Eq. (2) repeatedly (or by applying induction on $|\lambda \setminus \gamma|$) for $\gamma \subseteq \lambda$, we have

$$\frac{\mathsf{P}(\lambda)}{\mathsf{P}(\gamma)} \geq \left(1 - \frac{q\xi_{\max}^2}{N}\right)^{|\lambda \setminus \gamma|}. \tag{4}$$

We call this an initial condition that would be used later to prove Proposition 1.

3.2   Link-Deletion Equation and Proof Overview

Link-Deletion Equation. Let $x \in S \in \gamma \subseteq \lambda$. Let us write

$$\gamma = \{\gamma_1, \ldots, \gamma_\alpha\}$$

using an arbitrary ordering of the multiset γ, and let us assume $S = \gamma_1$ and $x = \gamma_{1,1}$. Then, the event $\mathsf{Disj}(\gamma)$ corresponds to the fact that all the $\mathsf{R}_i \oplus \gamma_{i,j}$ values are pairwise distinct, and the event $\mathsf{Disj}(\gamma_{-x|S})$ corresponds to the same event, where the conditions involving $R_1 \oplus \gamma_{1,1}$ are ignored. Hence, one has $\mathsf{Disj}(\gamma) \Rightarrow \mathsf{Disj}(\gamma_{-x|S})$. Suppose $\mathsf{Disj}(\gamma_{-x|S}) \wedge \neg \mathsf{Disj}(\gamma)$ holds. Then, there must exist $y \in S' \in \gamma_{-\gamma_1}$ such that $S' = \gamma_i$ for some integer $i \neq 1$, and $y \oplus R_i = x \oplus R_1$. As $(S \setminus x) \oplus R_1$ is disjoint from $S' \oplus R_i$ (same as $S' \oplus (x \oplus y \oplus R_1)$), $S \setminus x$ should be disjoint from $S' \oplus x \oplus y$. Let

$$I := \{(x \oplus y, S') : y \in S' \in \gamma_{-S}, \ S' \oplus (x \oplus y) \text{ is disjoint with } S \setminus x\}.$$

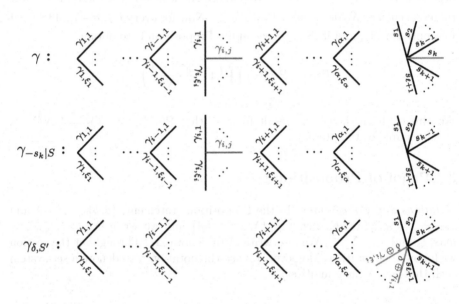

Fig. 1. Graphical depiction of the link-deletion operation. Here, we have represented graphs corresponding to the three types of terms appearing in the link-deletion equation, with $x = s_k$, $y = \gamma_{i,j}$, $\delta = s_k \oplus \gamma_{i,j}$, $S = \{s_1, \ldots, s_{\ell+1}\}$, and $S' = \gamma_i$. Central vertices correspond to the $R_1, \ldots, R_\alpha, R$ random variables.

Note that simultaneously $R_1 \oplus x = R_i \oplus y = R_j \oplus y'$ for some $y' \in \gamma_j \in \gamma_{-S}$ cannot hold. Since otherwise, the disjointness of $\gamma_{-x|S}$ cannot hold. Thus, we have established a useful relation, called **link-deletion equation**.

$$P(\gamma) = P(\gamma_{-x|S}) - \frac{1}{N} \sum_{(\delta, S') \in I} P(\gamma_{\delta, S'}) \tag{5}$$

where $\gamma_{\delta, S'} = \gamma_{-S-S'+S_1}$ and $S_1 = (\delta \oplus S') \sqcup (S \setminus x)$. This is because, the probability $P(\gamma_{-x|S})$ can be divided in two disjoint events:

- either adding x as a link to the set S does not create any collision (this happens with probability $P(\gamma)$), or

– a collision is created; all those collision events are disjoint, and correspond to
a unique element from the set I. For every $(\delta, S') \in I$, the probability that
such a collision occurs (while keeping all the other disjointness conditions),
is exactly $\mathsf{P}(\gamma_{\delta,S'})/N$, as this event corresponds to the event, $\mathsf{Disj}(\gamma_{\delta,S'}) \wedge$
$(R_1 = R_i \oplus \delta)$, where the sub-event $R_1 = R_i \oplus \delta$ occurs with probability $1/N$
independently of $\mathsf{Disj}(\gamma_{\delta,S'})$ (because $\gamma_{\delta,S'}$ does not involve S' and hence R_i).

Proof Strategy. In order to prove Proposition 1, we will prove that $|\mathsf{P}(\gamma_{\delta,S'}) -$
$\mathsf{P}(\gamma_{-x|S})|$ is small enough in front of $\mathsf{P}(\gamma_{-x|S})$, for all $(\delta, S') \in I$. This will be
done in the following steps.

1. Upper bound the size of the set I (in Sect. 3.3).
2. Establish a recursive inequality between the maximum difference between
   terms of the form $\mathsf{P}(\gamma'_{-x|S})$, and terms of the form $\mathsf{P}(\gamma'_{\delta,S'})$, with $\gamma'_{-S} \subset \lambda$,
   and S an arbitrary set of some fixed size (in Sect. A.2). This will be done by
   applying the link-deletion equation to the two probabilities that maximize
   the difference term, thus introducing new difference terms and an error term.
3. After applying this inequality a logarithmic number of times along with simple bounds on the probability ratios, prove that remaining terms become
   sufficiently small thanks to the geometric reduction offered by the recursive
   inequality (Sects. 3.5 and A.2).

Comparison with Previous Proofs. The main difference with previous proof
strategies is centered around the link-deletion equation. Indeed, previous works
started with the introduction of the so-called orange equation, which can be seen
as two consecutive applications of the link-deletion equations. Hence, instead of
always merging a single set $S' \in \gamma$ with the final set S, this could be seen as
merging two distinct sets $S', S'' \in \gamma$, which leads to a more complicated analysis.

3.3   Size Lemma

We also write the above set I as $I_{x|S}$ to emphasize that I depends on x, S.
Clearly, for all $x \in S \in \gamma$, $|I| \leq \|\gamma\|$. However, we establish an improved upper
bound for the size of $I_{a|T}$ where a and T are described in the statement of the
Proposition.

Lemma 1 (size lemma). *For a given $a \in T \in \lambda$ as described in the Proposi-
tion statement, we have $|I_{a|T}| \leq \|\lambda\| - \Delta - |T|/2$.*

Proof. Take any $S \in \lambda_{-T}$. Note that there are $\delta_S(a \oplus b)$ many 2-sets $\{w_1, w_2\} \subseteq S$
such that $w_1 \oplus w_2 = a \oplus b$ and hence $b = w_2 \oplus (a \oplus w_1) \in S \oplus (a \oplus w_1)$. So,
$(a \oplus w_1, S) \notin I_{a|T}$. So,

$$|I_{a|T}| \leq \sum_{S \in \lambda \backslash T} (|S| - \delta_S(a \oplus b)) = (\|\lambda\| - |T|) - \Delta_\lambda + \delta_T(a \oplus b) \leq \|\lambda\| - \Delta_\lambda - |T|/2,$$

as $\delta_T(a \oplus b) \le |T|/2$. Indeed, for every element, $x \in T$, there exists at most one element y in T such that $x \oplus y = a \oplus b$. In the case where it exists, then neither x nor y can be part of a different 2-set.   □

3.4   Recursive Inequality of D-Terms

In this section, we introduce D-terms, which correspond to the maximum difference between the two types of terms that can appear in the link-deletion equation. Formally, one has the following definition.

Definition 2. $\tau = \gamma_{+U}$ with $\gamma \subseteq \lambda$ where $|\gamma| = \alpha$ and $|U| = \ell + 1$. For any $S \in \gamma$ disjoint with U, let $\tau' := \gamma_{-S+(S \sqcup U)}$ (same as $\tau_{-S-U+S\sqcup U}$, i.e., we merge two disjoint elements of τ). We define

$$D(\alpha, \ell) = \max_{\gamma, U, S} \left| P(\tau) - P(\tau') \right|, \tag{6}$$

where the maximum is taken over all choices of $\gamma \subseteq \lambda$ of size α, $S \in \gamma$ and a set U of size $\ell + 1$ disjoint with S. For all $\ell < 0$, we define $D(\alpha, \ell) = 0$.

Now we state and prove the Recursive Inequality for D-terms:

Lemma 2 (Recursive Inequality of D-Terms). Let $\alpha \le q \le \frac{N}{12\xi_{\max}^2}$, $\ell \ge 0$. We write $\beta := \xi_{\max}/N$. Then,

$$D(\alpha, \ell) \le D(\alpha, \ell - 1) + \frac{\xi_{\max}}{N} \sum_{i=1}^{q} D(\alpha - 1, \ell + \xi_i - 1) + \frac{2\Delta \xi_{\max} \cdot P(\lambda)}{N\left(1 - q\xi_{\max}^2/N\right)^{q-\alpha}}. \tag{7}$$

Note, for $q \le \|\lambda\| \le N/12\xi_{\max}^2$, $\frac{\xi_{\max}}{N(1-q\xi_{\max}^2/N)} \le (4\xi eq)^{-1}$. Denoting $\beta := \xi_{\max}/N$, and $a_{d,\ell} = \frac{\beta^d}{2P(\lambda)} D(q - d, \ell)$ we have,

$$a_{d,\ell} \le a_{d,\ell-1} + \sum_{i=1}^{q} a_{d+1,\ell+\ell_i} + \beta\Delta \left(4e\xi_{\max}q\right)^{-d},$$

where $\ell_i = \xi_i - 1$.

The proof of this Lemma is postponed to Appendix A.1.

Remark 2. Note that the r.h.s. of the inequality contains three types of terms:

- $D(\alpha, \ell - 1)$ which will disappear after $\ell - 1$ applications of the recursive inequality,
- terms of the form $D(\alpha - 1, \ell + \xi_i - 1)$ which involve a smaller set-system, but a larger U set; however, those terms are multiplied by $\frac{\xi_{\max}}{N}$, which will ensure their geometric reduction,
- a parasite term that, as we will see, is small enough not to cause an issue after a logarithmic number of iterations.

Besides, in addition to the above recursive inequality, we also have the following bound, which follows from Eq. (4):

$$D(\alpha, \ell) = |P(\tau) - P(\tau')| \leq \frac{2P(\lambda)}{(1 - q \cdot \|\lambda\|_{\max}^2/N)^{|\lambda \setminus \gamma|}}$$

and so

$$a_{d,\ell} = \frac{\beta^d}{2P(\lambda)} D(q - d, \ell) \leq \left(\frac{\xi_{\max}}{N (1 - q\xi_{\max}^2/N)} \right)^d \leq 1/(4e\xi_{\max}q)^d$$

3.5 Final Wrap up of Proof

We can conclude the proof of Proposition 1 using Lemmas 1, 2, along with the following result that will be proven in Appendix A.2.

Lemma 3 (Recursive Inequality Lemma). *Suppose $a_{d,\ell} \geq 0$ such that: (i) $a_{d,k} := 0$ for all $k < 0$, and (ii) for all $0 \leq d \leq \xi n$ and $0 \leq \ell_i \leq \xi - 1$ for $i \in [q]$, we have*

$$a_{d,\ell} \leq (4\xi eq)^{-d} \qquad \text{(initial bound)} \qquad (8)$$

$$a_{d,\ell} \leq a_{d,\ell-1} + \sum_{i=1}^{q} a_{d+1,\ell+\ell_i} + C \cdot (4\xi eq)^{-d} \qquad \text{(recursive inequality)} \qquad (9)$$

for some $C > 0$. Then, for every $\ell \in [\xi - 2]$,

$$a_{0,\ell} \leq \frac{4}{N} + 4C\xi.$$

Let a, b, T, λ be as in the statement of Proposition 1, and let $\lambda_0 = \lambda_{-T}$. Note that one has $\xi_{\max}^2 n \leq \sqrt{N} - \xi_{\max} \leq \|\lambda_0\| \leq N/12\xi_{\max}^2$. Moreover, let $q = |\lambda_0|$. Similarly, one has $\xi_{\max}q \geq \|\lambda_0\| \geq \xi_{\max}^2 n$, which means that $q \geq \xi_{\max}n$. We are going to apply Lemma 3 to λ_0 as follows.

Let us take, $\xi = \xi_{\max}$, $C = \beta\Delta = \Delta_\lambda \xi_{\max}/N$ in the statement of the above Lemma 3. From the definition of $a_{d,\ell} = \frac{\beta^d}{2P(\lambda_0)} D(q - d, \ell)$, we must ensure that $q \geq d$ in order to apply Lemma 3. This can easily be seen to be true as $q \geq \xi n$ and $d \leq \xi n$. Then, for $(\delta, S) \in I_{a|T}$, we have

$$|P(\lambda_{\delta,S}) - P(\lambda_{-a|T})| \leq D(q, |T| - 2) \leq 2P(\lambda_0)a_{0,|T|-2} \leq \frac{8P(\lambda_0)}{N}(\Delta\xi_{\max}^2 + 1).$$

Note that one has

$$P(\lambda_{-a|T}) \geq P(\lambda_0)\left(1 - \frac{\|\lambda_0\|\xi_{\max}}{N}\right) \geq P(\lambda_0)\left(1 - \frac{1}{12\xi_{\max}}\right) \geq P(\lambda_0)\frac{23}{24}.$$

Thus, one has

$$\mathsf{P}(\lambda_{\delta,S}) \leq \frac{8\mathsf{P}(\lambda_0)}{N}(\Delta\xi_{\max}^2 + 1) + \mathsf{P}(\lambda_{-a|T}) \leq \left(\frac{8\mathsf{P}(\lambda_0)(\Delta\xi_{\max}^2 + 1)}{N \cdot \mathsf{P}(\lambda_{-a|T})} + 1\right)\mathsf{P}(\lambda_{-a|T})$$

$$\leq \left(\frac{24 \cdot 8}{23 \cdot N}(\Delta\xi_{\max}^2 + 1) + 1\right)\mathsf{P}(\lambda_{-a|T}) \leq \left(\frac{C'\Delta}{N} + 1\right)\mathsf{P}(\lambda_{-a|T}),$$

where $C' = 9(\xi_{\max}^2 + 1)$, as $\Delta \geq 1$. Using this bound in the appropriate link deletion equation we have:

$$\mathsf{P}(\lambda) = \mathsf{P}(\lambda_{-a|T}) - \frac{1}{N}\sum_{(\delta,S)\in I_{a|T}} \mathsf{P}(\lambda_{\delta,S}) \quad \text{(From Eq. (5))}$$

$$\geq \mathsf{P}(\lambda_{-a|T}) - \frac{1}{N}\sum_{(\delta,S)\in I_{a|T}} \mathsf{P}(\lambda_{-a|T})(1 + C'\Delta/N)$$

$$\geq \mathsf{P}(\lambda_{-a|T})\left(1 - \frac{\|\lambda\| - \Delta - |T|/2}{N}\left(1 + \frac{C'\Delta}{N}\right)\right) \quad \text{(From Lemma 1)}$$

$$\geq \mathsf{P}(\lambda_{-a|T})\left(1 - \frac{\|\lambda\| - 1}{N} + \frac{\Delta}{N}\left(1 - \frac{C'(\|\lambda\| - \Delta - 1)}{N}\right)\right)$$

$$\geq \mathsf{P}(\lambda_{-a|T})\left(1 - \frac{\|\lambda\| - 1}{N}\right).$$

The last inequality follows as $C'\|\lambda\| \leq N$, for $\|\lambda\| \leq N/12\xi_{\max}^2$, which concludes our proof of Proposition 1.   □

Remark 3. Note that the initial bound ensures only that $a_{0,\ell} \leq 1$. However, the presence of recursive inequality forces the value of $a_{0,\ell}$ to be very small.

4 Cryptographic Applications

In order to give an overview of how Mirror Theory can be used, and to illustrate the importance of the "$P_i \oplus P_j$ theorem" for any $\xi_{\max}$, we provide security proofs for a diverse set of constructions. Note that we focus on the parts of the proof that involve system of bivariate equations and omit the other parts, for which we cite the relevant results in the literature. We felt the need to add this section mainly to motivate the readers on the importance of the proof of this result.

4.1 The H Coefficients Technique

In this section, we consider one of the main applications of Theorem 1, which is proving the security of a pseudorandom function (PRF) F, or a pseudorandom permutation, P, based on a secret random primitive. Formally, for any information-theoretical adversary **A** that is allowed at most q oracle queries, we define its advantage in distinguishing F from a truly uniformly random oracle, denoted \$, as follows:

$$\mathbf{Adv}_F^{\mathrm{prf}}(\mathbf{A}) := \left| \Pr\left(\mathbf{A}^F = 1\right) - \Pr\left(\mathbf{A}^\$ = 1\right) \right|.$$

whereas, for any information-theoretical adversary $\mathbf{A}$ that is allowed at most q forward and backward oracle queries, we define its advantage in distinguishing P from a truly uniformly random permutation oracle, denoted \$\$, as follows:

$$\mathbf{Adv}_P^{\mathrm{sprp}}(\mathbf{A}) := \left| \Pr\left(\mathbf{A}^P = 1\right) - \Pr\left(\mathbf{A}^{\$\$} = 1\right) \right|.$$

One way of upper-bounding the prf-advantage of $\mathbf{A}$ is to use the H coefficients technique, which is tightly linked to Mirror Theory. To use this method, we summarize the interaction of $\mathbf{A}$ with its oracle in what we refer to as a transcript

$$\tau = \{(X_1, Y_1), \ldots, (X_q, Y_q)\},$$

where, for each pair (x_i, y_i), $\mathbf{A}$ made a query x_i and received y_i as an answer (or made a query y_i and received x_i as an answer, in case of backward queries). We also introduce two random variables $\mathrm{T}_{\mathrm{real}}$ and $\mathrm{T}_{\mathrm{ideal}}$ which correspond to the value of τ when $\mathbf{A}$ interacts respectively with the real world (the construction F or P) and the ideal world (resp., \$ or \$\$). We say that a transcript τ is *attainable* if it satisfies $\Pr(\mathrm{T}_{\mathrm{ideal}} = \tau) > 0$. The set of all attainable transcripts is written $\mathscr{T}$. One has the following result.

Lemma 4 ([38]). *Let $\mathscr{T}_{\mathrm{good}} \subset \mathscr{T}$ be a subset of the set of all attainable transcripts. Assume that, for every $\tau \in \mathscr{T}_{\mathrm{good}}$, one has*

$$\frac{\Pr\left(\mathrm{T}_{\mathrm{real}} = \tau\right)}{\Pr\left(\mathrm{T}_{\mathrm{ideal}} = \tau\right)} \geq 1 - \varepsilon.$$

Then, one has

$$\mathbf{Adv}_F^{\mathrm{prf}}(\mathbf{A}) \leq \Pr\left(\mathrm{T}_{\mathrm{ideal}} \in \mathscr{T} \setminus \mathscr{T}_{\mathrm{good}}\right) + \varepsilon.$$

Mirror Theory is generally used when computing the lower bound of the ratio $\Pr(\mathrm{T}_{\mathrm{real}} = \tau)/\Pr(\mathrm{T}_{\mathrm{ideal}} = \tau)$ by providing a lower bound for the number of intermediate values for the underlying random primitive. We now illustrate this technique by revisiting existing security proofs using Theorem 1.

4.2   The XORP Construction

In [21], Iwata introduced CENC, a beyond-birthday-bound secure mode of operation which uses an underlying permutation-based PRF dubbed XORP which is defined as follows:

$$\mathsf{XORP}[w] : \{0,1\}^{n-s} \longrightarrow \{0,1\}^{wn}$$
$$x \longmapsto \|_{i=1}^{w} \pi\left(\langle 0\rangle_s \| x\right) \oplus \pi\left(\langle i\rangle_s \| x\right),$$

where $s = \lceil \log_2(w+1) \rceil$, and π is a uniformly random secret n-bit permutation. Later, Iwata, Mennink, and Vizár [22] made the link between XORP and Mirror Theory explicit, and proved optimal security for the construction, using [40, Theorem 6]. We revisit their proof by applying Theorem 1 in order to demonstrate the following result[6].

Theorem 2. *Let* $\mathbf{A}$ *be an adversary against the prf-security of* XORP$[w]$, *which is allowed at most* q *queries. If* $q \leq 2^n/12(w+1)^2$, *one has*

$$\mathbf{Adv}^{\mathrm{prf}}_{\mathsf{XORP}[w]}(\mathbf{A}) \leq \frac{wq}{2^n} + \frac{w^2q}{2^{n+1}}.$$

Proof. We are going to rely on the H coefficients technique. Let us fix an adversary $\mathbf{A}$ against the prf-security of XORP$[w]$, which is allowed at most q queries. We assume without loss of generality that $\mathbf{A}$ is deterministic (as it is time-unbounded), never repeats queries, and always makes exactly q queries. The transcript τ of the interaction of $\mathbf{A}$ with its oracle can be written as

$$\tau = \{(X_1, Y_{1,1} \| \dots \| Y_{1,w}), \dots, (X_q, Y_{q,1} \| \dots \| Y_{q,w})\},$$

where, for $i = 1, \dots, q$ and $j = 1, \dots, w$, one has $|Y_{i,j}| = n$. We say that an attainable transcript τ is bad if at least one of those conditions is satisfied:

- there exists $(i,j) \in (q] \times (w]$ such that $Y_{i,j} = 0^n$;
- there exists $(i,j,j') \in (q] \times (w] \times (w]$ such that $j \neq j'$ and $Y_{i,j} = Y_{i,j'}$.

The set $\mathscr{T}_{\mathrm{good}}$ consists in all attainable transcripts which are not bad. Since the $Y_{i,j}$ values are uniformly random and independent in the ideal world, it is easy to see that one has

$$\Pr\left(\mathrm{T}_{\mathrm{ideal}} \in \mathscr{T} \setminus \mathscr{T}_{\mathrm{good}}\right) \leq \frac{wq}{2^n} + \frac{w^2q}{2^{n+1}}. \tag{10}$$

Let us fix any good transcript τ. By taking $X'_{i,j} = \pi\left(\langle j \rangle_s \| X_i\right)$, the event $\mathrm{T}_{\mathrm{real}} = \tau$ can easily be turned into the following system of bivariate affine equations:

$$X'_{1,0} \oplus X'_{1,1} = Y_{1,1} \qquad\qquad X'_{1,0} \oplus X'_{q,1} = Y_{q,1}$$
$$\vdots \qquad\qquad \dots \qquad\qquad \vdots$$
$$X'_{1,0} \oplus X'_{1,w} = Y_{1,w} \qquad\qquad X'_{1,0} \oplus X'_{q,w} = Y_{q,w}$$

Since τ is a good transcript, the corresponding graph clearly has q components, of size $w+1$, and the sum of labels of edges of any path in the graph is not 0^n. Let us denote N the number of pairwise distinct solutions of this system. Then the probability that $X'_{i,j} = \pi\left(\langle j \rangle_s \| X_i\right)$ for all pairs (i,j) is exactly $1/(2^n)^{\underline{(w+1)q}}$. Hence, one has

$$\frac{\Pr\left(\mathrm{T}_{\mathrm{real}} = \tau\right)}{\Pr\left(\mathrm{T}_{\mathrm{ideal}} = \tau\right)} \geq N\frac{(2^n)^{wq}}{(2^n)^{\underline{(w+1)q}}} \geq 1, \tag{11}$$

where the last inequality results from the application of Theorem 1. Combining Lemma 4 with Eqs. (10) and (11) ends the proof of Theorem 2.

---

[6] We do not claim novelty for this Theorem, but we present its proof for illustration purpose.

4.3 Optimally Secure Variable-Input-Length PRFs

In [7], Cogliati, Jha and Nandi propose several constructions to build optimally secure variable-input-length (VIL) PRFs from secret random permutations. Those schemes combine a diblock almost collision-free universal hash function with a finalization function based on the Benes construction [2]. The most
efficient variant, whose representation can be found in Fig. 2, relies on two independent permutations, and its security proof [7, Theorem 7.3] involves the use
of Mirror Theory for a single permutation.

First, let us recall the necessary definition for keyed hash function. A
$(\mathcal{K}, \mathcal{X}, \mathcal{Y})$-keyed function H is said to be ϵ-almost universal (AU) hash function
if for any distinct $X, X' \in \mathcal{X}$, we have

$$\mathsf{Pr}_{KK \leftarrow\!\!{}_\$ \, \mathcal{K}} \left(H_{KK}(X) = H_{KK}(X') \right) \leq \epsilon. \tag{12}$$

Let us fix a non-empty set $\mathcal{X} \subset \{0,1\}^*$, and let H be a $(\mathcal{K}, \mathcal{X}, \mathcal{Y})$-keyed function
that processes its inputs in n-bit blocks. H is said to be (q, σ, ϵ)-Almost θ-
Collision-free Universal (or ACU_θ) if, for every $X^q \in (\mathcal{X})_q$ such that X^q contains
at most σ blocks, one has $\Pr[C \geq \theta] \leq \epsilon$, where

$$C := |\{(i,j) : 1 \leq i < j \leq q, H_K(X_i) = H_K(X_j)\}|.$$

Finally, we say that a pair $H = (H_1, H_2)$ of two $(\mathcal{K}, \mathcal{X}, \mathcal{Y})$-keyed hash functions
H_1, H_2 is $(q, \sigma, \epsilon_2, \epsilon_1)$-Diblock ACU_q (or DbACU_q) if H is (q, σ, ϵ_2)-AU and H_1,
H_2 are (q, σ, ϵ_1)-ACU_q.

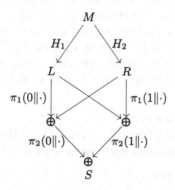

Fig. 2. Representation of the 2k-HtmB-p2$[H]$ based on two uniformly random and
independent n-bit permutations π_1, π_2. An edge (u, v) with label g denotes the mapping
$v = g(u)$. Unlabelled edges are identity mapping. The inputs to the functions $\pi_i(j\|\cdot)$
are first truncated before the application of π_i.

Having defined the required security notion for the underlying hash function,
the following result holds.

Theorem 3. *For* $\epsilon_1, \epsilon_2, \sigma \geq 0$, $q \leq 2^n/12n^2$, *and* $(q, \sigma, \epsilon_2, \epsilon_1)$-*DbACU$_q$ hash function H instantiated with key $K \xleftarrow{\$} \mathcal{K}$, the prf-advantage of any distinguisher* **A** *that makes at most q queries against* 2k-HtmB-p2$[H]$ *is given by*

$$\mathbf{Adv}_{\text{2k-HtmB-p2}[H]}^{\text{prf}}(\mathbf{A}) \leq \frac{128q^2}{2^{3n}} + \frac{136q^2}{2^{2n}} + \frac{8q}{2^n} + \epsilon_2 + 2\epsilon_1.$$

The complete proof of this result is exactly the same as the one of [7, Theorem 7.3] where [40, Theorem 6] is replaced with Theorem 1.

Proof Sketch. Let us denote with M_i, for $i = 1, \ldots, q$, the inputs from **A**. We introduce several random variables: $L_i = H_1(M_i)$, $R_i = H_2(M_i)$, $X_i = \text{trunc}_{n-1}(\pi_1(0\|L_i) \oplus R_i)$ and $Y_i = \text{trunc}_{n-1}(\pi_1(1\|R_i) \oplus L_i)$, so that

$$S_i = \pi_2(0\|X_i) \oplus \pi_2(1\|Y_i).$$

Additionally, at the end of the interaction of **A** with its oracle, we release the values of the L_is, R_is, X_is, and Y_is. In the real world, we release the actual values, while in the ideal world we simply draw uniformly random keys for H_1 and H_2, along with a lazily sampled uniformly random π_1. Note that this can only increase the advantage of an adversary, so this can be done without loss of generality.

In order to apply Theorem 1, we need to make sure that the system (S) consisting of the q equations

$$S_i = \pi_2(0\|X_i) \oplus \pi_2(1\|Y_i)$$

satisfies the initial conditions. We recall that an alternating trail of length k is a sequence $(i_1, \ldots, i_{k+1})$ such that either $X_{i_j} = X_{i_{j+1}}$ or $Y_{i_j} = Y_{i_{j+1}}$ for $j = 1, \ldots, k$, and consecutive equalities do not involve the same family of variables (i.e. an equality in X should be followed with an equality in Y). Moreover, an alternating cycle is a special type of alternating trail of even length, such that $i_{k+1} = i_1$. We say that a transcript τ is bad if at least one of the following conditions hold:

- τ contains an alternating cycle;
- τ contains an alternating trail $(i_1, \ldots, i_{k+1})$ such that $\oplus_{j=1}^{k+1} S_{i_j} = 0$;
- the largest block of equalities contains at least $n + 1$ variables.[7]

In [7], the authors prove that

$$\Pr\left(\text{T}_{\text{ideal}} \in \mathcal{T} \setminus \mathcal{T}_{\text{good}}\right) \leq \frac{128q^2}{2^{3n}} + \frac{136q^2}{2^{2n}} + \frac{8q}{2^n} + \epsilon_2 + 2\epsilon_1. \tag{13}$$

Moreover, for any good transcript τ, one has

$$\frac{\Pr\left(\text{T}_{\text{real}} = \tau\right)}{\Pr\left(\text{T}_{\text{ideal}} = \tau\right)} = \frac{s2^{nq}}{(2^n)^{q_X + q_Y}} \geq 1, \tag{14}$$

---

[7] We say that two variables are in the same block of equalities if there exists an alternating trail involving both variables.

where s denotes the number of p.d. solutions to the system (S) of equations, and q_X (resp. q_Y) the number of pairwise distinct X_i (resp. Y_i) values, and the last inequality results from the application of Theorem 1. Combining Lemma 4 with Eqs. (13) and (14) ends the proof of Theorem 3.

4.4 Feistel Schemes

In [41], Patarin introduced the study of beyond-birthday-bound security of balanced and unbalanced Feistel schemes using Mirror Theory. Since our work has improved upon the bounds of the '$P_i \oplus P_j$ Theorem for any $\xi_{\max}$' used by Patarin, we present here the proof sketch of security analysis of six-round balanced Feistel scheme with our new improved bounds.

Definition of ψ^k. Suppose Func_n is the collection of all n-bit functions from $\{0,1\}^n$ to itself, and Perm_{2n} be the collection of all permutations on $\{0,1\}^{2n}$. Then for $f \in \mathsf{Func}_n$ and $L, R \in \{0,1\}^n$, $\psi(f) \in \mathsf{Perm}_{2n}$ is defined as follows:

$$\psi(f)[L, R] := [R, L \oplus f(R)]$$

In general, for $f_1, \cdots, f_k \in \mathsf{Func}_n$, $\psi^k(f_1, \cdots, f_k) \in \mathsf{Perm}_{2n}$ is defined as,

$$\psi^k(f_1, \cdots, f_k) := \psi(f_k) \circ \cdots \circ \psi(f_1).$$

The permutation $\psi^k(f_1, \cdots, f_k)$ is called a *balanced Feistel scheme with k rounds*. When $f_1, \cdots, f_k$ are randomly and independently chosen in Func_n, $\psi^k(f_1, \cdots, f_k)$ is called a *random Feistel scheme with k rounds*.

To analyse the PRP security of k-round Feistel scheme via the H-coefficient technique, given a transcript containing q query-response pairs

$$\tau := \{([L_i, R_i], [S_i, T_i]) : L_i, R_i, S_i, T_i \in \{0,1\}^n, i \in [q]\},$$

we would like to find out the probability of realizing this transcript in the real world,

$$\Pr(T_{\text{real}} = \tau) = \Pr_{\substack{(f_1, \cdots, f_k) \\ \leftarrow\$\ \mathsf{Func}_n^k}} \left(\psi^k(f_1, \cdots, f_k)[L_i, R_i] = [S_i, T_i]\ \forall i \in [q]\right) = \frac{H_k(\tau)}{|\mathsf{Func}_n|^k}$$

where,

$$H_k(\tau) := \left|\{(f_1, \cdots, f_k) \in \mathsf{Func}_n^k : \psi^k(f_1, \cdots, f_k)[L_i, R_i] = [S_i, T_i]\ \forall i \in [q]\}\right|$$

Note that, here, irrespective of whether the transcript was realized in the real or the ideal world, we will have that $[L_i, R_i], i \in [q]$ are pairwise distinct, and $[S_i, T_i], i \in [q]$ are pairwise distinct. There are no bad transcripts in the following analysis.

In Fig. 3 we have denoted the outputs of the successive rounds as follows:

$$[L_i, R_i] \xrightarrow{\psi(f_1)} [R_i, X_i] \xrightarrow{\psi(f_2)} [X_i, Y_i] \xrightarrow{\psi(f_3)} [Y_i, Z_i] \xrightarrow{\psi(f_4)} [Z_i, A_i] \xrightarrow{\psi(f_5)} [A_i, S_i] \xrightarrow{\psi(f_6)} [S_i, T_i]$$

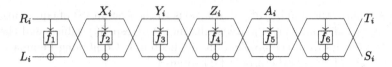

Fig. 3. Balanced Feistel scheme with 6 rounds

Viewing 6-round Feistel as $\psi^6(f_1, \cdots, f_6) = \psi(f_1) \circ \psi^4(f_2, \cdots, f_5) \circ \psi(f_6)$, we can write

$$H_6(\tau) = \sum_{f_1, f_6 \in \mathsf{Func}_n} H_4(\tau') \tag{15}$$

where

$$\tau' = \{([R_i, X_i], [A_i, S_i]) : X_i := L_i \oplus f_1(R_i), A_i := T_i \oplus f_6(S_i), i \in [q]\}$$

Frameworks for ψ^4. To calculate $H_4(\tau')$ we define a 'framework' as collection of equations of the form $Y_i = Y_j$ or $Z_i = Z_j$. We will say that two frameworks are equal if they imply exactly the same set of equalities in Y and Z. Let $\mathscr{F}$ be a framework. We will denote by $\mathsf{weight}(\mathscr{F})$ the number of $(Y_i, Z_i) \in (\{0,1\}^n)^2, i \in [q]$ that satisfy $\mathscr{F}$. If we denote $y_{\mathscr{F}}$ (resp., $z_{\mathscr{F}}$) the number of independent equalities of the form $Y_i = Y_j$ (resp., of the form $Z_i = Z_j$) in $\mathscr{F}$, then obviously we have $\mathsf{weight}(\mathscr{F}) = (N)^{\underline{q-y_{\mathscr{F}}}} \cdot (N)^{\underline{q-z_{\mathscr{F}}}}$

Note that, for a given framework $\mathscr{F}$, $Y_i = Y_j \in \mathscr{F} \implies f_3(Y_i) = f_3(Y_j)$, which is equivalent to saying $X_i \oplus Z_i = X_j \oplus Z_j$. Similarly, $Z_i = Z_j \in \mathscr{F} \implies Y_i \oplus A_i = Y_j \oplus A_j$. Moreover, $X_i = X_j \implies f_2(X_i) = f_2(X_j)$ which is equivalent to saying $R_i \oplus Y_i = R_j \oplus Y_j$. Similarly, $A_i = A_j \implies Z_i \oplus S_i = Z_j \oplus S_j$.

Let x be the number of independent equalities of the form $X_i = X_j, i \neq j$ and a be the number of independent equalities of the form $A_i = A_j, i \neq j$. Then by simple algebraic manipulation we have the following result.

Lemma 5 (exact formula for $H_4(\tau')$).

$$H_4(\tau') = |\mathsf{Func}_n|^4 \sum_{\mathscr{F}} \frac{[\#Y^q \ satisfying \ (C1)] \cdot [\#Z^q \ satisfying \ (C2)]}{N^{4q-x-y_{\mathscr{F}}-z_{\mathscr{F}}-a}} \tag{16}$$

where

$$(C1): \begin{cases} X_i = X_j \implies Y_i \oplus Y_j = R_i \oplus R_j \\ Z_i = Z_j \in \mathscr{F} \implies Y_i \oplus Y_j = A_i \oplus A_j \\ \text{The only equations } Y_i = Y_j, i < j, \text{ are exactly those implied by } \mathscr{F} \end{cases}$$

$$(C2): \begin{cases} A_i = A_j \implies Z_i \oplus Z_j = S_i \oplus S_j \\ Y_i = Y_j \in \mathscr{F} \implies Z_i \oplus Z_j = X_i \oplus X_j \\ \text{The only equations } Z_i = Z_j, i < j, \text{ are exactly those implied by } \mathscr{F} \end{cases}$$

The summation on the r.h.s. of Eq. (16) is taken over all possible frameworks $\mathscr{F}$.

A we can see $(C1)$ yields a system of difference equations in the variables Y^q, and $(C2)$ a system of difference equations in Z^q. To find the number of solutions to these systems of equations using Theorem 1, we have to ensure: (1) the systems are p.d.-consistent, (2) the conditions specified in the theorem, like the bound on the maximum component size, and that on the number of variables, is satisfied by the concerned systems.

Now the systems will be p.d. consistent if there is no cycle of non-zero label sum. To be on the safe side, we eliminate the possibility of any cycle whatsoever. Note that, there will be a cycle in the graph representing the system of difference equations in $(C1)$ (resp., $(C2)$) only if there is a 'circle in $X, Z_{\mathscr{F}}$' (resp., 'circle in $A, Y_{\mathscr{F}}$'), by which we mean that, for some $k \geq 3$, there is a cyclic tuple of indices $(i_1, \cdots, i_k)$, with $i_1, \cdots, i_{k-1}$ pairwise distinct and $i_k = i_1$, such that for all $j \in [k-1]$, either we have $X_{i_j} = X_{i_{j+1}}$ or we have $Z_{i_j} = Z_{i_{j+1}} \in \mathscr{F}$. We define a circle in $A, Y_{\mathscr{F}}$ similarly.

Following the same arguments there will be component of size ξ in the graph representing the system of difference equations in $(C1)$ (resp., $(C2)$) only if there is a 'line in $X, Z_{\mathscr{F}}$' (resp., 'line in $A, Y_{\mathscr{F}}$') of length ξ, by which we mean that, there are $\xi + 1$ distinct indices $i_1, \cdots, i_{\xi+1}$ such that for all $j \in [\xi]$, either $X_{i_j} = X_{i_{j+1}}$ or $Z_{i_j} = Z_{i_j} \in \mathscr{F}$. We define a line in $A, Y_{\mathscr{F}}$ similarly.

Good Framework. We call a framework for ψ^4, $\mathscr{F}$, a *good framework*, if it does not result in any of the following:

1. a circle in $X, Z_{\mathscr{F}}$
2. a circle in $A, Y_{\mathscr{F}}$
3. a line in $X, Z_{\mathscr{F}}$ of length $\geq n$
4. a line in $A, Y_{\mathscr{F}}$ of length $\geq n$

From elaborate probability calculations done in Appendix C of [41] we have the following result:

Lemma 6 ([41]). *For a realizable transcript* $\tau = \{([L_i, R_i], [S_i, T_i]) : i \in [q]\}$, *when* $f_1, f_6 \leftarrow_\$ \mathsf{Func}_n$ *and* $\mathscr{F}$ *is randomly chosen (i.e., with probability proportional to* $\mathsf{weight}(\mathscr{F})$*), then*

$$\Pr[\mathscr{F} \text{ is a good framework}] \geq 1 - \frac{8q}{N}.$$

If a good framework $\mathscr{F}$ is chosen, then the systems of difference equations in $(C1)$ and $(C2)$ are p.d.-consistent and satisfy the conditions of Theorem 1 with $\xi_{\max} \leq n$. Now the system of difference equations in $(C1)$ (resp., $C2$) has $x + z_{\mathscr{F}}$ equations in $q - y_{\mathscr{F}}$ variables (resp., $a + y_{\mathscr{F}}$ equations in $q - z_{\mathscr{F}}$ variables) and hence by Theorem 1 has at least $(N)^{\underline{q - y_{\mathscr{F}}}}/N^{x + z_{\mathscr{F}}}$ solutions (resp., $(N)^{\underline{q - z_{\mathscr{F}}}}/N^{a + y_{\mathscr{F}}}$ solutions) if $q \leq N/12(\log_2 N)^2$. Then from Eq. (15) and Eq. (16) we get that

$$H_6(\tau) \geq \frac{|\mathsf{Func}_n|^4}{N^{4q}} \sum_{f_1, f_6 \in \mathsf{Func}_n} \sum_{\text{good } \mathscr{F}} \underbrace{(N)^{\underline{q - y_{\mathscr{F}}}} \cdot (N)^{\underline{q - z_{\mathscr{F}}}}}_{\mathsf{weight}(\mathscr{F})} \overset{(\star)}{\geq} \frac{|\mathsf{Func}_n|^6}{N^{2q}}\left(1 - \frac{8q}{N}\right)$$

where ($\star$) follows from Lemma 6 and the fact that $\sum_{\mathcal{F}} \text{weight}(\mathcal{F}) = N^{2q}$. Thus, we have a for a realizable transcript τ

$$\frac{\Pr[T_{\text{real}} = \tau]}{\Pr[T_{\text{ideal}} = \tau]} = \frac{\frac{1}{N^{2q}}\left(1 - \frac{8q}{N}\right)}{1/(N^2)^{\underline{q}}} \geq 1 - \frac{8q}{N} - \frac{q^2}{N^2}.$$

Summarizing we have the following result.

Theorem 4. *If $q \leq \frac{2^n}{12n^2}$, then for every CPCA-2 adversary[8] $\mathbf{A}$ with q adaptive chosen plaintext or chosen ciphertext queries, we have*

$$\mathbf{Adv}^{\text{sprp}}_{\psi^6(f_1,\cdots,f_6)}(\mathbf{A}) \leq \frac{8q}{2^n} + \frac{q^2}{2^{2n}}.$$

where $f_1, \cdots, f_6 \leftarrow_{\$} \mathsf{Func}_n$.

4.5   A Comparative Study of the Security Bounds

First we consider the security bounds attainable for the above constructions without using Mirror Theory.

1. There exists another proof of optimal n-bit security for the XORP[w] construction [6], that does not rely on Mirror Theory. Instead, it uses the so-called χ^2 technique [11].
2. In [7] Cogliati et al. proposes several VIL PRF constructions from secret random permutations using the Hash-then-modified-Benes method. To obtain optimal security without using Mirror Theory they proposed the candidate 2k-HtmB-p1[H], which requires 6 secret random permutations. In comparison 2k-HtmB-p2[H] only needs 4 secret random permutations (obtained from domain separating two random permutations) to attain n-bit security. However, the only existing security proof of the latter depends crucially on Mirror Theory.
3. Six-round Feistel construction can only be shown to be birthday-bound secure without using Mirror Theory, no better security proof is known.

Also, the optimal n-bit security bounds for the above three constructions, are obtained in [7, 22] and [41], respectively, by using the following conjectured version of Mirror Theory [40, Theorem 6], whose proof is incomplete:

"Theorem $P_i \oplus P_j$" for any $\xi_{\max}$. *Let (A) be a set of a equation $P_i \oplus P_j = \lambda_k$ with α variables such that:*

1. *We have no circle in P in the equations (A).*
2. *We have no more than $\xi_{\max}$ indices in the same block.*
3. *By linearity from (A) we cannot generate an equation $P_i = P_j$ with $i \neq j$.*

---

[8] CPCA-2 adversary here means an adversary that adaptively queries Chosen Plaintexts and Chosen Ciphertexts.

Then: if $\xi_{\max}^2 \alpha \ll 2^n$, we have $H_\alpha \geq J_\alpha$. *More precisely the fuzzy condition* $\xi_{\max}^2 \alpha \ll 2^n$ *can be written with the explicit bound:* $(\xi_{\max} - 1)^2 \alpha \leq 2^n/67$.

In the above theorem conditions 1 and 3 correspond to the p.d.-consistency condition of this paper, and condition 2 correspond to the condition that the maximum component size of the corresponding graph is $\xi_{\max}$. α in the above theorem is replaced by p in Theorem 1 of this paper. Also using the notation of [40], $H_\alpha \geq J_\alpha$ translates to: the number of p.d. solutions of the system of equations (A) is $\geq (2^n)\underline{\alpha}/2^{nm} = (N)\underline{\alpha}/N^m$, which is exactly the bound obtained in this paper. However we notice the following important differences:

1. The above theorem is for any $\xi_{\max}$, while Theorem 1 of this paper works for $\xi_{\max}$ of the order $O(N^{1/4})$.
2. The bound on α or p in the above theorem is $N/67(\xi_{\max} - 1)^2$, while the one attained in Theorem 1 of this paper is $N/12\xi_{\max}^2$, which is slightly better.

5   Conclusion and Future Work

In this work, we present the first complete and verifiable proof of the $P_i \oplus P_j$ Theorem with any $\xi_{\max}$. Our proof builds on the previous works on this subject by reusing the overall strategy. However, our core novelty is the use of the link-deletion equation, which allows a better proof by induction that introduces a much smaller number of terms. This improvement leads to a shorter proof and a slightly better bound, as long as $\xi_{\max}$ is of the order $O(N^{1/4})$. As an application, we give proofs of n-bit security for the XORP and 2k-HtmB-p2 constructions, thus confirming the results from [22] and [7]. Theorem 1 is also used to revisit the security proofs of balanced Feistel schemes [32,41] and prove the optimal security of six rounds Feistel scheme [32,41]. Moreover, using our result, one can also show an asymptotically optimal security bound for DWCDM [15,16] construction. In fact, the H coefficients technique can be used to transform many cryptographic security proofs into Mirror Theory problems. However, these problems may sometimes be more general than the one we target in this work. For example, in this work we deal with pairwise distinctness of the solution to a system of equations, which is same as finding solutions to the given system of equations, along with a system of non-equations of the form $X_j \oplus X_k \neq 0^n$ for all $j \neq k$. However, when dealing with constructions like the Feistel cipher where the round functions are permutations, we find that in addition to the conditions of the form $(C1)$ obtained in Lemma 5, we also get that $X_i \neq X_j \implies Y_i \oplus Y_j \neq R_i \oplus R_j$, i.e. non-equations with non-zero labels. This indicates to the following more general problem, that is yet to be solved:

OPEN PROBLEM 1. Find the lower bound to the number of solutions to a system of equations and a *possibly non-homogeneous system of non-equations.*

Studying variants of Theorem 1, as the one mentioned above, would help to improve security bounds for current and future cryptographic constructions:

OPEN PROBLEM 2. Generalize Theorem 1 for *groups of exponent* $\neq 2$. Then it can be used for security proof of Feistel network whose operator is modular addition, and not $\oplus$ (which is important for Format-Preserving Encryption).

OPEN PROBLEM 3. Generalize Theorem 1 for $\xi_{max} > O(2^{n/4}/\sqrt{n})$. This might be used for optimal security proof of nonce misuse resistant MAC scheme nEHtM. Note that the bound does not always hold when ξ_{max} gets close to $2^{n/2}$. A counterexample can be found in [32, p. 225].

OPEN PROBLEM 4. Generalize Theorem 1 for the case when *the solutions are chosen from a proper subset of* $\{0,1\}^n$. This is applicable for ideal-permutation-based keyed constructions. As an adversary can make direct queries to the ideal permutation P, some inputs and outputs are fixed beforehand.

OPEN PROBLEM 5. Generalize for *systems of equations having more than just two variables*, for example, say, $X_1 \oplus X_2 \oplus X_3 \oplus X_4 = 0$. This will prove optimal security for constructions like the ones mentioned in [8].

Also, there are two other conjectured Mirror-Theory-like results [32, Conjecture 14.1 & 14.2] about the number of permutations g and h such that $g * h$ is equal to a given function f, for any commutative group law $*$.

Acknowledgements. Part of this work was carried out in the framework of the French-German-Center for Cybersecurity, a collaboration of CISPA and LORIA, while Benoît Cogliati was employed at the CISPA Helmholtz Center for Information Security.

A   Postponed Proofs

A.1   Proof of Lemma 2

We fix $S \in \gamma \subseteq \lambda$ where $|\gamma| = \alpha$ and a set U with $|U| = \ell + 1$ disjoint with S. Let $\tau := \gamma_{+U}$ and $\tau' := \gamma_{-S+(S \sqcup U)}$. In words, γ is a set-system that is included in λ, U is any subset of $\mathscr{G}$ of size $\ell + 1$, and S is an element of γ. Then, τ corresponds to the $\gamma \cup \{U\}$, while τ' corresponds to τ after S and U have been merged. Looking back at Fig. 1, τ and τ' would correspond respectively to the second and third graphs. We assume that γ, U, S are chosen in such a manner that $|P(\tau) - P(\tau')| = D(\alpha, \ell)$. Now we prove the inequality in two cases.

Case $|U| = 1$. In this case, let $U = \{x\}$. Then $P(\tau) = P(\gamma) \cdot (1 - \|\gamma\|/2^n)$ from Eq. (1). Also $\tau'_{-x|S \sqcup U} = \gamma$. Hence from link deletion equation, Eq. (5),

$$P(\tau') = P(\gamma) - N^{-1} \sum_{(\delta, S') \in I} P(\tau'_{\delta, S'})$$

where $I := I_{x,S} = \{(\delta, S') : x \oplus \delta \in S' \in \gamma_{-S}, S' \oplus \delta \text{ is disjoint with } S\}$. For $z' \in S' \in \gamma_{-S}$, $(x \oplus z, S') \notin I$ if and only if there exists $y \in S$ and $w \in S'$

such that $x \oplus y = z \oplus w$. Thus $|I| \geq \sum_{S' \in \gamma_{-s}} \left(|S'| - \sum_{y \in S} 2\delta_{S'}(x \oplus y) \right) = \|\gamma\| - |S| - \sum_{y \in S} 2\delta_{\gamma_{-s}}(x \oplus y) \geq \|\gamma\| - \|\gamma\|_{\max} \cdot 2\delta_\gamma$. Hence

$$D(\alpha, 0) = |P(\tau) - P(\tau')| = \left| \frac{\|\gamma\|}{N} P(\gamma) - N^{-1} \sum_{(\delta, S') \in I} P(\tau'_{\delta, S'}) \right|$$

$$\overset{(\star)}{\leq} N^{-1} \sum_{(\delta, S') \in I} |P(\gamma) - P(\tau'_{\delta, S'})| + \frac{2\Delta_\gamma \|\gamma\|_{\max} \cdot P(\lambda)}{N \left(1 - \frac{\|\lambda \backslash \gamma\|_{\max} \times \|\gamma\|}{N} \right)^{|\lambda \backslash \gamma|}}$$

$$\leq \frac{\|\gamma_{-s}\|_{\max}}{N} \sum_{S' \in \gamma \backslash S} D(\alpha - 1, |S'| - 1) + \frac{2\Delta_\gamma \|\gamma\|_{\max} \cdot P(\lambda)}{N \left(1 - \frac{\|\lambda \backslash \gamma\|_{\max} \times \|\gamma\|}{N} \right)^{|\lambda \backslash \gamma|}},$$

where the last term in $(\star)$ is obtained from the initial condition Eq. (4).

Case $|U| \geq 2$. Fix $x \in U$. By link-deletion equation, we have

$$P(\tau) = P(\tau_{-x|U}) - \frac{1}{N} \sum_{(\delta, S') \in I} P(\tau_{\delta, S'})$$

$$P(\tau') = P(\tau'_{-x|S \sqcup U}) - \frac{1}{N} \sum_{(\delta, S') \in I'} P(\tau'_{\delta, S'}),$$

where

$$I := I_{x|U} = \{(\delta, S') : x \oplus \delta \in S' \in \gamma, \ S' \oplus \delta \text{ is disjoint with } U \setminus x\},$$
$$I' := I_{x|S \sqcup U} = \{(\delta, S') : x \oplus \delta \in S' \in \gamma_{-s}, \ S' \oplus \delta \text{ is disjoint with } S \sqcup U \setminus x\}.$$

It is easy to see that $I' \subseteq I$. If $(\delta, S') \in I \setminus I'$, then,

- either $S' = S$ and $\delta = x \oplus y$ for some $y \in S$, such that $S \oplus (x \oplus y)$ is disjoint with $U \setminus x$ or
- $S' \in \gamma \setminus S$ and $\delta = x \oplus z$ for some $z \in S'$, such that $S' \oplus (x \oplus z)$ is disjoint with $U \setminus x$ but not disjoint with $S \sqcup (U \setminus x)$.

The first case can contribute at most $|S|$. The second case will happen if for some $z, w \in S'$, and $y \in S$, $z \oplus w = x \oplus y$. Thus

$$|I \setminus I'| \leq |S| + \sum_{y \in S} \delta_{\gamma_{-s}}(x \oplus y) \leq \|\gamma\|_{\max} \cdot 2\Delta_\gamma.$$

Hence, we have the following:

$$D(\alpha, \ell) = |\mathsf{P}(\tau) - \mathsf{P}(\tau')|$$

$$\leq |\mathsf{P}(\tau_{-x}) - \mathsf{P}(\tau'_{-x})| + N^{-1} \sum_{(\delta, S') \in I'} |\mathsf{P}(\tau_{\delta, S'}) - \mathsf{P}(\tau'_{\delta, S'})| + \sum_{(\delta, S') \in I \setminus I'} \mathsf{P}(\tau_{\delta, S'})/N$$

$$\leq D(\alpha, \ell - 1) + \frac{\|\gamma_{-S}\|_{\max}}{N} \sum_{S' \in \gamma_{-S}} D(\alpha - 1, \ell + |S'| - 1) + \frac{2\Delta_\gamma \|\gamma\|_{\max} \cdot \mathsf{P}(\lambda)}{N \left(1 - \frac{\|\lambda \setminus \gamma\|_{\max} \times \|\gamma\|}{N}\right)^{|\lambda \setminus \gamma|}}.$$

$$(17)$$

The last inequality follows from the observation that $\tau_{\delta, S'}$ and $\tau'_{\delta, S'}$ are considered when we take maximum to compute $D(\alpha - 1, \ell + |S'| - 1)$. Moreover, from our initial condition Eq. (4),

$$\mathsf{P}(\tau_{\delta, S'}) \leq \mathsf{P}(\gamma) \leq \mathsf{P}(\lambda) / \left(1 - \frac{\|\lambda \setminus \gamma\|_{\max} \times \|\gamma\|}{N}\right)^{|\lambda \setminus \gamma|}$$

Now, taking upper bounds of the total size terms, and adding some positive terms in the middle sum, and noting that $\Delta_\gamma \leq \Delta_\lambda$[9], the inequality, Eq. (17) can be easily modified to the theorem statement, Eq. (7).

A.2   Proof of Recursive Inequality Lemma

Let us denote by an ordered tuple of integers from $[q]$, as $i^k := (i_1, \cdots, i_k) \in [q]^k$. Note that, for all positive integer j, $e^j \geq \frac{j^j}{j!}$ and so $1/j! \leq (e/j)^j$, and we have

$$\binom{m}{j} \leq \frac{m^j}{j!} \leq (em/j)^j. \tag{18}$$

This inequality will be frequently used for the proof of this lemma. We also use the following fact extensively: for $r < 1$, $\sum_{j \geq i} r^j \leq \frac{r^i}{1-r}$.

We state the following claim, which follows from iterated applications of the recursive inequality.

Claim 1. *For any* $0 \leq d \leq \xi n$, *and* $0 \leq \ell < \xi - 1$ *we have*

$$a_{0, \ell} \leq \sum_{k=\lceil \frac{d-\ell}{\xi} \rceil}^{d} \binom{d}{k} \sum_{i^k \in [q]^k} a_{k, k + \sum_{j=1}^{k} \ell_{i_j} - d} + C \sum_{i=0}^{d-1} \sum_{j=\lceil \frac{i-\ell}{\xi} \rceil}^{i} \binom{i}{j} (4\xi e)^{-j}. \tag{19}$$

---

[9] Since $\gamma \subseteq \lambda$, we have $\sum_{S \in \gamma} \delta_S(z) \leq \sum_{S' \in \lambda} \delta_{S'}(z)$ for every $z \in \{0, 1\}^n$, since every $S \in \gamma$ is subset of some $S' \in \lambda$. So taking maximum over all $z \in \{0, 1\}^n$, on both sides would give us $\Delta_\gamma \leq \Delta_\lambda$.

Proof of the Claim. We prove the claim by induction on d. The result holds trivially for $d = 1$ (by applying $d = \ell = 0$ in Eq. (9)). Now we prove the statement for $d_0 + 1$, assuming it true for d_0. Therefore, we have

$$
a_{0,\ell} \leq \sum_{k=\left\lceil \frac{d_0-\ell}{\xi} \right\rceil}^{d_0} \binom{d_0}{k} \sum_{i^k \in [q]^k} a_{k,k+\sum_{j=1}^k \ell_{i_j} - d_0} + C \sum_{i=0}^{d_0-1} \sum_{j=\left\lceil \frac{i-\ell}{\xi} \right\rceil}^{i} \binom{i}{j} (4\xi e)^{-j}
$$

$$
\leq \sum_{k=\left\lceil \frac{d_0-\ell}{\xi} \right\rceil}^{d_0} \binom{d_0}{k} \sum_{i^k \in [q]^k} \left(\sum_{i_{k+1} \in [q]} a_{k+1,k+1+\sum_{j=1}^{k+1} \ell_{i_j} - (d_0+1)} + C \cdot (4\xi eq)^{-k} \right)
$$

$$
+ \sum_{k=\left\lceil \frac{d_0-\ell}{\xi} \right\rceil}^{d_0} \binom{d_0}{k} \sum_{i^k \in [q]^k} a_{k,k+\sum_{j=1}^k \ell_{i_j} - (d_0+1)} + C \sum_{i=0}^{d_0-1} \sum_{j=\left\lceil \frac{i-\ell}{\xi} \right\rceil}^{i} \binom{i}{j} (4\xi e)^{-j}
$$

$$
\leq \sum_{k=\left\lceil \frac{d_0+1-\ell}{\xi} \right\rceil}^{d_0+1} \binom{d_0}{k-1} \sum_{i^{k-1} \in [q]^{k-1}} \sum_{i_k \in [q]} a_{k,k+\sum_{j=1}^k \ell_{i_j} - (d_0+1)}
$$

$$
+ \sum_{k=\left\lceil \frac{d_0+1-\ell}{\xi} \right\rceil}^{d_0+1} \binom{d_0}{k} \sum_{i^k \in [q]^k} a_{k,k+\sum_{j=1}^k \ell_{i_j} - (d_0+1)} + C \sum_{i=0}^{d_0} \sum_{j=\left\lceil \frac{i-\ell}{\xi} \right\rceil}^{i} \binom{i}{j} (4\xi e)^{-j}.
$$

The range of the first and second summations has deliberately been taken to start from $\lceil (d_0+1-\ell)/\xi \rceil \leq \lceil (d_0-\ell)/\xi \rceil + 1$, because if $k < \lceil (d_0+1-\ell)/\xi \rceil$, then $k + \sum_{j=1}^k \ell_{i_j} - (d_0+1) \leq k\xi - (d_0+1) < 0$ and hence $a_{k,k+\sum_{j=1}^k \ell_{i_j} - (d_0+1)} = 0$. Now we can see that the coefficient of $\sum_{i^k \in [q]^k} a_{k,k+\sum_{j=1}^k - (d_0+1)}$ in the above summation is bounded by $\binom{d_0}{k-1} + \binom{d_0}{k} = \binom{d_0+1}{k}$. This concludes the proof of the claim. $\qquad\qquad\square$

Proof of Lemma 3. Let us take $d = \xi n$. In that case, Claim 1 becomes

$$
a_{0,\ell} \leq \sum_{k=\left\lceil \frac{\xi n-\ell}{\xi} \right\rceil}^{\xi n} \binom{\xi n}{k} \sum_{i^k \in [q]^k} a_{k,k+\sum_{j=1}^k \ell_{i_j} - \xi n} + C \sum_{i=0}^{\xi n-1} \sum_{j=\left\lceil \frac{i-\ell}{\xi} \right\rceil}^{i} \binom{i}{j} (4\xi e)^{-j}.
$$

We are going to upper bound both terms of the sum in subsequent turns. For the first term, note that one has $k \geq n - \frac{\ell}{\xi} > n - 1$ since $\ell < \xi - 1$ by definition. This implies that

$$
\binom{\xi n}{k} \leq \left(\frac{e\xi n}{k} \right)^k \leq \left(\frac{e\xi n}{n-1} \right)^k \leq (2e\xi)^k.
$$

Hence, using the initial bound, one has

$$
\sum_{k=\left\lceil \frac{\xi n-\ell}{\xi} \right\rceil}^{\xi n} \binom{\xi n}{k} \sum_{i^k \in [q]^k} a_{k,k+\sum_{j=1}^k \ell_{i_j} - \xi n} \leq \sum_{k=\left\lceil \frac{\xi n-\ell}{\xi} \right\rceil}^{\xi n} (2e\xi)^k q^k (4\xi eq)^{-k} \leq \frac{4}{2^n} \leq \frac{4}{N}
$$

As for the second term, we make the following observation: For $\xi k < i \leq \xi(k+1)$, $k \in (n-1]$, $j \geq \lceil \frac{i-\ell}{\xi} \rceil \geq k$, and hence

$$\binom{i}{j} \leq \left(\frac{ei}{j}\right)^j \leq \left(\frac{e\xi(k+1)}{k}\right)^j \leq (2e\xi)^j.$$

For $0 \leq i \leq \xi$ and $j \geq 1$, $\binom{i}{j} \leq \left(\frac{ei}{j}\right)^j \leq (e\xi)^j$. Thus, we are going to break the sum into two parts:

$$\sum_{i=0}^{\xi n-1} \sum_{j=\lceil \frac{i-\ell}{\xi} \rceil}^{i} \binom{i}{j}(4\xi e)^{-j} = \sum_{i=0}^{\xi} \sum_{j=\lceil \frac{i-\ell}{\xi} \rceil}^{i} \binom{i}{j}(4\xi e)^{-j} + \sum_{i=\xi+1}^{\xi n-1} \sum_{j=\lceil \frac{i-\ell}{\xi} \rceil}^{i} \binom{i}{j}(4\xi e)^{-j}$$

$$\leq \xi + 1 + \sum_{i=0}^{\xi} \sum_{j=1}^{i} (e\xi)^j (4e\xi)^{-j} + \sum_{i=\xi+1}^{\xi n-1} \sum_{j=\lceil i/\xi \rceil-1}^{i} (2e\xi)^j (4e\xi)^{-j}$$

$$\leq \xi + 1 + \frac{\xi+1}{3} + 4 \sum_{i=\xi+1}^{\xi n-1} \frac{1}{2^{\lceil i/\xi \rceil}}$$

$$\overset{(1)}{\leq} \frac{4}{3}(\xi+1) + 2\xi \overset{(2)}{\leq} 4\xi,$$

where the last inequality follows from the fact that $\xi \geq 2$.

References

1. Data encryption standard. Federal Information Processing Standards Publication 112 (1999)
2. Aiello, W., Venkatesan, R.: Foiling birthday attacks in length-doubling transformations. In: Maurer, U. (ed.) EUROCRYPT 1996. LNCS, vol. 1070, pp. 307–320. Springer, Heidelberg (1996). https://doi.org/10.1007/3-540-68339-9_27
3. Bellare, M., Krovetz, T., Rogaway, P.: Luby-Rackoff backwards: increasing security by making block ciphers non-invertible. In: Nyberg, K. (ed.) EUROCRYPT 1998. LNCS, vol. 1403, pp. 266–280. Springer, Heidelberg (1998). https://doi.org/10.1007/BFb0054132
4. Morris, B., Rogaway, P., Stegers, T.: How to encipher messages on a small domain. In: Halevi, S. (ed.) CRYPTO 2009. LNCS, vol. 5677, pp. 286–302. Springer, Heidelberg (2009). https://doi.org/10.1007/978-3-642-03356-8_17
5. Bhattacharjee, A., Dutta, A., List, E., Nandi, M.: Cencpp* - beyond-birthday-secure encryption from public permutations (2020)
6. Bhattacharya, S., Nandi, M.: Revisiting variable output length XOR pseudorandom function. IACR Trans. Symmetric Cryptol. **2018**(1), 314–335 (2018). https://doi.org/10.13154/tosc.v2018.i1.314-335
7. Cogliati, B., Jha, A., Nandi, M.: How to build optimally secure PRFs using block ciphers. In: Moriai, S., Wang, H. (eds.) ASIACRYPT 2020. LNCS, vol. 12491, pp. 754–784. Springer, Cham (2020). https://doi.org/10.1007/978-3-030-64837-4_25
8. Cogliati, B., Lampe, R., Patarin, J.: The indistinguishability of the XOR of k permutations. In: Cid, C., Rechberger, C. (eds.) FSE 2014. LNCS, vol. 8540, pp. 285–302. Springer, Heidelberg (2015). https://doi.org/10.1007/978-3-662-46706-0_15

9. Cogliati, B., Patarin, J.: Mirror theory: a simple proof of the pi+pj theorem with xi_max=2. Cryptology ePrint Archive, Report 2020/734 (2020). https://eprint. iacr.org/2020/734

10. Cogliati, B., Seurin, Y.: EWCDM: an efficient, beyond-birthday secure, nonce-misuse resistant MAC. In: Robshaw, M., Katz, J. (eds.) CRYPTO 2016. LNCS, vol. 9814, pp. 121–149. Springer, Heidelberg (2016). https://doi.org/10.1007/978-3-662-53018-4_5

11. Dai, W., Hoang, V.T., Tessaro, S.: Information-theoretic indistinguishability via the chi-squared method. In: Katz, J., Shacham, H. (eds.) CRYPTO 2017. LNCS, vol. 10403, pp. 497–523. Springer, Cham (2017). https://doi.org/10.1007/978-3-319-63697-9_17

12. Datta, N., Dutta, A., Dutta, K.: Improved security bound of (E/D)WCDM. IACR Trans. Symmetric Cryptol. **2021**(4), 138–176 (2021). https://doi.org/10.46586/tosc.v2021.i4.138-176

13. Datta, N., Dutta, A., Nandi, M., Paul, G.: Double-block hash-then-sum: a paradigm for constructing BBB secure PRF. IACR Trans. Symmetric Cryptol. **2018**(3), 36–92 (2018). https://doi.org/10.13154/tosc.v2018.i3.36-92

14. Datta, N., Dutta, A., Nandi, M., Paul, G., Zhang, L.: Single key variant of PMAC_plus. IACR Trans. Symmetric Cryptol. **2017**(4), 268–305 (2017). https://doi.org/10.13154/tosc.v2017.i4.268-305

15. Datta, N., Dutta, A., Nandi, M., Yasuda, K.: Encrypt or decrypt? To make a single-key beyond birthday secure nonce-based MAC. In: Shacham, H., Boldyreva, A. (eds.) CRYPTO 2018. LNCS, vol. 10991, pp. 631–661. Springer, Cham (2018). https://doi.org/10.1007/978-3-319-96884-1_21

16. Datta, N., Dutta, A., Nandi, M., Yasuda, K.: sfDWCDM+: a BBB secure nonce based MAC. Adv. Math. Commun. **13**(4), 705–732 (2019). https://doi.org/10.3943/amc.2019042

17. Dutta, A., Nandi, M., Saha, A.: Proof of mirror theory for $\xi_{max} = 2$. IEEE Trans. Inf. Theor. **68**(9), 6218–6232 (2022). https://doi.org/10.1109/TIT.2022.3171178

18. Dutta, A., Nandi, M., Talnikar, S.: Beyond birthday bound secure MAC in faulty nonce model. In: Ishai, Y., Rijmen, V. (eds.) EUROCRYPT 2019. LNCS, vol. 11476, pp. 437–466. Springer, Cham (2019). https://doi.org/10.1007/978-3-030-17653-2_15

19. Guo, C., Shen, Y., Wang, L., Gu, D.: Beyond-birthday secure domain-preserving PRFs from a single permutation. Des. Codes Crypt. **87**(6), 1297–1322 (2018). https://doi.org/10.1007/s10623-018-0528-8

20. Hall, C., Wagner, D., Kelsey, J., Schneier, B.: Building PRFs from PRPs. In: Krawczyk, H. (ed.) CRYPTO 1998. LNCS, vol. 1462, pp. 370–389. Springer, Heidelberg (1998). https://doi.org/10.1007/BFb0055742

21. Iwata, T.: New blockcipher modes of operation with beyond the birthday bound security. In: Robshaw, M. (ed.) FSE 2006. LNCS, vol. 4047, pp. 310–327. Springer, Heidelberg (2006). https://doi.org/10.1007/11799313_20

22. Iwata, T., Mennink, B., Vizár, D.: CENC is optimally secure. Cryptology ePrint Archive, Report 2016/1087 (2016). https://eprint.iacr.org/2016/1087

23. Iwata, T., Minematsu, K.: Stronger security variants of GCM-SIV. IACR Trans. Symmetric Cryptol. **2016**(1), 134–157 (2016). https://doi.org/10.13154/tosc.v2016.i1.134-157

24. Iwata, T., Minematsu, K., Peyrin, T., Seurin, Y.: ZMAC: a fast tweakable block cipher mode for highly secure message authentication. In: Katz, J., Shacham, H. (eds.) CRYPTO 2017. LNCS, vol. 10403, pp. 34–65. Springer, Cham (2017). https://doi.org/10.1007/978-3-319-63697-9_2

25. Jha, A., Nandi, M.: Tight security of cascaded LRW2 (2019). https://eprint.iacr.org/2019/1495
26. Kim, S., Lee, B., Lee, J.: Tight security bounds for double-block hash-then-sum MACs. In: Canteaut, A., Ishai, Y. (eds.) EUROCRYPT 2020. LNCS, vol. 12105, pp. 435–465. Springer, Cham (2020). https://doi.org/10.1007/978-3-030-45721-1_16
27. List, E., Nandi, M.: Revisiting full-PRF-secure PMAC and using it for beyond-birthday authenticated encryption. In: Handschuh, H. (ed.) CT-RSA 2017. LNCS, vol. 10159, pp. 258–274. Springer, Cham (2017). https://doi.org/10.1007/978-3-319-52153-4_15
28. List, E., Nandi, M.: ZMAC+ - an efficient variable-output-length variant of ZMAC. IACR Trans. Symmetric Cryptol. 2017(4), 306–325 (2017). https://doi.org/10.13154/tosc.v2017.i4.306-325
29. Mennink, B.: Towards tight security of cascaded LRW2. In: Beimel, A., Dziembowski, S. (eds.) TCC 2018. LNCS, vol. 11240, pp. 192–222. Springer, Cham (2018). https://doi.org/10.1007/978-3-030-03810-6_8
30. Mennink, B., Neves, S.: Encrypted Davies-Meyer and its dual: towards optimal security using mirror theory. In: Katz, J., Shacham, H. (eds.) CRYPTO 2017. LNCS, vol. 10403, pp. 556–583. Springer, Cham (2017). https://doi.org/10.1007/978-3-319-63697-9_19
31. Moch, A., List, E.: Parallelizable MACs based on the sum of PRPs with security beyond the birthday bound. In: Deng, R.H., Gauthier-Umaña, V., Ochoa, M., Yung, M. (eds.) ACNS 2019. LNCS, vol. 11464, pp. 131–151. Springer, Cham (2019). https://doi.org/10.1007/978-3-030-21568-2_7
32. Nachef, V., Patarin, J., Volte, E.: Feistel Ciphers - Security Proofs and Cryptanalysis. Springer, Cham (2017). https://doi.org/10.1007/978-3-319-49530-9
33. Naito, Y.: Full PRF-secure message authentication code based on tweakable block cipher. In: Au, M.-H., Miyaji, A. (eds.) ProvSec 2015. LNCS, vol. 9451, pp. 167–182. Springer, Cham (2015). https://doi.org/10.1007/978-3-319-26059-4_9
34. Naito, Y.: Blockcipher-based MACs: beyond the birthday bound without message length. In: Takagi, T., Peyrin, T. (eds.) ASIACRYPT 2017. LNCS, vol. 10626, pp. 446–470. Springer, Cham (2017). https://doi.org/10.1007/978-3-319-70700-6_16
35. Patarin, J.: Luby-Rackoff: 7 rounds are enough for $2^{n(1-\varepsilon)}$ security. In: Boneh, D. (ed.) CRYPTO 2003. LNCS, vol. 2729, pp. 513–529. Springer, Heidelberg (2003). https://doi.org/10.1007/978-3-540-45146-4_30
36. Patarin, J.: Security of random feistel schemes with 5 or more rounds. In: Franklin, M. (ed.) CRYPTO 2004. LNCS, vol. 3152, pp. 106–122. Springer, Heidelberg (2004). https://doi.org/10.1007/978-3-540-28628-8_7
37. Patarin, J.: On linear systems of equations with distinct variables and small block size. In: Won, D.H., Kim, S. (eds.) ICISC 2005. LNCS, vol. 3935, pp. 299–321. Springer, Heidelberg (2006). https://doi.org/10.1007/11734727_25
38. Patarin, J.: The "coefficients H" technique. In: Avanzi, R.M., Keliher, L., Sica, F. (eds.) SAC 2008. LNCS, vol. 5381, pp. 328–345. Springer, Heidelberg (2009). https://doi.org/10.1007/978-3-642-04159-4_21
39. Patarin, J.: A proof of security in $O(2^n)$ for the XOR of two random permutations. In: Safavi-Naini, R. (ed.) ICITS 2008. LNCS, vol. 5155, pp. 232–248. Springer, Heidelberg (2008). https://doi.org/10.1007/978-3-540-85093-9_22
40. Patarin, J.: Introduction to mirror theory: analysis of systems of linear equalities and linear non equalities for cryptography. Cryptology ePrint Archive, Report 2010/287 (2010). https://eprint.iacr.org/2010/287

41. Patarin, J.: Security of balanced and unbalanced feistel schemes with linear non equalities. Cryptology ePrint Archive, Paper 2010/293 (2010). https://eprint.iacr.org/2010/293
42. Patarin, J.: Security in $o(2^n)$ for the xor of two random permutations - proof with the standard H technique. Cryptology ePrint Archive, Report 2013/368 (2013). https://eprint.iacr.org/2013/368
43. Schneier, B., Kelsey, J.: Unbalanced Feistel networks and block cipher design. In: Gollmann, D. (ed.) FSE 1996. LNCS, vol. 1039, pp. 121–144. Springer, Heidelberg (1996). https://doi.org/10.1007/3-540-60865-6_49
44. Sorkin, A.: Lucifer, a cryptographic algorithm. Cryptologia 8(1), 22–42 (1984). https://doi.org/10.1080/0161-118491858746
45. Yasuda, K.: The sum of CBC MACs is a secure PRF. In: Pieprzyk, J. (ed.) CT-RSA 2010. LNCS, vol. 5985, pp. 366–381. Springer, Heidelberg (2010). https://doi.org/10.1007/978-3-642-11925-5_25
46. Yasuda, K.: A new variant of PMAC: beyond the birthday bound. In: Rogaway, P. (ed.) CRYPTO 2011. LNCS, vol. 6841, pp. 596–609. Springer, Heidelberg (2011). https://doi.org/10.1007/978-3-642-22792-9_34
47. Zhang, L., Wu, W., Sui, H., Wang, P.: 3kf9: enhancing 3GPP-MAC beyond the birthday bound. In: Wang, X., Sako, K. (eds.) ASIACRYPT 2012. LNCS, vol. 7658, pp. 296–312. Springer, Heidelberg (2012). https://doi.org/10.1007/978-3-642-34961-4_19
48. Zhang, P., Hu, H., Yuan, Q.: Close to optimally secure variants of GCM. Secur. Commun. Netw. **2018**, 9715947:1–9715947:12 (2018). https://doi.org/10.1155/2018/9715947

Non-adaptive Universal One-Way Hash Functions from Arbitrary One-Way Functions

Xinyu Mao[1(✉)], Noam Mazor[2(✉)], and Jiapeng Zhang[1(✉)]

[1] Department of Computer Science, University of Southern California, Los Angeles, USA
jiapengz@usc.edu

[2] The Blavatnik School of Computer Science, Tel-Aviv University, Tel-Aviv, Israel
noammaz@gmail.com

Abstract. In this work we give the first *non-adaptive* construction of *universal one-way hash functions* (UOWHFs) from arbitrary one-way functions. Our construction uses $O(n^9)$ calls to the one-way function, has a key of length $O(n^{10})$, and can be implemented in NC1 assuming the underlying one-way function is in NC1.

Prior to this work, the best UOWHF construction used $O(n^{13})$ *adaptive* calls and a key of size $O(n^5)$ (Haitner, Holenstein, Reingold, Vadhan and Wee [Eurocrypt '10]). By the result of Applebaum, Ishai and Kushilevitz [FOCS '04], the above implies the existence of UOWHFs in NC0, given the existence of one-way functions in NC1.

We also show that the PRG construction of Haitner, Reingold and Vadhan (HRV, [STOC '10]), with small modifications, yields a relaxed notion of UOWHFs, which is a function family which can be (inefficiently) converted to UOWHF by changing the functions on a negligible fraction of the inputs. In order to analyze this construction, we introduce the notion of *next-bit unreachable entropy*, which replaces the next-bit pseudoentropy notion used by HRV.

Keywords: universal one-way hash function · one-way function · non-adaptive

1 Introduction

A wide class of cryptographic primitives can be constructed from *one-way functions*, which is the minimal assumption for cryptography. Two important such primitives are *pseudorandom generators* (PRGs) [11,30] and *universal one-way hash functions* (UOWHFs) also known as, target-collision resistant (TCR) hash functions [26]. PRGs and UOWHFs are useful for constructing even more powerful primitives such as encryption, digital signatures and commitments. Yet, the optimal efficiency of black-box constructions of PRGs and UOWHFs from one-way functions is not fully understood. In this paper, we

© International Association for Cryptologic Research 2023
C. Hazay and M. Stam (Eds.): EUROCRYPT 2023, LNCS 14007, pp. 502–531, 2023.
https://doi.org/10.1007/978-3-031-30634-1_17

focus on constructions of UOWHF, a relaxation of *collision-resistant hash function* (CRHF) introduced by Naor and Yung [26]. Informally, a keyed function family $\mathcal{F} = \{f_k \colon \{0,1\}^n \to \{0,1\}^m\}_k$ is a UOWHF if $m < n$, and, for every poly-time algorithm A, and for every input $x \in \{0,1\}^n$, the following holds: with high probability over the choice of a uniformly random key k, A(k,x) cannot find a collision $x' \neq x$ with $f_k(x) = f_k(x')$.

There are several important efficiency measures to account for when considering black-box constructions of UOWHFs and PRGs form one-way functions. For PRG constructions, one aims to minimize the seed length and the number of calls to the one-way function f. For UOWHF constructions, there is a need to minimize the key length and the number of calls to f. Besides these two measurements, another important parameter is the *adaptivity* of the calls. That is, whether the invocations of the one-way function are independent of the output of previous calls. A non-adaptive construction naturally gives rise to a, more efficient, parallel algorithm. By contrast, if the calls are adaptive, one must make them sequentially.

The first UOWHF construction from arbitrary one-way functions is due to Rompel [27] (see [22] for a full proof of Rompel's construction). The efficiency was then improved by Haitner, Holenstein, Reingold, Vadhan and Wee (HHRVW [15]), who give a construction of UOWHF using $O(n^{13})$ *adaptive* calls, and with a key of size $O(n^7)$, which can be improved easily to size $O(n^5 \log n)$ (see Observation 1.3). Notably, prior to the work presented here, there was no non-adaptive UOWHF construction.

The above construction of HHRVW [15] uses ideas similar to the ones used in the constructions of PRGs. Still, the best PRG constructions from arbitrary one-way functions are more efficient. Currently, the state-of-the-art construction of PRGs uses $O(n^4 \log n)$ bits of random seed and $O(n^3 \log n)$ *non-adaptive* calls to the one-way function, or alternatively seed of size $O(n^3 \log^2 n)$ with $O(n^3 \log n)$ adaptive calls [17,29]. Constructing a UOWHF using $\widetilde{O}(n^3)$ calls to the one-way function is still an interesting open question.

These efficiency gaps between UOWHFs and PRGs constructions are even more surprising in the light of the similarities between the constructions. Specially, for more structured one-way functions such as permutations or regular functions, there is essentially no efficiency gap between PRG and UOWHF constructions.[1] Moreover, the constructions are very similar to each other and use similar techniques. For example, the method of *randomized iterate* is used for the constructions of both primitives from unknown-regular one-way functions [2,14,31]. Recently, Mazor and Zhang [25] introduced non-adaptive constructions for both UOWHF and PRG from an unknown-regular one-way function. Their constructions for both primitives have in common a similar structure and are composed of the same building-block operations.

---

[1] f is called *regular* if for every n and x, x' with $|x| = |x'| = n$ it holds that $|f^{-1}(f(x))| = |f^{-1}(f(x'))|$. We say that the function is *unknown-regular* if the *regularity parameter*, $|f^{-1}(f(x))|$, may not be a computable function of n.

Example 1.1 (Similarity between black-box construction of PRGs and UOWHFs, known-regular [19, 31]). For a concrete example, assume $f\colon \{0,1\}^n \to \{0,1\}^n$ is a regular one-way function with regularity parameter r, such that no poly-time algorithm can invert f with probability more than ϵ (for a negligible ϵ). Then

$$G(h_1, h_2, x) = (h_1, h_2, h_1(f(x)), h_2(x))$$

is a PRG, where the functions $h_1\colon \{0,1\}^n \to \{0,1\}^{n-r-\Theta(\log 1/\epsilon)}$ and $h_2\colon \{0,1\}^n \to \{0,1\}^{r+\Theta(\log 1/\epsilon)+\log n}$ are hash functions from appropriate hash families. Similarly, $\mathcal{C} = \{C_k = G(z \oplus k)\}_k$ is a UOWHF when taking $h_2\colon \{0,1\}^n \to \{0,1\}^{r+\Theta(\log 1/\epsilon)-\log n}$, and using the same function G.

Example 1.2 (Similarity between black-box construction of PRGs and UOWHFs, unknown regular [25]). Another example is the following. For an unknown-regular one-way function $f\colon \{0,1\}^n \to \{0,1\}^n$,

$$G(h, x_1, \ldots, x_n) = h(f(x_1), x_2), h(f(x_2), x_3) \ldots, h(x_{t-1}, f(x_n))$$

is a PRG for a hash function $h\colon \{0,1\}^{2n} \to \{0,1\}^{n+\log n}$ from a suitable family. The following similar function

$$C(h, x_1, \ldots, x_n) = f(x_1), h(f(x_1), x_2), h(f(x_2), x_3) \ldots, h(x_{t-1}, f(x_n)), x_n,$$

can be converted into a UOWHF by taking the family $\mathcal{C} = \{C_k = C(z \oplus k)\}_k$, when taking $h\colon \{0,1\}^{2n} \to \{0,1\}^{n-\log n}$.

Furthermore, the first constructions from (unstructured) arbitrary one-way functions of PRGs, by Hastad, Impagliazzo, Levin and Luby [19], and the constructions of UOWHFs by Rompel [27] and HHRVW [15], shared a similar framework. This framework includes first constructing a non-uniform version of the desired primitive, and then eliminating the non-uniform (short) advice by enumerating over all possible advices, and combining the constructions together. This enumeration and combining step has a significant efficiency cost for both primitives.

By contrast, in their beautiful work, Haitner, Reingold and Vadhan (HRV [17]) introduced a simpler and more efficient framework to construct PRGs from arbitrary one-way functions. By introducing a notion called *next-bit pseudoentropy*, they give a very efficient and simple non-adaptive construction of PRGs from one-way functions. This work starts by showing that the function $g(h, x) = (h, f(x), h(x))$, where h is a hash function from some appropriate 2-universal family, has non-trivial next-bit pseudoentropy. The work proceeds by describing a procedure that extracts pseudorandomness from next-bit pseudoentropy (see Fig. 1 for a sketch of the construction). As stated above, this construction has $O(n^4 \log n)$ random seed size with $O(n^3 \log n)$ calls, which is a significant improvement over [19]. One main reason for this efficiency improvement is that this framework no longer requires the non-uniformity elimination step. Unfortunately, there is no analog to this construction for UOWHFs. Adapting the framework of HRV [17] to improve the efficiency of UOWHF constructions is still an interesting open question.

1.1   Our Contribution

In this paper, we partially answer the last question above. Our first result is (the first) non-adaptive construction of UOWHF from arbitrary one-way functions. We achieve this by introducing a construction that does not have the non-uniformity elimination step. By the result of Applebaum, Ishai and Kushilevitz [4], the above implies the existence of UOWHFs in NC0, assuming the existence of one-way functions in NC1.[2] In addition, our construction reduces the call complexity over HHRVW [15], and uses $O(n^9)$ calls to the one-way function instead of $O(n^{13})$. On the negative side, the key length of our construction is $O(n^{10})$, instead of $O(n^5)$.

Next, aiming to close the still remaining gap between PRG and UOWHF constructions, we show that small modifications to the PRG construction of HRV [17] yield a relaxed notion of UOWHF, which we call "almost-UOWHF". Informally, a function family is almost-UOWHF if by changing the functions on a negligible fraction of the inputs, we can convert it into a (perfect) UOWHF. To analyze the almost-UOWHF construction, we introduce the notion of *next-bit unreachable entropy*, an analogue of *next-bit pseudoentropy* used in [17]. Similarly to the PRG construction, our almost-UOWHF construction uses $O(n^3 \log n)$ non-adaptive calls to the one-way function and has a key of size $O(n^4 \log n)$. More details below.

Non-adaptive UOWHF from One-Way Functions. In their construction of UOWHFs from one-way functions, HHRVW [15] define the notion of *accessible entropy*.[3] Informally, for a function g, the accessible entropy of g^{-1} is a bound on the entropy of the output of every *collision finder for g* (i.e., of every poly-time algorithm that, given an input x, always outputs a pre-image of $g(x)$).

HHRVW [15] show how a one-way function $f\colon \{0,1\}^n \to \{0,1\}^n$ can be used to construct a function $\rho\colon \{0,1\}^{n^5} \to \{0,1\}^{n^5}$ such that, for a uniformly chosen input $X \leftarrow \{0,1\}^{n^5}$, there is a gap between the *entropy* of X given $\rho(X)$, and the *accessible entropy* of ρ^{-1}. Namely, there exists some $\ell \in \mathbb{N}$, such that for every collision finder A for ρ, the following holds with all but a negligible probability: the size of $\rho^{-1}(\rho(X))$ is at least $2^{\ell + \omega(\log n)}$, while for every input X, the support size of the output of $A(X)$ is at most 2^ℓ.[4] When ℓ is known, it is not hard to convert such a function to UOWHF, but here the parameter ℓ depends on f and may be unknown. To overcome this obstacle, HHRVW construct UOWHF candidates $C_1, .., C_t$ from ρ, one for each $1 \le \ell \le t = n^2/\log n$, out of which

---

[2] The result of Applebaum, Ishai and Kushilevitz [4] implies that, using a method called randomized encoding, the existence of UOWHF in NC1 implies the existence of UOWHF in NC0.

[3] We use the term accessible entropy to denote accessible entropy of functions. Somewhat different notions of accessible entropy are used in other contexts, for example to construct statistically-hiding commitments from one-way functions [18].

[4] The actual definition of inaccessible entropy ignores some events that have a negligible probability.

at least one is an UOWHF. Then, for each ℓ, HHRVW feed the output of C_ℓ into itself repeatedly and obtain a new function $C'_\ell(x)$ which is also an UOWHF, but is additionally sufficiently compressing. Finally, the concatenation $C(x) := C'_1(x), .., C'_t(x)$ is a UOWHF if at least one of the C_ℓ is. The transformation from C_ℓ to C'_ℓ introduces adaptivity into the constructions by HHRVW and Rompel, and the combination of parallel and sequential composition increases the number of calls to f by a factor of n^9 in HHRVW, and increases the key length by a factor of $\log n$.

Observation 1.3 (The key-length in HHRVW [15]). *The described above step of removing non-uniformity in HHRVW actually increases the size of the key by a n^2 factor: while the transformation from C_ℓ to C'_ℓ only increases the key length by a factor of $\log n$ for each ℓ, HHRVW use a different key for each such candidate, and the key of the final construction is the concatenation of the t keys. Our observation is that it is possible to use the same key for all the candidates. This reduces the key-length from $O(n^7)$ to $O(n^5 \log n)$.*

By viewing ℓ as an unknown regularity parameter of ρ, we replace the parallel and sequential composition in HHRVW by applying the recent construction of [25] of non-adaptive UOWHF from (unknown) regular one-way functions. Namely, for $m = n^5$ hash functions $h_1, \ldots, h_m \colon \{0,1\}^{2m} \to \{0,1\}^{m-\log n}$ from a universal family $\mathcal{H}$, and inputs $z_1, \ldots, z_m$, let

$$C(h_1, \ldots, h_{m-1}, z_1, \ldots, z_m)$$
$$= h_1, \ldots, h_{m-1}, \rho(z_1), h_1(z_1, \rho(z_2)), \ldots, h_{m-1}(z_{m-1}, \rho(z_m)), z_m.$$

Following [25], we show that C is (length-decreasing) *collision resistant on random inputs*, and can be easily be converted to UOWHF (see Sect. 2 for the definition of collision resistant on random inputs and discussion). The above gives rise to the following result.

Theorem 1.4 (Non-adaptive UOWHF from OWF, informal). *There exists a black-box construction of UOWHF from any one-way function that uses $O(n^9)$ non-adaptive calls to the one-way function. Moreover, the construction has key length and output length of $O(n^{10})$, and is computable in $NC1$ using oracle calls to f.*

We note that, since ρ is not a regular function (indeed, there is a negligible fraction of inputs for which ρ may have fewer collisions), the use of [25] is not straightforward, and the security proof requires a new analysis. An overview of the proof is given in Sect. 2.1.

Next, using the result of Applebaum, Ishai and Kushilevitz [4], who construct a UOWHF in NC0 based on a UOWHF in NC1 and randomized encodings, we get the following corollary.

Corollary 1.5 (UOWHF in NC0, informal). *Assuming that one-way functions exist in NC1, there exists a UOWHF in NC0.*

Efficient Almost-UOWHF from One-Way Functions. Our second construction is inspired by the work of HRV [17] on PRG constructions from one-way functions. We show that small modifications to the PRG of [17] yield an *almost-UOWHF*. Informally, a shrinking, keyed function family

$$\mathcal{F} = \{f_k\colon \{0,1\}^n \to \{0,1\}^m\}_k$$

is an almost-UOWHF if, for every key k, there exists a negligible-sized set of inputs $\mathcal{B}_k$ such that the following holds for every poly-time algorithm A, and every input $x \in \{0,1\}^n$: With all but negligible probability over the choice of a uniformly random key k, $\mathsf{A}(k,x)$ cannot find a collision $x' \neq x$ with $f_k(x) = f_k(x')$, unless $x' \in \mathcal{B}_k$ (see Definition 5.1 for the formal definition).

We note that, similarly to the above definition of almost-UOWHF, we can also define an "almost-PRG". However, unlike UOWHF, it is easy to see that an almost-PRG is a (standard) PRG. Hence, viewing the HRV construction as an "almost-PRG", we believe that the UOWHF analog of the HRV construction is essentially our almost-UOWHF. While we do not know if an almost-UOWHF can be converted efficiently into a UOWHF, in our non-adaptive construction we are able to remove the negligible-sized set $\mathcal{B}_k$ (due to which the construction is only almost-UOWHF) at the cost of more repetitions and calls to the one-way function (see Sect. 2.1 for more details). Thus, the almost-UOWHF construction emphasizes that this need of eliminating the negligible-sized set is the *main efficiency gap* between the currently known constructions of PRGs and UOWHFs. We get the following theorem.

Theorem 1.6 *(Almost-UOWHF from OWF, informal).* *There exists a black-box construction of an almost-UOWHF with key length $O(n^4 \log n)$ from one-way functions with input length n. The construction makes $O(n^3 \log n)$ non-adaptive calls to the underlying one-way function.*

Next-Bit Unreachable Entropy. In their work, HRV [17] define the notion of *next-bit pseudoentropy*. HRV first show how to construct a function with non-trivial (i.e., larger than the input size) next-bit pseudoentropy. Then, using this function, HRV construct an efficient and simple PRG. To replace the notion of next-bit pseudoentropy in our construction, we define the notion of *next-bit unreachable entropy*, a variant of inaccessible entropy, defined by HHRVW [15], that allows us to achieve almost-UOWHF using a similar construction to the above PRG. We discuss the definition and the motivation behind it in detail in Sect. 2.2.

1.2 Additional Related Work

Next-Block Pseudoentropy and Inaccessible Entropy. A different variant of inaccessible entropy, for online generator, was defined and used by Haitner, Reingold, Vadhan and Wee [18] to construct statistically hiding commitments. Chen Horel and Vadhan [1] pointed out that the HRVW [18] notion of accessible entropy and next-block pseudoentropy are deeply related to each other. Recently, Haitner, Mazor and Silbak [16] showed that incompressibility implies next-bit pseudoentropy.

UOWHFs from Regular One-Way Functions. Constructions of UOWHF from *regular* one-way functions are more efficient. Besides the mentioned above constructions from unknown-rgular one-way functions [2,14,25,31], Naor and Yung [26] construct an UOWHF using 1 call to an 1-to-1 one-way functions, and [31] give a construction from known-regular one-way functions, using $\omega(1)$ non-adaptive calls.

Additionally, a few refinements of regularity were considered. Barhum and Maurer [8] show an adaptive construction for UOWHF that uses $O(ns^6(n))$ key-length under the assumption that $\left|f^{-1}(f(x))\right|$ is concentrated in an interval of size $2^{s(n)}$. Yu, Gu, Li and Weng [31] give adaptive constructions with key of length $O(n \log n)$, for functions with polynomial fraction of inputs x such that $\left|f^{-1}(f(x))\right|$ is maximal.

Lower Bounds. The lower bounds for black-box UOWHF and PRG constructions from one-way functions are relatively far from the upper bounds. Gennero, Gertner, Katz and Trevisan [12] prove that any black-box PRG construction $G \colon \{0,1\}^m \to \{0,1\}^{m+s}$ from f must use $\Omega(s/\log n)$ calls to f. Similarly, any black box UWOHF construction with input size m and output size $m - s$ must use $\Omega(s/\log n)$ calls. Holenstien and Sinha [20] prove that any black-box PRG construction from a one-way function f must use $\Omega(n/\log n)$ calls to f, even for 1-bit stretching. Barhum and Holenstein [7] give an analog lower bound of $\Omega(n/\log n)$ calls 1-bit compressing UWOHF constructions. These lower bounds hold even when the one-way function f is unknown-regular. In this case, these bounds are known to be tight [2,14,25,31].

(Multi)-collision Resistant Hash Functions (CRHFs). UOWHF is a relaxation of CRHF. In the latter, we require that for a random function from the family, no adversary can find a collision (x, x'). Constructing a CRHF is a more challenging task, and its complexity is still not clear. Asharov and Segev [6] prove that there is no black-box construction of CRHFs even from indistinguishable obfuscation (iO) additionally to a one-way permutation. Holmgren and Lombardi [21] show how to construct CRHF from exponentially secure OWF, under an assumption on the probability to invert two independent one-way function challenges. Recent works also study a relaxation of CRHF, called Multi-Collision Resistant hash functions (MCRH) [9,10,23]. Rothblum and Vasudevan [28] show a nonconstructive transformation from MCRH to CRHF for some range of parameters.

Low-Complexity Cryptography. As described above, Applebaum, Ishai and Kushilevitz [4] develop a general method to construct cryptographic primitives in NC0 based on primitives in higher complexity classes. HRV [17] use this method in order to prove the existence of PRG in NC0, assuming one-way function in NC1. Applebaum, Haramaty-Krasne, Ishai, Kushilevitz and Vaikuntanathan [3] show the existence of CRHF with low algebric degree and linear shrinkage based on a specific assumption. Based on the assumption that random local function is a one-way function (Goldreich [13]), Applebaum and Moses [5] construct a UOWHF with constant locality and linear shrinkage.

1.3 Paper Organisation

Section 2 gives a high-level description of our constructions and proof technique. Section 3 gives formal definitions. The non-adaptive UOWHF construction and its security reduction to one-way functions are in Sect. 4. Finally, Sect. 5 provides the formal definition of almost-UOWHF and next-bit unreachable entropy, as well as the almost-UOWHF construction. The security reduction from the almost-UOWHF construction to one-way functions is in the full version of this paper [24].

2 Our Technique

In this section, we provide a detailed description of our constructions and proof technique. In both of the proofs, we first construct a function that is *collision resistant on random inputs*, and then use known techniques to convert it into a UOWHF. Informally, a function C is collision resistant on random input if, given a random input x, no adversary can find $x' \neq x$ with $C(x') = C(x)$.

Definition 2.1 (Collision resistance on random inputs). *Let n be a security parameter. A function $f \colon \{0,1\}^{m(n)} \to \{0,1\}^{\ell(n)}$ is collision resistant on random inputs if for every probabilistic polynomial-time adversary A, the probability that A succeeds in the following game is negligible in n:*

1. *Choose $x \leftarrow \{0,1\}^{m(n)}$.*
2. *Let $x' \leftarrow \mathsf{A}(1^n, x) \in \{0,1\}^{m(n)}$.*
3. *A succeeds if $x \neq x'$ and $f(x) = f(x')$.*

In contrast, the security requirement in the definition of UOWHF is called *target-collision resistance* (see Definition 3.3), according to which the adversary can choose x, but without knowing the randomly chosen key for the function. It is well known that a collision resistant on random input function C that is length-decreasing (i.e., $\ell < m$) can be converted into a UOWHF defined by

$$\mathcal{C} = \Big\{ C_k \colon \{0,1\}^m \to \{0,1\}^\ell \Big\}_{k \in \{0,1\}^m},$$

for $C_k(x) = C(k \oplus x)$. The key length of the resulting UOWHF is the same as the input length of C, and the complexity of the UOWHF is similar to the complexity of C. It is not hard to see that the other direction also holds. That is, by adding the key to the input and output of the function, a UOWHF can be converted into a (shrinking) collision resistant on random input function. A similar notion and transformation can be defined also for the case of almost-UOWHFs. Below, we show how to construct collision resistant on random input functions.

2.1 Non-adaptive UOWHF

We start with a high-level description of the constructions of [15] and [25].

UOWHF from Unknown-Regular One-Way Functions. Mazor and Zhang (MZ [25]) showed how to construct a non-adaptive UOWHF from an unknown-regular one-way function $f : \{0,1\}^n \to \{0,1\}^n$. For hash functions $h_1, \ldots, h_{n-1} \colon \{0,1\}^{2n} \to \{0,1\}^{n-\log n}$ from a hash family $\mathcal{H}$, and n inputs $x_1, \ldots, x_n \in \{0,1\}^n$, MZ [25] show that, for the right choice of $\mathcal{H}$, the function $C \colon \mathcal{H}^n \times \{0,1\}^{n^2} \to \mathcal{H}^n \times \{0,1\}^{2n+(n-1)(n-\log n)}$, defined by

$$
\begin{aligned}
&C(h_1, \ldots, h_n, x_1, \ldots, x_n) \\
&= h_1, \ldots, h_n, f(x_1), h_1(x_1, f(x_2)), \ldots, h_{n-1}(x_{n-1}, f(x_n)), x_n
\end{aligned}
$$

is collision resistant on random inputs. Since this function is also shrinking, it can be converted into an UOWHF easily by a standard construction.[5]

Intuitively, for a regular function f and i.i.d uniform random variables X_1, X_2 over $\{0,1\}^n$, given any fixing of $f(X_1)$, the entropy of the pair $X_1, f(X_2)$ is exactly n. To see the above, recall that for a regular f with an (unknown) regularity parameter Δ, it holds that there are exactly Δ possible values for X_1 given $f(X_1)$, and exactly $2^n/\Delta$ possible values for $f(X_2)$. Thus, the regularity parameter Δ "cancels out" when considering the number of possible values (given $f(X_1)$) of the pair $X_1, f(X_2)$, as this number is $\Delta \cdot 2^n/\Delta = 2^n$. It follows that the compression of the pair $X_1, f(X_2)$ does not create too many collisions. This fact can be used in order to reduce the problem of inverting f, into finding a collision for C.

Inaccessible Entropy from One-Way Functions. In order to construct an UOWHF from an arbitrary one-way function, given a one-way function $f \colon \{0,1\}^n \to \{0,1\}^n$, HHRVW [15] first construct a function g, that takes as input an index $i \in [n]$, string $x \in \{0,1\}^n$ and a description of a random hash function h from a 3-wise independent hash family $\mathcal{H}$, and outputs h, together with the i first bits of $h(f(x))$. That is, $g(i, x, h) = (h, h(f(x))_{\leq i})$. HHRVW [15] showed that for every collision finder algorithm A, there are sets $\{\mathcal{L}_w\}_{w \in ([n] \times \{0,1\}^n \times \mathcal{H})}$, such that, for a random input $W \leftarrow ([n] \times \{0,1\}^n \times \mathcal{H})$,

1. $\mathbf{Pr}\,[\mathsf{A}(W) \notin \mathcal{L}_W] = neg(n)$, and,
2. $H(W \mid g(W)) - \mathbf{E}\,[\log(|\mathcal{L}_W|)] \geq \log n/n$,

where H is the entropy function. The above $\log n/n$ is a gap between the *entropy* of W given $g(W)$, to its *accessible average max entropy*.

HHRVW [15] then showed, using standard concentration bounds, that for $\rho = g^{n^4}$ (i.e., $\rho(w_1, \ldots, w_{n^4}) = g(w_1), \ldots, g(w_{n^4})$), the concatenation of the outputs

---

[5] MZ actually show it is enough to use a single hash function. The number of repetitions n is necessary only to make the function shrinking.

of n^4 independent invocations of g), both the entropy and the accessible entropy are highly concentrated around their means. That is, there exist some $\ell \in \mathbb{N}$ and $s = \omega(\log n)$ such that $|\rho^{-1}(\rho(z))| \geq 2^{\ell+s}$ for all but negligible fraction of z's, and the following holds. For every collision finder A for ρ, there exist sets $\{\mathcal{L}_z\}_{z \in \text{Domain}(\rho)}$ such that (1) $|\{\mathcal{L}_z\}| \leq 2^\ell$ for all but negligible fraction of z's, and (2), $\mathbf{Pr}\,[\mathsf{A}(z) \notin \mathcal{L}_z] = neg(n)$ for every collision finder A for ρ.

We now proceed to describing our construction. In the following we view ρ as a function from $\{0,1\}^m$ to $\{0,1\}^k$, for $m, k = O(n^5)$ (using a proper encoding of the input).

Our Construction. Thinking of ℓ as the regularity parameter of the function ρ, we use the MZ construction of in order to build a non-adaptive UOWHF. That is, for hash functions $h_1, \ldots, h_{m-1} \colon \{0,1\}^m \times \{0,1\}^k \to \{0,1\}^{m-\log n}$ from a universal family $\mathcal{H}$, and inputs $z_1, \ldots, z_m$, let

$$C(h_1, \ldots, h_{m-1}, z_1, \ldots, z_m)$$
$$= h_1, \ldots, h_{m-1}, \rho(z_1), h_1(z_1, \rho(z_2)), \ldots, h_{m-1}(z_{m-1}, \rho(z_m)), z_m.$$

We show that C is collision resistant on random inputs. Indeed, assume that $|\rho^{-1}(\rho(z))| \geq 2^{\ell+\omega(\log n)}$ for every $z \in \{0,1\}^m$. Then the image size of ρ is at most $2^m \cdot 2^{-\ell-\omega(\log n)}$. Thus, for $Z_1, Z_2 \leftarrow \{0,1\}^m$ and $H_1 \leftarrow \mathcal{H}$, any poly-time algorithm cannot find a collision for $\rho(Z_1), H_1(Z_1, \rho(Z_2))$, since it only has

$$|\mathcal{L}_{Z_1}| \cdot |\text{Image}(\rho)| \leq 2^\ell \cdot (2^m \cdot 2^{-\ell-\omega(\log n)}) = 2^{m-\omega(\log n)}$$

possible values to choose from, and the probability for each such value to collide with $Z_1, \rho(Z_2)$ on H_1 is $2^{-m+\log n}$. Thus, by the union bound, the probability that there is a collision for Z_1, Z_2 inside the set $\mathcal{L}_{Z_1} \times \text{Image}(\rho)$ is negligible. By a similar argument, the analysis shows that it is impossible to find a collision for the entire function C.

However, there is an issue with the above idea. Note that the condition concerning the pre-image size of an image of ρ holds only with overwhelming probability, which may pose a problem. Indeed, let

$$\mathcal{B} = \left\{ z \in \{0,1\}^m : |\rho^{-1}(\rho(z))| < 2^{\ell+\omega(\log n)} \right\}$$

be the set of all untypical inputs. The size of $\rho(\mathcal{B})$ can be much larger than $2^m \cdot 2^{-\ell-\omega(\log n)}$, the number of "typical" images. Thus, by choosing X_2' from this set, the adversary might be able to find a collision (Z_1', Z_2') for $\rho(Z_1), H_1(Z_1, \rho(Z_2))$. Fortunately, it turns out that this issue can be resolved by a more careful analysis, which yields the following key insight: for every collision $(z_1', \ldots, z_m')$ for C found by an efficient algorithm, it holds that if $z_i' \in \mathcal{B}$ for some i, it must hold that $z_{i+1}' \in \mathcal{B}$ as well. It follows from the above that in this case, z_m' is also in $\mathcal{B}$. Since C outputs its last input z_m, and with all but a negligible probability $z_m \notin \mathcal{B}$, we have that $(z_1', \ldots, z_m')$ is not a valid collision.

Remark 2.2 (Using a more shrinking hashing). The actual gap s between the accessible and real entropy of ρ^{-1} is $s \approx n^3$. Thus, the first part of the argument above will work even if the hash functions will output only $m - n^3 + \omega(\log n)$ bits. In this case, however, we will not be able to show that it is infeasible to find a collision inside $\mathcal{B}$. The above suggests the following construction of an *almost-UOWHF*: let $t \approx n^2$, and for $h_1, \ldots, h_{t-1}, z_1, \ldots, z_t$, consider

$$
\begin{aligned}
&C(h_1, \ldots, h_{t-1}, z_1, \ldots, z_t) \\
&= h_1, \ldots, h_{t-1}, \rho(z_1), h_1(z_1, \rho(z_2)), \ldots, h_{t-1}(z_{t-1}, \rho(z_t)), z_t,
\end{aligned}
$$

for $h_i \colon \{0,1\}^{m+k} \to \{0,1\}^{m-n^3/2}$.

For large enough t, the above function is shrinking. For a random input $(h_1, \ldots, h_{t-1}, z_1, \ldots, z_t)$ it is hard to find a collision $(z_1', \ldots, z_t')$, such that $z_i' \notin \mathcal{B}$ for every i. The latter implies that all the collisions that can be found by an efficient algorithm come from a negligible-sized set. Such a function can easily be converted into an almost-UOWHF, which yields a construction with $O(n^6)$ non-adaptive calls, and key length of $O(n^7)$ bits. It turns out, see next section, that there are better approaches for constructing almost-UOWHFs.

2.2   Next-Bit Unreachable Entropy

As mention above, HRV [17] defined the notion of *next-bit pseudoentropy*. Roughly, a function $g \colon \{0,1\}^m \to \{0,1\}^\ell$ has next-bit pseudoentropy k, if for random $X \leftarrow \{0,1\}^m$ and $I \leftarrow [\ell]$ the bit $g(X)_I$ has pseudoentropy k/ℓ given $g(X)_{<I}$.[6] HRV [17] used a one-way function to construct a function $g \colon \{0,1\}^m \to \{0,1\}^\ell$ with non-trivial (i.e., larger than m) next-bit pseudoentropy. This function g is then used to construct an efficient and simple PRG (see Sect. 2.3 for a high-lvel description of the construction).

To replace the notion of next-bit pseudoentropy in our construction, we define the notion of *next-bit unreachable entropy*, a variant of inaccessible entropy, defined by HHRVW [15], that allows us to achieve almost-UOWHF using a similar construction to the above PRG.

Remark 2.3 (Motivating the definition). Before presenting our definition, we start with some intuition. As in the case of next-bit pseudoentropy, we would like to say that a function g has non trivial "next-bit inaccessible entropy" if, for random X and I, the accessible entropy of $g(X)_I$ given $g(X)_{<I}$ is smaller than its real entropy. That is, for any adversary that, given X and I, outputs X' with $g(X)_{<I} = g(X')_{<I}$, it holds that the entropy of $g(X')_I$ is small (smaller than $H(g(X)_I \mid g(X)_{<I})$).

However, there is an issue with this definition: If for some fixing x, i of X, I, the accessible entropy of $g(X')_I$ is noticeable, the adversary can make it to be

---

[6] That is, $g(X)_I$ is indistinguishable from some random variable Z (jointly distributed with X and I), such that $H(Z \mid g(X)_{<I}) \geq k/\ell$. Here, $H(Z \mid g(X)_{<I})$ is the conditional Shannon entropy of Z given $g(X)_{<I}$ (see Sect. 3.5).

almost one. Indeed, assume that given i, x the adversary can find, with noticeable probability, $\hat{x}$ such that $g(\hat{x})_{<i} = g(x)_{<i}$ and $g(\hat{x}) \neq g(x)$. In this case, using simple amplification, the adversary can set its output x' to be equal to each one of x or $\hat{x}$ with probability $1/2$. In this case, the entropy of $g(X')_I$ can be arbitrarily close to 1. In particular, the entropy may be larger than the real entropy

$$H(g(X)_I \mid g(X)_{<I} = g(x)_{<i})$$

(which is at most $|g(X)_I| = 1$). For this reason, we only focus on inputs for which the entropy of $g(X')_I$ is negligible (that is, no PPT adversary can find an input X' such that $g(X)_{<I} = g(X')_{<I}$ and $g(X')_I \neq g(X)_I$).

Unfortunately, while the above gives a definition that is strong enough to work with, we are not able to construct it from a one-way function. Thus, we consider a weaker definition, in which we allow the above property to hold only for a large fraction of the inputs. That is, we define the sets $\mathcal{U} = \{\mathcal{U}_i\}_{i \in [\ell]}$ of inputs which are *unreachable* to the adversary in the following sense. First, we require that it is hard for every adversary to get inside $\mathcal{U}_i$. That is, for every $x \notin \mathcal{U}_i$, it is hard to find $x \in \mathcal{U}_i$ with $g(x)_{<i} = g(x')_{<i}$. Secondly, we require that the next-bit inaccessible entropy property will hold inside $\mathcal{U}$. That is, for every $x \in \mathcal{U}_i$ it is hard to find x' **inside** $\mathcal{U}_i$ such that $g(x)_{<i} = g(x')_{<i}$ and $g(x')_i \neq g(x)_i$. While it may be easy to find such an x' outside of $\mathcal{U}_i$, if the size of $\mathcal{U}_i$ is large enough, the above promises that every such collision will be a member of a (respectively) small set and will look (somewhat) untypical. This property will be useful in the construction. We give more examples below the definition.

We now define the notion of next-bit unreachable entropy. The formal definition is given in Definition 5.3.

Definition 2.4 (Unreachable entropy, informal). *A function* $g \colon \{0,1\}^m \to \{0,1\}^\ell$ *has next-bit unreachable entropy* v, *if for every* $i \in [\ell]$ *there exists a set* $\mathcal{U}_i \subseteq \{0,1\}^m$, *such that*

1. $\mathcal{U}_i$ are large:

$$\Pr_{x \leftarrow \{0,1\}^m, i \leftarrow [\ell]} [x \notin \mathcal{U}_i] \leq (m - v)/\ell.$$

2. Hard to get inside $\mathcal{U}_i$: *For every* PPT A,

$$\Pr_{\substack{x \leftarrow \{0,1\}^m, \\ i \leftarrow [\ell], x' \leftarrow \mathsf{A}(x,i)}} [((x' \in \mathcal{U}_i)) \wedge (g(x)_{<i} = g(x')_{<i}) \wedge (x \notin \mathcal{U}_i)] = \mathrm{neg}(n).$$

   That is, for $x \notin \mathcal{U}_i$, *it is hard to find a collision for* $g(x)_{<i}$ *inside* $\mathcal{U}_i$.

3. The entropy inside $\mathcal{U}_i$ is unreachable: *For every* PPT A,

$$\Pr_{\substack{x \leftarrow \{0,1\}^m, \\ i \leftarrow [\ell], x' \leftarrow \mathsf{A}(x,i)}} [((x' \in \mathcal{U}_i)) \wedge (g(x)_{<i} = g(x')_{<i}) \wedge (g(x)_i \neq g(x')_i)] = \mathrm{neg}(n).$$

   That is, even if $x \in \mathcal{U}_i$, *it is hard to flip the* i-*th bit of* g *while staying inside* $\mathcal{U}_i$.

For example, for every permutation $p\colon \{0,1\}^m \to \{0,1\}^m$, the function $g\colon \{0,1\}^m \to \{0,1\}^\ell$ defined by $g(x) = p(x)0^{\ell-m}$ has (trivial) next-bit unreachable entropy 0, as can been seen by setting $\mathcal{U}_i = \{0,1\}^m$ for every $i > m$, or the empty set for $i \leq m$. Note also that, without assuming computational hardness, the above sets $\mathcal{U}_i$ are the maximal that respect the definition of unreachable entropy.

More generally, for every *injective* function $g\colon \{0,1\}^m \to \{0,1\}^\ell$, we can define $\mathcal{U}_i$ to be the set of all inputs $x \in \{0,1\}^m$, such that there is no $x' \in \{0,1\}^m$ with $g(x)_{<i} = g(x')_{<i}$ while $g(x)_i \neq g(x')_i$.[7] In this case, it is not hard to see that the probability that a random x is outside of $\mathcal{U}_i$ (for any fixed i) is at least the entropy of $g(X)_i$ given $g(X)_{<i}$ (i.e., $H(g(X)_i \mid g(X)_{<i})$).[8] Using the chain rule of entropy, we get that for a random index I, the probability that X is outside of $\mathcal{U}_I$ is at least

$$1/\ell \cdot \sum_{i \in \ell} H(g(X)_i \mid g(X)_{<i}) = 1/\ell \cdot H(g(X)) = m/\ell.$$

By the above observations, it follows that a function g has $v > 0$ next-bit unreachable entropy if the "reachable entropy" of $g(X)_I$ given $g(X)_{<I}$ is smaller than its real entropy.[9] In this sense, our definition is a dual version of the next-bit pseudoentropy definition. We show that a very similar function to the function g used by HRV [17] has non-trivial next-bit unreachable entropy. More details on the constructions and the security proof are given below.

2.3   Almost-UOWHF

In this part, we show that small modifications to the PRG of HRV [17] yield an *almost-collision resistant on random inputs* function.

Definition 2.5 (Almost collision resistance on random inputs). *Let n be a security parameter. A function $f\colon \{0,1\}^{m(n)} \to \{0,1\}^{\ell(n)}$ is almost collision resistant on random inputs if there exists a set $\mathcal{B}_n \subseteq \{0,1\}^{m(n)}$, such that $|\mathcal{B}_n| / 2^{m(n)} = \mathrm{neg}(n)$, and for every probabilistic polynomial-time adversary A, the probability that A succeeds in the following game is negligible in n:*

1. *Choose $x \leftarrow \{0,1\}^{m(n)}$.*
2. *Let $x' \leftarrow \mathsf{A}(1^n, x) \in \{0,1\}^{m(n)}$.*
3. *A succeeds if $x' \notin \mathcal{B}_n$, $x \neq x'$ and $f(x) = f(x')$.*

---

[7] If the function g is not injective, it is natural to consider $g'(x) = (g(x), x)$. We use a similar construction in Sect. 5.

[8] Indeed, observe that $H(g(X)_i \mid g(X)_{<i} = g(x)_{<i})$ is zero iff $x \in \mathcal{U}_i$. Additionally, $H(g(X)_i \mid g(X)_{<i} = g(x)_{<i}) \leq 1$ for every x. It follows that $H(g(X)_i \mid g(X)_{<i}) = \mathbf{E}_{x \leftarrow \{0,1\}^m} [H(g(X)_i \mid g(X)_{<i} = g(x)_{<i})] \leq \mathbf{E}_{x \leftarrow \{0,1\}^m} [1_{x \notin \mathcal{U}_i}] = \mathbf{Pr}[X \notin \mathcal{U}_i]$.

[9] We use the term "reachable entropy" to denote the difference between the real entropy and the next-bit unreachable entropy of $g(X)$.

For a more formal definition, see Definition 2.5. As in the case of (perfect) UOWHF, such a shrinking function can be converted into almost-UOWHF. We start with a high-level description of the one-way function based pseudorandom generator of HRV [17]. The main building block of the construction is a function $g: \{0,1\}^m \to \{0,1\}^\ell$, with $k > m$ next-bit pseudoentropy. On a given input, their PRG starts by using g to construct the following matrix-like structure (see Fig. 1): the structure is composed of $q \approx m^2$ rows, where each row contains $t \approx m$ independent copies of $g(X)$, for $X \leftarrow \{0,1\}^m$, shifted by a random offset between 0 to ℓ. Every fully populated column is then hashed by a hash function $h: \{0,1\}^q \to \{0,1\}^a$, for $a \approx q \cdot k/\ell > q \cdot m/\ell$. Finally, the output of the PRG is the concatenation of the outputs of the hash function applied to every fully populated column (the non-fully populated columns are not part of the output).

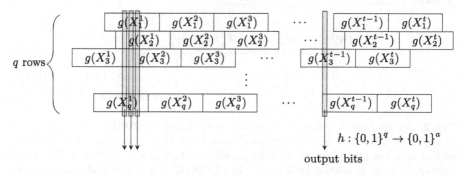

Fig. 1. The PRG construction of HRV [17], $G: \mathcal{H} \times (\{0,1\}^m)^{t \cdot q} \to \mathcal{H} \times (\{0,1\}^a)^{(t-1)\ell}$. There are $q \approx m^2$ rows, each row has $t \approx m$ i.i.d copies of $g(X)$, shifted by a random offset. Every fully populated column, marked in grey, is hashed by $h \in \mathcal{H}$. The almost-UOWHF construction also outputs the columns that are not fully populated.

We prove that slightly tweaking the above construction, and using a different function g, yields a function that is almost collision-resistant on random inputs. Specifically, the output of our construction contains not only the hashed fully populated columns, but also all the columns that are not fully populated (without hashing). Additionally, we choose the parameter a to be smaller than $q \cdot n/m$, in order to make the function length-decreasing. The function g we are using in our construction, is defined by

$$g(h_1, h_2, x) = (h_1, h_2, h_1(f(x)), h_2(x)),$$

for hash functions $h_1, h_2: \{0,1\}^n \to \{0,1\}^n$ from a 3-wise independent family. We prove in Sect. 5.2 that if f is a one-way function, the above function g has next-bit unreachable entropy $\log n$.[10]

---

[10] For the PRG construction, HRV [17] used $g(h,x) = (h, f(x), h(x))$ and Vadhan and Zheng [29] used $g(x) = (f(x), x)$. Observe that, since $h_1(f(x))$ is also a one-way function, our g can be used in the PRG construction.

Remark 2.6 (Similarities between our constructions). We note that the function ρ, defined in Sect. 2.1, is composed of n^4 independent repetitions of a simpler function with random shifts. Thus, our first construction of non-adaptive UOWHF can be modified to be an instantiation of the second (almost-UOWHF) construction, described above, where we apply the hash function on blocks of m columns, instead of hashing every single column (and by taking the number of rows to be larger). This equivalent construction is illustrated in Fig. 2, and its security can be proven using a similar proof to the one given in Sect. 4.

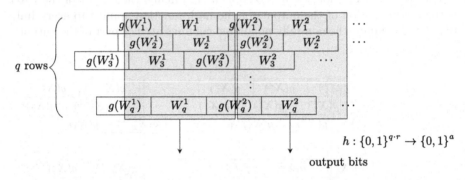

Fig. 2. An equivalent construction to our non-adaptive UOWHF, where $g(h, x) = (h, h(f(x)))$. There are $q \approx n^4$ rows, each row has $t \approx n^5$ i.i.d copies of $(g(W), W)$, shifted by a random offset. Every fully populated block of $r = |(g(W), W)|$ columns, marked in grey, is hashed by $h \in \mathcal{H}$. The UOWHF construction also outputs the columns that are not fully populated.

In the rest of this section we give some details on the security proof. Consider the function σ induced by taking the first hashed column in our almost-UOWHF construction (Fig. 1) together with the columns to the left of it. That is,

$$\sigma(h, i_1, \ldots, i_q, x_1, \ldots, x_q) = h, (g(x_1)_{<i_1}, \ldots, g(x_q)_{<i_q}), h(g(x_1)_{i_1}, \ldots, g(x_q)_{i_q}),$$

for a hash function $h: \{0, 1\}^q \rightarrow \{0, 1\}^a$ from a universal family $\mathcal{H}$.

Additionally, consider the function $\hat{\sigma}$, defined similarly to σ, but without applying the hash h on the column. That is,

$$\hat{\sigma}(h, i_1, \ldots, i_q, x_1, \ldots, x_q) = h, (g(x_1)_{<i_1}, \ldots, g(x_q)_{<i_q}), (g(x_1)_{i_1}, \ldots, g(x_q)_{i_q}).$$

It turns out, see detail below, that the following holds for a right choice of the parameter a and for some negligible-sized set of inputs $\mathcal{B}$: for a random input, every collision found by a collision finder to the function σ is either a collision for $\hat{\sigma}$, or it is inside the set $\mathcal{B}$. That is, the function h does not make the task of finding a collision (outside of $\mathcal{B}$) easier.

To see that the above is enough to prove the security of the construction, let C be the almost-UOWHF construction described above, and let $\widehat{C}$ be the function defined by the raw matrix-like structure (without applying the hash function on every fully-populated column). Observe that since the function g is (close to be) injective, the function $\widehat{C}$ is (not shrinking) collision-resistant on random inputs. A simple hybrid argument yields that every collision finder that, given an input w for C, is able to find a collision $w' \neq w$ for C that is not a collision for $\widehat{C}$ (namely, $C(w) = C(w')$ but $\widehat{C}(w) \neq \widehat{C}(w')$), can be used to find a collision for σ which is not a collision for $\widehat{\sigma}$.[11] Since the latter is hard to find, and since $\widehat{C}$ is collision-resistant, the above concludes the proof.

σ *is (almost) as hard as* $\widehat{\sigma}$. It thus left to prove that it is hard to find a collision for σ which is not a collision for $\widehat{\sigma}$, outside of the negligible sized set $\mathcal{B}$. let A be a collision finder for σ, and let $w' = (h, i_1, \ldots, i_q, x_1' \ldots, x_q')$ be a collision found by A(w), for some $w = (h, i_1, \ldots, i_q, x_1 \ldots, x_q)$. We show that either $\widehat{\sigma}(w) = \widehat{\sigma}(w')$, or w' is a member of a small set $\mathcal{B}$. To do so, we use the next-bit unreachable entropy property of g.

Let $\{\mathcal{U}_i\}_{i \in [\ell]}$ be the sets guaranteed by the next-bit unreachable entropy of g (these sets are independent from the choice of A). By the definition of next-bit unreachable entropy it holds that:

1. for every j such that $x_j \notin \mathcal{U}_{i_j}$, no collision finder can find $x_j' \in \mathcal{U}_{i_j}$ such that $g(x_j)_{<i_j} = g(x_j')_{<i_j}$, and thus it must hold that $x_j' \notin \mathcal{U}_{i_j}$.
2. Similarly, for every j with $x_j \in \mathcal{U}_{i_j}$, it holds that $g(x_j)_{i_j} = g(x_j')_{i_j}$, unless $x_j' \notin \mathcal{U}_{i_j}$.

Let $\mathcal{J}_w$ be the set of indices for which x_j is inside the set $\mathcal{U}_{i_j}$. Formally,

$$\mathcal{J}_w = \left\{ j \in [q] \colon x_j \in \mathcal{U}_{i_j} \right\}.$$

By Item 1 above, it holds that $\mathcal{J}_{w'} \subseteq \mathcal{J}_w$. Moreover, Item 2 implies that $g(x_j)_{i_j} = g(x_j')_{i_j}$ for every $j \in \mathcal{J}_{w'} \cap \mathcal{J}_w$. The above yields the key observation of the proof:

Claim 2.7. *For any collision* $w' = (h, i_1, \ldots, i_q, x_1' \ldots, x_q')$ *found by a collision finder* A, *unless* $|\mathcal{J}_{w'}|$ *is smaller than* $|\mathcal{J}_w|$, *there are* $|\mathcal{J}_w|$ *bits in* $g(x_1')_{i_1}, \ldots,$ $g(x_q')_{i_q}$ *that get the exact same value as in* $g(x_1)_{i_1}, \ldots, g(x_q)_{i_q}$ *(namely,* $g(x_j)_{i_j} = g(x_j')_{i_j}$ *for every* $j \in \mathcal{J}_w$*).*

Observe that for large enough q, the size of $\mathcal{J}_w$ (for a random w) is concentrated around its mean. Since g has $\log n$ next-bit unreachable entropy, its mean is at least $q \cdot (1 - \frac{m - \log n}{\ell})$. In the following, assume for simplicity that the size of $\mathcal{J}_w$ is equal to its mean, and that this mean is exactly $q \cdot (1 - \frac{m - \log n}{\ell})$. To conclude the proof, let $\mathcal{B}$ be the negligible-sized set of all inputs $w' = (h, i_1, \ldots, i_q, x_1' \ldots, x_q')$ for which $|\mathcal{J}_{w'}|$ is (much) smaller than $q \cdot (1 - \frac{m - \log n}{\ell})$, and set the length of the output of the hash function h to be $a \approx q \cdot \frac{m - \log n}{\ell} < q \cdot m / \ell$. It follows that the output of every collision finder for σ is either in $\mathcal{B}$, or agrees with $g(x_1)_{i_1}, \ldots, g(x_q)_{i_q}$ on (almost) all the indices in $\mathcal{J}_w$.

---

[11] Furthermore, the hybrid argument yields that w' must be from a small set if the collision for $\widehat{\sigma}$ is.

However, with all but a negligible probability, there is no string y' that agrees with $y = (g(x_1)_{i_1}, \ldots, g(x_q)_{i_q})$ on $q \cdot (1 - \frac{m - \log n}{\ell})$ bits, for which $h(y) = h(y')$, unless $y = y'$. In other words, any such collision for σ is also a collision for $\hat{\sigma}$.

3   Preliminaries

3.1   Notations

We use calligraphic letters to denote sets, uppercase for random variables, and lowercase for values and functions. For $n \in \mathbb{N}$, let $[n] := \{1, \ldots, n\}$. Given a vector $s \in \{0,1\}^n$, let s_i denote its i-th entry, and $s_{\leq i}$ denote its first i entries. Define $s_{<i}$, $s_{>i}$ and $s_{\geq i}$ similarly.

The support of a distribution P over a finite set $\mathcal{S}$ is defined by $\mathrm{Supp}(P) := \{x \in \mathcal{S} : P(x) > 0\}$. For a (discrete) distribution D let $d \leftarrow D$ denote that d was sampled according to D. Similarly, for a set $\mathcal{S}$, let $s \leftarrow \mathcal{S}$ denote that s is drawn uniformly from $\mathcal{S}$. For an event W, we use $\overline{W}$ to denote the complement event. For a function $f: \{0,1\}^n \to \{0,1\}^n$, let $\mathsf{Im}(f) := \{f(x): x \in \{0,1\}^n\}$ be the image of f.

Let poly denote the set of all polynomials, and let PPT stand for probabilistic polynomial time. A function $\mu: \mathbb{N} \to [0,1]$ is negligible, denoted $\mu(n) = neg(n)$, if $\mu(n) < 1/p(n)$ for every $p \in$ poly and large enough n. For a security parameter n, a function $f: \{0,1\}^{m(n)} \to \{0,1\}^{\ell(n)}$ is efficiently computable if it is computable in polynomial time in n.

3.2   One-Way Functions

We now formally define basic cryptographic primitives. We start with the definition of one-way function.

Definition 3.1 (One-way function). *A polynomial-time computable function* $f : \{0,1\}^* \to \{0,1\}^*$ *is called a* one-way *function if for every probabilistic polynomial time algorithm* A, *there is a negligible function* $\mu : \mathbb{N} \to [0,1]$ *such that for every* $n \in \mathbb{N}$

$$\Pr_{x \leftarrow \{0,1\}^n} \left[\mathsf{A}(f(x)) \in f^{-1}(f(x)) \right] \leq \mu(n)$$

For simplicity we assume that the one-way function f is length-preserving. That is, $|f(x)| = |x|$ for every $x \in \{0,1\}^*$. This can be assumed without loss of generality, and is not crucial for our constructions.

Immediately from the definition of a one-way function, we get the following simple observation.

Claim 3.2. *For every one-way function* $f: \{0,1\}^n \to \{0,1\}^n$ *there exists a negligible function* $\mu(n)$ *such that for every input* $x \in \{0,1\}^n$ *it holds that* $\left| f^{-1}(f(x)) \right| \leq 2^n \cdot \mu(n)$.

3.3   Universal One Way Hash Functions

We now formally define UOWHF.

Definition 3.3 (Universal one-way hash function). *Let n be a security parameter. A family of functions $\mathcal{F} = \left\{ f_z \colon \{0,1\}^{m(n)} \to \{0,1\}^{\ell(n)} \right\}_{z \in \{0,1\}^{k(n)}}$ is a family of* universal one-way hash functions *(UOWHFs) if it satisfies:*

1. *Efficiency: Given $z \in \{0,1\}^{k(n)}$ and $x \in \{0,1\}^{m(n)}$, $f_z(x)$ can be evaluated in time $\operatorname{poly}(n)$.*
2. *Shrinking: $\ell(n) < m(n)$.*
3. *Target Collision Resistance: For every probabilistic polynomial-time adversary A, the probability that A succeeds in the following game is negligible in n:*
   (a) Let $(x, \text{state}) \leftarrow \mathsf{A}(1^n) \in \{0,1\}^{m(n)} \times \{0,1\}^*$.
   (b) Choose $z \leftarrow \{0,1\}^{k(n)}$.
   (c) Let $x' \leftarrow \mathsf{A}(\text{state}, z) \in \{0,1\}^{m(n)}$.
   (d) A succeeds if $x \neq x'$ and $f_z(x) = f_z(x')$.

A relaxation of the target collision resistance property can be done by requiring the function to be collision resistant only on random inputs (see Definition 2.1). The following lemma states that it is enough to construct a function that is collision resistant on random inputs, in order to get UOWHF.

Lemma 3.4 (From random inputs to targets, folklore). *Let n be a security parameter. Let $F \colon \{0,1\}^{m(n)} \to \{0,1\}^{\ell(n)}$ be an efficiently computable length-decreasing function. Suppose F is collision-resistant on random inputs. Then $\left\{ F_y \colon \{0,1\}^{m(n)} \to \{0,1\}^{\ell(n)} \right\}_{y \in \{0,1\}^{m(n)}}$, for $F_y(x) := F(y \oplus x)$, is an UOWHF.*

3.4   Hash Families

2-universal and t-wise independent hash families are an important ingredient in our constructions. In this section, we formally define this notion, together with some useful properties of such families.

Definition 3.5 (2-universal and t-wise independent families)
A family of functions $\mathcal{F} = \left\{ f \colon \{0,1\}^n \to \{0,1\}^\ell \right\}$ is 2-universal *if for every $x \neq x' \in \{0,1\}^n$ it holds that $\mathbf{Pr}_{f \leftarrow \mathcal{F}}[f(x) = f(x')] \leq 2^{-\ell}$. $\mathcal{F}$ is t-wise independent if for all $x_1 \neq \cdots \neq x_t \in \{0,1\}^n$, the random variables $F(x_1), \ldots, F(x_t)$ for $F \leftarrow \mathcal{F}$ are independent and uniformly distributed over $\{0,1\}^\ell$.*

A family is explicit *if given a description of a function $f \in \mathcal{F}$ and $x \in \{0,1\}^n$, $f(x)$ can be computed in polynomial time (in n, ℓ). Such family is* constructible *if it is explicit and there is a PPT algorithm that given $x \in \{0,1\}^n$ and $y \in \{0,1\}^\ell$ outputs a uniform $f \in \mathcal{F}$, such that $f(x) = y$.*

It is well-known that for every constant t, there are constructible families of t-wise independent functions with description size $O(t \cdot (n + \ell))$ in NC1. The next lemma, proven in the full version of this paper [24], will be useful in the proof.

Lemma 3.6. *Let $f \colon \{0,1\}^n \to \{0,1\}^n$ be a function, and $\mathcal{H} = \{h \colon \{0,1\}^n \to \{0,1\}^n\}$ a two-wise independent family. For every $x \in \{0,1\}^n$ and $c \in \mathbb{N}$ the following holds.*

$$\Pr_{h \leftarrow \mathcal{H}} \left[|\{x' : h(f(x')) = h(f(x))\}| \geq |f^{-1}(f(x))| + n^{2c} \right] \leq 2/n^c.$$

3.5 Entropy and Accessible Entropy

The *Shannon entropy* of a random variable X is defined by

$$H(X) = - \sum_{x \in \text{Supp}(X)} \Pr[X = x] \cdot \log(\Pr[X = x]).$$

The conditional entropy of a random variable X given Y, is defined as $H(X \mid Y) = \mathbf{E}_{y \leftarrow Y}[H(X|_{Y=y})]$. For a number $p \in [0,1]$, we will use $H(p)$ to denote the entropy of a random variable distributed according to $Bernoulli(p)$. That is $H(p) = -p \log p - (1 - p) \log(1 - p)$.

The *min entropy* of a random variable X is defined by

$$\mathrm{H}_\infty(X) = \min_{x \in \text{Supp}(X)} \log \frac{1}{\Pr[X = x]},$$

and the *max entropy* of X is defined by $H_0(X) = \log |\text{Supp}(X)|$.

Lastly, for random variables X and Y, the sample entropy of $x \in \text{Supp}(X)$ (with respect to X) is defined by $H_X(x) = -\log \Pr[X = x]$, and the sample entropy of x given $y \in \text{Supp}(Y)$ is defined by $H_{X|Y}(x|y) = -\log \Pr[X = x|Y = y]$. The following equality is immediate from the definitions above.

$$H(X \mid Y) = \mathop{\mathbf{E}}_{x \leftarrow X, y \leftarrow Y} H_{X|Y}(x \mid y) \tag{1}$$

For a function g, we also use the following notation, defined in [15], for the entropy of g^{-1}.

Definition 3.7 (Real entropy). *Let n be a security parameter and $g \colon \{0,1\}^n \to \{0,1\}^m$ be a function.*

We say that g^{-1} has real Shannon entropy k if $H(X|g(X)) = k$, where X is uniformly distributed on $\{0,1\}^n$.

We say that g^{-1} has real min-entropy at least k if there is a negligible function $\varepsilon = \varepsilon(n)$ such that $\Pr_{x \leftarrow X} H_{X|g(X)}(x|g(x)) \geq k \geq 1 - \varepsilon(n)$.

We say that g^{-1} has real max-entropy at most k if there is a negligible function $\varepsilon = \varepsilon(n)$ such that $\Pr_{x \leftarrow X} H_{X|g(X)}(x|g(x)) \leq k \geq 1 - \varepsilon(n)$.

[15] also introduced the notion of accessible max-entropy. A collision finder for a function g is an algorithm that, given input x, always outputs x' such that $g(x) = g(x')$. g^{-1} has small accessible entropy, if the output of every collision finder for g comes from a small set.

Definition 3.8 (Collision finder). *For a function* $g\colon \{0,1\}^{m(n)} \to \{0,1\}^{\ell(n)}$, *an algorithm* A *is a* g-collision finder *if for every* $x \in \{0,1\}^{m(n)}$ *it holds that* $\Pr\left[g(\mathsf{A}(1^n, x)) = g(x)\right] = 1$.

Definition 3.9 (accessible max-entropy). *Let* n *be a security parameter and* $g\colon \{0,1\}^{m(n)} \to \{0,1\}^{\ell(n)}$ *be a function. We say that* g^{-1} *has accessible max-entropy at most* k *if for every* PPT g-collision finder A *and for every* $n \in \mathbb{N}$, *there exists a family of sets* $\{\mathcal{L}(x)\}_{x \in \{0,1\}^{m(n)}}$ *each of size at most* $2^{k(n)}$ *such that* $x \in \mathcal{L}(x)$ *for all* x, *and* $\Pr_{x \leftarrow \{0,1\}^{m(n)}}\left[\mathsf{A}(1^n, x) \in \mathcal{L}(x)\right] \geq 1 - neg(n)$.

The next theorems are implicit in [15] and will be useful in our constructions.

Theorem 3.10 (Entropy gap, implicit in [15]). *Let* $f\colon \{0,1\}^n \to \{0,1\}^n$ *be a one-way function. Then there exists* $\ell = \ell(n)$, $s = \omega(\log n)$ *and an efficiently computable function* $g\colon \{0,1\}^{n^5} \to \{0,1\}^{n^5}$ *such that:*

1. g^{-1} *has real min-entropy at least* $\ell + s$.
2. g^{-1} *has accessible max-entropy at most* ℓ.
3. g *is computable in* NC1 *using* $O(n^4)$ *non-adaptive oracle calls to the one-way function.*

Theorem 3.11 (Implied by Claim 4.9, [15]). *Let* $f\colon \{0,1\}^n \to \{0,1\}^n$ *be a one-way function and let* $\mathcal{H} = \{h\colon \{0,1\}^n \to \{0,1\}^n\}$ *be a family of constructible, three-wise independent hash functions.*[12] *Then, for every* PPT A, *every constant* $c > 0$ *and every* $i \in [n]$, *it holds that:*

$$\Pr_{\substack{h \leftarrow \mathcal{H}, \\ x \leftarrow \{0,1\}^n, \\ x' \leftarrow \mathsf{A}(1^n, h, x, i)}} \left[\begin{array}{c} (f(x') \neq f(x)) \wedge (h(f(x))_{<i} = h(f(x'))_{<i}) \\ \wedge\ i > n - (\log|f^{-1}(f(x'))| - c\log n) \end{array} \right] = neg(n).$$

3.6 Useful Facts

We will use the well known Chernoff bound in our proof.

Fact 3.12 (Chernoff bound). *Let* $A_1, ..., A_n$ *be independent random variables s.t.* $A_i \in \{0,1\}$ *and let* $\widehat{A} = \Sigma_{i=1}^n A_i$. *For every* $\epsilon \in [0,1]$ *It holds that:*

$$\Pr\left[\left|\widehat{A} - \mathbf{E}\left[\widehat{A}\right]\right| \geq \epsilon \cdot \mathbf{E}\left[\widehat{A}\right]\right] \leq 2 \cdot e^{-\epsilon^2 \cdot \mathbf{E}[\widehat{A}]/3}.$$

---

[12] Actually, the proof in [15] only requires two-wise independence.

4   Non-adaptive UOWHF from One-Way Functions

In this part we construct and prove the security of our non-adaptive UOWHF. This is done by combining the construction of [15] with the non-adaptive construction of UOWHF for unknown-regular one-way functions of [25].

We start with the construction. Let $g\colon \{0,1\}^{m(n)} \to \{0,1\}^{k(n)}$ be a function with a sufficient gap between the real min-entropy and the max accessible entropy of g^{-1}. Let $\mathcal{H}_n = \left\{ h\colon \{0,1\}^{m(n)+k(n)} \to \{0,1\}^{m(n)-\log n} \right\}$ be a 2-universal hash family. For every $t \in \mathbb{N}$, define the function $C_t\colon \mathcal{H}_n^{t-1} \times (\{0,1\}^{m(n)})^t \to \mathcal{H}_n^{t-1} \times \{0,1\}^{k(n)} \times (\{0,1\}^{m(n)-\log n})^{t-1} \times \{0,1\}^{m(n)}$, by

$$C_t(h_1,\ldots,h_{t-1},x_1,\ldots,x_t)$$
$$:= h_1,\ldots,h_{t-1}, g(x_1), h_1(x_1,g(x_2)),\ldots h_{t-1}(x_{t-1},g(x_t)), x_t.$$

Note that the above function is length decreasing when $(t-1)\log n > k(n)$. The next theorem states that, for the right choice of parameters, C_t is also collision resistant.

Theorem 4.1. *Let $\ell = \ell(n)$, $s = \omega(\log n)$ and let $g\colon \{0,1\}^{m(n)} \to \{0,1\}^{k(n)}$ be a function. Assume that g^{-1} has real min-entropy at least $\ell + s$ and accessible max entropy at most ℓ. Then the function C_t is collision resistant on random inputs, for every $t \in$ poly.*

Corollary 4.2. *There exists a black-box construction of UOWHF from any one-way function that uses $O(n^9)$ non-adaptive calls to the one-way function. Moreover, the construction has key length and output length of $O(n^{10})$, and is computable in NC1 using oracle calls to f.*

Proof. Let $k = m = n^5$ and $t = k/\log n + 2$. By Theorem 3.10, there is a efficiently computable (using $O(n^4)$ non-adaptive calls to the one-way function f) function $g\colon \{0,1\}^m \to \{0,1\}^k$ such that g^{-1} has real min-entropy at least $\ell + s$ and accessible max-entropy at most ℓ. The proof is now immediate from Theorem 4.1 and Lemma 3.4, together with the fact that there is an explicit 2-universal family $\mathcal{H} = \left\{ h\colon \{0,1\}^{m+k} \to \{0,1\}^{m-\log n} \right\}$ with description size $O(m+k)$ in NC1.

Using the general method of randomized encoding, Applebaum, Ishai and Kushilevitz [4] showed how to compile CRHF in NC1 to a CRHF in NC0. By observing their proof applies also for UOWHFs, we get the following corollary.

Corollary 4.3 *Assuming that one-way functions exist in NC1, there exists a UOWHF in NC0.*

We now prove Theorem 4.1. Let m, k, ℓ, g and t be as in Theorem 4.1. We will need the following two claims. The first, which is straight-forward from the definition of accessible entropy, states that every collision for C_t comes from a small set. The proof, which is a simple reduction, is given in the full version of this paper [24].

Claim 4.4. *For every collision-finder algorithm for C_t it holds that there exists a family of sets $\{\mathcal{L}(x)\}_{x \in \{0,1\}^m}$ each of size at most 2^ℓ such that*

$$\Pr_{\substack{h:=(h_1,\ldots,h_{t-1})\leftarrow\mathcal{H}_n^{t-1}, \\ x:=(x_1,\ldots,x_t)\leftarrow(\{0,1\}^{m(n)})^{t(n)} \\ (h,(x_1',\ldots,x_t'))\leftarrow\mathsf{A}(1^n,h,x)}} [\exists i \in [t] \text{ s.t. } g(x_i') = g(x_i) \wedge x_i' \notin \mathcal{L}(x_i)] = neg(n).$$

For the second claim we will need the following definition. Let

$$\mathcal{T}_n := \left\{ x \in \{0,1\}^{m(n)} : H_{X|g(X)}(x|g(x)) \geq \ell + s \right\}$$
$$= \left\{ x \in \{0,1\}^m : |g^{-1}(g(x))| \geq 2^{\ell+s} \right\}.$$

That is, $\mathcal{T}_n$ is the set of all "typical" inputs x for g, for which $H_{X|g(X)}(x|g(x))$ is large.

The second claim considers the function C_d for every $d \in$ poly. It states that for typical inputs, i.e., $x_1, \ldots, x_d \in \mathcal{T}$, there is no collision $x_1', \ldots, x_d'$ for C_d such that x_1' is from a small set $\mathcal{G}$.

Claim 4.5. *For every $d, n \in \mathbb{N}$, set $\mathcal{G} \subseteq \{0,1\}^{m(n)}$ of size at most $2^{\ell(n)}$ and $x = (x_1, \ldots, x_d) \in \mathcal{T}_n^d$ it holds that*

$$\Pr_{h=(h_1,\ldots,h_{d-1})\leftarrow\mathcal{H}_n^{d-1}} \left[\begin{array}{c} \exists x'=(x_1',\ldots,x_d') \text{ s.t} \\ x_1'\in\mathcal{G}\wedge(x_1',g(x_2'))\neq(x_1,g(x_2))\wedge C_d(h,x)=C_d(h,x') \end{array} \right]$$
$$\leq d \cdot \mu(n),$$

for some negligible function μ.

We prove Claim 4.5 below, but first we use them in order to prove Theorem 4.1.

Proof (Proof of Theorem 4.1). Let A be a PPT collision-finder algorithm of C_t such that

$$\Pr_{\substack{h=(h_1,\ldots,h_{t-1})\leftarrow\mathcal{H}_n^{t-1}, \\ x=(x_1,\ldots,x_t)\leftarrow(\{0,1\}^{m(n)})^{t(n)} \\ (h,x')\leftarrow\mathsf{A}(1^n,h,x)}} [x \neq x' \wedge C_t(h,x) = C_t(h,x')] = \alpha(n). \tag{2}$$

We will show that α must be negligible.

For $n \in \mathbb{N}$, let $\{\mathcal{L}(x)\}_{x\in\{0,1\}^{m(n)}}$ be the family promised by Claim 4.4. Let $H = (H_1, \ldots, H_{t-1}) \leftarrow \mathcal{H}_n^{t-1}$ and $X = (X_1, \ldots, X_t) \leftarrow (\{0,1\}^{m(n)})^{t(n)}$ be random variables, and let $(\cdot, X') \leftarrow \mathsf{A}(1^n, H, X)$ be the output of A. Let W_1^n be the event that A found a valid collision. By construction, this event can be written as follows: There exists $i \in [t(n)]$, such that,

1. $(X_i', g(X_{i+1}')) \neq (X_i, g(X_{i+1}))$, and
2.

$$(g(X_i), H_i(X_i, g(X_{i+1})), \ldots, H_{t-1}(X_{t-1}, g(X_t)), X_t)$$
$$= (g(X_i'), H_i(X_i', g(X_{i+1}')), \ldots, H_{t-1}(X_{t-1}', g(X_t')), X_t').$$

Observe that, by definition of the function C, the last condition is equivalent to
$C_{t-i+1}(H_{i,\ldots,t-1}, X_{i,\ldots,t}) = C_{t-i+1}(H_{i,\ldots,t-1}, X'_{i,\ldots,t})$.

Additionally, we define the following two events. Let W_2^n be the event that exists $i \in [t(n)]$ such that $X_i \notin \mathcal{T}_n$, and let W_3^n be the event that there exists $i \in [t(n)]$ such that $g(X_i) = g(X'_i)$ and $X'_i \notin \mathcal{L}(X_i)$.

It holds that,

$$\alpha \leq \mathbf{Pr}\left[W_2^n\right] + \mathbf{Pr}\left[W_3^n\right] + \mathbf{Pr}\left[W_1^n \wedge \overline{W_2^n} \wedge \overline{W_3^n}\right].$$

Finally, observe that $\mathbf{Pr}\left[W_2^n\right] = \text{neg}(n)$ by the assumption that g^{-1} has min-entropy at least $\ell + s$ and the union bound, and $\mathbf{Pr}\left[W_3^n\right] = \text{neg}(n)$ by Claim 4.4. Additionally, $\mathbf{Pr}\left[W_1^n \wedge \overline{W_2^n} \wedge \overline{W_3^n}\right] = \text{neg}(n)$ by Claim 4.5 and the union bound (choosing $\mathcal{G} = \mathcal{L}(X_i)$).

4.1   Proving Claim 4.5

Fix n, and omit it from the notation. Let $\mathcal{T} = \mathcal{T}_n$ and $\mathcal{B} := \{0,1\}^m \setminus \mathcal{T}$. Recall that, by Theorem 3.10 and the definition of real min-entropy, it holds that $|\mathcal{B}| = \varepsilon(n) \cdot 2^m$ for some $\varepsilon \in neg(n)$. Let $g(\mathcal{T}) := \{g(x) \colon x \in \mathcal{T}\}$. The next claim is the main part of the proof of Claim 4.5. It states that for every small set $\mathcal{G}$ and strings x_1, x_2, the following holds with overwhelming probability over $h \in \mathcal{H}$. For every x'_1, x'_2 such that $x'_1 \in \mathcal{G}$ and $h(x_1, g(x_2)) = h(x'_1, g(x'_2))$ it holds that x'_2 is non-typical (that is, $x'_2 \in \mathcal{B}$). Moreover, the number of such collision is small.

Claim 4.6. *Let $\mathcal{B} := \{0,1\}^m \setminus \mathcal{T}$. Let $x_1, x_2 \in \{0,1\}^m$, and let $\mathcal{G} \subseteq \{0,1\}^m$ be a set of size at most 2^ℓ. For $h \in \mathcal{H}$, let*

$$\mathcal{G}_h = \{x'_2 \colon \exists x'_1 \in \mathcal{G} \text{ s.t. } (x'_1, g(x'_2)) \neq (x_1, g(x_2)) \wedge h(x_1, g(x_2)) = h(x'_1, g(x'_2))\}.$$

Then, $\mathbf{Pr}_{h \leftarrow \mathcal{H}}\mathcal{G}_h \subseteq \mathcal{B} \wedge |\mathcal{G}_h| \leq 2^\ell \geq 1 - n(\varepsilon(n) + 2^{-s(n)})$.

Proof (Proof of Claim 4.6). We start with showing that $\mathbf{Pr}_{h \leftarrow \mathcal{H}}\mathcal{G}_h \subseteq \mathcal{B} \geq 1 - n \cdot 2^{-s(n)}$. Indeed,

$$\mathbf{Pr}_{h \leftarrow \mathcal{H}}[\mathcal{G}_h \not\subseteq \mathcal{B}]$$

$$= \mathbf{Pr}_{h \leftarrow \mathcal{H}}\left[\substack{\exists (x'_1, x'_2) \in \mathcal{G} \times \mathcal{T} \text{ s.t.} \\ (x'_1, g(x'_2)) \neq (x_1, g(x_2)) \wedge h(x_1, g(x_2)) = h(x'_1, g(x'_2))}\right]$$

$$= \mathbf{Pr}_{h \leftarrow \mathcal{H}}\left[\exists (x'_1, y') \in \mathcal{G} \times g(\mathcal{T}) \text{ s.t. } (x'_1, y') \neq (x_1, g(x_2)) \wedge h(x_1, g(x_2)) = h(x'_1, y')\right]$$

$$\leq n \cdot 2^{-m} \cdot |\mathcal{G}| \cdot |g(\mathcal{T})|$$

$$\leq n \cdot 2^{-m} \cdot 2^\ell \cdot 2^m / 2^{\ell+s}$$

$$= n \cdot 2^{-s(n)}$$

where the first inequality holds since $\mathbf{Pr}_{h \leftarrow \mathcal{H}}h(x_1, g(x_2)) = h(x'_1, y') \leq n \cdot 2^{-m}$ for every $(x'_1, y') \neq (x_1, g(x_2))$ together with the union bound. The second inequality holds since by definition of $\mathcal{T}$ it must hold that $|g(\mathcal{T})| \leq 2^m / 2^{\ell+s}$.

We next show that $\mathbf{Pr}_{h \leftarrow \mathcal{H}} |\mathcal{G}_h \cap \mathcal{B}| \geq 2^\ell \leq n \cdot \varepsilon(n)$, which concludes the proof. We start with computing the expectation of $|\mathcal{G}_h \cap \mathcal{B}|$:

$$\mathop{\mathbf{E}}_{h \leftarrow \mathcal{H}} |\mathcal{G}_h \cap \mathcal{B}| \leq n \cdot 2^{-m} \cdot |\mathcal{G}| \cdot |\mathcal{B}|$$

$$\leq n \cdot 2^{-m} \cdot 2^\ell \cdot \varepsilon(n) \cdot 2^m$$

$$\leq n \cdot \varepsilon(n) \cdot 2^\ell.$$

The claim now follows by Markov and the Union bound.

We are now ready to prove Claim 4.5 using Claim 4.6. Intuitively, Claim 4.6 shows that if x_1' is from a small set, x_2' is from a small set too. Thus, we can continue by induction, to prove that also x_d' is from the set $\mathcal{B}$. It follows that, $x_d' \neq x_d$ with overwhelming probability (as $x_d \in \mathcal{T}$), which is enough since the output of C_d includes x_d.

Proof (Proof of Claim 4.5). Fix $n \in \mathbb{N}$, $x = (x_1, \ldots, x_d) \in \mathcal{T}_n^d$ and a set $\mathcal{G} \subseteq \{0,1\}^m$. For $h = (h_1, \ldots, h_{d-1}) \in H^{d-1}$, let

$$\mathcal{COL}(h, x) = \left\{ x' = (x_1', \ldots, x_d') \in \mathcal{G} \times (\{0,1\}^m)^{d-1} : \begin{smallmatrix} (x_1, g(x_2)) \neq (x_1', g(x_2')) \\ \wedge C_d(h,x) = C_d(h,x') \end{smallmatrix} \right\}$$

be the set containing all the possible collision of h, x with $x_1' \in \mathcal{G}$ and $(x_1, g(x_2)) \neq (x_1', g(x_2'))$. Similarly, for every $i \in \{0, \ldots, d-1\}$, let

$$\mathcal{COL}_i(h_1, \ldots, h_i, x) = \left\{ x' \in \mathcal{G} \times (\{0,1\}^m)^{d-1} : \begin{smallmatrix} (x_1, g(x_2)) \neq (x_1', g(x_2')) \\ \wedge \forall j \in [i] \; h_j(x_j, g(x_{j+1})) = h_j(x_j', g(x_{j+1}')) \end{smallmatrix} \right\}$$

That is, all inputs with $x_1' \in \mathcal{G}$ and $(x_1, g(x_2)) \neq (x_1', g(x_2'))$ that collide with i blocks of C_d. It is clear that for every x and h,

$$\mathcal{COL}(h, x) \subseteq \mathcal{COL}_{d-1}(h, x) \subseteq \ldots \subseteq \mathcal{COL}_0(x) \tag{3}$$

We want to show that with high probability over the choice of h, it holds that $\mathcal{COL}(h, x)$ is empty.

For every $i \in [d-1]$, let W_i be the event (over the choice of $h_1, \ldots h_{i-1} \leftarrow \mathcal{H}^{i-1}$) that there exists a set $\mathcal{G}_i$ of size at most 2^ℓ, such that for every $x' \in \mathcal{COL}_{i-1}(h_1, \ldots, h_{i-1}, x)$, it holds that $(x_i', g(x_{i+1}')) \neq (x_i, g(x_{i+1}))$ and $x_i' \in \mathcal{G}_i$.

For $i \in [d]$, let $\widehat{W}_i$ be the event that there exists a set $\mathcal{G}_i$ of size at most 2^ℓ such that for every $x' \in \mathcal{COL}_{i-1}(h_1, \ldots, h_{i-1}, x)$, it holds that $x_i' \neq x_i$ and $x_i' \in \mathcal{G}_i$.

Observe that $\mathbf{Pr}\left[W_i \mid \widehat{W}_i \right] = 1$. We will show that, for every $1 \leq i < d$, it holds that

$$\mathbf{Pr}\left[\widehat{W}_{i+1} \mid W_{\leq i} \right] \geq 1 - n(\varepsilon(n) + 2^{-s(n)}) \tag{4}$$

Furthermore, $\mathbf{Pr}[W_1] = 1$. Indeed, let $\mathcal{G}_1 = \mathcal{G}$. By assumption $x_1 \in \mathcal{G}$ and $(x_1', g(x_2')) \neq (x_1, g(x_2))$ for every $x_1', x_2' \in \mathcal{COL}_0(x)$.

To see that Eq. (4) holds, fix $1 \leq i < d$. Let $H' \leftarrow \mathcal{H}^{d-1}|_{W_{\leq i}}$, and observe that H_i' is uniformly distributed over $\mathcal{H}$. By the definition of W_i, it holds that for every $x' \in \mathcal{COL}_{i-1}(H'_{<i}, x)$ it holds that $(x'_i, g(x'_{i+1})) \neq (x_i, g(x_{i+1}))$ and $x'_i \in \mathcal{G}_i$ for some set $\mathcal{G}_i$ of size at most 2^ℓ. Define

$$\mathcal{G}_{i+1} := \left\{ x'_{i+1} : \begin{smallmatrix} \exists x'_i \in \mathcal{G}_i \ s.t. \\ (x'_i, g(x'_{i+1})) \neq (x_i, g(x_{i+1})) \wedge H'_i(x_i, g(x_{i+1})) = H'_i(x'_i, g(x'_{i+1})) \end{smallmatrix} \right\}.$$

By definition $x'_{i+1} \in \mathcal{G}_{i+1}$ for every $x' \in \mathcal{COL}_i(H'_{\leq i}, x)$. Applying Claim 4.6 we get that with all but $n(\varepsilon(n) + 2^{-s(n)})$ probability over the choice of H'_i, it holds that $|\mathcal{G}_{i+1}| \leq 2^\ell$. Moreover, with the same probability $\mathcal{G}_{i+1} \subseteq \mathcal{B}$, which implies that $x'_{i+1} \neq x_{i+1}$ (since by assumption, $x_{i+1} \in \mathcal{T}_n$).

To conclude, we get that for every $x' \in \mathcal{COL}(h, x) \subseteq \mathcal{COL}_{d-1}(h, x)$ it holds that $x'_d \neq x_d$ with probability at least

$$\mathbf{Pr}\left[\widehat{W}_d\right] \geq \mathbf{Pr}\left[\widehat{W}_d \mid W_{<d}\right] \cdot \prod_{1 < i \leq d-1} \mathbf{Pr}\left[W_i \mid W_{<i}\right]$$

$$\geq \mathbf{Pr}\left[\widehat{W}_d \mid W_{<d}\right] \cdot \prod_{1 < i \leq d-1} \mathbf{Pr}\left[W_i, \widehat{W}_i \mid W_{<i}\right]$$

$$= \mathbf{Pr}\left[\widehat{W}_d \mid W_{<d}\right] \cdot \prod_{1 < i \leq d-1} \left(\mathbf{Pr}\left[W_i \mid \widehat{W}_i, W_{<i}\right] \cdot \mathbf{Pr}\left[\widehat{W}_i \mid W_{<i}\right] \right)$$

$$\geq (1 - n(\varepsilon(n) + 2^{-s(n)}))^d$$

$$\geq 1 - d \cdot n(\varepsilon(n) + 2^{-s(n)})$$

$$= 1 - d \cdot \mathrm{neg}(n).$$

where the penultimate inequality holds by Eq. (4) and the fact that $\mathbf{Pr}\left[W_i \mid \widehat{W}_i, W_{<i}\right] = 1$. Recall that C_d outputs x_d. Thus, the above implies that $C_d(h, x) \neq C_d(h, x')$, which implies that $\mathcal{COL}(h, x) = \emptyset$ with the same probability.

5   Almost-UOWHF from One-Way Functions

In this section we formally define almost-UOWHF and next-bit unreachable entropy, and show how to construct them from one-way functions.

5.1   Almost-UOWHF

In this part we formally define almost-UOWHF. The definition of almost-UOWHF is similar to the definition of almost collision resistance on random input (Definition 2.5).

Definition 5.1 (Almost universal one-way hash function). *Let n be a security parameter. A family of functions*

$$\mathcal{F} = \left\{ f_z \colon \{0,1\}^{m(n)} \to \{0,1\}^{\ell(n)} \right\}_{z \in \{0,1\}^{k(n)}}$$

is a family of almost universal one-way hash functions *(almost-UOWHF) if it satisfies:*

1. *Efficiency: Given* $z \in \{0,1\}^{k(n)}$ *and* $x \in \{0,1\}^{m(n)}$, $f_z(x)$ *can be evaluated in time* poly(n).
2. *Shrinking:* $\ell(k) < m(k)$.
3. *Almost Target Collision Resistance: There exist sets* $\{\mathcal{B}_z\}_{z \in \{0,1\}^{k(n)}}$ *such that* $|\mathcal{B}_z| / 2^{m(n)} = \text{neg}(n)$, *and for every probabilistic polynomial-time adversary* A, *the probability that* A *succeeds in the following game is negligible in* n:
   (a) *Let* $(x, state) \leftarrow A(1^n) \in \{0,1\}^{m(n)} \times \{0,1\}^*$.
   (b) *Choose* $z \leftarrow \{0,1\}^{k(n)}$.
   (c) *Let* $x' \leftarrow A(state, z) \in \{0,1\}^{m(k)}$.
   (d) A *succeeds if* $x' \notin \mathcal{B}_z$, $x \neq x'$ *and* $f_z(x) = f_z(x')$.

The proof of the next lemma is similar to the proof of Lemma 3.4.

Lemma 5.2 (From random inputs to targets, almost version). *Let* n *be a security parameter. Let* $F: \{0,1\}^{m(n)} \to \{0,1\}^{\ell(n)}$ *be an efficiently computable length-decreasing function. Suppose* F *is almost collision-resistant on random inputs. Then* $\left\{ F_y: \{0,1\}^{m(n)} \to \{0,1\}^{\ell(n)} \right\}_{y \in \{0,1\}^{m(n)}}$, *for* $F_y(x) := F(y \oplus x)$, *is an almost-UOWHF.*

5.2 Next-Bit Unreachable Entropy

In this section we present the notion of next-bit unreachable entropy, and construct a function with next-bit unreachable entropy from one-way functions. Intuitively, we say that a function $g: \{0,1\}^m \to \{0,1\}^\ell$ has next-bit unreachable entropy v if for every $i \in [\ell]$, there is a set $\mathcal{U}_i \subseteq \{0,1\}^m$, such that, on the average over x, each x is a member of $(\ell - m + v)$ such sets, and, given $x \in \{0,1\}^m$, a poly-time algorithm cannot find $x' \in \mathcal{U}_i$ with $g(x)_{<i} = g(x')_{<i}$, but $g(x)_i \neq g(x')_i$.

Definition 5.3. *A function* $g: \{0,1\}^{m(n)} \to \{0,1\}^{\ell(n)}$ *has next-bit unreachable entropy* v, *if the following holds. For every* $n \in \mathbb{N}$ *and* $i \in [\ell(n)]$ *there exists a set* $\mathcal{U}_{i,n} \subseteq \{0,1\}^{m(n)}$, *such that*

1. $\mathcal{U}_{i,n}$ *are large: For every* $n \in \mathbb{N}$,

$$\Pr_{x \leftarrow \{0,1\}^{m(n)}, i \leftarrow [\ell(n)]} [x \notin \mathcal{U}_{i,n}] \leq (m(n) - v(n))/\ell(n).$$

2. Hard to get inside $\mathcal{U}_{i,n}$: *For every* PPT A,

$$\Pr_{\substack{x \leftarrow \{0,1\}^{m(n)}, \\ i \leftarrow [\ell(n)], x' \leftarrow A(1^n, x, i)}} [((x' \in \mathcal{U}_{i,n})) \wedge (g(x)_{<i} = g(x')_{<i}) \wedge (x \notin \mathcal{U}_{i,n})] = \text{neg}(n).$$

3. The entropy inside $\mathcal{U}_{i,n}$ is unreachable: *For every* PPT A,

$$\Pr_{\substack{x \leftarrow \{0,1\}^{m(n)}, \\ i \leftarrow [\ell(n)], \\ x' \leftarrow A(1^n, x, i)}} [((x' \in \mathcal{U}_{i,n})) \wedge (g(x)_{<i} = g(x')_{<i}) \wedge (g(x)_i \neq g(x')_i)] = \text{neg}(n).$$

We stress that for $x \notin \mathcal{U}_i$, Item 2 is stronger compared to Item 3. While Item 2 implies that it is hard to flip the i-th bit of g with inputs from $\mathcal{U}_i$, Item 2 requires that it is hard to find (any) input from $\mathcal{U}_i$ that agrees with x on the $i - 1$ firs bits.

The definition above is especially useful when the function g is close to be injective. Formally,

Definition 5.4. *A function g is almost-injective if*

$$\Pr_{x \leftarrow \{0,1\}^m} |g^{-1}(g(x))| > 1 = neg(n).$$

We use the above definition for the construction of almost-UOWHF in Sect. 5.3. The following claim, proved in the full version of this paper [24], shows how to construct a function with non-trivial next-bit unreachable entropy from a one-way function.

Theorem 5.5. *Let $f\colon \{0,1\}^n \to \{0,1\}^n$ be a one-way function and let $\mathcal{H} = \{h : \{0,1\}^n \to \{0,1\}^n\}$ be a family of constructable, three-wise independent hash functions. Let $g\colon \mathcal{H}^2 \times \{0,1\}^n \to \mathcal{H}^2 \times \{0,1\}^{2n}$ be defined by $g(h_1, h_2, x) = (h_1, h_2, h_1(f(x)), h_2(x))$. Then g is an almost-injective function with next-bit unreachable entropy $c \log(n)$, for every constant $c > 0$.*

Moreover, the input and output size of g are of length $O(n)$.

5.3   Next-Bit Unreachable Entropy to Almost-UOWHF

The Construction. We now describe our main construction. We start with some notations.

A *position vector* $p \in [\ell]^q$ is just a vector of indexes from $[\ell]$. For a function $g\colon \{0,1\}^m \to \{0,1\}^\ell$, input vector $w = (x_1, \ldots x_q) \in (\{0,1\}^m)^q$ and a position vector $p = (i_1, \ldots, i_q) \in [\ell]^q$, let $g_p(w) := g(x_1)_{i_1}, \ldots, g(x_q)_{i_q}$. Similarly, define $g_{<p}(w) := g(x_1)_{<i_1}, \ldots, g(x_q)_{<i_q}$, and $g_{\geq p}(w)$ analogously. For a number $k \in \mathbb{N}$, let $p + k := (i_1 + k, \ldots, i_q + k)$. For a number t, let $g^t\colon \{0,1\}^{tm} \to \{0,1\}^{t\ell}$ be the t-fold repetition of g, i.e., $g^t(x_1, \ldots, x_t) = g(x_1), \ldots, g(x_t)$.

We are now ready to present the construction (see Fig. 1).

Construction 5.6 (Almost-UOWHF). *Let n be a security parameter, and let $q = q(n), t = t(n)$ and $k = k(n)$ be parameters. Let $g : \{0,1\}^{m(n)} \to \{0,1\}^{\ell(n)}$ be a function, and let $\mathcal{H}_n = \left\{ h : \{0,1\}^{q(n)} \to \{0,1\}^{k(n)} \right\}$ be a 2-universal hash family. Define the function $C\colon \mathcal{H}_n \times [\ell(n)]^{q(n)} \times (\{0,1\}^{m(n) \cdot t(n)})^{q(n)} \to \mathcal{H}_n \times [\ell(n)]^{q(n)} \times \{0,1\}^{\ell(n) \cdot q(n) + (t(n) - 1)\ell \cdot k(n)}$ by*

$$C(h, p, z) := p, g'_{<p}(z), h(g'_p(z)), h(g'_{p+1}(z)), \ldots, h(g'_{p+(t-1)\ell - 1}(z)), g'_{\geq p + (t-1)\ell}(z),$$

for $g' = g^t$.

The main theorem of this part is stated below and proven in the full version of this paper [24]. Informally, it states that when g is an almost-injective function with non-trivial next-bit unreachable entropy, and for the right choice of parameters, the above construction is almost-collision resistant on random inputs.

Theorem 5.7. *Let* $g\colon \{0,1\}^{m(n)} \to \{0,1\}^{\ell(n)}$ *be an efficient, almost-injective function with next-bit unreachable entropy* $v(n) \in \mathbb{N}$*. For every* $q \in poly$ *and* $\varepsilon \in 1/poly$ *such that* $H(4\varepsilon(n)) \leq 0.1v(n)/\ell(n)$*,* $q = \omega\left(\log n \cdot \max\left\{\ell, \frac{\ell}{\varepsilon^2(\ell-m-v)}\right\}\right)$ *and for* $k = q(m-v/3)/\ell$*,* $t = 3(\ell-m)/v+2$ *the function* C *as in Construction 5.6 is efficient, shrinking and almost collision resistant on random inputs.*

This gives the following corollary.

Corollary 5.8. *Let* $s = \omega(1)$*. Assuming that one-way functions exist, there exists an almost-UOWHF with key length* $O(n^4 \cdot s)$*. Moreover, the almost-UOWHF construction makes* $O(n^3 \cdot s)$ *non-adaptive calls to the underlying one-way function.*

Acknowledgments. We are very thankful to Iftach Haitner for very useful discussions, and to the anonymous referees for valuable comments and their significant help with improving the presentation of this work.

The research of X. Mao and J. Zhang is supported by NSF CAREER award 2141536. The research of N. Mazor is supported by Israel Science Foundation grant 666/19.

References

1. Agrawal, R., Chen, Y.-H., Horel, T., Vadhan, S.: Unifying computational entropies via Kullback–Leibler divergence. In: Boldyreva, A., Micciancio, D. (eds.) CRYPTO 2019. LNCS, vol. 11693, pp. 831–858. Springer, Cham (2019). https://doi.org/10.1007/978-3-030-26951-7_28
2. Ames, S., Gennaro, R., Venkitasubramaniam, M.: *The generalized randomized iterate* and its application to new efficient constructions of UOWHFs from regular one-way functions. In: Wang, X., Sako, K. (eds.) ASIACRYPT 2012. LNCS, vol. 7658, pp. 154–171. Springer, Heidelberg (2012). https://doi.org/10.1007/978-3-642-34961-4_11
3. Applebaum, B., Haramaty-Krasne, N., Ishai, Y., Kushilevitz, E., Vaikuntanathan, V.: Low-complexity cryptographic hash functions. In: 8th Innovations in Theoretical Computer Science Conference, ITCS 2017. Schloss Dagstuhl-Leibniz-Zentrum fuer Informatik (2017). https://doi.org/10.4230/LIPIcs.ITCS.2017.7
4. Applebaum, B., Ishai, Y., Kushilevitz, E.: Cryptography in NC⁰. SIAM J. Comput. **36**(4), 845–888 (2006). https://doi.org/10.1137/S0097539705446950
5. Applebaum, B., Moses, Y.: Locally computable UOWHF with linear shrinkage. J. Cryptol. **30**(3), 672–698 (2016). https://doi.org/10.1007/s00145-016-9232-x
6. Asharov, G., Segev, G.: Limits on the power of indistinguishability obfuscation and functional encryption. SIAM J. Comput. **45**(6), 2117–2176 (2016). https://doi.org/10.1137/15M1034064

7. Barhum, K., Holenstein, T.: A cookbook for black-box separations and a recipe for UOWHFs. In: Sahai, A. (ed.) TCC 2013. LNCS, vol. 7785, pp. 662–679. Springer, Heidelberg (2013). https://doi.org/10.1007/978-3-642-36594-2_37

8. Barhum, K., Maurer, U.: UOWHFs from OWFs: trading regularity for efficiency. In: Hevia, A., Neven, G. (eds.) LATINCRYPT 2012. LNCS, vol. 7533, pp. 234–253. Springer, Heidelberg (2012). https://doi.org/10.1007/978-3-642-33481-8_13

9. Berman, I., Degwekar, A., Rothblum, R.D., Vasudevan, P.N.: Multi-collision resistant hash functions and their applications. In: Nielsen, J.B., Rijmen, V. (eds.) EUROCRYPT 2018. LNCS, vol. 10821, pp. 133–161. Springer, Cham (2018). https://doi.org/10.1007/978-3-319-78375-8_5

10. Bitansky, N., Kalai, Y.T., Paneth, O.: Multi-collision resistance: a paradigm for keyless hash functions. In: Proceedings of the 50th Annual ACM SIGACT Symposium on Theory of Computing, pp. 671–684 (2018). https://doi.org/10.1145/3188745.3188870

11. Blum, M., Micali, S.: How to generate cryptographically strong sequences of pseudo random bits. In: Annual Symposium on Foundations of Computer Science (FOCS), pp. 112–117 (1982). https://doi.org/10.1109/SFCS.1982.72

12. Gennaro, R., Gertner, Y., Katz, J., Trevisan, L.: Bounds on the efficiency of generic cryptographic constructions. SIAM J. Comput. 35(1), 217–246 (2005). https://doi.org/10.1137/S0097539704443276

13. Goldreich, O.: Candidate one-way functions based on expander graphs. In: Goldreich, O. (ed.) Studies in Complexity and Cryptography. Miscellanea on the Interplay between Randomness and Computation. LNCS, vol. 6650, pp. 76–87. Springer, Heidelberg (2011). https://doi.org/10.1007/978-3-642-22670-0_10

14. Haitner, I., Harnik, D., Reingold, O.: On the power of the randomized iterate. In: Dwork, C. (ed.) CRYPTO 2006. LNCS, vol. 4117, pp. 22–40. Springer, Heidelberg (2006). https://doi.org/10.1007/11818175_2

15. Haitner, I., Holenstein, T., Reingold, O., Vadhan, S., Wee, H.: Universal one-way hash functions via inaccessible entropy. In: Gilbert, H. (ed.) EUROCRYPT 2010. LNCS, vol. 6110, pp. 616–637. Springer, Heidelberg (2010). https://doi.org/10.1007/978-3-642-13190-5_31

16. Haitner, I., Mazor, N., Silbak, J.: Incompressibility and next-block pseudoentropy. 14th Innovations in Theoretical Computer Science (2023)

17. Haitner, I., Reingold, O., Vadhan, S.: Efficiency improvements in constructing pseudorandom generators from one-way functions. SIAM J. Comput. 42(3), 1405–1430 (2013). https://doi.org/10.1137/100814421

18. Haitner, I., Reingold, O., Vadhan, S., Wee, H.: Inaccessible entropy. In: Proceedings of the 41st Annual ACM Symposium on Theory of Computing, pp. 611–620 (2009). https://doi.org/10.1145/1536414.1536497

19. Håstad, J., Impagliazzo, R., Levin, L.A., Luby, M.: A pseudorandom generator from any one-way function. SIAM J. Comput. 28(4), 1364–1396 (1999). https://doi.org/10.1137/S0097539793244708

20. Holenstein, T., Sinha, M.: Constructing a pseudorandom generator requires an almost linear number of calls. In: 2012 IEEE 53rd Annual Symposium on Foundations of Computer Science, pp. 698–707. IEEE (2012). https://doi.org/10.1109/FOCS.2012.51

21. Holmgren, J., Lombardi, A.: Cryptographic hashing from strong one-way functions (or: one-way product functions and their applications). In: 2018 IEEE 59th Annual Symposium on Foundations of Computer Science (FOCS), pp. 850–858. IEEE (2018). https://doi.org/10.1109/FOCS.2018.00085

22. Katz, J., Koo, C.Y.: On constructing universal one-way hash functions from arbitrary one-way functions. Cryptology ePrint Archive (2005)
23. Komargodski, I., Naor, M., Yogev, E.: Collision resistant hashing for paranoids: dealing with multiple collisions. In: Nielsen, J.B., Rijmen, V. (eds.) EUROCRYPT 2018. LNCS, vol. 10821, pp. 162–194. Springer, Cham (2018). https://doi.org/10.1007/978-3-319-78375-8_6
24. Mao, X., Mazor, N., Zhang, J.: Non-adaptive universal one-way hash functions from arbitrary one-way functions. Cryptology ePrint Archive, Paper 2022/431 (2022). https://eprint.iacr.org/2022/431
25. Mazor, N., Zhang, J.: Simple constructions from (almost) regular one-way functions. In: Nissim, K., Waters, B. (eds.) TCC 2021. LNCS, vol. 13043, pp. 457–485. Springer, Cham (2021). https://doi.org/10.1007/978-3-030-90453-1_16
26. Naor, M., Yung, M.: Universal one-way hash functions and their cryptographic applications. In: Proceedings of the 21st Annual ACM Symposium on Theory of Computing, pp. 33–43 (1989). https://doi.org/10.1145/73007.73011
27. Rompel, J.: One-way functions are necessary and sufficient for secure signatures. In: Proceedings of the 22nd Annual ACM Symposium on Theory of Computing, pp. 387–394 (1990). https://doi.org/10.1145/100216.100269
28. Rothblum, R.D., Vasudevan, P.N.: Collision-resistance from multi-collision-resistance. In: Advances in Cryptology-CRYPTO 2022: 42nd Annual International Cryptology Conference, CRYPTO 2022, Santa Barbara, CA, USA, 15–18 August 2022, Proceedings, Part III, pp. 503–529. Springer, Heidelberg (2022). https://doi.org/10.1007/978-3-031-15982-4_17
29. Vadhan, S., Zheng, C.J.: Characterizing pseudoentropy and simplifying pseudorandom generator constructions. In: Proceedings of the 44th Annual ACM Symposium on Theory of Computing, pp. 817–836 (2012). https://doi.org/10.1145/2213977.2214051
30. Yao, A.C.: Theory and application of trapdoor functions. In: 23rd Annual Symposium on Foundations of Computer Science, SFCS 1982, pp. 80–91. IEEE (1982). https://doi.org/10.1109/SFCS.1982.45
31. Yu, Yu., Gu, D., Li, X., Weng, J.: (Almost) optimal constructions of UOWHFs from 1-to-1, regular one-way functions and beyond. In: Gennaro, R., Robshaw, M. (eds.) CRYPTO 2015. LNCS, vol. 9216, pp. 209–229. Springer, Heidelberg (2015). https://doi.org/10.1007/978-3-662-48000-7_11

XOCB: Beyond-Birthday-Bound Secure Authenticated Encryption Mode with Rate-One Computation

Zhenzhen Bao$^{1,4(\boxtimes)}$ ⓘ, Seongha Hwang^2 ⓘ, Akiko Inoue^3 ⓘ, Byeonghak Lee^2 ⓘ, Jooyoung Lee^2 ⓘ, and Kazuhiko Minematsu^3 ⓘ

[1] Institute for Network Sciences and Cyberspace, BNRist, Tsinghua University, Beijing, China
zzbao@tsinghua.edu.cn
[2] KAIST, Daejeon, Korea
{mathience98,lbh0307,hicalf}@kaist.ac.kr
[3] NEC, Kawasaki, Japan
{a_inoue,k-minematsu}@nec.com
[4] Zhongguancun Laboratory, Beijing, China

Abstract. We present a new block cipher mode of operation for authenticated encryption (AE), dubbed XOCB, that has the following features: (1) beyond-birthday-bound (BBB) security based on the standard pseudorandom assumption of the internal block cipher if the maximum block length is sufficiently smaller than the birthday bound, (2) rate-1 computation, and (3) supporting any block cipher with any key length. Namely, XOCB has effectively the same efficiency as the seminal OCB while having stronger quantitative security without any change in the security model or the required primitive in OCB. Although numerous studies have been conducted in the past, our XOCB is the first mode of operation to achieve these multiple goals simultaneously.

Keywords: Authenticated encryption · Block cipher · OCB · Beyond-birthday-bound security

1 Introduction

AUTHENTICATED ENCRYPTION. Since the formalization of authenticated encryption (AE) [6,25,36], constructing an efficient and secure AE[1] scheme has been one of the central topics in symmetric-key cryptography for decades. OCB, first proposed by Rogaway et al. at CCS 2001 [38], has been known to be a seminal scheme for its efficiency and security. OCB operates at rate 1, *i.e.*, each input block needs only one block cipher call used inside[2]. In addition, it is parallelizable. XOCB is much more efficient than the generic composition schemes that

---

[1] We use the term AE to mean nonce-based AEAD [36] throughout the paper, unless otherwise stated.

[2] By convention, we ignore the constant number of block cipher calls per message.

ⓒ International Association for Cryptologic Research 2023
C. Hazay and M. Stam (Eds.): EUROCRYPT 2023, LNCS 14007, pp. 532–561, 2023.
https://doi.org/10.1007/978-3-031-30634-1_18

need at least two block cipher calls (thus rate $\leq 1/2$) and its variant, most notably GCM [1], which is specified by NIST SP800-38D and now quite widely deployed. The security of OCB can be reduced to the standard computational assumption on the block cipher used: namely, if the block cipher is a strong pseudorandom permutation (SPRP), OCB is shown to be provably secure. OCB has three versions [27,37,38], and the latest one (OCB3 [27]) is one of the winners of CAESAR competition[3] and is specified in RFC 7253. OCB3[4] has been implemented by OpenSSL and many other cryptographic libraries.

BEYOND OCB. The security guarantee of (any version of) OCB is up to the birthday bound (upBB)[5], that is, if the internal block cipher has n-bit block, OCB is broken by attacks of data complexity $O(2^{n/2})$. This significantly limits the practical value of OCB with a small – most typically 64-bit – block cipher, because the limit of $2^{n/2}$ data per each secret key can be too severe. A very impactful exposition of such a risk is Sweet32 attack against TLS/SSL using 64-bit block ciphers [7]. Even if we use 128-bit block ciphers, such as AES, this is not a threat to the distant future.

For example, NIST[6] has recently been reviewing FIPS 197 (specifying AES), and several comments received in conjunction with this review process, more specifically from Microsoft and Amazon, warn that continued use of 128-bit block ciphers with GCM will be a problem in the near future. In particular, it is mentioned that exabyte ($10^{18} \approx 2^{60}$) data is already in use and zettabyte ($10^{21} \approx 2^{70}$) in the near future.

Transitioning to a new (possibly wide-block) cipher would not be easy and take time. If one wants to use AES (or, more generally, any n-bit block cipher where $n/2$-bit security can be a concern), a promising approach is to employ a *beyond-birthday-bound* (BBB) secure AE mode that resists attacks of complexity $O(2^{n/2})$. Moreover, the advancement of lightweight cryptography produces many block ciphers having application/platform-specific advantage over AES, in terms of various metrics, such as hardware size [4,10], energy [3], latency [11], and software performance on low-end platforms [5]. To make it lightweight while achieving security equivalent to AES-128, it is quite often that these ciphers have key and block lengths at most 128 bits.

A BBB-secure AE mode has been extensively studied. Iwata proposed CHM [21], and CIP [22] that combine CENC [21], a BBB-secure nonce-based encryption mode, with a universal hash (UH) function using field multiplications. These schemes are provably secure under the standard pseudorandom assumption and roughly have $2n/3$-bit provable security. While the encryption part (CENC) is efficient, the need for the UH function makes the total cost (both for computation time and implementation memory) largely similar to GCM.

---

[3] https://competitions.cr.yp.to/caesar.html.

[4] We may simply write OCB to mean OCB3.

[5] The second version OCB2 is flawed and allows devastating attacks, though a simple fix is possible [20].

[6] https://csrc.nist.gov/News/2022/proposal-to-revise-sp-800-38a.

Another approach is to instantiate a tweakable block cipher (TBC) [28] using a block cipher and adopt a BBB-secure AE mode of a TBC as a template. The most popular template is ΘCB3, which has n-bit security using a TBC of n-bit block and about $3n$-bit tweak (required tweak length depends on the length of nonce and a maximum of message length etc.). If we instantiate such a TBC by an upBB-secure block cipher mode such as XEX, we obtain OCB3, and the resulting AE is also upBB-secure at best. Instantiating a BBB-secure TBC will break this barrier, however, is far from trivial. The cascaded LRW achieves BBB-security, but it needs two or more block cipher calls plus UH functions. Naito's XKX [32] requires a block cipher of more than n-bit keys and rekeying per nonce for BBB security. This allows us to use, say AES-256, but excludes a large number of lightweight ciphers for its key size as described above; hence it is not a perfect solution, and we cannot benefit from the state-of-the-art lightweight ciphers. Other TBC constructions, such as Mennink's F1 and F2 [29], or Jha et al.'s XHX [24] are efficient and work with a block cipher of about n-bit key. However, they need the ideal-cipher model for security reduction. Obtaining a standard security reduction for these constructions is considered to be hard [30]. This poses a non-trivial gap between GCM or OCB, which have been proved under the standard model. That is, the previous BBB-secure AE modes require either a significant increase in computation, making the rate close to $1/2$, or a change in the cryptographic primitive supported by OCB, that is, an n-bit SPRP of any key length. The natural question here is *if we can achieve a BBB-secure AE maintaining the advantages of* OCB *as much as possible.*

OUR CONTRIBUTIONS. In this paper, we present a solution that answers the above question positively. Our proposal, dubbed XOCB, is an AE mode that can be based on an n-bit block cipher, and achieves BBB, namely $2n/3$-bit security for a constant maximum input length, assuming that the block cipher is an SPRP (for its use of both block cipher forward and inverse operations). The rate is one. Unlike XKX, XOCB does not need a rekeying while operating, making it possible to be instantiated with ciphers of k-bit keys for any k, and $k = n = 128$ allows using AES-128. When the maximum input length is not a constant, XOCB still maintains upBB security. Namely, it can securely encrypt a message of $\ll O(2^{n/2})$ blocks. In addition, XOCB is fully parallellizable as OCB. Despite numerous previous works, XOCB is the first mode of operation that achieves these goals[7]. See Table 1 for comparison.

The main innovation of XOCB is an encryption part that can be seen as an amalgamation of CENC and OCB's encryption part. We add one more output-masking layer to (a variant of) OCB's internal XEX mode throughout encryption or decryption. This additional mask is computed once for each nonce. Hence the rate is one. In more detail, for m-block message and a-block associated data (AD), XOCB needs $m+a$ plus 7 to 8 calls. The security depends on the maximum input length l (in n-bit blocks) and ranges between $n/2$ to $2n/3$ bits depending on the maximum length of a message. In more detail, the concrete bound is

---

[7] In concurrent to our work, Bhattacharjee, Bhaumik, and Nandi [8] presented an AE scheme combining SPRP and PRF that has some structural similarity to XOCB.

shown at Theorem 1, and its leading terms are $l\sigma/2^n + l\sigma^3/2^{2n}$ ignoring the constants, where σ denotes the total number of input blocks and l denotes the maximum input length in n bits. At first glance, the security improvement of XOCB over OCB appears limited because of the length factor. I.e., it is birthday-secure concerning l. However, many practical communication protocols specify a maximum packet length, also known as a Maximum transmission unit (MTU), that is not large. For example, the Internet Protocol (IP) has an MTU of 65535 $(= 2^{15})$ bytes. With this limit, XOCB with AES-128 can encrypt at most around $2^{80.3}$ bytes of input blocks, while OCB is limited to 2^{68} bytes. For low-power communication protocols, MTU is much smaller, such as 257 bytes for Bluetooth (specifically BLE 4.2). We also point out that XKX includes $l^2 q/2^n$ [31,32] in its bound for q queries, that is, a birthday term for l. We provide a numerical bound comparison for practical message lengths at Table 1. This exhibits the stronger security of XOCB for real-world use cases.

While the main routine of XOCB is structurally similar to CENC, we need a quite different analysis. This is because (1) the block cipher inputs in CENC are all determined by a single variable (nonce), while in our case, all inputs are determined by message blocks, independently for each block, and (2) the decryption of XOCB involves a block cipher inverse, which is absent in CENC. Note that CENC implements a nonce-based additive encryption by a BBB-secure expanding PRF. Hence the encryption and decryption are symmetric and do not need the block cipher inverse. These differences require us to develop a dedicated security analysis, which is much more involved than the case of CENC. We employ the framework developed by Kim et al. [26] for analyzing DBHtS MAC [15] (that is also based on the standard Coefficient-H) for proofs. This helps to reduce the proof complexity and gains accessibility, but it remains a lot of involved bad cases, which turns out to be a challenging task.

Finally, we stress that our security goal is the standard AE security under nonce-respecting adversaries. Due to its online computation algorithm, the nonce-misuse resistance security [39] is impossible to achieve by nature. Similarly, we do not claim security under the release of unverified plaintext (RUP) introduced by Andreeva et al. [2]. We consider classical single-user security, and analyzing multi-user security is left open.

IMPLEMENTATIONS. We present implementations of XOCB's AES instantiation on both high-end CPUs and low-end microprocessors to show its practical relevance. The implementation results show that on a modern 64-bit CPU (Intel's Tiger Lake family), AES-XOCB can encrypt and authenticate a 4096-byte message plus a 16-byte AD at a speed of 0.5 cycles per byte (cpb), while AES-ECB runs at 0.3 cpb at the same platform. Comparatively, AES-OCB and AES-CIP with the same implementation of AES executed at a speed of 0.4 and 1.2 cpb, respectively. On an 8-bit AVR processor (AVR ATmega328P), AES-XOCB requires 8556 bytes of ROM to support both encryption and decryption, and processes a 128-byte message plus a 16-byte AD at a speed of 306 cpb; In contrast, an optimized implementation of AES-GCM requires 11012 bytes of ROM and executes at a speed of 880 cpb.

Table 1. Comparison of AE schemes that can use an n-bit block cipher of any key length. MUL denotes a field multiplication over $GF(2^n)$. The cost of MUL depends on the platform and implementation, and we simply assume it is equivalent to the block cipher used. The "Security" column denotes the bit security ignoring the contribution of the maximum input length. The "Lead Terms" column denotes the leading terms in the nAE advantage (Refer to the main texts for more details).

Scheme	Primitive	Rate	Security	Lead Terms*	Ref
OCB	SPRP	1	$n/2$	$\sigma^2/2^n + q/2^n$ †	[27]
GCM	PRP, MUL	1/2	$n/2$	$\sigma^2/2^n + q/2^n$	[23,33]
CHM,CIP	PRP, MUL	1/2	$2n/3$	$\sigma^3/2^{2n} + \sigma/2^n$	[21,22]
XOCB	SPRP	1	$2n/3$	$l\sigma^3/2^{2n} + l\sigma/2^n$	This paper

* σ: total queried blocks in n-bit blocks, q: total number of queries, and l: the maximum block length of a query. We assume $O(1)$ AD blocks

† Bhaumik and Nandi [9] improved the bound with respect to the decryption queries

2   Preliminaries

BASIC NOTATION. For a positive integer n, we write $N = 2^n$ and $[n] = \{1, \ldots, n\}$. For two nonnegative integers m and n such that $m \leq n$, we write $[m..n] = \{m, m+1, \ldots, n\}$. Given a nonempty set $\mathcal{X}$, $x \leftarrow_\$ \mathcal{X}$ denotes that x is chosen uniformly randomly from $\mathcal{X}$. The set of all functions from $\mathcal{X}$ to $\mathcal{Y}$ is denoted $\mathsf{Func}(\mathcal{X}, \mathcal{Y})$, and the set of all permutations on $\mathcal{X}$ is denoted $\mathsf{Perm}(\mathcal{X})$. For simplicity, $\mathsf{Perm}(n)$ denotes the set of all permutations on $\{0,1\}^n$. For integers a and b such that $1 \leq a \leq b$, we write $(b)_a = b(b-1)\ldots(b-a+1)$, and $(b)_0 = 1$ by convention.

For a positive integer n, let $\{0,1\}^n$ be the set of n-bit strings and $\{0,1\}^{\leq n} = \bigcup_{i \in [0..n]}\{0,1\}^i$. Let 0^n be the string of n zero bits. Note that $0^0 = \varepsilon$. We write $\{0,1\}^*$ to denote the set of all arbitrary-length strings, including the empty string, and let $\{0,1\}^+ = \{0,1\}^* \setminus \{\varepsilon\}$. The set $\{0,1\}^n$ is sometimes regarded as a set of integers $\{0,1,\ldots,2^n - 1\}$ by converting an n-bit string $a_{n-1}\ldots a_1 a_0 \in \{0,1\}^n$ to an integer $2^{n-1}a_{n-1} + \cdots + 2a_1 + a_0$. An element $x \in \{0,1,\ldots,2^c - 1\}$ for some positive integer c may be denoted by $\langle x \rangle_c \in \{0,1\}^c$ following the above (standard) encoding. We also identify $\{0,1\}^n$ with a finite field $GF(2^n)$ with 2^n elements, assuming that 2 cyclically generates all the nonzero elements of $GF(2^n)$.

For $X \in \{0,1\}^*$, let $|X|$ be the bit length of X. For a positive integer n and $X \in \{0,1\}^+$, let $|X|_n = \lceil |X|/n \rceil$ where $\lceil x \rceil$ is the smallest integer y such that $y \geq x$ and let $|\varepsilon|_n = 1$. For a positive integer n and a string $X \in \{0,1\}^*$,

$(X_1, X_2, \ldots, X_m) \xleftarrow{n} X$ denotes that X is partitioned into strings $X_1, \ldots, X_m$, where $m = |X|_n$, $|X_1| = \cdots = |X_{m-1}| = n$, and $0 < |X_m| \le n$ if $X \ne \varepsilon$, and $X_m = \varepsilon$ otherwise. For a positive integer n and $X \in \{0,1\}^*$, let $\mathsf{pad}(X) = X \parallel 1 \parallel 0^{n-(|X| \bmod n)-1}$. Note that pad is an injective function. For a positive integer n and $X \in \{0,1\}^*$, $\mathsf{ozp}(X)$ and $\overline{X}$ denote one-zero padding; $\mathsf{ozp}(X) = \overline{X} = X$ if $|X| = 0 \bmod n$, and $\mathsf{ozp}(X) = \overline{X} = \mathsf{pad}(X)$ if $|X| \ne 0 \bmod n$. For a positive integer $t \le n$ and $X \in \{0,1\}^n$, $\mathsf{msb}_t(X)$ denotes a string of the most significant t bits of X. For $X, Y \in \{0,1\}^*$, let

$$X \oplus_{\mathsf{msb}} Y = \begin{cases} X \oplus \mathsf{msb}_{|X|}(Y) & \text{if } |X| < |Y|. \\ \mathsf{msb}_{|Y|}(X) \oplus Y & \text{if } |X| \ge |Y|. \end{cases}$$

SECURITY NOTIONS. Let $E : \mathcal{K} \times \{0,1\}^n \to \{0,1\}^n$ be a keyed permutation with key space $\mathcal{K}$, where $E(K, \cdot)$ is a permutation for each $K \in \mathcal{K}$. We will denote $E_K(X)$ for $E(K, X)$. A (q, t)-distinguisher against E is an algorithm $\mathcal{D}$ with oracle access to an n-bit permutation and its inverse, making at most q oracle queries, running in time at most t, and outputting a single bit. The advantage of $\mathcal{D}$ in breaking the PRP-security of E, i.e., in distinguishing E from a uniform random permutation $\pi \leftarrow_\$ \mathsf{Perm}(n)$, is defined as

$$\mathsf{Adv}_E^{\mathsf{sprp}}(\mathcal{D}) = \left| \Pr\left[K \leftarrow_\$ \mathcal{K} : \mathcal{D}^{E_K, E_K^{-1}} = 1 \right] - \Pr\left[\pi \leftarrow_\$ \mathsf{Perm}(n) : \mathcal{D}^{\pi, \pi^{-1}} = 1 \right] \right|.$$

In our security proof, the underlying block cipher E will be replaced by a truly random permutation up to the above adversarial distinguishing advantage.

Given key space $\mathcal{K}$, nonce space $\mathcal{N}$, associate data (AD) space $\mathcal{A}$, message space $\mathcal{M}$, ciphertext space $\mathcal{C}$, and tag space $\mathcal{T}$, a nonce-based authenticated encryption (nAE) scheme is defined by a tuple

$$\Pi = (\mathcal{K}, \mathcal{N}, \mathcal{A}, \mathcal{M}, \mathcal{C}, \mathsf{Enc}, \mathsf{Dec}),$$

where Enc and Dec denote encryption and decryption schemes, respectively. More precisely,

$$\mathsf{Enc} : \mathcal{K} \times \mathcal{N} \times \mathcal{A} \times \mathcal{M} \longrightarrow \mathcal{C} \times \mathcal{T},$$
$$\mathsf{Dec} : \mathcal{K} \times \mathcal{N} \times \mathcal{A} \times \mathcal{C} \times \mathcal{T} \longrightarrow \mathcal{M} \cup \{\perp\},$$

where for $\mathsf{Enc}(K, N, A, M) = (C, T)$, we require $|C| = |M|$ and

$$\mathsf{Dec}(K, N, A, C, T') = \begin{cases} M & \text{if } T = T', \\ \perp & \text{otherwise.} \end{cases}$$

We will write $\mathsf{Enc}_K(N, A, M)$ and $\mathsf{Dec}_K(N, A, C)$ to denote $\mathsf{Enc}(K, N, A, M)$ and $\mathsf{Dec}(K, N, A, C)$, repectively. Throughout this paper, we will fix $\mathcal{N} = \{0,1\}^{n-2}$, $\mathcal{A} = \mathcal{M} = \mathcal{C} = \{0,1\}^*$ and $\mathcal{T} = \{0,1\}^n$.

Against the nonce-based authenticated encryption security of Π, an adversary $\mathcal{D}$ aims at distinguishing the real world $(\mathsf{Enc}_K, \mathsf{Dec}_K)$ and the ideal world $(\mathsf{Rand}, \mathsf{Rej})$, where Rand returns a random string of length $|M| + n$ for every encryption query $\mathsf{Enc}_K(N, A, M)$ and Rej always returns $\perp$ for every decryption query.

In this paper, we assume that $\mathcal{D}$ is nonce-respecting; it does not repeat nonces in *encryption* queries. Furthermore, $\mathcal{D}$ is non-trivial, i.e., $\mathcal{D}$ never repeats the same encryption/decryption query nor makes a decryption query (N, A, C, T) once (C, T) has been obtained by a previous encryption query $\mathsf{Enc}_K(N, A, M)$. Then the advantage of $\mathcal{D}$ against the nonce-based authenticated encryption security of Π is defined as

$$\mathsf{Adv}_{\Pi}^{\mathrm{nAE}}(\mathcal{D}) = \left| \Pr\left[K \leftarrow_{\$} \mathcal{K} : \mathcal{D}^{\mathsf{Enc}_K, \mathsf{Dec}_K} = 1\right] - \Pr\left[\mathcal{D}^{\mathsf{Rand}, \mathsf{Rej}} = 1\right] \right|.$$

We say that $\mathcal{D}$ is a (q_e, q_d, σ, l, t)-adversary against the nonce-based AE security of Π if $\mathcal{D}$ makes at most q_e encryption queries and at most q_d decryption queries, and running in time at most t, where the length of each encryption/decryption query (with a nonce and a tag excluded)[8] is at most l blocks of n bits. The total length of the encryption and decryption queries (with nonces and tags excluded) is at most σ blocks of n bits. When considering information-theoretic security, we will drop the parameter t.

COEFFICIENT-H TECHNIQUE. We will use Patarin's coefficient-H technique. The goal of this technique is to upper bound the adversarial distinguishing advantage between a real construction and its ideal counterpart. In the real (resp. ideal) world, an information-theoretic adversary $\mathcal{D}$ is allowed to make queries to a oracle denoted $\mathcal{O}_{\mathrm{real}}$ (resp. $\mathcal{O}_{\mathrm{ideal}}$). The interaction between $\mathcal{D}$ and the oracle determines a transcript. It contains all the information obtained during the interaction. We write that transcript τ is attainable if the probability of obtaining τ in the ideal world is non-zero. We also write T_{id} and T_{re} to denote the probability distribution of the transcript τ induced by the ideal world and the real world, respectively. By extension, we use the same notation to denote a random variable distributed according to each distribution.

We partition the set of attainable transcripts Γ into a set of "good" transcripts Γ_{good}, where the probability to obtain $\tau \in \Gamma_{\mathrm{good}}$ is close in the real world and the ideal world, and a set of "bad" transcripts Γ_{bad}, where the probability of obtaining $\tau \in \Gamma_{\mathrm{bad}}$ is small in the ideal world. Then the coefficient-H technique is summarized as the following lemma.

Lemma 1. *Let $\Gamma = \Gamma_{\mathrm{good}} \sqcup \Gamma_{\mathrm{bad}}$ be a partition of the set of attainable transcripts, where there exists a non-negative number ϵ_1 such that for any $\tau \in \Gamma_{\mathrm{good}}$,*

$$\frac{\Pr\left[\mathsf{T}_{\mathrm{re}} = \tau\right]}{\Pr\left[\mathsf{T}_{\mathrm{id}} = \tau\right]} \geq 1 - \epsilon_1,$$

---

[8] More precisely, the block length of an encryption (resp. decryption) query is defined as $|A|_n + |M|_n$ (resp. $|A|_n + |C|_n$), while the length of the "empty" query is 1.

and there exists a non-negative number ϵ_2 such that $\Pr\left[\mathsf{T}_{\mathrm{id}} \in \Gamma_{bad}\right] \leq \epsilon_2$. Then for any adversary $\mathcal{D}$, one has

$$\left|\Pr\left[\mathcal{D}^{\mathcal{O}_{real}} = 1\right] - \Pr\left[\mathcal{D}^{\mathcal{O}_{ideal}} = 1\right]\right| \leq \epsilon_1 + \epsilon_2,$$

where $\mathcal{D}^{\mathcal{O}_{real}}$ and $\mathcal{D}^{\mathcal{O}_{ideal}}$ denote the adversarial outputs in the real and the ideal worlds, respectively.

We refer to [19] for the proof of Lemma 1.

EXTENDED MIRROR THEORY. Patarin's Mirror theory [34,35] is a very powerful tool to estimate the number of solutions to a certain type of system of equations. At the beginning, there were some uncertainties in the proof of Mirror theory, but now there are several results on the full proof of Mirror theory up to n-bit security [13,14,17]. In this paper, we will use the *extended Mirror theory* [16,18], which is a variant of Mirror theory, and estimates the number of solutions to a system of equations as well as non-equations.

We will represent a system of equations and non-equations by a graph. Each vertex corresponds to an n-bit *distinct* unknown. We will assume that the number of vertices is at most $2^n/4$, and by abuse of notation, identify the vertices with the values assigned to them. We distinguish two types of edges, namely, $=$-labeled edges and $\neq$-labeled edges that correspond to equations and non-equations, respectively. Each of the edges is additionally labeled by an element in $\{0,1\}^n$. So, if two vertices P and Q are adjacent by an edge with label $(\lambda, =)$ (resp. $(\lambda, \neq)$) for some $\lambda \in \{0,1\}^n$, then it would mean that $P \oplus Q = \lambda$ (resp. $P \oplus Q \neq \lambda$).

Consider a graph $\mathcal{G} = (\mathcal{V}, \mathcal{E}^= \sqcup \mathcal{E}^{\neq})$, where $\mathcal{E}^=$ and $\mathcal{E}^{\neq}$ denote the set of $=$-labeled edges and the set of $\neq$-labeled edges, respectively. Then $\mathcal{G}$ can be seen as a superposition of two subgraphs $\mathcal{G}^= =^{\mathrm{def}} (\mathcal{V}, \mathcal{E}^=)$ and $\mathcal{G}^{\neq} =^{\mathrm{def}} (\mathcal{V}, \mathcal{E}^{\neq})$. Let $P \overset{\lambda}{-} Q$ denote a $(\lambda, =)$-labeled edge in $\mathcal{G}^=$. For $\ell > 0$ and a trail[9]

$$\mathcal{L} : P_0 \overset{\lambda_1}{-} P_1 \overset{\lambda_2}{-} \cdots \overset{\lambda_\ell}{-} P_\ell$$

in $\mathcal{G}^=$, its label is defined as

$$\lambda(\mathcal{L}) \overset{\mathrm{def}}{=} \lambda_1 \oplus \lambda_2 \oplus \cdots \oplus \lambda_\ell.$$

In this work, we will focus on a graph $\mathcal{G} = (\mathcal{V}, \mathcal{E}^= \sqcup \mathcal{E}^{\neq})$ with certain properties, as listed below.

1. $\mathcal{G}^=$ contains no cycle.
2. $\lambda(\mathcal{L}) \neq \mathbf{0}$ for any trail $\mathcal{L}$ in $\mathcal{G}^=$.
3. If P and Q are connected with a $(\lambda, \neq)$-labeled edge, then they are not connected by a λ-labeled trail in $\mathcal{G}^=$.

---

[9] A trail is a walk in which all edges are distinct.

Any graph $\mathcal{G}$ satisfying the above properties will be called a *nice* graph. Given a nice graph $\mathcal{G} = (\mathcal{V}, \mathcal{E}^= \sqcup \mathcal{E}^{\neq})$, an assignment of *distinct* values to the vertices in $\mathcal{V}$ satisfying all the equations in $\mathcal{E}^=$ and all the non-equations in $\mathcal{E}^{\neq}$ is called a *solution* to $\mathcal{G}$. We remark that if we assign any value to a vertex P, then =-labeled edges determine the values of all the other vertices in the component containing P in $\mathcal{G}^=$, where the assignment is unique since $\mathcal{G}^=$ contains no cycle. The values in the same component are all distinct since $\lambda(\mathcal{L}) \neq \mathbf{0}$ for any trail $\mathcal{L}$. Furthermore, any non-equation between two vertices in the same component will be redundant due to the third property above.

In the following lemma, we partition the set of vertices $\mathcal{V}$ into two disjoint sets, denoted $\mathcal{V}_{kn}$ and $\mathcal{V}_{uk}$, respectively, and fix an assignment of distinct values to the vertices in $\mathcal{V}_{kn}$. Subject to this assignment, the number of possible assignments of distinct values to the vertices in $\mathcal{V}_{uk}$ can be lower bounded (in a way that the entire assignment becomes a solution to $\mathcal{G}$).

Lemma 2. *For a positive integer q and a nonnegative integer v, let $\mathcal{G} = (\mathcal{V}, \mathcal{E}^= \sqcup \mathcal{E}^{\neq})$ be a nice graph such that $|\mathcal{E}^=| = q$ and $|\mathcal{E}^{\neq}| = v$. Suppose that*

1. *$\mathcal{V}$ is partitioned into two subsets, denoted $\mathcal{V}_{kn}$ and $\mathcal{V}_{uk}$;*
2. *there is no =-labeled edge that is incident to a vertex in $\mathcal{V}_{kn}$;*
3. *there is no $\neq$-labeled edge connecting two vertices in $\mathcal{V}_{kn}$.*

Suppose that $\mathcal{G}_{uk}^= = (\mathcal{V}_{uk}, \mathcal{E}^=)$ is decomposed into k components $\mathcal{C}_1, \ldots, \mathcal{C}_k$ for some k. Given a fixed assignment of distinct values to the vertices in $\mathcal{V}_{kn}$, the number of solutions to $\mathcal{G}$, denoted $h(\mathcal{G})$, satisfies

$$\frac{h(\mathcal{G})N^q}{(N - |\mathcal{V}_{kn}|)_{|\mathcal{V}_{uk}|}} \geq 1 - \frac{|\mathcal{V}|^2}{N^2} \sum_{i=1}^{k} |\mathcal{C}_i|^2 - \frac{2v}{N}.$$

We refer to [12] for the proof of Lemma 2.

3   Description of XOCB

We define our proposed scheme XOCB. The algorithms are shown in Figs. 1 and 2, and the figures are shown in Figs. 3 and 4. Below we describe the encryption of XOCB. For the decryption, please refer to Figs. 1 and 2.

Given an n-bit block cipher E, the encryption routine of XOCB takes a triple of nonce, associate data and message $(N, A, M) \in \{0,1\}^{n-2} \times \{0,1\}^* \times \{0,1\}^*$ by computing $(C, T) \in \{0,1\}^* \times \{0,1\}^n$ as follows. Here, $|C| = |M|$ holds for any M.

1. Break the associated data A and the message M into n-bit blocks:

$$(A[1], \ldots, A[a]) \xleftarrow{n} \mathsf{pad}(A),$$
$$(M[1], \ldots, M[m]) \xleftarrow{n} M.$$

Note that $0 \leq |M[m]| \leq n$ and $|M[\alpha]| = n$ for $\alpha \in [m - 1]$.

2. Compute masking values:

$$\Delta_1 = E_K(N \parallel \langle 0 \rangle_2) \oplus E_K(N \parallel \langle 1 \rangle_2),$$
$$\Delta_2 = E_K(N \parallel \langle 0 \rangle_2) \oplus E_K(N \parallel \langle 2 \rangle_2),$$
$$\Delta_3 = E_K(N \parallel \langle 0 \rangle_2) \oplus E_K(N \parallel \langle 3 \rangle_2).$$

3. Compute the inputs and the outputs for block cipher calls:

   (a) for $\alpha \in [0..m]$,

$$X[\alpha] = \begin{cases} 2^\alpha \Delta_1 \oplus \Delta_2 & \text{if } \alpha = 0, \\ 2^\alpha \Delta_1 \oplus \Delta_2 \oplus M[\alpha] & \text{if } \alpha > 0, \text{ and } |M[\alpha]| = n, \\ 2^\alpha \Delta_1 & \text{if } \alpha = m \text{ and } |M[m]| < n, \end{cases}$$

$$Y[\alpha] = E_K(X[\alpha]);$$

   (b) for $\alpha \in [a]$, $U[\alpha] = 2^\alpha \Delta_2 \oplus A[\alpha]$, and $V[\alpha] = E_k(U[\alpha])$;

   (c) for $\alpha \in \{0, 1\}$,

$$P[\alpha] = \begin{cases} 2^m \Delta_1 \oplus 2^\alpha \Delta_3 & \text{if } \alpha = 0, \\ 2^m \Delta_1 \oplus 2^\alpha \Delta_3 \oplus \bigoplus_{i \in [m]} \overline{M[i]}; & \text{if } \alpha = 1, \end{cases}$$

$$Q[\alpha] = E_K(P[\alpha]).$$

4. Compute ciphertext C and tag T:

   (a) for $\alpha \in [m]$,

$$C[\alpha] = \begin{cases} Y[0] \oplus Y[\alpha] \oplus (2^\alpha + 1)\Delta_1 & \text{if } |M[\alpha]| = n, \\ (Y[0] \oplus Y[m] \oplus (2^m + 1)\Delta_1 \oplus \Delta_2) \oplus_{\mathtt{msb}} M[m] & \text{otherwise}; \end{cases}$$

   (b) output (C, T) where

$$C = C[1] \parallel \dots \parallel C[m],$$
$$T = Q[0] \oplus Q[1] \oplus 3\Delta_3 \oplus \bigoplus_{\alpha \in [a]} V[\alpha].$$

XOCB AND OCB. The major difference between XOCB from OCB is its additional output masking. In more detail, in its message encryption, XOCB adds an extra masking to the ciphertext blocks so that each ciphertext block can be viewed as a sum of two XEX outputs:

$$C = E(M \oplus \Delta) \oplus \Delta \oplus E(\Delta') \oplus \Delta'.$$

Since each ciphertext block is built from two block cipher calls, unlike OCB, XOCB allows a single collision of input blocks between two queries. Instead, ciphertext blocks in a single query share additional masking, so one can break XOCB if there exists an input collision in a single query, and this is the fundamental reason why the security bound of XOCB is given as $\sigma l / 2^n$ instead of $\sigma^2 / 2^n$ for OCB.

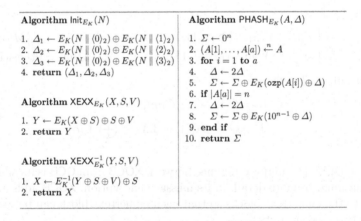

Fig. 1. Algorithms of XOCB. Subroutines are shown at Fig. 2.

Algorithm $\mathrm{Init}_{E_K}(N)$

1. $\Delta_1 \leftarrow E_K(N \| \langle 0 \rangle_2) \oplus E_K(N \| \langle 1 \rangle_2)$
2. $\Delta_2 \leftarrow E_K(N \| \langle 0 \rangle_2) \oplus E_K(N \| \langle 2 \rangle_2)$
3. $\Delta_3 \leftarrow E_K(N \| \langle 0 \rangle_2) \oplus E_K(N \| \langle 3 \rangle_2)$
4. **return** $(\Delta_1, \Delta_2, \Delta_3)$

Algorithm $\mathrm{XEXX}_{E_K}(X, S, V)$

1. $Y \leftarrow E_K(X \oplus S) \oplus S \oplus V$
2. **return** Y

Algorithm $\mathrm{XEXX}_{E_K}^{-1}(Y, S, V)$

1. $X \leftarrow E_K^{-1}(Y \oplus S \oplus V) \oplus S$
2. **return** X

Algorithm $\mathrm{PHASH}_{E_K}(A, \Delta)$

1. $\Sigma \leftarrow 0^n$
2. $(A[1], \ldots, A[a]) \xleftarrow{n} A$
3. **for** $i = 1$ to a
4. $\Delta \leftarrow 2\Delta$
5. $\Sigma \leftarrow \Sigma \oplus E_K(\mathrm{ozp}(A[i]) \oplus \Delta)$
6. **if** $|A[a]| = n$
7. $\Delta \leftarrow 2\Delta$
8. $\Sigma \leftarrow \Sigma \oplus E_K(10^{n-1} \oplus \Delta)$
9. **end if**
10. **return** Σ

Fig. 2. Subroutines for XOCB.

4 Security of XOCB

Let $\mathsf{XOCB}[\pi]$ denote an idealized version of XOCB where the underlying n-bit keyed block cipher E_K is replaced by a random n-bit (secret) permutation π. We can prove the security of $\mathsf{XOCB}[\pi]$ as follows. Deriving the standard model security bound by using a block cipher $E : \mathcal{K} \times \{0,1\}^n \to \{0,1\}^n$ (for a certain key space $\mathcal{K}$) instead of π is standard, thus omitted here.

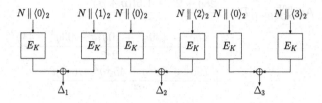

Fig. 3. Generation of masking values for XOCB.

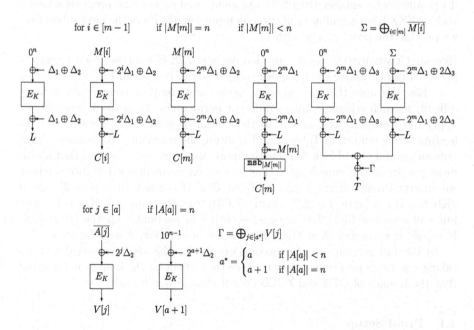

Fig. 4. Encryption of XOCB. (Top) Encryption of plaintext. (Bottom) Processing of Associated data. For $X \in \{0,1\}^{\leq n}$, $\overline{X}$ denotes the one-zero padding (see Sect. 2). The computation of T involves redundant output mask values, which is omitted in the text description of Sect. 3.

Theorem 1. *Let* $\mathcal{D}$ *be a* (q_e, q_d, σ, l)-*adversary against* nAE-*security of* XOCB$[\pi]$ *(see . Then we have*

$$\mathsf{Adv}^{\mathsf{nAE}}_{\mathsf{XOCB}[\pi]}(\mathcal{D}) \leq \frac{28q + 2\sigma + 1.5l(q + \sigma)}{2^n}$$
$$+ \frac{4q\sigma^2 + (30q^2 + 10q)\sigma + 93q^3 + 44q^2}{2^{2n}}$$
$$+ \frac{(9\sigma^3 + 8\sigma^2 q + 45\sigma q^2 + 6q^3)l}{2^{2n+1}},$$

where $q = q_e + q_d$.

As defined in Sect. 2 (Security Notion), q_e denotes the number of encryption queries, q_d denotes the number of decryption queries, l denotes the maximum query length in n-bit blocks, and σ denotes the total queried blocks in n-bit blocks.

The leading terms in the bound of Theorem 1 are $l \cdot \sigma/2^n + l \cdot \sigma^3/2^{2n}$, hence XOCB achieves $2n/3$-bit security if $l = O(1)$. In general, it achieves BBB security if l is sufficiently smaller than $2^{n/2}$. As mentioned earlier, the previous schemes such as XKX have a similar limitation on input length. From the next subsection, we provide the proof of Theorem 1.

BOUND COMPARISON. To get an idea on how XOCB improves security in the practical use cases, we show a quick comparison of bounds in Fig. 5 for the case $n = 128$. We note that providing a precise and compact comparison is fairly difficult as each scheme employs different parameters. To make it compact, we apply our notations of l and σ to the bound of each mode, focusing on the leading terms (shown in Table 1) and ignoring the constants. We assume no tag truncation and $O(1)$-block AD. Furthermore, we assume $q_e = q_d$ and that all the messages are of the same length, thus $lq = \sigma$. As we mentioned in Introduction, we observed a significant gain over GCM/OCB if l is not large ($l = 2^8$, about 4Kbyte). If l is large ($l = 2^{30}$, about 17 GBytes), the gain of XOCB is reduced but still remains. CIP offers stronger security, in particular for the latter case. However, it is costlier than XOCB for the use of a universal hash function.

In the full version, we also present graphs for the aforementioned settings taking constants into consideration to see their effect on the bound. It turns out that the bounds of OCB and XOCB do not change significantly.

4.1   Proof Setup

Let $\mathcal{D}$ be a (q_e, q_d, σ, l)-adversary against the nAE-security of XOCB$[\pi]$. We assume that $\mathcal{D}$ does not make any redundant query and makes exactly q_e encryption queries and q_d decryption queries without loss of generality. Let

$$\tau_e = (N_i, A_i, M_i, C_i, T_i)_{i \in [q_e]}$$
$$\tau_d = (N'_j, A'_j, C'_j, T'_j, b'_j)_{i \in [q_d]}$$

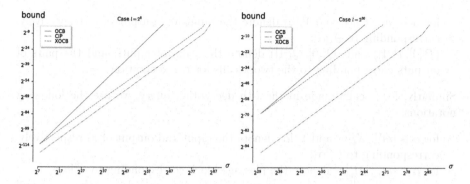

Fig. 5. nAE bound comparison. (Left) $l = 2^8$ (Right) $l = 2^{30}$. The bound of GCM is identical to that of OCB in our setting, hence omitted.

denote the list of encryption queries and decryption queries, respectively. Note that $\mathcal{D}$ always has $b'_j = \bot$ for $j \in [q_d]$ if $\mathcal{D}$ interacts with the ideal oracle. At the end of the game, we assume that the real world oracle reveals all the inputs and the outputs for π calls made during the query phase so the (extended) transcript is of the form $\tau = (\tau_e, \tau_d, \Pi)$, where Π denotes the set of the permutation input and output pairs on π. In the ideal world, the corresponding values should be carefully sampled and revealed to the adversary. The sampling process is described in Sect. 4.2.

For $i \in [q_e]$ (resp. $j \in [q_d]$), let $m_i = |M_i|_n$ (resp. $m'_j = |M'_j|_n$) be the number of blocks in M_i (resp. M'_j), and let $a_i = |\mathsf{pad}(A_i)|_n$ (resp. $a'_j = |\mathsf{pad}(A'_j)|_n$) be the number of blocks in A_i (resp. A'_j). Let $l_i = m_i + a_i$ and let $l'_j = m'_j + a'_j$. For $i \in [q_e]$, A_i, M_i and C_i are divided into n-bit blocks, written as follows.

$$(A_i[1], \ldots, A_i[a_i]) \xleftarrow{n} \mathsf{pad}(A_i),$$
$$(M_i[1], \ldots, M_i[m_i]) \xleftarrow{n} M_i,$$
$$(C_i[1], \ldots, C_i[m_i]) \xleftarrow{n} C_i.$$

Similarly, for $i \in [q_d]$, we write

$$(A'_i[1], \ldots, A'_i[a'_i]) \xleftarrow{n} \mathsf{pad}(A'_i),$$
$$(C'_i[1], \ldots, C'_i[m'_i]) \xleftarrow{n} C'_i.$$

Let $q = q_e + q_d$. We define N_i, A_i, and a_i for $i \in [q]$ by letting $N_{j+q_e} = N'_j$, $A_{j+q_e} = A'_j$, and $a_{j+q_e} = a'_j$ for $j \in [q_d]$. With this extension, we can write

$$(A_i[1], \ldots, A_i[a_i]) \xleftarrow{n} \mathsf{pad}(A_i)$$

for $i \in [q]$, where $A_{j+q_e}[\alpha] = A'_j[\alpha]$ for $j \in [q_d]$, and $\alpha \in [a'_j]$.

For π calls made in the i-th encryption query, we use the following notations:

- for $\alpha \in [m_i]$, $X_i[\alpha]$ and $Y_i[\alpha]$ denote the input and output of π, respectively, corresponding to $M_i[\alpha]$;

- for $\alpha \in [a_i]$, $U_i[\alpha]$ and $V_i[\alpha]$ denote the input and output of π, respectively, corresponding to $A_i[\alpha]$;
- $(P_i[0], P_i[1])$ and $(Q_i[0], Q_i[1])$ denote the pairs of inputs, and the pairs of outputs corresponding to the two π calls for tag generation.

Similarly, for π calls made in the i-th decryption query, we use the following notations:

- for $\alpha \in [m_i']$, $X_i'[\alpha]$ and $Y_i'[\alpha]$ denote the input and output of π, respectively, corresponding to $C_i'[\alpha]$;
- for $\alpha \in [m_i']$, $M_i'[\alpha]$ denote the message block corresponding to $C_i'[\alpha]$;
- for $\alpha \in [a_i']$, $U_i'[\alpha] (= U_{i+q_e}[\alpha])$ and $V_i'[\alpha] (= V_{i+q_e}[\alpha])$ denote the input and output of π, respectively, corresponding to $A_i'[\alpha]$;
- $(P_i'[0], P_i'[1])$ and $(Q_i'[0], Q_i'[1])$ denote the pairs of inputs, and the pairs of outputs corresponding to the two π calls for tag generation.

4.2 Simulating π in the Ideal World

In the ideal world, the underlying π is simulated at the end of the attack. The π-evaluations are recorded in a set Π, initialized as the empty set. The π-evaluations are sampled consistently with all the encryption and decryption queries made during the attack. In other words, such evaluations will uniquely determine all the queries. Whenever an evaluation $\pi(X) = Y$ is fixed, (X, Y) will be included in Π. In this way, Π grows. The set of inputs X (resp. outputs Y) of Π will be denoted $\mathsf{dom}(\pi)$ (resp. $\mathsf{rng}(\pi)$). We now describe the sampling process, which might abort if a certain bad event happens.

STEP 1. For each $i \in [q_e]$, $\Delta_{i,1}$, $\Delta_{i,2}$, $\Delta_{i,3}$ are sampled uniformly at random from $\{0,1\}^n$. For each $j \in [q_d]$, $(\Delta_{j,1}', \Delta_{j,2}', \Delta_{j,3}')$ is set to $(\Delta_{i,1}, \Delta_{i,2}, \Delta_{i,3})$ if $N_i = N_j'$ for some $i \in [q_e]$, and otherwise $\Delta_{j,1}', \Delta_{j,2}', \Delta_{j,3}'$ are sampled uniformly at random from $\{0,1\}^n$.

Let $(\Delta_{i+q_e,1}, \Delta_{i+q_e,2}, \Delta_{i+q_e,3}) = (\Delta_{i,2}', \Delta_{i,3}', \Delta_{i,3}')$ for $i \in [q_d]$. For $i \in [q]$ and $\alpha \in [0..3]$, we will write $N_{i,\alpha} = N_i \parallel \langle \alpha \rangle_2$. Let

$$\mathcal{P} \overset{\text{def}}{=} \{(i, \alpha) : i \in [q_e], \alpha \in [0..m_i]\},$$

$$\mathcal{P}_\$ \overset{\text{def}}{=} \{(i, m_i) : i \in [q_e], |M_i[m_i]| < n\},$$

$$\mathcal{P}_2 \overset{\text{def}}{=} \{(i, \alpha, \beta) : (i, \alpha), (i, \beta) \in \mathcal{P}, \alpha \neq \beta\},$$

$$\mathcal{N} \overset{\text{def}}{=} \{(i, \alpha) : i \in [q], \alpha \in [0..3]\},$$

$$\mathcal{N}_2 \overset{\text{def}}{=} \{(i, \alpha, \beta) : (i, \alpha), (i, \beta) \in \mathcal{N}, \alpha \neq \beta\}.$$

For each $(i, m_i) \in \mathcal{P}_\$$, $\mathbf{s}_i$ is sampled uniformly at random from $\{0,1\}^{n-|M_i[m_i]|}$. For $(i, \alpha) \in \mathcal{P}$, set:

$$X_i[\alpha] = \begin{cases} \Delta_{i,1} \oplus \Delta_{i,2} & \text{if } \alpha = 0, \\ 2^\alpha \Delta_{i,1} & \text{if } (i, \alpha) \in \mathcal{P}_\$, \\ 2^\alpha \Delta_{i,1} \oplus \Delta_{i,2} \oplus M_i[\alpha] & \text{otherwise;} \end{cases}$$

$$Z_i[\alpha] = \begin{cases} 0 & \text{if } \alpha = 0, \\ (2^\alpha + 1)\Delta_{i,1} \oplus \Delta_{i,2} \oplus ((C_i[\alpha] \oplus M_i[\alpha]) \parallel \mathbf{s}_i) & \text{if } (i, \alpha) \in \mathcal{P}_\$, \\ (2^\alpha + 1)\Delta_{i,1} \oplus C_i[\alpha] & \text{otherwise.} \end{cases}$$

We now define a bad event as follows.

$$\mathsf{badA} \Leftrightarrow \mathsf{badA}_1 \vee \mathsf{badA}_2 \vee \mathsf{badA}_3 \vee \mathsf{badA}_4 \vee \mathsf{badA}_5,$$

where

- $\mathsf{badA}_1 \Leftrightarrow$ there exists $(i, \alpha, \beta) \in \mathcal{P}_2$ such that $X_i[\alpha] = X_i[\beta]$;
- $\mathsf{badA}_2 \Leftrightarrow \mathsf{badA}_{2a} \vee \mathsf{badA}_{2b} \vee \mathsf{badA}_{2c} \vee \mathsf{badA}_{2d}$, where
  - $\mathsf{badA}_{2a} \Leftrightarrow$ there exist $(i, \alpha, \beta) \in \mathcal{P}_2$, $(j, \alpha'), (k, \beta') \in \mathcal{P}$ such that $X_i[\alpha] = X_j[\alpha']$ and $X_i[\beta] = X_k[\beta']$;
  - $\mathsf{badA}_{2b} \Leftrightarrow$ there exist $(i, \alpha, \beta) \in \mathcal{P}_2$, $(j, \alpha') \in \mathcal{P}$, $(k, \beta') \in \mathcal{N}$ such that $X_i[\alpha] = X_j[\alpha']$ and $X_i[\beta] = N_{k,\beta'}$;
  - $\mathsf{badA}_{2c} \Leftrightarrow$ there exist $(i, \alpha, \beta) \in \mathcal{P}_2$, $(j, \alpha'), (k, \beta') \in \mathcal{N}$ such that $X_i[\alpha] = N_{j,\alpha'}$ and $X_i[\beta] = N_{k,\beta'}$;
  - $\mathsf{badA}_{2d} \Leftrightarrow$ there exist $(i, \alpha, \beta) \in \mathcal{N}_2$, $(j, \alpha'), (k, \beta') \in \mathcal{P}$ such that $N_{i,\alpha} = X_j[\alpha']$ and $N_{i,\beta} = X_k[\beta']$;
- $\mathsf{badA}_3 \Leftrightarrow \mathsf{badA}_{3a} \vee \mathsf{badA}_{3b}$, where
  - $\mathsf{badA}_{3a} \Leftrightarrow$ there exist three distinct $(i, \alpha), (j, \beta), (k, \gamma) \in \mathcal{P}$ such that $X_i[\alpha] = X_j[\beta] = X_k[\gamma]$;
  - $\mathsf{badA}_{3b} \Leftrightarrow$ there exist distinct $(i, \alpha), (j, \beta), \in \mathcal{P}$ and $(k, \gamma) \in \mathcal{N}$ such that $X_i[\alpha] = X_j[\beta] = N_{k,\gamma}$;
- $\mathsf{badA}_4 \Leftrightarrow \mathsf{badA}_{4a} \vee \mathsf{badA}_{4b}$, where
  - $\mathsf{badA}_{4a} \Leftrightarrow$ there exists $(i, \alpha, \beta) \in \mathcal{P}_2$ such that $Z_i[\alpha] = Z_i[\beta]$;
  - $\mathsf{badA}_{4b} \Leftrightarrow$ there exist $i \in [q]$, $(\alpha, \beta) \in [3]^{*2}$ such that either $\Delta_{i,\alpha} = 0$ or $\Delta_{i,\alpha} = \Delta_{i,\beta}$;
- $\mathsf{badA}_5 \Leftrightarrow \mathsf{badA}_{5a} \vee \mathsf{badA}_{5b}$, where
  - $\mathsf{badA}_{5a} \Leftrightarrow$ there exist distinct $(i, \alpha, \alpha'), (j, \beta, \beta') \in \mathcal{P}_2$ such that $X_i[\alpha] = X_j[\beta]$ and $Z_i[\alpha] \oplus Z_i[\alpha'] = Z_j[\beta] \oplus Z_j[\beta']$;
  - $\mathsf{badA}_{5b} \Leftrightarrow$ there exist $(i, \alpha, \alpha') \in \mathcal{P}_2$, $(j, \beta, \beta') \in \mathcal{N}_2$ such that $X_i[\alpha] = N_{j,\beta}$ and

$$Z_i[\alpha] \oplus Z_i[\alpha'] = \begin{cases} \Delta_{j,\beta} & \text{if } \beta' = 0, \\ \Delta_{j,\beta'} & \text{if } \beta = 0, \\ \Delta_{j,\beta} \oplus \Delta_{j,\beta'} & \text{otherwise.} \end{cases}$$

If badA occurs, then the sampling process aborts.

STEP 2. In this step, we construct a system of equations in Y-variables, representing the images of X-variables under π. For $(i, \alpha) \in \mathcal{P}$, let $Y_i[\alpha] = \pi(X_i[\alpha])$. It should be the case that

$$Y_i[\alpha] \oplus Y_i[0] = Z_i[\alpha]$$

for each $\alpha > 0$. Let $\mathcal{L}$ denote a system of equations obtained by collecting all these equations, as well as

$$\pi(N_{i,0}) \oplus \pi(N_{i,1}) = \Delta_{i,1},$$
$$\pi(N_{i,0}) \oplus \pi(N_{i,2}) = \Delta_{i,2},$$
$$\pi(N_{i,0}) \oplus \pi(N_{i,3}) = \Delta_{i,3}$$

for $i \in [q]$. A solution to $\mathcal{L}$ is sampled uniformly at random from the set of all solutions to $\mathcal{L}$, and the corresponding π-evaluations are included in Π. We will show later that a solution to $\mathcal{L}$ does exist as long as badA does not happen.

STEP 3. In this step, we handle the associated data. For $i \in [q]$ and $\alpha \in [a_i]$, set $U_i[\alpha] = 2^{\alpha} \Delta_{i,2} \oplus A_i[\alpha]$ and

- $V_i[\alpha] = \pi(U_i[\alpha])$ if $U_i[\alpha] \in \text{dom}(\pi)$,
- $V_i[\alpha] \leftarrow_\$ \{0, 1\}^n \setminus \text{rng}(\pi)$ otherwise, where $\pi(U_i[\alpha]) = V_i[\alpha]$ is added to Π.

STEP 4. In this step, we handle the decryption queries. Let

$$\mathcal{P}' \stackrel{\text{def}}{=} \{(i, \alpha) : i \in [q_d], \alpha \in [m]\},$$
$$\mathcal{P}'_0 \stackrel{\text{def}}{=} \{(i, 0) : i \in [q_d]\},$$
$$\mathcal{P}'_\$ \stackrel{\text{def}}{=} \{(i, m'_i) \in \mathcal{P}' : i \in [q_d], |C'_i[m'_i]| < n\}.$$

For $(i, \alpha) \in \mathcal{P}'$, set:

$$Z'_i[\alpha] = \begin{cases} 0 & \text{if } \alpha = 0, \\ ((2^{\alpha} + 1)\Delta'_{i,1} \oplus \Delta'_{i,2}) \oplus_{\text{msb}} C'_i[\alpha] & \text{if } (i, \alpha) \in \mathcal{P}'_\$, \\ (2^{\alpha} + 1)\Delta'_{i,1} \oplus C'_i[\alpha] & \text{otherwise.} \end{cases}$$

For $(i, \alpha) \in \mathcal{P}'_\$ \cup \mathcal{P}'_0$, set $X'_i[\alpha] = \Delta'_i[\alpha]$ and

- $Y'_i[\alpha] = \pi(X'_i[\alpha])$ if $X'_i[\alpha] \in \text{dom}(\pi)$,
- $Y'_i[\alpha] \leftarrow_\$ \{0, 1\}^n \setminus \text{rng}(\pi)$ otherwise, where $\pi(X'_i[\alpha]) = Y'_i[\alpha]$ is added to Π.

Next, for $(i, \alpha) \in \mathcal{P}' \setminus (\mathcal{P}'_\$ \cup \mathcal{P}'_0)$, set $Y'_i[\alpha] = Y'_i[0] \oplus Z'_i[\alpha]$ and

- $X'_i[\alpha] = \pi^{-1}(Y'_i[\alpha])$ if $Y'_i[\alpha] \in \text{rng}(\pi)$,
- $X'_i[\alpha] \leftarrow_\$ \{0, 1\}^n \setminus \text{dom}(\pi)$ otherwise, where $\pi(X'_i[\alpha]) = Y'_i[\alpha]$ is added to Π.

Finally, for $(i, \alpha) \in \mathcal{P}'$, set

$$M'_i[\alpha] = \begin{cases} (Y'_i[\alpha] \oplus Y'_i[0]) \oplus_{\text{msb}} Z'_i[\alpha] & \text{if } (i, \alpha) \in \mathcal{P}'_\$, \\ X'_i[\alpha] \oplus 2^\alpha \Delta'_{i,1} \oplus \Delta'_{i,2} & \text{otherwise.} \end{cases}$$

STEP 5. In this step, we sample the π-evaluations needed for tag generation. For each $i \in [q_e]$, set:

$$P_i[0] = 2^{m_i} \Delta_{i,1} \oplus \Delta_{i,3};$$
$$P_i[1] = 2^{m_i} \Delta_{i,1} \oplus 2\Delta_{i,3} \oplus \bigoplus_{\alpha \in [m_i]} \overline{M_i[\alpha]};$$
$$Z_{i,*} = T_i \oplus 3\Delta_{i,3} \oplus \bigoplus_{\alpha \in [a_i]} V_i[\alpha].$$

For each $j \in [q_d]$, set:

$$P'_i[0] = 2^{m'_i} \Delta'_{i,1} \oplus \Delta'_{i,3};$$
$$P'_i[1] = 2^{m'_i} \Delta'_{i,1} \oplus 2\Delta'_{i,3} \oplus \bigoplus_{\alpha \in [m'_i]} \overline{M'_i[\alpha]};$$
$$Z'_{i,*} = T'_i \oplus 3\Delta'_{i,3} \oplus \bigoplus_{\alpha \in [a'_i]} V'_i[\alpha].$$

Let

$$\mathcal{P}^* \stackrel{\text{def}}{=} \{(i, \alpha) : i \in [q_e], \alpha \in \{0, 1\}\},$$
$$\mathcal{P}^*_{\text{coll}} \stackrel{\text{def}}{=} \{(i, \alpha) \in \mathcal{P}^* : P_i[\alpha] \in \text{dom}(\pi) \text{ or } (j, \beta) \in \mathcal{P}^* \setminus \{(i, \alpha)\}$$
$$\text{such that } P_i[\alpha] = P_j[\beta]\}.$$

We now define bad events badB and badC; let

$$\text{badB} \Leftrightarrow \text{badB}_1 \vee \text{badB}_2 \vee \text{badB}_3 \vee \text{badB}_4 \vee \text{badB}_5,$$

where

- $\text{badB}_1 \Leftrightarrow$ there exists $i \in [q_e]$ such that $(i, 0), (i, 1) \in \mathcal{P}^*_{\text{coll}}$.
- $\text{badB}_2 \Leftrightarrow$ there exists $i \in [q_e]$ such that $Z_{i,*} = 0$.

- $\mathsf{badB_3} \Leftrightarrow$ there exists $(i, \alpha) \in \mathcal{P}^*$ such that $P_i[\alpha] \in \mathrm{dom}(\pi)$ and $\pi(P_i[\alpha]) \oplus Z_{i,*} \in \mathrm{rng}(\pi)$.
- $\mathsf{badB_4} \Leftrightarrow$ there exist three distinct $(i, \alpha), (j, \beta), (k, \gamma) \in \mathcal{P}^*$ such that

$$P_i[\alpha] = P_j[\beta] = P_k[\gamma].$$

- $\mathsf{badB_5} \Leftrightarrow$ there exist $(i, \alpha), (j, \beta) \in \mathcal{P}^*$ such that $i \neq j$, $P_i[\alpha] = P_j[\beta]$, and $Z_{i,*} = Z_{j,*}$,

and let

$$\mathsf{badC} \Leftrightarrow \mathsf{badC_1} \vee \mathsf{badC_2} \vee \mathsf{badC_3} \vee \mathsf{badC_4},$$

where

- $\mathsf{badC_1} \Leftrightarrow$ there exists $i \in [q_d]$ such that $P_i'[0] \in \mathrm{dom}(\pi)$, $P_i'[1] \in \mathrm{dom}(\pi)$ and $\pi(P_i'[0]) \oplus \pi(P_i'[1]) = Z_{i,*}'$.
- $\mathsf{badC_2} \Leftrightarrow$ there exist $i \in [q_d]$, $\alpha \in \{0, 1\}$, and $(j, \beta) \in \mathcal{P}_{\mathrm{coll}}^*$ such that $P_i'[\alpha] \in \mathrm{dom}(\pi)$, $P_i'[1 - \alpha] = P_j[1 - \beta]$, and $\pi(P_i'[\alpha]) \oplus \pi(P_j[\beta]) = Z_{i,*}' \oplus Z_{j,*}$.
- $\mathsf{badC_3} \Leftrightarrow$ there exist $i \in [q_d]$, and $(j, \alpha) \in \mathcal{P}^*$ such that $P_i'[0] = P_j[\alpha]$, $P_i'[1] = P_j[1 - \alpha]$, and $Z_{i,*}' = Z_{j,*}$.
- $\mathsf{badC_4} \Leftrightarrow$ there exist $i \in [q_d]$, $(j, \alpha), (k, \beta) \in \mathcal{P}^*$ such that $j \neq k$, $P_i'[0] = P_j[\alpha]$, $P_i'[1] = P_k[\beta]$, $P_j[1 - \alpha] = P_k[1 - \beta]$, and $Z_{i,*}' = Z_{j,*} \oplus Z_{k,*}$.

Without badB, one can use Mirror theory in the ideal world, while the adversarial forgery is prevented by excluding badC. Assuming $\neg\mathsf{badB} \wedge \neg\mathsf{badC}$, we establish a system of equations in $\pi(P_i[0])$ and $\pi(P_i[1])$ and then sample one solution uniformly at random from the set of all possible solutions. The corresponding π-evaluations, namely $Q_i[\alpha] = \pi(P_i[\alpha])$ and $Q_j'[\beta] = \pi(P_j'[\alpha])$ are includeded in Π for $i \in [q_e]$ and $j \in [q_d]$. Let $\mathcal{L}'$ denote a system of equations and non-equations in Q-variables constructed by the following rules: for each $i \in [q_e]$,

- if $P_i[0] \in \mathrm{dom}(\pi)$, add $\pi(P_i[1]) = \pi(P_i[0]) \oplus Z_{i,*}$ to Π,
- if $P_i[1] \in \mathrm{dom}(\pi)$, add $\pi(P_i[0]) = \pi(P_i[1]) \oplus Z_{i,*}$ to Π,
- otherwise, add an equation $Q_i[0] \oplus Q_i[1] = Z_{i,*}$ to $\mathcal{L}'$,

and for each $i \in [q_d]$,

- if $P_i'[0] \in \mathrm{dom}(\pi)$ and $P_i'[1] \notin \mathrm{dom}(\pi)$, add $Q_i'[1] \neq \pi(P_i'[0]) \oplus Z_{i,*}'$ to $\mathcal{L}'$,
- if $P_i'[1] \in \mathrm{dom}(\pi)$ and $P_i'[0] \notin \mathrm{dom}(\pi)$, add $Q_i'[0] \neq \pi(P_i'[1]) \oplus Z_{i,*}'$ to $\mathcal{L}'$,
- otherwise, add $Q_i'[0] \oplus Q_i'[1] \neq Z_{i,*}'$ to $\mathcal{L}'$.

Once $\mathcal{L}'$ is established, one solution is sampled uniformly at random from the set of solutions to $\mathcal{L}'$ such that none of the values is contained in $\mathrm{rng}(\pi)$. There is at least one such solution assuming $\neg\mathsf{badB} \wedge \neg\mathsf{badC}$. For $i \in [q_e], j \in [q_d], \alpha \in \{0, 1\}$, the following π-evaluatoins are added to Π:

$$\pi(P_i[\alpha]) = Q_i[\alpha],$$
$$\pi(P_j'[\alpha]) = Q_j'[\alpha].$$

Once all the steps are finished without abortion, the following transcript is returned:

$$\tau = \left\{ (N_i, A_i, M_i, C_i, T_i)_{i \in [q_e]}, (N'_j, A'_j, C'_j, T'_j, b_j)_{j \in [q_d]}, \Pi \right\}.$$

4.3 Proof of Theorem 1

We are now ready to prove Theorem 1. The transcript τ will be called *bad* if badA, badB, or badC occurs. Let $\mathcal{T}_{\mathsf{bad}}$ be the set of all the bad transcripts. Then the probability that a transcript is bad in the ideal world is upper bounded as follows.

Lemma 3.

$$
\begin{aligned}
\Pr\left[\mathsf{T}_{\mathsf{id}} \in \mathcal{T}_{\mathsf{bad}}\right] &\leq \frac{25q + 2\sigma + 1.5l(q + \sigma)}{2^n} \\
&+ \frac{4q\sigma^2 + (30q^2 + 4q)\sigma + 93q^3 + 44q^2}{2^{2n}} \\
&+ \frac{(\sigma^3 + 8\sigma^2 q + 45\sigma q^2 + 6q^3)l}{2^{2n+1}}.
\end{aligned}
$$

Lemma 3 holds since

$$\Pr\left[\mathsf{T}_{\mathsf{id}} \in \mathcal{T}_{\mathsf{bad}}\right] \leq \Pr\left[\mathsf{badA}\right] + \Pr\left[\mathsf{badB}\right] + \Pr\left[\mathsf{badC}\right]$$

and by the following lemmas.

Lemma 4.

$$\Pr\left[\mathsf{badA}\right] \leq \frac{1.5l(q + \sigma) + 14q}{2^n} + \frac{(\sigma^3 + 8\sigma^2 q + 45\sigma q^2 + 6q^3)l}{2^{2n+1}}.$$

Lemma 5.

$$\Pr\left[\mathsf{badB}\right] \leq \frac{3q + 2\sigma}{2^n} + \frac{73q^3 + 22q^2\sigma + 4q^2}{2^{2n}}.$$

Lemma 6.

$$\Pr\left[\mathsf{badC}\right] \leq \frac{8q}{2^n} + \frac{4q\sigma^2 + 8q^2\sigma + 20q^3 + 4q\sigma + 40q^2}{2^{2n}}.$$

The proof of the above lemmas is given in the full version.

If a transcript is not bad, then such a transcript will be called *good*. The ratio of probabilities of obtaining any good transcript in the ideal and the real worlds is lower bounded as follows.

Lemma 7. *For any transcript $\tau \notin \mathcal{T}_{\mathsf{bad}}$,*

$$\frac{\Pr\left[\mathsf{T}_{\mathsf{re}} = \tau\right]}{\Pr\left[\mathsf{T}_{\mathsf{id}} = \tau\right]} \geq 1 - \frac{4\sigma^3 l + 6\sigma q}{2^{2n}} - \frac{3q_d}{2^n}.$$

Proof. Fix a transcript $\tau \notin \mathcal{T}_{\mathsf{bad}}$. Let $\mathcal{B} = \{ j \in [q_d] : N'_j \neq N_i \text{ for } \forall i \in [q_e] \}$. Let L denote the number of input/output pairs given to the adversary. Since the probability that $\mathcal{D}$ obtains $b_j = \perp$ is exactly $1 - \frac{1}{2^n}$ for each $j \in [q_d]$, we have

$$\Pr\left[\mathsf{T}_{\mathsf{re}} = \tau\right] = \frac{(2^n - L)!}{(2^n)!} \cdot \left(1 - \frac{1}{2^n}\right)^{q_d} \geq \frac{1}{(2^n)_L} \cdot \left(1 - \frac{q_d}{2^n}\right). \tag{1}$$

For the set of π-evaluations obtained in the ideal world Π, let

$$L_1 = \{ X_i[\alpha] : (i, \alpha) \in \mathcal{P}, i \in [q_e] \} \cup \{ N_i \parallel \langle \alpha \rangle : (i, \alpha) \in \mathcal{N} \},$$
$$L_2 = \{ U_i[\alpha] : (i, \alpha) \in [q] \times [a_i] \} \setminus L_1,$$
$$L_3 = \{ X'_j[\alpha] : (j, \alpha) \in \mathcal{P}' \} \setminus (L_1 \cup L_2),$$
$$L_4 = (\{ P_i[\alpha] : (i, \alpha) \in [q_e] \times \{0, 1\} \} \cup \{ P'_j[\alpha] : (j, \alpha) \in [q_d] \times \{0, 1\} \})$$
$$\setminus (L_1 \cup L_2 \cup L_3).$$

Note that $|L_1|, |L_2|, |L_3|, |L_4|$ are the number of π-evaluations determined by step 2, step 3, step 4 and step 5, respectively, and hence $|L_1| + |L_2| + |L_3| + |L_4| = L$. Then, we make the following observation.

1. Since s_i is sampled for each partial block $(i, m_i) \in \mathcal{P}_\$$, the probability that $\mathcal{D}$ obtains $(C_i[m_i], \mathsf{s}_i)$ is exactly $\frac{1}{2^n}$ for $(i, \alpha) \in \mathcal{P}_\$$. Since ciphertexts and tags are chosen uniformly and independently at random, the probability of $\mathcal{D}$ obtaining them is at most

$$\frac{1}{(2^n)^{\sigma_e}(2^n)^{q_e}}$$

   where $\sigma_e = \sum_{i \in [q_e]} m_i$.

2. At step 1, $\Delta_{i,1}, \Delta_{i,2}, \Delta_{i,3}$ are sampled uniformly and independently at random from $\{0, 1\}^n$ for each $i \in [q_e]$. Also, $\Delta'_{j,1}, \Delta'_{j,2}, \Delta'_{j,3}$ are sampled in the same way. Therefore, the probability that $\mathcal{D}$ obtains the masking values (in the transcript) is given as

$$\frac{1}{(2^n)^{3(q_e + |\mathcal{B}|)}}.$$

3. At step 2, we determine the π-evaluations used in the mask generations and message encryptions. For $i \in [q_e]$, let

$$\mathcal{V}_{i,\mathsf{X}} = \{ \pi(X_i[\alpha]) : (i, \alpha) \in \mathcal{P} \},$$
$$\mathcal{E}_{i,\mathsf{X}} = \{ (\pi(X_i[0]), \pi(X_i[\alpha])) : \alpha \in [m_i] \},$$
$$\mathcal{G}_{i,\mathsf{X}} = (\mathcal{V}_{i,\mathsf{X}}, \mathcal{E}_{i,\mathsf{X}})$$

   where $(\pi(X_i[0]), \pi(X_i[\alpha])) \in \mathcal{E}_{i,\mathsf{X}}$ has label $(Z_i[\alpha], =)$. For $i \in [q]$, let

$$\mathcal{V}_{i,\mathsf{N}} = \{ \pi(N_i[\alpha]) : \alpha \in \{0, 1, 2, 3\} \},$$
$$\mathcal{E}_{i,\mathsf{N}} = \{ (\pi(N_{i,0}), \pi(N_{i,\alpha})) : \alpha \in [3] \}$$
$$\mathcal{G}_{i,\mathsf{N}} = (\mathcal{V}_{i,\mathsf{N}}, \mathcal{E}_{i,\mathsf{N}})$$

where $(\pi(N_{i,0}), \pi(N_{i,\alpha})) \in \mathcal{E}_{i,\mathsf{N}}$ has label $(\varDelta_{i,\alpha}, =)$. Note that $\mathcal{G}_{i,\mathsf{X}}$ for $i \in [q_e]$ and $\mathcal{G}_{i,\mathsf{N}}$ for $i \in [q]$ are all connected graphs, and we will call these graphs by 'segments'. Now $\mathcal{G}$ be the union of all segments, i.e.,

$$\mathcal{G} = \left(\bigcup_{i \in [q_e]} \mathcal{G}_{i,\mathsf{X}} \right) \cup \left(\bigcup_{i \in [q]} \mathcal{G}_{i,\mathsf{N}} \right).$$

Then, $\mathcal{G}$ has the following properties.
- No more than two segments are included in a single connected component of $\mathcal{G}$. Otherwise, either there exist three segments meeting in one vertex, which implies badA_3, or three segments meeting in two different vertices, which implies badA_2.
- $\mathcal{G}$ does not have any cycle. If there exists a cycle in a single segment, then it implies badA_1, and if there exists a cycle contained in two (connected) segments, there should be at least two different collisions, which implies badA_2.
- Let u denote the number of components in $\mathcal{G}^=$, and let $\mathcal{C}_1, \ldots, \mathcal{C}_u$ be the components of $\mathcal{G}^=$. Then obviously $\sum_{i=1}^{u} |\mathcal{C}_i| = |L_1|$ and $|\mathcal{C}_i| \leq 4l$ for each $i = 1, \ldots, u$. Therefore we have

$$\sum_{i=1}^{u} |\mathcal{C}_i|^2 \leq 4l \, |L_1| . \tag{2}$$

- $\lambda(\mathcal{L}) \neq 0$ for any trail $\mathcal{L}$ in $\mathcal{G}(= \mathcal{G}^=)$ since otherwise such a trail will be included in a single segment or both the endpoints of the trails are included in the two different segments respectively. The former case implies badA_4, and the latter case implies badA_5. Recall that any three segments are not included in a single component.

By Lemma 2, we can lower bound the number of the possible assignments such that the evaluations sampled in step 2 are the same as the corresponding part of the transcript. Let $h(\mathcal{G})$ denote the possible assignments of distinct values to the vertices of $\mathcal{G}$. In step 2, one of the possible $h(\mathcal{G}')$ assignments is chosen uniformly at random. Note that $|\mathcal{E}^=| = \sigma_e + 3q_e + 3\,|\mathcal{B}|$. By Lemma 2 and (2),

$$h(\mathcal{G}) \geq \frac{(N)_{|L_1|}}{N^{\sigma_e + 3q_e + 3|\mathcal{B}|}} \times \left(1 - \frac{|L_1|^2}{N^2} \sum_{i=1}^{u} |\mathcal{C}_i|^2 \right)$$

$$\geq \frac{(N)_{|L_1|}}{N^{\sigma_e + 3q_e + 3|\mathcal{B}|}} \times \left(1 - \frac{4l \, |L_1|^3}{N^2} \right).$$

4. At step 3, the oracle samples $V_i[\alpha]$'s in the encryption queries and $V_j'[\beta]$'s in the decryption queries from $\{0,1\}^n$ excluding $|L_1|$ numbers of the evaluations determined in step 2. Therefore, the probability that $\mathcal{D}$ obtains $V_i[\alpha]$'s (in the transcript) is $\frac{1}{(2^n - |L_1|)_{|L_2|}}$.

5. At step 4, the oracle samples the primitive calls for the message blocks in the decryption queries. For $i \in [q_d]$, let $X_i'[0] = \Delta_i'[0]$. The oracle samples $Y_i'[0] = \pi(X_i'[0])$ from $\{0,1\}^n$ excluding $|L_1| + |L_2|$ numbers of evaluations determined in step 2 and step 3. Then $Y_i'[\alpha]$'s are determined by $Z_i'[\alpha] \oplus Y_i'[0]$. After that, $X_i'[\alpha]$'s are sampled uniformly at random from $\{0,1\}^n$. Therefore, the probability that $\mathcal{D}$ obtains $Y_i'[0]$'s and $X_i'[\alpha]$'s (in the transcript) is $\frac{1}{(2^n - |L_1| - |L_2|)_{|L_3|}}$.

6. At step 5, we determine the π-evaluations used to generate tags. Note that there is no successful forgery assuming $\neg\mathsf{badC}$. Let

$$W = \{\pi(P_i[\alpha]) : (i, \alpha) \in \mathcal{P}_*, P_i[\alpha] \in \mathsf{dom}(\pi)\}$$
$$\cup \left\{\pi(P_j'[\beta]) : (j, \beta) \in [q_d] \times \{0,1\}, P_j'[\beta] \in \mathsf{dom}(\pi)\right\},$$
$$\mathcal{V}_e' = \bigcup_{i \in [q_e]} \{\pi(P_i[0]), \pi(P_i[1])\} \setminus W,$$
$$\mathcal{V}_d' = \bigcup_{i \in [q_d]} \{\pi(P_i'[0]), \pi(P_i'[1])\} \setminus W,$$
$$\mathcal{V}' = \mathcal{V}_e' \cup \mathcal{V}_d',$$

where the elements of $\mathcal{V}'$ are unknown. Define a graph $\mathcal{G}' = (\mathcal{V}' \sqcup W, \mathcal{E}'^= \sqcup \mathcal{E}'^{\neq})$, where

$$\mathcal{E}'^= = \{(\pi(P_i[0]), \pi(P_i[1])) : i \in [q_e]\},$$
$$\mathcal{E}'^{\neq} = \{(\pi(P_i'[0]), \pi(P_i'[1])) : i \in [q_d]\},$$

$(P_i[0], P_i[1]) \in \mathcal{E}'^=$ has label $(Z_{i,*}, =)$, and $(P_i'[0], P_i'[1]) \in \mathcal{E}'^{\neq}$ has label $(Z_{i,*}', \neq)$. The graph $\mathcal{G}'$ has the following properties.

- $\mathcal{G}'$ contains no cycle since otherwise there should be two indices $(i, 0)$ and $(i, 1)$ that are contained in $\mathcal{P}_{\mathsf{coll}}^*$, which implies badB_1.
- No more than two edges are included in one component. Otherwise, either three edges should meet in one vertex which implies badB_4 or we have

$$(i, 0), (i, 1) \in \mathcal{P}_{\mathsf{coll}}^*,$$

which implies badB_1.

- Let u' denote the number of components in $\mathcal{G}'^=$, and let $\mathcal{C}_1', \mathcal{C}_2', \ldots, \mathcal{C}_{u'}'$ be the components of $\mathcal{G}'^=$. Then $\sum_{i=1}^{u'} |\mathcal{C}_i'| = |L_4|$ and $|\mathcal{C}_i'| \leq 3$ for each $i = 1, \ldots, u'$. Therefore we have

$$\sum_{i=1}^{u'} |\mathcal{C}_i'|^2 \leq 3|L_4|. \tag{3}$$

- For any trail $\mathcal{L}$ in $\mathcal{G}'^= = (\mathcal{V}' \sqcup W, \mathcal{E}'^=)$, $\lambda(\mathcal{L}) \neq 0$, since otherwise such a trail $\mathcal{L}$ is a single zero-labeled edge or both endpoints of the trail are included in the two different edges respectively. The former case implies badB_2, and the latter case implies badB_5. Recall that any three edges cannot be included in a single component.

Similarly to the analysis for step 2, we use Lemma 2 to lower bound the number of possible assignments such that the evaluations sampled in step 5 are the same as the corresponding part of the transcript. Let $h(\mathcal{G}')$ denote the possible assignments of distinct values to the vertices of $\mathcal{G}'$. In step 5, one of the possible $h(\mathcal{G}')$ assignments is chosen uniformly at random. Note that $|\mathcal{E}^=| \leq q_e$ and $|\mathcal{E}^{\neq}| \leq q_d$. By Lemma 2 and (3), we have

$$h(\mathcal{G}') \geq \frac{(N - |L_1| - |L_2| - |L_3|)_{|L_4|}}{N^{q_e}} \left(1 - \frac{L}{N^2} \sum_{i=1}^{k} |\mathcal{C}_i'|^2 - \frac{2q_d}{N} \right)$$

$$\geq \frac{(N - |L_1| - |L_2| - |L_3|)_{|L_4|}}{N^{q_e}} \left(1 - \frac{3L|L_4|}{N^2} - \frac{2q_d}{N} \right).$$

By the above argument, we have

$$\frac{1}{\Pr[\mathsf{T_{id}} = \tau]} = (2^n)^{\sigma_e} \cdot (2^n)^{q_e} \cdot (2^n)^{3(q_e + |\mathcal{B}|)} \cdot h(\mathcal{G}) \cdot (2^n - |L_1|)_{|L_2|}$$

$$\times (2^n - |L_1| - |L_2|)_{|L_3|} \cdot h(\mathcal{G}')$$

$$\geq (2^n)^{\sigma_e + q_e} \cdot (2^n)^{3(q_e + |\mathcal{B}|)} \cdot (2^n - |L_1|)_{|L_2| + |L_3|}$$

$$\times \frac{(2^n)_{|L_1|}}{(2^n)^{\sigma_e + 3q_e + 3|\mathcal{B}|}} \cdot \left(1 - \frac{4l |L_1|^3}{2^{2n}} \right)$$

$$\times \frac{(N - |L_1| - |L_2| - |L_3|)_{|L_4|}}{2^{nq_e}} \cdot \left(1 - \frac{3L|L_4|}{2^{2n}} - \frac{2q_d}{2^n} \right) \qquad (4)$$

$$\geq \frac{(2^n)^{3(q_e + |\mathcal{B}|)}}{(2^n)^{3(q_e + |\mathcal{B}|)}} \cdot (2^n)_L \cdot \left(1 - \frac{4l |L_1|^3 + 3L|L_4|}{2^{2n}} - \frac{2q_d}{2^n} \right)$$

$$\geq (2^n)_L \cdot \left(1 - \frac{4l |L_1|^3 + 3L|L_4|}{2^{2n}} - \frac{2q_d}{2^n} \right).$$

Therefore by (1) and (4), we have

$$\frac{\Pr[\mathsf{T_{re}} = \tau]}{\Pr[\mathsf{T_{id}} = \tau]} \geq \left(1 - \frac{4l |L_1|^3 + 3L|L_4|}{2^{2n}} - \frac{2q_d}{2^n} \right) \cdot \left(1 - \frac{q_d}{2^n} \right)$$

$$\geq 1 - \frac{4|L_1|^3 l + 3L|L_4|}{2^{2n}} - \frac{3q_d}{2^n}$$

$$\geq 1 - \frac{4\sigma^3 l + 6\sigma q}{2^{2n}} - \frac{3q_d}{2^n}$$

where the last inequality holds since $L < \sigma$ and $|L_4| \leq 2q$. □

5   On the Tightness of the Bound of XOCB

We show a brief analysis of the tightness of the bound in Theorem 1 by presenting an authentication attack against XOCB. The attack tries to invoke the event corresponding to badA_1. For a positive integer $s \geq 2$, the attack requires $l \approx 2^{n/s}$, $q_e \approx 2^{(s-2)n/s}$, and $\sigma_e = lq_e \approx 2^{(s-1)n/s}$. This is not tight for our claim of $2n/3$-bit security with $l = O(1)$. However, if l is not constant, especially when $s = 2$, the attack complexity is $l \approx 2^{n/2}$, $q_e = O(1)$, and $\sigma_e \approx 2^{n/2}$; thus, it is a tight attack. When $O(1) < l < 2^{n/2}$, the attack is not tight for our claim in Theorem 1. For example, if $s = 3$, the attack complexity is $l \approx 2^{n/3}$, $q_e \approx 2^{n/3}$, and $\sigma_e \approx 2^{2n/3}$. The gap from Theorem 1 increases as s increases.

The attack procedure is as follows:

1. The adversary queries (N, A, M) to the encryption oracle such that $M = M[1] \parallel M[2] \parallel \cdots \parallel M[m]$ and $|M[m]| = n - 1$. Then it obtains (C, T), where $C = C[1] \parallel C[2] \parallel \cdots \parallel C[m]$, and also obtains $(n-1)$-bit value $Z = M[m] \oplus C[m]$.
2. Assume that a collision $M[i] \oplus 2^i \Delta_1 \oplus \Delta_2 = M[j] \oplus 2^j \Delta_1 \oplus \Delta_2$ occurs for $i, j \in [m - 1]$ and $i \neq j$. Then, $M[i] \oplus M[j] = C[i] \oplus C[j]$ holds; thus, the adversary can detect the collision.
3. The adversary compute $\Delta_1 = (2^i \oplus 2^j)^{-1}(M[i] \oplus M[j])$.
4. The adversary queries (N', A', C', T') to the decryption oracle such that $N' = N$, $A' = A$, $T' = T$, $C' = C'[1] \parallel C'[2] \parallel \cdots \parallel C'[m]$, $C'[1] = 2\Delta_1$, $C'[2] = 2^2 \Delta_1$, $C'[i] = C[i]$ for $i \in [3..m-1]$, $|C'[m]| = n-1$, and $C'[m] = Z \oplus \mathsf{msb}_{n-1}(2\Delta_1 \oplus 2^2 \Delta_1 \oplus M[1] \oplus M[2]) \oplus M[m]$.

The last decryption query is accepted with a high probability. For $i \in [m]$, let $M'[i]$ and Σ' be a valid i-th decrypted plaintext block and a valid checksum of the last decryption query (N', A', C', T'), respectively.

$$
\begin{aligned}
\Sigma' &= \bigoplus_{i \in [m]} \mathsf{ozp}(M'[i]) = M'[1] \oplus M'[2] \oplus \mathsf{ozp}(M'[m]) \oplus \bigoplus_{i \in [3..m-1]} M'[i] \\
&= E_K^{-1}(\Delta_2 \oplus L) \oplus 2\Delta_1 \oplus \Delta_2 \oplus E_K^{-1}(\Delta_2 \oplus L) \oplus 2^2 \Delta_1 \oplus \Delta_2 \\
&\quad \oplus \mathsf{ozp}(\mathsf{msb}_{n-1}(2\Delta_1 \oplus 2^2 \Delta_1 \oplus M[1] \oplus M[2]) \oplus M[m]) \oplus \bigoplus_{i \in [3..m-1]} M[i]
\end{aligned}
$$

If the adversary has

$$
\begin{aligned}
&\mathsf{ozp}(\mathsf{msb}_{n-1}(2\Delta_1 \oplus 2^2 \Delta_1 \oplus M[1] \oplus M[2]) \oplus M[m]) \\
&= 2\Delta_1 \oplus 2^2 \Delta_1 \oplus M[1] \oplus M[2] \oplus \mathsf{ozp}(M[m]),
\end{aligned} \tag{5}
$$

it obtains $\Sigma' = \bigoplus_{i=1}^m \mathsf{ozp}(M[i]) = \Sigma$, and T becomes the valid tag for (N', A', C'). The adversary can check whether (5) holds before the last decryption query; thus, if (5) does not hold, the adversary can make a successful forgery by changing C' accordingly, for example, setting $C'[2] = 2^2 \Delta_1$, $C'[3] = 2^3 \Delta_1$, $C'[i] = C[i]$ for $i \in \{1\} \cup \{4, \ldots, m-1\}$, and $C'[m] = Z \oplus \mathsf{msb}_{n-1}(2^2 \Delta_1 \oplus 2^3 \Delta_1 \oplus M[2] \oplus M[3]) \oplus M[m]$, or changing the length of $C'[m]$ to smaller bits.

Next, we discuss the attack complexity. In step 2, the adversary requires the collision $M[i] \oplus 2^i \Delta_1 \oplus \Delta_2 = M[j] \oplus 2^j \Delta_1 \oplus \Delta_2$ for $i, j \in [m - 1]$ and $i \neq j$. To obtain this collision with a high probability, the adversary needs to query a sufficiently long plaintext M in step 1. Assuming that $m \approx 2^{n/s}$ for a positive integer s, the collision probability is approximately $m^2/2^n \approx 2^{(2-s)n/s}$. Repeating step 1 with $m \approx 2^{n/s}$ $q_e \approx 2^{(s-2)n/s}$ times, the adversary obtains the collision with a high probability. Thus, the attack requires $l \approx 2^{n/s}$, $q_e \approx 2^{(s-2)n/s}$, and $\sigma_e = lq_e \approx 2^{(s-1)n/s}$ when l is not a constant. If $l = O(1)$, the collision probability of step 2 is $\approx 1/2^n$ and the attack complexity is $q_e \approx \sigma_e \approx 2^n$, much larger than what the bound tells $(2^{2n/3})$. Further analysis is open.

6   Implementations of XOCB

This section presents the implementations for the instantiation of XOCB using AES – AES-XOCB[10].

ON 64-BIT HIGH-END PROCESSORS. Using the parallelizability of XOCB, our implementation of AES-XOCB can take advantage of the pipelined execution of AES-NI on high-end CPUs, resulting in an asymptotic speed of 0.5 cpb. This performance is as expected since the fully pipelined AES-ECB runs at 0.3 cpb and doubling in $GF(2^{128})$ runs at 0.2 cpb using SIMD instructions in our timing environment.

We compared the relative performance of AES-XOCB against AES-OCB and AES-CIP using the same AES-NI-based AES implementation, SIMD-based doubling in $GF(2^{128})$, and PCLMULQDQ-based multiplication in $GF(2^{128})$ supporting pipelined execution on multiple blocks. Our testing included the time cost of the entire procedure, including setting up keys, generating masks, and performing encryption and authentication. We used plaintexts of various lengths for testing, ranging from 16 to 4096 bytes (with a 16-byte AD).

Comparing the results, AES-XOCB has a slightly inferior performance compared to AES-OCB but is still close. AES-XOCB's initialization procedure uses five AES calls for computing mask initial values, which slightly impacts performance for short messages. However, for message lengths exceeding 512 bytes, the difference narrows to 0.1~0.2 cpb, which is the cost of a doubling. AES-XOCB outperforms AES-CIP for both short and long messages. Figure 6 shows how the performance of AES-XOCB changes with plaintext length, and how it compares to AES-OCB and AES-CIP.

ON 8-BIT LOW-END MICROPROCESSORS. We demonstrate the practical relevance of XOCB in constrained environments by implementing AES-XOCB on an 8-bit AVR. The simulation result on ATmega328P shows that AES-XOCB requires 8556 bytes of ROM and 672 bytes of RAM to support both encryption and decryption, including key setup and mask generation. Figure 7 shows concrete execution time for the entire procedure, including key setup, mask generation, encryption, and authentication. For a 128-byte message and a 16-byte AD, AES-XOCB processes at 306 cpb, while an optimized AES-GCM implementation requires 11012 bytes of ROM and runs at 880 cpb [40].

---

[10] The source codes can be found via https://www.dropbox.com/sh/k0y8h1boah072mn/AAAYPUr0j4MU9F3-w1k7U52Ha?dl=0.

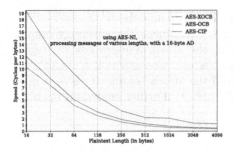

Fig. 6. Speeds on an x86-64 CPU   **Fig. 7.** Speeds on an 8-bit AVR

7 Conclusions

We have shown a new authenticated encryption mode XOCB. It has a quantitatively stronger security guarantee than the seminal OCB while inheriting most of the efficiency advantages. In particular, it is exactly rate-one and has beyond-birthday-bound security assuming SPRP for the underlying block cipher, if the maximum input length is sufficiently smaller than the birthday bound. The block cipher could be instantiated with an n-bit block cipher with a key of any length, allowing us to use AES-128 for a typical example. There are numerous works on BBB-secure AE modes, however, they rely on a stronger primitive (e.g. TBC) or stronger assumption (e.g. ideal cipher model), and XOCB is the first scheme that achieves the aforementioned goals without such a compromise. Several further research topics, such as optimizing the scheme to reduce computational overhead or reducing the length contribution to the bound, and a more comprehensive benchmark, would be interesting directions.

Acknowledgement. We thank the anonymous reviewers for their insightful comments that improved the presentation of our paper. Jooyoung Lee was supported by the National Research Foundation of Korea (NRF) grant funded by the Korea government (MSIT) (No.2021R1F1A1047146). Zhenzhen Bao was supported by the National Key R&D Program of China (Grant No. 2018YFA0704701), the Major Program of Guangdong Basic and Applied Research (Grant No. 2019B030302008), and the Shandong Province Key R&D Project (Nos. 2020ZLYS09 and 2019JZZY010133).

References

1. Recommendation for Block Cipher Modes of Operation: Galois/Counter Mode (GCM) and GMAC. NIST Special Publication 800–38D (2007), National Institute of Standards and Technology
2. Andreeva, E., Bogdanov, A., Luykx, A., Mennink, B., Mouha, N., Yasuda, K.: How to securely release unverified plaintext in authenticated encryption. In: Sarkar, P., Iwata, T. (eds.) ASIACRYPT 2014, Part I. LNCS, vol. 8873, pp. 105–125. Springer, Heidelberg (Dec 2014). https://doi.org/10.1007/978-3-662-45611-8_6

3. Banik, S., et al.: Midori: a block cipher for low energy. In: Iwata, T., Cheon, J.H. (eds.) ASIACRYPT 2015. LNCS, vol. 9453, pp. 411–436. Springer, Heidelberg (2015). https://doi.org/10.1007/978-3-662-48800-3_17

4. Banik, S., Pandey, S.K., Peyrin, T., Sasaki, Yu., Sim, S.M., Todo, Y.: GIFT: a small present. In: Fischer, W., Homma, N. (eds.) CHES 2017. LNCS, vol. 10529, pp. 321–345. Springer, Cham (2017). https://doi.org/10.1007/978-3-319-66787-4_16

5. Beierle, C., et al.: Alzette: a 64-Bit ARX-box. In: Micciancio, D., Ristenpart, T. (eds.) CRYPTO 2020. LNCS, vol. 12172, pp. 419–448. Springer, Cham (2020). https://doi.org/10.1007/978-3-030-56877-1_15

6. Bellare, M., Namprempre, C.: Authenticated encryption: relations among notions and analysis of the generic composition paradigm. In: Okamoto, T. (ed.) ASIACRYPT 2000. LNCS, vol. 1976, pp. 531–545. Springer, Heidelberg (2000). https://doi.org/10.1007/3-540-44448-3_41

7. Bhargavan, K., Leurent, G.: On the practical (in-)security of 64-bit block ciphers: Collision attacks on HTTP over TLS and OpenVPN. In: Weippl, E.R., Katzenbeisser, S., Kruegel, C., Myers, A.C., Halevi, S. (eds.) ACM CCS 2016, pp. 456–467. ACM Press (Oct 2016). https://doi.org/10.1145/2976749.2978423

8. Bhattacharjee, A., Bhaumik, R., Nandi, M.: Offset-based bbb-secure tweakable block-ciphers with updatable caches. In: INDOCRYPT. Lecture Notes in Computer Science, vol. 13774, pp. 171–194. Springer (2022). https://doi.org/10.1007/978-3-031-22912-1_8

9. Bhaumik, R., Nandi, M.: Improved security for OCB3. In: Takagi, T., Peyrin, T. (eds.) ASIACRYPT 2017. LNCS, vol. 10625, pp. 638–666. Springer, Cham (2017). https://doi.org/10.1007/978-3-319-70697-9_22

10. Bogdanov, A.: PRESENT: an ultra-lightweight block cipher. In: Paillier, P., Verbauwhede, I. (eds.) CHES 2007. LNCS, vol. 4727, pp. 450–466. Springer, Heidelberg (2007). https://doi.org/10.1007/978-3-540-74735-2_31

11. Borghoff, J.: PRINCE – a low-latency block cipher for pervasive computing applications. In: Wang, X., Sako, K. (eds.) ASIACRYPT 2012. LNCS, vol. 7658, pp. 208–225. Springer, Heidelberg (2012). https://doi.org/10.1007/978-3-642-34961-4_14

12. Choi, W., Lee, B., Lee, Y., Lee, J.: Improved security analysis for nonce-based enhanced hash-then-mask MACs. In: Moriai, S., Wang, H. (eds.) ASIACRYPT 2020. LNCS, vol. 12491, pp. 697–723. Springer, Cham (2020). https://doi.org/10.1007/978-3-030-64837-4_23

13. Cogliati, B., Dutta, A., Nandi, M., Patarin, J., Saha, A.: Proof of Mirror Theory for any xi_max. Cryptology ePrint Archive, Paper 2022/686 (2022), https://eprint.iacr.org/2022/686, https://eprint.iacr.org/2022/686

14. Cogliati, B., Patarin, J.: Mirror theory: A simple proof of the pi+pj theorem with xi_max=2. Cryptology ePrint Archive, Paper 2020/734 (2020). https://eprint.iacr.org/2020/734, https://eprint.iacr.org/2020/734

15. Datta, N., Dutta, A., Nandi, M., Paul, G.: Double-block hash-then-sum: A paradigm for constructing BBB secure PRF. IACR Trans. Symm. Cryptol. 2018(3), 36–92 (2018). https://doi.org/10.13154/tosc.v2018.i3.36-92

16. Datta, N., Dutta, A., Nandi, M., Yasuda, K.: Encrypt or decrypt? to make a single-key beyond birthday secure nonce-based MAC. In: Shacham, H., Boldyreva, A. (eds.) CRYPTO 2018. LNCS, vol. 10991, pp. 631–661. Springer, Cham (2018). https://doi.org/10.1007/978-3-319-96884-1_21

17. Dutta, A., Nandi, M., Saha, A.: Proof of mirror theory for xi_max=2. IEEE Trans. Inf. Theor. 68(9), 6218–6232 (2022). https://doi.org/10.1109/TIT.2022.3171178

18. Dutta, A., Nandi, M., Talnikar, S.: Beyond birthday bound secure MAC in faulty nonce model. In: Ishai, Y., Rijmen, V. (eds.) EUROCRYPT 2019. LNCS, vol. 11476, pp. 437–466. Springer, Cham (2019). https://doi.org/10.1007/978-3-030-17653-2_15

19. Hoang, V.T., Tessaro, S.: Key-alternating ciphers and key-length extension: exact bounds and multi-user security. In: Robshaw, M., Katz, J. (eds.) CRYPTO 2016. LNCS, vol. 9814, pp. 3–32. Springer, Heidelberg (2016). https://doi.org/10.1007/978-3-662-53018-4_1

20. Inoue, A., Iwata, T., Minematsu, K., Poettering, B.: Cryptanalysis of OCB2: attacks on authenticity and confidentiality. In: Boldyreva, A., Micciancio, D. (eds.) CRYPTO 2019. LNCS, vol. 11692, pp. 3–31. Springer, Cham (2019). https://doi.org/10.1007/978-3-030-26948-7_1

21. Iwata, T.: New blockcipher modes of operation with beyond the birthday bound security. In: Robshaw, M. (ed.) FSE 2006. LNCS, vol. 4047, pp. 310–327. Springer, Heidelberg (2006). https://doi.org/10.1007/11799313_20

22. Iwata, T.: Authenticated encryption mode for beyond the birthday bound security. In: Vaudenay, S. (ed.) AFRICACRYPT 2008. LNCS, vol. 5023, pp. 125–142. Springer, Heidelberg (2008). https://doi.org/10.1007/978-3-540-68164-9_9

23. Iwata, T., Ohashi, K., Minematsu, K.: Breaking and repairing GCM security proofs. In: Safavi-Naini, R., Canetti, R. (eds.) CRYPTO 2012. LNCS, vol. 7417, pp. 31–49. Springer, Heidelberg (2012). https://doi.org/10.1007/978-3-642-32009-5_3

24. Jha, A., List, E., Minematsu, K., Mishra, S., Nandi, M.: XHX a framework for optimally secure tweakable block ciphers from classical block ciphers and universal hashing. In: Lange, T., Dunkelman, O. (eds.) LATINCRYPT 2017. LNCS, vol. 11368, pp. 207–227. Springer, Cham (2019). https://doi.org/10.1007/978-3-030-25283-0_12

25. Katz, J., Yung, M.: Unforgeable encryption and chosen ciphertext secure modes of operation. In: Goos, G., Hartmanis, J., van Leeuwen, J., Schneier, B. (eds.) FSE 2000. LNCS, vol. 1978, pp. 284–299. Springer, Heidelberg (2001). https://doi.org/10.1007/3-540-44706-7_20

26. Kim, S., Lee, B., Lee, J.: Tight security bounds for double-block hash-then-sum MACs. In: Canteaut, A., Ishai, Y. (eds.) EUROCRYPT 2020. LNCS, vol. 12105, pp. 435–465. Springer, Cham (2020). https://doi.org/10.1007/978-3-030-45721-1_16

27. Krovetz, T., Rogaway, P.: The software performance of authenticated-encryption modes. In: Joux, A. (ed.) FSE 2011. LNCS, vol. 6733, pp. 306–327. Springer, Heidelberg (2011). https://doi.org/10.1007/978-3-642-21702-9_18

28. Liskov, M., Rivest, R.L., Wagner, D.: Tweakable block ciphers. J. Cryptol. 24(3), 588–613 (2011). https://doi.org/10.1007/s00145-010-9073-y

29. Mennink, B.: Optimally secure tweakable blockciphers. In: Leander, G. (ed.) FSE 2015. LNCS, vol. 9054, pp. 428–448. Springer, Heidelberg (2015). https://doi.org/10.1007/978-3-662-48116-5_21

30. Mennink, B.: Insuperability of the standard versus ideal model gap for tweakable blockcipher security. In: Katz, J., Shacham, H. (eds.) CRYPTO 2017. LNCS, vol. 10402, pp. 708–732. Springer, Cham (2017). https://doi.org/10.1007/978-3-319-63715-0_24

31. Naito, Y.: Improved XKX-based AEAD scheme: removing the birthday terms. In: Lange, T., Dunkelman, O. (eds.) LATINCRYPT 2017. LNCS, vol. 11368, pp. 228–246. Springer, Cham (2019). https://doi.org/10.1007/978-3-030-25283-0_13

32. Naito, Y.: Tweakable blockciphers for efficient authenticated encryptions with beyond the birthday-bound security. IACR Trans. Symm. Cryptol. 2017(2), 1–26 (2017). https://doi.org/10.13154/tosc.v2017.i2.1-26
33. Niwa, Y., Ohashi, K., Minematsu, K., Iwata, T.: GCM security bounds reconsidered. In: Leander, G. (ed.) FSE 2015. LNCS, vol. 9054, pp. 385–407. Springer, Heidelberg (2015). https://doi.org/10.1007/978-3-662-48116-5_19
34. Patarin, J.: Introduction to Mirror Theory: Analysis of Systems of Linear Equalities and Linear Non Equalities for Cryptography. IACR Cryptology ePrint Archive, Report 2010/287 (2010). https://eprint.iacr.org/2010/287
35. Patarin, J.: Mirror Theory and Cryptography. IACR Cryptology ePrint Archive, Report 2016/702 (2016). https://eprint.iacr.org/2016/702
36. Rogaway, P.: Authenticated-encryption with associated-data. In: Atluri, V. (ed.) ACM CCS 2002, pp. 98–107. ACM Press (Nov 2002). https://doi.org/10.1145/586110.586125
37. Rogaway, P.: Efficient instantiations of tweakable blockciphers and refinements to modes OCB and PMAC. In: Lee, P.J. (ed.) ASIACRYPT 2004. LNCS, vol. 3329, pp. 16–31. Springer, Heidelberg (2004). https://doi.org/10.1007/978-3-540-30539-2_2
38. Rogaway, P., Bellare, M., Black, J., Krovetz, T.: OCB: A block-cipher mode of operation for efficient authenticated encryption. In: Reiter, M.K., Samarati, P. (eds.) ACM CCS 2001, pp. 196–205. ACM Press (Nov 2001). https://doi.org/10.1145/501983.502011
39. Rogaway, P., Shrimpton, T.: A provable-security treatment of the key-wrap problem. In: Vaudenay, S. (ed.) EUROCRYPT 2006. LNCS, vol. 4004, pp. 373–390. Springer, Heidelberg (2006). https://doi.org/10.1007/11761679_23
40. Sovyn, Y., Khoma, V., Podpora, M.: Comparison of three CPU-core families for IoT applications in terms of security and performance of AES-GCM. IEEE Internet Things J. 7(1), 339–348 (2020). https://doi.org/10.1109/JIOT.2019.2953230

Side-Channels and Masking

Improved Power Analysis Attacks on Falcon

Shiduo Zhang[1], Xiuhan Lin[2], Yang Yu[3,4,5]([✉])[iD], and Weijia Wang[2][iD]

[1] Institute for Advanced Study, Tsinghua University, Beijing, China
zsd19@mails.tsinghua.edu.cn
[2] School of Cyber Science and Technology, Shandong University, Qingdao, China
xhlin@mail.sdu.edu.cn, wjwang@sdu.edu.cn
[3] BNRist, Tsinghua University, Beijing, China
yu-yang@mail.tsinghua.edu.cn
[4] Zhongguancun Laboratory, Beijing, China
[5] National Financial Cryptography Research Center, Beijing, China

Abstract. Falcon is one of the three post-quantum signature schemes selected for standardization by NIST. Due to its low bandwidth and high efficiency, Falcon is seen as an attractive option for quantum-safe embedded systems. In this work, we study Falcon's side-channel resistance by analysing its Gaussian samplers. Our results are mainly twofold.

The first result is an improved key recovery exploiting the leakage within the base sampler investigated by Guerreau et al. (CHES 2022). Instead of resorting to the fourth moment as in former parallelepiped-learning attacks, we work with the second order statistics covariance and use its spectral decomposition to recover the secret information. Our approach substantially reduces the requirement for measurements and computation resources: 220 000 traces is sufficient to recover the secret key of Falcon-512 within half an hour with a probability of $\approx 25\%$. As a comparison, even with 10^6 traces, the former attack still needs about 1000 h hours CPU time of lattice reduction for a full key recovery. In addition, our approach is robust to inaccurate leakage classification, which is another advantage over parallelepiped-learning attacks.

Our second result is a practical power analysis targeting the integer Gaussian sampler of Falcon. The analysis relies on the leakage of random sign flip within the integer Gaussian sampling. This leakage was exposed in 2018 by Kim and Hong, but it is not considered in Falcon's implementation and unexploited for side-channel analysis until now. We identify the leakage within the reference implementation of Falcon on an ARM Cortex-M4 STM32F407IGT6 microprocessor. We also show that this single bit of leakage is in effect enough for practical key recovery: with 170 000 traces one can fully recover the key of Falcon-512 within half an hour. Furthermore, combining the sign leakage and the aforementioned leakage, one can recover the key with only 45 000 signature measurements in a short time.

As a by-product, we also extend our power analysis to Mitaka which is a recent variant of Falcon. The same leakages exist within the integer Gaussian samplers of Mitaka, and they can also be used to mount key

© International Association for Cryptologic Research 2023
C. Hazay and M. Stam (Eds.): EUROCRYPT 2023, LNCS 14007, pp. 565–595, 2023.
https://doi.org/10.1007/978-3-031-30634-1_19

recovery attacks. Nevertheless, the key recovery in Mitaka requires much more traces than it does in Falcon, due to their different lattice Gaussian samplers.

1   Introduction

Recently, NIST announced the first post-quantum cryptography algorithms to be standardized. For digital signatures, two of the three selected algorithms are lattice-based: Dilithium [25] and Falcon [33], the third one is a hash-based signature scheme SPHINCS$^+$ [19]. In comparison, Dilithium and Falcon have better overall performance.

Dilithium and Falcon are constructed in two distinct frameworks. Dilithium uses "Fiat-Shamir with aborts" paradigm, developed by Lyubashevsky [23,24] and Falcon uses the hash-and-sign paradigm. Two schemes achieve acceptable overall performance for many use cases and also have their own advantages: Dilithium has a simpler implementation and more flexible parameter selections, while Falcon has a greatly smaller public key and signature sizes. For this, each of them would have potential applications in various situations and NIST eventually selected both schemes for standardization.

For a real-world deployed scheme, implementation security is of great importance. For insecure implementations, sensitive information may leak through side channels, e.g. execution time, power consumption, and electromagnetic emanations. These leakages may be exploited to mount devastating attacks that are the major threat to cryptographic embedded devices. The implementation security of Dilithium is relatively well-studied. The reference implementation of Dilithium is constant time, which eliminates side-channel vulnerabilities in former Fiat-Shamir lattice signatures [2,10,16,30,34]. Moreover, efficient masking of Dilithium at any order is proposed in [27], which protects Dilithium against stronger side-channel attacks.

In contrast, the implementation security of Falcon is intricate. Falcon follows the GPV framework [14] to prevent statistical attacks [7,9,28,37]. In the GPV signature scheme, signing requires Gaussian sampling which is a notorious target of side-channel attacks [10,13,16,21]. Furthermore, Falcon's sampling heavily relies on floating-point operations, which complicates the secure implementation. For the above reasons, while the implementation of Falcon is now secure against timing attacks [18,31], countermeasures against stronger side-channel attacks like power analysis remain a challenging open problem. The lack of side-channel protections provides an avenue for side-channel attacks. The first side-channel attack on Falcon is an electromagnetic attack presented by Karabulut and Aysu [20] that targets the floating-point multiplications within Falcon's Fast Fourier Transform. The Karabulut-Aysu attack is substantially improved later [17]: 5 000 power traces is sufficient for a full key recovery of Falcon-512 on ChipWhisperer. Also in [17], Guerreau et al. proposed another practical power analysis on Falcon based on a different side-channel leakage. It exploits the power leakage within the base Gaussian sampler to filter signatures in a secret-dependent region, and completes the key recovery by applying parallelepiped-learning attacks [7, 28]. As the very first side-channel attack targeting Falcon's Gaussian sampling, this attack is rather expensive in terms of computation resources and measurements: practical key recovery needs millions of traces.

Our Contributions. In this work, we develop several power analysis attacks on Falcon. Our contributions are mainly twofold.

We substantially improve the key recovery in the power analysis of Falcon's base sampler of [17]. The exploited leakage, called *half Gaussian leakage*, filters signatures in the slice $\{\mathbf{v} : |\langle \mathbf{v}, \mathbf{b} \rangle| \leq \|\mathbf{b}\|^2\}$ where $\mathbf{b}$ is the secret key. The key recovery is in essence to learn $\mathbf{b}$ from this secret-dependent slice, which was done by parallelepiped-learning attacks [7, 28] in [17]. Our main idea stems from the observation that the projection of filtered signatures tends to be unusually short in the direction of the slice. We therefore proceed to learn the direction and the width of the slice, i.e. $\frac{\mathbf{b}}{\|\mathbf{b}\|}$ and $\|\mathbf{b}\|$, through the spectral decomposition of the covariance of filtered signatures. Compared with the fourth moment considered in previous parallelepiped-learning attacks, covariance, as a lower order statistic, allows smaller measure errors and thus leads to a more accurate approximation of $\mathbf{b}$. As a result, our new key recovery algorithm significantly lowers the requirement of measurements and computation resources: 220 000 traces is sufficient for our algorithm to recover the secret key within half an hour with a probability of $\approx 25\%$; by contrast, even with 10^6 traces, the key recovery of [17] still requires around 1000 h CPU time of lattice reduction. Moreover, the effectiveness of our key recovery relies on the condition number and the measurement of the covariance of filtered signatures, thus our algorithm can even work with inaccurate leakage classification, say with accuracy 55%. In comparison, parallelepiped-learning attacks do not work well if the domain of filtered signatures has no clear boundary, which makes previous analysis reliant on accurate leakage classification. Therefore our result validates half Gaussian leakage to be a threat more serious than previously imagined.

We also propose a new power analysis of Falcon's integer sampler that is at the layer[1] above the base sampler investigated in [17]. To cope with variable parameters, Falcon's integer sampler first transforms a sample z^+ from fixed half integer Gaussian into a bimodal half Gaussian sample $z = b + (2b - 1)z^+$ with a random $b \in \{0, 1\}$ and then accepts z with corresponding probability. The random bit b can be retrieved via simple power analysis as shown in [21]. This leakage, called *sign leakage*, filters signatures in the halfspace $\{\mathbf{v} : \langle \mathbf{v}, \mathbf{b} \rangle \geq 0\}$. The aforementioned statistical attack can be directly applied to the case of halfspace in the same spirit, but the approximate direction, denoted $\mathbf{u}$, of $\mathbf{b}$ is less accurate. To refine the key recovery, we use the rough approximation $\mathbf{u}$ to filter signatures in the slice $\{\mathbf{v} : |\langle \mathbf{v}, \mathbf{b} \rangle| \leq b\}$ with a well-chosen b. Applying the former key recovery again, we can recover the key given 170 000 of traces. Moreover, the sign leakage can be combined with the previous half Gaussian

---

[1] There are 3 layers of Gaussian samplers in Falcon: lattice Gaussian sampler - integer Gaussian sampler - base sampler.

leakage and then filter a thinner slice. Focusing on the thinner slice, the statistical attack can be even more effective: only $45\,000$ traces is sufficient for a direct key recovery with a probability of $\approx 25\%$. Additionally, through simple power analysis, we practically identify the sign leakage in the reference implementation of Falcon. Furthermore, we also propose an efficient countermeasure to mitigate this leakage, which (based on our settings of leakage acquisition) decreases the sign classification accuracy to $\approx 52\%$ from almost 100%.

As an additional contribution, we extend the power analysis on Falcon to its recent variant Mitaka. Since Mitaka uses Falcon's integer sampler, both half Gaussian leakage and sign leakage exist within its reference implementation in the same manner. Different from Falcon, Mitaka uses the hybrid sampler [32] for lattice Gaussian sampling, in which the output is the sum of two samples from two ellipsoid Gaussians. This makes the domain of filtered signatures the ambient space rather than a slice or a half-space. Nevertheless, the distribution of filtered signatures is still secret-dependent, thus our aforementioned approach is able to recover the key with more traces.

Roadmap. We start in Sect. 2 with preliminary material. Section 3 introduces the Gaussian samplers of Falcon that are the targets of our side-channel attacks. We present in Sect. 4 an improved key recovery using the same side-channel leakage studied in [17]. Section 5 exhibits a new power analysis attack targeting the integer Gaussian sampling of Falcon and a countermeasure against this attack is provided. We extend the above power analysis to Mitaka in Sect. 6 and conclude in Sect. 7.

2   Preliminaries

We use bold lowercase (resp. uppercase) letters for vectors (resp. matrices). By convention, vectors are in column form. For a distribution D, we write $z \leftarrow D$ when the random variable z sampled from D and denote by $D(x)$ the probability of $z = x$. We denote by $z \sim D$ a random variable distributed as D. Let $\mathbb{E}[z]$ be the expectation of random variable z and $\mathbf{var}[z]$ be the variance. For a random vector $\mathbf{z} = (z_0, \cdots, z_{n-1}) \in \mathbb{R}^n$, its covariance is

$$\mathbf{Cov}[\mathbf{z}] = \begin{pmatrix} c_{0,0} & c_{0,1} & \cdots & c_{0,n-1} \\ c_{1,0} & c_{1,1} & \cdots & c_{1,n-1} \\ \vdots & \vdots & \vdots & \vdots \\ c_{n-1,0} & c_{n-1,1} & \cdots & c_{n-1,n-1} \end{pmatrix} \quad \text{where} \quad c_{i,j} = \mathbb{E}[z_i z_j] - \mathbb{E}[z_i]\,\mathbb{E}[z_j].$$

For a real-valued function f and a countable set S, we write $f(S) = \sum_{x \in S} f(x)$ assuming this sum is absolutely convergent. Let $\mathcal{N}(\mu, \sigma^2)$ be the normal distribution of the mean μ and the standard deviation σ.

2.1   Linear Algebra and Lattices

Let b_i (resp. $\mathbf{b}_i$) denote the i-th coordinate (resp. column) of $\mathbf{b}$ (resp. $\mathbf{B}$). Given $\mathbf{u}, \mathbf{v} \in \mathbb{R}^n$, their inner product is $\langle \mathbf{u}, \mathbf{v} \rangle = \sum_{i=0}^{n-1} u_i v_i$. When $\langle \mathbf{u}, \mathbf{v} \rangle = 0$, we call $\mathbf{u}$

and $\mathbf{v}$ are orthogonal. Let $\|\mathbf{v}\| = \sqrt{\langle \mathbf{v}, \mathbf{v} \rangle}$ be the ℓ_2-norm of $\mathbf{v}$, $\|\mathbf{v}\|_1 = \sum_i |v_i|$ be the ℓ_1-norm and $\|\mathbf{v}\|_\infty = \max_i\{|v_i|\}$ be the ℓ_∞-norm. Let $\mathbf{I}$ denote the identity matrix. For $\mathbf{H} \in \mathbb{R}^{n \times m}$, we let span($\mathbf{H}$) be the linear span of the rows of $\mathbf{H}$.

A symmetric matrix $\mathbf{\Sigma} \in \mathbb{R}^{n \times n}$ is positive definite, denoted $\mathbf{\Sigma} > 0$, if $\mathbf{x}^t \mathbf{\Sigma} \mathbf{x} > 0$ for all nonzero $\mathbf{x} \in \mathbb{R}^n$. The spectral decomposition of a positive definite matrix $\mathbf{\Sigma}$ is $\mathbf{\Sigma} = \mathbf{Q}\mathbf{D}\mathbf{Q}^{-1} = \mathbf{Q}\mathbf{D}\mathbf{Q}^t$ where $\mathbf{D} = \mathrm{diag}(\lambda_1, \cdots, \lambda_n)$ with $\lambda_1 \leq \cdots \leq \lambda_n$ being the eigenvalues of $\mathbf{\Sigma}$ and $\mathbf{Q}$ is an orthogonal matrix whose i-th column is the eigenvector corresponding to λ_i.

Let $\mathbf{B} = (\mathbf{b}_0, \cdots, \mathbf{b}_{n-1}) \in \mathbb{R}^{m \times n}$ of rank n. The Gram-Schmidt Orthogonalization (GSO) of $\mathbf{B}$ is the unique matrix $\widetilde{\mathbf{B}} = \left(\widetilde{\mathbf{b}}_0, \cdots, \widetilde{\mathbf{b}}_{n-1} \right) \in \mathbb{R}^{m \times n}$ such that $\mathbf{B} = \widetilde{\mathbf{B}}\mathbf{U}$ where $\widetilde{\mathbf{b}}_i$'s are pairwise orthogonal and $\mathbf{U}$ is upper-triangular with 1 on its diagonal. Let $\|\mathbf{B}\|_{GS} = \max_i \|\widetilde{\mathbf{b}}_i\|$.

A lattice $\mathcal{L}$ is the set of all integer linear combinations of linearly independent vectors $\mathbf{b}_0, \cdots, \mathbf{b}_{n-1} \in \mathbb{R}^m$, i.e. $\mathcal{L} = \left\{ \sum_{i=0}^{n-1} x_i \mathbf{b}_i \mid x_i \in \mathbb{Z} \right\}$. We call $\mathbf{B} = (\mathbf{b}_0, \cdots, \mathbf{b}_{n-1})$ a basis and n the dimension of $\mathcal{L}$. Let $\mathcal{L}(\mathbf{B})$ denote the lattice generated by a basis $\mathbf{B}$.

2.2 Gaussian Distributions

Let $\rho_{\sigma,\mathbf{c}}(\mathbf{x}) = \exp\left(-\frac{\|\mathbf{x} - \mathbf{c}\|^2}{2\sigma^2} \right)$ be the Gaussian function with center $\mathbf{c} \in \mathbb{R}^n$ and standard deviation σ. The discrete Gaussian over a lattice $\mathcal{L}$ with center $\mathbf{c}$ and standard deviation σ is defined by the probability function $D_{\mathcal{L},\sigma,\mathbf{c}}(\mathbf{v}) = \frac{\rho_{\sigma,\mathbf{c}}(\mathbf{v})}{\rho_{\sigma,\mathbf{c}}(\mathcal{L})}$ for any $\mathbf{v} \in \mathcal{L}$.

We call $D_{\mathbb{Z},\sigma,c}$ integer Gaussian that is of particular interest. It suffices to study the case where $c \in [0, 1)$, since $D_{\mathbb{Z},\sigma,c} = i + D_{\mathbb{Z},\sigma,c-i}$ for any $i \in \mathbb{Z}$. By restricting $D_{\mathbb{Z},\sigma,c}$ over $\mathbb{N}$, we get a half integer Gaussian $D_{\mathbb{Z},\sigma,c}^+$ satisfying $D_{\mathbb{Z},\sigma,c}^+(v) = \frac{\rho_{\sigma,c}(v)}{\rho_{\sigma,c}(\mathbb{N})}$ for any $v \in \mathbb{N}$.

2.3 NTRU

Typically, an NTRU-based scheme is defined over some polynomial ring $\mathcal{R}$ along with a modulus q. In this work, $\mathcal{R} = \mathbb{Z}[x]/(x^n + 1)$ with n a power-of-2. Let $\mathcal{K} = \mathbb{Q}[x]/(x^n + 1)$ and $\mathcal{K}_\mathbb{R} = \mathbb{R}[x]/(x^n + 1)$. The NTRU secret key consists of two short polynomials $f, g \in \mathcal{R}$ where f is invertible modulo q, and the public key is $h = f^{-1}g \bmod q$. The NTRU module determined by h is $\mathcal{L}_{NTRU} = \{(u, v) \in \mathcal{R}^2 \mid u + vh = 0 \bmod q\}$. From (f, g), by solving the NTRU equation $fG - gF = q$, one can compute $\mathbf{B}_{f,g} = \begin{pmatrix} g & G \\ -f & -F \end{pmatrix}$ a basis of $\mathcal{L}_{NTRU}$ that is called an NTRU trapdoor basis. When the context is clear, we simply denote $\mathbf{B}_{f,g}$ as $\mathbf{B}$. Elements in $\mathcal{R}$ are identified with their matrix of multiplication in a certain basis, thus the NTRU module is seen as a lattice of dimension $2n$ that is an NTRU lattice.

2.4   Falcon Signature Scheme

We now briefly describe the Falcon signature scheme. Some details that are unnecessary for understanding this work are omitted, and we refer to [33] for a complete description of Falcon.

Falcon is an instantiation of the GPV hash-and-sign framework [14] over NTRU lattices. The secret key of Falcon is an NTRU trapdoor basis $\mathbf{B}_{f,g}$ and the public key is $h = f^{-1}g \bmod q$. The secret polynomials f and g are drawn from $D_{\mathcal{R},\sigma,0}$ with $\sigma = 1.17\sqrt{\frac{q}{2n}}$ for nearly optimal parameters as per [6]. In addition, $\mathbf{B}_{f,g}$ is required to have a bounded Gram-Schmidt norm: $\|\mathbf{B}_{f,g}\|_{GS} \leq 1.17\sqrt{q}$. This work focuses on the parameters of Falcon-512 for NIST Level-I where $\mathcal{R} = \mathbb{Z}[x]/(x^n + 1)$, $n = 512$ and $q = 12289$.

Following the GPV hash-and-sign framework, the signing procedure of Falcon is in essence sampling a lattice point $\mathbf{v}$ from $D_{\mathcal{L}(\mathbf{B}),\sigma,\mathbf{c}}$ with a relatively small σ where $\mathbf{c}$ is the hashed message. The signature is $\mathbf{s} = \mathbf{v} - \mathbf{c}$ that is short: $\|\mathbf{s}\| \approx \sigma\sqrt{2n}$. To verify the signature, one just needs to compute the hashed message $\mathbf{c}$ and then check if $\mathbf{s} + \mathbf{c} \in \mathcal{L}$ and if $\|\mathbf{s}\|$ is less than the acceptance bound B. A simplified description of the signing and verification algorithms is given as follows:

Sign$(m, \mathsf{sk} = \mathbf{B})$	**Verify**$(m, s, \mathsf{pk} = h)$
Compute $c = \mathsf{hash}(m) \in \mathcal{R}$;	Compute $c = \mathsf{hash}(m) \in \mathcal{R}$;
Using sk, sample a short (s_1, s_2)	Compute $s_1 = c - sh \bmod q$;
such that $s_1 + s_2 h = c \bmod q$;	If $\|(s_1, s)\| > B$, reject.
If $\|(s_1, s_2)\| > B$, restart	Accept.
Return $s = s_2$.	

Falcon sets $\sigma = 1.17\sqrt{q} \cdot \eta_\epsilon(\mathcal{R}^2)$ where $\eta_\epsilon(\mathcal{R}^2)$ is the smoothing parameter with respect to $\mathcal{R}^2$ and a small $\epsilon > 0$. The acceptance bound is $B \approx 1.1\sqrt{2n}\sigma$.

3   Gaussian Samplers of Falcon

This section is dedicated to the presentation of the Gaussian samplers used in the signing procedure of Falcon. Indeed these samplers are the target of our side-channel attacks.

The signing procedure of Falcon relies on three layers of Gaussian sampling. At the top layer, the used sampler is FFOSampler and the output distribution is a lattice Gaussian $D_{\mathcal{L}(\mathbf{B}),\sigma,\mathbf{c}}$. At the intermediate layer, the sampler SamplerZ samples from some integer Gaussian $D_{\mathbb{Z},\sigma',c}$ where σ' and c are variable. At the bottom layer, the sampler BaseSampler samples from a fixed half integer Gaussian $D_{\mathbb{Z},\sigma_{\max},0}^+$.

3.1   FFOSampler

The FFOSampler algorithm is a ring variant of the KGPV sampler [14,22] based on fast Fourier nearest plane algorithm [8]. In FFOSampler, lattice Gaussian sampling is reduced to a series of integer Gaussian samplings, which is the same as

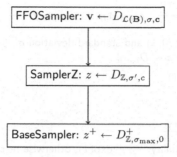

Fig. 1. Three layers of Gaussian samplers in Falcon signing algorithm.

———————— Algorithm 1: The KGPV sampler ————————

Input: a basis $\mathbf{B} = (\mathbf{b}_0, \cdots, \mathbf{b}_{n-1})$, a center $\mathbf{c}$ and $\sigma \geq \|\mathbf{B}\|_{GS} \cdot \eta_\epsilon(\mathbb{Z})$
Output: a lattice point $\mathbf{v}$ following a distribution close to $D_{\mathcal{L}(\mathbf{B}),\sigma,\mathbf{c}}$.

1   $\mathbf{v} \leftarrow 0, \mathbf{c}' \leftarrow \mathbf{c}$
2   **for** $i = n - 1, \cdots, 0$ **do**
3     $c_i'' = \langle \mathbf{c}', \widetilde{\mathbf{b}}_i \rangle / \|\widetilde{\mathbf{b}}_i\|^2, \sigma_i = \sigma/\|\widetilde{\mathbf{b}}_i\|$
4     $z_i \leftarrow \mathsf{SamplerZ}(\sigma_i, c_i'' - \lfloor c_i'' \rfloor) + \lfloor c_i'' \rfloor$
5     $\mathbf{c}' \leftarrow \mathbf{c}' - z_i \mathbf{b}_i, \mathbf{v} \leftarrow \mathbf{v} + z_i \mathbf{b}_i$
6   **end for**
7   **return** $\mathbf{v}$

---

the KGPV algorithm. Therefore we just describe the KGPV sampler in Algorithm 1.

3.2 SamplerZ

The integer Gaussian samplings in FFOSampler have variable standard deviations and centers, which complicates the implementation. To this end, SamplerZ uses rejection sampling to obtain target samples from a fixed half integer Gaussian. It first generates $z^+ \sim D_{\mathbb{Z},\sigma_{\max},0}^+$ by calling BaseSampler, then computes $z \leftarrow b + (2b-1)z^+$ with a random bit b, and finally outputs z with certain probability. A detailed algorithmic description is given in Algorithm 2 where $\sigma_{min} = 1.2778$ and $\sigma_{max} = 1.8205$ for Falcon-512. Particularly, SamplerZ is provably resistant against timing attacks [18].

3.3 BaseSampler

The BaseSampler algorithm for $D_{\mathbb{Z},\sigma_{\max},0}^+$ is implemented by table-based approach as described in Algorithm 3. Specifically, BaseSampler uses the (scaled) reverse cumulative distribution table (RCDT) of 18 items, which ensures the distribution sufficiently close to $D_{\mathbb{Z},\sigma_{\max},0}^+$. Also, the implementation of BaseSampler is constant time.

Algorithm 2: SamplerZ

Input: a center $c \in [0, 1)$ and standard deviation $\sigma' \in [\sigma_{min}, \sigma_{max}]$
Output: an integer $z \sim D_{\mathbb{Z}, \sigma', c}$

1 $z^+ \leftarrow \text{BaseSampler}()$
2 $b \xleftarrow{\$} \{0, 1\}$
3 $z \leftarrow b + (2b - 1)z^+$
4 $x \leftarrow -\frac{(z-c)^2}{2\sigma'^2} + \frac{(z^+)^2}{2\sigma_{max}^2}$
5 **return** z with probability $\frac{\sigma_{min}}{\sigma'} \cdot \exp(x)$, otherwise restart;

Algorithm 3: BaseSampler

Output: an integer $z^+ \sim D_{\mathbb{Z}, \sigma_{max}, 0}^+$

1 $u \xleftarrow{\$} \{0, 1\}^{72}$
2 $z^+ \leftarrow 0$
3 **for** $i = 0 \cdots 17$ **do**
4 $\quad | \quad z^+ \leftarrow z^+ + [\![u < RCDT[i]]\!]$
5 **end for**
6 **return** z^+

---

4 Improved Key Recovery from Half Gaussian Leakage

While the distribution of Falcon signatures is statistically independent of the secret key, the intermediate variables during Falcon's Gaussian sampling are sensitive, which poses a threat to the side-channel security. Recently, Guerreau et al. proposed a side-channel attack on Falcon exploiting power leakage within BaseSampler [17]. This attack is quite demanding in terms of computation resources and measurements: a direct key recovery for Falcon-512 needs ≈ 10 million of signature measurements, and with 1 million traces, the key recovery has to resort to lattice reduction requiring around 1000 h hours CPU time.

In this section, we propose an improved key recovery exploiting the same side-channel leakage exposed in [17]. With around 220 000 traces, our attack suffices to recover the key within half an hour with a probability of $\approx 25\%$. If lattice reduction is allowed, the number of required traces can be further reduced.

4.1 The Attack of [17]

Let us first recall the attack of [17] for better completeness and comparisons.

Half Gaussian Leakage. Falcon's BaseSampler uses a table-based approach that was shown to be vulnerable to simple power analysis in [21]. More precisely, through the power consumption of the comparison $[\![u < RCDT[i]]\!]$ (line 4, Algorithm 3), one can effectively determine the value of z^+. The attack of [17] exploits this leakage to classify if $z^+ = 0$ or not. When $z^+ = 0$, the corresponding output of SamplerZ belongs to $\{0, 1\}$. This allows to filter the signatures $\mathbf{s} = \sum_{i=0}^{2n-1} y_i \cdot \widetilde{\mathbf{b}}_i$ with $y_0 \in (-1, 1]$ where $\widetilde{\mathbf{b}}_0 = \mathbf{b}_0 = (g, -f)$ is the secret key. The region of filtered signatures is a slice in the direction of $\mathbf{b}_0$ (see Fig. 2). In this paper, the leakage used in [17] is called *half Gaussian leakage*.

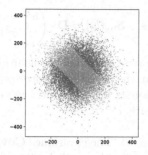

Fig. 2. Simplified 2-dimensional representation of Falcon signatures. Signatures with $y_0 \in (-1, 1]$ are in orange. (Color figure online)

The Key Recovery. The slice of filtered signatures can be seen as a deformed parallelepiped of $\mathbf{B}$. The authors of [17] thus propose to recover the secret key using a variant of the parallelepiped-learning attack, developed in [7,28]. Since only one direction of the parallelepiped of $\mathbf{B}$ is preserved in the slice, the key recovery of [17] needs much more signatures to reconstruct $\mathbf{B}$ compared with the previous attacks [7,28].

4.2 Our Key Recovery

Let us first formally define the *Learning Slice Problem*.

Definition 1 ($\text{LSP}_{b,\sigma,N}$). *Given $\mathbf{b} \in \mathbb{R}^n$, let $\mathcal{S}_{\mathbf{b}}(b) = \{\mathbf{v} : |\langle \mathbf{v}, \mathbf{b} \rangle| \leq b\}$. Let D_s be the conditional distribution of $\mathbf{z} \sim (\mathcal{N}(0, \sigma^2))^n$ given $\mathbf{z} \in \mathcal{S}_{\mathbf{b}}(b)$. Given N independent samples drawn from D_s, find an approximation of $\pm\mathbf{b}$.*

With half Gaussian leakage, we are able to identify signatures in $\mathcal{S}_{\mathbf{b}_0}(\|\mathbf{b}_0\|^2)$. Hence the key recovery now becomes to solve $\text{LSP}_{b,\sigma,N}$. Our idea stems from the geometric intuition that the projection of signatures in the slice on $\mathbf{b}_0$ tends to be unusually short. Instead of resorting to the fourth moment (known as kurtosis) as in parallelepiped-learning attacks, we discover that the covariance of the samples in the slice, i.e. filtered signatures, suffices to reveal the secret $\mathbf{b}_0$. Our LSP algorithm consists of two steps:

1. we learn the direction of $\mathbf{b}_0$;
2. we estimate $\|\mathbf{b}_0\|$;

Learning the slice direction. Let $\mathbf{B} = (\mathbf{b}_0, \mathbf{b}_1, \cdots, \mathbf{b}_{n-1})$ of full-rank where $\mathbf{b}_0$ is the solution to the LSP instance. Let $\mathbf{d}_i = \tilde{\mathbf{b}}_i / \|\tilde{\mathbf{b}}_i\|$, then $\mathbf{D} = (\mathbf{d}_0, \cdots, \mathbf{d}_{n-1})$ is orthogonal. For $\mathbf{s} \sim (\mathcal{N}(0, \sigma^2))^n$, let $\mathbf{s} = \sum_i y_i \mathbf{d}_i$, then the coefficients y_i independently follow $\mathcal{N}(0, \sigma^2)$ and $\mathbf{Cov}[\mathbf{s}] = \sigma^2 \mathbf{I}$. When $\mathbf{s} \in \mathcal{S}_{\mathbf{b}_0}(b)$, we have $|y_0| \leq \frac{b}{\|\mathbf{b}_0\|}$ and thus the variance of y_0 is $\sigma'^2 < \sigma^2$. Then the covariance of $\mathbf{s}$ given $\mathbf{s} \in \mathcal{S}_{\mathbf{b}_0}(b)$ becomes

$$\mathbf{Cov}[\mathbf{s}|\mathbf{s} \in \mathcal{S}_{\mathbf{b}_0}(b)] = \mathbf{D} \cdot \begin{pmatrix} \sigma'^2 & \\ & \sigma^2 \mathbf{I} \end{pmatrix} \cdot \mathbf{D}^t.$$

In the above covariance matrix, the smallest eigenvalue σ' is unique and clearly less than others. In addition, the eigenvector corresponding to the smallest eigenvalue is in the same direction as $\mathbf{b}_0$. Therefore, we can learn the direction of $\mathbf{b}_0$ through spectral decomposition.

Learning the norm of the secret. The covariance $\mathbf{Cov}[\mathbf{s}|\mathbf{s} \in \mathcal{S}_{\mathbf{b}_0}(b)]$ also leaks the information of $\|\mathbf{b}_0\|$. Specifically, the coefficient y_0 of samples in the slice follows the truncated normal distribution $\mathcal{N}(0, \sigma^2)$ over $\left[-\frac{b}{\|\mathbf{b}_0\|}, \frac{b}{\|\mathbf{b}_0\|} \right]$. Its variance is

$$\sigma'^2 = \frac{\int_{-b'}^{b'} x^2 \exp(-\frac{x^2}{2\sigma^2}) dx}{\int_{-b'}^{b'} \exp(-\frac{x^2}{2\sigma^2}) dx} \quad \text{where} \quad b' = \frac{b}{\|\mathbf{b}_0\|}. \tag{1}$$

that can be also computed through spectral decomposition. Then $\|\mathbf{b}_0\|$ can be numerically estimated given σ'.

With the approximate direction and the norm of $\mathbf{b}_0$, we can immediately construct a solution to the $\mathsf{LSP}_{b,\sigma,N}$ instance. A theoretical justification for the effectiveness of our LSP algorithm is provided in Appendix A.

Key recovery from approximate vectors. Up to now, we have shown that one is able to get an approximate secret key $\mathbf{b}_0'$ by solving the underlying LSP instance given by half Gaussian leakage. By rounding the coefficients of $\mathbf{b}_0'$, an integer vector $(g', -f') \in \mathcal{R}^2$ is recovered. As a certain number, denoted N_0, of signature measurements are performed, $(g', -f')$ is exactly the key with good probability, that is set around 25% throughout the paper, in practice. Even with fewer traces, the key can be fully recovered by combining exhaustive search or lattice reduction and the cost depends on the size of $\mathbf{e} = (g - g', f' - f) \in \mathcal{R}^2$. We further introduce N_1 and $N_1(x)$ as follows:

- N_1 : when the number of traces $\geq N_1$, $\|\mathbf{e}\|_\infty \leq 1$ with good probability;
- $N_1(x)$: when the number of traces $\geq N_1(x)$, $\|\mathbf{e}\|_\infty \leq 1$ and $\|\mathbf{e}\|_1 \leq x$ with good probability.

It is worth noting that when $\|e\|_\infty \leq 1$ and $\|e\|_1 \leq x$, either $g - g'$ or $f - f'$ has hamming weight $\leq \lfloor x/2 \rfloor$. In practice, it suffices to correct either g' or f': exploiting the NTRU public key h, it is easy to derive the other half and to check if the guess is correct or not.

Remark 1. We particularly treat the case where e is ternary, as this allows a practical key recovery by a simple exhaustive search. However, larger errors can also be corrected by expensive lattice reduction. (see Sect. 4.3 for details).

4.3 Experimental Results of Key Recovery

The experiments focus on the key recovery, since our attack uses the same side-channel leakage presented in [17]. In fact, [17] has shown that the leakage can be correctly identified in practice with a fairly high probability: 94% for Chip-Whisperer and 100% for ELMO. We did not repeat the measurements and just assumed a 100% accurate classification as done in [17].

We tested our key recovery attack over 40 Falcon-512 instances and 400 000 traces per instance. The practicality of our new key recovery is well supported by experimental results. More precisely, 360 000 traces suffices for our attack to directly recover the key. As a comparison, the attack in [17] requires about 10 000 000 traces. The value of $N_1(7)$ is around 220 000, and in this region, a certain proportion of keys can be recovered by combining a simple exhaustive search within half an hour. For clarity, we highlight that the trace number counts all signature measurements which is about twice the number of filtered signatures in the slice. Detailed experimental results are shown in Fig. 3. We also tested our attack on Falcon-1024 and Falcon-256, and experimental results are given in Appendix B.

Furthermore, there is a tradeoff between measurement and computation. The approximation obtained from fewer traces can be used by lattice reduction to effectively reduce the cost of key recovery. Figure 4 shows the bit security estimated by leaky LWE estimator [4] given a certain number of signature measurements. Given 20 000 traces, the security of Falcon-512 would decrease from 133 bits to 85 bits.

In practice, the half Gaussian leakage is noisy, inducing errors in the classification. The error can be further amplified in presence of side-channel protections. In this respect, we conduct the attack by emulating the case that the classification of $z^+ = 0$ or not only has imperfect accuracy. The result is shown in Fig. 5, where the required trace number increases with the classification accuracy. Notably, when the accuracy is 65%, an adversary is still able to practically recover the key using our attack with 10 million traces. In comparison, the attack in [17] cannot apply to inaccurate leakage classifications, because it requires that the domain of filtered signatures has a clear boundary.

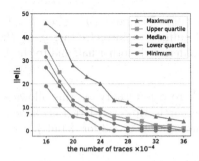

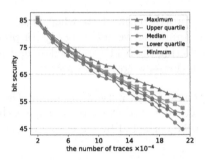

Fig. 3. The approximate error size $\|e\|_1$ measured over 40 Falcon-512 instances. The vector e is ternary for all 40 tested instances with 10^5 traces.

Fig. 4. The bit security estimated as per the approximate error. We use the Core-SVP model in classical setting, i.e. $2^{0.292\beta}$ where β is the required BKZ blocksize

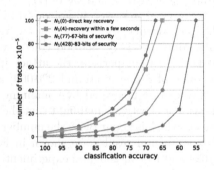

Fig. 5. The required trace numbers for different classification accuracies using half Gaussian leakage.

5   Power Analysis Using Sign Leakage

As outlined in Sect. 3.2, the integer Gaussian sampler SamplerZ requires transforming a half Gaussian sample into a bimodal one via a uniformly random sign flip and then accepting it with proper probability. While both the half Gaussian sample and the random sign can be revealed through single trace analysis as shown in [21], the sign leakage remains unexploited until now. Compared to the half Gaussian leakage, the sign flip seems to offer less information, as it can only help to filter signatures in a half-space instead of a slice.

In this section, we first identify the sign leakage in the reference implementation of Falcon. Then we show that sign leakage can indeed be used to mount effective key recovery attacks: about 170 000 traces is enough to fully recover the key. Perhaps counter-intuitively, the key recovery solely using sign leakage needs even fewer signature measurements than the one solely using half Gaussian leakage. Moreover, combining sign leakage with half Gaussian leakage, we can further reduce the requirements of measurements and computations for key recovery: a full key recovery needs only 45 000 signatures given two sources of leakage. At last, we propose a practical countermeasure to mitigate the sign leakage.

5.1 Side-Channel Analysis

As the goal of the side-channel analysis is to classify the sign of z (which is indicated by b), it is necessary to analyze its leakages. The most straightforward leakage of the sign should be directly from the generation of variable b, including the loading and storing process. We term this leakage type-1. Besides, the value of b also affects the intermediate variables in the Gaussian sampling. By its instruction, Falcon first performs half Gaussian sample to obtain the value z^+ and maps it to z using the sign-flip function based on a bit b, i.e., $[\![z \leftarrow b + (2b-1)z^+]\!]$ (line 3, Algorithm 2). Then, z is involved in the computation of x: $[\![x \leftarrow -\frac{(z-c)^2}{2\sigma'^2} + \frac{(z^+)^2}{2\sigma_{max}^2}]\!]$ (line 4, Algorithm 2). We term the sign leakage from the calculation of z and x type-2.

To better analyze the leakages of the above two types, we insert delay macros (by using an empty loop) between the generation of b, the calculation of $[\![z \leftarrow b + (2b-1)z^+]\!]$ and $[\![x \leftarrow -\frac{(z-c)^2}{2\sigma'^2} + \frac{(z^+)^2}{2\sigma_{max}^2}]\!]$. Thus, the power consumption before the first delay only contains the type-1 leakage. Meanwhile, the algorithm after the first delay comprises the loading of b and computation of z and x, thus containing both type-1 and type-2 leakages.

We run the reference implementation of Falcon (with the delay macro inserted) on an ARM Cortex-M4 STM32F407IGT6 microprocessor. The power traces are collected by using a PicoScope 3206D oscilloscope at a sampling rate of 1 GSa/s, equipped with a Mini-Circuits 1.9 MHz low pass filter. We collect 50 000 traces with different random seeds, and compute the Signal-to-Noise Ratio (SNR) with respect to the sign of z.

As shown in Fig. 6, we can identify the three regions, as well as the corresponding leakages by peak clusters. Moreover, the SNRs of regions B and C (containing type-1 and type-2 leakage) are much larger than those of region A (only containing type-1 leakage), showing that the type-2 leakage is much more significant than the type-1. It conveys that the calculations of z and x can amplify the leakage of the sign (i.e., the value of b). We attribute the leakage amplification to the following reasons.

– The first reason should be the power consumption of $((b \ll 1) - 1)$. Concretely, the corresponding register is assigned to the value of b, then adds itself and minus 1. The value in register turns into -1 (0xFFFFFFFF for complement) when $b = 0$ and 1 (0×00000001 for complement) when $b = 1$. The Hamming distance of two results is 31, which is sufficiently large to distinguish the sign of the output z. It should be noted that this type of leakage was detected in [21] and comprehensively analyzed in the very recent work by Wisiol et al. [36].

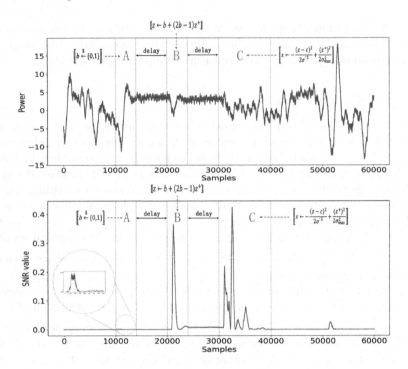

Fig. 6. Power traces and the corresponding SNR value.

- Another reason should be in $[\![x \leftarrow -\frac{(z-c)^2}{2\sigma'^2} + \frac{(z^+)^2}{2\sigma^2_{max}}]\!]$ (line 4, Algorithm 2). In the calculation of $z - c$, z is an integer while c is a floating point number. In most cases, z is first converted to the floating point number, and then the subtraction is performed. The former is essentially a conversion between complement and floating representations of z. If z is negative, the Hamming distance of complement and floating representation is relatively large. This eventually brings the sign leakage in the step of $[\![x \leftarrow -\frac{(z-c)^2}{2\sigma'^2} + \frac{(z^+)^2}{2\sigma^2_{max}}]\!]$.

To verify the vulnerabilities in practice, we conduct the Gaussian template attack [3], where the number of profiling traces varies from 70 to 100, 000. After the profiling, we repeat the single-trace attack 5, 000 times (with different attacking traces) to calculate the success rate. We perform the evaluation with four different configurations: 3 attacks targeting regions A, B, and C separately, and 1 attack targeting their combination. For each configuration, we apply the principal component analysis (PCA) to the samples before profiling and attacking, and then only target the points of the first 65 principal components.

Figure 7 presents the classification accuracy (as functions of the number of profiling traces). The results show that the attacks using samples in regions B and C (involving type-1 and type-2 leakages) are significantly better than those using region A (only involving type-1 leakages). The leakages in region C have led to an attack with an almost 1 classification accuracy, and using the leakages in region B can also achieve an accuracy ≈ 0.9. On the contrary, the classification accuracy corresponding to region A is up to 0.52. At last, using the combination of three regions leads to the best attack, which is slightly better than the attack using region C.

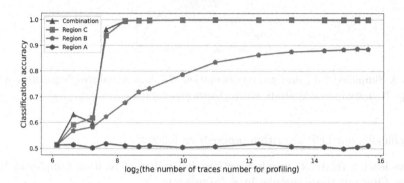

Fig. 7. The classification accuracy targeting the three regions and combination thereof.

5.2 Key Recovery Using Sign Leakage

Using the sign leakage, one can determine whether a signature $\mathbf{s}$ is in the halfspace $\mathcal{H}^+ = \{\mathbf{v} : \langle \mathbf{v}, \mathbf{b}_0 \rangle \geq 0\}$ or $\mathcal{H}^- = \{\mathbf{v} : \langle \mathbf{v}, \mathbf{b}_0 \rangle < 0\}$ (see Fig. 8). It is worth noting that one can transform a signature in $\mathcal{H}^+$ into one in $\mathcal{H}^-$ by multiplying -1. Therefore no waste of signature measurements occurs in this classification, which is different from the case presented in Sect. 4.

To study the key recovery, we define the *Learning Halfspace Problem*.

Definition 2 ($\mathsf{LHP}_{\sigma,N}$). *Given* $\mathbf{b} \in \mathbb{R}^n$, *let* $\mathcal{H}_{\mathbf{b}}^+ = \{\mathbf{v} : \langle \mathbf{v}, \mathbf{b} \rangle \geq 0\}$. *Let* D_h *be the conditional distribution of* $\mathbf{z} \sim (\mathcal{N}(0,\sigma^2))^n$ *given* $\mathbf{z} \in \mathcal{H}_{\mathbf{b}}^+$. *Given* N *independent samples drawn from* D_h, *find an approximate direction of* $\pm\mathbf{b}$.

Exploiting the sign leakage, signatures can be transformed into Gaussian samples in $\mathcal{H}_{\mathbf{b}_0}^+$. By solving $\mathsf{LHP}_{\sigma,N}$, we can get an approximate direction of $\mathbf{b}_0$.

The distribution of the given samples in the $\mathsf{LHP}_{\sigma,N}$ instance is determined by the secret $\mathbf{b}_0$. It is feasible to get a solution to $\mathsf{LHP}_{\sigma,N}$ through the spectral decomposition of $\mathbf{Cov}[\mathbf{s}|\mathbf{s} \in \mathcal{H}_{\mathbf{b}_0}^+]$ as done in Sect. 4. However, the accuracy of the solution is poor because the gap between the smallest eigenvalue and others is reduced. To overcome this issue, we propose to use a rough LHP solution to filter a slice and then apply the previous LSP algorithm to get an accurate solution. This can be roughly viewed as the following reduction:

$$\mathsf{LHP}_{\sigma,N} \rightarrow \mathsf{LSP}_{b,\sigma,N'}.$$

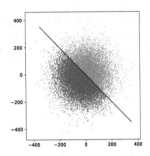

Fig. 8. Simplified 2-dimensional representation of Falcon signatures. Signatures in $\mathcal{H}^+$ (resp. $\mathcal{H}^-$) are in orange (resp. blue). (Color figure online)

Specifically, our LHP algorithm proceeds as follows:

1. we learn a relatively rough direction, denoted $\mathbf{v}$, of $\mathbf{b}_0$ from samples in $\mathcal{H}_{\mathbf{b}_0}^+$;
2. we filter out those samples in $\mathcal{S}_{\mathbf{v}}(b)$ using $\mathbf{v}$;
3. we learn the direction of $\mathbf{b}_0$ from the filtered samples in $\mathcal{S}_{\mathbf{v}}(b)$;

Learning a rough direction. By the same argument with Sect. 4, we have

$$\mathbf{Cov}[\mathbf{s}|\mathbf{s} \in \mathcal{H}_{\mathbf{b}_0}^+] = \mathbf{D} \cdot \begin{pmatrix} \sigma'^2 & \\ & \sigma^2\mathbf{I} \end{pmatrix} \cdot \mathbf{D}^t$$

where $\mathbf{D} = (\mathbf{d}_0, \cdots, \mathbf{d}_{n-1})$ with $\mathbf{d}_i = \widetilde{\mathbf{b}}_i / \|\widetilde{\mathbf{b}}_i\|$. The term σ'^2 equals the variance of half Gaussian, and a routine computation yields $\sigma'^2 = \sigma^2(1 - \frac{2}{\pi}) < \sigma^2$. Therefore the direction of $\mathbf{b}_0$ still corresponds to the eigenvector with respect to eigenvalue σ'^2.

Remark 2. The expectation of samples in $\mathcal{H}_{\mathbf{b}_0}^+$ is also the direction of $\mathbf{b}_0$. Nevertheless, the use of the expectation does not improve the learning accuracy as per our experimental results.

Filtering out a slice. To refine the learning accuracy, we attempt to amplify the distinction between σ' and σ. To do so, we use the above rough direction, denoted $\mathbf{v}$, to classify all samples into two sets $\mathcal{S} = \{\mathbf{s} \mid |\langle\mathbf{s},\mathbf{v}\rangle| \leq b\}$ and $\mathcal{C} = \{\mathbf{s} \mid |\langle\mathbf{s},\mathbf{v}\rangle| > b\}$ (see Fig. 9). The parameter b decides both the width of the approximate slice and the proportion of filtered samples. For a tradeoff, our key recovery sets $b = 1.17\sqrt{q}$ that is around the expectation of the secret key norm as per Falcon parameters. This actually corresponds to the case in Sect. 4. It should be noted here that the covariance of filtered samples is

$$\mathbf{Cov}[\mathbf{s}|\mathbf{s} \in \mathcal{H}_{\mathbf{b}_0}^+ \cap \mathcal{S}] = \mathbf{D}' \cdot \begin{pmatrix} \sigma'^2 & & & \\ & \sigma_1^2 & & \\ & & \ddots & \\ & & & \sigma_{n-1}^2 \end{pmatrix} \cdot \mathbf{D}'^t$$

where $\mathbf{D}'$ is slightly different from $\mathbf{D}$ due to the inaccuracy of $\mathbf{v}$ and $\sigma_1, \cdots, \sigma_{n-1}$ are no longer equal. Still, σ' is clearly less than others. As a consequence, its corresponding eigenvector is supposed to be in a very close direction of $\mathbf{b}_0$. Applying the LSP algorithm in Sect. 4 on filtered samples, one can obtain an approximate direction of $\mathbf{b}_0$ that is more accurate than $\mathbf{v}$.

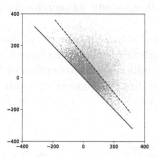

Fig. 9. Simplified 2-dimensional representation of Falcon signatures. Signatures in $\mathcal{H}_{\mathbf{b}_0}^+ \cap \mathcal{S}_{\mathbf{v}}(b)$ are in orange. (Color figure online)

Remark 3. Strictly speaking, the region $\mathcal{H}_{\mathbf{b}_0}^+ \cap \mathcal{S}_{\mathbf{v}}(b)$ is not an exact slice as the directions of $\mathbf{b}_0$ and $\mathbf{v}$ differ. But this region still maintains some information of $\mathbf{b}_0$ from $\mathcal{H}_{\mathbf{b}_0}^+$ that is captured by the LSP algorithm to refine the direction.

Remark 4. We can also use this idea to reduce the width of the slice in Sec. 4, but the effect is not good for our key recovery. The reason is that signatures in $\mathcal{S}$ are distributed densely, the reduction of slice width would eliminate a big number of signatures. In this section, the signature density in $\mathcal{C}$ is lower than that in $\mathcal{S}$. We therefore can reduce the slice width at the cost of fewer signatures.

Key recovery from an approximate direction. While $\|\mathbf{b}_0\|$ cannot be learnt purely from the sign information, we can still approximate $\|\mathbf{b}_0\|$ with some alternatives in $\{1.17\sqrt{q}, \cdots, 1.17\sqrt{q} - 10\}$. This works well in practice: one can always get one approximation well close to $\mathbf{b}_0$ using some alternatives to $\|\mathbf{b}_0\|$. In later experimental results, we shall present the best approximation for each tested instance.

5.2.1 Experimental Results

We use the same 40 Falcon-512 instances as in Sect. 4. Figure 10 shows the detailed experimental results. In the context of the key recovery in this subsection, $N_1(7)$ is around 170 000. This implies that one can recover the key from the approximation within half an hour with a probability of $\approx 25\%$ given a moderate number of traces. Compared with the key recovery presented in Sect. 4, the attack exploiting sign leakage seems more powerful, as it requires fewer traces to achieve the same size of the approximate error. A crucial reason for this is that the sign information of each signature contributes to the key recovery, at least to recover a rough direction, but in the attack in Sect. 4, about one half measured signatures are directly discarded in the first place. We also exhibit the tradeoff between measurements and the cost of key recovery combining lattice reduction in Fig. 11: 20 000 signature measurements would reduce the security of Falcon-512 by 50 bits.

Furthermore, we test our attack in the case of inaccurate sign classification. As shown in Fig. 12, our attack is robust to inaccurate classification: for 65% classification accuracy, 10 million traces are sufficient for key recovery in a short time. One can also observe that the number of required traces grows sharply as the accuracy gets below 65%.

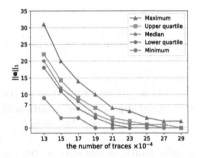

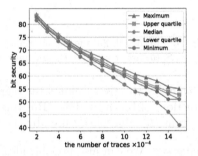

Fig. 10. The approximate error size $\|\mathbf{e}\|_1$ measured over 40 Falcon-512 instances solely using the sign leakage.

Fig. 11. The bit security estimated as per the approximate error. We use the Core-SVP model in classical setting, i.e. $2^{0.292\beta}$ where β is the required BKZ blocksize

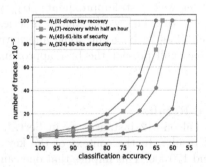

Fig. 12. The required trace numbers for different classification accuracies using sign leakage.

5.3   Key Recovery Using both Sign and Half Gaussian Leakages

It is natural to work with both sign leakage and half Gaussian leakage (presented in Sect. 4). Specifically, this allows filtering a slice that is only one half wide as the one filtered solely by half Gaussian leakage. Through spectral decomposition of the covariance, one can learn the secret key.

The combination of two leakages significantly improves the key recovery. When 20 000 signature measurements are available, the approximate error becomes ternary for all 40 tested instances. Detailed experimental results are presented in Figs. 13 and 14. In particular, with only 45 000 traces, one can fully recover the key with a probability of $\approx 25\%$ within half an hour. With around 12 000 traces, the attacker may reduce the security of Falcon-512 by 60 bits. Nevertheless, further tradeoff seems infeasible. As the number of traces is insufficient, the approximate error can enlarge quickly due to the measurement error, which makes the approximation ineffective.

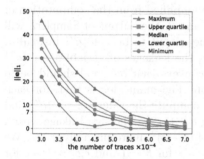

Fig. 13. The approximate error size $\|\mathbf{e}\|_1$ measured over 40 Falcon-512 instances using both sign and half Gaussian leakages.

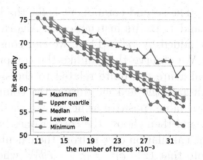

Fig. 14. The bit security estimated as per the approximate error. We use the Core-SVP model in classical setting, i.e. $2^{0.292\beta}$ where β is the required BKZ blocksize

5.4   A Countermeasure Against the Sign Leakage

We present a countermeasure to mitigate the leakage of the sign in the Gaussian sampling, which is made up of two components as follows.

The first component is for the direct leakage of the sign b. The leakage (e.g., power consumption) of a variable in software is largely related to its Hamming weight [26]. Thus, to eliminate the difference in Hamming weight between different values of b, the countermeasure encodes the sign by $\{1, 2\}$ instead of $\{0, 1\}$. Concretely, we first generate a 4-bit variable t by uniformly sampling a value in $\{0, \ldots, 15\}$, and map it to the variable b in $\{1, 2\}$ by using a look-up table with 16 entries in $\{1, 2\}$.

Algorithm 4: Protected SamplerZ

Input: a center c'' and standard deviation $\sigma' \in [\sigma_{min}, \sigma_{max}]$
Output: an integer $z \sim D_{\mathbb{Z}, \sigma', c''}$

1   $c \leftarrow c'' - \lfloor c'' \rfloor$
2   $z^+ \leftarrow \mathsf{BaseSampler}()$
3   $(\tilde{t}[0], \dots, \tilde{t}[15]) \leftarrow (2, 1, 1, 2, 2, 1, 1, 2, 2, 1, 2, 1, 1, 2, 1, 2)$
4   $t \xleftarrow{\$} \{0, \dots, 15\}$
5   $b \leftarrow \tilde{t}[t]$
6   $(\tilde{c}[0], \tilde{c}[1], \tilde{c}[2]) \leftarrow (0, c, 1 - c)$
7   $(\tilde{z}[0], \tilde{z}[1], \tilde{z}[2]) \leftarrow (0, \lfloor c'' \rfloor - z^+, \lfloor c'' \rfloor + 1 + z^+)$
8   $x \leftarrow -\frac{(z^+ + \tilde{c}[b])^2}{2\sigma'^2} + \frac{(z^+)^2}{2\sigma_{max}^2}$
9   **return** $\tilde{z}[b]$ with probability $\frac{\sigma_{min}}{\sigma'} \cdot \exp(x)$, otherwise restart;

The second component is for the leakage amplified from the computation of z and x. By its instruction in Algorithms 1 and 2, the output of SamplerZ will be added by $\lfloor c'' \rfloor$. Thus, we can consider the output to be $z + \lfloor c'' \rfloor$ instead of z. We observe that, unlike the computation, the leakages of variables $z + \lfloor c'' \rfloor$ and x are not quite related to the sign. It conveys that our goal should be to mitigate the leakage during the computation. The main idea is that, for each sign value (positive or negative), we directly compute the values of $z + \lfloor c'' \rfloor$ and x, and then choose the correct ones by using $b \in \{1, 2\}$. The sign leakage within the calculation of x is from the calculation of $(z - c)^2$, more precisely, $z - c$. We note that $(z - c)^2 = (z^+ + \tilde{c}[b])^2$ where $\tilde{c}[b] = c$ for $b = 1$ and $\tilde{c}[b] = 1 - c$ for $b = 2$. Instead of computing two x's for $b \in \{1, 2\}$, it suffices to compute two $\tilde{c}[b]$'s and to perform the calculation of x using $(z^+, \tilde{c}[b])$ only once.

The new SamplerZ equipped with the above components is provided in Algorithm 4. Lines 3-5 present the generation of $b \in \{1, 2\}$, and Lines 6-9 present the calculation of x and $z + \lfloor c'' \rfloor$.

To verify the effectiveness of the countermeasure, we implement the protected Gaussian sampling in C and collect the power traces using the same setup as in Sect. 5.1. The SNR for the sign value is depicted in Fig. 15, which is much lower than that of the unprotected algorithm (see Fig. 6). We conduct the template attack with 5 000 traces to calculate the classification accuracy. As shown in Fig. 16, with the increase of the number of profiling traces, the classification accuracy is growing up to ≈ 0.52.

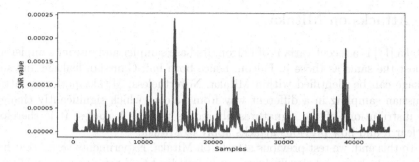

Fig. 15. SNR for the sign value of the Algorithm 4.

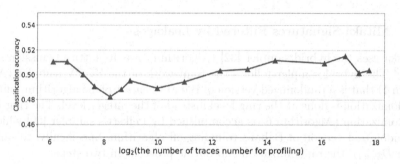

Fig. 16. Classification accuracy of the template attack on Algorithm 4.

Remarks. Our countermeasure can mitigate, but cannot prevent the leakage of the sign. As we can see from the experimental results, the accuracy of the template attack for sign classification is still significant (up to ≈ 0.52), and it is even possible to be higher if an adversary

1. adopts a more sophisticated setup for acquisition, or
2. exploits other targets than the direct leakage of b and the computation of x and z.

In this respect, we position our countermeasure as a (quite) efficient method to make the offline key recovery attack more difficult. As shown in Fig. 12, the number of required traces grows dramatically when the accuracy of the sign classification decreases. One can still conduct a successful attack if she can sign a lot of times (it usually can be avoided in practice by setting a counter for the maximum time of calls). A candidate of sufficiently secure countermeasures might be masking, with inevitably high overhead. Thus, we deem an efficient and provably secure countermeasure for Gaussian sampling as challenging and promising further work.

6 Attacks on Mitaka

Mitaka [11] is a recent variant of Falcon. Its base sampler and integer sampler are almost the same as those in Falcon, hence both half Gaussian leakage and sign leakage can be identified within Mitaka. Nevertheless, Mitaka performs lattice Gaussian sampling in a different way from Falcon, which significantly changes the distributions of the signatures filtered as per the leakages. It is therefore unclear if and how previous attacks apply to Mitaka.

To this end, we test previous attacks on Mitaka. Experiments verify that half Gaussian leakage and sign leakage can indeed lead to a key recovery in Mitaka, but the key recovery requires much more traces compared to the case of Falcon.

6.1 Mitaka Signatures Filtered by Leakages

Mitaka uses the hybrid sampler [32] (Algorithm 5) as its lattice Gaussian sampler.[2] The hybrid sampler follows the framework of the KGPV sampler (Algorithm 1) that is a randomized version of Babai's nearest plane algorithm, but the randomization is done at the ring level instead of the integer level. The ring-level randomization (Algorithm 6) is accomplished by Peikert's sampler [29] which is a randomized version of Babai's rounding-off algorithm. Specifically, to sample from $D_{\mathcal{R},\sigma,D}$, the randomization subroutine proceeds in two steps:

1. (perturbation sampling): it samples a perturbation $U \leftarrow \sigma_p \cdot \mathcal{N}_{\mathcal{K}_{\mathbb{R}},1}$ where $\sigma_p \overline{\sigma_p} = \sigma \overline{\sigma} - r^2$ and $\mathcal{N}_{\mathcal{K}_{\mathbb{R}},1}$ denotes the normal distribution over $\mathcal{K}_{\mathbb{R}}$.
2. (rounding-off): it samples the output $Z \leftarrow D_{\mathcal{R},r,D-U}$.

From Algorithms 5 and 6, it follows that the signature $\mathbf{s}$ can be written as $\mathbf{s} = \mathbf{v} - \mathbf{c} = \sum_{i=0}^{1} \widetilde{\mathbf{b}}_i (Z_i - D_i) = \sum_{i=0}^{1} \widetilde{\mathbf{b}}_i (Y_i + U_i)$ where $Y_i = Z_i - D'_i \in \mathcal{K}_{\mathbb{R}}$ and $U_i \in \mathcal{K}_{\mathbb{R}}$ is the perturbation. Then the signature is identified with $\mathbf{s} = \sum_{i=0}^{2n-1} (y_i + u_i) \mathbf{h}_i$ where $(y_0, \cdots, y_{2n-1})$ (resp. $(u_0, \cdots, u_{2n-1})$) is the coefficient vectors of (Y_0, Y_1) (resp. (U_0, U_1)) and $\mathbf{h}_i$'s correspond to $\widetilde{\mathbf{B}}$.

We target the integer Gaussian sampler called in the rounding-off step. Similar to the case of Falcon, half Gaussian leakage allows filtering signatures with $y_0 \in (-1, 1]$, while sign leakage allows distinguishing $y_0 > 0$ or not. Exploiting these leakages, one can actually distort the spherical Gaussian in the direction of $\mathbf{h}_0$ (See Fig. 17). This makes our previous attacks feasible. Note that the domain of filtered signatures is now the ambient space due to the perturbation u_0, thus parallelepiped-learning attacks do not seem to work.

---

[2] We do not discuss the integer arithmetic friendly version of Mitaka that uses the integral perturbation sampler [5,12] proceeding differently.

Algorithm 5: Hybrid sampler

Input: a basis $\mathbf{B} = (\mathbf{b}_0, \mathbf{b}_1) \in \mathcal{R}^{2 \times 2}$ and its GSO (over $\mathcal{K}$) $\widetilde{\mathbf{B}} = (\widetilde{\mathbf{b}_0}, \widetilde{\mathbf{b}_1})$, a center $\mathbf{c} \in \mathcal{K}^2$ and $\sigma > 0$

Output: a lattice point $\mathbf{v}$ following a distribution close to $D_{\mathcal{L}(\mathbf{B}), \sigma, \mathbf{c}}$.

1 $\mathbf{v}_1 \leftarrow \mathbf{0}, \mathbf{c}_1 \leftarrow \mathbf{c}$

2 $D_1 \leftarrow \frac{\langle \widetilde{\mathbf{b}_1}, \widetilde{\mathbf{c}_1} \rangle}{\langle \widetilde{\mathbf{b}_1}, \widetilde{\mathbf{b}_1} \rangle}, \sigma_1 \leftarrow \sqrt{\frac{\sigma^2}{\langle \widetilde{\mathbf{b}_1}, \widetilde{\mathbf{b}_1} \rangle}}$

3 $Z_1 \leftarrow \mathsf{RingPeikert}(D_1, \sigma_1)$

4 $\mathbf{v}_0 \leftarrow \mathbf{b}_1 Z_1, \mathbf{c}_0 \leftarrow \mathbf{c}_1 - \mathbf{b}_1 Z_1$

5 $D_0 \leftarrow \frac{\langle \widetilde{\mathbf{b}_0}, \widetilde{\mathbf{c}_0} \rangle}{\langle \widetilde{\mathbf{b}_0}, \widetilde{\mathbf{b}_0} \rangle}, \sigma_0 \leftarrow \sqrt{\frac{\sigma^2}{\langle \widetilde{\mathbf{b}_0}, \widetilde{\mathbf{b}_0} \rangle}}$

6 $Z_0 \leftarrow \mathsf{RingPeikert}(D_0, \sigma_0)$

7 $\mathbf{v} \leftarrow \mathbf{v}_0 + \mathbf{b}_0 Z_0$

8 **return** $\mathbf{v}$

Algorithm 6: RingPeikert

Input: a center $D \in \mathcal{K}$ and $\sigma \in \mathcal{K}_{\mathbb{R}}$.

Output: $z \in \mathcal{R}$ following a distribution close to $D_{\mathcal{R}, \sigma, D}$

1 Compute $\sigma_p \in \mathcal{K}_{\mathbb{R}}$ such that $\sigma_p \overline{\sigma_p} = \sigma \overline{\sigma} - r^2$ for some $r > 0$

2 $U \leftarrow \sigma_p \cdot \mathcal{N}_{\mathcal{K}_{\mathbb{R}}, 1}, D' \leftarrow D + U$

3 **for** $i = 0 \cdots n - 1$ **do**

4 $\quad z_i \leftarrow \mathsf{SamplerZ}(r, d_i' - \lfloor d_i' \rfloor) + \lfloor d_i' \rfloor$ $\qquad$ /** $D' = \sum_i d_i' x^i \in \mathcal{K}_{\mathbb{R}}$ **/

5 **end for**

6 **return** $Z = \sum_i z_i x^i \in \mathcal{R}$

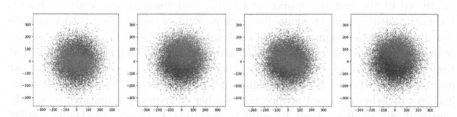

Fig. 17. Simplified 2-dimensional representation of Mitaka signatures. From left to right, the first graph is for half Gaussian leakage: signatures with $y_0 \in (-1, 1]$ in orange; the second graph is for sign leakage: signatures with $y_0 \in [0, +\infty)$ in orange; the third graph is for the combination of two leakages: signatures with $y_0 \in [0, 1]$ in orange; the fourth graph is for the combination of two leakages: signatures with $y_0 \in (1, +\infty)$ in orange. (Color figure online)

6.2   Experimental Results

Both half Gaussian leakage and sign leakage can be well detected as shown in [17] and Sect. 5. We thus only present the experimental results for the key recovery procedure.

6.2.1   Key Recovery Using Half Gaussian Leakage

We tested the attack in Sect. 4 and experimental results are shown in Fig. 18. Experiments validate the effectiveness of the attack: one can get a good approximation or a full recovery of the key with a certain number of Mitaka signatures. However, compared to the attack on Falcon, the key recovery on Mitaka requires much more signatures: the number of signatures required for a quick key recovery gets close to 9 million. This is because the condition number of the covariance of filtered signatures gets smaller due to the existence of the perturbation.

6.2.2   Key Recovery Using Sign Leakage

We can only partially apply the attack in Sect. 5.2 to Mitaka. Specifically, it is feasible to learn a relatively rough direction, denoted $\mathbf{h}'$, of $\mathbf{h}_0$ through the covariance as in the first step. However, refining $\mathbf{h}'$ via filtering out a slice does not work, as the domain of filtered signatures does not have a clear boundary. Hence we have to use $\mathbf{h}'$ directly for key recovery. We also observed that for Mitaka, using the expectation can give a better approximate direction than using the covariance, which is different from the case in Remark 2. For this, our test used the expectation to get $\mathbf{h}'$ and then used $\mathbf{h}'$ to recover the key. In this way, a practically efficient key recovery needs about 2.25 million signatures. Figure 19 shows the detailed experimental results.

6.2.3   Key Recovery Using Two Leakages

As shown in the last two graphs of Fig. 17, combining two leakages allows filtering signatures in two regions. For each region, we can obtain an approximate direction using the approach in the last subsection based on either the expectation or the covariance of filtered signatures. Extensive experiments suggested that using the expectation of the signatures with $y_0 \in (1, +\infty)$ gives the most accurate approximate direction. Different from the case in Sect. 5.3, using two leakages together does not reduce the number of required signatures so significantly: it still requires about 1.8 million signatures to recover the key in a short time. Detailed experimental results are shown in Fig. 20.

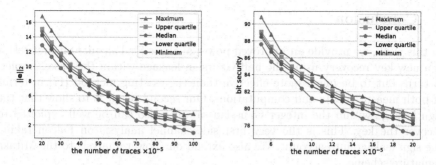

Fig. 18. Experimental results for the attack solely using half Gaussian leakage. The left figure shows the approximate error size $\|\mathbf{e}\|_2$, and the right one shows the bit security estimated as per $\|\mathbf{e}\|_2$. Experiments ran over 40 Mitaka-512 instances.

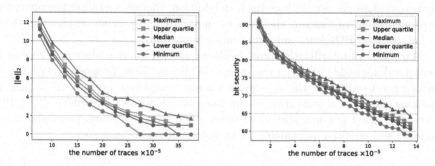

Fig. 19. Experimental results for the attack solely using sign leakage. The left figure shows the approximate error size $\|\mathbf{e}\|_2$, and the right one shows the bit security estimated as per $\|\mathbf{e}\|_2$. Experiments ran over 40 Mitaka-512 instances.

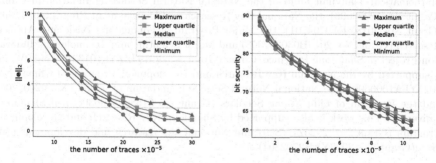

Fig. 20. Experimental results for the attack using both half Gaussian leakage and sign leakage. The left figure shows the approximate error size $\|\mathbf{e}\|_2$, and the right one shows the bit security estimated as per $\|\mathbf{e}\|_2$. Experiments ran over 40 Mitaka-512 instances.

7   Conclusion

In this work, we provide an improved power analysis for Falcon. Our first result is a new key recovery using the half Gaussian leakage within the base sampler. It turns out to be much more effective than the existing method [17] in terms of both measurements and computations. Our second result is to show that the sign leakage within the integer Gaussian sampler also can be well exploited to recover the key. This is the very first side-channel analysis on Falcon taking the sign leakage into account. We also extend our power analysis to the Mitaka signature scheme.

Our attacks are practical and powerful: only tens of thousand traces are enough to greatly weaken the security of Falcon; they can even work when leakage classification is inaccurate. This suggests that two exploited leakages are more dangerous than previously imagined. In addition, though we target the reference implementation of Falcon, the attacks apply to many other implementations including clean PQClean and pqm4 implementations.

With the standardization and deployment of Falcon underway, there is a clear need for side-channel protections. While we have proposed some countermeasure to mitigate the attacks, it cannot completely prevent the leakages. Masking might be a reassuring countermeasure. Despite some efforts [1,11,15], efficient masked implementation of integer Gaussian sampling, particularly for variable and sensitive parameters, remains a challenging problem.

Acknowledgements. The first two authors contributed equally to this work and are considered as co-first authors. We thank Pierre-Alain Fouque, Mélissa Rossi, Zongyue Wang, Yu Yu and Yuanyuan Zhou for valuable discussions. Yang Yu is supported by the National Natural Science Foundation of China (No. 62102216), the Mathematical Tianyuan Fund of the National Natural Science Foundation of China (Grant No. 12226006), the National Key Research and Development Program of China (Grant No. 2018YFA0704701), the Major Program of Guangdong Basic and Applied Research (Grant No. 2019B030302008) and Major Scientific and Technological Innovation Project of Shandong Province, China (Grant No. 2019JZZY010133). Weijia Wang is supported by the National Key Research and Development Program of China (No. 2021YFA1000600), the National Natural Science Foundation of China (No. 62002204) and the Program of Qilu Young Scholars (Grant No 61580082063088) of Shandong University. This work is also supported by Shandong Key Research and Development Program (Grant No. 2020ZLYS09) and National key research and development program(Grant No. 2022YFB2702804).

A   Theoretical Analysis for the LSP Algorithm

In this section, we will show that given a sufficiently large polynomial number of samples, our LSP algorithm finds a solution with constant approximation errors with some constant probability. This is formally described in Lemma 1.

Lemma 1. *Given an* $\mathsf{LSP}_{b,\sigma,N}$ *instance with exact solution* $\mathbf{b}$, *let* $\mathbf{b}'$ *be the output by our* LSP *algorithm. Let* $\sigma'^2 = \mathbf{var}\left[x \sim \mathcal{N}(0,\sigma^2) \mid -\frac{b}{\|\mathbf{b}\|} \leq x \leq \frac{b}{\|\mathbf{b}\|}\right]$. *Then*

$$\|\mathbf{b} - \mathbf{b}'\| \leq C_e \cdot \left(\sigma^2 + \frac{\sigma^2}{\sigma^2 - \sigma'^2} \cdot \|\mathbf{b}\|\right)\left(\sqrt{\frac{n+u}{N}} + \frac{n+u}{N}\right)$$

with a probability $\geq 1 - 4e^{-u}$ *for some constant* C_e.

To prove Lemma 1, we need the following theorems.

Theorem 1 (Weyl's inequality). *Let* $\mathbf{S}, \mathbf{T} \in \mathbb{R}^{n \times n}$ *be symmetric matrices. Then*

$$\max_i |\lambda_i(\mathbf{S}) - \lambda_i(\mathbf{T})| \leq \|\mathbf{S} - \mathbf{T}\|_2.$$

Here $\|\mathbf{S}\|_2$ *denotes the spectral norm of* $\mathbf{S}$.

Theorem 2 (Davis-Kahan [35]). *Let* $\mathbf{S}, \mathbf{T} \in \mathbb{R}^{n \times n}$ *be two symmetric matrices. Suppose that for some* i, *the* i-*th largest eigenvalue of* $\mathbf{S}$ *is well separated from the rest of the spectrum:*

$$\min_{j:j\neq i} |\lambda_i(\mathbf{S}) - \lambda_j(\mathbf{S})| = \delta > 0.$$

Then the unit eigenvectors $v_i(\mathbf{S})$ *and* $v_i(\mathbf{T})$ *satisfies:*

$$\exists \theta \in \{-1, 1\} : \|v_i(\mathbf{S}) - \theta v_i(\mathbf{T})\| \leq \frac{2^{\frac{3}{2}}\|\mathbf{S} - \mathbf{T}\|_2}{\delta}.$$

Theorem 3 (Adapted from Theorem 4.7.1 [35]). *Let* $\mathbf{X}$ *be a subgaussian random vector in* $\mathbb{R}^n$ *and* $\Sigma = \mathbf{Cov}[\mathbf{X}\mathbf{X}^t]$. *For independent samples* $\mathbf{X}_1, \cdots, \mathbf{X}_N$, *let* $\Sigma_N = \frac{1}{N}\sum_{i=0}^{N}\mathbf{X}_i\mathbf{X}_i^t$. *Then there exists a constant* K *(related to* $\mathbf{X}$) *and a universal constant* $C > 0$ *such that for any* $u \geq 0$,

$$\|\Sigma_N - \Sigma\|_2 \leq CK^2\left(\sqrt{\frac{n+u}{N}} + \frac{n+u}{N}\right)\|\Sigma\|_2$$

with probability at least $1 - 2e^{-u}$

Proof of lemma 1. Let $\mathbf{v} = \frac{\mathbf{b}}{\|\mathbf{b}\|}$ and $\mathbf{v}' = \frac{\mathbf{b}'}{\|\mathbf{b}'\|}$. We have

$$\mathbf{e} = \mathbf{b} - \mathbf{b}' = \|\mathbf{b}\| \cdot (\mathbf{v} - \mathbf{v}') + (\|\mathbf{b}\| - \|\mathbf{b}'\|) \cdot \mathbf{v}'$$

and then $\|\mathbf{e}\| \leq \|\mathbf{b}\| \cdot \|\mathbf{v} - \mathbf{v}'\| + |\|\mathbf{b}\| - \|\mathbf{b}'\||$.

Let $\Sigma = \mathbf{Cov}[\mathbf{s}|\mathbf{s} \in \mathcal{S}_\mathbf{b}(b)]$ and Σ_N be the covariance matrix measured over N given samples. Then $\mathbf{v}$ and $\mathbf{v}'$ are respectively the eigenvectors corresponding to the smallest eigenvalue of Σ and Σ_N. Since the smallest eigenvalue of Σ is σ'^2 and other eigenvalues are σ^2, Theorem 2 shows $\|\mathbf{v} - \mathbf{v}'\| \leq \frac{2^{\frac{3}{2}}\|\Sigma - \Sigma_N\|_2}{\sigma^2 - \sigma'^2}$.

By Theorem 3, we have $\|\mathbf{v} - \mathbf{v}'\| \leq 2^{\frac{3}{2}} CK^2 \frac{\sigma^2}{\sigma^2 - \sigma'^2} \cdot \left(\sqrt{\frac{n+u}{N}} + \frac{n+u}{N} \right)$ with probability at least $1 - 2e^{-u}$.

We next analyse the term $|\|\mathbf{b}\| - \|\mathbf{b}'\||$. Let $\sigma_N'^2$ be the smallest eigenvalue of Σ_N. By Theorems 1 and 3, we have $|\sigma'^2 - \sigma_N'^2| \leq \|\Sigma_N - \Sigma\|_2 \leq \sigma^2 CK^2 \left(\sqrt{\frac{n+u}{N}} + \frac{n+u}{N} \right)$ with probability at least $1 - 2e^{-u}$. Our LSP algorithm uses the equation

$$\sigma'^2 = \frac{\int_{-\frac{b}{\|\mathbf{b}\|}}^{\frac{b}{\|\mathbf{b}\|}} x^2 \exp(-\frac{x^2}{2\sigma^2}) dx}{\int_{-\frac{b}{\|\mathbf{b}\|}}^{\frac{b}{\|\mathbf{b}\|}} \exp(-\frac{x^2}{2\sigma^2}) dx}$$

to estimate $\|\mathbf{b}\|$, hence $\|\mathbf{b}\| = f(\sigma'^2)$ for some continuous function f determined by b, σ and σ'. Accordingly, $\|\mathbf{b}'\| = f(\sigma_N'^2)$. Therefore, there exists a constant C' such that $|\|\mathbf{b}\| - \|\mathbf{b}'\|| \leq C'|\sigma'^2 - \sigma_N'^2| \leq \sigma^2 CC'K^2 \left(\sqrt{\frac{n+u}{N}} + \frac{n+u}{N} \right)$. So far, we prove that $\|\mathbf{e}\| \leq C_e \left(\sigma^2 + \frac{\sigma^2}{\sigma^2 - \sigma'^2} \cdot \|\mathbf{b}\| \right) \left(\sqrt{\frac{n+u}{N}} + \frac{n+u}{N} \right)$ with probability at least $1 - 4e^{-u}$ where $C_e = \max\{CC'K^2, 2^{\frac{3}{2}}CK^2\}$. □

B   Attacks on Other Falcon Parameters

Our attacks easily apply to other Falcon parameter sets. The base sampler and the integer Gaussian sampler are exactly the same for different n, thus both leakages can be measured in the same way. Table 1 shows the experimental data for $n = 256, 512, 1024$, where $N_1(x)$ is the number of required traces to get an approximate error of hamming weight $\leq x$ with probability $\approx \frac{1}{4}$.

Table 1. Experimental data of $N_1(x)$ measured over 40 Falcon instances for each n. The item "A/B/C" represents the values for $n = 256/512/1024$.

	Half Gaussian leakage	Sign leakage	Two leakages
$N_1(0) \times 10^{-3}$	270 / 360 / 400	210 / 230 / 280	60 / 70 / 75
$N_1(5) \times 10^{-3}$	200 / 230 / 270	142.5 / 175 / 203	39 / 47 / 56
$N_1(7) \times 10^{-3}$	182.5 / 217 / 255	132.5 /164 / 188	37 / 45 / 54
$N_1(9) \times 10^{-3}$	175 / 201 / 240	127 / 155 / 184	35 / 43 / 50

References

1. Barthe, G., Belaïd, S., Espitau, T., Fouque, P.A., Rossi, M., Tibouchi, M.: Galactics: Gaussian sampling for lattice-based constant-time implementation of cryptographic signatures, revisited. In: ACM CCS 2019, pp. 2147–2164 (2019). https://doi.org/10.1145/3319535.3363223

2. Bootle, J., Delaplace, C., Espitau, T., Fouque, P.-A., Tibouchi, M.: LWE without modular reduction and improved side-channel attacks against BLISS. In: Peyrin, T., Galbraith, S. (eds.) ASIACRYPT 2018. LNCS, vol. 11272, pp. 494–524. Springer, Cham (2018). https://doi.org/10.1007/978-3-030-03326-2_17

3. Chari, S., Rao, J.R., Rohatgi, P.: Template attacks. In: Kaliski, B.S., Koç, K., Paar, C. (eds.) CHES 2002. LNCS, vol. 2523, pp. 13–28. Springer, Heidelberg (2003). https://doi.org/10.1007/3-540-36400-5_3

4. Dachman-Soled, D., Ducas, L., Gong, H., Rossi, M.: LWE with side information: attacks and concrete security estimation. In: Micciancio, D., Ristenpart, T. (eds.) CRYPTO 2020. LNCS, vol. 12171, pp. 329–358. Springer, Cham (2020). https://doi.org/10.1007/978-3-030-56880-1_12

5. Ducas, L., Galbraith, S., Prest, T., Yu, Y.: Integral matrix gram root and lattice gaussian sampling without floats. In: Canteaut, A., Ishai, Y. (eds.) EUROCRYPT 2020. LNCS, vol. 12106, pp. 608–637. Springer, Cham (2020). https://doi.org/10.1007/978-3-030-45724-2_21

6. Ducas, L., Lyubashevsky, V., Prest, T.: Efficient identity-based encryption over NTRU lattices. In: Sarkar, P., Iwata, T. (eds.) ASIACRYPT 2014. LNCS, vol. 8874, pp. 22–41. Springer, Heidelberg (2014). https://doi.org/10.1007/978-3-662-45608-8_2

7. Ducas, L., Nguyen, P.Q.: Learning a Zonotope and more: cryptanalysis of ntrusign countermeasures. In: Wang, X., Sako, K. (eds.) ASIACRYPT 2012. LNCS, vol. 7658, pp. 433–450. Springer, Heidelberg (2012). https://doi.org/10.1007/978-3-642-34961-4_27

8. Ducas, L., Prest, T.: Fast Fourier Orthogonalization. In: ISSAC 2016, pp. 191–198 (2016). https://doi.org/10.1145/2930889.2930923

9. Ducas, L., Yu, Y.: Learning strikes again: the case of the DRS signature scheme. J. Cryptol. **34**(1), 1–24 (2020). https://doi.org/10.1007/s00145-020-09366-9

10. Espitau, T., Fouque, P.A., Gérard, B., Tibouchi, M.: Side-channel attacks on BLISS lattice-based signatures: Exploiting branch tracing against strongswan and electromagnetic emanations in microcontrollers. In: ACM CCS 2017, pp. 1857–1874 (2017). https://doi.org/10.1145/3133956.3134028

11. Espitau, T., et al.: MITAKA: a simpler, parallelizable, maskable variant of FALCON. In: Eurocrypt 2022 (2022). https://doi.org/10.1007/978-3-031-07082-2_9

12. Fouque, P.A., Gérard, F., Rossi, M., Yu, Y.: Zalcon: an alternative FPA-free NTRU sampler for Falcon. In: Proceedings of 3rd NIST PQC Workshop, pp. 1–23 (2021)

13. Fouque, P.-A., Kirchner, P., Tibouchi, M., Wallet, A., Yu, Y.: Key recovery from gram–schmidt norm leakage in hash-and-sign signatures over NTRU lattices. In: Canteaut, A., Ishai, Y. (eds.) EUROCRYPT 2020. LNCS, vol. 12107, pp. 34–63. Springer, Cham (2020). https://doi.org/10.1007/978-3-030-45727-3_2

14. Gentry, C., Peikert, C., Vaikuntanathan, V.: Trapdoors for hard lattices and new cryptographic constructions. In: STOC 2008, pp. 197–206 (2008). https://doi.org/10.1145/1374376.1374407

15. Gérard, F., Rossi, M.: An efficient and provable masked implementation of qtesla. In: CARDIS 2019, pp. 74–91 (2019). https://doi.org/10.1007/978-3-030-42068-0_5

16. Groot Bruinderink, L., Hülsing, A., Lange, T., Yarom, Y.: Flush, gauss, and reload-a cache attack on the BLISS lattice-based signature scheme. In: CHES 2016, pp. 323–345 (2016). https://doi.org/10.1007/978-3-662-53140-2_16

17. Guerreau, M., Martinelli, A., Ricosset, T., Rossi, M.: The hidden parallelepiped is back again: power analysis attacks on falcon. IACR Trans. Cryptograp. Hardware Embedded Syst. (2022). https://doi.org/10.46586/tches.v2022.i3.141-164

18. Howe, J., Prest, T., Ricosset, T., Rossi, M.: Isochronous Gaussian Sampling: From Inception to Implementation. In: PQCrypto 2020, pp. 53–71 (2020). https://doi.org/10.1007/978-3-030-44223-1_4
19. Hulsing, A., et al.: SPHINCS+: Submission to the NIST's post-quantum cryptography standardization process (2020). https://csrc.nist.gov/Projects/post-quantum-cryptography/post-quantum-cryptography-standardization/roun.-3-submissions
20. Karabulut, E., Aysu, A.: Falcon down: breaking falcon post-quantum signature scheme through side-channel attacks. In: DAC 2021, pp. 691–696 (2021). https://doi.org/10.1109/DAC18074.2021.9586131
21. Kim, S., Hong, S.: Single trace analysis on constant time CDT sampler and its countermeasure. Appl. Sci. 8(10), 1809 (2018). https://doi.org/10.3390/app8101809
22. Klein, P.N.: Finding the closest lattice vector when it's unusually close. In: SODA 2000, pp. 937–941 (2000)
23. Lyubashevsky, V.: Fiat-shamir with aborts: applications to lattice and factoring-based signatures. In: Matsui, M. (ed.) ASIACRYPT 2009. LNCS, vol. 5912, pp. 598–616. Springer, Heidelberg (2009). https://doi.org/10.1007/978-3-642-10366-7_35
24. Lyubashevsky, V.: Lattice signatures without trapdoors. In: Pointcheval, D., Johansson, T. (eds.) EUROCRYPT 2012. LNCS, vol. 7237, pp. 738–755. Springer, Heidelberg (2012). https://doi.org/10.1007/978-3-642-29011-4_43
25. Lyubashevsky, V., et al.: Dilithium: Submission to the NIST's post-quantum cryptography standardization process (2020). https://csrc.nist.gov/Projects/post-quantum-cryptography/post-quantum-cryptography-standardization/round-3-submissions
26. Mangard, S., Oswald, E., Popp, T.: Power Analysis Attacks. Springer, Boston, MA (2007). https://doi.org/10.1007/978-0-387-38162-6
27. Migliore, V., Gérard, B., Tibouchi, M., Fouque, P.A.: Masking Dilithium. In: ACNS 2019, pp. 344–362 (2019). https://doi.org/10.1007/978-3-030-21568-2_17
28. Nguyen, P.Q., Regev, O.: Learning a parallelepiped: cryptanalysis of GGH and NTRU signatures. In: Vaudenay, S. (ed.) EUROCRYPT 2006. LNCS, vol. 4004, pp. 271–288. Springer, Heidelberg (2006). https://doi.org/10.1007/11761679_17
29. Peikert, C.: An efficient and parallel gaussian sampler for lattices. In: Rabin, T. (ed.) CRYPTO 2010. LNCS, vol. 6223, pp. 80–97. Springer, Heidelberg (2010). https://doi.org/10.1007/978-3-642-14623-7_5
30. Pessl, P., Bruinderink, L.G., Yarom, Y.: To BLISS-B or not to be: attacking strongswan's implementation of post-quantum signatures. In: ACM CCS 2017, pp. 1843–1855 (2017). https://doi.org/10.1145/3133956.3134023
31. Pornin, T.: New efficient, constant-time implementations of falcon. Cryptology ePrint Archive, Report 2019/893 (2019). https://ia.cr/2019/893
32. Prest, T.: Gaussian Sampling in Lattice-Based Cryptography. Ph.D. thesis, École Normale Supérieure, Paris, France (2015)
33. Prest, T., et al.: Falcon: Submission to the NIST's post-quantum cryptography standardization process (2020). https://csrc.nist.gov/Projects/post-quantum-cryptography/post-quantum-cryptography-standardization/round-3-submissions
34. Tibouchi, M., Wallet, A.: One bit is all it takes: a devastating timing attack on BLISS's non-constant time sign flips. J. Math. Cryptol. 15(1), 131–142 (2021). https://doi.org/10.1515/jmc-2020-0079
35. Vershynin, R.: High-dimensional probability: An introduction with applications in data science, vol. 47. Cambridge University Press (2018). https://doi.org/10.1080/14697688.2020.1813475

36. Wisiol, N., Gersch, P., Seifert, J.: Cycle-accurate power side-channel analysis using the chipwhisperer: a case study on gaussian sampling. IACR Cryptol. ePrint Arch, p. 903 (2022). https://eprint.iacr.org/2022/903
37. Yu, Y., Ducas, L.: Learning strikes again: the case of the DRS signature scheme. In: Peyrin, T., Galbraith, S. (eds.) ASIACRYPT 2018. LNCS, vol. 11273, pp. 525–543. Springer, Cham (2018). https://doi.org/10.1007/978-3-030-03329-3_18

Effective and Efficient Masking with Low Noise Using Small-Mersenne-Prime Ciphers

Loïc Masure[1], Pierrick Méaux[2], Thorben Moos[1(✉)],
and François-Xavier Standaert[1]

[1] Crypto Group, ICTEAM Institute, UCLouvain, Louvain-la-Neuve, Belgium
thorben.moos@uclouvain.be
[2] Luxembourg University, SnT, Luxembourg City, Luxembourg

Abstract. Embedded devices used in security applications are natural targets for physical attacks. Thus, enhancing their side-channel resistance is an important research challenge. A standard solution for this purpose is the use of Boolean masking schemes, as they are well adapted to current block ciphers with efficient bitslice representations. Boolean masking guarantees that the security of an implementation grows exponentially in the number of shares under the assumption that leakages are sufficiently noisy (and independent). Unfortunately, it has been shown that this noise assumption is hardly met on low-end devices. In this paper, we therefore investigate techniques to mask cryptographic algorithms in such a way that their resistance can survive an almost complete lack of noise. Building on seed theoretical results of Dziembowski et al., we put forward that arithmetic encodings in prime fields can reach this goal. We first exhibit the gains that such encodings lead to thanks to a simulated information theoretic analysis of their leakage (with up to six shares). We then provide figures showing that on platforms where optimized arithmetic adders and multipliers are readily available (i.e., most MCUs and FPGAs), performing masked operations in small to medium Mersenne-prime fields as opposed to binary extension fields will not lead to notable implementation overheads. We compile these observations into a new AES-like block cipher, called AES-prime, which is well-suited to illustrate the remarkable advantages of masking in prime fields. We also confirm the practical relevance of our findings by evaluating concrete software (ARM Cortex-M3) and hardware (Xilinx Spartan-6) implementations. Our experimental results show that security gains over Boolean masking (and, more generally, binary encodings) can reach orders of magnitude despite the same amount of information being leaked per share.

1 Introduction

Research Question. Masking is an important countermeasure against side-channel attacks. Introduced in [27,46], it has attracted significant attention thanks to the strong security guarantees it can provide [36,37,53,76]. Since leading to efficient implementations in software [13,79], bitslice software [47,49] and hardware [23,50], additive (Boolean) masking is for now the most investigated

© International Association for Cryptologic Research 2023
C. Hazay and M. Stam (Eds.): EUROCRYPT 2023, LNCS 14007, pp. 596–627, 2023.
https://doi.org/10.1007/978-3-031-30634-1_20

type of encoding. Concretely, assuming that the shares' leakage is sufficiently noisy and independent, Boolean masking can amplify the noise of an implementation (and therefore its security) exponentially in the number of shares.

Yet, and despite these strong theoretical guarantees, ensuring the noise and independence conditions may not be easy in practice. The independence issue is a well investigated one. Physical defaults such as glitches [61, 62] or transitions [8, 30] can cause leakage about re-combined shares. Fortunately, these defaults can be circumvented (at some cost) thanks to well understood design techniques [24, 44, 72]. To the best of our knowledge, the noise issue is for now a less investigated one. Concrete results of so-called horizontal attacks such as [12, 20] showed that a lack of noise can lead to devastating attacks against Boolean masking. Improved security against horizontal attacks has been captured with the notion of noise rate [5, 25]. But gadgets with limited noise rate only reduce the number of manipulations of the shares (in order to prevent reducing the noise by averaging). Therefore, they have limited impact when the noise level of an implementation is already small without averaging, as it is for example the case for small embedded devices (e.g., 32-bit ARM Cortex or similar cores). Another class of attacks which has been shown to threaten the security of Boolean masking by exploiting an insufficient noise level is based on leveraging the static power consumption of devices as a side-channel. In such attacks which, unlike horizontal attacks, are mostly a concern for hardware implementations, the adversary obtains the leakage of a halted computation state with almost arbitrarily low noise, which limits the effectiveness of Boolean encodings [66–68, 70, 75].

As a result, the main objective of this paper is to initiate a study of encodings and ciphers that can lead to secure and efficient low-noise implementations. Precisely, we question the possibility that increasing the number of shares in a masking scheme leads to security amplification without any noise.

Seed Results. Interestingly, the literature contains several hints that the answer to this question might be positive if changing the Boolean encoding into a more "complex" one. On the one hand, it has been observed that the Inner Product (IP) masking introduced in [40] can lead to significantly better security in low-noise settings than Boolean masking, for example in case of leakage functions that are close to the Hamming weight one (see for example [7], Figure 3 for an illustration with two shares). Unfortunately, computing on IP encodings generally leads to significant implementation overheads, and it remains an open question whether its security vs. efficiency trade-off can compare positively with the (simpler) multiplication algorithms of additive masking schemes.

On the other hand, Dziembowski et al. showed that the level of noise required for masking to amplify security can be significantly reduced if the encodings are defined in groups of prime orders [41]. Such an observation has the significant advantage of being valid for simple (additive) masking schemes that have been intensively studied in recent years and can benefit from increasingly efficient automated verification tools [9, 10, 17, 57]. However, the practical impact of these seed investigations has not been studied yet, leaving open questions like:

– How do these theoretical guarantees translate into concrete security guarantees for practically-relevant leakage functions and noise levels?

- What is the impact of increasing the prime size in these practical cases?
- Can masking with prime encodings be used to improve the side-channel security of block cipher implementations in software and hardware?
- What is the (software and hardware) cost of implementing masked block cipher operations in prime fields instead of binary extension fields?

Contributions. Based on this state of the art, we pick up on the challenge of better understanding masking in low-noise settings and propose encodings and ciphers that allow secure and efficient implementations in this context. More precisely, our contributions in this respect are in three parts:

First, we show in Sect. 2 that moving from Boolean encodings to arithmetic encodings, first in binary fields, then in prime fields, leads to gradual side-channel security improvements. We use the information theoretic framework put forward in [84] for this purpose, and consider both the standard Hamming weight leakage model and a (localized) model leaking the Least Significant Bit (LSB) of the target intermediate computations in our evaluations. It allows us to confirm Dziembowski et al.'s claimed gains in low-noise environments, but also to observe that these gains can be maintained without any noise (for these non-injective leakage functions) and are preserved as the noise increases. We additionally explain the low-noise weakness of Boolean encodings formally and show that for the practically-relevant Hamming weight leakage function, increasing the size of the prime moduli improves the side-channel security of masked encodings.

Next, we consider the question of efficiency. In Sect. 3, we show that by selecting small Mersenne primes to operate our masked computations, it is possible to implement them with performances that compare with binary fields, especially in case optimized arithmetic adders and multipliers are available (e.g., on most recent MCUs and FPGAs). Since standard symmetric designs are not directly suitable for efficient masked implementations with non-binary encodings, we then consider so-called **prime** ciphers in Sect. 4. A **prime** cipher is a cipher which performs all operations in $\mathbb{F}_p$ with p a prime modulus. In order to illustrate our results, we then consider **AES-prime** as a first example of such a **prime** cipher, where the S-box is based on a small power in $\mathbb{F}_p$ and the MixColumns operation is based on an MDS matrix in the same field.

Eventually, we move to the concrete evaluation of our designs in Sect. 5. Since our simulated evaluations in Sect. 2 are based on the Hamming weight and LSB leakage functions, and are limited to encodings, an important question is whether the security guarantees of these examples are observed when measuring concretely-relevant implementations with several exploitable target sensitive operations that may not exactly leak as assumed in our simulations. We answer this question positively by experimentally analyzing software (ARM Cortex-M3) implementations, where the (worst-case) adversary is first given full profiling access to the device to characterize its leakage behavior before performing the actual attack. Our results confirm that masking **prime** ciphers with prime encodings can significantly improve the security compared to Boolean masked designs in a low-noise setting. We also conduct a hardware (FPGA) case study, confirming the improved security provided for a naturally noisier target.

Cautionary Note: Why the `AES-Prime`? Initiating the investigation of new encodings naturally raises the question of what is the best cipher for evaluating them. As for example witnessed by the NIST Lightweight cryptography competition, the vast majority of the state-of-the-art ciphers designed for masking are bitslice ones.[1] Unfortunately, such ciphers cannot be easily turned into "prime equivalents". At the opposite side of the spectrum, the use of large prime moduli has recently attracted a lot of attention for the design of ciphers tailored for advanced cryptographic applications (e.g., multiparty computation, hybrid fully homomorphic encryption or zero knowledge proofs). Examples include MiMC [2] and its Feistel variant GMiMC [1], Rescue [4], HADESMiMC [48], CIMINION [34], HERA [28] or PASTA [35]. In general, these ciphers are not directly adapted to our goals either, since their proposed instances usually favor multiplications in large fields (in order to reduce their overall number) while embedded implementations crucially require small and well-chosen primes for efficiency. As a result, there is also little work on the secure implementation of such new ciphers. Given this state of the art, we turn back to AES-like ciphers for which it is easy to specify binary and prime versions. This allows us to leverage the wide body of research on countermeasures and evaluation tools tailored for the AES (which, we hope, can further stimulate external analyzes and follow up studies). It also allows us to work with primes that are well suited to the software and hardware implementations we target. We insist that the goal of the `AES-prime` cipher is only to illustrate the potential of prime masking. Since illustrating this potential requires mixing abstractions from different research fields, we admittedly do not claim that its security analysis is as comprehensive as if the very design of the `AES-prime` was our main contribution. So the security analysis we provide is only aimed to show that a prime cipher with an AES-like structure can be secure with a similar number of rounds as a binary cipher with an AES-like structure, based on the (standard) cryptographic properties of its components. Overall, the `AES-prime` may not be the best cipher for prime masking in the long run, but it is a suitable starting point for a comparison, since AES and `AES-prime` are the closest match between binary and **prime** cipher that we have at the moment. We hope that the promising results it leads to can motivate the design of new ciphers that are tailored for this specific application of prime-field masking and can compete with bitslice ciphers from an efficiency point of view.

2 From Boolean to Prime Field Arithmetic Masking

In this first section, we revisit the theoretical investigations of Dziembowsi et al. from a more practical viewpoint. Precisely, it is shown in [41] that masking with encodings in prime fields can lead to effective noise amplification. We next question the concrete security that can be observed for practically-relevant leakage

[1] https://csrc.nist.gov/Projects/lightweight-cryptography.

functions without any noise, and whether the gains of these prime encodings are maintained in high noise regimes. We additionally show the positive impact of increasing the size of the prime moduli and provide theoretical insights on our results and their generalization to parallel implementations.

2.1 Methodology

As a usual starting point to analyze the worst-case security provided by a countermeasure quantitatively, we use the information theoretic framework put forward in [84]. Namely, we will compute the mutual information between a target sensitive value $X \in \mathcal{X}$ and the leakage of its shares L, that is:

$$\mathrm{MI}(X; L) = \mathrm{H}(X) + \sum_{x \in \mathcal{X}} \mathsf{p}(x) \cdot \int_{l \in \mathcal{L}^d} \mathsf{f}(l|x) \cdot \log_2 \mathsf{p}(x|l), \qquad (1)$$

with $\mathsf{p}(x)$ the shortcut notation for $\Pr(X = x)$. Assuming uniformly distributed sensitive values, $\mathrm{H}(X) = \log_2(|\mathcal{X}|)$ and $\mathsf{p}(x|l)$ is computed as $\frac{\mathsf{f}(l|x)}{\sum_{x^* \in \mathcal{X}} \mathsf{f}(l|x^*)}$ where $\mathsf{f}(l|x)$ is the Probability Density Function (PDF) of the leakage samples. In the case of a masked implementation with d shares, this PDF then takes the shape of a mixture distribution defined as $\mathsf{f}(l|x) = \sum_{r \in \mathcal{X}^{d-1}} \mathsf{f}(l|x, r) \cdot \mathsf{p}(r)$.

In the following, we will make the standard assumption that the leakage of each component $\mathsf{p}(l|x, r)$ in the mixtures is a Gaussian distribution, so that the leakage of each share can be written as $\mathsf{L}(X_i) = \delta(X_i) + N_i$, the full leakage vector can be written as $L = (\mathsf{L}(X_1), \mathsf{L}(X_2), \ldots, \mathsf{L}(X_d))$ and the variance of the noise σ^2 is a security parameter. As for the deterministic part of the leakage function δ, we will consider both the standard Hamming weight function and a (more localized) bit leakage function leaking the LSB of X_i.

Note that directly computing the mutual information rapidly turns out to be computationally intensive as the number of shares increases. This is for example witnessed by the results of Fumaroli et al. [45, Fig. 2] and Standaert et al. [85, Fig. 7] which were limited to $d \leq 3$. We improve over these previous works by leveraging the fact that computing the mixture PDF of a masked encoding can be done without summing over all the terms of the mixture explicitly, because the leakage of such masked encodings can be written as a convolution product [63, Prop. 1]. Moreover, if several encodings of sensitive intermediate computations leak, the latter observation can be generalized as a Soft Analytical Side-Channel Attack (SASCA) without cycles [20,51], where the Belief Propagation (BP) algorithm efficiently provides an exact solution [86]. Therefore, the complexity of evaluating Eq. 1 actually scales in $\mathcal{O}(d \cdot n \cdot 2^n)$, instead of $\mathcal{O}(2^{2n \cdot d})$ for a naive approach. Concretely, we use the SCALib library for this purpose.[2] It allows us to analyze the leakage of up to 13-bit targets with up to 6 shares.

2.2 Information Theoretic Evaluation Results

The results of our information theoretic investigations are depicted in Fig. 1. Recall that the number of traces to perform a key recovery attack is inversely

---

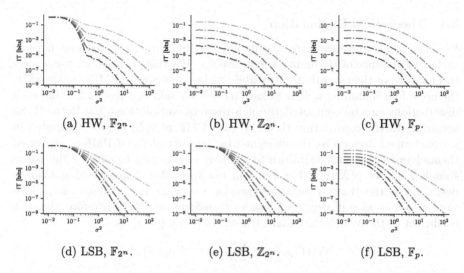

(a) HW, $\mathbb{F}_{2^n}$.   (b) HW, $\mathbb{Z}_{2^n}$.   (c) HW, $\mathbb{F}_p$.

(d) LSB, $\mathbb{F}_{2^n}$.   (e) LSB, $\mathbb{Z}_{2^n}$.   (f) LSB, $\mathbb{F}_p$.

Fig. 1. Information theoretic evaluation of different masked encodings for different numbers of shares. Top: Hamming weight leakage function, bottom: LSB leakage function. Left: Boolean encoding, middle: arithmetic encoding in $\mathbb{Z}_{2^n}$, right: arithmetic masking in $\mathbb{F}_p$. The X axis is the noise variance in log scale. The Y axis is the MI in log scale. The different curves are for increasing numbers of shares (from 2 to 6). The target sensitive variable is on 8 bits.

proportional to the MI [33]. So as expected in theory, all these curves have a slope $-d$ in the high noise regime [64]. The relevant observations for our investigations are twofold. First, arithmetic masking significantly improves the situation in low-noise regimes. This is reflected by the "stepped" regions of the curves. For Boolean masking, the left (low noise) parts of the figure show no reduction of the MI when increasing the number of shares. By contrast, arithmetic masking can lead to (exponential) security improvements (i.e., equidistant steps) in the same region. This only holds for the Hamming weight leakage function (on the top of the figure) when considering arithmetic masking in $\mathbb{Z}_{2^n}$ (in the middle plots) and it even holds for the LSB leakage function (on the bottom of the figure) when considering arithmetic masking in $\mathbb{F}_p$ (in the right plots). We insist that this exponential security amplification without noise of prime masking theoretically holds for any non-injective leakage function [41]. Our evaluations amplify this fact with the reassuring observation that its concrete impact is especially strong with leakage functions that are commonly considered to be suitable abstractions of real device behavior. Second, the gains that are obtained with low noise are maintained when increasing the noise, which was not studied by Dziembowski et al. So these results confirm that there is an interest to use prime encodings for better dealing with noise-free leakages, and put forward that such encodings can also lead to significant security improvements when leakages become noisy.

2.3   Theoretical Explanation

We now argue why increasing the number of Boolean shares without noise is useless in presence of Hamming weight leakage. For this purpose, we use a spectral analysis of the conditional Probability Mass Functions (PMFs) spanned by the noise-free Hamming weight leakage model. We said in Subsect. 2.2 that such distributions can be computed through discrete convolutions [63, Prop. 1]. So according to the convolution theorem, each PMF $\mathsf{p}(X|L)$ can be computed in a transformed domain as the element-wise product of the d PMFs—expressed themselves in the same transformed domain—associated to each of the corresponding shares $\mathsf{p}(X_i|L_i)$. For Boolean masking, this transformed domain is described by the *Walsh-Hadamard* transform over the input domain $\mathbb{F}_2^n$, which can be seen as an n-dimensional Fourier transform over $\mathbb{F}_2$. Therefore, the ω-th coefficient of the Walsh-Hadamard transform is computed as:

$$\mathsf{WHT}(\mathsf{p}, \omega) = \sum_{x \in \mathbb{F}_2^n} (-1)^{\langle \omega, x \rangle} \mathsf{p}(x|l), \tag{2}$$

where $\langle \omega, x \rangle$ is the inner product between ω and x. Figure 2 below depicts it when computed for Hamming weight leakages corresponding to a 4-bit target variable. It can be observed that for $l = 0$ or $l = n$ (i.e., the dotted gray curves in Fig. 2), the absolute value of the Walsh-Hadamard coefficients is a constant 1. This corresponds to values for which the leakage model is injective (i.e., the conditional probability distribution of the sensitive variable collapses to a single Dirac). Let us first consider the unrealistic assumption that these leakages are never observed – we will discuss the general case afterwards. For the remaining leakages that an adversary may observe, only the first and last coefficient of the Walsh-Hadamard transform are equal to 1 in absolute value. The first coefficient being equal to 1 is due to p being a probability distribution (i.e., all probabilities are summing to 1). For the last coefficient (i.e., for $\omega = 1^n$), the inner product $\langle 1^n, x \rangle$ coincides with the Hamming weight of x, *i.e.* $\mathrm{HW}(x) = \langle 1^n, x \rangle$. Hence:

$$\mathsf{WHT}(\mathsf{p}, 1^n) = \sum_{x \in \mathbb{F}_2^n} (-1)^{\langle 1^n, x \rangle} \mathsf{p}(x|l) = \sum_{x \in \mathbb{F}_2^n} (-1)^{\mathrm{HW}(x)} \frac{\mathbf{1}_{\mathrm{HW}(x)=l}}{\binom{n}{l}} = (-1)^l. \tag{3}$$

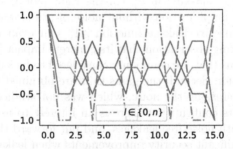

Fig. 2. Walsh-Hadamard transform of the conditional distribution $\mathsf{p}(X|L)$ for each hypothetical value of the Hamming weight leakage function.

As a consequence, any element-wise product between d Walsh-Hadamard transforms among the ones observable in a Hamming weight leakage model can only decrease all coefficients at an exponential rate, except the first and last ones. It results that when $d \to \infty$, the Walsh-Hadamard transform of the masked leakage distribution tends towards $(1, 0, \ldots, 0, \pm 1)$. Such asymptotic Walsh-Hadamard transforms correspond to uniform distributions over two non-overlapping supports of equal size 2^{n-1}, both leading to a conditional entropy of $n - 1$ bits.

Finally, we discuss our assumption that the adversary did not observe any sample such that $l = 0$ or $l = n$. As a consequence, d in our previous reasoning is replaced by the number of samples in the leakage that are neither null nor equal to n. Let us denote this number by the random variable T. Hereupon, we may notice that the marginal distribution of the leakage is such that T follows a binomial law of parameter $\mathcal{B}(d, \frac{1}{2^{n-1}})$. Such a law is known to concentrate exponentially fast towards its mean $\frac{d}{2^{n-1}}$. As a result, the probability to observe a number of null or full (equal to n) leakages becomes negligible when $d \to \infty$.

2.4   Intuitive Explanation

The theoretical explanation confirms our observations from the information theoretic analysis formally. To gain a more intuitive understanding of why the security level stagnates for binary masking (Boolean and arithmetic) when increasing the number of shares without noise we can also point to concrete properties of the considered leakage functions. If an adversary receives noise-free Hamming weight observations $\mathrm{HW}(x_1)$, ..., $\mathrm{HW}(x_n)$ of the Boolean shares x_1, ..., x_n of a secret variable x with $x_1 \oplus \ldots \oplus x_n = x$, then the parity-bit $b \equiv \mathrm{HW}(x_1) + \ldots + \mathrm{HW}(x_n) \bmod 2$ is also the parity of the Hamming weight of x. Likewise, the parity of noise-free LSB observations of all shares is also the LSB of the secret, since $\mathrm{LSB}(x) \equiv \mathrm{LSB}(x_1) + \ldots + \mathrm{LSB}(x_n) \bmod 2$. The latter equation holds for both Boolean masking and arithmetic encodings in binary fields. In all described cases the information learned about the secret variable is independent of the number of shares and the statistical security order. The order of the masking only becomes relevant when increasing the noise level. By contrast, for arithmetic encodings in prime fields no such relationships exist and an exponential decrease of the MI can be observed even in the no-noise scenario. This is true for any non-injective leakage model (i.e., in any case where not all shares and intermediates are already known to the adversary with probability 1).

2.5   Impact of the Prime Size

The results in Sect. 2.2 are for 8-bit targets. A natural further question is whether increasing the size of the prime modulus has any (positive or detrimental) effect on security. This investigation is especially interesting since the field size is a source of potential non-tightness in masking security proofs [54,64].

Using the same information theoretic approach as in Sect. 2.2, we can observe in Fig. 3 (especially in the bottom parts of the figure) that increasing the prime size significantly improves the security of the masked encodings for the Hamming weight leakage function, while it has no impact for the LSB leakage function.[3] Again, this is a quite positive outcome since the Hamming weight leakage function is commonly considered as a reasonable simplification of many leakage functions observed in practice. It also recalls that side-channel security against very localized leakage functions (e.g., the LSB one that corresponds to a probing attack) is very challenging to obtain. But as observed in [58], such models generally exploit significantly more powerful (and expensive) sources of leakage than the power consumption or electromagnetic radiation.

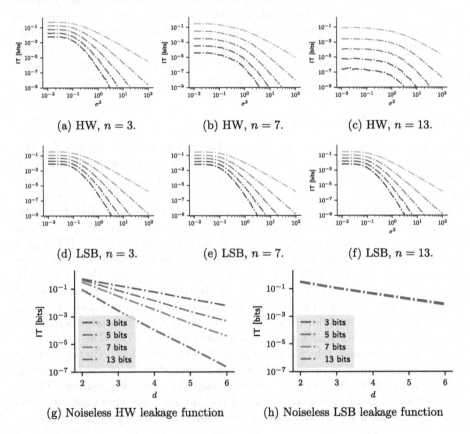

(a) HW, $n = 3$.   (b) HW, $n = 7$.   (c) HW, $n = 13$.

(d) LSB, $n = 3$.   (e) LSB, $n = 7$.   (f) LSB, $n = 13$.

(g) Noiseless HW leakage function   (h) Noiseless LSB leakage function

Fig. 3. Information theoretic evaluation of masked encodings with prime moduli $p = 2^n - 1$ of increasing sizes. Top: Hamming weight leakage function. Middle: LSB leakage function. The bottom figures are for the no-noise regime only.

---

[3] In fact, for the LSB leakage function and a fixed number of shares, it can even be shown that the $\mathrm{MI}(X; L)$ is lower bounded when increasing the size of p. For 2 shares the concrete lower bound is given by $\lim_{p \to \infty} \mathrm{MI}(X; L) = 0.2787$.

2.6 Parallel Leakage

By assuming that the adversary can observe the leakage of each share separately, our previous evaluations naturally correspond to a serial (e.g., software) implementation. Yet, the problem that we observe with low physical noise leakages actually holds even in the case of a parallel manipulation of the shares (more reflective of a hardware implementation). We analyzed this scenario by simply replacing the leakage vector L by the sum of its d elements. The resulting evaluation is depicted in Fig. 4 (for 8-bit targets). As expected, we see that the curves of the parallel implementation are always below (i.e., less informative) than the ones of the serial implementation, which is explained by the accumulation of the leakage of the shares processed in parallel, which leads to a loss of information available to the observer. More interestingly for our following investigations, we also see that the curves in Fig. 4b and Fig. 4d are stuck to the 1 bit threshold in the low-noise regime, matching the observations in [82].

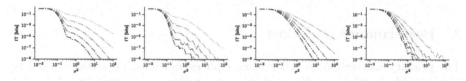

(a) HW, serial, $\mathbb{F}_{2^n}$.   (b) HW, par., $\mathbb{F}_{2^n}$.   (c) LSB, serial, $\mathbb{Z}_{2^n}$.   (d) LSB, par., $\mathbb{Z}_{2^n}$.

Fig. 4. Information theoretic evaluation of serial and parallel binary masking.

Here as well, our previous spectral analysis provides an explanation of our observations. In the serial case, the adversary is given a leakage tuple $l = (l_1, \ldots, l_d)$, so the PMF $x \mapsto \mathsf{p}(X = x|l)$ is the convolution product $x \mapsto (\mathsf{p}(X_1|l_1) * \ldots * \mathsf{p}(X_d|l_d))(x)$, as previously discussed [63, Prop.1]. In the parallel case, the adversary is only given the sum $\ell = \sum_i l_i$ of the tuple l, also denoted by $\mathcal{S}(l)$ hereafter. By applying the total probability formula over all the tuples l verifying $\mathcal{S}(l) = \ell$, and leveraging the mutual independence of the variables $L_1, \ldots, L_d$, the conditional PMF $\Pr(X|\mathcal{S}(L))$ verifies:

$$\Pr(X|\mathcal{S}(L) = \ell) = \sum_{l:\mathcal{S}(l)=\ell} (\mathsf{p}(X_1|l_1) * \ldots * \mathsf{p}(X_d|l_d)) \cdot \Pr(L = l|\mathcal{S}(l) = \ell) \ . \ (4)$$

In other words, the PMF becomes the averaged convolution product over all possible tuples verifying the constraint. Nevertheless, we argue that when $d \to \infty$, averaging does not affect the resulting PMF much. Indeed, for each tuple verifying the constraint, the parity of the number of odd values remains constant: if ℓ is even, there is always an even number of odd values in the tuple l. Likewise, if ℓ is odd, there is always an odd number of odd values in the tuple l. This ensures that all the convolution products that are averaged converge towards the same uniform distribution over a subset of size 2^{n-1}, as argued in Subsect. 2.3. Hence, the resulting conditional entropy (of $n - 1$ bits) remains unaffected.

2.7   Final Remark

While arithmetic masking in prime fields can be *sufficient* to deal with low-noise leakages, we may wonder whether it is *necessary* to consider groups of prime size, or if an odd modulus would suffice. This case has been discussed by Dziembowski et al. who showed that for groups of composite order, there exists some leakage models for which masking is ineffective [41, Prop. 1]. This result is actually closely linked to a wide literature studying the convergence of probability distributions through the iterative application of a self-convolution product [3,56]. For example, consider the group $\mathbb{Z}_{15}$, where the inner law is the addition modulo 15. Assuming that the target variable leaks such that $L(x) = x$ mod 3, the adversary will obtain $\log_2(3)$ bits. It can be verified that masking at any order keeps the conditional probability distribution of the target variable unchanged, up to a permutation, which in turn keeps the mutual information constant. Using prime orders avoids this theoretical possibility. As will be clear in Sect. 4, it also makes the cryptanalytic treatment of prime ciphers easier.

3   Performance and Cost

The primary motivation to tailor block ciphers and masking schemes towards binary fields is efficiency. From an implementation perspective the ability to perform field addition/subtraction using a simple bit-wise Exclusive-OR (XOR) operation is one of the core advantages of working in $\mathbb{F}_{2^n}$ compared to performing the equivalent tasks in $\mathbb{F}_p$. Field multiplication including the reduction using an irreducible polynomial can be implemented quite efficiently for small n as well. In hardware, XOR/AND sequences are used for this purpose, in software *log/alog* tables are one of the most efficient options [32]. In this section we argue that prime field arithmetic can be executed with similar (and sometimes even better) efficiency as (than) binary arithmetic on many platforms, due to a direct utilization of existing computation structures. In fact, devices like Micro-Controller Units (MCUs) and Field-Programmable Gate Arrays (FPGAs) are mostly developed with general purpose computing in mind. Hence, they often provide regular arithmetic operations like addition, subtraction and multiplication as dedicated and heavily-optimized hardware circuitry (for one specific size of operands). Many 32-bit micro-controllers for example include single-cycle arithmetic instructions for 32-bit operands. Yet, single-cycle multiplications sometimes produce only a 32-bit result, instead of a full 64-bit product (e.g., ARM Cortex-M0/M3). FPGAs on the other hand offer DSP slices which commonly include full 18×18-bit or 27×18-bit multipliers. Whenever such a hardware support is available, the heavy lifting for implementing prime field arithmetic is (at least for small primes) taken care of at the expense of occupying the integrated arithmetic accelerators (temporarily). The remaining element that might be a bottleneck in such implementations is the modular reduction. Yet, the efficiency of reduction algorithms modulo a prime is a well-studied subject in general and in Elliptic-Curve Cryptography (ECC) in particular.

3.1   Small Mersenne Primes

It is commonly known that reduction modulo a Mersenne prime, i.e., a prime of the form $p = 2^n - 1$, can be performed very efficiently on a binary computer. There are further categories of primes that emerged as particularly suitable choices for efficient modular reduction. These include generalized Mersenne primes, pseudo-Mersenne primes and Montgomery-friendly primes [6,18,19,52]. Yet, these alternatives are mostly needed because large Mersenne primes are sparsely distributed. In the range between $2^{127} - 1$ and $2^{521} - 1$ for example, there exist none. For our purposes, however, we are primarily interested in primes much smaller than that, namely with bit-lengths close to the size of binary extension fields that popular symmetric block ciphers operate in, e.g., $\mathbb{F}_{2^8}$ for the AES [32]. The Mersenne prime exponents closest to 8 are $n = 7$ and $n = 13$. In the following we extend this range a bit and compare the performance and cost of masked multiplication algorithms in fields $\mathbb{F}_{2^n}$ and $\mathbb{F}_{2^n-1}$ for all Mersenne exponents n with $3 \leq n \leq 31$. These sizes allow efficient implementation of field arithmetic both in software and hardware. Hence, they are relevant targets for the construction of cryptographic building blocks. Besides, Mersenne prime fields have the additional advantage that any multiplication of a field element by a power of 2 is merely a rotation of the bits, which is cheap in software and entirely free in hardware. As a result, also the Hamming weight of a value is preserved when it is multiplied by a power of 2. Eventually, when mapping messages into the desired prime field for encryption, Mersenne primes cause the minimum amount of unused bit strings (i.e., only the all-ones string).

3.2   Masked Multiplication in Binary Fields vs. Prime Fields

When masking a cryptographic primitive like a block cipher, the linear operations can trivially be extended and applied to each share individually. Therefore, the cost of masked linear operations grows linearly in the number of shares. The implementation of non-linear elements is less straightforward and requires dedicated gadgets which optimally offer (robust) probing security and, if desired, satisfy composability notions to enable their secure combination to construct larger (robust) probing secure circuits [11,44]. It is a common abstraction to estimate that the cost of masked non-linear operations grows quadratically in the number of shares [47]. This is traditionally motivated by the number of partial products required for executing the ISW multiplication algorithm [53]. Clearly, the main bottleneck for the efficiency of masked cipher implementations is the realization of the non-linear operations, or as commonly abstracted, the multiplications. In the following we therefore compare the performance and cost of masked multiplication algorithms and circuits. These gadgets are well-suited for a comparison as they not only consist of field multiplications but also require field addition and subtraction (which are equivalent in binary fields).

Software. First, we concentrate on software platforms. For the comparison we have chosen an STM32VLDISCOVERY board[4] with an STM32F100RB ARM

---

[4] https://www.st.com/en/evaluation-tools/stm32vldiscovery.html.

Table 1. Cycle counts of the ISW multiplication algorithm on an ARM Cortex-M3 MCU (STM32F100RB on STM32VLDISCOVERY) for binary and prime fields with small to medium Mersenne prime exponents $3 \leq n \leq 31$.

Field	n	Number of Shares						Field	n	Number of Shares					
		1	2	3	4	5	6			1	2	3	4	5	6
$\mathbb{F}_{2^n}$	3	24	73	173	330	656	956	$\mathbb{F}_{2^n-1}$	3	5	20	39	104	230	382
	5	26	75	215	388	672	968		5	5	20	39	104	230	382
	7	26	75	217	392	720	1032		7	5	20	39	104	230	382
	13	162	629	1429	2581	3933	6014		13	5	20	39	104	230	382
	17	210	821	1861	3349	5085	7758		17	17	82	224	468	804	960
	19	234	917	2077	3733	5661	8630		19	17	82	224	468	804	960
	31	378	1493	3373	6037	9117	13862		31	19	86	230	476	820	1262

Cortex-M3 32-bit micro-controller. It provides single-cycle addition, subtraction and multiplication instructions for 32-bit operands. However, the single-cycle multiplication instruction (MUL) only produces 32-bit results and is therefore effectively a 16×16-bit multiplier for our purposes. A multi-cycle 32×32-bit multiplication instruction (UMULL) producing a 64-bit result exists, but it does not execute in constant time and is therefore not considered in this work. All our software implementations are written in C and have been compiled and analyzed using Keil MDK for ARM (MDK-Lite Version 5.36.0.0). Table 1 compares the number of cycles required to execute an ISW multiplication in constant time in both binary and Mersenne-prime fields with up to six shares (providing fifth-order security). Up to $n = 7$, the masked binary ISW multiplication is quite efficient, as the partial products can be computed using *log/alog* tables [32]. The remaining operations in the masked multiplication algorithm are XORs. For $n = 13$ and larger fields, *log/alog* tables are too big to be hard-coded as static tables in the program and to be flashed onto the device. Thus, for 13×13-bit and larger multiplications, the partial products are computed using a regular constant-time Galois field multiplication based on shift, XOR and AND operations.[5]

The masked Mersenne-prime ISW multiplication is more efficient for any number of shares on this target platform since, unlike the binary field operation, it can leverage the arithmetic multiplication instructions. The subsequent modular reduction takes another 4 cycles for small n values. For $n = 17$ and larger Mersenne primes, the multiplication result does not fit into a single 32-bit word, implying the need for multi-precision arithmetic. Using the standard Karatsuba algorithm, at most three calls to the constant-time 16-bit multiplication instruction (MUL) are needed for $17 \leq n \leq 31$. Therefore, both the multiplication and the subsequent reduction require more cycles for these sizes. Nevertheless, compared to binary field multiplications of the same size they are still significantly more efficient, by up to one order of magnitude (for $n = 31$).

This comparison obviously neglects the significant performance improvements that can be achieved for binary field operations when making use of bit-slicing (first introduced in [14] to speed up DES implementations). Unfortunately

---

[5] It is possible to compute the tables on the device when they are needed. Yet, it creates additional (memory) overheads and complicates the comparison.

this technique can not be transferred to prime fields. By contrast, using medium-sized (e.g., 31-bit) primes that leverage the data width of the target platform optimally could serve as an alternative to build fast software implementations. A more detailed comparison including such considerations falls outside the scope of this work. Our point is anyway not that prime field operations are generally cheaper in software than binary field operations, but merely that Mersenne prime field arithmetic can be implemented very efficiently on such platforms too, mainly due to the existence of optimized arithmetic hardware support. Combining with their excellent side-channel security features, it makes them promising candidates for effective and efficient masking in low noise conditions.

Hardware. For hardware implementations it is usually distinguished between Application-Specific Integrated Circuits (ASICs) and Field-Programmable Gate Arrays (FPGAs). In this work we mainly consider FPGAs as a suitable target platform, since similar to MCUs they already come with optimized arithmetic hardware multipliers and adders on-board. If such resources are not available, the cost of building Mersenne-prime field multiplication from combinatorial logic cells (provided by a standard cell library) is, according to our estimation, about twice as high as for binary fields of the same size (this overhead shrinks for larger n). For addition and subtraction the resource overhead is even 3–4. However, when the FPGA includes DSP slices with multipliers and adders, the utilization of soft logic (LUTs, FFs, Slices) can be significantly reduced for prime field operations, at the cost of occupying the integrated arithmetic processors.

Table 2 shows the resource utilization of ISW multiplication circuits with up to 6 shares on a Xilinx Spartan-6 FPGA (XC6SLX75-2CSG484C) for both binary and Mersenne prime fields with exponents in the range $3 \leq n \leq 31$. This target FPGA offers 132 DSP48A1 slices with one 18×18-bit multiplier each. All circuits have been implemented using Xilinx ISE Design Suite 14.7 with synthesis parameters -keep_hierarchy set to yes and -use_dsp48 set to Auto. On average the masked prime field multiplications require less soft logic than the binary field equivalents, at the cost of using DSP48A1 slices. From the resource utilization figures, it becomes clear that $n = 5$ and $n = 19$ are sub-optimal choices for this target. For $n = 5$ the corresponding Mersenne prime $p = 31$ is still too small to effectively leverage the 18-bit multipliers (the synthesis tool then opted to not use a DSP slice), while its DSP-free implementation is already quite expensive. For $n = 19$ the multiplication cannot fit into an 18×18-bit multiplier, but it is also too small to effectively utilize a second instance for each multiplication, so the multiplier is extended by expensive soft logic. However, for $n = 7$, $n = 13$ and $n = 17$ (and even $n = 31$), efficient masked multiplications are found.

3.3 Larger Prime Ciphers

It is well-known from ECC-related research that performing cryptographic operations in larger prime fields requires expensive multi-precision arithmetic. For this reason, most existing prime-based block ciphers are not perfectly suited

Table 2. Resource consumption of the ISW multiplication algorithm on a Xilinx Spartan-6 FPGA (XC6SLX75-2CSG484C) for binary and prime fields with small to medium Mersenne prime exponents $3 \leq n \leq 31$. Note that 132 is the maximum number of available DSP48A1 slices on this target FPGA (*).

Shares	Field	n	LUTs	Slices	DSPs	Shares	Field	n	LUTs	Slices	DSPs
1	$\mathbb{F}_{2^n}$	3	3	3	0	2	$\mathbb{F}_{2^n}$	3	22	16	0
		5	12	6	0			5	64	41	0
		7	26	9	0			7	114	62	0
		13	81	35	0			13	382	157	0
		17	132	56	0			17	590	249	0
		19	166	71	0			19	742	322	0
		31	407	180	0			31	1722	802	0
	$\mathbb{F}_{2^n-1}$	3	3	3	0		$\mathbb{F}_{2^n-1}$	3	25	19	0
		5	34	13	0			5	197	79	0
		7	16	6	1			7	121	47	4
		13	27	12	1			13	216	80	4
		17	35	15	1			17	284	99	4
		19	116	36	1			19	623	183	4
		31	63	24	4			31	520	156	16

Shares	Field	n	LUTs	Slices	DSPs	Shares	Field	n	LUTs	Slices	DSPs
3	$\mathbb{F}_{2^n}$	3	57	46	0	4	$\mathbb{F}_{2^n}$	3	108	84	0
		5	156	102	0			5	294	168	0
		7	273	152	0			7	500	294	0
		13	862	440	0			13	1623	610	0
		17	1352	545	0			17	2414	1319	0
		19	1711	738	0			19	3060	1410	0
		31	3957	1904	0			31	7099	335	0
	$\mathbb{F}_{2^n-1}$	3	66	48	0		$\mathbb{F}_{2^n-1}$	3	126	85	0
		5	468	198	0			5	866	385	0
		7	327	123	9			7	600	254	16
		13	569	202	9			13	1082	386	16
		17	737	253	9			17	1428	467	16
		19	1512	444	9			19	2792	816	16
		31	1335	405	36			31	2527	768	64

Shares	Field	n	LUTs	Slices	DSPs	Shares	Field	n	LUTs	Slices	DSPs
5	$\mathbb{F}_{2^n}$	3	175	128	0	6	$\mathbb{F}_{2^n}$	3	258	200	0
		5	460	295	0			5	672	432	0
		7	821	446	0			7	1188	714	0
		13	2473	1237	0			13	3657	1653	0
		17	3761	1826	0			17	5469	2624	0
		19	4808	2201	0			19	6933	3182	0
		31	11217	5086	0			31	16237	7110	0
	$\mathbb{F}_{2^n-1}$	3	205	137	0		$\mathbb{F}_{2^n-1}$	3	303	211	0
		5	1369	575	0			5	1966	884	0
		7	984	381	25			7	1422	612	36
		13	1788	605	25			13	2625	891	36
		17	2284	769	25			17	3373	1131	36
		19	4468	1301	25			19	6532	1894	36
		31	4095	1295	100			31	9254	2369	132*

to deliver the desired efficiency for low-end embedded devices. For instance, a single unmasked 129×129-bit multiplication, as required 82 times in the MiMC-129/129 block cipher [2], already costs multiple hundreds of clock cycles (without modulo reduction) on devices where single-cycle 32-bit hardware multipliers are available [38]. On a Spartan-6 FPGA a single 129×129-bit unmasked multiplication without reduction is about as expensive as 16 31×31-bit multiplications or 64 17×17-bit (or smaller) multiplications. Considering additionally that no 129-bit Mersenne prime exists, the overheads for the modulo reduction will be even more significant. The same problems arise for all prime ciphers which are either based on operations in too large fields or which require reduction modulo an implementation-unfriendly prime (since integer division might be needed). We conclude that the design space for small to medium Mersenne-prime ciphers, dedicated to efficient masked implementations, is still mostly unexplored. We next show the interest of this design space by exhibiting the advantages of a first AES-prime cipher over its standard version for masked implementations.

4   AES-prime for Prime Encodings

Section 2 showed that prime encodings can improve the security of the masking countermeasure in low-noise settings. Section 3 showed that the resulting operations can be implemented efficiently in hardware and software. The next step in proving the utility of these encodings is to analyze concretely-relevant computations. Yet, as mentioned in the introduction, applying prime encodings to binary ciphers is expected to lead to large performance overheads. In general, prime ciphers, for which the key addition is in $\mathbb{F}_p$ and the diffusion layer is linear in this field, would be better suited to this goal. As a natural starting point, we propose an AES variant operating in prime fields, denoted as AES-prime.

4.1   AES-prime Design for $p = 2^7 - 1$

The main design guideline of AES-prime consists in adapting the standard AES design to $\mathbb{F}_p$ where p is a prime, using only additions and multiplications over the chosen prime field. The main design components are the same: the key is a vector of 16 elements of $\mathbb{F}_p$ and the state is considered as a table of 4 by 4 $\mathbb{F}_p$ elements. The round architecture is the same with the following adaptation on SubBytes, MixColumns and AddRoundKey. See [32] for details.

SubBytes. The non-linear substitution built upon the inverse function in $\mathbb{F}_{2^8}$ is replaced by a power function and the addition of a constant. The S-box is defined as $f(x) = x^e + c$ where e is the first integer such that e and $p - 1$ are co-prime, to ensure that the function mapping $x \in \mathbb{F}_p$ to x^e is a bijection, and c is the smallest positive integer such that $f(x)$ has no fix points (as in the original design). Then for $p = 2^7 - 1$ we have $e = 5$, $c = 2$ and $f(x) = x^5 + 2$.

Note that contrarily to the original AES nonlinear function this power map is not its own inverse. The main reason for this choice is that it allows reducing the number of multiplications in the S-box, which is the most expensive operation to mask. Concretely, the considered x^5 mapping can be performed with three multiplications. A counterpart of this choice is that the inverse will be less efficient. For now we therefore assume that AES-prime will be preferably used in an inverse-free mode of operation (e.g., CTR [59]), leaving the investigation of S-boxes in prime fields with efficient inverses as an open problem.

MixColumns. This part of the affine layer is replaced by a 4 by 4 Maximum Distance Separable (MDS) matrix over $\mathbb{F}_p$. The reason is to guarantee a branch number of 5 as in the original AES design (which is optimal for this size), for diffusion properties. To choose the MDS matrix, we start from a Vandermonde matrix and perform minor modifications to decrease the number of different elements. It is beneficial to choose elements which are powers of 2 when p is a Mersenne prime, since multiplication by such a value is merely a rotation of the bits. For $p = 2^7 - 1$ it leads to the following choice:

$$M = \begin{bmatrix} 1 & 1 & 1 & 1 \\ 1 & 2 & 4 & 16 \\ 1 & 4 & 16 & 2 \\ 1 & 16 & 2 & 4 \end{bmatrix}.$$

AddRoundKey. The bit-wise addition of the AES is replaced by the addition over $\mathbb{F}_p$ between the 16 elements of the round key and the state.

For completeness, we finally mention that AES-prime uses the key scheduling algorithm of the AES adapted with a prime S-box and additions modulo p. Its round constants are computed as multiples of 3 modulo p, resulting in the sequence 0x01, 0x03, 0x09, 0x1B, 0x74, 0x5E, 0x1C, 0x54 ...

4.2 Security Analysis

The proximity between the AES-prime and AES designs allows us to benefit from two decades of cryptanalysis in order to determine the security of the AES-prime to known attacks. For our choice of parameters, we can also lean on the security analysis of the HADES design strategy [48] that recently studied generalizations of SPN designs over prime fields. The main focus of [48] is on big prime sizes (where $\log_2(p)$ corresponds to the targeted security such as 128-bit) for MPC applications, but its security analysis also considers smaller sizes. For example, for $\log_2(p) = 8$ and a state of 16 words they advocate 14 rounds for a 128-bit security ($16 \times \log_2(p)$ more precisely). The main attacks exhibited against these prime designs are statistical attacks (mostly differential cryptanalysis), and algebraic attacks based on interpolation and Gröbner bases.

AES-prime has two main differences with the HADES ciphers. First, all rounds have a full S-box layer whereas HADES combines full S-box layers and partial S-box layers in order to decrease the total number of products. Second, the diffusion of AES-prime uses a 4 by 4 MDS matrix whereas HADES uses an MDS matrix on the whole state (16 by 16 in our case). We argue these differences have a limited impact on the security analyses, and a similar number of rounds could be considered. For statistical attacks, the strategy of HADES relies on the differential and linear probabilities of an S-box and the number of active S-boxes in the full layers. The S-box of `AES-prime` being a power function as in `HADES`, we can bound the statistical probabilities using the same arguments, and we can bound the number of active S-boxes from the diffusion properties proven for the regular `AES`. For algebraic attacks, the strategy of `HADES` is based on determining the degree of the polynomials obtained after r rounds, and the number of coefficients of such polynomials. The same strategy can be applied to `AES-prime`. We next give more details on these attacks on `AES-prime`.

Statistical Attacks. The most common attacks on block ciphers are linear [65] and differential cryptanalyses [16] and their variants. They consist in following how statistical biases from the S-boxes propagate along various rounds of the cipher in order to determine the key. Following the Wide Trail Strategy [31], we bound the linear and differential probability of the S-box function, and use the branch number to bound the number of active S-boxes over various rounds, in order to determine the minimal number of rounds preventing characteristics with probability higher than $2^{-\lambda}$, where λ is the security parameter. As in [48] we ensure that each characteristic has a probability smaller than $2^{-2\lambda}$ in order to avoid that a combination of various of them lead to an attack.

The differential probability of a 1-variable p-ary function f from a to b (both in $\mathbb{F}_p$) is defined as $|\{x : f(x + a) - f(x) = b\}|/|\mathbb{F}_p|$ and its linear probability relatively to a, b as $|\{x : f(x) = ax+b\}|/|\mathbb{F}_p|$.[6] Since $\mathbb{F}_p$ is a field, any polynomial of degree e has at most e roots, which gives the upper bound of $(\deg(f)-1)/p$ for the differential probabilities and $\deg(f)/p$ for the linear ones. Since in `AES-prime` ShiftRows is the one of the regular `AES` and MixColumns is based on an MDS matrix as for `AES` too, the number of active S-boxes in a four-round differential (or linear) trail is lower bounded by 25 (see [32], Theorem 9.5.1). Therefore, with 8 rounds the differential probabilities admit the upper bound:

$$\mathbf{p} \leq \left(\frac{\deg(f)}{p}\right)^{50}, \text{ hence for } p = 2^7 - 1 \text{ it gives } \mathbf{p} \leq \left(\frac{5}{127}\right)^{50} \approx 2^{-233}.$$

These probabilities are smaller than $2^{-2\lambda}$ and, as in [48], we add two rounds in order to guarantee that no differential attack can be set up by key guessing, which leads to a minimum of 10 rounds to avoid these attacks.

Algebraic Attacks. As for the `HADES` framework, we consider that the main algebraic attacks threatening `AES-prime` are the interpolation attack [55] and attacks exploiting Gröbner bases. In both cases, the goal of the analyses are to determine a minimum number of rounds such that the polynomial representations of the cipher that an adversary can build has a too high degree of too many monomials. First, we note that for a fixed key the encryption could be studied as a function (mapping each plaintext to a ciphertext) from $\mathbb{F}_{p^{16}}$ to $\mathbb{F}_{p^{16}}$. Then, even determining the polynomial corresponding to one full S-box layer is non-trivial. Accordingly, the basis field we consider for the cryptanalyses is $\mathbb{F}_p$, and polynomials built by the adversary belong to $\mathbb{F}_p[z_0, \cdots, z_{15}]/(z_0^p - 1, \cdots, z_{15}^p - 1)$.

---

[6] A n-variable p-ary function is a function from $\mathbb{F}_p^n$ to $\mathbb{F}_p$.

Since the degree in one variable is at most $p - 1$, the total degree is at most $16(p - 1)$ and there are p^{16} monomials. The S-box used in AES-prime being a power function x^e added to a constant, the total degree will therefore increase as e^r for the first r rounds, until reaching the maximum of $16(p - 1)$. For the number of monomials, most of the monomials will be present in each polynomial after a few rounds (most since even for a random polynomial each monomial is present with probability $(p - 1)/p$). Indeed, after $\lceil \log_e(p) \rceil$ rounds, all the univariate monomials (z_i^j) are obtained. Two more rounds ensure to have sums with each one of the 16 variables (at some power) as input of the S-box' f function (defined in Sect. 4.1). As a result, $\lceil \log_e(p) \rceil$ more rounds are sufficient to obtain all monomials. Overall, we obtain dense polynomials after $2\lceil \log_e(p) \rceil + 2$ rounds, which corresponds to 10 rounds for the chosen $p = 2^7 - 1$.

For the interpolation attack, the attacker aims at interpolating a polynomial from $\mathbb{F}_p^{16}$ to $\mathbb{F}_p$ corresponding to the encryption over all minus one rounds using known plaintext/ciphertext pairs. If such a polynomial has a low degree or few monomials, the adversary can guess the key of the final round, decrypt the ciphertexts, interpolate the polynomial corresponding to all minus one rounds and confirm it with an extra plaintext/ciphertext pair. The data cost is well approximated by the number of plaintext/ciphertext pairs necessary to build such a polynomial. Following the strategy of HADES, we consider that such an attack cannot succeed when the number of monomials in the cipher polynomial is equal to the full code book, since it corresponds to $p^{16} \approx 2^\lambda$ monomials which already meets the targeted security. Accordingly, we count $2\lceil \log_e(p) \rceil + 3$ rounds to rule out the interpolation attack, 11 for $p = 2^7 - 1$. Due to the proximity of design between SHARK [78] and AES-prime, we also consider the analysis of the first interpolation attack [55] on this block cipher. The principle of this attack is that even if the S-box corresponds to a function of high degree (maximal in the case of the inverse as in SHARK), it can be attacked more easily in another representation (e.g., as a fraction of low-degree polynomials). In this case, the complexity of the attack comes from the number of S-boxes rather than their size or degree. The complexity of the best attack is then at least $2(t^{r-3})^t$, where t is the number of S-boxes and r the number of rounds. For the AES-prime it corresponds to $2 \cdot 16^{16(r-3)}$, hence at least 5 rounds for $p = 2^7 - 1$.

For Gröbner bases attacks, the attacker aims at solving a system of multivariate polynomials over $\mathbb{F}_p$ in the key elements obtained with sufficient plaintext/ciphertext pairs. Determining the (tight) complexity of these attacks is impossible. Hence the security of ciphers against these attacks is usually based on the infeasibility of computing the Gröbner basis in degree reverse lexical order. We follow this strategy also used in HADES. Since the design differences (e.g., MDS matrix on partial or full state, full or partial S-boxes layers) have no influence on the final complexity, we respect the bound of at least $2 + \lceil \log_e(p)/2 \rceil + \lceil \log_e(16) \rceil$ rounds. For $p = 2^7 - 1$ it leads to a minimum of 6 rounds.

Number or Rounds. Based on the complexity of the different attacks considered, 11 rounds would be sufficient for the targeted security of $\lfloor 16 \log(2^7 - 1) \rfloor = 111$ bits for this value of p, which is coherent with the number of rounds in the AES. Since various improvement of the considered attacks, or attacks of the same families, are possible we take a more conservative approach and follow the estimations of HADES. Accordingly, we advocate the use of 14 rounds.

Before moving to the experimental validation of our findings, we re-insist that the proposed instance of the AES-prime cipher with $p = 2^7 - 1$ is only aimed to confirm the interesting design space that prime ciphers open. In particular, our following conclusions only require that AES-like ciphers operating in binary and prime fields of similar sizes require similar number of rounds (i.e., differ by factors that are covered by the physical security gains that the AES-prime provides). Besides, we note that this design is scalable. For example, if 128 bits of security or more are required, a 13-bit variant with $p = 2^{13} - 1$ can be considered. The S-box could then be based on $f(x) = x^{11} + 3$ while keeping the same MDS matrix as the 7-bit instance for MixColumns, and the same number of rounds.

5 Experimental Validation

In this last section, we finally consider the practical impact of prime encodings on the security of masked block cipher implementations in software and hardware. For this purpose we implement masked field multiplications in $\mathbb{F}_{2^7-1}$ based on the ISW multiplication algorithm [53] and construct probing secure implementations of the AES-prime S-box, i.e., $x^5 + 2$. We refrain from any comparison to masked versions of the standard AES S-box here, which is based on Galois field inversion in $\mathbb{F}_{2^8}$. The different bit lengths of inputs processed, the different number and size of field multiplications required and the various known implementation strategies for the standard AES S-box are among the reasons why any such comparison would depend a lot on the ad-hoc choices made along the way and indeed feel like comparing apples to oranges. Thus, we chose to compare the identical operations, i.e., multiplication and $f(x) = x^5 + 2$, in the corresponding fields $\mathbb{F}_{2^7-1}$ and $\mathbb{F}_{2^7}$. We stress that the following results are not meant as an efficiency comparison (which would favor binary fields for this choice of S-box since the squaring operation is linear in $\mathbb{F}_{2^7}$), but merely as a comparison of their side-channel leakage. For our software case study, we evaluate the security of these implementations for an increasing number of shares (up to 6) against a profiled SASCA attack (similar to the one considered in [20]). In this setting the adversary is given full profiling access to the device to characterize its leakage behavior and build optimal models for the attack. Furthermore, the chosen 32-bit MCU (specified next) has shown a low natural noise level when measuring its power consumption. As a second case study, we evaluate the leakage reduction offered by prime field operations in hardware compared to the equivalent binary field operations using a detection-based leakage assessment [81].

5.1 Target Devices and Experimental Setups

For the software-based investigations, we have targeted the same device as already described in Sect. 3, namely an STM32VLDISCOVERY board with an embedded STM32F100RB ARM Cortex-M3 32-bit micro-controller. Both the discovery board and the MCU are identical to the Cortex-M3 experiments presented in [20], where bitslice masked implementations have been analyzed. Also similar to [20], we have conducted a standard modification of the board for power measurements, namely carefully removing the decoupling capacitors in the power grid of the target chip to obtain improved results. The Cortex-M3 has been operated at 8 MHz throughout our experiments.

For the hardware-based investigation we have evaluated the masked implementations on a SAKURA-G FPGA board,[7] which employs two Xilinx Spartan-6 FPGAs: one as a target and one as a control unit. The target FPGA is the exact Spartan-6 device we have used for the estimation of the resource consumption of masked field multiplications in Sect. 3. We have operated the target implementations at 6 MHz. Low frequencies were selected since we are interested in conducting our comparisons at minimal noise levels.

In both cases, we have used the same measurement equipment and settings. In detail, we have placed a CT-1 current probe from Tektronix with a bandwidth up to 1 GHz in the power supply path of the target FPGA and acquired the measurements with a PicoScope 5244D digital sampling oscilloscope. The sampling rate was set to 250 MS/s and the vertical resolution was 12 bit.

5.2   Software Case Study

The goal of the software-based case study is to validate whether moving to encodings and operations in prime fields actually leads to concrete security improvements compared to standard Boolean masking in real-world experiments. To answer this question, we mount horizontal attacks against the AES-prime S-box for two different encodings and two implementation strategies realized on a small 32-bit micro-controller (known to provide limited natural noise).

Methodology. We implemented the S-box as a sequence of three ISW multiplications, as described in Sect. 4. It gives rise to intermediate computations x, x^2, x^4, x^5. We added refreshing gadgets according to the trivial composition strategy of [26,47]. We follow the attack of Bronchain and Standaert from CHES 2021 [20] to efficiently leverage the horizontal leakages and extend it to operations in prime fields. Concretely, this analytical attack targets all the encodings appearing in the multiplication chain, which has the significant advantage that the resulting factor graph does not have cycles and is guaranteed to converge.[8]

The procedure of the attack is as follows. We assume that the adversary can profile the leakage of the device while even knowing the random values used during the profiling phase. This is a standard assumption when trying to evaluate the security in the worst-case scenario for the designer by considering a very

---

[7] http://satoh.cs.uec.ac.jp/SAKURA/index.html.

[8] We also tested SASCA with the full factor graph, using the heuristic of running the BP algorithm for a number of steps corresponding to twice the diameter of the factor graph. This attack variant did not lead to significant improvements.

Table 3. Concrete cycle counts (left) and resource utilization figures (right) of the software and hardware implementations measured in this section. All values are for constant time implementations and exclude randomness generation.

	Field Arith.		log/alog			Binary Field $\mathbb{F}_{2^n}$			Prime Field $\mathbb{F}_{2^n-1}$		
d	$\mathbb{F}_{2^n}$	$\mathbb{F}_{2^n-1}$	$\mathbb{F}_{2^n}$	$\mathbb{F}_{2^n-1}$	d	LUTs	Slic.	DSPs	LUTs	Slic.	DSPs
2	1321	189	232	282	2	26	15	0	20	11	1
3	2902	334	448	535	3	126	77	0	131	70	4
4	5213	600	800	912	4	285	161	0	348	160	9
5	8255	1125	1340	1581	5	539	293	0	710	306	16
6	12038	1692	1988	2283	6	848	486	0	1096	515	25

strong attacker model [20]. The adversary uses the profiles subsequently to target each share and intermediate value separately and finally combines all acquired information to determine the underlying secrets. For this purpose, we first select representative Points-of-Interest (POIs) in the trace for each relevant intermediate value thanks to the standard Signal-to-Noise Ratio (SNR) metric [60]. The leakage distribution of each target intermediate value is then profiled thanks to a pooled template attack [29] after a dimensionality reduction step using Linear Discriminant Analysis (LDA) [83]. As a result, we obtain leakage models for all the target intermediate values of the factor graph and use them in place of the *a priori* (Hamming weight and LSB) ones of Sect. 2. These multivariate models can be superior to the previous HW and LSB models and may enable attacks with very few traces. Since we are interested in the practical interest of prime encodings, we also switch from (easier to estimate) information theoretic metrics to a security metric, namely the Guessing Entropy (GE) [84] that captures the average key rank and which we estimated based on 1,000 different attacks.

Experimental Results. We have implemented the masked computation of $x^5 + 2$ in both fields $\mathbb{F}_{2^7}$ and $\mathbb{F}_{2^7-1}$ using two different implementation strategies. First, using regular field arithmetic for the multiplication, which includes shift, XOR and AND operations for the binary field and single-cycle multiplication and addition instructions for the prime field. However, since these approaches show a vastly different leakage pattern, we have additionally realized a table-lookup based implementation using *log/alog* tables for both fields. The table-lookup based implementations are realized using very similar sequences of instructions and are therefore perfectly suited for a fair comparison. It is important to mention that all implementations work in constant time. For the *log/alog* table implementations we have only considered traces for the attack where the inputs to the lookup-based field multiplication are non-zero. Despite the fact that all our implementations execute in constant time (for any input), there is still an operation dependency in the case that one or both multiplication inputs are zero (see [32] for a description of the lookup function). This dependency, which is inherent to all *log/alog* table based implementations, allows to trivially identify all zero-inputs with probability one

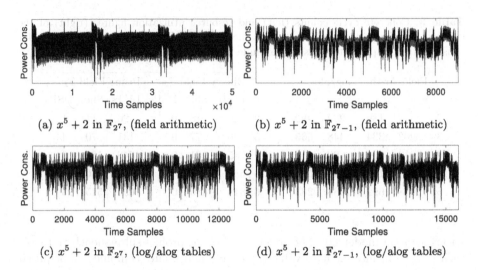

(a) $x^5 + 2$ in $\mathbb{F}_{2^7}$, (field arithmetic)   (b) $x^5 + 2$ in $\mathbb{F}_{2^7-1}$, (field arithmetic)

(c) $x^5 + 2$ in $\mathbb{F}_{2^7}$, (log/alog tables)   (d) $x^5 + 2$ in $\mathbb{F}_{2^7-1}$, (log/alog tables)

Fig. 5. Illustrative Cortex-M3 sample traces of a first-order masked implementation computing $x^5 + 2$ in binary field (left) and prime field (right) using regular field arithmetic operations (top) and log/alog tables (bottom).

in the traces. In order to avoid this special case in our comparison we have only considered non-zero inputs for *both* binary and prime fields. For our purposes this simple workaround was acceptable, for real implementations we recommend more prudent strategies such as presented in [80]. Sample traces of the acquired measurements from the Cortex-M3 for the four different implementations are shown in Fig. 5 for the case of 2 shares. We have repeated those measurements for 3, 4, 5 and 6 shares for each of the four cases. For completeness, we provide the concrete cycle counts and resource utilization figures of the analyzed implementations in Table 3. As detailed before, the cycle counts required for performing three consecutive masked multiplications are compared in the software case (which is clearly not the most efficient manner to compute x^5, especially in binary fields). Please note that log/alog table based prime implementations require slightly more cycles than the equivalent Boolean implementations, since only the partial multiplications are performed via table lookup, while additions are still performed using regular arithmetic (requiring a reduction in the prime case). Figure 6 for example shows the Signal-to-Noise Ratio (SNR) for one input share per implementation. As expected, the leakage patterns and magnitudes are different between binary and prime field computation when considering the regular field arithmetic implementations. However, they are strikingly similar for the table-based implementations.

In order to perform the attacks we have built profiles using 50,000 traces each, selected a maximum of 200 POIs per variable and set the number of dimensions after LDA projection to 2. The results are depicted in Fig. 7. As expected for a low-noise device, Boolean masking (in $\mathbb{F}_{2^7}$) with multiplication based on field arithmetic (Fig. 7a) leads to trivial attacks in less than 10 traces against all implementations with up to 6 shares using the profiled models. By contrast,

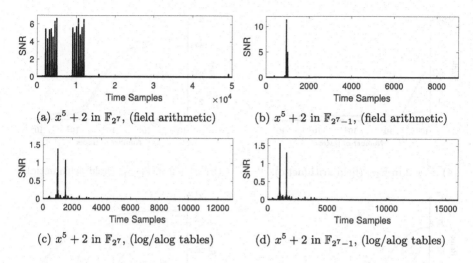

(a) $x^5 + 2$ in $\mathbb{F}_{2^7}$, (field arithmetic)   (b) $x^5 + 2$ in $\mathbb{F}_{2^7-1}$, (field arithmetic)

(c) $x^5 + 2$ in $\mathbb{F}_{2^7}$, (log/alog tables)   (d) $x^5 + 2$ in $\mathbb{F}_{2^7-1}$, (log/alog tables)

Fig. 6. Signal-to-Noise Ratio (SNR) of input share 0 for the traces in Fig. 5.

the corresponding SASCA against the AES-prime S-box (Fig. 7b) requires significantly more observations to succeed. Attacking the 6-share implementation requires around 4,000 traces. Yet, the differences between Fig. 7b and Fig. 7a could potentially be influenced by the way the field multiplication is implemented. Therefore, we repeated the attacks for the table-based implementations, where the leakage per share has been shown to be equivalent. The result is depicted in Figs. 7c and 7d. It can be observed that the attacks require more traces to succeed for both fields due to the lower SNR (c.f. Fig. 6). Yet, 50–60 traces still suffice to retrieve the key of the Boolean masked computation with 6 shares, while about 10,000 traces are required for the equivalent prime field masked S-box. These results confirm the interest of prime encodings. In particular, they show a significant security benefit when increasing the number of shares for prime field masking even in this challenging low-noise software context, which is a major advantage over Boolean masking.

5.3 Hardware Case Study

In order to investigate whether similarly impressive security improvements can be achieved for the (naturally more noisy) case of parallel hardware implementations, we have conducted a second case study. In this experiment, we implemented the ISW multiplication algorithm in hardware and, as for the previous case study, compare the security provided by Boolean (in $\mathbb{F}_{2^7}$) and prime field (in $\mathbb{F}_{2^7-1}$) masking. When implemented in two cycles (and synchronizing the outputs with a register [69]), the ISW multiplication algorithm leads to a robust probing secure and composable circuit gadget [44]. This is crucial to avoid a reduction of the statistical security order due to the presence of physical defaults in the hardware such as glitches. We implemented the ISW multiplication in both

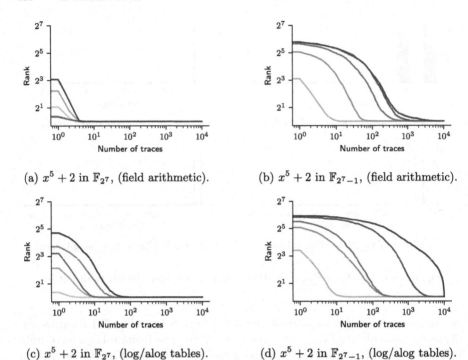

(a) $x^5 + 2$ in $\mathbb{F}_{2^7}$, (field arithmetic).   (b) $x^5 + 2$ in $\mathbb{F}_{2^7-1}$, (field arithmetic).

(c) $x^5 + 2$ in $\mathbb{F}_{2^7}$, (log/alog tables).   (d) $x^5 + 2$ in $\mathbb{F}_{2^7-1}$, (log/alog tables).

Fig. 7. Guessing Entropy of SASCA against a software implementation of the AES-prime S-box (top) and a binary variant (bottom) for 2 to 6 shares.

considered fields for up to five shares in a fully pipelined manner. A comparison of their resource utilization on the Spartan-6 FPGA is given in Table 3. As detailed in Sect. 3, the prime field multiplications are supported by DSP slices instead of pure soft logic implementations. We only execute and measure a single masked multiplication gadget to obtain relatively low noise levels (aside from the parallelism inside the gadget itself). Then we perform a Test Vector Leakage Assessment (TVLA)-based analysis [81] to verify the security order provided by the circuits and analyze the number of traces required to exceed the detection threshold. We chose to perform this analysis using two fixed classes $(0 \times 00 \cdot 0 \times 00$ vs. $0 \times 7E \cdot 0 \times 7E)$ to minimize the number of measurements required to detect data-dependent information, as suggested in [39]. Our results are depicted in Fig. 8. Table 4 lists the required amounts of traces to pass the detection threshold ($t > 4.5$) in the respective TVLA procedures.

Table 4. Required numbers of traces to pass the detection threshold.

Field $\backslash d$	1	2	3	4	5
$\mathbb{F}_{2^n}$	< 10	100	20,300	198,000	5,870,000
$\mathbb{F}_{2^n-1}$	< 10	3,700	128,100	$> 10,000,000$	$> 10,000,000$

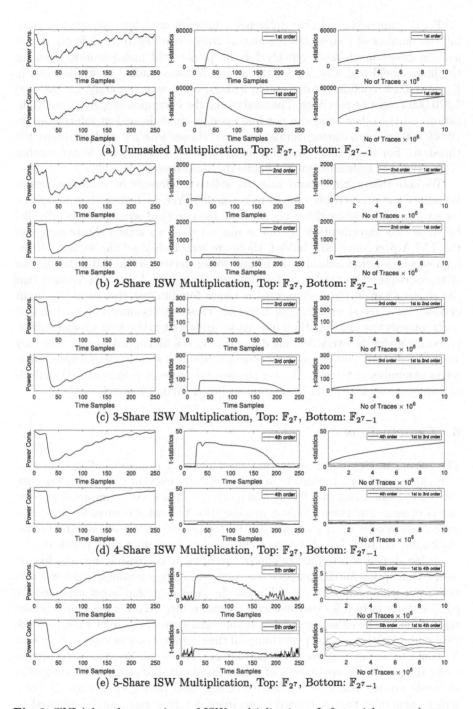

Fig. 8. TVLA-based comparison of ISW multiplications. Left to right: sample trace, TVLA over points, TVLA over traces.

For the unmasked case, the difference is insignificant. However, when increasing the number of shares, the amount of traces required to confidently detect leakage grows much more quickly for the prime field multiplication than for the binary field one. Concretely, the 4- and 5-share masked multiplications in $\mathbb{F}_{2^7}$ still show confidently detectable leakage after approximately 198,000 and 5,870,000 traces respectively. The analysis of the corresponding $\mathbb{F}_{2^7-1}$ multiplications on the other hand can not find enough input-dependent information in 10,000,000 traces to distinguish the two fixed classes with a confidence above the threshold. For the 4-share case this means that even a 50 times larger number of observations is insufficient to achieve the same detection result.

We note that in the 3-share case, the relative difference between the metrics for binary and prime fields appears to be smaller. Yet, we believe that it does not reflect a smaller relative difference between the practical security levels provided by these two implementations, but is instead owed to known shortcomings of the TVLA procedure [87]. Indeed, there are factors beyond the security of the implementation that influence the magnitude of the statistic and also the number of traces required to reach a certain magnitude in TVLA (e.g., we verified that the relative gap in the 3-share case is larger for different choices of the input classes). So as usual with leakage detection, these results should be used as first hints towards the significantly improved security that prime field masking offers, especially given the overwhelming differences in the higher order cases. But they are not a directly suitable way to conclude about a security level expressed in terms of number of traces to recover the key. We leave such an advanced analysis of worst-case attacks as an interesting scope for further research.

6   Conclusions

The results in this paper show that masking with prime encodings can lead to major security improvements in the practically-relevant case of devices with low noise. Evaluations in software and hardware show security improvements by orders of magnitude over Boolean masking (for targets of equivalent sizes). We hope these results open the way to a better understanding of masking in this challenging context. We also believe they lead to important open problems.

A first direction is to further improve security by decreasing the side-channel signal. One option for this purpose is to work with larger p values, which will also raise evaluation challenges, as it implies the need to profile larger intermediate computations (which is expensive with current tools). Another one is to leverage algorithmic noise, either by using random values that are larger than p in the ISW multiplications, or by performing all the computations modulo $p \cdot N$ (where N would be an algorithmic noise parameter). A second direction is to further study the physical cryptanalysis of prime encodings. For example, investigating algebraic attacks could be relevant (although also raising challenges, as these attacks generally have a limited noise tolerance that may not be adapted to masking) [22,73,77]. As mentioned in the introduction, assessing the interest of prime encodings in the context of static leakage is another interesting question.

And of course, the design of ciphers that are even better suited to masking in prime fields than the AES-prime, and their comparison with optimized bitslice ciphers implemented with Boolean masking is an important long-term goal.

Acknowledgments. François-Xavier Standaert is senior research associate of the Belgian Fund for Scientific Research (F.R.S.-FNRS). This work has been funded by the EU through the ERC project SWORD (724725).

References

1. Albrecht, M.R., et al.: Feistel structures for MPC, and more. In: ESORICS 2019 (2019). https://doi.org/10.1007/978-3-030-29962-0_8
2. Albrecht, M., Grassi, L., Rechberger, C., Roy, A., Tiessen, T.: MiMC: efficient encryption and cryptographic hashing with minimal multiplicative complexity. In: Cheon, J.H., Takagi, T. (eds.) ASIACRYPT 2016. LNCS, vol. 10031, pp. 191–219. Springer, Heidelberg (2016). https://doi.org/10.1007/978-3-662-53887-6_7
3. Aldous, D., Diaconis, P.: Shuffling cards and stopping times. Am. Math. Monthly **93**(5), 333–348 (1986). https://doi.org/10.1080/00029890.1986.11971821
4. Aly, A., Ashur, T., Ben-Sasson, E., Dhooghe, S., Szepieniec, A.: Design of symmetric-key primitives for advanced cryptographic protocols. ToSC (3) (2020). https://doi.org/10.13154/tosc.v2020.i3.1-45
5. Andrychowicz, M., Dziembowski, S., Faust, S.: Circuit compilers with $O(1/\log(n))$ leakage rate. In: EUROCRYPT 2016 [43], pp. 586–615. https://doi.org/10.1007/978-3-662-49896-5_21
6. Bajard, J.C., Duquesne, S.: Montgomery-friendly primes and applications to cryptography. J. Cryptogr. Eng. **11**(4), 399–415 (2021). https://doi.org/10.1007/s13389-021-00260-z
7. Balasch, J., Faust, S., Gierlichs, B., Paglialonga, C., Standaert, F.-X.: Consolidating inner product masking. In: Takagi, T., Peyrin, T. (eds.) ASIACRYPT 2017. LNCS, vol. 10624, pp. 724–754. Springer, Cham (2017). https://doi.org/10.1007/978-3-319-70694-8_25
8. Balasch, J., Gierlichs, B., Grosso, V., Reparaz, O., Standaert, F.: On the cost of lazy engineering for masked software implementations. In: CARDIS (2014). https://doi.org/10.1007/978-3-319-16763-3_5
9. Barthe, G., Belaïd, S., Cassiers, G., Fouque, P.A., Grégoire, B., Standaert, F.X.: maskVerif: automated verification of higher-order masking in presence of physical defaults. In: ESORICS 2019 (2019). https://doi.org/10.1007/978-3-030-29959-0_15
10. Barthe, G., Belaïd, S., Dupressoir, F., Fouque, P.A., Grégoire, B., Strub, P.Y.: Verified proofs of higher-order masking. In: Oswald and Fischlin [74]. https://doi.org/10.1007/978-3-662-46800-5_18
11. Barthe, G., et al.: Strong non-interference and type-directed higher-order masking. In: CCS 2016 (2016). https://doi.org/10.1145/2976749.2978427
12. Battistello, A., Coron, J.S., Prouff, E., Zeitoun, R.: Horizontal side-channel attacks and countermeasures on the ISW masking scheme. In: CHES 2016 (2016). https://doi.org/10.1007/978-3-662-53140-2_2
13. Belaïd, S., Benhamouda, F., Passelègue, A., Prouff, E., Thillard, A., Vergnaud, D.: Randomness complexity of private circuits for multiplication. In: EUROCRYPT 2016 [43]. https://doi.org/10.1007/978-3-662-49896-5_22

14. Biham, E.: A fast new DES implementation in software. In: Biham, E. (ed.) FSE 1997. LNCS, vol. 1267, pp. 260–272. Springer, Heidelberg (1997). https://doi.org/10.1007/BFb0052352

15. Biham, E. (ed.): FSE 1997, vol. 1267 (1997)

16. Biham, E., Shamir, A.: Differential cryptanalysis of DES-like cryptosystems. In: Menezes, A.J., Vanstone, S.A. (eds.) CRYPTO 1990. LNCS, vol. 537, pp. 2–21. Springer, Heidelberg (1991). https://doi.org/10.1007/3-540-38424-3_1

17. Bloem, R., Groß, H., Iusupov, R., Könighofer, B., Mangard, S., Winter, J.: Formal verification of masked hardware implementations in the presence of glitches. In: Nielsen and Rijmen [71]. https://doi.org/10.1007/978-3-319-78375-8_11

18. Bos, J.W., Costello, C., Hisil, H., Lauter, K.: Fast cryptography in genus 2. In: EUROCRYPT 2013 [42] (2013). https://doi.org/10.1007/978-3-642-38348-9_12

19. Bos, J.W., Costello, C., Longa, P., Naehrig, M.: Selecting elliptic curves for cryptography: an efficiency and security analysis. J. Cryptogr. Eng. 6(4), 259–286 (2015). https://doi.org/10.1007/s13389-015-0097-y

20. Bronchain, O., Standaert, F.X.: Breaking masked implementations with many shares on 32-bit software platforms. TCHES (3) (2021). https://doi.org/10.46586/tches.v2021.i3.202-234

21. Buhan, I., Schneider, T. (eds.): CARDIS 2022 (2023). https://doi.org/10.1007/978-3-031-25319-5

22. Carlet, C., Faugère, J.C., Goyet, C., Renault, G.: Analysis of the algebraic side channel attack. JCEN 2(1). https://doi.org/10.1007/s13389-012-0028-0

23. Cassiers, G., Grégoire, B., Levi, I., Standaert, F.: Hardware private circuits: from trivial composition to full verification. IEEE Trans. Comput. 70(10) (2021). https://doi.org/10.1109/TC.2020.3022979

24. Cassiers, G., Standaert, F.X.: Provably secure hardware masking in the transition- and glitch-robust probing model: better safe than sorry. TCHES (2) (2021). https://doi.org/10.46586/tches.v2021.i2.136-158

25. Cassiers, G., Standaert, F.X.: Towards globally optimized masking: from low randomness to low noise rate. TCHES (2) (2019). https://doi.org/10.13154/tches.v2019.i2.162-198

26. Cassiers, G., Standaert, F.: Trivially and efficiently composing masked gadgets with probe isolating non-interference. TIFS 15 (2020). https://doi.org/10.1109/TIFS.2020.2971153

27. Chari, S., Jutla, C.S., Rao, J.R., Rohatgi, P.: Towards sound approaches to counteract power-analysis attacks. In: Wiener, M. (ed.) CRYPTO 1999. LNCS, vol. 1666, pp. 398–412. Springer, Heidelberg (1999). https://doi.org/10.1007/3-540-48405-1_26

28. Cho, J., et al.: Transciphering framework for approximate homomorphic encryption. In: Tibouchi, M., Wang, H. (eds.) ASIACRYPT 2021. LNCS, vol. 13092, pp. 640–669. Springer, Cham (2021). https://doi.org/10.1007/978-3-030-92078-4_22

29. Choudary, O., Kuhn, M.G.: Efficient template attacks. In: CARDIS (2013). https://doi.org/10.1007/978-3-319-08302-5_17

30. Coron, J.S., Giraud, C., Prouff, E., Renner, S., Rivain, M., Vadnala, P.K.: Conversion of security proofs from one leakage model to another: a new issue. In: COSADE 2012 (2012). https://doi.org/10.1007/978-3-642-29912-4_6

31. Daemen, J., Rijmen, V.: The wide trail design strategy. In: IMACC (2001). https://doi.org/10.1007/3-540-45325-3_20

32. Daemen, J., Rijmen, V.: The Design of Rijndael: AES - The Advanced Encryption Standard. Information Security and Cryptography. Springer, Heidelberg (2002). https://doi.org/10.1007/978-3-662-04722-4

33. de Chérisey, E., Guilley, S., Rioul, O., Piantanida, P.: Best information is most successful. TCHES (2) (2019). https://doi.org/10.13154/tches.v2019.i2.49-79
34. Dobraunig, C., Grassi, L., Guinet, A., Kuijsters, D.: CIMINION: symmetric encryption based on toffoli-gates over large finite fields. In: Canteaut, A., Standaert, F.-X. (eds.) EUROCRYPT 2021. LNCS, vol. 12697, pp. 3–34. Springer, Cham (2021). https://doi.org/10.1007/978-3-030-77886-6_1
35. Dobraunig, C., Grassi, L., Helminger, L., Rechberger, C., Schofnegger, M., Walch, R.: Pasta: a case for hybrid homomorphic encryption. Cryptology ePrint Archive, Report 2021/731 (2021), https://eprint.iacr.org/2021/731
36. Duc, A., Dziembowski, S., Faust, S.: Unifying leakage models: from probing attacks to noisy leakage. In: Nguyen, P.Q., Oswald, E. (eds.) EUROCRYPT 2014. LNCS, vol. 8441, pp. 423–440. Springer, Heidelberg (2014). https://doi.org/10.1007/978-3-642-55220-5_24
37. Duc, A., Faust, S., Standaert, F.X.: Making masking security proofs concrete - or how to evaluate the security of any leaking device. In: Oswald and Fischlin [74]. https://doi.org/10.1007/978-3-662-46800-5_16
38. Düll, M., et al.: High-speed curve25519 on 8-bit, 16-bit, and 32-bit microcontrollers. Des. Codes Cryptogr. **77**(2-3) (2015). https://doi.org/10.1007/s10623-015-0087-1
39. Durvaux, F., Standaert, F.-X.: From improved leakage detection to the detection of points of interests in leakage traces. In: Fischlin, M., Coron, J.-S. (eds.) EUROCRYPT 2016. LNCS, vol. 9665, pp. 240–262. Springer, Heidelberg (2016). https://doi.org/10.1007/978-3-662-49890-3_10
40. Dziembowski, S., Faust, S.: Leakage-resilient circuits without computational assumptions. In: Cramer, R. (ed.) TCC 2012. LNCS, vol. 7194, pp. 230–247. Springer, Heidelberg (2012). https://doi.org/10.1007/978-3-642-28914-9_13
41. Dziembowski, S., Faust, S., Skórski, M.: Optimal amplification of noisy leakages. In: Kushilevitz, E., Malkin, T. (eds.) TCC 2016. LNCS, vol. 9563, pp. 291–318. Springer, Heidelberg (2016). https://doi.org/10.1007/978-3-662-49099-0_11
42. EUROCRYPT 2013 (2013)
43. EUROCRYPT 2016 (2016)
44. Faust, S., Grosso, V., Pozo, S.M.D., Paglialonga, C., Standaert, F.X.: Composable masking schemes in the presence of physical defaults & the robust probing model. TCHES (3) (2018). https://doi.org/10.13154/tches.v2018.i3.89-120
45. Fumaroli, G., Martinelli, A., Prouff, E., Rivain, M.: Affine masking against higher-order side channel analysis. In: SAC 2010 (2011). https://doi.org/10.1007/978-3-642-19574-7_18
46. Goubin, L., Patarin, J.: DES and differential power analysis (the "duplication" method). In: CHES 1999 (1999). https://doi.org/10.1007/3-540-48059-5_15
47. Goudarzi, D., Rivain, M.: How fast can higher-order masking be in software? In: Coron, J.-S., Nielsen, J.B. (eds.) EUROCRYPT 2017. LNCS, vol. 10210, pp. 567–597. Springer, Cham (2017). https://doi.org/10.1007/978-3-319-56620-7_20
48. Grassi, L., Lüftenegger, R., Rechberger, C., Rotaru, D., Schofnegger, M.: On a generalization of substitution-permutation networks: the HADES design strategy. In: Canteaut, A., Ishai, Y. (eds.) EUROCRYPT 2020. LNCS, vol. 12106, pp. 674–704. Springer, Cham (2020). https://doi.org/10.1007/978-3-030-45724-2_23
49. Grégoire, B., Papagiannopoulos, K., Schwabe, P., Stoffelen, K.: Vectorizing higher-order masking. In: COSADE 2018 (2018). https://doi.org/10.1007/978-3-319-89641-0_2
50. Groß, H., Mangard, S., Korak, T.: An efficient side-channel protected AES implementation with arbitrary protection order. In: CT-RSA 2017 (2017). https://doi.org/10.1007/978-3-319-52153-4_6

51. Grosso, V., Standaert, F.X.: Masking proofs are tight and how to exploit it in security evaluations. In: Nielsen and Rijmen [71]. https://doi.org/10.1007/978-3-319-78375-8_13

52. Hamburg, M.: Fast and compact elliptic-curve cryptography. IACR Cryptol. ePrint Arch, p. 309 (2012). http://eprint.iacr.org/2012/309

53. Ishai, Y., Sahai, A., Wagner, D.: Private circuits: securing hardware against probing attacks. In: Boneh, D. (ed.) CRYPTO 2003. LNCS, vol. 2729, pp. 463–481. Springer, Heidelberg (2003). https://doi.org/10.1007/978-3-540-45146-4_27

54. Ito, A., Ueno, R., Homma, N.: On the success rate of side-channel attacks on masked implementations: information-theoretical bounds and their practical usage. In: CCS 2022 (2022). https://doi.org/10.1145/3548606.3560579

55. Jakobsen, T., Knudsen, L.R.: The interpolation attack on block ciphers. In: Biham, E. (ed.) FSE 1997. LNCS, vol. 1267, pp. 28–40. Springer, Heidelberg (1997). https://doi.org/10.1007/BFb0052332

56. Kloss, B.M.: Probability distributions on bicompact topological groups. Theory Prob. Appl. 4(3) (1959). https://doi.org/10.1007/s10623-015-0087-1

57. Knichel, D., Sasdrich, P., Moradi, A.: SILVER – statistical independence and leakage verification. In: Moriai, S., Wang, H. (eds.) ASIACRYPT 2020. LNCS, vol. 12491, pp. 787–816. Springer, Cham (2020). https://doi.org/10.1007/978-3-030-64837-4_26

58. Krachenfels, T., Ganji, F., Moradi, A., Tajik, S., Seifert, J.P.: Real-world snapshots vs. theory: questioning the t-probing security model. In: 2021 Symposium on Security and Privacy (2021). https://doi.org/10.1109/SP40001.2021.00029

59. Lipmaa, H., Rogaway, P., Wagner, D.: Ctr-mode encryption. In: First NIST Workshop on Modes of Operation, vol. 39. Citeseer. MD (2000)

60. Mangard, S.: Hardware countermeasures against DPA - a statistical analysis of their effectiveness. In: CT-RSA 2004 (2004). https://doi.org/10.1007/978-3-540-24660-2_18

61. Mangard, S., Popp, T., Gammel, B.M.: Side-channel leakage of masked CMOS gates. In: CT-RSA 2005 (2005). https://doi.org/10.1007/978-3-540-30574-3_24

62. Mangard, S., Pramstaller, N., Oswald, E.: Successfully attacking masked AES hardware implementations. In: CHES 2005 (2005). https://doi.org/10.1007/11545262_12

63. Masure, L., Cristiani, V., Lecomte, M., Standaert, F.X.: Don't learn what you already know: scheme-aware modeling for profiling side-channel analysis against masking. TCHES (1) (2023). https://doi.org/10.46586/tches.v2023.i1.32-59

64. Masure, L., Rioul, O., Standaert, F.: A nearly tight proof of Duc et al'.s conjectured security bound for masked implementations. In: Buhan and Schneider [21]. https://doi.org/10.1007/978-3-031-25319-5_4

65. Matsui, M.: Linear cryptanalysis method for DES cipher. In: Helleseth, T. (ed.) EUROCRYPT 1993. LNCS, vol. 765, pp. 386–397. Springer, Heidelberg (1994). https://doi.org/10.1007/3-540-48285-7_33

66. Moos, T.: Static power SCA of sub-100 nm CMOS ASICs. TCHES (3) (2019). https://doi.org/10.13154/tches.v2019.i3.202-232

67. Moos, T., Moradi, A.: Countermeasures against static power attacks. TCHES (3) (2021). https://doi.org/10.46586/tches.v2021.i3.780-805

68. Moos, T., Moradi, A., Richter, B.: Static power side-channel analysis of a threshold implementation prototype chip. In: DATE, pp. 1324–1329. IEEE (2017). https://doi.org/10.23919/DATE.2017.7927198

69. Moos, T., Moradi, A., Schneider, T., Standaert, F.X.: Glitch-resistant masking revisited. TCHES **2019**(2), 256–292 (2019). https://doi.org/10.13154/tches.v2019.i2.256-292
70. Moradi, A.: Side-channel leakage through static power - should we care about in practice? In: CHES 2014 (2014). https://doi.org/10.1007/978-3-662-44709-3_31
71. Nielsen, J.B., Rijmen, V. (eds.): EUROCRYPT 2018, Part II, vol. 10821 (2018)
72. Nikova, S., Rijmen, V., Schläffer, M.: Secure hardware implementation of nonlinear functions in the presence of glitches. J. Cryptol. **24**(2), 292–321 (2010). https://doi.org/10.1007/s00145-010-9085-7
73. Oren, Y., Renauld, M., Standaert, F.X., Wool, A.: Algebraic side-channel attacks beyond the hamming weight leakage model. In: CHES 2012 (2012). https://doi.org/10.1007/978-3-642-33027-8_9
74. Oswald, E., Fischlin, M. (eds.): EUROCRYPT 2015, Part I, vol. 9056 (2015)
75. Pozo, S.M.D., Standaert, F., Kamel, D., Moradi, A.: Side-channel attacks from static power: when should we care? In: DATE. ACM (2015)
76. Prouff, E., Rivain, M.: Masking against side-channel attacks: a formal security proof. In: EUROCRYPT 2013 [42]. https://doi.org/10.1007/978-3-642-38348-9_9
77. Renauld, M., Standaert, F.X., Veyrat-Charvillon, N.: Algebraic side-channel attacks on the AES: why time also matters in DPA. In: CHES 2009, pp. 97–111 (2009). https://doi.org/10.1007/978-3-642-04138-9_8
78. Rijmen, V., Daemen, J., Preneel, B., Bossalaers, A., De Win, E.: The cipher SHARK. In: FSE 1996 (1996). https://doi.org/10.1007/3-540-60865-6_47
79. Rivain, M., Prouff, E.: Provably secure higher-order masking of AES. In: CHES 2010 (2010). https://doi.org/10.1007/978-3-642-15031-9_28
80. dos Santos, L.C., Gérard, F., Großschädl, J., Spignoli, L.: Rivain-prouff on steroids: faster and stronger masking of the AES. In: Buhan and Schneider [21]. https://doi.org/10.1007/978-3-031-25319-5_7
81. Schneider, T., Moradi, A.: Leakage assessment methodology. J. Cryptogr. Eng. **6**(2), 85–99 (2016). https://doi.org/10.1007/s13389-016-0120-y
82. Standaert, F.: How (not) to use welch's t-test in side-channel security evaluations. In: CARDIS (2018). https://doi.org/10.1007/978-3-030-15462-2_5
83. Standaert, F.X., Archambeau, C.: Using subspace-based template attacks to compare and combine power and electromagnetic information leakages. In: CHES 2008 (2008). https://doi.org/10.1007/978-3-540-85053-3_26
84. Standaert, F.-X., Malkin, T.G., Yung, M.: A unified framework for the analysis of side-channel key recovery attacks. In: Joux, A. (ed.) EUROCRYPT 2009. LNCS, vol. 5479, pp. 443–461. Springer, Heidelberg (2009). https://doi.org/10.1007/978-3-642-01001-9_26
85. Standaert, F.-X., et al.: The world is not enough: another look on second-order DPA. In: Abe, M. (ed.) ASIACRYPT 2010. LNCS, vol. 6477, pp. 112–129. Springer, Heidelberg (2010). https://doi.org/10.1007/978-3-642-17373-8_7
86. Veyrat-Charvillon, N., Gérard, B., Standaert, F.-X.: Soft analytical side-channel attacks. In: Sarkar, P., Iwata, T. (eds.) ASIACRYPT 2014. LNCS, vol. 8873, pp. 282–296. Springer, Heidelberg (2014). https://doi.org/10.1007/978-3-662-45611-8_15
87. Whitnall, C., Oswald, E.: A critical analysis of ISO 17825 ('testing methods for the mitigation of non-invasive attack classes against cryptographic modules'). In: Galbraith, S.D., Moriai, S. (eds.) ASIACRYPT 2019. LNCS, vol. 11923, pp. 256–284. Springer, Cham (2019). https://doi.org/10.1007/978-3-030-34618-8_9

One-Hot Conversion: Towards Faster Table-Based A2B Conversion

Jan-Pieter D'Anvers[✉] [ID]

imec-COSIC KU Leuven, Kasteelpark Arenberg 10 - bus 2452, 3001 Leuven, Belgium
janpieter.danvers@esat.kuleuven.be

Abstract. Arithmetic to Boolean masking (A2B) conversion is a crucial technique in the masking of lattice-based post-quantum cryptography. It is also a crucial part of building a masked comparison which is one of the hardest to mask building blocks for active secure lattice-based encryption. We first present a new method, called one-hot conversion, to efficiently convert from higher-order arithmetic masking to Boolean masking using a variant of the higher-order table-based conversion of Coron et al. Secondly, we specialize our method to perform arithmetic to 1-bit Boolean functions. Our one-hot function can be applied to masking lattice-based encryption building blocks such as masked comparison or to determine the most significant bit of an arithmetically masked variable. In our benchmarks on a Cortex M4 processor, a speedup of 15 times is achieved over state-of-the-art table-based A2B conversions, bringing table-based A2B conversions within the performance range of the Boolean circuit-based A2B conversions.

Keywords: Masking · A2B conversion · Side-Channel Protection · Post-Quantum Cryptography · Lattice-based Cryptography

1 Introduction

A majority of public key cryptographic algorithms are based on factoring or the discrete logarithm problem. These algorithms are no longer secure in the presence of a large-scale quantum computer. The field of Post-Quantum Cryptography (PQC) researches alternative cryptographic algorithms that remain secure in the presence of quantum computers. To replace the soon-to-be-insecure public-key standards, the National Institute of Standards and Technology (NIST) launched a standardization effort in 2016 [30]. In July 2022, NIST announced three lattice-based schemes to be standardized: Kyber [37], Dilithium [28] and Falcon [32].

One of the challenges in replacing the current standards with post-quantum standards is protecting their implementations against side-channel attacks. Side-channel attacks are attacks on a cryptographic implementation that use unwanted effects of computation leaking information, such as power usage, electromagnetic radiation and timing. Several side-channel attacks on lattice-based cryptographic implementations have been demonstrated, including timing attacks [19,25,38] or power consumption and electromagnetic radiation

© International Association for Cryptologic Research 2023
C. Hazay and M. Stam (Eds.): EUROCRYPT 2023, LNCS 14007, pp. 628–657, 2023.
https://doi.org/10.1007/978-3-031-30634-1_21

attacks [2,3,33,34,39,42,43]. These works illustrate the importance of protection mechanisms against side-channel attacks, and in its latest report NIST has emphasized the importance of these protection mechanisms [1], including them as a major evaluation criterion in the standardization process.

Masking is a popular tool to protect against side-channel attacks. The idea of masking is to split a sensitive variable into two or more shares, in such a way that an adversary that is able to see all but one share still can not infer any information about the sensitive value. The ideas behind masking were introduced by Chari et al. [9] and later extended by Barthe et al. [5] to include the notions of Non-Inference (NI) and Strong Non-Inference (SNI), which allow easier composition of building blocks.

To give an example of masking, a sensitive value x can be split into $x^{(1)}$ and $x^{(2)}$ so that $x = x^{(1)} \odot x^{(2)}$ where $\odot$ is a mathematical operation that depends on the type of masking. For Boolean masking $\odot$ is the XOR operation $\oplus$, while arithmetic masking chooses $\odot$ to be addition modulo a predefined integer q. In first-order masking, the sensitive value is split into 2 shares (i.e., an adversary can probe at most 1 share without compromised security), while higher-order masking splits the sensitive variable into more shares. One observation is that some efficient techniques have been developed specifically for first-order masking, which do not scale to higher masking orders.

Several masked implementations of lattice-based cryptographic schemes have been presented. For signature schemes, a masked implementation of the GLP signature scheme was presented by Barthe [6], followed by a Dilithium implementation by Migliore et al. [29]. Passively secure lattice-based encryption was first masked in [35], followed by an active secure scheme by Oder et al. [31] for first-order and Bache et al. [4] for higher-order. Van Beirendonck et al. [40] provided a first-order masked implementation of the NIST PQC finalist Saber [18], and Coron et al. [16], and later Kundu et al. [27] discussed a higher-order implementation. Kyber was implemented at arbitrary order by Bos et al. [8] and for first-order by Heinz et al. [26]. Fritzmann et al. [22] looked at making masked implementations of Saber and Kyber more effective using instruction set extensions. A masked NTRU implementation was proposed by Coron et al. [12].

A2B Conversion. One recurring property of most masked implementations of lattice-based cryptography is that both Boolean masking and arithmetic masking are used. To integrate both masking domains, arithmetic to Boolean (A2B) and Boolean to arithmetic (B2A) conversions are needed. In this paper, we are specifically interested in arithmetic to Boolean conversion. The first secure A2B conversion was proposed by Goubin [24], which was later extended by Coron et al. [10]. Both methods are focused on first-order and are based on writing the conversion as a Boolean circuit and implementing this Boolean circuit in a secure fashion.

A different approach to first-order A2B conversion is table-based conversion, where the Boolean result is stored in a table that is manipulated based on the arithmetic input. Coron and Tchulkine [14] were the first to propose such a conversion. Debraize [21] discovered a flaw in their algorithm and improved the overall efficiency of the Coron and Tchulkine approach. Later, Van Beirendonck et al. [41] discovered a security problem in one of the conversions of Debraize, and proposed two new A2B conversions to circumvent this problem.

Higher-order conversions were proposed in [10,11] for arithmetic masking modulo a power-of-two $q = 2^k$. These techniques were extended for arbitrary modulus by Barthe et al [6], which was later refined in [36]. Similar to the first A2B conversion algorithm by Goubin [24], the above techniques rely on a Boolean circuit methodology to perform the conversion.

Coron et al. [16] adapted the first-order table-based approach for higher orders both for A2B and B2A conversion. For large modulus q, the authors split the inputs into different chunks which are converted individually using A2B conversion, and the carries between the chunks are taken into account using an additional arithmetic to arithmetic (A2A with different moduli) conversion. While the B2A conversions in this work are generally efficient, the overall A2B conversions are only efficient in specific applications.

The increased importance of these conversions due to the rise of lattice-based cryptography is emphasized by the CHES 2021 Test of Time Award, which was awarded to Goubin [24] for introducing the first A2B and B2A conversion techniques.

Masked Comparison. One important application of A2B conversions is masked comparison, which is a vital building block in actively secure implementations of lattice-based cryptography. The goal of such a comparison is to validate an input ciphertext by comparing it with a recomputed ciphertext as part of the Fujisaki-Okamoto transformation [23].

For first-order masking, a hash-based approach was proposed by Oder et al. [31]. The main idea of this approach is to check if a sensitive array is zero by hashing both shares separately and checking the equality of the hash outputs. For schemes that perform ciphertext compression, this comparison additionally needs an arithmetic to arithmetic (A2A) conversion (i.e., a conversion between two arithmetic masking domains with different modulus). Such an A2A conversion can be implemented as a modified A2B conversion, where a table-based conversion is most efficient for first-order. A problem in the security of the hash-based method of [31] was discovered and fixed by Bhasin et al. [7].

Higher-order masked comparisons have to rely on different techniques, as the hash-based method is limited to two shares. The state-of-the-art conversion techniques to perform higher-order masked comparison first perform A2B conversion and then do the comparison in the Boolean domain. The approaches differ in pre- and postprocessing of the A2B conversion. Barthe et al. [6] perform a masked comparison by a simple approach: A2B conversion followed by a masked bitwise comparison. Bache et al. [4] introduced a method based on a random sum to reduce the number of coefficients. This method was broken by Bhasin et al. [7], who introduced a variant random sum compression that is secure but only applicable for cryptographic schemes without compression and with prime order moduli.

D'Anvers et al. [17] adapted the random sum method as a postprocessing method to reduce the cost of the final Boolean circuit. Bos et al. [8] looked at the preprocessing stage and proposed to decompress the input ciphertext instead of compressing the masked recomputed ciphertext. This approach was later adapted by Coron et al. [15] by combining the decompression idea, the random sum method, and some extra masked gadget into a new comparison. These methods were compared and improved in a later work by D'Anvers et al. [20], which we refer to to get an overview of higher-order masked comparison algorithms.

1.1 Our Contributions

In this paper, we introduce a new strategy to perform arithmetic to Boolean conversion. Although it is not exactly table-based, our method falls in the table-based category and is indebted to the higher-order table-based A2B conversions of [16], and more specifically to the register-based optimized arithmetic to 1-bit Boolean conversion. We start with introducing an arithmetic to Boolean conversion, and later introduce optimizations to more efficiently perform specific masked operations used in lattice-based cryptography.

Our method works on a register (which can be seen as a table with 1-bit entries). In contrast to previous table-based methods, where the table is used to encode the output values, our register is used as a one-hot encoding of the input values, with which we mean that a value x is represented with a register where the xþ bit is 1 and all others are 0. The first advantage of a one-hot encoding is that the register/table size does not grow with the output length, which would be the case in a table-based approach where all possible outputs are stored in the table. Secondly, the input has to be processed only once, and the result can be used to determine both a carry value (as a result of the arithmetic masking) and a Boolean masked output value. Thirdly, we introduce an efficient method to propagate carries by using the properties of the one-hot encoding. An intuitive introduction to these ideas is given in Sect. 3.

In Sect. 4 we formalize our arithmetic to Boolean conversion, followed by a generalization of our method and a security proof. In Sect. 5 we introduce an arithmetic to 1-bit Boolean function calculation. This is a generalization of the aforementioned register-based optimized arithmetic to 1-bit Boolean conversion of [16] in two ways: we allow an arbitrarily large arithmetic masking modulus (instead of 5 or 6 bits in previous works) and we allow multiple masked coefficients to be the input of the function. One of the use-cases of this algorithm is masked comparison, where multiple masked coefficients need to be compared with publicly known reference values and only one bit is returned that indicates whether all coefficients match their reference value(s).

Section 6 details how to obtain a more efficient implementation and how to achieve parallelism in our inherently sequential design at low cost. The resulting A2B implementation is then compared to the state-of-the-art algorithms in Sect. 7. Our measurements show a speedup of approximately a factor of 15 compared to the state-of-the-art table-based A2B comparisons. This brings higher-order table-based conversion to the performance range of Boolean circuit-based A2B conversions, in some cases outperforming the latter with a cycle count reduction of 27%. The implementations of our algorithms for Cortex M4 are made available at https://github.com/KULeuven-COSIC/One-hot-masking.

2 Preliminaries

2.1 Notation

Lists and matrices are denoted in bold text. These are indexed using a subscript, where $\mathbf{X}_i$ indicates the iþ element of the list $\mathbf{X}$ and where $\mathbf{X}_{i,j}$ indicates the element on the iþ row and jþ column of a matrix $\mathbf{X}$. We write $|\mathbf{X}|$ to denote the number of coefficients in the list $\mathbf{X}$. We denote with $\lfloor x \rfloor$ a flooring of a number x to the nearest integer less or equal to x, with $\lceil x \rceil$ ceiling x to the nearest integer greater or equal to x, and with $\lfloor x \rceil$ rounding to the nearest integer with ties rounded upwards. These operations are extended coefficient-wise to lists.

Positive integers are represented in unsigned binary representation unless stated otherwise, with the most significant bit (MSB) at the leftmost position and the least significant bit (LSB) at the rightmost position. $x[i]$ indicates the iþ bit of the binary representation of x starting from the least significant bit and $|R|$ indicates the number of bits in the representation of R.

The concatenation operator $x_1 \| x_0$ concatenates the bitstrings x_1 and x_0. This representation is extended for non-power-of-two p-ary numbers y_1, y_2 (i.e., numbers represented with an integer value between 0 and $p - 1$) as $y = y_1 \| y_0$. More precisely, the value of y equals $y_1 \cdot p + y_0$. In its most generalized sense we can concatenate numbers with different representations: for a p_2-ary number y_2, a p_1-ary number y_1 and a p_0-ary number y_0, we write $y = y_2 \| y_1 \| y_0$ to signify $y = y_2 \cdot (p_0 \cdot p_1) + y_1 \cdot p_0 + y_0$.

We denote with:

$$\underbrace{x_1}_{b_1} \| \underbrace{x_0}_{b_0} \leftarrow x, \tag{1}$$

splitting the binary representation of x in parts x_1 with bitsize b_1 and x_0 with bitsize b_0 so that $x = x_1 \| x_0$. This is generalized for p-ary numbers as:

$$\underbrace{x_1}_{p_1\text{-ary}} \| \underbrace{x_0}_{p_0\text{-ary}} \leftarrow x, \tag{2}$$

where x is split into a p_0-ary symbol x_0 and a p_1-ary symbol x_1 so that $x = x_1 \| x_0$. Note that this is a unique way of splitting a number x.

We denote with $x \ll i$ a shift of the binary representation of x to the left with i positions (which equals to $x \cdot 2^i$), and with $x \gg i$ a shift to the right with i positions (which equals $\lfloor x/2^i \rfloor$). A circular shift to the left with i positions is written as $x \overset{|R|}{\lll} i$, with $|R|$ the number of bits involved in the shift. More specifically, $x \overset{|R|}{\lll} i = (x \ll i) \| (x \gg (|R| - i))$.

Sampling a random value x from a distribution χ is denoted $x \leftarrow \chi$. Furthermore, $\mathcal{U}(S)$ denotes the uniform distribution over a set S.

2.2 Masking

In Boolean masking, a sensitive variable x is split into S shares $x^{[0]}$ to $x^{[S-1]}$, so that the XOR of the shares results in the original variable x (i.e., $x = \oplus_{i=0}^{S-1} x^{[i]}$). We write $x^{[i]}$ to denote the value of the iþ share of a masked variable x, and $x^{[\cdot]}$ to denote the value of x while explicitly making clear that x is shared. As such, the value $x^{[\cdot]}$ will not be physically represented in a secure implementation and is only implicitly present by combining the different shares.

One can perform Boolean operations on a Boolean masked variable: $z^{[\cdot]} = x^{[\cdot]} \oplus y^{[\cdot]}$ is calculated by an XOR on the corresponding shares as $z^{[i]} = x^{[i]} \oplus y^{[i]}$. An AND with an unmasked variable $z^{[\cdot]} = x^{[\cdot]}$ & m is calculated by applying m to each share individually $z^{[i]} = x^{[i]}$ & m. Similarly, shifts, rotations and concatenations on a Boolean masked variable are applied to each share individually.

Arithmetic masking splits a sensitive variable x in S shares $x^{(0)}$ to $x^{(S-1)}$ so that the sum of the shares modulo a given integer q equals the sensitive value ($x^{(\cdot)} = x^{(0)} + x^{(1)} \bmod q$). As before we denote with $x^{(i)}$ the iþ share of a masked variable, and with $x^{(\cdot)}$ the value of x while stressing that this value is not physically present in the implementation.

Arithmetic masking allows easy computation of arithmetic operations, where a sum $z^{(\cdot)} = x^{(\cdot)} + y$ can be calculated by summing y to the zeroþ share of $x^{(\cdot)}$ (i.e., $z^{(0)} = x^{(0)} + y$ and $z^{(i)} = x^{(i)}$ for other shares). Multiplication with an unmasked constant is performed on each share individually (i.e., $z^{(\cdot)} = c \cdot x^{(\cdot)}$ can be calculated as $z^{(i)} = c \cdot x^{(i)}$). Concatenation, flooring and rounding are calculated on each share individually. It is important to note that for arithmetic masking $\lfloor x^{(\cdot)} \rfloor$ is not necessarily equal to $\lfloor x \rfloor$ as the former is calculated on each share individually, while the latter is calculated on the unmasked variable. This is also true for rounding and concatenation.

3 Intuitive Introduction to One-Hot Conversion

The goal of our algorithm is to perform arithmetic to Boolean conversion. More specifically, the input is an arithmetically masked number $D^{(\cdot)}$, with masking modulus q. The output is a Boolean masked number $B^{[\cdot]}$ so that $B^{[\cdot]} = D^{(\cdot)}$. For the sake of simplicity, we will assume that the arithmetic masking modulus is a power of two unless stated otherwise. It is trivial to extend our method for different masking moduli and we will later show how to extend the method to non-power-of-two moduli.

We will first give an intuitive explanation of the algorithm before explaining the details in Sect. 4. The algorithm starts by preparing a Boolean masked register $R^{[\cdot]}$ with value 1, i.e., with a one in the zeroþ bit and zeros in all other bits. The algorithm then iteratively processes parts of $D^{(\cdot)}$, modifying the register $R^{[\cdot]}$ in two steps: in the first step, the register is converted to a one-hot encoding of the input coefficient $\mathbf{D}_i^{(\cdot)}$ (i.e., the value of $\mathbf{D}_i^{(\cdot)}$ is encoded by setting the register bit at position $\mathbf{D}_i^{(\cdot)}$ to 1, and all other bits to 0) and in the second step, the relevant information is extracted from the register in a sharewise fashion.

A Simple Example: $q = |R|$. First, imagine that the modulus q equals the number of bits in the register $|R|$. The algorithm first rotates the register with $\sum_k D^{(k)}$ positions using a variant of the secure rotation algorithm described in [16]. This corresponds in practice to a rotation of the register with $\sum_k D^{(k)} \bmod |R| = \sum_k D^{(k)} \bmod q = D^{(\cdot)}$ positions, where the $\bmod |R|$ operation is present due to the limited size of the register and the resulting wraparound. The output of this step can be seen as a one-hot encoding of the input $D^{(\cdot)}$ (i.e., the 1 in the register can be found on the $D^{(\cdot)}\text{þ}$ position).

After this operation we effectively associated each position in the register with one value of $D^{(\cdot)}$ (i.e., if the 1 is in the $t\text{þ}$ position, then $D^{(\cdot)} = t$ and vice versa). We then process the shares of the register individually to obtain the required result. For each share, we take the bit at position p (i.e., $D^{(i)}[t]$) and multiply it with t. The results are all XOR'ed together into a share of the output. The output is thus calculated as:

$$B^{[i]} = \bigoplus_{t=0}^{|R|-1} t \cdot R^{[i]}[t]. \tag{3}$$

Now remembering that $R^{[\cdot]}[t] = 1$ at position $t = D^{(\cdot)}$, but $R^{[\cdot]}[u] = 0$ at all other positions $u \neq t$, we can see that:

$$B^{[\cdot]} = \bigoplus_{i=0}^{S-1} B^{[i]} \tag{4}$$

$$= \bigoplus_{i=0}^{S-1} \left(\bigoplus_{t=0}^{|R|-1} t \cdot R^{[i]}[t] \right) = \bigoplus_{t=0}^{|R|-1} t \cdot \left(\bigoplus_{i=0}^{S-1} R^{[i]}[t] \right) \tag{5}$$

$$= \bigoplus_{t=0}^{|R|-1} t \cdot R^{[\cdot]}[t] \tag{6}$$

$$= D^{(\cdot)}. \tag{7}$$

Thus confirming that the output is indeed $B^{[\cdot]} = D^{(\cdot)}$ as required. In terms of masking security, the first operation can be instantiated as a variant of the secure rotation of [16], while the second operation is performed on each share separately and is thus inherently secure in the masking framework.

This simple example is depicted in Fig. 1 where in the first step the register is rotated with $\sum_k D^{(k)} \bmod |R| = 3$ positions, and in the second step the output is calculated following Eq. 3. Note that it is possible to implement the second operation as given in Eq. 3 more efficiently as will be discussed in Sect. 6.

More Complicated: $q > |R|$ The problem with the simple approach is that it is typically not efficient to allow an arbitrarily large register size. Therefore, we will adapt the previous algorithm to allow q to be bigger than the register size. We will do this by chopping the input coefficients $D^{(\cdot)}$ with bitlength $\log_2(q)$ in several smaller chunks with bitlength $\log_2(p)$, with $p < |R| < q$. These smaller

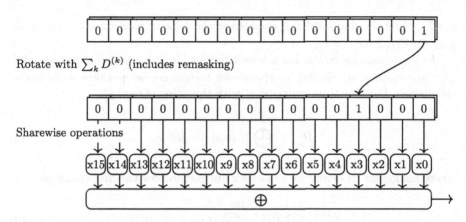

Fig. 1. Overview of the three steps in InnerLoop for $D^{(\cdot)} = 3$ and $q = 16$. In the first step the register is rotated with $D^{(\cdot)} = 3$ positions using the SecureRotate algorithm. In the second step, all elements of the register are multiplied with their position and the results are XOR'ed together to produce the output.

chunks are then processed iteratively, starting with the least significant chunk $D_0^{(\cdot)}$. Note that these chunks are not independent as the arithmetic masking entails that there are carries that need to be propagated from the less significant chunks to the more significant chunks. We will have to take care of these carries in our method.

First we choose the smaller power-of-two modulus p so that $p \cdot S < |R|$, with S the number of shares, and split the coefficients of $D^{(\cdot)}$ in chunks $\hat{D}_j^{(\cdot)}$ of $\log_2(p)$ bits. These chunks are then processed iteratively, starting with the least significant chunk. A depiction of the processing of the first chunk is given in Fig. 2.

To process a chunk $\hat{D}_j^{(\cdot)}$ we perform the following three operations: first, we rotate the register, then we compute the relevant output bits and finally we prepare the carry for the next iteration.

In the first operation, the register is rotated with $\sum_k \hat{D}_j^{(k)}$ positions. Note that in contrast to the previous method $\sum_k \hat{D}_j^{(k)} \bmod |R| \neq \hat{D}_j^{(\cdot)}$, more specifically, the modulo operation is no longer relevant and can be ignored as long as we choose p to be small enough to avoid any possible wrap-around of the 1 in the register.

The position of the one in the register can now be described in function of two components: the value of the chunk, $\hat{D}_j^{(\cdot)} = \sum_k \hat{D}_j^{(k)} \bmod p$, and the carry $c_j = \lfloor \sum_k \hat{D}_j^{(k)} / p \rfloor$ that needs to be propagated to the next chunk. These two components are represented in the position as follows: the register can be subdivided into multiple 'carry parts' of $\log_2(p)$ bits as given in Fig. 2 with the red lines. The carry is then encoded by the part containing the 1 (in Fig. 2,

$c = 2$), while the chunk value is encoded as the relative position of the one in its part (in Fig. 2, $\hat{D}_j^{(\cdot)} = 1$).

In the second operation, the relevant output bits corresponding to the chunk $\hat{D}_j^{(\cdot)}$ are calculated. Similar to the above technique, we perform a sharewise calculation, but this time multiplying with the value $(t \bmod p)$:

$$\hat{B}_j^{[i]} = \bigoplus_{t=0}^{|R|-1} (t \bmod p) \cdot R^{[i]}[t], \tag{8}$$

where analogous to before we can check our method for the first chunk as:

$$\hat{B}_0^{[\cdot]} = \bigoplus_{i=0}^{S-1} \hat{B}_0^{[i]} = \bigoplus_{t=0}^{|R|-1} (t \bmod p) \cdot R^{[\cdot]}[t] \tag{9}$$

$$= \hat{D}_0^{(\cdot)} \bmod p, \tag{10}$$

which means that the first $\log_2(p)$ bits are converted correctly. However, for subsequent iterations, we will have to take into account the carry c_j that needs to be propagated from chunk j to chunk $j+1$. This is done in the third operation.

The third operation propagates the carry and is again performed on each share separately. At the end of the third operation, the register contains a one-hot encoding of the carry c_j that needs to be propagated. This register is then used as the starting register in the next rotation. This means that the rotation already has an initial rotation with c_j, before the rotation with $\sum_k \hat{D}_{j+1}^{(k)}$ is applied. The total rotation is then $c_j + \sum_k \hat{D}_{j+1}^{(k)}$, thus effectively taking the carry into account.

The method to obtain the one-hot encoding of the carry can be best understood using Fig. 2. For each share of the register, we xor together all bits within the same carry bin c, and place it at position c in the register. Or more specifically, for each possible carry value c and each share k we calculate:

$$R^{[k]}[c] = \bigoplus_{m=0}^{p-1} R_{tmp}^{[k]}[c \cdot p + m] \tag{11}$$

The last iteration is slightly different, as the last chunk to be processed does not need to take into account further propagation of the carries. This case can thus be performed analogous to the simple example above (see Fig. 1) and can use any bitsize $\log_2(p_L)$ as long as $p_L \leq |R|$ (assuming the register size is also a power of two).

4   Arithmetic to Boolean Conversion

In this section, we will go into detail on the arithmetic to Boolean conversion technique, as well as generalize the technique and formulate a security proof.

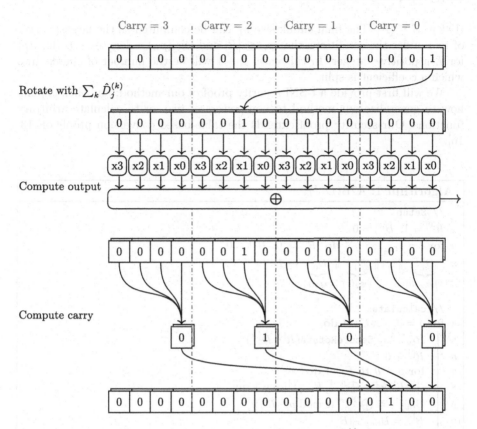

Fig. 2. Overview of an iteration of the A2B conversion for $\hat{D}_j^{(\cdot)} = 1$, with modulus $p = 4$, a carry value $c = \lfloor \sum_k \hat{D}_j^{(k)}/p \rfloor = 2$ and $S = 4$ shares. Note that all registers are masked during execution and that the values depicted are the corresponding unmasked values which should never be revealed during the computation. In the first step the register is rotated with $\sum_k \hat{D}_j^{(k)} = 9$ positions. In the second step the partial output is computed as in Fig. 1. In the third step the carry is propagated by XORing the values per carry and putting them in the relevant position of the output register. The latter step already gives an initial rotation of the register with 2, which is equal to the carry value and as such effectively propagates the carry to the next block.

Algorithm 1 gives a generalized algorithm to perform A2B conversion using the secure rotation method, which is given in Algorithm 2. Remember that operations on $R^{[\cdot]}$ are performed sharewise. A graphical overview of one iteration of the loop is given in Fig. 2, while the last iteration only performs the operations in Fig. 1.

For the parameter setting, we need to choose a register size $|R|$, which should be an integer of size at least S^2, with S the number of shares. For software implementations, one would typically choose $|R|$ to be the bit width of the processor. From $|R|$, we can derive the chunk modulus p as the largest power of two such that $p \cdot S \leq |R|$. The final chunk size p_L can be computed as the largest power of two under the conditions that $p_L \leq |R|$ and $\log_2(p_L) = \log_2(q) - L \cdot \log_2(p)$ for L a positive integer. In this case, $L + 1$ will be the number of chunks into which a coefficient is split.

We will first provide a t-SNI security proof of our method, and then explain how to generalize our method to non-powers of two, or to calculate arbitrary functions. Our security proof extends the table-based conversion proofs of [13, 16].

Algorithm 1: A2B($D^{(\cdot)}$)

    // Setup

1 $R^{[0]} = 1$; $B^{[0]} = 0$

2 for $i = 1, \ldots, S - 1$ do $R^{[i]} = 0$; $B^{[i]} = 0$

3 $\underbrace{\hat{D}_L^{(\cdot)}}_{<\log_2 |R|} \| \cdots \| \underbrace{\hat{D}_1^{(\cdot)}}_{\log_2(p)} \| \underbrace{\hat{D}_0^{(\cdot)}}_{\log_2(p)} \leftarrow D^{(\cdot)}$

    // calculate

4 for $j = 0, \ldots, L - 1$ do

5      $R_{tmp}{}^{[\cdot]} = \texttt{SecureRotate}(R^{[\cdot]}, \hat{D}_j^{(\cdot)})$

6      $R^{[\cdot]} = 0$

7   for $c = 0$ to $S - 1$ do

8          $R^{[\cdot]}[c] = \bigoplus_{m=0}^{p-1} R_{tmp}{}^{[\cdot]}[c \cdot p + m]$

9      $B_{tmp}{}^{[\cdot]} = \bigoplus_{t=0}^{|R|-1} (t \bmod p) \cdot R^{[\cdot]}[t]$

10    $B^{[\cdot]} = B_{tmp}{}^{[\cdot]} \| B^{[\cdot]}$

11 $R_{tmp}{}^{[\cdot]} = \texttt{SecureRotate}(R^{[\cdot]}, \hat{D}_L^{(\cdot)})$

12 $B_{tmp}{}^{[\cdot]} = \bigoplus_{t=0}^{|R|-1} t \cdot R^{[\cdot]}[t]$

13 $B^{[\cdot]} = B_{tmp}{}^{[\cdot]} \| B^{[\cdot]}$

14 return $B^{[\cdot]}$

Theorem 1 ($(S-1)$-SNI of Algorithm 1). *For any set of $t_c < S$ intermediate variables and for any subset $O \in [1, n]$ where $t_c + |O| < S$, we can perfectly simulate the output variables $R^{[O]}$ and the t_c intermediate values using the input values $D^{(i)}$ for each $i \in I$, with $|I| \leq t_c$.*

Proof. Within this proof we will refer to line x of Algorithm 1 with lx, and to line x of Algorithm 2 with l$_r$x. Before we delve into the details we choose which input coefficients will be used to simulate the intermediate values. All operations described in Algorithm 1 are performed sharewise, and so at most one share of the registers $R^{[\cdot]}$ and $R_{tmp}{}^{[\cdot]}$ is involved; and at most one share of $D^{(\cdot)}$ and $\hat{D}_j^{(\cdot)}$ is involved. For each probe during these lines, we will add the share number sh_R of the involved share of $R^{[\cdot]}$ or $R_{tmp}{}^{[\cdot]}$ (if applicable) to the set SHR; and similarly add the share number sh_D to the set SHD, if a share of $D^{(\cdot)}$ or $\hat{D}_j^{(\cdot)}$

Algorithm 2: SecureRotate($R^{[\cdot]}, \hat{D}^{(\cdot)}$)

// Rotate + remask

1 **for** $sh_D = 0$ **to** $S-1$ **do**

2      $R^{[0]} = R^{[0]} \overset{|R|}{\lll} \hat{D}^{(sh_D)}$

3   **for** $sh_R = 1$ **to** $S-1$ **do**

4          $R^{[sh_R]} = R^{[sh_R]} \overset{|R|}{\lll} \hat{D}^{(sh_D)}$

5          $U \leftarrow \mathcal{U}(2^{|R|})$

6          $R^{[sh_R]} = R^{[sh_R]} \oplus U$

7          $R^{[0]} = R^{[0]} \oplus U$

---

is involved. For the intermediate values in the rotation (Algorithm 2) we make the sets as described in Table 1.

Table 1. List of variables and their simulatability.

Variable:	Action: add $\cdots$	Simulated by:
$l_r 2/l_r 4$: $\hat{D}^{(sh_D)}$	sh_D to SHD	Corresponding bits of: $D^{(sh_D)}$
$l_r 2$: $R^{[0]}$	sh_D to SHD; 0 to SHR	$R_{in}^{(0)} \overset{q \cdot C}{\lll} \hat{D}^{(sh_D)}$
$l_r 4$: $R^{[sh_R]}$	sh_D to SHD; sh_R to SHR	$R_{in}^{(sh_R)} \overset{q \cdot C}{\lll} \hat{D}^{(sh_D)}$
$l_r 5$: U_{sh_D, sh_R}	sh_D to SHD; sh_R to SHR	U_{sh_D, sh_R}
$l_r 6$: $R^{[sh_R]}$	sh_D to SHD; sh_R to SHR	$(R_{in}^{(sh_R)} \overset{q \cdot C}{\lll} \hat{D}^{(sh_D)}) \oplus U_{sh_D, sh_R}$
$l_r 7$: $R^{[0]}$	sh_D to SHD; 0 to SHR	$(R_{in}^{(0)} \overset{q \cdot C}{\lll} \hat{D}^{(sh_D)}) \oplus_{k=1}^{sh_R} U_{sh_R, k}$

After building the sets SHD and SHR we know that $|SHD| \leq t_c$ and $|SHR| \leq t_c$, as each intermediate probe adds at most one item to each set. We then choose the input set to simulate all probed values as $D^{(sh_D)}$ for each share $sh_D \in SHD$. The set SHD then acts as the input set I and as such we have the asked condition $|I| \leq t_c$. Now rests to show that we can perfectly simulate all probed values.

The general overview of our proof will proceed as follows: first, we will argue that $R^{[\cdot]}$ and all other variables are simulatable during the setup of the algorithm, then we will argue that all asked intermediate values in the subblocks are simulatable if the input $R^{[\cdot]}$ is simulatable, and finally, we will show that $R^{[\cdot]}$ at the output of the block is simulatable if $R^{[\cdot]}$ at the input of the block (further denoted $R_{in}^{(\cdot)}$) is simulatable.

Simulatability of Variables During the Setup of the Algorithm (l1 to l3): This first step is easy, as $R^{[\cdot]}$ is deterministic and can thus be easily simulated by the adversary. The probed $\hat{D}_{i,j}^{(sh_D)}$ values can be simulated as $sh_D \in SHD$ due to our construction of SHD.

Simulatability of Variables During SecureRotate: This part will perform induction on the outer loop sh_D in SecureRotate. We will show that if we can simulate the values at the start of one loop iteration, we can also simulate the output variables of that loop iteration and all probed variables.

If $\mathbf{sh_D} \notin \mathbf{SHD}$, then the adversary has no information on the U_{sh_D,sh_R} and as such the output will look uniformly random, thus rendering $R^{[\cdot]}$ simulatable at the end of the iteration (i.e., it can be simulated by drawing from a uniformly random distribution $\mathcal{U}(\{0,1\}^{|R|})$).

If $\mathbf{sh_D} \in \mathbf{SHD}$, then we can simulate any probed intermediate variable as given in Table 1, where $R_{in}^{[\cdot]}$ is the value at the start of that outer loop iteration. For the latter two variables in the table, if the corresponding U_{sh_D,sh_R} is not probed we can replace it with a uniformly random value.

We have shown that if we can simulate the intermediate values at the start of the first loop iteration, then we can also simulate the intermediate values in the following loop iterations and therefore also at the end of the SecureRotate operation.

Simulatability of Variables After SecureRotate (l6–l10 and l12–13): Next we will show that if the register $R_{tmp}^{[\cdot]}$ is simulatable at the end of the SecureRotate then all variables at l6–l10 and l12–13 are simulatable. Note that the operations on these lines only work on one share at a time and are perfectly deterministic if the input $R_{tmp}^{[\cdot]}$ is known. As such, if $R_{tmp}^{[\cdot]}$ can be simulated, then any intermediate variable in these lines can be simulated.

To conclude, we have shown that $R^{[\cdot]}$ is simulatable at the start of the algorithm, that it is simulatable at the end of each block if it is simulatable at the start, and that all probed intermediate values can be simulated if $R^{[\cdot]}$ is simulatable at the start of the block. This means that both the probed intermediate values and the probed output variables are simulatable.

4.1   Generalization

The algorithm presented above can be generalized to have broader applicability. Firstly, the algorithm is not bound by calculating the identity function (i.e., $A^{(\cdot)} = B^{[\cdot]}$). Instead one can replace the multiplications with the value $(t \bmod p)$ in Eq. 8, which calculates a unity function, with any function $f()$ as:

$$\hat{B}_j^{[i]} = \bigoplus_{t=0}^{|R|-1} f(t \bmod p) \cdot R^{[i]}[t], \tag{12}$$

thus creating a more elaborate A2B conversion that allows calculating on the data for free.

Secondly, the modulus does not need to be a power of two but can be any positive integer q. In this case, we select different modulus p for each chunk. The selection of the p_i needs to fulfill the following conditions:

$$\prod_{i=0}^{L} p_i = q \tag{13}$$

$$\forall_{i=0}^{L} \, p_i \cdot S \leq |R| \tag{14}$$

Note that the latter condition can be relaxed for p_L, as we don't need to determine the carry location and can thus allow an overflow at positions that are a multiple of p_L. As such, a p_L value is also valid if p_L divides $|R|$.

Similar as before $D_i^{(\cdot)}$ is split into chunks. However, this time we represent $D^{(\cdot)}$ as a series of p_i-ary numbers:

$$\underbrace{\hat{D}_L^{(\cdot)}}_{p_L\text{-ary}} \| \dots \| \underbrace{\hat{D}_1^{(\cdot)}}_{p_1\text{-ary}} \| \underbrace{\hat{D}_0^{(\cdot)}}_{p_0\text{-ary}} \leftarrow D_i^{(\cdot)} \tag{15}$$

This representation immediately gives us the different chunks, as each symbol corresponds to a chunk $\hat{D}_j^{(\cdot)}$, with $\hat{D}_0^{(\cdot)}$ the least significant symbol.

5 Arithmetic to 1-Bit Boolean

In this section, we will specialize our method toward calculating a function $f()$ that takes one or more arithmetically masked variables and outputs one Boolean masked bit. Theoretically, our method can calculate any such function, however, when the input modulo q is split into smaller chunks modulo p (i.e. $L > 0$), only functions that can be described as:

$$f(D^{(\cdot)}) = f_L(\hat{D}_L^{(\cdot)}) \quad \& \quad \dots \quad \& \quad f_0(\hat{D}_0^{(\cdot)}), \tag{16}$$

are implementable. However, as we will show in Subsect. 5.3, this restriction does not pose a problem for typical applications in lattice-based encryption, such as masked comparison or extraction of the MSB.

Our method is similar to the arithmetic to Boolean conversion described above, where the calculation of $B^{[\cdot]}$ is not performed. The main idea is that in iteration i, if $f_i(\hat{D}_i^{(\cdot)}) = 1$, the register is propagated as before, while if $f_i(\hat{D}_i^{(\cdot)}) = 0$, a register with only zero is propagated. This can be achieved during a 'compute carry' step, by only propagating positions t where:

$$f_i(t \bmod p) = 1. \tag{17}$$

This means that if the 1 in the register is at a location where $f_i(t \bmod p) = 0$, the 1 in the register is not propagated and the register will have only 0's for the rest of the algorithm. At the end of the algorithm, we can check if the one is still present in the algorithm, which is the case if and only if $f(D^{(\cdot)}) = 1$. Note that the register remains masked throughout the algorithm and thus it is not revealed if and during which iteration the one is discarded.

642   J.-P. D'Anvers

5.1   Method Description

More specifically, the input is a list of arithmetically masked numbers $\mathbf{D}^{(\cdot)}$, with corresponding masking modulus q. The output is a boolean masked bit 1 if $\forall_i : f(\mathbf{D}_i^{(\cdot)}) = 1$, and 0 otherwise. The parameter setting (i.e., setting $|R|$, p, L and p_L) proceeds identical to the procedure explained in Sect. 4.

The setup phase of the algorithm similarly consists of two steps: initializing the Boolean masked register $R^{[\cdot]}$ to the value 1 and dividing each coefficient of $\mathbf{D}^{(\cdot)}$ into chunks of $\log_2(p)$ bits (with exception of the most significant chunk, which has $\log_2(p_L)$ bits).

The algorithm then iterates over all coefficients, and for each coefficient over all chunks starting with the least significant chunk. For each chunk first a secure rotation [16] is performed, as depicted in Algorithm 2. Then, instead of propagating all positions as in the full A2B conversion, only positions t where $f_i(t \bmod p) = 1$, are propagated to the output register in a step we will refer to as bit selection. More specifically, for each possible carry value c and each share k we calculate:

$$R^{[k]}[c] = \bigoplus_{t:f(t)=1} R_{tmp}^{[k]}[c \cdot p + t]. \tag{18}$$

The bit selection operation performs two functions: first, for all values of $\hat{\mathbf{D}}_{i,j}^{(\cdot)} \bmod p$ where $f(\hat{\mathbf{D}}_{i,j}^{(\cdot)}) = 1$, the 1 in the register is passed to the next iteration (othwerwise, the 1 is not passed to the next iteration). Secondly, the value of the carry (i.e., $c = \lfloor \sum_k \hat{\mathbf{D}}_{i,j}^{(k)}/p \rfloor$) is represented in the fact that the 1, if still present in the register, can be found at the cp position of the output register.

In the final iteration of a coefficient $\mathbf{D}_{i,L}^{(\cdot)}$, the carry is no longer relevant. We thus map all allowed positions to the zeroþ bit of $R^{[\cdot]}$ without distinguishing between the different carry values. Then the algorithm proceeds with the next coefficient in the input array. At the end of the algorithm, the zeroþ bit of $R^{[\cdot]}$ contains a Boolean masking of the output.

Side-Channel Security. Our security proof proceeds similarly to the security proof of the A2B conversion, as the secure-rotate function is still the only non-sharewise component that needs special attention.

Theorem 2 ($(S-1)$-SNI of Algorithm 3). *For any set of $t_c < S$ intermediate variables and for any subset $O \in [1, n]$ where $t_c + |O| < S$, we can perfectly simulate the output variables $R^{[O]}$ and the t_c intermediate values using the input values $\mathbf{D}^{(i)}$ for each $i \in I$, with $|I| \le t_c$.*

Proof. The t-SNI security proof of the Arithmetic to 1-bit Boolean function method is similar to the proof of the Arithmetic to Boolean conversion. The difference in both algorithms is only in the sharewise parts (l8 to l10 and l12-l13), which can be simulated deterministically using the knowledge on $R_{tmp}^{[\cdot]}$. As such one can essentially reuse the security proof of Theorem 1.

Algorithm 3: $A \rightarrow$ 1-bit $B(\mathbf{D}^{(\cdot)}, \mathbf{M})$

// Setup

1 $R^{[0]} = 1$

2 **for** $i = 1, \ldots, S - 1$ **do** $R^{[i]} = 0$

3 **for** $i = 1$ **to** $N - 1$ **do**

4 $\quad \underbrace{\hat{\mathbf{D}}_{i,L}^{(\cdot)}}_{<\log_2 |R|} \| \ldots \| \underbrace{\hat{\mathbf{D}}_{i,1}^{(\cdot)}}_{\log_2(p)} \| \underbrace{\hat{\mathbf{D}}_{i,0}^{(\cdot)}}_{\log_2(p)} \leftarrow \mathbf{D}_i^{(\cdot)}$

// calculate

5 **for** $i = 0, \ldots, N - 1$ **do**

6 $\quad$ **for** $j = 0, \ldots, L - 1$ **do**

7 $\quad\quad$ $R_{tmp}^{[\cdot]} = \texttt{SecureRotate}(R^{[\cdot]}, \hat{\mathbf{D}}_{i,j}^{(\cdot)})$

8 $\quad\quad$ $R^{[\cdot]} = 0$

9 $\quad\quad$ **for** $c = 0$ **to** $S - 1$ **do**

10 $\quad\quad\quad$ $R^{[\cdot]}[c] = \bigoplus_{\forall t: f_i(t)=1} R_{tmp}^{[\cdot]}[c \cdot p + t]$

11 $\quad$ $R_{tmp}^{[\cdot]} = \texttt{SecureRotate}(R^{[\cdot]}, \hat{\mathbf{D}}_{i,L}^{(\cdot)})$

12 $\quad$ $R^{[\cdot]} = 0$

13 $\quad$ $R^{[\cdot]}[0] = \bigoplus_{\substack{\forall t: f_i(t)=1 \\ \forall c \in [0, \ldots, |R|/p_L)}} R_{tmp}^{[\cdot]}[c \cdot p_L + t]$

14 **return** $R^{[\cdot]}$

5.2   Generalization

As with the arithmetic to Boolean conversion, our method can be generalized. First, the masking modulus q is not required to be a power of two. This generalization is similar to the non-power-of-two modulus generalization in Subsect. 4.1 and we refer to this section for an explanation on how to achieve this.

Secondly, the masking modulus q does not have to be equal for all coefficients. To allow different masking moduli q_i associated with their respective coefficients $D_i^{(\cdot)}$, one performs the determination of the parameters p, L, p_L for each coefficient separately. The rest of the algorithm then proceeds as usual, with each coefficient using its specific set of p, L, p_L.

5.3   Applications to Lattice-Based Encryption

The method presented above can be used as a building block for the masking of lattice-based encryption. In this section we will specifically look into two building blocks for lattice-based encryption: comparison of the (uncompressed) recomputed ciphertext with the input ciphertext in the Fujisaki-Okamoto transformation, and A2B for extraction of the most significant bit(s) during decryption. We will show how both these functionalities can be achieved using our methodology by choosing the appropriate input parameters.

Comparison. The comparison is an essential part of the Fujisaki-Okamoto transformation. The goal of this comparison is to validate the input ciphertext against a recomputed ciphertext. Several works have looked at optimizing higher-order masked comparison [4,7,16,17,20]. We will consider a recomputed ciphertext that has not been compressed, as the compression is generally expensive and we can include the compression in our solution at almost no cost. This is the same setup as used in previous works.

In previous works, the comparison is typically done in at least two steps containing an A2B conversion and the comparison itself. In this work, the comparison itself is already performed in the A2B conversion. Moreover, the adaptation of the A2B conversion even makes the A2B conversion more efficient as the Boolean output is not calculated.

The first input to the comparison is the input ciphertext, which consists of two arrays $(\mathbf{B}, \mathbf{C})$, with coefficients modulo q_b and q_c respectively. The second input is an uncompressed recomputed masked ciphertext $(\mathbf{B}^{*(\cdot)}, \mathbf{C}^{*(\cdot)})$, both with coefficients modulo q. The comparison then should return true if and only if:

$$\forall i : \lfloor q_b/q \cdot \mathbf{B}_i^{*(\cdot)} \rceil = \mathbf{B}_i \text{ and } \forall i : \lfloor q_c/q \cdot \mathbf{C}_i^{*(\cdot)} \rceil = \mathbf{C}_i \tag{19}$$

Power of Two q. For q, q_b and q_c powers of two, such a function can be instantiated by calculating the list with coefficients $\mathbf{D}_i^{(\cdot)}$:

$$\underset{i\in 0,\ldots,|B|-1}{\forall} : \mathbf{D}_i^{(0)} = \mathbf{B}_i^{*(0)} + \frac{q}{2q_b} - \frac{q}{q_b} \cdot \mathbf{B}_i \quad ; \qquad \underset{\substack{i\in 0,\ldots,|B|-1 \\ j>0}}{\forall} : \mathbf{D}_i^{(j)} = \mathbf{B}_i^{*(j)} ; \tag{20}$$

$$\underset{i\in 0,\ldots,|C|-1}{\forall} : \mathbf{D}_{i+|B|}^{(\cdot)} = \mathbf{C}_i^{*(0)} + \frac{q}{2q_c} - \frac{q}{q_c} \cdot \mathbf{C}_i \text{ and } \underset{\substack{i\in 0,\ldots,|C|-1 \\ j>0}}{\forall} : \mathbf{D}_{i+|B|}^{(j)} = \mathbf{C}_i^{*(j)}, \tag{21}$$

where the $\frac{q}{2q_b}$ and $\frac{q}{2q_c}$ terms are used to convert the rounding operation into a flooring operation. Note that this is the same input preparation as step 0 of Algorithm 7 in [17].

We furthermore prepare the functions $f_0, \ldots, f_L$ as:

$$f_{b,i}(x) = \begin{cases} 1 \text{ if: } x \leq (\frac{q}{q_b} - 1)/p^i \\ 0 \quad \text{otherwise} \end{cases} \text{ and: } f_{c,i}(x) = \begin{cases} 1 \text{ if: } x \leq (\frac{q}{q_c} - 1)/p^i \\ 0 \quad \text{otherwise} \end{cases},$$

$$\tag{22}$$

for the coefficients of $\mathbf{B}$ and $\mathbf{C}$ respectively.

Prime q. For prime moduli conversion, we follow the approach of Fritzmann et al. [22], where the compression is explicitly calculated for each share individually. This would result in an infinitely long bitstring, but Fritzmann et al. showed that it is sufficient to take into account a certain number of bits $f > \log_2(S) + \log_2\left(\frac{\lceil q/2 \rceil}{q} - 0.5\right)$, with S the number of shares. We end up with the following inputs:

$$\underset{i\in 0,\dots,|B|-1}{\forall: \mathbf{D}_i{}^{(0)}} = \lfloor \frac{q_b \cdot 2^f}{q} B_i^{*(0)} \rfloor + \frac{2^f}{2} - 2^f \cdot \mathbf{B}_i \ ; \quad \underset{\substack{i\in 0,\dots,|B|-1 \\ j>0}}{\forall: \mathbf{D}_i{}^{(0)}} = \lfloor \frac{q_b \cdot 2^f}{q} B_i^{*(j)} \rfloor \ ; \qquad (23)$$

$$\underset{i\in 0,\dots,|C|-1}{\forall: \mathbf{D}_{i+|B|}{}^{(\cdot)}} = \lfloor \frac{q_c \cdot 2^f}{q} C_i^{*(0)} \rfloor + \frac{2^f}{2} - 2^f \cdot \mathbf{C}_i \ \text{ and } \underset{\substack{i\in 0,\dots,|C|-1 \\ j>0}}{\forall: \mathbf{D}_{i+|B|}{}^{(0)}} = \lfloor \frac{q_c \cdot 2^f}{q} C_i^{*(j)} \rfloor, \qquad (24)$$

and moduli $q_b \cdot 2^f$ and $q_c \cdot 2^f$ respectively. The functions are constructed as:

$$f_{b,i}(x) = \begin{cases} 1 \text{ if: } x \le (2^f - 1)/p^i \\ 0 \quad \text{otherwise} \end{cases} \text{ and: } \quad f_{c,i}(x) = \begin{cases} 1 \text{ if: } x \le (2^f - 1)/p^i \\ 0 \quad \text{otherwise} \end{cases},$$
$$(25)$$

Again note that this is the same input preparation as step 0 of Algorithm 7 in [17].

A2B Compression/MSB Extraction. Our arithmetic to 1-bit Boolean can also be used to securely implement the A2B conversion in lattice-based encryption schemes. To be more precise, it can replace the A2B conversion where one is only interested in the most significant bit, which is typically the case in the decoding for schemes like Saber and Kyber. To find the most significant bit of a number $A^{(\cdot)}$ in case of a power of two moduli, one inputs $D_0{}^{(\cdot)} = A^{(\cdot)}$ with the modulus q equal to the arithmetic sharing modulus. The functions $f_0(), \dots, f_L()$ can be constructed as $f_i(x) = 1$, with the exception of $f_L()$, which equals:

$$f_{b,i}(x) = \begin{cases} 0 \text{ if: } x < p_L/2 \\ 1 \quad \text{otherwise} \end{cases} \qquad (26)$$

Note that the input $D^{(\cdot)}$ is in this case an array with only one coefficient.

Again, for prime moduli, we can perform a similar technique. The goal is to calculate the modulus switching function $\lfloor \frac{2}{q}x \rfloor$ on a masked variable. To do this, one also has the option to convert to power-of-two moduli using a trick similar to D'Anvers et al. [20] inspired by the technique of Fritzmann et al. [22]. In this case, we have:

$$D_0{}^{(\cdot)} = \lfloor \frac{2^{f+1}}{q} B^{(\cdot)} + S \rfloor \qquad (27)$$

with modulus 2^{f+1}. The function is calculated similar to before as $f_i(x) = 1$, again with the exception of $f_L()$, which equals:

$$f_{b,i}(x) = \begin{cases} 0 \text{ if: } x < p_L/2 \\ 1 \quad \text{otherwise} \end{cases} \qquad (28)$$

The reason for the multiplication with 2^{f+1} and addition of S is to preserve correctness even in the presence of flooring errors. The division with q creates an infinitely long fractional part, which the subsequent operation floors down. This means that an error in $(-1, 0]$ is introduced to all shares:

$$D_0^{(\cdot)} = \frac{2^{f+1}}{q} B^{(\cdot)} + S \cdot (1 + e) \tag{29}$$

To prove that this operation always gives the correct result, we investigate the border cases $B^{(\cdot)} = 0$ and $B^{(\cdot)} = \lfloor q/2 \rfloor$, which should result in $D_0^{(\cdot)} \in [0, 2^f)$; and $B^{(\cdot)} = \lceil q/2 \rceil$ and $B^{(\cdot)} = q - 1$, which should result in $D_0^{(\cdot)} \in [2^f, 2^{f+1})$. If these conditions are fulfilled the top bit is correct and the value of $D_0^{(\cdot)}$ will be valid. Note that since q is uneven we have $\lfloor q/2 \rfloor = (q-1)/2$ and $\lceil q/2 \rceil = (q+1)/2$.

The cases of $B^{(\cdot)} = 0$ and $B^{(\cdot)} = \lceil q/2 \rceil$ can only go wrong in negative wrap around, and so the worst-case scenario is $e = -1$. This results in:

$$D_0^{(\cdot)} = S \cdot (1 - 1) \geq 0 \quad \text{and} \quad D_0^{(\cdot)} = 2^f \frac{q+1}{q} + S \cdot (1 - 1) \geq 2^f \tag{30}$$

which is always fulfilled.

The cases of $B^{(\cdot)} = q - 1$ and $B^{(\cdot)} = \lfloor q/2 \rfloor$ can only go wrong in positive wrap around, and so the worst-case scenario is $e = 0$. This results in:

$$D_0^{(\cdot)} = 2^{f+1} \frac{q-1}{q} + S < 2^{f+1} \quad \text{and} \quad D_0^{(\cdot)} = 2^f \frac{q-1}{q} + S < 2^f \tag{31}$$

which results in conditions $S < \frac{2^{f+1}}{q}$ and $S < \frac{2^f}{q}$, of which the latter is the most restrictive. Therefore, as long as $f > \log_2(S) + \log_2(q)$ we have a correct most significant bit and thus a correct MSB extraction.

6   Implementation Aspects

The algorithms given above are not necessarily the most efficient way to implement one-hot conversions on a variety of computing platforms. In this section, we detail methods to speed up these conversion algorithms. We first look at possible tweaks in software implementations and then look at parallelization possibilities, which are typically more useful in hardware.

6.1   Software Optimizations

The inner loop of our technique consists of two parts: secure rotation and bit selection. The secure rotation itself consists of two main instructions: a rotation and an XOR operation on the register. As such it is relatively easy to optimize in both software and hardware. The bit selection warrants a more in-depth look, and we will first look into the bit selection of the arithmetic to 1-bit Boolean conversion, and then look into the A2B conversion.

Bit Selection. In this paragraph we will specifically look at the bit selection of $R^{[\cdot]}$ (line 11, and line 14 in Algorithm 3). In a hardware implementation, one can implement these operations using a simple Boolean hardware circuit.

For software implementations, as we are working within a register, an efficient implementation is more challenging. To get a feel for the cost we will describe the cost of algorithms in the number of XOR that needs to be performed, taking this measure because it is the main operation in the innermost loop in the code. We will specifically look at the power-of-two q case and a subfunction that considers each bit individually, i.e. a function $f_i(x)$ that can be written as:

$$f_i(x) = f_{i,0}^*(x[0]) \text{ AND } f_{i,1}^*(x[1]) \text{ AND } \ldots \text{ AND } f_{i,|X|-1}^*(x[|X|-1]). \quad (32)$$

This is the case that covers the typical applications from Subsect. 5.3.

A straightforward approach would be to perform the XORs one by one, which would lead to $S^2 \cdot (|f_i| - 1)$ XOR operations, where $|f_i|$ denotes the number of inputs to which the function f_i returns 1. This can be brought back to less than $S^2 + S \cdot \log_2(|f_i|)$ XOR operations using two tricks: exploiting inherent parallelism and a divide-and-conquer combination approach.

Firstly, the inherent parallelism comes from the fact that the XOR for positions in different carry bits but with the relative position can be calculated at the same time, by exploiting the fact that the different carry bins are exactly p positions separated. As such, when performing the XOR operation on the full register on line 11 and line 14, one is not only calculating the result for carry $c = 0$, but also for all other carries c, the result of which can be found $c \cdot p$ positions further in the register.

Secondly, one can speed up the calculations using a divide-and-conquer strategy. There are three possible instantiations for $f_i^*(x)$:

$$f_i^*(x) = x, \quad f_i^*(x) = NOT(x), \quad f_i^*(x) = 1 \quad (33)$$

Note that $f_i^*(x) = 0$ is not an option, as this would mean that $f(x) = 0$ which is a useless function to implement. The number of positions that needs to be propagated during bit selection in loop l can be calculated as:

$$\prod_{i=0}^{\log_2(p)-1} |f_i^*(x[i])| \quad (34)$$

For the functions $f_i^*(x[i]) = x$ and $f_i^*(x[i]) = NOT(x)$, $|f_i^*(x[i])|$ is one and thus the number of positions to be considered is not increased. However, for function of the form $f_i^*(x) = 1$, the number of positions is doubled. More specifically, for each position that is propagated, a position exactly 2^i further is also propagated.

We address such an instance by shifting the register $R^{[\cdot]}$ with 2^i positions and XORing it with the original register. This operation essentially combines the scenario where $x[i] = 0$, with the scenario where $x[i] = 1$, and puts both options at the position as if $x[i] = 0$. Thus, after this operation, the original function $f_i^*(x) = 1$ needs to be replaced with $f_i^*(x) = x$ to obtain the same result. Once all $f_i^*(x) = 1$ are replaced by $f_i^*(x) = x$, there is only one position left to be considered, more specifically this is position $F = \sum_{i=0}^{\log_2(p)-1} 2^i \cdot f_i^*(0)$.

Algorithm 4 gives a faster implementation of the bit selection, where in lines 1–6 the inherent parallelism and the divide-and-conquer combination are exploited. Line 7 is a cleanup where the XORed value for each carry c is placed at the $c \cdot p\mathfrak{p}$ position and all other positions are set to zero, after which lines 8–11 copy the carry bits to their final position c.

Postprocessing A2B The bit selection in the A2B conversion can be optimized in the same ways as in the arithmetic to 1-bit Boolean conversion detailed above. However, for the A2B conversion, there is an additional step to calculate $B_{tmp}^{[\cdot]}$ which can be optimized significantly. In this paragraph, we will discuss two optimizations.

The first algorithm uses the same divide-and-conquer combination to combine the different carry bins, after which the multiplication operation is calculated p times. This algorithm is depicted in Algorithm 5 and is efficient as long as p is a small value. It takes $S \cdot (p-1)$ multiplications and $S \cdot (S+p-2)$ XOR operations.

The second algorithm is aimed at a higher value p. For this, we take a step back at the bits of $B_{tmp}^{[\cdot]}$, which are calculated as:

$$B_{tmp}^{[\cdot]} = \bigoplus_{t=0}^{p-1} t \cdot \left(\bigoplus_{c=0}^{|R|/p-1} R_{tmp}^{[\cdot]}[c \cdot p_L + t] \right) \tag{35}$$

Note that the second term of the multiplication is a single bit with a value of 0 or 1. When looking at a specific bit of the output $B_{tmp}^{[\cdot]}[i]$, this equation can be further simplified:

$$B_{tmp}^{[\cdot]}[i] = \bigoplus_{\substack{\forall t=0,\ldots,p-1:t[i]=1 \\ c=0,\ldots,|R|/p_L-1}} R_{tmp}^{[\cdot]}[c \cdot p + t] \tag{36}$$

$$= \texttt{parity}(R^{[\cdot]} \,\&\, F_i) \quad \text{with: } F_i = \bigoplus_{\substack{\forall t=0,\ldots,p-1:t[i]=1 \\ c=0,\ldots,|R|/p_L-1}} 2^{c \cdot p+t}. \tag{37}$$

In essence, F_i is a mask that selects all terms involved in the XOR operation. For example, for $i = 0$, $F_i = 0101\ldots01$ and for $i = 1$, $F_i = 00110011\ldots0011$. The resulting algorithm is depicted in Algorithm 6.

The cost of this second algorithm heavily depends on the instruction set of the processor. If a parity instruction (or Hamming weight instruction) is present, the algorithm takes $S \cdot \log_2(p)$ parity instructions. If this instruction is not present, one can compute the parity with a divide-and-conquer strategy which would cost $\lceil \log_2(S \cdot p) \rceil$ operations.

6.2   Parallelization

Our algorithm is inherently serial, as the output $R^{[\cdot]}$ of the previous chunk is necessary to start the calculations on the next chunk. This might be a bottleneck

Algorithm 4:	Algorithm 5:

// Get valid positions
1 $F = 0$
2 **for** $i = 0$ **to** $\log_2(p) - 1$ **do**
3   **if** $f_i^*(x) = 1$ **then**
4      $R^{[\cdot]} \oplus= R^{[\cdot]} \gg 2^i$
5   **else if** $f_i^*(x) = NOT(x)$ **then**
6      $F = F + 2^i$
7 $R^{[\cdot]} = (R^{[\cdot]} \gg F) \,\&\, \sum_{i=0}^{S-1} 2^{i \cdot p}$
// Set carries
8 **for** $i = 1$ **to** $\log_2(S - 1)$ **do**
9   $R^{[\cdot]} \oplus= R^{[\cdot]} \gg (p - 1) \cdot i$
10 $R^{[\cdot]} = R^{[\cdot]} \,\&\, (2^S - 1)$
	1 **for** $i = 1$ **to** $\log_2(S - 1)$ **do**
	2 $R^{[\cdot]} \oplus= R^{[\cdot]} \gg 2^i \cdot p$
	3 **for** $i = 1$ **to** $p - 1$ **do**
	4 $R^{[\cdot]} \oplus= i \cdot R^{[\cdot]}[i]$
	
	Algorithm 6:
	1 **for** $i = 0$ **to** $\log_2(p) - 1$ **do**
	2 $B^{[\cdot]}[i] = \mathtt{parity}(R^{[\cdot]} \,\&\, F_i)$

for the masked comparison operation as used in lattice-based cryptography as described in Subsect. 5.3. In such a scenario one has typically an input array $\mathbf{D}^{(\cdot)}$ that has between 768 and 1280 coefficients that need to be validated. In this section, we will show how to make a parallel implementation on n 'cores' with minimal overhead.

At the start, one divides the array $\mathbf{D}^{(\cdot)}$ in n arrays of approximately $|\mathbf{D}^{(\cdot)}|/n$ elements. These sub-arrays are then validated separately on the n cores, which results in n registers $R_0^{[\cdot]}$ to $R_{n-1}^{[\cdot]}$. The LSB of each of these registers is a Boolean masked bit representing the result of the comparison of the corresponding sub-array (i.e., $R_i^{[\cdot]}[0] = 1$ if the corresponding sub-array was valid, and 0 if it was invalid).

To combine these registers, one can use the fact that one Boolean masked bit is essentially an arithmetic masked bit modulo 2. To combine $R_0^{[\cdot]}$ and $R_1^{[\cdot]}$ we perform another iteration of the arithmetic to 1-bit Boolean with these inputs: $\forall_k \mathbf{D}^{(k)} = R_1^{[k]}[0]$ with arithmetic masking modulus 2, $R^{[\cdot]} = R_0^{[\cdot]}$ and $f(x) = NOT(x)$. The output of this iteration is a register $R^{[\cdot]}$ that is 1 if both $R_0^{[\cdot]}$ and $R_1^{[\cdot]}$ were 1, and 0 otherwise.

Taking a step back we can see that the above paragraph uses the arithmetic to 1-bit Boolean technique to construct a masked AND gate on Boolean masked bits. By applying this AND gate on all $R_0^{[\cdot]}$ to $R_{n-1}^{[\cdot]}$ we end up with one register denoting the result of the masked comparison.

In a serial implementation, given $|\mathbf{D}^{(\cdot)}|$ coefficients and L chunks for each coefficient, the masked comparison takes $L \cdot |\mathbf{D}^{(\cdot)}|$ iterations (we count SecureRotate and the bit selection as one iteration). In the parallelized method we additionally have to perform $n - 1$ iterations to combine the sub-array $R_i^{[\cdot]}$, which increases the cost only slightly to $L \cdot |\mathbf{D}^{(\cdot)}| + n - 1$ iterations. For masked comparison of Saber, where $|\mathbf{D}^{(\cdot)}| = 1024$ and $L = 4$, performing the calculations in parallel on 4 cores would increase the cost from 4096 to 4099 iterations.

7 Validation

In this section, we compare the one-hot A2B conversion and masked comparison to state-of-the-art alternatives. We benchmarked the algorithms on an STM32F407 board with an ARM-Cortex M4F using `arm-none-eabi-gcc` version 9.2.1 with -O3. The system clock was set to 24 Mhz and TRNG clock to 48 Mhz, following the popular benchmarking framework PQM4 [KRSS]. One important factor in the benchmarking of these conversions is the limited throughput of the TRNG available on our processor. Therefore, we provide both benchmarks where the randomness cost is disregarded (i.e., it is sourced from a precomputed array of random elements), and where the randomness is sampled from the on-chip TRNG and its sampling cost is included in the cycle counts. Note that these implementations are only for reference and are not side-channel secured, as such implementations are outside the scope of this work but would be interesting for future work.

7.1 A2B Conversion

In Table 2 and Table 3, our one-hot A2B algorithm is compared with the state-of-the-art table-based conversion by Coron et al. [16], using their publicly available code. We also compare with the Boolean circuit-based A2B algorithm by Coron et al. [11], and additionally with the optimized bitsliced implementation of D'Anvers et al. [17]. The top results in the table give the cycle counts without the waiting effect of the TRNG, while the bottom results include the TRNG wait time.

Table 2. Cost to perform 32 A2B conversions on Cortex M4 in 1000 cycles. The top results ignore randomness sampling using the on-chip TRNG generator, the bottom results include the randomness sampling.

bits	8-bit		16-bit		32-bit	
order	2	3	2	3	2	3
Bool. circ. [11]	228.7	402.4	442.6	767.1	862.5	1484.7
Bool. circ. (optimized bitsliced) [11,17]	37.3	55.1	72.3	**108.2**	142.6	214.6
Table-based [16]	427.2	916.2	847.2	1806.6	1647.8	3514,8
One-hot [ours]	**27.3**	**51.2**	**54.3**	109.6	**103.3**	**206.4**
When sampling the randomness from the on-chip TRNG generator:						
Bool. circ. [11]	294.1	532.9	560.2	1002.0	1084.5	1928.6
Bool. circ. (optimized bitsliced) [11,17]	**43.2**	**67.1**	**84.8**	**133.3**	**168.2**	**265.9**
Table-based [16]	767.8	1617.4	1524.1	3213.0	3005,8	6338.3
One-hot [ours]	47.0	90.4	103.3	207.5	201.3	408.2

Table 3. Randomness cost to perform 32 A2B conversions in bytes.

bits	8-bit		16-bit		32-bit	
order	2	3	2	3	2	3
Bool. circ. [11]	5,120	10,240	9,216	18,432	17,408	34,816
Bool. circ. (opt. bitsliced) [11,17]	**464**	**928**	**976**	**1,952**	**2,000**	**4,000**
Table-based [16]	26,624	55,296	53,248	110,592	106,496	221,184
One-hot [ours]	1,536	3,072	3,840	7,680	7,680	15,360

We first compare our one-hot conversion to the state-of-the-art table-based conversion, as they are in the same family. As you can see from Table 2, our new conversion improves the state-of-the-art table-based conversion with approximately a factor of 15. Similarly, the randomness usage is also reduced with a factor of 15 in the one-hot encoding. From this, we can conclude that the one-hot conversion is an improved version of the table-based conversion of Coron [16] in both cycle count ($\times 15$) and randomness usage ($\times 15$), and as such it is the fastest table-based full A2B conversion algorithm available at the moment[1].

A comparison to the Boolean circuit method is more complex. First one can notice that the optimized and bitsliced method significantly outperforms a straightforward implementation of the Boolean circuit method. Note that in contrast to the optimized bitsliced implementation, the one-hot implementation provided in this paper is a proof of concept and not a fully optimized implementation, which we leave for future work.

Compared to the one-hot encoding, while reducing the randomness cost of table-based methods by around a factor of 15, the randomness required for the one-hot encoding is still approximately 4 times higher compared to the optimized bitsliced Boolean circuit implementation. Further reducing this randomness cost can thus be identified as an interesting focus for future work. Regarding the cycle count, the one-hot encoding is in most situations slightly faster (up to 27%) than the Boolean circuit method if the limited throughput of the TRNG is ignored. If using the on-chip TRNG, the Boolean circuit method becomes (up to 35%) faster.

The bitsliced optimized Boolean circuit implementation makes very efficient use of the processor instructions available through the use of the bitslicing. Similar optimizations are not implemented for the one-hot encoding. One example of an operation that could be optimized using the appropriate hardware support would be the sharewise operations. These operations are essentially a Boolean circuit with mostly (unmasked) XOR gates, which would be much more efficient in hardware or with the appropriate hardware support (e.g., a parity count or

---

[1] Note that the numbers given in [16] (Table 6) depict algorithmic operation counts and not cycles in an actual implementation. As there is no one-to-one match between the algorithmic operation count and the cycle count (e.g., memory accesses might be more expensive than local operations) one should be careful in comparing these numbers.

hamming weight instruction as discussion in Sect. 6). It would be interesting for future work to compare both techniques in a hardware implementation.

One advantage of the one-hot A2B over a Boolean circuit-based A2B is that the security-critical non-linear part is fully contained in the small and elegant SecureRotate function, as all other operations are linear and thus can be performed share-wise. As such, implementors have a more clear view of the security-critical parts of the algorithm, which should make side-channel secure implementations easier.

7.2   Masked Comparison

We compare our one-hot masked comparison with the state-of-the-art comparison techniques as identified in [20]. These implementations are optimized versions of the comparison by Barthe et al. [6] optimized in [20] (simple optimized) and Coron et al. [15] optimized in [20] (streamlined hybrid). Table 4 gives an overview of the cycle and randomness cost of the various comparison algorithm for usage in Saber and Kyber. For these techniques we use the optimized bitsliced A2B implementation of [17]. The implementation of the one-hot comparison follows the design of Algorithm 3 with the optimizations discussed in Sect. 6.

Table 4. Cycle and randomness cost of the state-of-the-art higher-order comparison methods

Order		Cycles w/o TRNG		Cycles with TRNG		Randomness	
		2	3	2	3	2	3
simple optimized [6,20]	Kyber	2.5M	4.1M	3.1M	5.3M	48K	100K
streamlined hybrid [15,20]	Kyber	2.4M	3.4M	3.3M	4.4M	80K	95K
one-hot (ours)	Kyber	2.3M	4.3M	4.6M	8.9M	184K	369K
simple optimized [6,20]	Saber	1.3M	2.0M	1.6M	2.6M	26K	53K
one-hot (ours)	Saber	1.0M	2.0M	2.2M	4.2M	92K	184K

Due to the improvements of the one-hot conversion, masked comparison based on table-based A2B now performs with similar performance to Boolean circuit A2B based solutions. However, the randomness consumption is still a factor 2 to 4 higher than the Boolean circuit A2B based conversions, which confirms the importance of future work on randomness reduction or reuse as stated above.

One difference between the techniques is the code complexity. The one-hot comparison only consists of one main loop that loops over all chunks and for each chunk performs a secure rotation and a bit selection. As such this technique has a low implementation complexity even compared to the simple optimized method. Moreover, the bit selection is performed share-wise and should therefore be relatively easy to implement securely. Therefore, the critical part for secure implementations is mainly contained in the secure rotation and as such limits the scope of critical code parts that need to be addressed for a secure implementation.

Additionally, the streamlined hybrid method is prone to a small collision probability in which the comparison returns an incorrect result. This probability can be made arbitrarily small at the cost of losing efficiency. The simple optimized and one-hot comparisons are always correct and thus do not suffer from collisions.

8   Conclusions and Future Work

In this paper, we introduced a new table-based arithmetic to Boolean conversion. We also showed how to adapt our new method to efficiently perform masked comparison or extraction of the most significant bit, operations which are important for the masking of lattice-based post-quantum schemes. Additionally, an interesting property of our conversion is that one can perform a wide range of functions on the masked data during the transformation at low to no cost, which could be useful in future applications.

Our A2B method is 15 times faster than state-of-the-art table-based conversions and reduces the randomness consumption by a factor of 15. The resulting scheme still consumes approximately 4 times more randomness than the state-of-the-art bitsliced optimized Boolean circuit based A2B, but can be (depending on the throughput of the TRNG) up to 27% faster. Given that higher-order A2B conversion algorithms using Boolean circuit-based A2B have been around for longer and that they have undergone more optimizations both on an algorithmic and implementation level, the relatively new higher-order table-based A2B conversions might be able to bridge the remaining performance gap in the future.

Future work could include looking at adaptations to make one-hot conversions more efficient, or to apply them in different contexts and for different types of conversions. Reduction of the randomness usage by the one-hot conversion might be an interesting research topic. One could also look at algorithmic or implementation optimizations. Note that possible optimizations to the algorithm will be different on different platforms, for example in a microprocessor the register size is typically fixed by the bitwidth of the processor, while hardware implementation has more slack in choosing the size. For hardware implementations, the Boolean circuit nature of the sharewise operations might lead to significant speedups. Implementing and lab verification of a practically secure one-hot conversion might also be interesting future work.

Another point of interest could be specific first-order versions of the one-hot conversion. In first-order table-based implementations, one can typically re-use randomness over multiple encodings, and thus the randomness cost can be reduced dramatically. As in this scenario the randomness is no longer a limiting factor, this could possibly lead to very efficient designs for first-order.

In terms of extending the reach of the algorithm, one could look into applying the one-hot conversion ideas to improve Boolean to arithmetic conversion or first-order comparison methods. In the future, other more exotic functions might be implementable using the technique (e.g., checking smallness of a vector). It would also be interesting to integrate the one-hot conversion algorithms in post-quantum schemes such as Kyber, Dilithium and Falcon.

Acknowledgements. I would like to thank Michiel Van Beirendonck for the interesting discussions on this topic. This work was supported in part by CyberSecurity Research Flanders with reference number VR20192203, the Research Council KU Leuven (C16/15/058) and the Horizon 2020 ERC Advanced Grant (101020005 Belfort). Jan-Pieter D'Anvers is funded by FWO (Research Foundation - Flanders) as junior post-doctoral fellow (contract number 133185 / 1238822N LV).

References

1. Alagic, G., et al.: Status Report on the Second Round of the NIST Post-Quantum Cryptography Standardization Process (2020). https://csrc.nist.gov/publications/detail/nistir/8309/final
2. Amiet, D., Curiger, A., Leuenberger, L., Zbinden, P.: Defeating NEWHOPE with a single trace. In: Ding, J., Tillich, J.-P. (eds.) PQCrypto 2020. LNCS, vol. 12100, pp. 189–205. Springer, Cham (2020). https://doi.org/10.1007/978-3-030-44223-1_11
3. Atici, A.C., Batina, L., Gierlichs, B., Verbauwhede, I.: Power analysis on ntru implementations for RFIDs: First results (2008)
4. Bache, F., Paglialonga, C., Oder, T., Schneider, T., Güneysu, T.: High-speed masking for polynomial comparison in lattice-based kems. IACR TCHES **2020**(3), 483–507 (2020). https://doi.org/10.13154/tches.v2020.i3.483-507, https://tches.iacr.org/index.php/TCHES/article/view/8598
5. Barthe, G., et al.: Strong non-interference and type-directed higher-order masking. In: Weippl, E.R., Katzenbeisser, S., Kruegel, C., Myers, A.C., Halevi, S. (eds.) ACM CCS 2016, pp. 116–129. ACM Press (2016). https://doi.org/10.1145/2976749.2978427
6. Barthe, G., et al.: Masking the GLP lattice-based signature scheme at any order. In: Nielsen, J.B., Rijmen, V. (eds.) EUROCRYPT 2018. LNCS, vol. 10821, pp. 354–384. Springer, Cham (2018). https://doi.org/10.1007/978-3-319-78375-8_12
7. Bhasin, S., D'Anvers, J.P., Heinz, D., Pöppelmann, T., Van Beirendonck, M.: Attacking and defending masked polynomial comparison. IACR TCHES **2021**(3), 334–359 (2021). https://doi.org/10.46586/tches.v2021.i3.334-359, https://tches.iacr.org/index.php/TCHES/article/view/8977
8. Bos, J.W., Gourjon, M., Renes, J., Schneider, T., van Vredendaal, C.: Masking kyber: first- and higher-order implementations. IACR TCHES **2021**(4), 173–214 (2021). https://doi.org/10.46586/tches.v2021.i4.173-214, https://tches.iacr.org/index.php/TCHES/article/view/9064
9. Chari, S., Jutla, C.S., Rao, J.R., Rohatgi, P.: Towards sound approaches to counteract power-analysis attacks. In: Wiener, M. (ed.) CRYPTO 1999. LNCS, vol. 1666, pp. 398–412. Springer, Heidelberg (1999). https://doi.org/10.1007/3-540-48405-1_26
10. Coron, J.-S., Großschädl, J., Tibouchi, M., Vadnala, P.K.: Conversion from arithmetic to boolean masking with logarithmic complexity. In: Leander, G. (ed.) FSE 2015. LNCS, vol. 9054, pp. 130–149. Springer, Heidelberg (2015). https://doi.org/10.1007/978-3-662-48116-5_7
11. Coron, J.-S., Großschädl, J., Vadnala, P.K.: Secure conversion between boolean and arithmetic masking of any order. In: Batina, L., Robshaw, M. (eds.) CHES

2014. LNCS, vol. 8731, pp. 188–205. Springer, Heidelberg (2014). https://doi.org/10.1007/978-3-662-44709-3_11

12. Coron, J.S., Gérard, F., Trannoy, M., Zeitoun, R.: High-order masking of ntru. Cryptology ePrint Archive, Paper 2022/1188 (2022). https://eprint.iacr.org/2022/1188, https://eprint.iacr.org/2022/1188

13. Coron, J.S., Rondepierre, F., Zeitoun, R.: High order masking of look-up tables with common shares. IACR TCHES **2018**(1), 40–72 (2018). https://doi.org/10.13154/tches.v2018.i1.40-72, https://tches.iacr.org/index.php/TCHES/article/view/832

14. Coron, J.-S., Tchulkine, A.: A new algorithm for switching from arithmetic to boolean masking. In: Walter, C.D., Koç, Ç.K., Paar, C. (eds.) CHES 2003. LNCS, vol. 2779, pp. 89–97. Springer, Heidelberg (2003). https://doi.org/10.1007/978-3-540-45238-6_8

15. Coron, J.S., Gérard, F., Montoya, S., Zeitoun, R.: High-order polynomial comparison and masking lattice-based encryption. Cryptology ePrint Archive, Report 2021/1615 (2021). https://ia.cr/2021/1615

16. Coron, J.S., Gérard, F., Montoya, S., Zeitoun, R.: High-order table-based conversion algorithms and masking lattice-based encryption. Cryptology ePrint Archive, Report 2021/1314 (2021). https://ia.cr/2021/1314

17. D'Anvers, J.P., Heinz, D., Pessl, P., van Beirendonck, M., Verbauwhede, I.: Higher-order masked ciphertext comparison for lattice-based cryptography. Cryptology ePrint Archive, Report 2021/1422 (2021). https://ia.cr/2021/1422

18. D'Anvers, J.P., Karmakar, A., Roy, S.S., Vercauteren, F.: SABER. Technical report, National Institute of Standards and Technology (2019). https://csrc.nist.gov/projects/post-quantum-cryptography/round-2-submissions

19. D'Anvers, J.P., Tiepelt, M., Vercauteren, F., Verbauwhede, I.: Timing attacks on error correcting codes in post-quantum schemes. In: Proceedings of ACM Workshop on Theory of Implementation Security Workshop, TIS 2019, pp. 2–9. Association for Computing Machinery, New York (2019). https://doi.org/10.1145/3338467.3358948

20. D'Anvers, J.P., Van Beirendonck, M., Verbauwhede, I.: Revisiting higher-order masked comparison for lattice-based cryptography: Algorithms and bit-sliced implementations. Cryptology ePrint Archive, Report 2022/110 (2022). https://ia.cr/2022/110

21. Debraize, B.: Efficient and provably secure methods for switching from arithmetic to boolean masking. In: Prouff, E., Schaumont, P. (eds.) CHES 2012. LNCS, vol. 7428, pp. 107–121. Springer, Heidelberg (2012). https://doi.org/10.1007/978-3-642-33027-8_7

22. Fritzmann, T., et al.: Masked accelerators and instruction set extensions for post-quantum cryptography. Cryptology ePrint Archive, Report 2021/479 (2021). https://eprint.iacr.org/2021/479

23. Fujisaki, E., Okamoto, T.: Secure integration of asymmetric and symmetric encryption schemes. In: Wiener, M. (ed.) CRYPTO 1999. LNCS, vol. 1666, pp. 537–554. Springer, Heidelberg (1999). https://doi.org/10.1007/3-540-48405-1_34

24. Goubin, L.: A sound method for switching between boolean and arithmetic masking. In: Koç, Ç.K., Naccache, D., Paar, C. (eds.) CHES 2001. LNCS, vol. 2162, pp. 3–15. Springer, Heidelberg (2001). https://doi.org/10.1007/3-540-44709-1_2

25. Guo, Q., Johansson, T., Nilsson, A.: A key-recovery timing attack on post-quantum primitives using the fujisaki-okamoto transformation and its application on FrodoKEM. In: Micciancio, D., Ristenpart, T. (eds.) CRYPTO 2020. LNCS,

vol. 12171, pp. 359–386. Springer, Cham (2020). https://doi.org/10.1007/978-3-030-56880-1_13

26. Heinz, D., Kannwischer, M.J., Land, G., Pöppelmann, T., Schwabe, P., Sprenkels, D.: First-order masked kyber on arm cortex-m4. Cryptology ePrint Archive, Report 2022/058 (2022). https://ia.cr/2022/058

27. Kundu, S., D'Anvers, J.P., Beirendonck, M.V., Karmakar, A., Verbauwhede, I.: Higher-order masked saber. Cryptology ePrint Archive, Paper 2022/389 (2022). https://eprint.iacr.org/2022/389, https://eprint.iacr.org/2022/389

28. Lyubashevsky, V., et al.: CRYSTALS-DILITHIUM. Technical report, National Institute of Standards and Technology (2020). https://csrc.nist.gov/projects/post-quantum-cryptography/round-3-submissions

29. Migliore, V., Gérard, B., Tibouchi, M., Fouque, P.-A.: Masking dilithium. In: Deng, R.H., Gauthier-Umaña, V., Ochoa, M., Yung, M. (eds.) ACNS 2019. LNCS, vol. 11464, pp. 344–362. Springer, Cham (2019). https://doi.org/10.1007/978-3-030-21568-2_17

30. NIST Computer Security Division: Post-Quantum Cryptography Standardization (2016). https://csrc.nist.gov/Projects/Post-Quantum-Cryptography

31. Oder, T., Schneider, T., Pöppelmann, T., Güneysu, T.: Practical CCA2-secure masked Ring-LWE implementations. IACR TCHES 2018(1), 142–174 (2018). https://doi.org/10.13154/tches.v2018.i1.142-174, https://tches.iacr.org/index.php/TCHES/article/view/836

32. Prest, T., et al.: FALCON. Technical report, National Institute of Standards and Technology (2020). https://csrc.nist.gov/projects/post-quantum-cryptography/round-3-submissions

33. Primas, R., Pessl, P., Mangard, S.: Single-trace side-channel attacks on masked lattice-based encryption. In: Fischer, W., Homma, N. (eds.) CHES 2017. LNCS, vol. 10529, pp. 513–533. Springer, Cham (2017). https://doi.org/10.1007/978-3-319-66787-4_25

34. Ravi, P., Roy, S.S., Chattopadhyay, A., Bhasin, S.: Generic side-channel attacks on CCA-secure lattice-based PKE and KEMs. IACR TCHES 2020(3), 307–335 (2020). https://doi.org/10.13154/tches.v2020.i3.307-335, https://tches.iacr.org/index.php/TCHES/article/view/8592

35. Reparaz, O., Sinha Roy, S., Vercauteren, F., Verbauwhede, I.: A masked ring-LWE implementation. In: Güneysu, T., Handschuh, H. (eds.) CHES 2015. LNCS, vol. 9293, pp. 683–702. Springer, Heidelberg (2015). https://doi.org/10.1007/978-3-662-48324-4_34

36. Schneider, T., Paglialonga, C., Oder, T., Güneysu, T.: Efficiently masking binomial sampling at arbitrary orders for lattice-based crypto. In: Lin, D., Sako, K. (eds.) PKC 2019. LNCS, vol. 11443, pp. 534–564. Springer, Cham (2019). https://doi.org/10.1007/978-3-030-17259-6_18

37. Schwabe, P., et al.: CRYSTALS-KYBER. Technical report, National Institute of Standards and Technology (2020). https://csrc.nist.gov/projects/post-quantum-cryptography/round-3-submissions

38. Silverman, J.H., Whyte, W.: Timing attacks on NTRUEncrypt via variation in the number of hash calls. In: Abe, M. (ed.) CT-RSA 2007. LNCS, vol. 4377, pp. 208–224. Springer, Heidelberg (2006). https://doi.org/10.1007/11967668_14

39. Ueno, R., Xagawa, K., Tanaka, Y., Ito, A., Takahashi, J., Homma, N.: Curse of re-encryption: a generic power/em analysis on post-quantum kems. Cryptology ePrint Archive, Report 2021/849 (2021). https://ia.cr/2021/849

40. Van Beirendonck, M., D'Anvers, J., Karmakar, A., Balasch, J., Verbauwhede, I.: A side-channel-resistant implementation of SABER. ACM JETC **17**(2), 10:1–10:26 (2021)
41. Van Beirendonck, M., D'Anvers, J.P., Verbauwhede, I.: Analysis and comparison of table-based arithmetic to boolean masking. IACR TCHES **2021**(3), 275–297 (2021). https://doi.org/10.46586/tches.v2021.i3.275-297, https://tches.iacr.org/index.php/TCHES/article/view/8975
42. Wang, A., Zheng, X., Wang, Z.: Power analysis attacks and countermeasures on ntru-based wireless body area networks. KSII Trans. Internet Inf. Syst. (TIIS) **7**(5), 1094–1107 (2013)
43. Xu, Z., Pemberton, O., Roy, S.S., Oswald, D.: Magnifying side-channel leakage of lattice-based cryptosystems with chosen ciphertexts: the case study of kyber. Cryptology ePrint Archive, Report 2020/912 (2020). https://eprint.iacr.org/2020/912

Author Index

Printed in the United States
by Baker & Taylor Publisher Services